Anthropology and History in Yucatán

The Texas Pan American Series

Anthropology

Edited by Grant D. Jones

and History

IN YUCATÁN

University of Texas Press/Austin and London

The Texas Pan American Series is published with the assistance of a revolving publication fund established by the Pan American Sulphur Company.

Library of Congress Cataloging in Publication Data
Main entry under title:
Anthropology and history in Yucatán.
(The Texas Pan American series)
Bibliography: p.
Includes index.
1. Mayas—Addresses, essays, lectures.
2. Yucatan Peninsula—History—Addresses, essays, lectures.
I. Jones, Grant D., 1941–
F1435.1.Y9A57   972′.6′00497   76–15243
ISBN 0–292–70314–7

To the memory of Sir Eric Thompson,
Maya archaeologist, ethnohistorian, and ethnologist
1898–1975

Contents

Introduction
Grant D. Jones   xi

Part One. Continuity and Change in Maya Ethnic Boundaries

1. A Proposal for Constituting a Maya Subgroup, Cultural and
Linguistic, in the Petén and Adjacent Regions
Sir Eric Thompson   3
2. The Francisco Pérez *Probanza* of 1654–1656 and the *Matrícula*
of Tipu (Belize)
France V. Scholes and Sir Eric Thompson   43
3. The Maya and the Colonization of Belize in the Nineteenth Century
O. Nigel Bolland   69

Part Two. Process of Adaptation in Maya Society

4. Independent Maya of the Late Nineteenth Century: Chiefdoms
and Power Politics
D. E. Dumond   103
5. Levels of Settlement Alliance among the San Pedro Maya
of Western Belize and Eastern Petén, 1857–1936
Grant D. Jones   139
6. Internal Migration in Yucatán: Interpretation of Historical
Demography and Current Patterns
James W. Ryder   191
7. The *Maestros Cantores* in Yucatán
Anne C. Collins   233

Part Three. Maya Views of History

8. The Caste War of Yucatán: The History of a Myth and the

Myth of History
Victoria Reifler Bricker   251
9. The Caste War in the 1970's: Present-Day Accounts from
Village Quintana Roo
Allan F. Burns   259
10. Historical Dimensions of Orientation to Change in a
Yucatec Peasant Community
Irwin Press   275
Notes on the Contributors   289
Bibliography   293
Index   317

Introduction

Grant D. Jones

● Such discoveries in colonial documents and in modern ethnological research are made because Maya culture did not die with the Spanish Conquest; it still persists. The Maya, an ultraconservative, deliberately
● conserved the past.
J. E. S. Thompson 1970:xv

The idea for this volume originated in a symposium on the anthropological history of Yucatán, organized by me for the 1972 Annual Meeting of the American Anthropological Association in Toronto. The anthropologists who participated in that symposium explored the use of historical sources and methodology in the study of sociocultural change in the Yucatán Peninsula. In early 1973 I invited the symposium participants and several additional scholars to submit contributions on this topic for inclusion in a collection. The book that has resulted represents a variety of approaches to the anthropological study of historical process in Yucatán. As such, it provides new methodological and empirical bases for the interpretation of the changes and continuities in lowland Maya culture and society from the earliest European contacts to the present.

For the most part, the common interests that integrate these articles reflect both a growing concern among anthropologists with the conceptual and methodological integration of ethnographic and historical approaches and the dissatisfaction among some lowland Mayanists with the static approach to cultural differentiation utilized in Redfield's influential studies of the folk-urban continuum in Yucatán (Dumond 1970; Redfield 1941). The variety of approaches to anthropological history is reviewed in depth in several recent publications (Hudson 1966, 1973; Lewis 1968; Smith 1962; Sturtevant 1966) and need not bear repetition here.

Cline's observations (1972) on the role of "ethnohistory" as a rapprochement of anthropological and historical perspectives in Mesoamerica capture the spirit of much recent thinking in this area (see also

Carmack 1971). While recognizing that ethnohistory can illuminate
both archaeological and ethnographic analyses, as well as provide a bridge
between the archaeological past and the ethnographic present, he observed that "ideally conceived and thoughtfully written ethnohistory has
an independent mission, quite as valid as that of archaeology or ethnology, in laying bare social dynamics, processes, adaptations, rejections,
syncretisms, and other topics in the 400-year colonial and national
periods" (1972:6). Underlying all recent writing on the relationships
between anthropology and history is this concern with processes of change
and adaptation in society and culture regardless of the period of time
involved. The growing concern in archaeology with processual analysis
(Binford 1968), the development of anthropologically oriented historical
analysis in Mesoamerica (Gibson 1952, 1964), and the writing of historical
analysis by social anthropologists (Lewis 1968) are examples of such
recent approaches.

Until recently, the lowland Maya region has been somewhat outside
the mainstream of such developments, although the studies in this book
clearly indicate a great debt to earlier writers. The years of Carnegie
Institution–sponsored research were a golden age of Maya studies, during
which great advances were made in the understanding of Maya society
before and during the Spanish conquest and of the nature of the impact
of Spanish colonialism. A number of classic studies were produced during
and shortly after that period that laid essential groundwork for all later
work on lowland Maya history and anthropology (including, among
others, Chamberlain 1948; Redfield and Villa Rojas 1934; Roys 1943,
1957; Scholes and Roys 1948; and Villa Rojas 1945). The focus of most
Carnegie-sponsored historical work in Yucatán was on the historiography
and historical ethnography (Cline 1972:11) of the early contact period
and the first two centuries of colonial rule (Carnegie Institution of
Washington 1930–1950, 1950–1958). Remarkable progress was made in
the discovery and analysis of native and European documentary sources,
many of which were published (e.g., Roys 1933, 1939; Scholes and Adams
1938; Scholes et al. 1936–1938). Little, however, was done to bridge the
gap between the late colonial period and the ethnographic present of the
1930's. The nineteenth century was poorly known, and Redfield began
his ethnographic research at Chan Kom in 1931 with little understanding
of the impact of the Caste War upon the vicinity of Ebtun, the parent
village of Chan Kom.

While Redfield and Villa Rojas's ethnography of Chan Kom (1934)
and Villa Rojas's study of the X-Cacal group (1945) have withstood the
test of time as the basic ethnographic sources on "traditional" Yucatec
Maya, Redfield's synchronic folk-urban continuum (Redfield 1941) apparently discouraged historically oriented anthropological studies of
Yucatán's recent past for some time. Ironically, Redfield's own restudy
of Chan Kom (1950) was the principal challenge to the simplicity of his

original model. Cline's writings on the disturbed state of nineteenth-century Yucatán (1947, 1948a, 1948b, 1950a–1950c) were the major corrective for the view that postcolonial change in Yucatán was little more than ripples of progress flowing from the urban centers. Reed's descriptive account of the Caste War (1964) and Strickon's interpretation of the changing cultural ecology of Yucatán (1965) likewise stimulated renewed interest in the recent history of Yucatán. Dumond surveys the recent literature in the appendix to his chapter in this volume.

The articles that follow comprise part of the continuing effort to fill the gap between the past and the present throughout the Yucatán Peninsula. The result is not an encyclopedic inventory of all regions but, rather, a series of case studies that utilize a wide variety of methodological orientations to broader questions of historical process. The inadequacy of our present knowledge would, in fact, make any integrative historical statement impossible to synthesize at this time. Nevertheless, there emerges from these studies the general consensus that lowland Maya society has maintained a remarkable degree of integrity and autonomy in the face of nearly overwhelming external pressure. Although this view of the Maya was implicit in the writing of Roys, especially in his analysis of the land-tenure archives of Ebtun (1939), the impact of his important contributions was somewhat limited by the poor state of knowledge of the recent historical past. New data and conceptual approaches make it essential to review Roys's work.

Whereas Redfield viewed historical process in Yucatán as the gradual outward spread of acculturative forces from the urban northwest, we now realize that the situation was far more complex and varied. Viewed regionally, the northwestern areas of the peninsula integrated the Maya into a succession of forms of plantation agriculture. To the east and south, within the Ticul-Tihosuco-Valladolid triangle, plantation systems met sporadic opposition by the native population. This opposition exploded in 1847 in the east and spread to the west like wildfire, dislocating the entire economy of Yucatán for many years to come. In the ensuing years of the Caste War the rebellious eastern Maya maintained their independence in the previously lightly inhabited forests southeast of Tihosuco, leaving a no man's land south of Valladolid that remained uninhabited until villages like Chan Kom were formed by migrants from settled areas to the north in the early part of the twentieth century. To the south, along the expanding borders of Belize, we now know that yet another stronghold of Maya autonomy was centered, in all probability, around the town of Chichanha. Long a point of articulation between the Maya to their north and the Belize Maya to their south, the Chichanhas and their allies played a major role as a semi-independent force in the struggles of the late nineteenth century.

While, as Redfield rightly observed, the process of acculturation affected all these groups to varying degrees, the complex dynamics of interaction between the various Maya groups, between the Maya and various forces of Yucatecan colonialism, and between the Maya and the forces of British colonialism make it clear that the folk-urban continuum is inadequate as an explanation of contemporary cultural variations. The lowland Maya in few cases submitted passively to the colonial or national society, as such a model inevitably implies. Even in pacified areas in the northwest, religious rituals and beliefs went underground, hidden from zealous missionaries. Dissatisfied and persecuted Maya migrated in large numbers throughout the colonial period and into the nineteenth century away from areas of Spanish and English control, forming groups of communities in the wilderness. Others, like the Itza of Petén, resisted conquest militarily for centuries. Even today, as several articles in this volume demonstrate, the Maya maintain a sense of their independent history and autonomy regardless of their degree of acculturation or the intensity of their experience with exploitive colonialism.

Maya independent political action during the nineteenth century became itself an ethnic tie with the past that remains alive in rural Quintana Roo and, like forms of religious belief, exhibits degrees of syncretization with the colonial society that vary over time and space. The Maya propensity to absorb alien dominant societies while maintaining sufficient symbolic and organizational identities to preserve a self-perception of autonomy, whether political or cosmological, must have been well established by the end of the Classic Period. It was manifested throughout the Postclassic, especially in northern Yucatán, providing Maya culture with "continuity from the first centuries of the Christian Era to the present day" (J. E. S. Thompson 1970:xvi).

Until the late colonial period, Spanish control over the vast hinterland of the Yucatán Peninsula was tenuous; and, even in areas where this control was more efficient, as was the case around Valladolid, administrative, economic, and ecclesiastical control by the colonial society was far less complete than it was, for example, in the central Mexican highlands. Added to the relative weakness of colonial control was the unique ecological character of the lowlands: a vast, untamed (from the perspective of the Spanish) wilderness where apostates and dissenters could seek refuge from all forms of external control. It was actually the British woodcutters who offered the greatest threat to what must have been a wilderness Maya population of considerable size, despite the inevitable depopulation of the postcontact period; for, as Bolland demonstrates in this volume, the logging operations increasingly threatened the refuge settlements in the southern areas.

Other factors related to the maintenance of Maya cultural and social autonomy were the adaptability of Maya cosmology in absorbing Christian elements into the preexistent pattern (D. E. Thompson 1954) and the failure of the Spanish *reducciones* to destroy completely either the Maya concept of political territoriality or the basic ceremonial center pattern. Roys noted the survival of political territories around Ebtun as late as the 1930's (1939:62), and the settlement patterns of the Santa Cruz– and Chichanha-derived groups of the nineteenth century conform with aspects of traditional patterns (Jones, this volume). As the Santa Cruz Maya demonstrate so vividly, the integration of the syncretized cosmology with the hierarchical political structure of centralized clusters of ceremonial centers and their village dependencies ultimately created a military force of formidable proportions. The comparative study of these features of lowland Maya society is in its infancy. While attention should not be drawn away from the implications of the Zinacantan data from highland Chiapas to questions of precontact Maya culture, lowland Maya archaeologists should recognize that there is much of interest to them in the ethnohistory and ethnography of their own territory (see Coe 1965 for a pioneering study along such lines).

The multiethnicity that has characterized the lowland Maya region since the Spanish conquest demands that any study of the area confront the question of ethnic boundaries (Barth 1969). Although nearly all the authors of this volume identify and analyze ethnic boundaries, the authors of the first part, "Continuity and Change in Maya Ethnic Boundaries," have jointly contributed to an understanding of the long-term changes in territorially defined ethnic boundaries within a specific area. Sir Eric Thompson defines this area, which he calls the Chan Maya region, in terms of its proto-historic roots. He suggests that this boundary, taken as a whole, was of political significance even in recent times. While emphasizing the speculative nature of his hypothesis, he cautions against an overemphasis upon changing local ceramic traditions in the face of Maya concepts of continuity in time. Because of the Maya view of history repeating itself and because of the conservatism of Maya thought, Thompson writes in this volume, "I readily accept continuity from past to present and so judge that where we have no reason to assess discontinuity, it is best to assume no break with the past. Thus events of A.D. 700 in the absence of contrary evidence are best explained in the light of happenings of, say, A.D. 1700 or A.D. 1900." If this hypothesis is correct, the longstanding conflict between Chichanha-affiliated Maya and those of Santa Cruz during the Caste War could be understood as a last chapter in efforts to maintain the northern Chan boundary. This view of nineteenth-century boundaries is less implausible when we recall that sixteenth-century Maya geographical affiliations were still of importance around Chan Kom during the 1930's (Roys 1939:62). Since northern Yucatec Maya surely joined those of Chichanha throughout the southern migrations of the colonial period, Thompson's views challenge any assumption that external intrusions completely destroy the sense of local ethnicity.

Thompson's review of the available documents, which will remain distressingly sketchy for this area until the archives are further combed, suggests, then, the basic and continuous cultural unity of the Mopan, the Itza, other Petén Maya, the Maya of western Belize, the Chichanha, the Chinamita, and the Yucatec-speaking Lacandon of Petén and Chiapas. Perhaps, like the territorial units of northern Yucatán at the time of the conquest, these were territorial groupings with varying degrees of political unity and ethnic identity. What Thompson has given us is a framework for investigating further the nature of ethnicity in this puzzling region. A central task of lowland Maya ethnohistory should be to test and expand his challenging ideas.

In "The Francisco Pérez *Probanza* of 1654–1656 and the *Matrícula* of Tipu (Belize)," Scholes and Thompson analyze one of the most important known Spanish documents concerning Maya ethnic boundaries in western Belize. Tipu was the most important Maya town along the Spanish route from Bacalar to Tayasal, and it played an important role throughout the seventeenth century in Spanish attempts to conquer spiritually and militarily their Itza neighbors and allies to their west. The authors conclude that Tipu was probably situated on the Eastern Branch of the Belize River. They also identify probable locations of several other Maya settlements visited by Pérez on his way south through Belize. Readers should refer to Sir Eric Thompson (1974) for a fuller account of early historic period Maya settlements in Belize. Of greatest interest in this article is the presence in the *matrícula* of Maya day names that occur as the first name in double surnames. These are limited to individuals identified as *indios del monte,* whom the authors identify as possibly Maya residing south of the Belize River. They suggest that Tipu itself had been ethnically Muzul, one of Thompson's Chan groups, until migrations from northern Yucatán of Maya fleeing Spanish rule changed the ethnic composition of the town. Either the more conservative Muzules fled into the forests, where they were picked up by Pérez's party, or by 1650 the Yucatecan immigrants had been absorbed by the previous inhabitants of Tipu, leaving the more remote Muzul unaffected.

In any event, the Tipu *matrícula* strongly suggests that at Tipu itself northern Yucatec migrants had made some ethnic inroads, whereas the impact of northern Yucatec culture had barely touched the more rural areas. It is unlikely, however, that the Tipuans lost their identity as a local power, for as late as 1696 marriage alliances still existed between the rulers of Tipu and Tayasal. Christianity was not taken seriously by the Tipuans, who managed to keep more Spanish outsiders—including Pérez the census taker—at a safe distance from their private activities.

Scholes and Thompson provide a marvelous account of the process by which the inhabitants of Tipu kept the Spanish at arm's length while giving verbal assurances of their loyalty as subjects. Tipu was too far from seats of colonial control for either secular or ecclesiastic authorities to know very much about goings on in the town. As in most remote areas, permanent priests could not be stationed there, and native assistants were undoubtedly given the responsibility of maintaining the faith (see Collins, this volume).

Although Tipu fades from sight after the 1697 conquest of Tayasal, there is reason to believe that inhabitants of the Tipu region remained in western Belize, probably into the nineteenth century. Bolland, shifting to British documentary sources, picks up the thread of Maya settlement in the late eighteenth century. He indicates that Maya settlement continued in western Belize, especially in the region southwest of New River Lagoon, as late as 1847. His documentation for the eighteenth and early nineteenth centuries makes this conclusion inescapable, although we have no way of knowing whether they were Tipu remnants, new migrants from northern Yucatán, groups affiliated with Chichanha, or perhaps a mosaic of all these.

The major emphasis of Bolland's article is on the effects of British colonialism on the Belize Maya. The British treatment of the native population was economically motivated. Unlike the Spanish, they were interested neither in tributaries nor in souls, nor even in laborers until the late nineteenth century. The extractive forest economy of Belize required undisturbed land. Any native inhabitant, especially a swidden cultivator, was regarded as a hindrance. Thus, the Maya-British boundary could not be mediated by religious syncretism or political inclusion. The ethnic boundary was the farthest extent of a given year's cutting. This boundary pushed the Maya ever deeper toward the Petén and was broken only by occasional Maya raids on the logging camps. Bolland identifies four stages in the history of Maya-British relations. From the late eighteenth century until about 1817 the encroachment of logging operations on Maya settlements resulted in raids on the camps. From 1817 until 1847, the second stage, little was heard of the Maya, who lived peacefully beyond European settlement. But from 1847 until 1867 the effects of the Caste War were to engage various Chichanha groups in open conflict with the British, ultimately resulting in Maya defeat. As the colony turned to agricultural settlement by importing whites in the late nineteenth century, the last stage witnessed the incorporation of the Maya into the colonial socioeconomic structure as a class of laborers.

Bolland describes the changing colonial image of the Maya as a reflection of the shifting political economy. In the late nineteenth century, for example, the Maya "were perceived in the colonial scheme, not as the agricultural pioneers that they in fact were, but merely as a potential source of 'tractable,' 'obedient,' and 'easily managed' labor for foreign-owned plantations" (see also G. D. Jones 1969:111–114). In nineteenth-century Belize, agricultural development was, as Bolland maintains, conceived in racist terms. In the northern region the effect was to stimulate foreign-owned plantation sugar. When the plantations failed during the 1880's, sugar production fell into the hands of elite mestizos, who, like the Maya, used swidden types of cultivation. Not until the late 1950's were the Maya of northern Belize given the opportunity to produce sugar cane on a significant scale, having been previously perceived as useful to the colonial economy only as wage laborers (see Abrams 1973; G. D. Jones 1969, 1971*b*). Yet, as Bolland maintains, the nineteenth-century Maya deeply affected the history of Belize, which gained status as a crown colony in 1862 largely as a result of the Maya military threat.

Each of the authors in the next part is concerned with particular ways in which Yucatec Maya society has adapted to externally imposed change. We learn from these articles that considerable variation existed both in local conditions and in resultant adaptive responses. In the northwest the response to intolerable native conditions was gradual and continuous migration, whereas in the more independent areas to the south and east adjustments were far more radical. It would appear that in areas of less-intense early colonial economic exploitation there was far greater potential for large-scale native political-military organization to arise in response to nineteenth-century increases in economic or other deprivations.

Dumond expands the earlier researches of Cline and Reed to present a synthesis of the history and organization of the nineteenth-century Maya groups that emerged from the ravages of the Caste War. Dumond's is the first major comparative study of all the independent groups. Previous studies have focused almost entirely upon the Santa Cruz, whereas Dumond has studied little-known sources from Yucatán and Campeche as well as from Belize in order to increase our knowledge of the poorly known *pacíficos del sur*. He has especially clarified the circumstances of the northern *pacífico* group at Lochha and Mesapich, which later shifted its political headquarters to Ixkanha. Relationships among all the independent Maya groups were highly complex and were further complicated by the conflicting policies and interests of the neighboring Mexican and British inhabitants. This article is an important step toward clarifying these problems.

Dumond views the major Maya groups as segmentary coalitions of semiautonomous minor groups. Although he notes that the Yucatecan militia system provided an important model for the organization and title system of these groups (p. 106), he later suggests that military principles of organization may not have been totally responsible for the nineteenth century Maya segmentary system (p. 127). He observes that the process of political fusion was often offset by processes of factionalism and segmentary fissioning. The structural basis for political fission and fusion is still not fully understood, although the basic unit was apparently the politically centralized chiefdom. In my article, I equate the chiefdom, as defined by Dumond, with a major cluster of settlements which, depending upon external or internal circumstances, could break up into its constituent minor clusters or strengthen its leadership by alliance with other major or minor settlement clusters.

Dumond has appended a synthesis of recent interpretations of the Caste War to his article. Those who are interested in carrying out further research on Caste War–related topics should read his remarks in conjunction with Cline's bibliographic essay (1945), which Dumond does not attempt to duplicate.

In my article I analyze one of the Chichanha subgroups in detail. Whereas some members of this group may have been indigenous to the Yalbac Hills area along upper Labouring Creek in Belize, the vast bulk of the one thousand or so who comprised the San Pedro Maya were a faction of migrants from the Chichanha region to the north. Eventually their settlements straddled the Belize-Petén boundary, creating a defensive ring with its headquarters in San Pedro village on the southeastern perimeter. The system of major and minor settlement clusters was segmentary, functioning politically, militarily, and possibly ceremonially at each level. The three principal villages were of ranked importance: a threatened attack on San Pedro would bring troops from the entire cluster to its defense, whereas threats to the two other village centers involved only troops from its own dependent settlements. This system may well be similar, if not virtually identical, to political systems of the other independent lowland Maya groups of the same period. Unlike Dumond, I believe that these systems are basically pre-Columbian, despite the heavy overlay of Spanish military titles.

A marked contrast exists between the factious Chichanha groups and the more permanently centralized Santa Cruz. Perhaps this reflects, in part, the positive integrative functions of the Talking Cross cult, which was absent at Chichanha (Zimmerman 1963). But sacred crosses were found throughout the independent Maya region, suggesting perhaps that the immense power of the cross at Santa Cruz was more a function of particular organizational pressures there than of the cult itself (G. D. Jones 1974:667–669). The military leaders of the northern rebels had a greater fear of alliance with Yucatán than did those of the southern Maya of Chichanha, whose location was far from any sizable white-controlled settlement other than Bacalar. Chichanha leaders were thus normally treaty makers, whereas peace seekers among the Santa Cruz were usually assassinated. Santa Cruz leaders developed in response to their circumstances a policy of aggressive expansion against the Chichanhas, who found themselves divided over the support of their Mexican allies, the Santa Cruz, and the British. It is no wonder that under these conditions Chichanha was unable to achieve a unified polity.

Ryder treats the problem of demographic change, especially that of migration, from a materialist theoretical perspective. His methodology, which combines an analysis of ethnohistorical, ethnographic, and demographic data, complements Cook and Borah's recent broad study (1974) of Yucatecan demographic history. Ryder's study is of interest for its careful, conservative reconstruction of the demographic profile of one Maya community (Pencuyut) from the sixteenth century to the present. Among his general conclusions is that Pencuyut experienced a high range of population loss through migration throughout most of its history. Migration, he suggests, was variously a mode of adaptation to external economic forces, population pressure on land, conflict, the fear and ravages of famine and epidemic, and, in modern times, the scarcity of local wage employment.

It is possible that some of Pencuyut's early migrants were moving southward, for, as Scholes and Thompson demonstrate in their analysis of the Tipu *matrícula*, Yucatec-speaking migrants were in western Belize by the seventeenth century. However, in later years the direction of movement may well have been quite different. Between 1846 and 1851 Pencuyut suffered a remarkable 88 percent drop in population. Skeptical of earlier beliefs that such losses were largely due to deaths suffered during the Caste War, Ryder estimates that such deaths actually accounted for only 20 to 30 percent of the loss. The rest, he believes, were mostly distributed among sugar and henequen haciendas, while a much smaller proportion moved to the independent Maya zone and to towns to the north and west.

Ryder also considers Pencuyut in the larger Latin American context, noting that the growth in the village's crude rate of natural increase after 1920 reflected the improved health conditions felt throughout the region. However, due to the economic attraction of the urban centers of Yucatán, particularly that of Mérida, the population of Pencuyut has remained stable. Whereas this rural-urban migration is stimulated by high fertility, also of importance is the small size and inferior political status of the rural village, which can provide its inhabitants with fewer services than they can obtain in the cities and larger towns.

In "The *Maestros Cantores* in Yucatán" Collins traces the history of a particular role that served different adaptive functions over the years. Initially a means by which the few missionaries that served Yucatán could bring Christianity to the native masses, the ecclesiastical role of *maestro* eventually served to aid in maintaining the religious systems of the independent Maya of the late nineteenth century (described for X-Cacal in Villa Rojas 1945:73). That the early *maestros cantores* were sons of nobles suggests the important role that the early Franciscans played, both in transforming the Maya nobility and in maintaining the high status of native religious leaders in Maya society. By allowing these ritual assistants increasing authority, even to administer sacraments, the missionaries were perhaps unwittingly aiding the process of religious syncretism, the results of which are so evident among the Santa Cruz Maya (Villa Rojas 1945). The utilization of native *maestros* to administer sacraments was probably unique in Mesoamerica. It was, as Collins is able to document, conditioned by the remote location of many of the native settlements and by the scarcity of missionaries. Thus, practical conditions probably rendered identical the originally distinguishable positions of *maestro de escuela, maestro de capilla,* and *maestro cantor.*

The articles in the last part emphasize the native's view of historical reality through the study of native texts and ethnographic data. They offer more than the study of oral tradition, for each author is concerned as well with the contrast between "internal" and "external" perceptions of historical process. They thus stress the relativity of both academic history and folk history, perhaps suggesting that the anthropologist's task is to explain and thereby mediate these discontinuities.

Bricker demonstrates that the contemporary X-Cacal Maya have faithfully and accurately preserved the myth that Juan de la Cruz was the Second Coming of Christ. She describes and translates, in part, a document in Maya, now in Mérida, which can be identified as a sermon written by a person who signed his name Juan de la Cruz. The sermon was delivered to the inhabitants of the Santa Cruz cult center on October 15, 1850, and is, in most respects, identical to the version of the sermon that is still consulted at X-Cacal. In this case a native document is of major importance for interpreting the inadequate white histories, which seem to confuse Juan de la Cruz with Venancio Puc, who by the late 1850's was the high priest of the Santa Cruz.

Since the sermon was probably an important foundation of the original cult of the cross, delivered perhaps by Juan de la Cruz himself, Bricker disputes Zimmerman's argument that Juan de la Cruz is an archaic, mythified memory of Jesus Christ as absorbed from early missionary teachings. A person named Juan de la Cruz may have been the first spokesman of the cult, as Bricker maintains, but it is also conceivable that his identity could have been the invention of secular military authorities who were anxious to unite the Maya refugees in the eastern wilderness (G. D. Jones 1974:667–669). Bricker is currently analyzing other Maya documents that bear the name of Juan de la Cruz. It is hoped that these will shed further light on the identity and role of Juan de la Cruz in the establishment of the Talking Cross cult.

Burns reinforces Bricker's observations of the strong sense of history possessed by contemporary Santa Cruz Maya in his analysis of spoken "counsels" that describe events of the nineteenth century and analyze conditions of the present. Like Bricker, he finds that these accounts keep alive this sense of history and thereby both symbolize and foster the autonomy of Santa Cruz culture. Indeed, in addition to the counsels, the ritual reading of the books of Chilam Balam during a period of "ritual, exchange, and entertainment, a time of unification and intensification," is reminiscent of Landa's accounts of priests reading sacred books four centuries ago (Tozzer 1941:153–154). The counsels themselves are of value in providing insight both into the Santa Cruz view of history and into our attempts to construct an "external" view of their history.

In one of the counsels, Juan de la Cruz speaks through a possessed Santa Cruz leader, Felipe Yama. We are reminded of the sixteenth-century Maya *chilans* who lay on the floor in a state of trance, communicating with voices emanating from the roof (Roys 1943:79), parts of which in Chan Kom are actually regarded as sacred crosses (Redfield and Villa Rojas 1934:147). It is hardly surprising that, in the Maya view, the "secular" general can easily play the "sacred" role of mouthpiece for Juan de la Cruz, who spoke as the cross through various mediums. (Since the cross is the most important medium through which the voice of Juan de la Cruz can be heard, Juan de la Cruz and the cross are often merged in Maya thought.) It is probable that, just as the cross could communicate to the X-Cacal scribes and to the *nohoch tata* during the 1930's, Juan de la Cruz could have communicated in the nineteenth century by means of the cross either to a scribe who on occasion wrote down his words or to a priest or military leader who might have dictated the message to a scribe.

In his observations on the relationships between past and present in Pustunich, Press seeks to identify the historical factors that determine the village's present orientations to change. He sees these factors as cumulatively situational while inevitably shaped by contemporary actors' selective interpretations of the past. Attitudes toward change are conditioned by the effects of "real" events as well as by a current world view whose memory is highly selective. He stresses what he regards to be the idiosyncratic and localized character of historical process in Yucatán, thus cautioning against temptations to overgeneralize.

Pustunich was part of the Mani province, which, unlike the Sotuta and Cupul provinces to the east, accepted Spanish colonialism on peaceful terms. The Xiu nobility ruled the village throughout the sixteenth century, and Pustunich remained politically subservient to the town of Mani and later to the town of Ticul. Such conditions provided the villagers with no historical precedent for self-determined change. Yet the village's political subservience contrasted with its early underground religious activities which led, in part, to the 1562 inquisition in Mani. It has maintained a spirit of religious independence throughout the colonial and national periods, preserving much that is Maya but selecting judiciously from the beliefs and rituals of formal Catholicism. This form of syncretism, in which "both Catholic and pagan rituals exist side by side," appears much like that of Chan Kom and X-Cacal to the east; but Press suggests that Pustunich is somewhat anomalous in the northwestern henequen zone, where few rituals of the field have survived. He explains that its conservatism is ecological, citing its location in the Puuc Hills, inaccessible to mechanized agriculture.

The self-image of Pustunich's history complements and reinforces this "real" history of political subjugation that resulted in local disinterest in political action and of anticlericalism that resulted in a sense of religious continuity with the Maya past. Historical change is seen as slow and gradual, with little sense of urgency about the future. Press contrasts Pustunich's historical experience and self-perception with Chan Kom, noting that Chan Kom had little of the objective basis for stability of self-image that characterizes Pustunich. We actually know very little about the view of the past in Chan Kom during the 1930's except from a handful of political leaders. Was Chan Kom's experience really a radical departure from a stable past or was its formation and its later political independence from Ebtun a continuation of ancient principles of community formation resulting from factionalism and migration? What Redfield regarded as "progressive" political change at Chan Kom may have been as conservative as Pustunich's political inactivity. However, in comparing Pustunich with Santa Cruz, the differences are indisputable. We find little vagueness or sense of stability in the Cruzob view of history. The unique Santa Cruz historical experience lives on in the constant recital and reinterpretation of specific past events. Here, too, the orientation to change is shaped by the composite effects of past events and self-perception, and the Cruzob approach the future at least as conservatively as do the Pustunicheños. The future presents, indeed, a far greater threat to the radical identity of the Quintana Roo Maya villages than it does to Maya villages that are as well adapted to the wider society as Pustunich appears to be.

The articles of this volume establish the continuity between the archaeological past and the uncertain future of the lowland Maya. They demonstrate some of the richness of the ethnohistorical data, much of which lies untapped in Old and New World archives. More significantly, they contribute toward closing the conceptual gap between the contemporary Maya and their historical past. But these articles are still only a small step toward closing either the empirical or the conceptual gaps in lowland Maya research. It is hoped that they will stimulate a continuing revival of interest in this region among ethnohistorians and ethnographers.

Postscript

Sir Eric Thompson died in Cambridge, England, on September 9, 1975. He had been planning further publications on Maya ethnohistory, a field to which he had brought great breadth of experience in Maya archaeology, hieroglyphic interpretation, and comparative ethnology. He will be remembered by his colleagues and admirers as a person who possessed remarkable intellectual energy and imagination, keen wit, and deep interest in the ideas of others. His encouragement was a continuing inspiration in the preparation of this book, which we have dedicated to his memory.

Note

While the authors of individual chapters have acknowledged support from many people, I wish to express my appreciation to the following individuals for their help in the preparation of this volume. The University of Texas Press staff has provided patient encouragement and support. Mrs. Carol Cratty, Mrs. June Darrow, and Mrs. Barbara Meelan typed much of the manuscript. Robert Kautz drew the maps for articles 1, 2, 3, and 5. Mrs. Virginia Vaughan drew the figures for article 6. David D. Earle compiled the index. Finally, I am grateful to Hamilton College for financial support in the preparation of the manuscript.

Part One

Continuity and Change in Maya Ethnic Boundaries

1

A Proposal for Constituting a Maya Subgroup,

Cultural and Linguistic,

in the Petén and Adjacent Regions

Sir Eric Thompson

It is here advocated that in vocabulary, pronunciation, personal names, religion, and religious practices the Maya speakers of variant forms of Yucatec in the Petén and adjacent Belize, including the so-called Itza, as known to us from colonial sources and present-day observation, are closer to the Mopan Maya than to the Maya of Yucatán. Consequently, it is proposed that those Petén Maya, the Mopan Maya, the Cehach, the Chinamita, and the Yucatec-speaking Lacandon should be constituted a subgroup, related rather closely to the Yucatec Maya but attached with considerably looser bonds to the Putun and Chol-speaking groups to their west, south, and southeast.

For this subgroup the name Chan Maya, or Chan, is suggested on the grounds that it is short, it is easily remembered, and it was a common, in some parts very common, surname in the area. Complete uniformity of culture within the subgroup is not implied. It must be emphasized that there are pitifully inadequate cultural and linguistic data for the greater part of the area. Consequently, the ground on which this subgroup rests is admittedly closer to sand than to rock; had it been firmer, some such regional division would have been proposed long ago. Despite those insubstantial foundations, archaeological data may warrant a backward extension of the subgroup into the Classic Period.

Area

Long-established linguistic boundaries are not like stone wall or clipped hedge. Rather, we should think in terms of tidal waters where man is hard put to say where fresh begins and brackish ends. That is particularly true of the northern frontier of our area. Including in Chan territory that strip in which tide and ebb mingle, one may suggest that the (northern) boundary with pure Yucatec culture ran west at about 18°30′ north across the northern tip of Belize, thence to the southern shore of Lake Bacalar and beyond just north of Tzibanche (map 1-1). Thence the boundary would turn southwesterly to pass north of Chichanha, then due west to pass just north of Oxpemul, continuing to about 90° west. The western boundary runs slightly west of south, passing at its northern part close to former Tzuctok as located by Scholes and Roys (1948:505, map 4). This, like so many settlements in the interior, had been overrun by refugees from Spanish rule, obscuring its original affiliations. It is called "the gateway to the Cehach." Indeed, Chunpich, 8 leagues south, was an important Cehach center. The boundary at that point probably lay about halfway between Chunpich, in the Aguada Cumpich region, and the former Putun capital of Itzamkanac, for Cortés seems to have entered Cehach territory not long after leaving the latter (Scholes and Roys 1948:map 3). One many suppose the boundary continued south-westerly as far as the Rio Usumacinta, for the Lacandon apparently once extended from Lake Izan to near Putun-speaking Tenosique (see below). South of the Usumacinta lay the seventeenth-century land of El Prós-pero, whose inhabitants may well have been ancestral to the present-day Lacandon of Lake Petha, and which should be included in Chan territory.

South of Lake Petén, settlements of the so-called Itza (here named Lake Petén Maya), extended in the nineteenth century to within 15–25 kil-ometers of the Río Pasión. Berendt gives these as Sacluk (now La Liber-tad), Ixpayac, Chachaclum and nearby El Cimarrón, San Juan de Dios, Santa Ana, and Juntecholol (1868a).

Thence the southern Chan boundary runs southeasterly, passing a little south of San Luis, then looping in a northeasterly direction to not far short of Stann Creek, on the Bay of Honduras. Campin, probably on Monkey River, was the northernmost Manche Chol–speaking town (J. E. S. Thompson 1974).

Inhabitants of the Area

Imposing lists of "nations" in the above area are given by Villagutierre Soto-Mayor (1933), but, for the most part, those are merely settlements or villages named for the ruling *cacique* and often, alas, wretchedly tran-scribed. The most important groups, some of which have preserved their entities to the present day, would appear to have been the following groups.

The Lake Petén Maya
The Lake Petén Maya is the group commonly called Itza following the Spanish colonial habit of naming a group after its ruling family (cf. use of the term *Inca*). The area directly under the rule of the Itza invaders at Tayasal is nebulous, but we are more certain about the territory when it is considered in terms of the Petén dialect. Lake Petén was the heart of

the concentration and Tayasal its most important entity until its downfall in 1697, hence the suggested name.

The Mopan Maya
The territory of the Mopan Maya, perhaps also known as Aycal, lay immediately north of the Manche Chol and southeast of Lake Petén. The
modern town of San Luis is probably the ancient Mopan. According to a
Mopan informant (Ximénez 1929–1971:bk. 5, chap. 65) all the Indians
of the coast (Bay of Honduras) were Mopan. He was happy when the
names of *caciques* and rivers in the itinerary of Fr. Joseph Delgado were
read to him. That was the journey made by the Dominican in 1677 from
the Moho to the Belize River. In fact, the first names were those of
Manche Chol, as far as Campin, almost surely on Monkey River (J. E. S.
Thompson [1974]). Beyond that Manche Chol town, Delgado gave an
itinerary leading northwest to Zaui, whose chief was Muzul and which
lay a day and a half by road (almost surely east) of Tipu, *"ranchería de
indios yucatecos."* From this we may deduce that the settlements passed
en route were not Yucatec. This conclusion is supported by the non-
Yucatec names of their chiefs. The Maya of Sittee, north of present-day
Stann Creek, are mentioned as part of the Muxunes (same as Muzules?)
who were rounded up in 1754 and settled at the Mopan town of Dolores
(Guatemala, Archivo General del Gobierno 1936:278). It was customary
to settle reduced Indians in towns of their own speech; thus, we may conclude that the Sittee valley was Mopan in speech.

To the Mopan, one can be reasonably certain, should be assigned the
indios del monte from the middle Belize who figure in the Pérez
matrícula of 1655 (Scholes and Thompson, this volume), as well as the
pagan Muzul, neighbors of the Tipuans who accompanied them to
Mérida to offer submission. They must have been the Maya of Zaui under
their chief Muzul.

The evidence suggests that the Belize River was the northern boundary
of the Mopan, though again one must not conceive of the boundary as
tightly drawn but, rather, as a zone of interpenetration.

It is highly unlikely that the use of Maya day names as the first part of
double surnames was restricted to that quite small group of pagan *indios
del monte*, apparently living immediately south of the middle Belize
River, whom Pérez chanced to catch in his net when fishing for Tipuans.
If, as seems reasonably certain, they were Mopan, one may perhaps assume that the use of day names was a Mopan custom. Only a handful of
surnames are recorded for Mopan itself, and, of those, none is a day name,
but it may well have been the custom to use only the second (paternal?)
name in everyday address.

Map 1-1
Over: The Chan area in the colonial period

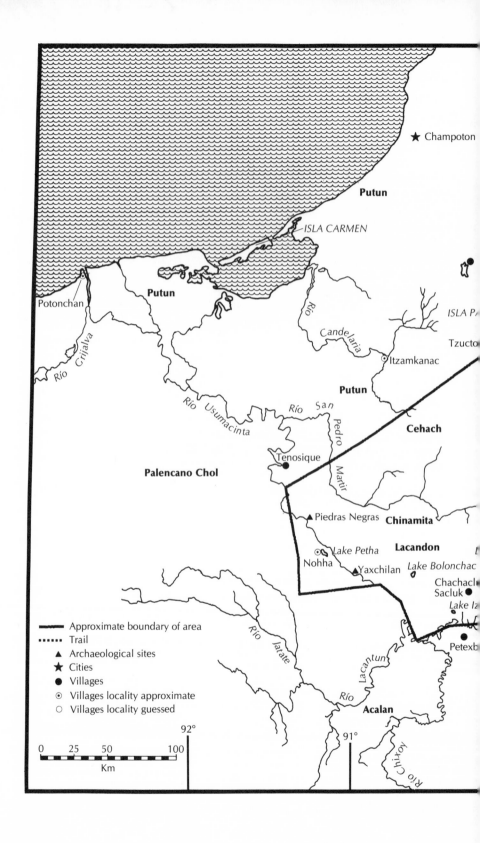

★ Champoton

Putun

ISLA CARMEN

Potonchan

Putun

Río Grijalva

Río Candelaria

Río

Itzamkanac

ISLA P

Tzucto

Putun

Río Usumacinta

Río San Pedro Mártir

Cehach

Tenosique

Palencano Chol

▲ Piedras Negras **Chinamita**

Lacandon

Lake Petha

Nohha ▲Yaxchilan Lake Bolonchac

Chachac

Sacluk ●

Lake Iz

Río Jatate

Petexb

Río Lacantun

Río

Acalan

Río Chixoy

—— Approximate boundary of area
••••• Trail
▲ Archaeological sites
★ Cities
● Villages
⊙ Villages locality approximate
○ Villages locality guessed

92°

91°

0   25   50   100
Km

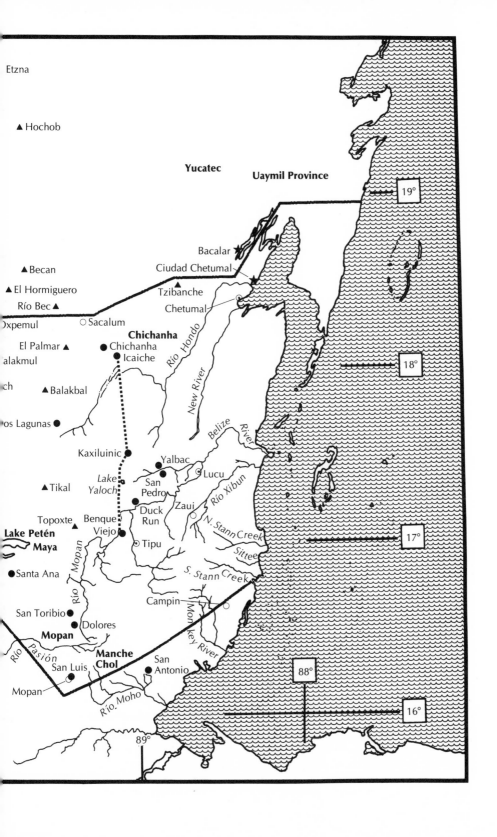

Etzna

▲ Hochob

Yucatec   **Uaymil Province**

19°

Bacalar
Ciudad Chetumal
▲ Becan
▲ El Hormiguero
Río Bec ▲   Tzibanche
                    Chetumal
Oxpemul   ○ Sacalum
El Palmar ▲   **Chichanha**   18°
alakmul   ● Chichanha
              ▲ Icaiche
ch
        ▲ Balakbal

os Lagunas ●

        Kaxiluinic   ● Yalbac
                     ● San   ○ Lucu
        Lake   Pedro
▲ Tikal *Yaloch* ○
                     ● Duck Zauí ○
Topoxte   Run
▲ Benque ○
Lake Petén Viejo ○ ○ Tipu   17°
Maya
● Santa Ana

● San Toribio
        ● Dolores   Campin
Mopan
                          Manche   San   88°
San Luis **Chol**   ● Antonio
○
Mopan   16°

89°

The Maya of Tipu

The Maya of Tipu and the upper Belize settlements had been swamped by refugees from Spanish rule, largely, perhaps almost entirely, from southern Quintana Roo, hence the description by Fr. Delgado of Tipu as a *rancheria de indios yucatecos*. By the mid-seventeenth century we find few surnames at Tipu that were not also found in Yucatán or Quintana Roo (Scholes and Thompson, this volume).

Tipu itself was, without much doubt, situated on the Macal or Eastern Branch of the Belize River, some few miles above San Ignacio el Cayo. Its relations with the Lake Petén Maya were close. Trade between the two groups was active, Tipu being an entrepôt for such desired Spanish products as machetes and steel axes. Tipuans lived in settlements of the Lake Petén Maya and intermarried with them. (Martin Can, leader of Can Ek's embassy to Mérida, was a son of the latter's sister; thus, a Tipuan could marry into Tayasal's royal family.) Relations generally seem to have been so close that a Mopan Maya testified, although incorrectly, that the Tipuans were Ah Itza. Those close ties presumably dated back prior to the big influx into Tipu from the north. Nevertheless, the people of Tayasal had no compunction in massacring Tipuans when they came to the lake as stooges of the Spaniards.

The principal settlements grouped with Tipu were Zaczuuz and Lucu, on the middle Belize, and Hubelna, probably on its tributary, now called Roaring Creek. Villages along what is now New River and New River Lagoon, north of the upper stretches of the Belize River, had close relations with Tipu. For instance, they joined the Tipu warriors threatening the Franciscans (López [de] Cogolludo 1867–1868:bk. 11, chap. 13).

Refugees tend to settle among their cultural kinsmen. That would suggest that the fugitives from the area south and southeast of Bacalar, presumably ancestors of the Chichanha-Icaiche Maya of the nineteenth century, took refuge among the people of the upper Belize because of close ties. Moreover, the southern boundary of the vicariate of Bacalar was the Belize valley. (Sibun and Sittee were nominally in the vicariate, although, in practice, the Maya there were left to their own devices.) There was a tendency for ecclesiastical boundaries to conform to ethnic divisions.

Significantly, the Maya revolt of 1636, sparked by the Sacalum massacre, kindled no flame to the north but eventually spread south to the Belize valley, surely indicative of regional solidarity.

The distribution of what I term Lacandon-type *incensarios* gives some support to the view that the ancestors of the Chichanha-Icaiche and the Maya of the middle and upper Belize valley formed a single group, for this type occurs from southeast Quintana Roo southward but ends abruptly in the vicinity of Tipu (see discussion below). If this view is acceptable, namely, that the Maya from Lake Bacalar to Tipu formed a related group, at least in the colonial period, one has an explanation of why the Maya of such villages as Yalbac, San Pedro, and San José allied themselves with Icaiche chiefs (Jones, this volume). Economic conditions, however, also played a part: encroachment of Belize mahogany cutters on Maya milpa.

It has been suggested that the present-day Maya of western Belize are descended from refugees from the Caste War. That is certainly true of some villages. Mazzarelli has shown through analysis of Roman Catholic church records that Benque Viejo and Socotz, founded in the 1860's, were very largely settled by refugees from Yucatán and Quintana Roo (1972). In fact, these immigrants, fleeing the Caste War, did not come directly to Belize but first sojourned in northeastern Petén. Without much doubt they were part of the large number which had migrated to the Petén in the middle of the last century, penetrating as far south as Dolores and the village of San Pedro, perhaps that on the San Pedro Martir. The settlers of Benque Viejo and Socotz apparently crossed into Belize following disturbances in mahogany camps in 1866 (González 1961:92, 93, 97, 99, 101). Some Chan Maya of the Petén were probably among them. Socotz is named for a plant of the Petén used to cure diarrhea (Soza 1957:55), which I believe is unknown in Yucatán. Also, non-Yucatec family names occur in Socotz, for example, Cunil, the name of my foreman and friend.

The problem is whether all the Maya of western Belize, such as the villagers of Kaxiluinic, San José, San Pedro, Yalbac, Bullet Tree Falls, and San Antonio, Cayo District, are descendants of the indigenous population of Belize or of recent immigrants from Yucatán or Quintana Roo or are an admixture of the two. The second view has been advanced partly, it would appear, because of the belief that by the middle nineteenth century no indigenous Maya population survived in western Belize. We have good evidence from British sources that that belief is incorrect.

The Bay-man's map of 1787 has written across the area of the upper Belize valley the words "Indios bravos in friendship with the Baymen." Below, the words "Indios bravos" ("wild Indians") appear south of the western drainage area of that river. Probably because of encroachments on the Indians' lands by British woodsmen, the friendly relations came to an end, as the following items in the Belize archives make manifest (cf. Bolland, this volume).

In 1802 a petition was presented to the magistrates that a detachment of soldiers be sent upriver to punish Indians committing depredations on mahogany works, and in 1807 twenty stands of arms and ammunition were requested for a gang working upriver at Hogstye Bank who had been attacked by the Indians (Burdon 1931–1935:II, 58, 101).

In 1821, in the course of a trial of a man accused of killing an Indian woman, justification was claimed on the grounds that "retaliation against the Indians has been hitherto encouraged on account of the many murders and depredations committed by these same inhabitants of the woods. And the same warfare has been (until now) sanctioned by custom and usage in the Settlement, and no proclamation has been promulgated to the contrary" (Burdon 1931–1935:II, 243–248). One is glad to read that this plea "was rejected with indignation."

Henderson writes: "Not many years passed numerous tribes of hostile Indians left their recesses in the woods for the purpose of plundering. This they often accomplished, and if resistance were offered, not unfrequently committed the most sanguinary murders. The habitations of these people have never been traced" (1809:20).

The Honduras Almanack for 1830 takes a more friendly position: "Those [Indians] who visit the British settlement are in general a timid, inoffensive race . . . they travel independent of either track or guide through woods and brush impervious to others and perform their journies with a rapidity and correctness of direction that almost set other modes and marks at defiance . . . [they] wander over wilds unknown to other men" (1830:12).

Crowe mentions Indians living in close proximity to the British settlement, the boundary of which he places at Duck Run (1850:234, 494). For him and almost everyone in the settlement, the Belize valley and the settlement were almost synonymous.

The authors of the Caddy-Walker expedition of 1839 recruited three Indians living on the left-hand (Macal) branch of the Belize River. There is also mention of the wild Indians who infest the vicinity of Tiger Run (a short distance below Duck Run) and who "during the night or in the absence of the proprietor, at various times emerge from the secret recesses of the forest for the purpose of plundering any domestic animals or domestic articles they can lay their hands upon" (Pendergast 1967:54, 159).

All these references predate Yucatec immigration resulting from the Caste War, and some deal with the vicinity of the Maya villages of San Pedro and Yalbac. They provide convincing proof of a continuity to the present day of an indigenous Maya population in western Belize, no doubt reinforced by refugees from the north in the nineteenth century. Those refugees, being largely, perhaps exclusively, Chichanha-Icaiche (again excepting Benque Viejo, Socotz, and San Ignacio el Cayo), came among their kinsmen, who, emboldened and led by the new arrivals (cf. Jones 1973), were ready to take on the might of the British Empire (they had no respect for Queen Victoria as had their enemies the Santa Cruz de Bravo Maya.)*

The Northern Frontier
Nothing of substance is known of the ethnography of the Maya who, in the colonial period, lived immediately south of the postulated northern

* Another analysis maintains that the early settlers of Benque Viejo and Socotz were of Chichanha-Icaiche origin (see Jones, this volume, pp. 167–168).—Ed.

boundary of the Chan subgroup. Immediately prior to the Spanish conquest, the eastern half of that zone was dominated by the Putun-influenced, or Putun-ruled, city of Chetumal, situated at or near the archaeological site of Santa Rita, in northern Belize (J. E. S. Thompson [1974]). One may suppose that the peasant population was Chan. It certainly had close ties with the middle and upper Belize valley in the colonial period. The whole area was involved in the 1636 revolt.

That revolt seems to have been the delayed outcome of the massacre of Francisco de Mirones and his party at Sacalum in 1624. The precise location of that town is unknown. Scholes and Roys, tentatively and noting their doubts, situate it east of Río Bec and some way north of Chichanha (1948:280, map 4). Moved 25–30 kilometers south of that tentative location, Sacalum would have lain close to Chichanha and so within postulated Chan territory. As Scholes and Roys point out, Father Delgado passed from Sacalum to Tipu without touching Bacalar. In fact, in the nineteenth century a trail ran from Icaiche through Chunhuas, Kaxiluinic, and Yaloch to Benque Viejo, a few miles west of where Tipu once stood (it may still exist; Blom [1929:19] seems to refer to it). I suspect this was an ancient route—probably pre-Columbian—down which the refugees fled. A branch from Laguna Yaloch passed via Plancha de Piedra to Lake Petén.

Sacalum, inhabited by a mixture of pagans (the high priest retained his Maya title of *ah kin*) and Yucatec Maya refugees, was a *visita* of the short-lived Franciscan *guardianía* of Tzuctok. Fray Juan de Santa María described Tzuctok in 1605 as "the gateway to all heathendom"; it was the last settlement north of Cehach territory and might have once been a Cehach town (Scholes and Roys 1948:272, 279). The location of Sacalum here suggested would lie about 95 kilometers due east of Tzuctok as tentatively proposed by Scholes and Roys (1948:map 4, 279–280). Both sites would appear to fall in the indeterminate boundary zone between Yucatec and Chan Maya.

The northern boundary of the Chan remains unsatisfactorily delineated. Near the eastern end it follows the poorly defined nineteenth-century division between the Santa Cruz de Bravo and the Chichanha-Icaiche Maya. I suggest that the marked hostility between the groups had its roots in ethnic differences stretching into the past, the former being true Yucatec, the latter of the Chan subgroup. For the western end we are dependent on the doubtful northern borders of the Cehach. The delineation of the central part has been influenced by data from the Classic Period in the absence of any satisfactory information from the colonial period.

The Cehach

A felicitous summary of the little known about the Cehach, a strategically important group of western Petén and adjacent southeast Campeche comes from the pen of Villa Rojas (1962*b*). The name means abundance of deer: *ceh*, "deer"; suffix *ach*, "abundance of or imbued with." Cortés, in his fifth letter, uses the Nahuatl equivalent, *Mazatlan*, "land of deer." Díaz del Castillo says that in Cehach territory the Spaniards hunted deer with ease because they were so tame they did not run (1908–1916:chap. 178). The guides, on being questioned, said the natives there considered the deer to be gods; their idol had ordered them neither to frighten nor to kill the deer. For that reason they had become so tame. At first sight this seems like some totemic cult, but Cortés, who wrote very shortly after the journey (Díaz del Castillo set down his account in his old age), places the deer hunt after leaving Tayasal; and that may well be true, for the land beyond Tayasal was savanna, whereas that of the Cehach was forest. Nevertheless, a deer totem fits a deer people. Perhaps Díaz's long memory was better than Cortés's short one.

The northern and northeastern boundaries Villa Rojas assigns the Cehach are open to question. He includes within their domains the archaeological sites of Becan and El Hormiguero, which lie north of the proposed Chan territory. Villa Rojas also regards as Cehach the Mocu-Civiltuk-Isla Pac region, presumably because Scholes and Roys speculated that Mazatlán, visited by Dávila on his journey from Acalan to Champoton, might have been in the general region of Lakes Mocu and Civiltuk (1948:128, 467, 469). Scholes and Roys were probably governed by the statement that Mazatlán was 30 leagues from both Itzamkanac and Champoton. However, *every* distance given in Lujan's account of the journey from Chiapas is given as 30 leagues (Oviedo y Valdés 1851–1855: bk. 32, chap. 5); so the term obviously means no more than several days' journey. They may be right, but, as Cehach territory seemingly did not extend north of Tzuctok in the seventeenth century, I am reluctant to suppose on such weak evidence that it embraced Mocu-Civiltuk at an earlier date. Nothing is actually known of the affiliations of the inhabitants of that area.

How far south the Cehach extended is in doubt; I would guess to the Río San Pedro Martir. From the very few names of places, objects, and persons which have survived, there is no doubt that the language was a dialect of Yucatec Maya. Villa Rojas believes the modern Lacandon are descended from the Cehach, who moved south shortly before the Spanish conquest.

The Chinamita
We are dependent upon Fr. Bartolomé Fuensalida (in López [de] Cogolludo 1867–1868:bk. 9, chaps. 8, 14; Villagutierre Soto-Mayor 1933:bk. 8, chap. 11; bk. 9, chap. 3) for the scant data available on the Chinamita. They were deadly enemies of the Itza rulers, being continually at war with them. Each side ate its captured enemies, and the Itza rulers went so far as to refer to the Chinamita as *ma uinicob*, not men, that is, as in-

human. Their chief town, Tulunqui (Tulumci) was said to have had more than eight thousand inhabitants, including, it was reputed, some Spanish men and women captives. The number eight thousand, the third multiple in the Maya vigesimal system, no doubt indicates merely a very large number. Tulumci signifies agave wall (*ci* in Yucatan is the henequen plant), and, in fact, Fuensalida says it was defended by a maguey hedge as well as a moat with a single narrow entrance. *Chinamitl* is a Nahuatl term denoting cane hedge. Villagutierre Soto-Mayor was under the impression that the Chinamita and the Tulunquies were two distinct "nations," but obviously the first is merely a Nahuatl translation of the second.

The Chinamita are said to have been the nearest neighbors of the inhabitants of Tayasal. People of the latter island habitually carried bows and arrows when they passed to the mainland for defense against Chinamita raiders. Fuensalida writes that the Chinamita inhabited the cordillera running east–west south of the Petén. Villagutierre Soto-Mayor, in a later passage (1933:bk. 9, chap. 3), contradicting his earlier acceptance of the Fuensalida location, would place the Chinamita in the same area as the Mopan, nine days' journey east of Tayasal. That is surely incorrect; eastern and southeastern Petén, fully explored by the Spaniards, contained no such group. Moreover, moated and fenced strongholds are typical of western, not eastern, Petén.

I believe we can safely accept Fuensalida's location save that the cordillera is not south of Tayasal, but southwest. In parts rising to 300 meters, it extends from north of Altar de Sacrificios nearly to Tenosique, paralleling the Río Usumacinta. The Río San Pedro Martir perhaps divided the Chinamita from the Cehach, but culturally the two groups were probably quite close; they certainly shared fortified towns. Incidentally, that is about the only location for Tulumci which would account for Spanish captives reported in their midst; it was within raiding distance of such lower Usumacinta towns as Tenosique.

The Chinamita seem to have practiced an unusual form of burial. The roped corpse, with legs bent and face over knees, was placed upright with food offerings in a round hole. At any rate, that rite was attributed to "a nation of highlanders [*serranos*] whom they call the people up above" and who lived somewhere east of El Próspero (López [de] Cogolludo 1867–1868:bk. 12, chap. 7). The term *nación de serranos* suggests they are the Chinamita, inhabitants of the cordillera, as described by Fuensalida. That is the only sierra north of the Río Usumacinta.

The Chinamita almost surely spoke a Yucatec dialect. Avendaño y Loyola, in a single reference, gives the impression he thought the "Tuluncies" were part of the Petén Maya or even Itza (1696:42v). Fr. Simon Villasis, missionary in the El Próspero in 1646, says they spoke Yucatec (López [de] Cogolludo 1867–1868:bk. 12, chap. 7).

The Lacandon

Lacandon, as used here, covers those of Yucatec speech, for we can reasonably assume that mention of the Lacandon by other Chan Maya groups does not refer to those of Chol speech in distant Acalan-Dolores-Miramar. In fact, the word *Lacandon* was probably put in the mouths of Itza informants by their Spanish interrogators. Quite likely they learned the term from the Spaniards and with similar ill definition.

Until about 1880, when mahogany cutters moved into the area and the Lacandon retired deeper into the forest—particularly that lying south of the river—to avoid them, the Lacandon were fairly numerous along both banks of the river. In addition to the move into deeper parts of Chiapas, many Lacandon died from smallpox and respiratory diseases (Sapper 1891). Now no Lacandon lives close to the great river.

From nineteenth-century accounts one can get an incomplete idea of the distribution of Lacandon settlements along the Usumacinta and Pasión rivers in that century. Unfortunately, I have not had access to the report describing the visit of Benito Gálvez to the Lacandon of the Petén in 1835 and the treaty of May 21, 1837 with Mencha (Menche?), "chief of the principal Lacandon tribe."

The data which follow refer to the Lacandon living along the Usumacinta and Pasión rivers, with special reference to those on the north banks and inland from there. They are arranged from southeast to northwest.

The southeasternmost Lacandon group appears to have been at Petexbatum, 6 miles south of Sayaxche on the Pasión. It was at one time a missionary center of the Capuchin friars, who were active in the Petén in the middle of the nineteenth century. A very short biography in Yucatec Maya of a Lacandon, José Sabino Ul Ahna Couoh Uc, dated 1871, states that "he was born *tetuhi* (tela?, there) the great river or lake Akul, in the land of Petén, as it is called" (Berendt 1868a:I). The year was 1856. When the priest Don Pedro came with the other Capuchins to Petén, his father and brothers were baptized (Berendt 1868:I). The settlement San Juan Acul on the Pasión just below Paso Real may well be the same place. *Akul* (with *a-ü* shift) may be *Akal*, "swamp."

A few miles farther downstream and on the north bank is Lake Izan, a Lacandon settlement which Sapper (1891) visited and briefly described. Yet a few more miles is a little logging camp settlement called Caribe, on the south bank. Caribe is the common Petén name for Lacandon. This site must commemorate an earlier Lacandon settlement.

Valenzuela, writing in 1879, reported the first Lacandon settlement 4–5 leagues below the mouth of the Lacantun (1951:406), about where Maudslay reported them three years later (1889–1902:pt. 3, 40). Valenzuela writes that they had moved there from the Lacantun because of logging operations along that river—a doubtful statement, for that would have been a case of out of the frying pan into the fire.

At Lake Bolonchac, about 8 miles east, northeast of Filadelfia, Maler reported a Lacandon group and vestiges of earlier settlements (1903: 201). Maudslay reported a Lacandon settlement on the Yalchilan River, east of Yaxchilan (1889–1902:pt. 3, 42), and Charnay writes of passing through huts and milpas of the Lacandon on the day he reached Chotal en route from Tenosique to Yaxchilan (1887:428). Such abandoned settlements would have lain about 8 miles north of the Usumacinta. The great ceremonial importance of Yaxchilan to the Lacandon south of the Usumacinta is good evidence that those groups once lived in the vicinity of that archaeological site.

Those ruins, most unwarrantably called Yaxchilan by Maler, were named Menche by their discoverer, Edwin Rochstroh, in memory of Bol Menche, ancestor of the Lacandon living in the vicinity (J. E. S. Thompson 1946:72–73). As we have seen, Menche (written *Mencha*) was the leader of the principal Lacandon tribe with whom a treaty was signed in 1837. It would appear that the chief concentration of Lacandon in the early nineteenth century was in the vicinity of Yaxchilan.[1]

Near Piedras Negras is the only Lacandon group still living north of the Usumacinta (Bruce S. 1968:13). It appears to have connections with the Lacandon of Lake Petha for, as Bruce observes, the two groups have the *maax*, "spider monkey" "totem" in common. In the 1930's there were Lacandon at Lake Texcoco, about 12 kilometers southeast of Piedras Negras and north of the Usumacinta (personal communication from L. Satterthwaite). There is dubious evidence that the Lacandon may have been long in the region of Piedras Negras. Excavation of Structure J-2 at that site uncovered five typical Lacandon incense burners. Two had been crushed by falling vault stones. They had stood on a stone slab which in turn rested on about 20 centimeters of debris. The remaining three were intact because they had been covered by a soft limy stratum that had washed down from the higher debris in front, accumulated after partial collapse of the building but before the vault collapse found by the university museum expedition in the early 1930's (Satterthwaite 1935:10; Butler 1935:pl. 6, no. 17). Other *incensarios* of the same type were found in Structure J-4. All one can say is that the *incensarios* in Structure J-2 may have been deposited quite some time ago.

Over seventy years ago Maler reported an abandoned Lacandon settlement on the south bank between El Cayo and La Mar (1903:90, 88), about 8 miles southwest of Piegras Negras and some considerable distance nearer the Usumacinta than Petha, now the nearest Lacandon settlement. He also found Lacandon incense burners in the ruins of El Cayo. These vestiges would tend to confirm Bruce's evidence for a connection between the present-day Piedras Negras Lacandon and those of Petha and, since the Lacandon movement seems to have been generally southward, perhaps indicate that the ancestor of the Petha Lacandon formerly lived along the Usumacinta.

We have indirect evidence for former Lacandon occupation upstream from Tenosique, which, having been a Putun settlement (Scholes and Roys 1948:24–27), presumably delimits the northwestern extension of the Lacandon. Tozzer states that the Lacandon god Yant'o had his home in a high cliff near Tenosique, which, as he writes, is undoubtedly in the gorge a few miles above that town (1907:94). One does not locate the terrestrial homes of gods outside one's territory; thus we may assume that the Lacandon once reached almost to Tenosique. Seler notes the presence of a Lacandon variant-type incense burner (the attached head is vertical) in the Copenhagen museum from an unknown locality in Tabasco (1904:83), presumably in the small wedge of the state east of Tenosique.

The above review would indicate a former Lacandon occupation of the Usumacinta-Pasión valley with definite evidence for north-bank settlements from Sayaxche, 35 miles southwest of Tayasal, almost to Tenosique. It is interesting that this area corresponds quite closely with that assigned by Stoll to the north-bank occupation of the Lacandon (1884, map 2). Stoll almost certainly depended for that datum on his old friend Edwin Rochstroh, who had been working along the Pasión and Usumacinta rivers immediately prior to Stoll's publication, and who almost certainly knew more about the Lacandon than anyone then living.

Previously, like others, I had entertained the view that the ancestors of the Yucatec-speaking Lacandon had entered the Usumacinta valley in post-Columbian times, in response to pressure from the southward exodus from Yucatán reacting to Spanish repression. I no longer accept that explanation. There are elements in their culture alien to the northern half of the peninsula, to wit:

Speech • Substitution of *ü* for *a* and a tendency to shift from *l* to *r*. As in other Chan dialects often a final *h* is absent in true Yucatec (e.g., *uh, kuh, beh, nah*), and final *b* is not sounded as a rule.

Vocabulary • Glottochronology produces a 600-year separation of Lacandon speech from Yucatec of Yucatán, with an inferred language divergence of 20 percent. This is greater than the probable divergence of Lake Petén Maya from Yucatec of Yucatán. Although glottochronology must be treated with considerable caution, the above findings suggest that Lacandon speech was separated longer from Yucatec of Yucatán than was Lake Petén Maya, and that, in turn, would indicate that the geographical relationship of the two southern groups has not changed markedly since pre-Columbian times.

Relationship names • The modern Lacandon call the first-born son and daughter *kin* and *na kin*; the second-born, *kayum* and *na kayum*; the third-born, *chankin* and *na chankin*. Nothing similar is known in the north of the peninsula.

The animal *onen* of the Lacandon has no parallels in the peninsula.

Were one to suppose some former relationship between the *onen* and Yucatec patronymics, it should be remembered that the former is confined to fauna; the latter includes fauna, flora, household utensils, and other minor groupings.

Religion • The Lacandon divine organization differs fundamentally from that of Yucatán.

Mythology • One important incident in Nuxi's descent to the underworld—his becoming a hummingbird, being taken to bed by his lover (Bruce S., Robles, and Ramos 1971:23), and resuming his human shape to make love to her—is taken from the sun and moon creation legend of the Mopan, Kekchi, and Cakchiquel and, in all probability, originated among the Manche Chol (J. E. S. Thompson 1970:363–366, 372). One may guess that the incident was borrowed by the Yucatec Lacandon, perhaps via the Chol Lacandon, centuries ago; only some 90 kilometers lay between western Manche and the eastern limits of Yucatec Lacandon of the late nineteenth century, all seemingly once held by Chol speakers. The incident is unreported from the north of the peninsula.

Present-day Lacandon of the Petha region have Cizin, their underworld and death god, inflict horrible tortures on the souls of the wicked. I suspect such ideas derive from Christian contacts. Indeed, the Petha Lacandon pop in and out of Las Casas. Could there be an illustrated copy of Dante's *Inferno* in the Fray Bartolomé library? If those tortures of the damned should represent an indigenous concept, it is another feature separating the modern Lacandon from the northern Yucatec, where no such ideas existed.

The Lacandon poncho, or smock • Tozzer gives for this the term *xicul* (1907:29), of Nahuatl derivation; Soustelle has *nok* (1937:58), but that is a general word for clothing; Cline has *coton* for the garment (1944:109–110). The Mopan of Belize use *coton* for the European-type shirt they wear with tails outside trousers. *Coton* is also a Spanish term for printed cotton, but I think it is a recent borrowing from English, coming with cotton goods imported from Victorian Lancashire. Modern Lacandon, until recently, wore smocks of woven cotton or, more rarely, of bark cloth. The Chol Lacandon seemingly used bark-cloth smocks but perhaps only in ritualistic settings. A boy captured near Coban in 1678 by Chol Lacandon had been dressed by his captors in a dalmatic (*vestidura dalmatica*) of bark cloth with painting on it and had been tied to a stake, both acts seemingly preliminaries to being sacrificed (Ximénez 1929–1971:bk. 4, chap. 70). The Cehach appear also to have used a ritual smock, but they used the work *kub*, which in Yucatán named a woman's *huipil* (Scholes and Roys 1948:344). The sharing of the term *coton*—for a long-tailed shirt may be deemed a sort of smock—by Mopan and Lacandon suggests the two groups were not too distant one from another. One may note that, in their ceremonies, Manche Chol priests wore bark-cloth garments with much painted design. The Spanish term *vestidura* often signifies a religious robe.

Hammock • The Lacandon hammock with its parallel knotted cords is completely different from the net type of most of the Yucatán Peninsula; it is of South American, not Yucatán, style. There is no information on hammock types among the extinct Manche and Lacandon Chol (the Lake Petén Maya and Mopan use the net type). Unless this is a Lacandon invention, it argues against northern origins.

Couoh • This name for one of the Lacandon "moieties" is a common Maya patronymic with greatest density in the south and southwest of the peninsula. The Couoh occupied territory between Lake Petén and the sierra to the west. They ruled Champoton at the Spanish conquest; a Couoh was chief of a village west of Isla Pac (Scholes and Roys 1948:505). The prominence of that name among the Lacandon gives slight support to their being indigenous to the region.

The above arguments of varying weight sustain the view that the modern Lacandon have lived north of the middle Usumacinta for many centuries and, therefore, must have had contact with the Chol Lacandon south of the river.

At this point we should perhaps consider the Yucatec-speaking settlement of Nohha, visited by Franciscans 1646–1648 (López [de] Cogolludo 1867–1868:bk. 12, chap. 3–7). This recently formed town in all probability lay south of the Usumacinta, perhaps not far from present-day Petha; but it conceivably was situated north of the river in the region of Piedras Negras. Features of Nohha culture argue against their being apostate refugees from the north, although the two or three known surnames are also Yucatec. Their painted (tattooed?) naked bodies, their long hair decorated with feathers, their ear and nose ornaments, their lack of hens and pigs, the non-Yucatec titles of their priests, and their women's enormous hair arrangements, tied with twisted cotton, do not accord with a settlement of rounded-up apostates. They were probably an indigenous group of south Chan Maya culture.

Surely we must see those southern Chan Maya—Nohha, Chinamita, Lake Petén Maya, and other long-lost groups—not as distinct cultural entities but in terms of the spectrum, with similarities far outweighing minor differences. Such local divergencies among the southwestern and northeasten Lacandon have been given too much weight by modern writers. They are such as one finds in almost any long-established group without control authority and good communications. Such differences are seemingly greater among the Palencano Chol, who occupy far less territory than do or did the Lacandon.

It would appear most logical to see the modern Lacandon as descendants of the Chinamita, perhaps mixed with other small groups in the
upper Usumacinta basin. The distance from the cordillera, almost certainly home of the Chinamita, to Yaxchilan is under 15 kilometers. Indeed,
Charnay observed abandoned Lacandon huts almost at the foot of the
cordillera (1887:428), and Stoll includes that ridge in Lacandon territory
(maps in Stoll 1884 and 1958).

Disease and Spanish harassment in the eighteenth century doubtlessly
caused the loss of many elements in the old culture (e.g., human sacrifice,
belligerency, and a stratified political organization). That is the fate of
refugees the world over. A glimpse at an earlier stage of disintegration is
afforded us by the willingness of Petén authorities to negotiate a treaty
with the Lacandon chief Menche early in the nineteenth century. He could
hardly have been a *halach uinic*, but he must have been quite a step above
the highest present-day Lacandon "authority," the leader of a single encampment.

Accepting the above, one sees the Lacandon as having moved downward
culturally in the past 275 years, but physically remaining within a good
day's walk of their ancient homeland.

Population

Early accounts make patent that parts of the Chan region were heavily
populated in the seventeenth century. Villagutierre Soto-Mayor gives the
impression that the area circumscribing Lake Petén was then densely
populated. Along the western route of the conquerors of Tayasal, population seems to have been far less, but absence of sizable villages may have
distorted the picture. Spanish chroniclers would not know of the perhaps
numerous four- or five-house hamlets, because logistically they were near
valueless. Yet, scattered hamlets were the pattern of settlement in much of
the Petén.

Reports vary with their purposes. Fray Joseph Delgado's account of the
many small settlements he visited or heard of along the Moho River of
Belize, indicative of an almost dense population, was detailed because it
was a survey of souls to be harvested (Ximénez 1929–1971:bk. 5, chap. 33).
Army reports may give quite different impressions; small settlements do
not feed an army nor give lodgment and so may be ignored. Cortés, crossing the same corner of Belize, leaves us with the impression it was almost
uninhabited; he lacked guides. I am persuaded that had Delgado or Francisco Morán followed that eastern route opened to Tayasal seeking souls
to save, their reports would have indicated a far higher population than do
those of the amateur soldiers who led the invasion of Tayasal.

In the eighteenth and nineteenth centuries a very sharp drop in population occurred in the Chan area, presumably because of the ravages of introduced diseases, such as hookworm, malaria, and smallpox. Disease on a large scale decimated the Spanish force in Tayasal almost as soon as the conquest was completed. That near extermination of indigenous population impeded ethnological investigation, for cultures disintegrate when their bearers are almost wiped out.

Another factor affecting our study is population movement. As already noted, there was a large immigration from Yucatán and Campeche into the Petén and Belize in the second half of the nineteenth century consequent on the Caste War. This was by no means confined to the northern Petén. In the south the Kekchi Maya expanded northward from Cajabon and other parts of the Alta Verapaz into southeastern Petén and southern Belize. Kekchi settlers in the Mopan villages of San Luis, Petén, and San Antonio, Belize, appear to have modified facets of Mopan culture, particularly the religion. We have reasons to believe that the Kekchi-speaking Cajaboneros are in fact originally of Manche Chol blood and culture; so here we have a strange situation of Manche Chol, bereft of their language and, to a large extent, of their old culture, returning to their homeland. Such movements of population do not exalt every valley or lay low every mountain and hill for the modern investigator.

Speech

That our Chan region spoke Yucatec or a dialect thereof is certain. We shall attempt to show that, in much of the region, differences in pronunciation and vocabulary justify constituting this tongue as a dialect or subdivision of the Yucatec of Yucatán. As one might expect, the transition is gentle; the exiguous evidence indicates that the speech of the northern frontier was the Yucatec of Yucatán, but, farther south, differences are apparent.

We will start with the southern half of the region. First, it is necessary to establish that, linguistic maps to the contrary, Lake Petén Maya and Mopan spoke the same dialect.

The Mopan guide of the force under the ill-fated Díaz de Velasco, which attempted to reach Tayasal in 1695 from the southeast, declared under official interrogation, "Que ellos [los mopanes] y los Ahitzaes tienen una misma lengua, pero que [los Ahitzaes] son distinta nación que los mopanes y que todos los indios de la costa son mopanes . . . que los del Tipu son Ahitzaes." He added that the Ahitzaes fought against the Lacandon and Mopan (Ximénez 1929–1971:bk. 5, chap. 65).

Fr. Agustín Cano, O.P., who had extensive first-hand knowledge of southeastern Petén, wrote, "la lengua del Ahitzá . . . es la misma de los mopanes y muy distinta de la lengua chol" (ibid.:bk. 5, chap. 71). It is true that in another passage in which he repeats the above statement, he adds that the Mopan were subject to a *cacique* of (Lake) Petén: "y asi quien vió Mopanes, vió Ahitzaes, porque Mopán es nombre de lugar o territorio que pertenece a el Ahitzá" (ibid.:bk. 5, chap. 68). He is definitely in error in stating that the Mopan were subject to Tayasal, but he surely hits the nail on the head when he maintains that *Mopan* was a territorial, not a linguistic, term in Maya mouths. The Maya clearly did not distinguish between the speech of Lake Petén, of the town of Mopan, and that of such coastal settlements as Sittee and Xibun. He also writes of Mopan as a mixture of Chol and Yucatec (ibid.:bk. 5, chap. 58), which is incorrect but nevertheless suggestive. Chol and Mopan understood each other to a small extent.

In 1866, when Maya was still widely spoken in the Petén, the linguist Carl Herman Berendt made a short vocabulary and phrase list of "*el dialecto del Petén*" (1868:I), published with many misreadings, mistranslations, and omissions in Means (1917:188–191). Among the villages south and east of Lake Petén he enumerates as speaking that dialect (also Santo Toribio, Yaxche, Dolores, Poctun, Petenzuc, and Machaquila, ibid.: 188) is San Luis, the principal Mopan-speaking town. Berendt, therefore, confirms the earlier statements of the friars that Mopan and the language of Lake Petén were one and the same. He is careful to distinguish the villages speaking the Petén dialect from those in which the Yucatec of Yucatán was used (all seemingly founded as a result of immigration from the horrors of the Caste War).

In the southern half of the Peten the *a* of Yucatán shifts to a sound close to our *u* in *urgent* or *further*. This sound occurs in Lake Petén speech (Schumann 1971*a*), in Berendt's dialect of the Petén, in Mopan (J. E. S. Thompson 1930:204; Schumann 1971*b*), and among some Yucatec-speaking Lacandon, notably those of Naha, Chiapas (Bruce S. 1968), of the Petha group. The Naha Maya appear to belong with the Lacandon group still north of the Usumacinta.

The same sound as a replacement (not invariable) for Yucatec *a* is extensive in Palencano Chol (Aulie and Aulie 1951), less extensive in the Yucatán dialect of Putun, but absent in Manche Chol and Tzeltal. In the Putun dialect of Tamulte (Hasler, n.d.) Yucatec *a* shifts to a sound which Hasler writes *i* with umlaut in a fair number of cases; in Tzotzil the shift from *a* to *o* is common.

Only a scattering of Cehach words in personal and place names and a few objects survive. Several place names are pure Yucatán Yucatec (e.g., Chunpich). However, Avendaño y Loyola speaks of crossing a little stream called Chinchinukum and 2 leagues on a large one named Nohukum (1696:23v). *Ukum* is "river" and *noh* is "big," but a Yucatec term for "little" is *chanchan*, not *chinchin*. Avendaño y Loyola also writes of Lake Yavilain, which surely corresponds to Yucatec Yabalain, "many crocodiles." Those two words supply evidence that the Cehach, like the Putun of Tamulte, at times employed the *a*-to-*i* shift.

There is no evidence that Chan of the northern frontier or in northern Belize differed from Yucatán in pronunciation of the *a*.

Vocabulary

The lengthiest vocabulary of the Petén dialect, under the name Maya Itza, was compiled by Schumann at San José, Petén (1971*a*). He notes that the speech of San Andrés is adulterated with Yucatec brought by immigrants fleeing the Caste War. However, he groups Socotz, Belize, with San José as speaking Itza, perhaps misled by statements of various persons, myself included, that Socotz was populated by migrants from the vicinity of Lake Petén. In fact, the Maya of Socotz is primarily Yucatec and the influence of the Petén dialect is at best very weak. The *u* sound, present in Schumann's San José vocabulary, is absent in Socotz and nearby Benque Viejo.

Among terms in Schumann's vocabulary which are not reported from Yucatán itself are a handful that I had recorded at the Mopan-speaking village of San Antonio in southern Belize. There would doubtless be many more had I made a vocabulary of San Antonio speech. This again is evidence supporting the identity of the Lake Petén and Mopan dialects, for which I suggest the term *Chan dialect*.

Of the just under 1,000 terms in Schumann's San José vocabulary, I found 124 either not recorded in Yucatec vocabularies or used in different senses or different constructions. A few represented flora or fauna absent or very rare in Yucatán. The shorter Berendt vocabulary has a few words not in the Schumann vocabulary, which are likewise unreported from Yucatán. One supposes there is no standard measure for what constitutes a dialect, but the difference noted is perhaps sizable enough to justify us in constituting Petén Maya and Mopan as a definite subdivision of Yucatec and naming it Chan.

There are few swallows indicative of a linguistic summer for the Cehach. A few place names and other terms come from the quills of Avendaño y Loyola, Villagutierre Soto-Mayor, and Cortés—nothing else.

Among Cehach terms also current in Yucatán are *alkalche, batcab, chac ekel, Chunpich, Chuntuki*[*l*], *Ixban, Kamaz, Pan* and *punab*. Cehach or Petén dialect words include *zib* (Avendaño y Loyola also gives *cib*, presumably missing a cedilla [1696]), a broad sharp-edged aquatic sedge or grass, as well as *zibal*, "a swampy area filled with such grass." The term was probably current in the Petén dialect, for the Urrutía map marks a settlement Sibal, south of Lake Yaloch in eastern Petén (1923). Villagutierre Soto-Mayor names as *moces* the troublesome (botlas?) flies which bothered the friars by day (1933:bk. 5, chap. 8). *Moc* or *moz* seems to be unknown in Yucatán. *Hulbalex* is noted by Avendaño y Loyola (1696) as a local term for swamps (in places, a terminal *s* is written *x*). Maler defines *hulek* as a calm sheet of water, applied to "mountain" (mistranslation of *montaña*, "forest") lakes in the Petén (1908:126) . *Ek* is a term for lake or pond and appears in the compound *kaxek*. The Urrutía map marks a little settlement, Hulec, beside Lake Machanche immediately east of Lake Petén. Morelet mentions another Hulek as a *ranchería* between Juntecholol and Santo Toribio (1871), southeast of Lake Petén and again in the area of Berendt's dialect of the Petén. The Urrutía map has yet another Hulec. This lies between Lake Petén and Paso Caballos on the upper San Pedro Martir and very probably is situated in what was once the southern limits of Cehach territory. Accordingly, *hul* would seem to be a term applied in both Cehach and the Petén dialect to denote areas of calm water. Schumann gives the meaning *abismo* to *hulek* (1971a), perhaps a misunderstanding of his informant.

Em, as a noun for "descent" (Avendaño y Loyola has *noh em*, "great ravine" [1696]) is a Cehach term. In Yucatán tradition the great descent or invasion was *noh emel*; *emel* is "descend," and *eemec* refers to something on a slope. The Cehach term is clearly a dialectal variation.

Ch'uy, "something hanging from on high" in Yucatec, was the term Avendaño y Loyola's Cehach informants gave him for the well-known *bromelia*, growing usually where branch meets tree trunk, and which stores water where its fleshy leaves join the plant's stalk. On balance, the informants would seem to have been naming the plant, not merely something pendent from on high, for the plant does not normally hang down; in that position it would retain no water.

Again, according to Avendaño y Loyola, *tocolche* was land covered with a confused mass of all sorts of weeds and thorny plants "so that I do not know how we brought our clothes and legs out from their midst" (1696). This description surely applies to abandoned milpa or unintentionally burned forest in the first stages of reverting to forest. Indeed, *tocolche* means forest razed by tools or fire (Motul dictionary S.V. *toc* and *tooc* [Martínez Hernández 1929]).

The above words in Cehach dialect are pitifully few; yet they must form not less than 15 to 20 percent of all linguistic survivals in what was once Cehach territory, the remainder being terms shared with Yucatec proper. As was to be expected, there is a scrap of evidence that the Cehach and Petén dialects were close.

As to Lacandon, Swadesh claimed that in his glottochronology system the separation of Lacandon from Yucatec proper dated back six centuries (1961:235), which, as his assumed rate of divergence would indicate, is a 20 percent difference in his word list. One must, however, bear in mind that his lists were of basic words, whereas our Petén and Cehach differences from Yucatec proper cover less-common terms including those of plants and animals which in part reflect environmental differences. Moreover, Lacandon twentieth century words were compared with those of seventeenth-century Yucatán. We find, accordingly, greater divergences from

Yucatec in the case of Lacandon than in the cases of Petén and Cehach dialects. That was to be expected since geographically Lacandon was farther removed than the other two from Yucatán.

As noted, the vocabulary of the present-day Maya of the Cayo district of Belize appears to vary very little, indeed, from that of Yucatán. Whether that is due to the influx of recent immigrants from the north is not clear. Unfortunately, almost no words have survived from the seventeenth-century speech of the country. A final *b* often becomes a *p* (e.g., *hatzcap*, "very early morning").

Berendt gives a *doctrina* owned by a priest, Ignacio Verzunza (1868:I, no. 10), said to be written in the dialect of the Petén forest (*montaña del Petén*). In the introduction to his manuscript of the Petén dialect, Berendt remarks that the dialect of the east is spoken in the Partido de la Montaña or of Holmul. Accordingly, this *doctrina* must be from northeastern Petén. It does not seem to differ from Yucatec Maya and may be referable to recent immigrants into the area from the north or possibly earlier settlers of the northern frontier of Chan territory.

On the matter of grammatical differences between Chan and true Yucatec I am totally unqualified to write.

Names of Individuals

In the territory controlled by the Itza group around Lake Petén and eastward therefrom, two features in the naming of individuals are patent: many persons have double names, but the prefix *na*, "mother," commonly prefixed in Yucatec to this first name to indicate it derives from the mother, is not found among the Lake Petén Maya. Furthermore, many of the names are unreported from Yucatán. It is noteworthy that, of twenty-five names of *caciques* of Lake Petén listed by Avendaño y Loyola (1696), thirteen are not Yucatec. Yet one would expect names in that group to have been predominantly the same as those current in Yucatán, in view of the fact that the ruling family asserted that its forebears came from Yucatán and even claimed lands its ancestors had once held there (Avendaño y Loyola 1696:34ᵛ).

The Couoh of Chakan Itza, immediately west of Lake Petén, seemingly were under the dominion of Can Ek and the Itza rulers of Tayasal but showed considerable hostility to Can Ek. One has the impression that they were an aboriginal group conquered by the immigrant Itza rulers. They take their name from their chief. Couoh is found as a surname in Yucatán and, Roys notes, is the term for a black poisonous spider (1940:42). It is also a Lacandon name and occurs as that of a *cacique*, seemingly known as Napol Couoh, of a village west of Isla Pac (Scholes and Roys 1948:505). As this chief lacks a baptismal name, one assumes he was not a refugee from Yucatán or Campeche. On balance, it would appear that Couoh was a Chan name which may have been introduced to Yucatán by immigrants from Chan territory. Appellations of the chiefs under Couoh are supplied, doubtlessly with misspellings, by Villagutierre Soto-Mayor (1933:bk. 9, chap. 3). There appear to be fourteen of these appellatives (six of eight chiefs seemingly had double-barreled names). Three of them are shared with Yucatán; one (Kua) is probably the same as Putun Cua; the remainder seem indigenous to the Petén. In Chan names we find no evidence of a shift from Yucatec *a* to *u* or *i*.

Clearly, Lake Petén names for the most part were not those of Yucatán. Many are double, but the matronymic *na* prefix of pre-Columbian Yucatán is absent.

Hardly a handful of Mopan surnames are known from the contact period, and spelling of those varies from one source to another (Cano 1942; Ximénez 1929–1971:bk. 5, chap. 58). They are Taxim Chan, Tezecum, Zuzben or Zulben, Tzac or Zac, Yaxcab or Yalbac, Zibac, and Tzuc. The *cacique* of San Luis, almost surely the former Mopan, was in 1754 a certain Francisco Sunkal; his predecessor was Martin Chan. Joseph Delgado, in describing the journey from Campin northeastward across what is now central Belize, mentions two other *caciques* of what were almost certainly Mopan-speaking settlements (J. E. S. Thompson [1974]). They were Chan and Ziken. The appellation Tesecum is still found at the Mopan village of San Antonio in southern Belize. Possibly the Lake Petén chief Tesucan is the name, misspelled by Villagutierre Soto-Mayor (1933:bk. 9, chap. 3). Unhappily, many Kekchi-speaking Maya have settled in San Antonio, and it is impossible to tell which surnames are Kekchi and which Mopan. Moreover, as many of those immigrants came from Cajabon, the situation is further confused, for the Cajaboneros, now Kekchi speaking, are believed to be largely of Manche Chol descent, settling there in the seventeenth century to secure themselves to mother church and their new fatherland.

Far and away the most interesting aspect of Chan appelatives was the use of Maya day names among a group of pagan Maya, labeled *indios del monte*, apparently from immediately south of the middle Belize River, brought to Chunukum in a roundup of Maya in 1655, and who are possibly to be identified with the Muzul (Scholes and Thompson, this volume). As the term Mopan was applied to the Maya of central Belize north of Campin, it is reasonable to accept these as Mopan. The statement that Tipu was Yucatec Maya (the flood of immigrants from the north had drastically altered its original composition), made by Joseph Delgado (Ximénez 1929–1971:bk. 5, chap. 33), implies that the other groups north of the Campin were recognized as non-Yucatec.

With the one probable exception of IxTinal (Ix could be the day name; IxIxTinal would sound strange), all the *indios del monte* have double names. As among the Lake Petén Maya, the matronymic *na* prefix is absent.

The full *matrícula* of Tipu and other settlements of the Belize valley is in the Scholes and Thompson article in this volume. Suffice it to say that surnames, other than day names, not reported from Yucatán form slightly over 16 percent of the total. However, Chan, found also in Yucatán but quite probably of Petén origin, is the commonest surname in the *matrícula* (nearly 8 percent). In a count of totals of surnames, it would sensibly increase the non-Yucatán percentage.

The vast majority of Yucatán appellatives along the upper Belize doubtlessly reflects the constant increment by Yucatec Maya fleeing the exactions of "many a knight from tawny Spain." Excepting again the forest Indians, no name is double-barreled; all are preceded by a baptismal name, which undoubtedly replaced a matronymic.

Information in early sources on names of the northern frontier amounts to a case of "plenty of nothing." Icaiche appellatives of the nineteenth century are overwhelmingly Yucatec. They include Chan. In all cases a baptismal name has replaced a matronymic.

Knowledge of Cehach names is of shrunken bikini size. The large settlement of Pachechem was inhabited by Chanes, regarded as a subdivision of the Cehach (Villagutierre Soto-Mayor 1933:bk. 5, chap. 9; bk. 7, chap. 8). The title Chanes may merely indicate that the local *cacique* was called Chan.

In 1604 two of the rulers of Chunpich, perhaps the northernmost Cehach town, were Aca and Namay Keb; and of the Cehach settlement of Petox, Cholo, Chac, Zel or Tzel, and Nabon Cacaalezuc (Scholes and Roys 1948:506–507). These are a mixture of Yucatán and Petén names. Nakeb and Nabon incorporate the matronymic *na*, common in pre-Columbian Yucatán but seemingly absent in other parts of the Petén. *Keb* is shared with Yucatán; *bon* is not. Nabon Cacaalezuc suggests a triple name.

Nomenclature of the present-day Lacandon is *sui generis* (Tozzer 1907: 40–43; Soustelle 1935; Bruce S. 1968:13–18). A survey of the systems would not be of value here except for the facts that *na* is not used as a matronymic prefix but in a quite different way and that we have no evidence of matronymics among those scattered groups, features which would argue against a Cehach ancestry.

Our brief survey exposes a lack of cohesion in personal-name systems among the Chan group but identifies features markedly different from the system in use in sixteenth century Yucatán.

Titles of Rank

Twelve of the Lake Petén chiefs listed by Avendaño y Loyola (1696:38[r], [v]) carry the title *ach cat*; three are designated *dz'o can* or *noh*, "great," *dz'o can*. Neither title to the best of my knowledge has been reported from Yucatán. However, the Motul dictionary (1929) gives *ch'ele kat* as a designation for a great chief or high priest, and *can* enters into the Yucatec name accorded the high priest, *ahau can (mai* coupled with this was probably the name of an individual holding that position).

Chomach was another term of respect applied to priests. Chomach Zulu was priest of Yalain, and Chomach Punab of a nearby town, both in the Lake Petén area. Avendaño y Loyola, who was, of course, a priest, tells that the Maya of Tayasal named him *Chomach Ahau*, for which he offered the translation "Great Lord [*ahau*] worthy of reverence" (1696:39ʳ, 49ᵛ, 51ʳ). Schumann has the entry *chümach*, "old man" (1971a), the *ü* element indicating a shift from Yucatec *a*. Villagutierre Soto-Mayor paraphrases Avendaño y Loyola but, apparently using a different version from that in the Newberry Library, writes the term as *chamax* (1933:bk. 7, chap. 2). Neither *chamach* nor *chomach* occurs as a Yucatec title.

This is one of two surviving examples of the well-known title of respect *ahau*. This precedes the individual's name in Yucatán but follows it in Putun and Manche Chol, and here follows the *chomach*; but the second example, *ahau can ek*, is the reverse (Ximénez 1929–1971:bk. 5, chap. 65).

Ah kin, "priest," seems to have been current all over the peninsula. *Batab*, "town chief" in Yucatán, with a meaning something like wielder of the axe, was the title of one of the rulers of the Cehach settlement of Petox. The title was presumably current in other parts of the Petén. Unfortunately, Avendaño y Loyola and other early writers use the term *cacique*. El Próspero priests were called *ah kulel*, "mediator," and *ah kayon*, "singer"; these are Yucatec terms but with different usage in Yucatán.

The Chan group, on the basis of the above limited data, had some local titles while sharing others with Yucatán.

Religion

Material on religion other than generalities is confined to observations on the Lake Petén Maya and present-day Mopan and Lacandon. Those on the former are summarized below.

Itzam Na Kauil (written Ytzimna Kauil and confused with the horse, *tzimin*, Cortés left at Tayasal) was worshipped by the Petén Maya. That is not surprising, for Itzam Na was the supreme god of the ruling families of most, perhaps all, lowland Maya groups.

Placed in the open at Tayasal was a flaring stone and mortar column resembling a table on a round pedestal. This represented Yaxcheelcab, the ceiba tree of the world. In its base was set the mask of Ah Cocahmut, identified as son of the very wise god. Again, the ceiba was a focal point of worship throughout the Maya lowlands, in Chiapas, and probably in most of highland Guatemala. Cocahmut, on the other hand, is definitely a divine name in Yucatán, seemingly an aspect of Itzam Na.

Apart from those three, our limited coverage of Lake Petén deities informs us only of local deities.

There were four very large idols and a fifth, Pecoc (Pakoc?), who resided in a cave. They had mouths and arms open and spoke to the people (Ximénez 1929–1971:bk. 5, chap. 66). Pakoc (Pecoc?) and Hexchunchan, war gods, were taken into battle. We are told that the god of battle was about 20 centimeters high *(un geme)*, of jade or greenstone *(esmeralda bruta)*, and was kept in the temple of the high priest. Above this was the figure of another god but of stucco with appliqué work and a corona with rays. Both were of mother-of-pearl; teeth in the idol's mouth were those of slain Spaniards. Suspended from the temple ceiling by multicolored cotton ribbons was the shin bone of Cortés's famed steed.

Hobo *(hobon,* a hollow object) was an idol, said to have been of metal, in whose interior victims were burned alive to music amid an encircling congregation of dancers (Villagutierre Soto-Mayor 1933:bk. 8, chaps. 11, 13). There are no parallels in Yucatán sources to this fire cult. In Tenochtitlan victims were thrown into a fire and then dragged out and sacrificed by removal of the heart in an annual ceremony in honor of the fire god, Xiuhtecutli, but that seems to have been quite different from this Lake Petén ceremony. Bolon Hobon was a Yucatec bee god, but in Yucatán *hobon* referred to the hollow-log hives and has no connection with this horrendous fire cult.

Another object of worship of the Lake Petén Maya was a figure of stone and mortar set on top of a small hill. He was known as Kinchilcoba, "who, they say, is their watchman and sentinel who defends them from all misfortunes" (Avendaño y Loyola 1696:29ᵛ). Kinchil Coba survives as the name of a shadowy figure in Yucatán history, but at Lake Petén I suspect that it was a deified anthropomorphic *chachalaca* bird *(Ortalis vetula pallidiventris)*, commonly known in Yucatán as *bach* but having a second and probably ritualistic name of *ah coba. Chachalacas* move in flocks and, on any danger signal, create an ear-splitting din which alerts all animals within half a mile. I suggest that Kinchil, "solar," Coba *(ah* is merely the masculine prefix) was a sentinel which, like Rome's geese, sounded the alert when any strangers approached. Nothing similar in Yucatán has been disclosed.

The strange skull cult at the Lake Petén village of San José (Reina 1962) and its association with new-made *(zuhuy,* "virgin") pottery surely represents a graft on a paganism not nurtured by Yucatán's rocky soil. San José is perhaps the old pagan village of the Tut family which was refounded under the patronage of San José.

Two Dominicans, captured when Díaz's impetuous advance on Lake Petén from Mopan territory ended in the massacre of the whole company of fencibles, were tied in the form of, or to a sort of, wooden(?) cross, in which position their hearts were removed (Villagutierre Soto-Mayor 1933: bk. 8, chap. 10). When Mirones's party was massacred at Sacalum in 1624, over seventy years earlier, Captain Mirones and the Franciscan priest were tied to forked mainposts of the church and their hearts were then removed.

Apparently, the rest of the party, caught unarmed in the church, was sacrificed in the same way. The bodies of the captain and priest were thrown into a hole in the ground; those of the others were impaled on stakes set up at the entrance to the village to greet oncoming Spaniards (López [de] Cogolludo 1867–1868:bk. 10, chap. 3). Sacalum, I have suggested (above), was in the indeterminate zone where the salt and fresh waters of Yucatec and Chan mingled. As the Maya leader Ah Kin P'olom was a pagan priest, tying to a stake before taking out the heart and impaling bodies on other stakes may well be attributable to the Chan rather than to Yucatec refugees there. Tying to a stake for removal of the heart was also the practice at Nohha, El Próspero (ibid.:bk. 12, chap. 7), confirmation of this being a Chan custom.

The natives of Tayasal sacrificed a party of Spaniards in the previous year of 1623. The head of each victim was impaled on a stake, and these were set up on a small hill in view of the town (ibid.:bk. 10, chap. 2).

Removal of the heart of a victim tied to a cross was relatively common in the early colonial period (Scholes and Adams 1938:various passages). In many, perhaps all, cases the rite was definitely associated with the Crucifixion, but that could also have been a mutation of an old pagan rite under Christian influence. No definite evidence exists that the practice was pre-Columbian in Yucatán. Accordingly, stake sacrifice may have been a Chan rite not shared with pre-Columbian Yucatán.

The impaling of heads or bodies on stakes is reminiscent of the Mexican *tzompantli,* or skull rack, for which there is archaeological evidence at Chichen Itza, but that grizzly custom had probably fallen into desuetude by the time the Spaniards reached Yucatán; had it still existed, it could hardly have escaped the notice of the Castillians. It is not clear whether the Itza took the rite to Tayasal when they left Chichen Itza, around A.D. 1200 in my opinion, or whether the Petén ceremony was indigenous. In favor of the second interpretation is the apparent Petén custom of placing head (or body at Sacalum) on an individual stake rather than the hurdle-like *tzompantli* of Chichen Itza. Impaling on individual stakes is unreported from Yucatán.

In connection with disposal of the remains of sacrificial victims, one may note that setting their teeth in the mouth of a stucco idol seemingly was not a custom in Yucatán. Pendergast, Bartley, and Armelagos discuss the recovery of 379 human teeth in accumulated soil at the base of a retaining wall of a platform that was almost surely in use during the proto-historic period at Yakalche in northeastern Belize (1968) and, so, within the Chan area. However, Pendergast informs me that there was no possibility that they were once set in masks.

In summary, Lake Petén religion shared the general Maya lowland pattern but differed from that of Yucatán in important features. As the available information on Petén religion is minute, those differences take on significance.

Present-day Lacandon share many religious ideas with Yucatec Maya, but those are largely those common to most lowland Maya groups. There are others not practiced in both areas, most important being the Chac cult with its associated world directions and colors, so ubiquitous in Yucatán but vestigial or absent among the Lacandon and the Mopan, as well as among other lowland Maya groups south of the Usumacinta valley. Among the Mopan, as well as among the Choloid and Tzeltal-Tzotzil groups, the functions of the Chacs are largely assumed by mountain-valley gods (J. E. S. Thompson 1970:272–276, 314–318). It may therefore be important that no Chac cult is reported from Tayasal, but, again, the reason may be the few data on divine cults from there. We have no information on Cehach religion and nothing specific on practices in the Belize valley.

There are rather firm grounds for positioning Mopan and present-day Lacandon mythology much closer to that of the Maya of Chiapas than to that of the Yucatec Maya. Unfortunately, we have no mythological corpus from the Lake Petén Maya.

As to religious structures, clearly the type of thatched(?) and open-sided temple with its two-tiered bench forming a sort of low enclosing wall (Avendaño y Loyola 1696:30ʳ) has no reported parallel in Yucatán. On the other hand, Bullard, in reviewing late proto-historic architecture at Topoxte, east of Lake Petén, cites for comparison Avendaño y Loyola's description, thus suggesting that this kind of temple occurred elsewhere in the Chan area (1970:266).

The hall attached to the residence of the Tayasal ruler Can Ek, Avendaño y Loyola tells us, was of the same type as the temple but with the added feature of a stone table (*mayactun*) standing in (inside?) the entrance. This was 2 *varas* long and proportionally wide and stood on stone columns. Twelve seats of the same (stone? or stone columns?) around it were for the priests. Avendaño y Loyola says this was a sacrificial table, but the term merely indicates it was a stone table. Nothing corresponding to this feature with its seats has been reported from Yucatán or anywhere else for that matter.

Elsewhere in the Chan region there is only an abbreviated description of a Mopan structure, perhaps a temple. It had been burned, which would indicate it was thatched; but its columns (*pilares*) survived, with the implication that they were of stone. Indeed, *pilar* primarily applies to a stone erection. These columns were worked and turned with such elegance that the observer realized that their makers were of advanced culture (Ximénez 1929–1971:bk. 5, chap. 80).

As adjuncts to religion, the distribution of Lacandon-type *incensarios* (Seler 1904:figs. 13, 14; Tozzer 1907:pls. 15, 17, nos. 2–4, 21, 27) presents us with an enigma. The standard type, still used by the Lacandon of Chiapas and found in ruins and caves of the Usumacinta valley and in northeastern Chiapas, is a bowl of unslipped pottery, standing on a flaring pedestal base. A variant is squat cylindrical, rounding to juncture with a ring base with little to almost no flare. The chief characteristic is a modeled head, identified as portraying a god by modern Lacandon, positioned in relief on the vessel's side so that the top of the head or headdress rises above the rim.

Outside Lacandon territory this distinctive type occurs along a narrow corridor following the boundary between Belize and southernmost Quintana Roo and the continuing frontier between northern Petén and Belize as far south as the vicinity of Benque Viejo and El Cayo, with greatest concentrations at the northern and southern extremes. South of the Benque Viejo area the type has not been reported. All such vessels with data on their finding were on the surface or in caves. Thus, as in the cases from the Usumacinta area, these almost certainly represent a late horizon, in all probability post-Columbian.

Gann illustrates one, a surface find, from "the country of the Icaiche Indians" (1918:fig. 69; 1934:fig. 11). Icaiche is in southeastern Quintana Roo, about 18°05' north and 89°25' west. Two others, one with a beard, from a cave at the head waters of the Río Hondo, which could mean about at the boundary of northeastern Petén and Quintana Roo, are in the National Museum of Natural History, Washington, D.C. (Pls. 1-1, 1-2).

One complete vessel of this type and five heads with parts of the vessel attached were found when making the aviation camp at Dos Lagunas over thirty years ago (Pl. 1-3). This lies about 12 kilometers south of the Campeche-Petén boundary, between two tributaries of Río Azul, a name applied to the upper Río Hondo.

Pieces of another *incensario* lay on the surface and up to 5 centimeters below in front of Stela 3, La Honradez, about 15 kilometers west of the Petén-Belize boundary, near the Río Bravo, another tributary of the Río Hondo. This vessel, now in the Field Museum of Natural History, Chicago, differs from the general run in having wings on each side of the head and a higher than usual conical headdress (Pl. 1-4). This headdress is studded with clay disks, strongly reminiscent of the single line of nodules on Lacandon *incensarios* from the Usumacinta valley (Seler 1904:figs. 13, 14).

From north of the Hondo drainage but within the suggested buffer region between Yucatec and Chan Maya come four other examples. One from close to the large Petén-style site of Tzibanche, Quintana Roo, lay uncovered on a small mound. The nearly straight sides flare slightly with a barely perceptible entasis with a consequently gentle join to the low pedestal base (Gann 1927:88, opp. 56). No doubt this is a mere variant with slight deviation, perhaps the work of an unskilled potter from the type under discussion.

The second vessel, from the outskirts of Ciudad Chetumal (Noguera 1940:pl. 15; Escalona Ramos 1946:pl. 6) appears to be of standard type except that the pedestal base is higher than usual and a global attachment represents the navel. Noguera described it as "un alto brasero con figuras humanas y de animal adheridas al cuello" (1940:13). Escalona Ramos, the excavator, states that the finds remained in Chetumal; so Noguera's description was founded on the poor photograph or a misunderstanding of what was told him. The vessel has no *cuello,* and the head rising above the rim and the small clay globe at the navel appear to be the only attachments. A necklace of stone beads and what seem to be worked shell is draped over the vessel, obscuring detail. A dim shadow at the back of the photograph conceivably represents another head, but the shape looks wrong for that. Also, an *incensario* with a second head in the rear is unknown. Cuidad Chetumal lies 50 kilometers east-southeast of Tzibanche.

Ian Graham saw five Lacandon-type *incensarios* in the home of Señor A. Boettiger, chief of the Policía Federal de Caminos in Quintana Roo. Four are said to have come from the vicinity of Bacalar; a fifth from Laguna Soh. Three are very similar, having a "tusk" projecting upward from each corner of the mouth and a protruding lower lip (or tongue?) reaching the chin. They also have lateral flanges incorporating ear-buttons (pl. 1-5). The long protruding lower lip is a diagnostic of Maya merchant gods (J. E. S. Thompson 1966:166–168) and reminds us of the strong cult of merchant gods at Chetmul, surely a Putun-Maya introduction, but other characteristics of Maya merchant gods are not present. However, another *incensario* (pl. 1-6) has a "pinocchio" nose, attribute of Maya merchant gods, although it lacks the lower lip protrusion. The last in this group has a sort of ropelike headdress or coiffure (pl. 1-7), perhaps related to the twisted rope design of the example from San Antonio, Cayo district (pl. 1-8). Merchant god features suggest the vessels which show them might be pre-Spanish. Equally, they could represent blind copying in the colonial period of, by then, meaningless attributes. So much for the known distribution of these *incensarios* in southeastern Quintana Roo.

A number of these same Lacandon-type *braseros* have been found in the vicinity of Benque Viejo and San Ignacio el Cayo, western Belize. Gann reports the find of what must surely be such vessels in a group of three mounds 14 or 15 kilometers northeast of Benque Viejo, that is to say, not far east of the Macal or Eastern Branch of the Belize River, about 3 kilometers above San Ignacio el Cayo. The mounds were "covered with bush amongst which we found several hour-glass shaped vases made of a very rough pottery, all having a hole in the bottom, evidently made at the time when the vase was fired. Several of these vases were decorated with human faces, others have little conical pieces of pottery stuck on all over them" (1895–1897:311). The presence of those hourglass vessels with spikes all over the surface is of interest, for similar vessels have been found under conditions indicating a late date.[2]

Peabody Museum, Harvard University, has two fine examples of Lacandon-type *braseros* from Negroman, on the Macal or the Eastern Branch of the Belize River, very close to the supposed site of Tipu (pl.

1-9); another from near Benque Viejo; and a fourth, somewhat squat, from San Antonio, Cayo District, not far from Gann's finds (pl. 1-8). Two others, from near Socotz, are in the University Museum of Archaeology and Ethnology, Cambridge, England. Weathering indicates that they, too, are surface finds (pl. 1-10). Garbutt's Falls, near Benque Viejo, yielded an atypical example (Lefroy 1884).

It is noteworthy that no examples have been found along New River or the Belize River below Duck Run. Thus, one supposes that communication lines between southern Quintana Roo and the vicinity of Tipu when these vessels were being made ran west of the Petén-Belize boundary, and not down the New and Belize rivers, as in the seventeenth century. The western route presumably was that from Icaiche via Yaloch to Plancha de Piedra, Benque Viejo's twin city, probably taken in 1623 by Fr. Diego Delgado and by nineteenth-century refugees from Yucatán. It is marked on several maps.

Exclusive of the Quintana Roo–El Cayo route and the upper Usumacinta valley, there is a scattering of *braseros* of this type.[3] Those from Yucatán and Campeche probably can be explained as resulting from the rounding up by Spanish authorities of refugees from their rule who had settled in what is now southeastern Quintana Roo and there largely reverted to paganism. Among those forcibly sent back to "civilization" may have been some who brought back the tradition of that type of *brasero* and produced it from memory for surreptitious pagan rites to which they returned, as the friars would have said, like dogs to their vomit.

How the Lacandon-type *brasero* spread from the vicinity of San Ignacio el Cayo to the territory of modern Lacandons is hard to explain, but it is stretching credulity to the breaking point to suppose that this type rose independently in the two areas at about the same time. Distance as the *zopilote* flies between Benque Viejo and Yaxchilan is a soar or two less than 200 kilometers. Excavation may some day give the answer.

The Calendar

It is certain that the Petén Maya had the katun count and that its calibration was at least roughly that of Yucatán. Fuensalida reports that a katun 3 Ahau was running its course when he and Fr. Orbita visited Tayasal in late October 1618. According to the 11.16.0.0.0. correlation, a katun 3 Ahau (12.1.0.0.0.) started on September 20, 1618, give or take a day.

Avendaño y Loyola tried to persuade the rulers of Tayasal that a katun which seemingly would foretell their acceptance of Spanish rule and Christianity would start about the end of August of 1696 (1696:35ᵛ). He explained, at great length, the calculations which led to that conclusion, naturally using Yucatec material, but one can't imagine how he made them clear to his auditors. He writes that they had been skeptical at the outset but were finally convinced by his argument. Anyone acquainted

with the inevitably affirmative reaction of a Maya to a white man's pronouncements may be so bold as to express deep skepticism that the Maya
were convinced.[4]

However, there is hitherto unreported evidence that the Petén Maya
were shortly expecting a new katun. Cehach Maya of the Chan group
somewhere around November 1695 stated that Petén Maya traders had
told them about six months earlier that they awaited the Spaniards in
Tayasal "because they knew that the time had come to have friendly relations with them" (Villagutierre Soto-Mayor 1933:bk. 5, chap. 9).

According to the 11.16.0.0.0. correlation, a katun 8 Ahau would start
about July 28, 1697. Katun 8 Ahau was generally recognized as a katun of
marked change.

I have a profound belief that the calendar was standardized and syn-
chronized throughout the Maya lowlands, but evidence on that point
regarding the Petén Maya is insufficient.

Fortified Towns

The defended towns of the Cehach described by Cortés, Bernal Díaz del
Castillo, and Dávila appear to mark a unique regional development, reported from no part of the Yucatán Peninsula outside Chan territory.
Archaeology will not expose watchtowers and palisades of perishables,
although post holes could supply partial proof.

Cortés passed through three such towns in Cehach territory. Of the first,
unnamed, he wrote:

● The town is situated on a lofty rock, having a great lake on one side and
on the other a deep stream which empties into the lake; there is but one
accessible entrance, and all is surrounded by a deep moat behind which
there is a palisade breast high; and beyond this palisade there is an en-
closure of very thick planks, two fathoms high, with loop-holes at all points
from which to shoot arrows; its watch towers rise seven or eight feet higher
than the said wall, which was also provided with towers, on the top of
which were many stones with which to fight from above. All the houses of
● the town had loop-holes and were fortified. (MacNutt 1908:II, 267–269)

Seven leagues beyond was the town of Tiac (place of the turtle), "which
was much larger than the former and equally well fortified, though not so
strong as it was situated in a plain. Like the other town, it had strong palisades, a deep moat, and watch towers, and each of the three quarters into
which it was divided had its own fortifications, while the whole was en-
circled by an outer wall stronger than the others" (ibid).

A day's journey brought the Spaniards to Yasuncabil (Yaxumcabil, land of the *cotingas*), last of the Cehach settlements. This was surrounded with palisades, as were the other two.

Cortés was impressed by these fortifications, clearly for him a novelty, as was, too, his soldier comrade Bernal Díaz del Castillo (1908–1916:chaps. 177, 178), who still had a vivid memory of them when he sat down to write his *True History of the Conquest of New Spain* in his old age. He adds that his fellow soldiers called the place the walled village. That name alone shows the fortifications were out of the ordinary.

Dávila, who passed through Cehach territory on his march from Itzam-kanac to Champoton, describes the town of Mazatlan ("place of the deer") as "strongly defended . . . by heavy well-hewn timbers fastened together with fibre ropes with a barbican and embrazures" (Chamberlain 1948:89–90), as well as a dry moat crossed by means of a narrow drawbridge. Dávila was proceeding, like Cortés, from Itzamkanac; but his route was north-easterly, following a circular route to Champoton, whereas Cortés marched south-southeast to Tayasal. Accordingly, it seems unlikely that both men were describing the same place. Clearly, all Cehach towns were thus defended.

These three old campaigners went out of their way to describe those fortified towns, whereas no writer has reported anything similar from out-side Chan territory. The conclusion is inescapable that they had encountered a unique regional specialization.

Palisades were also a prominent feature of Tulumci, as the names of the place and the people, the Chinamita, disclose. Those people were the southern neighbors of the Cehach, and doubtless the system passed from one group to the other. Unfortunately, we have no eyewitness account of the fortifications.

It is of interest that the only moated site discovered in modern times is that of Becan, Campeche, in Río Bec style, but lying only some 30 kilometers north of the suggested boundary with Chan territory. More-over, Petén ceramic influence was strong in the Preclassic and Classic pe-riods (Ball 1971).

Dependence on islands for defense is another Chan feature, but that may well have been a matter of taking advantage of geographical condi-tions absent in Yucatán. The crowded small island of Tayasal is the best-known example. This had defenses, some of which had obviously been prepared when the Spanish attack was imminent, but others may have been permanent. Villagutierre Soto-Mayor calls the island a fortress and writes that the Indians were in fortified positions behind barricades (*trincheras* here obviously not to be translated as trenches) of mud and stone on the lake shore, around the whole mass of the island, on the sum-mits of the many pyramids, and on the steps and retaining walls of stone and mortar (1933:bk. 8, chap. 9). From these fortifications they shot their arrows. Fortifying temple-pyramids reminds one of the Mexican conven-tion of showing conquest by a burning temple or one pierced by a spear.

Chanlacam, apparently south or southeast of Lake Bacalar, has been described as a once highly fortified island (López [de] Cogolludo 1867–1868:bk. 5, chap. 4). It is suggested that it might be the island, now called Albion Island, in the Río Hondo (Scholes and Thompson, this volume). In any case it supplies an example of a fortified island in northern Chan territory under Icaiche control in the nineteenth century.

Topoxte, in Lake Yaxha, east of Lake Petén, was certainly occupied in proto-historic times, although with a history of Classic-Period occupation. There is a good deal of terracing, and the main group rises abruptly from the surrounding land. Whether that was for purposes of defense is not clear; as such it did not impress visitors to the island, notably Bullard (1970), whose investigation is easily the most thorough. Probably the steepness largely reflects the nature of the terrain. Island settlements of the Chol-speaking Lacandon, surely chosen in part for defense, occur in Lake Miramar, archaeology confirming historical accounts. These settlements, of course, lie outside Chan territory.

Political and Social Organization

In contrast to Yucatán, divided into well-organized provinces, each with its ruler, *halach uinic,* "man who commands," governing through his town chiefs, *batabs,* Chan territory lacked central government except in the case of Tayasal. There cohesion had been imposed by invaders from Yucatán, the Itza. At that, Avendaño y Loyola gives the impression that the ruler Can Ek did not exercise complete control; the Couoh, for instance, seem to have largely gone their own way, paying scant attention to the Can Ek.

Among other Chan groups towns were very rare, the Cehach strongholds, Tulunci and Topoxte, being the only ones reported. Generally, each village, comprising clusters of huts scattered over a large area, was independent under its local chief and sometimes local priest, a situation in strong contrast to that obtaining in the Classic Period.

Centralized rule also existed in Chetumal, but, again, well-organized invaders (Putun) are the explanation. Representations of merchant gods at Santa Rita (J. E. S. Thompson 1966) supply archaeological evidence supporting statements in colonial documents.

Among the Lacandon, for whom alone information is forthcoming, there was some sort of totemic "clan" structure, something unreported from Yucatán. The possibility of a kind of "tribal totemism" among the Cehach has been noted.

The Classic Period

Like Peter timidly venturing on the waters of Galilee, I hazard myself on a sea of speculation.

Grant D. Jones (this volume) clearly shows that Chichanha-Icaiche had closer ties with the Chan of Belize and Petén than with the north. Other lines of inquiry in this article establish that those ties go back to the sixteenth and seventeenth centuries. We have a hint of a line of demarcation between antagonistic Yucatec and Chan Maya in the proto-historic period: chiefs of Uaymil, which did not resist Dávila's invasion of 1531–1533, are said to have asked him to let them fight on his side against Chetumal (Chamberlain 1948:102). We have also a hint of a linguistic fence— *boundary* is too strong a term—thereabouts between the two groups. Ciudad Real relates that the Spaniards of Bacalar had in *encomienda* some small towns of Indians of the "language of Uaymil which is almost like that of Campeche" (1873:II, 468). Campeche Maya is known to have differed somewhat from that of Yucatán.

I would go so far as to suggest that those provinces of Uaymil and Chetumal reflected political groupings of the Classic Period, the former recognizable by Río Bec and probably Chenes architecture (we do not know Uaymil's western boundaries); Chetumal, by Petén affiliations. Indeed, I had that in mind in drawing the central portion of the Chan northern border, for colonial sources tell nothing on that matter.

Yet linguistic or cultural demarcations are blurred and seldom static the world over; one side may drive a salient deep into the other's territory. Art and architecture of the Classic Period at Coba are such that one cannot doubt that Petén Maya long dominated it. Indeed, one can pinpoint the Petén source: Coba shares an Initial Series date, 9.12.10.5.12. 4 Eb 10 Yax (Stela 1) with Naranjo (Stelae 24 and 29). This is probably the most important one in Naranjo's history for it commemorates the marriage of a "princess" of Tikal to its ruler. Unfortunately, the Coba glyphic comment on that event is too weathered to yield information. That salient deep in Yucatec territory displays an exceptional degree of Petén influence. It seems to have been wiped out long before the end of the Classic Period.

How the line between the architectural styles meandered, two or three examples make clear: Oxpemul, a Petén site, lies perchance 18 kilometers west and fractionally south of San Lorenzo, a Río Bec site; Tzibanche, in Petén architectural and glyphic traditions, is about 11 kilometers south-southeast of the Río Bec site of Las Higueras (Lizardi 1939) but also some 50 kilometers northeast of the Río Bec site of Ceibarico (Merwin 1913).

Interestingly, Roys tentatively runs the southern boundary of the Yucatecan province of Uaymil westward from the south end of Lake Bacalar (1957:map 15). Whatever his grounds for that placement, they surely were not archaeological, but that line, extended a short way westward, would pass just south of Tzibanche, the northernmost known site save Coba in which Petén architecture dominates.

Information on pottery of large sites of Petén architecture and Petén-style stelae in the border area, such as Calakmul and Oxpemul, is negligible; but a longer stay than at those sites enabled a fair collection of sherds to be made at El Palmar, a large site with very marked Petén affiliations close to Icaiche. Sherds from El Palmar closely resembled those of the middle and late Classic at San José, Belize (J. E. S. Thompson 1936:126), whereas pottery of the Classic horizon at some Río Bec and Chenes sites appears to have few links with Petén. Coba pottery, on the other hand, had strong Petén affiliations during the Classic Period as the architecture and sculpture would lead one to expect (Brainerd 1958:10–11). At Becan, somewhat north of our postulated border, where only Río Bec architecture occurs (the three carved stelae are too weathered to be of any help), Petén-like pottery of the Classic Period is sufficiently dominant as to lead Ball to expand the "spheres" of Petén horizons from Mamon to Tepeu to include Becan (1971:22). Here, too, is the moat reminiscent of Cehach defenses.

Clearly then, in this postulated frontier zone between Yucatec and Chan territories, northern and southern ceramic traditions mingle (see also Fry 1973).

In hieroglyphic texts dissimilarities between Yucatec and Chan (as well as other lowland groups) are marked. Dating by the Initial Series is rare in the north. Large sites, such as Uxmal, Labna, Kabah, Hochob, and Dzibilchaltun, have yielded no Initial Series, but there is a scattering of a single Initial Series per site, for example, at Chichen Itza, Jaina, Oxkintok, and Xcalumkin; two were found at Santa Rosa Xtampak. The only northern site with a concentration of Initial Series is Petén-like Coba. One may say that, with the exception of Coba, the Initial Series in the north seems to have been something alien which never caught on.

Río Bec itself may mark a temporary Petén salient into northern territory, for one architectural grouping in Group II appears to be Petén inspired (Ruppert and Denison 1943:7), and, E. W. Andrews V informs me, Petén-style vaulting occurs in Group B. Stelae were located in Groups II and V. Denison reports that the carving of figures and glyphs on Stelae 5 and 6 of Group V are "distinctly Old Empire in feeling" (ibid.:1943:33). By that, of course, he meant the Maya central area during the Classic Period. Stelae 4 and 5 had carried Initial Series. Stela 5 of Group II may well have carried an Initial Series. Only the lower part of the stela was found; it had been reset upside down, presumably by latecomers.

Nowhere in the north, again excepting Coba, was the linking of dates by distance numbers practiced. Similarly, records of so-and-so, end of n katuns, so common in the south, are unknown in the north. Instead, a katun was marked by recording the day n Ahau with affixes 168 and 130, with the probable meaning "Lord owner" (J. E. S. Thompson 1972:65), here with reference to the katun over which the day Ahau ruled and which was named after him. Again, the system of fixing the long count position of a date by specifying that it falls in n tun or haab of a katun ending on *n* Ahau is common in texts of the Maya lowlands. Finally, one may note the marked stylistic differences in carving glyphs between the two areas and the painted capstone usually with accompanying date, a feature confined to the north (ibid.:1973).

Architectural, ceramic, and epigraphic evidence supports the suggestion that this division between Yucatán and the south may well have already been in existence during the Classic Period of Maya history. I am aware that archaeologists do not relish the employment of data recovered from colonial or modern sources to interpret cultural patterns in the Classic Period, particularly if those backward projections conflict with cherished theories.

Perhaps the archaeologist's reluctance to interpret the past from the present or from information of four centuries ago arises from the tendency of some of the brethren to augment the number of ceramic stages and to justify those by magnifying the differences they detect. The division of Tzakol into three sequential parts supplies an example. It doubtlessly is helpful to the ceramicist, but it may distort the view of one conditioned to those categories who seeks a wide vista of Maya history.

Were stylistical and technical changes in eighteenth century china of western Europe thus used as historical indicators, the student would be left with a decidedly false notion of that century. Neither they nor—to give other examples—the evolution from Early English through Decorated to Perpendicular architecture in England or the rise of the Impressionist school of painting in France directly reflects national history, political, social, or economic, but similar features are given much weight in archaeological contexts. Yet such innovations usually are inspired by individuals or very small groups of artists by profession recognizably volatile; they seldom influence or are influenced by national history.

Magnified by the importance with which he endows them, the temporal dams of the ceramicist's creation loom overlarge in the riverscape he has created. Unwittingly, he has misrepresented the flow of history's stream; some of his dams are at best sluice gates.

Perhaps because the Maya philosophy of time has so long interested me, I see time through Maya eyes as something both ongoing and static, the latter because, in the Maya view, history repeats itself: the future is in the past (no good Maya would approve of the above stream-of-history simile). For that reason and because of Maya conservative thinking, I readily accept continuity from past to present and so judge that, where we have no reason to assess discontinuity, it is best to assume no break with the past. Thus events of A.D. 700 in the absence of contrary evidence are best explained in the light of happenings of, say, A.D. 1700 or A.D. 1900.

Accordingly, I would interpret the archaeological picture of a cleavage between Río Bec—Chenes and the south as an early stage of Yucatec versus Chan differentiation.

Summary

From the sixteenth century onward, groups speaking variants of Yucatec Maya have occupied territory from southeastern Campeche and southern Quintana Roo southward, embracing most of the Petén and western Belize (but excluding southeastern Petén), and extending as far south as the Río Usumacinta and lower Río Pasión. It is proposed that they differed or differ sufficiently from the Yucatec Maya to their north as to justify constituting them a subgroup of the latter, for which the name Chan is suggested. The differences, while not great, might be compared to those between lowland Scots and English or between Austrians or Bavarians and Prussians (religion, architecture, speech, etc.). There appears not to have been a hard and fast cultural boundary between those two Maya groups. One might think, rather, in terms of the gradualness of the spectrum. The farther south one proceeds, the stronger are the deviations. The former Chichanha-Icaiche Maya in the extreme north of Chan territory show almost no cultural deviation from their northern kinsmen although politically antagonistic to them, but their political ties are with the Chan Maya; the Mopan and Yucatec-speaking Lacandon are spatially and culturally far more removed from the Maya of Yucatán.

The groups forming the proposed subdivision are or were the Chichanha-Icaiche, the Maya of Lake Petén and surrounding territory including the so-called Itza, those of the upper Belize River, the Cehach, Chinamita, Yucatec-speaking Lacandon (including those who have established themselves in Chiapas), and the Mopan.

The dissimilarities are based on observations of Chan groups from the sixteenth century to the present day, which, as far as the colonial period is concerned, are unfortunately scarce; modern studies are handicapped in most parts by deculturization.

Unfortunately, we can draw on no Sahagún, Motolinía, or Landa for a record of the culture of this vast area at the period of contact stretching from the sixteenth to the end of the seventeenth century. The Franciscans Fuensalida and Avendaño y Loyola supply a fair amount of information on the Maya of Lake Petén, but, apart from them, we are dependent on little asides of historians in their chronicles of the efforts of the Spaniards to subdue those lands. Even those asides are seldom informative for they usually refer to such practices as human sacrifices, blood-drawing, body painting, tattooing, carrying stools, worshiping idols, and so on, which are common to all the Maya lowlands. For instance, almost nothing specific is reported of the Cehach except their unusual fortified towns and their Maya speech. For the Chinamita, information is even scantier.

Nevertheless, scattered data, notably on language, personal names, titles of rank, religious ideas, temples, and fortifications, seem of sufficient importance to warrant the constitution of the Chan group.

A good case can be made out for projecting back to the Classic Period this cleavage between true Yucatec and Chan Maya, for north of the proposed border one finds a local architectural style (Río Bec–Chenes), local ceramic traditions, and noticeably distinct ways and methods of presenting calendrical matters and of recording hieroglyphs. Local variations in expressing the passage of time cut close to the bone; time in all its aspects was supremely important in the spiritual outlook of the lowland Maya ruling class in the Classic Period. Changes in methods of recording dates could have been as divisive as the *filioque* clause which has cloven Christianity for over a millennium and, by encouraging the Turks to invade Europe, changed history.

I make no large claim for the thesis here advanced. Yet I cherish the hope that it may affect thinking on territorial division in the Maya lowlands, a subject which emblem glyphs of the Classic Period and the provinces of the proto-historic period invite us to explore.

Notes

1.
Present-day Lacandon call the ruins Yachilan (Petryshyn 1968:19). The small stream which enters the Río Usumacinta on its north bank, 3–4 miles above Yaxchilan, is called Yalchilan (Maler, in his folly, corrected this to Yaxchilan). This clear Maya term must surely have been the Lacandon name for the stream, for nineteenth-century loggers were overwhelmingly of Spanish speech. The letter *l* at times drops out before a consonant in Yucatec (J. E. S. Thompson 1950:145–146; quotation from R. L. Roys). The same occurs in the Lacandon dialect of Yucatec even where an *r* now replaces the *l* (Bruce S. 1968:24; Petryshyn 1968:16). It is therefore a fair assumption that Lacandon Yalchilan was earlier Yalchilan. It is perhaps not too speculative to suggest that oral tradition may have preserved, perhaps with slight distortion, the original Classic-Period name of the site which may have been Chol. One may suppose that the clerical term *chilan* was common to various lowland Mayan languages. Admittedly, the Yaxchilan emblem glyph seems not to represent the chilan with their prophetic functions. *Yal* is "water of."
2.
Surface finds: in room of Structure A-XV and surface of Structure A-1, Uaxactun (Smith 1955:101–102); in a room doorway at Mountain Cow, alongside incense burners of earlier (Tepeu 1 or 2) date (J. E. S. Thompson 1931:257); surface material, mostly Tepeu 3 at Benque Viejo (Thompson 1940:fig. 45). As all three cases are of surface material, they could fall any time between the close of the Classic Period and the present day. Similar spiked vessels, complete or fragmentary, have been found in caves on Río Frio, only some 15 kilometers south of Gann's find (Mason 1928: fig. 20; Pendergast 1970: fig. 12g). It is uncertain that all the fragmentary pieces were of hourglass shape.

3.

One, in Peabody Museum, Harvard University, from Ticul, Yucatán, is atypical, for the head is not in full relief and the rim rises to form an unusually high headdress. One from the ruins of Labna is again atypical (Tozzer 1907:pl. XV, 1). A third is from Hochob, Campeche, with neck and arms in low relief, but hourglass shaped and face in crude relief with simple headdress rising above the rim, again aberrant (Miller and Carter 1932:pl. 46). One, typical modern Lacandon, was part of a collection said to have come from San José, Lake Petén. The remaining four pieces were later established as types found at San Agustín Acasaguastlan (Smith 1944: fig. 2*f*; 1954:27). Accordingly, the San José provenience is dubious; the piece probably came from a modern Lacandon settlement. Conceivably, a modern Lacandon family could have settled in San José, for three Lacandon families were living at Tikal in the nineteenth century. These last pieces may account for a fragmentary Lacandon-style *brasero* recently found there. Unfortunately, I have not seen a picture of it. A typical Lacandon *brasero,* to which Dr. Clifford Evans has called my attention, was excavated on Isla de Carmen and is now in the National Museum of Natural History, Washington, D.C. (cat. no. 325912). Did some Lacandon family move there in the colonial period? Ian Graham has told me of two other Lacandon-type *braseros* from an unidentified locality in El Quiche. Were they brought there in modern times?

4.

Avendaño y Loyola probably knew the new katun would start on 11 Imex 19 Uo but used the Landa year in which that month position fell on August 23. Somehow, by apostolic zeal perhaps, he was led to give the year as 1696, not 1697; ten thousand pagan souls weighed against a tun?

Plate 1-1

Opposite: Lacandon-type Incense Burner. From headwaters of Río Hondo, Quintana Roo-Petén border, height 20.5 cm. Courtesy of Department of Anthropology, Smithsonian Institution.

Plate 1-2
Lacandon-type Incense Burner. From headwaters of Río Hondo, Quintana
Roo-Petén border, height 21 cm. Courtesy of Department of
Anthropology, Smithsonian Institution.

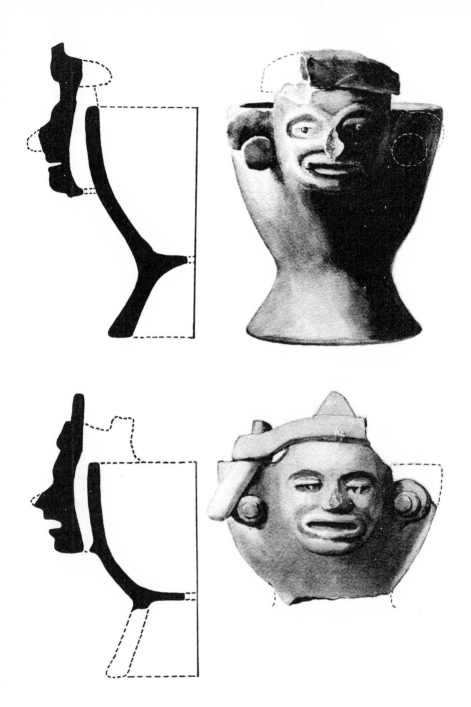

Plate 1-3
Lacandon-type Incense Burners. Complete and fragmentary vessels found
in making the aviation camp, Dos Lagunas, N.E. Petén. Height of complete vessel 15.3 cm. From watercolors by A. Tejeda F. Courtesy of
Peabody Museum, Harvard University.

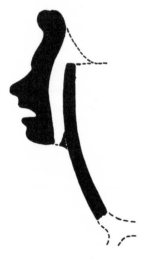

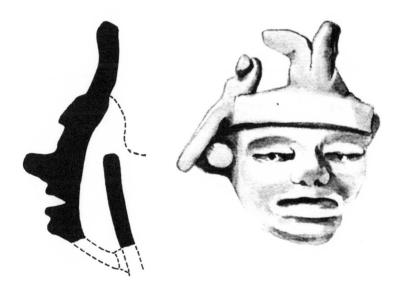

189214

Plate 1-4
Lacandon-type Incense Burner. From surface before stela, La Honradez,
N.E. Petén. Courtesy of Field Museum of Natural History, Chicago.

Plate 1-5
Lacandon-type Incense Burner. Bacalar region, height 16 cm. Courtesy
of Ian Graham, photographs of Eric von Euw.

Plate 1-6
Lacandon-type Incense Burner. Laguna Soh, height 16.5 cm. Courtesy
of Ian Graham, photographs of Eric von Euw.

Plate 1-7
Lacandon-type Incense Burner. Bacalar region, height 13.5 cm.
Courtesy of Ian Graham, photographs of Eric von Euw.

Plate 1-8
Lacandon-type Incense Burner. From San Antonio, Cayo District, Belize.
Courtesy of Peabody Museum, Harvard University.

Plate 1-9
Lacandon-type Incense Burner. From Negroman, Cayo District, Belize.
Courtesy of Peabody Museum, Harvard University.

Plate 1-10
Lacandon-type Incense Burner. From near Socotz, Cayo District, Belize.
Courtesy of Museum of Archaeology and Ethnology, Cambridge
University.

2

The Francisco Pérez Probanza of 1654–1656

and the Matrícula of Tipu (Belize)

France V. Scholes and Sir Eric Thompson

This article is the somewhat tardy outcome of the finding in 1933–1934 by one author of the above *probanza* and of the interest of the other in the Yucatec-speaking Maya of the Petén and Belize. The *probanza* recounts the efforts of Captain Francisco Pérez in 1654–1656 to restore the revolted Maya of a large area south of Bacalar, Quintana Roo, to obedience to the crown of Spain and the triple tiara of the papacy. With the papers is a *matrícula,* or census, of the inhabitants of Tipu and neighboring settlements, the importance of which lies in the appearance of a number of Maya day names used as surnames.

The Pérez documents comprise manuscripts totaling fifty-eight folios lodged in the Archivo General de Indias, Seville (Audiencia de México, Legajo 158). First, however, Tipu and other villages must be placed in space and history.

Location of Tipu and Other Belize Sites

Tipu can be located quite closely and other villages downstream from Tipu with rather less accuracy because of the good description Fr. Bartolomé de Fuensalida left of the journey he and Fr. Juan de Orbita made in 1618 from Salamanca de Bacalar to Tipu (in López [de] Cogolludo 1867–1868:bk. 9, chap. 6). Note that Salamanca de Bakhalal, Salamanca de Bacalar, and Bacalar are one and the same place; the last is present-day usage and will be used in this article except in formal contexts.

The friars left Bacalar in canoe and, paddling down the lake of the same name on which the town stands, they entered the Nohukum, now Chac River, which flows from the southeast end of the lake to enter the Río Hondo a short way above its mouth. From the mouth of the Hondo the route was southeastward across Chetumal Bay and following the north coast of what is now Belize to the mouth of the Dzuluinicob, now New River. Incidentally, as Fuensalida notes, they passed close to the site of the great proto-historic site of Chetumal, almost certainly close to present-

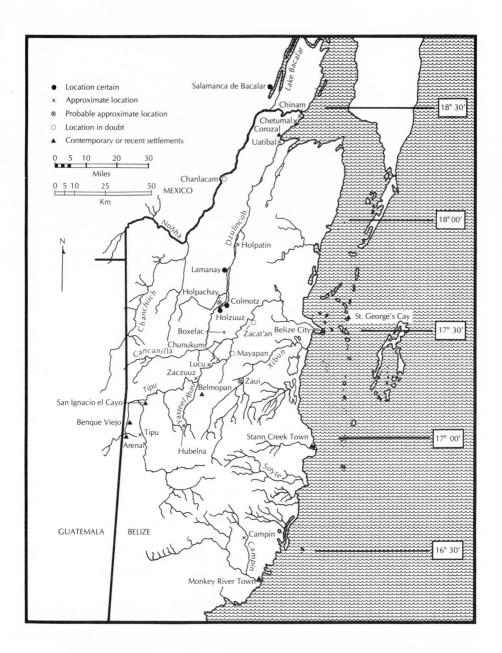

● Location certain
× Approximate location
⊗ Probable approximate location
○ Location in doubt
▲ Contemporary or recent settlements

0 5 10   20   30
            Miles

0 5 10   25   50   MEXICO
            Km

N

Salamanca de Bacalar ●
Lake Bacalar
Chinam
18° 30'
Chetumal ×
Corozal
Uatibal ⊗
Chanlacam ○
18° 00'
Nohha
Dzulincob
× Holpatin
Lamanay ●
Chanchich
Holpachay
⊗ Colmotz
Holzuuz ●
Boxelac ── ×   ⊗ Zacat'an   Belize City
St. George's Cay
17° 30'
Cancanilla
Chunukum
○ Mayapan
Xibun
Lucu ×
Zaczuuz
Tipu
⊗ Zaui
Belmopan ▲
San Ignacio el Cayo ▲
Yaxteel Ahau
Benque Viejo ▲
× Tipu
Arenal ▲
Hubelna
Stann Creek Town ▲
17° 00'
Soyte
GUATEMALA   BELIZE
× Campin
Campin
16° 30'
Monkey River Town ▲

Map 2-1
Settlements and rivers referred to in Pérez *probanza* and other
colonial documents

day Corozal (J. E. S. Thompson 1974), and probably partly corresponding to the site of Santa Rita, excavated by Gann (1900).

Passing various towns or villages on New River, the friars entered New River Lagoon, with the settlement of Lamanay on its bank, identified by the remains of the colonial church as present-day Indian Church. Disembarking at the south end of New River Lagoon at a place called Colmotz, they continued southward on foot. A journey of 6 leagues, largely through pine woods, brought them to a natural bridge over the Cancanilla River (now Labouring Creek) and another 6 leagues to the site of Lucu on the banks of the Tipu River, the present-day Belize River, which probably lay somewhere about where the modern settlements of Never Delay or Mount Pleasant now stand. The pine ridge, in fact, stretches south from the southeast corner of New River Lagoon. Its modern name is Ramgoat Creek Pine Ridge.

Fuensalida's description of the journey upstream from Lucu, 12 leagues to Tipu, agrees completely with actual conditions on the upper Belize. There were 190 rapids to be negotiated, and the stream was so fast that the canoes had often to be poled, and frequently the Indians threw themselves into the water to haul the canoes over the rapids by hand. It took Fuensalida and his party three days to cover those 12 leagues to Tipu, the *cacique* and other leaders of which had paddled 2 leagues downstream to meet them.

It is highly probable that Tipu was on the west bank of the Macal or Eastern Branch of the Belize River, above San Ignacio el Cayo and in the neighborhood of present-day Negroman or Macaw Bank. It almost surely was not on the Mopan or West Branch because Bullet Tree Falls, just above the junction of that river with the Belize River, prevents navigation. Moreover, the padres, on their subsequent journey to Lake Yaxha en route to Lake Petén, reached a wide river 2 leagues from Tipu, and that surely must have been the Mopan. A direct line from the vicinity of Macaw Bank or Negroman to Lake Yaxha would cross the Mopan near Arenal or Benque Viejo, about 1.5 Guatemalan leagues (6.5 km) west of the starting point, a good agreement with the padres' route.

The *matricula* itself was made at Chunukum, a place not directly located by the *probanza*. It was clearly beyond Holzuuz, at the bottom of New River Lagoon, the farthest point reached on Pérez's second trip, and we can infer that it was on the Belize River, then called the Tipu; for Pérez wrote that he could not go up (*subir*) because of the flooded rivers and roads and so sent messengers to the Indians of the three principal pueblos (Tipu, Zaczuuz, and Lucu [Luku]) that they should come to meet him at Chunukum. Other mentions of going up to the three towns and coming down from them to Chunukum make it evident that Chunukum was downstream from Lucu, the town at which Fuensalida took a canoe to ascend the Belize River. The name means source of a river or swamp, and appears on the Gonsález map of 1766 as Estero Chuncum, a stretch of water connecting the western end of Spanish Creek (written Yspaniscrik) with the Belize River due south. One must not expect accuracy, and, indeed, no stream unites Spanish Creek with the upper Belize, but the general position, south of New River Lagoon and Ramgoat Creek, Pine Ridge, is about where one would expect the Chunukum of Pérez's days to have been—on the Belize River in the general vicinity of Rock Dondo or Never Delay. There may have been another Chunukum, perhaps on Chac River (Roys 1957:161, 164).

Our Chunukum is called a town and small settlement (*pueblo y paraje*) in the Pérez documents but clearly was of little consequence. As none of its twenty-three inhabitants are listed as from Chunukum in the *matrícula,* one may perhaps infer that it was possibly a large center for cacao orchards and that its inhabitants were merely temporary residents. The leaders of Tipu offered to build a church there and to go there whenever church or lay officials required their attendance. Tipu chiefs, one suspects, were not anxious to have Spanish representatives visiting their village and decided the long journey to Chunukum on the rare occasions they were summoned was the lesser of two evils.

Zaczuuz, on the Belize River close to where Roaring Creek joins it, produced only thirteen adults and five children, presumably because its inhabitants had moved south to Hubelna some eighteen years earlier, as recounted by Fuensalida.

Zacatan (Zacat'an) is listed as one of the deserted towns Fuensalida passed on his journey of 1641 from Bacalar to Zaczuuz (López [de] Cogolludo 1867–1868: bk. 11, chap. 13). Avendaño y Loyola gives Zacatan as a district adjoining the province of Yucatán and inhabited by English logwood cutters who were driven out that same year in which he wrote (1696:2ᵛ). The logwood cutters operated along the Belize River and north and south of it. They had not apparently at that date extended operations to New River. Zacat'an would seem, then, to have been on the Belize River. However, the Gonsález map of 1766 labels as Sactham what must be North River, flowing into the Caribbean some way north of Belize, a region Fuensalida never visited. As Tisactan (*ti* signifies *at*) it appears as a *visita* of the *curato* of Salamanca de Bacalar in the Guillen de las Casas *Memoria de los conventos, vicarías y pueblos . . . de Yucatán, Cozumel y Tabasco* of 1582 (Scholes et al. 1936–1938: II, 63). The thirty-seven who called Zacat'an their home are of sufficient number to suggest that they were not refugees from a distant town but that Zacat'an was near Chunukum and on the Belize River, agreeing with Fuensalida's datum.

Holpatin, Fuensalida informs us, was on New River; perhaps it was near the site of present-day Orange Walk Town. With other villages it had been burned and abandoned in the uprising of the 1630's. Its eleven natives in the *matrícula* presumably had settled on the Belize River.

Chalacam is surely Chanlacam (Showy Standard) of the 1582 *visita* and the place López [de] Cogolludo spells Chanlacao (1867–1868:bk. 5, chap.

4). This town, he informs us, took part in the revolts of 1546 and the 1630's, when its apostastizing inhabitants fled to join the Itza. It was in the province of Chetumal and at the time of the conquest on a highly fortified island. The Spaniards who crushed its rebellion in 1646 traveled from Bacalar in canoes by rivers and lagoons, presumably down Chac River, which joins the south end of Lake Bacalar with the Río Hondo. Chanlacam could have been on an island in that region of swamps and lagoons, but good agricultural land does not lie nearby. It might even have been on Albion Island, in the Río Hondo, above Douglas. From this island, 5 miles long, comes a small collection of artifacts, now in Bristol City Museum, England, those identifiable being of the period immediately prior to, or contemporary with, the Spanish conquest. The two couples who gave Chanlacam as their home were undoubtedly refugees who settled in the Belize valley when the town was abandoned in the 1630's. More were found at Holzuuz.

Mayapan also appears in the 1582 *visita*. Roys speculated that it might have been the walled site of Ichpatun, in southern Quintana Roo (1957: 162), but our *matrícula,* unknown to him, is evidence that it was on the Belize River. Its seventeen inhabitants, one supposes, are rather numerous to have been refugees from a considerable distance.

Chinam is located by Fuensalida in northern Belize, 5 leagues east of the mouth of the Hondo. It was not abandoned during the troubles of 1630, when it was estimated by him to have had forty *vecinos.* The single couple in the *matrícula* presumably left as individuals, settling in the Belize Valley.

The same explanation accounts for the couple Diego Malah of Soyte and his wife from Xibun (present-day Sittee and Sibun rivers).

Lucu, as we have seen, was upstream from Chunukum. Only four adults and two children are enrolled from there. Since earlier it had been rated an important settlement, most of its inhabitants must have played truant.

Everyone in the middle Belize valley must have known by bush telegraph of Pérez's summons to come in, but the *matrícula* makes clear that few outside Tipu responded. Most of the population probably decided rightly that Pérez had no intention of making an extensive roundup—friendly Maya with Pérez may have weighed him up and passed on their conclusions to the apostates—and so stayed home. As an estimate of the population of the middle and upper Belize valley and a listing of the settlements, the *matrícula* is next door to worthless.

Tipu and the Belize River Settlements before 1650

Tipu and other Maya settlements on the banks of the upper Belize and New rivers (then called the Tipu and Dzuluinicob rivers) are named as *visitas* of the *curato* of Salamanca de Bacalar in the Guillen de las Casas *Memoria* of 1582 (Scholes et al. 1936–1938:II, 51–65). Because of the difficult and very long journey by land and water which separated those out-lying settlements from Bacalar, the inhabitants were long left almost to their own devices, for Bacalar was assigned to secular clergy who, at least in Yucatán, were hardly renowned for either apostolic energy or zeal in learning Maya.

Two factors brought Tipu out of its quiet obscurity. The first was the interruption to sea communications between Yucatán and both Mexico and Guatemala caused by corsairs lurking on both coasts of the peninsula. That factor was a growing incentive during the whole seventeenth century for the conquest, spiritual and temporal, of the independent and still pagan Maya whose lands lay athwart an alternative land route. Endless forests and swamps, disease (largely of European introduction), and lack of natural resources attractive to the Spaniards had combined to preserve those strongholds of paganism for 150 years after Spanish arms had triumphed to north and south. With the growing need for the conquest of the center of the peninsula, Tipu assumed strategic importance as the last outpost of Christianity on the eastern road to Tayasal, on Lake Petén, capital of the Can Ek dynasty, at the heart of a vast concourse of heathen-dom.

The second factor which brought Tipu into prominence was the south-ern drift of long-established Christian, tribute-paying Maya from Yucatán to escape Spanish rule. Often these refugees relapsed into outright or crypto-paganism. Certainly, historical data and evidence of surnames make clear that a considerable proportion of Tipu's inhabitants were refugees from Yucatán or were their descendants. Specifically, Francisco Cumux, a *principal* of Tipu in the early seventeenth century, was descended from the *halach uinic* of Cozumel Island when Cortés was there. The choir-master of Tipu, apparently accused of idolatry, had fled from Xecchakan, near Campeche.

In 1618 the first attempt to evangelize the pagans of eastern and north-eastern Petén was made; the Franciscans Bartolomé de Fuensalida and Juan de Orbita, both good speakers of Maya, accompanied by the *alcalde* of Bacalar, traveled from that town to the south end of the lake of that name and thence via the Nohukum, now Chac River, to the lower reaches of the Río Hondo. After following the coast of what is now northern Belize eastward, they ascended New River and continued southward across New River Lagoon. From there, as already noted, they traveled overland to the Tipu (now Belize) River, reaching it at the settlement of Lucu, or Luku, about where the rapids of Never Delay are situated or, perhaps, a short distance upstream from there. Thence they went in other canoes to Tipu, which then had a hundred *vecinos* and a church. There they were well received, but, while the friars carried out their religious duties, with the festival of Pentecost celebrated with all pomp possible, procession and dances, the *alcalde* of Bacalar reminded the Maya of Tipu of their civic duties by collecting back taxes, doubtlessly something which did not contribute to the joy of the Tipu Maya at being reincorporated in the Spanish polity.

Following the return to Tipu with encouraging messages of emissaries to Can Ek, ruler of Tayasal, the friars proceeded to the island in Lake Petén. There, Fr. Orbita, clearly an impetuous priest, quickly lost the goodwill of their hosts by smashing one of their most important idols. The friars were thrown out of Tayasal and their escort of Tipuans ordered never more to guide Spaniards there. The party returned to Tipu having accomplished nothing.

Because of jealousy of the secular priest of Bacalar at this Franciscan trespass in his bailiwick, Fuensalida returned almost immediately to Mérida to smooth relations, leaving Orbita in charge at Tipu. The latter in short time succeeded in alienating his not overly Christian flock. Fuensalida returned to Tipu early in 1619, and, soon thereafter, evidence of large-scale idolatry in Tipu was uncovered. The *cura* and *alcalde* of Bacalar arrived at that time, and the friars requested the *cura* to institute a minor, but illegal, *auto de fe*. Idols were consumed in a great bonfire; more serious offenders were whipped, and others suffered lighter punishment.

Later, the two friars revisited Tayasal but, again, after a friendly reception, were ignominiously expelled. Realizing that the conversion of the Petén pagans was not then possible, they returned to Mérida after tarrying a while in Tipu, and that town and the neighboring settlements were left to their own devices, probably unholy. After the Franciscans withdrew, those settlements were again under the lax religious ministrations of the secular priest at Bacalar.

In 1622 Francisco de Mirones made his disastrous *entrada* aimed at the conquest of Tayasal by way of Oxkutzcab and Sacalum (Scholes and Adams 1936). Before Mirones had advanced far, the Franciscan Diego Delgado, one of his party but on bad terms with him, slipped off to Tipu with the intention of forestalling the military invasion of Tayasal. With a band recruited in Tipu reported to number eighty—surely an exaggeration since the total number of *vecinos* of that town was around one hundred—and with a small military escort, Delgado set out for Tayasal, where yet again the visitors were received in peace. Later, warriors of Tayasal, falling upon the party lulled into a false sense of security, captured and sacrificed the lot. That was in July 1623 (López [de] Cogolludo 1867–1868: bk. 10, chap. 2).

On Candlemas Day, 1624, Mirones and his whole force were massacred while at mass.

Those two setbacks to Spanish authority and prestige ultimately resulted in an uprising of the Maya in the Bacalar-Chetumal area, which extended as far as the Belize valley. In 1631 the Maya of the Bacalar region began fleeing in the direction of Tipu. The movement grew, and three years later, as López [de] Cogolludo put it, the Maya of that area "refused all obedience to God and king and returned to the vomit of the idolatries and abominations of their forbears, outraging the images, burning the temples consecrated to the Divine Majesty, and later their towns, fleeing to the distant forests" (1867–1868:bk. 11, chap. 12). Messengers to the *alzados* were told that, should they return, they would be slain.

Nevertheless, in 1641 another attempt was made to pacify the revolted Maya. The Bacalar curacy was turned over to the Franciscans, the secular priest, Gregorio de Aguilar, moving to Valladolid. Fuensalida, veteran of the 1618–1619 missions, set forth in an attempt to win back Tipu and the villagers of the New and Belize rivers. He was accompanied by Juan de Estrada, a lay friar who had lived many years in Bacalar—he had been *alcalde* and *justicia mayor* there—and was godfather to many Tipuans, perhaps evidence that Tipu had not been completely isolated after the withdrawal of the friars in 1619.

Following the route of 1618–1619, apparently an old Maya route probably of pre-Columbian times, they found Lamanay deserted, its church and huts burned. They reached the Belize River at a cacao orchard called Chantome. Thence the party traveled by canoe to Zaczuc (Zaczuuz), which they found also burned and abandoned, the bell of the burned church thrown into the bush. The Maya of Zaczuuz ("White Sand"; this is surely the correct rendering of the place name) had retreated to a place called Hubelna, apparently some way up Roaring Creek and in the vicinity of the new capital of Belize, Belmopan.

After waiting in vain for an invitation to proceed upstream to Tipu, the friars persuaded the *cacique* of Hubelna to allow them to proceed to his town. There they witnessed idolatry and a mock mass celebrated with *posole* and tortillas.

Next morning the Maya, apparently from Tipu and other villages, advanced to the friars' hut with boys in front blowing conch shells, such as they used in war, and behind men with lances, bows and arrows, and faces painted red. They threatened to kill the missionaries, abused them, and smashed a crucifix and their images. Finally, they drove them from Hubelna with many shouts and whistles as though running a bull out of the bullring, with grimaces, insults, and so on. The fathers and their comrades fled back to Bacalar (López [de] Cogolludo 1867–1868:bk. 11, chaps. 12–15).

Meanwhile, the second prong of the Franciscan attack on paganism, that along the coast of Belize as far south as Campin, almost certainly on Monkey River (J. E. S. Thompson [1974]), had equally ended in disaster. But this time the successful counterattack of the powers of darkness took the forms of corsairs who pillaged the newly resettled Maya villages and even seized Salamanca de Bacalar itself.

In 1643 the Franciscans, in view of the total collapse of their mission, withdrew from Bacalar, having arranged with the bishop that a secular priest should once again take over that curacy (Lopez [de] Cogolludo 1867–1868:bk. 11, chaps. 16–17).

The Probanza of Francisco Pérez

The *probanza,* which lacks an official title, consists of a certified copy of a series of separate documents setting forth the claims of Captain Francisco Pérez, *vecino de la* Villa de Salamanca de Bacalar, for remuneration for services rendered to the crown in his capacity of leader of three expeditions from Bacalar to the forests to the south to search out and "reduce" to crown and church Maya Indians living there in a state of rebellion.

The first two folios record the petition and council action concerning the same. The *probanza* itself comprises three separate and short reports on those journeys, made in 1645–1655 to what is now west central Belize. Each report opens with a summary of the journey and a petition presented, on return from each journey, to Juan Gómez Santoya, *alcalde ordinario* and *capitán a guerra* of Salamanca de Bacalar, asking that witnesses be examined as to the veracity of the facts set forth in the report. In each case Spaniards and Indians who had accompanied Captain Pérez testified. In some cases their testimony was supplemented with additional documents.

Finally, a single document relates that in the latter part of April 1656, Pérez, accompanied by Fr. Pedro Juan Fernández, secular priest of Bacalar, made a final trip apparently to Chunukum to receive back the apostates into the bosom of the church.

The *probanza* also gives the information that in October 1661, Pérez, then in Mérida, asked and received authorization for the making of a certified copy of the documents. This copy was made and certified by public notary in Mérida on November 11, 1661, and this was presented in 1668 to the Council of the Indies in support of Pérez's petition for an annual pension of two thousand pesos for two lives, that is, for himself and his heir, to be paid from the tribute collected from *indios reducidos* in Yucatán or from income of *encomiendas* that might become vacant.

The petition was accorded the usual bureaucratic treatment; it was referred to a council member who finally recommended, in June 1668, that a royal *cédula* of recommendation for Pérez be dispatched to the governor of Yucatán, instructing him to take into account Pérez's services when making appointments to local offices. This was routine procedure by the council in cases of claims for reward when services were not particularly distinguished. Probably a *cédula* to that effect was sent in due course and is probably on record in the register of royal *cédulas* in Seville.

Whether Pérez did receive a reward is not known. His expenditure of effort was small and of money probably not great. The results of his journeys appear to have been minimal, although admittedly Tipu was still officially in the bosom of the church at the close of the century, as we shall see. A place somewhat low down in the bureaucratic pecking order of Yucatán would, one supposes, have been ample reward.

Aside from what the *probanza* reveals, nothing is known of Francisco Pérez. How he came to be awarded the rank of captain is uncertain; he can hardly have been thus honored for valor in defending Bacalar from the corsairs in 1641, for the town was sacked without the slightest resistance, the inhabitants fleeing to the woods.

Pérez's Journeys into the Interior

As noted, the *probanza* is extremely repetitious, with each witness covering the same ground. However, occasionally, one witness or another gives a detail not in Pérez's account. Such details are added to Pérez's description in the summaries that follow.

The immediate cause of the first journey made by Pérez was that perhaps in the second half of 1653 or early in 1654 the Maya of Chalacam and Hautila in the general area of Bacalar had burned and abandoned their villages and fled to the forest, apparently in the general direction of Tipu. This must have been seen by the Spanish authorities as a dangerous recrudescence of the apostasies of 1636–1639.

The location of Chalacam (Chanlacam) has been reviewed. Hautila is very probably a wrong transcription of a town or village of the Bacalar vicariate given as Guatibal in the 1582 list of *visitas*. As Uaitibal it figures as an abandoned town visited by Fuensalida, who locates it near the shore beyond the abandoned site of Chetumal but some distance short of the mouth of the Dzuluinicob (New) River (Lopez [de] Cogolludo 1867–1868: bk. 9, chap. 6). It must have lain near present-day Corozal. Pérez was taken ill there, the distance from Bacalar being given as 8 leagues. That is surely an underestimate. Uatibal would seem the preferable spelling.

In answer to an appeal by the local authorities in Bacalar, the governor of Yucatán sent a detachment of troops to bring the revolted Indians back to their two towns. The force was unable to reach Bacalar because of flooding and had to return to Chunhuhub. Indeed, the road south of Chunhuhub was impassable in the rainy season; swamps there were nicknamed "Horse Bones" because of pack animals sucked into the morasses. Thereupon Pérez offered to lead a small force to discover and restore the villagers to obedience. On October 24, 1654, Captain Juan Gómez Santoya of Bacalar appointed Pérez leader of such a detachment. Some of the fugitives from Hautila were said to be in some lagoons called Kantenal, 20 leagues from Bacalar.

Pérez refurbished two old canoes and, before the end of that same month, set forth with five Spaniards and fifteen friendly Indians. Going by water he and his men found most of the fugitives in various small settlements (*parajes*) in the forest. Unfortunately, we have no information as to where these were.

The *probanza* states that a small group of the fugitives had fled farther into the interior and were living at places named as Holpachay and Holsuzil, far from Bacalar and near Tipu (note that throughout, *c* with cedilla is here rendered as *z*). *Hol* is without serious doubt a Maya term for landing place, and survives in Putun as *holtun* (Scholes and Roys 1948:81). As *tun* means stone, *holtun* presumably was a landing place with stone wharves, such as have been found sporadically in the Maya area. Holsuzil is variously named Holsuzil, Holtzuc, Holsucil, Holsus, Holzuc, and Holcuc. Cedillas have clearly been omitted by the scribe. The termination *il* is a term indicating relationship, here translatable as *of*. As *suz* (more correctly transcribed *zuz* or *zuuz*) means sand, the term signified sandy landing place. In the *probanza* the place is once called Puerto (harbor) of Holsus, and once "the harbor where they disembarked to go to the *rancherías* and pueblo of Tipu."

From this last description one may conclude with fair certainty that Holzuuz was at the southeast end of New River Lagoon, where, as we know from the Fuensalida *relación*, travelers disembarked to cross via Ramgoat Creek Pine Ridge and over Labouring Creek to the Belize River. The Pérez *relación* says Holzuuz was 70 leagues from Bacalar, a gross exaggeration, but we must remember that the more the captain emphasized (to put it politely) the length and hazards of his journey, the more pecuniary a reward he might expect to get.

Accordingly, it would seem that on his first entry, Captain Pérez probably penetrated only a short distance up New River. The date of his return to Bacalar is not known, although it was before January 10, 1655, for on that date he submitted an account of his expedition to Gómez Santoya and asked him to take the testimony of witnesses who had accompanied him.

The witnesses included three Indians—Fernando Coboh (Couoh) of Pacha, a village 15 leagues north of Bacalar on the road to Chunhuhub; Gaspar Uc, *alcalde ordinario* of the same village; and Gaspar Chan, *alcalde ordinario* of the Barrio de San Juan Extramuros of Salamanca (Bacalar) —and an interesting reference to a Maya quarter outside the walls of Bacalar.

The petition and testimony point out that the Maya of Tipu and other towns had been in revolt for the past seventeen or eighteen years and that the Franciscan mission (the *entradas* of Fuensalida, Becerril, and Tejero of 1641) to restore them to crown and church had achieved nothing. The argument was advanced that, unless those revolted Indians were reincorporated in the Christian community, their independence was a constant temptation to settled Maya to flee Spanish rule. Captain Pérez was the man to do that, which his first journey showed. Incidentally, it is recorded that on that occasion he had suffered chills and fever, presumably malaria. No doubt, royal bounty would prove an efficacious medicament.

Captain Pérez received orders on January 16, 1655, from Captain Gómez Santoya to make another *entrada*, and presumably he set forth soon after that date. His force this time comprised 10 Spaniards and no less than 60 friendly Indians.

The force reached the *rancherías* ("small settlements") of Holtzuc (Holzuuz) and Holpachay, the former, as noted above, probably at the southeast end of New River Lagoon, and there they found 48 men, women, and children from Chalacam (Chanlacam) and Hautila (Uatibal) and also 62 men, women, and children from the town of Tipu. These 110 Maya they took back with them to Bacalar; they do not figure in the *matrícula*. Pérez sent 6 of the Indians in his force to summon the *caciques* and principal men of Tipu to come to Holzuuz to meet him within six days. Presumably those messengers would have gone overland to Tipu as it was in the dry season; there would hardly have been time for the arrangements to be made had the journeys been via the middle Belize settlements.

In fact, Pérez waited twelve days for them. Then, being afflicted by mosquitoes and short of supplies, he returned to Bacalar. However, he left some of his friendly Indians at Holzuuz with orders to bring any Indians from Tipu who might arrive in response to his summons.

After his return to Bacalar, Pérez gave a short official report of his journey and asked for witnesses to be examined. On April 20, 1655, three Indian witnesses testified. They were Andrés Pech, Francisco Cocom, and Francisco Kan, all leading men of the same San Juan Extramuros quarter of Bacalar.

In the last days of July, ten of the *indios alzados* of Tipu arrived at Bacalar. They stated that, in answer to Pérez's summons, a large group of Tipu Maya reached Holzuuz a few days after Pérez had set off from there on his return journey to Bacalar. They were disappointed not to find him there because they wished to offer obedience, to return to Spanish rule, once more to have relations with the Spaniards, to serve His Majesty, and to enter again the fold of Mother Church. Not finding Pérez at Holzuuz, they had sent these ten men to Bacalar to find him and tell him that, whenever he chose to return and settle them in towns, they would come at his summons and that after a settlement had been made they would send for the padre at Bacalar to administer the sacraments to them. This information was sent to the governor of Yucatán in letters of the third and fourth of August signed by the *cabildo* and the parish priest. López [de] Cogolludo added a couple of lines to his completed book, noting that in the previous year of 1655, Indians had arrived from Tipu offering their submission (1867–1868:bk. 11, chap. 16).

Pérez himself took the letters to the governor and, no doubt, gave fuller details of the events. In response, the latter gave him a formal commission to lead a new expedition to "reduce" the Maya of Tipu. He also wrote a letter to its leaders calling on them to renew their obedience to church and state.

Pérez set out on his third journey on October 5, 1655, at the very height of the rainy season, as he carefully points out, when rivers and swamps were full and the land under water. The party got as far as the "town and settlement" of Chunukum, "one of the said pueblos" (of Tipu). This, as noted previously, was on the Belize River, probably in the neighborhood of Rock Dondo or Never Delay. Because he could not ascend to the towns (*subir a los pueblos*) farther on because the roads were under water and the rivers in flood, Pérez sent messengers to the three chief towns (identified above as Tipu, Zaczuuz, and Lucu) and all the other Indians that they should come to meet him and see the governor's letter. The use here of the word *subir* is reasonable evidence that Chunukum was indeed on the Belize River and downstream from those three towns on its banks.

In response to the summons, the chiefs and other Indians of the Tipu settlements, save those absent, sick, or for other reasons unable to make the trip, came to Chunukum. There were 110 men and numbers of women and children. In addition, 23 Indians were already at Chunukum. This figure fails to agree with the *matrícula*, which gives 141 male residents of Tipu, unless we make the highly doubtful assumption that those of Tipu found at Holzuuz are included. In fact, unless disease had swept off many youngsters, many children must have been left at home; they are outnumbered by adults by three to one.

An interpreter read in Maya to the assembled Indians Pérez's commission and the governor's letter. The *matrícula* was then made. All were listed without anyone hiding, according to the *probanza*, but, as we have seen, that was a highly optimistic appraisal of the operation. The date we know from the *matrícula* itself was November 6, 1655.

The Indians promised, as Pérez reported on his return to Bacalar, that on his next visit he would find a church built at Chunukum, in which the priest of Bacalar could say mass, and that whenever they were summoned they would come gladly. "With this agreement all the said Indians remained peaceful and pacified," commented Pérez. His task superficially accomplished, he returned to Bacalar. He became so ill on the journey that the priest of Bacalar was summoned to Hautila (Uatibal?), 8 leagues distant, to give him the sacraments (extreme unction?), but he recovered and was carried safely to Bacalar in a hammock.

Whether the mission was as successful as Pérez claimed one may doubt. Why should the people of Tipu have been anxious to build a church at Chunukum? It lay about 28 miles in direct line from Tipu and perhaps 40 miles by trail; by river the distance must have been a good 50 miles with innumerable small rapids to negotiate. Such a journey by land or water would have been an ordeal for whole families. A church at Chunukum would have been convenient to the padre coming from Bacalar, but one suspects that the reason behind the offer to build there was to keep priest and government official from poking around Tipu, where some highly unchristian practices might have come to light. There had been a church at Tipu when Fuensalida was there in 1619. Whether it was still standing in 1655 is not evident.

On November 28, 1655, after his return to Salamanca de Bacalar, Pérez made the usual report in the form of a petition to Gómez Santoya. Several witnesses testified to the facts presented.

Although the *probanza* speaks of three journeys, a certified declaration attached to the *probanza* makes a fourth clear. This, dated July 16, 1656, was a deposition made by *licenciado* Pedro Juan Fernández, secular priest (*beneficiado, cura y vicario*) of Bacalar. In this he states that he set forth from Bacalar on April 25, 1656, in the company of Pérez with the purpose of administering to and restoring to Spanish control the Indians of the Tipu who had been in rebellion for twenty years. The use of *the* (*el*) before Tipu is not uncommon in Spanish writings—in Villagutierre Soto-Mayor, for instance—and we think refers to the River Tipu, that is, the upper Belize River, but possibly refers to the Tipu district.

Before starting, Pérez sent ahead two Indians to warn those of Tipu of their visit and when they might be expected so that the Indians should gather to receive them (presumably at Chunukum), coming down from the towns above (*arriba*). "That is what they did, chiefs and a number of Indians coming down from their towns and bringing everything necessary for our maintenance." The *cura* calls attention to Pérez's expenditure of money and effort to bring the Indians once more into the fold. Unfortunately, he gives no other details. We do not know, for instance, how many came to meet Pérez and the padre; numbers seem to have been small. Neither are we informed whether the promised church had been built. As we shall see, the Tipu towns did not take seriously their reconciliation with church and state.

This is the last document directly bearing on Pérez's travels.

Tipu after 1656

For subsequent information about the Tipu towns we are dependent on Villagutierre Soto-Mayor (1933:bk. 5, chaps. 10–12; bk. 6, chaps. 3–5; bk. 7, chaps. 4, 11) and the Avendaño y Loyola *relación* of 1696.

In the mid 1690's plans were set afoot for what was to prove the conquest of the Itza of Tayasal and the whole Petén, with armies advancing from Guatemala and Yucatán. Although the main invasion from Yucatán followed the western route down the peninsula, Tipu played an important part. It should be noted that Villagutierre Soto-Mayor uses the term *El Tipu*, and one is not always certain whether he refers to the town of Tipu specifically or the towns of the upper Belize (Tipu) valley.

A visit by Capt. Francisco de Hariza, *alcalde* of Bacalar, to the Tipu towns, perhaps early in 1695, coincided, doubtlessly not by chance, with the opening of the road down the west side of the peninsula, preliminary to invasion. The Maya, both heathen and apostates, gave Hariza to understand that they were willing to submit to Spanish crown and papal tiara. Clearly Pérez's journeys had had no lasting effect. Hariza brought in a priest who baptized many and gave instruction to seven chiefs, all over sixty years old, of the heathen "nation" called Muzulules (written elsewhere Muzules), who had no knowledge of Christianity.

At the same time Hariza sent a message of amity to the ruler of Tayasal by Mateo Bichab (Uicab?), a Tipuan. Not awaiting a reply, he left for Mérida with twenty newly baptized Maya of the Tipu to offer obedience to the governor. The governor promised four secular priests for the evangelization of the area, and those were subsequently sent. Of the success of their work, nothing is known.

During Hariza's absence, a delegation sent by Can Ek, ruler of Tayasal, reached Tipu en route to Mérida to discuss his submission to Spanish rule. Two of its members, later known as Martin Can and Pedro Miguel Can, figured prominently in the later history of the conquest of Tayasal. They were nephews of Can Ek, their mother, Cante, being a sister of Can Ek. I assume the younger brother, Pedro, had the same mother; their father, Can, was a native of Tipu, and they lived in Yalain, at the end of Lake Petén (Avendaño y Loyola 1696:50ʳ; Villagutierre Soto-Mayor 1933:bk. 5, chap. 12; bk. 6, chap. 4; bk. 8, chap. 4). Unlike Bertha, wife of pagan Ethelbert of Canterbury, whose Christian religion was guaranteed in her marriage settlement, Can surely discarded his Christianity upon marriage into heathen "royalty." Apart from the historical romance of this Tipuan abjuring Christianity, which probably sat lightly on him, the prosaic fact that a man of Tipu could marry the sister of the ruler of Tayasal and settle in his territory is evidence of the close bonds between Tipu and the Petén Maya, deeper than commercial relations (Tipu traded machetes and axes for textiles of Tayasal).

Villagutierre Soto-Mayor writes that this delegation came to the town of Achamabux of El Tipu, where the *alcaldes* of the town of Tipu, as well as some of the neighboring heathen Muzul, awaited them to act as interpreters. Towns were often given the name of the chief. The first part of this name can probably be reconstructed as Ah Chan; no worthwhile guess can be made as to the second half (Villagutierre Soto-Mayor's transcriptions of Maya names are wretched). Note that the baptismal name is absent and apparently the old Maya prefix *ah* appears. One supposes that the settlement lay on the Tipu-Tayasal trail and probably not far west of Tipu.

Can Ek's delegates with their Muzul companions, after an enthusiastic reception in Mérida, stopped at Tipu on their return journey.

Hariza, who, with a small force, had been ordered to proceed to Tayasal to receive the surrender of Can Ek, prudently remained at Tipu when he learned that a force under Zubiaur had been attacked at Lake Petén and forced to retreat after suffering casualties. He confined his activities to attacks on a subordinate, blaming him for the failure of the Indian surrender mission to Mérida. The luckless victim spent several months in jail before he could establish his innocence. Nothing more is heard of Hariza; he seems to have had no part in the final capture of Tayasal.

One is left with the impression that those two captains of Castille, or, rather, of Bacalar, Pérez and Hariza, were mightiest when it came to bombast.

With Captain Hariza waiting prudently in Tipu, conclude the references to that small town thrust into the foreground by economic forces from outside. The text of Pérez's *matrícula* of Tipu follows (quoted directly from the *probanza* of Captain Francisco Pérez, A.G.I., Audiencia de México, Legajo 158).

●   Matrícula del Pueblo de Tipu, 1655

Hoy que se contaron seis días del mes de noviembre de mil seiscientos cincuenta y cinco años en este pueblo de Chunukum reduje, congregué y junté todos los indios que están en esta matrícula para llevarla al señor gobernador y capitán general como me lo tiene ordenado y mandado, y es como se sigue:

Juan May, Ana Na del pueblo de Tipu	2 – 0
Bernardino Ek, Ana Ɔiu de Tipu con dos hijos	2 H 2
Juan Ku, Susana Tut de Tipu con una hija	2 H 1
Baltasar May, Ana Cumun, Tipu con un hijo	2 H 1
Francisco Ku, Francisca Uc, Tipu con un hijo	2 H 1
Francisco Ku, Angelina Tut, Tipu con dos hijos	2 H 2
Fernando Boh huido Tipu	2 H 0 [sic]
Andrés Ku, Catalina Hau, Tipu	2 H 0
Lorenzo Chable, Magdalena Uc, Tipu con un hijo	2 H 1
Juan Chable, Catalina Canche, Tipu con un hijo	2 H 1
Luis Uc, Magdalena Can, Tipu	2 H 0
Andrés Cauil, Viviana Puc, Tipu con dos hijos	2 H 2
Simon Can, Elena Mux, Tipu con un hijo	2 H 1
Cristóbal Nauat, Francisca Can, Tipu con un hijo	2 H 1
Gerónimo Ppol, María Cocom, Tipu con un hijo	2 H 1
Jua[n] Euan, Tipu con un hijo	1 H 1
Andrés Peche, Ana Canche, Tipu con un hijo	1 H 1 [sic]
Baltasar Cen, Tipu con un hijo	2 H 1 [sic]
Angelina Chan, Tipu	2 H 0 [sic]
Lorenzo Itza, Juana Chan, Tipu con un hijo	1 H 1 [sic]

Francisco Canche, Elena Tun, Tipu con un hijo	1 H 1 [*sic*]
Bartolomé Mo, Ana Mamaçun, Tipo con un hijo	2 H 1
Juan Nauat, Viviana Hau, Tipu con un hijo	2 H 1
Pablo Cocom, Juana Puc, Tipu con un hijo	2 H 1
Pedro Tzuc, Andrea Chel, Tipu	2 H 0
Melchor Uc, Ana Cab, Tipu con un hijo	2 H 1
Joseph Tzuc, Catalina Uc, Tipu con un hijo	2 H 1
Andrés Balan, viudo	1 H 0
Simon Ku, Juana Mo, Tipu con dos hijos	2 H 2
George Chan, Clara Balan, Tipu con un hijo	2 H 1
Gaspar Itza con un hijo	1 H 1
Juan Can, Magdalena May, Tipu con un hijo	2 H 1
Juan Cuioc, Ana Can, Tipu con dos hijos	2 H 2
Fabian Tut, Andrea May, Tipu con un hijo	2 H 1
Baltasar Pat, Tipu	1 H 0
Diego Ppol, Magdalena Balan, Tipu con un hijo	2 H 1
Francisco Balan, Tipu	1 H 0
Pedro Uc, María Tut, Tipu	2 H 0
Luis Macun, Juana Ku, Tipu	2 H 0
Diego Maçum, Francisca Chuc, Tipu con un hijo	2 H 1
Andrés Ku, Clara Cima, Tipu con un hijo	2 H 1
Gaspar Chicil, Tipu	1 H 0
Francisco Chan, Andrea Mux, Tipu con un hijo	2 H 1
Fabian Mux, Tipu	1 H 0
Pedro Canul, Petrona Chable, Tipu	2 H 0
Fernando Ucan, viudo, Tipu	1 H 0
Andrés Can, María Ceh, Tipu con un hijo	2 H 1
Juan Can, Juliana Canche, Tipu con un hijo	2 H 1
Juan Cetzal, viudo, Tipu	1 H 0
Francisco Cetzal, Petrona Malah, Tipu	2 H 0
Gaspar Keb, Tipu con un hijo	1 H 1
Juan Pix, Magdalena Balan, Tipu	2 H 0
Fernando Pix, Tipu	1 H 0
Gaspar Mil, Juan Tzuc, Tipu	2 H 0
Mateo Cupul, Beatriz Ku, Tipu	2 H 0
Juan Maz, Juliana Chi, Tipu	2 H 0
Gaspar Maz, Tipu	1 H 0
Francisco Mo, Clara Ba, Tipu con dos hijos	4
Aparicio Pat, Tipu	1
Juan Maz, viudo, Tipu	1
Gaspar Chan, Lucía Tuz, Tipu con un hijo	4 [*sic*]
Pedro Cante, viudo, Tipu	1
Gabriel Chan, Tipu	1
Juan Euan, María Mo, Tipu con un hijo	3

Juan Maz, María Yam, Tipu con un hijo	3
Diego Uc, Ana Panti, Tipu	2
Sebastián Uc, viudo, Tipu	1
Andrés Balan, Marta Pat, Tipu	2
Andrés Uc, Tipu	1
Clemente Chan, Ana Can, Tipu	2
Bartolomé May, Juliana Tun, Tipu	2
Juan Tun, viudo, Tipu	1
Pedro May, Beatriz May, Tipu con un hijo	3
Juan Bicab, Juana Puc, Tipu	2
Juan Pol, Ana Cumun, Tipu con un hijo	3
Pablo Cob, Juana May, Tipu con un hijo	3
Juan May, Tipu	1
Bartolomé Ceh, María Mukul, Tipu con un hijo	3
Gerónimo Coyi, Clara Yan, Tipu	1
Pedro Coyi	1
María Vicab, Tipu	1
Alonso Chan, Magdalena Cob, Tipu con un hijo	3
Melchor Chan, María Mo, Tipu	2
Gregorio Chan, Tipu	1
Pedro Cumun, Isabel Ttax, Tipu con un hijo	3
Lucas Chim, Tipu	1
Mateo May, Juana Chan, Tipu con una hija	3
Juan Xix, María Kuk, con un hijo	3
Pedro Chi, Ana Tzuc, Tipu	2
Baltasar Ek, Paulina Cab, Tipu con dos hijos	4
Simon Ek, Catalina Cabal, Tipu con un hijo	3
Juan Canche, viudo, Tipu	1
Francisco Canche, María Noh, Tipu con tres hijos	5
Pedro Canche, viudo, Tipu	1
Juan Noh, viudo, Tipu	1
Juan Puc, viudo, Tipu con tres hijos	1
	4 [sic]
Juan Coboh Lamayna Clara Pol, Tipu con un hijo	3
Cristóbal Chuc, Maria Coboh, Tipu con tres hijos	5
Francisca Chay con un hijo, Tipu	2
Andrés Chi, Tipu	1
Diego Peche, viudo, con un hijo, Tipu	2
Juan Ceh, Clara Çel, Tipu con un hijo	3
Juan Antonio Chan, María Chuc, Tipu	2
Pedro Xol, viudo, Tipu	1
Pedro Puc, viudo, Tipu	1
Lorenzo Pat, Catarina Ma, Tipu	2
Antonio Pat, Lucía Balan, Tipu	2

Gaspar Ma, Tipu	1
Gaspar Chan, viudo, Tipu	1
Gregorio Puc, María Ayl, Tipu	2
Francisco Xol, Lucía Chim, Tipu	2
Bartolomé Poot, Ursula Xol, Tipu	2
Isabel Xol, viuda, Tipu	1
Mateo Cime, Tipu	1
Juan Habnal, Juliana Cech, Tipu	2
Francisco Chuc, viudo, Tipu	1
Joseph Poot, viudo, Tipu	1
Diego Poot, Ursula Tuyu, Tipu	2
Juan Canche, viudo, Tipu	1
Luis Maz, Juana Tzuc, Tipu	2
Juan Chuc, Francisca Ttun	2
Antonio Chuc, Juana Ek, Tipu	2
Lucas Chuc, Juana Tep, Tipu con un hijo	3
Pedro Mil, Andrea Can, Tipu con 1	2 [sic]
Lorenzo Kauil, Tipu	1
Antonio Chi, viudo, Tipu	1
Agustina Puc, viuda, Tipu	1
Cristóbal Ek, viudo, Tipu	1
Cristóbal Chan, Tipu	1
Cristóbal Pat, viudo, Tipu	1
Pablo Habnal, Tipu con un hijo	2
Pablo Habnal, viudo Tipu	1
Juan Ku, Juana Uh, Tipu	2
Lucas Tian Ku, Tipu	1
Clemente Canul, viudo, Tipu	1
Pedro Cakin, Ana Na, Tipu	2
Juan Uicab, Andrea Chan, Tipu con un hijo	3
Joseph Chi, Francisco Pat, Tipu con tres hijos	5
Antonio Chi, Andrea Pat, Tipu con un hijo	3
Francisco Na, viudo, Tipu	1
Pablo Cen, Marta Chan, Tipu	1 [sic]
Pedro Tamay, Catalina Ceb, Tipu	2
Francisco Chin, viudo, Tipu	1
Juan Cauich, Tipu	1
Francisco Na, Ursala Çel, Tipu	1 [sic]
Gaspar Mis, Andrea Coboh, Tipu	2

Son el pueblo de Tipu doscientos treinta y nueve grandes, y muchachos setenta y seis.

Cacçuuz
Francisco Kuxeb, Clara Ek, Çacçuz con una hija

Luis May, María Xiu
Gaspar Maz, Catalina Cupul con un hijo
Juan Chi, Francisca Uc con un hijo
Juan Uicab, Andrea Uc con una hija
Pedro Keb, María Vicab con un hijo
Juan Tzuc, viudo
    Hay es este pueblo trece grandes y cinco muchachos.

Çacatan
Lorenzo Puc, María Sima con un hijo
Pedro Sima, María Chi con dos hijos
Juan Malah, Juliana Hau con un hijo
Francisco Malah
Juana Chan
María Sima
Fernando Çima, viudo
Diego Malah
Felipe Çima
Rodrigo Puc, Juliana Çima
Juan Çima, Francisca Puc con un hijo
Pedro Chan, viudo
Francisco Çima, Agustina Malah
Francisco Puc, Ana Malah con dos hijos
Juan Chan, Francisca Çima, con un hijo
Sicilia Chan
Fernando Chan, Francisca Chan con dos hijos
María Çima
    Son veinte y siete grandes los de este pueblo y diez muchachos.

Holpattin
Pablo Can, Isabel Maz
Juan Tun, Andrea Cetzal con un hijo
Juan Hau, Paulina Chan
Juan Canche, Clara Chable con dos hijos
    Son de Holpatín ocho grandes y tres muchachos.

Chalacam
Gaspar Chan, Angelina Canche
Juan Chan, Juana Noh
    Son cuatro grandes de Chalacam.

Mayapan
Juan Chan, viudo
Diego Mo, viudo

Pablo Mo, María Chacxib con dos hijos
Andrés Mo con un hijo
Diego Mo, Andrea Yatz con un hijo
Juan Vicab, Angelina Hau
Andrés Cab, Juana Chan con un hijo
   Item, otra llamada María Chan, con que son doce grandes y cinco
   muchachos.

Chinam
Clara Mo, Juana Chim

Coyte y Xibun
Diego Malah de Soyte y su mujer de Xibun

Indios del monte
Chuen Caan, varón, Ixmen Caan de Tipu
Xoc Ku, hembra, Tipu
Ixcan Hau, hembra, Tipu
Xoc Ku, hembra, Tipu
Ic Kib, varón, Tipu
Çalpuc, hembra, Tipu
Ah Canchi, varón, Ekmaz, hembra, Tipu
Ixci May, hembra, Tipu
Ixcaban Ppol, hembra
Ixcib Chable, hembra, Tipu
Ixetzpix, Tipu, hembra
Ixca Vac Cavih, hembra, Tipu
Ixben Can, Tipu, hembra
Ixcaban Mo, hembra, Tipu
Chuen Can, varón, Ixetznab ca Vih, hembra, Tipu
Ixmen Kante, Tipu, hembra, Tipu
Ixcam Balam, hembra, Tipu
Ixmen Can, hembra, Tipu
Ixmen Çima, Çacatan, hembra
Ixmuluc Chan, Tipu, hembra
Ixcau Cech, Tipu, hembra
Ixtutzpix, hembra, Tipu
Ixtinal, hembra, Tipu
Ixmuluc Mukul, Tipu, hembra
Ixcab Uz, Tipu, hembra
Ixcan Chan, hembra, Tipu
Ixmen Cob, Tipu, hembra
   Estas treinta almas dejé pobladas con los demás indios en el pueblo de
   Tipu.

Lucu
Gregorio Chable, Inés Ku con un hijo
Francisco Chable, Francisca Coyi con un hijo
  Hay en esta matrícula trescientos cuarenta y uno grandes y muchachos
  ciento y uno.
● Francisco Pérez.

Surnames in the Matrícula

The scribe who copied the *probanza* had the habit of doubling consonants, for example, *ttrayendo ttodo lo nessesario, cappitan,* and *confforme.* Tipu is frequently written *Ttipu.* Accordingly, doubling of *t* and *p* in Maya surnames almost certainly is not to indicate fortis consonants.

Of the approximately ninety-two names in the *matrícula,* excluding those under the heading *Indios del monte,* all but fifteen appear in Roys's (1940) lists of personal names in Yucatán. Names not on those lists are Ayl, Boh, Caan, Cabnal, Cakin, Cech, Chacxib, (but note Chac Xib Chac, defeated ruler of Chichen Itza), Ma, Malah, Mil, Mux, Peche, Tian, Tutz, and Yatz. Some of the following could be in the group, but most probably were carelessly recorded: Bicab for Uicab, Cima for Zima, Chel for Ch'el, Kante for Cante, Macum for Mazum, Yan for Yam, and Dziu for Tziu.

This great preponderance of names found also in Yucatán, no doubt, reflects to a considerable extent the southward movement of Maya from Yucatán and Quintana Roo to escape Spanish rule. Indeed, Fuensalida reported that Francisco Cumux, one of Tipu's *principales,* was descended from the former ruling family of Cozumel (López [de] Cogolludo 1867–1868:bk. 9, chap. 7). On the other hand, some names common to Yucatán and upper Belize valley may represent families who moved—presumably in pre-Columbian times—in the opposite direction. Chan, for instance, far the commonest name in the Tipu region and common in much of the Petén, may have been introduced into Yucatán by immigrants, as indeed, Roys has suggested (1940:36).

Compound or double-barreled surnames, rare in colonial Yucatán but common in parts of the southern lowlands, are rare in the Tipu region, there being only three examples: Ma Mazum, Chac Xib, and Tian Ku. It is significant that in all three cases one of the names is not found in Yucatán.

Nevertheless, compound names may have been common or even universal in pre-Columbian Yucatán but were reduced to a single (paternal) surname when baptismal names were introduced. Indeed, Landa records that both paternal and maternal names were used (1938:113). Roys established that in Yucatán the latter, which came first, was preceded by *na,* "mother," in contrast to the use of straight compound names. Contrary to pre-Columbian usage, two couples have the same surname.

Day Surnames of the Indios del Monte

In contrast to other entries in the *matrícula*, the names of the thirty *indios del monte*, that is, forest Indians, synonymous with wild Indians (twenty-six women; four men), have these unusual features: with one exception (Ix Tinal), all are double-barreled names; all lack baptismal names; nearly all names of women carry the female prefix *ix*, and one of the four names of men has the masculine prefix *ah*; finally, and most important of all, half of the group has a Maya day name which, in every case, precedes the other name. Those fifteen are named:

Ix Muluc Chan, Ix Muluc Mukul
Chuen Caan, Chuen Can
Ix Ben Can
Ix Men Caan, Ix Men Kante, Ix Men Cah, Ix Men Cob, Ix Men Zima
Ix Cib Chable
Ix Caban Mo, Ix Caban Ppol
Ix Etznab Cauih
Ix Cauac (written Ixca Vac) Cauih

Possibly the list yields two more day names. Xoc, which appears twice as the first part of a woman's double name, might be a contraction of Ix Oc or X'Oc, Oc being the tenth of the twenty Maya day names. The Maya female prefix is more correctly transcribed as *x*, but the Spaniards, having difficulty with that *sh* sound without an opening vowel (cf. *e* before *sc* or *st* in Spanish), usually pronounced it as English *ish* and transcribed it *ix*, but by no means always (cf. place names, such as Xlabpak, Xcalac, Xpukil). Moreover, if this is a day name, in both cases it conforms to the custom of placing the day name first in a compound surname. Xoc is a Yucatec surname but does not appear elsewhere in the Tipu *matrícula*. Finally, as all other women's names with one exception carry the *ix* prefix, were the surname Xoc, one would expect it to be written Ix Xoc.

Another candidate for this group is Ic Kib. Ic as a surname has not been reported, but Ik is the second of the twenty Maya day names.

If these three dubious cases are accepted 60 percent of the *indios del monte* had day names. A Maya calendar may well have still functioned among this group in the 1630's (all bearers of day names were adults in 1655). Certainly, a Maya calendar flourished among the Manche Chol in 1631 (Scholes and Adams 1960:184), and that group and the *indios del monte* may well have been neighbors, as we shall see.

The fact that the day name is invariably the first name is good evidence that it was not inherited but given because the owner was born on the day in question, for under the usual compound-name structure one name is of one parent; the other, of the second. With such an arrangement, a day name should statistically appear as often for a second name as it does for a first. That is not so with our *indios del monte;* the day name is always the first. A run of fifteen (perhaps eighteen) reds and no blacks is very rare in a game of chance. Moreover, were day names inherited, one would expect at least one case of a double day name. On the other hand, no less than five of the day names are men. As spelled, eleven of thirty nonday names of this group are not in Roys's Yucatec name lists.

Distribution of Day Names

The use of Maya day names, with the added feature of numbers, was common—at least among the nobility—in the Quiche and Cakchiquel parts of highland Guatemala (e.g., persons named Oxib Ceh, Beleheb Tzi, and Hun Igh). Day names and numbers also occur among the Mixtec and on reliefs in Veracruz. In the Maya lowlands they are probably confined to a few glyphic representations, not in Maya style, on reliefs at Chichen Itza.

Interestingly, the only reported case of a day name in colonial Yucatán is that of a certain Ah Chuen Chay. This name deviates from the general run of Yucatec names in three respects: it carries the masculine *ah* prefix; it is a double-barreled name without the *na* prefix; and it is the name of a slave (Roys 1940:40). As rank-and-file prisoners of war were commonly enslaved in Yucatán, most probably this slave was a non-Yucatec Maya taken prisoner of war. He may well have belonged to the group of which our *indios del monte* formed a part.

Among the Putun Maya of the Itzamkanac area, the only Putun for whom a reasonably long list of surnames has been published, the day name Lamat appears by itself or in the compound names Bolon Lamat and Lamat Azel (Scholes and Roys 1948:482, 484). As Bolon signifies the number 9, it has been suggested that this might represent a day name with number, 9 Lamat, but Bolon is also a name among these Putun (Bolon Pacha and Pax Bolon) and among the Mopan Maya. Accordingly, it seems more probably that Bolon Lamat was a son of parents called Bolon and Lamat.

Another possible day name with number in this same group is Buluch Atzi (Scholes and Roys 1948:65). Buluch is number 11 and Atzi conceivably might be Tzi, tenth day in some Maya calendars, but that leaves the opening *a* unexplained. Oc, Yucatec name for the tenth day, also occurs in this Putun list. Perhaps the best explanation is that Lamat and Oc were inherited day names perhaps deriving from non-Putun Maya absorbed by the Putun.

The Maya day name Cib, already noted in the *matrícula*, was borne by the chief of Canizan (Villagutierre Soto-Mayor 1933:bk. 6, chap. 5) on the Río Usumacinta, below Tenosique, and is probably Putun in speech (Scholes and Roys 1948:25, 26, 445–446).

We know of no other Maya day names in the lowlands. One must, however, bear in mind that for large areas few names have been recovered. A fair assortment has been recorded for Lake Petén and the surrounding area, but these include no day names. Accordingly, we can be confident that this day name practice was unknown in northern Petén.

Identity of the <u>Indios del Monte</u>

Pérez lists the *indios del monte* as being, for the most part, from Tipu (one from Zacat'an), but that is impossible to accept; their names are completely distinct from those of Tipu. One suspects he added that locality together with the statement "I left them settled at the town of Tipu" as a bit of eyewash, for certainly he never set foot in that town. Probably Tipu is given as the place of origin and final destination of this group because he did not want to leave himself open to censure for having allowed those heathen to escape from the fold by returning to the forest.

The fact that the group comprised twenty-six women but only four men and no children suggests that it had been rounded up by a detachment of Pérez's force while the men were out hunting or elsewhere engaged and the children had been left behind with the infirm and aged. In that case their homes would have been in the vicinity of Chunukum, presumably south of the Belize River. One may suggest that they were part of the Muzul nation, often mentioned by Villagutierre Soto-Mayor, but without the slightest information about them save that they were heathen and that they spoke Yucatec since they offered to accept Spanish rule through interpreters in Mérida.

Fr. Joseph Delgado, O.P., in his account of the peoples, places, and rivers of what is now Belize, reports that in 1677 the town of Zaui, one and a half day's journey by road from Tipu, was governed by a certain Juan Muzul (Ximénez 1929–1971:bk. 5, chap. 33). Muzul is not a Yucatec name. Zaui lay on a route leading from Campin, almost certainly some way upstream on the Monkey River (J. E. S. Thompson [1974]), in a northwesterly direction. Accordingly, we may locate it roughly as about half way between Tipu and the mouth of Mullins River, which would not be far south of where we place Chunukum (close to Rock Dondo or Never Delay). From other sources we know that Yucatec or a dialect thereof was the speech north of Manche Chol–speaking Campin.

A document (Guatemala, Archivo General del Gobierno 1936) tells of a roundup in the same general region in 1754. A group called Muxun, one of whose towns was Siytee (cf. Zoite and its modern equivalent, the Sittee River of Belize) was settled after reduction at Dolores, Mopan, or perhaps the closely related Petén Maya in speech. If the Muxun can be identified with the Muzul—Villagutierre Soto-Mayor once calls them Muzulun—a possibility in view of the hash Spanish writers so often made of Maya names, then the name Muzul applied to the occupants of a band of territory stretching from the middle Belize valley to the Sittee River.

The case is far from proven but is reasonably strong that Pérez's *indios del monte* were Muzul, and perhaps it is not too implausible to see Tipu and the other villages of the upper Belize valley as having been part of the Muzul group before their culture was disrupted first by Spanish crown and church and later by Maya refugees from the north. Conceivably, the parents or grandparents of the *indios del monte* were, indeed, born near Tipu but, resisting settlement in the town, had fled farther into the forest, which would explain Pérez's entries that many of them were from Tipu.

Epilogue

The *probanza* of Francisco Pérez, undisturbed for three centuries in the Archive of the Indies, is a good example of the workings of the Spanish bureaucratic system. It gives us glimpses of an ambitious man with an eye to the main chance. Above all, it lifts a curtain on seventeenth-century interplay between Maya and hispanic cultures.

Those Maya of the upper Belize valley realized that direct confrontation would surely have led to subjection. Instead, they made promises with tongue in cheek and relied on such allies as distance, forest and swamp, malaria, and dysentery to keep Spanish control minimal. In that type of amorphous resistance we may perhaps see a rough parallel to recent events in Vietnam.

3

The Maya and the Colonization of Belize
in the Nineteenth Century

O. Nigel Bolland

Introduction: "The Owl of Minerva Spreads Its Wings
Only with the Falling of the Dusk"

It has been stated that "there is no record of any indigenous population
and no reason to believe that any such existed except far in the interior [of
Belize]. There are traces of extensive Maya Indian population . . . all over
the Colony . . . but this occupation was long before British settlement"
(Burdon 1931–1935:I, 4). Sir John Alder Burdon, who knew the records
better than anyone else at the time, was the governor of British Honduras
from 1925 to 1931. His view that the area was uninhabited at the time of
British settlement was convenient because it removed some of the stigma
attached to the process of conquest, dispossession, and colonization.
Stephen L. Caiger, an amateur historian and colonial apologist, wrote of
the Maya as "aboriginals" but asserted that they "had abandoned the
Belize district long before the seventeenth century. Afterwards, however,
hearing of the mild rule of the logwood-cutters as contrasted with Spanish
arrogance and cruelty, they percolated over the frontiers from Mexico and
Guatemala, in such large numbers that today these Indians compose more
than one sixth of the total population, with a culture, industrial life, and
a Reservation of their own" (Caiger 1951:126–127). Caiger, who wrote during the period of emerging nationalism in Belize (see Shoman 1973), was
arguing, first, that the British occupation did not *displace* any indigenous
population and, second, that the Maya *chose* the "mild rule" of the British.

It is only now, when the sun is finally setting on the British Empire,
that it is possible to perceive and understand the meaning of the colonial
myths. Historical events can be interpreted only when enough further
events have unfolded for the total historical framework, within which the
earlier ones occurred, to be revealed. The meaning of history, therefore,
progressively unfolds itself, and it is only toward the end of a historical
epoch that we can achieve sufficient wisdom to penetrate the gloom of preceding events. Now, for example, it is possible to expose the ideological

nature of Caiger's shadowy argument. The view that Maya-British relations in Belize were nonantagonistic, while convenient from the standpoint of colonial ideology, is contrary to the historical record.

This article presents evidence to demonstrate that the territory now
known as Belize (map 3-1) was definitely occupied by Maya who were displaced and dispossessed by the British, that relations between the Maya
and the British were generally antagonistic in nature, and that the rule of
the British, neither mild nor chosen, was imposed upon the Maya in the
nineteenth century by force of arms. Finally, this article examines the
changing image held by the British of the Maya and relates the changes to
phases of the colonization process.

Early Encounters between the Maya and the British Woodcutters

The first British settlers who arrived on the coast of Belize to cut logwood,
about the middle of the seventeenth century, have left no record of contact
with Maya for the first century of their occupation, though we know from
Spanish records that Maya did live in the interior during that century (see
Bolland 1974). The Maya who inhabited the coast at the time of Dávila's
forays in 1530 may have succumbed to epidemics in the interim, or they
may have retreated to less-vulnerable sites. Alternatively, or in addition,
they may have retired at the sight of the returning white men, keeping out
of the way of the British logwood cutters as the latter worked their way up
the various rivers, creeks, and lagoons. There is, in any case, such a paucity
of early British records that evidence of early contacts is unlikely to be un-
earthed. The first British settlers were pirates and adventurers, probably
mostly illiterate, who, unlike the Spanish missionaries, would not be inclined to keep accounts of their encounters with the indigenous people.
Moreover, if any accounts existed, they are unlikely to have survived, as
the constant harassment of the early settlement by the Spaniards provided
little security for historical records. For example, when St. George's Key,
the British settlers' principal residence, was captured by Spaniards from
Bacalar on September 15, 1779, it was recorded that all "the Books and
Papers of the Merchants and principal Inhabitants should be put into
Chests . . . and delivered to . . . Merida."[1] Just prior to this attack, however, a description of the state of the settlement had mentioned the presence of small numbers of Maya in the area: "The Indians who live near
the English are so inconsiderable that it is unnecessary to take any notice
of them."[2]

Up to this time there would have been little cause for contact, the British obtaining most of their logwood near the coast, where it could be easily
loaded on their ships, and the Maya probably preferring to retire and keep

Map 3-1
Opposite: Some principal locations in late nineteenth century Belize

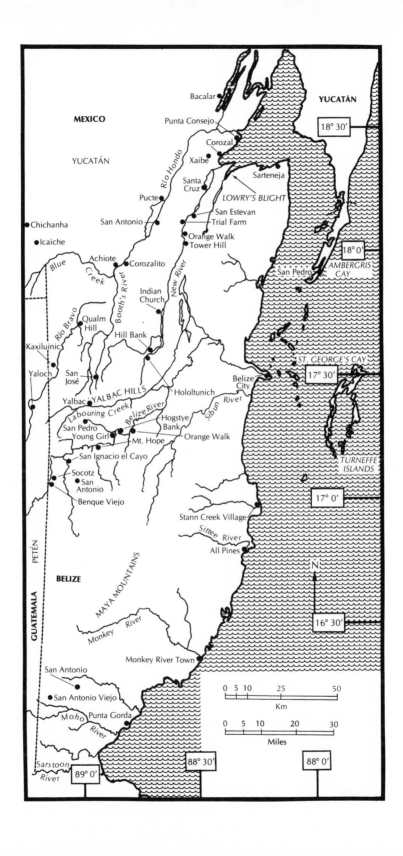

out of their way. As the accessible timber became exhausted, however, the British penetrated farther inland, and in the 1770's the demand for mahogany created by the English luxury furniture industry enticed the British woodcutters into the Maya forests of what is now central and northwest Belize. As the frontier of British exploitation moved inland, contacts between the two peoples increased, the Maya forcing the British to "take notice" of them.

From maps of the late eighteenth and early nineteenth centuries it is observed that the frontier of the British timber reserve at that time lay from the Río Hondo south through New River Lagoon and Roaring Creek to the Sibun River.[3] The Maya who lived to the west of this line responded to British encroachments upon their territory with vigorous military action. Thus an "attack of the Wild Indians"[4] was reported as having occurred on the New River in 1788, and in 1802 a detachment of troops was requested to "be sent up river to punish the Indians who are committing depredations upon the Mahogany works" (Burdon 1931–1935: II, 58). Unfortunately it is not recorded which river was involved in that case, but a request in 1807 for "arms and ammunition for gangs working up the River at Hogstye Bank, who have been attacked by Indians" (ibid.: II, 101) is more helpful in locating the frontier, for Hogstye Bank was a little above Orange Walk on the Belize River, probably close to Roaring Creek.

Though they ultimately failed to check the expansionism of the British, these Maya were certainly seen by the British as a serious threat to their settlement. Capt. George Henderson, who was stationed in Belize with the Fifth West India Regiment at the beginning of the nineteenth century, stated that "not many years past, numerous tribes of hostile Indians often left their recesses in the woods for the purpose of plunder. This they often accomplished; and if resistance were offered, not infrequently committed the most sanguinary murders. The habitations of these people have never been traced. Their dispositions are peculiarly ferocious. . . . the dread of the military, whom it has been found expedient frequently to dispatch in pursuit of these fugitives, has latterly operated as a very effectual check" (Henderson 1809:18–19). Contrary to Henderson's assurances, the Maya continued to fight back, despite the employment of regular troops against them. As late as 1817 "the exposed and unprotected state of the settlers, surrounded by vast hordes of Indians who are all in the constant habit of breaking in upon their works" was feared as placing the British settlers "entirely at the mercy of the Slave Population."[5] Supt. George Arthur also reported in 1817 that "we are surrounded by Tribes of Indians who occasionally commit great depredations upon the Cutters."[6] Though "vast hordes" can be assumed to be an exaggeration resulting from fear, there can be no doubt that the number of Maya encountered by the British was no longer "inconsiderable" as it had been in 1779. Neither can it be doubted that the relations between the Maya and the British, far from being as cordial as has been suggested, were extremely hostile and antagonistic.

The cultural identity of these Maya is in doubt, however. They may have included some Tipu Maya[7] and, possibly, refugees from Spanish oppression in the Petén and Yucatán (the Maya revolt at Quisteil under Jacinto Canek had been savagely suppressed by the Spaniards in 1761). Though we cannot be certain regarding the origin or identity of these Maya, they were probably living in small towns, similar to Tipu, and in little villages and homesteads scattered around the upper Belize River valley and in the bush and forest to the north. Their political decentralization meant that they were unable to mount a massive attack, but it also meant that they could not be decisively beaten. How many Maya there were in the Belize area early in the nineteenth century cannot be estimated, and no attempt was made to enumerate them in the early censuses.

The British settlers' fears of a link between the Maya and the African slaves proved groundless, no mention being made of the Maya when a slave uprising occurred on the Belize River in 1820. By that time, in fact, the Maya seem to have been on the wane; and in the 1820's and 1830's, unable to overcome the woodcutters' invasion, the Maya had retired deeper into the forests and rarely appeared to the British settlers. Walker and Caddy, in their expedition to Palenque in 1839, described Duck Run (just east of present-day San Ignacio el Cayo) as "the highest inhabited spot" up the Belize River, and there they employed three Indians to accompany them to the Petén. They referred to the presence of "wild Indians in the vicinity, who . . . at various times emerge from the secret recesses of the Forest for the purpose of plundering" (Pendergast 1967:52, 159), Maya settlements in the upper Belize River valley having by then been pushed back to the limits of present-day Belize.

The Maya of the Belize area were adversely affected by Spanish expeditions of the sixteenth and seventeenth centuries, but these *entradas* were so sporadic, the Spaniards showing no interest in settling in the area, that they were much less socially disruptive than was the case in, say, Yucatán. The Spaniards passed through the Belize area simply because it was on their route to Tayasal, and, after making a few vain attempts at converting the Maya of Tipu, they left them to their isolated independence. The effect of the British colonizers was to prove far more serious.

For the first century after the arrival of the British little or no contact took place between them and the Maya. During most of the eighteenth century we can assume that the Maya in the west of present-day Belize were relatively unaffected by the British woodcutting operations near the coast (though the British occupation would have disrupted their traditional maritime trade) and that they continued to live in small villages or isolated homesteads throughout the area. Only when the British penetrated farther inland in search of mahogany late in the eighteenth and early in the nineteenth centuries were these Maya settlements seriously affected. The British, whose sole concern was then the extraction of timber, perceived the Mayas' swidden agriculture as a threat to the forest reserves, while the Maya viewed British expansionism as a threat to their territory and their independence.

The fresh evidence presented here proves not only that the British displaced the Maya in the territory of Belize but also that the Maya resisted the rule of the British in this period, fighting frequent skirmishes along the frontier of British occupation. Despite their spirited resistance, the Maya were forced back into the forests of the interior. When they re-emerged later in the nineteenth century from "the secret recesses of the Forest" into which they had been driven, they were decisively beaten by the British, who then incorporated them into the social structure of the colony as a dominated and dispossessed people.

The Resurgence and Defeat of the Maya, 1847–1872

The resurgence of the Maya of Yucatán that began in 1847 was paralleled by a revival of anticolonial activity among the Maya in the west of Belize. A newspaper report of June 12, 1847, states that, while Bacalar was threatened in the north, "on several occasions recently we have heard of depredations being committed on the property of the Mahogany Cutters in the Belize River, and in one or two instances attacks on individuals, by what are called the 'wild Indians.' We learn that some two or three weeks since, a party of them attacked and plundered several of the storehouses of the gangs employed on the Eastern and Western Branches, and fears are entertained that unless some effectual means are at once resorted to, this system of pillage will be continued."[8]

A raid on a mahogany camp on the Río Bravo was reported later in 1847,[9] and in March 1848 it was reported that "the Indians are surrounding and attacking the Gangs in the New River pilfering our working tools [and] destroying our cattle."[10] Another letter states that "we have engaged in the Mahogany Works in the New River Lagoon and Irish Creek about 100 Men with their families . . . Indians are supposed to have crossed from the Rio Hondo and are armed with bows & arrows, several arrows were fired at the people in charge of our provisions at Hill Bank . . . Indians were kept off by firearms in possession of the men."[11]

Though it was "supposed" that the last raid originated from north of the Río Hondo, it is quite possible that this, and the raids of the preceding year on the Belize River and Río Bravo, came from Maya settlements in the western forests. If there were Maya settlements in the Yalbac Hills area at this time, these three raids were directed toward the most advanced penetration of mahogany camps to the south, north, and east of that region. It can be surmised that this may have been an attempt, possibly in coordination with Maya groups north of the Río Hondo, of Maya settlements in the Yalbac Hills region to preserve their territorial integrity against the continually expanding woodcutting frontier. However, the events then taking place in Yucatán were to profoundly influence the pattern of Maya settlement and the nature of their relations with the British in the west and north of Belize.

The Santa Cruz Maya, who were engaged in the prolonged war with the Spanish Mexicans known as the Guerra de las Castas (see Reed 1964), made a few raids across the Río Hondo into the northern districts of Belize but never attempted to lay claim to any of the territory. The Santa Cruz preferred generally to keep good relations with the British as they needed the supply of arms and ammunition that came to them from the merchants of Belize. The British colonial officials were frequently willing to turn a blind eye to this munitions trade, despite complaints from the Mexican government, as long as the Santa Cruz were the de facto rulers of the territory just north of the settlement's border. The British were very apprehensive of the dangers of alienating their powerful neighbors who had forcefully demonstrated their dislike of *los blancos* in Yucatán. Throughout the Guerra de las Castas, therefore, the British and the Santa Cruz, with brief exceptions, perceived a mutual interest in keeping the Río Hondo a peaceful channel of communication. Not so the Mexicans, however, who wished to cut off the war supplies of their enemies, the Santa Cruz Maya.

In 1853, apparently on the intervention of Supt. Philip Wodehouse, who had succeeded Col. St. John Fancourt in a mediating role between the Santa Cruz and the Mexicans, a section of Maya to the south and west of Santa Cruz submitted to the Mexican authorities. These Maya, known as *los pacíficos del sur,* consisted of various groups, including the Xkanha, the Lochha, and the Chichanha, who formed and re-formed in a series of alliances, splits, and reachlliances between the two centers of power, the Mexicans of Campeche and the Maya of Santa Cruz. At one time, Pablo Encalada, the leader of the Lochha, claimed control over all *los pacíficos,* with the support of the Mexicans but basing his authority on the "votes of the Indians in the different villages."[12] One group of Maya, the Chichanha, located close to the northwest border of Belize, proved particularly independent of any such alliances, however.

Chichanha was a Maya settlement with a long history. In 1695 the Maya of Chichanha were discovered plotting to massacre the Spaniards who resided in their town. The leader was executed in the town plaza and many of the Maya scattered into the surrounding jungle (Villa Rojas 1945: 17). Said to have been reestablished in 1733, it was first referred to in the British records as "a considerable Town named Chechenha" in 1826.[13] In 1813 it had been mentioned in a Spanish dispatch, two escaped Belizean slaves having been "sent by the alcalde of Chicanha, Miguel Navaez," to Bacalar, but it is not clear whether "the authorities of Chicanha" referred to were Maya or Spanish.[14] The Maya of Chichanha had been among the first to sign a treaty of peace in 1851, but peace with the Mexican authorities meant war with the Santa Cruz. José María Barrera, founder of the cult of the Talking Cross, marched on Chichanha with about five hundred men, burned the village, and captured the head, Angelino Itza (Reed 1964:141). Through signing the treaty the Chichanha Maya had gained no protection from remote Campeche or Mérida but had brought the wrath of the Santa Cruz upon themselves. By the treaty of 1853 *los pacíficos del sur* were to fight against the Santa Cruz, Maya against Maya, the Chichanha agreeing to furnish four hundred men for the Mexican cause. In particular, the Mexicans wanted the Chichanha to cut the trade in war materials between Belize and Santa Cruz.

The Chichanha Maya, led by Luciano Tzuc, raided the mahogany works of Young, Toledo and Company at Blue Creek in September 1856. They demanded rent for cutting on Mexican territory and ransom for the prisoners they had taken.[15] This action, which was repeated in May the following year, appears to have been motivated not so much by Mexican interests as by a desire for gain on the part of the Chichanha themselves. In 1857 the Santa Cruz again attacked the Chichanha, and the village divided, "nearly one half . . . of the whole force accompanied by women & children, under the guidance of Asunsión Ek march southward & settle in the territory of Guatemala and of British Honduras."[16] These latter Chichanha Maya appear to have been motivated by a desire for peace, retiring from the struggles of Yucatán and settling in an area which was probably thinly populated by other Maya.

On May 15, 1857, Supt. Frederick Seymour reported: "On a visit which I recently made to the Northern & Western frontiers of this settlement I fell in with some Indian residents of British Honduras, who communicated to me the intelligence that several bodies of Indians of another tribe; the Chichenhas, numbering in the aggregate . . . 8000 individuals, forsaking the neighbouring province of Yucatan have immigrated to our side of the Hondo where they are employed in burning & otherwise destroying bush & mahogany trees with a view to the cultivation of the soil, contemplating permanent occupation."[17] Seymour himself stated an unwillingness "to make myself responsible for the accuracy of the numbers reported," and eight thousand is certainly an overestimation. At the time of Seymour's report these Maya were settling near "the remoter mahogany works" from New River Lagoon west to Booth's River and over the boundary in the Petén.

After Bacalar fell to the Santa Cruz Maya in 1858, the Chichanha lacked any buffer between themselves and their eastern neighbors. In 1860 the Santa Cruz burned Chichanha, and the village disintegrated, Tzuc establishing the survivors at a new site nearer the border of Belize at Icaiche. In the meantime, Ek's group of Chichanha drifted farther south, away from Tzuc, who seemed anxious to reestablish his authority over them. In 1862 a commissioner sent by Seymour found them in the Yalbac Hills area, just north of the Belize River valley.[18] Their main village was San Pedro, lying less than 10 miles northwest of Young Girl, and inhabited by about 350 people. Their villages extended northward, to include San José, Chunbalche, and Naranjal, and Ek's authority extended west, beyond Chorro and San Domingo, to villages within the Petén. The population of ten of the villages was estimated by the commissioner to amount to over 900 persons.

The area into which Ek's Maya migrated may have been already populated, though we do not yet have sufficient evidence to prove a continuous Maya occupation since the seventeenth century. A distinction must be made between the Maya who may have already inhabited the area (though not necessarily uninterruptedly since Tipu) and those who migrated with Ek from north of the Río Hondo and who may have borne no relation whatever to the Tipu Maya. That Ek may have settled in an area that was already inhabited by Maya is indicated by a reference to the village of "San Pedro on the River Belize" shown in a Guatemalan map of 1832[19] to be in the vicinity of Ek's village. Moreover, in 1834 it was stated that the Belize River became navigable at San Pedro,[20] which would place this village close to the branch and, hence, the old site of Tipu. So, while it cannot be denied that there *may* have been some continuity between Tipu and the nineteenth-century settlements, first, there is no evidence to support such a claim, and, second, we do know that considerable numbers of the Maya in that area had migrated from the north.

Ek's group had moved into the last area of western Belize that had not been penetrated by the woodcutters—the Yalbac Hills region. British settlers, the sole goal of whom was the extraction of timber, had always restricted themselves to camps on the rivers and creeks, down which they could float the huge mahogany logs to the coast. The frontier of their exploitation, for it was hardly a settlement in any permanent sense,[21] had moved west from New River Lagoon and Roaring Creek since the early nineteenth century. By the middle of the century, the mahogany cutters had penetrated the northwest up the Río Bravo and Booth's River, and the west along Labouring Creek to Yalbac and up the Belize River as far as Duck Run, near present-day San Ignacio el Cayo. The Maya settled just beyond this frontier, in the Yalbac Hills region, but they were close enough to the mahogany camps to make the mahogany cutters and the colonial administrators apprehensive about them. Superintendent Seymour attempted to control these new immigrants and to bring them under the authority of the colonial administration by appointing Asunción Ek as their *comandante* and appointing other individuals in the various villages as *alcaldes,* giving them all symbols of their offices.[22] Though, in fact, this amounted merely to a recognition of Ek's own previously established authority among the Maya, Seymour attempted to make them dependent upon British protection. The superintendent's intention was only fulfilled with difficulty, however, after a period of struggle and armed conflict.

The Icaiche Maya had been led, since the death of Tzuc in 1864, by

Marcos Canul, a man who showed little respect for British authority and did not recognize British territorial claims in the northwest of the colony. Canul's raid on a mahogany camp at Qualm Hill on the Río Bravo in April 1866 was considered very serious by the timber companies and the colonial administration. Two men had lost their lives, rent was demanded for the use of land considered to be British territory, and a considerable ransom was demanded for the prisoners taken in the raid.[23] Six months later the administration was afraid that the Icaiche Maya were about to join those in western Belize, thereby threatening the Belize River camps. It appears that Canul was under some pressure from both the Santa Cruz and the Lochha Maya in the north,[24] while Ek expressed apprehension of the approach of the Icaiche,[25] probably fearing that he would be displaced if the two groups of the Chichanha Maya became reunited. In any case, a hasty march on San Pedro by one Capt. Peter Delamere actually precipitated the very realliance it had been intended to prevent. The San Pedro Maya, feeling they had somehow earned the disapproval of the British, could only turn to Canul for support. Canul and his troops arrived in San Pedro early in December, promptly demanded rent from a mahogany camp,[26] and protested to Lt. Gov. John G. Austin "that English troops had been scouring the country . . . with a view of molesting the Indians."[27] A detachment of British troops was sent up the Belize River under the command of Major McKay, but on the morning of December 21 they were routed on their way to San Pedro by the combined Maya forces led by Canul's second-in-command, Rafael Chan.[28] The British casualties were five dead and sixteen wounded, and the civil commissioner, Mr. Edward L. Rhys, was abandoned in the precipitate retreat and never heard from again. Though the situation appeared serious to the British at the time and caused considerable panic throughout the colony,[29] the repercussions were in fact to prove far more serious for the Maya.

After troop reinforcements arrived in Belize early in 1867, a field force of over three hundred soldiers, complete with incendiary rockets, was organized and led by Lt. Col. Robert William Harley. Entering San Pedro without opposition on February 9, they burnt the village to the ground. San Pedro had been a village "of some 50 houses most of them well built and substantial, beside larger buildings, which were of a solid construction, such as the Fiesta House, Chapel, etc.—but nothing of San Pedro now remains except the Chapel, its population . . . was not less than between 3, and 400 people."[30] Harley went on to destroy "the rich and ample provision grounds of San Pedro covering a large extensive plain, about 3 or 4 miles from the Town . . . as also their corn houses."[31] The British troops also destroyed the Maya villages of Santa Teresa, San José, Naranjal, Cerro, Santa Cruz, and Chunbalche, burning the adjacent corn and provision grounds and the granaries, in order to drive the Maya out of the district.[32] This they appeared to have done, the area remaining sparsely occupied for a while, but soon the Maya drifted back, rebuilding and reoccupying some of their old villages.

Canul kept up his struggle against the British during the next five years. In April 1870, Canul and his men marched into Corozal, occupied the town, and on August 31, 1872, leading about 150 men, Canul attacked the barracks at Orange Walk (New River). After several hours of fighting, the Icaiche were unable to dislodge the garrison, so they retired. Canul, who had been fatally wounded, was carried over the Hondo where he died on September 1, 1872.[33] That was the last serious attack on the colony, and more peaceable, but still uneasy, relations continued between the Icaiche Maya and the British throughout the 1870's.

In 1875 it was reported that the Icaiche Maya had joined those of San Pedro at Hololtunich and laid claim to the whole of the north bank of the Belize River down to Black Creek.[34] In 1879 the Icaiche made another raid across the Río Hondo, but by this time their strength had diminished. On October 13, 1882, there was a meeting at Government House, Belize, between General Santiago Pech, head of the Icaiche Maya, and Governor Harley. Pech began by stating that "he had Alcaldes, appointed by him, stationed at Holotonich, San José and San Pedro, and had always understood that his jurisdiction extended to those places."[35] But Harley, threatening to maintain a trade blockade with the Icaiche, managed to extract from Pech a declaration of willingness to respect the boundaries claimed by the British.

The British, having resolved the problem posed by the Icaiche in 1882, no longer found it necessary to maintain their unofficial alliance with the Santa Cruz Maya. Following the submission of the Icaiche and intense diplomatic pressure from the Mexican government, British relations with the Santa Cruz deteriorated, and in 1886 Great Britain and Mexico reopened negotiations for fixing the northern frontier of the colony. The Mexican conditions for entering into negotiations were that the British should stop supplying Santa Cruz with arms, whereas the British conditions were that Mexico should control both the Santa Cruz and the Icaiche Maya and prevent Indian raids upon the colony. When the treaty was signed on July 8, 1893, the first article concerned the location of the boundary and the fourth was purely procedural. The remaining two articles concerned the mutual control of the Maya near the frontier—an agreement to prohibit the supply of arms and ammunition to the Maya and to prevent the Maya within each territory from raiding the other (see Humphreys 1961:145–147). In this way the governments of Mexico and Great Britain reached a mutual agreement concerning the "pacification" of the Maya on their common border.

The Maya who had migrated to the Yalbac Hills in the mid-nineteenth century were a splinter from one of the several groups of the Maya of Yucatán who had been divided against each other during the Guerra de las Castas. But this group, the San Pedro Maya under Ek, had avoided one area of conflict only to be drawn into another. Escaping the conflict between the Spanish Mexicans and the Santa Cruz Maya, which had developed into a fraternal struggle between groups of Maya, Ek and his followers were unable to remain neutral in the conflict between the British and the Icaiche Maya, despite the fact that they had settled in a relatively remote region. The realliance between the San Pedro Maya and the Icaiche Maya was a temporary affair, at first precipitated but later destroyed by British military action. When the San Pedro Maya were joined by the Icaiche, they were able to win the battle of San Pedro in 1866, but they were to lose the subsequent war. Driven out of the Yalbac Hills area in 1867, these Maya, upon their return, were dominated by the British colonialists, while the Icaiche Maya were beaten back across the northern border during the following five years.

The Place of the Maya in the British Colony

It can now be seen that there were four phases of Maya-British relations in nineteenth-century Belize. The first of these went back into the eighteenth century, at least to 1788, and lasted until about 1817. During this period Maya settlements in the interior of Belize, which may have been occupied more or less continuously since the Spanish visits to Tipu in the late seventeenth century, were encroached upon by the intruding British mahogany camps. The Maya, in a series of small, but persistent, raids upon these camps, resisted the British occupation. The second phase lasted from 1817 until 1847, three decades during which little was recorded of the Maya who had retreated into "the secret recesses of the Forest" in the interior. The reemergence of the Maya of western Belize in 1847 occurred simultaneously with the resurgence of the Maya of Yucatán. The third phase, from 1847 to 1872, was characterized by periodic and violent military activity throughout the western and northern parts of the colony, resulting, in 1867 and 1872, in decisive defeats of the San Pedro and Icaiche Maya. The remainder of the nineteenth century, constituting the fourth phase, witnessed the consolidation of British jurisdiction over the Maya within Belize and the incorporation of these Maya into the colonial social structure.

The images held by the British of the Maya changed considerably during the nineteenth century, and it is possible to associate these changing images with the different phases of the colonization process. Thus, during the first phase, when the Maya undertook vigorous and spirited resistance against the British woodcutters, they were perceived, in the words of Captain Henderson, as a "hostile" and "peculiarly ferocious" people who "not infrequently committed the most sanguinary murders" (Henderson 1809: 18–19). In other words, the image of the Maya which the British held in the early nineteenth century was that of a warlike and hostile people, the "vast hordes" of whom were feared and had to be checked by the military.

During the second phase of colonization, when the Maya were secluded in the unknown interior, the image of them changed dramatically, as is apparent from this anonymous description in *The Honduras Almanack for 1830*:

●   With respect to the Indians, the real aborigines of the South American continent . . . they are in general a timid, inoffensive race; they seem to be guided as much by instinct as by reason; they travel independent either of track or of guide, through woods and bush impervious to others, and perform their journeys with a rapidity and correctness of direction, that almost set other modes and marks at defiance. A small bag of maize, slung over their shoulder . . . is all the subsistence they need; and thus, in a state of nature, they wander . . . over wilds unknown to other men, and through forests. . . . Their greatest luxury is composed of rind of limes with corn and allowed to ferment, which they term Pesso; this, with a mixture of a little honey, forms a beverage of which they are particularly fond. They are almost without exception addicted to drunkenness to an excessive degree, but appear to be entirely free from vindictive or malicious propensi-
● ties. (*Honduras Almanack* 1830:11–13)

By this time, then, the Maya, though still perceived as "savage," are somewhat ennobled. This Rousseauian vision of the noble savage "in a state of nature," at peace with his primitive and wild environment, contrasts greatly with Henderson's emphasis. After more than a decade of peaceful relations (or, more precisely, an absence of relations), the Maya in 1830 were perceived as "timid," "inoffensive," and "free from vindictive or malicious propensities."

In the second half of the nineteenth century, as relations between the Maya and the British became closer, the British image of the Maya became more complex. In particular, the changing perception of the Maya after 1847 is related to the actions of the Maya throughout Yucatán and the changing character of British colonialism in Belize, as the raison d'être of the settlement shifted from forestry toward agriculture.

In the last quarter of the eighteenth century the demand for mahogany by the English luxury furniture industry sent the British woodcutters farther up the rivers and creeks of the interior, thereby rousing the Maya to resistance. Similarly, the demand for mahogany to be used for coach construction in the European railway boom of the 1830's and 1840's led to a further expansion of woodcutting, the export of mahogany rising from 4.5 million feet in 1830 to 8.5 million feet in 1837. In 1846, the year before the report of a recurrence of raids upon the camps up the Belize River, mahogany exports peaked at almost 14 million feet.[36] It is surely not the result of chance that the periods of increased mahogany production, which entail the penetration of the interior by the woodcutters, coincide with the reports of Maya raids upon the most advanced mahogany camps.

Although from about 1850 the mahogany trade entered a more or less permanent depression, the big landowners and the colonial administrators in the next decade remained primarily concerned with timber production, a concern which affected their perception of the Maya. Thus, when the immigrants from Chichanha moved south into western Belize in 1857, Superintendent Seymour made a point of insisting that they "must not be allowed to destroy the trees which alone give value to the land on which they are squatted,"[37] the exploitation of Belize's timber resources remaining the sole raison d'être of the British settlement's existence at that time. Seymour perceived these immigrants, whose swidden agriculture may have affected the valuable trees, chiefly as a nuisance. Nevertheless, he also wanted "to persuade them to accept work & wages in the interior,"[38] believing that by incorporating them into the labor force "much ultimate benefit to the settlement" might ensue.[39]

The image of the Maya as a potential agricultural wage laborer, which became the dominant image in the last half of the nineteenth century, had been foreseen as early as 1835 when a memorandum "relating to the labour which might be made available for the proposed cultivation of the soil in Honduras" suggested the importation of labor from "the adjoining countries":

● But a further supply could be obtained from the adjoining countries. Those which are contiguous to Honduras although not densely populous, are still well peopled. The population is native consequently they are inured to the climate. They are poor and therefore would be disposed to go where the wages would be good. The intercourse between Honduras and those countries is now so great that considerable numbers of the people have already hired themselves to the Mahogany cutters, and work on their Banks . . . Already there is an extensive and lucrative trade carried on with Belize by the Spaniards from the Northern town and port of Bacalar, in poultry etc.; and there can be no doubt that if inducements were held out to them, the native Americans would come up to Belize in
● great numbers.[40]

When the Maya came to Belize "in great numbers," however, it was not as a result of any "inducements" being offered them but, rather, in order to escape the strife of the Guerra de las Castas. Moreover, far from the Maya being imported in order to cultivate the soil, their pioneering agricultural efforts were often viewed initially, as by Seymour, to be a nuisance. It was only after the Yucatecan refugees in the Corozal area themselves began to cultivate, and even export, sugar that the big landowners began to consider the agricultural potential of the soil and, consequently, to perceive the Maya, as agriculturalists who were "inured to the climate," as their potential laborers.

In 1847 the superintendent had to report that "of Agriculture in British Honduras little that is satisfactory can be said." He reported that, though "two or three individuals have recently applied themselves to the manufacture of rum," sugar was still "almost exclusively derived from the Town of Bacalar in Yucatan." He concluded that "the existing body of Merchants & Mahogany Cutters" would probably never invest capital in the cultivation of the soil, despite the fact that "sugar cane grows luxuriantly."[41] The prospects for agricultural development were thus very dim in 1847 at a time when mahogany exports were at their peak.

However, as a result of the chaos and bloodshed of the Guerra de las Castas, thousands of Maya and mestizos fled south into Belize. Many of these refugees returned to Yucatán, but a large number remained and settled, some, as has been described, in the west, but most in the north. The report on the Blue Book for 1856,[42] which estimated a total permanent population of about twenty thousand, stated that over a quarter of the people, or about 5,500, were in the Northern District, and most of these would have been Yucatecan refugees. In 1857 it was reported that the town of Corozal "now in the sixth year of its existence already possesses 4500 inhabitants"[43] and that the population of the Northern District, excluding Indians, was between 10,000 and 12,000. "Tickets of residence" were issued at Corozal to 2,000 adult male immigrants in 1857, it being estimated that they were only a quarter of the refugees.[44]

In 1858 a census taken by the Fathers of the Society of Jesus "of such towns villages & mahogany works as are partially or entirely inhabited by Roman Catholics"[45] showed the enormous growth of villages in the Northern District, populated by Yucatecan refugees. Corozal, which contained 4,500 people, "Yucatecos principally but some Indians & Creoles," and San Estevan, populated by 1,300 "Yucatecos" were the second and third largest towns in the country. A number of villages, such as San Pedro, Sarteneja, Punta Consejo, Lowry's Bight, Orange Walk, San Antonio, and Corozal Chico, each contained 200 or more persons, mostly from Yucatán. Though many of the Maya who came into the Northern District settled as domestic servants and agricultural laborers in mestizo communities, it was at about this time that the Maya villages of Xaibe and Patchakan were settled (Jones 1971b:10). In the first of the regular modern censuses, taken in 1861, the total population was said to be 25,635, of which 13,547, over half of the total, lived in the Northern District,[46] a high proportion of them having come from Yucatán.

The Maya and mestizo refugees who came to Belize in the decade or so after 1848 had been, for the most part, small-scale cultivators in Yucatán. The value of their continuing agricultural activity and their potential value as laborers was recognized as early as 1852 by the superintendent: "They have already commenced the cultivation of Sugar, Corn, Tobacco, and other articles for which there must always be great demand in this market; and looking to the almost entire absence of agricultural undertakings in the other Districts, as well as to the general scarcity of labour which exists here, it cannot be disputed that the retention of these settlers, and their general absorption into the permanent population of our territory, is a matter of great importance to this community."[47] Four years later, in 1856, Superintendent Stevenson urged support of the Northern District, "the first . . . in which there has been any attempt at establishing villages, peopled by small and independent cultivators." He spoke of them growing "considerable quantities" of rice, corn, and vegetables, for which "we are at present wholly dependent on neighbouring countries." Since any break in the fragile friendly relations with those neighbors would create problems of supply, Stevenson concluded, "It requires but little forsight to encourage Agricultural Industry, wherever it can be profitably pursued."[48]

The Guerra de las Castas introduced uncertainties in this supply situation, and, since the Yucatecan refugees no doubt included some of the very people who had been engaged in such trade with Belize, the superintendents perceived it to be in the interests of the settlement to allow and encourage them to continue to supply the market from within the settlement itself. Moreover, when the Yucatecans began to produce sugar, as well as vegetables and other subsistence crops, the superintendent was plainly overjoyed at the development, for sugar was a tropical export crop *par excellence*. In 1856 Stevenson reported that, apart from subsistence plots, agriculture had never been successfully pursued.

● But within the last few years—the cultivation of the cane has been attempted by the recent Spanish and Indian Settlers in the Northern District, who, by their own rough means have succeeded very fairly in establishing small but rather profitable plantations near Corosal on the margins of the principal Rivers in that district,—and, although in no one place is there a large field of cultivation or anything like scientific agriculture or Manufacture, yet the result has shown . . . a pressure on the Revenue on "Spirits" and "Sugar." The aggregate amount produced and sent in small
● quantities from time to time to Belize being very considerable.[49]

The following year Stevenson reported that eight hundred acres were under cane cultivation in the north, and that "the wants of the Settlement, in the two articles of Sugar and Rum, will soon be more than fully supplied by the Northern District alone."[50] In fact, production increased so that, later in 1857, the new superintendent was able to report: "The first shipment to Europe of sugar the produce of Honduras was made, to the extent of a hundred barrels, about a fortnight ago, in the ship 'Byzantium' for Liverpool. It is but very recently that our planters were able to satisfy the demands of our own market."[51]

The Yucatecan refugees, with their little ranchos on rented lands, had shown that sugar could be successfully cultivated and exported, and before long the big landowners followed in the footsteps of these small farmers, their tenants, and took over the business. This development was foreseen by the settlement's treasurer, who predicted in 1860 that agricultural enterprises "will soon be valued by Capitalists, now that the capabilities of the Soil have been practically tested by small Planters."[52] Thus the big landowners, who were then suffering from the depression in the mahogany trade, became agricultural entrepreneurs, forcing some of their tenants into wage labor and quickly dominating the production of sugar.

Between 1862 and 1868 the export of sugar from Belize was more than quadrupled, from less than 400,000 pounds to 1,706,880 pounds.[53] Lt. Gov. James R. Longden stated that, in 1867, 3,000 acres of land were under cane, that 868 tons of sugar were produced, 544 tons being exported, and that 53,914 gallons of rum were produced, of which 4,800 were exported.[54] In 1868, 1,033 tons of sugar were produced, of which 762 tons were exported.[55] In the report on 1868 it was stated that "there are Ten Estates, devoted to the cultivation of Sugar, on which steam machinery has been erected. . . . the present acreage is only a small part of that which it is intended to cultivate." These ten estates with steam machinery had an estimated total of 1,683 acres in cane, of which 1,176 acres were in the north and 507 in the south. By far the biggest sugar producer was the British Honduras Company, whose four estates at Santa Cruz, Trial Farm, Tower Hill, and Indian Church had an estimated 746 acres in cane. The report added: "Besides these ten large Estates there are 32 small estates or Milpas cultivated partly in Sugar and partly in Indian corn by the Spaniards who immigrated into the Northern District from Yucatan. On these 'Milpas' as they are called the extent of land in cane varies from 5 acres to 110 acres. In the whole of the Milpas together there are 1,015 acres of cane land giving an average of nearly 32 acres to each Milpa."[56] There can be no question but that, within a decade of the first export of sugar from Belize by the mestizo rancheros, the production and export of sugar had become dominated by the five companies which had steam machinery on their extensive estates.

The system of production on the ranchos was quite different from that on the plantations. Whereas the former utilized traditional swidden techniques of cultivation, associated with the Maya milpa, animal power, and simple processing equipment, the plantations used a short-term fallow system, steam power, and more sophisticated machinery. Both plantations and ranchos cultivated sugar cane and subsistence crops, such as corn and vegetables, though one may expect that the development of the prime concern of the enterprise from subsistence toward cash crops was associated with increase in the size of the production unit. Only a little space of the smallest milpas was devoted to cash crops, but the largest plantations were primarily involved in the production of sugar.

The growing dominance of the plantations over the ranchos and milpas caused changes in the cultural ecology and social structure of the Northern District. Much of the traditional Maya culture in craft production, for example, was neglected as the Maya became increasingly dependent upon goods bought from the company store. Many of the Maya and mestizos became a rural proletariat dependent entirely upon the wages, in cash and goods, provided for plantation work. Others, however, became part proletariat and part peasantry, their low cash wages being underwritten by their continued subsistence agriculture on small plots of rented land. So long as the population remained small and the expansion of sugar production did not strain land resources, this arrangement suited the employers who could thereby reduce the wages and simultaneously collect rents.[57] With the consolidation of agricultural estates in the 1860's, therefore, the Maya and mestizo settlers were perceived by the big landowners chiefly as a potential source of cheap labor for the developing plantation system.

Within two decades of the reemergence of the Maya onto the colonial stage of Belize, the very foundations of this stage had changed dramatically, thereby creating a new situation into which the Maya become incorporated. The export of mahogany, which had been the basis of the settlement's economy since the 1770's, declined rapidly after its peak of nearly 14 million feet in 1846. In 1868 only 3 million feet of mahogany were exported,[58] and in 1870 only 2.75 million feet were exported,[59] the lowest recorded annual figure since the beginning of the century. But mahogany declined in value as well as in volume, so that in 1866 the 5,167,167 feet of mahogany exported, valued at 4½d. per foot, was worth £96,884, but only two years later the price had dropped to 2¼d. per foot, so the 3,006,619 feet exported in 1868 was worth only £28,187. The effect of this great fall in demand for the colony's staple product would have been completely catastrophic had it not been for a temporary increase in the volume of logwood exported. Nevertheless, the value of logwood was also declining, so that the combined value of logwood and mahogany, which together accounted for 82 percent of the total value of the colony's products exported in 1868, dropped from about £140,000 in 1866 to a mere £56,000 in 1868.[60]

It was in this context of a drastic decline in the value and volume of the colony's chief exports that agriculture was first seen as a serious alternative economic basis. Though an agricultural company had been formed in 1839,[61] it was unsuccessful in encouraging and promoting agricultural activity. It was not until the Yucatecan refugees demonstrated the agricultural potential of the land, particularly after they first exported sugar in 1857, that the big landowners, experiencing difficulty with the mahogany trade, looked to sugar production as an alternative. And as they looked to sugar production, the landowners perceived the Maya and mestizo immigrants as their chief potential labor supply.

A report of 1859 had distinguished between the Maya and the mestizo refugees in terms of their characteristic economic activities. The Maya were said to be either employed in mahogany gangs or engaged on their own account in logwood cutting, "which has passed principally into their hands," and in milpa farming and pig raising. The mestizos, on the other hand, were described as those "who, with a sprinkling of Indians, are our sugar growers." The report, heavy in its degree of racial stereotyping, concluded that the Maya, "more robust than the Spaniard, less addicted to pleasure than the negro . . . are admirably adapted to the monotonous drudgery of logwood cutting."[62]

In the 1860's, when sugar estates were expanding in the north, the question of a labor supply became of great concern. In 1864 Lieutenant Governor Austin reported that there were 2,883 people on the Río Hondo and 10,664 on the New River and that "of these 3933 are pure Indians, 1129 Spanish and 6737 Mixed, and consequently with exception of the wood cutting gangs which are migratory, & consist to a great extent of Creoles, there is but little labour available in the rivers, save for the Yucatecan & Indian villages scattered here and there on the banks."[63] Austin commented that both "Medical & Magisterial supervision in the New River . . . are even now lamentably deficient," and he expressed his desire "of placing the rights of employers & employed generally on a more satisfactory basis. I had several opportunities of observing how at such a distance masters could be successfully defied by their people, & how in many ways the labourer was completely at the mercy of his employer."[64] It is apparent from the report of Edwin Adolphus, the magistrate at Corozal, on "the general treatment of the Indian labourers" five years later that "Magisterial supervision" meant enforcing "the rights of employers," not of the employed. *All* of the 286 cases decided by him under the colony's labor laws in 1869 consisted of discipline imposed upon the employees: 245 for "absenting themselves from work without leave," 30 for "insolence and disobedience," 6 for "assaults on masters and book-keepers," and 5 for "entering into second contracts before the expiry of the period of former ones."[65]

Though the magistrate clearly functioned in his legal capacity as an instrument of discipline for the employers against the employed, his report on labor conditions is not uncritical of the behavior of the employers and particularly of the advance and truck systems whose use had been extended from the mahogany cutters to the Maya and mestizo agricultural laborers. Adolphus stated that the *mozos,* or "Indian labourers," are, "without exception, always in debt to their Employers," and he described the causes and effects of their indebtedness:

During the annual fair, held in Corozal at Christmas, when much carousing takes place, the greater part of the mozos squander their money advances for the following year: the advances in goods are usually supplied after Christmas on their proceeding to work.

The system of advances to which they have become so accustomed, and without which the Indians cannot be got to hire, is the main drawback to their regular attendance to work; for, knowing at the commencement of their engagements that they already are in debt, the chief incentive to labour is thereby removed. The Employer, though able of course to cause the idle to be arrested and punished by the Magistrate, is frequently deterred from so doing by reason of the great probability that, on liberation from gaol, the recently punished Indians will take the earliest opportunity of crossing the border into Yucatan, but a few miles distant, where the Indian Commandants gladly receive them . . . There are at present scores of runaway mozos living on the opposite bank of the Río Hondo, who are largely indebted to their former masters, some of whom have actually been ruined by this practice. Another reason that they are so seldom imprisoned for misconduct, as compared with the black laborers, is that they are paid by the task and not by the month as are the latter. . . .

The Spanish system of hiring, or as I may truly call it semi-slavery, was originally brought to this Colony by the Yucatecans when they took refuge here, some twenty years back, after having been driven out of Bacalar by the Indians. It is still practised to a great extent. The Indian laborers, all being overwhelmed with debt, become regarded, in course of time, as a portion of the value of the various ranchos or Estates on which they live and work, and actually themselves imagine, in many instances, that they have no right to leave the same unless they satisfy their Master's heavy claims against them, which belief is naturally of course much fostered by the employers, as it is their principal security for the payment of the servants' debts. . . . but if the mozo fails to obtain, within a limited period, a new master, who will pay the debt for him, he unhesitatingly returns to the old service under the impression that there, and no where else, is he obliged to work. . . . it is always clearly understood between the Indian and the Ranchero when the latter pays the debt of the former, that before he can leave his new Master's service he must repay either in cash or by labour the heavy money advance made. . . . a complaint by an Indian against his master is a matter of very rare occurrence indeed.[66]

The debt peonage created by the advance system, combined with rents for annual tenancies in a context of land monopolization, and a truck system in which "they must receive the greater portion of their wages in goods" amounted to a situation of "semi-slavery." But Adolphus was wrong in placing the responsibility for the introduction of this system upon the Yucatecan refugees. Though a similar system had been practiced in Yucatán, it also existed in the settlement long before the immigration of the Yucatecans. The combination of the advance and truck systems had been utilized by employers to control the Creole laborers in mahogany gangs even before, but particularly after, emancipation in 1838. In fact, Adolphus stated that "the Creoles and Caribs receive about the same advances as the Indians, from three to four months—half goods, half cash," but that their contracts were attested before a magistrate. When breaking the contract, they were likely to be brought to the Summary Court, charged with "non-performance of tasks, disobedience, absenting themselves from their work, sick and idle time etc." (ibid). The Creoles and Caribs were actually more likely to be punished for such labor indiscipline because escape was more difficult for them than for the Indians. Thus we see that the prevalence of escape, the deterrent which had to some extent inhibited the masters' treatment of slaves, also inhibited the employers of the *mozos* in the 1860's.

The living conditions of Maya and Creole laborers were said to be similar: "Their houses, or rather hovels, are . . . entirely devoid of any [of] the slightest appearance of comfort." Adolphus stated that the Creoles and Caribs received more substantial rations than the *mozos*, "four pounds of salt pork or fish and fifty plantains per week," but that they also received "nominally much larger tasks than the Indians." According to Adolphus, "The Indian labourers . . . are much sought after," and he gave four reasons: first, "cheapness—their rations consisted of only twelve quarts of corn per week; second, they were considered to be "tractable and obedient . . . more easily managed than the Creoles and Caribs"; third, "they finish their work in a better style than the other laborers, although they perform less"; fourth, "they will work at night willingly where but seldom the blacks can be got to do so. In fact they will attend for weeks together, during the night, at the mill without murmuring" (ibid.).

The problem facing the employers was the organization of a plantation labor force from among people whose experience had been either one of slave labor in the mahogany forests or primitive subsistence cultivation. While the laborers could be made thoroughly dependent upon their employers through the imposition of rents and the use of the advance and truck systems to induce indebtedness, such dependency did not ensure their regular attendance or disciplined behavior at work. The employers seem to have preferred the *mozos* for plantation labor because they perceived them as more amenable to discipline, though less susceptible to punishment, than the blacks. The employers, judging that the blacks would quit at the end of their contract whether they remained in debt or not, did not extend advances exceeding the value of their labor, with the result that the blacks were generally free from debt at the termination of their contracts. "The black labourers . . . knowing full well that, at the expiry of their contracts, they cannot be detained cause, but too frequently, considerable trouble by impertinence and disobedience," while the *mozos*, encouraged to believe that they had "to continue working in the respective estates until the debts they have contracted are liquidated," were more easily intimidated and disciplined (ibid.). However, it was thought that there was a limit on the punishment it was profitable to apply to the Maya, as a "runaway *mozo*" was of no value to a plantation.

The magistrate at Orange Walk on New River, Robert T. Downer, wrote a similar report of labor conditions in 1869. He emphasized, however, that the Mayas' "love of independence" and "reluctance to enter into written contracts of service" made them "not so easily imposed upon, as some persons are inclined to think . . . Those that seek employment, or are prevailed upon to undertake it, are perhaps barely equal, numerically, to those that remain at home."[67] Downer also described wages, indebtedness, and the functioning of the truck system:

● The average rate of wages paid to Indian laborers varies with the nature of the work they are required to perform. For cutting logwood, which is their principal occupation, they are paid at the rate of three dollars per ton with rations, or four dollars, they feeding themselves. The mule drivers, or those employed in bringing out the logwood, are paid at the rate of ten dollars and sometimes as high as twelve dollars per month with rations. For ordinary labor, such as working on the ranchos etc. the are paid according to the work done . . . average at the rate of from $7 to $8 per month, and rations . . .

There is . . . a considerable percentage charged upon goods supplied to a laborer . . . the Indian laborer is scarcely ever out of debt . . . even where an estate laborer signs for all cash, he generally places himself in the same position as one who hires "half and half," by taking from the Estates's
● store such goods as he stands in need of.[68]

The wages were not only low, they were also frequently paid partly in rations, or "half and half," a practice which was obviously to the advantage of the employer. But even when the laborer was paid entirely in cash, the charges for goods at the estate's store would be excessive, thereby benefiting the employer and leading inevitably to the indebtedness and further dependency of the employees. Though the Maya were often perceived as "tractable," "obedient," and "easily managed," they did repeatedly demonstrate their "love of independence." Consequently it suited their employers to develop mechanisms of labor control so that the Maya *mozos*, "being overwhelmed with debt," would come to regard themselves as "a portion of the value of the various ranchos or Estates on which they live and work . . ."[69]

When, in 1857, Superintendent Seymour considered the Chichanha Maya immigrants to be merely a nuisance to the mahogany business, unless they could be persuaded to become wage laborers, "British Honduras" was still not officially a colony, little interest existed in agricultural development, and even the registration of land titles had not been instituted. Within the next decade, however, all this was to change and the place of the Maya within the colonial structure had to be more defined and systematized. The north and west of Belize were being colonized by the British in the last half of the nineteenth century, and a suitable administrative system had to be devised. Thus, even before the declaration of colonial status in 1862, an act was passed in Belize "to provide for the more speedy Administration of Justice in the rural districts of British Honduras" (Laws of British Honduras 1882[?]) giving a legal basis to the position of *alcalde*, which had been adopted from the Spanish colonial system.

The settlement of the Maya in the north and west of Belize in the third quarter of the nineteenth century took place within the discriminatory restrictions of a colonial framework. Thus, the zeal with which the British crushed the San Pedro Maya in 1867 is in part explained by their desire to revenge the rout of the preceding year, but it was also caused by the desire to secure the extremities of the colony for the settlement of potential immigrant Confederate refugees from the American Civil War.[70] Most of those immigrants who came stayed only a few years in the south of the colony, but the policy of attracting white settlers remained. This policy was not based solely on a desire to develop agriculture but also on the hope that the number of whites in the population, which in 1881 was a mere 375, or 1.4 percent of the total (Gibbs 1883:158), would increase. The Maya, who were trying to develop the interior of Belize for their own agricultural purposes, were thus the victims of a racial scheme of colonization. They were perceived in the colonial scheme, not as the agricultural pioneers that they in fact were, but merely as a potential source of "tractable," "obedient," and "easily managed" labor for foreign-owned plantations.

In 1867 Lieutenant Governor Austin issued the following regulation: "No Indian will be at liberty to reside upon or occupy, or cultivate any land without previous payment or engagement to pay rent whether to the Crown or the owner of the land."[71] The following year, in a lengthy "Report on the Land Question," Lieutenant Governor Longden discussed what could be done with the Maya villages which had been reestablished in the western district: "Several of these villages are situate upon the lands claimed either by the British Honduras Company or Messrs. Young Toledo and Company, but whenever they are situate on Crown Lands I think the villages and a sufficient surrounding space should be reserved *in the hands of the Crown* for the use of the Indians,—no marketable titles being issued to them to enable them to dispose of such lands."[72] Thus it was made clear that, whereas the largest landowners of the country, who only a few years before had obtained firm titles to their vast lands, were not to be disturbed, the Maya should not be allowed to own land but were to be confined to reservations, the latter being created by the Crown Lands Ordinance in 1872.

The Maya, although made the objects of this discriminatory colonial scheme of things, were also significant subjects of Belizean history in the nineteenth century. They were, of course, pioneer settler–agriculturalists in the west and north of the colony, thereby having an effect, in part by their example, upon the economy. But more dramatically, the military activities of the Maya had an impact upon the politics of the colony in the late 1860's, the result being a major constitutional change.

In the late 1860's the expenses of administering the colony had increased, largely as a result of having to pay for the military expeditions against the Maya, at a time when the economy was severely depressed. As a result the public debt, being "chiefly for military expenditure" (Gibbs 1883:155), rose to about $150,000 by 1870. The great landowners, whose mahogany camps in the west and northwest had been attacked and were continually threatened by the Icaiche Maya under Marcos Canul, were at last moved by this state of affairs to allow the Legislative Assembly to impose a land tax in 1867. However, its operation was limited to only two years to meet the immediate emergency, and it was based on terms which were actually very favorable to the big landowners.[73] In the particular crisis of 1866–1867 the great mahogany companies were willing to support a temporary measure for raising revenue by the taxation of land, but they had no intention of continuing to pay such a tax.

The Legislative Assembly, which determined the colony's revenue and expenditure, was controlled by the great landowners and the merchants. Though the landowners were also involved in commerce, some antagonism existed between them and the other merchants of Belize Town. Whereas the former resisted the taxation of land and favored an increase on import duties, the latter preferred the opposite. Moreover, the merchants of Belize Town felt relatively secure from the Maya attacks and were therefore unwilling to contribute toward the military expenditure necessary to resist them. At the same time the landowners were unwilling to bear the expense themselves and held the view that it was unjust to require them to pay taxes for lands that were given inadequate protection. These conflicting interests produced a stalemate in the Legislative Assembly, which failed to authorize the raising of sufficient revenue.

Unable to agree among themselves but pressed by the necessity to raise additional revenue, the members of the assembly attempted to convert British Honduras into a crown colony in 1869 so that the imperial government would bear more of the burdens of defense. In 1870 the assembly agreed to surrender its privilege of self-government in return for greater security against the persistent Maya threat, in much the same way as the Jamaican assembly had abolished itself after the crisis of the Morant Bay rebellion in 1865. The Legislative Assembly having "committed political suicide" (Gibbs 1883:152), the new colonial constitution was inaugurated in April 1871. A year later Canul was killed, and the Maya threat was annulled.

The fact that the Maya had made themselves the subjects, as well as being the objects, of Belizean history, introduced a new complexity into the colonial image of the Maya. Though white colonizers wished to perceive the Maya only as agricultural wage laborers, the Maya had thrust themselves into the colonial consciousness as a military force with which the colonizers had to reckon. The British in the latter half of the nineteenth century tended to hold two conflicting images of the Maya—one of the "tractable," "obedient," and "easily managed" agricultural laborer and the other of an independent fighter whose resistance to colonial rule commanded at least a modicum of respect.

An ambivalence in the perception and characterization of the Maya had developed shortly after the outbreak of the Guerra de las Castas. Frederick Crowe, who was attached to the Baptist mission in Belize, wrote of the Maya in 1850: "In disposition, their leading characteristics are docility and timidity. When aroused, however, they are fierce, cruel, and implacable. Generally industrious, though not aspiring, they often amass wealth . . . In their dealings they are shrewd, but not dishonest, and their word may generally be relied on. Long subjection has taught them a cringing servility and low cunning, probably foreign to their original character" (Crowe 1850:42–43). In 1850 the Maya were still seen as "noble savages," alternately docile and fierce, timid and cruel, and it was not until the development of agriculture had created a greater need for labor and the expansionist British had encountered organized Maya military resistance that the images of the Maya as tractable plantation laborers and hardy warriors emerged. Thus, in 1883, Gibbs, in his *British Honduras: An Historical and Descriptive Account of the Colony from Its Settlement, 1670*, wrote two descriptions which illustrate the ambivalent colonial images of the Maya in the late nineteenth century. On the one hand, he emphasized their potential as cheap plantation labor: "The Indians . . . are baptized, but mix up idolotrous rites and superstitious beliefs with the Christian creed and ceremonies. . . . They live industriously and inoffensively in villages scattered over the district, cultivating their patches of maize and pulse, their pigs and poultry . . . The indigenous Indian . . . might be made available to some extent could he be induced to quit his scattered village-homes, and this is perhaps the cheapest labour to be procured" (1883:162, 176). On the other hand, Gibbs, who had been the commissariat officer in the field force which destroyed the Maya villages in

1867, wrote of the Maya troops with a degree of respect:[74] "The 'Indios bravos' . . . are trained to arms and discipline, are capable of enduring much fatigue . . . are wiry, hardy, and courageous" (1883:140).

With the wisdom that comes with hindsight, we can see that these images of the Maya, like the preceding ones, are something less than half-truths. They are distorted stereotypes of a colonized people, produced by the circumstances of a historically specific social situation.

Summary and Conclusions

The British settlement at Belize was first established as a base from which to export timber, and Belize grew as the center of the exploitation of the country's timber reserves using African slave labor. When the settlement's raison d'être shifted from the export of logwood to that of mahogany in the last quarter of the eighteenth century, the British woodcutters, penetrating farther inland, encountered resistance from the Maya. Displaced by the British occupation, the Maya remained in the forests of the interior until the middle of the nineteenth century when, simultaneously with the Guerra de las Castas in Yucatán, they once more resisted the colonial invasion.

The history of the Maya in the Belize area in the second half of the nineteenth century is inextricably linked with that of the larger Mesoamerican context, particularly the migrations and military activities connected with the political changes and shifts in the loci of power north of the Río Hondo. But the Maya within Belize were also affected by, and themselves in turn affected, major developments in the colonial political economy. With the decline of the timber trade after midcentury, the land itself began to be perceived by the colonizers as being intrinsically valuable, and the interior was seen as a potential site of agricultural development, especially after the Yucatecan refugees successfully exported sugar in 1857. In the 1860's the western and northern frontiers of the colony had to be "secured" and the Maya "pacified" in order to make the interior attractive as an area for white settlement. In the colonialists' racialist scheme of things, only white settlers, whether humble homesteaders or big planters, were considered to be valuable from the point of view of agricultural development or to be reliable in relation to defense.

Within this evolving colonial framework, the Maya, who had first been driven back and kept away from the valuable mahogany trees, came to be perceived as potential agricultural wage laborers to be exploited by immigrant white capitalists. The Maya, in this scheme, had to be "induced to quit his scattered village-homes" and denied the right to own land, in order to deprive him of his independent means of livelihood and make him dependent upon his employers. Defeated in military action in 1867 and 1872, dispossessed and denied the right to own land by colonial legislation, many Maya did become dependent upon wage labor. For the last century, therefore, the Maya have been integrated into the capitalist-colonialist society of Belize as a defeated, dispossessed, and dependent people.[75]

Notes

Abbreviations: AB   Archives of Belize, Belmopan
               CO   Colonial Office Records, Public Records Office, London

1.
Edward Felix Hill, "An account of the Spaniards landing at and taking of St. George's Key, by the subscriber, who was then on the place, and an inhabitant," October 1, 1779, CO 137/76.
2.
Unsigned letter to Governor Dalling, September 3, 1779, CO 137/75.
3.
See, e.g., two maps: Thomas Jefferys, "The Bay of Honduras," February 20, 1775, CO 123/14/1, and H. C. Du Vernay, "A sketch of the British settlement of Honduras and course of the southern coast to the River Dulce," March 9, 1814, CO 123/23.
4.
Thomas Graham, "Journal of my visitation of part of the district granted by His Catholic Majesty for the occupation of British settlers . . . , October 27, 1790, CO 123/9, and Edward Marcus Despard, "A narrative of the publick transactions in the Bay of Honduras from 1784 to 1790," March 8, 1791, CO 123/10.
5.
Minutes from the public record, February 25, 1817, CO 123/26.
6.
Arthur to Major Fraser, June 12, 1817; see also Magistrates to Earl Bathurst, February 26, 1817, and Arthur to Earl Bathurst, June 12, 1817, CO 123/26.
7.
Thompson's statement suggesting that "British logwood cutters working on the Belize River in the eighteenth century employed Indians . . . [who] were probably descendents of the Maya of Tipu culture" (J. E. S. Thompson 1970:71) is misleading. The Indian slaves used by the British in the late eighteenth and early nineteenth centuries were brought from the Mosquito Shore when it was evacuated in 1787, and they were not indigenous to the Belize area (see memorandum from Despard to the committee, August 18, 1789, minutes of public meeting, August 22, 1789, CO 123/12, and Settlers of Honduras, 1845–46; for a general discussion of the settlement in the eighteenth century, see Bolland 1973:1–42). We have no record of the Maya having been enslaved by the British or employed by them in the eighteenth century, though some were employed in cutting

logwood and mahogany later in the nineteenth century.

8.
Honduras Observer and Belize Gazette, June 12, 1847.

9.
Ibid., October 30, 1847.

10.
Letter to Charles St. John Fancourt, March 16, 1848, AB, R. 28.

11.
Letter to Major General Berkley, March 17, 1848, AB, R. 28.

12.
Statement of Encalada's commissioners, February 1867, AB, R. 89.

13.
George Hyde to Marshall Bennett, February 12, 1826, CO 123/37.

14.
Manuel Melendez to Manuel Artazo, March 15, 1813, in Work Projects Administration 1939:120–121.

15.
Stevenson to Maj. Gen. E. Wells Bell, September 9, 1856, and October 16, 1856, AB, R. 55.

16.
Seymour to Gen. Edward John Eyre, November 12, 1862, AB, R. 81.

17.
Seymour to Bell, May 15, 1857, AB, R. 52.

18.
Rhys to Seymour, November 3, 1862, AB, R. 78.

19.
"Departamento de Verapaz, Año de 1832," CO 123/47.

20.
Frederick Chatfield to Viscount Palmerston, November 7, 1834, CO 123/47.

21.
This kind of frontier, which was not supported by extensive rural settlement, has been referred to as a "hollow" frontier (see Humphreys 1961:17–18).

22.
Rhys to Seymour, November 3, 1862, AB, R. 78.

23.
See AB, R. 93, passim.

24.
Delamere to Austin, October 4, 1866, and Encalada to Austin, November 8, 1866, AB, R. 89.

25.
Ek to Austin, November 9, 1866, AB, R. 89.

26.
J. Swasey to Young, Toledo and Co., December 5, 1866, AB, R. 89.

27.
Canul and Chan to Austin, December 9, 1866, AB, R. 89.
28.
McKay to Austin, December 24, 1866, AB, R. 95; R. Williamson to Austin, December 26, 1866, AB, R. 89.
29.
A later account stated that "the inhabitants, Governor Austin's family, at least included, if not himself, were all packed up ready to take to the shipping. . . . Christmas was anything but a holiday in Belize that year" (Gibbs 1883:138).
30.
Harley to Austin, February 9, 1867, AB, R. 95.
31.
Harley to Austin, February 15, 1867, AB, R. 95.
32.
John Carmichael, Jr., to Graham, March 30, 1867, and Harley to Austin, September 7, 1867, AB, R. 95; see also the account by Lt. Col. E. Rogers, "British Honduras: Its resources and development," delivered before the Members of the Society at the Manchester Atheneum, October 14, 1885 (Rogers 1885).
33.
Maj. William Johnston to Gov. William Wellington Cairns, September 11, 1872, and Serapio Ramos to Major Johnston, September 15, 1872, AB, R. 111.
34.
Phillips and Co. to Graham, March 22, 1875, AB, R. 119.
35.
Memorandum, October 13, 1882, AB, R. 93.
36.
Figures from quarterly returns of exports from Belize, CO 123/41–42; Gibbs 1883:93, 102.
37.
Seymour to Bell, May 15, 1857, AB, R. 52.
38.
Ibid.
39.
Seymour to Bell, June 17, 1857, AB, R. 52.
40.
Thomas Miller to William E. Gladstone, February 13, 1835, CO 123/47.
41.
Fancourt to Gov. Sir Charles Edward Grey, June 19, 1847, AB, R. 25.
42.
Stevenson to Bell, March 2, 1857, AB, R. 55.
43.
Seymour to Gov. Charles Henry Darling, November 16, 1857, AB, R. 55.

44.

Edmund Burke to Seymour, November 2, 1857, AB, R. 58.

45.

Seymour to Darling, March 1858, AB, R. 55.

46.

April 8, 1861, AB, R. 74.

47.

Superintendent to Chairman, public meeting, January 20, 1852, AB, R. 20.

48.

Votes of the Honourable House of Assembly, sessions 1854–1859, January 22, 1856.

49.

Stevenson to Sir Henry Barkly, April 5, 1856, AB, R. 55.

50.

Stevenson to Darling, March 2, 1857, AB, R. 55.

51.

Seymour to Darling, August 1857, AB, R. 55.

52.

Treasurer to Acting Supt. Thomas Price, April 4, 1860, AB, R. 66.

53.

Longden to Gov. Sir John Peter Grant, June 19, 1868, and May 17, 1869, AB, R. 98.

54.

Longden to Grant, June 19, 1868, AB, R. 98.

55.

Longden to Grant, May 17, 1869, AB, R. 98.

56.

Ibid.

57.

The maintenance of this form of land use and land tenure enabled the Maya to develop into small-scale cash crop producers when the plantations declined and also established a precedent for the coexistence of peasant-milpa and industrial-estate types of agriculture when the plantations were reintroduced in the twentieth century (see G. D. Jones 1969 for a discussion of these cultural ecological changes).

58.

Longden to Grant, May 17, 1869, AB, R. 98.

59.

Hooper's report, 1887, cited in Hummel 1921:12.

60.

Longden to Grant, May 17, 1869, AB, R. 98.

61.

Col. Alexander Macdonald to Chairman, public meeting, March 4, 1839, AB, R. 16.

62.

Seymour to Darling, June 22, 1859, AB, R. 65.

63.

Austin to Eyre, May 26, 1864, AB, R. 81.

64.

Ibid.

65.

Adolphus to Longden, January 15, 1870, AB, R. 105.

66.

Ibid.

67.

Robert T. Downer to Longden, January 27, 1870, AB, R. 105.

68.

Ibid.

69.

Adolphus to Longden, January 15, 1870, AB, R. 105.

70.

For example, one J. C. McRae, an ex-Confederate general, purchased a
large tract of land up the Belize River in 1868; see Clegern 1967:43.

71.

February 28, 1867, AB, R. 96.

72.

Longden to Grant, March 6, 1868, AB, R. 98.

73.

Longden to Grant, December 4, 1867, AB, R. 98.

74.

This emphasis on the martial qualities of the Maya was repeated a few
years later in *Report of Indian Soldiery*: "The Indians are masters in the
use of cover, and in the bush are redoubtable enemies" (Allen 1887:3).

75.

I gratefully acknowledge the support of the Institute of Social and Economic Research of the University of the West Indies and of the Research
Council of Colgate University and the assistance of the officials of the
Public Records Office, London, and of the Archives and National Collection, Belize.

Part Two

Process of Adaptation in Maya Society

4

Independent Maya of the Late Nineteenth Century:

Chiefdoms and Power Politics

D. E. Dumond

After the outbreak in 1847 of the massive rebellion known commonly in Yucatán as the Guerra de las Castas—the Caste War or, better, the Race War—several autonomous Indian political units arose in the southern and eastern portions of the Yucatán Peninsula as outgrowths of the rebel army. Organized in quasi-military fashion, fluctuating in number to some extent and varying in their affiliations both with one another and with the governments of Yucatán and Campeche, these units persisted throughout the second half of the nineteenth century.

This article reports on a continuing study of the history and organization of these various chiefdoms, a study that is focused in two directions: on the one hand, toward various factors in the local milieu that influenced the development of the chiefdoms and their relationships both to one another and to the national polities around them and, on the other hand, toward changes that occurred in the Maya social units as the Indians responded to these conditions and to each other. The eventual aim of the study is to provide certain analyses of the formation and persistence of the independent Maya political units within the context of anthropological theory. The present effort, however, stops little beyond the bare outline of the histories of the units, a function both of space and of the unfinished state of the research. Nevertheless, I believe that much of the emphasis and many of the facts are new.[1]

In addition to sources that are listed in the bibliography by Howard Cline (1945), I draw particularly upon documents in the Archives of Belize and upon material published in contemporary newspapers, especially the official gazettes of Yucatán and Campeche—material that was gathered between 1971 and 1973 in Belize and in various libraries and repositories in Mexico.[2] The use to which these are put should be evident from the citations. I have ended the account about 1901, the year in which Chan Santa Cruz was permanently occupied by Mexican troops. The locations of the more important places mentioned are shown on map 4-1.

At the request of the editor of this volume, I have also undertaken a

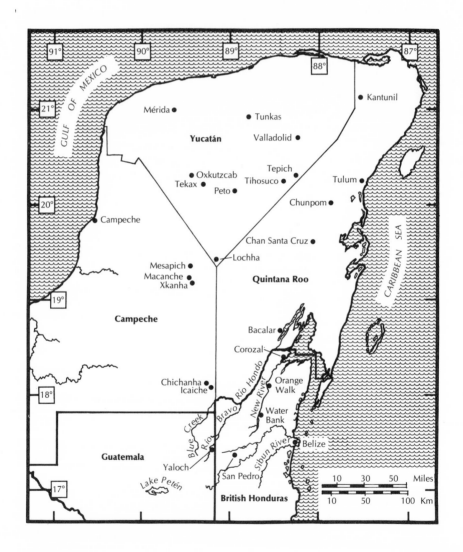

Map 4-1
The Yucatán Peninsula

brief survey of some earlier uses of Caste War historical materials, which is included as an appendix to this article.

The Rebel Background

In the mid-nineteenth century the economic exploitation of Yucatecan territory varied considerably. The zone around Mérida, the northern strip as far east as Valladolid, and the western coastal strip south to Campeche were established colonial regions of haciendas, plantations, ranchos, and—in the last area mentioned—coastal fishermen (Cline 1950c:chaps. 3, 4). The least progressive of these three zones was that centering on Valladolid (Cline 1950b:311–335), an area which also had the highest ratio of Indians to whites (five to one) of any region in Yucatán (Cline 1950c:table 15).

Toward the geographical center of the peninsula and radiating south and east from the newly important centers of Tekax and Peto was land that in the early nineteenth century was being brought under cultivation in sugar cane, the newly established plantations spreading into territory previously exploited only by swidden-farming Indians. Still farther south and east was the area reputedly inhabited by the semiwild Maya known to Yucatecans as *huites,* some of whom were said to be the offspring of refugees from an Indian uprising of 1761 (Cline 1950c:335–369); this was a region found by Stephens in 1842 to be without roads, never visited by whites (Stephens 1963:II, 229).

The distribution of population reflected the exploitation of the land. In 1845 nearly 70 percent of the population lived in the colonial areas of the north and west, more than 30 percent in the developing commercial sector of the sugar-producing borderlands. Available figures reflect little more than 1 percent (fewer than 8,000 people) in the southeastern zone (Cline 1950c:tables 18, 28; Regil and Peón 1853), although some estimates have been said to place the total number of the southern *huites* at twenty thousand or more (Cline 1950c:364).

In that southern area the only European center was Bacalar, founded as a town in the 1540's (Ancona 1889:I, 266) and around 1730 reestablished as an outpost against English piratical incursions (ibid.:II, 413). The southern Indian center of Chichanha was also reportedly "repopulated" at this last date, as certain previously rebellious Maya were induced to submit to government control (ibid.:415).

Thus at the outbreak of the war the native peoples of Yucatán varied from long-time hacienda and plantation laborers in the north and west to newly recruited sugar workers and free Maya of varying degrees of wildness in the south and east. As the rebellion spread in 1848, only the most settled workers of the old colonial areas remained loyal to their Creole masters. Although one may suppose that a part of the rebel army was composed of free Maya of the southeast, a numerically more significant portion was almost certainly made up of former agricultural workers of hacienda and plantation.

Of the four men usually presumed to be the original leaders of the revolt, three bore Maya surnames; two of these latter, Jacinto Pat and Antonio Ay, were landholders and official *caciques*—leaders responsible to the central Yucatecan government—of Indian settlements, and the third, Cecilio Chi, had seen militia service in the early 1840's with Creole forces. Pat and Chi were from the eastern edge of the commercial sugar zone—the towns of Tihosuco and Tepich—and Ay was from a village in the near neighborhood of Valladolid. The fourth man, Bonifacio Novelo, was from Valladolid itself (Baqueiro 1878–1887:I, 226–239). From the frequency of Spanish surnames among other rebel leaders, it seems clear that the leadership in general was fairly heavily mestizo, and persistent Yucatecan reports alleged a certain component of British Hondurans (e.g., Hübbe 1940:123). Thus there is every reason to think of the leadership as at least moderately sophisticated—if not always literate—products of centuries of European acculturation. Nevertheless, the rebels spoke Maya and identified themselves as Indians.

From all this, it is no surprise that, although the rebels came to demand the ownership of all of Yucatán as the heritage of their putative Indian forefathers,[3] nothing appeared in the movement that derived from ancient social forms. Even the nativistic cult of the miraculous Talking Cross, around which the most militant of the rebels were to rally after 1850, was derivatively Roman Catholic in form; and, although its practitioners eschewed intercourse with the established priesthood, they never gave up their own identification as Christians, albeit, in effect, protestant ones.

The Rebel Secular Organization and Its Prototype

When the remnant of the most militant of the chiefdoms was studied in the 1930's (Villa Rojas 1945), the secular organization was headed by men with military titles—major, captain, lieutenant, sergeant, and corporal—who directed quasi-military "companies" composed of all able-bodied males with their female and juvenile affiliates, and around which the entire society was organized. This is the obvious heritage of the nineteenth-century rebel organization, which in turn was apparently derived from the organization of the Yucatecan militia.

As had been provided nationally by law in 1827 (Mexico 1829:134–138) and implemented in Yucatán by laws of 1828 (Yucatán 1832:108–123) and 1832 (Aznar Pérez 1849:54–66), each of fifteen districts was required to organize one or more battalions of local militia, each batallion to be composed of eight companies numbering between about 800 and 1,200 men. The commander of each battalion (a colonel) and his staff (a lieutenant colonel, a captain, a lieutenant, a sublieutenant, and lesser officials) were appointed by the Yucatecan government. Companies, on the other hand, were organized by individual towns and were officered by local individuals selected by the towns; these minimally included a captain as commander, a lieutenant, two sublieutenants, four sergeants, eight corporals, and three drummers. No military rank between that of captain and lieutenant colonel was established. Membership in this *milicia local* was mandatory for all able-bodied white male Yucatecans between the ages of sixteen and fifty. Although Indians were exempt from compulsory military service, they could be enlisted as volunteers, and for certain intra-Yucatecan campaigns preceding the Caste War, they were actively recruited (e.g., Baqueiro 1878–1887:I, 32, 180).

The first rebel attack of the war is usually said to be that on Tepich of July 30, 1847. In the months that followed, the rebels were consistently successful. By April of 1848 when they took the town and fortress of Bacalar—generously permitting the garrison and inhabitants to withdraw to nearby British Honduras—the rebel organization had already assumed something of its later form. According to the report of one English observer, "the Indians seem to have no regular form of government—it appears to be a kind of military dictatorship, under which the authority of the Chiefs is not always respected, in fact the Indians appear to be runaway schoolboys who try to do the most with their momentary liberty."[4]

Immediately afterward, the higher rebel officers were writing to the superintendent of British Honduras for a variety of reasons (and especially to complain against the removal of logs without payment of tax from the now Indian north side of the Río Hondo), signing themselves variously in Spanish as *general, comandante general, comandante general del oriente, comandante de Bacalar,* and *capitán.*[5] Although it is doubtful that any of them had previous experience with the military other than through local militia companies commanded by captains, they had already—and quite reasonably—borrowed other current Yucatecan military terms to designate the higher ranks.

At this time, the term *comandante* appears to have been used by the rebels only in its functional sense (i.e., for one who commands) rather than to designate a specific rank in the military hierarchy. By the 1860's, however, this term *comandante* would become a specific designator for a rank intermediate between that of captain and general (e.g., Trebarra 1864). Although the British translators usually rendered it simply as "commandant," the term can also be properly translated "major," as it was rendered by Villa Rojas (1945). The designation *coronel*, on the other hand, appears to have been used by no Indians earlier than the 1870's, and even then it appears only sporadically and in connection with the pacified chiefdoms most closely connected with Yucatán and Campeche.[6]

An additional and consistently prominent position was also established in that of the secretary, literate in Spanish, who had responsibility for communications with the outside world. At times this office would achieve the formal dignity of "Secretary General," and at others it would provide a scapegoat when an illiterate commander would want to elude the responsibility for any particular action that had involved written communications.

Thus the rebel acquisition of military titles, while presumably fairly true to the militia model in ranks of captain and below, apparently involved more selective borrowing and possibly some gradual innovation in the designations applied to the highest of the secular leaders. The annexation of spouses and children to the companies such as was reported much later by Villa Rojas (1945) was, of course, the expectable result in a society long under total military mobilization; indeed, the appearance of such companies would represent no great departure from that of any army abundantly supplied with female and juvenile camp followers, as were the Yucatecan armies of the period.

Early Independence and Fission

Despite their initial success, during which the very city of Mérida had been threatened, by 1849 the war was running strongly against the rebels, who were pushed east and south, away from the settled portions of the peninsula. Attempts by both sides to arrange a truce had been unsuccessful. After Bacalar was retaken by the Yucatecans in May of 1849, the only population center remaining to the Maya was the old southern Indian town of Chichanha, reportedly now the magazine for munitions purchased in British Honduras (Hübbe 1940:132) and transported thither through ports on the upper Río Hondo,[7] out of reach of the Yucatecan garrison at Bacalar.

The lack of an eastern center began to be remedied in late 1850 with the rise of a new and militant religious movement that had its focus at a previously uninhabited *cenote*—that is, a natural well—in eastern Yucatán. The standard accounts are that in late 1850 a small cross carved on a tree at the *cenote*—or crosses set up near a tree that had small crosses carved upon it—began to speak in Maya, promising relief to the hard-pressed rebels. The speech was reputed to be through the agency of one Manuel Nahuat, an Indian ventriloquist working at the direction of the rebel general José María Barrera (Baqueiro 1878–1887:II, 388; Villa Rojas 1945:20–21). Whatever the details, the site became the immediate focus of new settlement. In January 1851, Barrera, on behalf of the miraculous cross, wrote his only known letter to the Belize government, exhorting it to send powder and to come and receive a benediction from the "Holy Cross Three Persons."[8]

By March of that year, when the new center was attacked by Yucatecan forces, its population was reported to be more than two thousand. Crosses were confiscated; Manuel Nahuat died in their defense; Barrera escaped. The miraculous cross was replaced; the new one was silent for a time, then reportedly began to communicate anew by letter (Baqueiro 1878–1887: II,

390, 391); this means of communicating, in turn, was apparently super-
seded by the use of a resonating chamber concealed beneath the altar of
the chapel that was built at the spot.[9] At any rate, the militant cult of the
Talking Cross and the new eastern capital of Santa Cruz—or Chan Santa
Cruz as it came to be called—were born together.

Later that year, 1851, while the militant fire was kindling at Santa Cruz,
the southern rebels around Chichanha signed a tentative agreement with
Guatemalan intermediaries, promising to resubmit themselves to Yucatecan rule (Baqueiro 1878–1887:II, 429; Burdon 1931–1935:III, September
9, 1851; Hübbe 1940:133). The people of the new Santa Cruz retaliated
for this show of disloyalty by attacking and occupying the southern capital, which was shortly freed from their control by a Yucatecan column that
arrived in March 1852 (Baqueiro 1878–1887:II, 440; Hübbe 1940:133).[10]
The southern secessionist movement did not end. Led now by José María
Tzuc, who had been commandant of Bacalar during its earlier occupation
by the Indians, and who since its recapture had commanded Indian forces
sitting in siege around the same fortress, the southern troops met those of
Santa Cruz a second time at Chichanha in December 1852. The Santa Cruz
soldiers were defeated, and one of their most prominent commanders was
killed (Baqueiro 1878–1887:II, 445; Hübbe 1940:133). According to at
least one version, an important element in the southern defection was the
unwillingness of the Chichanha people to submit themselves to the miraculous Talking Cross (Baqueiro 1878–1887:II, 445; cf. Berendt 1872).

In September of 1853, Tzuc and Andrés Zima, acting on behalf of themselves and ten other Indian leaders, met with Yucatecan commissioners in
Belize and signed a treaty of peace by the terms of which the Chichanha
party submitted themselves to the government of Yucatán, promised to
provide 400 men to fight the remaining rebels, were permitted to retain
their arms while the war should last, were permitted to reside where they
wished, and were substantially exempted from taxes (Ancona 1889:IV,
434–442; Hübbe 1940:136–137). Even though no provision was made in
the treaty for military or quasi-military appointments for the Indian leaders or for independent local government, a substantial measure of the
latter was already provided for in the ancient institution of the *repúblicas
indígenas,* which remained in existence and in which Indian *caciques* were
appointed by the state governor to be responsible for both the protection
and the direction of their Indian subjects (Ancona 1889:II, 186–190; see
also González Navarro 1970:55).[11] The treaty of 1853 was never ratified by
the government of Yucatán, but it was fairly consistently observed by both
parties and was credited with a significant diminution of hostilities.[12]

Thus was effected a permanent division in the rebel ranks—between
sublevados pacíficos in the south and *sublevados bravos* in the east. There
is every reason to believe that at this time the rudimentary organizations of
the *pacíficos* and the *bravos* were substantially identical. Both were organized in military fashion. Both were at least nominally commanded by one

or more leaders to whom might be applied the title *general*. Beneath them were a number of officers who, although nominally supportive of the general, apparently had considerable autonomy. The impression conveyed by the list of leaders on whose behalf Tzuc signed the treaty of 1853 is that of relatively independent *caudillos,* each with his personal following, who had coalesced into an ephemeral union. It is certain that at least three of the ten were residents of the area around Mesapich and Lochha.[13] That virtually all of the treating Indians may in fact have lived dispersed throughout a broad area extending north from Chichanha finds reinforcement in the relatively small size of that settlement: Chichanha was said in 1852 to consist of some 200 houses and to have 700 or 800 inhabitants.[14]

For the people of the Santa Cruz group, more complete information of slightly later times clearly suggests dispersed residence, and there is a tendency for letters from the leaders to bear multiple signatures. Although the presence of the militant cross cult might provide a force for greater unity among the Santa Cruz, there is no evidence that by the early 1850's that cult had been solidly integrated into the political hierarchy.

Situational Factors

With the permanent division between the Chichanha and Santa Cruz parties, the subsequent development and interaction of the various Indian political units were influenced strongly by two additional factors: the availability to Indians of munitions through merchants of English-controlled territory, and the dispute between Great Britain and Mexico regarding the sovereignty over that same territory.

The Powder Trade
In general, the British Honduras government favored the avoidance of direct involvement of any kind in commerce with the Indians—of which trade in munitions was only a part—on the ground of complete neutrality in the war. By most of the English governors, the private trade in powder —but not that in other commodities—was decried, and relations between a trader and his Indian customers were at the complete risk of the trader. Factors against an outright ban on the powder trade in the early decades of the war included both the substantial popular sympathy in the colony for the side of the Indians and the fear that Santa Cruz forces would make retaliatory raids on the English settlement. In the view of the Yucatecans, however, the British position was one of open support for the rebels.[15]

The Territorial Claims
Anglo-Spanish treaties of 1783 and 1786 had established British rights to settle and cut wood between the Sibun River and the Río Hondo, while recognizing ultimate Spanish sovereignty to that area in the years before

the Mexican war of independence (Clegern 1967:6). In 1826, the British recognized Mexican independence, and the Mexican diplomatic position then became that this recognition constituted the acceptance of Mexican sovereignty over all the Yucatán Peninsula, including the territory of British Honduras. The British position was that it had recognized Mexican sovereignty over only that area under direct Mexican control—which did not include British Honduras—and in 1862 Britain declared British Honduras its colony (Gibbs 1883:142–143). Two years later Maximilian's government formally claimed sovereign rights to all former Spanish territory on the Yucatán Peninsula, including the Petén and British Honduras. Thus, the first area of dispute regarded the ultimate ownership of the entire zone of British occupancy.

The British chose to consider Blue Creek, one of the westernmost tributaries of the Hondo system, to be the upper Río Hondo and therefore their boundary with Mexico; the Mexicans chose to consider the Río Bravo, a more easterly tributary, to be the upper Río Hondo and the boundary of the zone under British control. To make matters worse, in the early 1850's a Belize logging firm had contracted with the government of Yucatán for rights to cut mahogany in lands of that state on the left bank of the main Río Hondo—the location of which was under no dispute—over a period of fifteen years and in exchange for a substantial rent (Hübbe 1940:140). Before that period was up, control of the left bank of the Hondo had shifted to rebelling Indians, who as new masters of the land felt themselves entitled to a continuation of the rent, regardless of the feelings of either the British Hondurans or the Yucatecans.[16] Thus the second area of dispute concerned both the definition of the territory within which payments for cutting could legitimately be charged and the identity of the legitimate recipient of such payments.

Both the territorial dispute and the differences regarding the powder trade persisted until they were settled by a treaty ratified in 1897, a settlement which finally served to bring about the end of the Caste War.

It is now possible to turn to the political histories of the Indian groups themselves.

Independent Chiefdoms

Bellicose Pacíficos
José María Tzuc, signatory of the treaty with Yucatán of 1853 and first general of the independent and pacified Chichanha Maya, died in October of that same year, to be succeeded by his second-in-command, Andrés Zima, who was chosen by Chichanha leaders and ratified in the position by a Yucatecan emissary, despite the preference of some of the people for Tzuc's son.[17]

How long Zima held the post is not clear, but by 1856 the Chichanha leader was Luciano Tzuc—presumably that favored son of José María—and shortly afterward Zima went to British Honduras, where he apparently settled permanently.[18]

As far as the English were concerned, Luciano Tzuc made his debut in 1856 when he and his followers occupied logging works on Blue Creek and extorted money on threat of firing the logs. Although Tzuc was deposed shortly afterward—reportedly because of his failure to distribute the extorted money fairly—and took refuge in British Honduras, his raid set the tone for relations between British Honduras and the southern *pacíficos* for the next several decades, and British complaints to the Mexican authorities received no satisfaction.[19]

In 1857, the Chichanha district was invaded yet again by Santa Cruz forces, and a number of the *pacíficos* (as many as 8,000 by some highly inflated reports) defected southward along the British Honduras–Guatemala border, where they settled quietly.[20] At the end of the year Pablo Encalada, a *pacífico* leader from Lochha and one of the principals listed in the treaty of 1853, was said to be at Chichanha gathering 500 troops with which to oppose Santa Cruz.[21] In 1860, however, the town of Chichanha was burned by Santa Cruz forces, and prisoners were carried off and slaughtered; later that year the rebels threatened the *pacíficos* around Mesapich.[22]

About this same time Luciano Tzuc was again accepted as leader by the Chichanha people, and in 1861 he visited Campeche, where he presented a plan for a campaign against the Santa Cruz, and received arms. But his attempt at mobilization apparently only intensified defections from Chichanha.[23] By June 1863 letters from Tzuc carried the dateline "Santa Clara" or "Icaiche,"[24] indicating the abandonment of Chichanha and the establishment of a new capital, Santa Clara Icaiche, a short distance away and more difficult of access for Santa Cruz soldiers.

That not all Chichanha defections were toward the south, however, is suggested by reports that in the early sixties Lochha to the north was peopled largely by Chichanha remnants.[25] Although earlier there was some population in this northern zone, it is probable that, after having been the focus of a Yucatecan campaign in 1852—indeed, Lochha was occupied by government forces throughout most of that year (Baqueiro 1878–1887:II, 481)—and after having been pacified by the agreement of 1853, that zone was steadily reoccupied by *pacífico* immigrants, many of them from the south. According to the leader Pablo Encalada, the site of Lochha counted only five people in 1849 and was part of an area inhabited by scattered rebels under the leadership of José María Cocom, the largest settlement being then Macanche, a town of about 500.[26] Population grew steadily thereafter, however, and in the census of 1861, taken upon the occasion of the formal separation of Campeche from Yucatán, two *pacífico* municipalities are shown, consisting of the *cabeceras* Lochha and Mesapich, with twenty-four subsidiary settlements, having a total population of 14,400 (Aznar Barbachano and Carbó 1861).

Naturally enough, this growing area was, like Chichanha to the south, a focus of Santa Cruz military pressure in the middle and late 1850's, and in 1863 Lochha was taken and held a short time by the rebels.[27]

By the early sixties, then, three major groups of Chichanha remnants and their pacified affiliates existed: those in the far south in British Honduras and Guatemala, those at Icaiche, and those in the north around Lochha. These will be taken up briefly, in turn.

The Southern Group • By 1862 the southern refugees were under the leadership of Asunción Ek, who now lived at San Pedro in British Honduras, but who as recently as 1860 had been a Chichanha official, protesting the presence in British Honduras of people with unpaid debts to the Indians.[28] That he was broadly recognized as a leader by the Chichanha immigrants to the south was indicated by an incident in which an unpopular representative of the Petén government was seized by some of them in Guatemala and transported across the border to be turned over to Ek in San Pedro.[29] Shortly thereafter, when the superintendent of British Honduras named *alcaldes* and sub-*alcaldes* for a number of the refugee towns, Ek was given the special title of *comandante* of the Indians of the entire region, "in consideration of his having been a general amongst them."[30]

It is reasonable to think, therefore, that the quasi-military organization of Chichanha and Icaiche was replicated among the southern refugees, although the appointments by the superintendent of British Honduras served to alter their organizational nomenclature to some extent. Despite the earlier excessive estimates of the number of refugees moving into the south, mentioned previously, none of the later accounts ever placed the total southern strength at more than about a thousand.

This southern unit was to attract the attention of the English only into early 1867. In 1866, apparently in part as a result of Maximilian's claim to sovereignty over all British Honduras, the current Icaiche leader and his men raided on the English side of the Río Bravo, killing two people and kidnapping sixty-eight;[31] in the English response, a supply of arms was sent to Asunción Ek and the fifty or sixty men he could then marshal.[32] And when a few months later the English received word that the Icaiche leader would appear near Ek's center of San Pedro, presumably in order to raid nearby English mahogany works, a British military force was dispatched to the area. Although it made no contact with the Icaiche force, it apparently succeeded in frightening Ek and his men.[33]

But the following month, December, extortionary letters from Icaiche leaders were sent to English logging interests under the dateline "San Pedro."[34] Whatever Asunción Ek's real attitude toward Icaiche might have been a few months earlier, this clearly suggested a merging of Indian interests, in opposition to English political stability and commercial enterprise. A second British force was dispatched immediately to San Pedro. To British mortification it was completely routed by an Indian night attack.[35]

But, shortly afterward, San Pedro men were thought implicated in a raid on an English settlement, and in a harsh retaliatory attack a British detachment destroyed San Pedro and its allied towns.[36]

For a period thereafter, people of the San Pedro area seem to have acted in concert with Icaiche; indeed, a San Pedro sub-*alcalde* whose behavior toward Icaiche was suspiciously friendly in 1866 would become the commanding general at Icaiche in 1877.[37] As the furor quieted in the years after the British attack, the destroyed towns appear to have been reoccupied. As late as 1888 Asuncíon Ek was reported to be *alcalde* of San Pedro, although two years later he was no longer in office (Bristowe and Wright 1888:133, 1890:123).

Icaiche • In 1864, Luciano Tzuc had become involved in an altercation with a Yucatecan refugee (said to owe him money) in British Honduras, which resulted in a raid by Icaiche men on the refugee's establishment in English-controlled territory, where they took hostages. This occasioned strong complaints by the British colonial governor in Jamaica to Yucatán on the ground that Tzuc claimed to act on behalf of the Yucatecan government.[38] The reply was that the Yucatecans were powerless, that the *pacíficos* governed themselves independently, and that "if their Principal Chief has any appointment from Campeche or from Yucatán it is certain that he does not derive his authority more than from the personal influence which he exercises over the Indians."[39] At the end of 1864 Tzuc was dead and succeeded by Marcos Canul, who, following in the footsteps of his predecessor, immediately registered claims for rents on logging between Río Bravo and Blue Creek, allegedly on behalf of Mexico, which claimed that territory as part of Yucatán. Protests to Mexico again resulted in a response that "the government of Yucatán has given neither orders nor appointment of any kind whatever to the Indian Canul."[40]

Nevertheless, by the late 1860's Canul was recognized by the governor of Campeche as commandant of the Cantón of Icaiche, a quasi-independent polity that remitted no taxes to any higher government but collected taxes on its own account, yet which was at certain times supplied with Mexican arms, presumably for defense against the rebels of Santa Cruz. Icaiche demands continued to trouble English settlers, although Canul was inclined to try to blame some of it upon his secretary, who he said was acting without his knowledge.[41]

Be that as it may, with a party of 116 men Canul took forcible possession of the British Honduras town of Corozal for a brief period in 1870 but departed without doing harm to persons (Burdon 1931–1935:III, 320–323). In August 1872 he made the fatal mistake of leading his men against the British Honduras towns of Water Bank and Orange Walk; in the gunfight he was mortally wounded.[42]

After his death his second-in-command, Comandante Rafael Chan, was elevated to leadership at Icaiche, claiming the title of "General in

Chief."[43] Relationships with the English became less violent, although they were marred periodically by Indian claims for rent. Toward the end of that decade, apparently in 1877, Chan was succeeded by General Santiago Pech, the former sub-*alcalde* of San Pedro referred to previously, who was no consistent respector of English territory. In late 1882 Pech was prevailed upon to meet with the governor of British Honduras, at which time he expressed a desire for friendship, denied complicity in certain extortionate threats made earlier that year (which he blamed upon his literate secretary), and admitted that he had appointed Indian *alcaldes* at certain British Honduras towns to which he felt his jurisdiction extended. He agreed at least tentatively to respect British territorial claims in an agreement signed at that time, in which he was seconded by his subordinate, Col. Gabriel Tamay. Apparently his motive in completing the agreement was the reinstatement of trade between Icaiche and British Honduras, which had been ended by governmental decree as a result of Icaiche depredations.[44]

The Northern Group • Sometime during the late 1850's José María Cocom was assassinated in the course of a minor uprising of *pacíficos* said to be in sympathy with the rebels of Santa Cruz (Baqueiro 1878–1887:III, 133), and Pablo Encalada was elected by the commanders of the *pacífico* settlements to replace him as *gobernador*.[45] By this time the position at least nominally included hegemony over Icaiche as well, and in 1866 a British estimate indicated Encalada to control territory stretching from the Hondo almost to the city of Campeche, with a total population in excess of thirty thousand.[46] Whatever this control may have amounted to, Encalada had no noticeable success when he attempted in 1864 and 1867 to curb the predations of Tzuc and Canul against British Honduras.[47]

Late in 1864 the imperial government of Maximilian was formally recognized by the *pacíficos,* and, in a move to regularize the government of the Indians, it appointed one José María Arredondo to be prefect over them; shortly thereafter Arredondo and nine *pacífico* commanders journeyed to Mexico, where the Indians presented their felicitations to the emperor (Hübbe 1940:151).[48] Encalada remained at the top of the Indian leadership as subprefect.

In 1866 Arredondo was assassinated—by one account as a reaction to his having done physical injury to the Indian commandant of Mesapich—and, in a meeting of Indian commanders called in order both to establish an agreement for self-government and to assuage the imperial authorities, Encalada was selected *gobernador* and Antonio Uc was designated military leader with the title of *general*. Whatever the explanation they provided for Arredondo's death, it was apparently acceptable to the imperial commissary in Mérida, who was already busy with various cracks in the imperial edifice; the government made no attempt to intervene (Hübbe 1940: 159).[49]

Tranquility did not last, however. In mid-1867 the rebels of Santa Cruz succeeded in subverting a substantial number of *pacíficos* who rose up in concert with an invasion by Santa Cruz forces. Lochha was taken, and Encalada was imprisoned and deposed in favor of Santa Cruz sympathizers. Although Encalada was released and the Santa Cruz puppets were shortly captured by Uc and hanged, the rebellion continued. According to one account, it involved all but some two hundred of the *pacífico* troops and was a direct aftermath of the killing of Arredondo.[50]

As a result of the disturbance, Encalada and his family moved permanently westward to the protection of government troops, whither they were accompanied by a large number of residents of the *pacífico* settlements around Lochha and Mesapich. At the same time, a large number of people of the same area with opposing sympathies took up residence around Bacalar in Santa Cruz territory.[51]

Led by Uc and the brothers Andrés and Eugenio Arana, loyal *pacíficos* continued desultory fighting around Lochha and Mesapich until pacification was achieved again in 1868. In 1869 Eugenio Arana was *general* and overall leader of the *pacíficos,* a post he was to retain until the end of the century. He was shortly to be in amiable correspondence with the British government in Belize, using on his letters a stamp with the Mexican eagle and the title "Canton General de Xkan-ha."[52] With his headquarters established at Xkanha, that settlement eclipsed Lochha as the northern *pacífico* capital.

Although after the 1860's provisions for the existence of the *repúblicas indígenas* did not occur in the laws covering the internal governance of the states of Campeche and Yucatán, and the Indians were at least theoretically subject to the same annual election of officials that was required of other towns,[53] there is no indication that any change was made in their governments before the end of the century. At the same time, the *pacíficos* remained generally unpredictable in the view of the central government and unpopular in the eyes of their ladino neighbors.

In 1878, in an unusually frank exposition, the Mexican minister of external relations admitted that the submission of the *pacíficos* was far from complete and that the governments of Yucatán and Campeche received only the degree of obedience from the Indians that the Indians cared to give. He went on to acknowledge that the nominal appointments given to the Indian "generals" were a matter of simple convenience, in recognition of their de facto position as chiefs, and that far from being loyal subjects these "generals" felt themselves free to treat with foreign governments— that is, British Honduras—without need of consultation with any Mexican authority. The government hoped, however, that with increased contact and with the development of schools in the *pacífico* zone—he stated that three had already been established, one of them in Xkanha—the Indians would gradually be won over (Sociedad Tipográfica 1878:29–84).

In a description published the same year, the *jefe político* of the *partido* of Bolonchenticul, of which the *pacífico* zone in Campeche was a part, spoke more strongly, referring to the Indian *cantones* and "their inhabitants living without laws to govern their actions, with a theocratic-military government . . . more despotic than that established in Poland by the Czar of Russia, directed only by the will of the so-called General Eugenio Arana, . . . a man of vicious antecedents, customarily drunk and capable . . . of any disorder" (Solis 1878:43). Conditions of substantial peace prevailed through the rest of the century, however.

Thus, in addition to those settlements made in the early 1860's in British Honduras and Guatemala, the decades of the 1860's and 1870's saw two important centers of relatively independent *pacíficos*—at Chichanha and then Ichaiche in the south, and at Mesapich, Lochha, and then Xkanha in the north. In the early part of this period hostility against the people of Santa Cruz was intense. By the late sixties a degree of rapprochement was effected between Santa Cruz and rebellious elements of Lochha, but this cooperation was short lived; and by the end of the decade the *pacíficos* were again pacific, holding themselves in constant readiness to do battle with the rebels of the east.

During the last two decades of the century, Icaiche was visited sporadically by outsiders, chiefly religious, who braved the week's journey across country either from Xkanha or British Honduras. Since Xkanha itself was isolated from major settlements, the result was that most spiritual care was from Belize, even though Icaiche was located within the diocese of Yucatán and, later, Campeche.[54] Accounts by these visitors indicate that the town itself was near the Lago Santa Clara on a hill surrounded by a thicket of bamboo; one indicated it to be divided into four *barrios*. Population was estimated between seventeen hundred and thirty-five hundred. The leader was Gen. Gabriel Tamay, who consulted a council of subordinate chiefs in major decisions but served as supreme judge in criminal matters. He worked hard in his own fields. A secretary handled written communications. All adult males over fifteen years of age composed the army, and sentries were always on guard around the town, allegedly to protect against surprise attack by the enemies of Santa Cruz. *Maestros* performed routine services—novenas, ceremonies of Holy Week, baptisms—but priests were welcomed; those who came performed many marriages and baptisms and heard great numbers of confessions.[55]

Xkanha was more accessible, requiring a journey of about a week from Oxkutzcab, which in the 1890's was reached by rail from Mérida. Trade with Yucatán and Campeche was effected by traveling peddlers, and priests visited regularly from Campeche. In addition to Xkanha itself, General Arana counted thirteen major settlements in his control, each of them commanded by an individual with military rank ranging from sergeant to colonel. In 1895 Arana indicated that his people remained independent chiefly because they were unable to obtain assistance from the government of Campeche when they asked for it and complained that, although a school building was ready, they had never received a teacher. Arana himself dressed as any other Indian, in white cotton trousers and shirt, distinguished from his escort when seen by one reporter only by his painted canvas shoulder bag which bore the words "te amo."[56]

In 1894 and 1895 both Icaiche and Xkanha were visited by the German geographer Carl Sapper (1904). At that time he estimated the population of Icaiche—after a serious epidemic—at about five hundred and that of the entire polity of Xkanha at about eight thousand. In both, the chief was titled *general* and he was assisted by a *comandante*. In both, the offices were said to be confirmed by the governor of Campeche, who after election of a new office holder by the Indians would appoint him to minor administrative, military, and legal positions. Both used a stamp with the Mexican eagle. In both centers military service was compulsory. Judgment in criminal cases was said to be prompt and summary, with punishment by flogging or in serious cases by shooting. In both, of course, the language was Maya. Xkanha, which traded primarily with Campeche, was said to exhibit more obvious Mexican influence than did Icaiche, where trade was greater with people of British Honduras.

Taking all of this together, there is little reason to think that any major organizational changes occurred within either of these units during the decades following the signing of the treaty of 1853, except that the use of military titles may have become somewhat more regularized, and at times the title *comandante* appears to have been replaced by the term *coronel*. In both, succession to leadership appears to have been orderly, and at Chichanha and Icaiche it is especially clear that succession to the supreme leadership tended to follow relatively strict military order, with the second-in-command—usually termed *comandante*—assuming the lead as *general*. By the late nineteenth century, if not considerably earlier, Mexican government appointments served to legitimize the leadership.

In the 1890's, when it became clear that Yucatán would receive significant help from the central Mexican government in the pacification of the rebel Indians of Santa Cruz, interest in all uncontrolled Indians in both Campeche and Yucatán revived. The legal basis for the continuation of *pacífico* autonomy gone with the defunct *repúblicas indígenas,* the process of incorporating these people became simply one of a gradual extension of networks of communication and administration, which would lead eventually, it was hoped, to taxation and the other benefits of civilization. Although this process had scarcely begun by 1900, certain moves in the direction had been made. In 1897 Arana himself had visited Mérida, where he was welcomed by the commandant of the military zone and was lodged in style in the home of the *alférez*. In that same decade Xkanha was visited by military emissaries and, in 1898, by the Bishop of Campeche. In 1899 a new church was begun in Xkanha, and funds for it were solicited by means of advertisements in major newspapers.[57] By 1903 the Campeche government could claim the investigation of serious crimes in the area were under its control.[58]

Despite its difficult access, Icaiche also received its apostolic visit—the first time a bishop had ever been there—in 1898 from the same active Bishop of Campeche, who was able to marry both General Tamay and an aide, Captain May, to their current spouses; he confirmed three hundred.[59] In 1901, General Tamay paid a friendly visit to the Mexican general who by then had reoccupied Bacalar for the government. On his departure up-river on the Río Hondo, the steamer on which he and his party traveled as passengers hit a log and sank.[60]

He did not drown, however, and in 1902 was claimed to be involved in an attempt to extort $200 from a resident of British Honduras who was bleeding chicle in the vicinity of Yaloch in Guatemala. The affair occasioned official correspondence between British Honduras and Mexico over the next two years, correspondence in which the virtual absence of any Mexican control over Icaiche was made clear.[61]

Theocratic Bravos

For several years after the unsuccessful attack on Chichanha in 1852, the Santa Cruz rebels were hard pressed in defending themselves against Yucatecan campaigns directed at Chan Santa Cruz itself, and they did little fighting in the south; Bacalar remained an isolated outpost of Yucatecans, relieved occasionally by military columns. Barrera died—apparently not violently—at the close of 1852 (Baqueiro 1878–1887:II, 445), and for a time thereafter the identity of the supreme leader or leaders is not clear. During this period communications purporting to come from the cross were signed simply "Juan de la Cruz."[62]

The first indication of renewed rebel interest in the south occurred in May 1857, when a Santa Cruz force occupied an English mahogany works on the Río Hondo and extorted a money payment.[63] This was at about the time of their renewal of pressure on Chichanha and the *pacíficos*, as described previously. In September of 1857 a Santa Cruz force made a daring raid on the important Yucatecan town of Tekax, committed massacre, and shortly afterward arrived at the Hondo to trade the spoils.[64]

In February of 1858 Bacalar was retaken by Santa Cruz soldiers; this time the prisoners were held, and shortly afterward the rebels offered to trade them to the English in exchange for the Yucatecan commander of the fort, who had escaped across the border to British territory. The English refused, and in the face of an offer of ransom by a private citizen of British Honduras, the fate of the prisoners was decided at night by the Talking Cross itself, consulted by the Santa Cruz *patrón* (as the religious leader was now called) Benancio Puc,[65] in a house converted to a shrine; the cross responded with whistling and other noises, while the answers were interpreted to the prisoners, the Indian soldiers, and the visiting English commissioners of mercy outside. By command of the cross the cash ransom was spurned and all adult prisoners, male and female, were put to the machete within earshot of the English negotiators.[66]

After this there ensued a period of coolness between the Santa Cruz and the Belize governments, a period in which the cross cult reached its apparent apex as an integral element in the Santa Cruz government and the truculence of the Santa Cruz leadership was at its height. Late in 1858 ransomed juvenile prisoners reported both that the Santa Cruz people had formally renounced the Roman Catholic Church and that they had begun the construction of a large masonry church building for their cult.[67]

Despite the general health of the Santa Cruz polity, some notable losses occurred. In 1859 the rebels at Kantunil, well to the north, negotiated a separate peace with the central government under terms similar to, although somewhat less generous than, those of the earlier treaty with the southerners.[68] Thereafter the Kantunil people joined the official ranks of the *pacíficos,* although their remoteness from those of the south and from any major settled center meant that they were to receive little public attention in ensuing years. They would occasionally be forced to ask for defensive help from the Yucatecan government.

Despite verbal assurances by the Santa Cruz leaders that they intended no harm to the English, for some time following the Bacalar massacre the British Honduras government saw them as sullen, and kept a watchful eye upon the permanent Santa Cruz garrison of four hundred men now located at Bacalar.[69] And, indeed, border violations began to trouble Belize—the results both of hot pursuit by Santa Cruz soldiers of their Chichanha *pacífico* enemies, and of armed Santa Cruz attempts to collect debts said to be owed them by various people who had previously cut logs or farmed in territory north of the Hondo, and who had taken refuge in the English colony.[70]

The violations finally in March 1861 resulted in the deputation by the Belize government of British Army Lieutenants James J. Plumridge and J. Y. Twigge to go to Santa Cruz and demand a formal apology from the *patrón.* Upon their arrival they were disarmed, detained, manhandled, interrogated by the cross in the dark of night, and subjected to various indignities by the drunken Benancio Puc; they were, however, allowed to return to Belize with their lives (Rogers 1885).[71] Whatever may have been the obfuscating role of an unscrupulous interpreter in the affair,[72] the aggressiveness of Benancio Puc and the followers of the cross was clear. The English took no action in reprisal.

From the period following 1860 comes the description of the Santa Cruz hierarchy that has been most frequently quoted (Aldherre 1869; cf. Trebarra 1864). In the management of the cult were said to be three persons: a supreme priest, the *patrón* (or *tatich,* in Maya), Benancio Puc, who conducted the actual interviews with the cross; the "Interpreter of the Cross" (*Tata Polin*), a person named Apolinar Sánchez, who interpreted the noises of the cross; and the "Organ of the Divine Word" (no Maya equivalent given), José Na, who apparently was responsible for the voice and noises of the cross. Beneath the *patrón* stood a supreme general (*Tata Chikiuic*), who commanded a number of lesser generals and *comandantes*. Military duties were arranged so that a guard of four hundred men was present in the capital at all times. There was also an office of chief spy (*Tata Nohoch Dzul*), said to be filled by Bonifacio Novelo.

Although after the Plumridge and Twigge affair border incidents apparently diminished along the Río Hondo, excesses continued to be committed against the Yucatecan enemy. An attack on Tunkás in September 1861 was said to have resulted in the massacre of some six hundred prisoners (Baqueiro 1878–1887:III, 227–229). Finally, in December 1863, as an avowed reaction to the bloody rule of the cross and Benancio Puc (and brought on, it was said, by the discovery that the speaking of the cross was a hoax), a coup was engineered in which Puc and his two priest cohorts were killed. The leaders were two Santa Cruz generals, Dionisio Zapata and Leandro Santos, who immediately upon assuming control wrote to the superintendent at Belize, described the coup and its background, and indicated a desire for peace and tranquility.[73] Word of the coup and of the inclinations of the new leaders electrified Mérida and Campeche, and a commission was shortly sent to Belize to treat with them for peace.[74] But the new regime was never firmly in control, and in March 1864 its leaders were dead in a countercoup that brought to power the triumvirate of Bonifacio Novelo, Bernabé Ken, and José Crescencio Poot, reputedly an antipeace party (Hübbe 1940:150).[75]

Thereupon ensued a period of instability, as partisans of Puc and of Zapata and Santos continued in turmoil. Government peace overtures were rejected.[76] Nevertheless, the newest leaders endured, and Santa Cruz hostilities continued against the Yucatecans. Between Santa Cruz and Belize, however, there followed a time of relatively stable relations. A number of border incidents still occurred—incidents consisting of the seizures on British territory of debtors or Yucatecan refugees or of rebel visits in force to buy powder.[77] But the English view had become more liberal, for "it would be absurd to expect of the Indians a scrupulous regard of international law. They simply have no idea of it."[78] And in their turn the Santa Cruz leadership offered to go to British assistance against elements among the *pacíficos* who were troubling Belize[79] and became convinced that their defense against Yucatán was to be gained only through English friendship.

Periodic visits of traders from British Honduras to Chan Santa Cruz were apparently routine. According to John Carmichael, one such visitor in 1867, Novelo was *patrón*, or head of the church, and administrator of civil justice. Bernabé (or Bernardino, in some correspondence) Ken, the second chief, commanded the army, which was claimed to consist of eleven thousand fighting men, of whom four thousand were said to be furnished by allies of Macanche and Lochha; José Crescencio Poot was third chief. Each Indian soldier was required to give fifteen days military service per month, during which time he fed himself and received no pay; but he was allowed to keep his spoils (except for a mandatory portion offered to the church), which, when his turn came to be assigned to the garrison at Bacalar, he could sell to the English traders. Permanent buildings in Chan Santa Cruz included the church, where the miraculous cross was said to be kept; the barracks and prison flanking it; and the house of the *patrón* facing it across the plaza. Population of the rather dispersed town alone was estimated at seven thousand. The mummery of the Talking Cross was said to have been stopped, and the treasure of the church was claimed by Novelo to exceed $200,000, not including jewels and gold ornaments.[80]

It may be that these figures for population and wealth were somewhat inflated, inasmuch as it is clear that Carmichael was in favor of annexing eastern Yucatán to British Honduras, and his report is intended to show that eventuality in the best possible light. Six years earlier Plumridge and Twigge had estimated the Santa Cruz military force, without allies, to consist of about five thousand men. Taking both estimates, it would seem possible to guess the total population loyal to Chan Santa Cruz, not including allied *pacíficos* (who, as relayed by Carmichael, included those of the Lochha region who cooperated with Santa Cruz only briefly in 1867 and 1868), at somewhere between twenty-five thousand and thirty thousand,[81] of whom as many as seven thousand could have formed the army, and a relative few may have been full-time nonagricultural specialists in religion, government, or crafts. These figures seem in at least rough accord with reports of a prisoner taken in fighting at Tihosuco in 1869, who said that about forty-five hundred *sublevados* (the implication is soldiers, although it could conceivably apply to total population) were then in Chan Santa Cruz, while others were fighting elsewhere. But none of these reports accords with that of one escaped Santa Cruz prisoner in 1861 that the army consisted of no more than one thousand armed men[82] nor with the estimate of the unsuccessful Yucatecan peace commissioners of 1864: these reported that their inquiries in British Honduras revealed Chan Santa Cruz to consist of some two hundred houses, which were inhabited only by the leaders and by a few of the relatively rich, and that the total population of the polity did not exceed four thousand people.[83] Surely the period of the 1860's, despite the internal troubles, was that of maximum strength, affluence, and stability for the polity centered at Chan Santa Cruz. Granted the tendency for a number of the estimates to be inflated, it is difficult to conceive of the Santa Cruz success in controlling most of the eastern portion of Yucatán with a population of less than, say, fifteen thousand.

Carmichael's statement regarding the silence of the once voluble cross might also be qualified. Whatever the behavior of the cross at Santa Cruz itself during his visit, one account indicates that shortly after the countercoup of 1864 attempts were being made to revive the oracular practice near Tulum (Trebarra 1864). In 1866 at least one report from Santa Cruz states that a cross at Tulum was offering pronouncements on matters important to the Santa Cruz people. In 1871 a talking cross at Tulum was under the direct control of a priestess, and much later—in 1890—a Santa Cruz resident was forced to flee for his life because he indicated he did not believe the cross could talk.[84]

By mid-1868, José Crescencio Poot was supreme head of the Santa Cruz government (the fate of his colleagues is not clear), and in 1869 he was signing communications as "Gobernador y Comandante en Jefe."[85] In 1871 Santa Cruz encroachments toward the *pacíficos* of Kantunil in the north were in some part responsible for a Yucatecan expedition that attacked into their territory as far as Chunpom. In July of the following year Santa Cruz forces assaulted Kantunil, the people of which being quickly aided by Yucatecan troops. The combined Yucatec and Kantunil force counterattacked, repulsing the rebels, and took and burned the rebel town of San Antonio.[86] Later that same year British officials expressed the opinion that discipline in Santa Cruz was growing lax and that the polity might fragment with little provocation.[87]

It did not do so, however, and Poot remained at its head throughout the 1870's, although his earlier sanguinary spirit must have mellowed, for, after the unsuccessful Kantunil attack, the rebels made no more major excursions. At the beginning of 1884 Poot acquiesced in an abortive peace treaty with Yucatán, which was signed in Belize but never ratified because one of the Indian commissioners—Aniceto Dzul—was insulted by the Yucatecan representative in the postsigning festivities.[88] The following year Poot was killed together with seven other leaders and sixty-seven soldiers in a coup that brought power to that same Aniceto Dzul, who reportedly had formed a force of six hundred men in Tulum and had fallen on Chan Santa Cruz.[89]

In January 1888, at the time of a visit by an English surveyor, William Miller (1889), *Gobernador* Dzul lived, not in Chan Santa Cruz, but at San Pedro 4 leagues distant. By this time Chan Santa Cruz was said to have no permanent residents, although it provided a place for the chiefs periodically to assemble, and it was guarded by a military force of some one hundred and fifty men. About this time there was also a separate chief at Tulum, who was known independently to the Belize government, although he was apparently allied with the hierarchy at Santa Cruz.[90] The cross was also still talking in the Tulum vicinity, and it was alleged to interrogate all visitors and to appoint the chiefs of Santa Cruz. Miller was unable to visit it, because his guides refused to take him there (Miller 1889).

Not long afterward Dzul reportedly fell on Tulum and did much killing, ostensibly because the people there had received a Yucatecan hospitably and had even allowed him to marry one of their women. As a result of the attack, that center was said to be almost depopulated, many of the people having fled to British Honduras.[91] Thereafter the people of Tulum held themselves away from Santa Cruz, and by the late 1890's they were said to be substantially independent, maintaining commercial relations with the *pacíficos* of Kantunil.[92]

By early 1890 Dzul was dead, succeeded by José Crescencio Puc and Román Pec.[93] Pec remained in power until 1896, when one account indicates he was killed by his second-in-command, who was horrified at his bloody attack made on Tulum in response to word that people of the place were preparing to submit to the Yucatecan government; a story by a somewhat more credible witness is that Pec died of sickness.[94] In any event, he was succeeded by Felipe Yama, already an old man, who was apparently assassinated in 1901, virtually on the eve of the occupation of Chan Santa Cruz by the Mexican army, when he became finally convinced that the Indians must surrender and urged his companions to do so.[95]

Despite the maintenance of a spirit of rebellion and despite some attacks on trespassers,[96] incursions into their territory were increasingly tolerated by the rebels, as woodcutters expanded their operations around Bacalar and some Yucatecan colonization and woodcutting was initiated in locations on the east coast. A number of Santa Cruz people, soldiers included, were said to be working as woodcutters for these outsiders, most of whom were careful to pay rents to the Santa Cruz leaders.[97] It is clear that the days of the fearsome military power of Santa Cruz were waning and the rebel population was scattering and in decline. When it became evident that the central Mexican government under Porfirio Díaz would support a final campaign to pacify the rebels, the information of these outside events as usual reached Chan Santa Cruz immediately and accelerated emigration from rebel territory, especially toward Belize. By 1895 some apparently informed sources suggested that the Santa Cruz leadership could not field as many as one thousand armed men,[98] although other estimates were as high as three thousand.

In 1897 ratification of the Spencer-Mariscal treaty settled the territorial dispute between Mexico and British Honduras and made possible the placement of a Mexican barge and customs force in the Río Hondo, which inhibited the commercial traffic of Santa Cruz. Towns long abandoned in the no man's land west of the rebel zone were refurbished by the government, and tax exemptions and other inducements were offered to encourage their resettlement. Railroads, roads, and telegraph lines were driven from western Yucatán toward the east, under military protection when necessary. On March 31, 1901, Bacalar was reoccupied by government forces. On May 4 of the same year the Mexican army entered Santa Cruz, and in July a detachment occupied Tulum. Although the spirit of rebellion and the cult of the cross were to continue, the rebel polity of Santa Cruz was thus ended after a continuous and fairly stable life of half a century.

This is not to say that the organization of the Santa Cruz group did not undergo significant internal change during that span. Perhaps most evident is the strong suggestion of a fundamental shift in the place of the religious cult in the society.

In the early 1850's Chan Santa Cruz was the site of a genuine nativistic religious movement within which a surge of blind devotion resulted in increased ferocity and suicidal military raids against the Yucatecans; military efforts were also made to bring the Chichanha defectors back into line. By the end of that decade—with the rise of Benancio Puc—the workings of the cross had been routinized, priestly roles had been formalized, and the military hierarchy was subordinated to the religious leadership. Interrogations of the cross were clearly a part of regular political decision making, and the powers of cult and military were united in Puc, the high priest and supreme political head.

But, with the overthrow of Puc in 1864, manipulations of the cult for direct political ends were apparently considerably lessened. Despite some recent accounts that seem to imply that the form of Puc's religious triumvirate endured throughout the late nineteenth century (e.g., Cline 1950b: 173–175; Reed 1964:161; Villa Rojas 1945:23)—during a time well after Santa Cruz seems to have lost its own Talking Cross—there seems to be no evidence for the continuation of any such organization. There is no further reference in contemporary documents to either an "Interpreter of the Cross" or an "Organ of the Divine Word," although, of course, the office of *tatich* or *patrón* has continued to the present (e.g., Machlin and Marx 1971; Reed 1964:271–280). The term *triumvirate,* which has been used by these later writers to refer to the religious hierarchy, appears in contemporary British documents only to describe the Santa Cruz leadership during the joint rule of Novelo, Ken, and Poot, during which time the "triumvirs" were those three—one of them reputedly the religious *patrón,* the others secular (i.e., military) leaders. It is therefore tempting to conceive of the Santa Cruz government at this time as finally professionalized, with the cross cult and secular leadership representing approximately coordinate parts. This decade was also the only time when the size of the polity was such that at least a small nonagricultural population may have been supported, but from the indications of instability reported from that time onward, it seems certain that the leadership never managed a successful monopoly of the use of force—that is, Santa Cruz could not reasonably be called a state, as states are commonly defined.

By the 1870's the florescence of Chan Santa Cruz had passed, and in the 1880's virtually no resident town population existed. The supreme political leader, now known as *gobernador,* was clearly secular and military and remained so thereafter. Although Miller (1889) is not explicit on this point, it appears from his wording that the *gobernador* in 1888 may have worked his own fields, as did the military chief—but not the *patrón*—of the X-Cacal polity of the 1930's (Villa Rojas 1945). At any rate, the presence at Tulum of a talking cross over which the *gobernador* apparently had no immediate and direct control suggests that civil and religious administration and aims had somehow become still further separated one from another (cf. Reed 1964:223–224); it is fitting that the sacred Chan Santa Cruz had by then become a vacant town.

Whatever its decadence by the end of the century, the rebel movement of Santa Cruz with its cult of the Talking Cross appears to have followed the course of revitalistic movements as they were formulated by Wallace (1956): the appearance of a new code was spread broadly among converts, leading to a new organization, to efforts to maintain the organization and the code, and, finally, to the formation of a new and integrated society.

Concluding Discussion

I have attempted to sketch the main features of the development of the relatively independent Indian political units following the outbreak of the Caste War of Yucatán. After the early years of the revolt, the rebels split into two major groups, one of which continued the rebellion and embraced a revitalistic religious cult featuring a miraculous Maya-speaking cross, while the second submitted to the Yucatecan government and throughout the rest of the nineteenth century remained at peace, if occasionally obnoxious, in a condition of de facto independence.

At the outset, these two groups were organized in identical fashion, following the model of the local militia of mid-nineteenth-century Yucatán. The pacified faction rapidly experienced a number of further fragmentations, resulting in separate units in three distinct areas: one (rather ephemeral) in the south, in British Honduras and Guatemala; one at Chichanha and then Icaiche; and one in the north, focused variously around the centers of Mesapich, Lochha, and Xkanha. In two of these areas the rebel military organization was retained to perfection, whereas the southern unit was influenced by the nomenclature introduced by the superintendent of British Honduras for local officials. In later years the leadership of the two northern units came to be legitimized by appointments from the government of Campeche.

Except for the comparatively minor Kantunil defection, fragmentation of the rebel Santa Cruz faction took a different course. Despite upheavals as leaders fought sporadically for supreme position, an overall unity was maintained in most periods. Meanwhile, although the revitalizing religious cult of the miraculous cross was persistent, the relationship of that cult to the politico-military leadership of the rebels underwent changes from outright supremacy of the cult toward an accommodation in which the cult and the military leadership were more nearly coordinate and then finally became distinct from one another. This last stage seems to have coincided with the appearance of two separated centers—Chan Santa Cruz and Tulum.

In this article all these societies have been referred to as chiefdoms. That term is used substantially as it has been defined by Service, as a society that is characterized by "centers which coordinate economic, social, and religious activities" (1962:143), and by the office of chief, yet which lacks a clear monopoly by the leader of the legitimate use of force.

It also seems reasonable to describe all these societies as segmental, as that term has been used to describe social units that exhibit ease in fragmenting and realigning (e.g., Sahlins 1961; cf. Dumond 1970). I believe it would be erroneous to conclude that the military nature of the organization was responsible for the segmentary nature of these units. Rather, it appears simply that the hierarchical terminology that is used by the military throughout the world is uniquely suited for use by segmentary organizations. On the other hand, the formal chain of authority and responsibility that is inherent in the military ranking system—some of which seems to have been retained by the rebels—may reflect a degree of organization beyond that to be found in many aboriginal segmental societies.

Zimmerman has argued that the cult of the cross was responsible for the ability of the rebels to continue their resistance (1963). In opposition, G. D. Jones has insisted that the significant feature in the maintenance of independence by the people of Chan Santa Cruz lay in the relatively unrestricted availability to them of powder through merchants of British Honduras (1971a). It seems obvious that this last situational factor was permissive in the evolution of the Indian chiefdoms. Plainly, the Santa Cruz people could not have continued the rebellion, in an age in which fighting required gunpowder, without a convenient magazine. But the same source was open just as consistently to the other Indian units, the *pacíficos*, who did not choose to maintain their independent and rebellious stand. Although it is doubtful that the cause is as simple as Zimmerman seems to propose, it seems clear that the possession of the cult of the cross by the Santa Cruz rebels was related intimately to their continued rebelliousness. In any comparison of the Indian polities, then, the possession by the Santa Cruz rebels of the miraculous cult, formally separated as it was from institutional Catholicism, must assume importance as a psychological centrum around which the rebels rallied themselves in the fight for their very lives, a mechanism indispensable to the maintenance of unity and a decidedly revolutionary spirit through half a century and more.[99]

To this continued belligerence of the Santa Cruz group, in turn, was owed the existence of the *pacífico* chiefdoms. The large and dispersed *pacífico* unit at Lochha and Xkanha, in particular, stood as a guardian backwoods hinterland to the civilized zone of Campeche and Yucatán, on the one hand, and as a relatively unfriendly, but not altogether unsympathetic, frontier neighbor to the Santa Cruz, on the other. Despite some sharp ideological differences between the leadership of the *pacíficos* and the rebels, the common, swidden-farming adherents apparently found little difficulty in changing allegiance from one to the other as it seemed convenient. Clearly, without the existence of Santa Cruz, the *pacífico* territory would shortly have been colonized and absorbed by Yucatán or Campeche; and without the continuing activities of the latter, the interests of the *pacíficos* would almost certainly have merged again with those of Santa Cruz.

Last of all, the boundary dispute between Mexico and British Honduras served to bolster the faltering, often diminishing chiefdom of Icaiche, the farthest both from civilized Yucatán and Campeche and from the Santa Cruz capital. For, while claims on former Yucatecan territory northwest of the Río Hondo provided the Santa Cruz with occasional income, the collection of these extortionary "rents" in a fluctuating territory and the concomitant belligerence against Belize seem to have provided Icaiche with much of the unification it managed.

I conclude, then, that following the outbreak of the Caste War, Indian political units developed that were essentially new, that were segmentary in form and chiefdoms in political organization, and that worked out the relationships between themselves and adjoining societies in a milieu in which the availability of powder and the continuation of a territorial dispute between England and Mexico were both permissive and necessary conditions.

Appendix

A Brief Review of Literature Useful in the Study of the Caste War

Any student who approaches the Caste War is fortunate in having available the excellent bibliographical essay by Cline (1945), which, although confined to sources available in the United States, happily renders unnecessary further extensive bibliographic discussion. Here I mention only a few later writings and point out some of the more obvious problems faced by the anthropologist who turns to these historical works for his own ends. Discussion of relatively primary sources is avoided, for such sources will vary substantially according to the problem that is addressed.

Although the kinds of specific, localized social data that anthropologists tend to be in search of are seldom to be found in the obvious secondary sources, adequate secondary treatments are invaluable in the elimination of the need for extensive research in the general Yucatecan milieu, for they will at least provide a usable outline of political and institutional history.

Thrusting itself upon Yucatecans as the salient fact of the mid-nineteenth century, the war naturally enough became the subject of local historians. Even though they wrote as contemporaries of—often participants in—events fraught with a mutual aggressiveness that resolved itself into ideologies of race hatred, many of them maintained admirable balance and impartiality. The works of Baqueiro (1878–1887) and Ancona (1889)

are noteworthy in this regard. Baqueiro devoted himself entirely to the
Caste War and various contemporaneous intrigues in Yucatán, and Ancona devoted to the period one entire volume of his history. Unfortunately, their detailed coverage of events ends respectively in 1863 and 1864,
with the rise of Maximilian's empire. An apparently lesser known book by
Molina Solís (1921) ends in 1867, with the downfall of that same imperial
government. The very useful, if relatively short and undetailed, volume
by Hübbe (1940)—a compilation of newspaper articles that were published in 1880 and 1881—extends coverage only through the 1870's. The
first two of these authors append useful documents, published in support
of their accounts. Unfortunately, as with most such works of the time and
the place, citations appear relatively seldom, so that it is impossible for the
modern student to find an easy guide into primary materials.

Although the independence of the Maya and the attendant warfare endured through the remainder of the nineteenth century, and had only a
little earlier been interesting enough to the popular mind to provide the
subject of several romances (e.g., Castillo 1883; Trebarra 1864), such summary histories of these later decades as are generally available (Acereto
1947; Urzaiz R. 1946) devote almost no attention at all to the lagging
hostilities. Fortunately, the entry of the federal government into the war
in the 1890's created a resurgence of Yucatecan interest in the rebellion
(by then localized in the extreme east of Yucatán), and a rash of historical
reminiscences and other discussions of the war appeared in local newspapers. Few of these are of high quality, but some are useful for accounts
of specific incidents, as well as for the broad chronicling of local events at
the end of the century; unfortunately, foreign holdings of Mexican newspapers are such that access to these is virtually impossible outside of
Mexico. One rather good example is the series by F. Pérez Alcalá, "Guerra
social en Yucatán," published in *La Revista de Mérida* between July 24
and September 19, 1899, and then republished as a part of a collection
(Pérez Alcalá 1914) that seems scarcely more readily available than the
newspapers.

Still later works that refer extensively to the Caste War or to events related to it tend to abandon chronicle for polemic, picking up threads of
nineteenth-century argument, sometimes intermingling them with thought
of later decades: the interests of Mexico and Yucatán were dealt with un-
fairly in the settlement of territorial differences with the English in the
matter of Belize (e.g., Fabela 1944); the Indian uprising resulted directly
from an abiding Indian hatred for whites that stemmed from three centuries of colonial oppression, and the Caste War was the expiation of
white Yucatecan sin (e.g., Berzunza Pinto 1965); the war and the ensuing
rise and fall of henequen production coincided to bring about Yucatán's
economic ruin, exacerbated by shortsighted government policies (e.g.,
Molina Font 1941).

One exception is the *Enciclopedia Yucatanense*, a set of eight volumes on Yucatecan history, geography, and culture published by the Yucatán government between 1944 and 1947, in which articles (of diverse authorship) display restraint and balance, although coverage of the war and its effects are sometimes sketchy. A second obvious exception is the recent work of González Navarro (1970), a socioeconomic history of Yucatán that focuses sharply upon the nineteenth century and after. Excellent for attitudinal and institutional background, and scrupulously equipped with all the scholarly appurtenances, the book is especially useful, even though the scope is such that the section on the Caste War is necessarily abbreviated.

Contemporary accounts in English of events related to the Caste War are few, and these appear chiefly as incidental portions of works dealing with British Honduras (e.g., Burdon 1931–1935; Fowler 1879; Gibbs 1883). Similar information is also contained in recent historical treatments of the same colony (Clegern 1967; Dobson 1973; Humphreys 1961; Waddell 1961).

The first modern description in English specifically of the Caste War was by an anthropologist, appearing in the introductory section of the Villa Rojas (1945) monograph devoted to the X-Cacal Maya, the most militant twentieth-century remnant of the Caste War rebels. One village of the X-Cacal group, Tusik, was also used by Redfield in the original illustration of his hypothesized folk-urban continuum (e.g., Redfield 1941), together with Chan Kom, Dzitas, and Mérida. The war, however, is so far in the background of Redfield's interest that it is possible to cover his material with some care and never realize that Chan Kom was established by migrants in a great depopulated no man's land laid waste in the fighting of the Caste War, or that Tusik was peopled with self-isolating remnants of the same rebellion who felt themselves still at war against the central government.

The first comprehensive attention in English to the background and cause of the war was by the historian Cline (1950b, 1950c), unfortunately in a form that has made for little dissemination. In his work the socioeconomic background of mid-nineteenth-century Yucatán unfolds to demonstrate that the Caste War followed upon the development of a pronounced regionalism, its beginnings coinciding with the encroachment of the sugar plantation system in eastern and southern Yucatán. His approach was then taken up by the anthropologist Strickon, who emphasizes some of Cline's minor themes—that the containment of the warring Maya coincided with the growth of the monocrop henequen industry in the northwest, and that this in turn served to restore to the southeast its viability as an area of independent corn farmers—and develops from them an ecological explanation of the nature of the four settlements in Redfield's folk-urban formulation (1965).

In addition to works in the present volume, there have been a few other relatively restricted uses of Caste War material in an anthropological vein: Zimmerman has focused upon the religious cult of the remaining rebels

(1963). In one paper Grant D. Jones has concentrated upon the role of the English in the support of the rebels during the war (1971a), and in a second he has described and discussed a number of important events in the history of the Santa Cruz polity, which he argues to be best viewed as a recent adaptation of a traditional lowland Maya political system (1974). I have presented a very brief account of the war and of the Indian chiefdoms, as part of a discussion of organizational factors within the X-Cacal group and in Yucatecan peasant communities (Dumond 1970). Cook and Borah have devoted some attention to the demographic effects of the war (1974).

By far the most ambitious treatment of the Caste War in English is that of Reed, who consulted primary materials in British Honduras and made some use of Yucatecan newspapers (1964). Exciting and readable, the book is generally accurate, although lacking in the usual scholarly adjuncts. Unfortunately for the serious student, errors appear in some of the bibliographic listings that he does provide, as well as in a few sequential details (relatively unimportant, to be sure), and certain of the incidents seem to have been dramatized somewhat past the point of accuracy. Nevertheless, it provides a fascinating full-length portrait of the war and its milieu and is written as trippingly as the tale deserves.

With the exception of a section in the book by Reed and of a pair of papers by Cline that suffer from limited source material (1950a, 1950b), none of these accounts has focused specifically upon the course of development of the several chiefdoms of the nineteenth century and upon their shifting interrelationships, which is the subject of the present work.

Notes

1.
I am grateful to Alfredo Barrera Vásquez, director of the Instituto Yucateco de Antropología é Historia, for his assistance in locating various sources in Mérida and for his generosity with those under his control. I also thank the late Antonio Canto López, former director of the Museo de Arqueología de Yucatán, for interesting insights into certain aspects of the Caste War. Grant D. Jones most generously shared with me his knowledge regarding the location of various documents in the Archives of Belize in preparation for my own visit to Belize in 1971, and C. T. Brockmann kindly checked forgotten items for me there in 1973. Victoria Reifler Bricker furnished helpful information regarding material in the Biblioteca Carrillo y Ancona in Mérida and also provided invaluable documents from the Public Records Office in London. I am most of all grateful to Carol Steichen Dumond, who spent interminable hours in archives and libraries of varying degrees of darkness and discomfort, screening and copying documents in unending multitudes, and who still rallied to do much of the specific research for the map in this article.

2.

These archival, newspaper, and official periodical sources are listed below with abbreviations as cited throughout this article.

Unpublished Materials

AB Archives of Belize. Belmopan. Terminal numbers in citations refer to bound volumes.

CCA Collection of the Biblioteca Crescencio Carrillo y Ancona. Mérida.

BFO British Foreign Office documents. Public Records Office, London. Citations include volume and folio number.

Newspapers and Official Periodicals

C *El Constitutional*. 1857–1863. Official gazette of Yucatán. Mérida.

DY *Diario de Yucatán*. 1925–present date. Mérida.

EC *El Eco del Comercio*. 1880–1900. Mérida.

EP *El Espíritu Público*. 1857–1863, 1867–1870. Official gazette of Campeche. Campeche.

ER *El Regenerador*. 1852–1855. Official gazette of Yucatán. Mérida.

GS *Las Garantías Sociales*. 1855–1856. Official gazette of Yucatán. Mérida.

LR *La Restauración*. 1864–1865. Official gazette of Campeche. Campeche.

RM *La Revista de Mérida*. 1869–1914. Mérida.

NE *La Nueva Era*. 1877–1883. Official gazette of Campeche. Campeche.

S *El Siglo XIX*. 2nd series. 1850–1852. Official gazette of Yucatán. Mérida.

3.

E.g., John Kingdon to Col. Charles St. John Fancourt, March 9, 1849, AB, R. 28.

4.

J. W. Faber to Fancourt, December 4, 1848, AB, R. 29.

5.

Various letters of 1848, 1849, AB, R. 28.

6.

Eugenio Arana to Lieutenant Governor, April 13, 1875, AB, R. 119; memorandum of agreement between Harley and Pech, October 13, 1882, AB, R. 93.

7.

Faber to Superintendent, July 6, 1860, AB, R. 71.

8.

Barrera and José V. Reyes to Superintendent, January 1851, AB, R. 33.

9.

Juan María Novelo despatch, S, April 4, 1851; F. de la Cámara Zavala, "Memorias," DY, September 16, 1928.

10.

"Noticias de la campaña," S, October 8, 1851; J. T. Cervera, "Chichanhá," RM, October 8, 1895.

11.
Articles 93–97, "Law for interior government of Yucatán," November 23, 1853, LR, March 11, 1864.
12.
Antonio Meda to E. Eyre, July 6, 1864, AB, R. 86; Rómulo Díaz de la Vega to José Cadenas, ER, November 29, 1854.
13.
Díaz de la Vega to Governor of Yucatán, March 18, 1853, ER, March 23, 1853; Encalada statement, EP, September 24 and 27, 1867.
14.
F. de la Cámara Zavala, "Memorias," DY, October 14, 1928.
15.
E.g., despatch 55, September 14, 1858, AB, R. 55; despatch 10, February 17, 1858, AB, R. 55; despatch 111, July 25, 1868, AB, R. 98.
16.
Despatches 32, September 16, 1857, and 72, September 9, 1856, AB, R. 55; despatch 41, June 1, 1866, AB, R. 92.
17.
Díaz de la Vega to Cadenas, ER, November 29, 1854; Novelo despatch, ER, January 21, 1855 and March 7, 1855.
18.
Faber to Frederick Seymour, December 20, 1857, AB, R. 58; García to Canul, n.d., AB, R. 93.
19.
Despatch 72, September 9, 1856, AB, R. 55; confidential despatch 3, July 14, 1857, AB, R. 52; despatches 32, September 16, 1857, and 34, October 17, 1857, AB, R. 55.
20.
Confidential despatches 1, May 15, 1857, and 2, June 17, 1857, AB, R. 52.
21.
Faber to Seymour, December 20, 1857, AB, R. 58.
22.
Faber to Superintendent, July 6, 1860, AB, R. 71; despatch 50, July 9, 1860, AB, R. 68; "Los indios bárbaros," EP, December 25, 1860.
23.
Despatches 127, November 12, 1862, and 15, February 13, 1863, AB, R. 81.
24.
Luciano Tzuc to S. General, June 15, 1863, and untranslated Tzuc letter in Maya, June 20, 1863, AB, R. 83.
25.
Despatch 29, April 13, 1863, AB, R. 81.
26.
Encalada statement, EP, September 24, 1867.
27.
Gumesindo Ruiz to the Comandant of the Brigada Cadenas, GS, January

2, 1856; Peraza report, GS, January 4, 1856; LGS, September 24, 1856; "Los indios bárbaros," EP, December 25, 1860; May statement, EP, February 3, 1863.

28.

Despatch 127, November 12, 1862, AB, R. 81; E. P. Burke to T. Price, June 15, 1860, AB, R. 71.

29.

Despatch 117, October 8, 1862, AB, R. 81.

30.

Edward M. Rhys to Seymour, November 3, 1862, AB, R. 78.

31.

Despatch 21, May 6, 1866, AB, R. 92; Coroner's reports of May 19 and 21, 1866, AB, R. 93.

32.

Thomas Graham to J. Gardner Austin, August 2, 1866, AB, R. 93.

33.

Despatches 100, November 1, 1866, and 26, January 12, 1867, AB, R. 92.

34.

Canul and Chan to James Swasey, Canul and Chan to George Elliott, December 3, 1866, AB, R. 93.

35.

Despatch 133, December 28, 1866, AB, R. 92.

36.

Austin to Harley, February 5, 1867, AB, R. 91; despatch 35, February 25, 1867, AB, R. 92.

37.

José Carmen Hernández statement, October 29, 1866, AB, R. 93; Henry Fowler to Magistrate, Orange Walk, January 9, 1878, AB, R. 120a.

38.

John Hodge to the Director, British Honduras Co., September 20, 1864, AB, R. 86; Eyre to the Governor of Yucatán, June 22, 1864, AB, R. 86.

39.

Meda to Eyre, July 6, 1864, AB, R. 86.

40.

Despatch 123, December 14, 1864, AB, R. 81; despatch 19, March 18, 1865, AB, R. 92; José F. Ramírez to P. Campbell Scarlett, October 17, 1865, AB, R. 90.

41.

Despatches 111, July 25, 1868, and 127, August 12, 1868, AB, R. 98.

42.

William Johnson statement, September 11, 1872, AB, R. 111.

43.

Chan to Lieutenant Governor, September 26, 1872, AB, R. 111.

44.

Memorandum of agreement between Harley and Pech, October 13, 1882,

AB, R. 93; NE, November 17, 1882.
45.
Encalada statement, EP, September 24, 1867.
46.
Despatch 24, February 6, 1867, AB, R. 92.
47.
Military letter 82, May 19, 1867, and Austin to Harley, May 20, 1867, AB, R. 91; despatch 55, April 9, 1867, AB, R. 98; Dionisio Valencia letter, LR, August 12, 1864.
48.
LR, January 17, 1865; Encalada statement, EP, September 24, 1867.
49.
Encalada statement, EP, September 24 and 27, 1867.
50.
José Luis Santini despatches, EP, August 9, 1867.
51.
Encalada statement, EP, September 24 and 27, 1867; B. H. Mitchell to Magistrate, Orange Walk, April 28, 1873, AB, R. 119a.
52.
Santini and José Leandro Solís despatches, EP, May 19 and 22, 1868; Arana to Pablo García, October 6, 1869, EP, October 19, 1869; Arana to *Gobernador,* June 29, 1878, AB, R. 116; Arana to Lieutenant Governor, March 16, 1874, AB, R. 119a.
53.
"Law for interior government" of August 30, 1877, NE, September 4, 1877; Cervera, "El nombre Maya batab," RM, July 30, 1895.
54.
RM, August 11, 1895.
55.
Aristarco, "Icaiché," RM, September 29, 1895; Severo, "Icaiche," RM, June 29, 1898; "Icaiché," unattributed newspaper clipping in "Breve reseña de Yucatán," vol. 2, a collection of Yucatecan memorabilia compiled for the Paris exposition of 1900 by José Antonio Alayón, CCA.
56.
"La Comisión del Gral. Canto," RM, November 14, 1895; "La llegada del gobernador de Xkanhá," RM, August 5, 1897.
57.
"La llegada del gobernador de Xkanhá," RM, August 5, 1897; RM, February 10, 1898; "El templo de Xkanhá," RM, March 17, 1899.
58.
García to the Secretary of State and Foreign Relations, April 11, 1903, BFO 50, folio 547.
59.
RM, June 26, 1898.

60.
RM, June 15, 1901.
61.
Alonzo Lewis statement, March 19, 1902, and García to Secretary of State
and Foreign Relations, April 11, 1903, BFO 50, folio 547.
62.
Juan de la Cruz to Miguel Barbachano, August 24 and 28, 1851, CCA; GS,
October 18, 1855; "El Cristo de los bárbaros," EP, July 19, 1867.
63.
Young, Toledo and Co. to Seymour, June 15, 1857, AB, R. 58.
64.
Despatch 36, November 17, 1857, AB, R. 55.
65.
Although the present customary literate spelling of this given name is
Venancio, the form Benancio is used here to accord with the consistent
usage of Puc's own secretaries and contemporaries.
66.
Despatch 11, March 13, 1858, AB, R. 55.
67.
Despatch 69, November 17, 1858, AB, R. 65.
68.
Acereto and Vicente Marín to the Governor, October 3, 1859, C, October
10, 1859.
69.
Despatches 66, October 17, 1858, and 62, September 15, 1859, AB, R. 65.
70.
Despatch 50, May 1, 1861, AB, R. 68.
71.
Plumridge and Twigge to Superintendent, April 12, 1861, José María
Trejo statements, April 9 and 12, 1861, and Arcadio Orio statement, April
9, 1861, AB, R. 71; Loeza statement, August 26, 1861, AB, R. 74.
72.
Despatch 50, May 1, 1861, AB, R. 68.
73.
Burke to George Berkeley, January 25, 1864, and José Dionisio Zapata and
José Leandro Santos to Superintendent, January 1, 1864, AB, R. 84.
74.
LR, February 19, 1864 and April 29, 1864.
75.
Burke to Berkeley, March 5, 1864, AB, R. 84; Manuel A. Sierra O'Reilly
and R. Barrera report, LR, July 1 and 5, 1864.
76.
O'Reilly and Barrera report, LR, July 1 and 5, 1864.
77.
E.g., despatch 41, June 1, 1866, AB, R. 92; despatches 5, June 11, 1868,

and 128, November 13, 1869, AB, R. 98.
78.
Despatch 12, January 30, 1868, AB, R. 98.
79.
Novelo, Ken, Poot to Carmichael, October 30, 1867, AB, R. 93.
80.
Carmichael to Superintendent, November 15, 1867, AB, R. 93.
81.
Cf. despatch 6, November 28, 1867, AB, R. 93.
82.
Loeza statement, August 26, 1861, AB, R. 74.
83.
O'Reilly and Barrera report, LR, July 1 and 5, 1864.
84.
Edwin Adolphus to Graham, December 4, 1866, AB, R. 93; D. Traconís, "Diario de la columna de operaciones," RM, February 26, 1871; "Noticias de los bárbaros," RM, August 12, 1890.
85.
"Gacetilla," EP, July 27, 1869.
86.
D. Traconís, "Diario de la columna de operaciones," RM, February 24 and 26, and March 1, 1871; F. Pérez Alcalá, "Guerra social en Yucatán," RM, September 13, 1899.
87.
Mitchell to William W. Cairns, October 30, 1872, AB, R. 111.
88.
Treaty of January 10, 1884, Poot to Fowler, January 30, 1884, AB, R. 118.
89.
"Chan Santa Cruz," EC, February 13, 1886; "Ecos de la excursión," RM, July 3, 1901.
90.
Administrator to Aniceto Dzul, April 12, 1887, Administrator to Pech, May 1887, AB, R. 117.
91.
"Ecos de la excursión," RM, July 3, 1901.
92.
Remegio Pool and Romualdo Cab statement, RM, August 12, 1897.
93.
"Noticias de los bárbaros," RM, August 12, 1890; J. H. Rosado, "Bacalar histórico," RM, May 11, 1899.
94.
RM, February 23, 1897; "Indios sublevados," RM, August 12, 1897.
95.
" 'El General' Felipe Yama asesinado," RM, April 19, 1901.

96.
E.g., "Los asesinatos cometidos por los indios," RM, May 18, 1899.
97.
Felipe Ibarra statement, RM, June 23, 1895; "Colonos contratados," RM, July 12, 1896; "Importantes noticias de Bacalar," RM, June 4, 1895.
98.
Ibarra statement, RM, June 23, 1895; Pool and Cab statement, RM, August 12, 1897.
99.
In a second article, appearing since this was written, Grant D. Jones is more nearly in accord with this view (1974). In contrast to the overall emphasis here, however, he stresses continuity between the Santa Cruz (and X-Cacal) polity and more ancient forms of political organization of the lowland Maya.

5

Levels of Settlement Alliance
among the San Pedro Maya of Western Belize
and Eastern Petén, 1857–1936

Grant D. Jones

Introduction

This article describes the structure of settlement alliance among the San Pedro Maya, a little known Yucatec-speaking population of the late nineteenth and early twentieth centuries.[1] The San Pedro settlements were composed of migrants who about 1857 began to move southward from Chichanha into a territory that eventually covered a significant portion of the headwaters of the Río Bravo (including Booth's River) and Labouring Creek. At their height they comprised about about twenty settlements widely dispersed over an area of some 1,100 square kilometers, straddling the boundary between Belize and the district of Petén, Guatemala. Their total population, which probably never exceeded twelve hundred persons, had significantly declined by the early twentieth century due to epidemic diseases. The only other inhabitants within this territory were the gangs of the seasonal mahogany camps.

The San Pedro Maya settlements were organized at three levels of integration which incorporated increasingly larger territories. I designate these as the village, the minor settlement cluster, and the major settlement cluster. The major settlement cluster included the entire San Pedro population. It was a loosely centralized unit that functioned as a polity primarily during periods of intense military activity. Within the major cluster were three minor settlement clusters. The political-military hierarchy, which on certain occasions controlled the affairs of the entire major settlement cluster, was located at the village of San Pedro in Belize. Thus, San Pedro was the principal village of the major cluster as well as the center of political-military activities within a minor cluster of settlements. Each of the other two minor clusters had their headquarters at settlements which I refer to as secondary village centers. The name of each minor cluster is derived from its village center (San Pedro, San José, and Holmul), while the major cluster is named for the principal village center, San Pedro.

In addition to the principal and secondary village centers, there were a number of other settlements which may also be called villages. All villages had a permanent authority structure under one or two elected *alcaldes*. In some villages the *alcaldes* carried the additional or substitute title of *capitán* in accordance with the system of military titles that characterized all the independent Maya groups of the Caste War period. In later years *alcaldes* were also known as *comandantes*. The *alcaldes* within a minor cluster presumably formed a governing council that was internally ranked like that described by Villa Rojas for the "sub-tribe" of X-Cacal (1945:92). However, there is little direct evidence pertaining to this level of political organization for the San Pedro Maya. San Pedro village itself was the residence of the chief political-military authority of the entire major cluster, referred to as the *general* or *comandante*. Similarities in the overall social systems lead me to presume that the role of this principal *comandante* was not unlike that of the "supreme chief" of X-Cacal (Villa Rojas 1945:91), who served as the nominal head of a council of titled military officers. In the case of the major cluster of San Pedro, this council would have been drawn from each of the minor cluster councils. Village government was identical on both sides of the international frontier and was recognized in their respective territories by both Guatemalan and British officials.

The "military" organization may also have been similar to the primarily village-based *compañía* system of X-Cacal (Villa Rojas 1945:91). Although the available data focus upon the political and military functions of the principal and secondary village centers, these settlements probably functioned as ceremonial centers as well. This was the case with X-Cacal *guardia*, which was, and indeed still is, the ceremonial as well as the political-military center of all the X-Cacal settlements.

Attached to some villages were settlements that I call hamlets. These, in most cases, probably comprised one or two extended families. Each hamlet was subject to the adjacent village's authorities, especially during times of military activities. They tended to be ephemeral and often evaporate from the historical record, presumably having been incorporated into associated settlements following periods of epidemic disease or warfare. Villages frequently migrated as units during such periods of stress. In some cases villages fissioned, and one faction would migrate to form a new village or to join an established one. Village locations were seldom abandoned permanently. The secondary village center of San José survived for more than seventy years, and several other villages are known to have lasted nearly this long.

At the end of this article I draw some tentative conclusions about the broader significance of the San Pedro data. Going beyond the obvious similarities in the overall structures of the San Pedro and X-Cacal groups, I suggest that all the nineteenth-century independent Yucatec Maya groups may have had similar settlement alliance patterns and military-political organizations. Each of these groups, including Santa Cruz,

Lochha-Xkanha, Icaiche, and San Pedro, possessed one or more settlement clusters. Each cluster had a central village that served ceremonial and political functions. Where the group comprised more than one minor settlement cluster, one such central village or town served as the principal settlement of the major cluster. This system, organized by means of a village-based hierarchical "military" structure, was a highly flexible adaptive mechanism in times of armed conflict with neighboring populations. Preliminary historical analysis shows, in fact, that the basic structure common to all of these groups may have been of preconquest origins. If this is the case, we may thus be able to gain new insight into preconquest processes of migration and cycles of political centralization and decentralization.

Although these wider issues are of major importance for understanding the processes of lowland Maya politics and settlement organization, I attempt here only to lay out some initial comparative observations. The purpose of this article is largely empirical. The problems of generalization are highly complex and will be dealt with in a subsequent publication.

Settlement Location

San Pedro, the principal village center, was located near the mahogany bank of Yalbac, just south of Labouring Creek in western Belize (see map 5-1). Its minor cluster satellites were scattered in a generally western direction along the upper tributaries of Labouring Creek and the small creeks that feed into the Belize River to the south. San José, a secondary village center, was to the northeast of San Pedro on an upper tributary of Booth's River. Unlike San Pedro, its satellite settlements, primarily of hamlet status, were tightly clustered around the central village. Holmul, the other secondary village center, was on the Río Holmul (the upper extension of Blue Creek–Río Hondo) within the district of Petén. Its satellite villages were scattered primarily along this river and its feeder creeks to the north and south of the central village. Some 90 kilometers to the north of Holmul was Santa Clara Icaiche, a principal ceremonial and political center of the northern Chichanhas after 1863.

The San Pedro Maya occupied a zone that had previously been nearly uninhabited, difficult of access, and far beyond the principal population centers of Yucatán, Petén, and Belize. It was the last possible refuge zone for a peaceably inclined, independent Maya group in the southern Yucatán Peninsula. To the north of the San Pedro Maya were Chichanha remnants anxious to press the fugitives into military service against the more powerful Santa Cruz Maya. To the west was the Guatemalan town of Flores and its surrounding cattle ranches. To the south in Guatemala was a small group of so-called Mopan Maya around San Luis and Dolores and a number of scattered ladino-operated cattle ranches. To the south in Belize was the Belize River valley, occupied by seasonal mahogany gangs and a steady stream of traders passing between Flores and Belize. South of that were the Maya Mountains, an area generally avoided by swidden

San Pedro Maya Settlements:

● Location known

○ Location approximate

■ Settlements primarily non-Maya
  in composition

▲ Settlements composed primarily of
  Holmul cluster refugees after 1866

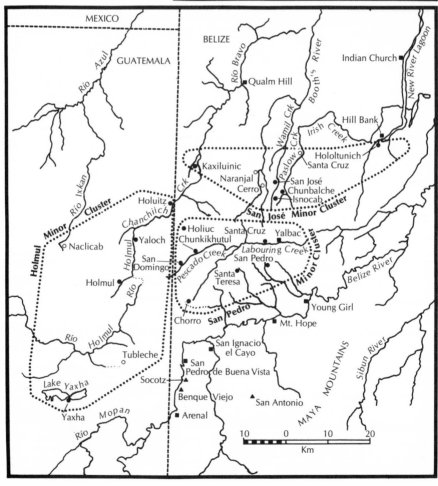

cultivators. To the east were the timber operations on the swamps of lower Labouring Creek and along New River Lagoon. The San Pedro Maya clearly chose a refuge zone beyond which they could not easily expand but within which they could maintain an effective defense against potential enemies.

The factor of defensive effectiveness becomes clearer when we examine the minor clusters. San Pedro village was located on the southeastern extremity of the new Maya settlements. This position provided the San Pedro leadership with close access to British military cooperation in the event of attacks from either the Santa Cruz or the northern Chichanha and with a direct opportunity to legitimize its authority with officials in Belize. This legitimacy eventually provided the San Pedro leaders with British arms and ammunition. The secondary village centers were also strategically located. San José served as a defensive frontier post near the limits of British settlement along the New River Lagoon, thus protecting the frontier on the east and north. Holmul, on the eastern frontier of Petén settlement north of the main road between Flores and Belize, safeguarded the western boundary. With San Pedro protecting the southeast and southern frontier, the ring around the entire territory was completed.

The San Pedro zone was characterized by moderate seasonal rainfall, generally well-drained limestone soils (although shallow in hilly areas), and numerous rivers and streams. Such conditions were, on the whole, suitable for the swidden cultivation that the Maya practiced (Romney 1959:111, 196–204). The area was certainly capable of supporting a far greater population than these few settlements represented, even under conditions of highly extensive land use. The San Pedro Maya often settled near the Maya ceremonial center ruins that cover much of the area, indicating, perhaps, that the environmental factors favoring Classic Period subsistence continued to be important during the nineteenth century. Villages and hamlets were nearly all on or near a stream or small river; wells were used as supplementary water supplies, since many of these bodies of water dried out during several months of each year.

Historical Sketch of the San Pedro Maya
The region later occupied by the San Pedro Maya was off the main sixteenth- and seventeenth-century European routes to the Petén.[2] Refugee Maya from northern Yucatán, however, must have passed through this zone on their way south to Tipu on the West Branch of the Belize River. As Thompson has shown in article one, Tipu and its nearby settlements were a haven for such fugitives. Following the apparent abandonment of Tipu shortly after the 1697 conquest of Tayasal, the Maya gave up their

Map 5-1
Opposite: The San Pedro settlements and other locations mentioned in text

control of the upper Belize River valley. It is possible that at least a portion of the Tipu population moved northeastward to the remote and uninhabited Labouring Creek–Yalbac Hills area. The existence of a Laguna de Tipu in the latter region during the mid-eighteenth century, on the frontiers of British logwood operations, suggests such a possibility.[3] San Pedro was the patron of the original Tipu (Roys 1957:164), offering a conceivable, although shaky, connection between the seventeenth and nineteenth centuries.

Whatever their origins, independent Maya certainly occupied portions of the San Pedro region during the eighteenth and nineteenth centuries. Whether these inhabitants maintained relationships with the Chichanha Maya to their north will probably never be known. However, it is likely that the area continued to be a refuge zone for northern Maya fugitives who passed through the Chichanha region. The 1857 migration from the Chichanha region into the San Pedro region, which continued on a smaller scale for many years thereafter, would thus have been a continuation of a pattern that had been established in the sixteenth century.

The bulk of the San Pedro migration took place in 1857, when it was reported that eight thousand Maya (a gross overestimate) from the Maya town of Chichanha had crossed the frontier with Mexico and were settling along Booth's River.[4] This was a vague location, for the upper tributaries of this river, which bore the same name, cover an extensive region to the west and southwest of New River Lagoon. The causes of the migration are not yet completely understood, but it is clear that they involved both a crisis of leadership at Chichanha and increased military pressures from the Santa Cruz Maya (see Dumond, this volume, for a general discussion of the history of Chichanha). In 1856 Luciano Tzuc, *comandante general* of Chichanha, demanded payment in firearms from Young, Toledo and Company for mahogany they had cut along Blue Creek, threatening to embargo the timber and set fire to the works.[5] Later that year Tzuc led an attack on these works,[6] claiming lands along the east bank of Blue Creek.[7] The southern migration was first reported the following May, eight months later. By that time the Santa Cruz Maya were pressing through Chichanha territory. The migrant Chichanhas claimed to be seeking refuge from these Santa Cruz Maya, who promptly occupied the Blue Creek mahogany bank earlier threatened by the Chichanhas. The Santa Cruz kidnapped some of the workers, removed the cattle, and killed four Chichanhas in the vicinity. Finally they demanded and received a ransom from the company, which thereupon closed its bank.[8] The superintendent, regretting the weakness of British claims to the lands between the Río Bravo and Blue Creek, now recognized the Santa Cruz as "the real masters of the country adjoining us."[9]

This period of Santa Cruz aggression exacerbated the division of the Chichanhas into two groups: peace-seeking fugitives who fled to the Booth's River area and a more stubborn, militaristic remnant group that remained for a time at Chichanha. Still later a third group migrated to the northwest and established a headquarters at Lochha. The leadership of the southern group, if such actually existed, is unknown for this early period. Among the remnants at Chichanha, however, the political process is better known. Since it was intimately concerned with events among the San Pedro Maya in later years, it deserves a brief summary:

Luciano Tzuc was out of power by July 1857, only shortly after the initial southern migration.[10] In December the Chichanhas were said to hold him "in disgrace" because of his hostile activities on the Blue Creek the year before.[11] Perhaps his failure to prevent Santa Cruz incursions was a more important factor. At the same time, Pablo Encalada, who was now apparently the military head of all the *pacíficos del sur,* was reportedly massing forces along the Río Hondo. It was believed that he was attempting to intercept further Santa Cruz southward movements, perhaps to prevent Santa Cruz attempts to retake Bacalar.[12] Tzuc had been replaced by Feliciano Ya as *comandante general* of Chichanha. Notwithstanding Encalada's military efforts, the Santa Cruz recaptured Bacalar from the Yucatecans in 1858. Their southern front strengthened, the Santa Cruz went on to attack Chichanha itself in 1860[13] and again in 1861.[14] During the latter year, Tzuc, who had been working for a British mahogany gang, returned to power with promises of arms from Campeche.[15] Through early 1863 he served under José Uluac, the "nominal chief" of the Chichanhas, both as military commandant and as the "director of [Uluac's] Council."[16] Uluac is not heard from again. It was Tzuc who must have masterminded the permanent abandonment of Chichanha in early 1863, leading his followers to a new and better-protected site to the southeast, known as Santa Clara de Icaiche.[17] Tzuc died in 1864[18] and was succeeded as *comandante general* by one of his faithful officers, Marcos Canul.[19] Canul remained in power until 1872, when he succumbed to wounds received when the Icaiche attacked Orange Walk (New River). His successor was his principal subordinate officer, Rafael Chan.

During the period between 1862 and 1867 the San Pedro Maya were caught between the dual forces of the Icaiche to their north and the British who surrounded their eastern settlements. In order to present details concerning San Pedro settlement distribution and intervillage relationships, I must first briefly outline the history of their interaction with these forces.

Very little is known of the early years of the early southern Chichanha settlers. Their first political center was apparently at Santa Cruz on Labouring (or Yalbac) Creek, under the leadership of Juan Can. Conflict existed between Santa Cruz and nearby San Pedro in 1860 when Juan Can cooperated with the British in arresting individuals at San Pedro who had threatened the Yalbac mahogany bank. Asunción Ek, who was later the chief political figure (*general* or *comandante*) of the San Pedro Maya, first appeared in June 1860, collecting rents on the Río Hondo and signing his name as *general* at Chunaba, the "General Command of Chichanja."[20] He wrote of a "separation" within Chichanha. This separation almost certainly referred to the long-standing division between those who supported a militaristic policy at Chichanha and those who were seeking refuge from such conditions by migrating southward. Despite his rent demands, which were for lands on the left bank of the Hondo, he apparently belonged to the latter division.[21] Ek must have established his headquarters at San Pedro in 1861 or early 1862.[22]

By 1862 British officials had discovered that Ek was recognized as chief authority over all the southern Chichanha settlements on both sides of the frontier. Prisoners captured within his territory were brought to his headquarters at San Pedro, and he would thereupon turn them over to British officials. Anxious to foster a friendly Maya group on their beseiged western frontier, colonial officers recognized Ek as *comandante* over the southern Chichanhas within their territory and presented *alcaldes* in the villages under his jurisdiction with commissions and staffs of office.[23] The population of the settlements within Belize was estimated at about nine hundred persons at that time.[24] By this date the organization of the southern Chichanhas was already apparent. The Holmul cluster in the Petén maintained direct relationship with the *corregidor* at Flores; yet they also recognized Ek's authority. Although the affiliations of the satellite settlements of San José and San Pedro minor clusters were not yet clear, the relative independence of the two village centers had been established.

The principal events leading to increased British awareness of the structure of the migrant Maya settlements may be summed up in a remarkable case study which I refer to throughout this article as the Lino Lara affair. As an example of the kinds of processual data that allow the reconstruction of San Pedro alliance structure, I summarize this case study below:

Case Study: The Lino Lara Affair

Lino Lara, according to one source, was the "Patron, or elected Headman" of Chunbalche (a hamlet of San José).[25] In 1862 British officials were informed of a "conspiracy" by Lara and others, identified as Indians, to rob and burn the British Honduras Company's banks at Yalbac and Irish Creek. The informer claimed that Lara and his followers had tried to assassinate him for refusing to participate in the "conspiracy." The plot having been exposed, Lara and some of his party fled to Flores, Petén.

While at Flores, Lara and one Juan José Que approached the *corregidor* of Petén, José Vidaurre, apparently informing him of the considerable number of Chichanha refugees in the eastern part of the district. According to Vidaurre, they claimed to represent the villages of Holmul, Chunbalche, Tulines, Naclicab, and Tubleche, which, they said, had commissioned them "to solicit for their inhabitants a reincorporation with this District."[26] On August 23 Vidaurre appointed Lara as commissioner to collect taxes in several of these villages.[27] At the same time he appointed Que "as a commissioner to arrange on the best mode of management or of government which ought to be established among all these my beloved inhabitants of those mountains."[28] The "captains" of the villages of Chunbalche, Holuitz, and Naclicab were to be assembled by Que and taken to Holmul for the "elections of governors who are to command in each village." The elected officials were then to proceed to Flores, where they would be bestowed with "tithes" and staffs of office. Lara and Que were to be accompanied by Martin Sosa, who was to serve as their secretary. Que claimed to be *"capitan antigua entre los indios"* and lived at Holmul.[29]

About September 12 the inhabitants of Tubleche captured Lara, Que, and Sosa, who were "taking the census" in that village, along with three men from Yaxha.[30] The prisoners were taken by some inhabitants of Tubleche to Asunción Ek, then *comandante* at San Pedro.[31] Ek released one of the Yaxha men and named one Antonio Quetzal to replace Que as *alcalde* of Holmul.[32] He took the others to Yalbac and turned them over to G. W. Hulse of the British Honduras Company on September 14. Hulse released Que and the other men from Yaxha but sent Lara and Sosa under guard to Belize.[33] Sosa was soon released. Lara was jailed after trial as a conspiracy suspect, but he escaped in April 1863.[34]

Unaware of the events taking place in the Petén, Supt. Frederick Seymour dispatched Police Inspector Cunningham and six constables to the Yalbac area on September 5, 1862, with a warrant for the arrest of "conspirators" still remaining in the hamlet of Chunbalche. Accompanied by Ek and the *alcalde* of San Pedro, along with about seventy men from that village, this party passed through San José on the morning of the thirteenth, occupied Chunbalche, and took five prisoners. At that time Ek declared his friendship with the British, and Lara was said to have been planning to attack San Pedro because of such friendly overtures.[35] One of the prisoners, José Pech, later escaped from jail with Lino Lara.[36]

British officials then began to unravel the complexity of these simultaneous events, further confused by rumors of a pending visit from Icaiche to collect rents from the British Honduras Company. Seymour spoke in glowing terms of the friendly Maya at San Pedro and reported that they, along with other villages,

● wish me to adopt the plan in use in the Altos of Guatemala, which works there admirably under the Indian Carrera; that of conferring recognition on the Headman of each village, allowing direct communication between him and the Administrator of the Government and giving orders to all Indians (only) within a limited circuit to obey the recognized Chief.

Their authority would be doubled and consolidated, they think, if I
would both present each of them with a staff of office such as I have seen
used in Santa Catalina & the mountains of Quesaltenango . . . Once
adopted . . . we shall probably have an extremely sensitive machinery at
our extreme limits which will make known in Belize with extraordinary
rapidity any suspicious movements of the formidable tribes beyond.[37]

It was with such goals in mind that Seymour sent Edward L. Rhys as a
commissioner to San Pedro to appoint *alcaldes* in the villages said to be
under Ek's control. Rhys did appoint officials at the principal villages on
the British side but did not visit the villages of Tubleche, Holmul,
Holuitz, Chunbalche, and Naclicab, as they were said to be on the Guatemalan side of the frontier.[38] Seymour stressed his belief that all the villages, including those in Guatemala, recognized the authority of Ek.[39]

It is difficult to assess the accuracy of the reports on which this case
study is based. I find it hard to believe that Lara was the elected headman
of Chunbalche or that he represented the interests of Holmul and the
other Guatemalan villages. These questions aside, it is nevertheless clear
that the villages of Holmul, Tubleche, Naclicab, and Chunbalche had an
identity quite distinct from those on the British side of the boundary.
Lara and Que obviously represented Holmul to Vidaurre as principal
among these villages, and it is reasonable to suppose that Que actually
hoped to utilize his Guatemalan commission in order to legitimize his
authority as *"capitán antigua entre los indios,"* headquartered at Holmul.
Ek challenged Que's local authority by packing him off to the Belize jail
and replacing him as headman (synonymous with *capitán, gobernador,*
and *alcalde*). Nor is it unreasonable to suppose that these simultaneous
attempts by Ek to gain British legitimacy and by Que to gain Guatemalan
legitimacy were actually part of a general struggle over the central control
of the San Pedro major cluster itself. The rumors of Lara's intention to
attack San Pedro (surely with the aid of the Holmul settlements) would
be consistent with this assumption.

Over the next several years Asunción Ek maintained friendly relations
with the authorities in Belize. His motive for doing so was, in part, as a
means of obtaining ammunition "for the safety of this District in case of
some treason that may happen in this mountain or some faction of
Chichanha that may surprise me empty handed."[40] While Ek feared
both internal factions and interference from Tzuc at Icaiche (Chichanha
remained a generic reference for the northern group), he also reported
difficulties with the mahogany gangs, whose cattle were ruining the milpas
at San Pedro.[41] Upon his request, Lieutenant Governor Seymour supplied
Ek with ammunition in 1863. For his part, Ek was expected "to catch all
runaways accused of murder or escape from the Belize gaol gang. To re-

spect the mahogany trees. To keep the peace, and to punish Indians who ill treated women or committed theft."[42]

In 1865 Marcos Canul, following the earlier lead of Luciano Tzuc, demanded rent for trees cut on lands between Río Bravo and Blue Creek.[43] The following year, on April 27, Canul and his followers raided the British Honduras Company's mahogany bank at Qualm Hill on the Río Bravo, kidnapping the foreman and about eighty inhabitants.[44] The captives were taken to Icaiche and held until June 30, 1866. They were released for a ransom of $3,000 amid severe criticism of John Hodge, the manager of the British Honduras Company. Hodge had reportedly broken an earlier rental agreement with Canul for his Río Bravo works. Such actions were considered incautious, as the lieutenant governor was willing to entertain the idea that Qualm Hill might have been beyond the British western frontier.[45]

Ek was still considered friendly to British interests. In fact, even after sales of powder and arms were prohibited to Icaiche and Santa Cruz due to Canul's aggressiveness, British authorities sent arms and ammunition to Ek at San Pedro.[46] There is evidence of factionalism among the San Pedro leaders in mid-1866, at least in part over the issue of relations with mahogany gangs in the immediate vicinity of San Pedro village. Ek remained in control of the situation as "governor" (frequently used as a title of importance), but José Domingo Vela, the previous first *alcalde* of San Pedro, was out of office. A faction reportedly led by Juan Balam and José María Dzul made its first appearance as strong opponents of the mahogany gangs.[47] In early September a visit from the leaders of Icaiche to San Pedro was reported, possibly indicating that conflicts at San Pedro were not locally confined.[48]

On October 29 two employees of Florencio Vega, a former Yucatecan who maintained a mahogany bank near San Pedro, approached Capt. Peter Delamere at Orange Walk (New River) with claims that San Pedro had suddenly turned against the British.[49] They maintained that Santiago Pech, Ek's second *alcalde*,[50] had recently returned from a visit to Icaiche with a report that the Icaiches were coming to San Pedro on November 1 in order to lead raids against the mahogany banks in the vicinity. The visit was to coincide with the fiesta of All Souls' Day being held at San Pedro.[51] Delamere, who commanded the troops of the Second West India Regiment at Orange Walk, took these rumors seriously and headed off the next morning with forty-three men and Capt. John Carmichael, Jr., of the British Honduras Militia in order to head off the rumored "invasion" of British territory.[52]

As Ek learned of the approaching troops, he apparently believed that he was about to be arrested. He warned Carmichael's advance messenger that the appearance of British troops at San Pedro, which he said was under arms, might lead to open conflict.[53] Delamere, although disappointed by the intelligence that Canul and his followers had not arrived for Ek's fiesta of November 1, nevertheless entered San Pedro on the morning of November 6 with his troops. He found San Pedro guarded by two hundred to three hundred men, obviously well prepared for an attack. Although Ek told him that they were armed in preparation for the approach of the Icaiches, Delamere was convinced that "Asumpcion Ek and his Indians are traitors and are only awaiting Kanul's at San Pedro to join him in a raid on English settlements, the limits of which cannot be foreseen."[54]

Reports soon emerged of a pro-Icaiche faction at San Pedro led by Pech, Balam, and others and that these planned to kill Ek, "as he was too much a friend of the English."[55] It was clear that San Pedro was being armed by men from other southern Chichanha settlements who were reportedly arriving in large numbers each day.[56] By the end of December armed representatives from virtually every village under its control, including all three minor settlement clusters, were standing guard over San Pedro.[57]

Lt. Gov. John Gardiner Austin was convinced that the rumors of a San Pedro–Icaiche conspiracy were falsely contrived by the woodcutters, noting that Ek had earlier threatened retaliation for the seizure of their cattle by the British Honduras Company foreman at Yalbac.[58] Later reports by priests who interviewed Balam and others at San Pedro confirmed his suspicions and clarified that Ek had been convinced by Vega's foreman that Delamere intended to arrest him due to his conflicts with the mahogany cutters. Only after Delamere's visit did the San Pedro Maya request military aid from Canul.[59] Even after that visit, Ek claimed that San Pedro was still threatened by an Icaiche attack, whereupon Austin gave Ek "permission" to defend his villages from Canul.[60]

Marcos Canul, Rafael Chan, and Virginia Cámara, their secretary, finally arrived in San Pedro with a few armed men on December 1.[61] Ek, long considered an English sympathizer by the Icaiches, was reportedly powerless by December 5, serving as a sentry under Rafael Chan.[62]

On December 11, after frenetic planning in Belize, Major McKay left with 446 troops and Edward L. Rhys, who was to serve as a peace commissioner should a confrontation at San Pedro not materialize.[63] McKay's troops did meet those of San Pedro outside the village on December 21. After a brief battle, Major McKay inexplicably sounded a retreat and fled with his officers and men back to Orange Walk (Belize River) in total disarray.[64] Rhys was lost in the fray and was never heard from again.

Panic struck the town of Belize, sending Austin to wait in a ship offshore in preparation for a retreat from a full-scale Indian invasion. Troop reinforcements arrived from Jamaica on January 19, 1867, under the command of Lt. Col. Robert William Harley and accompanied by Gov. Sir John Peter Grant himself. Harley, promoted to brigadier general for the auspicious occasion, left with his troops on the twenty-ninth "with orders to retake and destroy San Pedro, and to drive off any hostile Indians who

might be found within our boundaries."[65] Anxious to overcome the
shame of McKay's retreat, Harley carried out his mission to excess. San
Pedro, still under arms, was now controlled by Juan Balam as a "department" of Icaiche.[66] Ek's political status was uncertain.[67] However, Harley
and his troops met no opposition, the inhabitants of every settlement re-
treating before them. The entering troops burned all buildings (but
reverently saving the "chapels" found in most villages) and destroyed all
else that was left behind, including the stored corn and the fields. Most of
the victims retreated to the Petén, although those of San José hid for a
time at the new settlement of Cerro and attempted to rebuild San José
itself. Captain Carmichael finally led a second mission of destruction
against the San José settlements later in February, pushing the last of the
stubborn defenders across the frontier line.[68]

This, however, was not the end of the San Pedro Maya settlements in
Belize. Most of the settlements were repopulated, and reasonably neutral
relations with the British were reestablished. Although the Icaiche leaders made occasional demands for rents through the inhabitants of San
José, and although they claimed jurisdiction over the San Pedro settlements for many years thereafter, these claims had little effect upon either
the resident Maya or their neighbors the woodcutters. In the last years of
the nineteenth century devastating epidemics passed through the Maya
settlements of western Belize and Petén, resulting in the concentration of
population in fewer communities. Those of the Holmul cluster were virtually depopulated by 1900, some having migrated to settlements along
the Belize River and others having joined the villages of the eastern
minor clusters. The latter appear to have been abandoned during the late
1920's and early 1930's; some joined the Belize River settlements (Romney 1959:189), while those at San José were removed by the Belize Estate
and Produce Company to Orange Walk Town (J. E. S. Thompson
1939:4).

In the section that follows I detail the known evidence concerning
settlement location and intersettlement affiliations among the San Pedro
Maya, focusing upon the period between 1860 and 1880. I discuss each
minor cluster—San Pedro, San José, and Holmul—in turn.

The San Pedro Minor Cluster

Three of the San Pedro villages (San Pedro, Santa Teresa, and Chorro)
were remarkably stable, surviving into the 1920's. Early in the cluster's
history there had been three additional villages (Santa Cruz, San Domingo, and Chunkikhutul), but these were abandoned after 1862, presumably having been absorbed into the three surviving villages.

The San Pedro settlements were aligned in a northeast-southwest arc
from a point south of Labouring Creek near Yalbac to a point next to the

western frontier. They thus marked the southern boundary of the major cluster, protecting an area largely remote from permanent British settlement.

San Pedro • The easternmost of the San Pedro settlements, this village center of San Pedro was located among a small group of hills south of Labouring (Yalbac) Creek, almost due south of the mahogany bank of Yalbac. Immediately by its central "plaza" ran a small creek over which a bridge had been built.[69] This may have been Stump Creek, a tributary of Quacco Creek, which has its outlet in the Belize River above Young Girl. About 100 yards beyond the plaza was a small hill which served during 1866 as a fortification for some two hundred armed men "strongly posted behind fallen timber."[70] San Pedro was connected by paths to all the other settlements of its own minor cluster, to those of San José to its north, and to the mahogany banks farther down Labouring Creek and on New River Lagoon. Paths from the Holmul cluster led indirectly to San Pedro village through villages on the western frontier.

The village of San Pedro was in existence at least by 1860,[71] and by 1862 it was seen by the British authorities as being the political and military headquarters, under Asunción Ek, of the entire southern Chichanha faction in Belize and Petén.[72] In 1862 San Pedro had a population of about 350.[73] By 1867 it straddled both sides of the creek[74] and consisted of fifty houses, a "fiesta house," a "chapel,"[75] and possibly some other "large buildings."[76] The "fiesta house" and perhaps the other "large buildings" may well have served as barracks for soldiers from other villages during periods of military activity.[77] British troops destroyed the entire village except for the church in February 1867. The lieutenant governor was later to regret this act, for "the Fiesta Hall . . . would have accommodated fully 100 men most comfortably and all the other buildings . . . would have been useful for officers, Hospital, Magistrate and Police."[78]

The milpas of San Pedro were described in glowing terms by the British officer who destroyed them: "The rich and ample provision ground of San Pedro—covering a large extensive plain—about 3 or 4 miles from the Town—were destroyed by me on the line of march to 'Young Girl,' as also their Corn Houses, but as the crop of corn was still standing they were empty. Corn in abundance and ready to be gathered. Sugar Canes in luxuriant growth, Eddoes, Yams, and even raddishes and chalots filled these plantations."[79] Although the brigadier general was surely exaggerating his conquest, this description would seem to indicate that the San Pedro Maya were planting a winter crop of corn and that the area of cultivation was concentrated and continuous. The practice of planting large milpas cooperatively is still carried out by the Maya of northern Belize but only when special expeditions to cut high bush at considerable distances from the home village are undertaken.[80] The description might thus indicate that the San Pedro Maya still had available large tracts of high forest a decade or so after their settlement in this area.

During the 1866–1867 crisis, San Pedro was joined by armed recruits from nearly every village in its own minor cluster as well as from the principal settlements of the San José and Holmul minor clusters.[81] By December 1866, two hundred to three hundred men in arms were guarding the village. The *alcaldes* of several villages had apparently accompanied the visiting troops. During this period the women and children of the village were removed to safer places in the forest.[82] After the British destroyed the village in February, it was abandoned, and the inhabitants fled with those of Santa Teresa and Chorro to the Petén.[83] It was reoccupied before 1872, when the Icaiches again claimed rents from the mahogany houses cutting near San Pedro, Santa Teresa, and San José.[84]

San Pedro remained under Icaiche pressures over the next several years and, at one point, joined Icaiche in claiming lands north of the left bank of the Belize River up to the mouth of Black Creek.[85] Eventually General Eugenio Arana of Xkanha stepped in and claimed these lands for the state of Campeche, but apparently the rents were never paid.[86] As late as 1880 Santiago Pech, then *comandante general* of Icaiche, maintained "that he had alcaldes appointed by him, stationed at Holotunich, San José, and San Pedro, and has always understood that his jurisdiction extended to those places."[87] However, Icaiche's claim of control over San Pedro and its satellites may have been more symbolic than practical, for its threats to exercise force in the San Pedro region were not seriously exercised after 1867.

Asunción Ek was still San Pedro's first *alcalde* in 1888 (Bristowe and Wright 1888:113). His son, Timoteo, had married a young woman from Icaiche in 1883.[88] Gann found that a settlement at San Pedro was still in existence as late as 1924 (1925:102) near a related Maya settlement at Yalbac, the previous site of the mahogany bank. The British Honduras Land Use Survey Team learned that some of the inhabitants of Benque Viejo had originally come from Yalbac (Romney 1959:189). It is possible that in the 1930's the San Pedro and Yalbac villagers were together moved from their settlements on lands of the Belize Estate and Produce Company to Benque Viejo, just as those of San José were resettled at Orange Walk in 1936 (J. E. S. Thompson 1939:4).

San Pedro may have also been the principal ceremonial center of the major settlement cluster, although there is little evidence for the ritual functions of the village. Armed men from throughout the major cluster were on hand at San Pedro for the All Souls' Day fiesta held there on November 1, 1867. Such a fiesta was held simultaneously at Icaiche, suggesting perhaps that the subsequent alliance between Icaiche and San Pedro had ideological, as well as militarily strategic, goals.[89] Could this fiesta have represented a deeply significant event involving beliefs concerning the return of ancestral spirits from the ruins and from the possibly sacred hills near San Pedro? San Pedro, like Santa Cruz, was built among hills which, among highland Maya, are considered sacred dwelling places of ancestral spirits and other supernatural beings.[90] All Souls' Day of 1867 might have been the climax of prophecies that the ancestors would return to demand the occupation of the San Pedro hills as the ritual center of the Icaiche as well as the San Pedro Maya (see Redfield and Villa Rojas 1934:202–204 for a description of the "days of the dead" at Chan Kom). Such an occurrence would have paralleled the removal of the eastern Maya rebel leadership to Santa Cruz following the discovery of the talking crosses in 1850 (see G. D. Jones 1974:667).

Although the above must remain at the level of speculation, a comparison of the known characteristics of San Pedro village with better-documented "ceremonial centers" elsewhere in the Caste War independent Maya zone suggests that this central village must have had at least certain ritual functions. From the sketches we have of San Pedro's barracks, church, and recreation hall, we may surmise that Larsen's (1964: 23) and Villa Rojas's (1945:43) descriptions of X-Cacal, the principal surviving Santa Cruz *guardia* settlement and ceremonial center in 1936, might well fit the nineteenth-century village in western Belize. At X-Cacal's center was a sacred area consisting of the church and a community building (*corredor*). Around these two buildings were four crosses set at the intercardinal points. Surrounding this area were the five barracks that housed visiting *compañías,* and beyond were the houses of the officers who lived in X-Cacal. This pattern seems virtually identical to that of Santa Cruz in the 1850's and 1860's. Santa Cruz was said to have two plazas, one containing the church and the house of the *patrón* of the cross and the other containing the house of the principal military officer (Aldherre 1869:73–74). Also in the first plaza were the barracks, the "council house" (*corredor?*) and a jail.[91]

At Icaiche in the 1890's there were also two plazas. The "Plaza de la Iglesia" contained the church, a single barracks, and a bullfight ground.[92] The "Plaza de Armas" contained the houses of the general and his principal commandant (*The Angelus* 1895:87; cf. Sapper 1895: 198, 1904:627).

Similarities existed, then, in the physical layout of certain villages of the independent Maya and in the functions of these settlements as military, political, and, in some cases, ceremonial centers. Such similarities probably indicate further likenesses in other social institutions. I believe that we can learn something about San Pedro social structure by a comparative and historical approach to Yucatecan town and village organization, a topic to which I return at the end of this article.

Santa Cruz • Santa Cruz was located on Labouring Creek about 5 kilometers northwest of San Pedro (Fowler 1879:map). With San Pedro, it is one of the first of the migrant settlements referred to by name in the historical record,[93] but it disappears from sight shortly afterward. In April

1860 Acting Lt. Gov. Thomas Price visited Yalbac and Santa Cruz in an effort to assert a bit of British justice in the colonial hinterlands.[94] His visit was caused by a recent attack upon three "tame Indians" by four "wild Indians" downstream from Yalbac. Two of the former were killed, but the third returned wounded to Santa Cruz, apparently his village. Shortly thereafter the *alcalde* of Santa Cruz, one Juan Can, took six "wild Indians" subsequently captured by his village to the bank foreman at Yalbac. The foreman refused to send them on to Belize, so Can sent them to Chichanha. They were later released by the authorities at Chichanha, who refused to recognize offenses committed on British territory. Price regarded the inhabitants of Santa Cruz as "tame Indians" who had "attached themselves to mahogany gangs." His garbled account does not clarify where the "wild Indians" resided, although it was apparently at San Pedro. During Price's visit, San Pedro was surrounded by his police constable and a party from Santa Cruz in the hopes of capturing an "Indian ruffian" who had tried to burn one of the buildings of the British Honduras Company.

It is unlikely that Santa Cruz village was in close contact with the military faction still at Chichanha in April 1860, as Price's report would seem to indicate.[95] It is more plausible to assume that the prisoners were sent by Juan Can to Chunaba, then Ek's separatist headquarters on the Río Hondo. At this early date, then, Can's village was probably allied with Ek in the southern separatist movement. Can, like Ek after him, sought British support in legitimizing his local authority against that of the northern Chichanhas by sending prisoners to British authorities. By 1862 Ek and his supporters at Santa Cruz had apparently united with the residents of San Pedro, abandoning both Chunaba and Santa Cruz and establishing a headquarters at San Pedro.

Chunkikhutul • The early settlement of Chunkikhutul[96] was located on Pescado Creek, the northern branch of upper Yalbac Creek, about 10 kilometers due north of Chorro and 3–4 kilometers from the western border (Fowler 1879:map). In 1862 its population was about seventy. Near Chunkikhutul to the northwest (ibid.) was its hamlet of Holiuc, which had a population of thirty.[97] Commissioner Rhys appointed one Juan Mo as *alcalde* for the two settlements but noted that "all the Inhabitants are about removing nearer San Pedro and will come under their jurisdiction."[98] It is possible that those of Chunkikhutul moved to the site of Santa Teresa, which Rhys did not include in his exhaustive survey of 1862. Chunkikhutul disappears from the documents at my disposal after Rhys's survey. Holiuc, however, was still in existence in 1868, having sent armed men to San Pedro in 1866.[99]

San Domingo • San Domingo was visited by Commissioner Rhys in 1862. He appointed first and second *alcaldes* and noted that the village, which had a population of 150, was only one mile from the border line.[100] This position corresponds with a contemporary map, which shows it on Pescado Creek, somewhat above Chunkikhutul (Fowler 1879:map). I have discovered no later references to San Domingo except for its appearance, accurately located, on Berendt's map based on an 1867 visit to the area (1879). Berendt indicates that it was connected by direct paths to Holmul, Santa Teresa, and Chorro. Like Chorro, San Domingo probably served as a frontier point through which east–west migrations within the San Pedro major cluster took place during the 1866–1867 hostilities. In later years it may have been absorbed by other villages in Belize.

Santa Teresa • The village of Santa Teresa was located about 6 kilometers southwest of San Pedro on Santa Teresa Creek, a small tributary of Iguana Creek, which joins the Belize River just below Mount Hope. The path from San Pedro descended from the hills south of Labouring Creek to a relatively flat area surrounding Santa Teresa. Although the inhabitants of Santa Teresa played an active role in the events of 1866–1867, there is no reference to the village before 1866. I suspect that it was populated by the inhabitants of Chunkikhutul and Holiuc, which were apparently abandoned after 1862 in order to be closer to San Pedro village.

In late 1866 Santa Teresa was described as a "small hamlet" of about ten to fifteen houses or families.[101] In 1867, Capt. Thomas Edmunds burned the entire village sparing only the "chapel." To the east of the village was "a large hut full of corn," which Edmunds also burned.[102] Somewhere in the vicinity the villagers also had a store of rock salt, also destroyed by the British troops.[103]

Santa Teresa was almost always mentioned in terms of its close association with San Pedro village. Its *alcalde* and a number of its adult males were present at San Pedro while the latter was being fortfied in late 1866.[104] After the villages were destroyed, the residents of Santa Teresa were said to have fled with those of San Pedro and Chorro to Santa Rita in the Petén.[105] Like San Pedro, Santa Teresa was later resettled and in the 1870's remained the subject of territorial claims made by the Icaiche leaders.[106] The settlement was described by Gann as a "little village" in 1924, and he noted that a young man there had a *compadre* at San Pedro (1925:102). It is clear from his discussion that Santa Teresa, San Pedro, Chorro, and a village of Indians at Yalbac itself had very close interconnections. The San Pedro minor cluster seems, then, to have remained a culturally recognized entity more than sixty years after its formation.

Chorro • About 15 kilometers southwest of Santa Teresa, across a level stretch of forest, was the village of Chorro. The settlement, located on Billy White Creek, which joins the Belize River below Duck Run, was about 3 kilometers from the western boundary of British Honduras (Fowler 1879:map).

When Chorro was visited by Edward L. Rhys, it had a population of 140. Nearby was the hamlet of Tumbul, with 15 persons. Rhys appointed a first and second *alcalde* at Chorro itself.[107] Chorro, like Santa Teresa, sent armed men to guard San Pedro in late 1866.[108] Although its inhabitants fled with those of Santa Teresa and San Pedro to the Petén after these two villages were destroyed by British troops in February 1867,[109] the settlement itself was not destroyed. Maya, escaping British attacks on San José and Naranjal to the north during February, fled through this western retreat, presumably along with those of Santa Teresa and San Pedro.[110]

Chorro appears to have been one of the first of the San Pedro villages in British Honduras to have been resettled after the 1867 hostilities. In April 1868, armed Icaiche Maya joined those of Chorro to demand rent payments at Young, Toledo and Company's mahogany works at Turnbull Bank near Chorro.[111] There was still a "small, exclusively Maya village, containing from forty to fifty huts" and a church at Chorro in the early 1920's (Gann 1925:97, 100). Gann described the village as being overcrowded, apparently due to the migration of Maya from the Petén villages to Chorro during this period (ibid.:98–99). It would thus appear that the settlement continued to function as a frontier point through which the Maya of the vicinity passed.[112]

The San José Minor Cluster

In 1862 the small group of San José settlements comprised a single village (San José) and three hamlets (Chunbalche, Isnocab, and Naranjal), rather closely grouped in the headwaters of Booth's River and Irish Creek. This area was north of San Pedro and southwest of New River Lagoon. In later years Naranjal was abandoned, concentrating the population around San José and Chunbalche. In 1866 there was also a settlement at Santa Cruz, to the northeast of San José and Chunbalche. During the 1870's a second village was established at the old mahogany bank of Hololtunich. Finally, during the 1880's, a third village, Kaxiluinic, joined the cluster farther to the north on the Río Bravo. As in the San Pedro minor cluster, we find evidence of internal mobility among settlements. In addition, there was a tendency to form new, temporary settlements during periods of stress. From the perspective of the defensive posture of the major cluster, the San José group formed a northeastern front against British mahogany works on the south end of New River Lagoon. In the long run, it served as a defense against a major British military access route to the western interior from Orange Walk along the New River.

San José • The village center, San José, was located on hilly ground along Wamil Creek, the easternmost of several upper branches of Booth's River. The village was about 18 kilometers north of San Pedro and 27 kilometers southwest of Hill Bank on the southern end of New River Lagoon. Five kilometers to the east of the village were the ruins known as San José, excavated by J. E. S. Thompson in 1938 (1939).[113]

San José first appears in the historical record in connection with the Lino Lara affair in September 1862. At that time Police Inspector Patrick Cunningham found the San José villagers to be on "very friendly terms" with those of San Pedro.[114] He estimated the population of San José at 150. When Commissioner Rhys visited the village two months later, he indicated a population of only 60, although the combined population of the surrounding hamlets totaled 152.[115]

While at San José, Rhys appointed first and second *alcaldes*. He appointed no officials at Chunbalche, Isnocab, or Naranjal, obviously regarding these settlements as satellites of San José. At that time the San José Maya were in conflict with the neighboring British and "Spanish" woodcutters, who, he reported, sometimes frightened the villagers and caused them to run into the bush so that the vandals might rob the deserted settlement. One mahogany cutter had recently taken possession of cornfields at San José, preventing the owners from gathering in their crops.[116]

When San José assisted with armed men in the defense of San Pedro later in 1866, it was by virtue of its location a supply station for San Pedro, providing aniseed, gunpowder, and general provisions. These items, we may assume, were originally purchased by San José villagers at Orange Walk, New River, a colonial town which also served as a supply station for Icaiche.[117] Nevertheless, San José remained on hostile terms with the neighboring woodcutters and with the British Honduras Company's large sugar estate at Indian Church on New River Lagoon. San José was among the villages burned by British troops in February 1867, approximately a week after a party from the settlement terrorized Indian Church, demanding that rent payments be delivered to San Pedro or to Hill Bank.[118] Harley did not burn Chunbalche, but Captain Carmichael of the British Honduras Militia carried out an unauthorized destruction of Chunbalche and "what had been rebuilt of San José" later that month.[119] Shortly after the first destruction of San José, it would appear that its inhabitants, along with those of Naranjal (and probably Chunbalche), moved to a new site on a hill not far to the northwest of San José. The new settlement, which they appropriately named Cerro, was burned by Captain Delamere's troops on March 9, "together with a large granary of about 100 cargoes of corn, a milpa, and extensive provision grounds."[120] Lt. Gov. James R. Longden was later pleased to report that this campaign of village destruction had resulted in "the total expulsion of the Indians from our Territory."[121]

San José was fully reestablished by 1872, when the Icaiche chiefs claimed rents for wood cut in the vicinity of San José, San Pedro, and Santa Teresa.[122] In 1875 San José and Chunbalche were notably uncooperative in police attempts to expel from the colony one Sico Figueroa of Hololtunich.[123] Eugenio Arana, the Xkanha general, claimed in 1877 that the San José lands belonged to Mexico.[124] Icaiche later claimed to have political supremacy over San Pedro, San José, and Santa Teresa.[125] By 1885 San José had apparently become more cooperative with British authorities, and the *alcalde* was called upon to aid in the arrest of Mexican murderers possibly escaping to Icaiche via Kaxiluinic.[126]

San José remained a village until 1936, when it was removed by the Belize Estate and Produce Company (the successors of the British Honduras Company), on whose lands it was situated, to the town of Orange Walk. As J. Eric S. Thompson observed, "The removal was partly the result of friction between the Maya and negro lumbermen of the company, and partly because of damage done to young timber by the villagers in their indiscriminate felling and burning of forest for milpa cultivation" (1939:4). Thus ended the last chapter in the history of British–San José relations, although the last residents of the village may still be found in a *barrio* of Orange Walk Town.

Chunbalche • San José's principal hamlet, Chunbalche, was on Paslow Creek, a short distance north of the San José ruins (Fowler 1879:map). In 1862 the settlement was under the authority of San José's two *alcaldes*. Rhys noted that its population had been "formerly abt. 50," implying that people were moving out, perhaps to San José.[127] Two months before Rhys's census, Police Inspector Cunningham, with aid from San Pedro and San José, occupied the hamlet and arrested five men believed to be involved in the plot to burn and "plunder" the British Honduras Company's works at Yalbac and on Irish Creek (see Lara affair above).[128]

In December 1866 Chunbalche was temporarily abandoned, its inhabitants having presumably moved to San José in preparation for a confrontation with the British.[129] Some of the men of the hamlet may have joined in the defense of San Pedro as well. Since Chunbalche was on the path from San José to Hill Bank and Hololtunich, it would have been in the direct line of any attack by the British from Orange Walk, New River. Chunbalche was still in existence in 1876, when it figured in the attempted arrest of Sico Figueroa, another "Spaniard" who, like Lara, attempted to utilize the smaller Maya settlements as refuges from British authorities.[130]

Isnocab • Rhys identified Isnocab in 1862 as being under the authority of San José. It appears only once in the archives, and its population was at that time only eighteen.[131] This hamlet is found on one map, appearing southeast of San José, perhaps on Paslow Creek, a short distance below the ruins (Fowler:1879). I presume that it was later absorbed into San José itself or that it maintained an existence too insignificant for British recognition.

Naranjal and Cerro • Naranjal was also identified by Rhys as falling under the jurisdiction of the *alcaldes* of San José and had a population of twenty-four.[132] The most reliable contemporary map (Fowler:1879) located the settlement about 8 kilometers northwest of San José, west of the "no. 1 branch" of Booth's River. This places it in the hills that rise in the western area of the headwaters of this river. By 1867 the settlement had grown to some sixty houses, perhaps having taken on the status of a separate village. Captain Delamere's troops found only a few men guarding Naranjal in March 1867, and these ran along the "San José and Chorro road," presumably toward Chorro. Delamere learned that the bulk of the population had "removed all their domestic and other utensils to a new town called Cerro built on a hill about midway between here and San José, after the capture of that town on the 14th of last month."[133] Anxious to capture some prisoners, he moved on to Cerro before setting fire to Naranjal. The inhabitants of the latter settlement were indeed surprised, but, like those of Naranjal, they fled along the road toward Chorro. Cerro was a well-established community "with a large granary of about 100 cargoes of corn, a milpa, and extensive provision grounds."[134] Delamere destroyed the houses, granary, and subsistence grounds of Cerro and returned to Naranjal to destroy that settlement the next morning.

As mentioned above, Cerro almost certainly included persons from San José as well as Naranjal. The inhabitants of San José remained somewhere in the immediate vicinity following the burning of that village on February 14, for the village was partially rebuilt by the time of Carmichael's expedition later that month.[135] Cerro was thus a retreat settlement for the population of the minor cluster and remained unknown to the British until Delamere's expedition of March 9. The only hills roughly between San José and Naranjal, where Cerro was said to be located, are about 6 kilometers due west of San José, south of the presumed location of Naranjal.

Santa Cruz • Santa Cruz was a settlement of undetermined size to the northeast of San José and Chunbalche. It was apparently included in the San José minor cluster, for it was abandoned along with Chunbalche by December 24, 1866. Its inhabitants had presumably joined those of San José in the defense of that village as well, perhaps, as that of San Pedro.[136] This Santa Cruz is not to be confused with the settlement of that name known to have been above Yalbac on Labouring Creek in 1860 (see above). It appears on a poor sketch map drawn by John Carmichael, Jr., presumably in late 1866, along a path connecting Hololtunich and Chunbalche, directly east of Naranjal.[137]

Hololtunich • Hololtunich was located on Ramgoat Creek, which flows into the south end of the New River Lagoon. Until 1867 it was solely a mahogany bank. However, after the resettlement of the San José minor cluster, a small Maya settlement was established at the site, perhaps supplying laborers for the nearby banks of Phillips and Company and the British Honduras Company (at Hill Bank). Lieutenant M. B. Salmon of the Second West Indies Regiment made a reconnaissance of this area, then being claimed by the government of Campeche through Xkanha,[138] and described it as follows:

● Indian Village is about ¾ of a mile from D. O'Brien's Bank (Phillips and Company), and is approached by a narrow path through thick woods and undergrowth, the village cannot be seen until the wood is left and the clear ground round the houses entered, in fact a person might be 10 yards from the first house on the N.E. side without knowing there was a village there at all. About 12 houses constitute the village, and contain not more than eight families of Indians at present. Ram Goat Creek winds round it, but does not approach nearer than 600 yards. And the ground between the village and the creek is covered with thick forest. A small creek running from the high ridge on the N.W. side flows through the village and joins Ram Goat Creek. The way out of Indian Village resembles nearly the entrance, being a very narrow path which bends
● suddenly into a thick wood and the village is out of sight.[139]

This rare description of an Indian settlement is of special interest, as it emphasizes the defensive nature of its location: hidden by forest and well away from the main branch of the creek. Its small size was typical of Maya hamlets throughout the San Pedro cluster.

Hololtunich was claimed by Canul and Chan of Icaiche, along with Hill Bank, as early as 1868.[140] Icaiche repeated these claims in 1875[141] and was supported by General Arana of Xkanha, who maintained that Hololtunich belonged to Campeche.[142] These claims appear to have been an extension of Ichaiche's 1872 demands for rent in the area of San José, which were discussed earlier. The hamlet at Hololtunich thus seems to have been established as the eastern front of the San José minor cluster, directly adjacent to the British mahogany works.

Kaxiluinic • Kaxiluinic was on the Río Bravo, about 19 kilometers west-northwest of San José and about 5 kilometers from the western boundary line. It does not appear in the historical record until January 1885, when Mexicans were said to have escaped through the settlement following some grisly murders committed by them at a mahogany bank near San José.[143] Later that year a British party under William Miller began to resurvey the western boundary line and ran into difficulty with the inhabitants of Kaxiluinic, who apparently considered themselves to be on

Mexican territory.[144] Gov. Roger Tucksfield Goldsworthy asked Gen. Gabriel Tamay of Icaiche to order the *alcalde* of Kaxiluinic, one Antonio Baños, to put a stop to these disturbances. Tamay, however, had already denied knowledge of the settlement.[145] Tamay's denial was false, for in July there were futher "disquieting rumours from the village of Kaxi Venic regarding the attitude of the Indians of Ycaiche towards the Survey Party,"[146] and the survey party later crossed an "old trail that was supposed to lead from Xaxe-Venic to Ycaiche."[147] Miller's map of the western frontier shows Kaxiluinic connected with both Icaiche and San José by this path (1887:421). Entering Kaxiluinic from the west is a path marked "From Peten." Maler found in 1905 that the people of Chuntuci in the Petén still knew of a route leading from Santa Rita, northwest of Flores, to Kaxiluinic (1910:151).

Kaxiluinic may have originally been settled by migrants from Holuitz, a Holmul cluster village that was abandoned sometime after 1868 (see below). In later years its own population began to migrate to San José. In fact, its few remaining families abandoned the village and moved to San José in 1931 (J. E. S. Thompson 1939:4).

Comments • The San José minor cluster differed from the San Pedro cluster in at least two major features. Until 1867 the cluster consisted of only a single village, unless we include Naranjal, whereas the San Pedro cluster had several villages. Corresponding with this feature was a greater concentration of settlements in the San José cluster within short distances of the principal village.

These differences may have been primarily a function of size, for the total population of the San Pedro settlements was certainly greater than that of the San José cluster. They may also have been related to San José's relationship with the mahogany banks south of New River Lagoon. These relationships were hostile from the earliest years of San José's history into the 1880's, in contrast to San Pedro's somewhat more peaceful experience with the Yalbac area works. The tight concentration of the cluster's small population around a central village thus appears to have been a defensive strategy. The removal of the cluster's population to a more remote location at Cerro in 1867 strengthens this interpretation, for the new village was clearly designed to be a centralized defensive village.[148]

The Holmul Minor Cluster

The Holmul cluster seems to have functioned independently in situations of political and military stress, although, like San José, it did cooperate in the defense of the village of San Pedro in 1866. Like those of the San Pedro minor cluster, the Holmul settlements were, for the most part, dispersed semiautonomous villages, spread along a waterway and its surrounding lands and tributaries. Just as Labouring Creek and its head-waters formed the east–west axis for the San Pedro settlements, the upper Río Bravo was the primary axis for the Holmul villages. This river is known as Chanchiich Creek near the western border of Belize, and its upper stream in the Petén is known as Río Holmul. The Holmul villages extended southward along or near the Río Holmul from a point near the eastern Petén boundary. Several of the settlements were located south of the river along the road that passed from Benque Viejo to Lake Yaxha and on to Flores.

The Holmul settlements formed the western front of the major cluster, although I have seen no evidence that defenses against Guatemalan elements were ever needed. Like the San José cluster, these villages maintained close contacts with Icaiche due to their proximity to that settlement. These contacts, however, were not always friendly, and the principal military orientation of the Holmul cluster was toward the defense of San Pedro. From San Pedro's perspective, the northern villages of the Holmul cluster may have formed part of a defensive line against potential incursions by the Icaiches, just as the San José cluster served to defend the principal village from British incursions from the direction of New River Lagoon.[149]

Holmul • Holmul was apparently located near the ruins later identified by the same name, about 15 kilometers northwest of Chorro.[150] It first appears in the historical record in 1862 in its key connection with the Lino Lara affair, summarized earlier.

Holmul disappears from the record until December 1866, when it was said to have had representatives, along with Naclicab and most of the San José and San Pedro settlements, guarding San Pedro.[151] A few months later it was listed along with Tubleche, Naclicab, Holuitz, and Yaloch as having participated in the burning of Benque Viejo, Socotz, and a settlement called "Clarissee" some time before.[152] This information indicates that the Holmul cluster had remained distinguishable over the intervening years, although it does not clarify whether Holmul village itself remained the principal settlement. The latest reference to Holmul in my possession is from 1868.[153]

Tubleche • Tubleche (Tubulche, perhaps?) was located by Berendt south-southwest of Holmul, near a lake along the road leading from San Ignacio el Cayo via Yaxha to Flores (1879). He apparently passed through the village as did Maudslay some years later (Maudslay 1883: map following p. 248). Maudslay's map shows Tubleche to be on the east end of a lake connected by a stream to what must be Río Holmul. These locations lead me to believe that the village was located on the large *aguada* near the ruins of Naranjo (Maler 1908:119), as Berendt's map indicates a sharp turn to the southwest from Tubleche, just as a route that went from Naranjo to Yaxha would require. Maler, who visited Naranjo in 1905, heard that in the mid-nineteenth century a settlement of "a few Indian of half-African families" had existed near the large *aguada* and that the citrus trees planted by them earned the place its name (ibid.). It seems more likely that the place was called El Naranjo only after its original inhabitants abandoned it (sometime between Maudslay's visit in the early 1880's and Maler's 1905 expedition) and migrated to British territory.

The inhabitants of Tubleche were, of course, those who took Lara, Que, and Sosa to Ek at San Pedro, having first confiscated their clothes, arms, and the taxes they had collected.[154]

Naclicab was located by Berendt northwest of Holmul, situated on "Rio Acan" (1879), which flows into Lake Tipu. This lake, presumably misplaced here, must refer to the *bajos* along Blue Creek not far to the south of the correct location of Icaiche. The Río Acan would be Río Ixkan, the eastern branch of upper Blue Creek (Río Azul), which flows northwest of Holmul.

Holuitz • Holuitz[155] was near Chanchiich Creek (the upper Bravo), just to the west of the point where the river crosses the boundary. Berendt indicated a Lake Holuitz at this point (1879), which certainly refers to the extensive *bajo* that covers this area, flooding extensive portions in the rainy season (W. Miller 1887:422). In 1868 Holuitz and Holmul sent representatives to Icaiche to discuss Icaiche's plans to collect rents at Blue Water. Holuitz would have been on one of the direct paths from Icaiche to San José, just as Kaxiluinic was in later years. In fact, such a path passes just to the south of Lake Holuitz on Berendt's map. I suspect that inhabitants of Holuitz may have migrated to Kaxiluinic sometime after 1868, for Holuitz is not heard from again, and nearby Kaxiluinic was established on British soil sometime prior to 1885.

Xbalche • Xbalche was one of the Petén settlements that was consistently grouped with the Holmul cluster during the Lino Lara affair. Nothing is known concerning its location, however. It does not appear in any later historical records, suggesting that its inhabitants abandoned the site and migrated elsewhere.

Yaloch • Yaloch first appears in connection with the burning of Socotz and Benque Viejo by a group of Holmul cluster villages.[156] It is especially interesting as a well-documented case of village migration. The original village was a place marked on modern maps as Yaloch Viejo, situated on the Río Holmul, about 8 kilometers north of the supposed location of the village of Holmul, and about 7 kilometers west of the boundary line. To the southeast of this location is a lake known by the same name.

During July 1868, one Domingo Tzuc of Yaloch entered British terri-

tory with twenty-five men, claiming on behalf of Campeche a large por-
tion of the western section of the colony.[157] Marcos Canul of Icaiche
denied any knowledge of the affair and announced that he would punish
Tzuc for acting without proper authority.[158] In September, John Samuel
August, the foreman at Benque Viejo, received a remarkable letter from
Yaloch, signed by José Justo Chan.[159] Chan claimed that Captain
Domingo Tzuc had been taken to Icaiche, where he had been shot by
Canul's orders.[160] Chan stated that he wished to move the families of
Yaloch to the British side now that Tzuc was gone. Claiming to be *"el
Capitán grande,"* whose every order was obeyed, he wrote that he and the
villagers were tired of the military pressures they had suffered under
Tzuc's command. He wanted August to ask the *alcalde* of Socotz (near
Benque Viejo) to send him twenty-five men to help with the move, and
he requested that August find them a place to live. August asked the
lieutenant governor for help, and Longden requested officials of Young,
Toledo and Company and the British Honduras Company to make available some of their land for the use of the Yaloch migrants. Hodge of the
British Honduras Company would have welcomed them. He had had
previous experience with the Yaloch Maya as laborers at the Indian
Church sugar estate, and having them nearer New River Lagoon would
have stabilized his labor force.[161] McDonald of Young, Toledo and Company would have approved of their settlement on the company's lands as
long as the migrants did not interfere with Confederate Americans
settling near the western frontier.[162]

Chan, however, chose instead to move to Benque Viejo, where in 1878
Colonial Secretary Fowler found him to be the *alcalde* of that settlement,
"as fine a specimen of a pure Indian as one may wish to meet" (1879:5).
Chan died shortly after Fowler's visit. In 1880 a representative from
Icaiche demanded $100 from his widow for having broken an unspecified
oath.[163] Chan's migration to British territory was apparently not looked
upon with favor by Icaiche.

Yaloch continued to be occupied in later years, indicating that Chan
migrated with a faction, not with the entire village.[164] Maler found a
small settlement still there in 1905 and identified among its inhabitants
a man with the title of *sargento segundo,* indicating that the tradition of
military titles inherited from Icaiche was still in effect (1908:123).

Yaxha • There were Maya, almost certainly Yucatecan migrants, living in
a settlement on Lake Yaxha in 1862.[165] There is reason to believe that
Yaxha was involved with the attempts by Lara and Que to gain control
over the Holmul villages, but its role appears to have been minimal.[166]

Maler visited the village of Yaxha in 1904 and wrote: "I found everything on the eve of a general breaking up. Most of the cabins were
already abandoned, and now only served travellers and muleteers as a
shelter or as fuel, the inhabitants having either died or emigrated to

British Honduras. The last three remaining families were making their arrangements to remove to Benque Viejo" (1908:61). This small settlement, which still had its own *alcalde,* was on the east end of Lake Yaxha. Maler learned, however, that earlier there had been another settlement on the northeastern end of Lake Sacnab, just to the east of Lake Yaxha. The inhabitants of this place had "either died out or emigrated to British Honduras" (Maler 1908:72).[167]

Abandonment of the Holmul Villages

After 1867 and continuing into the twentieth century, the San Pedro–affiliated settlements in the Petén were gradually and almost completely abandoned, the inhabitants migrating eastward into Belize. The settlements of Holmul, Holuitz, Tubleche, Naclicab, and Chunbalche disappear from the historical record shortly after the 1868 hostilities. While the San Pedro and San José minor clusters were being reestablished, numerous Maya settlers began to appear about 1868 along the eastern and western branches of the Belize River. They established new villages, such as Santa Cruz and Arenal, and they joined old ones, such as Benque Viejo and Socotz. The case of the Yaloch migration may have been typical for this period. Later writers observed that these Maya, particularly those at Socotz, had migrated from the Flores area, suggesting that they were indigenous Petén Maya (J. E. S. Thompson 1930:37). Whereas the migration had indeed been from the Petén, the first inhabitants were apparently southern Chichanhas of the Holmul cluster.[168]

Holmul cluster migrants may also have been absorbed into the San Pedro and San José clusters. As already stated, the close proximity of Holuitz and Kaxiluinic, coupled with their succession in time, suggests that Kaxiluinic may have been settled by Holuitz migrants between 1868 and 1880. Kaxiluinic at first displayed strong Icaiche sympathies, which is what we might expect of a northern Holmul cluster village. Eventually it was absorbed into the San José cluster, and its inhabitants actually migrated to San José village in 1931. Further evidence of population movements in the area is indicated by a trio of closely related settlements near the western frontier. These included in 1882 the remnants of the village of Yaloch, the San Pedro–affiliated village of Chorro, and a recently established village known as Santa Cruz on the Belize River (location uncertain).[169] The direction of migration was probably from Yaloch through the frontier San Pedro settlement of Chorro. Given the substantial connections between the San Pedro clusters up to 1867, I believe that we may reasonably assume that movements such as these were typical of the entire late nineteenth century.

The settlement of southern Chichanhas along the upper Belize River had actually begun before 1867. Berendt's observations on the Maya living on the western branch in early 1866 indicate that *pacífico*-affiliated

Maya were already living along the river, employed as carriers and as agricultural laborers for a "Spanish"-owned farm at San Pedro de Buena Vista (1868b:422–423). In 1867 Young, Toledo and Company moved one of their principal foremen, John August, from a bank at Duck Run to the branch, or Benque Viejo.[170] August's new bank attracted Maya settlers who soon came into open conflict with some of the Creole and Spanish (the local term for *ladino*) laborers. This conflict resulted in the murder of a Spanish employee by one Pedro Tun, apparently one of the new Maya settlers.[171] The residents of Benque Viejo were harassed by "Indian thieves, who have been invading their properties" during 1867.[172] These "Indian thieves" must have been the more militant Icaiche-sympathizing Maya of the Holmul cluster, such as those under Domingo Tzuc at Yaloch, whereas those Maya who settled at Benque Viejo were those who sought refuge from Icaiche pressures. The migration of José Justo Chan and his followers from Yaloch to Benque Viejo in 1868 would have been a continuation of this pattern. Chan, as mentioned earlier, later became *alcalde* of Benque Viejo, which Fowler described in 1878 as an "Indian village," Maya being the principal language. Along with Socotz, its population was "increasing rapidly, as there is better security for life and property on this side" (1879:5)— clearly an indication that the migration from the Petén villages had not yet ceased. Three years later the village was characterized as being more "Spanish" than Maya in culture.[173] The population of Benque Viejo, frontier settlement that it was, was certainly ethnically mixed despite its Maya core.

A short distance downstream from Benque Viejo was Socotz, a village which always was and still remains strongly Maya in composition. Socotz was in existence in 1867, when it was burned along with Benque Viejo by a party of Maya from the Holmul cluster settlements.[174] Apparently the village then split into two factions which fled into the Petén. One of these factions was later convinced to return by an agent of the colonial government.[175] Records of marriages performed in Socotz in 1875 and 1876 indicate that the population of the village was largely Chichanha in origin (Marcella Mazzarelli, personal communication, 1974). It is thus reasonable to postulate that the original settlers of Socotz were migrants from the dwindling Holmul settlements.[176] The burning of this village along with Benque Viejo by Holmul inhabitants in 1867, despite their postulated common origins, may be explained by the negative view in which the Maya who worked for the British were held by the strong Icaiche sympathizers among the Holmul villages—as the Domingo Tzuc– José Justo Chan conflict at Yaloch so clearly demonstrated in 1868. Chan, leader of a Yaloch faction that had apparently earlier approved of wage labor at Indian Church, called upon the support of the *alcalde* of Socotz in moving his allies from Yaloch to British territory.[177] The Icaiche interference at San Pedro in 1866–1867 was likewise, in part, due to dislike of Ek's overly friendly dealing with British officials. The Maya at Socotz and Benque Viejo, it might be added, remained friendly toward the British in later years.[178]

Colonial Secretary Fowler also visited the Maya village of San Antonio in 1878. Situated 10 kilometers southeast of San Ignacio el Cayo, the village had "only recently been located, in consequence of an epidemic breaking out among the Indians in their former village on Barton Creek. They removed here about two years ago, and are the purest Indians in the district" (Fowler 1879:20).

Barton Creek joined the Belize quite far downstream from San Ignacio el Cayo. At this juncture was the site of Mount Hope, a mahogany bank operated by Young, Toledo and Company in the late 1860's. Originally San Antonio was presumably near the mahogany bank because of the opportunities for employment and for selling produce. Socotz was near Benque Viejo for similar reasons. I possess no evidence that its inhabitants, like those of Socotz and Benque Viejo, migrated from the Holmul cluster. However, their location leads me to suspect that they did. I was told by an elderly inhabitant of San Antonio in 1966 that his ancestors were from Icaiche and that they migrated to British territory in order to escape fighting conditions.

By the turn of the century most of the Holmul villages were deserted. Maler, who traveled widely over the eastern Petén in 1904–1905, was impressed by the general abandonment of this region. He referred to "the social disintegration, prevailing throughout the southern portion of the peninsula of Yucatan and the greater part of the Department of Peten," noting that most of the inhabitants of Yaxha had already migrated to Belize (1908:61) and that all the inhabitants of Naranjo (Tubleche?) had done the same (1908:119). From Morley's descriptions of the Holmul region in 1916, it may be concluded that by that time its only inhabitants were *chicleros* (1965). What caused this remarkable migration of the Holmul villages to Belize over the years between 1867 and the early years of the present century? Although this question can never be satisfactorily resolved, I believe that we may identify some of the principal factors involved.

Most significant among these factors may have been the impact of a series of epidemics that severely reduced the population of the San Pedro cluster as a whole. With their villages decimated and their subsistence potential weakened, many Petén Maya sought refuge in Belize, where wage labor was available as a supplement to subsistence production. Some chose to settle near or among the mahogany banks or close to other elements of the Belize River population. Others established new villages in more isolated regions of the colony, usually near preexistent independent communities, such as San José, San Pedro, and Chorro.

A number of serious epidemics spanning the second half of the nineteenth century and the first quarter of the twentieth century are documented for a region that included the San Pedro Maya. In 1867–1868 a cholera epidemic spread throughout the British colony.[179] It had been fourteen years since the last such epidemic.[180] In 1891–1892 a serious smallpox epidemic struck the northern and western districts as well as the territory of Icaiche and Xkanha.[181] The disease apparently spread from the Corozal area through Icaiche and from there into the western district. By late March 1892 there were serious outbreaks in San José and "not less than" thirty deaths in Kaxiluinic. A priest reported that "some 300" persons at Icaiche died during the epidemic (*The Angelus* 1895: 87).[182] In 1918 the worldwide influenza epidemic struck the Corozal area with severity, leaving hundreds of victims dead.[183] Certainly the disease spread throughout the Maya area beyond Corozal. A smallpox epidemic is known to have decimated the population of the Santa Cruz Maya in Yucatán after 1915, perhaps shortly before the influenza epidemic (Villa Rojas 1945:30–31). Finally, Thomas W. F. Gann, a medical officer, reported that in 1924 smallpox had "decimated" a village about 20 miles across the border in the Petén, sending a young couple in fear for their lives to Chorro. The husband shortly died from the disease himself; the disease spread throughout the village "and carried off a number of population, hardly a house but was left mourning the loss of some member of the family" (Gann 1925:99).

Sir Eric Thompson has shown that epidemic diseases had seriously affected the demography of the Maya throughout the colonial period (1970:48–83). The effect of the late epidemics in the San Pedro region was that of migration to areas of economic security. A succession of epidemics in a small community would have left extended families, the principal cooperative subsistence units, economically incapacitated. Before the development of chicle enterprises in the Petén in the early twentieth century, little existed in the form of wage labor to attract the Maya.[184] However, in Belize there still remained active mahogany banks, opportunities to serve as carriers on the trade routes between Belize and Flores, and opportunities to raise produce for sale to nonagriculturalists along the Belize River.[185] Disease did not always lead to migration to well-settled areas, as the case of San Antonio demonstrates. But even this relatively isolated village was close enough to El Cayo to engage in trade and other economic activities.

Another factor related to the migration to Belize was the poor state of Indian-government relations in late nineteenth-century Guatemala. Thompson cited as the cause of the migration of Mopan-speaking Maya from San Luis (Petén) to the Toledo District in 1883 the fact that they were "irked by constant taxation and military service" (J .E. S. Thompson 1930:38). Referring to this migration in 1884, the *Colonial Guardian* noted that "they give as their reason for leaving their native place, the oppression of the government officials."[186] The editor opposed government proposals to create reservations, resting his case on maintaining good relations with the Guatemalans. Since the "Indians of the Department of Peten are flying from the exactions of the authorities of that district and settling in our territory," he felt that any major land concessions would exacerbate hostile relations with Guatemala.[187] Conditions for Maya on British territory were certainly not ideal either, and the British destruction of the San Pedro villages in 1867 resulted in what Berendt, then in Flores, referred to as "a general stampede of the Indians of the montaña of the Peten" (1868:426). And while the Maya may have paid taxes to the Guatemalans, they also grudgingly paid rent to their British landlords.[188] Forced military service, however, was not practiced in Belize. This fact might well have induced the Holmul Maya, their numbers reduced by disease and their military ties with Icaiche considerably less effective than in 1866–1867, to seek more favorable conditions on British territory.

It is important to view the dissolution of the Holmul sector in the wider context of the decline of the military and political structure of the San Pedro major cluster. The impact of epidemic disease, increased dependence on wage labor, and acceptance of British political authority by nearly all the Maya in the Western District: all these factors were jointly responsible for the decline of the effectiveness of the centralized structure of the San Pedro settlements. Although the boundaries of the original minor clusters continued to be recognized into the 1920's, by 1888 San Pedro was no longer the center of a military hierarchy that could call upon support for its defense from villages covering a large territory to its north and west. San Pedro was just another village, and Asunción Ek, once *comandante* of the combined San Pedro forces, was just another *alcalde* in an efficient system of British colonial jurisdiction.

Conclusions and Comparative Implications

Three of the San Pedro settlements were village centers wherein military decisions were made. These centers were ranked, the principal village center serving as the military and probably the ceremonial headquarters of the entire group of settlements. Within and between the minor clusters there was a high degree of internal mobility, villages and factions frequently migrating in the face of various external forces. While we know relatively little about the political system that corresponded to this pattern of settlement affiliation, it is apparent that this system comprised village *alcaldes* who formed councils at both the minor and major cluster levels. The major cluster council was headed, at least nominally, by the *comandante* or *comandante general* who was resident in the principal village center.

Even the most cursory glance at comparative Yucatec Maya data will indicate the continuity of this system with those described elsewhere in the peninsula, even for much earlier periods. Roys concluded that the sixteen "native states" or "provinces" (a better term) into which the population of the Yucatán Peninsula was divided at the time of the conquest fell into three principal types (1957:6). First, there were territorial units under hereditary rulers known as *halach uinic* who exacted moderate tribute from those under his control; the *halach uinic* served as the local head, or *batab*, of his town, "but all the other batabs of his province were subject to him" (ibid.). Second, there were territorial units with no single ruler but with *batabs* who belonged for the most part to a single patronymic group. Third, some named territorial units appear to have had few formal principles of organization, consisting "apparently of loosely allied groups of towns which managed to keep from being incorporated by their better organized neighbors" (ibid.). Roys's three types form a continuum characterized by varying degrees of political centralization in which the town functioned as the basic structural unit. Some degree of independent town organization was found at all three levels, as was some degree of intertown alliance. Variation existed in the degree to which town organization was itself subject to higher levels of formal organization.

Through his study of the land title archives of Ebtun, Roys was able to describe the effects of the Spanish colonial system on town and intertown organization in the province of Cupul and, to a lesser extent, in the province of Sotuta to its west (1939). The substance of his analysis indicates that the changes introduced in town organization, while significant, preserved many of the basic functions of Maya town government through even the early nineteenth century. Furthermore, while the structure of supratown organization changed significantly, towns within the province continued to be allied for the purpose of working out boundary agreements.

Sotuta (with its famous *halach uinic*, Nachi Cocom) fell into Roys's centralized type 1 territory, and Cupul was ruled by an alliance of Cupuls, *batabs* of their respective towns, fitting his type 2 territory. The principal effect of the conquest was to eliminate the position of *halach uinic* in Sotuta and gradually to erode the importance of lineage affiliation among the Cupul town heads (1939:48–49, table I). The town *batab*, freed of direct institutional ties with either a higher Maya authority or a lineage council of town heads, remained, in effect, the surviving locus of Maya leadership under the Spanish colonial system. The *halach uinic* "seems to have been primarily a war chief" (Roys 1943:59), and his disappearance corresponded with the declining military functions of the province as Spanish control became more fully entrenched in the late sixteenth century. We may assume that the Cupul lineage council of *batabs* had similar military functions, rendered equally impotent by Spanish colonial control. However, the survival of the local *batab* under the title of *gobernador* reflected the Spanish preservation of his original functions as the administrative, judicial, and military head of his town (Roys 1939: 43–45; 1943:169). His military duties, in fact, continued to be recognized "by the appearance of a number of town governors as captains of the local Indian militia," although the position of town war chief (*nacom*) had disappeared (Roys 1939:45). Roys hypothesized that the *ah cuch cabs,* the town councillors next in importance to the *batab* and his war chief, became *alcaldes* and *regidores.* The *ah kulels,* also subsidiary functionaries of the *batab,* may also have been included in the office of *alcalde* (also called *justicia* or magistrate). Also under the *gobernador* were a *teniente* and several lesser officers (1939:44–45). By 1814 the position of *gobernador* came occasionally to be known as *alcalde constitucional* at Ebtun (1939:49).

The "titles of Ebtun" demonstrate that the officials of the various towns of southwest Cupul both bickered and cooperated in the matter of land boundaries. Meetings of officials were frequently held, and at times several towns would present a joint case to the Spanish officials as a joint council. Conflicts over interprovince boundaries were met with solid alliance of the litigant towns. Intraprovince boundaries, on the other hand, were often disputed among towns. The five Cupul towns that were most frequently the subjects of litigation in the titles of Ebtun seem themselves to have made up a sort of "minor cluster" in terms of territorial claims as distinct from the surrounding Cupul towns (Roys 1939:19).

I have suggested elsewhere that during the Caste War of Yucatán the Maya inhabitants of the Cupul province fought as town or village units under traditional local leaders (1974). The town became the *compañia,* while the *batab* or *gobernador* functioned as its *capitán.* The title of *capitán* was assumed by the town head participating in Indian militia units in the eighteenth century (see Roys 1939:doc. 267–268, 394–397; also, 1943: chap. 22). Under the *capitanes* were lesser military officials, presumably derived from the lower town offices with titles modeled after the Yucatecan military system. Integrating these town units were councils of the principal officers under a *comandante* or *comandante general.* The resemblance of this system to that reconstructed for the conquest period in certain provinces—a militarily powerful *halach uinic* and his multifunction town heads—is, I believe, too close to deny the historical antiquity of the Caste War period system of leadership. Whereas Cupul did not have a *halach uinic* at the time of the conquest, a centralized system of priestly and military leadership did arise during the 1547 rebellion in that province; a province's degree of centralization may thus have been flexible, responding to perceptions of the seriousness of external threats.

The organizational effect of the appearance of the Talking Cross cult in 1850 was to concentrate several of the eastern rebel units under rather factious *comandantes* in a small area at Santa Cruz under a powerful priest who claimed divine inspiration for his military orders. The original units may have maintained their autonomy at the six "dependencies" of Santa Cruz, which were probably centers of minor settlement clusters (Aldherre 1869:74). In the late nineteenth century, however, the seams of this ritually based alliance began to come apart. A second ceremonial-political center established at Tulum clashed with Santa Cruz about 1890 and eventually became independent of the principal center (Dumond, this volume). Likewise, following the abandonment of Santa Cruz de Bravo by federal troops and an ensuing smallpox epidemic, the Santa Cruz divided into three "sub-tribes," as Villa Rojas called them, eventually establishing "ceremonial centers" at X-Cacal, Chancah, and Chunpom. Chancah had been a "dependency" of Santa Cruz for half a century (see Aldherre 1869:74). Recent visitors to the X-Cacal group indicate that the divisions that Villa Rojas described for these three settlement clusters have mellowed in recent years, resulting in increased intercluster visiting and meeting of joint councils of the three groups (Ira R. Abrams and Allan F. Burns, personal communications, 1974).

X-Cacal was the ceremonial and political center of a cluster of nine settlements at the time of Villa Rojas's study (1945). Every person belonged to one of five *compañías,* in which membership passed from father to child, females joining their husband's *compañía* at marriage. Although not strictly localized, *compañías* nevertheless had strong village identifications (1945:91). Each *compañía* was housed in a barracks at X-Cacal during the two-week period in which it fulfilled its *guardia* duty, a combination of ritual and military responsibilities (1945:76–77). Each company participated in the two principal religious fiestas of the year at X-Cacal (1945:129). The principal officers of the *compañías* made up a governing council which met occasionally at X-Cacal under the leadership of a "supreme chief" and a ritual leader known as *nohoch tata* (1945:73, 91, 93).

The X-Cacal social system is assumed to be a continuation of that practiced at Santa Cruz during the second half of the nineteenth century. It also conforms in many respects with our analysis of San Pedro and with what little we know of Icaiche and Lochha (see references in Dumond, this volume). As I noted earlier, the physical layouts of the principal settlements of Icaiche, San Pedro, Santa Cruz, and X-Cacal were similar. Icaiche was also certainly a ceremonial center, the residence of an important sacred cross taken by Canul from Xaibe, a settlement of refugee Cruzob near Corozal (*The Angelus* 1895:87). Ichaiche's adult male population was militarily organized under a *comandante general* (and his second-in-command), *capitanes,* and lesser officers. After 1870 there was apparently a restructuring of the military system, and the *capitanes* came to be known as *comandantes*.[189] The settlements of Icaiche were apparently tightly clustered around the main village, except for small outposts along the Río Hondo, indicating, perhaps, a compact defensive pattern similar to that of the San José minor cluster (*The Angelus* 1901:206).

Icaiche itself was defensively situated on a hillside protected on the lower side by "a living fortification of impenetrable bamboo" (*The Angelus* 1889). Little is understood of the military organization of Icaiche, although the presence of a multiplicity of *capitanes* or *comandantes* in conjunction with evidence of required *guardia* duty at Ichaiche (Sapper 1904:627) implies a *compañía* organization similar to that of X-Cacal.

Lochha, which was considerably larger than Icaiche, was said to be composed in 1866 of four *cantones*, each under a chief officer commanding some five hundred troops.[190] Every village was said to have a *capitán* and lieutenants "who act as magistrates."[191] Pablo Encalada was the commander in chief of all four *cantones* as well as, apparently, the chief authority in the *canton* of Lochha.[192] In later years the principal headquarters were moved to Xkanha where Sapper described a ceremonial-military *guardia* center similar to that of Icaiche (1904:627).

From this superficial survey several broad generalizations may be made. The similarity of settlement alliance and organization throughout the independent Maya groups of the Caste War and post–Caste War period is remarkable. The San Pedro minor clusters, the Lochha and Xkanha *cantones,* and the Santa Cruz subtribes (as recently demonstrated by X-Cacal, Chancah, and Chunpom) were all loosely allied multivillage clusters, each with a principal village having special military and political functions. San Pedro, Lochha, and nineteenth-century Santa Cruz were centralized under a chief military authority whose settlement of residence was the principal political and military center and, at least in the case of Santa Cruz, the principal ceremonial center as well. In 1936 the Santa Cruz groups lacked such centralization due to political factionalism. In each of these three Maya groups, villages maintained local "military" units with broad sociopolitical functions that were under the leadership of village officials (*gobernadores, comandantes, alcaldes, capitanes,* or other titles of military office). Each local unit was expected to defend the central village of the minor cluster at any time and, in certain cases, the principal village of the major cluster as well. While I am less certain about Icaiche's village organization, its system of military titles and *guardia* duty imply a similar, although truncated, version of the same pattern exhibited by the larger groups.

Further analysis will clarify the details and may require revising this argument. At this point, I believe that we may reasonably hypothesize that the widespread system thus described for the Maya of the southern Yucatán Peninsula may be explained as the common heritage of a system whose roots are preconquest, despite the later obvious adaptations to Spanish colonialism. A direct relationship exists between the military-political organization of the eastern rebels and the local and territorial organization in the Cupul region dating from the early colonial period. Roys demonstrated that the latter was a rather close modification of the preconquest system. The simultaneous appearance throughout southern

Yucatán of this system of levels of multivillage alliance based on traditional patterns of local leadership indicates that it was shared by all groups on the eve of the Caste War. It may, in fact, be instructive to view variations in the Caste War groups along the same centralization continuum as that proposed by Roys for the territories of Yucatán at the time of the conquest. Finally, I would suggest that both Roys's continuum and variations in the nineteenth-century groups were processual, not static, features of Maya political organization. Both were indicative of the high degree of flexibility in the adaptational features of lowland Maya political and settlement organization.

While space limitations have prevented an adequate analysis of the roles of the village *alcaldes* and the *comandante general* in the San Pedro major cluster, I should note in closing that *alcaldes* functioned both as military heads of their respective villages[193] and as magistrates for petty village disputes. They accompanied their armed villagers to San Pedro in late 1866 and served there as an advisory council to Asunción Ek, the principal *comandante*. Ek, like the *comandantes generales* of Xkanha and Icaiche, heard cases of greater importance, either passing a sentence immediately or referring the case to the magistrates in Belize. It is not clear whether cases heard by Ek were also decided by a council of *alcaldes* as at X-Cacal, where important cases were tried by the entire governing council. We know virtually nothing concerning the nature of the minor cluster military-political hierarchies, of the principle of succession to office, or of the length of tenure in office. Much of the primary source material on these and related aspects of San Pedro political structure is still incompletely analyzed and will be discussed in a future publication. Adding to the difficulty of this task is the problem of specifying the historical roots of certain roles. While the village *alcalde* may indeed be the descendant of the Yucatecan *batab* (later *gobernador* and sometimes *alcalde* and *capitán*), it is clear that the concept also entered the British colonial system through Guatemala, where the role had a somewhat different history. Further complicating the situation was the 1858 passage of an act in Belize that defined the duties of rural *alcaldes* (Grant 1967: 62–65). This legislation was almost certainly a response to the 1857 Chichanha migration.

There is need for further locational analysis of settlement patterns among the San Pedro and other nineteenth-century Maya. I have already suggested that the San Pedro village arrangement suggests placement in a defensive ring around a cultivable hinterland, the major defensive centers positioned near areas of non-Maya settlement or movement. A defensive strategy may account for the highly dispersed quality of settlement in all but the very small San José minor cluster. Now that village locations are fairly well established for the San Pedro major cluster, it will also be possible to analyze the ecological concomitants that have been treated cursorily in the present article. Until comparative analysis of these lowland ecological and social structural problems has been more fully developed, I shall refrain from the temptation of generalizing from the present case to the broader issues of archaeological settlement patterns in the lowland Maya area.

Notes

1.

Research in the Archives of Belize was carried out primarily during the summer of 1972 under a grant from Hamilton College, to which I extend my gratitude. Mr. Leo Bradley, then the archivist, was most helpful. I thank Marcella Mazzarelli, Anthony Short, S.J., and Richard Buhler, S.J., for bringing valuable additional information to my attention. Conversations and correspondence with the late Sir Eric Thompson and with Ira R. Abrams, O. Nigel Bolland, Allan F. Burns, Marcella Mazzarelli, James Ryder, Norman Schwartz, and Robert S. Thompson were of major inspiration during the preparation and revision of this article; however, I accept complete responsibility for its weaknesses.

2.

Most of the evidence presented here is found in the Archives of Belize (abbreviated AB throughout notes), a vast storehouse of data on British interaction with Maya groups around the frontiers of the colony during the latter half of the nineteenth century. The quality and reliability of this information is highly variable, ranging from clearly biased statements by mahogany gang foremen who were hostile to the Maya to carefully considered intelligence reports from rural magistrates—often reinterpreted by the lieutenant governors in dispatches to their superiors in Jamaica. Despite the caution with which most intelligence was gathered, more often than not information of interest to the ethnologist is missing from the historical record. Therefore the analysis presented here is actually quite skeletal in character, and inference from incomplete data plays a more important role than one would wish.

It is impossible, unfortunately, to reconstruct even a sketchy demographic profile of the San Pedro Maya. A census of sorts was made of the villages and hamlets by a British commissioner in 1862 (Rhys to Seymour, 11 November 1862, AB, R. 78), and visitors occasionally would guess at a settlement's population. Official censuses did not, however, cover the scattered Maya villages effectively. Even the detailed 1921 census (British Honduras 1921: table 3) ignored the existence of several settlements of the San Pedro minor cluster that are known to have been in existence at that time.

3.

"Memoria" by Lorenzo Hermoso de Mendoza, AGI, quoted in Calderon Quijano 1944:440–441.

4.

Seymour to Lt. Gov. E. Wells Bell (Jamaica), May 15, 1857, AB, R. 52.

5.

Superintendent Stevenson to Bell, September 9, 1856, AB, R. 55; Tzuc, Fernando Chable, and Canul to Toledo[?], August 20, 1856, AB, R. 26; Tzuc to Toledo, September 2, 1856, AB, R. 26.

6.

Young, Toledo and Co. to Seymour, June 15, 1857, AB, R. 58.

7.

Stevenson to Percy W. Doyle, October 7, 1856, AB, R. 54.

8.

Seymour to Bell, June 17, 1857 (confidential no. 1 and no. 20), AB, R. 52; Seymour to Charles Henry Darling (Jamaica), May 17, 1858, AB, R. 55.

9.

Seymour to Bell, July 14, 1857, AB, R. 55.

10.

Ibid.

11.

J. H. Faber to Seymour, December 20, 1857, AB, R. 58.

12.

Ibid.

13.

Faber to Price, June 7, 1860, AB, R .71.

14.

Faber to Price, April 27, 1861, AB, R. 74.

15.

Seymour to Lt. Gov. Edward John Eyre (Jamaica), February 13, 1863, AB, R. 81.

16.

Ibid.

17.

Stephen Panting to Toledo, April 26, 1863, AB, R. 83; Tzuc to Seymour, June 15, 1863, AB, R. 83; Tzuc to Seymour, June 20, 1863, AB, R. 83. *Icalche* refers to the spirit of a tree or of wood, signifying perhaps the sacred cross known to have existed as Icaiche.

18.

Statement of Santiago Cervera, May 16, 1866, AB, R. 93.

19.

Canul and Rafael Chan to Edwin Adolphus, January 18, 1867, AB, R. 89.

20.

Asunción Ek to Corozal Magistrate, June 6, 1860, AB, R. 71.

21.

Commissioner Rhys found in late 1862 that Ek's followers still feared that the leaders at Chichanha would compel them "to return to Yucatan and fight those of Santa Cruz" (Seymour to Eyre, November 12, 1862, AB, R. 81).

22.
The Santa Cruz Maya attacked Chichanha in April 1861, vowing to return in a month to "rout them [the Chichanhas] out even from Yalbac. Juan Can is at a place called Santa Rita somewhere near Yalbac and has three hundred men under his orders" (Faber to Price, April 27, 1861, AB, R. 74). This was probably a reference to Santa Cruz, for there is no record of a Santa Rita in this area. Ek was obviously not yet in control of the Yalbac area Maya.
23.
Rhys to Seymour, November 3, 1862, AB, R. 78.
24.
Lieutenant Governor Seymour actually considered pressing the San Pedro Maya with two hundred British troops against the Santa Cruz Maya along Blue Creek in 1863 (Seymour to Eyre, June 14, 1863, AB, R. 81).
25.
Seymour to Eyre, October 8, 1862, AB, R. 81; unless otherwise indicated, this dispatch serves as the documentation for the description of the Lino Lara affair.
26.
Vidaurre to Seymour, October 7, 1862, AB, R. 78.
27.
Vidaurre to Lino Lara, August 23, 1862, AB, R. 78.
28.
Vidaurre to the inhabitants of Tolmul, n.d., AB, R. 78.
29.
Declaration of Juan José Que and Martin Sosa, September 22, 1862, AB, R. 78.
30.
Petén investigation, testimony of Andrés Chan, Francisco Lara, and Miguel Mo, residents of the lagoons of San Pedro, Yaxha of Petén, Primary Court of the District of Petén, October 6, 1862, Flores, AB, R. 78.
31.
Ibid.; Hulse to Cunningham, September 14, 1862, AB, R. 78; declaration of Que and Sosa, September 22, 1862, AB, R. 78.
32.
Petén investigation, testimony of Chan, Lara, and Mo.
33.
Hulse to Cunningham, September 14, 1862, AB, R. 78.
34.
James Hume Blake to Seymour, April 30, 1863, AB, R. 83.
35.
Cunningham to A. W. Moir, September 1862, AB, R. 78.
36.
Blake to Seymour, April 30, 1863, AB, R. 83.

37.
Seymour to Eyre, October 8, 1862, AB, R. 81.
38.
Rhys to Seymour, November 3, 1862, AB, R. 78.
39.
Seymour to Eyre, November 12, 1862, AB, R. 81.
40.
Ek to "Superior yntendente de Belize, honduras," May 8, 1863, AB, R. 83; translation in AB.
41.
Ek to Señor Majistrado de la Suprema Corte de Belize, June 26, 1863, AB, R. 83.
42.
Seymour to Eyre, July 13, 1863, AB, R. 81.
43.
Austin to Eyre, March 18, 1865, AB, R. 92.
44.
Austin to Gov. Sir Henry Storks (Jamaica), May 8, 1866, AB, R. 92; Hodge to Austin, May 2, 1866, AB, R. 93.
45.
Austin to Storks, August 2, 1866, AB, R. 92.
46.
Ek to Governor, May 10, 1866, AB, R. 93; Austin to Storks, August 2, 1866, AB, R. 92; Thomas Graham to Austin, August 2, 1866, AB, R. 93.
47.
Claudio Manriquez to Vega, July 11, 1866, AB, R. 93.
48.
Adolphus to Thomas Graham, September 11, 1866, AB, R. 93.
49.
Statements of José Carmen Hernandez and Agustín Ongay, October 29, 1866, AB, R. 93.
50.
Ek apparently bore the title of first *alcalde* of San Pedro. Santiago Pech replaced Rafael Chan as *comandante general* of Icaiche in 1877, remaining in that position until his death in 1883.
51.
Austin to Gov. Sir John Peter Grant (Jamaica), November 1, 1866, AB, R. 92.
52.
Delamere to Major Molesworth, October 29, 1866, AB, R. 93.
53.
Ek to Carmichael, November 5, 1866, AB, R. 93.
54.
Delamere to Austin, November 11, 1866, AB, R. 93.

55.
Statement of Lorenzo Ortiz, November 10, 1866, AB, R. 93.
56.
Statement of Manuel Isama, November 10, 1866, AB, R. 93.
57.
Statement of Felipe Fuentes, January 25, 1867, AB, R. 89.
58.
Austin to Grant, November 1, 1866, AB, R. 92.
59.
Statement of Eugenio Biffi, January 23, 1867, AB, R. 89; report (unidentified) of George M. Avraro's interview with the Indians at San Pedro, n.d., AB, R. 89; Avraro to Austin, January 25, 1867, AB, R. 89.
60.
Ek and Calistro Medina to Lieutenant Governor, November 13, 1866, AB, R. 89; Austin to Ek, November 20, 1866, AB, R. 89.
61.
Cañul, Chan, and Cámara to Governor of Belize, December 9, 1866, AB, R. 89 and R. 93.
62.
J. M. Swasey to Young, Toledo and Co., December 5, 1866, AB, R. 89 and R. 93; statement of James Phillips, December 14, 1866, AB, R. 93.
63.
Austin to Grant, December 12, 1866, AB, R. 92; Rhys to Austin, December 20, 1866, AB, R. 89.
64.
Austin to Grant, December 28, 1866, AB, R. 92; statement of James Haylock, December 24, 1866, AB, R. 89; R. Williamson to Austin, December 26, 1866, AB, R. 89.
65.
British Honduras Colonist and Belize Advertiser, December 28, 1867.
66.
Balam to Commander General of Belize, January 19, 1867, AB, R. 86.
67.
Avraro to Lieutenant Governor, January 26, 1867, AB, R. 89.
68.
Longden to Grant, December 27, 1867, AB, R. 98.
69.
Delamere to Austin, November 11, 1866, AB, R. 93.
70.
Ibid.
71.
Price to Darling, May 3, 1860, AB, R. 68.
72.
Seymour to Eyre, November 12, 1862, AB, R. 81; February 13, 1863, AB, R. 81.

73.

Rhys to Seymour, November 3, 1862, AB, R. 78.

74.

Statement of Biffi, January 23, 1867, AB, R. 89.

75.

Harley to Austin, February 9, 1867, AB, R. 95.

76.

Austin to Grant, February 25, 1867, AB, R. 92; Harley to Austin, February 9, 1867, AB, R. 95.

77.

Ek was later reported to have said that he had invited Captain Delamere and his troops to stay in a "large house," presumably one of these barracks, but that Delamere had insultingly refused (Avraro to Austin, January 25, 1867, AB, R. 89).

78.

Austin to Grant, April 8, 1867, AB, R. 98.

79.

Harley to Austin, February 15, 1867, AB, R. 95.

80.

Grant D. Jones, unpublished field notes on the Corozal region, 1967.

81.

Statement of Fuentes, January 25, 1867, AB, R. 89.

82.

Delamere to Austin, November 11, 1866, AB, R. 93; declaration of José Medina, November 10, 1866, AB, R. 93; statement of Isama, November 10, 1866, AB, R. 93.

83.

Edmunds to Samuel Cockburn, May 31, 1867, AB, R. 96.

84.

Icaiche chiefs to Administrator (Harley), January 2, 1872, AB, R. 110.

85.

Phillips and Co. to Graham, March 22, 1875, AB, R. 119.

86.

R. M. Mundy to Eugenio Arana, March 3, 1875, AB, R. 114; Arana et al. to Governor of Belize (Mundy), April 13, 1875, AB, R. 114; cf. Arana to Magistrate (Ohlafen), December 8, 1877, AB, R. 119.

87.

Interview between Harley and Pech, Belize, October 13, 1882, AB, R. 93. Shortly before this claim, Pech had apparently sent a representative from Icaiche with a letter to show to the "commandants of Yaloch, Ycash [Yaxha?], San José, San Pedro, and Sta. Teresa", indicating that he did indeed attempt to exercise authority over the San Pedro major cluster (Frederick P. Barlee to Pech, March 8, 1880, AB, R. 120).

88.

Benque Viejo marriage records: Marcella Mazzarelli, personal communication, 1974.

89.

It was later learned that the Icaiches were celebrating a "grand fiesta" at their own community on All Souls' Day (Austin to Grant, December 12, 1866, AB, R. 92).

90.

Hills are considered the dwelling places of gods and ancestors among many highland Maya groups. See, e.g., Vogt on the Zinacantecos (1970:6) and Wisdom on the Chorti (1940:394). Sir J. Eric S. Thompson notes that the Lacandon associate rain gods with hills, caves, and bodies of water, whereas the absence of mountains in Yucatán precludes supernatural associations of land forms (1970:267). I can only suspect that the Lacandon belief was widespread in such hilly lowland areas as that occupied by the San Pedro Maya. Thompson reported that the Mopan Huitz-Hok was a "mountain-valley god" at San Antonio in the Toledo district (J. E. S. Thompson 1930:42).

In this context it may be noted that San Pedro was often known as San Pedro de Siris. Rhys, in fact, stated that the village had formerly been known as "ceris" (Rhys to Seymour, November 3, 1862, AB, R. 78). Given its location in the midst of small hills, could this alternative name have been a Maya corruption of the Spanish *cerros* ("hills")? If so, this might strengthen the argument that the village had a unique and possibly sacred location. The ruins were at Yalbac, a short distance away (J. E. S. Thompson 1939:282).

91.

Carmichael to Longden, November 15, 1867, AB, R. 93.

92.

Icaiche was devastated by a smallpox epidemic in 1893, probably accounting for the reduction in defensive quarters.

93.

Price to Darling, May 3, 1860, AB, R. 68.

94.

Price to Darling, May 14, 1860, AB, R. 68.

95.

Ibid.

96.

Spelled *Chunquijudio* by Rhys. The present spelling, referring to a felled rubber tree, is a guess.

97.

Rhys to Seymour, November 3, 1862, AB, R. 78.

98.

Ibid.

99.

Statement of Fuentes, January 25, 1867, AB, R. 89; notes of meeting of Lieutenant Governor Longden et al., July 13, 1868, AB, R. 102.

100.

Rhys to Seymour, November 3, 1862, AB, R. 78.

101.

Statement of Lorenzo Santos, December 18[?], 1866, AB, R. 93.

102.

Edmunds to Harley[?], February 13, 1867, AB, R. 95.

103.

Harley to Austin, February 15, 1867, AB, R. 95. Salt was an important trade item among the frontier Maya around this time. Icaiche, for example, bought salt for sale to the Río Hondo (statement of Daniel Clarke, March 5, 1868, AB, R. 97).

104.

Delamere to Austin, November 11, 1866, AB, R. 93; statement of Fuentes, January 25, 1867, AB, R. 89.

105.

Edmunds to Cockburn, May 31, 1867, AB, R. 96.

106.

Icaiche chiefs (Canul and Chan) to Señor General of Belize (Harley), January 2, 1872, AB, R. 110; cf. Barlee to Pech, March 8, 1880, AB, R. 120, in which the lieutenant governor complains of an Icaiche representative sent with a letter to show the "commandants" of Santa Teresa, San Pedro, San José, and some of the western settlements.

107.

Rhys to Seymour, November 3, 1862, AB, R. 78.

108.

Vidaurre to Austin, December 27, 1866, AB, R. 89; statement of Fuentes, January 25, 1867, AB, R. 89.

109.

Edmunds to Cockburn, May 31, 1867, AB, R. 96.

110.

Delamere to Harley, March 9, 1867, AB, R. 95.

111.

George Gillett to Young, Toledo and Co., April 19, 1868, AB, R. 97.

112.

Berendt visited this area in 1867 and estimated the location of many of the San Pedro settlements on his famous 1879 map (1868, 1879). Although his locations are somewhat inaccurate, it is interesting to note the path that he drew from Holmul through Chorro (misprinted as Chohha) directly to San Pedro.

113.

Like Icaiche, San José was situated on hilly terrain (Great Britain, Ministry of Defense 1970:sheet 9). Icaiche was also located near ruins. A Jesuit priest visited Icaiche in 1894 and made the following comments about attitudes toward the ruins:

● I may as well remark here that Indian Mounds abound all around about Icaiche; in fact many of the present huts are built upon these mounds thus securing a good dry spot for the inhabitants. We did not trouble ourselves about examining the mounds as General Tamay and the others did not seem to care for such sacrilegious tomb-breaking. A sort of idea exist here, that if you open up these mounds a pack of devils gets loose upon them working much mischief. I for my part think that in spite of scientific hobbies the dead of our Indian ancestors have just as much
● right to rest in peace as we have. (*The Angelus* 1895:87)

Perhaps the priest was informed that the ancestors of the present inhabitants lived in the mounds, just as Zinacantecos believe that their ancestors inhabit the surrounding sacred mountains (Vogt 1970:3–16).
114.
Cunningham to Moir, September 1862, AB, R. 78.
115.
Rhys to Seymour, November 3, 1862, AB, R. 78.
116.
Ibid.
117.
Statement of Fuentes, January 25, 1867, AB, R. 89.
118.
Harley to Austin, February 9, 1867, AB, R. 95; Chief Justice Richard James Corner to Austin, May 18, 1867, AB, R. 96.
119.
Lieutenant Governor Longden to Governor Grant, December 27, 1867, AB, R. 98.
120.
Delamere to Harley, March 9, 1867, AB, R. 95.
121.
Longden to Grant, June 19, 1868, AB, R. 98.
122.
Icaiche chiefs to Administrator (Harley), January 2, 1872, AB, R. 110.
123.
Various letters, e.g., Acting Colonial Secretary Graham to Gustav von Ohlafen, January 1, 1877, AB, R. 120.
124.
Arana to Magistrate (Ohlafen), December 8, 1877, AB, R. 119.
125.
Barlee to Pech, March 8, 1880, AB, R. 120; interview between Harley and Pech, Belize, October 13, 1882, AB, R. 93.
126.
F. E. Gabb to Inspector of Police, January 13, 1885, AB, R. 121.
127.
Rhys to Seymour, November 3, 1862, AB, R. 78.

128.
Seymour to Eyre, October 8, 1862, AB, R. 81; Cunningham to Moir, September 1862, AB, R. 78.
129.
Statement of Fuentes, January 25, 1867, AB, R. 89.
130.
The origins of ladinos, or "Spaniards," in western Belize were various: from Yucatán, the Petén, and Honduras. Flores was a Guatemalan penal colony for a time, and Spanish Hondurans were hired by the mahogany banks (Gonzáles 1961:76, 101).
131.
Rhys to Seymour, November 3, 1862, AB, R. 78.
132.
Ibid.
133.
Delamere to Harley, March 9, 1867, AB, R. 95. Chorro appears to have served as a funnel through which the escaping Maya passed on their way into the Petén. It was the principal link between the Holmul and the San Pedro–San José clusters.
134.
The number of houses is mentioned in Delamere's letter but is illegible due to water damage.
135.
Longden to Grant, December 27, 1867, AB, R, 98.
136.
Statement of Fuentes, January 25, 1867, AB, R, 89.
137.
"Sketch map made from personal observation by J. Carmichael Junr.," n.d., AB, R. 93. This location seems accurate, as it conforms with the only other description of the settlement which places Santa Cruz between Francisco Pat's mahogany work at Hololtunich and Chunbalche (statement of Fuentes, January 25, 1867, AB, R. 89).
138.
Arana et al. to Governor of Belize (Mundy), April 13, 1875, AB, R. 114.
139.
"Abstract of reconnaissance made by Lieutenant M. B. Salmon, Second W. I. Regt., of the country and roads between the Boom, Old River, and Hill Bank, British Honduras," n.d. (ca. September 25, 1876), AB, R. 114.
140.
"Cuenta de los Venques que trabajan en las Tierras de Ucatan Como Facultado por el Gobierno a cobrar los derichos de sus trabajos al SS. Ynglésese," signed by Marcos Canul and Rafael Chan, April 20, 1868, Icaiche, AB, R. 97.
141.
Mundy to Arana, March 3, 1875, AB, R. 114; Phillips and Company to

Graham, March 22, 1875, AB, R. 119.
142.
Arana et al. to Governor of Belize (Mundy), April 13, 1875, AB, R. 114.
143.
Gabb to Inspector of Police, January 13, 1885, AB, R. 121; statement by
F. Vernon, ca. January 15, 1885, AB, R. 121.
144.
Governor Goldsworthy to Gabriel Tamay, January 6, 1886, AB, R. 121.
145.
Tamay to Governor, December 19, 1885, AB, R. 121. Gabriel Tamay had
succeeded Santiago Pech as general of Icaiche by January 10, 1884
(Teodosio Canto, Vice Governor of Yucatán, to General Gabriel Tamay,
January 10, 1884, AB, R. 118).
146.
Lloyd Cuthbert to District Magistrate, O.W., July 17, 1886, AB, R. 121.
147.
William James McKinney to Orange Walk Magistrate, ca. December 20,
1886, AB, R. 121.
148.
This relocation of a principal village under conditions of military stress
was probably quite a common phenomenon throughout the independent
Maya groups of the period, e.g., the removal from Chichanha to Icaiche
about 1860 and from Lochha to Xkanha in the early 1870's.
149.
This overland route from Icaiche to San Pedro with a branch to San José
appears to have been used more frequently than the more circuitous path
along Booth's River on the Río Bravo.
150.
The village suffers from a wide variety of misspellings in the primary
documentation (e.g., Tolmul, Tulmul, Tobmul, Xmul, Chumul), which
were apparently not always recognized as the same village by the British.
The name refers to a hill or mound with an entrance (*hol*, "door"; *mul*,
"mound"), translated by Maler as *"Cerro con entradas"* (1908:56), almost
certainly referring to the ruin itself.
151.
Statement of Fuentes, January 25, 1867, AB, R. 89.
152.
Edmunds to Cockburn, May 31, 1867, AB, R. 96. The burning, I assume,
was carried out because of the presence of British sympathizers in the
latter three settlements.
153.
Liberato Robelo to British Honduras Company, April 27, 1868, AB, R.
97.
154.
Declaration of Que and Sosa, September 22, 1862, AB, R. 78.

155.
Also spelled Tolhuito, Holuib, Alwitz, and Höll Wects!
156.
Edmunds to Cockburn, May 31, 1867, AB, R. 96.
157.
Notes of meeting of Lieutenant Governor Longden et al., July 13, 1868, AB, R. 102.
158.
Canul to Governor (Longden), July 24, 1868, AB, R. 102.
159.
Chan to August, September 20, 1868, AB, R. 102.
160.
Later reports indicated that Tzuc had been punished but not killed (Hodge to Longden, October 10, 1868, AB, R. 102).
161.
Hodge to Longden, October 10, 1868, AB, R. 102.
162.
H. McDonald to Longden, October 12, 1868, AB, R. 102.
163.
Barlee to Pech, March 8, 1880, AB, R. 120.
164.
In 1882 the *alcalde* of Yaloch, convinced by Col. Sec. Henry Fowler that his village was on British soil, actually swore allegiance to the queen (*Colonial Guardian,* August 5, 1882).
165.
Petén investigation, testimony of Chan, Lara, and Mo.
166.
See declaration of Que and Sosa, September 22, 1862, AB, R. 78.
167.
Maler's general comments on these settlements are of considerable interest (1908:58, 61, 70–73). If Yaxha was abandoned shortly after Maler's visit, it was repopulated in later years, for a small settlement was photographed from the air in 1929 on what appears to be the east end of Lake Yaxha (Ricketson and Kidder, 1930:191).
168.
This is not to deny that immigrants from San José near Flores settled at Socotz in later years, however.
169.
Colonial Guardian, July 22, July 29, August 5, and August 12, 1882.
170.
Vidaurre to Governor, December 15, 1866, AB, R. 89; statement of John Samuel August, December 27, 1866, AB, R. 89; Francisco May to Commandant of Petén (Vidaurre), January 29, 1867, AB, R. 102 (enclosed with Manuel María Cifuentes to Magistrate of the Settlement of Belize, July 28, 1868, AB, R. 102).

171.
De Ayurena to Superintendent [sic], April 27, 1867, AB, R. 96.
172.
Cifuentes to Magistrate of . . . Belize, July 28, 1868, AB, R. 102.
173.
Colonial Guardian, July 22, 1882.
174.
Edmunds to Cockburn, May 31, 1867, AB, R. 96.
175.
Ibid.
176.
Maler noted that Socotz and Arenal were "inhabited by Indian families who have migrated from Peten villages" (1908:76). Sir J. Eric S. Thompson pointed out that socotz is a local Petén tree (personal communication, 1974).
177.
Chan to August, September 20, 1868, AB, R. 102.
178.
By 1905 additional Petén migrants had established another Maya settlement above Benque Viejo. This village, Arenal, was apparently later absorbed by surrounding communities (Maler 1908:76).
179.
Longden to Grant, June 19, 1868, AB, R. 98 (report on the Blue Book for 1867); Robert T. Downer to Longden, February 9, 1868, AB, R. 97.
180.
As recalled by a Maya laborer: statement of Juan Chable, December 28, 1867, Corozal, AB, R. 96.
181.
Colonial Guardian, November 7, 1891, November 14, 1891, December 12, 1891, February 13, 1892, March 12, 1892; Sapper 1904:627.
182.
The effects of this epidemic, as well as others, are not recorded for the Holmul villages, but the constant social intercourse among the Maya villages would have spread the disease throughout the area.
183.
Historia Domus, Xavier Parish, Corozal Town, October 1917–January 1918.
184.
Chicle enterprises in the Petén were largely British operations. Later spread of such activities into the Petén was thus a westward expansion of colonial extractive operations.
185.
Fowler 1879:16–17. Trade was going on between the village of Santa Cruz on the Belize River and El Cayo in 1882 (Colonial Guardian, August 12, 1882). Trade contacts might explain the late survival of Yaxha, which was

situated directly on the Flores-Belize route.
186.
Colonial Guardian, July 19, 1884.
187.
Colonial Guardian, June 14, 1884.
188.
Colonial Secretary Fowler's notorious government-paid military expedition to the Western District in 1882 was later said to have been in response to the refusal of his Maya tenants to pay rent on his land (*Colonial Guardian*, June 14, 1884).
189.
Canul, Chan, et al. to William W. Cairns[?], April 10, 1871, AB, R. 109; cf. *The Angelus* 1901:206.
190.
Statement of Mariano Medina, December 14, 1866, AB, R. 89.
191.
Notes taken from a meeting between the commissioners of Pablo Encalada and Lieutenant Governor Austin, February 4, 1867, AB, R. 89.
192.
Encalada to Austin, March 4, 1867, AB, R. 89.
193.
There was a reference to the *comandantes* of a number of San Pedro villages in 1880, certainly a reference to the *alcaldes* (Barlee to Pech, March 8, 1880, AB, R. 120). As in the Cupul territory in the eighteenth century, village heads were also called *capitanes* (Chan to August, September 20, 1868, AB, R. 102).

6

Internal Migration in Yucatán:

Interpretation of Historical Demography and

Current Patterns

James W. Ryder

Introduction

This article is a materialist analysis of data derived through the use of a combination of method and theory from anthropology, ethnohistory, and demography.[1] The analysis traces the evolution of a form of adaptation—*migration*—under differing conditions, from pre-Columbian times to the present. With regard to Yucatán I quantify rates of internal migration, establish causal factors and, for the 1901–1970 period, demonstrate the relationship between rural-urban migration and the rate of urbanization in Yucatán. In a broader context the data and analysis demonstrate the necessity of examining phenomena that appear to have only isolated or regional determinants as part of a pervasive network of relationships which are closely integrated with the world economic system.

Therefore, single-factor explanations, such as Davis's recent hypothesis that the primary cause of migration is the "technological inequality between one group and another" (1974:93), are considered inadequate. The problem lies in the formulation of the hypothesis. Specifically, technological inequality is certainly a primary determinant of a group's or a society's potential to migrate into the territory of another group or society or into unoccupied territory. However, technology alone is an inadequate indicator of potential for migration or expansion. It is necessary to examine the predominant mode of production in both groups or societies. Such an examination includes technology as one aspect of the forces of production and also stresses the study of the means and the social relations of production.[2] This approach deals with the important question of how technological inequality develops rather than accepting its existence as given. From this perspective it is insufficient to deal with the "institutional framework" (Davis and Blake 1956) as the primary determinant of fertility, maintaining fertility at high levels in the face of changing socioeconomic conditions. In addition to the effects of the institutional framework on individuals,[3] the influence of a capitalist system of production which reaches into every part of the world must also be considered.

As might be anticipated by anyone with an acquaintance with demographic literature, migration data, both international and internal, are frequently the least accessible and reliable of the demographic statistics necessary for accurate analysis of population history and trends. In fact, there are no statistics on migration for small jurisdictions anywhere in Mexico unless they are derived from ethnographic data, usually over very short periods. Such data would be interesting as qualitative examples of a phenomenon, but, because of random fluctuations in a small population over time, they could not be considered dependable as the basis for calculating long-term rates or changes over time. However, in dealing with the principal interests of anthropological ethnohistory, historical ethnography, and historiography (Sturtevant 1966; Cline 1972), findings at the village level can be integrated with vital statistics and a knowledge of the social, economic, and political conditions prevailing at the regional, state, and national levels, as well as in the world market, in order to derive reliable estimates of the varying importance of migration through time.

The data upon which this study is based are fragmentary through the initial 350 years under consideration. Therefore, various clearly labeled assumptions are made about crude birth and death rates (births and deaths per thousand total population, respectively) in order to derive the crude rates of natural increase (difference between crude birth and crude death rates) which are used to calculate net migration (difference between immigration and emigration). Thus, if the population of a village is known at two dates and the crude rate of natural increase is known for the interval between those dates, the population which would have been expected at the second date, if there had been no net migration, can be calculated. If the observed population at the second date is greater than the expected population, the difference is due to positive net immigration. If the observed population is smaller, the difference is due to positive net emigration. Conservative assumptions are made concerning the crude birth and death rates to avoid generating statistics whose sole purpose is to support the argument.

The role of migration in the demographic history of Yucatán has been virtually ignored, primarily because of the obvious influence of mortality on the postconquest indigenous populations (see Cook and Borah 1974, González Navarro 1970, and Hunt 1974 for exceptions). This article, on the contrary, demonstrates the importance of migration in the demographic history of one Yucatecan village and in Yucatán from 1900 until the present. Therefore, instead of assuming high rates of natural increase, which would increase the importance of migration in the overall equation, assumptions about crude birth and death rates are made which produce conservative rates of natural increase, while at the same time approximating actual conditions of fertility and mortality as closely as possible.

I begin with a brief description of the pueblo and its areal integration, followed by the population statistics, which are discussed in historical perspective. The reliability of the demographic data is tested in several ways, one of which is new to the anthropological literature. The actual analysis of the data with regard to migration follows in a separate section in order to avoid intertwining ethnohistorical analysis and evaluation of the data with the methodology and conclusions concerning migration. In addition, consideration of the assumptions used to derive rates and test reliability occurs throughout the article.

Pencuyut: Physical Geography

Pencuyut is a small pueblo in south central Yucatán, under the administrative jurisdiction of the *municipio* of Tekax. Pencuyut lies 8 kilometers east of both a major highway, Mexico 180, which connects Chetumal and Belize with the Mérida-Campeche highway at Muna, and the railroad connecting Peto to Mérida, both of which run through the pueblo of Akil (lat. 20°16′N, long. 89°21′W). Pencuyut is 14 kilometers north of the city of Tekax (lat. 20°12′N, long. 89°17′W), the principal city of the *municipio*. The name Pencuyut, or Ppencuyut, is said to have been changed from Chheenyuc.[4]

Physically, Pencuyut is typical of the orderly, gridded communities imposed by the Spaniards and found throughout Latin America. The grid pattern is an ancient Mediterranean trait predating the Roman era (Stanislawski 1946, 1947). The plaza is central to the entire pueblo, with houses radiating out in all directions. Fruit trees, chili peppers, and maize are frequently planted in the yards; the yards and streets are cleanly weeded. The plaza is actually a grassy block with the Catholic church at the east end. The church was partially destroyed during the Caste War. The plaza is surrounded by the larger, more prestigious houses of *mamposteria* ("rubble masonry"), the municipal building, the schools, and by several of the typical Yucatec Maya wooden (wattle and daub) apsidal houses.

The new school is identical to the hundreds of rural schools completed or being constructed in Yucatán. Opposite the Catholic church is the Protestant (Presbyterian) church, which used to be the nuns' convent prior to the Caste War. Conversion to Protestanism began in the late 1930's and met with considerable resistance. The Protestant congregation recently cleared an airstrip in the far north to enable the missionaries to land, both for continued contact and for flying out seriously ill members of the congregation. Only one plane landed during my residence. Once beyond the pueblo boundaries, one enters the forest (*monte*) which is primarily *ejidal* land with some private property.

Evidence pertaining to the antiquity and the size of Pencuyut through time comes both from present-day informants and from physical remains. First, there are artificial water tanks (*chaltunob*), mounds of stone rubble (*moolob*), and the stone and ceramic images in the milpas of Pencuyute-ños. As for Pencuyut's previous size, older residents point out the over-grown streets and abandoned house lots as proof of Pencuyut's diminish-ing size. In fact, my mapping of the entire pueblo uncovered enough additional streets with overgrown house lots and platforms to demonstrate that Pencuyut was easily twice as large in the not too distant past as it is today. Additional mapping into even more overgrown areas would, I be-lieve, lead to additional streets and house sites.

Yucatán and Pencuyut: Socioeconomic History

A skeletal outline of the development of colonial Yucatán, its distinct regional variations, and changes specific to Pencuyut follows.[5] Yucatán can be divided on the basis of economic, productive, or cultural-ecological zones. The significant divisions depend upon the time period selected be-cause the socioeconomic conditions have changed dramatically from region to region over time.

For the colonial and early independence period I will follow Cline (1950c) and divide Yucatán into four sections: Old Colonial, West Coast, East Colonial, and Borderlands. The parallels of their development, as well as their differentiations, are traced by Cline from the conquest of Yucatán in 1542 through the development of cattle raising, followed by the increasing production of sugar, then henequen. Parallels in the devel-opment of the peninsula are found in such institutions as the church, the early dominance of the *encomenderos*, and the stabilizing factor of central authority residing in Spain.

Yucatán had no mineral wealth. In fact, Yucatán's primary value was found in the exploitation of its large indigenous population. The *en-comienda* remained a powerful asset one hundred years longer in Yucatán than in other parts of Mexico because of this economic situation (Cook and Borah 1974). This same lack of wealth and Yucatán's relative physical isolation resulted in a degree of autonomy of social development in the peninsula. However, development followed the same patterns found throughout Hispanic America, merely being retarded in pace. For exam-ple, production of specific items was either permitted or denied on the basis of peninsular Spanish needs; and markets were regulated, taxes levied, and legislation controlled by Spain.

Encomenderos everywhere in the peninsula were the aristocratic elite of the upper class. Bureaucratic officials from Spain and elsewhere in New Spain were rapidly assimilated into the upper class of Yucatecan society and correspondingly had a vested interest in the advancement of upper-class aims. The church in Yucatán was controlled by the secular clergy, who were, in turn, brothers or close relatives of *encomenderos* (Hunt 1974).

In contrast to these peninsula-wide similarities, the sectional differences were extremely important in the development of Yucatán. The Old Colonial section was centered around and extended out from Mérida, the political center of the peninsula. This same area is the center of the present-day henequen zone. Mérida was established within a region which had a high-density indigenous population. The Old Colonial section was an important maize region, and cattle for the domestic market became important almost immediately. As the Spanish population increased and began moving into the countryside in order to further exploit Indian surplus production, reverse migration streams of Maya artisans and laborers came to the cities. Merchants, closely allied to *encomenderos*, if not actually *encomenderos* themselves, became more important as they accumulated capital which provided them the opportunity to move into promising new enterprises, such as cattle *estancias* and, later, sugar and henequen haciendas. Economic ties between the Old Colonial section and Mexico were minimal. Trade based first on maize, cattle and leather goods, and cotton and wax was with Cuba and Europe. Later, with sugar and henequen products, important markets were Cuba, Europe, and the United States.

Henequen was the most significant factor in the revival of Yucatán. After the devastation of the first year of the Caste War, henequen served as a resource of badly needed revenue. It united the area socially and economically, formed a protective barrier against attack, was responsible for an improved communications network, and returned the northern and western regions of Yucatán to total social, economic, and political dominance. Henequen also brought Yucatán into dependence on a monocrop economy over which Yucatecans have almost no control. Henequen is profitable as a source of state revenues and "is easily manipulated for the benefit of those in control" (Raymond 1971:17–18). Despite lowered demand (prior to the present increase in oil prices), "until such time as henequen no longer is a source of revenue, it will never be in the interest of those who control production to diversify production" (ibid.). González Navarro sums up the situation thus: "The importance of henequen is still fundamental in the Yucatecan economy: half of the inhabitants are directly dependent upon this fiber, and the remainder indirectly" (1970: 273).

The West Coast was dominated by its port, Campeche. Fewer *encomenderos* were active in this section because it had fewer Indians, and, although *encomenderos* were important, that importance was related to their early reliance upon commercial activity. Economically, the West Coast was dependent upon salt, logwood (for dyes), hardwoods, and, later, sugar. Campeche became a bustling port because of its favorable position on trade routes between gulf ports, Cuba, and Spain. Therefore, its economic advantages were also tied to commercial shipping, shipbuilding, and its peninsula-wide trade networks for supplying goods required for the exploitation of Indians through the *repartimiento* system. Commercial links were primarily with Veracruz and other gulf ports that connected the West Coast with Mexico. The economic and demographic differences between the Old Colonial and West Coast sections, especially with regard to their foreign and domestic trade networks and their later investments in sugar, were significant in Campeche's rivalry with Mérida and the division of the peninsula into the states of Campeche and Yucatán in 1858. The Caste War resulted in initial economic losses to Campeche, especially in terms of capital invested in sugar in the Borderlands. However, sugar became more important in the West Coast after 1852–1853 than it had been before the Caste War and more important than its post–Caste War significance in the Borderlands. Henequen, although economically important for a short period, never achieved a dominant position in Campeche's economy.

The East Colonial section was centered around Valladolid, whose *encomenderos* maintained absolute social, economic, and political control. This section had a large indigenous population and was an important maize-producing region. Cattle raising became important only after the Caste War, although the area between Mérida and Valladolid became one of the most important cattle areas early in the colonial period. Wealth in the East Colonial section was even more dependent upon the Indian tribute and *repartimiento* systems than in the Old Colonial section. The region produced more cotton than did the Old Colonial and West Coast sections combined. This section was in a sharp decline, in all respects, prior to 1700. Some investment was made in sugar, but lack of roads and port facilities made this enterprise, as well as the logging, rice, and tobacco enterprises, unprofitable. It was due to the conservative, even reactionary, behavior of the Creole population in its attempts to maintain a landed aristocracy and feudal relations which was responsible for the section being "socially decadent, economically unintegrated and politically impotent" (Cline 1950c:335) at the outbreak of the Caste War. These same social relations have helped maintain the backwardness of this region to the present day.

The Borderlands, in which Pencuyut was located, was a frontier zone in the process of differentiation and rapid economic development on the eve of the Caste War. This section had a numerous, though dispersed, indigenous population. It was an important maize-producing region and had the most fertile land on the peninsula. Throughout the colonial period the frontier zones of the south and east served as population reservoirs for *encomenderos* because thousands of Indians fled into these areas to escape epidemics, famine, warfare, and exploitation. Economic development in the Borderlands was a result of heavy capital investment in the cultivation of sugar by the wealthy upper class of Mérida and Campeche (Cline 1948b,

1950*c*). The development and prosperity of the Borderlands effected a tremendous population increase in the Borderlands and relative changes in the population distribution within the peninsula. Cultivation of sugar cane came into direct conflict with subsistence maize cultivation. Cultivation of sugar is capital and labor intensive. Investment in sugar required ownership of large areas of land, which was gained through the alienation of communal lands, a process which took several forms. A permanent labor force was also required. The end results were the formation of a new, capitalistic unit of production, similar to the more slowly developing henequen haciendas which began to flourish after the most violent years of the Caste War, increased debt peonage (both in extent and severity of obligations), and the impetus for the outbreak of the Caste War.[6] By the time peace was restored to the Borderlands (after 1860), Yucatecan economic development had become synonymous with henequen, a fact which has not changed to the present day. The Borderlands section, or more appropriately today, the "southern indigenous zone" (Villa Rojas 1962*a*), has unobtrusively returned to its earlier colonial status of a backward, predominantly rural, maize-producing zone.

The contemporary appearance of Pencuyut's physical isolation should not be confused either with its previous position or with its present relationships vis-à-vis Mérida, Mexico, or the world market system. Pencuyut was one of the earliest *encomiendas* and, with Ixil, was granted to the *conquistador* Julian Donzel before 1549. Pencuyut remained in private *encomienda* until the crown assumed control of all *encomiendas* in 1785. This means that, from shortly after the conquest of Yucatán, Pencuyuteños were required to pay tributes to *conquistadores* and their descendants and to suffer the additional burden of the *repartimiento* trade. They were under the influence of priests, including the payment of *obvenciones* and fees for baptisms, marriages, and other pious acts, and they were involved in the periodic roundups of Maya who had fled to the frontier or of previously unacculturated Maya, all of whom were used to replenish the *encomienda* and church pueblos.[7] Throughout the colonial period Pencuyut was on a main line of communication which ran from Mérida to Mani, Teabo, Pencuyut, Tekax, and on south to Bacalar.

During the colonial period Pencuyuteños were dependent on maize cultivation for subsistence and on cloth mantas, which with maize constituted the primary items of tribute. Chamberlain demonstrates that, although the tribute system was well known in preconquest Yucatán, the Spanish version was far more onerous, especially when combined with the obligations of *repartimiento* trade and church tributes and fees (1951). However, the Maya status of subsistence cultivator was not greatly changed. What did change significantly was that under Spanish feudalism in Yucatán the indigenous population was brought directly into a world market system but at a level of economic and political impotency.

From the brief sketch presented here it is clear that the greatest changes for Pencuyuteños as a result of the conquest occurred immediately after the conquest and then during the "sugar episode." In the former period, the indigenous population suffered the effects of warfare, famine, epidemic, forced migration (civil congregation), and exploitation at the hands of *encomenderos*, priests, officials, and merchants. During the latter period, changing economic conditions, including the loss of communal lands and increasing debt peonage, were among the primary causes of the Caste War. It was precisely during these two distinct periods that the greatest demographic changes also occurred.

Contemporary inhabitants of Pencuyut are primarily dependent upon maize cultivation, both for subsistence and for cash, through the sale of any surplus. A varying number of men, approximately ten to thirty per year, leave Pencuyut for anywhere from two to six weeks in order to earn cash as agricultural laborers. They clear, burn, sow, and harvest milpa in southern Yucatán and in Quintana Roo. Some additional changes are obvious. Today almost every household has a transistor radio. Several individuals read a newspaper regularly, although no one in the pueblo has more than a primary education. Pencuyut has four small stores, two of which have gasoline-engine maize grinders. The stores stock an extremely limited supply of goods. Many of the commercial dealings are based on the exchange of maize rather than cash. Not many visitors come to Pencuyut, but those who do enter are usually buying or selling something; the most frequent items are maize, pigs, turkeys, and fruit. Others come to play baseball, to show an occasional movie, to recruit labor for the construction of a road or a telephone line, or to gain political support. The recruitment of labor for projects was always intimately related to local and regional politics.

Pencuyut has no classes in the strict sense of social and economic classes, but it does have relatively wealthier and poorer inhabitants. In contemporary Pencuyut not even segments of a lower class exist, although they almost certainly did in pre–Caste War days when there were resident artisans and several larger landowners. Goldkind confuses stratification and class, which leads him to misinterpret his findings in Chan Kom (1965, 1966).[8]

Pencuyut may or may not be a typical Yucatecan pueblo with regard to ethnographic content. I have found much concurrence with the ethnographic data for Chan Kom in the 1930's and 1940's (Redfield and Villa Rojas 1934; Redfield 1941) and with Pustunich in the 1960's (Press 1968). The intrapueblo conflict and factionalism reported by Goldkind (1965, 1966) are similar to what I found in Pencuyut. The Protestant religion is stronger numerically (25%) than is general in Yucatán. But at the most fundamental levels—social, economic, and political—Pencuyut is like other pueblos of its size in Yucatán; it is powerless to act decisively in its own interest.[9]

Pencuyut: Demographic History

Ethnohistorical research has resulted in the location of Pencuyut with a prominent church on the Mani Land Treaty map of 1557 (Stephens 1963; I, 264), which attests to the antiquity of Pencuyut as a pre-Columbian population center. The first mention of Pencuyut I have located is a calculation of population from the 1549 tax list cited by both Roys, Scholes, and Adams (1959) and Paso y Troncoso (1938). Roys, Scholes, and Adams believe that there had been no civil congregation (Simpson 1934; Cline 1949) in Pencuyut at the time of the 1583 census and that the 1549 and 1583 counts represent a population relatively undisturbed by forced emigration or immigrations (1959). The 1549 tax list gives a total of 250 tributaries (individuals from whom standard rates of tribute are collected). Earlier research by Roys yields an estimate of 4.0 inhabitants for every registered tributary in the 1570's (1957). If Roys's ratio is accepted, Pencuyut would have had a population of 1,000 in 1549. Paso y Troncoso estimates 4.5 inhabitants per tributary (1938), which would have yielded a population of 1,125 in 1549. In 1583 the census gives a population of 684 and the number of tributaries as 164, a ratio of 4.2 inhabitants per tributary (table 6-1). This is the highest ratio of inhabitants to tributaries among the six census reports cited by Roys, Scholes, and Adams (1959), but Pencuyut falls in the center of the range on the average number of inhabitants per household. This suggests a breakup of multiple-family households in Pencuyut by 1583, a point reinforced by the number of houses with fewer than two married couples. In Pencuyut there were a large number of single-family households, whereas in Cozumel in 1570, "where there had been comparatively little Spanish supervision" (Roys, Scholes, and Adams 1959:204), no household had fewer than two couples. Gates (1937) and several of the *Relaciones de Yucatán* (Colección de Documentos Inéditos 1898–1900) report a diminution of the population by two-thirds between the 1540's and 1597 for many parts of Yucatán. Pencuyut appears to have lost between 30 to 40 percent of its inhabitants between 1549 and 1583, with a diminution of between 50 and 65 percent by 1606. Kurjack has proposed not only that it was the conquest, disease, and civil congregation that *caused* depopulation but also that conceivably the early and extensive civil congregation in Yucatán was made possible *because* of the tremendous depopulation (1974). That is, if depopulation had not occurred, the Spanish would have been unable to congregate numerous large pueblos. The populations would have been too large for social and physical control by the small number of Spaniards, and such large populations would have been disruptive of agricultural production. The available series of population figures stress both the similarities and the differences between Pencuyut and Yucatán as a whole. By 1606 (Paso y Troncoso 1940) there were between 400 and 500 inhabitants in Pencuyut (calculation based on the amount of tribute in mantles of cloth and the ratios of inhabitants to tributaries cited above). A gap exists between 1606 and the end of the eighteenth century so that one does not know whether the population continued to decrease, leveled off, or increased. However, in 1794 (Rubio Mañé 1942) Pencuyut had again grown to a sizable pueblo of 1,629 inhabitants. If Cook and Borah's (1974) analysis of the growth and decline of population within the territorial entity demarcated as the Alta, of which Pencuyut is a part, is accurate and if that

Table 6-1

Census dates and population of Pencuyut, 1549–1972

Date	Population	Corrected Population
1549	1,000–1,125[b]	
1583	684	
1606	400–500[b]	
1794	1,629	
1828	2,186–2,421[c]	
1846	2,000–2,075[c]	
1851	242	
1900*	559	
1910*	430	524[d]

(continued)

demographic pattern is applicable to Pencuyut, the population of Pencuyut continued to decrease through 1736. Therefore, the curve in Figure 6-1 should continue downward, and then increase more sharply between 1736 and 1794.

In 1822 in the parish of Pencuyut and its auxiliary of Akil, there was a single *ministro* for each pueblo plus the administrative head (a priest) of the parish. In 1828 the parish of Pencuyut, including Akil and all the haciendas and ranchos under their jurisdiction, recorded a total popula-

Hypothesized reason for population change	*Source*[a]
First recorded population	Spanish tax list
Decrease due to introduced disease and possible emigration	Spanish census/tax list
Decrease due to introduced disease and possible emigration	Spanish tax list
Increase due to natural increase; limited by possible emigration, famine, and epidemic	Spanish census
Increase due to natural increase; limited by possible emigration, famine, and epidemic	Church census
Decrease due to famine, epidemic, war, and emigration	Yucatán census
Decrease due to Caste War–related mortality and emigration	Yucatán census
Increase due to natural increase and possible immigration	Mexican census
Decrease due to emigration	Mexican census

[a]Pencuyut was not enumerated in the 1970 Mexican Census, which gave data for larger jurisdictions only.
[b]The population is dependent upon the number of dependents per tributary (see text).
[c]The number of inhabitants excluding/including the ranchos, respectively (see text).
[d]These population figures omit several of the ranchos pertaining to Pencuyut (see text) and are corrected through examination of inhabitants listed for those ranchos in the censuses.
[e]The mean population for the years 1970 and 1972 is assumed for 1971.
*Census populations used to calculate mean population for Pencuyut for 1901 to 1970.

Date	Population	Corrected Population
1921*	491	
1930*	433	
1935*	481	
1936	490	
1940*	534	
1950*	497	
1960*	400	517[d]
1964*	524	
1966	526	
1970*	590	
1971[e]	530	593
1972	595	

tion of 5,073 (the unpublished originals are in the archives of Sr. Joaquín de Arrigunaga, Mérida, Yucatán; the numbers were added incorrectly and should have read 5,086).* A priori I would expect the parish (Pencuyut) to have been larger and more important than its auxiliary (Akil) at the time Pencuyut was designated head of the parish. During this epoch and as late as 1930, correspondence from Mérida to Tekax and farther south and back to Mérida passed through Pencuyut. However, Pencuyut alone, without its outlying haciendas and ranchos, had a popu-

* Three documents, each titled "Curato de Pencuyut," were found in the files of Sr. Arrigunaga; these files include documents from most of the parishes of Yucatán and are in an alphabetical file. Sr. Arrigunaga's help is here gratefully acknowledged.

Hypothesized reason for population change	*Source*[a]
Decrease due to revolution and emigration	Mexican census
Decrease due to emigration	Mexican census
Increase due to natural increase; limited by emigration	Steggerda census
Increase due to natural increase	Steggerda census
Increase due to natural increase	Mexican census
Decrease due to emigration and possible underenumeration	Mexican census
Increase due to natural increase; limited by emigration	Mexican census
Increase due to natural increase; limited by emigration	Pencuyut archives
Increase due to natural increase; limited by emigration	Pencuyut archives
Increase due to natural increase; limited by emigration	Ryder census
Increase due to natural increase; limited by emigration	Pencuyut archives
Increase due to natural increase; limited by emigration	Ryder census

[a]Pencuyut was not enumerated in the 1970 Mexican Census, which gave data for larger jurisdictions only.
[b]The population is dependent upon the number of dependents per tributary (see text).
[c]The number of inhabitants excluding/including the ranchos, respectively (see text).
[d]These population figures omit several of the ranchos pertaining to Pencuyut (see text) and are corrected through examination of inhabitants listed for those ranchos in the censuses.
[e]The mean population for the years 1970 and 1972 is assumed for 1971.
*Census populations used to calculate mean population for Pencuyut for 1901 to 1970.

lation of 2,186, 138 fewer than Akil. This could indicate that at this early date Akil was growing more rapidly than Pencuyut or that Pencuyut had begun its final decline, documented in later censuses below.

A document dated 1832 (Arrigunaga archives) records the births and deaths for 1830 and 1831 for Pencuyut and Akil jointly, based upon the total population. I will assume zero net migration and use the crude natural increase derived from the excess of births over deaths in both 1830 and 1831 to calculate the base population (using the 1828 population of

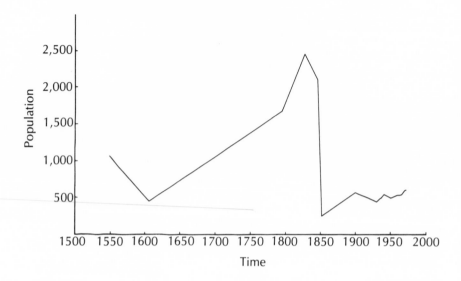

Figure 6-1
Population change in Pencuyut, 1549–1972

5,086) with which crude birth, death, and natural increase rates can be calculated. Births and deaths are averaged for the two-year period in order to smooth the fluctuation between 1830 and 1831. The 1829 population will be taken as the figure for 1828 plus the average natural increase for 1830–1831.

	Births	Deaths
1830	244	103
1831	181	137
Total	*425*	*240*

Using the vital registration and census data for Pencuyut between 1901 and 1970, a comparison between 1830–1831 and 1901–1970 can be made. During the seventy-year interval of the latter period, 1,657 births were recorded, or 23.7 per year. There were 897 deaths recorded, or 12.8 per year, resulting in a natural increase of 10.9 persons annually. In 1830–1831, Pencuyut plus the haciendas and ranchos under its jurisdiction constituted 48 percent of the population of the parish, or 2,421 inhabitants, and, assuming that Pencuyut and Akil had identical birth and death rates, there would have been an average of 102.0 births and 57.6

deaths per year. The natural increase for Pencuyut would have been 44.4 persons per year. The birth, death, and natural increase figures for 1830–1831 are in striking contrast to those for 1901–1970 until the total populations are compared. The 1830–1831 population was 4.7 times larger than the average population between 1901 and 1970, while there were 4.3 times as many births and the deaths were 4.5 times greater. The data have a high degree of internal consistency.

The average crude birth rate for Pencuyut during 1830–1831 was 39.9, compared to 46.0 per thousand between 1901 and 1970 (table 6-2). The average crude death rates were 22.6 and 24.9 per thousand, respectively. The average crude rates of natural increase were 17.3 and 21.1 per thousand, respectively. The crude birth rates for the two periods are high but are comparable with rates for other high fertility populations who practice little or no contraception.[10] At this first level of analysis the full seventy-year period has been used in order to reduce the fluctuations in numbers and rates due to the small numbers of vital events. In fact, the absolute numbers of births, as well as the crude birth rate, were almost constant during the ten-year intervals between 1901 and 1970. However, deaths and the crude death rate varied immensely between 1901–1930 and 1931–1970 (see table 6-4). This latter fact clearly indicates that it is reasonable to compare the 1830–1831 birth rates with those of 1901–1970 but that the earlier death rate must be compared with the death rates of 1901–1930. When this is done, it is clear that the 1830–1831 death rate is low and suspect. There are several potential explanations. First, under-

Table 6-2

Crude rates of birth, death, and natural increase, Pencuyut, 1830–1831 and 1901–1970

	1830–1831	1901–1970
Crude birth rate *births per 1,000 total population*	39.9	46.0
Crude death rate *deaths per 1,000 total population*	22.6	24.9
Crude rate of natural increase *CBR minus CDR*	17.3	21.1

Note: The census figures used to calculate the average population for Pencuyut are listed with an asterisk in table 6-1. Corrected population figures are used in these and all succeeding calculations.
Total population for 10 census years = 5,150
Average population per year = 515

reporting of deaths, especially infant deaths, is a strong possibility at this early date. Second, it is possible that the births and deaths, as well as total population, should be distributed differently between Pencuyut and Akil, thus changing the rates. It is also possible that these two years were particularly good years with regard to mortality and would have been balanced by heavier mortality over a five- or ten-year interval.

Returning to the sequence of data on population size through time, further confirmation of the consistency of this series is found in the Memoria of 1846 (Yucatán, Secretario General de Gobierno 1846), which credits Pencuyut with 2,000 or 2,075 inhabitants, excluding and including haciendas and ranchos, respectively. The results of the Caste War, begun in 1847, one year after the Memoria census, can be seen in the 1851 census of Pencuyut (México, Archivo General de la Nación 1948), which lists a population of 242. One of the older men of the village reported that during the first year of the Caste War the government ordered or kidnapped by force of arms 1,000 men from Pencuyut, of whom only a few ever returned. This number is surely an exaggeration, but the difference between the census populations of 1846 and 1851 indicates a tremendous depopulation. However, mortality-related depopulation is not the only, or necessarily best, explanation. Throughout Yucatán, but especially in the eastern and southern indigenous zones, thousands of Maya fled into the forests either to take up arms or to avoid being conscripted by one side or killed by the other.

The long-term fluctuations in population documented for Pencuyut between 1549 and the present are not atypical for a village or for Yucatán in general. Historically, migration and flight have occurred in response to diverse circumstances: to avoid upheaval and revolution,[11] to find fertile lands when population pressure or loss of soil fertility necessitates, to avoid intrapueblo conflict,[12] to escape epidemic and famine (see Redfield and Villa Rojas 1934 and quotes below from Molina Solis 1896), as well as to find employment in modern times. The following passage from Landa demonstrates the time depth of migration as a mode of adaptation: "Before the Spaniards had conquered that country, the natives lived together in towns in a very civilized fashion. They kept the land very well cleared and free from weeds, and planted very good trees. . . . And the wells, if there were but few of them, were near the houses of the lords; and they had their improved lands planted with wine trees and they sowed cotton, pepper and maize, and they lived thus close together for fear of their enemies, who took them captive, and it was owing to the wars of the Spaniards that they scattered in the woods" (Tozzer 1941: 62–64).

Migration, voluntary or forced, is thus seen to be a primary factor in the population distribution through space and time in Pencuyut and in Yucatán.

Migration in Pencuyut and Yucatán

If we accept the 1549 population of Pencuyut, estimated to fall within
the range of 1,000 to 1,125 inhabitants, as our baseline, and further accept
the census total of 684 in 1583, it would be reasonable to attribute the
majority of the 30-to-40-percent decrease in population to disease-related
mortality. It would be reasonable because even higher mortality has been
documented, including the excellent account of the Putun Maya of
Acalan-Tixchel (Scholes and Roys 1948), whose population declined 60
percent between 1525 and 1553 and by 90 percent by 1561. On the other
hand, additional factors must have played varying roles in the dynamics
of the demographic history of Pencuyut. Intermittent warfare between the
native states of Sotuta and Mani (the Cocom and Xiu, respectively), as
well as conflict between Spaniards and Maya contributed to mortality and
probably migration. The burdens of *encomienda* and *repartimiento* were
variables in the demographic equation throughout New Spain (Chamberlain 1939; Hanke 1949; Hunt 1974). More important as an alternative
cause of mortality and migration during this period (and later) were
famines, which also increased epidemic mortality. The effects of famine
on a peninsula-wide scale are difficult to measure at the local level since
small, scattered areas frequently receive sufficient rain to produce crops.
Juan Francisco Molina Solis described a drought-induced famine, followed by a plague of locusts in 1535 (just prior to our first population
estimate), and then famines in 1551–1552 and 1571 (1896). Tomás López,
a judge (*oidor*) of the Royal Audiencia of Guatemala, whose inspection
visit in 1552 initiated the early efforts toward civil congregation in
Yucatán, also left orders to remedy conditions of starvation which he
encountered, but they were insufficient (Molina Hübbe 1941). One of the
measures was the establishment of public granaries, which were expro-
priated in time of need by *encomenderos* and government officials. The
following quotation vividly portrays the consequences of drought.

● The desperate, starving people went into the countryside in search of
roots and the bark of trees with which to satiate their hunger: a tree
named *kumche* whose cooked, bland center was eaten as if it were bread,
served primarily as a great aid, in such terrible necessity. Neither the
roots nor the bark, nor the wild fruits could mediate the misery and total
lack of substantial nourishment which afflicted the population; men died
from necessity in the plazas, streets and roads; a great number went into
the forests searching for something to eat, and they never returned from
there, because they fell exhausted in the countryside, and gave up life in
● complete feebleness. (Molina Solis 1896:514–515)

A specific tree was used for subsistence in times of need, which indicates that famine was recurrent and that the Maya fled to the forests in search of food as well as in search of refuge in time of warfare.

Returning to the sequence of population data we note a further population loss, to a total of between 400 and 500 inhabitants by 1606. This constitutes a depopulation of between 50 and 65 percent in less than sixty years. By 1605 the major administrative efforts toward civil congregation had taken place (Cline 1949). It is thus apparent that, unless a higher mortality is assumed, in addition to very small populations being congregated there, Pencuyut had not been augmented by civil congregation in 1606. In our series the next figure occurs in 1794 and gives a total of 1,629 inhabitants. During the years between 1606 and 1794 seven famines were recorded (1628, 1648, 1651, 1692, 1725–1727, 1765, and 1769–1770) in Yucatán (González Navarro 1970; Molina Hübbe 1941), but we have no evidence concerning their severity or, more specifically, their effects on Pencuyut. Mortality certainly increased at these times, not only because of starvation but also because of lowered resistance to infectious and parasitic diseases. Fertility may also have decreased. There had been several rebellions, the bloodiest in 1761, but these various insurrections appear to have been localized, without affecting Pencuyut. Additional ethnohistorical research could yield data on disturbances directly affecting the Tekax area. The lack of such data does not deny their existence.

In an attempt to identify the variables responsible for the observed population increase during the interval 1606–1794, alternative sets of assumptions will be examined with regard to our knowledge of Pencuyut during these years. Of course, the ultimate objective is to attempt an estimate of net migration and derive a rate of migration which corresponds to the situation which, to the best of our knowledge, prevailed. The assumptions used compare what actually happened, in terms of growth, with a statistical procedure which uses known rates of natural increase for the 1606–1794 interval and calculate expected growth. Both of these results are then compared with findings based upon assumptions concerning observed crude birth and death rates, given a constant rate of growth. Each method accepts the population figures for 1606 and 1794 because those figures are consistent with census populations preceding and following them. Each method also assumes that a constant rate of growth prevailed during the interval. Barclay cautions against assuming constant growth rates over long intervals, because the longer the interval, the less realistic the assumption (1958). Barclay's argument is conceded and, in fact, strengthened by our knowledge of the seven famines. However, we have no evidence to help adjust the rate of change according to different postulated mortality conditions of periodic nature and unknown duration.

To determine what actually happened in Pencuyut, we take the difference between the two census figures ($P_2 - P_1$), which represents the amount of growth; the ratio between the two figures $\dfrac{P_2}{P_1}$ measures their relative

size. This ratio may be computed as a percentage also $(\dfrac{P_2}{P_1} - 1) \times 100$.

The population of Pencuyut in 1606 will be taken as 450, the mean of the two estimates cited above, and as 1,629 in 1794. This represents a growth of 262 percent in 188 years, which is equal to a constant yearly growth rate of 6.9 persons per thousand total population. These calculations do not give any hint concerning birth or death rates or migration levels, however.

Several statistical methods exist for calculating the crude rate of natural increase, using the data from 1830 to 1831 and from 1901 to 1970 to derive the rate for 1606 to 1794. The method selected is the "average rate of change," chosen because it assumes a constant growth rate. This method yields a crude rate of natural increase of 13.5 per thousand (table 6-3). Assuming a constant rate of growth and no net migration, Pencuyut would have had a population of 5,599[13] in 1794. If the crude rate of natural increase had been 13.5 per thousand over the entire interval, which is not very probable, the annual rate of emigration from Pencuyut would have been 6.6 per thousand, a rate almost equal to the actual observed rate of increase (6.9 per thousand).

Alternatively, let us assume that fertility between 1606 and 1794, measured by the crude birth rate, was high, although not unusually high. A rate of 45.0 per thousand will be assumed, a rate falling between the 1830–1831 and the 1901–1970 levels. The high level of fertility is assumed

Table 6-3

Crude rates of natural increase, Pencuyut, 1606–1794, 1830–1831, and 1901–1970

	Mid-interval year	Interval years	CRNI
X_1	1935		21.1
		105	
X_2	1830		17.3
		130	
X_3	1700		(13.5)

Note: The following equation was used to calculate the estimated crude rate of natural increase for 1606–1794:

$X_3 = X_2 \cdot (1+r)$ $t23/t12$ where $(1+r) = \dfrac{X_2}{X_1}$; r=rate; t=time

because the population under consideration is a noncontracepting population with documented high fertility. In fact, a crude birth rate of 45.0 is not only reasonable but also conservative, since in five of the seven decades between 1901 and 1970 the crude rates were higher than 45.0 and the average for the entire period was 46.0 per thousand (see table 6-4).

Let us further assume that mortality, measured by the crude death rate, was 35.0 per thousand. This crude death rate is higher than the 1830–1831 and 1901–1970 levels and is higher than the crude death rate during any decade in the latter interval, except that which prevailed during the Revolution (see table 6-4). The crude death rate is assumed to be high as a conservative measure to yield a low estimate for the crude rate of natural increase. In fact, a crude rate of 35.0 per thousand is consonant with the rates experienced in Pencuyut between 1901 and 1930, before imported public health programs affected the level of mortality. During those thirty years the crude death rate averaged 35.4 per thousand. Other evidence which supports the level of the rate assumed comes from Mexican data. Between 1893 and 1908 the Mexican rates fluctuated between 31.0 and 39.9 and averaged 34.0 per thousand (México, Dirección General de Estadística 1939). Therefore, the conservative estimates of crude birth and death rates used to derive a crude rate of natural increase of 10.0 per thousand also fit the most probable conditions of fertility and mortality during the period being considered. This rate of natural increase is 53 percent lower than the 1901–1970 rate, almost identical to the low rate which prevailed from 1901 to 1930, but 31 percent higher than the observed rate of 6.9 per thousand. If the estimated crude rate of 10.0 per thousand had prevailed, and assuming a constant rate of growth in a closed population, in 1794 Pencuyut would have had 2,922 inhabitants instead of 1,629. There would have been a positive net migration rate of 3.1 per thousand, a very significant rate, almost half as large as the observed rate of natural increase. If Arriaga's assessment of Latin America before the 1930's is accurate (1970) and can be projected back to the early period under consideration, his moderate population growth rate of between 11.0 and 13.0 per thousand is close to both the rate of 13.5 derived by standard statistical procedures and my own calculation of 10.0 per thousand. It should be noted here, however, that we are dealing with a primarily indigenous population, and the Latin American rates may not be entirely appropriate for comparison.

It is clear that Pencuyut did not grow at even the moderate rates suggested as alternatives to the observed rate, at least for any extended period. In fact, it is probable that growth rates were variable, depending primarily on the level of mortality and migration. The value of estimating the rate of increase that one could reasonably expect is found precisely in the comparison of observed and expected behavior. The differences require a careful consideration of the variables which could affect the rates. In this example the crude death rate almost certainly fluctuated around the observed rates for Pencuyut and for Mexico during the late nineteenth and early twentieth centuries, that is, around 34.0 to 35.0 per thousand. Therefore, if either the statistical method of extrapolation or the method based upon assumptions concerning known crude rates and postulated conditions approximates reality, migration played a significant role in the demographic history of Pencuyut between 1606 and 1794.

By 1828 Pencuyut had increased in population to 2,186—2,421 including the ranchos within its registrational jurisdiction—an increase of between 34 and 49 percent (depending upon the base population) within thirty-four years. The latter percent increase is almost identical to that observed between 1606 and 1794. Moreover, this increase parallels the increase experienced by the Borderlands during this period. Between 1794 and 1828 famine and epidemics extracted a heavy mortality toll across the peninsula. Famines due to drought were recorded in 1805 and 1809, and excessive rains brought the same result in 1807, 1817, and 1827. In 1826 an estimated 49,000 persons were killed by smallpox (González Navarro 1970; Molina Hübbe 1941). We have no mortality figures specific to Pencuyut.

In 1846 the population numbered between 2,000 and 2,075. Mortality between 1828 and 1846 was again heavy, with the causes including civil war and a cholera epidemic (52,000 cholera victims) in 1832, famine in 1834–1835, and excessive rains and starvation in 1837 and 1846, sandwiched around another civil war in 1843 (González Navarro 1970; Molina Hübbe 1941). The most probable single cause for the loss of population in Pencuyut between 1828 and 1846 was the increasing incorporation of pueblo Indians into the ranks of peons on the sugar haciendas (González Navarro 1970:173).

The Caste War, which was a peasant rebellion to regain alienated land rather than a race war, had complex antecedents. Nevertheless, the social, political, religious, and economic causes which are outlined by students of the Caste War have a common denominator which should be explicitly recognized: the exploitation of the lower class. The most important cause, however, was the rapid and intensifying loss of productive lands in the Borderlands and East Colonial sections due to the expansion of sugar cultivation.[14]

The Caste War broke out in 1847, and at first glance the decrease to 242 inhabitants recorded in 1851 does not appear to require much explanation. It has generally been accepted that the Caste War was responsible for a tremendous mortality, especially in the east and south centering around Valladolid/Tihosuco and Tekax/Peto. In fact, we have no reason to question the assumption of heavy mortality. The question revolves around quantifying "heavy." González Navarro, relying on previous investigators and census data, has arrived at a figure of 64,904 as the total number of deaths and emigrants attributable to the Caste War (1970:173). He recognized Tekax as one of the areas which suffered the greatest population loss. However, González Navarro does not attempt to separate the 64,904 figure into the categories of deaths, emigrants to Belize, Cuba, Guatemala, Honduras, and the rest of Mexico, and the sale of Maya slaves in Cuba. This diminution, based upon the total population of the peninsula (504,635 in 1846 and 439,731 in 1856), is a 13 percent loss. These figures also include a five-year period of rebellion beyond the 1846–1851 period under consideration. In 1846, 27 percent of the peninsula's population was in the district of Tekax, which included the *partidos* of Tekax, Sotuta, Peto, and Bacalar. If we attribute 40 percent of the total mortality between 1846 and 1851 to the district of Tekax (an arbitrary and probably high estimate) and assume that the entire 64,904 diminution was due to mortality (a very high estimate), the population loss for the district still amounts to only 19 percent. It is, of course, difficult to proceed from the total population of the district to the population of one pueblo for purposes of analogy, but the magnitude of loss is so strikingly different that the analogy will be made. Whereas the loss to the district, using assumptions which almost certainly increased mortality (possibly doubling the percent of loss), was calculated at 19 percent, Pencuyut apparently lost 88 percent of its population. It is clear that more than mortality is involved and that migration is the logical explanation.

There is no way to determine how many Pencuyuteños fled into the forests, to the pueblos in the north or west, and to join the rebellious Maya. However, traditionally, at the end of famine or warfare the inhabitants of Pencuyut, as in other pueblos, returned to their homes. This had not happened by 1851 or soon thereafter, or to the present day. Today there are sufficient, open lands to support a population three to four times as large as that found in Pencuyut, using swidden technology and maintaining the present standard of living. The original *ejidos* ("communal lands") granted in 1925 and enlarged in 1945 are ample, according both to the copies of *ejidal* maps in my possession and to discussions with the *comisario ejidal* of Pencuyut. In addition, for a small amount of money or maize per *mecate*, the *milperos* of Pencuyut can (and do) clear milpa in primary scrub forest belonging to ranchos which are interspersed with the *ejidos*. Therefore, we have to examine conditions immediately before and after the heaviest fighting of the Caste War to account for the observed population decline. Caution must be observed, of course, when "the end" of the Caste War is considered. For example, in 1857 the eastern Maya attacked Tekax and killed an estimated one thousand inhabitants, and in 1884 large garrisons of Mexican and Yucatecan soldiers were still maintained in Tekax and Valladolid to protect both the cities and rural areas (González Navarro 1970; Reed 1964).

Prior to 1847 sugar cane was the largest and most important commercial crop in Yucatán, although a distant second in importance when compared with maize cultivation. In 1844 almost 95 percent of all cultivated land (6,000,159 of a possible 6,330,478 *mecates*) was in maize, while almost

2 percent was in sugar cane. Henequen, tobacco, cotton, rice, and beans accounted for nearly 3 percent. On the eve of the Caste War, Tekax, it will be recalled, had become an economic center of the southeast, dependent primarily on sugar cane. A large number of ranchos, 705, were recorded in the district, the majority being owned by *cañeros*. The sugar cane was fabricated into sugar and *aguardiente* for local sale and consumption, as well as for export. From the 1840's through the 1880's, Tekax produced from one-third to more than one-half of the sugar cane grown in Yucatán. After 1858, however, this percentage does not include the new state of Campeche's production. During the initial year of the Caste War all production and cultivation suffered severely. This condition persisted in the sugar zones long after the henequen zone had begun to recover. Between 1847 and 1850 Yucatán changed from an exporter of sugar to an importer. By 1851 sugar cane cultivation began to increase in Tekax. The significance and seemingly inevitable augmentation of henequen production had already commenced. Thus, despite a tripling of *mecates* of sugar cane under cultivation from 1844 to 1854, sugar cane was displaced by henequen to third in importance after 1850. Henequen continued to increase in importance, not only becoming the principal export of Yucatán but also passing maize in total cultivation, 59 to 36 percent of cultivated land, by 1883 (González Navarro 1970).

Population distribution was affected by state fiscal policy from 1855 through the 1890's by means of eliminating taxes in frontier pueblos to encourage the repopulation of southeastern Yucatán. But changing patterns of social relations and production were also primary determinants of population distribution after the Caste War. An intensification of programs and legislation permitting the appropriation of uncultivated land (*terrenos baldíos*) and the redistribution of communal (*ejido*) lands brought more land and power to the *hacendado* class. Debt servitude increased not only in absolute numbers but also in amount of debt. Cline reports that by 1880 at least 20,767 men had that status and, with their families, totaled more than 100,000 individuals (1950c:550). In Pencuyut the period following the Caste War is today recalled as the time of "slavery." During this period the *partido* of Tekax slowly increased its sugar cane production to a level almost equal to its pre–Caste War production. At the same time henequen became commercially important to the south central region. By 1877 the *partido* of Tekax produced 1,740,000 kilograms of henequen, only 4 percent below the mean production of all *partidos*.

The conclusion of this part of my argument depends upon ethnographic fact and inference. Population redistribution is the only means through which the increased production of sugar cane and henequen could have been achieved in such a short period of time. That is, the primarily pueblo-living agriculturalists of the district had to be redistributed on the haciendas, recently enlarged by the alienation of 20 percent of the entire area of the state of Yucatán. In fact, several informants of present-day Pencuyut, whose births were not registered there, reported their place of birth as San Diego Tekax, a sugar hacienda in the vicinity. If not born in San Diego themselves, they reported that parents or siblings had been. In addition, other informants reported living in San Juan, a local henequen hacienda, where they worked as day laborers (*jornaleros*) or lived in "slavery" (depending on the informant). The interpretation of the population decline of Pencuyut between 1846 and 1851 is that on the order of 20 to 30 percent died from starvation and war-related factors, whereas the remaining 70 to 80 percent were redistributed among either the rebellious Indians (probably a small number), the towns farther north and west (probably 25–50 percent), or the sugar and henequen haciendas (probably the largest percent).

Table 6-4 presents the numbers of births and deaths per year and the crude rates for Pencuyut in ten–year intervals, from 1901 to 1970, in order to facilitate the reader's evaluation of the discussion and to permit alternative conclusions. However, emphasis must be placed on the fact that the numbers involved are small, cover a long time period, and should be considered as showing trends rather than absolute values or rates upon which all arguments rest.

Relatively constant numbers of births were recorded during each ten-year interval in a population whose crude birth rate appeared to be rising. The crude birth rate for 1931–1940 is especially high but not unreasonable in an underdeveloped region where contraception is almost

Table 6-4

Births, deaths, and crude rates, Pencuyut 1901–1970

	1901–1910	*1911–1920*
Mid-interval population	541.0	507.0
Births/year	22.3	23.6
Deaths/year	17.9	20.0
Natural increase/year	4.4	3.6
Crude birth rate	41.2	46.5
Crude death rate	33.1	39.4
Crude rate of natural increase	8.1	7.1

universally unused. If this rate actually prevailed, such factors as the age structure and mortality decline (discussed below) could be partially responsible. However, the crude birth rate for Yucatán during this interval averaged 42.4, while for Mexico the rate was 43.5 per thousand. Another explanation could be that the population of Pencuyut was underenumerated in 1930, producing a higher rate for the interval than actually occurred.

The crude death rate was consistently high between 1901 and 1930. Then, paralleling the absolute reduction of annual deaths, it fell precipitously between 1930 and 1960 and possibly again during the 1961–1970 interval. The factors involved have been dealt with in considerable detail (Arriaga 1970; Arriaga and Davis 1969; Davis 1956; Stolnitz 1965) and will be treated only briefly here. Comparable Mexican rates for 1901–1910 and 1922–1930 were 32.7 and 25.8 per thousand, respectively. No data for 1911 to 1921 are available because of the Revolution. For Yucatán the available data indicate a crude death rate of 33.0 for 1928 to 1930 (México, Dirección General de Estadística 1941). Taken together, the rates for Pencuyut, Yucatán, and Mexico appear consistent.

Although the crude death rate increased during 1910 to 1921, the crude birth rate did not decrease, as would be expected during times of warfare. However, in opposition to Mexico as a whole, whose population decreased 5.5 percent (15,160,369 in 1910 to 14,334,780 in 1921), Yucatán increased in population by 5.2 percent (339,613 in 1910 to 358,221 in 1921). It is clear that the effects of the Revolution were not felt in the same

1921–1930	*1931–1940*	*1941–1950*	*1951–1960*	*1961–1970*
461.0	481.0	515.0	507.0	552.0
21.7	26.4	22.4	23.2	26.1
15.5	11.0	10.5	9.8	5.0
6.2	15.4	11.9	13.4	21.1
47.1	54.9	43.5	45.8	47.3
33.6	22.9	20.4	19.3	9.1
13.5	32.0	23.1	26.5	38.2

Notes:

The 1921 census was used for the 1920 population.

The mid-interval population is Steggerda's (1941) population for 1935, which very closely approximates a mid-interval calculation derived from the 1930 and 1940 censuses.

magnitude in Yucatán as in the southern escarpment, central plateau, and north. It is probable that the increase in the Pencuyut crude death rate was distributed throughout the age and sex categories. In fact, infant mortality (under one year) was lower between 1911 and 1920 than between 1901 and 1910. Furthermore, more female than male deaths were recorded in Pencuyut during the Revolution, although the major registered causes of death did not vary significantly from either the preceding or succeeding intervals. Restraint in drawing conclusions from these data is cautioned, however, since no physician was involved in the determination of cause of death. Moreover, additional males fighting in the Revolution could have been killed and their deaths not recorded in Pencuyut. The population of Pencuyut declined during the succeeding interval (1921–1930), but we have no evidence to indicate that mortality was more responsible than migration. In fact, the opposite is indicated by the positive crude rate of natural increase (see discussion below). The internal consistency between crude birth and death rates and the population increase and decrease for Yucatán, Pencuyut, and Mexico lends support to the reliability and accuracy of the Pencuyut records.

The sudden, rapid decline in the crude death rate in Pencuyut coincides not only with a sharp decline in Yucatán and Mexico but also with the unprecedented decline, unaccompanied by substantial economic development, throughout Latin America. There was far greater economic development in Mexico as a country than in Pencuyut, whose economy remained at a subsistence level. Mexican economic development was uneven and has benefited the upper and middle classes almost to the exclusion of the lower class. The explanation for the decline is not difficult. Lowered mortality was dependent almost entirely upon imported public health programs. Of primary importance to Pencuyut were programs for the eradication of malaria and mass vaccinations, neither of which required the education of the masses. To a lesser degree, greater availability of medicine and medical facilities made their contributions, as did the increasing knowledge of their utility on the part of Pencuyuteños. Improved knowledge of sanitary and hygienic precautions still lags, although probably because of the living conditions per se as much as the ignorance. The decline of mortality was not compensated for by a drop in fertility, as indicated by increasing crude birth rates. In fact, for Latin America, the constant or slightly increasing crude birth rates have masked the fact that the actual trend has been an increase in the number of children per female in the fertile ages (Arriaga 1970), while the expected reduction in fertility due to the effects of mortality decline on the age structure (a decreasing proportion in the reproductive ages) never occurred. Therefore, the rapidly expanding populations found today are structurally explainable almost entirely in terms of declining mortality.[15]

The following statistics again demonstrate the consistency between the data for Pencuyut, Yucatán, and Mexico. Between 1931 and 1960 the crude death rates for Pencuyut ranged between 19.3 and 22.9 per thousand. In Yucatán the range was greater, 13.0 to 26.0, for the three ten-year intervals, but the overall mean was 21.6 compared to 20.9 per thousand for Pencuyut. The Yucatecan crude death rate was divided into urban and rural for a number of years, with a lower rural rate averaging 16.9 per thousand for the thirty years. Arriaga (1967) has determined that this result, with regard to developing countries, is not due either to differential rural-urban age structure or to rural deaths being registered as urban. The principal cause is attributed to rural underregistration of deaths. For Mexico the mean of the yearly averages was 19.2 per thousand. The apparent conclusion to be drawn from this evidence is that the Pencuyut records were maintained within a reasonable degree of completeness.

Infant mortality declined from 166.9 per thousand in 1901–1935 to 106.6 per thousand in 1936–1970 in Pencuyut. Such a decline would be expected, especially if the overall mortality decline were attributed to improved medical programs. The infant mortality rate for Yucatán between 1936 and 1969 was 86.7 per thousand, compared with 94.6 for Mexico between 1936 and 1967. These data are consistent with the crude death rates, Pencuyut experiencing both higher infant and general mortality than either Yucatán or Mexico, as would be expected considering their superior economic and medical conditions. Male infant mortality is higher than female infant mortality in both the 1901–1935 (92.2 vs. 74.4 per thousand) and the 1936–1970 (59.7 vs. 46.8 per thousand) intervals.

The crude death rate for 1961–1970 in Pencuyut declined sharply to 9.1 per thousand. The small numbers involved do not permit generalization, although the previously experienced mortality decline would have affected the age structure in a manner favorable to low crude death rates. By comparison, the crude death rate for Yucatán between 1961 and 1969 was 9.8 and for Mexico from 1961 to 1967, 9.9 per thousand.

Table 6-4 gives rates of natural increase for Pencuyut by ten-year intervals. Rates of migration were estimated by analyzing population trends over long intervals through the use of crude rates of natural increase derived in table 6-4. However, since we have annual numbers of births and deaths for each year between 1901 and 1970, a different method can be used to calculate migration rates. This method, expressed by the equation $P_2 = P_1 + B - D$, is simple, straightforward, and uses data in which I have confidence. An interval with known population size at two dates is necessary. The population at the end of the interval is compared with the population which is calculated by adding the difference between the total number of births and deaths which occurred during that interval to the population at the beginning of the interval. Any difference between the observed and expected population is due to migration. Table 6-5 gives the estimated rates of migration calculated for Pencuyut by this method. The alternative method, using the rate of natural increase, was also used to calculate migration rates for the same intervals. The results were very similar. However, the former method gave more consistent and somewhat smaller average rates of migration (20.5 vs. 21.8 per thousand over the seventy-year period) and is, therefore, preferable for this discussion.

The most obvious point to be drawn from table 6-5 is that a continuous and consistently high rate of net migration from Pencuyut has occurred since 1901. In fact, Pencuyut has lost more inhabitants (723) through out-migration in the past seventy years than the pueblo has recorded in any census since 1846. The fluctuations seen in table 6-5 are explainable in terms of patterns which have been established for Mexico in general. Rural-urban migration has been heavy since 1900. The first three decades of this century show a moderately heavy out-migration, which fits the pattern, with 1921–1930 higher than 1900–1920. Between 1930 and 1940 an extensive program of agrarian reform was carried out, with the consequence that rural-urban migration slowed more rapidly during this decade than during any other decade this century (México, Centro de Estudios Económicos y Demográficos 1970). For Mexico, 1940–1950 showed the highest rural-urban migration of any decade, although the estimated 1960–1970 migration was even higher. Between 1950 and 1960 another slowdown in rural-urban migration occurred, but not as great as that between 1930 and 1940. These generalizations for Mexico absolutely parallel the pattern found in the Pencuyut data.

The explanation for the out-migration during recent years revolves primarily around economic factors, although intrapueblo factionalism has had its role. The data upon which this conclusion is based are derived

Table 6-5

Estimated rates of net annual migration, Pencuyut, 1901–1970

(1) Interval	(2) Population at beginning of interval	(3) Mid-interval population	(4) Population at end of interval
1900–1910	559	541	524
1911–1921	524	507	491
1922–1930	491	461	433
1931–1940	433	481	534
1941–1950	534	515	497
1951–1960	497	507	517
1961–1970	517	525	590

from ethnographic research. Between 1970 and 1972 I observed two young men and their families move to Mérida when they obtained jobs. Another man moved permanently when he obtained a job in Mérida, but his family remained in Pencuyut. A family moved to Akil in order that the man could get permanent wage labor as a mason. Several young men work part-time in Akil, and one of them married an Akileña, and moved to Akil permanently. One young woman went to Mexico City as a domestic. The civil registrar moved to Akil, remarried, and works part-time as a carpenter. Another man moved to Oxkutzcab and started a profitable store there. Two older couples moved to Mérida and Acanceh for reasons of comfort and to be near medical facilities. The previous *comisario municipal* and the civil registrar were both involved in factional disputes, which made their decisions to move an easy task.

These are several of the more familiar and better-investigated cases from recent years. Details change, but additional examples of similar nature were recorded among now departed families, as well as among several families who have now returned. In past years more families emigrated to other pueblos and remained agriculturalists.

Two important facts are established by these data: (1) the primary reason for leaving Pencuyut is economic, and (2) the primary recipient of most emigrants has been Mérida. Mérida is often the ultimate destination, although Tekax, Akil, or Oxkutzcab may become an intermediate place of residence for the emigrants. In this regard, Pencuyut can be demonstrated to be typical of other pueblos in Yucatán by examining census figures for Mérida, the other cities of the state, and for Yucatán as a

(5) *Expected population at end of interval with no net migration* $P_2 = P_1 + B - D$	(6)=(4)−(5) *Estimated net migration*	(7)=(6)/(3) *Rate of net annual migration per 1,000*
607	− 83	15.3
566	− 75	15.3
547	−114	24.7
587	− 43	8.9
653	−156	30.3
631	−114	22.5
728	−138	26.3

Note: Compiled from census and vital statistics data.

whole. Of the eight localities (Izamal, Mérida, Motul, Progreso, Tekax, Ticul, Tizimin, and Valladolid) designated as cities in one or more censuses between 1900 and 1970, the following comparisons can be made:
1.
In 1900 the eight localities constituted 23.1 percent of the population of the state, while Mérida alone accounted for 61 percent of the total.
2.
In 1970 the population of the state had increased 1.4 times, while the seven localities had increased 2.5 times and Mérida had increased 3.9 times.
Mérida has acted like a magnet, siphoning off the population of the hinterland and maintaining a high rate of natural increase.

A different method has been used to calculate trends and rates of rural-urban migration for Mérida, since reliable data over the 1901–1970 period are not available. The method used assumes that Yucatán was a closed population, that is, a population with no net migration. This assumption is justifiable, at least until 1950. The percentage of resident Yucatecans who were born in other Mexican states or foreign countries was very small and remained nearly constant through 1970. A negative net migration occurred between 1930 and 1960, with an increase in absolute numbers between 1950 and 1960, but the percentage of emigrants to total population was still small, especially in comparison with other Mexican states. The magnitude of emigration during the latter decade would have almost no effect on our assumption of a closed population for Yucatán. However, if a sizable proportion of the emigrants had been residents of Mérida, the results of applying methods of natural increase based upon Yucatán, to the population of Mérida, could be significant.

At any rate, with a closed population, the difference between any two census populations is due to natural increase. The census populations of Yucatán were compared, and crude rates of natural increase were calculated by ten-year intervals. These rates were then applied to the census data for Mérida and to the populations of the other seven urban localities taken together as a unit (see table 6-6).

The trends of rural-urban migration for Mérida and for the other seven localities are similar but have somewhat different patterns. These variations are explained in terms of regional and national conditions which had differential effects on Mérida and the other cities. The data for Mérida are examined first. Mérida experienced moderate to high rates of positive net migration between 1900 and 1930. The rates were highest in the first and second decades, in opposition to the pattern experienced in Pencuyut, where the rate of emigration increased in each decade from 1900 to 1930. Between 1931 and 1940 Mérida experienced a period of negative net migration. Throughout Mexico there had been a slowdown in rural-urban migration in this decade, attributed to the vast agrarian reform program being carried out. The lower rate of emigration in Pencuyut for 1931–1940 has been explained in terms of agrarian reform, which would also explain the out-migration experienced in Mérida. The new upsurge in rural-urban migration in Mexico between 1941 and 1950 was mirrored in the positive rate of net migration in Mérida. The proportion of rural-urban migration in Mexico dropped between 1951 and 1960, although absolute numbers remained nearly constant. The rate for Mérida, as calculated from the rate of natural increase for Yucatán, decreased sharply to 1.0 per thousand. Estimates by Mexico's Centro de Estudios Económicos y Demográficos indicate a small, negative net migration (1970:109), equal to a rate of approximately 2.0 per thousand. Despite the change in sign, this difference is not too great, especially considering the greater sensitivity of the Centro's method. In fact, their calculation of net migration for 1930–1940 and my own for 1931–1940 were 4,418 and 4,044 respectively. The difference between our calculations for 1940–1950 (1941–1950) was approximately equal to the difference between our 1950–1960 rates. These data reinforce my confidence in the method selected to analyze migration in Mérida and in the results discussed above.

The data for Izamal, Motul, Progreso, Tekax, Ticul, Tizimin, and Valladolid, taken as a unit, offer several variations to all other cases previously examined. The first interval shows a small net rate of emigration. The explanation, I believe, is that, despite attracting a small stream of rural migrants themselves, these cities lost an even greater number of inhabitants to Mérida. Such an explanation is consistent with the extremely high migration rate experienced by Mérida between 1900 and 1910. In contrast to Mérida, the other seven localities had the greatest rate of positive net migration experienced in any decade during the Revolution. Taking the prevailing social conditions into consideration, I hypothesize that the majority of the emigrants sought safer living conditions in the more protected urban areas of the state. Between 1922 and 1970 these small cities maintained a small and relatively constant positive rate of net migration, in addition to high rates of natural increase. In fact, they grew more rapidly, on the whole, than did Mérida between 1951 and 1970.

Figure 6-2 clearly demonstrates the significance of migration for population distribution in Yucatán. During 1900–1930 the cities show a clear and consistent pattern of growth, whereas rural Yucatán grew much more slowly and actually suffered a loss of population between 1910 and 1921. This figure also shows the tremendous increase in population, rural and urban, from 1940 to 1970, as a result of greatly reduced mortality and continued high fertility.

In summary, this section demonstrates clearly that migration has been significant in the history of Pencuyut and in the redistribution of population in the entire state of Yucatán. It also demonstrates the consistency of the Pencuyut data with the social, economic, and demographic conditions which prevailed in Yucatán and in Mexico.

Vital Statistics and Reliability

While comparing the results of the two censuses which I conducted (July 1970 and May 1972) with civil registry records, several discrepancies were discovered. The errors were found in the first census and resulted from a lack of knowledge of custom concerning naming of the newborn and registration practices. Two infants were not enumerated because the names of the children were requested in the census and the infants (both less than one week old) had not yet been named. Two elderly residents in two separate households were also missed because questions concerning distant collateral kinsmen had not been asked in one household and non-

Table 6-6

Estimated rates of net annual migration, 1900–1970

(1) Interval	(2) Population at beginning of interval	(3) Population at end of interval	(4) Annual rate of NI per 1,000
Mérida			
1900–1910	43,630	62,447	8.4
1911–1921	62,447	79,225	4.8
1922–1930	79,225	95,015	8.3
1931–1940	95,015	98,852	8.0
1941–1950	98,852	142,858	21.2
1951–1960	142,858	170,834	17.2
1961–1970	170,834	212,097	21.1
Izamal, Motul, Progreso, Tekax, Ticul, Tizimin, and Valladolid			
1900–1910	27,873	29,375	8.4
1911–1921	29,375	41,891	4.8
1922–1930	41,891	45,611	8.3
1931–1940	45,611	50,863	8.0
1941–1950	50,863	63,566	21.2
1951–1960	63,566	76,438	17.2
1961–1970	76,438	97,889	21.1

related residents were not requested in the other. The 1972 census was taken with greater knowledge, experience, and care. The results were compared with genealogies constructed from the civil registry and from the previous census. There were no omissions in the civil registry of either children or adults (if born within the past seventy years) who reported their birthplace as Pencuyut. The census and the civil registry showed 100 percent comparability between birth and death registration of spouses and children reported to have been born and to have died in Pencuyut within the past seventy years.

In addition, the census elicited data on stillbirths and spontaneous abortions. The majority of the stillbirths reported had been recorded, although admittedly several were missed. This form of omission, however, is common in even the most sophisticated and complete registration systems. The collected data are from 132 women aged fifteen to forty-nine, for whom birth and marriage dates are known and fertility histories are

(5) Expected population at end of interval (no net migration)	(6)=(3)−(5) Estimated net migration	(7)=(6)/(2) Rates of net annual migration per 1,000
47,835	14,612	33.5
65,824	13,401	21.5
85,343	9,672	12.2
102,896	− 4,044	− 4.3
121,925	20,983	21.2
169,421	1,413	1.0
210,502	1,595	0.9
30,559	− 1,184	− 4.2
30,964	10,927	37.2
45,126	485	1.2
49,394	1,469	3.2
62,735	831	1.6
75,386	1,052	1.7
94,187	3,702	4.8

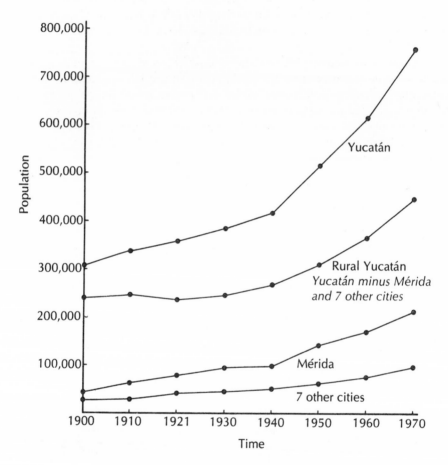

Figure 6-2
Growth curves for Yucatán, rural Yucatán, Mérida,
and the 7 other cities, 1900–1970.

available and who presently reside in Pencuyut. Forty of these women
(30 percent) reported having had a total of 83 spontaneous abortions,
accounting for 13.2 percent of the total pregnancies reported. Seventeen
women (13 percent) reported 21 stillbirths, or 3.3 percent of the total
pregnancies. This amounts to a pregnancy loss of 16.6 percent. However,

the age of these women precludes further analysis, except to note that even larger numbers of stillbirths and spontaneous abortions would have been recorded if women of completed fertility were used. This is clear in that the group aged fifteen to forty-nine averaged 4.8 pregnancies and 3.9 live births, whereas women over 44 averaged 7.1 pregnancies and 5.9 live births.

The registration of births, deaths, and marriages is a very old tradition in Pencuyut, begun with the ecclesiastical records in the sixteenth century and maintained through various state and national systems to this day. The indigenous population of Yucatán has used the present civil registry system since the 1870's, and the records have been maintained in Pencuyut since 1901. The most important reasons for registering births and deaths are compelling. For example, in order to be legally married, a birth certificate from the local civil registry must be presented. More importantly, today mandatory military service (one year) requires a birth certificate. A death must be registered in order to use the cemetery, and it is mandatory to have a burial within one to three days after death. Despite arguments concerning the prevalence of consensual union which would negate the need for a birth certificate (130 of 135 first unions for both spouses of present residents of Pencuyut were legal unions) or that the Maya do not strongly adhere to their formal religious burial practices (such an argument merely overlooks the importance of overt compliance and symbolism), the data have shown that the inhabitants do record their vital events. I believe that 95 percent or more of all births and deaths (except spontaneous abortions) are recorded. This argument is of sufficient complexity to deserve separate treatment in another article.

I believe that the accuracy of the data reported is related to the degree of completeness of the data. Although I have no way to quantify such a proposed correlation, it is certain that if the reported data were found to be accurate, less doubt would be cast upon their completeness. Inaccurate records simply do not inspire confidence. A suggestion was made that I take a one-in-twenty sample census of households and ask the following question: how many births, deaths, and marriages have occurred within your respective families of orientation and your family of procreation within the past five years? This was asked of both the household head and spouse. Then they were requested to furnish (1) the present age of all children born within that interval, (2) the age of the parents at the birth of the first child born within the five-year interval, (3) the age of anyone who died and, if a child, the age of the parents at the time of the child's death, and (4) the age of the newly married husband and wife.

These data were cross-referenced with genealogical files which had birth, death, and marriage dates taken from the civil registry. The results were then compared with what was reported with regard to each age and person in the actual household in which the event occurred, as elicited in the 1972 census. An additional 34 ages or events were reported in the actual census households. There were 124 vital events or ages in the sample. Fifty-six exact ages were given. The sample respondents missed the exact age by only 1.1 years on the average. In the census families 106 exact ages were given, and the mean error was a mere 0.4 years per event. This degree of accuracy indicates a reliable vital registry system in Pencuyut, lending credence to the statistics upon which the preceding analyses have been based.

Conclusions

A number of conclusions have been reached in the analysis of each of the intervals from 1549 to 1970, in the analyses of the vital rates, and in considering the accuracy and reliability of the vital statistics for Pencuyut. A considerable degree of reconstruction has been proposed on the basis of fragmentary data, dealing with birth, death, natural increase, and migration rates, and also with the social and economic conditions which prevailed during the successive intervals. The primary importance of migration in the redistribution of population in Yucatán from pre-Columbian times to the present has been demonstrated through the use of ethnohistoric, demographic, and ethnographic data.

The hypothesis that the primary determinant of migration was technological inequality between groups (Davis 1974) was selected for critical evaluation because it is the best single-factor explanation I have seen. It was rejected in the introduction on the bases of theoretical and empirical inadequacy and will now be examined in light of data specific to Yucatán. Numerous Maya were forced to migrate into the frontiers of Yucatán at the conquest. The conquest, however, was accomplished through the formation of alliances with several of the factional Maya states. The technological superiority of the Spaniards could never have secured them victory without their exploitation of the weaknesses of the Maya. Francisco de Montejo's conquest thus parallels Cortés's methods in his conquest of the Aztecs. Moreover, the Spanish technological superiority was developed through, and in conjunction with, the social relations of production. To use technology as an independent variable rather than to see how it interacts with other variables within a social system is to see social evolution as determined by external variables, to mistake effect for cause (Faris 1975).

This may be seen more clearly if the migration which occurred during the Caste War is examined. Creole domination on the eve of the Caste War, including technological superiority, could do nothing to stem the onslaught of the rebellious Maya. Rebel successes came from their organization of large numbers and the peasants' goal of regaining their lands and removing the bonds of peonage (no overall strategy was possible because of internal conflicts between leaders and geographical groups). Creoles were forced to migrate with mestizos and nonrebellious Maya.

Yucatecan successes in the war resulted less from improving their technological superiority than from internal conflict among the rebels, the failure of the northern and western Maya to revolt (they instead fought for
their exploiters in exchange for promises of reduced taxes, elimination of
debts, honorary titles, and other benefits), and the rebels' return to make
milpa when complete victory was within reach (González Navarro 1970;
Cline 1950b). Other migrations, such as those resulting from famine and
the civil congregations, also resulted from the complete domination of
Creole over Maya.

Much of the more recent rural-urban migration has resulted from the
attraction of superior economic, social, and health conditions achieved in
the cities through the process of modernization. The improved economic
conditions of the numerically small upper and middle classes has come at
the expense of the continued poverty of the numerically large lower class.
This is to be expected, especially in Latin America, where the city had its
origins connected to a position of privilege. The Spanish founded their
regional cities to incorporate the indigenous population into the Spanish
economy, and those same cities today remain instruments of domination
(Frank 1970). In addition,

● . . . the mestizo population, in fact, always lives in a city, a center of an
intercultural region, which acts as a metropolis of a zone of indigenous
population and which maintains with the underdeveloped communities
an intimate relation which links the center with the satellite communities.
(Furthermore) between the mestizos who live in the nuclear city of the
region and the Indians who live in the peasant hinterland there is in reality a closer economic and social interdependence than might at first glance
appear "and that the provincial metropolises" by being centers of intercourse are also centers of exploitation. (Instituto Nacional Indigenista, as
● quoted in Frank 1970:67)

The provincial towns are satellites of the regional cities, which are in turn
satellites of the national metropolis, which in its turn is a satellite to the
international metropolises. "Thus, a whole chain of constellations of
metropolises and satellites relates all parts of the whole system from its
metropolitan center in Europe or the United States to the farthest outpost
in the Latin American countryside" (Frank 1970:7). It is through these
means, a combination of social, political, and economic pressures, rather
than technology per se, that migration has been facilitated and through
which migration should be studied.

The preceding analysis has shown the adaptive or the survival value of
migration under changing conditions through time. But what do the vital
statistics, assumptions, and rates discussed in this article mean to the cur-

rent residents of Pencuyut? Personal observation indicates that towns and villages of sufficient size, usually larger than two thousand inhabitants, or smaller if they happen to lie on direct routes of transportation and communication between larger cities, are the only towns and villages which have paved roads, cheap public transportation, telephone and telegraph facilities, a post office, schools with more than three or four grades and resident teachers, markets and accompanying cheaper prices on most produce, entertainment (movies, regular dances, bars), libraries, purified water, electricity, doctors, dentists and clinics, frequent public health services, and a myriad of other advantages, the most important of which are the combined opportunities in nonagricultural labor. The political importance of the larger towns can never be underestimated; great effort is expended to improve conditions in those towns. There is no desire to deprive the smaller villages of these same advantages. However, it is more costly per person to provide services to small, isolated communities, and it is also difficult to service such communities before improvements are completed in the towns and cities.

The constant out-migration experienced by Pencuyut during the past seventy years and longer has resulted in a loss of political and economic leverage. If Pencuyut were again a pueblo of two thousand inhabitants, as it was before 1847, I believe more of the services and advantages available in other pueblos of similar size would also be available in Pencuyut.

On the other hand, many of those Pencuyuteños who did migrate to Mérida and other towns and cities have benefited from the greater availability of goods and services found there and from increased standards of living resulting from nonagricultural employment. There is a negative aspect to this phenomenon as well, however. Migrants who fall into the category of rural, unskilled labor have been necessary in the industrialization and modernization processes, but they have also created the peripheral slums found in most rapidly expanding cities. They are the residents who require, but only occasionally effectively demand, that huge sums be invested by the city and state in education, housing, electricity, employment, and other basic improvements. Laborers from the country who have found work in the city become alienated rapidly. They are placed in daily contact, on a personal level, with discrimination, prejudice, and uncertainty with regard to dress, custom, and manners. It is precisely this alienation which brings an awareness of the laborers' relation to the workers of the henequen zone. In other words, there are two sides to the coin of rural-urban migration, neither side being entirely positive or entirely negative. The objective, therefore, must be an understanding of the conditions which motivate migration and a policy to maximize the benefits not only for the migrants but, also, for those who choose not to migrate.

Given the data presented here, it would appear that such an enlightened policy would be difficult to formulate and impossible to implement unless continued exploitation of the lower class (peasants and laborers) is recognized as an intrinsic part of the structure of the social system. Anything less than dramatic structural change will enable only scattered improvement in the lower-class standard of living and will increase the differential between the upper and lower classes.

Notes

1.
I wish to thank Prithwis Das Gupta, Kingsley Davis, Grant D. Jones, Edward B. Kurjack, Rosemary Lee, and Sarah Tsai for critical comments and methodological contributions used in the several revisions of this article. Funds in support of various phases of the study upon which this article is based came from the Population Council, Fellowship No. 83.71.033, Wenner-Gren Foundation for Anthropological Research, Grant No. 2739, a National Science Foundation Traineeship, and from The Explorer's Club, and are gratefully acknowledged.
2.
A classic example of the importance of the social relations of production with regard to migration is described by Sahlins (1961), who demonstrates the effectiveness of segmentary lineage organization to expand into territory held by groups which cannot compete with the massing effect enabled by such segmentary organization.
3.
Davis and Blake chose to deal with the institutional framework rather than the underlying mode of production which plays the determinant role in the development of the institutional framework. Mamdani (1972) and Faris (1975) discuss the necessity of viewing decisions concerning fertility with regard to economic conditions which are beyond the control of individuals. My thesis (Ryder n.d.) also deals at length with this problem.
4.
Chheenyuc "literally translates, *well of the goat* (diminutive)" (Pacheco Cruz 1959:247). Contemporary Pencuyuteños recall that their parents referred to Pencuyut as Chenyuc. However, Pacheco Cruz mistranslates *yuc*, both in the quoted passage and in his *Diccionario de la Fauna Yucateca* (1958:312), mistaking the small species of deer, common to Yucatán, for the wild goat principally found south of the Puuc and farther east. The correct translation of *yuc* is "deer" (diminutive) or "small deer" (Swadesh, Alvarez, and Bastarrachea 1970:94), thus making *Chenyuc*, "well of the deer" (diminutive) or "well of the small deer."
5.
A detailed description and analysis of seventeenth-century Yucatán is available in Hunt (1974). Other important references include Cline (1950*a,b,c*), González Navarro (1970), Lee (n.d.), Raymond (1971), and Redfield and Villa Rojas (1934).

6.

The evolution of capitalistic units of production in Yucatán is a complex problem. The following sources are recommended, although many others could supplement them: Strickon (1965), Raymond (1971), González Navarro (1970), and Lee (n.d.). In addition, Wolf and Mintz (1957) and, especially, Kay (1974) are recommended. Cline (1950c) is recommended for a detailed discussion of the development of sugar in Yucatán.

7.

Hunt describes the relations among *encomenderos*, the church, bureaucratic officials, and the ethnic components of the population of the peninsula, including an analysis of the increasing influence of Spanish and Yucatecan institutions and exploitation on the indigenous population (1974).

8.

Several references deal specifically with Yucatán and clarify the confusion which Goldkind introduces (Redfield 1938; Raymond 1971; Lee n.d.).

9.

Although the point is not elaborated, Raymond comments that the size of towns affects their access to resources (1974).

10.

The following populations have crude birth rates of 40.0 or above and are considered reliable, although several of the calculations are based upon small samples: Eskimo, 46.5; Hutterite, 45.9; Puerto Rico, 40; Tepoztlan, 41.3; Korea, 45.8; North Chinese, 40.1; Sinhalese, 40.1; Taiwan, 45.3; and Tikopia, 43.0 (Nag 1962:174). Miro also lists the countries of Latin America whose crude birth rates are in the 40's in fifteen of twenty countries for which she presents statistics (1964:35, 39). The majority of these Latin countries have crude death rates significantly below those of Pencuyut, but seven countries had comparable rates between 1945 and 1950, and three still had comparable rates between 1955 and 1960.

11.

See González Navarro concerning the depopulation of the eastern and southern frontiers during the Caste War (1970).

12.

See Redfield and Villa Rojas concerning the relationship between population pressure and factionalism as they affected the foundation of Chan Kom (1934).

13.

This and succeeding calculations of population increase, based upon a known rate of natural increase and known interval, are derived from the following equation:

$$\frac{P_2}{P_1} = (1+r)^n$$

P_2 = population at end of interval
P_1 = population at beginning of interval
n = interval
r = rate of increase

14.

In addition to the articles in this volume, important references include Cline (1950c), González Navarro (1970), and Lee (n.d.). To deal with the analysis presented here, but in more depth, it is necessary to include Ryder (n.d.).

15.

The underlying causes of these structural features are dealt with in Mamdani (1972) and Faris (1975). Simply stated, the position of these authors is that rapidly expanding populations are not the primary contradiction to be resolved, but, rather, production for exchange rather than for consumption is the most significant issue. Rapidly expanding populations will not take care of themselves, but without radical structural changes in the capitalistic-dominated world economic system, it is impossible for increased production (such as has occurred in China) to be distributed equitably, eliminating poverty and far outdistancing population growth (which has also occurred in China).

7

The <u>Maestros Cantores</u> in Yucatán

Anne C. Collins

The Caste War of 1847–1853 and its aftermath encompass one of the most turbulent periods in Yucatán's history. An aspect of this conflict, which has always held particular interest for the anthropologist, concerns the emergence and subsequent importance of the Talking Cross cult among one of the rebel Indian groups, the Chan Santa Cruz *cacicazgo* of Quintana Roo. Serving initially as a rallying device for the Maya during a period of serious military setbacks, the Talking Cross soon came to occupy a position of primary importance as the central organizing element of Chan Santa Cruz society. Around the miraculous cross, and often in response to its direct commands, a strong politico-religious organization was developed and elaborated, with the *patrón* of the cross becoming the supreme authority in not only religious but political and military matters as well. Serving as the first and most important of a three-man inter-mediary group (the other two were an interpreter, or organ, of the cross and a secretary), the *patrón* received and interpreted the will of God as conveyed by the cross and implemented supernatural decisions and com-mands bearing on the current political and military maneuvers of the rebel Maya group (Reed 1964; Villa Rojas 1945).

Although including a number of essentially non-Christian ideas, the new cult nevertheless retained many of the organizational aspects of village Catholicism as introduced by the early Spanish missionaries and practiced by the Maya throughout the colonial period. Catholic rituals, for example, continued to be favored, and compulsory attendance at mass, a carry-over from colonial days, was still required of all the cult's mem-bers. Yet the Maya now found themselves in a position quite different from any which had existed during the colonial period: they no longer had access to that most essential of all Catholic functionaries, the ladino priest.[1] The Mayas' response to this situation is hardly surprising: selected members of their own group began to take over the responsibility of say-ing masses, novenas, and rosaries and performing other ritual duties formerly associated with the ladino priesthood. José María Rosado, who spent nine months as a captive in Chan Santa Cruz in 1858, gives a first-hand description of the activities of one of these early native priests: "A large Church was being built by the prisoners taken from the towns raided from time to time . . . An old Indian called Tata Naz (Nazareo) was in charge and as a priest (under the control of the Tatich) he led the prayers and rosary. . . . All Baptisms and marriages are performed by Tata Naz, the former to infants using the prescribed words and pouring water on the head, the latter simply saying in Maya 'Yo te case [*sic*] en el nombre de la Santa Cruz Amen' " (1931).

Another account from the same general time period describes the functions of these native religious specialists in the *cacicazgo* of Icaiche (to the southwest of Chan Santa Cruz):

● It may not unnaturally occur to ask how have these Indians managed to carry on so long without a pastor. There exist among them a class of men whom they designate *Maestros* on whom fall all the duties which necessitate a Book and who between them divide the various novenas and public services which may require a leader. These *maestros* are not backward, but conduct service for the people in their own simple way—perform all the ceremonies of the Holy Week and of "Fiestas mayores."

Nay some are bold enough to administer baptism . . . instead of adhering to the prescribed form they have, for greater solemnity, added prayers and ceremonies of their own rubric to the detriment of the legitimate
● sacramental form. (Molina 1889:277)

This account constitutes the earliest mention in the literature known to me of the specific title (i.e., *maestro*) of these native religious specialists. Their continuation into the present day is well attested among the descendants of the rebel Maya where, with their duties and responsibilities largely unchanged, they are known as *maestros cantores*. (See, e.g., Redfield and Villa Rojas 1934:73, 367; and Villa Rojas 1945:73 for an account of the *maestros cantores* as they function in modern Maya society.)

The fact that the *maestros* are referred to only by their Spanish titles, coupled with the Catholic-derived nature of their religious duties, has led some researchers (e.g., Redfield and Villa Rojas 1934) to suggest a colonial period origin for these native functionaries, particularly since *maestros* of various types, including *maestros cantores*, are known to have been introduced by the early Franciscan missionaries. These colonial period *maestros* are generally described in the literature as "lay assistants to the priests" and their special training in church doctrine and ritual is seen as making them the most likely prototypes of the present-day *maestros cantores*, who likewise must be familiar with church ritual and proficient in the recitation of Catholic prayers and chants. Beyond this, little inquiry has been made into either the origins of this group of native religious assistants or into their subsequent role in colonial society. What were the duties of the *maestro cantor* as a "lay assistant"? How was he trained? What was his status within the local community? An inquiry into these and other points is best approached through a brief review of historical events, particularly those related to the spiritual conquest of Yucatán and to the methods of conversion utilized by the early Catholic missionaries.

The Spiritual Conquest of Yucatán

The account of the spiritual conquest of Yucatán is largely an account of the Franciscan order. Franciscan friars were the first to begin mission work on the peninsula, and, while many of their missions were eventually taken over by the secular clergy (a pattern which can be observed throughout Mesoamerica), they were almost everywhere responsible for the initial conversion and baptism of the Indians and for their education in the basic tenets of the Catholic faith. The early Franciscans' efforts were, by all accounts, quite successful, and the crown soon rewarded them with exclusive rights to the Christianization of the peninsula.

The first Franciscan mission had been established on the western coast of Yucatán, at Champoton, perhaps as early as 1535.[2] This mission, however, was a short-lived one, its failure owing not so much to the unreceptivity of the Indians as to the untimely arrival of Spanish land troops involved in Francisco de Montejo's third *entrada* into the peninsula (Chamberlain 1948:312–313). The friars, who had promised the Indians that no Spaniards other than themselves would enter the area, suddenly found themselves in an untenable position; and, seeing that further efforts under the circumstances would be fruitless, they abandoned the mission and returned to New Spain.

A second attempt to missionize was not made until 1545 when, the worst of the fighting over, Yucatán was settling down into an uneasy peace. In that year two groups of friars[3] arrived at Campeche, a town which had been founded and abandoned during the second phase of the conquest and which was now being resettled by thirty *conquistadores* (Cárdenas Valencia 1937:89). Here the eight friars established a base mission from which they began an expansion into the surrounding countryside. Again, there does not appear to have been much initial resistance to their efforts and, according to López [de] Cogolludo, within eight months of their arrival the Franciscans had succeeded in baptizing over twenty thousand adults in the region of Campeche (1957:256). In addition, a church had been built and a school founded where the Indian children could be taught to read, write, and sing and, most importantly, to recite the Catholic prayers.

Meanwhile, some of the friars had moved inland to Mérida, Montejo's newly established capital city, where they began similar conversion efforts. At Mérida the first clear outlines of a well-tested operational pattern begin to emerge, a pattern characteristic of early Catholic missionary activity throughout the densely populated regions of Mesoamerica. With such vast numbers of souls to save but so few to attend to the actual work at hand, the missionaries were forced to devise a conversion plan which would produce exponential returns in terms of man-hours of missionary activity. This plan, in Yucatán, involved two main components: the *caciques* and the *maestros,* each of crucial importance at a particular stage of the conversion process.

Initial conversions in a new area were sought (and, more often than not, obtained) among the native nobility.[4] These influential men, by their example, were then instrumental in attracting their subjects to the new religion. Most of the mass baptisms referred to in the early Franciscan chronicles were undoubtedly made possible by this type of cooperation on the part of the native lords. The Franciscans realized, of course, that some type of systematic follow-up work was required if the new gains were to be consolidated, and to this end they promoted the *maestros* to a position of central importance. The *maestros* were sons of native lords who had received special instruction in the Franciscan schools. After a period of study in which they learned reading and writing and, especially, Catholic doctrine and ritual, they were sent back to their native towns (or sometimes to other villages in the hinterland) where they were expected to set up schools of their own and to promote the acceptance of Christianity and the observation of Catholic ritual by their teaching and example (Lizana 1893:50–51; Scholes and Adams 1938:I, xx). Thus, from the beginning the *maestros* constituted an extremely vital link in the Franciscan organization, serving more often than not as the only official representatives of Christianity in their local communities.

In 1547, with their work at Campeche and Mérida well under way, the friars undertook to establish a third mission, this time at Mani. Mani was the home territory of the Xiu, Montejo's oldest and staunchest allies; it was also the site of Montejo's hereditary grant; and these facts undoubtedly influenced the friars in their selection of a suitable location for their first mission in a non-Spanish town.

Two Franciscans, Fray Luis de Villalpando—a fluent Maya speaker by this time—and Fray Melchor de Benavente, were entrusted with the early missionary activity at Mani. At first their work proceeded as smoothly as before: the initial reception was warm and the natives set about erecting a convent, a church, and a school for the friars' use. Then, prebaptismal instruction was begun, and the Indians received the unwelcome news that becoming a Christian involved giving up their slaves. This unpopular condition met with considerable resistance. A conspiracy to kill the missionaries was hatched and uncovered; and twenty-seven of the instigators were identified and carried off to Mérida for trial. There they were sentenced to death by fire, the harshest measures taken so far in the conversion campaign and extremely effective, as no doubt they were intended to be, in impressing upon the Indians the seriousness with which the civil authorities viewed such resistance to the friars. However, Montejo, most certainly fearing the consequences of mass executions in a newly pacified and still hostile country, secretly conspired with Villalpando to release the prisoners in response to a public plea by the friar on the day of the executions. This plan was carried out and achieved its desired results—a potential uprising was avoided and the friars' prestige among the natives enjoyed a considerable increase (Chamberlain 1948:316–317).

After this temporary setback it does not appear that the friars were further impeded in their territorial expansion (at least within the well-controlled northwestern sector of the peninsula) by overtly hostile native activities. Rather, from this point on a more serious limitation to their expansion became the shortage of missionary personnel. As early as 1547 Friar Nicholas de Albalate had been sent to Spain to recruit additional Franciscans, and in late 1548, while Villalpando and Benavente were consolidating their triumph in Mani, he returned to Yucatán with six or seven friars, among them Diego de Landa.[5]

These new additions were temporarily divided up between the existing missions (at Campeche, Mérida, and Mani), while plans were laid for the establishment of two new missions at Izamal and Conkal. López [de] Cogolludo indicates that these two missions were in existence by 1549 (1957:269), whereas Lizana places the founding date somewhat later, in 1552 (1893:61). In any event, after these new missions were in operation, still further expansion began to be contemplated, and twice during the 1550's Friar Lorenzo de Bienvenida was sent to Spain to recruit the personnel necessary to make such plans a reality. On his first trip Bienvenida was given permission to recruit fifteen Franciscans; however, the exact number which he actually brought with him on his return to Yucatán is not known (Scholes and Adams 1938:I, xiii n.). These Franciscans arrived in 1553 and were followed in 1561 by ten more friars, recruited by Bienvenida on his second trip to Spain.

With the influx of additional personnel, the Franciscans now began to expand more rapidly into new territory. In their first twenty years of missionary activity (1535–1555), the friars had only been able to staff six base missions (the latest one being Valladolid, founded in 1553). Now in a period of only eight years they managed to double this number: by 1563 six missions (those mentioned above) had convents erected; two new missions at Homun and Calkini had building programs under way; and the remaining four, probably located at Sotuta, Motul, Dzidzantun, and Tizimin (Scholes and Adams 1938:I, xiv), were still operating out of "ranchos de pajo" (Scholes and Adams 1938:I, doc. 32).

Expansion continued at this rate over the next twenty years or so, and by 1582 twenty-two Franciscan missions existed in Yucatán, each serving a major town and its outlying area. Table 7-1 lists these missions, the approximate number of friars working out of each one, and the number of outlying towns under their jurisdiction.

In many respects this period represents the apogee of Franciscan influence in Yucatán. Up until this time the friars had faced little competition

Table 7-1

Franciscan missions, 1582

Mission seat*	Approximate number of friars**	Number of towns served
Calkini	3	13
Campeche	3	11
Chancenote		8
Conkal	3	6
Dzidzantun	3	8
Hecelchakan	1	4
Hocaba	2	8
Homun	2	6
Hunucma	2	3
Ichmul	2	7
Izamal	4	15
Mani	4	10
Mérida	13	12
Motul	3	7
Oxkutzcab	2	4
Sotuta		9
Tekanto	2	7
Tekax	2	2
Tinum	2	5
Tixkokob	1	5
Tizimin	4	22
Valladolid	4	14
Total/22 missions:	62+	186

*Information on the sites of Franciscan missions and the number of towns which they served in 1582 in found in Scholes et al. 1936–1938:II, doc. 29.
**Information on the number of friars serving each mission is taken from the Ponce *relación* of 1588 (Noyes 1932). Between 1582 and 1588 Chancenote and Sotuta had become secular parishes and thus did not figure in his account.

from the secular clergy and even less from other regular orders. Secular priests had of course been present in Yucatán since the conquest, but their activities had been largely confined to towns with predominantly Spanish populations. Thus, in 1582, secular parishes existed only in Mérida, Campeche, Valladolid, and Bacalar, all Spanish towns, and in Cozumel and Peto. Map 7-1, which shows the extent of missionary activity (both secular and regular) in Yucatán in 1582, illustrates the relative unimportance of the secular clergy at this time in terms of total spheres of influence.

Within the next few years, however, the secular clergy began to make inroads into the Franciscan-dominated Indian areas of the peninsula. This movement was given considerable impetus by the appointment of Yucatán's first resident non-Franciscan bishop, Gregorio de Montalvo, who upon his arrival in Yucatán in 1581 initiated a long, organized, and at times vigorous, campaign to provide more positions for the secular clergy, many of them Yucatecan Creoles. Although the Franciscans were bitterly opposed to relinquishing any of their posts to the secular branch of the church and fought this challenge to their authority tooth and nail,[6] the weight of public opinion favored secularization, and over the years the friars found themselves eliminated from one area after another.

It should be emphasized that this process of secularization was a gradual one. Over fifty years after the first serious attempts to secularize were begun, the influence of the secular clergy was just beginning to be felt throughout the peninsula. Of the forty-eight centers of religious activity in existence in 1639 (see map 7-2), only eight formerly Franciscan parishes were in the hands of secular priests, these in addition to the six parishes traditionally under their control. The trend toward secularization continued, however, and by 1759 the Franciscans were active in only twenty-six parishes; the secular clergy by this time had fifty parishes under its control (Lopetegui and Zubillaga 1965:854).

It is hoped that this rather detailed account of the spiritual conquest and pacification of the Yucatán Peninsula has provided the reader with a useful point of reference for the discussion which follows. The foregoing should clearly demonstrate, for example, that, even at the height of their numerical strength, the Franciscans did not have the personnel needed for adequate coverage of the entire area under their jurisdiction. Ten to twenty towns were often assigned to one mission center, and, despite constant efforts to recruit additional friars, the available supply was never able to keep up with demand. In fact, one of the chief arguments put forward by the Creole priests in their campaign for secularization hinged on the need to release the friars from their responsibilities in the well-established parishes so that they might be free to move into the more isolated and less-Christianized regions of the peninsula! It may be supposed too that the *maestros*, introduced to solve some of the problems arising out of Franciscan personnel shortages, continued to play an important

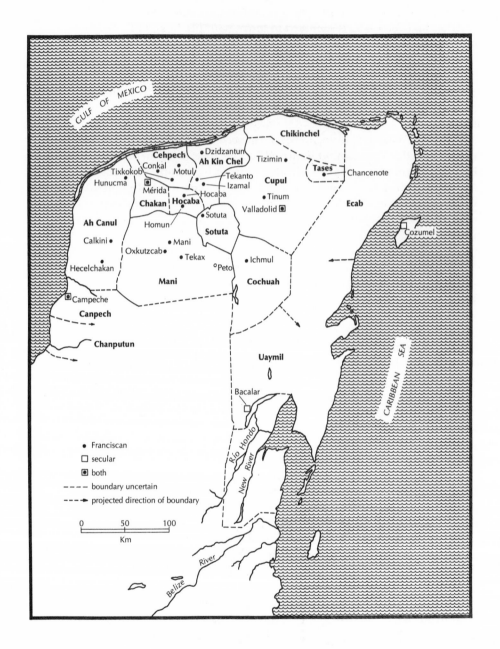

Map 7-1
Seats of missionary activity, Yucatán Peninsula, 1582

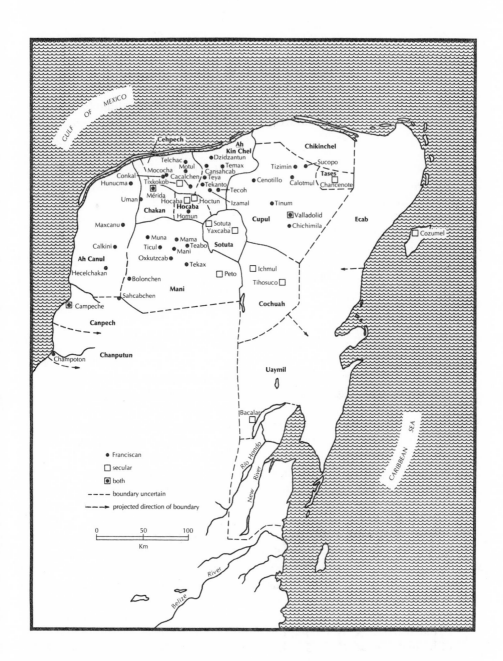

Map 7-2
Seats of missionary activity, Yucatán Peninsula, 1639

role in the Christianization process as long as the original situation persisted. With these points in mind, let us move on to a closer examination of the *maestro* and his role in colonial society.

The Maestro Cantor in Colonial Society

It was not until 1618 that the crown provided formal guidelines for the local organization of the church in the colonies:

● En todos los Pueblos que pasaren de cien Indios, haya dos, ó tres Cantores, y en cada Reduccion un Sacristan, que tenga cuidado de guardar los ornamentos, y barrer la Iglesia, todos los quales sean libres de tase, y servicios personales. (*Recopilación de leyes de los reynos de las Indias* 1943: libro VI, titulo III, ley VI)
[In all towns of one hundred or more Indians there shall be two or three *cantores* and in each reduction one *sacristan,* who is to take care of the ornaments and sweep the church. All of the above shall be free of taxes and personal services.]

Si el Pueblo fuere de hasta cien Indios, haya un Fiscal, que los junte, y convoque á la Doctrina; y si pasare de cien Indios, dos Fiscales, y no sean mas, aunque exceda el número de Indios, los quales han de ser de edad de cincuenta á sesenta años, y los Curas no los podrán ocupar fuera de su oficio, si no fuere pagándolos su trabajo, y ocupacion. (Ibid., ley VII)
[If a town has up to one hundred Indians, there shall be one *fiscal* who is to gather them together for *doctrina*; and if more than one hundred Indians, two *fiscales,* and there shall not be more even though the number of Indians is excessive. The above must be between fifty and sixty years old, and the priests will not be allowed to give them extraneous
● work, unless they are paying them for their work and occupation.]

It is almost certain that these laws merely provided official sanction for a type of organization which was already in widespread use by this time. In Yucatán, for example, there are clear indications that this form of organization was in existence on the local level from an early date. Landa states that "the *adelantado* and the judges of the king have always appointed *fiscales* to the friars to bring the Indians together for the teaching of the *doctrina,* as well as to punish those who returned to their old way of living" (Tozzer 1941:73). López [de] Cogolludo indicates that it was the custom to elect these *fiscales* on the same day that the civil officers—the *alcaldes* and *regidors*—of a town were chosen (1957:226). Also selected at this time were the *alguaciles de doctrina,* whose principal function was to assist the *fiscal* in carrying out his duties. The *alguaciles* were responsible for gathering together all the children of the town for *doctrina* instruction and for enforcing the compulsory church attendance rule.

Each town also had a number of *sacristanes* whose duties, according to López [de] Cogolludo, were to take care of the ornaments, keep the church clean, and serve at the altar during mass (1957:230). Bishop Toral, in his instructions to the clergy (ca. 1563), made provision for a *sacristan mayor* in each town whose function would be to train young men as altar boys and as general church custodians (Scholes et al. 1936–1938:II, doc. 18). In connection with their duties as altar attendants, the *sacristanes* were responsible for leading the adult Indians in reciting certain prayers and responses. These sessions were usually held immediately before or after mass and served as a sort of review for the Indians, who often had difficulty committing the liturgy to memory.

The third and most important category of local church officials were the *maestros*. At least three types of *maestros* are mentioned in the literature: *maestros de canto (maestros cantores), maestros de capilla,* and *maestros de escuela.* Often these terms appear to be used interchangeably, thus making the exact functions of each difficult to delineate and raising the question of whether or not each was indeed a separate position. Reed translates *maestro de capilla* as "choirmaster" and *maestro cantor* as "lay assistant to the priest" but does not cite any references (1964:214). Roys considers the *maestro de capilla* and the *maestro de escuela* to have been the same person (1939:117 n), citing as evidence the fact that in some of the titles of Ebtun the same person is referred to as schoolmaster (*ah cambezah*)[7] in Maya and as *maestro de capilla* in Spanish (see, e.g., Roys 1939:46 n; docs. 28, 30). López [de] Cogolludo, in describing a typical mass in an Indian town, relates, "demas de rezar el oficio divino los sacerdotes, el maestro de capilla y la mitad de los cantores a semanas . . . rezan las cuatro horas menores de el oficio de nuestra Señora, despues cantan la tercia de la festividad de el día . . . y a la tarde vísperas." Here we see the *maestro de capilla* leading the *cantores* in various chants and prayers and thus fulfilling the role of *maestro cantor.* In the next paragraph, however, López [de] Cogolludo says, "los maestros de capilla enseñan a leer, escribir, y cantar a algunos muchachos: con que no solo se provee de quien sirva el culto divino, si no que de alli salen escribanos para los pueblos (1957:230–231). This statement, then, combines the functions of the *maestro de escuela* with those of the *maestro cantor* under the title of *maestro de capilla.* On the basis of this evidence, we are led to conclude that *maestro cantor, maestro de escuela,* and *maestro de capilla* were merely three different titles for what in reality was one position. It is possible that the particular aspect of the *maestro*'s duties being emphasized influenced the selection of terms in each individual case. However, this is difficult to document from the existing evidence.

The *maestros*, as stated previously, received their training in the Franciscan schools where they were instructed in reading and writing and in church doctrine and ritual. Upon graduation they returned to their own communities where the were accorded important leadership roles in the local religious organization. It is interesting to note the striking resemblance which these *maestros* bear to the pre-Columbian priests-teachers described by Landa in the following passage:

> ... they had a high priest whom they called *Ah Kin Mai* and by another name *Ahau Can Mai* ... In him was the key of their learning and it was to these matters that they dedicated themselves mostly. ... They provided priests for the towns when they were needed, examining them in the sciences and ceremonies, and committed to them the duties of their office, and sent them forth. And they employed themselves in the duties of the temples and in teaching their sciences as well as in writing books about them.
>
> They taught the sons of the other priests and the second sons of the lords who brought them for this purpose from their infancy, if they saw that they had an inclination for this profession. (Tozzer 1941:27)

Catholic *maestros* were taught by the high priests of the new religion (who were in fact referred to as *ah kines* [Lizana 1893:5]); they returned to their villages with the essentials for serving as religious specialists; and they combined religious duties and educative roles in carrying out their everyday duties. The similarity is striking and becomes even more so when one realizes that these new religious specialists were drawn from the same class of people who had provided their pre-Columbian counterparts.

Furthermore, it should be noted that, at least in the early days of Franciscan activity, the *maestros* were accorded a good deal more responsibility than is commonly credited to them. Bishop Toral (ca. 1563), in his instructions to the clergy of Yucatán (Scholes et al. 1936–1938: II, doc. 18), delineates for them the duties of a group of people whom he refers to as *ahcambecahes*.[8] Under Toral's ordinances the *ahcambecahes*, or *maestros*, were granted the authority to catechize, baptize the sick, administer extreme unction, and hear confessions from (and presumably absolve) the sick and dying. These added responsibilities place them somewhat more on a par with their pre-Columbian counterparts in terms of importance of duties and degrees of access to the supernatural.

There is, then, some basis for hypothesizing a degree of kinship between the pre-Columbian priests-teachers and the Catholic *maestros*. The question now becomes: what was the nature of this relationship? My feeling is that during the early colonial period a great deal of continuity existed between the two posts at the local level, both in terms of the personnel filling the positions and in terms of how these men viewed themselves and were viewed by others in the community. This contention receives some support from the evidence gathered at Landa's inquisition in 1562. A perusal of the inquisition documents reveals that in several of the testimonies the *maestros* were portrayed as having actively participated in a wide variety of pagan rites and ceremonies. And in at least one case the *maestro* was also referred to as an *ah kin*. This particular individual, one "Juan Pech, *ah-kin y maestro de escuela*" of Sotuta, was accused of and admitted to officiating at the crucifixion of two sacrificial victims (Scholes and Adams 1938:I, doc. 12).

Clearly the *maestros* were not functioning exactly as the Franciscans had envisioned. For, in addition to their Catholic duties, they were involved in a variety of activities closely associated with the native priesthood. If we assume that the same people who at one time would have become priests-teachers were now becoming *maestros*, this functional duality becomes somewhat more understandable. The Maya religion was inclusive in nature, and Catholic gods (Trinity, saints, etc.) and rituals could be incorporated without violation to any deep-seated religious principles. Thus, it is quite possible that neither the *maestros* nor the people in general saw any great incompatibility in the two roles.

It was only after *reducción* was achieved (ca. 1560) that the Franciscans began to see the extent to which Catholicism was being syncretized with the old religion. And Landa's inquisition (1562), directly following this discovery, can be seen not only as an attempt to extirpate idolatry but as an attack on this emerging syncretic pattern as well (Victoria Reifler Bricker, personal communication, 1974). No doubt it was only at this point that the natives became fully aware of the implications of the new religion's most foreign characteristic—its exclusive nature. The inquisition also revealed the extent to which the new religious authorities were interested in purely local affairs. It may be suspected that up to this time the natives had assumed that, just as the pre-Columbian civil government had been maintained by the Spanish authorities, so the local religious organization would be able to persist without excessive outside influence.

The inquisition, then, changed a number of native conceptions about the new religion; and it undoubtedly served to curtail any incipient tendencies, such as the one postulated above, to combine Christian and pagan duties in the person of the *maestro*. It should be noted, however, that as late as 1579 the *maestros* were still being accused of being idolaters and of keeping idols in their schoolhouses (*Relaciones de Yucatán* 1898–1900: 190, 213). And Scholes and Roys believe that the schoolmasters "continued to carry on the old traditions for a long time and were the men who compiled the so-called Books of Chilam Balam and kept them in circulation" (1938:605; see also Sanchez de Aguilar 1892:115).

Conclusion

This article has attempted to describe and analyze the role of the *maestro cantor* in Yucatán, as instituted by the early Franciscan missionaries. We have seen that, throughout the early colonial period, the friars were constantly plagued by a shortage of personnel and that effective, direct control of all the areas under their jurisdiction was never a realistic possibility. Under the circumstances they were forced to rely rather heavily on a specially created and trained group of native assistants, the *maestros cantores,* who, ideally, saw to the day-to-day observations of Catholic ritual at the local level and involved themselves in the conversion and education activities advocated by the friars.

That the *maestros* themselves were not always fully committed to Christianity is clearly indicated by the evidence obtained at Landa's inquisition. It has been suggested that this situation is explainable, at least in part, by the fact that the *maestros* were recruited from the same class of people which had traditionally provided the priests-teachers of the native religion. Rather close similarities in training and subsequent duties served to blur even more the distinctions between the old and the new religious specialists, particularly at a time when the exclusive nature of Catholicism was still poorly understood.

Landa's inquisition, while exposing the dual activities of many of the *maestros,* did not, however, lead to their abolition as a functioning body. Bishop Toral's instructions, issued the following year, make it clear that the *maestros* continued to occupy a position of uppermost importance in the Franciscan organization. Toral's directives, as discussed earlier, accorded the *maestros* an impressive range of responsibilities at the local level, including the all-important power to administer some of the church sacraments in the absence of a regular priest.

Given, then, this history of specialized knowledge and major community responsibility dating back to the early colonial period, it is hardly surprising that it was the *maestros* who replaced the ladino priests in free Maya society. Indeed, in light of the foregoing evidence, it is quite possible that the transition involved little more than the full-time assumption of those duties which, under other circumstances, had long been performed by the *maestros* on a part-time basis within their local community.

Notes

1.

A document recording secular clergy deaths between 1796 and 1887 in the bishopric of Yucatán (Archivo de la Secretaría del Arzobispado [Yucatán], Asuntos Terminados, 1887–1891) indicates that, of the 1,069 deaths occurring during this period, 22, or 2 percent, were of Maya surnamed individuals. (I am indebted to Philip C. Thompson and to Victoria Reifler

Bricker for bringing this document to my attention.) Thus, a small proportion of the secular priesthood was being recruited from the native population at this time. There is, however, no evidence to indicate that these ordained Indian priests were ever involved in rebel Maya society.
2.
Sources disagree on the exact date of this first mission, although it was almost certainly no earlier than 1535 and no later than 1537. See Chamberlain for a more complete discussion of the question (1948:311).
3.
Four friars from Guatemala and four from New Spain.
4.
Montejo, a firm supporter of the Franciscans, undoubtedly applied political pressure in many cases. It must be remembered too that the nobility accrued certain advantages from conversion. See Wolf for an elaboration of the latter point (1959:173).
5.
The exact number is unclear; see Scholes and Adams for a further discussion of this point (1938:I, xiii).
6.
See, e.g., Carrillo y Ancona for an account of some of the tactics and countertactics employed in this struggle (1908:7–13).
7.
Literally, "he who causes to learn."
8.
The Motul dictionary defines *ahcambecah* as "maestro de la escuela" (Martínez Hernández 1929).

Part Three

Maya Views of History

8

The Caste War of Yucatán:

The History of a Myth and the Myth of History

Victoria Reifler Bricker

In this article I consider the historical value of oral traditions concerning the Caste War of Yucatán (1847–1853). Until recently, both historians and social anthropologists have refused to consider oral tradition as a valid source of historical information. Under the influence of A. R. Radcliffe-Brown (1965:3), social anthropologists have denounced historical reconstructions based on oral traditions as "conjectural" history and have limited themselves to strictly synchronic investigations of nonliterate peoples. This synchronic bias was reflected in the work of Robert Redfield when he tried to reconstruct the history of culture change in the Yucatán Peninsula, not by consulting historical documents and informants, but by translating "space into time and differences between communities into history" Strickon 1965:37).

Implicit in the differential evaluation of the validity of oral and written traditions is the premise that facts that are transmitted orally are necessarily subject to distortion. But even written sources can distort events in terms of the conscious or unconscious biases of their authors: "Each type of historical source not only has its own limitations, but also its own particular way of seeing things—its own particular bias" (Vansina 1965:141). For, as Jan Vansina has pointed out, history "is always an interpretation" (1965:183) and "no more than a calculation of probabilities" (1965:185); for these reasons oral traditions may be no less valid a source of historical data than written documents.

According to Vansina, the best way to assess the validity of an oral tradition is to compare it with other types of historical evidence, such as archaeology, written documents, and linguistics (Vansina 1965:182). If an oral tradition is in agreement with, or complements other sources of evidence, then it is unlikely that history has been distorted through oral transmission. On the other hand, if two types of evidence yield discrepant or conflicting kinds of information, then one or both accounts must be distorted and other types of evidence must be brought into the picture to determine which account has been distorted.

The Caste War of Yucatán is both recent enough to be well-documented historically and remote enough for legends about it to have developed. The historical materials include documents written in Maya and Spanish. The Maya documents consist of about two hundred letters written in the Latin-based alphabet introduced by Spanish priests during the sixteenth century; they were written by the Indian leaders of the rebellion to each other and to the Yucatecan authorities. The Spanish sources include letters, military reports, eyewitness descriptions, and newspaper reports, as well as several substantial general historical accounts which synthesize, summarize, and interpret the documentary sources (Ancona 1889; Baqueiro 1878–1887; González Navarro 1970). The published interpretative histories, which are written by whites, are based primarily on documents in Spanish.

Maya oral traditions about the Caste War of Yucatán agree remarkably well with the written histories of whites in all but one respect: the role they assign to a man named Juan de la Cruz. Historians are very vague about the identity of this man, whom they refer to as Juan de la Cruz Puc. They say only that he served as the interpreter or scribe for the Talking Cross, which was the religious focus of the uprising (Baqueiro 1878–1887: II, 390–391; González Navarro 1970:97–98; Reed 1964:137, 161). Historians pay much more attention to José María Barrera, who they believe invented the cult of the Talking Cross (Baquerio 1878–1887:II, 388; González Navarro 1970:97; Reed 1964:135–136). Yet Barrera is never mentioned in folk history, while Juan de la Cruz often is.

Juan de la Cruz plays an important part in Indian legends about the Caste War. For example, descendants of the rebel Maya who live in the village of X-Cacal identify him with Jesus Christ. They say that Juan de la Cruz is the Son of God, who was crucified but returned to earth to lead the Maya to victory in the Caste War. In their version of the Crucifixion they explain how Juan de la Cruz was persecuted by government troops, whom they refer to as Jews (Villa Rojas 1945:100).

This legend illustrates a type of distortion that is frequently found in oral tradition, namely, the telescoping of time (Vansina 1965:102). In the legend, time differences have apparently been ignored and sequential events separated by almost two thousand years have been treated as equivalent and interchangeable. The legend emphasizes structural similarities between the persecution of Christ and white efforts to subdue the rebel Maya, one of whose leaders was Juan de la Cruz.

The Maya legend of Juan de la Cruz makes him out to be more central a figure in the Caste War of Yucatán than white historians do. Given the apparent temporal distortion evident in the legend, must we necessarily conclude that, in this case, written history is right and oral tradition is wrong?

I think not. On the basis of a document that I discovered in the library of the state museum of Yucatán in Mérida, I am now convinced that, in addition to his other roles, Juan de la Cruz was an impersonator of Christ and that therefore the temporal distortion in the legend is more apparent than real.

The document in question is a Maya sermon that was written by someone who signed his name as Juan de la Cruz and which was delivered to the inhabitants of Chan Santa Cruz, the cult center, on October 15, 1850. The year 1850 is also usually cited by historians as the year in which the cult of the Talking Cross was founded. Juan de la Cruz makes it clear at the beginning of his sermon that he will be speaking for himself and not for the cross. The sermon is full of passages in which he clearly identifies himself with Christ and His Passion. Let me quote two examples:

● 1.
t u mèen tèen t in sihsé?eš;
Because I it was who caused you to be created;
tèen t in lohé?eš;
I it was who redeemed you;
tèen t in w ekah in kilí?ìč k'i?ik'el t a w ó?olalé?eš.
I it was who shed my precious blood on your behalf.
bey túuno?, in yàamah winkilé?eš,
Thus, then, o ye who are my beloved people,
táan wáah a w ilké?eš biš in k'amik bahá?anil in w òok
do you see how I receive nails in my feet
y éetel aniyos?
and shackles?
táan wáah a w ilké?eš bahun ȼ'aplik in sùunil k'ašá?anilen
Do you see how many ropes are tied around me
likil in kastigartá?al t u mèen in kí?ič kelmil
with which I am being punished by my most magnificent
in yùum t a w ó?olalé?eš?
Lord on your behalf?

2.
le ?ó?olal k in ȼ'aik té?eš hun p'éel senyal
This is the reason I am giving you a sign
u tiá?al č'iklá?al la bá?al t a puksi?ik'alé?eš,
as a thing to be guarded in your hearts,
t u mèen tene?, t u láakal òorah táan in lúubul,
because as for me, I am falling all the time,
táan in č'á?akal,
I am being cut,
táan in ló?omol.
I am being nailed.

táan u hǎʔahatiken k'iʔiš,
Thorns are piercing me,
táan y òokol tèen čeʔ
sticks are punching me
likil in manel,
while I am traveling through
in šíimbat yukatan;
[while] I am visiting Yucatán;
likil in lohkéʔeš,
while I am redeeming you,
in yàamahil winkéʔeš.
● o ye who are my beloved men.

To the person untrained in theology, this sermon suggests that Juan de la Cruz viewed himself as the Second Coming of Christ. Of course, one cannot infer from the text alone what his motives were or whether or not he himself believed that he was Christ. But that is not the point. The point is that Juan de la Cruz's followers were almost all uneducated men and women who were not trained to consider the possible symbolic implications of his sermon. They could only take his text at face value, and if they did so, then Juan de la Cruz *was* Christ.

If this interpretation of the "Sermon of John of the Cross" is correct, then the fact that the descendants of the original believers in the cross cult equate Juan de la Cruz with Christ does not necessarily mean that they have distorted history by telescoping time. The myth *is* history—it is one of the doctrines of the religious cult and not a distorted relic of the history of that movement. The true mythmaker was Juan de la Cruz, not his followers or their descendants. The oral tradition of the people of X-Cacal and Carrillo Puerto (formerly the cult center of Chan Santa Cruz) simply faithfully preserves the myth he passed off on them as history.

Professor D. E. Dumond (personal communication, December 5, 1973), has brought to my attention the fact that Juan de la Cruz never used the surname Puc in any document bearing his signature. Yet historians usually refer to him as "Juan de la Cruz Puc" (Baqueiro 1878–1887:II, 390–391; González Navarro 1970:97–98; Reed 1964:137, 287). It may be that they regard the name "Juan de la Cruz" as a pseudonym for Venancio Puc, who was a leader of the movement until 1864. If so, they cite no evidence for this association, and I have found none either. In the absence of conclusive evidence, the implication that Juan de la Cruz was Venancio Puc may be as mythical as his identification with Christ.

A version of the document I found in Mérida exists also in X-Cacal, where it is treated as a sacred book. Alfonso Villa Rojas published an English translation of this document in an appendix to his ethnographic monograph on X-Cacal (1945:161–164). A copy of this manuscript was photographed by Milt Machlin and Bob Marx, who led an expedition to Quintana Roo for *Argosy* magazine in 1971 (Machlin and Marx 1971). Nelson Reed, the author of a well-known history of the Caste War of Yucatán (1964), served as consultant for the expedition; he very kindly arranged for me to receive a Xerox copy of the manuscript.

The X-Cacal manuscript, which is originally dated 1887, is almost identical to the manuscript I found in Mérida. The two manuscripts differ in only one important respect: the 1887 version includes several passages which do not appear in the 1850 version. The extra sections in the 1887 version include (1) an introduction which is a historical account of events which occurred between 1850 and 1887, bringing the document up to date; (2) an excerpt from a letter written to Miguel Barbachano, the governor of Yucatán, in 1851 (an "epistle"), a copy of which I also found in Mérida; and (3) several epilogues, or addenda, dated serially 1887, 1903, 1944, and 1957. The wording in all other sections of the two manuscripts is virtually identical. Such minor differences as exist may be attributed to copying errors or to attempts to improve the style and adapt to changes in orthographic conventions (see Bricker 1974:384–387).

According to Villa Rojas, in X-Cacal this sacred document is read "during the solemn Mass which closes the annual fiesta of the sanctuary. The attendance of this Mass is exceptionally large, and everyone listens to the reading on bended knees and with lowered heads" (1945:161). The Maya of X-Cacal believe that "Juan de la Cruz is still keeping in touch with 'his children' (the Indians), through Yum Pol [the man who was scribe when Villa Rojas was conducting his field work in X-Cacal], to whom he dictates letters, orders, and requests" (ibid.).

Two other villages in Quintana Roo are populated by Indians who left Chan Santa Cruz, the cult center, after it was captured by General Ignacio Bravo in 1901. According to Charlotte Zimmerman (1963:53 n), the scribe of one of these villages, Chunpom, also has a copy of the document; it, too, is read aloud on "special holy days" (1963:63). The other town is Chancah, which I visited in August 1971. When I inquired about the possible existence of such a manuscript there as well, I was informed that no copy of the manuscript exists in Chancah, but that every two years, the religious leaders of the village travel to X-Cacal in order to attend the fiesta of the cross and what has now become the biennial reading of the sermon of Juan de la Cruz.

The document I found in Mérida, then, is most likely the original version of the manuscript which Villa Rojas has called the "Sermons of the Talking Cross" (1945:161). I have argued that it is really a sermon of Juan de la Cruz, an impersonator of Christ. Juan de la Cruz is identified with Christ in the original version, and annual or biennial readings of the text have kept that association alive. It is therefore not surprising that the legend of Juan de la Cruz agrees so closely with the original text of the sermon.

By showing that the sermon of Juan de la Cruz was first written and delivered in 1850, the year in which the cult of the Talking Cross was supposedly founded, I have ruled out the possibility that it was merely a legendary document first put in writing in 1887, almost forty years after the new religious cult was invented. Charlotte Zimmerman, who has studied the X-Cacal version of the sermon, has also noted that Juan de la Cruz seemed to identify himself with Christ, but she argues that "as historical personage he does not appear in the sermon at all, he appears only as 'mythified'; he is absorbed and understood by the Maya popular memory and the individual, perhaps the amanuensis, who wrote down this Sermon or composed it, by the archaic and cosmological memory only insofar as he participates in *its understanding* of a god named Jesus Christ, who had been absorbed by them from the teaching of the Christian missionaries" (1963:69). She believes that

● for the Maya Indians of the cult and for those who began it, Christ's life and Passion and death became the archetypal reality in which all other priests or religious individuals would acquire meaning. . . . no religious personality is or has meaning except as he participates in this model.

Hence, all priests who are religious heroes must be Christ because he is the paradigm by which popular memory understood and transmitted the actions and life of Juan de la Cruz Puc, outside of this paradigm, this archetype, his life has no meaning. . . . Juan de la Cruz Puc is only real, only remembered, as he is mythified as Christ, as he too participates in the
● life, death, and the Passion. (1963:69–70)

It is clear that Zimmerman regards the sermon of Juan de la Cruz as something that was produced long after the religious movement began. She believes that his identity became "mythified" during the thirty-seven years which separated the founding of the movement and the writing of the 1887 version of the sermon, and she appeals to Eliade's concept of the structure of the "archaic mentality" (1959) to explain this transformation of history into myth.

But since, as I have shown, the sermon was originally written in the same year that the cult of the Talking Cross was supposedly founded, we cannot attribute the identification of Juan de la Cruz with Christ to the "archaic mentality" of his followers. If it was Juan de la Cruz who wrote the sermon it was he who "mythified himself as Christ."

Juan de la Cruz's impersonation of Christ, whether or not it fits the eschatological category of "the second coming" (Zimmerman 1963:63), makes a great deal of sense in terms of Anthony F. C. Wallace's typology of "revitalization movements," which he has defined as ". . . deliberate, organized, conscious effort[s] by members of a society to construct a more satisfying culture" (1956:265). All Maya efforts to revitalize their culture included (1) an attempt to throw off what they considered the yoke of "foreign" domination, and (2) an attempt to reinterpret (i.e., "revitalize") the symbols of the Catholic cult which had been forced on them by their Spanish conquerors, in order to make them more relevant to the Indian experience. By posing as the Indian Christ, Juan de la Cruz obviated the need for white priests. In his sermon to the people of Chan Santa Cruz in 1850, he made the Passion of Christ meaningful in terms of the ethnic conflict represented by the Caste War of Yucatán. Under his leadership, a "more satisfying culture" developed in which the Indian was master and the white prisoner was slave (Reed 1964:175).

In conclusion, I believe that the historical syntheses of white historians are biased because they are based almost exclusively on Spanish sources. Of course, if the oral traditions about Juan de la Cruz are evaluated solely in terms of the written histories of whites, they are only quaint legends which telescope time and "confuse" Juan de la Cruz with Christ. But if the oral traditions of the Maya are compared with Maya documents written during the Caste War of Yucatán, then there is no discrepancy between legend and history. In this particular case, the legend apparently has greater validity than history books based on Spanish sources.

The history of the Caste War of Yucatán needs to be rewritten with more attention paid to the Maya version of the conflict. The Maya of nineteenth-century Yucatán were literate, and in about two hundred letters and other documents they wrote eloquently about their reasons for rebelling against the whites, their day-to-day needs and hardships, their military strategies, and their victories and losses in battle. Juan de la Cruz's role in the development of the religious revitalization movement needs to be spelled out in more detail than I have had time to do here. There are other documents written in Maya that bear his signature which may provide information about his activities. It is possible that it was he who masterminded the cult of the Talking Cross, for, to my knowledge, no documentary evidence exists that Barrera was the person who invented it. And just as oral traditions must be weighed against written documents, so also must the written documents of both sides in the conflict be weighed against each other in order to determine what is history and what is myth.

Notes

1.
The research here reported was assisted by a grant awarded by the Joint Committee on Latin American Studies of the Social Science Research Council, by Wenner-Gren Foundation Grant No. 2807, and by a grant from the Tulane University Council on Research. I am deeply grateful to these institutions for making the research possible.

I owe a great debt to Professor Alfredo Barrera Vásquez for bringing the Yucatecan documents to my attention and for giving me the opportunity to read them. To Professor Munro S. Edmonson go my special thanks for his advice in translating those documents. I am grateful also to Eleuterio Póot Yah, who spent many hours helping me elicit, transcribe, and translate the Yucatecan data. Finally, I would like to express my appreciation to Professor Gary H. Gossen, who first made me aware of Vansina's work on the potential value of folklore for history, and to Professors John D. Early and D. E. Dumond for their helpful comments on an earlier version of the article.

9

The Caste War in the 1970's:

Present-Day Accounts from Village Quintana Roo

Allan F. Burns

By far one of the most profound influences on present-day Yucatec Maya life since the Spanish conquest of the sixteenth century has been the Caste War. As has been outlined by Reed (1964), this revolution came very close to reversing the first three hundred years of Spanish hegemony on the Yucatán Peninsula. By the end of 1848, the Spanish population had been driven to the capital city of Mérida by the Maya, ready at a moment's notice to desert it in favor of the security of Campeche and Veracruz.

But the Spaniards[1] did not have to leave. The coming of the rainy season signaled to the Maya that the circle of the year continued whether or not a Caste War was going on. The rebel Maya returned to their milpas to plant new fields of corn, the "sacred grace" of their existence. The Spaniards, aided by reinforcements from other parts of Mexico, began a slow process of reclaiming the peninsula once again. For the next fifty years, a guerrilla war between some of the Maya and the Spaniards continued, neither side admitting defeat or victory. At the close of the nineteenth century the Caste War was officially declared at an end by the Spaniards. The entrance of General Ignacio Bravo into the town of Santa Cruz (present-day Carillo Puerto) is usually taken as the final official event of the war. During the twentieth century, the events of the agrarian revolution of 1915–1920 overshadowed the continuing struggle of the Caste War in Yucatán.

Anthropologists and historians who have concerned themselves with the war have been content to deal with it up to the end of the nineteenth century. Reed, for example, describes the post-1900 period as a time when the symbol of Maya resistance, the "Cross," was "sleeping" (1964:250). He describes only one minor skirmish between the remaining rebel Maya and the federal government in Quintana Roo during this time (1964:255). Villa Rojas has a short section dealing with the aftermath of the Caste War on the X-Cacal villages (1945:28). In keeping with tradition, he excludes this section from the ethnological discussion of Tusik and places it under the division of his work dealing with the historical background.

Villa Rojas's visit to Tusik in the 1930's seemed to open the door for the influx of modern Mexican life into the last of the *separado* villages, and enthusiasm about the struggle appeared to be steadily diminishing (cf. Redfield 1941:57; Villa Rojas 1945:34–37). Accounts of the Caste War collected by Redfield in Chan Kom have been relegated to an appendix in the ethnography of the villages and referred to as examples of Maya folk tales (Redfield and Villa Rojas 1934).

In 1959, Nelson Reed traveled to Carrillo Puerto to conclude his historical research on the Caste War. He sought out the landmarks of the struggle, asked about the cross, and met with elder Maya in the town of Chancah. The elders of Chancah complained that villagers lacked interest in the war and that traditional "guard service" to the shrines of the war was difficult to sustain. The perceived dismay of the Maya affected Reed. He concluded his discussion by describing Carrillo Puerto, the old capital of the rebel Maya, as typical of "any small Central American town" (1964:273). The cross seemed to be sleeping soundly.

In 1971, I undertook field work in a village[2] not far from Tusik which had earlier been studied by Villa Rojas. Like Tusik, this village formed one of the satellite communities around the civil and religious center of X-Cacal *guardia*. One reason I undertook a study of this area was that it was the last stronghold of the rebel Maya. I wondered if the Caste War had any lasting effects on the villagers in the present time, over a hundred years from its beginning. I was interested in how the people themselves perceived a struggle which may have ended seventy years ago. I quickly learned that the war was not over; the rebel Maya of east central Quintana Roo are still involved in the Caste War.

To be sure, the actual fighting had ceased. But the Maya are still prepared. Ceremonies are performed to honor the cross; guard duty is carried out around the sacred temples; and discussions about antagonism between Mexico and the Maya nation are heard with surprising frequency. A real reminder of the importance of the war during the time I was there was the arrival of federal troops to X-Cacal during one of the annual ceremonies when thousands of Maya had assembled from villages within an eighty-mile radius. I asked one of the civil and religious leaders (*tatich*) of X-Cacal why they had been sent. He replied that the arrival of the federal troops was a regular occurrence and that he would send someone over to give the soldiers some soft drinks. He said that they generally do not stay for more than a few hours. In discussing the matter with other people at the ceremony, I found that the soldiers still ask about the sacred cross; they wonder if it might be hidden in the village, if it is truly covered with jewels, and if it has magical powers.

The Caste War in east central Quintana Roo is an ongoing concern. It is not an esoteric belief of the old people in the villages but touches everyone living in the area. The appearance of federal troops at Maya ceremonies provides a very real reminder that the war is more than past history. I will convey some of this reality as it exists in the 1970's by discussing a number of verbal descriptions of events of the war recorded in the field. Translations of spoken Maya "counsels,"[3] or statements about the historical world, will be presented with exegesis as a description of a portion of contemporary Maya world view. The narratives themselves are highly refined; they represent countless reinterpretations of events, ideas, and possibilities which make up an elaborate philosophical system of Maya thought.

I have chosen to concentrate on those statements which deal with the Caste War because it is seldom recognized that a people's world view has a historical dimension. The concept is most often used to refer to the "enduring patterns," the "existential postulates" of a society which are seldom, if ever, articulated (cf. W. T. Jones 1972:83). Through the discussions of basic patterns and regular features, the concept of world view quickly becomes associated with a timeless, if not static, description of society and culture. Interviews with villagers in Quintana Roo have convinced me that the Yucatec Maya recognize an extremely rich historical and archaeological record. Any description of their world view as "timeless" or unarticulated distorts the reality as spoken by the Maya themselves.

Examples of contemporary Maya counsels illustrate world view in action. The Maya utilize ethnohistorical events and characters to generate descriptions of how societies and individuals are related. The counsels form a didactic function by bringing up beliefs, attitudes, and values for public discussion. Characters within the counsels serve as models of appropriate and inappropriate behavior. Social relations described within the texts illustrate that the current world has meaning given the events of the past. As I have already noted, the present-day Maya continue to define themselves and "the Spaniards" as opposing groups. The counsels describe why this is true today and how other societies are incorporated into a system which allows this conflict to continue. The counsels also illustrate the importance of the transcending power of "the cross". That the cross speaks to the Maya of today through the vehicle of counsels is instructive of the place the cross held in Maya society during the 120 years of the Caste War. Maya world view is, then, explicit, as it is found in verbal accounts; it is historical, as these accounts link historical events with the present; and it is generative, as the accounts incorporate modern knowledge of the political world into the genre of counsels.

In the X-Cacal villages, the Chilam Balam[4] are still read at yearly ceremonies (cf. Villa Rojas 1945:161; Barrera Vásquez and Rendón 1948). The reading of these sacred books culminates a week-long event of ritual, exchange, and entertainment. The yearly ceremonies are times of unification and intensification for the several thousand Maya who attend. The books themselves contain a variety of subjects including syncretic accounts of Christian and Maya mythology, and their reading or performance by the two "scribes" of X-Cacal is an all-night affair. The books are a charter of the Maya today, a link with the ancient, or pre-Columbian, as well as the recent basis of Maya society. During the time of their performance, audience members do not interrupt the reading.

Throughout the rest of the year, however, portions of the sacred books of Chilam Balam are commented on quite regularly. Episodes are retold by older men of the villages, and criticism, skepticism, and other commentary greet the performances. Performers who initiate the telling of these counsels (referred to in Yucatec Maya as *ʔalmaxikiʔin* or *teʔeskunah*) are highly skilled at narrating and explaining the episodes contained in the Chilam Balam. The advice and counsel of the elders are often greeted with suspicion by younger audience members. The suspicion, and at times hostility, to the "old ways" are not as serious as some of the younger people would have one believe, however. Even among those who profess to have given up traditional Maya life, the counsels are listened to with considerable interest. In addition, even the highly acculturated young people continue to attend the yearly ceremonies where the Chilam Balam is read. Their distrust of the Mexican "outsider" is as real today as it was at the turn of the century.

In January of 1972, I recorded one of these counsels from a respected narrator. Tape recording was new to him, but he understood that I would be retelling his words in English to a different audience. His first question posed to me as we began the recording signifies this understanding.

● WHAT,[5] what is the name of the president of the United States?
[*Response*: Nixon.]
Nixon, ahah.
MISTER PRESIDENT NIXON: You are the United States.
You have the power within you.
Your town was marked by Beautiful True God.
Not in time will you come apart;
● Not in time will you lose.

This counsel begins, quite naturally, with a greeting. Unlike tales and other myths told for entertainment, narratives of this class begin with a recognition of the audience. According to native exegesis, the performer here is "offering his hand" to the president. He is acknowledging a fellow leader's symbolic position ("You *are* the United States") and at the same time signifying that a commonality exists between the United States and the Maya nation: the "town" of each was marked by the same Beautiful True God. In keeping with real life tradition of ritual greeting (Burns 1973:331), the narrator shows his verbal expertise by speaking three short poems before introducing the subject of his counsel.

● The first time Wonderful True God was given,
 It went to Wonderful Heaven.
 Yum[6] Jesucristo and Beautiful Woman
 Honored María went to the Sacred Town of Jerusalem,
 To heaven . . . they left us again.
 Truly no man is going to put the tower on the church.
 The one there in *Nohcah Santa Cruz Balam Nah.*
 The building there is a huge ancient work of the people . . . NO:
 It is the building of the Spirits.

 That's who did some of the building of the church.
 That one there;
● The one without a tower.

    The church referred to here is the same one which stands today in the town of Carrillo Puerto. The narrative at this point is necessarily obscure. The reference to the tower alludes to the ending of the counsel, and I will discuss its importance there. Stylistically, the performer is introducing the end of the narrative at its inception. When the tower is referred to later, the counsel will have completed a symbolic circle. In this way the performer cues the audience to the direction the counsel will take.

    The first real episode of the counsel is introduced with a pure couplet. This couplet names the principal character in the episode.

● Venancio Puc,
● Venancio Puc.

    The episode then continues with an account of Puc's actions during the Caste War.

● He did a lot of killing.
 He did a lot of killing, he did.
 He always looked for ways of being a traitor, besides. [A traitor] to the
     governor . . .
 To the governor, the commander, to the captain, to all of the officials.
 They met every day for nine days.
 There was a meeting held every day at sunset.
 Well, every month Venancio Puc,
 Every month, each month didn't end before
 He brought together six hundred people.

Then he picked the ones to be killed at random.
● That's what scared the governors.

Venancio Puc was a historic figure in the Caste War. An early leader who later became *tatich* of the rebel Maya in the 1850's, Puc's career in the later part of that decade was highlighted by a massacre he perpetrated on the captives taken at Bacalar in 1858 (G. D. Jones 1974:671–673). The wanton killing indeed put his fellow leaders on edge. Here was a person in the highest position of political and religious leadership in Maya society who was acting contrary to moral law. The counsel at this early stage is presenting a view of the inner workings of Maya society in the 1850's. Puc's excesses cannot be tolerated; his killings serve no purpose, even at the height of the early period of the Caste War. The importance attached to this problem within the counsel is signified by the description of *nine* meetings held by the other leaders. The number nine has a high ritual value in Maya, outside of narrative context, and generally connotes importance and finality to a situation.

Along with this moral message, the reference to the killing of 600 people is well grounded in historic fact. Reed notes the number of captives taken by Puc at Bacalar in 1858 to be about 550 (1964:170).

Within this short passage, a historic figure has been introduced; a leadership system has been described (the positions of governor, commander, and captain still exist today in the area); a statement about the necessary order of society even in the traumatic time of war has been made; and a historic event 120 years in the past has been alluded to. The episode continues.

● The generals thought in their hearts,
"How can we put Venancio Puc to the side?
He's gone too far killing people;
He's become a traitor."
Then the next day they held another meeting.
A mule with a saddle and bridle [was prepared].
Well, after nine days, Venancio Puc said,
"Well, Wonderful God, I guess my time has come. What more?"
They came and tied a rope around his head,
They then tied a flag around his neck.
They brought him to where the governors wanted.
Well, then he bowed down and asked for mercy from the taata yum
    governor.
When he asked for mercy from the governor,
CHAH! The people grabbed him.

They beat and kicked him.
He ran to find the mule with the bridle;
He jumped on it and got his foot tangled in the ropes, that Venancio Puc.
The mule was hit. It began to run.
The mule ran about seventy feet and dragged him there.
His leg was pulled out.
That's how Venancio Puc was killed.
● Then Venancio Puc was dead all right.

Venancio Puc's death here in the counsel presents a problem. It is obvious that he was out of favor with the leadership of the Maya at that time, but it is unclear whether he died by execution or unfortunate mishap. A mule with a saddle and bridle was mentioned at the beginning of this section. The mule was probably being prepared for his execution, although it may have been prepared in order to allow him to be banished from the area. But when Venancio Puc dies, it is as he is trying to escape on this same mule. Other historical accounts of this event, which constituted one of the first conflicts over power among the rebel Maya, state clearly that he was executed along with two of his assistants (G. D. Jones 1974:675). This counsel, however, is offering an interpretation which excuses the other leaders from the actual killing of Puc. Since Puc was responsible for so many deaths, this counsel argues that he was also responsible for his own death.

The line between what is done at the hands of fate (in this case Wonderful True God) and what is done at the hands of men is not always exact in Maya thought. The "Speaking Cross" itself was subject to much suspicion in this regard (Reed 1964:150), and present-day discussions about the cross are replete with skepticism about its divine nature.

The counsel continues with a short "intermission" of sorts before introducing the next episode.

● Well, they let the people go, then, to make a little milpa.
The first milpa the people made was 120 feet by 120 feet.
The people made the milpa.
That's how the people found their lives in times past.

It was told to Wonderful True God;
He was told what happened.
Don Felipe Yama was governor.
He said to his generals, "If you are killed, then it is not your fault if you
    don't have eyes.

Well, I'm going to have real justice. Who will be afraid?
Now I'm going to ask whose fault it is.
        I'll ask He who bled, He who sanctified himself."
He then asked.
Lightning flashed in his eyes! Whose?
The official. The one who was killed was General Felipe Yama.
He was dead.
He was down.
● He lay there on the ground for three days.

Like Venancio Puc of the last episode, Felipe Yama was an important leader during the war. Yama served the Maya during the 1890's (Reed 1964:227). The problem of human versus supernatural control and leadership is again brought up in this episode. Felipe Yama was the governor, but he seeks supernatural guidance during the days of rapid decline in the Maya population which occurred at the end of the nineteenth century. The description of Yama lying on the ground dead for three days is an obvious parellel to the death of Christ in European thought. It represents the type of blending of religious concepts and ideas from Christianity and Maya religion which Zimmerman described for another Maya village, Chunpom (1963).

The counsel continues by describing the subsequent possession of Felipe Yama.

● He got up and rubbed his eyes.
He began to say his name.
Lightning flashed in his eyes.
LEEM! He was down;
He fell.
Well then mister,
True God said, "My name is the General Felipe Yama.
There is my temple.
No one is going to put up that tower
Except those that are called English,
And those that are called Americans, red-red men.
They will put up the tower on my temple.
That is the only truth.

I've made it true until the sun ends.
There you will get whatever things you need, there with those who are
        called English,
With those who are called American, red-red men.

They are my servants;
They are my sacred people.
I am Juan de la Cruz,
I am the Noh Cah Santa Cruz Balam Nah.
● *There isn't anyone else!"*

Like Christ, Felipe Yama arises after three days, but then falls again.
When he awakens the second time, he is possessed by Wonderful True
God. In addition, the voice within him later states that it is Juan de la
Cruz, an ambiguous figure who may have been the secretary or founder of
the cross during 1850–1855 (Reed 1964:287, Bricker, this volume). This
voice also says that it is the Noh Cah Santa Cruz Balam Nah, the "Large
Town of Santa Cruz of the House of God," one of the ritual names of
Santa Cruz or Carrillo Puerto. In short, the "voice" of Wonderful True
God is pervasive. The cross speaks; it can speak through any number of
channels or doors, including people. There is no ambiguity between the
cross speaking as Felipe Yama or Juan de la Cruz. The cross can also
speak through the *town* of Santa Cruz, and it can also speak through the
wooden crosses that were housed there. The pervasiveness of the cross was
not understood by the Spaniards who fought the Maya. They discredited
the cross as a "trick" when it became apparent that it was speaking
through many individuals and even writing letters (Reed 1964:161).

The shift from secular to sacred leadership through possession under
conditions of great social stress is a common feature of Maya history.
Another counsel recorded in the field describes the arrival of the first
Spaniards on the shores of Yucatán. The counsel describes how Titul
Xiu, the Maya leader at that time, and his people undergo a similar possession and transformation. The *Itzamna* of Chichen Itza are regarded by
the villagers as magicians who could transform themselves at will into
other than human forms in times of social or political stress.

Rather than a strict line between the sacred and the secular, this counsel illustrates that things and people can be one or the other, depending
on the circumstances. The cross is only wood when it is captured by the
Spaniards during the Caste War, as explained in another counsel recorded
in the field. But it is carried away by nine angels when the Spaniards
subsequently attempt to burn it.

At a more mundane level, the corn planted in present day milpas is
referred to as plain "corn" (*ʔixiʔim*) or "sacred grace" (*santo gracia*), depending on the situation.

Within this period of the counsel, the "tower" of the church or temple
is mentioned again. Here it is explained that the English and the Americans (the "red-red men," or *chachak wiinkoʔob*) will rebuild the tower.
The tower and, in fact, the building itself refer back to the first episode
of the counsel, as they were most likely built under the auspices of

Venancio Puc (cf. G. D. Jones 1974:674; Villa Rojas 1945:22). The cross is saying here that the allies of the Maya, the English to the south and the Americans to the north, will form the triad with the Maya which will reclaim the Yucatán Peninsula as the rightful territory of the Maya once again. The association of the Americans with the "red-red men" from the north is of preconquest origin, but reports of the successes of the United States in two world wars have reached the Maya of Quintana Roo, and thus the contemporary association of *chachak wiinko²ob* with Americans seems as valid as the mythological association of these people. Reed found this association in use when he traveled to some of the smaller villages around Carillo Puerto (1964:278). The Maya asked him for guns and ammunition. This same kind of request was made to me many times while I was in the area. Rounds of ammunition, material aid, and money to fight off the Mexicans from Mayan territory were regularly requested. The counsel presented here is, as evidenced by the opening statement, a portion of one of those requests, directed to the president of the United States.

A definite stylistic change took place in the voice quality of the narrator as he performed the last portion of the counsel. The speed of his delivery slowed, and the words and phrases of the narrative were articulated with care. He seemed almost to be speaking a prayer rather than a narrative.

Later I recorded another counsel which gave further evidence to the use of a special voice style when a narrator spoke the words of the cross. An audience member remarked at the time that the counsel indeed sounded like a prayer. He later requested I play back the counsel for other people so that they might hear the beautiful words that came out of the narrator. In this counsel, the performance itself embodied the cross. The counsel had no episodes as the previous one but, rather, appeared to be the cross itself speaking directly into the microphone.

● THAT PATRÓN,
The Patrón remains with us.
[It] isn't ordered to remain with the *English,*
[It] isn't ordered to remain with the *French,*
[It] isn't ordered to remain with the *Turks,*
[It] isn't ordered to remain with the *Spaniards,*
[It] isn't ordered to remain with the *Mexicans.*
ORDERED, ORDERED by God
To remain with the People.
Ahah.
Then who will win? No one will win.
    God will win
With the People.
Well now,

The thing is, the Sacred Cross is confused,
    I tell you. Listen now while I tell you:
You don't serve a Patrón like this.
It was truly ordered to REMAIN WITH YOU
By . . . really ordered to remain . . . by Yum Jesucristo.
Really ordered by Rey de Dios Padre
To remain with you.
THAT'S WHY, if you let it go, if you suspend service, if you abandon it,
It will just abandon you too.
It will lose you too.
That's why you ought to listen to the counsel I'm giving you.
Believe what I'm telling you. This isn't just playing.
I'm not just breathing air;
I'm not just breathing for you.
You won't be left behind,

● Nor will you be ground into the dirt.

The *Patrón* referred to here is the cross. The admonition to serve it
better has a familiar sound to it. Reed quotes the cross in 1887 as writing:
"I am therefore calling you one by one to punish you . . . because you are
talking about mixing with the enemy . . . I am advising you my children,
don't say that . . . but even so I will not abandon you into his hands, my
children" (Reed 1964:227).

This counsel, like the previous one, indicates that the cross (Noh Cah
Santa Cruz, Juan de la Cruz, Wonderful True God, etc.) is not a thing of
the past with modern Maya of Quintana Roo. The cross does not "sleep";
it actually talks with people and continues to admonish them to serve it
better. The genre of counsels often forms the vehicle for the cross today,
and the events and lessons of the Caste War continue to be a vital reminder of its place in Maya society. But just as the cross can choose from
events from a hundred years ago to illustrate a point, it can also describe
events from the more recent past. The following counsel is similar to the
first in that it begins with a stylized opening, but its content is based on
recent history. This counsel translates some of the ideas about the place
of the Maya vis-à-vis other political groups in the Western Hemisphere
into language perhaps better understood by a non-Maya audience than
the other counsels.

● The . . . the . . . the PATRÓN,
The Patrón of my town,
Noh Cah Santa Cruz, the real town.
The real towns of Xoken, Chindzonot town.
There it appeared; there it came out of a cave.

My town is Noh Cah Santa Cruz Balam Nah Kampocolche Town.
Now,
THE LAND HERE HAS BEEN DIVIDED by the Mexican masters.
Well now, I'm thinking . . . I'm thinking that
It isn't very legal. It isn't legal because they don't care about us.
They don't like us; they don't give us any respect. They don't AID US
    like they should.
Well whatever . . . all the conversations that are heard now
Are understood. A long time ago, long ago, we were all VERY
    IGNORANT. ALL IGNORANT. Our eyes were closed, as they
    ought to be. Now, in the time we are living,
WE ARE ALL "*campesinos* of the Maya zone." All of our eyes are open.
    All of them.

Well now,
We're thinking about all the things that have happened, all that has been
    told to us.
Like what happened in Havana, Cuba.
Havana, Cuba, in the time of . . . what, what, what was his name?
    [*Response*: Batista.]
Batista was overthrown, overthrown by Fidel Castro. Beaten by Fidel
    Castro.
Well, all of the . . . all of the THINGS that were put on those streets by
    the Americans were left there.
They were all taken by Fidel Castro.
Since the Americans didn't want anything, didn't want to fight,
All of the goods were left. Left there,
Left for Fidel Castro.

We are POOR now. Well, now we are thinking that the SAINT,
The Noh Cah Santa Cruz, ought to be served.
It ought to be respected. It ought not . . . not to be left to become old and
    useless. We ought not sleep through the dusk. It ought to be
    respected.
Even before sunset it ought to be lit up with lights. How good that would
    be! How beautiful that would be!
All of the Sacred Candles
Ought to be given to . . . to . . . to the SAINT. And all of the Sacred
    Incense ought to serve the SAINT as it should.
If it is served as it should be,
Even Old One Rey de Dios Padre would SEE. The Wonderful Father,
    Yum Jesucristo WOULD SEE. Beautiful Woman Venerable María
    WOULD SEE, if it were rightfully respected.

Respected as it ought to be.

We are in poverty.
Well now, we, The People,
Are poor. That is how the Most Sacred Patrón is also, poor.
A leader hasn't arisen to HELP US AS HE SHOULD.
Well, as we are now,
The Mexicans HAVE ENTERED Noh Cah Santa Cruz Xbalam Nah.
    They have TAKEN EVERYTHING. Everything has been grabbed
    by them, everything has been eaten.
Who owns the land? Who? The People, the "*campesinos* of the Maya
    Zone."
They get nothing. They aren't paid a good wage.
They are in real Poverty. All poor. Well, we are taking all of this into
    account.
When will we be given respect? When will we be helped?
We are serving the Patrón who was left to us here on earth.
We have no STRENGTH,
We are POOR: in POVERTY. We don't have BOWLS, we don't have
    CAULDRONS, we don't have anything.
Well now,
We are thinking to ask
And from Mister President . . . Mister Governor, because they have the
    territory.
They hold everything in the territory.
Where else can we ask for help?
We cannot ask any other nation. We cannot ask the English, we cannot
    ask the Americans, not them.
They are not the ones who are eating our food, they are not the ones who
    are holding the territory.
The President and the Governor, they are the ones holding the territory.
    They have robbed us of everything. They ought to give us ALL the
    implements, everything.
Things like the
 .   .
ORCHESTRA that is needed for the Sacred Ceremonies.
Everything like TRUMPETS. Everything.
They ought to give us everything, so we can serve the Patróns of our town.
 .   .
● That is it.

   I have utilized these counsels here in order to illustrate that the system
of knowledge about the social and historical world of Maya of today in-

cludes events and ideas generated during the last 120 years. The counsels which deal with the Caste War look upon it as an aspect of Maya life which is in need of interpretation and consideration today just as it was in the past. What is significant about the counsels presented here is the place of the cross. Rather than emerging as a self-servicing "trick" which different political leaders used during the war on their fellow citizens, the cross is better understood as a central charter or consciousness of Maya society. The cross seeks to make itself clear, much the same way anthropologists seek to make clear a theory of culture. The world view of the Maya is present in the narratives. At times the texts seem almost purposefully obscure and vague, but this, too, is in keeping with a tradition of Maya mythology which goes back far into preconquest times. If their vagueness is indeed intentional, then it is produced in order to invite audience members present at their telling to be involved with the topics of the counsels. In this sense, the obscurity in the texts can be seen as a motivating device of their style.

The three counsels presented here in full, and the others referred to, illustrate that contemporary Maya world view is an articulated system. The counsels verbalize a system for categorizing and thinking about social and natural relationships found in the Maya world. Through the counsels, the church at Carrillo Puerto is related to the coming of the "red-red men" from the north who will aid the Maya in reclaiming their territory. These counsels describe the reasons for the continuing opposition between the Maya and the rest of Mexico (Mexicans have control of Maya resources) and describe a solution to this conflict, the joining of Americans and English to the Maya cause. The counsels are not "folk tales." Instead, they can best be considered maps which are continuously redrawn and reinterpreted, showing where the Maya have been, where they are now, and hopefully where they will be in the future.

Notes

1.
The term *Spaniards* will be used here to refer to non-Maya speakers of the Yucatán Peninsula. Technically Mexicans, these people are referred to as Spaniards by the Maya even today, a usage I will follow here.
2.
I wish to acknowledge the support of the National Science Foundation and the University of Washington Department of Anthropology, which support was given for field work in Yucatán. The friendship and assistance of officials and residents of the *municipios* of Ticul, Yucatán, and Carrillo Puerto, Quintana Roo, have made this study possible. The support of Abt Associates during the writing of this article is also greatly appreciated. Terry Hays and Grant D. Jones offered many useful comments on

earlier drafts of the work. I retain responsibility for the interpretations and conclusions given here.

3.

"Counsels" are one of the many types of speech that occur in the village. An explanation of taxonomies of speech in Yucatec Maya can be found in Burns (1973:58–76).

4.

The writings were referred to as "sacred books" in the village. I refer to them here as Chilam Balam, the common name given to all such books found in the Yucatán Peninsula.

5.

The translations given here utilize pause length as the defining feature of a line. Dots between lines refer to pauses longer than one second. Capital letters denote portions spoken louder than normal, and italics are used to show portions spoken softer than normal. Discussions of this type of translation can be found in Tedlock (1972) and Burns (1973).

6.

Some words and phrases are left in Maya or Spanish because of the difficulty in providing succinct translations which fit the rhythmic confines of the lines. Their meaning can be readily judged from their context. *Yum*, for example, refers to a term of address such as "mister" and has some of the same connotations as the Spanish term *señor*.

10

Historical Dimensions of Orientation to Change in a Yucatec Peasant Community

Irwin Press

History and Change

There are two histories. One is the "actual" or scientifically determinable past (Malinowski 1945:29)—the sum of all events preceding the present instant. Such historical events shape the present and attitudes toward it. There is yet a second history, which includes those events remembered, reinterpreted, invented, or assumed to have occurred. This, too, serves as a referent and mechanism for judging and validating present acts. "History written from the inside view," said Redfield, "is the temporal dimension of world view" (1958:111).

At various times in anthropology's past, one or the other of these two histories has been given preference in explaining contemporary world views and attitudes toward change. Not infrequently, too, historical phenomena have been largely ignored in explaining present social structural phenomena. In spite of his lip service to "inside" history, one of the more glaring examples of this latter is, pertinently enough, Redfield's Yucatán work (1934, 1941).

Although Redfield's folk-urban scheme is no longer of major interest, his description and analysis of peasant social change still remains influential. Quite ahistorical, it suggests that outside contact in itself exerts inexorable pressures upon—or attractions to—the peasant. The less folk-like the community, the greater must have been the outside contact. Redfield chose Yucatán as a locus for his study in that it ostensibly presented

Note:
Reprinted by permission of the publisher, Greenwood Press, a division of Williamhouse-Regency Inc., 51 Riverside Avenue, Westport, Conn. 06880 and the author, Irwin Press, from his TRADITION AND ADAPTA-TION: Life in a Modern Yucatan Maya Village, published by Greenwood Press in September, 1975.

a single, homogeneous cultural zone with a single colonial overlay. Differences among communities (in terms of folk-nonfolk characteristics) must therefore be due to differential contact with outside elements, as opposed to idiosyncratic local development or cultural variation. These elements emanated, by and large, from the single city Mérida.

Today, of course, we are aware that the events which entered into the creation of modern Yucatán were far from evenly distributed in time or space. The conquest was easier for some native groups (the Xiu, for example) than others (such as the Cocom or Itzas). Some villages experienced more-threatening, others less-threatening contact with colonial Europeans. The northern zone suffered far more disruption from commercial henequen than did the central and southern portion of Yucatán. The Caste War dislocated some communities, whereas others experienced minimal violence or factionalism.

Each microarea of the state (if not each community) thus exhibits a variant historical configuration. Each community, furthermore, interprets this history idiosyncratically, inventing some elements, misinterpreting or forgetting others. The combination of actual and remembered events is the base upon which local self-image and orientation toward continuity or change are built. All outside influences, regardless of urban or other provenience, must confront this orientation and undergo evaluation with reference to it.

The following examines both real and recalled local events in terms of their effects upon orientation toward change in one Maya village.

Politics and Leadership

Pustunich is a contemporary Yucatec peasant community some 2 kilometers east of Ticul, on the Muna-Peto road to British Honduras. With few exceptions, all males make milpa in the old way, dress mestizo, speak Maya in street and home, and protect their crops with an annual round of traditional Maya ritual. The village sports a *h-men*, or Maya priest, and two well-known *curanderos*, and it still engages in large-scale communal hunts. At the same time, Technicolor movies, radios, bicycles, plastic hair curlers, enamel pans, almost universal literacy, and a top-notch traveling baseball team have been part of the village life for decades.

One of the earliest references to Pustunich occurs in the *Chilam Balam of Chumayel*. Both the village and nearby Xocnaceh are mentioned in legend as way points on the twelfth-century migration from the south (Roys 1933:72). Today, it should be mentioned, Xocnaceh is a ruined sugar plantation with crumbling buildings, and no one can recall when it might have been a settlement in its own right. As early as 1557, however, Pustunich is recorded as a distinct town with a church of its own (Roys 1957).

Prior to the conquest, Pustunich was almost certainly a small tributary of the ruling Xiu family. The Xiu were apparently latecomers to Yucatán and established themselves in Uxmal, some 12 kilometers to the southwest of Pustunich. Subsequently, they managed to gain considerable influence in the territory to the north, governed by the Cocom family out of the temple center of Mayapan. When Mayapan was destroyed in the midfifteenth century, the Xiu subsequently moved to the Mani area, 5 short kilometers northeast of Pustunich. Village contact with the ruling bureaucracy likely increased considerably at this time. In 1536, approximately eight years after Francisco de Montejo's disastrous first sortie into Yucatán, the Xiu leadership, on a pilgrimage to Chichen Itza, was betrayed and decimated by the Cocom (Roys 1957:61–63, 69–70). When Montejo's son arrived in Yucatán to finish the work of his father, the Xiu voluntarily united with him, ostensibly to revenge themselves further upon the Cocom (Blom 1936). It is also possible that cooperation with the Spanish was encouraged by an oracle who resided in Mani around 1500. This famous priest (named Chilam Balam) is said to have predicted, prior to the conquest, that fair-skinned, bearded strangers would come to convert the people and that they should be met with cooperation (*Relaciones de Yucatán* 1898–1900:XI, 44–45). Regardless of the cause, the Xiu and their tributary villages, such as Pustunich, suffered little during the actual conquest.

Both because of its location at the southern fringe of the populous flatlands and because of Xiu cooperation with the colonial regime, Mani was made a separate province and administrative center of southern Yucatán. Once again, Pustunich was hard by a major bureaucratic headquarters.

Shortly after the conquest, Montejo the younger made a *repartimiento* of the Mani province, portioning out lands and inhabitants in a number of *encomiendas*. Rather than the limited grants made in Mexico, the *encomiendas* of Yucatán were made in perpetuity (cf. Simpson 1950). Ticul (2 miles west of Pustunich) was created an *encomienda* in 1549, with 3,555 inhabitants listed as residing in 790 locations (Roys 1957:70). Pustunich, however, though but several kilometers from Ticul, fell to a separate *encomendero*, Francisco Arzeo, who also received tribute from the towns of Chaltum and Xanaba (*Relacions de Yucatán* 1898–1900:XI, xvii). In that Arzeo's three towns are scattered around the peninsula, it is unlikely that he resided in any of them. Unfortunately Arzeo was one of nine who failed to respond to the crown's amazing socioeconomic questionnaire of 1577 which was sent to thirty-three Yucatec *encomenderos*. We thus know nothing of the town's earliest colonial appearance. It was, however, a thriving distinct community even at that early date. In 1588, Pustunich, as an autonomous political entity, executed a land treaty with Ticul over water holes at least 10 kilometers distance (Roys 1943:190). This autonomy, however, was incomplete.

Prior to the conquest, individual towns of the area were governed by local, permanent chieftans (*batabs*) appointed by the Xiu ruler of Mani. Often, the *batab* was a son or close relative of the ruler. Advising the *batab* was a town council. Following the conquest, a new governmental form was imposed upon Yucatec towns, consisting of a governor chosen by the townsmen (yet confirmed by the Spanish authority), two *alcaldes*, a justice, and three or more councillors (*regidores*). In many villages, however, this elected hierarchy was actually subservient to a *cacique*—usually charismatic, often an old *batab* or son of the preconquest *batab*—and permanent in his position. Pustunich oldsters still refer to leaders of their parents' generation as *batabs*. In the Mani area, *caciques* almost always appeared from the ranks of remaining Xiu (Roys 1943:140). Because of their obvious utility as local leaders and opinion makers, Spaniards relied heavily upon *caciques*, often granting them special privileges. Thus, where they existed, *caciques* were the major (though unofficial) local power figures. In the treaty of 1588, the "principal man" of Pustunich is listed as Alonso Xiu. Following his name are those of the "official" *alcaldes* who are listed as such (Roys 1943:190). In other words, the new political machinery itself was "run" by such a *cacique*—and one of the old royal family, at that.

Because of its proximity to the larger and more important centers of Ticul and Mani and because of the presence of a Xiu *cacique*, Pustunich had little opportunity to govern many of its affairs, less even than more isolated towns governed by elected *alcaldes* and councils.

The *encomienda* system ended, and the political center of the immediate area passed from Mani to Ticul. Though always a separate town, Pustunich's political life was controlled by Ticul through several centuries. Prior to 1939, the town leader (called *cabo*) was appointed directly from Ticul. He and his council held but moderate authority, limited to the adjudication of minor torts. Older Pustunicheños tell of the 1939 visit to the village by Mexican President ("general") Lázaro Cardenas, who spent an hour in the pueblo "with his *mariachis*." He stressed the *campesino*'s right to elect his own *comisario* ("mayor") and put the best men in office. With this incentive, the schoolteacher helped organize a "league of workers" upon which to base future "election" of village officials. However, indirect pressure soon limited candidates to those "friendly" to the *presidente* of Ticul. Often but one candidate was nominated. The present school head has persistently stressed the necessity for autonomous elections with at least two candidates. Indeed, two candidates have frequently been nominated—and in 1961 both sent turkeys surreptitiously to the Ticul president a week prior to the vote. Pustunich, it must be stressed, controls no important natural resources, nor does it provide significant taxes to the Ticul treasury. Its political subservience to Ticul has been one of simple tradition—for both towns. For years the proceeds of the lucrative annual fiesta (in honor of the Virgin Assumption) had been confiscated by the county president, with small gratuity to the mayor of Pustunich. "The town isn't ready to handle its own affairs," was the excuse reportedly given. No one cared or dared to oppose this.

Disinterest in and distrust of politics is traditional in Pustunich. Within memory there have been no "political" deaths. While many towns suffered bloodshed during the Yucatec Socialist-Liberal dispute of the 1920's, Pustunich endured a few fistfights and one man reportedly left town in fear of his life. Only a minority of Pustunicheños actively seek office—the clandestine "deals" with the president of Ticul, the modicum of judicial power over one's neighbors. One mayor held office continually from 1924 to 1935 and is referred to as a *"cacique."* The town still recalls (unemotionally, jestingly) the time Comisario Uinic ordered a lime-burning *fagina* ("for school improvements"). One night, it is said, he sold the entire pile for a tidy personal profit. The last mayor's term was his second. The first time, it is maintained, he was thrown out of office for robbing a poor old villager's house of cash and goods. Yet no loud protest went up when he was reelected after some ten years out of office. There is no rush among Pustunicheños to stand for election.

Though always a distinct community, under *batabs, caciques, cabo,* and Ticul, Pustunich has had little opportunity to control its important affairs. Always a small—yet centrally located—cog within larger political networks, the village long ago abandoned its direction to others. Others have done its official thinking. Villagers do not view outside political intervention as unusual or disruptive. Nor do they view local governmental representatives as leaders, nor have they come to expect innovative behavior of them. Continuously lacking has been a precedent for self-determination and change-oriented action.

Ritual and Religious Hierarchy

As part of the Xiu empire, Pustunich owed both political and religious allegiance to Uxmal. The closest large ruin complex is that of Xcorralche, 10 kilometers to the south and roughly contemporary with Uxmal. Smaller temple ruins can be seen in Dzan, Mani, and on the outskirts of Ticul. Pustunich, however, has no such remains, nor does anyone know of any in the immediate vicinity. As vassal of Mayapan, Uxmal, and Mani, Pustunich undoubtedly had to supply labor and (occasionally) sacrifices to the priesthood in the capitals. In that the village lies but three hours' walk from Uxmal and twenty minutes from Mani, it is unlikely that any major ceremonials were carried out within it. The simple milpa ritual, however, was most likely performed autonomously even during the Xiu epoch. In 1548, Yucatán's first Catholic priests settled in the new Xiu capital of Mani. After initial hostility on the part of certain noble factions in Mani, the province settled down to ostensibly voluntary practice of Christianity. By 1557 a monastery had appeared in Mani and a church in Pustunich itself (Roys 1957).

The new priesthood outlawed pagan ritual; though, as Wolf demonstrates, predominantly the more overt, permanently organized and public spectacles were immediately displaced (1959:69–70). Covert field and house ritual, being less visible, continued to thrive or went underground. After the centralized Maya priesthood was disbanded, local curers and practitioners took up the thread of religious leadership. For the small peasant communities, this was not overly difficult. Polytheistic Maya belief further syncretized easily with the multiplicity of Catholic saints. Monopoly of esoteric knowledge and literacy merely passed from one set of priests to another.

Regardless of the presence of a church, however, the conversion of Pustunich was still incomplete. As early as 1558, Bishop Diego de Landa found that many newly Christianized natives in Yucatán were "perverted by the native priests and reverted to idolatry" (Tozzer 1941:76). In 1561 or 1562, a certain priest of Sacaba sent several principals to "the town of Quicucche and to the town of Pustuniche, and in these two towns they purchased two small boys which had just begun to walk, and who were bought from Juan Puc, principal Indian and powerful person of the said town of Pustuniche" (Scholes and Adams 1938:101). The sacrifice took place one league from the present hacienda of Tabi, 12 kilometers south of Pustunich.

Appalled by such incidents (which were beginning to multiply), Landa initiated an inquisition in the Mani territory in early May 1562. It was discovered that village leaders (*caciques* appointed by trusting *encomenderos*), as well as poor farmers, were involved. Landa states in his defense that his friars killed or maimed no one intentionally and that many natives "hung themselves in the bush and uninhabited sites and hidden places in order not to give [up] the idols nor abandon their evil ways as two or three did [hang themselves] in the province of Sotuta and as many more in that of Mani in the Pueblo of Tekax and Pustuniche" (Scholes and Adams 1938:294). Though such spectacular phenomena as sacrifice were soon suppressed, the basic field ritual of Pustunich survived, a remnant of the early tenacity of the town. Centuries later, Catholic Pustunich put as much effort into preserving its saints during the anti-cleric era. The image of the Virgin was secreted in a cave, and, even today, the mildew streaks across her face are pointed out with pride as the story is told.

The religious autonomy of Pustunich is of considerable antiquity and continuity. Fray López [de] Cogolludo, writing in the mid-seventeenth century, reports that Pustunich's patroness even then was the Virgin Assumption, leading to the conclusion that she has been the only patron saint since the conversion of the village began in the 1540's. Furthermore, the image was important enough to engage in a relationship of "visits" (*visitas*) with the Ticul patron, Saint Anthony of Padua (López [de] Cogolludo 1957:236).

The present church was completed by the Franciscans in 1779. It is typical of many small-town Mexican churches—single naved, with an ancient stone baptismal font to the right of the main entrance. Midway to the altar are two side entrances across from one another. Just beside the church stands a small ruined building, which villagers think was once a monastery. Within memory of the oldest inhabitant, no priest ever resided in Pustunich, however. Ticul is the religious center of the *municipio* with at least one and sometimes two priests. Unlike the general practice in Guatemala, villages of the *municipio* pay homage to their particular *santos* only and do not regard the *cabecera*'s saints as important to their welfare.

Today both Catholic and pagan rituals exist side by side. Neither complex has threatened the other for centuries. Both are under almost complete direction of the village. Seldom does a priest visit Pustunich and then only at the request of someone with the required fee. Because of the expense of priest-directed masses, Pustunich has done without many of the formal trappings of orthodox Catholicism. The most progressive of priests are viewed with suspicion, and tales of "slavery epoch" abuses are common.

There has been little change in either Catholic or pagan ritual since the postconquest conversion was effected. The village has held tenaciously to both and views each as generally distinct, albeit complementary in certain functions and somewhat syncretistic in form. Saint Michael the Archangel directs the four ancient *balams* of the cardinal directions. On the other hand, offerings to the dead on All Souls' Day are those of the milpa and its deities. Should the Cha Chaac ritual in late spring fail to produce rain, San Antonio's day on June 10 serves as a backstop.

The Economic Past

Pustunich is fortuitously located. It lies snuggling the Puuc Hill range on the fringe of an area which is rocky, generally inaccessible, and impractical to farm on a large mechanized scale. Here, in and beyond the Puuc, the village makes its milpas. As sugar and later henequen plantations ate up the flat, arable land to the north, Pustunich suffered no land pressure. Towns surrounded by large haciendas soon found their croplands dissipated and their residents forced wholesale into peonage. Furthermore, as traditional Maya ritual and the making of milpa are mutually dependent, disappearance of one almost inevitably meant destruction of the other. The displaced Indian seemed unable to transfer a ritual attachment focused on milpa to the paid production of yet another crop—henequen or sugar. Today, few towns in the henequen zone hold the annual Cha Chaac ceremony unless a good proportion of the men make some milpa on the side. Even so, many towns must import a *h-men* from other areas. In some instances Maya ritual is a *recent* phenomenon in henequen zone communities, for government redistribution of former plantation lands has permitted newly formed cooperative henequen villages to allocate some plots for home-use corn planting.

Some Pustunicheños were certainly caught in debt servitude to local plantations, due largely to extra cash needs. However, village milpa remained untouched in the vast and fairly inaccessible region south of the Puuc. Plantation work for Pustunicheños thus generally meant extra cash rather than actual subsistence. Frequently, one day a week would be given in exchange for cash or debt cancellation. Such service was given on Mondays, and thus nonresident workers became known as *luneros*. For those who worked part-time on plantations, milpa time-requirements were not severely challenged. Until late in the nineteenth century, sugar was the major cash crop of Puuc region plantations. Unlike henequen, the sugar labor-requirement calendar does not compete directly with corn production. It should be stressed that many Pustunicheños, having a solid autonomous milpa base, simple *chose* to work part-time for plantations, particularly during periods of peak labor needs. Thus wage labor was established early and existed side by side with the traditional milpa.

Shortly before the Revolution and breakup of the haciendas, Pustunich had a population of 283 (México, Dirección General de Estadística 1905). By 1940 the population has less than doubled to only 541 (ibid., 1943), indicating natural growth rather than wholesale immigration from haciendas. Since 1943 immigration has been practically negligible, and the population has more than doubled. In the census of 1900 the nearby hacienda of Tabi is listed as a rural *finca* of 851 population—513 males and 338 females. All other towns in the vicinity exhibit greater numbers of females than males. This suggests that possibly one-third of Tabi's work force represented males commuting for varying periods from their native villages of Pustunich, Santa Elena, Ticul, Dzan, and others. Today's Pustunich population of about 1,000 is largely a result of internal growth rather than migration from other towns. And migrants bring variant values with them. Slightly over 88 percent of all males are village-born. Approximately 75 percent of the women are locals.

The "epoch of slavery," as Pustunicheños refer to it, was ended by such state-level heroes as the martyred Carillo Puerto, who, to hear the villagers tell of it, "personally came to this area and hanged hacienda owners." Such statements help explain Pustunich antipathy toward local power figures and genuine respect for state-level politicians.

When, following the revolution of 1910, *ejidos* (community land grants) were established for peasant use, Pustunich merely received *formal* authority over rather marginally located farmlands which it had been using exclusively for centuries. Now, however *ejidal* status carried the added advantage of legal status with it, giving Pustunicheños the hitherto unavailable "clout" to collect damages from cattle ranchers whose beasts trampled milpa.

Pustunich was located fortuitously from another point of view. It is in the center of the state's only *juano* palm region. *Juano* is an excellent roof thatching and early became the raw material for a local hat-making industry. Significant extra income is obtained through selling crude and plaited *juano* palm. Every village woman and child earns daily *juano* money. Thus Pustunich has had an income insurance lacking in many other communities. Lastly, the vast bush south of Pustunich is fairly rich in small game. Even today a man can turn to hunting in an emergency, and all families have owned shotguns for generations.

Continuity and security are thus major themes of Pustunich economic history. Milpa, wage labor, and small-scale (palm industry) entrepreneurship have long coexisted in harmony. All are thus "traditional" and, never having been seriously threatened, are presently taken for granted. Similarly taken for granted are the functionally related elements of social class (mestizo dress), pagan ritual (milpa offerings and communal rain purchase), and possession of "modern" goods via cash.

Outside Contact

As part of the colonial Mani province, 4 miles from Mani and 2 from Ticul, Pustunich became an early way station for trade, missionaries, and diplomatic intercourse with Mérida. The Ticul-Pustunich land treaty of 1588 indicates an early introduction to Spanish bureaucratic mechanisms. The Puuc, as a natural barrier to southward travel and colonization, became the frontier zone of Yucatán. Important settlements, such as Ticul, Oxkutzcab, Tekax, and Peto, flourished, linked along with Pustunich by a single road—all lying in the shadow of the hills like knots on a string. The zone was more fluid than other areas, its Spaniards "mixing more easily with the indios" (Reed 1964:18–19). In the Valladolid district (near Chan Kom), natives far outnumbered the Spanish Creoles. Yet in 1881 the Ticul district contained roughly equal numbers of Indians and whites (Cline 1963:136). At the same time, traditional activities appeared to have continued. During the early nineteenth century, the zone raised two-thirds of Yucatán's corn crop, indicating not only a heavy and continuing reliance upon milpa but also long familiarity with broader cash-based market requirements (Reed 1964:18).

Good roads have linked the village to other towns and to the capital for centuries. The railroad from Mérida to Peto runs through the village outskirts. It has offered an inexpensive four-hour means of contact with (and transportation of goods to) the capital for over eighty years. General literacy has been part of Pustunich life since at least 1893, when the first school opened. Movies have been shown by the town's wealthiest storekeeper since the 1930's (power supplied by a gasoline generator). Traveling circuses, curers, hucksters, credit salesmen, and confidence men have made Pustunich a regular stop for unknown decades. For over fifty years motorized corn mills have freed village women from the time-consuming task of hand grinding. In the early 1930's, a telephone line linked Pustunich with Ticul and several other nearby towns. It was abandoned, however, insofar as there was nothing much to talk about. The phone hangs today in the *comisaria,* a mute reminder that the village had once sampled this particular element of modernity and found it wanting.

As a town on a main road, only several miles from important administrative centers, and as a village supplying workers to haciendas, Pustunich had centuries of opportunity for viewing the Spaniard and the latest of "Western culture" as it appeared in Yucatán. Pustunich was able to see innovations as they appeared among the Spaniards of Mani and the ladinos of Ticul and hacienda—innovations in logical sequence, with subsequent understanding of their development and relationship to one another. Modernism has not burst upon the village with the opening of a road nor trickled to it with an itinerant backwoods merchant. For centuries, in a mainstream of social and political movement, Pustunich has had the opportunity to pick and choose what it would—or, more realistically, *could*—of "modern" ways.

The Inside View

What of Pustunich's own view of the past? Some villagers say that the town was first settled by the *huites,* who subsequently fled during the wars between the Xiu and other royal groups. No one is sure who the *huites* were, though possibly they were Indians. Others claim that the first inhabitants were the *ppuses,* who preceded even the Indians. In fact, the Xiu are the "legitimate" descendants of the ppuses. The ppuses, who were dwarfs, occupied all of Yucatán. Once it is said, at Xocnaceh plantation several miles down the road, sixteen stone coffins were discovered which could only have held midgets. The ppuses (*not* the Franciscans) built the Pustunich church in only two days, as rock was softer then (thus the Catholic hierarchy is effectively dissociated from its own works). Later the Franciscans came and rebuilt it. It is said that when the Spanish arrived, they considered making Pustunich the capital of Yucatán but decided upon Mérida because it was closer to the coast.

Spaniards, maintain several old villagers, first came to Pustunich around 1800. After mining iron,* forging weapons, and taking Pustunich women to wife (thus the present Spanish surnames entered the village), they left, promising to return one day and make a grand city of the village. One of the Spaniards stayed to become *encomendero,* and it was he, it is said, who built the first masonry houses in the village square. This story is, in turn, contradicted by two rival oldsters, each of whom claims that his own great grandfather, and no "outsider" Spaniard, built

* There are no known iron deposits in Yucatán.

the first masonry houses in Pustunich. Interestingly enough, both of these old men bear Spanish surnames (though not of the alleged *encomendero*).

It is certain that village life was disrupted during the Caste War of the past century when less-acculturated, more-isolated Maya groups rose in rebellion against the Yucatec colonial masters and Hispanicized town Maya. Many communities, particularly in the north central portion of the state, were emptied and their populations driven into the bush. Being neither bush Maya nor Spanish nor landless plantation workers, Pustunich was ostensibly "neutral" and an unlikely target for specific attack by either side. Major battles, however, were fought in Ticul, and, indeed, the city was under siege during most of the month of May 1848 before falling to Maya attackers (Reed 1964:91–92). It is doubtful whether Pustunicheños could have remained wholly neutral yet safe during such a period; they may have taken to the bush or joined the native forces or, more likely, simply provided shelter and food for the Maya who were fighting less than a mile away.

Pustunich's own history of this era is sketchy yet important. The war was between the "Indians and the Castillians." The town itself was threatened by the "Indians," some of whom even occupied the northern periphery. However, three famous Pustunich witches came to the rescue and sent magical plagues of bats, bees, and *balancabs* (large stinging insects) to drive them off. The people of Pustunich at that time were neither "Indians" nor "Castillians," but *mayeros. Mayero,* like the Spanish terms *molinero* ("miller"), *carpintero* ("carpenter"), and so on, indicates professional status or expertise—in this case, expertise in the "Maya" life style. The Maya of those days are also referred to by villagers as "legitimate Maya." The Pustunich version of the Caste War thus turns inward, denying disruption, stressing continuity and magical events. It further attributes to Pustunich cultural descendancy from a specific, orthodox (*mayero*) life style (rather than ethnic or racial group) from which it has somehow diverged.

The plantation era, or "epoch of slavery," is recalled but hazily, and destinies of rich and poor merge in an aura of past subjugation to secular and religious authority. "I was a slave in the old days," recalls an eighty-year-old man, who neglects to add that he and his father also made milpa. "Yes, we were all slaves," sighs the town's richest man, whose family was long wealthy and never involved in anything but full-time milpa and entrepreneurial activity. Thus grows a tale of homogeneity, uniting rich and poor alike in a past of partial domination by others.

An ancient relates that, during the epoch of slavery

● all the priests made slaves of the people. All the people—even the young —were told when they were to marry, because they didn't [simply] fall in love with their wives. This was permitted because they [the priests] were the authorities. The boy met his wife in front of the authorities; he met her for the first time. The priests who directed marriages said to them, "There once was the Holy Inquisition, which says to the parents that a woman who marries must wait eighteen days before the mass can be performed." So [they took the bride off and] at the passage of eighteen days the bride was delivered to the groom and the priests said, "She is now crossed with Spanish blood," for they had lain with her, "and all your children will be Spanish." All are mixed, all. The bishops were first to get the girl during these eighteen days, and then she was passed on to the lower-ranking priests. "Afterward we will deliver her to you," [said the priests]. "You will go and say nothing because you are a slave." This was said to all boys who would marry. Such were the times. I had not been born yet. My grandfather told me about this. Probably took place before the revolution for independence.

In 1901, when the last of the rebel Maya were finally mopped up in Chan Santa Cruz, several presently living Pustunicheños were present. Typically, they were not even given the responsibility of bearing arms. Instead they were bearers and saw no action. This occurred about the time the revolution began. No one recalls any difficulties in the village during the revolution years of 1910–1920. During the rise to importance of the Yucatec socialists, in the twenties, oldsters recall some mild factionalism, and one man was reportedly forced to "flee for his life." No deaths, injuries, or physical clashes are remembered.

History and Orientation to Change

The two histories of Pustunich complement one another. They paint a picture of a community with autonomous identity, whose ways and families merge in a distant past. At the same time, a clear tradition of political subjugation exists. Leaders came from outside, not inside, and neither a tradition nor precedent for innovation exists. The great age, the continuity of economic and ritual institutions, and the assumed lack of serious threat to village life have all combined to produce a self-view of Pustunich as relatively timeless and slow to change. Many present phenomena have the authority of tradition whose roots are lost in time, legend, misinterpretation, falsification, claim, and counterclaim. There is little possibility of anyone's stating with unimpeachable conviction what "things were once like." Even Pustunicheños hasten to qualify most tales of the past with the phrase "it is said that . . . ," or "so they say." "I think so, but who knows?" they answer, when pressed about whether such and such an event really occurred.

Chan Kom, it must be recalled, was an isolated community *less than forty-five years old* when Redfield arrived in 1930. It was originally and subsequently settled by individuals discontented with or routed from their previous communities. In terms of world view and self-image, Chan Kom lacked a specific tradition and a "personality" of its own, as compared with Pustunich, whose traditions and families were solidified through over four hundred years of nonisolated existence. Any middle-aged resident of Chan Kom could say, with authority and experience, that "things were once different." For Pustunicheños of any age, things were always pretty much the same. Yet Chan Kom is still viewed by many as the archetype of Yucatec peasant communities, and its experience with change as representative of the problems to be faced by others. It is thus of relevance to note that, whereas 5 percent of the Chan Kom population dressed in the ladino manner in 1950, less than 3 percent of Pustunicheños were so garbed fourteen years later (Redfield 1950:40).

As one of the earliest towns to fall beneath Spanish rule in Yucatán, and being so near administrative centers, early contact and overt adoption of required European and Catholic socio-religious forms meant earlier readjustment and a longer subsequent period of untraumatic "simmering." During this period, Pustunich experienced more or less continuous and relatively unthreatening contact with the European settler. Pustunich views outside forces as paternalistic, self-serving, and generally avaricious —but not as ultimately dangerous. The village thus exhibits no "cultural paranoia." It is not consciously protecting its life style from encroachment by nonintelligible forces bent upon its destruction. In fact, it hardly admits to influence from "outside" sources. Its marvelous hunchbacked ancestors built the church overnight. Its witches saved the day during the Caste War, preventing possible destruction of the village. The "epoch of slavery," though ostensibly an imposition upon village autonomy, was a period less of disruption than stabilization in a configuration of dependency. And dependency is hardly new to Pustunich.

Although feeling itself to possess a quite specific life style, Pustunich does admit to having deviated from some now forgotten standard of cultural orthodoxy established by its *mayero* ancestors. In short, while there is some precedent for change, the precedent is unclear (no one knows how the "legitimate Maya" lived) and its advocates are unspecified. The various "histories" contribute to a self-view which is neither conducive to novel behavior nor necessarily threatening to it. This is not a "nonstatement." It describes a specific situation where innovation is possible yet where abrupt change is unanticipated and traditional role incumbents— both within and from outside the village—are not looked to for initiation of change.

Thus we can comprehend how, some twenty-five years ago, a Pustunich boy was able to initiate a vigorous committee system of village communal labor which paralleled the preexisting political organization. This young man was the first non-*milpero* ever produced—a schoolteacher, son of a highly conservative family. He had created an unprecedented role for himself and organized activity for unprecedented goals (See Press 1969 for an intensive analysis of the teacher's role and career). At the same time, we can understand the minimal use and respect for priests in the village. Tales of past abuse by the religious hierarchy and of earlier ppus (as opposed to Franciscan) architectural ingenuity serve to reinforce old attitudes toward the church and its priests as superfluous or self-seeking. This in turn prevents Pustunich from maintaining regular contact with young and eager new clerics whose nutrition-oriented sermons, cooperative produce-marketing projects, credit unions, and so on, might serve as stimuli for significant economic change.

Pustunich has a pragmatic view of "outside" role incumbents and physical trappings. Where such trappings could be utilized, they were. In its baseball team, basketball court, radios, bicycles, plastic hair curlers, general literacy, weekly cinema, and defunct telephone, Pustunich feels itself to be, if not terribly modern, at least one of the less "hickish" villages in the area. In its ubiquitous milpa, mestizo dress, pagan ritual, *curanderismo*, and Maya language, Pustunich feels itself to be linked with a fairly stable, nonthreatening past.

These views, and their effect upon orientation toward change, are products of historical manufacture. Pustunich's "verifiable" history is unique or, at most, shared by a handful of villages in the same microarea of Yucatán. Its myths and personal recollections are certainly shared by no others. Thus, the village's experiences cannot be generalized directly to other communities confronting the present. Nonetheless, we profit by the example. Reinforced is the obvious—and for that reason easily ignored—principle that specific historical events play a major role in the development of any community's world view and, ultimately, orientation toward stability and change. Further, we must remember that quantity and frequency of "outside" contact are but two among a host of variables which affect orientation to change. Pustunich's experience demonstrates that centuries of outside contact, if not directly threatening to the economic or social system, may create a stable *modus vivendi*, enabling the community to confront the world with pragmatism and self-confidence. This, after all, is what Foster meant when he described the peasant community as a perennial part-society, a result of long "simmering" of inside and outside phenomena (1967:2). This, too, is what Wolf meant when he suggested that peasants, at whatever point in their history, are "neither simple 'survivals,' nor the results of 'culture lag.' . . . They exist, because their functions are contemporaneous" (1957:13). It is particularly important to keep this in mind when dealing with Yucatecan peasantry, whose experience with change and urban influences has been viewed for so long through lenses colored by Redfield's largely ahistorical approach.

Notes on the Contributors

O. Nigel Bolland

(Ph.D., University of Hull, 1976) is assistant professor of sociology in the Department of Social Relations, Colgate University. He was a research fellow in the Institute of Social and Economic Relations, Jamaica, from 1968 to 1972. He has carried out extensive archival research on the social and economic history of Belize and has published several articles on colonialism and decolonization in the Caribbean. Coauthor with Assad Shoman of *Land in Belize: 1765–1871*, he has also written *The Formation of a Colonial Society: Belize, from Conquest to Crown Colony*.

Victoria Reifler Bricker

(Ph.D., Harvard University, 1968) is associate professor of anthropology at Tulane University. She was book review editor of the *American Anthropologist* from 1971 through 1973 and editor of the *American Ethnologist* from 1973 through 1976. She conducted archival research in Yucatán during the summers of 1971 and 1972, in Belize during the summer of 1972, and in the Public Record Office in London during the summer of 1973. Her publications include *Ritual Humor in Highland Chiapas* and articles on Mayan linguistics, humor, and rebellions. She is currently writing a book which will be a comparative study of Maya rebellions, including the Caste War of Yucatán.

Allan F. Burns

(Ph.D., University of Washington, 1973) is currently a research associate with Abt Associates, Inc., of Cambridge, Massachusetts. He has carried out eighteen months of sociolinguistic research in Yucatán, Quintana Roo, and Chiapas, Mexico (1970–1972), and has recently conducted ethnographic research on bilingualism and education in Arizona. He has published several articles on contemporary Maya folklore in *Alcheringa, Ethnopoetics.*

Anne C. Collins

is currently preparing a Ph.D. dissertation in the Department of Anthropology, Tulane University, on the ethnohistory of the Jacaltec Maya of Guatemala. As a fellow of the Matilda Geddings Gray Foundation (1974 and 1975), she conducted extensive research in the Archivo General del Gobierno in Guatemala City. Her field experience was gained from 1966 to 1969 when she resided in the Jacaltenango area. Some of the results of her research at that time have been published in *Guatemala Indígena.*

Don E. Dumond

(Ph.D., University of Oregon, 1962) is professor of anthropology and head of the Department of Anthropology at the University of Oregon. Although most of his research has focused upon the archaeology of Arctic America, his interests in Mexican prehistory and ethnohistory are indicated in such publications as "Swidden Agriculture and the Rise of Maya Civilization," "Competition, Cooperation, and the Folk Society," and "Demographic Aspects of the Classic Period in Puebla-Tlaxcala," in *Southwestern Journal of Anthropology;* "Classic to Postclassic in Highland Central Mexico" (with Florencia Muller), in *Science;* and "An Outline of the Demographic History of Tlaxcala."

Grant D. Jones

(Ph.D., Brandeis University, 1969) is chairman and associate professor of anthropology at Hamilton College. He has carried out field research among Mopan and Yucatec Maya in Belize and has studied documentary sources for the ethnohistory of the independent Maya of Yucatán during the nineteenth-century Caste War period. He is the author of *The Politics of Agricultural Development in Northern British Honduras* and several articles on the political organization of the Maya during the Caste War of Yucatán. In addition to continuing research on Maya ethnohistory, he is currently carrying out ethnohistoric research on the Guale Indians of the Georgia coast during the sixteenth and seventeenth centuries.

Irwin Press

(Ph.D., University of Chicago, 1968) is associate professor of anthropology in the Department of Sociology and Anthropology, University of Notre

Dame. He has conducted extensive field research in the United States, Mexico, Colombia, and Spain, with emphasis upon sociocultural change. He is author of numerous papers and articles relating to peasant and urban social structure and to the adaptation of folk medical practices to urban milieus. He most recently published *Tradition and Adaptation: Life in a Modern Yucatán Maya Village.*

James W. Ryder

a Ph.D. candidate in anthropology at Ohio State University, has completed two years of anthropological and demographic field work in Yucatán. During 1974–1975 he served as a research associate with the International Population and Urban Research Program, University of California at Berkeley. He is the author of "Interrelations between Family Structure and Fertility in Yucatán," in *Human Biology.* In addition to his theoretical concerns with the social structural aspects of demographic phenomena, he is also focusing his current interests on problems of political and economic development in Latin America.

France V. Scholes

(Ph.D., Harvard University, 1943) is research professor emeritus of history at the University of New Mexico. He served as investigator for the Carnegie Institution of Washington from 1931 to 1936 and became professor of history at the University of New Mexico in 1946. He conducted extensive research on the colonial history of Mexico and the United States Southwest. His writings on Yucatán are among the most important contemporary resources for Maya ethnohistory. Among his publications are *The Maya Chontal Indians of Acalan-Tixchel: A Contribution to the History and Ethnography of the Yucatán Peninsula* (with Ralph L. Roys), *Documentos para la historia de Yucatán* (three volumes, with Carlos R. Menéndez, J. I. Rubio Mañé, and Eleanor Adams), and *Troublous Times in New Mexico, 1659–1670.*

Sir Eric Thompson

who died in 1975, devoted his life to the study of the Maya and made major contributions to this end through his research and extensive writings in the fields of ethnology, ethnohistory, archaeology, and epigraphy. He was assistant curator at the Field Museum of Natural History, Chicago, from 1926 to 1935 and was archaeologist with the Carnegie Institution of Washington from 1935 to 1958. He was a fellow of the British Academy, a commander of the Spanish Order of Isabel la Católica, and had been awarded the Mexican Order of the Aztec Eagle and a Honorary Doctorate of Letters (Tulane University, 1972). Among his writings are *The Rise and Fall of Maya Civilization, Maya Archaeologist* (an autobiography), *Maya History and Religion, Maya Hieroglyphic Writing: An Introduction*, and *A Commentary on the Dresden Codex, a Maya Hieroglyphic Book.*

Bibliography

Abrams, Ira R.
 1973 Cash crop farming and social and economic change in a Yucatec Maya community in northern British Honduras. Ph.D. dissertation, Department of Social Relations, Harvard University.

Acereto, Albino
 1947 Historia política desde el descubrimiento Europeo hasta 1920. In *Enciclopedia Yucatanense* 3:5–388. Mexico City: Government of Yucatán.

Aldherre, Fred
 1869 Los indios de Yucatán. *Sociedad de Geografía y Estadística de la República Mexicana. Boletín.* IIa época, 1:73–76.

Allen, Capt. D. M.
 1887 *Report of Indian soldiery.* Belize: Government Press.

American Geographical Society of New York
 1935–1936 World (North America), 1:1,000,000, series 1301. Sheets of Belize N.E.-16 (1935), Istmo de Tehuantepec N.F.-15 (1938), Yucatan N.F.-16 (1956). New York.

Ancona, Eligio
 1889 *Historia de Yucatán desde la época mas remota hasta nuestros días.* 4 vols. Barcelona: Imprenta de Jaime Jepus Roviralta.

The Angelus [Belize]
 1889 Icaiche 5(7, supp.); (9):277–279; (10):298–301.
 1895 Icaiche 11:87–88.
 1901 A visit to Ycaiche 17:179–184, 202–206.

Arriaga, Eduardo E.
 1967 Rural-urban mortality in developing countries: An index for detecting rural underregistration. *Demography* 4:90–107.
 1970 *Mortality decline and its demographic effects in Latin*

America. Institute of International Studies. Population Monograph Series, no. 6. Berkeley and Los Angeles: University of California Press.

Arriaga, Eduardo E., and Kingsley Davis
1969   The pattern of mortality change in Latin America. *Demography* 6:223–242.

Aulie, Wilbur, and Evelyn Aulie
1951   Palencano-Chol vocabulary and folk-tales with English translation. MS.

Avendaño y Loyola, Andrés de
1696   Relación de las entradas que hize a la conversión de los gentiles Ytzaex. Original MS in Newberry Library, Chicago.

Aznar Barbachano, Tomás, and Juan Carbó
1861   *Memoria sobre la conveniencia, utilidad y necesidad de la erección constitucional del estado de Campeche*. Mexico City: Imprenta de Ignacio Cumplido.

Aznar Pérez, Alonso
1849   *Colección de leyes, decretos y órdenes o acuerdos de tendencia general del poder legislativo del estado libre y soberano de Yucatán*. Vol. 1. Mérida: Rafael Pedrera.

Ball, J. W.
1971   A preliminary report on the ceramic sequence at Becan, Campeche, Mexico. *Cerámica de Cultura Maya* 7:16–30. Philadelphia.

Baqueiro, Serapio
1878–1887   *Ensayo histórico sobre las revoluciones de Yucatán desde el año de 1840 hasta 1864*. 3 vols. Mérida: Imprenta de Manuel Heredia Arguelles.

Barclay, George W.
1958   *Techniques of population analysis*. New York: John Wiley & Sons.

Barrera Vásquez, Alfredo, and Silvia Rendon
1948   *El libro de los libros de Chilam Balam*. Mexico City: Fondo de Cultura Económica.

Barth, Fredrik, ed.
1969   *Ethnic groups and boundaries: The social organization of culture difference*. Boston: Little, Brown & Co.

Bay-Man
1787   A map of a part of Yucatán or that part of the eastern shore within the bay of Honduras alloted to Great Britain for the cutting of logwood in consequence of the convention signed with Spain on the 14th July 1786. By a Bay-Man. London.

Berendt, Carl Herman
 1868 Lengua maya. Miscelanea. 3 vols. MS in University Museum, Philadelphia.
 1872 *Report of explorations in Central America.* Smithsonian Institution. Annual Report . . . for the year 1867, pp. 420–426. Washington, D.C.: Government Printing Office.
 1879 Karte der Halbinsel Yucatán, Hauptsächlich Nach der von Joachim Hübbe und Andrés Aznar Pérez . . . Gotha: Justus Perthes. *Petermann's Geographische Mittheilungen,* tafel 11. [See also Hübbe and Pérez 1878.]

Berzunza Pinto, Ramón
 1965 *Guerra social en Yucatán.* Mérida: Costa-Amic.

Binford, Lewis R.
 1968 Some comments on historical versus processual archaeology. *Southwestern Journal of Anthropology* 24(3):267–275.

Blom, Franz
 1929 *Preliminary report of the John Geddings Gray Memorial Expedition, 1928.* New Orleans: Department of Middle American Research, Tulane University.
 1936 *The conquest of Yucatán.* Cambridge, Mass.: Riverside Press.

Bolland, O. Nigel
 1973 The social structure and social relations of the settlement in the Bay of Honduras (Belize) in the eighteenth century. *Journal of Caribbean History* 6:1–42.
 1974 Maya settlements in the upper Belize River valley and Yalbac Hills: An ethnohistorical view. *Journal of Belizean Affairs,* no. 3, 3–23.

Brainerd, George W.
 1958 *The archaeological ceramics of Yucatán.* Anthropological Records 19. Berkeley and Los Angeles: University of California Press.

Bricker, Victoria Reifler
 1973 Algunas consecuencias religiosa y sociales del nativismo maya del siglo XIX. *América Indígena* 33(2):327–348.
 1974 The ethnographic context of some traditional Mayan speech genres. In *Explorations in the ethnography of speaking,* edited by R. Bauman and J. Sherzer, pp. 368–388. Cambridge: At the University Press.

Bristowe, Lindsay W., and Philip B. Wright
 1888 *Handbook of British Honduras for 1888–89.* Edinburgh and London: William Blackwood & Sons.
 1890 *Handbook of British Honduras for 1890–91.* Edinburgh and London: William Blackwood & Sons.

British Honduras, Government of
> 1921   *Report on the census of 1921.* Belize: Government Printing Office.

Bruce S., Roberto D.
> 1968   *Gramática del Lacandón.* Instituto Nacional de Antropología e Historia, Publicaciones 26. Mexico City.

————, C. Robles, and E. Ramos
> 1971   *Los lacandones* 2. Cosmovisión maya. Instituto Nacional de Antropología e Historia, Publicaciones 26. Mexico City.

Bullard, William R.
> 1970   *Topoxte: A Postclassic Maya site in Peten, Guatemala.* Monographs and Papers in Maya Archaeology. Papers 61: 245–307. Cambridge, Mass.: Harvard University, Peabody Museum of Archaeology and Ethnology.

Burdon, Sir John Alder
> 1931–1935   *Archives of British Honduras.* 3 vols. London: Sifton Praed.

Burns, Allan F.
> 1973   Pattern in Yucatec Mayan narrative performance. Ph.D. dissertation, Department of Anthropology, University of Washington.

Butler, Mary
> 1935   *Piedras Negras pottery.* Piedras Negras Preliminary Papers 4. Philadelphia: University Museum.

Caiger, Stephen L.
> 1951   *British Honduras, past and present.* London: Allen & Unwin.

Calderon Quijano, José Antonio
> 1944   *Belize, 1663(?)–1821: Historia de los establecimientos británicos del Rio Valis hasta la independencia de Hispanoamérica.* Escuela de Estudios Hispanoamericanos de la Universidad de Sevilla. Publications 5. Seville.

Campeche, Estado de
> n.d.   Untitled map of roads, 1:500,000. Secretaria de Obras Públicas, Dirección General de Carreteras en Cooperación (Junta Local de Caminos). [Obtained January 1972; boundaries shown are those of the 1960's and later.]

Cano, Agustín
> 1942   Informe dado al Rey por el Padre Fray Agustín Cano sobre la entrada que por la parte de la Verapaz se hizo al Petén en el año de 1695, y fragmento de una carta al mismo, sobre el propio asunto. Sociedad de Geografía e Historia de Guatemala. *Anales* 18:75–79. Guatemala City: Tipografía Nacional. [Original MS dated 1696.]

Cárdenas Valencia, Francisco de
> 1937 *Relación historical eclesiastica de la provincia de Yucatán de la Nueva España.* Edited with introduction by F. Gómez de Orozco. Biblioteca Historia de México. Obras Inéditas 3. Mexico City. [Original MS dated 1639.]

Carmack, Robert M.
> 1971 Ethnography and ethnohistory: Their application in Middle American studies. *Ethnohistory* 18(2):127–145.

Carnegie Institution of Washington
> 1930–1950 *Reports of the Division of Historical Research.* Yearbooks 29–49. Washington, D.C.
> 1950–1958 *Reports of the Department of Archaeology.* Yearbooks 50–57. Washington, D.C.

Carrillo y Ancona, Crescencio
> 1908 *Biografía del illmo. y revmo. Sr. Dr. D. Fray Luis de Cifuentes y Sotomayor, obispo de Yucatán.* Edición del Gremio de Profesores y Estudiantes. Mérida.

Castillo, José Severo del
> 1883 *Cecilio Chi.* Mérida: G. Canto.

Chamberlain, Robert S.
> 1939 *Castilian backgrounds of the repartimiento-encomienda.* Carnegie Institution of Washington. Publication 509. Washington, D.C.
> 1948 *The conquest and colonization of Yucatán, 1517–1550.* Carnegie Institution of Washington. Publication 582. Washington, D.C.
> 1951 *The pre-conquest tribute and service system of the Maya as preparation for the Spanish repartimiento-encomienda in Yucatán.* Hispanic-American Studies 10. Coral Gables: University of Miami Press.

Charnay, Désiré
> 1887 *The ancient cities of the New World.* London: Chapman & Hall.

Ciudad Real, Antonio de
> 1873 *Relación breve y verdadera de algunas cosas de las muchas que sucedieron al Padre Fray Alonso Ponce en las provincias de Nueva España* . . . 2 vols. Madrid: Imprenta de la Viuda de Calero. [Original MS dated 1588.]
> 1929 *Diccionario de Motul.* [See Martínez Hernández, ed., 1929.]

Clegern, Wayne M.
> 1967 *British Honduras: Colonial dead end, 1859–1900.* Baton Rouge: Louisiana State University Press.

Cline, Howard F.
> 1944 The lore and deities of the Lacandon Indians, Chiapas,

Mexico. *Journal of American Folklore* 56–57:107–115.

1945 Remarks on a selected bibliography of the Caste War and allied topics. In Villa Rojas 1945:165–178.

1947 The Aurora Yucateca and the spirit of enterprise in Yucatan, 1821–1847. *Hispanic American Historical Review* 27:30–60.

1948a The henequen episode in Yucatan. *Inter-American Economic Affairs* 2(2):30–51.

1948b The sugar episode in Yucatan, 1825–1850. *Inter-American Economic Affairs* 1(4):79–100.

1949 Civil congregation of the Indians of New Spain, 1598–1606. *Hispanic American Historical Review* 29:349–369.

1950a *War of the castes and the independent Indian states of Yucatán*. Related Studies in Early Nineteenth Century Yucatecan Social History, pt. 1, no. 1. Microfilm Collection of Manuscripts on Middle American Cultural Anthropology, no. 32. Chicago: University of Chicago Library.

1950b *The war of the castes and its consequences*. Related Studies in Early Nineteenth Century Yucatecan Social History, pt. 1, no. 2. Microfilm Collection of Manuscripts on Middle American Cultural Anthropology, no. 32. University of Chicago Library.

1950c *Regionalism and society in Yucatán, 1825–1847: A study of "progressivism" and the origins of the Caste War*. Related Studies in Early Nineteenth Century Yucatecan Social History, pt. 3. Microfilm Collection of Manuscripts on Middle American Cultural Anthropology, no. 32. University of Chicago Library.

1963 *The United States and Mexico*. Cambridge, Mass.: Harvard University Press.

1972 Introduction: Reflections on ethnohistory. In *Guide to ethnohistorical sources*, edited by Howard F. Cline, pt. 1. Handbook of Middle American Indians 12:3–16. Austin: University of Texas Press.

Coe, Michael D.

1965 A model of ancient community structure in the Maya lowlands. *Southwestern Journal of Anthropology* 21(2):97–114.

Colonial Guardian (Belize)

1882–1913 Microfilm, Bancroft Library, University of California, Berkeley.

Cook, Sherburne, F., and Woodrow Borah

1974 The population of Yucatán, 1517–1960. In *Essays in population history: Mexico and the Caribbean*, by S. F. Cook and W. Borah, vol. 2, pp. 1–170. Berkeley and Los Angeles: University of California Press.

Crowe, Frederick
  1850   *The gospel in Central America.* Containing a Sketch of the Country . . ., a history of the Baptist mission in British Honduras . . . London: Charles Gilpin.

Davis, Kingsley
  1956   The amazing decline of mortality in underdeveloped areas. *American Economic Review* 46:305–318.
  1974   The migrations of human populations. *Scientific American* 231(3):92–107.

———, and Judith Blake
  1956   Social structure and fertility: An analytic framework. *Economic Development and Cultural Change* 4:211–235.

Díaz del Castillo, Bernal
  1908–1916   *The true history of the conquest of New Spain.* Translated and edited by Alfred P. Maudslay. Vols. 23–25, 30, 40. London: Hakluyt Society.

Dobson, Narda
  1973   *A history of Belize.* Trinidad and Jamaica: Longman Caribbean.

Dumond, D. E.
  1970   Competition, cooperation, and the folk society. *Southwestern Journal of Anthropology* 26:261–286.

Eliade, Mircea
  1959   *Cosmos and history: The myth of the eternal return.* New York: Harper & Row.

Escalona Ramos, Alberto
  1946   Algunas ruinas prehispánicas en Quintana Roo. *Sociedad Mexicana de Geografía y Estadística. Boletín.* IIa época, 61:515–628.

Fabela, Isidro
  1944   *Belice: Defensa de los derechos de México.* Mexico City: Editorial Mundo Libre.

Faris, James
  1975   Social evolution, population, and production. In *Population, ecology, and social evolution*, edited by Stephen Polgar. The Hague: Mouton.

Foster, George M.
  1967   What is a peasant? In *Peasant society: A reader*, edited by Jack M. Potter, May N. Diaz, and George M. Foster, pp. 2–14. Boston: Little, Brown & Co.

Fowler, Henry
  1879   *A narrative of a journey across the unexplored portion of British Honduras with a short sketch of the history and*

resources of the colony. Belize: The Government Press.

Frank, Andre Gunder

1970 The development of underdevelopment. In *Imperialism and underdevelopment: A reader.* New York: Monthly Review Press.

Fremont, H.

1868 *Plano del estado de Campeche.* Campeche: Agencia del Ministerio de Fomento.

Fry, Robert E.

1973 The archaeology of southern Quintana Roo: Ceramics. *Proceedings of the 40th International Congress of Americanists, Rome-Genoa, 1972* 1:487–93.

Gann, Thomas W. F.

1895–1897 The contents of some ancient mounds in Central America. *Proceedings of the Society of Antiquaries of London* 16:308–16.

1900 *Mounds in northern Honduras.* Smithsonian Institution. Bureau of American Ethnology. Annual Report 19:655–692. Washington, D.C.: U.S. Government Printing Office.

1918 *The Maya Indians of southern Yucatan and northern British Honduras.* Smithsonian Institution. Bureau of American Ethnology. Bulletin 64. Washington, D.C.: U.S. Government Printing Office.

1925 *Mystery cities: Exploration and adventure in Lubaantun.* London: Duckworth.

1927 *Maya cities: A record of exploration and adventure in Middle America.* London: Duckworth.

1934 Changes in the Maya censor [*sic*] from the earliest to the latest times. *Verhandlungen des XXIV. Internationalen amerikanisten-kongresses, Hamburg, 7. bis 13, September 1930.* Hamburg: Friederichsen, de Gruyter & co.

Gates, William E.

1937 *Yucatan before and after the conquest by Friar Diego de Landa with other related comments, maps, and illustrations.* Baltimore: The Maya Society.

Gibbs, Archibald R.

1883 *British Honduras: An historical and descriptive account of the colony from its settlement, 1670.* London: Sampson Low, Marston, Searle, and Rivington.

Gibson, Charles

1952 *Tlaxcala in the sixteenth century.* Yale Historical Publications. Miscellany 56. New Haven: Yale University Press.

1964 *The Aztecs under Spanish rule: A history of the Indians of the valley of Mexico, 1519–1810.* Stanford: Stanford University Press.

Goldkind, Victor
>1965   Social stratification in the peasant community: Redfield's
Chan Kom reinterpreted. *American Anthropologist* 67:
863–884.
>1966   Class conflict and cacique in Chan Kom. *Southwestern
Journal of Anthropology* 22:325–345.

Gonsález, J. de D.
>1766   Plano de la provincia de Yucatán. [Original MS in British
Museum, London.]

González, Manuel S.
>1961   Memorias sobre el departamento del Petén. *Guatemala
Indígena* 1(2):75–102. [Originally published in 1867.]

González Navarro, Moisés
>1970   *Raza y tierra: La guerra de castas y el henequén.* Mexico
City: El Colegio de México.

Grant, C. H.
>1967   Rural local government in Guyana and British Honduras.
Social and Economic Studies 16(1):57–76.

Great Britain. Directorate of Overseas Surveys
>1964   [Map of] British Honduras. 1:250,000. 2d ed. D.O.S. 649.
Series E552. Tolworth, Surrey.
>1965   [Map of] British Honduras. 1:800,000. 2d ed. D.O.S. 958.
(n.p.)

———. Ministry of Defence
>1970   [Map of] British Honduras. 1:50,000. 1st ed. Series D.O.S.
4499. Director of Military Survey. London.

Guatemala. Archivo General del Gobierno
>1936   Autos hechos en virtud de la real cédula de S.M. en que
se ordena . . . que se saquen de los montes los indios que
han huido. *Boletín* 1:257–293.

———. Dirección General de Cartografía
>1959   Mapa preliminar de la República de Guatemala, 1:750,-
000.

Hanke, Lewis
>1949   *The Spanish struggle for justice in the conquest of Amer-
ica.* Washington, D.C.: American Historical Association.

Hasler, J. A.
>n.d.   Vocabulario español-chontal recogido en Tamulte, Tab.
[approximately 650 words]. MS.

Henderson, Capt. George
>1809   *An account of the British settlement of Honduras* . . .
London: C. & R. Baldwin.

Honduras Almanack
>1830   *The Honduras almanack for 1830.* Belize.

Hübbe, Joaquin
>1940   *Belice.* Edited by C. R. Menéndez. Mérida: Tipográfica
>Yucateca.
———, and Andrés Aznar Pérez
>1878   *Mapa de la peninsula de Yucatán, comprendiendo los
>estados de Yucatán y Campeche.* Revised and augmented
>by Carl Herman Berendt. Paris: Prevel; Mérida: B. Aznar
>Pérez y Cía; New York: Geo. E. Shiels. [See also Berendt
>1879.]

Hudson, Charles
>1966   Folk history and ethnohistory. *Ethnohistory* 13:52–70.
>1973   The historical approach in anthropology. In *Handbook
>of social and cultural anthropology,* edited by John J.
>Honigmann, pp. 111–141.

Hummel, C.
>1921   *Report on the forests of British Honduras.* London:
>Crown Agents for the Colonies.

Humphreys, R. A.
>1961   *The diplomatic history of British Honduras, 1638–1901.*
>London: Oxford University Press.

Hunt, Marta Espejo-Ponce
>1974   Colonial Yucatán: Town and region in the seventeenth
>century. Ph.D. dissertation, University of California, Los
>Angeles.

Jones, Grant D.
>1969   Los Cañeros: Sociopolitical aspects of the history of agri-
>culture in the Corozal region of British Honduras. Ph.D.
>dissertation, Department of Anthropology, Brandeis
>University.
>1971a   La estructura política de los Mayas de Chan Santa Cruz:
>El papel del respaldo inglés. *América Indigena* 31(2):415–
>428.
>1971b   *The politics of agricultural development in northern
>British Honduras.* Developing Nations Monograph Series
>1, no. 4. Overseas Research Center. Winston-Salem, N.C.:
>Wake Forest University.
>1973   Maya intergroup relations in nineteenth century Belize
>and southern Yucatan. *Journal of Belizean Affairs,* no. 1,
>3–13.
>1974   Revolution and continuity in Santa Cruz Maya society.
>*American Ethnologist* 1(4):659–683.

Jones, W. T.
>1972   World views: Their nature and their function. *Current
>Anthropology* 13(1):79–109.

Kay, Cristobal
    1975   Comparative development of the European manorial
           system and the Latin American hacienda system. *Journal
           of Peasant Studies* 2(1):69–98.

Kurjack, Edward B.
    1974   *Prehistoric lowland Maya community and social organi-
           zation: A case study at Dzibilchaltun, Yucatán, Mexico.*
           Publications 38. New Orleans: Middle American Re-
           search Institute, Tulane University.

Landa, Diego de
    1938   *Relación de las cosas de Yucatán.* Introduction and notes
           by H. Pérez Martínez. Mexico City: Pedro Robredo. [See
           also Gates 1937 and Tozzer 1941.]

Larsen, Helga
    1964   Trip from Chichen-Itzá to Xcacal, Q.R., Mexico. *Ethnos*
           29:5–42.

Laws of British Honduras
    1882[?]   *Laws of British Honduras in force on 31 Dec. 1881.* N.p.

Lee, Rosemary
    n.d.   The tourist industry in Yucatan: A case study in the
           interaction between economic development and social
           structure in an underdeveloped region. Unpublished MS,
           University of California, Irvine.

Lefroy, H.
    1884   On some pottery, flint implements, and other objects from
           British Honduras. *Archaeological Journal* 41:47–53.

Lewis, I. M., ed.
    1968   *History and social anthropology.* A.S.A. Monographs 7.
           London: Tavistock.

Lizana, Bernardo de
    1893   *Historia de Yucatán. Devocionario de nuestra Señora de
           Izamal y conquista espiritual.* Mexico City: Museo
           Nacional de México. [Originally published in 1633.]

Lizardi Ramos, Cesar
    1939   Exploraciones arqueológicas en Quintana Roo. *Revista
           Mexicana de Estudios Antropológicos* 3:46–53.

Lopetegui, Leon, and Felix Zubillaga
    1965   *Historia de la iglesia en la América española.* Madrid:
           La Editorial Católica.

López [de] Cogolludo, Fr. Diego
    1867–1868   *Historia de Yucatán escrita en el siglo XVII por el
           reverendo padre Fr. Diego López Cogolludo.* 2 vols. 3rd
           ed. Mérida: Manuel Aldana Rivas. [Originally published
           in 1688.]

1957   *Historia de Yucatán.* Prologue by J. Ignacio Rubio Mañé.
        5th ed. Mexico City: Editorial Academia Literaria.
        [Originally published in 1688.]

Machlin, Milt, and Bob Marx
1971   First visit to three forbidden cities. *Argosy* 372(5):18–28.

MacNutt, Francis Augustus, ed. and trans.
1908   *Letters of Cortes: The five letters of relation from
        Fernando [sic] Cortes to the Emperor Charles V.* New
        York and London: G. P. Putnam's Sons.

Maler, Teoberto
1903   *Researches in the central portion of the Usumacinta
        valley.* Reports of Explorations for the Museum. Mem-
        oirs 2 (2). Cambridge, Mass.: Peabody Museum of Archae-
        ology and Ethnology, Harvard University.
1908   *Explorations in the department of Peten, Guatemala, and
        adjacent regions: Topoxte, Yaxha, Benque Viejo,
        Naranjo.* Memoirs 4(2)53–127. Cambridge, Mass.: Pea-
        body Museum of Archaeology and Ethnology, Harvard
        University.
1910   *Explorations in the department of Peten, Guatemala, and
        adjacent regions: Motul de San José, Peten-Itza.* Mem-
        oirs 4(3):131–170. Cambridge, Mass.: Peabody Museum
        of Archaeology and Ethnology, Harvard University.

Malinowski, B.
1945   The dynamics of culture change. In *An inquiry into race
        relations in Africa,* edited by Phyllis M. Kaberry. New
        Haven: Yale University Press.

Malte-Brun, V. A.
1864   Carte de Yucatan et des regions voisines (n.d.). In *Un
        coup d'oeil sur de Yucatan, geographie, histoire et monu-
        ments.* Paris: Libraire de la Société de Géographie.

Mamdani, Mahmood
1972   *The myth of population control: Family, caste, and class
        in an Indian Village.* New York: Monthly Review Press.

Martínez Hernández, Juan, ed.
1929   *Diccionario de Motul: Maya Español.* Atribuido a Fray
        Antonio de Ciudad Real y arte de la lengua maya por
        Fray Juan Coronel. Mérida. [MS ca. 1585 in John Carter
        Brown Library, Providence, R.I.]

Mason, Gregory
1928   *Pottery and other artifacts from caves in British Honduras
        and Guatemala.* Indian Notes and Monographs 47. Heye
        Foundation. Museum of the American Indian, New York.

Maudslay, A. P.
1883   Explorations in Guatemala and examination of the

newly-discovered Indian ruins of Quirigua, Tikal, and the Usumacinta. *Proceedings of the Royal Geographical Society* 5:185–204; map, 248. London.

1889–1902 *Archaeology*. Biologia Centrali-Americana. 5 vols. London: Porter & Dulau.

Mazzarelli, Marcella
1972 Maya Settlement in the Cayo District, British Honduras: Nineteenth century. Paper presented at the American Anthropological Association meetings, November 30, 1972, Toronto.

Means, Philip Ainsworth
1917 *History of the Spanish Conquest of Yucatan and of the Itzas*. Papers 7. Cambridge, Mass.: Peabody Museum of Archaeology and Ethnology, Harvard University.

Merwin, Raymond E.
1913 The ruins of the southern part of the peninsula of Yucatan with special reference to their place in the Maya area. [Original MS in Widener Library, Harvard University, Cambridge, Mass.]

México. Archivo General de la Nación
1948 *Situación estadística de Yucatán en 1851*. Mexico City: Secretaria de Gobernación, Dirección General de Información.

———. Centro de Estudios Económicos y Demográficos
1970 *Dinámica de la población de México*. Mexico City: El Colegio de México.

———. Dirección General de Estadística
1905 II censo general de población 1900. Mexico City.
1917–1918 III censo general de población 1910. Mexico City.
1928 IV censo general de población 1921. Mexico City.
1934 V censo general de población 1930. Mexico City.
1939 Anuario estadístico 1938. Mexico City.
1941 Anuario estadístico 1939. Mexico City.
1943 VI censo general de población 1940. Mexico City.
1952 VII censo general de población 1950. Mexico City.
1963 VIII censo general de población 1960. Mexico City.
1971 IX censo general de población 1970. Mexico City.

———. Gobierno de
1829 *Colección de órdenes y decretos de la soberana junta provisional gubernativa, y soberanos congresos generales de la nación mexicana*. Vol. 4. Mexico City: Galvan.

———. República de
1957–1958 [Map of] Estados Unidos Mexicanos, 1:500,000. Comisión Intersecretarial Coordinadora del Levantamiento de la Carta Geográfica de la República Mexicana.

Sheets of Campeche 15Q-VI(1957), Chetumal 16Q-V y Río Azul 16Q-VII (1958), Mérida 16Q-III y Cozumel 16Q-IV (1958), 15Q-IV Triángulos (1958).

1963–1969 [Map of] Estados Unidos Mexicanos, 1:1,000,000. Secretaria de Agricultura y Ganadería, Departamento Geográfico. Sheets of Campeche (1963), Quintana Roo (1969), Yucatán (n.d.).

Miller, L. K., and J. R. Carter

1932 *Maya artifacts . . . largely from the Cámara and Rafael Regil collections.* Edition of 90 copies privately printed. Cleveland, Ohio.

Miller, William

1887 Notes on a part of the western frontier of British Honduras. *Proceedings of the Royal Geographical Society of London,* n.s., 9:420–423.

1889 A journey from British Honduras to Santa Cruz, Yucatan. *Proceedings of the Royal Geographical Society of London,* n.s., 11:23–28.

Miro, Carmen

1964 The population of Latin America. *Demography* 1:15–41.

Molina, Rev. Pastor

1889 Icaiche. *The Angelus,* Calendar and Monthly Notes, September 1889. [See also *The Angelus* 1889.]

Molina Font, Gustavo

1941 *La tragedia de Yucatán.* Mexico City: Revista de Derecho y Ciencias Sociales.

Molina Hübbe, Ricardo

1941 *Las hambres de Yucatán.* Mexico City: Editorial Orientaciones.

Molina Solis, Juan Francisco

1896 *Historia del descrubrimiento y conquista de Yucatán con una reseña de la historia antigua de esta península.* Mérida: Imprenta y Litografía R. Caballero.

1904–1913 *Historia de Yucatán durante la dominación española.* 3 vols. Mérida: Imprenta de la Lotería del Estado.

1921 *Historia de Yucatán desde la independencia de España hasta la época actual.* 2 vols. Mérida: Talleres Gráficos de "La Revista de Yucatán."

Morelet, Arthur

1871 Travels in Central America, including accounts of some regions unexplored since the conquest. New York: Leypoldt, Holt, & Williams.

Morley, Sylvanus G.

1965 Murder on the trail. In *They found the buried cities: Exploration and excavation in the American tropics,* edited by Robert Wauchope, pp. 231–240. Chicago: University of Chicago Press. [Original MS dated 1916.]

Motul Dictionary. *See* Martínez Hernández 1929.

Nag, Moni
1962　*Factors affecting human fertility in nonindustrial societies: A cross-cultural study.* Publications in Anthropology 66. New Haven: Yale University.

Noguera, Eduardo
1940　Expedición científica mexicana, 1937. *Cerámica de Quintana Roo. El México Antiguo* 5:9–17.

Noyes, Ernst, ed. and trans.
1932　*Fray Alonso Ponce in Yucatan, 1588.* Publications 4 (Middle American Papers): 297–372. New Orleans: Middle American Research Institute, Tulane University.

Oviedo y Valdés, Gonzalo Fernández de
1851–1855　*Historia general y natural de las Indias, islas y tierra firme del mar océano.* 4 vols. Madrid: Real Academia de la Historia.

Pacheco Cruz, Santiago
1958　Diccionario de la fauna Yucateca. Mérida: Editorial Zamná.
1959　Diccionario de etimologías toponómicas Mayas. Mérida: Imprenta de Don Antonio Ortega.

Paso y Troncoso, Francisco de, comp.
1938　*Epistolario de Nueva España, 1505–1818.* Vol 5. Mexico City: Antigua Librería Robredo de José Porrua e Hijos.
1940　*Epistolario de Nueva España, 1505–1818.* Vol 15. Mexico City: Antigua Librería Robredo de José Porrua e Hijos.

Pendergast, David M.
1967　*Palenque: The Walker-Caddy Expedition to the ancient Maya city, 1839–1840.* Norman: University of Oklahoma Press.
1970　*A. H. Anderson's excavations at Rio Frio Cave E, British Honduras (Belize).* Occasional Papers 20. Toronto: Royal Ontario Museum.

———; Murray H. Bartley; and George J. Armelagos
1968　A Maya tooth offering from Yakalche, British Honduras. *Man* n.s. 3:635–643.

Peniche, Manuel
1869　Carta del territorio de Belice. Historia de los relaciones de España y México con Inglaterra sobre el establicimiento de Belice. *Sociedad Mexicana de Geografía y Estadística. Boletín.* Epoca 2, 1:217–256, 377–402. [With notation that it is "una copia del que dirigió al gobierno del principe Maximiliano el enviado

extraordinario de Inglaterra . . . Mr. Campbell Scarlet, adjunto a su comunicación de 6 de marzo de 1866."]

Pérez Alcalá, Felipe
1914   *Ensayos biográficos, cuadros históricos, hojas dispersas.* Mérida: La Revista de Mérida.

Petryshyn, Jaroslaw T.
1968   El panteón maya de los lacandones en Najá: Relación preliminar sobre la expedición a la selva lacandona. San Cristóbal Las Casas.

1969   Ein Lakandonischer Gottesdienst en der Höhle des Gottes Tsibana am Heiligen See von Mensabok . . . Chiapas. *Archiv fur Völkerkunde* 23:169–176.

Press, Irwin
1968   Continuity in transition: The anatomy of a Yucatec peasant community. Ph.D. dissertation, Department of Anthropology, University of Chicago.

1969   Ambiguity and innovation: Implications for the genesis of the culture broker. *American Anthropologist* 71:205–217.

Quintana Roo, Territorio de
n.d.   Quintana Roo, red de carreteras. Secretaria de Obras Públicas, Junto Local de Caminos. [Obtained January 1972; boundaries shown are those of the 1950's.]

Radcliffe-Brown, A. R.
1965   *Structure and function in primitive society.* New York: The Free Press. [Originally published in 1952.]

Raymond, Nathaniel Curtis
1971   The impact of land reform in the monocrop region of Yucatán, Mexico. Ph.D. dissertation, Department of Anthropology, Brandeis University.

1974   Revolución, reforma agraria y población. *Anuario Indigenista* 34:173–182.

Recopilación de leyes de los reynos de las Indias
1943   3 vols. 4th ed. Madrid. [Originally published in 1791.]

Redfield, Robert
1934   Culture change in Yucatan. *American Anthropologist* 36:57–69.

1938   *Race and class in Yucatan.* Cooperation in Research. Carnegie Institution of Washington. Publications 501. Washington, D.C.

1941   *The folk culture of Yucatan.* Chicago: University of Chicago Press.

1950   *A village that chose progress: Chan Kom revisited.* Chicago: University of Chicago Press.

1958   *The little community.* Chicago: University of Chicago Press.

Redfield, Robert, and Alfonso Villa Rojas
1934   *Chan Kom: A Maya village.* Publication 448. Washington, D.C.: Carnegie Institution of Washington.

Reed, Nelson
1964   *The Caste War of Yucatan.* Stanford: Stanford University Press.

Regil, José María, and Alonso Manuel Peón
1848   Plano de Yucatán. In *Regil and Peón* 1853.
1853   Estadística de Yucatán. *Sociedad Mexicana de Geografía y Estadística. Boletín.* Época 1, 3:237–240.

Reina, Ruben E.
1962   The ritual of the skull in Peten, Guatemala. *Expedition* (4):25–35.

Relaciones de Yucatán
1898–1900   *Colección de documentos inéditos relativos al descubrimiento, conquista y organización de las antiguas posesiones españolas de Ultramar.* 2nd series. Vols. 11, 13. Madrid: Real Academia de la Historia.

Ricketson, Oliver, Jr., and A. V. Kidder
1930   An archaeological reconnaissance by air in Central America. *Geographical Review* 20(2):177–206.

Rogers, E.
1885   British Honduras: Its resources and development. *Journal of the Manchester Geographical Society* 1 (July): 197–227 (including Appendix: "The Santa Cruz Indians").

Romney, D. H., ed.
1959   *Land in British Honduras: Report of the British Honduras Land Use Survey Team.* Colonial Office. Colonial Research Publications 24. London: Her Majesty's Stationery Office.

Rosado, José María
1931   The Indian rising in Bacalar, as told in a letter (1915) to Bishop Murphy, S.J. *Clarion,* June 25, 1931. Belize.

Roys, Ralph L.
1933   *The Book of Chilam Balam of Chumayel.* Publication 438. Washington, D.C.: Carnegie Institution of Washington.
1939   *The titles of Ebtun.* Publication 505. Washington, D.C.: Carnegie Institution of Washington.
1940   *Personal names of the Maya of Yucatan.* Publication 523. Contribution 31. Washington, D.C.: Carnegie Institution of Washington.

1943   *The Indian background of colonial Yucatan.* Publication
        548. Washington, D.C.: Carnegie Institution of
        Washington.

1957   *The political geography of the Yucatan Maya.* Publica-
        tion 613. Washington, D.C.: Carnegie Institution of
        Washington.

Roys, Ralph L.; France V. Scholes; and Eleanor B. Adams

1959   Census and inspection of the town of Pencuyut, Yucatan,
        in 1583 by Diego García de Palacio, Oidor of the
        Audiencia of Guatemala. *Ethnohistory* 6:195–225.

Rubio Mañé, J. Ignacio, ed.

1942   *Archivo de la historia de Yucatán, Campeche y Tabasco.*
        3 vols. Mexico City.

Ruppert, Karl, and J. H. Denison

1943   *Archaeological reconnaissance in Campeche, Quintana
        Roo, and Peten.* Publication 543. Washington, D.C.:
        Carnegie Institution of Washington.

Ryder, James W.

n.d.   Interrelations between family structure and level of fer-
        tility: A conceptual and methodological clarification.
        Unpublished MS, Ohio State University, Columbus.

Sahlins, Marshall D.

1961   The segmentary lineage: An organization of predatory
        expansion. *American Anthropologist* 63:322–345.

Sanchez de Aguilar, Pedro

1892   Informe contra idolorum cultores del obispado de
        Yucatán. Museo Nacional de México. *Anales* 6:13–122.

Sapper, Karl

1891   Ein Besuch bei den östlichen Lakandonen. *Ausland*
        64:892–895. Stuttgart.

1895   Die Unabhängigen Indianerstaaten von Yucatan. *Globus*
        67(13):197–201 (includes map).

1904   Independent Indian states of Yucatan. In *Mexican and
        Central American antiquities, calendar systems, and
        history.* Smithsonian Institution. Bureau of American
        Ethnology. Bulletin 28:625–634. Washington, D.C.: U.S.
        Government Printing Office.

Satterthwaite, Linton S.

1935   Palace Structures J2 and J6. Piedras Negras Preliminary
        Papers 3. University Museum, University of Pennsylvania.

Scholes, France V., and Eleanor B. Adams

1936   Documents related to the Mirones Expedition to the
        interior of Yucatan, 1621–1624. *Maya Research*
        3:153–176, 251–276.

1938   *Don Diego Quijada, alcalde mayor de Yucatán, 1561–*

       1565. 2 vols. Documentos sacados de los archivos de España. Biblioteca Histórica Mexicana de Obras Inéditos, nos. 14–15. Mexico City: Antigua Librería Robredo.

1960   *Relaciones histórico-descriptivas de la Verapaz, el Manche y Lacandón, en Guatemala.* Guatemala: Editorial Universitaria.

————, and Ralph L. Roys

1938   *Fray Diego de Landa and the problem of idolatry in Yucatán.* Cooperation in Research. Publication 501:585–620. Washington, D.C.: Carnegie Institution of Washington.

1948   *The Maya Chontal Indians of Acalan-Tixchel: A contribution to the history and ethnography of the Yucatan Peninsula.* Publication 560. Washington, D.C.: Carnegie Institution of Washington.

————; Carlos R. Menéndez; J. Ignacio Rubio Mañé; and Eleanor B. Adams, eds.

1936–1938   *Documentos para la historia de Yucatán.* Vol. 1, *1550–1561.* Vol. 2, *La iglesia en Yucatán, 1560–1610.* Vol. 3, *Discurso sobre la constitución de las provincias de Yucatán y Campeche.* Mérida: Compañía Tipográfica Yucateca.

Schumann, Otto

1971*a*   *Descripción estructural del Maya Itzá del Petén, Guatemala, C. A.* Centro de Estudios Mayas. Cuaderno 6. Mexico City: Universidad Nacional Autónoma de México, Coordinación de Humanidades.

1971*b*   El origen del maíz en Maya-Mopan. *Tlalocan* 6:305–311. México.

Seler, Eduard

1904   *Antiquities of Guatemala.* Smithsonian Institution. Bureau of American Ethnology. Bulletin 28:75–121. Washington, D.C.: U.S. Government Printing Office.

Service, Elman R.

1962   *Primitive social organization.* New York: Random House.

Settlers of Honduras

1824   *The defence of the settlers of Honduras against the unjust and unfounded representations of Colonel George Arthur . . .* Kingston: Alex. Aikman.

Shoman, A.

1973   The birth of the nationalist movement in Belize, 1950–1954. *Journal of Belizean Affairs,* no. 2, 3–40.

Simpson, Lesley Byrd

1934   *Studies in the administration of the Indians in New Spain: I, the laws of Burgos; II, the civil congregation.*

Ibero-Americana 7. Berkeley and Los Angeles: University of California Press.

1950   *The encomienda in New Spain.* Berkeley and Los Angeles: University of California Press.

Smith, Michael G.
1962   History and social anthropology. *Journal of the Royal Anthropological Institute* 92:72–85.

Smith, Robert E.
1944   *Archaeological specimens from Guatemala.* Carnegie Institution of Washington. Notes on Middle American Archaeology and Ethnology 37. Cambridge, Mass.

1954   *Pottery specimens from Guatemala: 1.* Carnegie Institution of Washington. Notes on Middle American Archaeology and Ethnology 118. Cambridge, Mass.

1955   *Ceramic sequence at Uaxactun, Guatemala.* Tulane University. Middle American Research Institute. Publication 20. 2 vols. New Orleans.

Sociedad Tipográfica
1878   *Correspondencia diplomática cambiada entre el gobierno de la república y el de su Majestad Britanica con relación al territorio llamado Belice, 1872–1878.* Campeche: Imprenta de la Sociedad Tipográfica.

Solis, José Leandro
1878   *Memoria del partido de los Chenes: Presentado por su jefe político.* Campeche: Imprenta de la Sociedad Tipográfica.

Soustelle, Jacques
1935   Le totémisme des lacandons. *Maya Research* 2(4):235–244.
1937   La culture matérielle des Indiens Lacandons. *Journal Société des Américanistes de Paris* 24:1–95.

Soza, José María
1957   *Pequeña monografía del Departamento del Petén.* Guatemala: Editorial del Ministerio de Educación Pública.

Stanislawski, Dan
1946   The origin and spread of the grid-pattern town. *Geographical Review* 36:105–120.
1947   Early Spanish town planning in the New World. *Geographical Review* 37:94–105.

Steggerda, Morris
1941   *Maya Indians of Yucatan.* Publication 531. Washington, D.C.: Carnegie Institution of Washington.

Stephens, John L.
1841   *Incidents of travel in Central America, Chiapas, and Yucatan.* 2 vols. New York: Harper and Brothers.

1963 *Incidents of travel in Yucatan.* 2 vols. New York: Dover Publications. [Originally published in 1843.]

Stoll, Otto

1884 *Zur Ethnographie der Republik Guatemala.* Zürich: Druck von Orell Füssli & Co.

1958 *Ethnografía de Guatemala.* Guatemala: Editorial del Ministerio de Educación Pública.

Stolnitz, George

1965 Recent mortality trends in Latin America, Asia, and Africa. *Population Studies* 19:117–138.

Strickon, Arnold

1965 Hacienda and plantation in Yucatan: An historical-ecological consideration of the folk-urban continuum in Yucatan. *América Indígena* 25(1):35–63.

Sturtevant, William C.

1966 Anthropology, history, and ethnohistory. *Ethnohistory* 13:1–51.

Swadesh, Mauricio; María Cristina Alvarez; and
Juan Ramón Bastarrachea

1970 *Diccionario de elementos del Maya yucateco colonial.* Centro de Estudios Mayas. Cuadernos 3. Mexico City: Universidad Nacional de México, Coordinacíon de Humanidades.

Swadesh, Morris

1961 Interrelaciones de las lenguas mayenses. Instituto Nacional de Antropología e Historia. *Anales* 13:231–267.

Tedlock, Dennis

1972 On the translation of style in oral narrative. In *Toward new perspectives in folklore,* edited by Americo Paredes and Richard Bauman. Austin: University of Texas Press.

Thompson, Donald E.

1954 *Maya paganism and Christianity: A history of the fusion of two religions.* Tulane University. Middle American Research Institute. Publications 19:1–35. New Orleans.

Thompson, J. Eric S.

1930 *Ethnology of the Mayas of southern and central British Honduras.* Field Museum of Natural History. Publications 274. Anthropological Series 17:(2). Chicago.

1931 *Archaeological investigations in the southern Cayo District, British Honduras.* Field Museum of Natural History. Publications 301. Anthropological Series 17:(3). Chicago.

1936 *Exploration in Campeche and Quintana Roo and excavations at San José, British Honduras.* Yearbook 35:125–

128. Washington, D.C.: Carnegie Institution of
Washington.

1937   *A new method of deciphering Yucatecan dates with
special reference to Chichen Itza.* Publication 483.
Contributions 22. Washington, D.C.: Carnegie
Institution of Washington.

1939   *Excavations at San José, British Honduras.* Publication
506. Washington, D.C.: Carnegie Institution of
Washington.

1940   *Late ceramic horizons at Benque Viejo, British Honduras.*
Publication 528. Contributions 35. Washington, D.C.:
Carnegie Institution of Washington.

1946   *The dating of structure 44, Yaxchilan, and its bearing on
the sequence of texts at that site.* Carnegie Institution of
Washington. Notes on Middle American Archaeology
and Ethnology 71. Cambridge, Mass.

1950   *Maya hieroglyphic writing: An introduction.* Carnegie
Institution of Washington. Publication 589. Washington,
D.C. (3rd ed., Norman: University of Oklahoma Press,
1971).

1966   Merchant gods of Middle America. In *Summa anthro-
pologica: Homenaje a Roberto J. Weitlaner,* edited by
A. Pompa y Pompa, pp. 159–172. Mexico City: Instituto
Nacional de Antropología e Historia.

1970   *Maya history and religion.* Norman: University of
Oklahoma Press.

1972   *Maya hieroglyphs without tears.* London: British
Museum.

1973   The painted capstone at Sacnicte, Yucatan, and two
others at Uxmal. *Indiana* 1:59–64.

[1974] *The Maya of Belize: Historical chapters since Columbus.*
Belize City: Benex Press.

Tozzer, Alfred M.

1907   *A comparative study of the Mayas and the Lacandones.*
New York: Macmillan Co.

———, ed. and trans.

1941   *Landa's relación de las cosas de Yucatán.* Peabody
Museum of Archaeology and Ethnology. Papers 18.
Cambridge, Mass.: Harvard University.

Trebarra, Napoleon

1864   *Los misterios de Chan Santa Cruz.* Mérida: M. Aldama
Rivas.

Urrutía, C.

1923   *Mapa del estado de Guatemala, República de Centro
América.* Hamburg: L. Freiderichsen y Cia.

Urzaiz R., Eduardo
  1946   *Del Imperio a la Revolución, 1865–1910.* Mérida: Government of Yucatán.

Valenzuela, Salvador
  1951   Informe sobre al departamento del Petén, dirijido al Ministerio de Fomento. Sociedad de Geografía e Historia de Guatemala. *Anales* 25(4):397–410. Guatemala: Tipografía Nacional.

Vansina, Jan
  1965   *Oral tradition: A study in historical methodology.* Translated by H. M. Wright. Chicago: Aldine.

Villagutierre Soto-Mayor, Juan de
  1933   *Historia de la conquista de la provincia de el Itzá, reducción y progresos de la de el Lacandón.* Biblioteca.. "Goathemala" de la Sociedad de Geografía e Historia. Vol. 9. Guatemala: Tipografía Nacional. [Originally published in 1701.]

Villa Rojas, Alfonso
  1945   *The Maya of east central Quintana Roo.* Publication 559. Washington, D.C.: Carnegie Institution of Washington.
  1962a Cultural-ecological map of Yucatán. Mexico City: Instituto Nacional de Antropología e Historia.
  1962b Los Quehaches: Tribu olivadada del antiguo Yucatán. *Revista Mexicana de Estudios Antropológicos* 18:97–116.

Vogt, Evon Z.
  1970   *The Zincantecos of Mexico: A modern Maya way of life.* New York: Holt, Rinehart, & Winston.

Waddell, D. A. G.
  1961   *British Honduras: A historical and contemporary survey.* London: Oxford University Press.

Wallace, Anthony F. C.
  1956   Revitalization movements. *American Anthropologist* 58:264–281.

Wisdom, Charles
  1940   *The Chorti Indians of Guatemala.* Chicago: University of Chicago Press.

Wolf, Eric R.
  1957   Closed corporate peasant communities in Meso-America and central Java. *Southwestern Journal of Anthropology* 13:7–12.
  1959   *Sons of the shaking earth.* Chicago: University of Chicago Press.

———, and Sidney Mintz
  1957   Haciendas and plantations in Middle America and the Antilles. *Social and Economic Studies* 6:380–412.

Works Projects Administration, Professional and Service Division, the Historical Records Survey

1939 *An inventory of the collections of the Middle American Research Institute.* Calendar of the Yucatecan Letters, no. 2. Tulane University. Middle American Research Institute. New Orleans.

Ximénez, Francisco

1929–1971 *Historia de la provincia de San Vincente de Chiapa y Guatemala de la Orden de Predicadores.* Biblioteca "Goathemala" de la Sociedad de Geografía e Historia, vols. 1–3, 24, 25. Guatemala: Tipografía Nacional.

Yucatán. Estado de

1832 *Colección de leyes, decretos y órdenes del Augusto Congreso del Estado de Yucatán.* Vol. 2. Mérida: Lorenzo Segui.

1944 *Enciclopedia Yucatanense.* 8 vols. C. A. Echanove T., director. Mexico City: Government of Yucatán.

1971 *Estado de Yucatán, red de caminos.* Mérida: Secretaria de Obras Públicas, Junta Local de Caminos de Yucatán.

———. Secretaria General de Gobierno

1846 *Memoria: Leida ante el augusto congreso extraordinario de Yucatán.* Mérida: Imprenta de Castillo y Compañía.

Zimmerman, Charlotte

1963 The cult of the holy cross: An analysis of cosmology and Catholicism in Quintana Roo. *History of Religions* 3(1):50–71.

Index

Human settlements (villages, towns, cities, missions, mahogany banks) are identified in main entries by an asterisk (*).

Aca, Chunpich ruled by, 26. *See also* Namay Keb
Acalan,* journey of Dávila from, 12
Acalan-Tixchel Maya. *See* Putun Maya
Acanceh,* 219
Achamabux, possible Tipu chief, 57
Achamabux of El Tipu,* 57
Ach cat, Lake Petén Maya chiefs, 26
Adelantado, 242
Adolphus, Edwin (magistrate), 87
Advance system, in Belize, 88–89
Agriculture: commercial, in Belize, xvii–xviii, 83–94; Maya, in Belize, 98n, 152. *See also* Cacao; Cotton; Henequen production; Pustunich, agriculture in; Sugar production; Swidden agriculture; Tobacco
Aguada Cumpich,* within Chan Maya boundary, 4
Aguardiente, 213
Aguilar, Gregorio de, 50
Ahau Can Mai, Maya priest, 244
Ahcambecahe, maestro designation, 244
Ah Chuen Chay, as Maya day name, 66
Ah Cocahmut, mask of, at Tayasal, 27
Ah cuch cab, in colonial Yucatán, 172
Ahitzaes. *See* Itza Maya; Lake Petén Maya
Ah kin: Catholic priests as, 244; distribution of title, 27; at Sacalum, 11
Ah Kin Mai, Maya priest, 244

Ah Kin P'olom, priest at Sacalum, 29
Ah kulel, 172
Akil,* 201–204, 206, 219
Albalate, Fr. Nicholas de, 237
Albion Island, as possibly Chanlacam, 36, 47
Alcaldes, 140, 189n; adaptation of office, 175; at Benque Viejo, 165, 167; British Honduras appoints for San Pedro Maya, 113, 146; at Chorro, 157; in colonial Yucatán, 278; at Holmul, 147; at Hololtunich, 79; internal ranking among, 140; in laws of British Honduras, 91; in Maya minor cluster, 140; at Pacha, 53; at Pustunich, 278; at San Domingo, 155; at San José, Belize, 79, 158–159; at San Pedro, 79, 113–115, 147, 149, 153, 156; in San Pedro major cluster, 175; San Pedro Maya sociopolitical organization and, 153, 170; at Santa Cruz, Labouring Creek, 155; among Santa Cruz "subtribes," 174; at Santa Teresa, 156; at Socotz, 165; at Tipu, 57; among Yucatán Maya, 175, 242, 278
Alcaldes ordinarios, 53
Alguaciles de doctrina, 243
All Soul's Day: at Icaiche, 153, 182n; at San Pedro, 149, 153
Altar de Sacrificios, site, 13
Alta Verapaz, Kekchi Maya migration from, 20
Anthropological history: application of, in Yucatán, xi–xxi; native views of history and, xxi–xxiii, 251, 275

Arana, Andrés, Lochha-Mesapich *pacíficos* led by, 116. *See also* Arana, Eugenio

Arana, Eugenio: Belize government and, 116; claims to Belize lands by, 153, 159, 161; description of, 118; settlements controlled by, 117; visits Mérida, 118; Xkanha headquarters established by, 116

Arenal:* migrants from Holmul cluster at, 166, 188n; on Negroman–Lake Yaxha route, 45

Arredondo, José María, 115

Arthur, Supt. George, 72

Arzeo, Francisco, 277

August, John, 165, 167

Austin, Lt. Gov. John G.: labor relations in Belize and, 87; Marcos Canul and, 78; Maya rent payments and, 91; San Pedro–Icaiche conspiracy and, 150

Auto de fe, at Tipu, 49

Avendaño y Loyola, Andrés de, 33–34, 42n

Ay, Antonio, as Caste War leader, 106

Aycal, name for Mopan Maya, 5

Bacalar,* xvi, 88, 105, 197; *alcalde* of, 48, 56; alternate names of, 43; attempts to ransom prisoners from, 119; Barrio de San Juan Extramuros of, 53; *cabildo* of, 54; Frs. Fuensalida and Estrada flee to, 50; Lacandon-type *incensarios* from, 32; massacre by Santa Cruz at, 119–120, 264; Maya capture of, 107; Maya threat to (1847), 74; Mexican army reoccupies, 124; *partido* of, 212; refugee Maya taken to, 54; retaking by Yucatecans of (1849), 108; sacked by corsairs, 50, 52; Santa Cruz occupation of, 76, 119–126, 145; secular priest of, 49–50, 54–55; Yucatecans hold, 119

Bacalar, Lake. *See* Lake Bacalar

Bacalar region: Lochha-Mesapich faction at, 116; rebellion of Maya in, 49

Bacalar vicariate, southern extent of, 8

Bakhahal. *See* Bacalar

Balam, Juan, 150–151

Balancabs, 285

Baptism: Icaiche Maya priests perform, 235; Santa Cruz priests perform, 234; of Tipu Maya, 57

Baptismal names. *See* Names, baptismal

Baptist mission in Belize, 93

Barbachano, Gov. Miguel, 255

Barrera, José María: death of, 119; leads Santa Cruz against Chichanha, 76; Maya oral tradition and, 252; Talking Cross cult and, 251–252

Barrios: at Bacalar, 53; at Icaiche, 117

Barton Creek,* epidemic at, 168

Batabs: Xiu rulers and, 278; in Yucatán, 27, 36, 171–172, 279

Bay of Honduras, Mopan speakers on, 4, 5

Becan, site, and Chan Maya boundary, 12, 35, 38

Becerril, Fr. Bartolomé, 53

Belize, 22, 25, 128, 141, 152, 189n, 193, 212, 276; agriculture in, xvii–xviii, 83–94, 98n, 152; Chan Maya in western, 40; colonial ideology in, history of, 69–70; corsairs on coast of, 50; creation of, as colony, 91, 111; economic conditions in, 81, 84, 86–94; ethnic composition of, 91; importation of food to, 84; labor laws of, 87; labor relations in, 87–92; man-land relations in, 86, 152–153; migration to, from Yucatán, 20; munitions trade and, 75, 108, 110; population of, 83; sugar cultivation in, xvii–xviii, 83–90; Yucatán refugees in, 83–85. *See also* British Honduras, government of; Maya of Belize; San Pedro Maya; Timber industry, British

Belize,* Yucatecan peace commission at, 121

Belize Estate and Produce Co., 151, 153

Belize River, 77–78, 152–153, 156, 168–169; Bacalar *visitas* and *curatos* on, 47; boundary of Mopan Maya at, 5; Chunukum on, 55; Delgado's trip to, 5; eighteenth-century Maya on, 9; in Fuensalida *relación*, 45, 50, 53; Holmul migrants settle along, 166; Icaiche claims to, 79; Maya attack woodcutters on, 72, 74; Maya settlements on, 8, 73; San Pedro and, 141; slave uprising on, 73; Yucatecan Maya presence along, 26

Belize River, eastern branch. *See* Eastern branch, Belize River

Belize River, western branch. *See* Mopan River

Belize valley, 10, 141

Belmopan,* as site of Hubelna, 50
Benavente, Fr. Melchor de, 236
Benque Viejo,* 22, 153, 163, 166–167,
188n; burned by San Pedro Maya,
163; Icaiche faction and conflict in,
167; Lacandon-type *incensarios* from,
31–33; location of, 45; migration to,
from Yaloch, 165–167; settled by Caste
War refugees, 9; trail from Icaiche to,
11
Bichab, Mateo, 57
Bienvenida, Fr. Lorenzo de, 237
Billy White Creek, 156
Birth rate, 209; in Akil, 204; in
Pencuyut, 204, 226
Birth rate, crude, 208; definition of,
192; in Pencuyut, 205, 209–210, 214,
216; in Yucatán, 215
Bishop of Campeche, 118–119
Black Creek, 153
Blue Creek, 145, 164; attack on
mahogany works at, 76, 144; as
Belize-Mexico boundary, 111; Icaiche
rent demands on, 114; Santa Cruz
occupy mahogany bank at, 112, 144.
See also Río Azul
Bol Menche, ancestor of Yaxchilan
Lacandon, 15
Bolon, 66
Bolonchac, Lake. *See* Lake Bolonchac
Bolonchenticul, 117
Bolon Hobon, Yucatec bee god, 28
Boom,* 185n
Booth's River, 157, 160, 186n;
Chichanha refugee group on, 76–77,
144; San José location and, 141; San
Pedro Maya territory and, 139
Borderlands section of Yucatán. *See*
Campeche; Yucatán, Borderlands
section of
Bow and arrow: Belize Maya use, 74;
Maya at Hubelna use, 50; at Tayasal,
13
Braseros, Lacandon. *See* Lacandon-type
incensarios
Bravo, Gen. Ignacio, capture of Santa
Cruz by, 255, 259
Bravo, Río. *See* Río Bravo
British colonialism: Belize River Maya
of early nineteenth century and, 9;
campaign against San Pedro Maya
and, 91; Confederate refugee
settlement and, 91, 93; demand for
wage labor and, 94; image of Maya of

Belize and, xvii, 80–82, 93–94;
recognition of Asunción Ek and, 146.
See also Timber industry, British
British colonialism, and Maya of Belize,
xiv, xvii–xviii, 9, 69, 80–94
British colonial policy: fear of Santa
Cruz and, 75; Icaiche Maya and, 79;
munitions trade and, 75; San Pedro
Maya and, 77. *See also* British
colonialism; British Honduras,
government of; Munitions trade
British Empire, 69; and defense of
British Honduras, 92–93
British Honduras: missionaries from, at
Icaiche, 117; munitions trade with
Santa Cruz Maya and, 127. *See also*
Belize; British Honduras, government
of
British Honduras, government of:
alcalde position created by, 91;
alteration of constitution of, 92–93;
appointment of San Pedro officials by,
113, 126, 146, 148; arrests at San
Pedro and, 145; complaints about
Chichanha by, 112, 114; crown colony
status and, 91–92; delegation to Santa
Cruz from, 120; dispatches force
against San Pedro, 78, 113; fiscal crisis
of, 92; Icaiche–San Pedro Maya
alliance and, 78; Icaiche treaty with
(1882), 115; labor legislation of, 87;
legislative assembly of, 92; Maya land
tenure and, 91; munitions trade and,
108, 110, 149; ransom attempts at
Bacalar and, 119; relations with
Mexico of, 79, 110–112, 114, 124, 128;
San Pedro Maya supplied arms by,
113; and Santa Cruz border violations,
120–121, 144; Spencer-Mariscal treaty
(1897) and, 124; trade embargo with
Icaiche and, 115. *See also* British
Empire; British military
British Honduras, governor of, 115
British Honduras Company, 85, 159,
161, 165
British Honduras Militia, 149
British military: action of, against San
Pedro–Icaiche Maya, 78, 80, 113, 170;
and early Maya attacks in Belize, 72;
expenses of, in Belize, 92. *See also*
Fifth West India Regiment; Second
West India Regiment
Bullet Tree Falls,* origins of Maya of,
9, 45

Burdon, Gov. Sir John Alder, 69

Cabo, at Pustunich, 278–279
Cacaalezuc, Nabon. See Nabon
  Cacaalezuc
Cacao: at Chantome, 50; at Chunukum,
  46
Cacicazgo, 233. See also Caciques
Caciques: of Chanes, 26; in colonial
  Yucatán, 109, 278; early use of term,
  27; Franciscan missionaries' use of,
  236; at Hubelna, 50; among Manche
  Chol Maya, 5; in Mani region, 278;
  Maya town names and, 4, 57; among
  Mopan Maya, 25; at Petox, 26; at
  Pustunich, 278–279; at Tipu, 45–46,
  54–55, 57; Xiu as, 278
Caddy-Walker expedition, 10, 73
Cajabon,* Kekchi Maya migration from,
  20, 25. See also Kekchi Maya
Cakchiquel, mythology of, 17
Calakmul, site, 37
Calendar, Maya: Chan-Yucatec Maya
  cleavage and, 41; among colonial
  Manche Chol, 65; and day names, 65;
  and interpretation of dates in, 34,
  38–39
Calendrical prophecies, at Tayasal,
  33–34, 42n
Calkini,* Franciscan mission at, 237
Cámara, Virginia, 150
Campeche, 11, 40, 105, 128, 194–196,
  259; Borderlands development and,
  196; diocese of, 117; Mérida versus,
  196; migration to Petén and Belize
  from, 20; settlement of, 235; Xkanha
  territory and, 115
Campeche, Bishop of. See Bishop of
  Campeche
Campeche:* Franciscan mission at, 235,
  237; Xecchakan located near, 48
Campeche, government of, 103, 107, 126;
  Chichanha Maya supported by, 112,
  114; creation of, 112; jurisdiction of,
  at Xkanha, 119; pacifico political
  organization and, 114
Campeche-Petén boundary, 33
Campin:* Delgado at, 25; language of,
  67; location of, 4, 5, 67; Manche Chol
  at, 4–5; as southern limit of
  Franciscan activity, 50
Can, Tipuan, brother-in-law of Can Ek,
  57

Can, Juan, San Pedro Maya leader, 145,
  155, 178n
Can, Martin, nephew of Can Ek, 8, 57
Can, Pedro Miguel, nephew of Can Ek,
  57
Cancanilla River (Labouring Creek), 45
Can Ek: attempts to arrange submission
  of, 49, 57–58; marriage relationship
  of, with Tipu, 8, 57; political
  hegemony of, 36; relationship with
  Couoh and Chakan Itza Maya, 24;
  ruler of Tayasal, 30, 57; sends envoys
  to Mérida, 57
Canizan,* 61, 66
Cano, Fr. Agustín, 20–21
Cante, sister of Can Ek, 57
Cantón: Icaiche as, 114; Lochha and,
  174
Cantores, 243
Canul, Marcos, 149–150; attacks Orange
  Walk (1872), 79, 114, 145; attacks
  Qualm Hill, 78, 149; Campeche
  government recognizes, 114; claims
  Hololtunich, 161; claims land rents in
  Belize, 114, 149; death of, 79, 114,
  145; at San Pedro, 150; Santa Cruz
  and Lochha Maya pressure on, 78;
  and his secretary, 114; seizure of
  Corozal by, 79, 114; succeeds L. Tzuc
  at Icaiche, 114, 145; on D. Tzuc
  invasion, 165
Capitanes, 172, 174, 189n, 264
Capuchin missions, at Petexbatum, 14
Cárdenas, Pres. Lázaro, visits Pustunich,
  278
Caribe, term for Lacandon, 14
Caribe,* Lacandon settlement at, 14
Caribs, as laborers, 89
Carillo Puerto.* See Felipe Carillo
  Puerto
Carillo Puerto, Felipe, 282
Carmichael, Capt. John J., 149; San
  Pedro raid led by, 151; visits Santa
  Cruz, 121–122
Carnegie Institution of Washington, xii
Caste War of Yucatán, xiii, xvii–xix, 45,
  82, 93–94, 103, 105–130, 172, 174,
  195–196, 198, 226, 233, 252, 255–256,
  259, 276; Borderlands economic
  conditions and, 197; British-Mexican
  treaty and, 111, 124; casualty and
  migration estimates for, 211–212;
  causes of, 197, 211; contemporary
  Santa Cruz Maya view of, 260;

historical interpretation of, 257;
Maya language documents on,
252–257; Maya loyal to whites during,
105; Maya military organization
during, 106–108, 172–175; Maya oral
tradition concerning, 261, 285;
mestizos and Maya leadership during,
106; migration from Yucatán and, 9,
20; Pencuyut population and, 193,
206, 211; Pustunich and, 285; sources
for, xix, 128–131, 251–257, 261, 285.
See also Chichanha Maya;
Independent Maya; Lochha Maya;
Rebel Maya of Yucatán, 1847–1850;
Santa Cruz Maya, pre-1901; Xkanha
Maya
Catholicism, 127; Independent Maya of
Yucatán and, 106; Mani resistance to,
279; at Pustunich, 280–281, 285–286,
288; Santa Cruz Maya and, 120, 233;
Tipu Maya and, xvi, 8, 47–52, 73; and
Yucatán Missions, xx–xxi, 234–239
Cattle raising: in Petén, 141; in Yucatán,
195–196
Cayo district, Belize, 24
Cehach Maya, 11–12, 17, 30, 34;
boundaries of, 11–12, 23, 26; as Chan
Maya subgrouping, 3, 40; Chinamita
Maya and, 13, 35; Chunpich
inhabited by, 4, 26; Cortés travels
among, 12; fortified towns of, 13,
34–35; Lacandon as descendants of,
12; language of, 12, 21–23; names
among, 26; sources for, 40; totemism
among, 36; at Tzuctok, 4. *See also*
Chanes
Ceibarico, site, 37
Ceiba tree, Maya worship at, 27
Censuses. *See* Jesuits, census of 1858;
Population; Tipu *matrícula*
Ceremonial centers: of
nineteenth-century Maya, xv, 140,
154, 170, 172, 175; of
twentieth-century Maya, 172–173
Cerro,* 151; destroyed by British forces,
78, 158, 160
Chac, Petox *cacique*, 26
Chac cult, among Lacandon and
Mopan, 30
Cha Chaac ritual, 281
Chachaclum, Petén Maya settlement at,
4
Chac River, 46–47. *See also* Nohukum
River

Chakan Itza Maya, Can Ek's domination
over, 24
Chalacam. *See* Chanlacam
Chaltum,* *encomendero* of, 277
Chaltunob, 194
Champoton:* Dávila visits, 12, 35;
Franciscan mission at, 235; location
of Mazatlán and, 12
Chan, Mopan Maya *cacique*, 25
Chan, Gaspar, as *alcalde ordinario* of
Barrio de San Juan Extramuros, 53
Chan, José Justo: as *alcalde* of Benque
Viejo, 167; and migration from
Yaloch to Benque Viejo, 164–165, 167
Chan, Martin, *cacique* at San Luis, 25
Chan, Rafael, 179n; British-Icaiche
relations and, 115; claims
Hololtunich, 161; as Icaiche leader,
78, 114–115, 145; at San Pedro, 150
Chan, surname: *matrícula* of Tipu and,
26; in Petén, 64; in Tipu area, 64
Chancah: attitudes on Caste War at,
260; Juan de la Cruz sermon and,
255; as Santa Cruz ceremonial center,
173–174
Chanchiich Creek, 163. *See also* Río
Bravo; Río Holmul
Chanes, subdivision of Cehach Maya, 26
Chan Kom, xii, 130, 154, 283; attitudes
on Caste War at, 260; compared with
Pustunich, xxiii, 286–287;
development of, xiii, 286–287;
survival of political territories
around, xv
Chanlacam:* fortifications at, 36, 47;
migrations of inhabitants of, 47, 52;
rebellions at, 47; refugees from, 47, 54
Chanlacao.* *See* Chanlacam
Chan Maya, 3–42; boundaries of, xv,
3–4, 11–12; Chichanha-Icaiche Maya
and, 11; during Classic period, 36–39;
fortified towns of, 34–36; human
sacrifice among, 17, 28–29;
identification of, 3; language of, 22,
24, 40; personal name systems among,
24–26; population of region of, 19;
religion among, 27–33; Sacalum and,
11; settlement distribution among,
36; sociopolitical organization of, 36;
subgroupings of, xv–xvi, 3; titles of
rank among, 26–27; Yucatec Maya
and, 40–41; Yucatec speech of, 3, 20.
See also Cehach Maya; Chichanha
Maya; Chinamita Maya; Itza Maya;

Lacandon Maya; Lake Petén Maya;
Maya of Belize; Mopan Maya; Muzul
Maya
Chan Santa Cruz. *See* Santa Cruz,
Quintana Roo
Chantome, cacao orchard at, 50
Chenes sites, 38
Chetumal,* 193; Chan Maya affiliation
of, 11; location of, 43–45; Maya revolt
of 1636 and, 11; political organization
of, 36; Putun influence at, 11, 32, 36
Chetumal, Ciudad, Lacandon-type
incensario from, 31
Chetumal Bay, 43
Chetumal province: Maya rebellion in,
49; Petén affiliations of, 37
Chheenyuc,* former name of Pencuyut,
193
Chi, Cecilio, Caste War Maya leader, 106
Chichanha,* xiii, 117, 126, 146, 155,
186n; abandoned, 141; attacked by
Santa Cruz, 76, 112, 119, 145; Chan
Maya boundary and, 4, 11; Maya
revolt at (1695), 75; migration of
refugee group from, 144; munitions
magazine at, 108; political factions at,
144–146; pre–Caste War history of,
75–76; San Pedro Maya and, 139, 141;
Santa Cruz defeated at, 109; as
southern Indian center, 105, 108;
Spanish settlement at, 75, 105
Chichanha Maya, 10, 75, 91, 120, 125;
Blue Creek logging works occupied
by, 76, 112; Chan Maya and, xv, 11,
37, 40; and cutting of Santa
Cruz–Belize trade, 76; demand
ransom from British, 76; as
descendants of Bacalar region
refugees, 8–9; hostility between Santa
Cruz and, 11, 75–76, 109–112; Icaiche
becomes capital of, 112, 145;
migration of segment of, to Belize,
10, 76, 112, 144–145; sign treaty with
Mexicans, 75–76, 109; sociopolitical
organization of, xv, xviii–xix,
109–112, 144–145; Tipu Maya and, 8;
Zima replaces Tzuc as head of, 111.
See also Icaiche Maya; Independent
Maya; Lochha Maya; San Pedro Maya
Chichanha Maya at Yalbac Hills. *See*
San Pedro Maya
Chichen Itza, site, 277; initial series
date at, 38; *Itzamna* of, 267;
tzompantli at, 26

Chicle extraction, in Petén, 188n
Chiefdoms: defined, 127; of
Independent Maya, 103, 111–126
Chiefs. *See Caciques*
Chilam Balam, oracle at Mani, 277
Chilam Balam books, 273n; paganism
of *maestros* and, 245; Pustunich
mentioned in, 276; read among
contemporary Santa Cruz Maya, xxi,
261–262
Chilans, xxii, 41n
Chinam,* population of, 47
Chinamita Maya, 19, 40; as Chan Maya
subgrouping, xvi, 3, 18, 40; discussed,
12–13
Chindzonot,* 269
Chol, Manche. *See* Manche Chol Maya
Chol Maya: Chan Maya and, 3; gods of,
30; location of, 4, 17. *See also*
Lacandon Chol Maya; Manche Chol
Maya; Palencano Chol Maya
Chol Maya language, 14, 20, 41n
Cholo, Petox chief, 26
Chomach, priestly title, 27
Chomach Ahau, Avedaño y Loyola as,
27
Chomach Punab, priest of town near
Yalain, 27
Chomach Zulu, priest of Yalain, 27
Chorro,* 77, 151, 155–157, 160, 163, 169,
183n, 185n; British-Icaiche
confrontation and, 157; Ek's authority
over, 77; population of, 157. *See also*
San Pedro minor cluster
Christianity. *See* Catholicism; Churches;
Franciscan missionaries; Fuensalida,
Fr. Bartolomé de; Idolatry; Paganism;
Syncretism, religious
Chunaba,* Asunción Ek at, 146
Chunbalche,* 77, 147–148, 160, 185n;
abandonment of, 159, 166; destroyed
by British, 78, 158; Lino Lara affair
and, 146; population of, 159; in San
José minor cluster, 146, 157–159
Chunhuas,* 11
Chunhuhub,* 52–53
Chunkikhutul,* 151, 156; population
of, 155
Chunpich,* Cehach center at, 4, 26
Chunpom, 123, 174; as ceremonial
center, 173; Juan de la Cruz
manuscript at, 255. *See also* Santa
Cruz Maya, post-1901
Chuntuci,* 162

Chunukum,* 67; description of, 46; expeditions of Pérez and, 55–56; Tipu region Maya summoned to, 25, 45–46. See also Estero Chuncum

Churches: burning of, at Lamanay, Zaczuc, and Bacalar region, 50; at San Pedro, 151–152, 154; at Santa Cruz, Quintana Roo, 109; at Tipu, 48, 56; at Xkanha, 174

Civil congregation: idolatry uncovered through, 245; at Pencuyut, 198–199, 208; in Yucatán, 198, 207, 242; Yucatán population loss and, 199. See also Reduction

Civiltuk region, as Cehach territory, 12

Cizin, Lacandon god of underworld, 17

Clan structure, among Lacandon, 36

Clarissee,* San Pedro Maya burn, 163

Classic period, Maya lowlands, 11, 39

Coba, site: calendrical dates at, 38; Petén Maya influences at, 37–38

Coban, site, 17

Coboh, Fernando, 53

Cocahmut, aspect of Itzam Na in Yucatán, 27

Cocom, Francisco, leader of Bacalar barrio, 54

Cocom, José María, leader at Macanche, 112, 115

Cocom, Nachi, halach uinic of Sotuta, 171

Cocomes, 207, 276; Mayapan ruled by, 277

Colmotz,* 45

Colonialism. See British colonialism; Spanish colonial policy

Comandantes, 140, 189n, 264; at Icaiche, 118, 174; military title of, 107; and preconquest halach uinic, 172; among San Pedro Maya, 170, 175; among Santa Cruz Maya, 174; at Xkanha, 118. See also Military titles

Comandantes generales: at Icaiche, 175; in San Pedro major cluster, 175; at Xkanha, 175. See also Military titles

Comisario, at Pustunich, 278

Communal labor, at Pustunich, 287–288

Communication routes: from Bacalar area to Tipu, 50; Icaiche–Benque Viejo trail, 11; Mérida-Pustunich-Peto railroad, 283; Pencuyut and Mérida-Bacalar route, 197; of San Pedro Maya with Belize, 143; of San Pedro Maya with Petén, 162; among

San Pedro settlements, 152, 156, 159, 162, 164; to Santa Cruz, Q.R., 124; from southern Quintana Roo to Tipu, 33; Ticul-Pustunich-Peto road, 283

Compadrazgo, 50

Compañías: Independent Maya, at Icaiche, 174; Maya social organization and, 107–108, 126; San Pedro Maya social organization and, 140; traditional Maya town units and, 172; at X-Cacal, 154, 173

Compound names. See Names, compound; Names, day

Conch shells, as trumpets, 50

Confederate refugees, settle in western Belize, 165

Congregaciones. See Reduction

Conkal,* Franciscan mission at, 237

Corozal,* 52, 89; epidemics at, 169; fair at, 88; Marcos Canul occupies (1870), 79, 114; population composition of, 83

Corozal Chico,* population of, 83

Cortés, Hernán, in Cehach territory, 4, 34–35

Cotton, production of, in Yucatán, 196, 206, 213

Councils: of major and minor clusters, 140; of major cluster, 170; in Mani area, 278; of minor cluster, 170; at Pustunich, 278; among San Pedro Maya, 140, 175; at X-Cacal, 140, 175

Counsels on Maya history: Americans in, 266–268; Caste War and, 261, 272; English in, 266–268; Maya and non-Maya discussed by, xxi–xxii, 261, 269–272; Maya world view and, 261; performers of, 262; ritual greeting in, 262; Spanish conquest in, 267

Couoh: as Chan Maya name, 18, 24–25; rulers of Champoton, 18; as surname in Yucatán, 24

Couoh, Fernando. See Coboh, Fernando

Couoh, Napol, chief near Isla Pac, 18, 24–25

Couoh Maya, relations of, with Can Ek, 24, 36

Cozumel,* household organization at, 199

Cozumel Island, Tipu nobility descended from, 48

Creoles, Belizean, as laborers, 87–89

Cross, sacred, 269–272; festivals to honor, 255, 260; guardia duty for,

260; Maya "counsels" and, 267;
skepticism concerning, 265. *See also*
Crosses, sacred; Talking Cross;
Talking Cross cult
Crosses, sacred: at Chancah, 260;
Christian influence and, 29; human
sacrifice in colonial Yucatán and,
28–29; Maya priests communicate
through, xxii
Crown Lands Ordinance, Maya land
tenure and, 92
Crucifixion, of Juan de la Cruz, 252
Cruzob. See Santa Cruz Maya, pre-1901
Cuba: Campeche and, 195; Maya slaves
sold to, 212; trades with Yucatán, 195
Cultural change: peasantry and, 288;
Pustunich exposure to, 284, 286–288;
Redfield on, 275–276
Cultural ecology, of Yucatán, xiii
Cumpich. *See* Aguada Cumpich
Cumux, Francisco, Tipu noble of
Cozumel ancestry, 48, 64
Cunil, non-Yucatec name in Socotz, 9
Cunningham, Police Insp. Patrick,
158–159
Cupul province, 171–172, 174

Dancers, among Lake Petén Maya, 28
Dávila, Capt. Alonso, *entradas* of, 12,
34–35, 37, 70
Day names. *See* Names, day
Death rate, 209; in Akil, 204; in
Pencuyut, 204, 226
Death rate, crude, 208; definition of,
192; in Latin America, 216; in
Mexico, 210, 215–217; in Pencuyut,
205, 210, 214–217; in Yucatán,
215–217
Debt peonage, 88, 90, 198, 213;
Pustunich residents and, 282
Deer, 12
Delamere, Capt. Peter, 149–150, 181n
Delgado, Fr. Diego, Mirones *entrada*
and, 11, 33, 49
Delgado, Fr. Joseph: Belize description
by, 62; population of Petén and, 19
Demography. *See* Birth rate; Birth rate,
crude; Death rate; Death rate, crude;
Fertility; Migration; Mortality;
Population; Rate of natural increase;
Rate of natural increase, crude
Díaz, Porfirio, 124
Díaz del Castillo, Bernal, description of
Cehach by, 34

Díaz de Velasco, Juan, Tayasal *entrada*
of, 20, 28
Disease: cholera in British Honduras,
169; cholera in Yucatán, 211; colonial
Maya affected by, 169; colonial
Pencuyut and, 198–199; conquest of
Petén and, 48; influenza epidemic of
1918, 169; at Pencuyut, 211; in Petén,
20; among San Pedro Maya, 139, 151,
168–169; smallpox among *pacíficos*
and San Pedro Maya, 168–169;
smallpox among Santa Cruz Maya,
169, 173; smallpox in Yucatán, 211;
in Yucatán, 206, 208
Distilling, Supt. Stevenson on, 84
Dolores:* Caste War refugees at, 9;
Mopan town at, 5; Muxun (Soyte)
Maya reduced at, 5, 67; Petén dialect
spoken at, 21
Donzel, Julian, 197
Dos Lagunas, Lacandon-type *incensario*
from, 31
Douglas,* 47
Downer, Robert T. (magistrate), 90
Drought, and famine in Yucatán, 211
Duck Run,* 156, 167; as British-Maya
frontier, 10, 73, 77
Dzan, site, 279–282
Dzibilchaltun, site, 38
Dzidzantun,* Franciscan mission at, 237
Dzitas,* 130
Dzul, Aniceto, Santa Cruz Maya leader,
123–124
Dzul, José María, San Pedro Maya
faction leader, 149
Dzuluinicob River, 43, 47, 52. *See also*
New River

Eastern branch, Belize River, 10;
Lacandon-type *incensarios* found
near, 52; Tipu probably on, xvi, 8, 45
Ebtun:* Chan Kom and, xii–xiii; land
tenure archives of, xiii, 171–172;
survival of Maya political territories
around, xv, 172
Economic conditions: demographic
history and, xx; and Maya of Belize,
9, 80–82, 86–95; Maya rebellions and,
xviii, 80–82, 94, 105–106, 197, 211; in
Pencuyut, 197–198, 216; in Pustunich,
281–283; San Pedro Maya and, 9,
80–82, 94, 149, 158; in Yucatán, 48,
105, 129–130, 194–198, 213, 218,
281–283

Edmunds, Capt. Thomas, 156
Ejidos: alienation of, 213; at Pencuyut,
    193, 212; at Pustunich, 282
Ek, Asunción, 152, 170, 175, 179n, 181n;
    as British ally, 77–78, 113, 146–149;
    Chichanha refugees under, 76, 113;
    collects rent at Río Hondo, 145–146;
    as general at Chunaba, 146; Icaiche
    threat and, 148, 150; mahogany gangs
    and, 148, 150; as San Pedro Maya
    leader, 77, 113–114, 146–147, 150, 153
Ek, Timoteo, son of A. Ek, 153
El Cayo,* Lacandon occupation and, 15,
    31
El Cimarrón,* Lake Petén Maya at, 4
El Hormiguero, site, 12
El Palmar, site, 38
El Próspero,* 4; language of, 13; titles
    of priests of, 27
El Quiche,* 42n
Encalada, Pablo, 145, 174; authority of,
    at Icaiche, 115; as Lochha and
    pacíficos del sur leader, 75, 112,
    115–116, 145; Santa Cruz Maya and,
    112, 145
Encomenderos, 51, 194–198, 207, 277–278
Encomiendas: in Mani province, 277; in
    Mexico, 174; at Pencuyut, 197;
    population loss and, 207; at
    Pustunich, 277–278
Entradas: of Avendaño y Loyola, 33–34,
    42n; of Dávila, 12, 34–35, 37, 70; of
    Fr. Diego Delgado, 11, 33, 49; of Fr.
    Joseph Delgado, 19, 67; of Díaz de
    Velasco, 20, 28; of Fuensalida, 33–34,
    43–45, 48–50; of Hariza, 56–58; of
    Hernán Cortés, 4, 34–35; of Pérez, 43,
    45, 52–56
Estero Chuncum, 45
Estrada, Juan de, 50
Ethnic boundaries: of Cehach and
    Chinamita Maya, 12–13; Chan and
    Yucatec Maya and, 11, 25, 37, 39–40;
    ecclesiastical boundaries and, 8; of
    Lacandon Maya, 16; among lowland
    Maya, xv; in western Belize, xvi–xvii,
    10, 73, 77
Ethnohistory, Maya counsels and, 261.
    See also Anthropological history;
    History

Factionalism: at Chichanha, 144; among
    Independent Maya groups, 126;
    migration and, 206; at San Pedro,

148–150, 170; at Santa Cruz, 121,
    123–124, 264; at Socotz, 167; among
    twentieth-century Santa Cruz Maya,
    174
Famine, in Yucatán, 206–208, 211
Fancourt, Col. St. John, 75
Felipe Carillo Puerto,* 254, 259–260,
    263, 267–268, 272. See also Santa Cruz,
    Quintana Roo
Fernández, Pedro Juan, secular priest
    of Bacalar, 56
Fertility, 193; in Latin America, 216;
    migration dynamics and, 191; in
    Pencuyut, 208–210
Fiesta house, at San Pedro, 152
Fiestas. See All Soul's Day; Corozal, fair
    at
Fifth West India Regiment, in Belize,
    72
Figueroa, Sico, 158
Filadelfia,* 14
Fiscal, in colonial Yucatán, 242–243
Floods, 52, 55, 211
Flores,* 141, 146, 163, 169–170, 185n,
    187n, 189n
Folk-urban continuum, xi–xiv, 275–276
Fortresses, of Maya of Petén, 13, 34–36,
    46–47
Fowler, Henry, 165, 168, 187n, 189n
Franciscan missionaries: failure of, in
    Belize, 48–51, 53; missions of, in
    Yucatán, 236–241; public opinion
    and, 239; secular clergy and, 235, 239;
    shortage of, 237, 239; use of caciques
    by, 236; use of maestros by, xx–xxi,
    234, 236, 239
Fuensalida, Fr. Bartolomé de:
    calendrical computations by, at
    Tayasal, 33–34; entradas of, to Tipu
    and Tayasal, 8, 43, 45, 48–50; route
    of Bacalar-Tipu entrada of, 43–45,
    50. See also Orbita, Fr. Juan de

Gálvez, Benito, 14
Gann, Thomas, 153
Garbutt's Falls, 33
Generales, at Icaiche and Xkanha, 118.
    See also Military titles
Gibbs, Archibald R., 93–94
Glottochronology, Lacandon Maya and,
    16, 23
Gobernador, title: among Caste War
    Maya, 172; in colonial Yucatán, 172,

278; at Holmul, 147; among Santa
Cruz Maya, 125, 174, 264–265
Goldsworthy, Gov. R. T., 162
Gómez Santoya, Capt. Juan, Pérez
expedition and, 51–54, 56
Governor, local title. See Gobernador
Grant, Gov. Sir John P., 150
Great Britain, government of: British
Honduras and, 110–111; treaties of,
79, 110
Guatemala, 27, 56, 109, 113, 212. See
also Petén
Guatibal.* See Uatibal
Guerra de Castas. See Caste War of
Yucatán

Haciendas. See Henequen production;
Sugar production
Halach uinic: decline of role of, 171; in
Yucatán, 36
Hamlets, 140
Hammock, 18
Hariza, Capt. Francisco de, entrada to
Tipu of, 56–58
Harley, Lt. Col. Robert W., Icaiche–San
Pedro Maya and, 78–79, 150–151
Hautila.* See Uatibal
Henderson, Capt. George, 72
Henequen production, in Yucatán,
194–197, 213, 276, 281–282
Henequen zone, Yucatán, Maya ritual
in, xxii, 281–282
Hexchunchan, Lake Petén Maya war
god, 28
Hieroglyphic texts, 38. See also
Calendar, Maya
Hill Bank,* 158–159, 161, 185n; Maya
attack, 74
Hills, in Maya religion, 182n
History: Maya concept of, xv, xxi–xxiii,
39, 251–257, 261, 271–272, 284–288;
and microregional analysis, 276. See
also Anthropological history
H-men, 276, 281
Hobo, metal idol of Lake Petén Maya,
28
Hobon, Bolon. See Bolon Hobon
Hochob, site, 38, 42n
Hodge, John, Qualm Hill attack and,
149
Hogstye Bank,* Maya attack (1807),
xvii, 72
Holcuc.* See Holzuuz
Holiuc,* 155

Holmul,* 141, 156, 183n, 185n, 186n,
188n; abandonment of, 166; as center
of minor cluster, 139, 148; defense of
San Pedro and, 163; election of
governors at, 147; Icaiche and, 164;
language of, 24; Lino Lara affair and,
146, 163; migration from, 151
Holmul, Río. See Río Holmul
Holmul minor cluster, 152–153, 164–169;
abandonment of, 151; Ek's authority
recognized by, 146; Icaiche and, 163;
migration to Belize by, 170;
settlement patterns of, 162
Hololtunich,* 159, 185n; Icaiche
authority at, 79, 153; population of,
161; in San José minor cluster, 157;
Xkanha-Icaiche claim lands around,
161
Holpachay:* fugitive Bacalar Maya at,
53; Pérez expedition at, 54
Holpatin,* Maya rebellion at, 46
Holsucil.* See Holzuuz
Holsus.* See Holzuuz
Holsuzil.* See Holzuuz
Holtzuc.* See Holzuuz
Holuitz,* 147–148; burning of Benque
Viejo and, 163; migrants from, at
Kaxiluinic, 162, 164, 166;
representatives of, at Icaiche, 164
Holuitz, Lake. See Lake Holuitz
Holzuc.* See Holzuuz
Holzuuz:* Bacalar Maya flee to, 53;
Chunukum and, 45; Pérez expedition
arrives at, 54; refugees from
Chanlacam at, 47
Homun,* Franciscan mission at, 237
Hondo River. See Río Hondo
Honduras, 212
"Horsebones," swamp, 52
Hubelna:* Tipu Maya at, 8, 50;
Zaczuuz inhabitants retreat to, 46, 50
Huites, 105, 284
Hulek,* 23
Hunting, at Pustunich, 283

Icaiche,* 126, 128, 159, 183n, 186n; as
cantón, 114; as ceremonial-political
center, 141; Chan and, 165; Chichanha
headquarters moved to, 112;
Chichanha refugees at, 76, 113;
council chiefs at, 117; defensive layout
of, 173–174; description of, 117,
173–174; epidemics at, 118, 169, 182n;

fiestas led by *maestros* at, 234;
Holmul minor cluster contact with,
163; location of, 38, 141; Mexican
government and leaders of, 118–119;
on north-south migrant route, 11, 33;
political succession at, 118; population
of, 117–118; Qualm Hill captives at,
149; San Pedro Maya alliance with,
89; secretary at, 117; Talking Cross
at, 173; town layout of, 154, 173–174;
L. Tzuc moves headquarters to, 145;
visits of outsiders to, 117–118

Icaiche Maya: attack Orange Walk, 79,
114, 145; attack Qualm Hill works,
78, 113, 149; British defeat of, 80;
British-Mexican boundary dispute
and, 128; British-Mexican treaty on
pacification of, 79; British relations
with, 79–80, 93, 115; British trade
embargo against, 115; claim lands in
Belize, 79, 113, 153, 161; claim rents
in Belize, 114, 147, 153, 157–158, 164;
compared with other Independent
Maya, 174; occupy Corozal, 79, 114;
raid across Río Hondo by (1879), 79;
relations with San Pedro Maya, 113,
149, 151, 153, 159, 167–168; settlement
clusters among, 141; sociopolitical
organization of, 114, 117–119, 141,
151, 173; visit San Pedro, 113, 149.
See also Canul, Marcos; Chan, Rafael;
Chichanha Maya; Independent Maya;
San Pedro Maya; Tzuc, José María;
Tzuc, Luciano

Icaiche region, Lacandon-type *incensario*
from, 31

Ichpatun,* same as Mayapan, 47

Idolatry: choirmaster of Tipu accused
of, 48; Maya *maestros* and, 245; Maya
of Bacalar region and, 49; in
sixteenth-century Yucatán, 280; at
Tayasal, 49; at Tipu, 49; in Tipu
region, 50; at Xecchakan, 48. *See also*
Paganism

Imperial commissary, at Mérida, 115

Independent Maya: continuity in
sociopolitical organization of, 171;
discontinuity in sociopolitical
organization of, 106; military titles
among, 109–110; preconquest
sociopolitical roots of, 141, 172. *See
also* Chichanha Maya; Icaiche Maya;
Lochha Maya; Mesapich; San Pedro
Maya; Santa Cruz Maya, post-1901;

Santa Cruz Maya, pre-1901; Xkanha
Maya

Indian Church sugar estate, 85, 165;
San José Maya terrorize, 158; San
Pedro Maya work for, 167. *See also*
Lamanay

Indios del monte: accept Spanish rule
in Mérida, 67; day names among, 5,
65–66; identity and location of, 5, 25,
67–68; as original residents of Tipu
area, 68; in Tipu *matricula*, 65, 67; as
Yucatec speakers, 67

Initial series dates, 38

Inquisition: impact on Maya of, 245; by
Landa (1562), 245; Maya *maestros*
and, 246; Maya religious syncretism
and, 245

Interpreter of the Talking Cross, 125,
233; Apolinar Sánchez as, 121; Juan
de la Cruz Puc as, 252

Interpreters: at Chunukum, 55; from
Tipu region, 57

Irish Creek, 157, 159; British Honduras
Company's banks at, 146; Maya
attacks on mahogany works at, 74

Isla de Carmen, 42n

Isla Pac, 12, 24

Isnocab:* population of, 159; in San
José cluster, 157–159

Itza, Angelino, Chichanha leader, 76

Itza Maya, 276; anthropophagy among,
12; centralized government brought
to Tayasal by, 36; as Chan Maya
subgrouping, xvi, 40; as enemies of
Chinamita, 12; language of, 20;
migration of, from Chichen Itza, 29;
Mopan and Lacandon fought against,
20; Mopan distinct from, 20; Mopan
subject to, 21; names among, 24;
territory of, 4; Tipu Maya and, xvi,
20. *See also* Can Ek; Late Petén
Maya; Tayasal

Itzamkanac:* journey of Dávila from,
35; location of, 4, 12; Putun capital
at, 4

Itzamkanac region, Putun Maya names
in, 66

Itzamna, of Chichen Itza, 267

Itzam Na: as supreme Maya god, 27;
worshiped by Petén Maya, 22

Ixil, Yucatán,* 197

Ixkan, Río. *See* Río Ixkan

Ixpayac,* Lake Petén Maya settlement
at, 4

Izamal:* Franciscan mission at, 237; migration and, 220–221
Izan, Lake. *See* Lake Izan

Jaina, site, initial series date at, 38
Jamaica, governor of, Icaiche kidnapings protested by, 114
Jesuits, census of 1858, northern Belize, 83
Juan de la Cruz, 267, 269; Jesus Christ as, 252–253, 256; as Maya military leader, 252; meaning of, 252–253; ritual possession and, xxii; sacred cross and, 119, 267; sermon of, 253–256; sources for sermon of, 252, 255
Juan de la Cruz Puc, identity of, xxi, 252, 254, 256
Juano palm, exploitation of, 283
Judicial procedure: at Icaiche, 117–118; at Xkanha, 118
Juntecholol:* Lake Petén settlement at, 4; location of, 23
Justicia mayor, at Bacalar, 50

Kabah, site, 38
Kan, Francisco, leader of Bacalar *barrio*, 54
Kantenal,* refugees from Hautila at, 54
Kantunil:* *pacífico* status of, 120; Santa Cruz Maya conflicts with, 120, 123, 126
Kaxiluinic,* 159; location of, 11, 161; migration to San José from, 162, 166; Miller survey party and, 161–162; origins of, 9, 166; in San José minor cluster, 157; smallpox at, 169
Keb, Namay. *See* Namay Keb
Kekchi Maya: as Manche Chol descendants, 20, 25; mythology of, 17; northward migration of, 20; in southern Belize, 20
Ken, Bernabé, Santa Cruz Maya leader, 121, 125
Ken, Bernardino. *See* Ken, Bernabé
Kinchil Coba, sentinel god among Lake Petén Maya, 28
Kinship terms, of Lacandon Maya, 16

Labna, site, 38, 42n
Labor conditions. *See* Belize, labor laws of; Belize, labor relations in; Debt peonage

Labouring Creek, xix, 77, 156, 160, 162–163; in Fuensalida *relación*, 53; hardwood production on, 143; San Pedro settlements and, 139, 141, 151, 152, 154
Lacandon, Mayan language, 14, 16, 24
Lacandon, as term used by Spanish, 14
Lacandon Chol Maya: in Acalan-Dolores-Miramar region, 14; bark-cloth smocks among, 17; contact of, with Lacandon Yucatec Maya, 18; hammock among, 18; island settlements of, 36
Lacandon Maya, 41n, 182n; Cehach possible ancestors of, 12; Cehach unlikely ancestors of, 26; Chac cult absent among, 30; as Chan Maya subgrouping, 3, 40; Chinamita possible ancestors of, 19; compared with other Yucatec Maya, 16; creation myth of, 17; disease among, 14, 19; dress of, 17; former location of, 16; glottochronology and, 16, 23; *halach uinic* and, 19; hammocks among, 18; kinship terms of, 16; Lacandon Chol Maya and, 18; language of, 14, 16; locations of settlements of, 14–19; mahogany cutting and, 14; Mencha (Menche) leader of, 14, 19; "moieties" of, 18; mythology of, 17, 30; names of, 26; religion of, 17, 27; totemic clans among, 36; Yant'o a god of, 16; Yucatán Maya and, 40; Yucatán origin theory for, 16; Yucatec Maya religion and, 30
Lacandon Maya incense burners. *See* Lacandon-type *incensarios*
Lacandon-type *incensarios*, distribution and discussion of, 8, 15–16, 31–33, 41n, 42n
Lacandon Yucatec Maya. *See* Lacandon Maya
Lacantun River. *See* Río Lacantun
Lago Santa Clara, at Icaiche, 117
Laguna de Tipu, 164; location of, 144
Laguna Soh, Lacandon-type *incensario* from, 32
Laguna Yaloch, 11
La Honradez, site, Lacandon-type *incensarios* at, 31
Lake Bacalar: Chan Maya boundary and, 3; route to Tipu region and, 43, 47–48; Uaymil province and, 37

Lake Bolonchac, Lacandon settlement at, 14–15
Lake Holuitz, 164
Lake Izan, Lacandon settlement at, 4, 14
Lake Macanche, 23
Lake Miramar, 36
Lake Mocu, 12
Lake Petén, 11, 23, 25; and Díaz expedition, 28; language of, 21; location of Tayasal at, 4–5, 49; population of region of, 19
Lake Petén Maya, 4–5, 24–25; calendrical prophecies and, 33–34; as Chan Maya subgrouping, 3, 40, 78; conquest of, 48; deities of, 27–28; hammocks among, 18; language of, 16, 20–21; mythology lacking for, 30; priests among, 27; relations with Tipu and, 8; religion of Yucatán and, 29; rulers of, and Yucatán origins, 24; sources for, 40; southern extent of, 4; titles of rank among, 26. See also Chakan Itza Maya; Couoh Maya; Itza Maya; Tayasal
Lake Petén region, migrants from, at Socotz, 22
Lake Petha, Lacandon of, 4, 15
Lake Sacnab, 166
Lake Texcoco, Lacandon at, 15
Lake Yavilain, 21
Lake Yaxha, 163, 166, 187n; Topoxte located in, 36
La Libertad,* present name of Sacluk, 4
Lamanay:* burning of, by Maya, 50; as Indian Church, 45; location of, 45. See also Indian Church
La Mar, Lacandon settlement near, 15
Lances, 50
Landa, Fray Diego de: arrives in Yucatán, 237; and Mani inquisition, 245, 280
Land tax, in Belize, 92
Land tenure, Maya: archives of Ebtun and, xiii, 171–172; in Belize, 91–92
Language. See under various Maya groups and Mayan languages
Lara, Lino, Chunbalche leader, 146. See also Lino Lara affair
Las Higueras, site, 37
Lino Lara affair, 146–151
Loccha,* 117, 126, 143–144, 186n; Chichanha remnants at, 112; pacífico polity at, xviii, 112, 127; population of (1861), 112; resettlement of, 112; Santa Cruz allied forces from, 122; Santa Cruz capture twice, 113, 116; Santa Cruz sympathizers captured at, 116; Yucatecan forces occupy, 112
Lochha Maya: cantones of, 174; as Chichanha subgrouping, xviii, 113; migrations of, 112–113, 116, 144; pacífico rebellion among, 115; as pacífico subgroup, 75; Santa Cruz military pressure on, 113; settlement clusters among, 174; sociopolitical organization of, 174. See also Chichanha Maya; Xkanha Maya
Locusts, 207
Logwood, in economy of Yucatán, 195. See also Timber industry, British
Longden, Lt. Gov. James R.: Indian land tenure report by, 91; San Pedro Maya and, 158, 165; sugar production report by, 85
Lowland Maya: calendar synchronization among, 34, 38–39; ceiba tree worshiped among, 27; cultural conservatism of, xiv–xv; ethnic boundaries of, xv; rebellions of, xiv; sociopolitical organization of, 141; stability of society of, xiii. See also Independent Maya; names of various groups
Lowry's Bight, population of, 83
Lucu,* 8, 45, 48; Pérez expedition and, 45, 55; in Tipu matricula, 47
Luku.* See Lucu

Macal Branch of Belize River. See Eastern branch, Belize River
Macanche:* location of, 112; Santa Cruz allies at, 122
Macanche, Lake. See Lake Macanche
Macaw Bank,* location of Tipu near, 45
Machaquila,* language of, 21
McKay, Major, 78, 150
Maestros: at Icaiche, 117; among Independent Maya, 246; introduced by Franciscan missionaries, 234; native nobility trained as, 236, 244; paganism among, 245–246; pre-Columbian priests and, 244–245; roles of, 236, 244; in Titles of Ebtun, 243; types of, 243
Maestros cantores, xx–xxi, 234–235, 242–243, 246

Maestros de canto. See Maestros cantores
Maestros de capilla, xxi, 48, 243
Maestros de escuela, xxi, 243
Maize: in Maya religion, 267;
  production of, in Belize, 84;
  production of, in Yucatán, 195–197,
  206, 212, 259
Manche Chol, Mayan language, 21, 67
Manche Chol Maya: bark-cloth
  garments among priests of, 18;
  caciques of, 5; hammocks among, 18;
  indios del monte and, 65; Kekchi
  Maya and, 20; location of, 5, 17;
  Maya calendar among, 65; mythology
  of, 17; title *ahau* among, 27
Mani,* 197, 283; *caciques* in region of,
  278; Franciscan mission at, 236–237,
  279; inquisition of 1562 in, xxii;
  Maya conspiracy at, 236–237; oracle
  at, 277; Xiu occupy, 277
Mani, site, 279
Mani Land Treaty Map, Pencuyut and,
  199
Mani province, xxii, 207, 283;
  encomiendas in, 277; suicides of
  idolaters in, 280
Marriage alliances: between Tikal and
  Naranjo, 37; between Tipu and
  Tayasal, 8, 57
Mass, mock, at Hubelna, 50
Massacre: at Bacalar by Santa Cruz,
  264; of Delgado party at Tayasal, 49;
  of Díaz de Velasco expedition to
  Tayasal, 28; of Mirones party at
  Sacalum, 28; of Tipuans at Tayasal, 8
Matronymics. *See* Names
Maximilian, Emperor of Mexico, 129;
  appoints *pacífico* prefect, 115; claim
  to Belize by, 113; visited by *pacífico*
  chiefs, 115
Maya groups. *See* Cehach Maya;
  Chichanha Maya; Chinamita Maya;
  Icaiche Maya; Independent Maya;
  Indios del monte; Itza Maya;
  Lacandon Chol Maya; Lacandon
  Maya; Lake Petén Maya; Lochha
  Maya; Lowland Maya; Manche Chol
  Maya; Maya of Belize; Maya of
  Yucatán; Mopan Maya; Muzul Maya;
  Pacíficos del sur; Palencano Chol
  Maya; Putun Maya; Rebel Maya,
  1847–1850; San Pedro Maya; Santa
  Cruz Maya, post-1901; Santa Cruz
  Maya, pre-1901; Tipu Maya; X-Cacal

Maya; Xkanha Maya; Yucatec Maya
Maya Mountains, 141
Maya of Belize, 67–68, 91; agricultural
  labor conditions of, xvii–xviii, 86–91,
  94, 152; attacks on Río Bravo and
  New River (1847–1848) and, 74;
  British timber interests and, xiv, xvii,
  69–70, 72–74, 78, 95n, 148–150,
  158–159; as Caste War refugees in
  north, 83, 94; colonial images of, xvii,
  80–82, 93–94; conditions attracting,
  170; continuous settlement of, 9–10,
  70, 73; corsair attacks and, 50;
  declining craft production of, 86;
  dependent status of, 94–95; early
  rebellions of, 43; in Fuensalida-Orbita
  entrada, 43; land tenure and, 91–92,
  170; language of, 21; as logwood
  producers, 87; pacification of, along
  New River, 50; sociopolitical
  organization of, 73. *See also* Muzul
  Maya; San Pedro Maya; Tipu Maya
Maya of Yucatán, 259; Caste War and
  migration of, 206; Chan Maya and, 3;
  conquest of, 226; Franciscans and
  nobility of, 236; migration of, to
  Belize, xvi, xx, 9–10, 20, 26, 48–49, 64;
  migration of, to San Pedro, 144;
  settlement patterns among, 206;
  starvation among, 207; world view of,
  261. *See also Huites*; Pencuyut;
  Pustunich; Yucatec Maya
Mayapan,* Tipu *matricula* and location
  of, 47
Mayapan, site: destruction of, 277;
  Pustunich and, 279
Mayeros, at Pustunich, 285, 287
Mazatlán:* alternate designation for
  Cehach, 12; fortifications at, 35;
  meaning of name of, 12
Mencha, Lacandon chief, 14
Menche: as Lacandon chief, 15, 19; as
  possible rendering of Mencha, 14
Menche, Bol. *See* Bol Menche
Merchant gods, 36
Merchants of Belize, timber industry
  and, 92
Mérida,* 130, 193, 195–197, 202, 219,
  284; Borderlands development and,
  196; Campeche versus, 196; Can Ek's
  delegation visits, 57; Caste War and,
  259; Franciscan mission at, 235–237;
  imperial commissary at, 115; *indios
  del monte* visit, 5, 67; Mani

conspirators tried at, 236–237; migration and, 220–221; threatened during Caste War, 108; Tipu Maya visit, 5, 67

Mesapich,* 117, 126; migration from, 116; *pacíficos* at, xviii, 110; population of, 112; Santa Cruz threaten *pacíficos* around, 112. *See also* Lochha

Mexican Revolution, 221, 282; Caste War and, 259; population dynamics and, 210, 215–216; at Pustunich, 286

Mexico, 128–129, 196–197, 211–212, 259–260, 277; crude death rate in, 210; economic development in, 216; migration data in, 192; Yucatán and, 195

Mexico, government of: Belize boundary disputes and, 111, 113, 128; and Belize-Chichanha relations, 112; British–Santa Cruz munitions trade and, 79; campaign against Santa Cruz and, 118, 124; *pacífico* independence and, 116; Santa Cruz Maya and, 75, 79, 124; Spencer-Mariscal treaty and, 124; territorial dispute with Great Britain, 110–111; treaty with Great Britain of, 79

Mexico City,* 219

Migration: Belize Maya names in Yucatán and, 64; calculation of net, 192; Caste War and, 206; causes of, 191; from Chichanha to Icaiche, 76, 145; from Chichanha to San Pedro region, 76–77, 139, 145; from Chichen Itza to Tayasal, 29; civil reduction and, 227; of colonial Maya artisans, 195; data for study of, 192–193; encouraged by rebellious Belize Maya, 53; famine and, 227; from Icaiche to Chichanha, 76, 112–113; of Kekchi Maya to Petén, 20; of Kekchi Maya to San Antonio, Toledo district, Belize, 25; of Lacandon, from Yucatán, considered, 15; of Lacandon to Chiapas, 14; from Lochha to Bacalar region, 116; Muzul Maya affected by, at Tipu, 68; Pencuyut and, xx, 208, 210–212, 218–219; from Petén to western Belize, 151, 165–166, 168–169; preconquest processes of, 141; public policy toward, 229; rural-urban, 191; rural-urban in Mexico, 218, 220–221; rural-urban in Yucatán, 220, 227–228; from San José to Cerro, 158; among San Pedro Maya settlements, 157–158, 162, 164, 166; San Pedro Maya sociopolitical organization and, 140, 170; from San Pedro to Benque Viejo, 153; from San Pedro to Petén, 153, 156; of Santa Cruz Maya, 125; from Santa Cruz region to northern Belize, 83, 94; technological inequality and, 191, 227; in Tipu region, 46, 52–53; from Tulum to Belize, 124; Valladolid and, 220–221; in Yucatán, 195, 207, 213, 226; between Yucatán and Mexico, 220; from Yucatán to Belize, xx, 9, 20, 26, 64; from Yucatán to Petén, 20, 22; from Yucatán to Tipu, xvi, 10, 25, 48–49, 68. *See also* Refugees

Military titles: among Icaiche Maya, 118; among Independent Maya, 109–110; among rebel Maya, 106; among San Pedro Maya, 113; among Santa Cruz Maya, 174; among Xkanha Maya, 118

Miller, William: survey party under, 161; visit to Santa Cruz by, 123

Miramar, Lake. *See* Lake Miramar

Mirones, Francisco de, Sacalum massacre and, 28, 49

Missionaries, Spanish. *See* Franciscan missionaries

Mo, Juan, *alcalde* of Chunkikhutul and Holiuc, 155

Mocu, as Cehach territory, 12

Moho River, 5, 19

Monkey River: Campin located on, 50; Zaui located on, 67

Montalvo, Gregorio de, Bishop of Yucatán, 239

Montejo, Francisco de (elder), 226, 247n; first *entrada* of, 235, 277; Mani Indian conspirators and, 237; Mani land grant of, 236

Montejo, Francisco de (son), Mani divided in *encomienda* by, 277

Mopan:* site of, probably at San Luis, 5; speech of, 21

Mopan, as territorial term, 21

Mopan Maya: Aycal as name for, 5; boundaries of, 5; *caciques* of, 25; Chacs and mountain-valley gods of, 30; as Chan Maya subgrouping, xvi, 3, 40; day names among, 66; hammock among, 18; language of,

20–21; Maya of Yucatán and, 40; migration from San Luis of, 109; Muzul as designation for, 25; mythology of, 17, 30; names among, 25; religion of, 27; at San Antonio, Toledo district, 25, 109; at San Luis and Dolores, 109, 141; subject to Itza Maya, 20–21. *See also Indios del monte*; Muzul Maya

Mopan River, location of Tipu and, 45, 143

Morán, Francisco, 19

Mortality, 193; epidemic-related, 207; in Latin America, 216; in Pencuyut, 207–208, 210–212, 215, 217; in Yucatán, 207

Mosquito Shore, Indian slaves from, 95n

Motul:* Franciscan mission at, 237; migration and, 220–221

Mountain Cow, site, 41n

Mount Hope,* 156, 168

Mozos, 87–90

Mullins River, Zaui located near, 67

Muna,* 193, 276

Munitions trade: between British and Independent Maya, 108; between British and Santa Cruz Maya, 75, 110, 121, 127–128; and British-Maya relations, 108, 110; Mexican complaints concerning, 75; San Pedro Maya and, 143, 148

Muxun Maya, 5, 67. *See also* Muzul Maya

Muzul, as non-Yucatec name, 67

Muzul, Juan, Zaui ruler, 5, 67

Muzul Maya: as Chan Maya subgrouping, xvi, 5, 67; as designation for Mopan Maya, 25; *indios del monte* as, 67–68; paganism and, 25, 57; territory of, 25, 67; Tipu chiefs as, 57; visit Mérida, 5, 57. *See also Indios del monte*

Muzulules. *See* Muzul Maya

Muzulun Maya. *See* Muzul Maya

Nabon Cacaalezuc, Petox chief, 26

Naclicab:* abandonment of, 166; burning of Benque Viejo and, 163; in Holmul minor cluster, 163–164; Lino Lara affair and, 146–148

Naha, Chiapas,* Lacandon Maya at, 21

Nahuat, Manuel, as voice of Talking Cross, 108

Namay Keb, Chunpich ruler, 26

Names: of Cehach Maya, 26; of Chan Maya, 3, 24–26; compound, in Belize, Petén, and Yucatán, 64; compound, of *indios del monte*, 25–26; compound, of Lake Petén Maya, 24–25; day, distribution of, among Maya groups, 65–67; day, among *indios del monte*, xvi, 5, 25, 43, 64–66; day, inheritance of, 65; day, in Tipu *matrícula*, 26, 43, 64–66; of Lacandon, 18; matronymic, 26; of Mopan Maya, 5, 25; non-Yucatec, in Socotz, 9; patronymic, 17; Spanish use of, 4; Yucatec, in Tipu *matrícula*, 26; of Yucatec Maya at Tipu, 8

Names, baptismal: and *indios del monte*, 65; in *matrícula* of Tipu, 64–65; as replacement for matronymic, 26; among Yucatec refugees in Belize, 26

Naranjal:* abandonment of, 157; burned by British, 78, 157, 160; flight from, 158; inhabitants of, 77; location of, 166; population of, 160; as San José minor cluster village, 158, 160

Naranjo, site, 37; royal marriage alliance with Tikal and, 37; Tubleche located near, 163–164, 168

Negroman,* 45; Lacandon-type *incensarios* from, 32

Never Delay,* Chunukum in vicinity of, 46, 55, 67

New River, 79, 90, 140, 149; Maya attacks on woodcutters, 72, 74; Maya of, to be pacified, 50; population of, 87; reached on first Pérez expedition, 53; on route to Tipu, 48; Tipu Maya related groups on, 8

New River Lagoon, xvii, 77, 152, 157–158, 162, 165; Chichanha refugees settle near, 76, 144; hardwood cutting on, 143; Holpachay located on, 54; Holsuzil located on, 53; limit of British settlement along, 143; logwood cutting on, 72; Maya attacks on mahogany works at, 74; on route to Tipu, 45, 48; Tipu Maya related groups on, 8. *See also* Hill Bank; Hololtunich; Indian Church; Lamanay; New River

New Spain, 194, 235

Nohha, El Próspero,* description of, as Chan Maya settlement, 18, 29

Nohoch tata, xxii, 173. *See also Patrón*

Nohukum,* on route to Tipu, 43, 48
Nohukum River, 21, 43, 48
Northern district, Belize: establishment of villages in, 84; labor conditions in, 87; population of, 83, 87
Novelo, Bonifacio: as early Caste War leader, 106; as Santa Cruz "chief spy" and *patrón*, 121, 125
Nuxi, Lacandon mythic figure, 17

O'Brien's Bank,* 161
Onen, among Lacandon, 16–17
Oral tradition: Caste War history and, 251–252; Maya documents and, 257. *See also* Counsels on Maya history
Orange Walk, Belize River:* Hogstye Bank and, 72; McKay's force retreats to, 150
Orange Walk, New River,* 149, 152–153; Icaiche attack, 79, 114; population of, 83
Orbita, Fr. Juan de: *entradas* to Tayasal by, 48–49; *entrada* to Tipu by, 43–45
Oxkintok, site, initial series date at, 38
Oxkutzcab,* 49, 219, 283

Pacíficos. See Pacíficos del sur
Pacíficos del sur, xviii, 110, 112, 114; alliances among, 75; British relations with, 75; as buffer for Yucatán, 127; commanders of, 115; Maximilian's government recognized by, 115; Mexican government and, 116; Mexican interest in, 118; rebellion of, in Lochha area, 115; Santa Cruz Maya relations with, 75, 119, 127; submission to Mexicans of, 75; Yucatán and Campeche governments and, 114. *See also* Chichanha Maya; Icaiche Maya; Independent Maya; Lochha Maya; Mesapich; Xkanha Maya
Paganism: attempts to eliminate in Petén, 48; of Belize River Maya, 25; in colonial Yucatán, 280; among Maya *maestros*, 245–246; and migration of apostasized Maya to Belize, 48; at Sacalum, 11, 28–29; in southeastern Quintana Roo, 33; suicides by Maya and, 280; Tipu Maya and, 56–57. *See also* Idolatry
Pakoc, Lake Petén Maya war god, 28

Palencano Chol Maya: compared with Lacandon, 19; language of, 21
Palisades, 34–35
Pasión River. *See* Río Pasión
Paslow Creek, 159
Paso Caballos, 23
Paso Real, 14
Pat, Jacinto, early Caste War Maya leader, 106
Patchakan,* founding of, 83
Patrón, of Santa Cruz Maya, 119, 125, 233
Patronymics. *See* Names
Pec, Román, Santa Cruz Maya leader, 124
Pech, Andrés, leader of Bacalar *barrio*, 54
Pech, José, 147
Pech, Juan, *ah kin* and *maestro* at Sotuta, 245
Pech, Santiago, 176n, 181n; British Honduras government and, 79, 115; as Icaiche *general*, 79, 115, 153; as San Pedro Maya leader, 114, 149
Pecoc. *See* Pakoc
Pedro, Don, Capuchin missionary, 14
Pencuyut,* 204, 213, 219, 229n; agricultural labor and, 198; Caste War and, 193; Caste War and population of, 206, 212, 214; Catholic priests at, 197; civil congregations and, 197; consensual unions in, 225; demographic data for, 199, 217, 222–226; demographic processes of, xix–xx, 203, 205, 215; description of, 193, 198; economic conditions in, 197–198, 216; *ejido* land at, 193; *encomienda* at, 197; history of, 194; household organization at, 199; location of, 193, 196; migration and, xx, 209, 211, 218, 221, 228; peonage increase at, 211; population of, colonial, 199–201, 208–209; population of, postcolonial, 201–202, 206–207, 210–211; Protestantism at, 193, 198; regional politics and, 198; *repartimiento* trade and tribute at, 197; sociopolitical organization of, 198; spontaneous abortions at, 224; stillbirths at, 223; town layout of, 193
Pérez, Capt. Francisco, 51, 68; *entradas* of, to Tipu region, xvi, 43, 45, 52–53, 55–57. *See Probanza* of Francisco Pérez; Tipu matrícula

Pescado Creek, 155–156
Petén, 25–26, 40, 143, 152; Caddy-Walker expedition to, 73; Cehach Maya in, 11; Chichanha refugees settle in, 9, 20, 76–77, 139; chicle extraction in, 188n; Classic period styles in, 37–38; Holmul minor cluster in, 141; Kekchi Maya in, 20; Maya language of, 21–24; population of, 19–20; religious architecture in, 30; San Pedro Maya abandon, 168; settlement patterns in, 19. See also Holmul minor cluster; Itza Maya; Lake Petén Maya; Lino Lara affair; Mopan Maya
Petén Lake. See Lake Petén
Petenzuc,* 21
Petexbatum,* Lacandon mission settlement, 14
Petha, Lake. See Lake Petha
Plazas. See Town layout
Plumridge, Lt. James J., as British envoy to Santa Cruz, 120–122
Poot, José Crescencio, as Santa Cruz Maya leader, 121, 123, 125
Population: of Belize, 83; of Chan Maya region, 19; of Chinam, 47; of Chorro, 157; of Chunbalche, 159; of Chunkikhutul, 155; of Corozal, 83; of Corozal Chico, 83; distribution of, in Yucatán, xiii, 221; of Holiuc, 155; of Hololtunich, 161; of Icaiche, 117–118; of Lake Petén region, 19; of Lowry's Bight, 83; of Mesapich, 112; of Naranjal, 160; of New River, 87; of Orange Walk, New River, 83; of Pencuyut, 199–202, 206–211; of Petén, 19–20; of Punta Consejo, 83; of refugee Chichanha Maya, 76; on Río Hondo, 87; of San Antonio, Río Hondo, Belize, 83; of San Domingo, 155–156; of San José, Belize, 158; of San Pedro, 77, 83, 152; of San Pedro Maya, 113, 139, 146, 176n; of Santa Cruz Maya, 122, 127; of Sarteneja, 83; of Ticul, 277; of Tipu, 48; of Tulunqui, 13; of Xkanha, 118; in Yucatán, 195
Posole, in mock mass, 50
Powder trade. See Munitions trade
Ppuses, building of Pustunich church by, 284
Price, Acting Lt. Gov. Thomas, 155
Priests, Maya: among Lake Petén Maya, 27; among Manche Chol Maya, 18;
pre-Columbian, 244; at Sacaba, 280; at Sacalum, 11; among Santa Cruz Maya, 234; temple of, at Tayasal, 28
Probanza of Francisco Pérez: discovery of, 43; entradas to Belize and, 45–47, 51–56. See also Pérez, Capt. Francisco; Tipu matrícula
Production: capitalist system of, 192; social relations of, 191
Progreso,* migration and, 220–221
Próspero, El.* See El Próspero
Protestantism, at Pencuyut, 193, 198
Puc, Benancio. See Puc, Venancio
Puc, José Crescencio, Santa Cruz Maya leader, 124
Puc, Juan, leader at Pustunich, 280
Puc, Venancio: death of, 121, 125, 264–265; Juan de la Cruz confused with, xxi, 254; massacre at Bacalar and, 264; in Maya oral tradition, 263–265; Plumridge-Twigge delegation and, 120; as Santa Cruz Maya leader, 119–120, 125, 263–264, 268
Puerto of Holsus.* See Holzuuz
Punab, Chomach. See Chomach Punab
Punta Consejo,* population of, 83
Pustunich:* agriculture in, 276, 281–283; alcaldes at, 278; Caste War and, 285; Catholic rituals at, 280–281; in Chilam Balam of Chumayel, 276; church at, 276, 279, 281; communal labor at, 287–288; compared with Chan Kom, xxiii; compared with contemporary Santa Cruz Maya, xxiii; conquest and, 277; economic conditions at, 281–283; education at, 276, 283, 287–288; ejido lands of, 282; encomienda of, 277; endogamy of, 282; "epoch of slavery" at, 282, 285, 287; historical interpretations of, xxii–xxiii; historical self-perspective of, 284–288; hunting at, 276, 283; Juan Puc leader at, 280; Mérida and, 283; pagan rituals at, 280–281, 288; plantations and, 281; political dependency of, 279, 286–287; population of, 282; relations of, with Ticul, 277–278, 283; saints of, 280; suspicion of priests at, 281, 285–286, 288; Uxmal and, 279; as Xiu family dependency, 277–278
Putun Maya: absorption of non-Putun and, 66; ahau as title among, 27; Chan Maya and, 3; day names among, 66; of Itzamkanac region, 66; language of,

21; names among, 25; population loss among, 207; at Tenosique, 4
Puuc Hills, xxii, 281, 283

Quacco Creek, 152
Qualm Hill,* Icaiche raid on, 78, 149
Que, Juan José, Lino Lara affair and, 147
Quetzal, Antonio, *alcalde* of Holmul, 147
Quicucche,* 280
Quintana Roo, xvi, 9, 64, 198, 255, 259–261, 269
Quisteil,* Maya revolt at (1761), 73, 105

Ramgoat Creek, 160–161
Ramgoat Creek, Pine Ridge, on route to Tipu, 43, 45–46, 53
Rate of natural increase, 208; in Pencuyut, 226; in Yucatán, 220
Rate of natural increase, crude: calculation of, 209; definition of, 192; in Pencuyut, 209–210, 217
Rebellions: in Belize and Bacalar-Chetumal region (after 1624), 8, 11, 47, 49–50, 52–53, 56; at Chichanha (1693), 75; of Maya in Yucatán, 208; Morant Bay rebellion, Jamaica (1865), 93; Quisteil uprising of 1761, 73, 105, 208; Sacalum massacre (1624), 8, 11, 28; in Tipu region, 8, 53, 56. *See* Caste War of Yucatán; Maya of Belize, British timber interests and
Rebel Maya, 1847–1850, 74–75, 105–109, 226, 259
Redfield, Robert, xi–xiii, 130, 275–276. *See also* Folk-urban continuum
Reducción. *See* Civil congregation; Reduction
Reduction: Maya languages and, 5; of Muxun Maya, 67; in Quintana Roo, 33; in Yucatán, 51. *See also* Civil congregation
Refugees: as ancestors of Chichanha Maya, 8; from Bacalar area (seventeenth century), 8, 49, 53; from Bacalar (*mestizo*) in Corozal, 83, 107; in Belize due to post-1624 Maya rebellion, 53; Caste War Maya in Belize as, 9–10, 76, 83–84, 112, 139, 144, 151, 206; Confederate, in Belize, 91, 165; from Holpatin, 46; at Hubelna, 50; *indios del monte* as, 68; Lacandon Maya as,

19; from Quintana Roo in Tipu region, 8, 48, 143; from Petén and Yucatán, 73; route of Caste War Maya, 33; at Sacalum, 11; at Tzuctok, 4. *See also* Migration
Regidores, among Maya of Yucatán, 242, 278
Religion, Christian. *See* Catholicism; Ceremonial centers; Churches; Franciscan missionaries; Fuensalida, Fr. Bartolomé de; Protestantism; Syncretism, religious
Religion, Maya, xiv–xv, xx, xxii, 3, 28, 245, 267, 281. *See also* Ceremonial centers; Cross, sacred; Crosses, sacred; Idolatry; Juan de la Cruz; *Maestros*; Paganism; Sacrifice, human; Syncretism, religious; Talking Cross; Talking Cross cult; and under various Maya groups
Religious architecture, among Petén Maya, 30
Repartimiento, 196, 207, 277
Repartimiento trade, 192
Repúblicas indígenas: Chichanha-Yucatán relations and, 109; laws concerning, 116; legal termination of, 118
Reservations, Indian, in Belize, 92, 169–170. *See also* Crown Lands Ordinance; Land tenure, Maya
Revitalization movements, 256
Rhys, Edward L., 155; appoints *alcaldes* among San Pedro Maya, 148; death and disappearance of, 78, 150; as peace commissioner to San Pedro Maya, 150
Rice, in Belize, 84
Río Acan. *See* Río Ixkan
Río Azul, 31. *See also* Blue Creek
Río Bec–Chenes sites: Chan-Yucatec boundary and, 39, 41; as Petén influence in Yucatán, 38
Río Bravo, 31, 77, 111, 157, 186n; Holmul villages and, 141, 163; Icaiche raid on, 113; Icaiche rent demands and, 114; Maya attacks on woodcutters on, 74; Qualm Hill on, 78; San Pedro Maya territory and, 139
Río Frio, 41n
Río Holmul, 163
Río Hondo, 47, 79, 119, 128, 145, 155; Albion Island and, 36; Belize-Mexico boundary and, 111; Chichanha

migration across, 77; Lacandon-type *incensario* from headwaters of, 31; on limit of logwood cutting, 72; mahogany cutting on north bank of, 111; Mexican customs barge on, 124; population on, 87; rebel Maya cross, 74–75; rebel Maya ports on, 108; on route to Tipu, 48; runaway Maya workers cross, 89; Santa Cruz Maya–British relations and, 75; Santa Cruz occupy mahogany works at, 119; Santa Cruz trade spoils at, 119; territory of Encalada and, 115

Río Ixkan, western branch of Blue Creek, 164

Río Lacantun, Lacandon settlements on, 14

Río Pasión, 14; Chan Maya at, 40; Lacandon Maya and, 16; Lake Petén Maya boundary and, 4

Río San Pedro Martir, Chinamita-Cehach boundary and, 12–13

Río Usumacinta, 13, 19, 21, 41n, 66; Chan Maya at, 40; as Chan Maya boundary, 4; Lacandon settlement and, 15–16; Lacandon-type *incensarios* in region of, 30–31

Río Yalchilan, 15

Roaring Creek, 77; Hubelna on, 50; on limit of logwood cutting, 72; Tipu Maya settlements on, 8

Rock Dondo,* 46, 55, 67

Roman Catholicism. See Catholicism

Roys, Ralph L., xiii, xv, 64, 171–172

Sabino Ul Ahna Couoh Uc, José, Lacandon, biography of, 14

Sacaba,* human sacrifice by priest of, 280

Sacalum:* Chan boundary and, 29; description of, 11; massacre of Mirones party at, 11, 28, 49

Sacalum massacre, later Maya revolts and, 8, 11

Sacluk (La Libertad),* Lake Petén Maya at, 4

Sacnab, Lake, 166

Sacrifice, human: Christian crucifixion and use of cross in, 29; of Fr. Delgado's party at Tayasal, 49; Díaz expedition victims of, 28; impaling of victims and, 29; among Lacandon near Coban, 17; at Nohha, El Próspero, 29; removal of heart in, 28–29; ritual use of teeth in,

29; by Sacaba priest, 280; at Sacalum, 28–29; at Tayasal, 29, 49

Sacristan, colonial role of, 242–243

Sacristan mayor, 243

Sactham.* See Zacat'an

St. George's Key, Maya in vicinity of (ca. 1779), 70

Salamanca de Bacalar. See Bacalar

Salmon, Lt. M. B., report on Hololtunich area by, 161

Salt, 195

San Agustín Acasaguastlan,* 42n

San Antonio, Cayo district, Belize;* Lacandon-type *incensario* from, 33; settled by Petén Chichanha, 168–169

San Antonio, Quintana Roo,* Santa Cruz outpost at, burned, 123

San Antonio, Río Hondo, Belize,* population of, 83

San Antonio, Toledo district, Belize: Kekchi at, 25; Kekchi modify Mopan culture of, 20; Mopan vocabulary from, 22; names at, 25

Sánchez, Apolinar, interpreter of the cross, 121

San Diego Tekax,* sugar hacienda, 214

San Domingo:* *alcaldes* at, 155; authority of Asunción Ek over, 77; as frontier migration point, 156; population of, 155–156; refugee population of, 83; as San Pedro minor cluster village, 151

San Ignacio el Cayo,* 10, 73, 77, 163, 168, 188n; Lacandon-type *incensarios* from, 32; location of Tipu and, 45

San José, Belize, 147, 152, 160–161, 181n, 183n, 185n, 186n; *alcaldes* of, 79, 158–159; attacked by British, 157; Chichanha Maya at, 77; destroyed by British, 78, 151, 158; Icaiche relations with, 79, 151, 153; Lino Lara affair and, 158; location of, 141, 157; migration from, to Cerro, 158; as minor cluster center, 139, 141, 157; population of, 158; removed to Orange Walk, 151, 158–159; San Pedro and, 158; satellite communities and, 139, 141, 157; smallpox at, 169; strategic location of, 143; Tipu Maya and, 8–9. See also San José Maya; San José minor cluster

San José, Petén,* 42n, 187n; skull cult at, 28; vocabulary from, 22

San José, site, 38, 158

San José Maya: claim rent at Indian Church, 158; origins of, 9; purchase supplies at Orange Walk, 158; removed to Orange Walk, 151, 158–159. *See also* San José, Belize; San Pedro Maya

San José minor cluster, 153, 157–162

San Juan, Pencuyut residents at, 214

San Juan Acul,* 14

San Juan de Dios,* Lake Petén Maya at, 4

San Juan Extramuros,* *barrio* of Salamanca de Bacalar, 53

San Lorenzo, site, 37

San Luis, Petén,* 169; *caciques* of (1754), 25; within Chan Maya boundary, 4; Kekchi influence Mopan culture of, 20; language of, 21, 141; Mopan Maya at, 21, 141; as town of Mopan, 5

San Pedro,* 181n, 182n, 183n, 185n, 186n; agriculture at, 98n, 152; *alcaldes* at, 79, 147; bivouac facilities at, 152; British appoint officials at, 113; Canul arrives at, 78; as ceremonial center, 153–154; Chichanha refugees at, 113; Chunkikhutul and, 155; church at, 151–152, 154; decline of, 170; Capt. Delamere marches on, 78; description of, 152; destroyed by British, 78, 114, 151, 153; early references to, 77; fiesta hall at, 152, 154; fortification at, 152, 163; Icaiche arrive at, 149; Icaiche influence over, 79, 153; location of, 77, 141, 152, 156; major cluster political-military hierarchy at, 76–77, 139–140, 150, 152, 170; military activities at, 150, 153; as minor cluster center, 139, 153; plaza at, 154; population of, 77, 83, 152; possible removal of, to Benque Viejo, 153; pre–Caste War Maya near, 10; resettlement of, 114; return of ancestors and, 154; San José and, 157–159; Santa Cruz Maya and, 155; Santa Teresa and, 156; stability of, 151; Tipu Maya and, 8–9; town layout of, 173; X-Cacal compared with, 154. *See also* San Pedro Maya; Yalbac Hills

San Pedro, patron saint of Tipu, 144

San Pedro de Buena Vista, 167

San Pedro Martir River. *See* Río San Pedro Martir

San Pedro Maya, 189n; Asunción Ek leader of, 80; British appoint officials of, 113; British destroy villages of, 78–80, 114, 150–151, 170; British relations with, 82, 113–114, 145, 149, 151; British supply munitions to, 143, 148; burning of Benque Viejo and, 163; Chichanha relations with, xix, 141; decline of, 170; defeat British troops, 78; environmental conditions and, 143; Icaiche relations with, 78, 80, 114, 145, 149–150, 153; mahogany gangs and, 82, 149; migration from Chichanha by, 77, 144; migration to Petén by, 151, 157; military strategy of, 143; population of, 76, 113, 139, 146, 176n; reestablishment of settlements of, 79, 114, 151; settlement organization of, 139, 141, 163, 170, 174–175; sociopolitical organization of, xix, 113, 139–140, 170–171; subsistence among, 143; territory of, xix, 79–80, 139, 141, 143; Tipu Maya and, 8–9; titles of office among, 140. *See also* Holmul minor cluster; San José, Belize; San José Maya; San José minor cluster; San Pedro; San Pedro minor cluster

San Pedro minor cluster, 151–157, 166

San Pedro region, early Maya occupation of, 8–9, 77, 143–144

Santa Ana,* Lake Petén settlement at, 4

Santa Clara, Lago. *See* Lago Santa Clara

Santa Clara Icaiche.* *See* Icaiche

Santa Cruz, Belize River,* 166, 188n

Santa Cruz,* Labouring Creek: abandoned, 155; *alcalde* of, 155; location of, 154–155; as San Pedro minor cluster village, 145, 151, 154–155

Santa Cruz, Northern district, Belize,* sugar estate at, 85

Santa Cruz, Quintana Roo,* 126, 185n, 254–255, 267, 269–270; attack from Tulum on, 123; Belizian traders at, 121; church at, 120, 122; early rebel settlement around *cenote* at, 108–109; Icaiche plans for campaign against, 112; Juan de la Cruz's sermon at, 253–254; migration from, 125; occupation by Mexican army, 124, 126; population of, 127; Talking Cross cult at, 108, 110, 154; town layout of, 122, 154, 173. *See also* Felipe Carillo Puerto; Santa Cruz de Bravo; Santa

Cruz Maya, post-1901; Santa Cruz
Maya, pre-1901; Talking Cross cult
Santa Cruz, San José vicinity, Belize,*
78, 157, 160
Santa Cruz de Bravo,* 173. See also
Felipe Carillo Puerto; Santa Cruz,
Quintana Roo
Santa Cruz Maya, post-1901: attitudes
toward Mexicans of, 260; compared
with Pustunich, xxiii; oral traditions
of, xxi–xxii, 259–273; request aid,
268; resistance of, 259; subtribes of,
173–174; Venancio Puc and, 264;
Wonderful True God in religion of,
264–265, 267, 269. See also Chancah;
Chunpom; Felipe Carillo Puerto;
Tusik; X-Cacal; X-Cacal Maya
Santa Cruz Maya, pre-1901: attack
Chichanha Maya, 76, 109, 112; attack
Lochha, 116; attack Tekax, 119;
British-Mexican treaty on pacification
of, 79; British relations with, 75, 79,
120–121, 131, 145; Catholicism and,
120, 233; Chichanha-Icaiche Maya
boundary with, 11; Chichanha Maya
and, 11, 76, 112, 119–120, 141, 144–145;
claim rent on Blue Creek mahogany
works, 144; collect debts in Belize, 120,
128; defeated at Kantunil, 123;
factional conflict among, 121, 126;
fighting forces of, 121–122, 124;
imprison Encalada, 116; Juan de la
Cruz and, xxi, 251–257; Kantunil
rebels desert, 120; Lochha Maya and,
113, 115–116, 122; Maya priests among,
234; Mexican campaigns against, 88,
119, 286; munitions trade and, 75, 121,
127; nonagricultural specialists among,
122, 125; occupy Blue Creek, 145;
occupy Río Hondo works, 119;
pacíficos del sur and, 128; political
headquarters of, moved, 123;
population distribution of eastern
Yucatán and, xiii; population of, 122;
ritual possession among, xxii;
secularization of leadership at,
125–126; settlement clusters among,
140, 173–174; sociopolitical
organization of, xv, xix, 106–107,
122–123, 125–126, 173–174, 233, 264;
tolerance of outsiders by, 124; treaty
(1884) with Yucatán, 123. See also
Juan de la Cruz; Santa Cruz, Quintana
Roo; Talking Cross cult

Santa Elena, 282
Santa María, Fr. Juan de, Txuctok and,
11
Santa Rita, Petén,* San Pedro Maya
Lake refuge at, 156
Santa Rita, site: Chetumal located near,
11; merchant god representations
found at, 36
Santa Rosa Xtampak, site, initial series
date at, 38
Santa Teresa,* 181n, 183n; alcalde of, at
San Pedro fortifications, 156;
description of, 156; destroyed by
British, 78; location of, 156;
population of, flees to Petén, 156;
resettlement of, 156; in San Pedro
minor cluster, 156; settlement of, 155;
stability of, 151, 156–157
Santa Teresa Creek, 156
Santos, Leandro, Santa Cruz Maya leader,
121
Santo Toribio:* language of, 21;
location of, 23
Sarteneja,* population of, 83
Sayaxche,* Lacandon settlement at, 14,
16
Scribes. See Secretaries
Second West India Regiment, 149, 161
Secretaries: at Icaiche, 117; among
Independent Maya, 107; sacred cross
and, xxii; of the Talking Cross, 233;
at X-Cacal, 255, 262–263
Segmental societies, Independent Maya
sociopolitical organization and, 127
Sermon of the Talking Cross. See Juan
de la Cruz
Settlement clusters, 139–143, 171–175
Settlement patterns: of Holmul minor
cluster, 162–170; of Hololtunich,
161; among Maya of Yucatán,
xviii–xix, 206; in Petén, 19; of San José
minor cluster, 141, 157–162; of San
Pedro major cluster, 139–143, 173–175;
of San Pedro minor cluster, 152–157;
of Santa Cruz Maya, 122, 154, 173; of
X-Cacal Maya, 154, 173; of Xkanha
Maya, 174. See also Town layout
Seymour, Supt. Frederick: Maya
agricultural activities and, 83, 91; San
Pedro Maya and, 76–77, 82, 91,
147–148
Sibal,* 22
Sibun.* See Xibun
Sibun River, 47, 72

Sittee,* 5, 8, 21. *See also* Soyte
Sittee River, 67
Sittee valley, 5
Siytee.* *See* Sittee; Soyte
Slaves, Maya, and revolts in Belize, 72–73
Smallpox, 14, 20, 169
Sociopolitical organization: of Chan
  Maya, 36, 115–117; of Chichanha
  Maya, xv, xviii–ix, 109–112, 144–145;
  of colonial Yucatán, 278; of Icaiche
  Maya, 114, 117–119, 141, 151, 173; of
  Independent Maya, 106, 141, 171–172;
  of Lochha Maya, 174; Maya cultural
  conservatism and, xiv–xv; of Pencuyut,
  198; of preconquest Yucatán, 141, 171;
  of San Pedro Maya, xix, 113, 139–140,
  170–171; of Santa Cruz Maya, xv, xix,
  106–107, 122–123, 125–126, 173–174,
  233, 264; of Sotuta province, 171; of
  X-Cacal Maya, 125, 140, 173–174; of
  Xkanha Maya, 117–118. *See also*
  Settlement clusters
Socotz,* 187n, 188n; *alcalde* of, 165;
  burned by Holmul Maya, 163, 167;
  Chichanha origins of, 9–10, 167;
  Lacandon-type *incensario* found near,
  33; language of, 22; migration to and
  from, 166–168; origin of name of, 9;
  Yaloch migration and, 165
Sosa, Martin, 147
Sotuta,* Franciscan mission at, 237
Sotuta, *partido* of, 212
Sotuta province, 207; sociopolitical
  organization of, 171; suicides of Maya
  idolaters in, 280
Southern Chichanha Maya. *See* Icaiche
  Maya; San Pedro Maya
Soyte:* language of, 67; Muzul (Muxun)
  Maya reduced from, 67; Tipu
  matrícula and, 47
Soyte River. *See* Sittee River
Spain: Campeche and, 194–195; and
  treaties with Great Britain, 110
Spanish colonial policy, 68; and the
  Maya, xiv, 52–53, 174, 197
Spanish Creek, 46
Spencer-Mariscal treaty, 111, 124
Stann Creek, Chan Maya boundary and,
  4
Stevenson, Supt. William, on refugee
  agriculture in Belize, 84
Stump Creek, 152
Sublevados bravos. See Santa Cruz Maya
Sublevados pacíficos. See Chichanha

Maya; Icaiche Maya; Lochha Maya;
  Mesapich; *Pacíficos del sur*; Xkanha
  Maya
Subtribes, of Santa Cruz Maya, 173. *See*
  also Settlement clusters
Sugar production: in Borderlands
  section, Yucatán, 197, 213; Caste War
  impact on, 213; communal land tenure
  and, 197; conflict of, with maize, 287;
  debt peonage and, 87–88, 197; export
  and, 84–85, 94; in northern Belize,
  xvii–xviii, 83–90; San Pedro Maya and,
  152; in Yucatán, 194–196, 212–213, 282
Sunkal, Francisco, *cacique* of San Luis,
  25
Swidden agriculture: in Northern
  district, Belize, 84–85; at Pencuyut,
  212; at Pustunich, 276, 281–283;
  among San Pedro Maya, 76–78, 152
Syncretism, religious: at Chunpom, 266;
  in contemporary Santa Cruz thought,
  266; and inquisition in Yucatán, 245;
  among Lacandon Maya, 17; among
  Yucatán Maya, 280. *See also* Cross,
  sacred; Crosses, sacred; *Maestros*;
  Talking Cross; Talking Cross cult

Tabi:* hacienda, 282; human sacrifice
  at, 280
Talking Cross, 122–123; Bacalar massacre
  and, 119; confiscated at Santa Cruz
  (1851), 108; disappearance of, at Santa
  Cruz, 125; discovery of, at *cenote*, 108;
  interpreter of, 121, 125, 233, 252;
  letter in name of, 108; *patrón* of, 233;
  resonating chamber used with, 109;
  Santa Cruz sociopolitical organization
  and, 233; secretary of, 233; at Tulum,
  122–123, 125–126. *See also* Cross,
  sacred; Crosses, sacred; Talking Cross
  cult
Talking Cross cult, 106; as alleged hoax,
  121; Caste War and, 252; Catholicism
  and, 233; decline of, at Santa Cruz,
  173; height of, 120; Juan de la Cruz
  and, 252; reestablished at Santa Cruz,
  108–109; as revitalization movement,
  126; ritual specialists for, 233–234;
  Santa Cruz Maya independence and,
  127; Santa Cruz Maya sociopolitical
  organization and, xix, 172–173; at
  Tulum, 122–123, 125–126, 173. *See also*
  Cross, sacred; Crosses, sacred; Juan de
  la Cruz

Tamay, Gabriel: at Bacalar, 119; Belize survey disturbances and, 162; lack of Mexican control over, 119; as leader at Icaiche, 117; monetary demands by, at Yaloch, 119; works in own fields, 117

Tata Chikiuic, 121

Tata Nohoch Dzul, 121

Tatich, at X-Cacal, 260. *See also Patrón*

Taxation, Yucatán frontier zones and, 213

Tayasal,* xvi; calendrical prophecy and conquest of, 33–34; Can Ek Itza dynasty at, 4–5, 30, 48; Chac cult absent from, 30; Chinamita raid population of, 13; column of Yaxcheelcab at, 27; conquest of, 19–20, 33–34, 56, 143; Cortés marches to, 35; defensive use of island at, 35; delegation from, to Mérida, 57; emissaries to Tipu from, 49; fortifications at, 35; Fuensalida and Orbita visit, 48–49; human sacrifice at, 29; invader-imposed central government at, 36; massacres at, 8, 28–29, 49; migration of Itza to, 29; missionary efforts abandoned at, 49; refusal of, to submit to Spanish, 57–58; Tipu trade and, 57; weakened controls of, 36

Teabo,* 197

Tejero, Fr. Martin, 53

Tekax,* 193, 197, 202, 208, 283; Caste War mortality around, 211; migration and, 220–221; nineteenth-century development and, 105; Santa Cruz Maya attacks on, 119, 212; sugar production centered around, 213; suicides of Maya idolaters in, 280; Yucatán garrison at, 212

Tekax: *municipio* of, 193; *partido* of, 212; sugar and henequen production in, 213

Tenochtitlán, site, fire cult at, 128

Tenosique,* 15; Lacandon settlement at, 16; and location of Canizan, 66; Putun Maya at, 4, 16; Tulumci and raids against, 13

Tepich,* Maya attack on, 107

Terrenos baldíos, 213

Tesekum, Mopan name, 25

Tesucan, Lake Petén Maya chief, 25

Texcoco, Lake. *See* Lake Texcoco

Tiac,* fortified town at, 34

Ticul,* 276, 282; Caste War siege of, xiii, 285; *encomienda* at, 277;

migration and, 220–221; patron saint of, 280; population of, 277; *presidente* of, 278; priests resident at, 281; relations of, with Pustunich, xxii, 277–279, 283

Ticul district, Indian-Mexican population ratio in, 283

Tiger Run,* Maya at, 10

Tihosuco,* Caste War and, xiii, 122, 211

Tikal, site, 42n

Timber industry, British: in Belize valley, 141; and conflict with merchants, 92; decline of, 82, 86, 94; and disruption of Maya maritime trade, 73; eighteenth-century limits of, 144; exhaustion of coastal timber by, 72; expansion of, toward interior, 72–74, 77; and government of Yucatán, 111; Icaiche attacks on, 78, 149; land tax and, 92; logwood in Belize settlement and, 46; Maya labor used by, 94n; Maya of Belize and, xvii, 9, 69–70, 72–74, 78, 82, 148–150, 158–159; Maya swidden agriculture and, 74, 158–159; railway boom and, 81; San Pedro–Icaiche "conspiracy" and, 150; San Pedro Maya and, 77, 82, 148–150, 158–159; Santa Cruz Maya and, 119, 124

Tipu:* abandonment of, 143; *alcaldes* of, 57; Bacalar priest at, 49; *caciques* of, 45–46, 55, 57; Chanlacam and Hautila Maya flee toward, 52; choirmaster of, 48; Christianized refugees at, 48; Chunukum as possible administrative outpost of, 46; church at, 48, 56; conquest of Tayasal and, 48; dances at, 48; delegation from, to Mérida, 57; delegation of Can Ek at, 57; delegation to Tayasal from, 49; Fr. Delgado visits, 11; Frs. Fuensalida and Orbita visit, 43, 48, 56; history of, after 1656, 56; idolatry at, 49; *indios del monte* and, 67; Itza Maya said to inhabit, 20; Lacandon-type *incensarios* found near, 32; Lake Petén Maya marriage alliances with, 8; Lake Petén Maya trade relations with, 8, 57; language of, 25; location of, xvi, 8, 11, 43, 45, 48, 77; migration to Yalbac Hills from, considered, 143–144; Muzul Maya as early inhabitants of, 68; Pérez's expeditions and, 54–56; population of (1618), 48; *principal* of,

64; rebellions at, 8, 53, 56; representatives of, massacred at Tayasal, 8; significance of, xvi–xvii; taxes collected from, 48; ties of nobility of, to Yucatán, 48; as *visita* and *curato* of Bacalar, 47; Yucatán refugees at, xvi, 8, 143. *See also* Tipu *matrícula*; Tipu Maya

Tipu, Laguna de. *See* Laguna de Tipu

Tipu *matrícula*: day names in, xvi, 25–26, 43, 64–66; *indios del monte* and, 5, 65–68; migrations inferred from, 64; text of, 58–64. *See also Probanza* of Francisco Pérez

Tipu Maya, 77, 95n; apostasy of, 50; at Bacalar, Holpachay, and Holzuuz, 54; boundary of Bacalar vicariate and, 8; brought to Chunukum, 55; Chichanha Maya and, 8; as Christians, 51–52; discussed, 8–10; as Itza Maya ally, xvi; Maya revolt of 1636 and, 8; at Mérida, 5; missionary activities and, 73; rebellions of, 8, 53, 56; submission of, 54–55, 57; summoned by Pérez, 45; Yucatán refugees among, xvi, 8, 143. *See also* Tipu; Tipu *matrícula*

Tipu region: and coastal corsair threat, 48; during early nineteenth century, 73; Hubelna apostasy and, 50; known as "El Tipu," 56; later mission activity in, 57; secular clergy and, 48

Tipu River: as Belize River, 45, 47; "El Tipu" as, 56; on route to Tipu, 45, 48

Tisactan,* 46. *See also* Zacat'an

Tixchel. *See* Acalan; Putun Maya

Tizimin:* Franciscan mission at, 237; migration and, 220–221

Tobacco, 84

Topoxte:* as Cehach fortified island, 36; religious architecture at, 30

Toral, Bishop Francisco de, instructions on *maestros* by, 243–244, 246

Tortillas, in mock mass, 50

Totemism: among Cehach, 12, 36; among Lacandon, 15, 36

Tower Hill,* sugar estate at, 85

Town layout: of Icaiche, 154, 173–174; of Pencuyut, 193; of San Pedro, 173; of Santa Cruz, Q.R., 122, 154, 173. *See also* Settlement patterns

Trade: between Campeche and Veracruz, 196; embargo against Icaiche, 115; between Flores and Belize, 141; Maya maritime, 48; between Tayasal and

Tipu, 8, 57; between Yucatán and other countries, 191, 195. *See also* Munitions trade

Transcription, 53, 65

Treaty: Chichanha-Yucatán (1853), 109; of 1786, Anglo-Spanish, 110; of 1783, Anglo-Spanish, 110; Spencer-Mariscal, 124

Trial Farm,* sugar estate of, 85

Tributary-inhabitant ratio at Pencuyut, 199–200

Tribute, Indian, in Yucatán, 196

Triumvirate, at Santa Cruz, 125

Truck system, 86–90. *See also* Belize, labor laws of; Belize, labor relations in; Debt peonage

Tubleche:* abandonment of, 166; burning of Belize villages and, 163; in Holmul minor cluster, 163–164; Lino Lara affair and, 146–148, 164; location of, 163

Tulum:* alleged attack by Pec on, 124; attack on Santa Cruz from, 123; Mexican Army occupies, 124; political split between Santa Cruz and, 124; refugees from, in British Honduras, 124; relations of, with Kantunil, 124; separate leadership at, 123; Talking Cross at, 123, 126

Tulumci.* *See* Tulunqui

Tulunqui:* Cehach stronghold at, 36; Chinamita settlement at, 13; fortified town at, 35

Tumbul,* 157

Tun, Pedro, 167

Tunkás,* massacre at, 121

Tusik:* Caste War and, 130, 259–260; Redfield and, 130; as satellite of X-Cacal, 260. *See also* Santa Cruz Maya, post-1901; X-Cacal; X-Cacal Maya

Tut family, San José, Petén, 28

Twigge, Lt. J. Y., as British representative at Santa Cruz, 120

Tzakol, site, 39

Tzeltal, Mayan language, 21

Tzeltal Maya, Chacs and mountain/ valley gods of, 30

Tzibanche, site: Chan Maya boundary and, 3, 37; Lacandon-type *incensarios* found near, 31

Tzompantli, 29

Tzotzil, Mayan language, 21

Tzotzil Maya, Chacs and mountain/valley gods of, 30
Tzuc, Domingo, Yaloch faction leader, 164–165, 167, 187n
Tzuc, José María, as Chichanha leader, 109–111
Tzuc, Luciano: abandons site of Chichanha for Icaiche, 76, 112, 145; assumed son of José María Tzuc, 112; as Chichanha leader, 111–112, 114, 144–145; Chichanha under Ek flee control of, 76; death of (1864), 114, 145; leads attack on Blue Creek works, 76, 112, 144; as refugee in Belize, 112, 145
Tzuctok,* Cehach mission settlement at, 4, 11–12

Uaitibal.* See Uatibal
Uatibal:* burned and abandoned, 52; location of, 52, 55; refugees from, 52, 54
Uaxactun, site, 41n
Uaymil province, Chan boundary question and, 37
Uc, Antonio, Lochha-Mesapich faction leader, 115–116
Uc, Gaspar, alcalde ordinario of Pacha, 53
Uluac, José, Chichanha leader, 145
United States of America, Yucatán trade with, 195
Urban development, 227
Usumacinta River. See Río Usumacinta
Uxmal, site, 38, 277, 279

Valladolid,* 191, 196; Caste War and, xiii, 211; ethnic composition of, 105; Franciscan mission at, 237; haciendas and plantations around, 105; migration and, 220–221; Yucatán garrison at, 212
Valladolid district, ethnic population ratio in, 283
Vela, José Domingo, San Pedro alcalde, 149
Veracruz,* 259; Campeche trade with, 196
Vidaurre, José, Lino Lara affair and, 146–148
Villalpando, Fr. Luis de, Franciscan at Mani, 236
Villa Rojas, Alfonso, xii, 130, 173

Wamil Creek, 157

Water Bank,* Icaiche Maya attack, 114
Western branch, Belize River. See Mopan River
Wharves, stone, 53
Wodehouse, Supt. Philip, 75
Woodcutting gangs. See Timber industry, British
World view, 261, 272

Xaibe,* Santa Cruz refugee village, 83, 173
Xanaba,* 277
Xbalche,* 164
X-Cacal:* Caste War aftermath and, 259; as ceremonial center, 140, 173; Chilam Balam book read at, 261–262; guardia at, 260; Mexican troops visit, 260; pilgrimage to, 260; scribe of, 255; sermon of Juan de la Cruz read at, 255–256
X-Cacal Maya, 130–131; compañia organization of, 140; Juan de la Cruz and, xxi, 252, 254–256; settlement patterns of, 173; sociopolitical organization of, 125, 140, 173–174
Xcalumkin, site, 38
Xcorralche, site, 279
Xecchakan,* 48
Xibun:* in Bacalar vicariate, 8; language of, 21; Sibun River and, 47; Tipu matrícula and, 47
Xiu, Maya group, 207, 276, 284; as caciques in Mani area, 278; control over Pustunich by, xxii, 277; Mani mission and, 236; polity of, 279; Spanish alliance with, 277
Xiu, Titul, preconquest Maya leader, 267
Xiuhtecutli, Nahuat fire god, 28
Xkanha,* 126, 153, 186n; ceremonial-military center at, 174; pacifico headquarters at, 116; pacifico polity and, 127; school at, 116, 118; smallpox at, 169; visitors to, 117–118
Xkanha Maya: cantones of, 174; claims to Hololtunich and, 161; Mexican government and, 118; miltary service and titles among, 118; non-Maya society and, 118; as pacifico subgrouping, 75; population of, 118; settlement clusters among, 174; sociopolitical organization of, 117–118
Xocnaceh,* 276, 284
Xoken,* 269

Ya, Feliciano, Icaiche leader, 145

Yakalche, site, 29

Yalain:* Lake Petén Maya at, 57; Maya priest of, 27

Yalbac,* 77, 155, 160; mahogany bank at, 141, 146, 153, 159; pre–San Pedro Maya and, 8–9; San Pedro and, 141, 152; San Pedro Maya and woodcutters at, 150

Yalbac Creek, 155. See Labouring Creek

Yalbac Hills: indigenous Maya in, xix, 74; San Pedro Maya in, 76–77, 79–80

Yalchilan River, 15, 41n

Yaloch,* 167, 181n, 187n; in burning of Benque Viejo, 163; José Justo Chan leader of, 165; laborers from, 165; migration from Yaloch Viejo to, 164–166; military titles at, 165; on old north-south trail, 11, 33

Yaloch, Laguna. See Laguna Yaloch

Yaloch Viejo,* 164

Yama, Felipe, Santa Cruz Maya leader, xxii, 124, 265–267

Yant'o, Lacandon god, 16

Yasuncabil,* 35

Yavilain, Lake, 21

Yaxche,* 21

Yaxcheelcab, Tayasal idol, 27

Yaxchilan, site, 19, 41n; Lacandon Maya and, 15

Yaxha,* 147, 163, 181n, 187n, 188n; migration from, to Belize, 5, 165

Yaxha, Lake. See Lake Yaxha

Yaxumcabil,* 34–35

Young, Toledo, and Co., 157, 165, 167–168

Young Girl,* 77, 152

Yspaniscrik (Spanish Creek), 46

Yucatán, 9, 20, 22, 24–25, 57–58, 64, 88, 94, 103, 128, 141, 191–192, 216–217; *ahau* title used in, 27; attitudes toward British-Maya relations, in, 110; Borderlands region of, 194, 196–197, 211; cattle raising in, 194; the church in, 194–195; Classic Petén influence in, 37; conquest of, 194, 235, 276; creoles of, 196, 227; demographic history of, 192, 199; diocese of, 117; East Colonial section of, 196, 211; economic conditions in, 48, 105, 129–130, 194–196, 213, 218; *encomienda* grants in, 277; henequen production of, 129–130, 194; historical interpretations of, 194–197, 276; Maya as economic

base of, 194; militia of, and Maya, xviii–xix, 106–108; Old Colonial section of, 194–196; political economy of, 105; population distribution in, 105, 213; population growth in, 197, 211, 221; preconquest polities in, 171; preconquest provinces of, 171; regional variations in, 195; resettlement of war zone in, 124; revival of interest in Maya in, 129; schools in, 193; sea communications with, 48; secular clergy in, 239; social development of, 174; Socialist-Liberal conflict in, 279, 286; social services in, 228; sociopolitical organization of, 36, 196, 278; sugar production in, 194, 211; Tayasal conquest and, 56; theory of Lacandon migration from, 16; tribute systems in, 197; urbanization in, 191; West Coast section of, 194–196; whites of, 75; world market system and, 191, 195, 197. See also Caste War of Yucatán; Migration

Yucatán, government of, 103, 107; British logging contracts with, 111; Campeche separated from, 112; Chichanha and, 109, 111; expeditions against Santa Cruz by, 108, 123; Icaiche kidnaping and, 114; *pacifico* political organization and, 114; and peace efforts with Santa Cruz, 121, 123

Yucatán, governor of: Beliza Maya and, 54–55; dispatches troops to Bacalar area, 52; Tipu Maya and, 54, 57

Yucatec, Mayan language, 21, 24; biography in, 14; Lacandon Maya and, 16; phonetic shifts in, 25; among San Pedro Maya, 139; spoken by Independent Maya leaders, 106; spoken counsels in, 261; spoken in northeastern Petén, 24; spoken north of Manche Chol, 67; Talking Cross speaks in, 108

Yucatec Lacandon Maya. See Lacandon Maya

Yucatec Maya: Chan Maya and, 11, 40; hammock among, 18; Itza rulers claim to be, 24; migration of, to Belize, 10; mythology of, 30; in Petén due to Caste War, 21; Santa Cruz Maya as, 11; sociopolitical organization of, xix; at Tipu, 25. See also Independent Maya; Maya groups; Maya of Belize; Maya of Yucatán

Yum Pol, scribe at X-Cacal, 255

Zacat'an,* 46
Zaczuc.* *See* Zaczuuz
Zaczuuz:* burned and abandoned, 50;
  location of, 8; meaning of, 50;
  migration from, to Hubelna, 46;
  Pérez expedition and, 45, 55; in Tipu
  matrícula, 46
Zapata, Dionisio, Santa Cruz Maya
  leader, 121
Zaui,* 5, 67
Zima, Andrés, Chichanha leader, 109, 111
Zinacantan,* as model for lowland Maya,
  xv
Zoite.* *See* Sittee River; Soyte
Zubiaur, Capt. Pedro, 58
Zulu, Chomach. *See* Chomach Zulu

Complete Reference

to the Built-In Functions

and Formulas in

Microsoft Excel

Microsoft®
Excel
Worksheet Function
Reference Second Edition

PUBLISHED BY
Microsoft Press
A Division of Microsoft Corporation
One Microsoft Way
Redmond, Washington 98052-6399

Library of Congress Cataloging-in-Publication Data
Microsoft Excel worksheet function reference / Microsoft Corporation.
    -- 2nd ed.
        p.   cm.
    Includes bibliographical references and index.
    ISBN 1-55615-878-5
    1. Microsoft Excel (Computer file)   2. Business--Computer
programs.   3. Electronic spreadsheets.   I. Microsoft Corporation.
HF5548.4.M523M543   1995
005.369--dc20   95-34447
                                                           CIP

Printed and bound in the United States of America.

1 2 3 4 5 6 7 8 9   MLML   0 9 8 7 6 5

Distributed to the book trade in Canada by Macmillan of Canada, a division of Canada Publishing Corporation.

A CIP catalogue record for this book is available from the British Library.

Microsoft Press books are available through booksellers and distributors worldwide. For further information about international editions, contact your local Microsoft Corporation office. Or contact Microsoft Press International directly at fax (206) 936-7329.

Apple and Macintosh are registered trademarks of Apple Computer, Inc. dBASE is a registered trademark of Borland International, Inc. Microsoft and Windows are registered trademarks and Windows NT is a trademark of Microsoft Corporation in the U.S. and/or other countries. ORACLE is a registered trademark of Oracle Corporation.

Acquisitions Editor: Casey D. Doyle
Project Editor: Brenda L. Matteson

Contents

Introduction   v

What Are Worksheet Functions?   v

The Anatomy of a Function   v

Find Answers by Combining Functions   vi

Entering Functions Easily: The Function Wizard   vii

Conventions Used in This Book   vii

Learning More About Functions   viii

All Worksheet Functions Listed by Category   ix

Database & List Management Functions   ix

Date & Time Functions   ix

DDE & External Functions   x

Engineering Functions   xi

Financial Functions   xii

Information Functions   xv

Logical Functions   xvi

Lookup & Reference Functions   xvi

Math & Trigonometry Functions   xvii

Statistical Functions   xix

Text Functions   xxii

Function Reference   1

(Functions are listed alphabetically)

Appendix: Using the CALL and REGISTER Functions   308

For More Information   313

Introduction

This book explains the worksheet functions included in Microsoft® Excel version 5.0 and Microsoft Excel for Windows® 95. Except for a few differences, worksheet functions are identical for all operating systems supported by Microsoft Excel. Whenever information pertains to a specific operating system, such as the Apple® Macintosh®, the operating system is mentioned.

What Are Worksheet Functions?

Worksheet functions are the calculations built into Microsoft Excel for you. Each function calculates a different type of value. For example, you can use functions to calculate sums, averages, loan payments, and slopes of lines. Microsoft Excel includes hundreds of functions for financial, statistical, mathematical, trigonometric, and other types of calculations.

Using these functions saves you the time and effort of knowing, calculating, and recalculating many different mathematical equations. Functions can tell you whether a condition is true or false, whether one number is greater than another, or whether two words are exactly the same. Functions also help you to sort through data by identifying and calculating minimum, maximum, average, percentile, and rankings of values.

The Anatomy of a Function

Each function has two parts: the name of the function and its *arguments*. The name of a function always appears in uppercase letters and describes what the function does. For example, the AVERAGE function calculates the average of all the arguments included with the function.

Arguments are the numbers, cell references, worksheet names, or other information that a function needs to calculate a value for you. An argument can be any one of the following:

- Numbers, such as −5, 11, and 63.2.

- Text, such as "a", "Word", and "w/punc." If the text you want to use contains quotation marks, use two double quotation marks (""text"") for each double quotation mark.

- Logical values, such as TRUE or FALSE, or a statement that creates a logical value when calculated, such as B10>20.

- Error values, such as #REF!.

- References, such as D12 or C4:C6.

Arguments follow the name of the function and are enclosed in parentheses. Multiple arguments are separated by commas. For example, if you wanted to find the average of the numbers 5, 11, and 63, plus the numbers included in the range C4:C6, you would enter the AVERAGE function and the following arguments into a cell:

```
=AVERAGE(5, 11, 63, C4:C6)
```

When you enter a function, you must precede it with an equal sign (=).

The functions, equal sign, and numbers, text, or references entered in a cell are referred to as a *formula*. After you enter a formula, Microsoft Excel calculates the formula and displays the resulting value in the cell. However, your formula isn't erased when a cell displays the value calculated from the formula. You can see your formula by selecting the cell and looking at the formula bar. Microsoft Excel recalculates the formula every time an argument changes.

Find Answers by Combining Functions

Functions can be used as arguments to other functions. Combining functions in this way helps you to make the most of the data entered on your worksheet. It also takes advantage of the ability of Microsoft Excel to quickly calculate and recalculate formulas. Remember to type an equal sign at the beginning of every formula, but not before functions used as arguments to other functions.

For example, suppose you want to estimate your income tax bill for the next year based on your last three years' worth of tax records. The cells A1:A3 on your worksheet contain your taxable income for the last three years and the cells B1:B3 contain your tax rates for those years. Without re-entering any data that is already on your worksheet, you can estimate the tax you will owe next year by using the formula:

```
=PRODUCT(AVERAGE(A1:A3), AVERAGE(B1:B3))
```

Entering Functions Easily: The Function Wizard

Keeping track of all the names, arguments, commas, and parentheses in a function can be confusing. The simplest way to enter functions into cells is by using the Microsoft Excel Function Wizard. The Function Wizard presents all the functions in categorical lists, and then leads you through each of the arguments. Along the way, it fills in all the needed commas and parentheses for you.

To use the Function Wizard, choose the Function command from the Insert menu or click the button on the Standard toolbar. The Function Wizard button also appears on the formula bar while you are editing a cell.

To learn more about using the Function Wizard, look up Function Wizard in Help.

Conventions Used in This Book

Each function description in this book contains a section called Syntax, which shows the name of the function, the order of its arguments, and which arguments are required. Function names appear in uppercase letters without an equal sign (=). Required arguments are shown in **bold** and optional arguments are in plain text (not bold). Where functions and arguments are discussed in the text, all arguments are shown in plain text (not bold), whether they are required or optional.

Argument names use underline characters to separate the parts of the argument name. For example, num_chars is the name of an argument specifying the number of characters (letters) in a word or phrase.

In addition to the Syntax section, each function description might also include other information, such as:

- Explanation about a function and its use
- Examples showing how to use a function in a formula
- Related functions that are similar or complimentary to the one described
- Return values, the possible values calculated by the function

Learning More About Functions

The documentation included with Microsoft Excel contains additional information about using functions. For more information, including how to enter worksheet functions, how to use the Function Wizard, how Microsoft Excel calculates worksheet functions, and how to create your own worksheet functions, look up Worksheet functions in Help.

Worksheet Functions Listed by Category

Database & List Management Functions

DAVERAGE   Returns the average of selected database entries.

DCOUNT   Counts the cells containing numbers from a specified database and criteria.

DCOUNTA   Counts nonblank cells from a specified database and criteria.

DGET   Extracts from a database a single record that matches the specified criteria.

DMAX   Returns the maximum value from selected database entries.

DMIN   Returns the minimum value from selected database entries.

DPRODUCT   Multiplies the values in a particular field of records that match the criteria in a database.

DSTDEV   Estimates the standard deviation based on a sample of selected database entries.

DSTDEVP   Calculates the standard deviation based on the entire population of selected database entries.

DSUM   Adds the numbers in the field column of records in the database that match the criteria.

DVAR   Estimates variance based on a sample from selected database entries.

DVARP   Calculates variance based on the entire population of selected database entries.

SQLREQUEST   Connects with an external data source and runs a query from a worksheet, then returns the result as an array without the need for macro programming.

Date & Time Functions

DATE   Returns the serial number of a particular date.

DATEVALUE   Converts a date in the form of text to a serial number.

DAY   Converts a serial number to a day of the month.

x Microsoft Excel Worksheet Function Reference

DAYS360   Calculates the number of days between two dates based on a 360-day year.

EDATE   Returns the serial number of the date that is the indicated number of months before or after the start date.

EOMONTH   Returns the serial number of the last day of the month before or after a specified number of months.

HOUR   Converts a serial number to an hour.

MINUTE   Converts a serial number to a minute.

MONTH   Converts a serial number to a month.

NETWORKDAYS   Returns the number of whole workdays between two dates.

NOW   Returns the serial number of the current date and time.

SECOND   Converts a serial number to a second.

TIME   Returns the serial number of a particular time.

TIMEVALUE   Converts a time in the form of text to a serial number.

TODAY   Returns the serial number of today's date.

WEEKDAY   Converts a serial number to a day of the week.

WORKDAY   Returns the serial number of the date before or after a specified number of workdays.

YEAR   Converts a serial number to a year.

YEARFRAC   Returns the year fraction representing the number of whole days between start_date and end_date.

DDE & External Functions

CALL   Calls a procedure in a dynamic link library or code resource.

REGISTER.ID   Returns the register ID of the specified dynamic link library (DLL) or code resource that has been previously registered.

SQL.REQUEST   Connects with an external data source and runs a query from a worksheet, then returns the result as an array without the need for macro programming.

Engineering Functions

BESSELI   Returns the modified Bessel function $I_n(x)$.

BESSELJ   Returns the Bessel function $J_n(x)$.

BESSELK   Returns the modified Bessel function $K_n(x)$.

BESSELY   Returns the Bessel function $Y_n(x)$.

BIN2DEC   Converts a binary number to decimal.

BIN2HEX   Converts a binary number to hexadecimal.

BIN2OCT   Converts a binary number to octal.

COMPLEX   Converts real and imaginary coefficients into a complex number.

CONVERT   Converts a number from one measurement system to another.

DEC2BIN   Converts a decimal number to binary.

DEC2HEX   Converts a decimal number to hexadecimal.

DEC2OCT   Converts a decimal number to octal.

DELTA   Tests whether two values are equal.

ERF   Returns the error function.

ERFC   Returns the complementary error function.

GESTEP   Tests whether a number is greater than a threshold value.

HEX2BIN   Converts a hexadecimal number to binary.

HEX2DEC   Converts a hexadecimal number to decimal.

HEX2OCT   Converts a hexadecimal number to octal.

IMABS   Returns the absolute value (modulus) of a complex number.

IMAGINARY   Returns the imaginary coefficient of a complex number.

IMARGUMENT   Returns the argument theta, an angle expressed in radians.

IMCONJUGATE   Returns the complex conjugate of a complex number.

IMCOS   Returns the cosine of a complex number.

IMDIV   Returns the quotient of two complex numbers.

IMEXP   Returns the exponential of a complex number.

IMLN Returns the natural logarithm of a complex number.

IMLOG10 Returns the base-10 logarithm of a complex number.

IMLOG2 Returns the base-2 logarithm of a complex number.

IMPOWER Returns a complex number raised to an integer power.

IMPRODUCT Returns the product of two complex numbers.

IMREAL Returns the real coefficient of a complex number.

IMSIN Returns the sine of a complex number.

IMSQRT Returns the square root of a complex number.

IMSUB Returns the difference of two complex numbers.

IMSUM Returns the sum of complex numbers.

OCT2BIN Converts an octal number to binary.

OCT2DEC Converts an octal number to decimal.

OCT2HEX Converts an octal number to hexadecimal.

SQRTPI Returns the square root of (number * PI).

Financial Functions

ACCRINT Returns the accrued interest for a security that pays periodic interest.

ACCRINTM Returns the accrued interest for a security that pays interest at maturity.

AMORDEGRC Returns the depreciation for each accounting period.

AMORLINC Returns the depreciation for each accounting period.

COUPDAYBS Returns the number of days from the beginning of the coupon period to the settlement date.

COUPDAYS Returns the number of days in the coupon period that contains the settlement date.

COUPDAYSNC Returns the number of days from the settlement date to the next coupon date.

COUPNCD Returns the next coupon date after the settlement date.

COUPNUM   Returns the number of coupons payable between the settlement date and maturity date.

COUPPCD   Returns the previous coupon date before the settlement date.

CUMIPMT   Returns the cumulative interest paid between two periods.

CUMPRINC   Returns the cumulative principal paid on a loan between two periods.

DB   Returns the depreciation of an asset for a specified period using the fixed-declining balance method.

DDB   Returns the depreciation of an asset for a spcified period using the double-declining balance method or some other method you specify.

DISC   Returns the discount rate for a security.

DOLLARDE   Converts a dollar price, expressed as a fraction, into a dollar price, expressed as a decimal number.

DOLLARFR   Converts a dollar price, expressed as a decimal number, into a dollar price, expressed as a fraction.

DURATION   Returns the annual duration of a security with periodic interest payments.

EFFECT   Returns the effective annual interest rate.

FV   Returns the future value of an investment.

FVSCHEDULE   Returns the future value of an initial principal after applying a series of compound interest rates.

INTRATE   Returns the interest rate for a fully invested security.

IPMT   Returns the interest payment for an investment for a given period.

IRR   Returns the internal rate of return for a series of cash flows.

MDURATION   Returns the Macauley modified duration for a security with an assumed par value of $100.

MIRR   Returns the internal rate of return where positive and negative cash flows are financed at different rates.

NOMINAL   Returns the annual nominal interest rate.

NPER   Returns the number of periods for an investment.

NPV   Returns the net present value of an investment based on a series of periodic cash flows and a discount rate.

ODDFPRICE   Returns the price per $100 face value of a security with an odd first period.

ODDFYIELD   Returns the yield of a security with an odd first period.

ODDLPRICE   Returns the price per $100 face value of a security with an odd last period.

ODDLYIELD   Returns the yield of a security with an odd last period.

PMT   Returns the periodic payment for an annuity.

PPMT   Returns the payment on the principal for an investment for a given period.

PRICE   Returns the price per $100 face value of a security that pays periodic interest.

PRICEDISC   Returns the price per $100 face value of a discounted security.

PRICEMAT   Returns the price per $100 face value of a security that pays interest at maturity.

PV   Returns the present value of an investment.

RATE   Returns the interest rate per period of an annuity.

RECEIVED   Returns the amount received at maturity for a fully invested security.

SLN   Returns the straight-line depreciation of an asset for one period.

SYD   Returns the sum-of-years' digits depreciation of an asset for a specified period.

TBILLEQ   Returns the bond-equivalent yield for a Treasury bill.

TBILLPRICE   Returns the price per $100 face value for a Treasury bill.

TBILLYIELD   Returns the yield for a Treasury bill.

VDB   Returns the depreciation of an asset for a specified or partial period using a declining balance method.

XIRR   Returns the internal rate of return for a schedule of cash flows that is not necessarily periodic.

XNPV   Returns the net present value for a schedule of cash flows that is not necessarily periodic.

YIELD   Returns the yield on a security that pays periodic interest.

YIELDDISC   Returns the annual yield for a discounted security. For example, a treasury bill.

YIELDMAT   Returns the annual yield of a security that pays interest at maturity.

Information Functions

CELL   Returns information about the formatting, location, or contents of a cell.

COUNTBLANK   Counts the number of blank cells within a range.

ERROR.TYPE   Returns a number corresponding to an error type.

INFO   Returns information about the current operating environment.

ISBLANK   Returns TRUE if the value is blank.

ISERR   Returns TRUE if the value is any error value except #N/A.

ISERROR   Returns TRUE if the value is any error value.

ISEVEN   Returns TRUE if the number is even.

ISLOGICAL   Returns TRUE if the value is a logical value.

ISNA   Returns TRUE if the value is the #N/A error value.

ISNONTEXT   Returns TRUE if the value is not text.

ISNUMBER   Returns TRUE if the value is a number.

ISODD   Returns TRUE if the number is odd.

ISREF   Returns TRUE if the value is a reference.

ISTEXT   Returns TRUE if the value is text.

N   Returns a value converted to a number.

NA   Returns the error value #N/A.

TYPE   Returns a number indicating the data type of a value.

Logical Functions

AND   Returns TRUE if all its arguments are TRUE.

FALSE   Returns the logical value FALSE.

IF   Specifies a logical test to perform.

NOT   Reverses the logic of its argument.

OR   Returns TRUE if any argument is TRUE.

TRUE   Returns the logical value TRUE.

Lookup & Reference Functions

ADDRESS   Returns a reference as text to a single cell in a worksheet.

AREAS   Returns the number of areas in a reference.

CHOOSE   Chooses a value from a list of values.

COLUMN   Returns the column number of a reference.

COLUMNS   Returns the number of columns in a reference.

HLOOKUP   Looks in the top row of an array and returns the value of the indicated cell.

INDEX   Uses an index to choose a value from a reference or array.

INDIRECT   Returns a reference indicated by a text value.

LOOKUP   Looks up values in a vector or array.

MATCH   Looks up values in a reference or array.

OFFSET   Returns a reference offset from a given reference.

ROW   Returns the row number of a reference.

ROWS   Returns the number of rows in a reference.

TRANSPOSE   Returns the transpose of an array.

VLOOKUP   Looks in the first column of an array and moves across the row to return the value of a cell.

Math & Trigonometry Functions

ABS   Returns the absolute value of a number.

ACOS   Returns the arccosine of a number.

ACOSH   Returns the inverse hyperbolic cosine of a number.

ASIN   Returns the arcsine of a number.

ASINH   Returns the inverse hyperbolic sine of a number.

ATAN   Returns the arctangent of a number.

ATAN2   Returns the arctangent from x- and y- coordinates.

ATANH   Returns the inverse hyperbolic tangent of a number.

CEILING   Rounds a number to the nearest integer or to the nearest multiple of significance.

COMBIN   Returns the number of combinations for a given number of objects.

COS   Returns the cosine of a number.

COSH   Returns the hyperbolic cosine of a number.

COUNTIF   Counts the number of non-blank cells within a range which meet the given criteria.

DEGREES   Converts radians to degrees.

EVEN   Rounds a number up to the nearest even integer.

EXP   Returns e raised to the power of a given number.

FACT   Returns the factorial of a number.

FACTDOUBLE   Returns the double factorial of a number.

FLOOR   Rounds a number down, toward zero.

GCD   Returns the greatest common divisor.

INT   Rounds a number down to the nearest integer.

LCM   Returns the least common multiple.

LN   Returns the natural logarithm of a number.

LOG   Returns the logarithm of a number to a specified base.

LOG10   Returns the base-10 logarithm of a number.

MDETERM   Returns the matrix determinant of an array.

MINVERSE   Returns the matrix inverse of an array.

MMULT   Returns the matrix product of two arrays.

MOD   Returns the remainder from division.

MROUND   Returns a number rounded to the desired multiple.

MULTINOMIAL   Returns the multinomial of a set of numbers.

ODD   Rounds a number up to the nearest odd integer.

PI   Returns the value of Pi.

POWER   Returns the result of a number raised to a power.

PRODUCT   Multiplies its arguments.

QUOTIENT   Returns the integer portion of a division.

RADIANS   Converts degrees to radians.

RAND   Returns a random number between 0 and 1.

RANDBETWEEN   Returns a random number between the numbers you specify.

ROMAN   Converts an Arabic numeral to Roman, as text.

ROUND   Rounds a number to a specified number of digits.

ROUNDDOWN   Rounds a number down, toward zero.

ROUNDUP   Rounds a number up, away from zero.

SERIESSUM   Returns the sum of a power series based on the formula.

SIGN   Returns the sign of a number.

SIN   Returns the sine of the given angle.

SINH   Returns the hyperbolic sine of a number.

SQRT   Returns a positive square root.

SQRTPI   Returns the square root of (number * PI)

SUM   Adds its arguments.

SUMIF   Adds the cells specified by a given criteria.

SUMPRODUCT   Returns the sum of the products of corresponding array components.

SUMSQ   Returns the sum of the squares of the arguments.

SUMX2MY2   Returns the sum of the difference of squares of corresponding values in two arrays.

SUMX2PY2   Returns the sum of the sum of squares of corresponding values in two arrays.

SUMXMY2   Returns the sum of squares of differences of corresponding values in two arrays.

TAN   Returns the tangent of a number.

TANH   Returns the hyperbolic tangent of a number.

TRUNC   Truncates a number to an integer.

Statistical Functions

AVEDEV   Returns the average of the absolute deviations of data points from their mean.

AVERAGE   Returns the average of its arguments.

BETADIST   Returns the cumulative beta probability density function.

BETAINV   Returns the inverse of the cumulative beta probability density function.

BINOMDIST   Returns the individual term binomial distribution probability.

CHIDIST   Returns the one-tailed probability of the chi-squared distribution.

CHIINV   Returns the inverse of the one-tailed probability of the chi-squared distribution.

CHITEST   Returns the test for independence.

CONFIDENCE   Returns the confidence interval for a population mean.

CORREL   Returns the correlation coefficient between two data sets.

COUNT   Counts how many numbers are in the list of arguments.

COUNTA   Counts how many values are in the list of arguments.

COVAR   Returns covariance, the average of the products of paired deviations.

CRITBINOM   Returns the smallest value for which the cumulative binomial distribution is less than or equal to a criterion value.

DEVSQ   Returns the sum of squares of deviations.

EXPONDIST   Returns the exponential distribution.

FDIST   Returns the F probability distribution.

FINV   Returns the inverse of the F probability distribution.

FISHER   Returns the Fisher transformation.

FISHERINV   Returns the inverse of the Fisher transformation.

FORECAST   Returns a value along a linear trend.

FREQUENCY   Returns a frequency distribution as a vertical array.

FTEST   Returns the result of an F-test.

GAMMADIST   Returns the gamma distribution.

GAMMAINV   Returns the inverse of the gamma cumulative distribution.

GAMMALN   Returns the natural logarithm of the gamma function, $\Gamma(x)$.

GEOMEAN   Returns the geometric mean.

GROWTH   Returns values along an exponential trend.

HARMEAN   Returns the harmonic mean.

HYPGEOMDIST   Returns the hypergeometric distribution.

INTERCEPT   Returns the intercept of the linear regression line.

KURT   Returns the kurtosis of a data set.

LARGE   Returns the k-th largest value in a data set.

LINEST   Returns the parameters of a linear trend.

LOGEST   Returns the parameters of an exponential trend.

LOGINV   Returns the inverse of the lognormal distribution.

LOGNORMDIST   Returns the cumulative lognormal distribution.

MAX   Returns the maximum value in a list of arguments.

MEDIAN   Returns the median of the given numbers.

MIN   Returns the minimum value in a list of arguments.

MODE   Returns the most common value in a data set.

NEGBINOMDIST   Returns the negative binomial distribution.

NORMDIST   Returns the normal cumulative distribution.

NORMINV   Returns the inverse of the normal cumulative distribution.

NORMSDIST   Returns the standard normal cumulative distribution.

NORMSINV   Returns the inverse of the standard normal cumulative distribution.

PEARSON   Returns the Pearson product moment correlation coefficient.

PERCENTILE   Returns the k-th percentile of values in a range.

PERCENTRANK   Returns the percentage rank of a value in a data set.

PERMUT   Returns the number of permutations for a given number of objects.

POISSON   Returns the Poisson distribution.

PROB   Returns the probability that values in a range are between two limits.

QUARTILE   Returns the quartile of a data set.

RANK   Returns the rank of a number in a list of numbers.

RSQ   Returns the square of the Pearson product moment correlatin coefficient.

SKEW   Returns the skewness of a distribution.

SLOPE   Returns the slope of the linear regression line.

SMALL   Returns the k-th smallest value in a data set.

STANDARDIZE   Returns a normalized value.

STDEV   Estimates standard deviation based on a sample.

STDEVP   Calculates standard deviation based on the entire population.

STEYX   Returns the standard error of the predicted y-value for each x in the regression.

TDIST   Returns the Student's t-distribution.

TINV   Returns the inverse of the Student's t-distribution.

TREND   Returns values along a linear trend.

TRIMMEAN   Returns the mean of the interior of a data set.

TTEST   Returns the probability associated with a Student's t-Test.

VAR   Estimates variance based on a sample.

VARP   Calculates variance based on the entire population.

WEIBULL   Returns the Weibull distribution.

ZTEST   Returns the two-tailed P-value of a z-test.

Text Functions

CHAR   Returns the character specified by the code number.

CLEAN   Removes all nonprintable characters from text.

CODE   Returns a numeric code for the first character in a text string.

CONCATENATE   Joins several text items into one text item.

DOLLAR   Converts a number to text, using currency format.

EXACT   Checks to see if two text values are identical.

FIND   Finds one text value within another (case-sensitive).

FIXED   Formats a number as text with a fixed number of decimals.

LEFT   Returns the leftmost characters from a text value.

LEN   Returns the number of characters in a text string.

LOWER   Converts text to lowercase.

MID   Returns a specific number of characters from a text string starting at the position you specify.

PROPER   Capitalizes the first letter in each word of a text value.

REPLACE   Replaces characters within text.

REPT   Repeats text a given number of times.

RIGHT   Returns the rightmost characters from a text value.

SEARCH   Finds one text value within another (not case-sensitive).

SUBSTITUTE   Substitutes new text for old text in a text string.

T   Converts its arguments to text.

TEXT   Formats a number and converts it to text.

TRIM   Removes spaces from text.

UPPER   Converts text to uppercase.

VALUE   Converts a text argument to a number.

ABS

Returns the absolute value of a number. The absolute value of a number is the number without its sign.

Syntax

ABS(number)

Number   is the real number of which you want the absolute value.

Examples

ABS(2) equals 2

ABS(-2) equals 2

If A1 contains −16, then:

SQRT(ABS(A1)) equals 4

Related Functions

IMABS	Returns the absolute value (modulus) of a complex number
SIGN	Returns the sign of a number

List of Math & Trigonometry Functions

ACCRINT

Returns the accrued interest for a security that pays periodic interest.

If this function is not available, run the Setup program to install the Analysis ToolPak. After you install the Analysis ToolPak, you must select it in the Add-In Manager. For more information, look up Add-ins in Help.

Syntax

ACCRINT(issue, first_interest, settlement, rate, par, frequency, basis)

Issue   is the security's issue date, expressed as a serial date number.

First_interest   is the security's first interest date, expressed as a serial date number.

Settlement   is the security's settlement date, expressed as a serial date number.

Rate   is the security's annual coupon rate.

Par   is the security's par value. If you omit par, ACCRINT uses $1000.

Frequency   is the number of coupon payments per year. For annual payments, frequency = 1; for semiannual, frequency = 2; for quarterly, frequency = 4.

Basis   is the type of day count basis to use.

Basis	Day count basis
0 or omitted	US (NASD) 30/360
1	Actual/actual
2	Actual/360
3	Actual/365
4	European 30/360

Remarks

- If any argument is non-numeric, ACCRINT returns the #VALUE! error value.
- Issue, first_interest, settlement, frequency, and basis are truncated to integers.
- If issue, first_interest, or settlement is not a valid serial date number, ACCRINT returns the #NUM! error value.
- If coupon ≤ 0 or if par ≤ 0, ACCRINT returns the #NUM! error value.
- If frequency is any number other than 1, 2, or 4, ACCRINT returns the #NUM! error value.
- If basis < 0 or if basis > 4, ACCRINT returns the #NUM! error value.
- If issue ≥ settlement, ACCRINT returns the #NUM! error value.
- ACCRINT is calculated as follows:

$$ACCRINT = par \times \frac{rate}{frequency} \times \sum_{i=1}^{NC} \frac{A_i}{NL_i}$$

where:

A_i = number of accrued days for the ith quasi-coupon period within odd period.

NC = number of quasi-coupon periods that fit in odd period. If this number contains a fraction, raise it to the next whole number.

NL_i = normal length in days of the ith quasi-coupon period within odd period.

Example

A Treasury bond has the following terms:

February 28, 1993 issue date
May 1, 1993 settlement date
August 31, 1993 first interest date
10.0% coupon
$1000 par value
Frequency is semiannual
30/360 basis

The accrued interest (in the 1900 Date System) is:

`ACCRINT(34028,34212,34090,0.1,1000,2,0)` equals 16.85083.

| **Related Functions** | ACCRINTM | Returns the accrued interest for a security that pays interest at maturity |
| | DATE | Returns the serial number of a particular date |

List of Financial Functions

ACCRINTM

Returns the accrued interest for a security that pays interest at maturity.

If this function is not available, run the Setup program to install the Analysis ToolPak. After you install the Analysis ToolPak, you must select it in the Add-In Manager. For more information, look up Add-ins in Help.

Syntax

ACCRINTM(issue, maturity, **rate**, par, basis)

Issue   is the security's issue date, expressed as a serial date number.

Settlement   is the security's maturity date, expressed as a serial date number.

Rate   is the security's annual coupon rate.

Par   is the security's par value. If you omit par, ACCRINTM uses $1000.

Basis   is the type of day count basis to use.

Basis	Day count basis
0 or omitted	US (NASD) 30/360
1	Actual/actual
2	Actual/360
3	Actual/365
4	European 30/360

Remarks

- Issue, settlement, and basis are truncated to integers.
- If any argument is non-numeric, ACCRINTM returns the #VALUE! error value.
- If issue or settlement is not a valid serial date number, ACCRINTM returns the #NUM! error value.
- If rate ≤ 0 or if par ≤ 0, ACCRINTM returns the #NUM! error value.

- If basis < 0 or if basis > 4, ACCRINTM returns the #NUM! error value.
- If issue ³ settlement, ACCRINTM returns the #NUM! error value.
- ACCRINTM is calculated as follows:

$$ACCRINTM = par \times rate \times \frac{A}{D}$$

where:

A = Number of accrued days counted according to a monthly basis. For interest at maturity items, the number of days from the issue date to the maturity date is used.

D = Annual Year Basis.

Example

A note has the following terms:

April 1, 1993 issue date
June 15, 1993 maturity date
10.0% coupon
$1000 par value
Actual/365 basis

The accrued interest (in the 1900 Date System) is:

`ACCRINTM(34060,34135,0.1,1000,3)` equals 20.54795

Related Functions

ACCRINT	Returns the accrued interest for a security
DATE	Returns the serial number of a particular date

List of Financial Functions

ACOS

Returns the arccosine of a number. The arccosine is the angle whose cosine is number. The returned angle is given in radians in the range 0 to π.

Syntax

ACOS(number)

Number   is the cosine of the angle you want and must be –from –1 to 1.

If you want to convert the result from radians to degrees, multiply it by 180/PI().

Examples	ACOS(-0.5) equals 2.094395 (2π/3 radians)
	ACOS(-0.5)*180/PI() equals 120 (degrees)
Related Functions	COS Returns the cosine of a number
	PI Returns the value π

List of Math & Trigonometry Functions

ACOSH

Returns the inverse hyperbolic cosine of a number. Number must be greater than or equal to 1. The inverse hyperbolic cosine is the value whose hyperbolic cosine is number, so ACOSH(COSH(number)) equals number.

Syntax	**ACOSH(number)**
	Number is any real number equal to or greater than 1.
Examples	ACOSH(1) equals 0
	ACOSH(10) equals 2.993223
Related Functions	ASINH Returns the inverse hyperbolic sine of a number
	ATANH Returns the inverse hyperbolic tangent of a number
	COSH Returns the hyperbolic cosine of a number

List of Math & Trigonometry Functions

ADDRESS

Creates a cell address as text, given specified row and column numbers.

Syntax	**ADDRESS(row_num, column_num,** abs_num, a1, sheet_text)
	Row_num is the row number to use in the cell reference.
	Column_num is the column number to use in the cell reference.

Abs_num   specifies the type of reference to return.

Abs_num	Returns this type of reference
1 or omitted	Absolute
2	Absolute row; relative column
3	Relative row; absolute column
4	Relative

A1   is a logical value that specifies the A1 or R1C1 reference style. If a1 is TRUE or omitted, ADDRESS returns an A1-style reference; if FALSE, ADDRESS returns an R1C1-style reference.

Sheet_text   is text specifying the name of the worksheet or macro sheet to be used as the external reference. If sheet_text is omitted, no sheet name is used.

Examples

ADDRESS(2,3) equals "$C$2"

ADDRESS(2,3,2) equals "C$2"

ADDRESS(2,3,2,FALSE) equals "R2C[3]"

ADDRESS(2,3,1,FALSE,"[Book1]Sheet1") equals "[Book1]Sheet1!R2C3"

ADDRESS(2,3,1,FALSE,"EXCEL SHEET") equals "'EXCEL SHEET'!R2C3"

Related Functions

COLUMN	Returns the column number of a reference
ROW	Returns the row number of a reference
OFFSET	Returns a reference offset from a given reference

List of Lookup & Reference Functions

AMORDEGRC

Returns the depreciation for each accounting period. This funcion is provide for the French accounting system. If an asset is purchased in the middle of the accounting period, then the prorated depreciation is taken into account. The function is similar to AMORLINC, except that a depreciation coefficient is applied in the calculation depending on the life of the assets.

If this function is not available, run the Setup program to install the Analysis ToolPak. After you install the Analysis ToolPak, you must select it in the Add-In Manager. For more information, look up Add-ins in Help.

Syntax	**AMORDEGRC(cost, purchase, first_period, salvage, period, rate, year_basis)**

Cost   is the cost of the asset.

Purchase   is the date of the purchase of the asset.

First_period   is the date of the end of the first period

Salvage   is the salvage value at the end of the life of the asset.

Period   is the period.

Rate   is the rate of depreciation.

Year_basis   is the year_basis to be used.

Year_Basis	Date System
0	360 days (NASD method).
1	Actual
3	365 days in a year
4	360 days in a year (European method)

Remarks

- This function will return the depreciation until the last period of the life of the assets or until the cumulated value of depreciation is greater than the cost of the assets minus the salvage value.

- The depreciation coefficients are:

Life of Assets (1/rate)	Depreciation Coefficient
Between 3 and 4 years	1.5
Between 5 and 6 years	2
More than 6 years	2.5

- The depreciation rate will grow to 50 percent for the period preceding the last period, and will grow to 100 percent for the last period.

- if the Life of Assets is between 0 and 1, 1 and 2, or 2 and 3, or 4 and 5, the #NUM! error value is returned.

Related Functions

AMORLINC	Returns the depreciation for each accounting period
DAYS360	Returns the number of days between two dates based on a 360-day year (twelve 30-day months

AMORLINC

Returns the depreciation for each accounting period. This function is provided for the French accounting system. If an asset is purchased in the middle of the accounting period, then the prorated depreciation is taken into account.

If this function is not available, run the Setup program to install the Analysis ToolPak. After you install the Analysis ToolPak, you must select it in the Add-In Manager. For more information, look up Add-ins in Help.

Syntax

AMORLINC(cost, purchase, first_period, salvage, period, rate, year_basis)

Cost   is the cost of the asset.

Purchase   is the date of the purchase of the asset.

First_period   is the date of the end of the first period

Salvage   is the salvage value at the end of the life of the asset.

Period   is the period.

Rate   is the rate of depreciation.

Year_basis   is the year_basis to be used.

Year_Basis	Date System
0	360 days (NASD method).
1	Actual
3	365 days in a year
4	360 days in a year (European method)

Related Functions

AMORDEGRC	Returns the depreciation for each accounting period
DAYS360	Returns the number of days between two dates based on a 360-day year (twelve 30-day months)

AND

Returns TRUE if all its arguments are TRUE; returns FALSE if one or more arguments is FALSE.

Syntax

AND(logical1, logical2, ...)

Logical1, logical2,...   are 1 to 30 conditions you want to test that can be either TRUE or FALSE.

- The arguments should be logical values or arrays or references that contain logical values.
- If an array or reference argument contains text or empty cells, those values are ignored.
- If the specified range contains no logical values, AND returns the #VALUE! error value.

Examples

AND(TRUE, TRUE) equals TRUE

AND(TRUE, FALSE) equals FALSE

AND(2+2=4, 2+3=5) equals TRUE

If B1:B3 contains the values TRUE, FALSE, and TRUE, then:

AND(B1:B3) equals FALSE

If B4 contains a number between 1 and 100, then:

AND(1<B4, B4<100) equals TRUE

Suppose you want to display B4 if it contains a number strictly between 1 and 100, and you want to display a message if it is not. If B4 contains 104, then:

IF(AND(1<B4, B4<100), B4, "The value is out of range.") equals "The value is out of range."

If B4 contains 50, then:

IF(AND(1<B4, B4<100), B4, "The value is out of range.") equals 50

Related Functions

NOT	Reverses the logic of its argument
OR	Returns TRUE if any argument is TRUE

List of Logical Functions

AREAS

Returns the number of areas in a reference. An area is a range of contiguous cells or a single cell.

Syntax

AREAS(reference)

Reference   is a reference to a cell or range of cells and can refer to multiple areas. If you want to specify several references as a single argument, then you must include extra sets of parentheses so that Microsoft Excel will not interpret the comma as a field separator. See the second example following.

Tip   This function is useful in a macro for testing whether or not a reference is a nonadjacent selection. See the fourth example following.

Examples

AREAS(B2:D4) equals 1

AREAS((B2:D4,E5,F6:I9)) equals 3

If the name Prices refers to the areas B1:D4, B2, and E1:E10, then:

AREAS(Prices) equals 3

The following macro formula branches to an error routine if the current selection is not contiguous:

IF(AREAS(SELECTION())>1,GOTO(Error))

Related Functions

ADDRESS	Returns a reference as text to a single cell in a worksheet
CELL	Returns information about the formatting, location, or contents of a cell
COLUMN	Returns the column number of a reference
COLUMNS	Returns the number of columns in a reference
INDEX	Uses an index to choose a value from a reference or array
ROW	Returns the row number of a reference
ROWS	Returns the number of rows in a reference

List of Lookup & Reference Functions

ASIN

Returns the arcsine of a number. The arcsine is the angle whose sine is number. The returned angle is given in radians in the range $-\pi/2$ to $\pi/2$.

Syntax

ASIN(number)

Number   is the sine of the angle you want and must be from -1 to 1.

Remarks	To express the arcsine in degrees, multiply the result by 180/PI( ).
Examples	ASIN(-0.5) equals −0.5236 (−π/6 radians)
	ASIN(-0.5)*180/PI() equals −30 (degrees)

Related Functions	ASINH	Returns the inverse hyperbolic sine of a number
	PI	Returns the value π
	SIN	Returns the sine of the given angle

List of Math & Trigonometry Functions

ASINH

Returns the inverse hyperbolic sine of a number. The inverse hyperbolic sine is the value whose hyperbolic sine is number, so ASINH(SINH(number)) equals number.

Syntax	**ASINH(number)**
	Number is any real number.
Examples	ASINH(-2.5) equals −1.64723
	ASINH(10) equals 2.998223

Related Functions	ACOSH	Returns the inverse hyperbolic cosine of a number
	ATANH	Returns the inverse hyperbolic tangent of a number
	SINH	Returns the hyperbolic sine of a number

List of Math & Trigonometry Functions

ATAN

Returns the arctangent of a number. The arctangent is the angle whose tangent is number. The returned angle is given in radians in the range −π/2 to π/2.

Syntax	**ATAN(number)**
	Number is the tangent of the angle you want.

Remarks	To express the arctangent in degrees, multiply the result by 180/PI( ).
Examples	ATAN(1) equals 0.785398 (π/4 radians)
	ATAN(1)*180/PI( ) equals 45 (degrees)

Related Functions		
	ATAN2	Returns the arctangent from x- and y- coordinates
	ATANH	Returns the inverse hyperbolic tangent of a number
	PI	Returns the value π
	TAN	Returns the tangent of a number

List of Math & Trigonometry Functions

ATAN2

Returns the arctangent of the specified x- and y- coordinates. The arctangent is the angle from the x-axis to a line containing the origin (0, 0) and a point with coordinates (x_num, y_num). The angle is given in radians between –π and π, excluding –π.

Syntax

ATAN2(x_num, y_num)

X_num is the x-coordinate of the point.

Y_num is the y-coordinate of the point.

Remarks

- A positive result represents a counterclockwise angle from the x-axis; a negative result represents a clockwise angle.
- ATAN2(a,b) equals ATAN(b/a), except that a can equal 0 in ATAN2.
- If both x_num and y_num are 0, ATAN2 returns the #DIV/0! error value.
- To express the arctangent in degrees, multiply the result by 180/PI( ).

Examples

ATAN2(1, 1) equals 0.785398 (π/4 radians)

ATAN2(-1, -1) equals –2.35619 (–3π/4 radians)

ATAN2(-1, -1)*180/PI( ) equals –135 (degrees)

Related Functions	ATAN	Returns the arctangent of a number
	ATANH	Returns the inverse hyperbolic tangent of a number
	PI	Returns the value π
	TAN	Returns the tangent of a number

List of Math & Trigonometry Functions

ATANH

Returns the inverse hyperbolic tangent of a number. Number must be between –1 and 1 (excluding –1 and 1). The inverse hyperbolic tangent is the value whose hyperbolic tangent is number, so ATANH(TANH(number)) equals number.

Syntax   **ATANH(number)**

Number   is any real number between 1 and –1.

Examples   ATANH(0.76159416) equals 1, approximately

ATANH(-0.1) equals –0.10034

Related Functions	ACOSH	Returns the inverse hyperbolic cosine of a number
	ASINH	Returns the inverse hyperbolic sine of a number
	TANH	Returns the hyperbolic tangent of a number

List of Math & Trigonometry Functions

AVEDEV

Returns the average of the absolute deviations of data points from their mean. AVEDEV is a measure of the variability in a data set.

Syntax   **AVEDEV(number1**, number2, ...)

Number1, number2,...   are 1 to 30 arguments for which you want the average of the absolute deviations. You can also use a single array or a reference to an array instead of arguments separated by commas.

Remarks
- The arguments should be numbers, or names, arrays, or references that contain numbers.
- If an array or reference argument contains text, logical values, or empty cells, those values are ignored; however, cells with the value zero are included.
- The equation for average deviation is:

$$\frac{1}{n}\sum\left|x - \bar{x}\right|$$

AVEDEV is influenced by the unit of measurement in the input data.

Example   AVEDEV(4, 5, 6, 7, 5, 4, 3) equals 1.020408

Related Functions

DEVSQ	Returns the sum of squares of deviations
STDEV	Estimates standard deviation based on a sample
STDEVP	Calculates standard deviation based on the entire population
VAR	Estimates variance based on a sample
VARP	Calculates variance based on the entire population

List of Statistical Functions

AVERAGE

Returns the average (arithmetic mean) of the arguments.

Syntax   **AVERAGE(number1**, number2, ...)

Number1, number2,...   are 1 to 30 numeric arguments for which you want the average.

Remarks

- The arguments should be numbers, or names, arrays, or references that contain numbers.
- If an array or reference argument contains text, logical values, or empty cells, those values are ignored; however, cells with the value zero are included.

Tip   When averaging cells, keep in mind the difference between empty cells and those containing the value zero, especially if you have cleared the Zero Values check box in the View tab of the Options dialog box. Empty cells are not counted, but zero values are. To see the Options dialog box, choose the Options command from the Tools menu.

Examples

If A1:A5 is named Scores and contains the numbers 10, 7, 9, 27, and 2, then:

AVERAGE(A1:A5) equals 11

AVERAGE(Scores) equals 11

AVERAGE(A1:A5, 5) equals 10

AVERAGE(A1:A5) equals SUM(A1:A5)/COUNT(A1:A5) equals 11

If C1:C3 is named OtherScores and contains the numbers 4, 18, and 7, then:

AVERAGE(Scores, OtherScores) equals 10.5

Related Functions

DAVERAGE	Returns the average of selected database entries
GEOMEAN	Returns the geometric mean
HARMEAN	Returns the harmonic mean
MEDIAN	Returns the median of the given numbers
MODE	Returns the most common value in a data set
TRIMMEAN	Returns the mean of the interior of a data set

List of Statistical Functions

BESSELI

Returns the modified Bessel function, which is equivalent to the Bessel function evaluated for purely imaginary arguments.

If this function is not available, run the Setup program to install the Analysis ToolPak. After you install the Analysis ToolPak, you must select it in the Add-In Manager. For more information, look up Add-ins in Help.

Syntax

BESSELI(x, n)

X is the value at which to evaluate the function.

N is the order of the Bessel function. If n is not an integer, it is truncated.

Remarks

- If x is non-numeric, BESSELI returns the #VALUE! error value.
- If n is non-numeric, BESSELI returns the #VALUE! error value.
- If n < 0, BESSELI returns the #NUM! error value.
- The n-th order modified Bessel function of the variable x is:

$$I_n(x) = (i)^{-n} J_n(ix)$$

Example

BESSELI(1.5, 1) equals 0.981666

Related Functions

BESSELJ	Returns the Bessel function
BESSELK	Returns the modified Bessel function
BESSELY	Returns the Bessel function

List of Engineering Functions

BESSELJ

Returns the Bessel function.

If this function is not available, run the Setup program to install the Analysis ToolPak. After you install the Analysis ToolPak, you must select it in the Add-In Manager. For more information, look up Add-ins in Help.

Syntax

BESSELJ(x, n)

X is the value at which to evaluate the function.

N is the order of the Bessel function. If n is not an integer, it is truncated.

Remarks
- If x is non-numeric, BESSELJ returns the #VALUE! error value.
- If n is non-numeric, BESSELJ returns the #VALUE! error value.
- If n < 0, BESSELJ returns the #NUM! error value.
- The n-th order Bessel function of the variable x is:

$$J_n(x) = \sum_{k=0}^{\infty} \frac{(-1)^k}{k!\,\Gamma(n+k+1)}\left(\frac{x}{2}\right)^{n+2k}$$

where:

$$\Gamma(n+k+1) = \int_0^{\infty} e^{-x}\,x^{n+k}\,dx$$

is the Gamma function.

Example   BESSELJ(1.9, 2) equals 0.329926

Related Functions

BESSELI	Returns the modified Bessel function
BESSELK	Returns the modified Bessel function
BESSELY	Returns the Bessel function

List of Engineering Functions

BESSELK

Returns the modified Bessel function, which is equivalent to the Bessel functions evaluated for purely imaginary arguments.

If this function is not available, run the Setup program to install the Analysis ToolPak. After you install the Analysis ToolPak, you must select it in the Add-In Manager. For more information, look up Add-ins in Help.

Syntax   **BESSELK(x, n)**

X   is the value at which to evaluate the function.

N   is the order of the function. If n is not an integer, it is truncated.

Remarks
- If x is non-numeric, BESSELK returns the #VALUE! error value.
- If n is non-numeric, BESSELK returns the #VALUE! error value.

- If n < 0, BESSELK returns the #NUM! error value.
- The n-th order modified Bessel function of the variable x is:

$$K_n(x) = \frac{\pi}{2} i^{n+1} [J_n(ix) + iY_n(ix)]$$

where J_n and Y_n are the J and Y Bessel functions, respectively.

Example   BESSELK(1.5, 1) equals 0.277388

Related Functions

BESSELI	Returns the modified Bessel function
BESSELJ	Returns the Bessel function
BESSELY	Returns the Bessel function

List of Engineering Functions

BESSELY

Returns the Bessel function, which is also called the Weber function or the Neumann function.

If this function is not available, run the Setup program to install the Analysis ToolPak. After you install the Analysis ToolPak, you must select it in the Add-In Manager. For more information, look up Add-ins in Help.

Syntax   **BESSELY(x, n)**

X   is the value at which to evaluate the function.

N   is the order of the function. If n is not an integer, it is truncated.

Remarks

- If x is non-numeric, BESSELY returns the #VALUE! error value.
- If n is non-numeric, BESSELY returns the #VALUE! error value.
- If n < 0, BESSELY returns the #NUM! error value.
- The n-th order Bessel function of the variable x is:

$$Y_n(x) = \lim_{v \to n} \frac{J_v(x)\cos(v\pi) - J_{-v}(x)}{\sin(v\pi)}$$

where:

$$J_{-n}(x) = (-1)^n J_n(x)$$

Example BESSELY(2.5, 1) equals 0.145918

Related Functions

BESSELI	Returns the modified Bessel function
BESSELJ	Returns the Bessel function
BESSELK	Returns the modified Bessel function

List of Engineering Functions

BETADIST

Returns the cumulative beta probability density function. The cumulative beta probability density function is commonly used to study variation in the percentage of something across samples, such as the fraction of the day people spend watching television.

Syntax **BETADIST(x, alpha, beta, A, B)**

X is the value between A and B at which to evaluate the function.

Alpha is a parameter to the distribution.

Beta is a parameter to the distribution.

A is an optional lower bound to the interval of x.

B is an optional upper bound to the interval of x.

Remarks
- If any argument is non-numeric, BETADIST returns the #VALUE! error value.
- If alpha ≤ 0 or beta ≤ 0, BETADIST returns the #NUM! error value.
- If x < A, x > B, or A = B, BETADIST returns the #NUM! error value.
- If you omit values for A and B, BETADIST uses the standard cumulative beta distribution, so that A = 0 and B = 1.

Example BETADIST(2,8,10,1,3) equals 0.685470581

Related Functions

BETAINV	Returns the inverse of the cumulative beta probability density function

List of Statistical Functions

BETAINV

Returns the inverse of the cumulative beta probability density function. That is, if probability = BETADIST(x,...), then BETAINV(probability,...) = x. The cumulative beta distribution can be used in project planning to model probable completion times given an expected completion time and variability.

Syntax

BETAINV(probability, alpha, beta, A, B)

Probability   is a probability associated with the beta distribution.

Alpha   is a parameter to the distribution.

Beta   is a parameter to the distribution.

A   is an optional lower bound to the interval of x.

B   is an optional upper bound to the interval of x.

Remarks

- If any argument is non-numeric, BETAINV returns the #VALUE! error value.
- If alpha ≤ 0 or beta ≤ 0, BETAINV returns the #NUM! error value.
- If probability ≤ 0 or probability > 1, BETAINV returns the #NUM! error value.
- If you omit values for A and B, BETAINV uses the standard cumulative beta distribution, so that A = 0 and B = 1.
- BETAINV uses an iterative technique for calculating the function. Given a probability value, BETAINV iterates until the result is accurate to within $\pm 3 \times 10^{-7}$. If BETAINV does not converge after 100 iterations, the function returns the #N/A error value.

Example

BETAINV(0.685470581,8,10,1,3) equals 2

Related Functions   BETADIST   Returns the cumulative beta probability density function

List of Statistical Functions

BIN2DEC

Converts a binary number to decimal.

If this function is not available, run the Setup program to install the Analysis ToolPak. After you install the Analysis ToolPak, you must select it in the Add-In Manager. For more information, look up Add-ins in Help.

Syntax	**BIN2DEC(number)**

Number   is the binary number you want to convert. Number may not contain more than 10 characters (10 bits). The most significant bit of number is the sign bit. The remaining 9 bits are magnitude bits. Negative numbers are represented using two's-complement notation.

Remarks

- If number is not a valid binary number, or if number contains more than 10 characters (10 bits), BIN2DEC returns the #NUM! error value.

Examples

`BIN2DEC(1100100)` equals 100

`BIN2DEC(1111111111)` equals −1

Related Functions

DEC2BIN   Converts a decimal number to binary

HEX2BIN   Converts a hexadecimal number to binary

OCT2BIN   Converts an octal number to binary

List of Engineering Functions

BIN2HEX

Converts a binary number to hexadecimal.

If this function is not available, run the Setup program to install the Analysis ToolPak. After you install the Analysis ToolPak, you must select it in the Add-In Manager. For more information, look up Add-ins in Help.

Syntax   **BIN2HEX(number**, places)

Number   is the binary number you want to convert. Number may not contain more than 10 characters (10 bits). The most significant bit of number is the sign bit. The remaining 9 bits are magnitude bits. Negative numbers are represented using two's-complement notation.

Places   is the number of characters to use. If places is omitted, BIN2HEX uses the minimum number of characters necessary. Places is useful for padding the return value with leading 0s (zeros).

Remarks

- If number is not a valid binary number, or if number contains more than 10 characters (10 bits), BIN2HEX returns the #NUM! error value.
- If number is negative, BIN2HEX ignores places and returns a 10-character hexadecimal number.

- If BIN2HEX requires more than places characters, it returns the #NUM! error value.
- If places is not an integer, it is truncated.
- If places is non-numeric, BIN2HEX returns the #VALUE! error value.
- If places is negative, BIN2HEX returns the #NUM! error value.

Examples

BIN2HEX(11111011, 4) equals 00FB

BIN2HEX(1110) equals E

BIN2HEX(1111111111) equals FFFFFFFFFF

Related Functions

DEC2BIN	Converts a decimal number to binary
HEX2BIN	Converts a hexadecimal number to binary
OCT2BIN	Converts an octal number to binary

List of Engineering Functions

BIN2OCT

Converts a binary number to octal.

If this function is not available, run the Setup program to install the Analysis ToolPak. After you install the Analysis ToolPak, you must select it in the Add-In Manager. For more information, look up Add-ins in Help.

Syntax

BIN2OCT(number, places)

Number   is the binary number you want to convert. Number may not contain more than 10 characters (10 bits). The most significant bit of number is the sign bit. The remaining 9 bits are magnitude bits. Negative numbers are represented using two's-complement notation.

Places   is the number of characters to use. If places is omitted, BIN2OCT uses the minimum number of characters necessary. Places is useful for padding the return value with leading 0s (zeros).

Remarks

- If number is not a valid binary number, or if number contains more than 10 characters (10 bits), BIN2OCT returns the #NUM! error value.
- If number is negative, BIN2OCT ignores places and returns a 10-character octal number.
- If BIN2OCT requires more than places characters, it returns the #NUM! error value.

- If places is not an integer, it is truncated.
- If places is non-numeric, BIN2OCT returns the #VALUE! error value.
- If places is negative, BIN2OCT returns the #NUM! error value.

Examples

BIN2OCT(1001, 3) equals 011

BIN2OCT(01100100) equals 144

BIN2OCT(1111111111) equals 7777777777

Related Functions

DEC2BIN	Converts a decimal number to binary
HEX2BIN	Converts a hexadecimal number to binary
OCT2BIN	Converts an octal number to binary

List of Engineering Functions

BINOMDIST

Returns the individual term binomial distribution probability. Use BINOMDIST in problems with a fixed number of tests or trials, when the outcomes of any trial are only success or failure, when trials are independent, and when the probability of success is constant throughout the experiment. For example, BINOMDIST can calculate the probability that two of the next three babies born are male.

Syntax

BINOMDIST(number_s, trials, probability_s, cumulative)

Number_s   is the number of successes in trials.

Trials   is the number of independent trials.

Probability_s   is the probability of success on each trial.

Cumulative   is a logical value that determines the form of the function. If cumulative is TRUE, then BINOMDIST returns the cumulative distribution function, which is the probability that there are at most number_s successes; if FALSE, it returns the probability mass function, which is the probability that there are number_s successes.

Remarks

- Number_s and trials are truncated to integers.
- If number_s, trials, or probability_s is non-numeric, BINOMDIST returns the #VALUE! error value.
- If number_s < 0 or number_s > trials, BINOMDIST returns the #NUM! error value.

- If probability_s < 0 or probability_s > 1, BINOMDIST returns the #NUM! error value.
- The binomial probability mass function is:

$$b(x;n,p) = \binom{n}{x} p^x (1-p)^{n-x}$$

where:

$$\binom{n}{x}$$

is COMBIN(n,x).

The cumulative binomial distribution is:

$$B(x;n,p) = \sum_{y=0}^{x} b(y;n,p)$$

Example

The flip of a coin can only result in heads or tails. The probability of the first flip being heads is 0.5, and the probability of exactly 6 of 10 flips being heads is:

`BINOMDIST(6,10,0.5,FALSE)` equals 0.205078

Related Functions

COMBIN	Returns the number of combinations for a given number of objects
CRITBINOM	Returns the smallest value for which the cumulative binomial distribution is less than or equal to a criterion value
FACT	Returns the factorial of a number
HYPGEOMDIST	Returns the hypergeometric distribution
NEGBINOMDIST	Returns the negative binomial distribution
PERMUT	Returns the number of permutations for a given number of objects
PROB	Returns the probability that values in a range are between two limits

List of Statistical Functions

CALL

Calls a procedure in a dynamic link library or code resource. There are two syntax forms of this function. Use syntax 1 only with a previously registered code resource, which uses arguments from the REGISTER function. Use syntax 2a or 2b to simultaneously register and call a code resource.

For more information about DLLs and code resources, see the "Using the CALL and REGISTER Functions" in the Appendix.

Important This function is provided for advanced users only. If you use the CALL function incorrectly, you could cause errors that will require you to restart your computer.

Syntax 1

Used with REGISTER

CALL(register_id, argument1, ...)

Syntax 2a

Used alone (in Microsoft Excel for Windows)

CALL(module_text, **procedure**, **type_text**, argument1, ...)

Syntax 2b

Used alone (in Microsoft Excel for the Macintosh)

CALL(file_text, **resource**, **type_text**, argument1, ...)

Register_id   is the value returned by a previously executed REGISTER or REGISTER.ID function.

Argument1,...   are the arguments to be passed to the procedure.

Module_text   is quoted text specifying the name of the dynamic link library (DLL) that contains the procedure in Microsoft Excel for Windows.

File_text   is the name of the file that contains the code resource in Microsoft Excel for the Macintosh.

Procedure   is text specifying the name of the function in the DLL in Microsoft Excel for Windows. You can also use the ordinal value of the function from the EXPORTS statement in the module-definition file (.DEF). The ordinal value should not be in the form of text.

Resource   is the name of the code resource in Microsoft Excel for the Macintosh. You can also use the resource ID number. The resource ID number should not be in the form of text.

Type_text   is text specifying the data type of the return value and the data types of all arguments to the DLL or code resource. The first letter of type_text specifies the return value. The codes you use for type_text are described in detail in, "Using the CALL and REGISTER Functions" in the Appendix. For stand-alone DLLs or code resources (XLLs), you can omit this argument.

**Example
Syntax 1 (32-bit)**

In 32-bit Microsoft Excel for Windows 95 and Windows NT™, the following macro formula registers the GetTickCount function from 32-bit Microsoft Windows. GetTickCount returns the number of milliseconds since Microsoft Windows was started. (In 16-bit Microsoft Excel, substitute "User" for "Kernel32".)

```
REGISTER("Kernel32","GetTickCount","J")
```

Assuming that this REGISTER function is in cell A5, after your macro registers GetTickCount, you can use the CALL function to return the number of milliseconds that have elapsed:

```
CALL(A5)
```

**Example
Syntax 2a (32-bit)**

On a worksheet, you can use the following CALL formula (syntax 2a) to call the GetTickCount function:

```
CALL("Kernel32","GetTickCount","J!")
```

The ! in the type_text argument forces Microsoft Excel to recalculate the CALL function every time the worksheet recalculates. This updates the elapsed time whenever the worksheet recalculates.

Tip You can use optional arguments to the REGISTER function to assign a custom name to a function. This name will appear in the Paste Function dialog box, and you can call the function by using its custom name in a formula.

Related Functions REGISTER.ID   Returns register ID of a DLL or code resource

List of DDE & External Functions

CEILING

Returns number rounded up, away from zero, to the nearest multiple of significance. For example, if you want to avoid using pennies in your prices and your product is priced at $4.42, use the formula =CEILING(4.42,0.05) to round prices up to the nearest nickel.

Syntax	**CEILING(number, significance)**

Number   is the value you want to round.

Significance   is the multiple to which you want to round.

Remarks

- If either argument is non-numeric, CEILING returns the #VALUE! error value.
- Regardless of the sign of number, a value is rounded up when adjusted away from zero. If number is an exact multiple of significance, no rounding occurs.
- If number and significance have different signs, CEILING returns the #NUM! error value.

Examples

CEILING(2.5, 1) equals 3

CEILING(-2.5, -2) equals –4

CEILING(-2.5, 2) equals #NUM!

CEILING(1.5, 0.1) equals 1.5

CEILING(0.234, 0.01) equals 0.24

Related Functions

EVEN	Rounds a number up to the nearest even integer
FLOOR	Rounds a number down, toward zero
INT	Rounds a number down to the nearest integer
ODD	Rounds a number up to the nearest odd integer
ROUND	Rounds a number to a specified number of digits
ROUNDDOWN	Rounds a number down, toward zero
ROUNDUP	Rounds a number up, away from zero
TRUNC	Truncates a number to an integer

List of Math & Trigonometry Functions

CELL

Returns information about the formatting, location, or contents of the upper-left cell in a reference.

Syntax   **CELL(info_type, reference)**

Info_type   is a text value that specifies what type of cell information you want. The following list shows the possible values of info_type and the corresponding results.

Info_type	Returns
"address"	Reference of the first cell in reference, as text.
"col"	Column number of the cell in reference.
"color"	1 if the cell is formatted in color for negative values; otherwise returns 0.
"contents"	Contents of the upper-left cell in reference.
"filename"	Filename (including full path) of the file that contains reference, as text. Returns empty text ("") if the worksheet that contains reference has not yet been saved.
"format"	Text value corresponding to the number format of the cell. The text values for the various formats are shown in the following table. Returns "-" at the end of the text value if the cell is formatted in color for negative values. Returns "()" at the end of the text value if the cell is formatted with parentheses for positive or all values.
"parentheses"	1 if the cell is formatted with parentheses for positive or all values; otherwise returns 0.
"prefix"	Text value corresponding to the "label prefix" of the cell. Returns single quotation mark (') if the cell contains left-aligned text, double quotation mark (") if the cell contains right-aligned text, caret (^) if the cell contains centered text, backslash (\) if the cell contains fill-aligned text, and empty text ("") if the cell contains anything else.
"protect"	0 if the cell is not locked, and 1 if the cell is locked.
"row"	Row number of the cell in reference. .
"type"	Text value corresponding to the type of data in the cell. Returns "b" for blank if the cell is empty, "l" for label if the cell contains a text constant, and "v" for value if the cell contains anything else.
"width"	Column width of the cell rounded off to an integer. Each unit of column width is equal to the width of one character in the currently selected font size.

Reference   is the cell that you want information about. If reference is a nonadjacent selection, CELL returns the #VALUE! error value.

The following list describes the text values CELL returns when info_type is "format" and reference is a cell formatted with a built-in number format.

If the Microsoft Excel format is	CELL returns
General	"G"
0	"F0"

If the Microsoft Excel format is	CELL returns
#,##0	",0"
0.00	"F2"
#,##0.00	",2"
$#,##0_);($#,##0)	"C0'
$#,##0_);[Red]($#,##0)	"C0-"
$#,##0.00_);($#,##0.00)	"C2"
$#,##0.00_);[Red]($#,##0.00)	"C2-"
0%	"P0"
0.00%	"P2"
0.00E+00	"S2"
# ?/? or # ??/??	"G"
m/d/yy or m/d/yy h:mm or mm/dd/yy	"D4"
d-mmm-yy or dd-mmm-yy	"D1"
d-mmm or dd-mmm	"D2"
mmm-yy	"D3"
mm/dd	"D5"
h:mm AM/PM	"D7"
h:mm:ss AM/PM	"D6"
h:mm	"D9"
h:mm:ss	"D8"

If the info_type argument in the CELL formula is "format", and if the cell is formatted later with a custom format, then you must recalculate the worksheet to update the CELL formula.

Remarks   The CELL function is provided for compatibility with other spreadsheet programs.

Examples   CELL("row",A20) equals 20

If B12 has the format "d-mmm", then:

CELL("format",B12) equals "D2"

If A3 contains TOTAL, then:

CELL("contents", A3) equals "TOTAL"

Related Functions   List of Information Functions

CHAR

Returns the character specified by the code number. Use CHAR to translate code numbers you might get from files on other types of computers into characters.

Syntax

CHAR(number)

Number   is a number between 1 and 255 specifying which character you want. The character is from the character set used by your computer.

Operating environment	Character set
Macintosh	Macintosh character set
Windows	ANSI

Examples

CHAR(65) equals "A"

CHAR(33) equals "!"

Related Functions   CODE   Returns a numeric code for the first character in a text string

List of Text Functions

CHIDIST

Returns the one-tailed probability of the chi-squared distribution. The χ^2 distribution is associated with a χ^2 test. Use the χ^2 test to compare observed and expected values. For example, a genetic experiment might hypothesize that the next generation of plants will exhibit a certain set of colors. By comparing the observed results with the expected ones, you can decide if your original hypothesis is valid.

Syntax

CHIDIST(x, degrees_freedom)

X   is the value at which you want to evaluate the distribution.

Degrees_freedom   is the number of degrees of freedom.

Remarks

- If either argument is non-numeric, CHIDIST returns the #VALUE! error value.
- If x is negative, CHIDIST returns the #NUM! error value.
- If degrees_freedom is not an integer, it is truncated.

- If degrees_freedom < 1 or degrees_freedom ^{3} 1010, CHIDIST returns the #NUM! error value.
- CHIDIST is calculated as CHIDIST = P(X>x), where X is a χ^2 random variable.

Example   CHIDIST(18.307,10) equals 0.050001

Related Functions CHIINV   Returns the inverse of the chi-squared distribution

CHITEST   Returns the test for independence

List of Statistical Functions

CHIINV

Returns the inverse of the one-tailed probability of the chi-squared distribution. If probability = CHIDIST(x,…), then CHIINV(probability,…) = x. Use this function to compare observed results with expected ones to decide if your original hypothesis is valid.

Syntax   **CHIINV(probability, degrees_freedom)**

Probability   is a probability associated with the chi-squared distribution.

Degrees_freedom   is the number of degrees of freedom.

Remarks
- If either argument is non-numeric, CHIINV returns the #VALUE! error value.
- If probability < 0 or probability > 1, CHIINV returns the #NUM! error value.
- If degrees_freedom is not an integer, it is truncated.
- If degrees_freedom < 1 or degrees_freedom $\geq 10^{10}$, CHIINV returns the #NUM! error value.

CHIINV uses an iterative technique for calculating the function. Given a probability value, CHIINV iterates until the result is accurate to within $\pm 3 \times 10^{-7}$. If CHIINV does not converge after 100 iterations, the function returns the #N/A error value.

Example   CHIINV(0.05,10) equals 18.30703

Related Functions CHIDIST   Returns the one-tailed probability of the chi-squared distribution

CHITEST   Returns the test for independence

List of Statistical Functions

CHITEST

Returns the test for independence. CHITEST returns the value from the chi-squared (χ^2) distribution for the statistic and the appropriate degrees of freedom. You can use χ^2 tests to determine if hypothesized results are verified by an experiment.

Syntax

CHITEST(actual_range, expected_range)

Actual_range   is the range of data that contains observations to test against expected values.

Expected_range   is the range of data that contains the ratio of the product of row totals and column totals to the grand total.

Remarks

- If actual_range and expected_range have a different number of data points, CHITEST returns the #N/A error value.

- The χ^2 test first calculates a χ^2 statistic and then sums the differences of actual values from the expected values. The equation for this function is CHITEST=p(X>χ^2), where:

$$\chi^2 = \sum_{i=1}^{r} \sum_{j=1}^{c} \frac{\left(A_{ij} - E_{ij}\right)^2}{E_{ij}}$$

and where:

A_{ij} = actual frequency in the i-th row, j-th column

E_{ij} = expected frequency in the i-th row, j-th column

r = number or rows

c = number of columns

CHITEST returns the probability for a χ^2 statistic and degrees of freedom, df, where df = (r − 1)(c − 1).

Example

	A	B	C
1	Actual		
2		Men	Women
3	Agree	58	35
4	Neutral	11	25
5	Disagree	10	23
6			
7	Expected		
8		Men	Women
9	Agree	45.35	47.65
10	Neutral	17.56	18.44
11	Disagree	16.09	16.91

The χ^2 statistic for the data above is 16.16957 with 2 degrees of freedom.

CHITEST(B3:C5,B9:C11) equals 0.000308

Related Functions

CHIDIST	Returns the one-tailed probability of the χ^2 distribution
CHIINV	Returns the inverse of the χ^2 distribution

List of Statistical Functions

CHOOSE

Uses index_num to return a value from the list of value arguments. Use CHOOSE to select one of up to 29 values based on the index number. For example, if value1 through value7 are the days of the week, CHOOSE returns one of the days when a number between 1 and 7 is used as index_num.

Syntax

CHOOSE(index_num, value1, value2, ...)

Index_num   specifies which value argument is selected. Index_num must be a number between 1 and 29, or a formula or reference to a cell containing a number between 1 and 29.

- If index_num is 1, CHOOSE returns value1; if it is 2, CHOOSE returns value2; and so on.

- If index_num is less than 1 or greater than the number of the last value in the list, CHOOSE returns the #VALUE! error value.

- If index_num is a fraction, it is truncated to the lowest integer before being used.

Value1, value2,...   are 1 to 29 value arguments from which CHOOSE selects a value or an action to perform based on index_num. The arguments can be numbers, cell references, defined names, formulas, macro functions, or text. For information about using value arguments, see "Converting Data Types" in the first section, "About Functions."

Remarks

- If you are using CHOOSE in a macro, the value arguments can be GOTO functions or action-taking functions. For example, the following formulas are allowed in a macro, where Level is a name referring to a value or a cell containing a value between 1 and 3:

CHOOSE(Level,GOTO(Begin),GOTO(Intermed),GOTO(Adv))

CHOOSE(Level,ACTIVATE.NEXT(),ACTIVATE.PREV())

- If index_num is an array, every value is evaluated when CHOOSE is executed. If some of those value arguments are action-taking functions, all the actions are taken. For example, the following formula opens both a new worksheet and a new chart:

  CHOOSE({1,2},NEW(1),NEW(2))

- The value arguments to CHOOSE can be range references as well as single values. For example, the formula:

  SUM(CHOOSE(2,A1:A10,B1:B10,C1:C10))

  evaluates to:

  SUM(B1:B10)

  which then returns a value based on the values in the range B1:B10.

  The CHOOSE function is evaluated first, returning the reference B1:B10. The SUM function is then evaluated using B1:B10, the result of the CHOOSE function, as its argument.

Examples

CHOOSE(2,"1st","2nd","3rd","Finished") equals "2nd"

SUM(A1:CHOOSE(3,A10,A20,A30)) equals SUM(A1:A30)

If A10 contains 4, then:

CHOOSE(A10,"Nails","Screws","Nuts","Bolts") equals "Bolts"

If A10-3 equals 3, then:

CHOOSE(A10-3,"1st","2nd","3rd","Finished") equals "3rd"

If SalesOld is a name defined to refer to the value 10,000, then:

CHOOSE(2,SalesNew,SalesOld,SalesBudget) equals 10,000

Related Function

INDEX   Uses an index to choose a value from a reference or array

List of Lookup & Reference Functions

CLEAN

Removes all nonprintable characters from text. Use CLEAN on text imported from other applications which contains characters that may not print with your operating system. For example, you can use CLEAN to remove some low-level computer code that is frequently at the beginning and end of data files and cannot be printed.

Syntax	**CLEAN(text)**

Text   is any worksheet information from which you want to remove nonprintable characters.

Example   Since CHAR(7) returns a nonprintable character:

`CLEAN(CHAR(7)&"text"&CHAR(7))` equals "text"

Related Functions

CHAR	Returns the character specified by the code number
TRIM	Removes spaces from text

List of Text Functions

CODE

Returns a numeric code for the first character in a text string. The returned code corresponds to the character set used by your computer.

Syntax   **CODE(text)**

Operating environment	Character set
Macintosh	Macintosh character set
Windows	ANSI

Text   is the text for which you want the code of the first character.

Examples   `CODE("A")` equals 65

`CODE("Alphabet")` equals 65

Related Function

CHAR	Returns the character specified by the code number

List of Text Functions

COLUMN

Returns the column number of the given reference.

Syntax   **COLUMN(reference)**

Reference   is the cell or range of cells for which you want the column number.

- If reference is omitted, it is assumed to be the reference of the cell in which the COLUMN function appears.
- If reference is a range of cells and if COLUMN is entered as a horizontal array, COLUMN returns the column numbers of reference as a horizontal array.
- Reference cannot refer to multiple areas.

Examples

COLUMN(A3) equals 1

When entered as an array in any three horizontally contiguous cells:

COLUMN(A3:C5) equals {1,2,3}

If COLUMN is entered in C5, then:

COLUMN() equals COLUMN(C5) equals 3

Related Functions

| COLUMNS | Returns the number of columns in a reference |
| ROW | Returns the row number of a reference |

List of Lookup & Reference Functions

COLUMNS

Returns the number of columns in an array or reference.

Syntax

COLUMNS(array)

Array   is an array or array formula, or a reference to a range of cells for which you want the number of columns.

Examples

COLUMNS(A1:C4) equals 3

COLUMNS({1,2,3;4,5,6}) equals 3

The following macro formula returns the number of columns in a contiguous selection:

COLUMNS(SELECTION())

If the selection is not contiguous, the following macro formula returns the number of columns in a particular area (specified by AreaNum) of the selection. An "area" is a contiguous region within a nonadjacent selection, so a nonadjacent selection consists of multiple areas.

```
COLUMNS(INDEX(SELECTION(),,,AreaNum))
```

Related Functions	COLUMN	Returns the column number of a reference
	ROWS	Returns the number of rows in a reference

List of Lookup & Reference Functions

COMBIN

Returns the number of combinations for a given number of objects. Use COMBIN to determine the total possible number of groups for a given number of objects.

Syntax

COMBIN(number, number_chosen)

Number   is the number of objects.

Number_chosen   is the number of objects in each combination.

Remarks

- Numeric arguments are truncated to integers.
- If either argument is non-numeric, COMBIN returns the #NAME? error value.
- If number < 0, number_chosen < 0, or number < number_chosen, COMBIN returns the #NUM! error value.
- A combination is any set or subset of objects, regardless of their internal order. Combinations are distinct from permutations, for which the internal order is significant.
- The number of combinations is as follows, where number = n and number_chosen = k:

$$\binom{n}{k} = \frac{P_{k,n}}{k!} = \frac{n!}{k!(n-k)!}$$

where:

$$P_{k,n} = \frac{n!}{(n-k)!}$$

Example   Suppose you want to form a two-person team from eight candidates and you want to know how many possible teams can be formed. COMBIN(8, 2) equals 28 teams.

Related Functions

BINOMDIST	Returns the individual term binomial distribution probability
CRITBINOM	Returns the smallest value for which the cumulative binomial distribution is less than or equal to a criterion value
FACT	Returns the factorial of a number
HYPGEOMDIST	Returns the hypergeometric distribution
NEGBINOMDIST	Returns the negative binomial distribution
PERMUT	Returns the number of permutations for a given number of objects

List of Math & Trigonometry Functions

COMPLEX

Converts real and imaginary coefficients into a complex number of the form x + yi or x + yj.

If this function is not available, run the Setup program to install the Analysis ToolPak. After you install the Analysis ToolPak, you must select it in the Add-In Manager. For more information, look up Add-ins in Help.

Syntax   **COMPLEX(real_num, i_num, suffix)**

Real_num   is the real coefficient of the complex number.

I_num   is the imaginary coefficient of the complex number.

Suffix   is the suffix for the imaginary component of the complex number. If omitted, suffix is assumed to be "i".

Note All complex number functions accept "i" and "j" for suffix, but neither "I" nor "J". Using uppercase results in the #VALUE! error value. All functions that accept two or more complex numbers require that all suffixes match.

Remarks
- If real_num is non-numeric, COMPLEX returns the #VALUE! error value.
- If i_num is non-numeric, COMPLEX returns the #VALUE! error value.
- If suffix is neither "i" nor "j", COMPLEX returns the #VALUE! error value.

Examples	COMPLEX(3,4) equals 3 + 4i
	COMPLEX(3,4,"j") equals 3 + 4j
	COMPLEX(0,1) equals i
	COMPLEX(1,0) equals 1
Related Functions	Related functions include other complex number functions such as IMABS, IMAGINARY, IMREAL, and so on.
	List of Engineering Functions

CONCATENATE

Joins several text items into one text item.

Syntax	**CONCATENATE (text1, text2, ...)**
	Text1, text2,... are 1 to 30 text items to be joined into a single text item. The text items can be text strings, numbers, or single-cell references.
Remarks	The "&" operator can be used instead of CONCATENATE to join text items.
Examples	CONCATENATE("Total ", "Value") equals "Total Value". This is equivalent to typing "Total"&" "&"Value".
	Suppose in a stream survey worksheet, C2 contains "species", C5 contains " brook trout", and C8 contains the total 32.
	CONCATENATE("Stream population for ",C5," ",C2," is ",C8,"/mile") equals "Stream population for brook trout species is 32/mile"
Related Functions	List of Text Functions

CONFIDENCE

Returns the confidence interval for a population mean. The confidence interval is a range on either side of a sample mean. For example, if you order a product through the mail, you can determine, with a particular level of confidence, the earliest and latest the product should arrive.

Syntax

CONFIDENCE(alpha, standard_dev, size)

Alpha   is the significance level used to compute the confidence level. The confidence level equals 100(1 - alpha)%, or in other words, an alpha of 0.05 indicates a 95% confidence level.

Standard_dev   is the population standard deviation for the data range, and is assumed to be known.

Size   is the sample size.

Remarks

- If any argument is non-numeric, CONFIDENCE returns the #VALUE! error value.
- If alpha ≤ 0 or alpha ≥ 1, CONFIDENCE returns the #NUM! error value.
- If standard_dev ≤ 0, CONFIDENCE returns the #NUM! error value.
- If size is not an integer, it is truncated.
- If size < 1, CONFIDENCE returns the #NUM! error value.
- If we assume alpha equals 0.05, we need to calculate the area under the standard normal curve that equals (1 - alpha), or 95%. This value is ± 1.96. The confidence interval is therefore:

$$\bar{x} \pm 1.96 \left(\frac{\sigma}{\sqrt{n}} \right)$$

Example

Suppose we observe that, in our sample of 50 commuters, the average length of travel to work is 30 minutes with a population standard deviation of 2.5. We can be 95 percent confident that the population mean is in the interval:

$$30 \pm 1.96 \left(\frac{2.5}{\sqrt{50}} \right)$$

or:

CONFIDENCE(0.05,2.5,50) equals 0.692951.

= 30 ± 0.692951 minutes,

= 29.3 to 30.7 minutes.

Related Function

ZTEST   Returns the two-tailed P-value of a z-test

List of Statistical Functions

CONVERT

Converts a number from one measurement system to another. For example, CONVERT can translate a table of distances in miles to a table of distances in kilometers.

If this function is not available, run the Setup program to install the Analysis ToolPak. After you install the Analysis ToolPak, you must select it in the Add-In Manager. For more information, look up Add-ins in Help.

Syntax

CONVERT(number, from_unit, to_unit)

Number   is the value in from_units to convert.

From_unit   is the units for number.

To_unit   is the units for the result.

CONVERT accepts the following text values for from_unit and to_unit:

Weight and mass	From_unit or to_unit
Gram	"g"
Slug	"sg"
Pound mass (avoirdupois)	"lbm"
U (atomic mass unit)	"u"
Ounce mass (avoirdupois)	"ozm"

Distance	From_unit or to_unit
Meter	"m"
Statute mile	"mi"
Nautical mile	"Nmi"
Inch	"in"
Foot	"ft"
Yard	"yd"
Angstrom	"ang"
Pica (1/72 in.)	"Pica"

Time	From_unit or to_unit
Year	"yr"
Day	"day"

Time	From_unit or to_unit
Hour	"hr"
Minute	"mn"
Second	"sec"

Pressure	From_unit or to_unit
Pascal	"Pa"
Atmosphere	"atm"
mm of Mercury	"mmHg"

Force	From_unit or to_unit
Newton	"N"
Dyne	"dyn"
Pound force	"lbf"

Energy	From_unit or to_unit
Joule	"J"
Erg	"e"
Thermodynamic calorie	"c"
IT calorie	"cal"
Electron volt	"eV"
Horespower-hour	"HPh"
Watt-hour	"Wh"
Foot-pound	"flb"
BTU	"BTU"

Power	From_unit or to_unit
Horsepower	"HP"
Watt	"W"

Magnetism	From_unit or to_unit
Tesla	"T"
Gauss	"ga"

Temperature	From_unit or to _unit
Degree Celsius	"C"
Degree Fahrenheit	"F"
Degree Kelvin	"K"

Liquid measure	From_unit or to_unit
Teaspoon	"tsp"
Tablespoon	"tbs"
Fluid ounce	"oz"
Cup	"cup"
Pint	"pt"
Quart	"qt"
Gallon	"gal"
Liter	"l"

The following abbreviated unit prefixes can be prepended to any metric from_unit or to_unit.

Prefix	Multiplier	Abbreviation
exa	1E+18	"E"
peta	1E+15	"P"
tera	1E+12	"T"
giga	1E+09	"G"
mega	1E+06	"M"
kilo	1E+03	"k"
hecto	1E+02	"h"
dekao	1E+01	"e"
deci	1E-01	"d"
centi	1E-02	"c"
milli	1E-03	"m"
micro	1E-06	"u"
nano	1E-09	"n"
pico	1E-12	"p"
femto	1E-15	"f"
atto	1E-18	"a"

Remarks

- If the input data types are incorrect, CONVERT returns the #VALUE! error value.

- If the unit does not exist, CONVERT returns the #N/A error value.

- If the unit does not support an abbreviated unit prefix, CONVERT returns the #N/A error value.

- If the units are in different groups, CONVERT returns the #N/A error value.

- Unit names and prefixes are case-sensitive.

Examples	CONVERT(1.0, "lbm", "kg") equals 0.453592
	CONVERT(68, "F", "C") equals 20
	CONVERT(2.5, "ft", "sec") equals #N/A
Related Functions	Related functions include all base conversion functions such as BIN2DEC, BIN2HEX, BIN2OCT, HEX2BIN, OCT2BIN, and so on.
	List of Engineering Functions

CORREL

Returns the correlation coefficient of the array1 and array2 cell ranges. Use the correlation coefficient to determine the relationship between two properties. For example, you can examine the relationship between a location's average temperature and the use of air conditioners.

Syntax	**CORREL(array1, array2)**
	Array1 is a cell range of values.
	Array2 is a second cell range of values.
Remarks	▪ The arguments should be numbers, or names, arrays, or references that contain numbers.
	▪ If an array or reference argument contains text, logical values, or empty cells, those values are ignored; however, cells with the value zero are included.
	▪ If array1 and array2 have a different number of data points, CORREL returns the #N/A error value.
	▪ If either array1 or array2 are empty, or if s (the standard deviation) of their values equals zero, CORREL returns the #DIV/0! error value.
	▪ The equation for the correlation coefficient is:

$$\rho_{x,y} = \frac{Cov(X,Y)}{\sigma_x \cdot \sigma_y}$$

where:

$$-1 \le \rho_{xy} \le 1$$

and:

$$Cov(X,Y) = \frac{1}{n} \sum_{i=1}^{n} (x_i - \mu_x)(y_i - \mu_y)$$

Example

CORREL({3,2,4,5,6},{9,7,12,15,17}) equals 0.997054

Related Functions

COVAR	Returns covariance, the average of the products of paired deviations
FISHER	Returns the Fisher transformation
FISHERINV	Returns the inverse of the Fisher transformation

List of Statistical Functions

COS

Returns the cosine of the given angle.

Syntax

COS(number)

Number is the angle in radians for which you want the cosine. If the angle is in degrees, multiply it by PI()/180 to convert it to radians.

Examples

COS(1.047) equals 0.500171

COS(60*PI()/180) equals 0.5, the cosine of 60 degrees

Related Functions

ACOS	Returns the arccosine of a number
COSH	Returns the hyperbolic cosine of a number
PI	Returns the value π

List of Math & Trigonometry Functions

COSH

Returns the hyperbolic cosine of a number.

Syntax

COSH(number)

The formula for the hyperbolic cosine is:

$$\text{COSH}(z) = \frac{e^z + e^{-z}}{2}$$

Examples

COSH(4) equals 27.30823

COSH(EXP(1)) equals 7.610125, where EXP(1) is e, the base of the natural logarithm.

Related Functions

ACOSH	Returns the inverse hyperbolic cosine of a number
SINH	Returns the hyperbolic sine of a number
TANH	Returns the hyperbolic tangent of a number

List of Math & Trigonometry Functions

COUNT

Counts how many numbers are in the list of arguments. Use COUNT to get the number of entries in a number field in a range or array of numbers.

Syntax

COUNT(value1, value2, ...)

Value1, value2,...   are 1 to 30 arguments that can contain or refer to a variety of data types, but only numbers are counted.

- Arguments that are numbers, null, logical values, dates, or text representations of numbers are counted; arguments that are error values or text that cannot be translated into numbers are ignored.

- If an argument is an array or reference, only numbers in that array or reference are counted. Empty cells, logical values, text, or error values in the array or reference are ignored.

Examples

If A3 contains "Sales," A4 contains "12/8/90," A6 contains "19," A7 contains "22.24," and A9 contains "#DIV/0!", then:

COUNT(A6:A7) equals 2

COUNT(A4:A7) equals 3

COUNT(A2, A6:A9, "Twelve", 5) equals 3

COUNT(A1:A9, , "2"), where "2" is a text representation of a number, equals 5

COUNT(0.1, TRUE, "three", 4, , 6.6666, 700, , 9, #DIV/0!) equals 8

Related Functions

AVERAGE	Returns the average of its arguments
COUNTA	Counts how many values are in the list of arguments
DCOUNT	Counts the cells containing numbers from a specified database and criteria
DCOUNTA	Counts nonblank cells from a specified database and criteria
SUM	Adds its arguments

List of Statistical Functions

COUNTA

Counts the number of nonblank values in the list of arguments. Use COUNTA to count the number of cells with data in a range or array.

Syntax

COUNTA(value1, value2, ...)

Value1, value2,...   are 1 to 30 arguments representing the values you want to count. In this case, a value is any type of information, including empty text ("") but not including empty cells. If an argument is an array or reference, empty cells within the array or reference are ignored.

Examples

If A3 contains "Sales," A4 contains "12/8/90," A6 contains "19," A7 contains "22.24," and A9 contains "#DIV/0!", then:

COUNTA(A6:A7) equals 2

COUNTA(A4:A7) equals 3

COUNTA(A3, A6:A9) equals 4

COUNTA(A1:A9) equals 5

COUNTA(1, , 1) equals 3

COUNTA(A4:A7, 10) equals 4

Related Functions	AVERAGE	Returns the average of its arguments
	COUNT	Counts how many numbers are in the list of arguments
	DCOUNT	Counts the cells containing numbers from a specified database and criteria
	DCOUNTA	Counts nonblank cells from a specified database and criteria
	PRODUCT	Multiplies its arguments
	SUM	Adds its arguments

List of Statistical Functions

COUNTBLANK

Counts blank cells in the specified range.

Syntax **COUNTBLANK(range)**

Range   is the range from which you want to count the blank cells.

Remarks Cells with formulas that return "" (or empty text) are also counted. Cells with zero values are not counted.

Example

	A	B	C	D
1				
2		6		
3			27	
4		4	34	
5		4	0	
6				

Suppose in the above worksheet, B3 contains the following formula:
IF(C3<30,"",C3), which returns "" (empty text).

COUNTBLANK(B2:C5) equals 2

Related Functions	COUNTIF	Counts the number of non-blank cells within a range which meet the given criteria

List of Information Functions

COUNTIF

Counts the number of non-blank cells within a range which meet the given criteria which meet the given criteria.

Syntax

COUNTIF(range, criteria)

Range   is the range of cells from which you want to count non-blank cells.

Criteria   is the criteria in the form of a number, expression, or text that defines which cells will be counted. For example, criteria can be expressed as 32, "32", ">32", "apples".

Examples

Suppose A3:A6 contains "apples", "oranges", "peaches", "apples", respectively.

`COUNTIF(A3:A6,"apples")` equals 2

Suppose B3:B6 contains 32, 54, 75, 86, respectively.

`COUNTIF(B3:B6,">55")` equals 2

Related Functions

SUMIF	Adds the cells specified by a given criteria
COUNTBLANK	Counts blank cells in the specified range

List of Math & Trigonometry Functions

COUPDAYBS

Returns the number of days from the beginning of the coupon period to the settlement date.

If this function is not available, run the Setup program to install the Analysis ToolPak. After you install the Analysis ToolPak, you must select it in the Add-In Manager. For more information, look up Add-ins in Help.

Syntax

COUPDAYBS(settlement, maturity, frequency, basis)

Settlement   is the security's settlement date, expressed as a serial date number.

Maturity   is the security's maturity date, expressed as a serial date number.

Frequency   is the number of coupon payments per year. For annual payments, frequency = 1; for semiannual, frequency = 2; for quarterly, frequency = 4.

Basis   is the type of day count basis to use.

Basis	Day count basis
0 or omitted	US (NASD) 30/360
1	Actual/actual
2	Actual/360
3	Actual/365
4	European 30/360

Remarks

- All arguments are truncated to integers.
- If any argument is non-numeric, COUPDAYBS returns the #VALUE! error value.
- If settlement or maturity is not a valid serial date number, COUPDAYBS returns the #NUM! error value.
- If frequency is any number other than 1, 2, or 4, COUPDAYBS returns the #NUM! error value.
- If basis < 0 or if basis > 4, COUPDAYBS returns the #NUM! error value.
- If settlement ≥ maturity, COUPDAYBS returns the #NUM! error value.

Example

A bond has the following terms:

January 25, 1993 settlement date
November 15, 1994 maturity date
Semiannual coupon
Actual/actual basis

The number of days from the beginning of the coupon period to the settlement date (in the 1900 Date System) is:

COUPDAYBS(33994,34653,2,1) equals 71

Related Functions

COUPDAYS	Returns the number of days in the coupon period that contains the settlement date
COUPDAYSNC	Returns the number of days from the settlement date to the next coupon date
COUPNCD	Returns the next coupon date after the settlement date
COUPNUM	Returns the number of coupons payable between the settlement date and maturity date
COUPPCD	Returns the previous coupon date before the settlement date
DATE	Returns the serial number of a particular date

List of Financial Functions

COUPDAYS

Returns the number of days in the coupon period that contains the settlement date.

If this function is not available, run the Setup program to install the Analysis ToolPak. After you install the Analysis ToolPak, you must select it in the Add-In Manager. For more information, look up Add-ins in Help.

Syntax

COUPDAYS(settlement, maturity, frequency, basis)

Settlement   is the security's settlement date, expressed as a serial date number.

Maturity   is the security's maturity date, expressed as a serial date number.

Frequency   is the number of coupon payments per year. For annual payments, frequency = 1; for semiannual, frequency = 2; for quarterly, frequency = 4.

Basis   is the type of day count basis to use.

Basis	Day count basis
0 or omitted	US (NASD) 30/360
1	Actual/actual
2	Actual/360
3	Actual/365
4	European 30/360

Remarks

- All arguments are truncated to integers.
- If any argument is non-numeric, COUPDAYS returns the #VALUE! error value.
- If settlement or maturity is not a valid serial date number, COUPDAYS returns the #NUM! error value.
- If frequency is any number other than 1, 2, or 4, COUPDAYS returns the #NUM! error value.
- If basis < 0 or if basis > 4, COUPDAYS returns the #NUM! error value.
- If settlement ≥ maturity, COUPDAYS returns the #NUM! error value.

Example

A bond has the following terms:

January 25, 1993 settlement date
November 15, 1994 maturity date
Semiannual coupon
Actual/actual basis

The number of days in the coupon period that contains the settlement date (in the 1900 Date System) is:

COUPDAYS(33994,34653,2,1) equals 181

Related Functions

COUPDAYBS	Returns the number of days from the beginning of the coupon period to the settlement date
COUPDAYSNC	Returns the number of days from the settlement date to the next coupon date
COUPNCD	Returns the next coupon date after the settlement date
COUPNUM	Returns the number of coupons payable between the settlement date and maturity date
COUPPCD	Returns the previous coupon date before the settlement date
DATE	Returns the serial number of a particular date

List of Financial Functions

COUPDAYSNC

Returns the number of days from the settlement date to the next coupon date.

If this function is not available, run the Setup program to install the Analysis ToolPak. After you install the Analysis ToolPak, you must select it in the Add-In Manager. For more information, look up Add-ins in Help.

Syntax

COUPDAYSNC(settlement, maturity, frequency, basis)

Settlement   is the security's settlement date, expressed as a serial date number.

Maturity   is the security's maturity date, expressed as a serial date number.

Frequency   is the number of coupon payments per year. For annual payments, frequency = 1; for semiannual, frequency = 2; for quarterly, frequency = 4.

Basis   is the type of day count basis to use.

Basis	Day count basis
0 or omitted	US (NASD) 30/360
1	Actual/actual
2	Actual/360
3	Actual/365
4	European 30/360

Remarks
- All arguments are truncated to integers.
- If any argument is non-numeric, COUPDAYSNC returns the #VALUE! error value.
- If settlement or maturity is not a valid serial date number, COUPDAYSNC returns the #NUM! error value.
- If frequency is any number other than 1, 2, or 4, COUPDAYSNC returns the #NUM! error value.
- If basis < 0 or if basis > 4, COUPDAYSNC returns the #NUM! error value.
- If settlement ≥ maturity, COUPDAYSNC returns the #NUM! error value.

Example

A bond has the following terms:

January 25, 1993 settlement date
November 15, 1994 maturity date
Semiannual coupon
Actual/actual basis

The number of days from the settlement date to the next coupon date (in the 1900 Date System) is:

COUPDAYSNC(33994,34653,2,1) equals 110

Related Functions

COUPDAYBS	Returns the number of days from the beginning of the coupon period to the settlement date
COUPDAYS	Returns the number of days in the coupon period that contains the settlement date
COUPNCD	Returns the next coupon date after the settlement date
COUPNUM	Returns the number of coupons payable between the settlement date and maturity date
COUPPCD	Returns the previous coupon date before the settlement date
DATE	Returns the serial number of a particular date

List of Financial Functions

COUPNCD

Returns the next coupon date after the settlement date.

If this function is not available, run the Setup program to install the Analysis ToolPak. After you install the Analysis ToolPak, you must select it in the Add-In Manager. For more information, look up Add-ins in Help.

Syntax

COUPNCD(settlement, maturity, frequency, basis)

Settlement   is the security's settlement date, expressed as a serial date number.

Maturity   is the security's maturity date, expressed as a serial date number.

Frequency   is the number of coupon payments per year. For annual payments, frequency = 1; for semiannual, frequency = 2; for quarterly, frequency = 4.

Basis   is the type of day count basis to use.

Basis	Day count basis
0 or omitted	US (NASD) 30/360
1	Actual/actual
2	Actual/360
3	Actual/365
4	European 30/360

Remarks

- All arguments are truncated to integers.
- If any argument is non-numeric, COUPNCD returns the #VALUE! error value.
- If settlement or maturity is not a valid serial date number, COUPNCD returns the #NUM! error value.
- If frequency is any number other than 1, 2, or 4, COUPNCD returns the #NUM! error value.
- If basis < 0 or if basis > 4, COUPNCD returns the #NUM! error value.
- If settlement ≥ maturity, COUPNCD returns the #NUM! error value.

Example

A bond has the following terms:

January 25, 1993 settlement date
November 15, 1994 maturity date
Semiannual coupon
Actual/actual basis

The next coupon date after the settlement date (in the 1900 Date System) is:

`COUPNCD(33994,34653,2,1)` equals 34104 or May 15, 1993

Related Functions

COUPDAYBS	Returns the number of days from the beginning of the coupon period to the settlement date
COUPDAYS	Returns the number of days in the coupon period that contains the settlement date

COUPDAYSNC	Returns the number of days from the settlement date to the next coupon date
COUPNUM	Returns the number of coupons payable between the settlement date and maturity date
COUPPCD	Returns the previous coupon date before the settlement date
DATE	Returns the serial number of a particular date

List of Financial Functions

COUPNUM

Returns the number of coupons payable between the settlement date and maturity date, rounded up to the nearest whole coupon.

If this function is not available, run the Setup program to install the Analysis ToolPak. After you install the Analysis ToolPak, you must select it in the Add-In Manager. For more information, look up Add-ins in Help.

Syntax

COUPNUM(settlement, maturity, frequency, basis)

Settlement   is the security's settlement date, expressed as a serial date number.

Maturity   is the security's maturity date, expressed as a serial date number.

Frequency   is the number of coupon payments per year. For annual payments, frequency = 1; for semiannual, frequency = 2; for quarterly, frequency = 4.

Basis   is the type of day count basis to use.

Basis	Day count basis
0 or omitted	US (NASD) 30/360
1	Actual/actual
2	Actual/360
3	Actual/365
4	European 30/360

Remarks

- All arguments are truncated to integers.
- If any argument is non-numeric, COUPNUM returns the #VALUE! error value.
- If settlement or maturity is not a valid serial date number, COUPNUM returns the #NUM! error value.

- If frequency is any number other than 1, 2, or 4, COUPNUM returns the #NUM! error value.
- If basis < 0 or if basis > 4, COUPNUM returns the #NUM! error value.
- If settlement ≥ maturity, COUPNUM returns the #NUM! error value.

Example

A bond has the following terms:

January 25, 1993 settlement date
November 15, 1994 maturity date
Semiannual coupon
Actual/actual basis

The number of coupon payments (in the 1900 Date System) is:

COUPNUM(33994,34653,2,1) equals 4

Related Functions

COUPDAYBS	Returns the number of days from the beginning of the coupon period to the settlement date
COUPDAYS	Returns the number of days in the coupon period that contains the settlement date
COUPDAYSNC	Returns the number of days from the settlement date to the next coupon date
COUPNCD	Returns the next coupon date after the settlement date
COUPPCD	Returns the previous coupon date before the settlement date
DATE	Returns the serial number of a particular date

List of Financial Functions

COUPPCD

Returns the previous coupon date before the settlement date.

If this function is not available, run the Setup program to install the Analysis ToolPak. After you install the Analysis ToolPak, you must select it in the Add-In Manager. For more information, look up Add-ins in Help.

Syntax

COUPPCD(settlement, maturity, frequency, basis)

Settlement   is the security's settlement date, expressed as a serial date number.

Maturity   is the security's maturity date, expressed as a serial date number.

Frequency   is the number of coupon payments per year. For annual payments, frequency = 1; for semiannual, frequency = 2; for quarterly, frequency = 4.

Basis   is the type of day count basis to use.

Basis	Day count basis
0 or omitted	US (NASD) 30/360
1	Actual/actual
2	Actual/360
3	Actual/365
4	European 30/360

Remarks

- All arguments are truncated to integers.
- If any argument is non-numeric, COUPPCD returns the #VALUE! error value.
- If settlement or maturity is not a valid serial date number, COUPPCD returns the #NUM! error value.
- If frequency is any number other than 1, 2, or 4, COUPPCD returns the #NUM! error value.
- If basis < 0 or if basis > 4, COUPPCD returns the #NUM! error value.
- If settlement ≥ maturity, COUPPCD returns the #NUM! error value.

Example

A bond has the following terms:

January 25, 1993 settlement date
November 15, 1994 maturity date
Semiannual coupon
Actual/actual basis

The previous coupon date before the settlement date (in the 1900 Date System) is:

COUPPCD(33994,34653,2,1) equals 33923 or November 15, 1992

Related Functions

COUPDAYBS	Returns the number of days from the beginning of the coupon period to the settlement date
COUPDAYS	Returns the number of days in the coupon period that contains the settlement date
COUPDAYSNC	Returns the number of days from the settlement date to the next coupon date
COUPNCD	Returns the next coupon date after the settlement date
COUPNUM	Returns the number of coupons payable between the settlement date and maturity date
DATE	Returns the serial number of a particular date

List of Financial Functions

COVAR

Returns covariance, the average of the products of deviations for each data point pair. Use covariance to determine the relationship between two data sets. For example, you can examine whether greater income accompanies greater levels of education.

Syntax

COVAR(array1, array2)

Array1   is the first cell range of integers.

Array2   is the second cell range of integers.

Remarks

- The arguments should be numbers, or names, arrays, or references that contain numbers.
- If an array or reference argument contains text, logical values, or empty cells, those values are ignored; however, cells with the value zero are included.
- If array1 and array2 have a different number of data points, COVAR returns the #N/A error value.
- If either array1 or array2 are empty, COVAR returns the #DIV/0! error value.
- The covariance is:

$$Cov(X, Y) = \frac{1}{n} \sum_{i-1}^{n} (x_i - \mu_x)(y_i - \mu_y)$$

Example

COVAR({3, 2, 4, 5, 6}, {9, 7, 12, 15, 17}) equals 5.2

Related Functions

CORREL	Returns the correlation coefficient between two data sets
FISHER	Returns the Fisher transformation
FISHERINV	Returns the inverse of the Fisher transformation

List of Statistical Functions

CRITBINOM

Returns the smallest value for which the cumulative binomial distribution is less than or equal to a criterion value. Use this function for quality assurance applications. For example, use CRITBINOM to determine the greatest number of defective parts that are allowed to come off an assembly line run without rejecting the entire lot.

Syntax	**CRITBINOM(trials, probability_s, alpha)**
	Trials is the number of Bernoulli trials.
	Probability_s is the probability of a success on each trial.
	Alpha is the criterion value.
Remarks	■ If any argument is non-numeric, CRITBINOM returns the #VALUE! error value.
	■ If trials is not an integer, it is truncated.
	■ If trials < 0, CRITBINOM returns the #NUM! error value.
	■ If probability_s is < 0 or probability_s > 1, CRITBINOM returns the #NUM! error value.
	■ If alpha < 0 or alpha > 1, CRITBINOM returns the #NUM! error value.
Example	CRITBINOM(6,0.5,0.75) equals 4
Related Functions	

BINOMDIST	Returns the individual term binomial distribution probability
COMBIN	Returns the number of combinations for a given number of objects
FACT	Returns the factorial of a number
HYPGEOMDIST	Returns the hypergeometric distribution
NEGBINOMDIST	Returns the negative binomial distribution
PERMUT	Returns the number of permutations for a given number of objects
PROB	Returns the probability that values in a range are between two limits

List of Statistical Functions

CUMIPMT

Returns the cumulative interest paid on a loan between start_period and end_period.

If this function is not available, run the Setup program to install the Analysis ToolPak. After you install the Analysis ToolPak, you must select it in the Add-In Manager. For more information, look up Add-ins in Help.

Syntax	**CUMIPMT(rate, nper, pv, start_period, end_period, type)**

Rate   is the interest rate.

Nper   is the total number of payment periods.

Pv   is the present value.

Start_period   is the first period in the calculation. Payment periods are numbered beginning with 1.

End_period   is the last period in the calculation.

Type   is the timing of the payment.

Type	Timing
0	Payment at the end of the period
1	Payment at the beginning of the period

Remarks

- Make sure that you are consistent about the units you use for specifying rate and nper. If you make monthly payments on a four-year loan at 12% annual interest, use 12%/12 for rate and 4*12 for nper. If you make annual payments on the same loan, use 12% for rate and 4 for nper.
- Nper, start_period, end_period, and type are truncated to integers.
- If any argument is non-numeric, CUMIPMT returns the #VALUE! error value.
- If rate ≤ 0, nper ≤ 0, or pv ≤ 0, CUMIPMT returns the #NUM! error value.
- If start_period < 1, end_period < 1, or start_period > end_period, CUMIPMT returns the #NUM! error value.
- If type is any number other than 0 or 1, CUMIPMT returns the #NUM! error value.

Example

A home mortgage loan has the following terms:

Interest rate, 9.00% per annum (rate = 9.00% ÷ 12 = 0.0075)
Term, 30 years (nper = 30 × 12 = 360)
Present value, $125,000

The total interest paid in the second year of payments (periods 13 through 24) is:

`CUMIPMT(0.0075,360,125000,13,24,0)` equals –11135.23

The interest paid in a single payment, in the first month, is:

`CUMIPMT(0.0075,360,125000,1,1,0)` equals –937.50

Related Function   CUMPRINC   Returns the cumulative principal paid on a loan
                                                     between two periods

                        List of Financial Functions

CUMPRINC

Returns the cumulative principal paid on a loan between start_period and
end_period.

If this function is not available, run the Setup program to install the Analysis
ToolPak. After you install the Analysis ToolPak, you must select it in the Add-In
Manager. For more information, look up Add-ins in Help.

Syntax   **CUMPRINC(rate, nper, pv, start_period, end_period, type)**

Rate   is the interest rate.

Nper   is the total number of payment periods.

Pv   is the present value.

Start_period   is the first period in the calculation. Payment periods are numbered
beginning with 1.

End_period   is the last period in the calculation.

Type   is the timing of the payment.

Type	Timing
0	Payment at the end of the period
1	Payment at the beginning of the period

Remarks
- Make sure that you are consistent about the units you use for specifying rate and
  nper. If you make monthly payments on a four-year loan at 12% annual interest,
  use 12%/12 for rate and 4*12 for nper. If you make annual payments on the
  same loan, use 12% for rate and 4 for nper.
- Nper, start_period, end_period, and type are truncated to integers.
- If any argument is non-numeric, CUMPRINC returns the #VALUE! error value.
- If rate $\leq$ 0, nper $\leq$ 0, or pv $\leq$ 0, CUMPRINC returns the #NUM! error value.

- If start_period < 1, end_period < 1, or start_period > end_period, CUMPRINC returns the #NUM! error value.
- If type is any number other than 0 or 1, CUMPRINC returns the #NUM! error value.

Example

A home mortgage loan has the following terms:

Interest rate, 9.00% per annum (rate = 9.00% ÷ 12 = 0.0075)
Term, 30 years (nper = 30 × 12 = 360)
Present value, $125,000

The total principal paid in the second year of payments (periods 13 through 24) is:

`CUMPRINC(0.0075,360,125000,13,24,0)` equals –934.1071

The principal paid in a single payment, in the first month, is:

`CUMPRINC(0.0075,360,125000,1,1,0)` equals –68.27827

Related Function   CUMIPMT   Returns the cumulative interest paid on a loan between two periods

List of Financial Functions

Database Functions

This section describes the 12 worksheet functions used for Microsoft Excel database (or list) calculations. Each of these functions, referred to collectively as Dfunction, uses three arguments: database, field, and criteria. These arguments refer to the worksheet ranges that are used in the database function.

Syntax   **Dfunction(database, field, criteria)**

Database   is the range of cells that make up the database.

- In all database functions, if the database reference is to a cell inside a pivot table, then the calculation is done on only the pivot table data.

- A Microsoft Excel database is a contiguous range of cells organized into records (rows) and fields (columns). The database reference can be entered as a cell range, or as a name assigned to a range.

Tips

- You can use any range that includes field headings at the top of each row of data as the database argument. This is useful if you want to perform Dfunction calculations on more than one range of data on a worksheet.

- When you use a field heading, you must use double quotation marks.

- If all you want to do is generate subtotals within your list, use SUBTOTAL instead of these database functions.

Field   indicates which field is used in the function. Database fields are columns of data with an identifying field name in the first row. The field argument can be given as text, such as "Age" or "Yield" in the example database table below or as a field number: 1 for the first field (Tree), in the example below, 2 for the second (Height), and so on.

Criteria   is the range of cells that contains the database criteria. The criteria reference can be entered as a cell range, such as A9:F10 in the example database table below, or as a name assigned to a range.

Tips

- You can use any range for the criteria argument, as long as it includes at least one field name and at least one cell below the field name for specifying a criteria comparison value.

- For example, if the range G1:G2 contains the field heading Income in G1 and the amount 10,000 in G2, you could define the range as MatchIncome and use that name as the criteria argument in your database functions.

- To perform an operation on an entire column in a database, enter a blank line below the field names in the criteria range.

Examples

The following illustration shows a database for a small orchard. Each record contains information about one tree. The database is defined as A1:E7, and the criteria are defined as A9:F11.

	A	B	C	D	E	F
1	**Tree**	**Height**	**Age**	**Yield**	**Profit**	
2	Apple	18	20	14	$105.00	
3	Pear	12	12	10	$96.00	
4	Cherry	13	14	9	$105.30	
5	Apple	14	15	10	$75.00	
6	Pear	9	8	8	$76.80	
7	Apple	8	9	6	$45.00	
8						
9	**Tree**	**Height**	**Age**	**Yield**	**Profit**	**Height**
10	Apple	>10				<16
11	Pear					

`DCOUNT(Database,"Age",A9:F10)` equals 1. This function looks at the records of apple trees between a height of 10 and 16 and counts how many of the Age fields in those records contain numbers.

`DCOUNTA(Database,"Profit",A9:F10)` equals 1. This function looks at the records of apple trees between a height of 10 and 16 and counts how many of the Profit fields in those records are not blank.

`DMAX(Database,"Profit",A9:A11)` equals $105.00, the maximum profit of apple and pear trees.

`DMIN(Database,"Profit",A9:B10)` equals $75.00, the minimum profit of apple trees over 10.

`DSUM(Database,"Profit",A9:A10)` equals $225.00, the total profit from apple trees.

`DSUM(Database,"Profit",A9:F10)` equals $75.00, the total profit from apple trees with a height between 10 and 16.

`DPRODUCT(Database,"Yield",A9:F10)` equals 10, the product of the yields from apple trees with a height between 10 and 16.

`DAVERAGE(Database,"Yield",A9:B10)` equals 12, the average yield of apple trees over 10 feet in height.

`DAVERAGE(Database,3,Database)` equals 13, the average age of all trees in the database.

DSTDEV(Database,"Yield",A9:A11) equals 2.97, the estimated standard deviation in the yield of apple and pear trees if the data in the database is only a sample of the total orchard population.

DSTDEVP(Database,"Yield",A9:A11) equals 2.65, the true standard deviation in the yield of apple and pear trees if the data in the database is the entire population.

DVAR(Database,"Yield",A9:A11) equals 8.8, the estimated variance in the yield of apple and pear trees if the data in the database is only a sample of the total orchard population.

DVARP(Database,"Yield",A9:A11) equals 7.04, the true variance in the yield of apple and pear trees if the data in the database is the entire orchard population.

DGET(Database,"Yield",Criteria) returns the #NUM! error value because more than one record meets the criteria.

Related Functions AVERAGE, COUNT, COUNTA, COUNTBLANK, COUNTIF, MAX, MIN, PRODUCT, STDEV, STDEVP, SUM, SUMIF, VAR, and VARP perform the same operations as the corresponding database functions. However, they operate on their lists of arguments instead of on selected database entries.

List of Statistical Functions

DATE

Returns the serial number of a particular date. For more information about serial numbers, see NOW.

Syntax **DATE(year, month, day)**

Year is a number from 1900 to 2078 in Microsoft Excel for Windows™ or 1904 to 2078 in Microsoft Excel for the Macintosh.

Month is a number representing the month of the year. If month is greater than 12, then month adds that number of months to the first month in the year specified. For example, DATE(90,14,2) returns the serial number representing February 2, 1991.

Day is a number representing the day of the month. If day is greater than the number of days in the month specified, then day adds that number of days to the first day in the month. For example, DATE(91,1,35) returns the serial number representing February 4, 1991.

Remarks
- Microsoft Excel for Windows and Microsoft Excel for the Macintosh use different date systems as their default. For more information, see NOW.
- The DATE function is most useful in formulas where year, month, and day are formulas, not constants.

Examples

Using the 1900 Date System (the default in Microsoft Excel for Windows), DATE(91, 1, 1) equals 33239, the serial number corresponding to January 1, 1991.

Using the 1904 Date System (the default in Microsoft Excel for the Macintosh), DATE(91, 1, 1) equals 31777, the serial number corresponding to January 1, 1991.

Related Functions

DATEVALUE	Converts a date in the form of text to a serial number
DAY	Converts serial numbers to days
MONTH	Converts serial numbers to months
YEAR	Converts serial numbers to years
NOW	Returns the serial number of the current date and time
TIMEVALUE	Converts a time in the form of text to a serial number
TODAY	Returns the serial number of today's date

List of Date & Time Functions

DATEVALUE

Returns the serial number of the date represented by date_text. Use DATEVALUE to convert a date represented by text to a serial number.

Syntax

DATEVALUE(date_text)

Date_text   is text that returns a date in a Microsoft Excel date format. Using the default date system in Microsoft Excel for Windows, date_text must represent a date from January 1, 1900 to December 31, 2078. Using the default date system in Microsoft Excel for the Macintosh, date_text must represent a date from January 1, 1904 to December 31, 2078. DATEVALUE returns the #VALUE! error value if date_text is out of this range.

If the year portion of date_text is omitted, DATEVALUE uses the current year from your computer's built-in clock. Time information in date_text is ignored.

Remarks
- Microsoft Excel for Windows and Microsoft Excel for the Macintosh use different date systems as their default. For more information, see NOW.
- Most functions automatically convert date values to serial numbers.

Examples

The following examples use the 1900 Date System:

DATEVALUE("8/22/55") equals 20323

DATEVALUE("22-AUG-55") equals 20323

Assuming your computer's built-in clock is set to 1993 and you are using the 1900 Date System:

DATEVALUE("5-JUL") equals 34155

Related Functions

NOW	Returns the serial number of the current date and time
TIMEVALUE	Converts a time in the form of text to a serial number
TODAY	Returns the serial number of today's date

List of Date & Time Functions

DAVERAGE

Averages the values in the field column of records in the database which match the criteria. For more information about Microsoft Excel database functions, see "Database Functions".

Syntax

DAVERAGE(database, field, criteria)

Database   is the range of cells that make up the database.

Field   indicates which field is used in the function.

Criteria   is the range of cells that contains the database criteria.

Related Functions   List of Database & List Management Functions

DAY

Returns the day of the month corresponding to serial_number. The day is given as an integer ranging from 1 to 31.

Syntax

DAY(serial_number)

Serial_number   is the date-time code used by Microsoft Excel for date and time calculations. You can give serial_number as text, such as "4-15-93" or "15-Apr-1993", instead of as a number. The text is automatically converted to a serial number. For more information about serial_number, see NOW.

Remarks

Microsoft Excel for Windows and Microsoft Excel for the Macintosh use different date systems as their default. For more information, see NOW.

Examples

DAY("4-Jan") equals 4

DAY("15-Apr-1993") equals 15

DAY("8/11/93") equals 11

Related Functions

NOW	Returns the serial number of the current date and time
TODAY	Returns the serial number of today's date
YEAR, MONTH, WEEKDAY, HOUR, MINUTE, and SECOND	Convert serial numbers into years, months, days of the week, hours, minutes, and seconds

List of Date & Time Functions

DAYS360

Returns the number of days between two dates based on a 360-day year (twelve 30-day months). Use this function to help compute payments if your accounting system is based on twelve 30-day months.

Syntax

DAYS360(start_date, end_date, method)

Start_date   and end_date   are the two dates between which you want to know the number of days.

- The arguments can be either text strings using numbers to represent the month, day, and year (for example, "1/30/93" or "1-30-93"), or they can be serial numbers representing the dates.

- If start_date occurs after end_date, DAYS360 returns a negative number.

Method   is a number that specifies whether the European or US method should be used in the calculation

Method	Defined
1 or omitted	US (NASD)
2	European method. If the starting date is the 31st of the month, it becomes equal to the 30th of the same month. If the ending date is the 31th of the month, it becomes equal to the 1st of the next month, except when the starting date is the 30th. February 28 and 29 become equal to February 30.

Tip To determine the number of days between two dates in a normal year, you can use normal subtraction—for example, "12/31/93"–"1/1/93" equals 364.

Example

DAYS360("1/30/93", "2/1/93") equals 1

Related Function

DAY   Converts a serial number to a day of the month

List of Date & Time Functions

DB

Returns the depreciation of an asset for a specified period using the fixed-declining balance method.

Syntax

DB(cost, salvage, life, period, month)

Cost   is the initial cost of the asset.

Salvage   is the value at the end of the depreciation (sometimes called the salvage value of the asset).

Life   is the number of periods over which the asset is being depreciated (sometimes called the useful life of the asset).

Period   is the period for which you want to calculate the depreciation. Period must use the same units as life.

Month   is the number of months in the first year. If month is omitted, it is assumed to be 12.

Remarks

The fixed-declining balance method computes depreciation at a fixed rate. DB uses the following formulas to calculate depreciation for a period:

(cost – total depreciation from prior periods) * rate

where:

rate = 1 – ((salvage / cost) ^ (1 / life)), rounded to three decimal places

Depreciation for the first and last periods are special cases. For the first period, DB uses this formula:

cost * rate * month / 12

For the last period, DB uses this formula:

((cost – total depreciation from prior periods) * rate * (12 – month)) / 12

Examples

Suppose a factory purchases a new machine. The machine costs $1,000,000 and has a lifetime of six years. The salvage value of the machine is $100,000. The following examples show depreciation over the life of the machine. The results are rounded to whole numbers.

```
DB(1000000,100000,6,1,7) equals $186,083
DB(1000000,100000,6,2,7) equals $259,639
DB(1000000,100000,6,3,7) equals $176,814
DB(1000000,100000,6,4,7) equals $120,411
DB(1000000,100000,6,5,7) equals $82,000
DB(1000000,100000,6,6,7) equals $55,842
DB(1000000,100000,6,7,7) equals $15,845
```

Related Functions

DDB	Returns the depreciation of an asset for a spcified period using the double-declining balance method or some other method you specify
SLN	Returns the straight-line depreciation of an asset for one period
SYD	Returns the sum-of-years' digits depreciation of an asset for a specified period
VDB	Returns the depreciation of an asset for a specified or partial period using a declining balance method

List of Financial Functions

DCOUNT

Counts the cells that contain numbers that match the criteria in the field column of records in the database.

The field argument is optional. If field is omitted, DCOUNT counts all records in the database which match the criteria. For more information about Microsoft Excel database functions, see "Database Functions".

Syntax

DCOUNT(database, field, criteria)

Database   is the range of cells that make up the database.

Field   indicates which field is used in the function.

Criteria   is the range of cells that contains the database criteria.

Related Functions

COUNTBLANK and COUNTIF, perform similar operations; however, they operate on their lists of arguments instead of on selected database entries.

List of Database & List Management Functions

DCOUNTA

Counts the cells that are not blank and that satisfy the criteria in the field column of records in the database. For more information about Microsoft Excel database functions, see "Database Functions".

Syntax

DCOUNTA(database, field, criteria)

Database   is the range of cells that make up the database.

Field   indicates which field is used in the function.

Criteria   is the range of cells that contains the database criteria.

Related Functions

COUNTBLANK and COUNTIF, perform similar operations; however, they operate on their lists of arguments instead of on selected database entries.

List of Database & List Management Functions

DDB

Returns the depreciation of an asset for a specified period using the double-declining balance method or some other method you specify.

Syntax

DDB(cost, salvage, life, period, factor)

Cost   is the initial cost of the asset.

Salvage   is the value at the end of the depreciation (sometimes called the salvage value of the asset).

Life   is the number of periods over which the asset is being depreciated (sometimes called the useful life of the asset).

Period   is the period for which you want to calculate the depreciation. Period must use the same units as life.

Factor   is the rate at which the balance declines. If factor is omitted, it is assumed to be 2 (the double-declining balance method).

All five arguments must be positive numbers.

Remarks

The double-declining balance method computes depreciation at an accelerated rate. Depreciation is highest in the first period and decreases in successive periods. DDB uses the following formula to calculate depreciation for a period:

cost – salvage(total depreciation from prior periods) * factor / life

Change factor if you do not want to use the double-declining balance method.

Examples

Suppose a factory purchases a new machine. The machine costs $2400 and has a lifetime of 10 years. The salvage value of the machine is $300. The following examples show depreciation over several periods. The results are rounded to two decimal places.

DDB(2400,300,3650,1) equals $1.32, the first day's depreciation. Microsoft Excel automatically assumes that factor is 2.

DDB(2400,300,120,1,2) equals $40.00, the first month's depreciation.

DDB(2400,300,10,1,2) equals $480.00, the first year's depreciation.

DDB(2400,300,10,2,1.5) equals $306.00, the second year's depreciation using a factor of 1.5 instead of the double-declining balance method.

DDB(2400,300,10,10) equals $22.12, the 10th year's depreciation. Microsoft Excel automatically assumes that factor is 2.

Related Functions   SLN   Returns the straight-line depreciation of an asset
                                                  for one period

                         SYD   Returns the sum-of-years' digits depreciation of an
                                                  asset for a specified period

                         VDB   Returns the depreciation of an asset for a specified
                                                  or partial period using a declining balance method

                         List of Financial Functions

DEC2BIN

Converts a decimal number to binary.

If this function is not available, run the Setup program to install the Analysis
ToolPak. After you install the Analysis ToolPak, you must select it in the Add-In
Manager. For more information, look up Add-ins in Help.

Syntax   **DEC2BIN(number**, places)

Number   is the decimal integer you want to convert. If number is negative, places
is ignored and DEC2BIN returns a 10-character (10-bit) binary number in which
the most significant bit is the sign bit. The remaining 9 bits are magnitude bits.
Negative numbers are represented using two's-complement notation.

Places   is the number of characters to use. If places is omitted, DEC2BIN uses the
minimum number of characters necessary. Places is useful for padding the return
value with leading 0s (zeros).

Remarks
- If number < -512 or if number > 511, DEC2BIN returns the #NUM! error
  value.
- If number is non-numeric, DEC2BIN returns the #VALUE! error value.
- If DEC2BIN requires more than places characters, it returns the #NUM! error
  value.
- If places is not an integer, it is truncated.
- If places is non-numeric, DEC2BIN returns the #VALUE! error value.
- If places is negative, DEC2BIN returns the #NUM! error value.

Examples	`DEC2BIN(9, 4)` equals 1001	
	`DEC2BIN(-100)` equals 1110011100	
Related Functions	BIN2DEC	Converts a binary number to decimal
	HEX2DEC	Converts a hexadecimal number to decimal
	OCT2DEC	Converts an octal number to decimal

List of Engineering Functions

DEC2HEX

Converts a decimal number to hexadecimal.

If this function is not available, run the Setup program to install the Analysis ToolPak. After you install the Analysis ToolPak, you must select it in the Add-In Manager. For more information, look up Add-ins in Help.

Syntax

DEC2HEX(number, places)

Number   is the decimal integer you want to convert. If number is negative, places is ignored and DEC2HEX returns a 10-character (40-bit) hexadecimal number in which the most significant bit is the sign bit. The remaining 39 bits are magnitude bits. Negative numbers are represented using two's-complement notation.

Places   is the number of characters to use. If places is omitted, DEC2HEX uses the minimum number of characters necessary. Places is useful for padding the return value with leading 0s (zeros).

Remarks

- If number < –549,755,813,888 or if number > 549,755,813,887, DEC2HEX returns the #NUM! error value.
- If number is non-numeric, DEC2HEX returns the #VALUE! error value.
- If DEC2HEX requires more than places characters, it returns the #NUM! error value.
- If places is not an integer, it is truncated.
- If places is non-numeric, DEC2HEX returns the #VALUE! error value.
- If places is negative, DEC2HEX returns the #NUM! error value.

Examples

`DEC2HEX(100, 4)` equals 0064

`DEC2HEX(-54)` equals FFFFFFFFCA

Related Functions	BIN2DEC	Converts a binary number to decimal
	HEX2DEC	Converts a hexadecimal number to decimal
	OCT2DEC	Converts an octal number to decimal

List of Engineering Functions

DEC2OCT

Converts a decimal number to octal.

If this function is not available, run the Setup program to install the Analysis ToolPak. After you install the Analysis ToolPak, you must select it in the Add-In Manager. For more information, look up Add-ins in Help.

Syntax

DEC2OCT(number, places)

Number   is the decimal integer you want to convert. If number is negative, places is ignored and DEC2OCT returns a 10-character (30-bit) octal number in which the most significant bit is the sign bit. The remaining 29 bits are magnitude bits. Negative numbers are represented using two's-complement notation.

Places   is the number of characters to use. If places is omitted, DEC2OCT uses the minimum number of characters necessary. Places is useful for padding the return value with leading 0s (zeros).

Remarks

- If number < –536,870,912 or if number > 536,870,911, DEC2OCT returns the #NUM! error value.
- If number is non-numeric, DEC2OCT returns the #VALUE! error value.
- If DEC2OCT requires more than places characters, it returns the #NUM! error value.
- If places is not an integer, it is truncated.
- If places is non-numeric, DEC2OCT returns the #VALUE! error value.
- If places is negative, DEC2OCT returns the #NUM! error value.

Examples

DEC2OCT(58, 3) equals 072

DEC2OCT(-100) equals 7777777634

Related Functions	BIN2DEC	Converts a binary number to decimal
	HEX2DEC	Converts a hexadecimal number to decimal
	OCT2DEC	Converts an octal number to decimal

List of Engineering Functions

DEGREES

Converts radians into degrees.

Syntax **DEGREES(angle)**
Angle   is the angle in radians that you want to convert.

Example DEGREES(PI()) equals 180

Related Function RADIANS   Converts degrees to radians

List of Math & Trigonometry Functions

DELTA

Tests whether two values are equal. Returns 1 if number1 = number2; returns 0 otherwise. Use this function to filter a set of values. For example, by summing several DELTA functions you calculate the count of equal pairs. This function is also known as the Kronecker Delta function.

If this function is not available, run the Setup program to install the Analysis ToolPak. After you install the Analysis ToolPak, you must select it in the Add-In Manager. For more information, look up Add-ins in Help.

Syntax **DELTA(number1**, number2)

Number1   is the first number.

Number2   is the second number. If omitted, number2 is assumed to be zero.

Remarks ▪ If number1 is non-numeric, DELTA returns the #VALUE! error value.

▪ If number2 is non-numeric, DELTA returns the #VALUE! error value.

Examples DELTA(5, 4) equals 0

DELTA(5, 5) equals 1

DELTA(0.5, 0) equals 0

Related Functions EXACT   Checks to see if two text values are identical

GESTEP   Tests whether a number is greater than a threshold value

List of Engineering Functions

DEVSQ

Returns the sum of squares of deviations of data points from their sample mean.

Syntax   **DEVSQ(number1**, number2, ...)

Number1,number2,...   are 1 to 30 arguments for which you want to calculate the sum of squared deviations. You can also use a single array or a reference to an array instead of arguments separated by commas.

Remarks
- The arguments should be numbers, or names, arrays, or references that contain numbers.
- If an array or reference argument contains text, logical values, or empty cells, those values are ignored; however, cells with the value zero are included.
- The equation for the sum of squared deviations is:

$$DEVSQ = \sum (x - \bar{x})^2$$

Example   DEVSQ(4,5,8,7,11,4,3) equals 48

Related Functions

AVEDEV	Returns the average of the absolute deviations of data points from their mean
STDEV	Estimates standard deviation based on a sample
STDEVP	Calculates standard deviation based on the entire population
VAR	Estimates variance based on a sample
VARP	Calculates variance based on the entire population

List of Statistical Functions

DGET

Extracts single values from a database. Use DGET to extract a single field that matches the criteria from a database. For more information about Microsoft Excel database functions, see "Database Functions".

Syntax   **DGET(database**, **field**, **criteria**)

Database   is the range of cells that make up the database.

Field   indicates which field is used in the function.

Criteria   is the range of cells that contains the database criteria.

Remarks

- If no record matches the criteria, DGET returns the #VALUE! error value.
- If more than one record matches the criteria, DGET returns the #NUM! error value.

Related Functions   List of Database & List Management Functions

DISC

Returns the discount rate for a security.

If this function is not available, run the Setup program to install the Analysis ToolPak. After you install the Analysis ToolPak, you must select it in the Add-In Manager. For more information, look up Add-ins in Help.

Syntax   **DISC(settlement, maturity, pr, redemption**, basis)

Settlement   is the security's settlement date, expressed as a serial date number.

Maturity   is the security's maturity date, expressed as a serial date number.

Pr   is the security's price per $100 face value.

Redemption   is the security's redemption value per $100 face value.

Basis   is the type of day count basis to use.

Basis	Day count basis
0 or omitted	US (NASD) 30/360
1	Actual/actual
2	Actual/360
3	Actual/365
4	European 30/360

Remarks

- Settlement, maturity, and basis are truncated to integers.
- If any argument is non-numeric, DISC returns the #VALUE! error value.
- If settlement or maturity is not a valid serial date number, DISC returns the #NUM! error value.

- If pr ≤ 0 or if redemption ≤ 0, DISC returns the #NUM! error value.
- If basis < 0 or if basis > 4, DISC returns the #NUM! error value.
- If settlement ≥ maturity, DISC returns the #NUM! error value.
- DISC is calculated as follows:

$$DISC = \frac{redemption - par}{par} \times \frac{B}{DSM}$$

Where:

B = number of days in a year, depending on the year basis.

DSM = number of days detween settlement and maturity.

Example

A bond has the following terms:

February 15, 1993 settlement date
June 10, 1993 maturity date
$97.975 price
$100 redemption value
Actual/360 basis

The bond discount rate (in the 1900 Date System) is:

DISC(34015,34130,97.975,100,2) equals 0.063391 or 6.3391%

Related Functions

DATE	Returns the serial number of a particular date
PRICEDISC	Returns the price per $100 face value of a discounted security
YIELDDISC	Returns the annual yield for a discounted security

List of Financial Functions

DMAX

Returns the largest number in the field column of records in the database that match the criteria. For more information about Microsoft Excel database functions, see "Database Functions".

Syntax

DMAX(database, field, criteria)

Database   is the range of cells that make up the database.

Field   indicates which field is used in the function.

Criteria   is the range of cells that contains the database criteria.

Related Functions   List of Database & List Management Functions

DMIN

Returns the smallest number in the field column of records in the database that match the criteria. For more information about Microsoft Excel database functions, see "Database Functions".

Syntax   **DMIN(database, field, criteria)**

Database   is the range of cells that make up the database.

Field   indicates which field is used in the function.

Criteria   is the range of cells that contains the database criteria.

Related Functions   List of Database & List Management Functions

DOLLAR

Converts a number to text using currency format, with the decimals rounded to the specified place. The format used is $#,##0.00_);($#,##0.00).

Syntax   **DOLLAR(number, decimals)**

Number   is a number, a reference to a cell containing a number, or a formula that evaluates to a number.

Decimals   is the number of digits to the right of the decimal point. If decimals is negative, number is rounded to the left of the decimal point. If you omit decimals, it is assumed to be 2.

Remarks   The major difference between formatting a cell containing a number with the Cells command from the Format menu and formatting a number directly with the DOLLAR function is that DOLLAR converts its result to text. A number formatted with the Cells command is still a number. You can continue to use numbers formatted with DOLLAR in formulas, because Microsoft Excel converts numbers entered as text values to numbers when it calculates.

Examples	DOLLAR(1234.567, 2) equals "$1234.57"	
	DOLLAR(1234.567, -2) equals "$1200"	
	DOLLAR(-1234.567, -2) equals "($1200)"	
	DOLLAR(-0.123, 4) equals "($0.1230)"	
	DOLLAR(99.888) equals "$99.89"	
Related Functions	FIXED	Formats a number as text with a fixed number of decimals
	TEXT	Formats a number and converts it to text
	VALUE	Converts a text argument to a number
	List of Text Functions	

DOLLARDE

Converts a dollar price expressed as a fraction into a dollar price expressed as a decimal number. Use DOLLARDE to convert fractional dollar numbers, such as securities prices, to decimal numbers.

If this function is not available, run the Setup program to install the Analysis ToolPak. After you install the Analysis ToolPak, you must select it in the Add-In Manager. For more information, look up Add-ins in Help.

Syntax

DOLLARDE(fractional_dollar, fraction)

Fractional_dollar   is a number expressed as a fraction.

Fraction   is the integer to use in the denominator of the fraction.

Remarks

- If either argument is non-numeric, DOLLARDE returns the #VALUE! error value.
- If fraction is not an integer, it is truncated.
- If fraction ≤ 0, DOLLARDE returns the #NUM! error value.

Examples

DOLLARDE(1.02,16) equals 1.125

DOLLARDE(1.1,8) equals 1.125

Related Functions   DOLLAR   Converts a number to text, using currency format

DOLLARFR   Converts a dollar price, expressed as a decimal
                      number, into a dollar price, expressed as a fraction

List of Financial Functions

DOLLARFR

Converts a dollar price expressed as a decimal number into a dollar price expressed as a fraction. Use DOLLARFR to convert decimal numbers to fractional dollar numbers, such as securities prices.

If this function is not available, run the Setup program to install the Analysis ToolPak. After you install the Analysis ToolPak, you must select it in the Add-In Manager. For more information, look up Add-ins in Help.

Syntax   **DOLLARFR(decimal_dollar, fraction)**

Decimal_dollar   is a decimal number.

Fraction   is the integer to use in the denominator of a fraction.

Remarks
- If either argument is non-numeric, DOLLARFR returns the #VALUE! error value.
- If fraction is not an integer, it is truncated.
- If fraction ≤ 0, DOLLARFR returns the #NUM! error value.

Examples   DOLLARFR(1.125,16) equals 1.02

DOLLARFR(1.125,8) equals 1.1

Related Functions   DOLLAR   Converts a number to text, using currency format

DOLLARDE   Converts a dollar price, expressed as a fraction,
                      into a dollar price, expressed as a decimal number

List of Financial Functions

DPRODUCT

Multiplies the values in the field column of records in the database that match the criteria. For more information about Microsoft Excel database functions, see "Database Functions".

Syntax   **DPRODUCT(database, field, criteria)**

Database   is the range of cells that make up the database.

Field   indicates which field is used in the function.

Criteria   is the range of cells that contains the database criteria.

Related Functions   List of Database & List Management Functions

---

DSTDEV

Estimates the standard deviation of a population based on a sample, using the numbers in the field column of records in the database that match the criteria. For more information about Microsoft Excel database functions, see "Database Functions".

Syntax   **DSTDEV(database, field, criteria)**

Database   is the range of cells that make up the database.

Field   indicates which field is used in the function.

Criteria   is the range of cells that contains the database criteria.

Related Functions   List of Database & List Management Functions

---

DSTDEVP

Calculates the standard deviation of a population based on the entire population, using the numbers in the field column of records in the database that match the criteria. For more information about Microsoft Excel database functions, see "Database Functions".

Syntax   **DSTDEVP(database, field, criteria)**

Database   is the range of cells that make up the database.

Field   indicates which field is used in the function.

Criteria   is the range of cells that contains the database criteria.

Related Functions   List of Database & List Management Functions

DSUM

Adds the numbers in the field column of records in the database that match the criteria. For more information about Microsoft Excel database functions, see "Database Functions".

Syntax   **DSUM(database, field, criteria)**

Database   is the range of cells that make up the database.

Field   indicates which field is used in the function.

Criteria   is the range of cells that contains the database criteria.

Related Functions   SUMIF   Adds the cells specified by a given criteria

List of Database & List Management Functions

DURATION

Returns the annual duration of a security with periodic interest payments. Duration is defined as the weighted average of the present value of the cash flows, and is used as a measure of a bond price's response to changes in yield.

If this function is not available, run the Setup program to install the Analysis ToolPak. After you install the Analysis ToolPak, you must select it in the Add-In Manager. For more information, look up Add-ins in Help.

Syntax   **DURATION(settlement, maturity, coupon, yld, frequency,** basis)

Settlement   is the security's settlement date, expressed as a serial date number.

Maturity   is the security's maturity date, expressed as a serial date number.

Coupon   is the security's annual coupon rate.

Yld   is the security's annual yield.

Frequency   is the number of coupon payments per year. For annual payments, frequency = 1; for semiannual, frequency = 2; for quarterly, frequency = 4.

Basis   is the type of day count basis to use.

Basis	Day count basis
0 or omitted	US (NASD) 30/360
1	Actual/actual
2	Actual/360
3	Actual/365
4	European 30/360

Remarks

- Settlement, maturity, frequency, and basis are truncated to integers.
- If any argument is non-numeric, DURATION returns the #VALUE! error value.
- If settlement or maturity is not a valid serial date number, DURATION returns the #NUM! error value.
- If coupon < 0 or if yld < 0, DURATION returns the #NUM! error value.
- If frequency is any number other than 1, 2, or 4, DURATION returns the #NUM! error value.
- If basis < 0 or if basis > 4, DURATION returns the #NUM! error value.
- If settlement ≥ maturity, DURATION returns the #NUM! error value.

Example

A bond has the following terms:

January 1, 1986 settlement date
January 1, 1994 maturity date
8% coupon
9.0% yield
Frequency is semiannual
Actual/actual basis

The duration (in the 1900 Date System) is:

DURATION(31413,34335,0.08,0.09,2,1) equals 5.993775

Related Functions

| DATE | Returns the serial number of a particular date |
| MDURATION | Returns the Macauley modified duration for a security with an assumed par value of $100 |

List of Financial Functions

DVAR

Estimates the variance of a population based on a sample, using the numbers in the field column of records in the database that match the criteria. For more information about Microsoft Excel database functions, see "Database Functions".

Syntax

DVAR(database, field, criteria)

Database   is the range of cells that make up the database.

Field   indicates which field is used in the function.

Criteria   is the range of cells that contains the database criteria.

Related Functions   List of Database & List Management Functions

---

DVARP

Calculates the variance of a population based on the entire population, using the numbers in the field column of records in the database that match the criteria. For more information about Microsoft Excel database functions, see "Database Functions".

Syntax

DVARP(database, field, criteria)

Database   is the range of cells that make up the database.

Field   indicates which field is used in the function.

Criteria   is the range of cells that contains the database criteria.

Related Functions   List of Database & List Management Functions

EDATE

Returns the serial number date that is the indicated number of months before or after start_date. Use EDATE to calculate maturity dates or due dates that fall on the same day of the month as the date of issue.

If this function is not available, run the Setup program to install the Analysis ToolPak. After you install the Analysis ToolPak, you must select it in the Add-In Manager. For more information, look up Add-ins in Help.

Syntax

EDATE(start_date, months)

Start_date   is a serial date number that represents the start date.

Months   is the number of months before or after start_date. A positive value for months yields a future date; a negative value yields a past date.

Remarks

- If either argument is non-numeric, EDATE returns the #VALUE! error value.
- If start_date is not a valid serial date number, EDATE returns the #NUM! error value.
- If months is not an integer, it is truncated.

Examples

EDATE(DATEVALUE("01/15/91"),1) equals 33284 or 02/15/91

EDATE(DATEVALUE("03/31/91"),-1) equals 33297 or 02/28/91

Related Functions

DATE	Returns the serial number of a particular date
EOMONTH	Returns the serial number date for the last day of the month before or after a specified number of months
NETWORKDAYS	Returns the number of whole workdays between two dates
WORKDAY	Returns the serial number of the date before or after a specified number of workdays

List of Date & Time Functions

EFFECT

Returns the effective annual interest rate, given the nominal annual interest rate and the number of compounding periods per year.

If this function is not available, run the Setup program to install the Analysis ToolPak. After you install the Analysis ToolPak, you must select it in the Add-In Manager. For more information, look up Add-ins in Help.

Syntax	**EFFECT(nominal_rate, npery)**

Nominal_rate   is the nominal interest rate.

Npery   is the number of compounding periods per year.

Remarks
- Npery is truncated to an integer.
- If either argument is non-numeric, EFFECT returns the #VALUE! error value.
- If nominal_rate ≤ 0 or if npery < 1, EFFECT returns the #NUM! error value.
- EFFECT is calculated as follows:

$$EFFECT = (1 + \frac{Nominal\_Rate}{Npery})^{Npery} - 1$$

Example   EFFECT(5.25%,4) equals 0.053543 or 5.3543%

Related Function   NOMINAL   Returns the annual nominal interest rate

List of Financial Functions

EOMONTH

Returns the serial number date for the last day of the month that is the indicated number of months before or after start_date. Use EOMONTH to calculate maturity dates or due dates that fall on the last day of the month.

If this function is not available, run the Setup program to install the Analysis ToolPak. After you install the Analysis ToolPak, you must select it in the Add-In Manager. For more information, look up Add-ins in Help.

Syntax   **EOMONTH(start_date, months)**

Start_date   is a serial date number that represents the start date.

Months   is the number of months before or after start_date. A positive value for months yields a future date; a negative value yields a past date.

Remarks

- If either argument is non-numeric, EOMONTH returns the #VALUE! error value.

- If start_date is not a valid serial date number, EOMONTH returns the #NUM! error value.

- If months is not an integer, it is truncated.

- If start_date plus months yields an invalid serial date number, EOMONTH returns the #NUM! error value.

Examples

EOMONTH(DATEVALUE("01/01/93"), 1) equals 34028 or 2/28/93

EOMONTH(DATEVALUE("01/01/93"), -1) equals 33969 or 12/31/92

Related Functions

DATE	Returns the serial number of a particular date
EDATE	Returns the serial number of the date that is the indicated number of months before or after the start date
NETWORKDAYS	Returns the number of whole workdays between two dates
WORKDAY	Returns the serial number of the date before or after a specified number of workdays

List of Date & Time Functions

ERF

Returns the error function integrated between lower_limit and upper_limit.

If this function is not available, run the Setup program to install the Analysis ToolPak. After you install the Analysis ToolPak, you must select it in the Add-In Manager. For more information, look up Add-ins in Help.

Syntax

ERF(lower_limit, upper_limit)

Lower_limit   is the lower bound for integrating ERF.

Upper_limit   is the upper bound for integrating ERF. If omitted, ERF integrates between zero and lower_limit.

Remarks

- If lower_limit is non-numeric, ERF returns the #VALUE! error value.
- If lower_limit is negative, ERF returns the #NUM! error value.
- If upper_limit is non-numeric, ERF returns the #VALUE! error value.
- If upper_limit is negative, ERF returns the #NUM! error value.

$$ERF(z) = \frac{2}{\sqrt{\pi}} \int_0^z e^{-t^2} dt$$

$$ERF(a,b) = \frac{2}{\sqrt{\pi}} \int_a^b e^{-t^2} dt = ERF(b) - ERF(a)$$

Examples   ERF(0.74500) equals 0.70793

ERF(1) equals 0.84270

Related Function   ERFC   Returns the complementary error function

List of Engineering Functions

ERFC

Returns the complementary ERF function integrated between x and ∞.

If this function is not available, run the Setup program to install the Analysis ToolPak. After you install the Analysis ToolPak, you must select it in the Add-In Manager. For more information, look up Add-ins in Help.

Syntax   **ERFC(x)**

X   is the lower bound for integrating ERF.

Remarks   ▪ If x is non-numeric, ERFC returns the #VALUE! error value.
▪ If x is negative, ERFC returns the #NUM! error value.

$$ERFC(x) = \frac{2}{\sqrt{\pi}} \int_x^\infty e^{-t^2} dt = 1 - ERF(x)$$

Example   ERFC(1) equals 0.1573

Related Function   ERF   Returns the error function

List of Engineering Functions

ERROR.TYPE

Returns a number corresponding to one of Microsoft Excel's error values. Use ERROR.TYPE to determine what type of error occurred so that your macro can run an appropriate error-handling subroutine. ERROR.TYPE can also be used on a worksheet.

Syntax

ERROR.TYPE(error_val)

Error_val   is the error value whose identifying number you want to find. Although error_val can be the actual error value, it will usually be a reference to a cell containing a formula that you want to test.

If error_val is	ERROR.TYPE returns
#NULL!	1
#DIV/0!	2
#VALUE!	3
#REF!	4
#NAME?	5
#NUM!	6
#N/A	7
Anything else	#N/A

Example

The following macro formula checks the cell named Ratio to see if it contains a #DIV/0! error value. If it does, a subroutine named DivisionByZero is run.

```
IF(ERROR.TYPE(Ratio)=2,DivisionByZero())
```

Related Functions

ISERR	Returns TRUE if the value is any error value except #N/A
ISERROR	Returns TRUE if the value is any error value

List of Information Functions

EVEN

Returns number rounded up to the nearest even integer. You can use this function for processing items that come in twos. For example, a packing crate accepts rows of one or two items. The crate is full when the number of items, rounded up to the nearest two, matches the crate's capacity.

Syntax	**EVEN(number)**
	Number is the value to round.
Remarks	▪ If number is non-numeric, EVEN returns the #VALUE! error value.
	▪ Regardless of the sign of number, a value is rounded up when adjusted away from zero. If number is an even integer, no rounding occurs.
Examples	EVEN(1.5) equals 2
	EVEN(3) equals 4
	EVEN(2) equals 2
	EVEN(-1) equals –2

Related Functions

CEILING	Returns the number rounded up to the nearest multiple of significance
FLOOR	Rounds a number down, toward zero
INT	Rounds a number down to the nearest integer
ISEVEN	Returns TRUE if the number is even
ISODD	Returns TRUE if the number is odd
ODD	Rounds a number up to the nearest odd integer
ROUND	Rounds a number to a specified number of digits
TRUNC	Truncates a number to an integer

List of Math & Trigonometry Functions

EXACT

Compares two text strings and returns TRUE if they are exactly the same, FALSE otherwise. EXACT is case-sensitive but ignores formatting differences. Use EXACT to test text being entered onto a document.

Syntax	**EXACT(text1, text2)**
	Text1 is the first text string.
	Text2 is the second text string.

Examples	EXACT("word", "word") equals TRUE	

EXACT("Word", "word") equals FALSE

EXACT("w ord", "word") equals FALSE

To make sure that a user-entered value matches a value in a range, enter the following formula as an array in a cell. To enter a formula as an array in a single cell, press CTRL+SHIFT+ENTER (in Microsoft Excel for Windows) or COMMAND+ENTER (in Microsoft Excel for the Macintosh). The name TestValue refers to a cell containing a user-entered value; the name CompareRange refers to a list of text values to be checked.

{=OR(EXACT(TestValue, CompareRange))}

Related Functions	DELTA	Tests whether two values are equal
	LEN	Returns the number of characters in a text string
	SEARCH	Finds one text value within another (not case-sensitive)

List of Text Functions

EXP

Returns e raised to the power of number. The constant e equals 2.71828182845904, the base of the natural logarithm.

Syntax

EXP(number)

Number   is the exponent applied to the base e.

Remarks

- To calculate powers of other bases, use the exponentiation operator (^).
- EXP is the inverse of LN, the natural logarithm of number.

Examples

EXP(1) equals 2.718282 (the approximate value of e)

EXP(2) equals e^2, or 7.389056

EXP(LN(3)) equals 3

Related Functions	IMEXP	Returns the exponential of a complex number
	LN	Returns the natural logarithm of a number
	LOG	Returns the logarithm of a number to a specified base
	POWER	Returns the result of number raised to power

List of Math & Trigonometry Functions

EXPONDIST

Returns the exponential distribution. Use EXPONDIST to model the time between events, such as how long an automated bank teller takes to deliver cash. For example, you can use EXPONDIST to determine the probability that the process takes at most one minute.

Syntax

EXPONDIST(x, lambda, cumulative)

X   is the value of the function.

Lambda   is the parameter value.

Cumulative   is a logical value that indicates which form of the exponential function to provide. If cumulative is TRUE, EXPONDIST returns the cumulative distribution function; if FALSE, it returns the probability density function.

Remarks

- If x or lambda is non-numeric, EXPONDIST returns the #VALUE! error value.
- If x < 0, EXPONDIST returns the #NUM! error value.
- If lambda ≤ 0, EXPONDIST returns the #NUM! error value.
- The equation for the probability density function is:

$$f(x;\lambda) = \lambda e^{-\lambda x}$$

- The equation for the cumulative distribution function is:

$$F(x;\lambda) = 1 - e^{-\lambda x}$$

Examples

EXPONDIST(0.2,10,TRUE) equals 0.864665

EXPONDIST(0.2,10,FALSE) equals 1.353353

Related Functions

GAMMADIST	Returns the gamma distribution
POISSON	Returns the Poisson probability distribution

List of Statistical Functions

FACT

Returns the factorial of a number. The factorial of a number is equal to 1*2*3*...* number.

Syntax

FACT(number)

Number   is the nonnegative number you want the factorial of. If number is not an integer, it is truncated.

Examples

FACT(1) equals 1

FACT(1.9) equals FACT(1) equals 1

FACT(0) equals 1

FACT(-1) equals #NUM!

FACT(5) equals 1*2*3*4*5 equals 120

Related Functions

DPRODUCT	Multiplies the values in a particular field of records that match the criteria in a database
FACTDOUBLE	Returns the double factorial of a number
PRODUCT	Multiplies its arguments

Returns the Poisson probability distributionList of Math & Trigonometry Functions

---

FACTDOUBLE

Returns the double factorial of a number.

If this function is not available, run the Setup program to install the Analysis ToolPak. After you install the Analysis ToolPak, you must select it in the Add-In Manager. For more information, look up Add-ins in Help.

Syntax

FACTDOUBLE(number)

Number   is the value for which to return the double factorial. If number is not an integer, it is truncated.

Remarks	■ If number is non-numeric, FACTDOUBLE returns the #VALUE! error value.
	■ If number is negative, FACTDOUBLE returns the #NUM! error value.
	■ If number is even:

$$n!! = n(n-2)(n-4)\ldots(4)(2)$$

■ If number is odd:

$$n!! = n(n-2)(n-4)\ldots(3)(1)$$

Examples	FACTDOUBLE(6) equals 48
	FACTDOUBLE(7) equals 105

Related Functions	FACT	Returns the factorial of a number
	MULTINOMIAL	Returns the multinomial of a set of numbers

List of Math & Trigonometry Functions

FALSE

Returns the logical value FALSE.

Syntax	**FALSE( )**
Remarks	You can also type the word FALSE directly into the worksheet or formula, and Microsoft Excel interprets it as the logical value FALSE.
Related Functions	List of Logical Functions

FDIST

Returns the F probability distribution. You can use this function to determine whether two data sets have different degrees of diversity. For example, you can examine test scores given to men and women entering high school and determine if the variability in the females is different from that found in the males.

Syntax	**FDIST(x, degrees_freedom1, degrees_freedom2)**

X   is the value at which to evaluate the function.

Degrees_freedom1   is the numerator degrees of freedom.

Degrees_freedom2   is the denominator degrees of freedom.

Remarks
- If any argument is non-numeric, FDIST returns the #VALUE! error value.
- If x is negative, FDIST returns the #NUM! error value.
- If degrees_freedom1 or degrees_freedom2 is not an integer, it is truncated.
- If degrees_freedom1 < 1 or degrees_freedom1 $\geq 10^{10}$, FDIST returns the #NUM! error value.
- If degrees_freedom2 < 1 or degrees_freedom2 $\geq 10^{10}$, FDIST returns the #NUM! error value.
- FDIST is calculated as FDIST = P(F<x), where F is a random variable that has an F distribution.

Example FDIST(15.20675,6,4) equals 0.01

Related Functions

FINV	Returns the inverse of the F probability distribution
FTEST	Returns the results of an F-test

List of Statistical Functions

FIND

Finds one string of text within another string of text and returns the number of the character at which find_text first occurs. You can also use SEARCH to find one string of text within another, but unlike SEARCH, FIND is case-sensitive and doesn't allow wildcard characters.

Syntax **FIND(find_text, within_text, start_num)**

Find_text   is the text you want to find.

- If find_text is "" (empty text), FIND matches the first character in the search string (that is, the character numbered start_num or 1).
- Find_text cannot contain any wildcard characters.

Within_text   is the text containing the text you want to find.

Start_num   specifies the character at which to start the search. The first character in within_text is character number 1. If you omit start_num, it is assumed to be 1.

Remarks

- If find_text does not appear in within_text, FIND returns the #VALUE! error value.
- If start_num is not greater than zero, FIND returns the #VALUE! error value.
- If start_num is greater than the length of within_text, FIND returns the #VALUE! error value.

Examples

`FIND("M","Miriam McGovern")` equals 1

`FIND("m","Miriam McGovern")` equals 6

`FIND("M","Miriam McGovern",3)` equals 8

Suppose you have a list of parts and serial numbers in a worksheet, and you want to extract the names of the parts, but not the serial numbers, from each cell. You can use the FIND function to find the # symbol, and the MID function to omit the serial number. A2:A4 contain the following parts with serial numbers, respectively: "Ceramic Insulators #124-TD45-87", "Copper Coils #12-671-6772", "Variable Resistors #116010".

`MID(A2,1,FIND(" #",A2,1)-1)` returns "Ceramic Insulators"

`MID(A3,1,FIND(" #",A3,1)-1)` returns "Copper Coils"

`MID(A4,1,FIND(" #",A4,1)-1)` returns "Variable Resistors"

Related Functions

EXACT	Checks to see if two text values are identical
LEN	Returns the number of characters in a text string
MID	Returns a specific number of characters from a text string
SEARCH	Finds one text value within another (not case-sensitive)

List of Text Functions

FINV

Returns the inverse of the F probability distribution. If p = FDIST(x,...), then FINV(p,...) = x.

The F distribution can be used in an F-test that compares the degree of variability in two data sets. For example, you can analyze income distributions in the United States and Canada to determine whether the two countries have a similar degree of diversity.

Syntax   **FINV(probability, degrees_freedom1, degrees_freedom2)**

Probability   is a probability associated with the F cumulative distribution.

Degrees_freedom1   is the numerator degrees of freedom.

Degrees_freedom2   is the denominator degrees of freedom.

Remarks
- If any argument is non-numeric, FINV returns the #VALUE! error value.
- If probability < 0 or probability > 1, FINV returns the #NUM! error value.
- If degrees_freedom1 or degrees_freedom2 is not an integer, it is truncated.
- If degrees_freedom1 < 1 or degrees_freedom1 $\geq$ 10^10, FINV returns the #NUM! error value.
- If degrees_freedom2 < 1 or degrees_freedom2 $\geq$ 10^10, FINV returns the #NUM! error value.

FINV can be used to return critical values from the F distribution. For example, the output of an ANOVA calculation often includes data for the F statistic, F probability, and F critical value at the 0.05 significance level. To return the critical value of F, use the significance level as the probability argument to FINV.

FINV uses an iterative technique for calculating the function. Given a probability value, FINV iterates until the result is accurate to within $\pm$ 3x10^-7. If FINV does not converge after 100 iterations, the function returns the #N/A error value.

Example   FINV(0.01,6,4) equals 15.20675

Related Functions   FDIST   Returns the F probability distribution

FTEST   Returns the result of an F-test

List of Statistical Functions

FISHER

Returns the Fisher transformation at x. This transformation produces a function that is approximately normally distributed rather than skewed. Use this function to perform hypothesis testing on the correlation coefficient.

Syntax   **FISHER(x)**

X   is a numeric value for which you want the transformation.

Remarks
- If x is non-numeric, FISHER returns the #VALUE! error value.
- If $x \leq -1$ or if $x \geq 1$, FISHER returns the #NUM! error value.

The equation for the Fisher transformation is:

$$z' = \frac{1}{2} \ln\left(\frac{1+x}{1-x}\right)$$

Example   FISHER(0.75) equals 0.972955

Related Functions

CORREL	Returns the correlation coefficient between two data sets
COVAR	Returns covariance, the average of the products of paired deviations
FISHERINV	Returns the inverse of the Fisher transformation

List of Statistical Functions

FISHERINV

Returns the inverse of the Fisher transformation. Use this transformation when analyzing correlations between ranges or arrays of data. If y = FISHER(x), then FISHERINV(y) = x.

Syntax   **FISHERINV(y)**

Y   is the value for which you want to perform the inverse of the transformation.

Remarks
- If y is non-numeric, FISHERINV returns the #VALUE! error value.

The equation for the inverse of the Fisher transformation is:

$$x = \frac{e^{2y} - 1}{e^{2y} + 1}$$

Example   FISHERINV(0.972955) equals 0.75

Related Functions

CORREL	Returns the correlation coefficient between two data sets
COVAR	Returns covariance, the average of the products of paired deviations
FISHER	Returns the Fisher transformation

List of Statistical Functions

FIXED

Rounds a number to the specified number of decimals, formats the number in decimal format using a period and commas, and returns the result as text.

Syntax

FIXED(number, decimals, no_commas)

Number   is the number you want to round and convert to text.

Decimals   is the number of digits to the right of the decimal point.

No_commas   is a logical value that, if TRUE, prevents FIXED from including commas in the returned text. If no_commas is FALSE or omitted, then the returned text includes commas as usual.

- Numbers in Microsoft Excel can never have more than 15 significant digits, but decimals can be as large as 127.
- If decimals is negative, number is rounded to the left of the decimal point.
- If you omit decimals, it is assumed to be 2.

Remarks

The major difference between formatting a cell containing a number with the Cells command from the Format menu and formatting a number directly with the FIXED function is that FIXED converts its result to text. A number formatted with the Cells command is still a number.

Examples

FIXED(1234.567, 1) equals "1234.6"

FIXED(1234.567, -1) equals "1230"

FIXED(-1234.567, -1) equals "–1230"

FIXED(44.332) equals "44.33"

Related Functions

DOLLAR	Converts a number to text, using currency format
ROUND	Rounds a number to a specified number of digits
TEXT	Formats a number and converts it to text
VALUE	Converts a text argument to a number

List of Text Functions

FLOOR

Rounds number down, toward zero, to the nearest multiple of significance.

Syntax

FLOOR(number, significance)

Number   is the numeric value you want to round.

Significance   is the multiple to which you want to round.

Remarks

- If either argument is non-numeric, FLOOR returns the #VALUE! error value.
- If number and significance have different signs, FLOOR returns the #NUM! error value.
- Regardless of the sign of number, a value is rounded down when adjusted away from zero. If number is an exact multiple of significance, no rounding occurs.

Examples

FLOOR(2.5, 1) equals 2

FLOOR(-2.5, -2) equals –2

FLOOR(-2.5, 2) equals #NUM!

FLOOR(1.5, 0.1) equals 1.5

FLOOR(0.234, 0.01) equals 0.23

Related Functions

CEILING	Returns the number rounded up to the nearest multiple of significance
EVEN	Rounds a number up to the nearest even integer
INT	Rounds a number down to the nearest integer
ODD	Rounds a number up to the nearest odd integer
ROUND	Rounds a number to a specified number of digits
ROUNDDOWN	Rounds a number down, towards zero
ROUNDUP	Rounds a number up, away from zero
TRUNC	Truncates a number to an integer

List of Math & Trigonometry Functions

FORECAST

Returns a predicted value for x based on a linear regression of known x- and y-arrays or ranges of data. You can use this function to predict future sales, inventory requirements, or consumer trends.

Syntax

FORECAST(x, known_y's, known_x's)

X   is the data point for which you want to predict a value.

Known_y's   is the dependent array or range of data.

Known_x's   is the independent array or range of data.

Remarks

- If x is non-numeric, FORECAST returns the #VALUE! error value.
- If known_y's and known_x's are empty or contain a different number of data points, FORECAST returns the #N/A error value.
- If the variance of known_x's equals zero, then FORECAST returns the #DIV/0! error value.
- The equation for FORECAST is a+bx, where:

$$a = \overline{Y} - b\overline{X}$$

and:

$$b = \frac{n\Sigma xy - (\Sigma x)(\Sigma y)}{n\Sigma x^2 - (\Sigma x)^2}$$

Example

FORECAST(30,{6,7,9,15,21},{20,28,31,38,40}) equals 10.60725

Related Functions

GROWTH	Returns values along an exponential trend
LINEST	Returns the parameters of a linear trend
LOGEST	Returns the parameters of an exponential trend
TREND	Returns values along a linear trend

List of Statistical Functions

FREQUENCY

Returns a frequency distribution as a vertical array. For a given set of values and a given set of bins (or intervals), a frequency distribution counts how many of the values occur in each interval.

Syntax

FREQUENCY(data_array, bins_array)

Data_array   is an array of or reference to a set of values for which you want to count frequencies. If data_array contains no values, FREQUENCY returns an array of zeros.

Bins_array   is an array of or reference to intervals into which you want to group the values in data_array. If bins_array contains no values, FREQUENCY returns the number of elements in data_array.

Remarks

- FREQUENCY is entered as an array formula after selecting a range of adjacent cells into which you want the returned distribution to appear.

- The number of elements in the returned array is one more than the number of elements in bins_array.

- FREQUENCY ignores blank cells and text.

- Formulas that return arrays must be entered as array formulas.

Example

Suppose a worksheet lists scores for a test. The scores are 79, 85, 78, 85, 83, 81, 95, 88, 97, and are entered into A1:A9, respectively. The data_array would contain a column of these test scores. The Bins_array would be another column of intervals by which the test scores are grouped. In this example, Bins_array would be C4:C6 and would contain the values 70, 79, 89. When entered as an array, you could use FREQUENCY to count the number of scores corresponding to the letter grade ranges 0-70, 71-79, 80-89, and 90-100.This example assumes all test scores are integers. The following formula is entered as an array formula after selecting four vertical cells adjacent to your data.

FREQUENCY(A1:A9,C4:C6) equals {0;2;5;2}

Related Functions

COUNT	Counts how many numbers are in the list of arguments
DCOUNT	Counts the cells containing numbers from a specified database and criteria

List of Statistical Functions

FTEST

Returns the result of an F-test. An F-test returns the one-tailed probability that the variances in array1 and array2 are not significantly different. Use this function to determine if two samples have different variances. For example, given test scores from public and private schools, you can test if these schools have different levels of diversity.

Syntax

FTEST(array1, array2)

Array1   is the first array or range of data.

Array2   is the second array or range of data.

Remarks

- The arguments should be numbers, or names, arrays, or references that contain numbers.

- If an array or reference argument contains text, logical values, or empty cells, those values are ignored; however, cells with the value zero are included.

- If the number of data points in array1 or array2 is less than 2, or if the variance of array1 or array2 is zero, FTEST returns the #DIV/0! error value.

Example

FTEST({6,7,9,15,21},{20,28,31,38,40}) equals 0.648318

Related Functions

FDIST   Returns the F probability distribution

FINV   Returns the inverse of the F probability distribution

List of Statistical Functions

FV

Returns the future value of an investment based on periodic, constant payments and a constant interest rate.

Syntax

FV(rate, nper, pmt, pv, type)

For a more complete description of the arguments in FV and for more information on annuity functions, see PV.

Rate   is the interest rate per period.

Nper   is the total number of payment periods in an annuity.

Pmt   is the payment made each period; it cannot change over the life of the annuity. Typically, pmt contains principal and interest but no other fees or taxes.

Pv   is the present value, or the lump-sum amount that a series of future payments is worth right now. If pv is omitted, it is assumed to be 0.

Type   is the number 0 or 1 and indicates when payments are due. If type is omitted, it is assumed to be 0.

Set type equal to	If payments are due
0	At the end of the period
1	At the beginning of the period

Remarks

- Make sure that you are consistent about the units you use for specifying rate and nper. If you make monthly payments on a four-year loan at 12 percent annual interest, use 12%/12 for rate and 4*12 for nper. If you make annual payments on the same loan, use 12% for rate and 4 for nper.

- For all the arguments, cash you pay out, such as deposits to savings, is represented by negative numbers; cash you receive, such as dividend checks, is represented by positive numbers.

Examples

FV(0.5%, 10, -200, -500, 1) equals $2581.40

FV(1%, 12, -1000) equals $12,682.50

FV(11%/12, 35, -2000, , 1) equals $82,846.25

Suppose you want to save money for a special project occurring a year from now. You deposit $1000 into a savings account that earns 6 percent annual interest compounded monthly (monthly interest of 6%/12, or 0.5%). You plan to deposit $100 at the beginning of every month for the next 12 months. How much money will be in the account at the end of 12 months?

FV(0.5%, 12, -100, -1000, 1) equals $2301.40

Related Functions

FVSCHEDULE	Returns the future value of an initial principal after applying a series of compound interest rates
IPMT	Returns the interest payment for an investment for a given period
NPER	Returns the number of periods for an investment
PMT	Returns the periodic payment for an annuity
PPMT	Returns the payment on the principal for an investment for a given period
PV	Returns the present value of an investment
RATE	Returns the interest rate per period of an annuity

List of Financial Functions

FVSCHEDULE

Returns the future value of an initial principal after applying a series of compound interest rates. Use FVSCHEDULE to calculate future value of an investment with a variable or adjustable rate.

If this function is not available, run the Setup program to install the Analysis ToolPak. After you install the Analysis ToolPak, you must select it in the Add-In Manager. For more information, look up Add-ins in Help.

Syntax

FVSCHEDULE(principal, schedule)

Principal   is the present value.

Schedule   is an array of interest rates to apply.

Remarks

- If principal is non-numeric, FVSCHEDULE returns the #VALUE! error value.
- The values in schedule can be numbers or blank cells; any other value produces the #VALUE! error value for FVSCHEDULE. Blank cells are taken as zeros (no interest).

Example

FVSCHEDULE(1,{0.09,0.11,0.1}) equals 1.33089

Related Function

FV   Returns the future value of an investment

List of Financial Functions

GAMMADIST

Returns the gamma distribution. You can use this function to study variables that may have a skewed distribution. The gamma distribution is commonly used in queuing analysis.

Syntax

GAMMADIST(x, alpha, beta, cumulative)

X   is the value at which you want to evaluate the distribution.

Alpha   is a parameter to the distribution.

Beta   is a parameter to the distribution. If beta = 1, GAMMADIST returns the standard gamma distribution.

Cumulative   is a logical value that determines the form of the function. If cumulative is TRUE, GAMMADIST returns the cumulative distribution function; if FALSE, it returns the probability mass function.

Remarks
- If x, alpha, or beta is non-numeric, GAMMADIST returns the #VALUE! error value.
- If x < 0, GAMMADIST returns the #NUM! error value.
- If alpha ≤ 0 or if beta ≤ 0, GAMMADIST returns the #NUM! error value.
- The equation for the gamma distribution is:

$$f(x;\alpha,\beta) = \frac{1}{\beta^{\alpha}\Gamma(\alpha)} x^{\alpha-1} e^{-\frac{x}{\beta}}$$

The standard gamma distribution is:

$$f(x;\alpha) = \frac{x^{\alpha-1}e^{-x}}{\Gamma(\alpha)}$$

- When alpha = 1, GAMMADIST returns the exponential distribution with:

$$\lambda = \frac{1}{\beta}$$

- For a positive integer n, when alpha = n/2, beta = 2, and cumulative = TRUE, GAMMADIST returns (1 - CHIDIST(x)) with n degrees of freedom.
- When alpha is a positive integer, GAMMADIST is also known as the Erlang distribution.

Examples

GAMMADIST(10,9,2,FALSE) equals 0.032639

GAMMADIST(10,9,2,TRUE) equals 0.068094

Related Functions

CHIDIST	Returns the one-tailed probability of the chi-squared distribution
EXPONDIST	Returns the exponential distribution
GAMMAINV	Returns the inverse of the gamma cumulative distribution

List of Statistical Functions

GAMMAINV

Returns the inverse of the gamma cumulative distribution. If p = GAMMADIST(x,...), then GAMMAINV(p,...) = x

You can use this function to study a variable whose distribution may be skewed.

Syntax

GAMMAINV(probability, alpha, beta)

Probability   is the probability associated with the gamma distribution.

Alpha   is a parameter to the distribution.

Beta   is a parameter to the distribution. If beta = 1, GAMMAINV returns the standard gamma distribution.

Remarks

- If any argument is non-numeric, GAMMAINV returns the #VALUE! error value.

- If probability < 0 or probability > 1, GAMMAINV returns the #NUM! error value.

- If alpha ≤ 0 or if beta ≤ 0, GAMMAINV returns the #NUM! error value.

- If beta ≤ 0, GAMMAINV returns the #NUM! error value.

- GAMMAINV uses an iterative technique for calculating the function. Given a probability value, GAMMAINV iterates until the result is accurate to within $\pm 3 \times 10^{-7}$. If GAMMAINV does not converge after 100 iterations, the function returns the #N/A error value.

Example

GAMMAINV(0.068094,9,2) equals 10

Related Function

GAMMADIST   Returns the gamma distribution

List of Statistical Functions

GAMMALN

Returns the natural logarithm of the gamma function, $\Gamma(x)$.

Syntax

GAMMALN(x)

X   is the value for which you want to calculate GAMMALN.

Remarks
- If x is non-numeric, GAMMALN returns the #VALUE! error value.
- If x ≤ 0, GAMMALN returns the #NUM! error value.
- The number e raised to the GAMMALN(i) power, where i is an integer, returns the same result as (i − 1)!.
- GAMMALN is calculated as follows:

$$GAMMALN = LN(\Gamma(x))$$

where:

$$\Gamma(x) = \int_0^\infty e^{-u} u^{x-1} du$$

Examples

GAMMALN(4) equals 1.791759

EXP(GAMMALN(4)) equals 6 or (4 − 1)!

Related Function

FACT   Returns the factorial of a number

List of Statistical Functions

GCD

Returns the greatest common divisor of two or more integers. The greatest common divisor is the largest integer that divides both number1 and number2 without a remainder.

If this function is not available, run the Setup program to install the Analysis ToolPak. After you install the Analysis ToolPak, you must select it in the Add-In Manager. For more information, look up Add-ins in Help.

Syntax

GCD(number1, number2, ...)

Number1, number2,...   are 1 to 29 values. If any value is not an integer, it is truncated.

Remarks	■ If any argument is non-numeric, GCD returns the #VALUE! error value.
	■ If any argument is less than zero, GCD returns the #NUM! error value.
	■ One divides any value evenly.
	■ A prime number has only itself and one as even divisors.
Examples	GCD(5, 2) equals 1
	GCD(24, 36) equals 12
	GCD(7, 1) equals 1
	GCD(5, 0) equals 5
Related Function	LCM Returns the least common multiple

List of Math & Trigonometry Functions

GEOMEAN

	Returns the geometric mean of an array or range of positive data. For example, you can use GEOMEAN to calculate average growth rate given compound interest with variable rates.
Syntax	**GEOMEAN(number1**, number2, ...)
	Number1,number2,... are 1 to 30 arguments for which you want to calculate the mean. You can also use a single array or a reference to an array instead of arguments separated by commas.
Remarks	■ The arguments should be numbers, or names, arrays, or references that contain numbers.
	■ If an array or reference argument contains text, logical values, or empty cells, those values are ignored; however, cells with the value zero are included.
	■ If any data point ≤ 0, GEOMEAN returns the #NUM! error value.
	■ The equation for the geometric mean is:

$$GM_{\bar{y}} = \sqrt[n]{y_1 y_2 y_3 \ldots y_n}$$

Example	GEOMEAN(4,5,8,7,11,4,3) equals 5.476987

Related Functions

AVERAGE	Returns the average of its arguments
HARMEAN	Returns the harmonic mean
MEDIAN	Returns the median of the given numbers
MODE	Returns the most common value in a data set
TRIMMEAN	Returns the mean of the interior of a data set

List of Statistical Functions

GESTEP

Returns 1 if number $\geq$ step; returns 0 otherwise. Use this function to filter a set of values. For example, by summing several GESTEP functions you calculate the count of values that exceed a threshold.

If this function is not available, run the Setup program to install the Analysis ToolPak. After you install the Analysis ToolPak, you must select it in the Add-In Manager. For more information, look up Add-ins in Help.

Syntax

GESTEP(number, step)

Number   is the value to test against step.

Step   is the threshold value. If you omit a value for step, GESTEP uses zero.

Remarks

If any argument is non-numeric, GESTEP returns the #VALUE! error value.

Examples

GESTEP(5, 4) equals 1

GESTEP(5, 5) equals 1

GESTEP(-4, -5) equals 1

GESTEP(-1, 0) equals 0

Related Function

DELTA	Tests whether two values are equal

List of Engineering Functions

GROWTH

Fits an exponential curve to the data known_y's and known_x's, and returns the y-values along that curve for the array of new_x's that you specify.

Syntax

GROWTH(known_y's, known_x's, new_x's, const)

Known_y's   is the set of y-values you already know in the relationship $y = b*m^x$.

- If the array known_y's is in a single column, then each column of known_x's is interpreted as a separate variable.

- If the array known_y's is in a single row, then each row of known_x's is interpreted as a separate variable.

- If any of the numbers in known_y's is 0 or negative, GROWTH returns the #NUM! error value.

Known_x's   is an optional set of x-values that you may already know in the relationship $y = b*m^x$.

- The array known_x's can include one or more sets of variables. If only one variable is used, known_y's and known_x's can be ranges of any shape, as long as they have equal dimensions. If more than one variable is used, known_y's must be a vector (that is, a range with a height of one row or a width of one column).

- If known_x's is omitted, it is assumed to be the array {1,2,3,...} that is the same size as known_y's.

New_x's   are new x-values for which you want GROWTH to return corresponding y-values.

- New_x's must include a column (or row) for each independent variable, just as known_x's does. So, if known_y's is in a single column, known_x's and new_x's should have the same number of columns. If known_y's is in a single row, known_x's and new_x's should have the same number of rows.

- If new_x's is omitted, it is assumed to be the same as known_x's.

- If both known_x's and new_x's are omitted, they are assumed to be the array {1,2,3,...} that is the same size as known_y's.

Const   is a logical value specifying whether to force the constant b to equal 1.

- If const is TRUE or omitted, b is calculated normally.

- If const is FALSE, b is set equal to 1 and the m-values are adjusted so that $y = m^x$.

Remarks

- Formulas that return arrays must be entered as array formulas after selecting the correct number of cells.

- When entering an array constant for an argument such as known_x's, use commas to separate values in the same row and semicolons to separate rows.

Examples

This example uses the same data as the LOGEST example. The sales for the 11th through the 16th months are 33,100, 47,300, 69,000, 102,000, 150,000, and 220,000 units, respectively. Assume that these values are entered into six cells named UnitsSold.

When entered as an array formula, the following macro formula predicts sales for months 17 and 18 based on sales for the previous six months:

GROWTH(UnitsSold,{11;12;13;14;15;16},{17;18}) equals {320,197;468,536}

If the exponential trend continues, sales for months 17 and 18 will be 320197 and 468536 units, respectively.

You could use other sequential numbers for the x-value arguments, and the predicted sales would be the same. For example, you could use the default value for known_x's, {1;2;3;4;5;6}:

GROWTH(UnitsSold,,{7;8},) equals {320197;468536}

Related Functions

LOGEST	Also calculates a regression curve, but returns the parameters of that curve instead of an array of y-values along the curve
TREND	Similar to GROWTH and LOGEST, but fits your data to a straight line
LINEST	Similar to GROWTH and LOGEST, but fits your data to a straight line

List of Statistical Functions

HARMEAN

Returns the harmonic mean of a data set. The harmonic mean is the reciprocal of the arithmetic mean of reciprocals.

Syntax

HARMEAN(number1, number2, ...)

Number1,number2,...   are 1 to 30 arguments for which you want to calculate the mean. You can also use a single array or a reference to an array instead of arguments separated by commas.

Remarks
- The arguments should be numbers, or names, arrays, or references that contain numbers.
- If an array or reference argument contains text, logical values, or empty cells, those values are ignored; however, cells with the value zero are included.
- If any data point ≤ 0, HARMEAN returns the #NUM! error value.
- The harmonic mean is always less than the geometric mean, which is always less than the arithmetic mean.
- The equation for the harmonic mean is:

$$\frac{1}{H_y} = \frac{1}{n} \sum \frac{1}{Y_i}$$

Example   HARMEAN(4,5,8,7,11,4,3) equals 5.028376

Related Functions

AVERAGE	Returns the average of its arguments
GEOMEAN	Returns the geometric mean
MEDIAN	Returns the median of the given numbers
MODE	Returns the most common value in a data set
TRIMMEAN	Returns the mean of the interior of a data set

List of Statistical Functions

HEX2BIN

Converts a hexadecimal number to binary.

If this function is not available, run the Setup program to install the Analysis ToolPak. After you install the Analysis ToolPak, you must select it in the Add-In Manager. For more information, look up Add-ins in Help.

Syntax   **HEX2BIN(number**, places)

Number   is the hexadecimal number you want to convert. Number may not contain more than 10 characters. The most significant bit of number is the sign bit (40th bit from the right). The remaining 9 bits are magnitude bits. Negative numbers are represented using two's-complement notation.

Places   is the number of characters to use. If places is omitted, HEX2BIN uses the minimum number of characters necessary. Places is useful for padding the return value with leading 0s (zeros).

Remarks
- If number is negative, HEX2BIN ignores places and returns a 10-character binary number.
- If number is negative, it cannot be less than FFFFFFFE00, and if number is positive, it cannot be greater than 1FF.
- If number is not a valid hexadecimal number, HEX2BIN returns the #NUM! error value.
- If HEX2BIN requires more than places characters, it returns the #NUM! error value.
- If places is not an integer, it is truncated.
- If places is non-numeric, HEX2BIN returns the #VALUE! error value.
- If places is negative, HEX2BIN returns the #NUM! error value.

Examples

HEX2BIN("F", 8) equals 00001111

HEX2BIN("B7") equals 10110111

HEX2BIN("FFFFFFFFFF") equals 1111111111

Related Functions

BIN2HEX	Converts a binary number to hexadecimal
DEC2HEX	Converts a decimal number to hexadecimal
OCT2HEX	Converts an octal number to hexadecimal

List of Engineering Functions

HEX2DEC

Converts a hexadecimal number to decimal.

If this function is not available, run the Setup program to install the Analysis ToolPak. After you install the Analysis ToolPak, you must select it in the Add-In Manager. For more information, look up Add-ins in Help.

Syntax

HEX2DEC(number)

Number   is the hexadecimal number you want to convert. Number may not contain more than 10 characters (40 bits). The most significant bit of number is the sign bit. The remaining 39 bits are magnitude bits. Negative numbers are represented using two's-complement notation.

Remarks

If number is not a valid hexadecimal number, HEX2DEC returns the #NUM! error value.

Examples   HEX2DEC("A5") equals 165

HEX2DEC("FFFFFFFF5B") equals −165

HEX2DEC("3DA408B9") equals 1034160313

Related Functions

BIN2HEX	Converts a binary number to hexadecimal
DEC2HEX	Converts a decimal number to hexadecimal
OCT2HEX	Converts an octal number to hexadecimal

List of Engineering Functions

HEX2OCT

Converts a hexadecimal number to octal.

If this function is not available, run the Setup program to install the Analysis ToolPak. After you install the Analysis ToolPak, you must select it in the Add-In Manager. For more information, look up Add-ins in Help.

Syntax   **HEX2OCT(number**, places)

Number   is the hexadecimal number you want to convert. Number may not contain more than 10 characters. The most significant bit of number is the sign bit. The remaining 39 bits are magnitude bits. Negative numbers are represented using two's-complement notation.

Places   is the number of characters to use. If places is omitted, HEX2OCT uses the minimum number of characters necessary. Places is useful for padding the return value with leading 0s (zeros).

Remarks

- If number is negative, HEX2OCT ignores places and returns a 10-character octal number.
- If number is negative, it cannot be less than FFE0000000, and if number is positive, it cannot be greater than 1FFFFFFF.
- If number is not a valid hexadecimal number, HEX2OCT returns the #NUM! error value.
- If HEX2OCT requires more than places characters, it returns the #NUM! error value.
- If places is not an integer, it is truncated.
- If places is non-numeric, HEX2OCT returns the #VALUE! error value.
- If places is negative, HEX2OCT returns the #NUM! error value.

Examples	HEX2OCT("F", 3) equals 017
	HEX2OCT("3B4E") equals 35516
	HEX2OCT("FFFFFFFF00") equals 7777777400

Related Functions	BIN2HEX	Converts a binary number to hexadecimal
	DEC2HEX	Converts a decimal number to hexadecimal
	OCT2HEX	Converts an octal number to hexadecimal

List of Engineering Functions

HLOOKUP

Searches the top row of an array for a particular value, and returns the value in the indicated cell. Use HLOOKUP when your comparison values are located in a row across the top of a table of data and you want to look down a specified number of rows. Use VLOOKUP when your comparison values are located in a column to the left or right of the data you want to find.

Syntax

HLOOKUP(lookup_value, table_array, row_index_num, range_lookup)

Lookup_value   is the value to be found in the first row of the table. Lookup_value can be a value, a reference, or a text string

Table_array   is a table of information in which data is looked up. Use a reference to a range or a range name.

- The values in the first row of table_array can be text, numbers, or logical values.

- If range_lookup is TRUE, the values in the first row of table_array must be placed in ascending order: ...–2, –1, 0, 1, 2,... , A-Z, FALSE, TRUE; otherwise, HLOOKUP may not give the correct value.

- Uppercase and lowercase text are equivalent.

- You can put values in ascending order by selecting the values, choosing the Sort command from the Data menu, and selecting Sort By Columns and Ascending.

Row_index_num   is the row number in table_array from which the matching value should be returned. A row_index_num of 1 returns the first row value in table_array, a row_index_num of 2 returns the second row value in table_array, and so on. If row_index_num is less than 1, HLOOKUP returns the #VALUE! error value; if row_index_num is greater than the number of rows on table_array, HLOOKUP returns the #REF! error value.

Range_lookup   Is a logical value that specifies whether you want HLOOKUP to find an exact match or an approximate match. If TRUE or omitted, an approximate match is returned; in other words, if an exact match is not found, the next largest value that is less than lookup_value is returned. If FALSE, HLOOKUP will find an exact match. If one is not found, the error value #N/A is returned.

Remarks

- If HLOOKUP can't find lookup_value, and range_lookup is TRUE, it uses the largest value that is less than lookup_value.

- If lookup_value is smaller than the smallest value in the first row of table_array, HLOOKUP returns the #N/A error value.

Examples

Suppose you have an inventory worksheet of auto parts. A1:A4 contain "Axles", 4, 5, 6. B1:B4 contain "Bearings", 4, 7, 8. C1:C4 contain "Bolts", 9, 10, 11.

HLOOKUP("Axles", A1:C4,2,TRUE) equals 4

HLOOKUP("Bearings",A1:C4,3,FALSE) equals 7

HLOOKUP("Bearings",A1:C4,3,TRUE) equals 7

HLOOKUP("Bolts",A1:C4,4,) equals 11

Table_array can also be an array constant:

HLOOKUP(3,{1,2,3;"a","b","c";"d","e","f"},2,TRUE) equals "c"

Related Functions

INDEX	Uses an index to choose a value from a reference or array
LOOKUP	Looks up values in either a vector or an array
MATCH	Looks up values in a reference or array
VLOOKUP	Looks in the first column of an array and moves across the row to return the value of a cell

List of Lookup & Reference Functions

HOUR

Returns the hour corresponding to serial_number. The hour is given as an integer, ranging from 0 (12:00 A.M.) to 23 (11:00 P.M.).

Syntax

HOUR(serial_number)

Serial_number   is the date-time code used by Microsoft Excel for date and time calculations. You can give serial_number as text, such as "16:48:00" or "4:48:00 PM", instead of as a number. The text is automatically converted to a serial number. For more information about serial numbers, see NOW.

Note   Microsoft Excel for Windows and Microsoft Excel for the Macintosh use different date systems as their default. For more information, see NOW.

Examples

HOUR(0.7) equals 16

HOUR(29747.7) equals 16

HOUR("3:30:30 PM") equals 15

Related Functions

NOW	Returns the serial number of the current date and time
YEAR, MONTH, DAY, WEEKDAY, HOUR, and MINUTE	Convert serial numbers into years, months, days, days of the week, hours, and minutes

List of Date & Time Functions

HYPGEOMDIST

Returns the hypergeometric distribution. HYPGEOMDIST returns the probability of a given number of sample successes, given the sample size, population successes, and population size. Use HYPGEOMDIST for problems with a finite population, where each observation is either a success or a failure, and where each subset of a given size is chosen with equal likelihood.

Syntax

HYPGEOMDIST(sample_s, number_sample, population_s, number_population)

Sample_s   is the number of successes in the sample.

Number_sample   is the size of the sample.

Population_s   is the number of successes in the population.

Number_population   is the population size.

Remarks

- All arguments are truncated to integers.
- If any argument is non-numeric, HYPGEOMDIST returns the #VALUE! error value.

- If sample_s < 0 or sample_s is greater than the lesser of number_sample or population_s, HYPGEOMDIST returns the #NUM! error value.

- If sample_s is less than the larger of 0 or (number_sample – number_population + population_s), HYPGEOMDIST returns the #NUM! error value.

- If number_sample < 0 or number_sample > number_population, HYPGEOMDIST returns the #NUM! error value.

- If population_s < 0 or population_s > number_population, HYPGEOMDIST returns the #NUM! error value.

- If number_population < 0, HYPGEOMDIST returns the #NUM! error value.

- The equation for the hypergeometric distribution is:

$$P(X = x) = h(x;n, M, N) = \frac{\binom{M}{x}\binom{N - M}{n - x}}{\binom{N}{n}}$$

where:

x = sample_s

n = number_sample

M = population_s

N = number_population

HYPGEOMDIST is used in sampling without replacement from a finite population.

Example

A sampler of chocolates contains 20 pieces. Eight pieces are caramels, and the remaining 12 are nuts. If a person selects 4 pieces at random, the following function returns the probability that exactly 1 piece is a caramel.

`HYPGEOMDIST(1,4,8,20)` equals 0.363261

Related Functions

BINOMDIST	Returns the individual term binomial distribution probability
COMBIN	Returns the number of combinations for a given number of objects
FACT	Returns the factorial of a number
NEGBINOMDIST	Returns the negative binomial distribution
PERMUT	Returns the number of permutations for a given number of objects

List of Statistical Functions

IF

Returns one value if logical_test evaluates to TRUE and another value if it evaluates to FALSE.

There are two syntax forms of the IF function. Syntax 1 can be used on worksheets and macro sheets. Syntax 2 can only be used on macro sheets in conjunction with the ELSE, ELSE.IF, and END.IF functions.

Use IF to conduct conditional tests on values and formulas and to branch based on the result of that test. The outcome of the test determines the value returned by the IF function.

Syntax 1

Worksheets and macro sheets

IF(logical_test, value_if_true, value_if_false)

Logical_test   is any value or expression that can be evaluated to TRUE or FALSE.

Value_if_true   is the value that is returned if logical_test is TRUE. If logical_test is TRUE and value_if_true is omitted, TRUE is returned.

Value_if_false   is the value that is returned if logical_test is FALSE. If logical_test is FALSE and value_if_false is omitted, FALSE is returned.

Remarks

- Up to seven IF functions can be nested as value_if_true and value_if_false arguments to construct more elaborate tests. See the following last example.

- If you are using IF in a macro, value_if_true and value_if_false can also be GOTO functions, other macros, or action-taking functions.

  For example, the following formula is allowed in a macro:

  IF(Number>10,GOTO(Large),GOTO(Small))

  In the preceding example, if Number is greater than 10, then logical_test is TRUE, the value_if_true statement is evaluated, and the macro function GOTO(Large) is run. If Number is less than or equal to 10, then logical_test is FALSE, value_if_false is evaluated, and the macro function GOTO(Small) is run.

- When the value_if_true and value_if_false arguments are evaluated, IF returns the value returned by those statements. In the preceding example, if the number is not greater than 10, TRUE is still returned if the second GOTO statement is successful.

- If any of the arguments to IF are arrays, every element of the array is evaluated when the IF statement is carried out. If some of the value_if_true and value_if_false arguments are action-taking functions, all of the actions are taken. For example, the following macro formula runs both ALERT functions:

  IF({TRUE,FALSE},ALERT("One",2),ALERT("Two",2))

Examples   In the following example, if the value referred to by the name File is equal to "Chart", logical_test is TRUE and the macro function NEW(2) is carried out, otherwise, logical_test is FALSE and NEW(1) is carried out:

IF(File="Chart",NEW(2),NEW(1))

Suppose an expense worksheet contains in B2:B4 the following data for "Actual Expenses" for January, February, and March: 1500, 500, 500. C2:C4 contains the following data for "Predicted Expenses" for the same periods: 900, 900, 925.

You could write a macro to check whether you are over budget for a particular month, generating text for a message with the following formulas:

`IF(B2>C2,"Over Budget","OK")` equals "Over Budget"

`IF(B3>C3,"Over Budget","OK")` equals "OK"

Suppose you want to assign letter grades to numbers referenced by the name Average. See the following table.

If Average is	Then return
Greater than 89	A
From 80 to 89	B
From 70 to 79	C
From 60 to 69	D
Less than 60	F

You could use the following nested IF function:

```
IF(Average>89,"A",IF(Average>79,"B",
IF(Average>69,"C",IF(Average>59,"D","F"))))
```

In the preceding example, the second IF statement is also the value_if_false argument to the first IF statement. Similarly, the third IF statement is the value_if_false argument to the second IF statement. For example, if the first logical_test (Average>89) is TRUE, "A" is returned. If the first logical_test is FALSE, the second IF statement is evaluated, and so on.

Related Functions
AND	Returns TRUE if all its arguments are TRUE
FALSE	Returns the logical value FALSE
NOT	Reverses the logic of its argument
OR	Returns TRUE if any argument is TRUE
TRUE	Returns the logical value TRUE

List of Logical Functions

IMABS

Returns the absolute value (modulus) of a complex number in x + yi or x + yj text format.

If this function is not available, run the Setup program to install the Analysis ToolPak. After you install the Analysis ToolPak, you must select it in the Add-In Manager. For more information, look up Add-ins in Help.

Syntax

IMABS(inumber)

Inumber   is a complex number for which you want the absolute value.

Remarks

- Use COMPLEX to convert real and imaginary coefficients into a complex number.
- If inumber is not in the form x + yi or x + yj, IMABS returns the #NUM! error value.
- The absolute value of a complex number is:

$$\text{IMABS}(z) = |z| = \sqrt{x^2 + y^2}$$

where:

z = x + yi

Example

IMABS("5+12i") equals 13

Related Functions

Related functions include other complex number functions such as IMSUM, IMAGINARY, IMREAL, and so on.

List of Engineering Functions

IMAGINARY

Returns the imaginary coefficient of a complex number in x + yi or x + yj text format.

If this function is not available, run the Setup program to install the Analysis ToolPak. After you install the Analysis ToolPak, you must select it in the Add-In Manager. For more information, look up Add-ins in Help.

Syntax

IMAGINARY(inumber)

Inumber   is a complex number for which you want the imaginary coefficient.

Remarks	▪ Use COMPLEX to convert real and imaginary coefficients into a complex number.
	▪ If inumber is not in the form x + yi or x + yj, IMAGINARY returns the #NUM! error value.
Examples	IMAGINARY("3+4i") equals 4
	IMAGINARY("0-j") equals –1
	IMAGINARY(4) equals 0
Related Functions	Related functions include other complex number functions such as IMABS, IMSUM, IMREAL, and so on.
	List of Engineering Functions

IMARGUMENT

Returns the argument θ, an angle expressed in radians, such that:

$$x + yi = |x + yi| \times e^{i\theta} = |x + yi|(\cos\theta + i\sin\theta)$$

If this function is not available, run the Setup program to install the Analysis ToolPak. After you install the Analysis ToolPak, you must select it in the Add-In Manager. For more information, look up Add-ins in Help.

Syntax

IMARGUMENT(inumber)

Inumber   is a complex number for which you want the argument θ.

Remarks

▪ Use COMPLEX to convert real and imaginary coefficients into a complex number.

▪ If inumber is not in the form x + yi or x + yj, IMARGUMENT returns the #NUM! error value.

▪ IMARGUMENT is calculated as follows:

$$\text{IMARGUMENT}(z) = \tan^{-1}\left(\frac{y}{x}\right) = \theta$$

where:

$$z = x + yi \quad \text{and}$$

$$z = x + yi$$

Example IMARGUMENT("3+4i") equals 0.927295

Related Functions Related functions include other complex number functions such as IMSUM, IMAGINARY, IMREAL, and so on.

List of Engineering Functions

IMCONJUGATE

Returns the complex conjugate of a complex number in x + yi or x + yj text format.

If this function is not available, run the Setup program to install the Analysis ToolPak. After you install the Analysis ToolPak, you must select it in the Add-In Manager. For more information, look up Add-ins in Help.

Syntax **IMCONJUGATE(inumber)**

Inumber   is a complex number for which you want the conjugate.

Remarks
- Use COMPLEX to convert real and imaginary coefficients into a complex number.
- If inumber is not in the form x + yi or x + yj, IMCONJUGATE returns the #NUM! error value.
- The conjugate of a complex number is:

$$\text{IMCONJUGATE}(x + yi) = \bar{z} = (x - yi)$$

Example IMCONJUGATE("3+4i") equals 3 – 4i

Related Functions Related functions include other complex number functions such as IMSUM, IMAGINARY, IMREAL, and so on.

List of Engineering Functions

IMCOS

Returns the cosine of a complex number in x + yi or x + yj text format.

If this function is not available, run the Setup program to install the Analysis ToolPak. After you install the Analysis ToolPak, you must select it in the Add-In Manager. For more information, look up Add-ins in Help.

Syntax

IMCOS(inumber)

Inumber   is a complex number for which you want the cosine.

Remarks

- Use COMPLEX to convert real and imaginary coefficients into a complex number.
- If inumber is not text, IMCOS returns the #VALUE! error value.
- If inumber is not in the form x + yi or x + yj, IMCOS returns the #NUM! error value.
- The cosine of a complex number is:

$$\cos(x + yi) = \cos(x)\cosh(y) - \sin(x)\sinh(y)i$$

Example

IMCOS("1+i") equals 0.83373 – 0.988898i

Related Functions

Related functions include other complex number functions such as IMSUM, IMAGINARY, IMREAL, and so on.

List of Engineering Functions

IMDIV

Returns the quotient of two complex numbers in x + yi or x + yj text format.

If this function is not available, run the Setup program to install the Analysis ToolPak. After you install the Analysis ToolPak, you must select it in the Add-In Manager. For more information, look up Add-ins in Help.

Syntax

IMDIV(inumber1, inumber2)

Inumber1   is the complex numerator or dividend.

Inumber2   is the complex denominator or divisor.

Remarks

- Use COMPLEX to convert real and imaginary coefficients into a complex number.
- If inumber1 or inumber2 is not in the form x + yi or x + yj, IMDIV returns the #NUM! error value.
- The quotient of two complex numbers is:

$$\text{IMDIV}(z_1, z_2) = \frac{(a + bi)}{(c + di)} = \frac{(ac + bd) + (bc - ad)i}{c^2 + d^2}$$

Example IMDIV("-238+240i","10+24i") equals 5 + 12i

Related Functions Related functions include other complex number functions such as IMSUM, IMAGINARY, IMREAL, and so on.

List of Engineering Functions

IMEXP

Returns the exponential of a complex number in x + yi or x + yj text format.

If this function is not available, run the Setup program to install the Analysis ToolPak. After you install the Analysis ToolPak, you must select it in the Add-In Manager. For more information, look up Add-ins in Help.

Syntax **IMEXP(inumber)**

Inumber   is a complex number for which you want the exponential.

Remarks

- Use COMPLEX to convert real and imaginary coefficients into a complex number.
- If inumber is not in the form x + yi or x + yj, IMEXP returns the #NUM! error value.
- The exponential of a complex number is:

$$\text{IMEXP}(z) = e^{(x+yi)} = e^x e^{yi} = e^x (\cos y + i \sin y)$$

Example IMEXP("1+i") equals 1.468694 + 2.287355i

Related Functions Related functions include other complex number functions such as IMSUM, IMAGINARY, IMREAL, and so on.

List of Engineering Functions

IMLN

Returns the natural logarithm of a complex number in x + yi or x + yj text format.

If this function is not available, run the Setup program to install the Analysis ToolPak. After you install the Analysis ToolPak, you must select it in the Add-In Manager. For more information, look up Add-ins in Help.

Syntax

IMLN(inumber)

Inumber   is a complex number for which you want the natural logarithm.

Remarks

- Use COMPLEX to convert real and imaginary coefficients into a complex number.
- If inumber is not in the form x + yi or x + yj, IMLN returns the #NUM! error value.
- The natural logarithm of a complex number is:

$$\ln(x + yi) = \ln\sqrt{x^2 + y^2} + i\tan^{-1}\left(\frac{y}{x}\right)$$

where:

$$z = x + yi$$

Example

IMLN("3+4i") equals 1.609438 + 0.927295i

Related Functions

Related functions include other complex number functions such as IMSUM, IMAGINARY, IMREAL, and so on.

List of Engineering Functions

IMLOG10

Returns the common logarithm (base 10) of a complex number in x + yi or x + yj text format.

If this function is not available, run the Setup program to install the Analysis ToolPak. After you install the Analysis ToolPak, you must select it in the Add-In Manager. For more information, look up Add-ins in Help.

Syntax	**IMLOG10(inumber)**

Inumber   is a complex number for which you want the common logarithm.

Remarks
- Use COMPLEX to convert real and imaginary coefficients into a complex number.
- If inumber is not in the form x + yi or x + yj, IMLOG10 returns the #NUM! error value.
- The common logarithm of a complex number can be calculated from the natural logarithm as follows:

$$\log_{10}(x + yi) = (\log_{10} e)\ln(x + yi)$$

Example   IMLOG10("3+4i") equals 0.69897 + 0.402719i

Related Functions   Related functions include other complex number functions such as IMSUM, IMAGINARY, IMREAL, and so on.

List of Engineering Functions

IMLOG2

Returns the base-2 logarithm of a complex number in x + yi or x + yj text format.

If this function is not available, run the Setup program to install the Analysis ToolPak. After you install the Analysis ToolPak, you must select it in the Add-In Manager. For more information, look up Add-ins in Help.

Syntax   **IMLOG2(inumber)**

Inumber   is a complex number for which you want the base-2 logarithm.

Remarks
- Use COMPLEX to convert real and imaginary coefficients into a complex number.
- If inumber is not in the form x + yi or x + yj, IMLOG2 returns the #NUM! error value.
- The base-2 logarithm of a complex number can be calculated from the natural logarithm as follows:

$$\log_{2}(x + yi) = (\log_{2} e)\ln(x + yi)$$

Example   IMLOG2("3+4i") equals 2.321928 + 1.337804i

Related Functions   Related functions include other complex number functions such as IMSUM, IMAGINARY, IMREAL, and so on.

List of Engineering Functions

IMPOWER

Returns a complex number in x + yi or x + yj text format raised to a power.

If this function is not available, run the Setup program to install the Analysis ToolPak. After you install the Analysis ToolPak, you must select it in the Add-In Manager. For more information, look up Add-ins in Help.

Syntax   **IMPOWER(inumber, number)**

Inumber   is a complex number you want to raise to a power.

Number   is the power to which you want to raise the complex number.

Remarks
- Use COMPLEX to convert real and imaginary coefficients into a complex number.
- If inumber is not in the form x + yi or x + yj, IMPOWER returns the #NUM! error value.
- If number is non-numeric, IMPOWER returns the #VALUE! error value.
- Number can be either an integer, fractional or negative.
- A complex number raised to a power is calculated as follows:

$$(x + yi)^n = r^n e^{in\theta} = r^n \cos n\theta + ir^n \sin n\theta$$

where:

$$r = \sqrt{x^2 + y^2}$$

and:

$$\theta = \tan^{-1}\left(\frac{y}{x}\right)$$

and:

$$z = x + yi$$

Example

IMPOWER("2+3i", 3) equals −46 + 9i

Related Functions

Related functions include other complex number functions such as IMSUM, IMAGINARY, IMREAL, and so on.

List of Engineering Functions

IMPRODUCT

Returns the product of 2 to 29 complex numbers in x + yi or x + yj text format.

If this function is not available, run the Setup program to install the Analysis ToolPak. After you install the Analysis ToolPak, you must select it in the Add-In Manager. For more information, look up Add-ins in Help.

Syntax

IMPRODUCT(inumber1, inumber2,...)

Inumber1, inumber2   are 1 to 29 complex numbers to multiply.

Remarks

- Use COMPLEX to convert real and imaginary coefficients into a complex number.
- If inumber1 or inumber2 is not in the form x + yi or x + yj, IMPRODUCT returns the #NUM! error value.

The product of two complex numbers is:

$$(a + bi)(c + di) = (ac - bd) + (ad + bc)i$$

Examples

IMPRODUCT("3+4i","5-3i") equals 27 + 11i

IMPRODUCT("1+2i",30) equals 30 + 60i

Related Functions

Related functions include other complex number functions such as IMSUM, IMAGINARY, IMREAL, and so on.

List of Engineering Functions

IMREAL

Returns the real coefficient of a complex number in x + yi or x + yj text format.

If this function is not available, run the Setup program to install the Analysis ToolPak. After you install the Analysis ToolPak, you must select it in the Add-In Manager. For more information, look up Add-ins in Help.

Syntax

IMREAL(inumber)

Inumber   is a complex number for which you want the real coefficient.

Remarks

- Use COMPLEX to convert real and imaginary coefficients into a complex number.
- If inumber is not in the form x + yi or x + yj, IMREAL returns the #NUM! error value.

Example

`IMREAL("6-9i")` equals 6

Related Functions

Related functions include other complex number functions such as IMSUM, IMAGINARY, IMABS, and so on. .

List of Engineering Functions

IMSIN

Returns the sine of a complex number in x + yi or x + yj text format.

If this function is not available, run the Setup program to install the Analysis ToolPak. After you install the Analysis ToolPak, you must select it in the Add-In Manager. For more information, look up Add-ins in Help.

Syntax

IMSIN(inumber)

Inumber   is a complex number for which you want the sine.

Remarks

- Use COMPLEX to convert real and imaginary coefficients into a complex number.
- If inumber is not in the form x + yi or x + yj, IMSIN returns the #NUM! error value.
- The sine of a complex number is:

$$\sin(x + yi) = \sin(x)\cosh(y) - \cos(x)\sinh(y)i$$

Example   IMSIN("3+4i") equals 3.853738 − 27.016813i

Related Functions   Related functions include other complex number functions such as IMSUM, IMAGINARY, IMREAL, and so on.

List of Engineering Functions

IMSQRT

Returns the square root of a complex number in x + yi or x + yj text format.

If this function is not available, run the Setup program to install the Analysis ToolPak. After you install the Analysis ToolPak, you must select it in the Add-In Manager. For more information, look up Add-ins in Help.

Syntax   **IMSQRT(inumber)**

Inumber   is a complex number for which you want the square root.

Remarks   ▪ Use COMPLEX to convert real and imaginary coefficients into a complex number.

▪ If inumber is not in the form x + yi or x + yj, IMSQRT returns the #NUM! error value.

▪ The square root of a complex number is:

$$\sqrt{x + yi} = \sqrt{r}\cos\left(\frac{\theta}{2}\right) + i\sqrt{r}\sin\left(\frac{\theta}{2}\right)$$

where:

$$r = \sqrt{x^2 + y^2}$$

and:

$$\theta = \tan^{-1}\left(\frac{y}{x}\right)$$

and:

$$z = x + yi$$

Example   IMSQRT("1+i") equals 1.098684 + 0.45509i

Related Functions   Related functions include other complex number functions such as IMSUM, IMAGINARY, IMREAL, and so on.

List of Engineering Functions

IMSUB

Returns the difference of two complex numbers in x + yi or x + yj text format.

If this function is not available, run the Setup program to install the Analysis ToolPak. After you install the Analysis ToolPak, you must select it in the Add-In Manager. For more information, look up Add-ins in Help.

Syntax   **IMSUB(inumber1, inumber2)**

Inumber1   is the complex number from which to subtract inumber2.

Inumber2   is the complex number to subtract from inumber1.

Remarks   ▪ Use COMPLEX to convert real and imaginary coefficients into a complex number.

▪ If either number is not in the form x + yi or x + yj, IMSUB returns the #NUM! error value.

▪ The difference of two complex numbers is:

$$(a + bi) - (c + di) = (a - c) + (b - d)i$$

Example   IMSUB("13+4i","5+3i") equals 8 + i

Related Functions   Related functions include other complex number functions such as IMSUM, IMAGINARY, IMREAL, and so on.

List of Engineering Functions

IMSUM

Returns the sum of two or more complex numbers in x + yi or x + yj text format.

If this function is not available, run the Setup program to install the Analysis ToolPak. After you install the Analysis ToolPak, you must select it in the Add-In Manager. For more information, look up Add-ins in Help.

Syntax

IMSUM(inumber1, inumber2,...)

Inumber1,inumber2,...   are 1 to 29 complex numbers to add.

Remarks

- Use COMPLEX to convert real and imaginary coefficients into a complex number.
- If any argument is not in the form x + yi or x + yj, IMSUM returns the #NUM! error value.
- The sum of two complex numbers is:

$$(a + bi) + (c + di) = (a + c) + (b + d)i$$

Example

IMSUM("3+4i","5-3i") equals 8 + i

Related Functions

Related functions include other complex number functions such as IMABS, IMAGINARY, IMREAL, and so on.

List of Engineering Functions

INDEX

Returns the reference of the cell at the intersection of a particular row and column. If the reference is made up of nonadjacent selections, you can pick the selection to look in.

The INDEX function has two syntax forms: reference and array. The reference form always returns a reference; the array form always returns a value or an array of values.

Syntax

Reference form

INDEX(reference, row_num, column_num, area_num)

Reference   is a reference to one or more cell ranges.

- If you are entering a nonadjacent selection for reference, enclose reference in parentheses. For an example of using INDEX with a nonadjacent selection, see the fifth example following.

- If each area in reference contains only one row or column, the row_num or column_num argument, respectively, is optional. For example, for a single row reference, use INDEX(reference,,column_num).

Row_num   is the number of the row in reference from which to return a reference.

Column_num   is the number of the column in reference from which to return a reference.

Area_num   selects a range in reference from which to return the intersection of row_num and column_num. The first area selected or entered is numbered 1, the second is 2, and so on. If area_num is omitted, INDEX uses area 1.

For example, if reference describes the cells (A1:B4,D1:E4,G1:H4), then area_num 1 is the range A1:B4, area_num 2 is the range D1:E4, and area_num 3 is the range G1:H4.

After reference and area_num have selected a particular range, row_num and column_num select a particular cell: row_num 1 is the first row in the range, column_num 1 is the first column, and so on. The reference returned by INDEX is the intersection of row_num and column_num.

If you set row_num or column_num to 0, INDEX returns the reference for the entire column or row, respectively.

Remarks

- Row_num, column_num, and area_num must point to a cell within reference; otherwise, INDEX returns the #REF! error value. If row_num and column_num are omitted, INDEX returns the area in reference specified by area_num.

- The result of the INDEX function is a reference and is interpreted as such by other formulas. Depending on the formula, the return value of INDEX may be used as a reference or as a value. For example, the macro formula CELL("width",INDEX(A1:B2,1,2)) is equivalent to CELL("width",B1). The CELL function uses the return value of INDEX as a cell reference. On the other hand, a formula such as 2*INDEX(A1:B2,1,2) translates the return value of INDEX into the number in cell B1.

Examples

In the following worksheet, the range A2:C6 is named Fruit, the range A8:C11 is named Nuts, and the range A1:C11 is named Stock.

	A	B	C
1		**Price**	**Count (lbs.)**
2	Apples	$0.69	40
3	Bananas	$0.34	38
4	Lemons	$0.55	15
5	Oranges	$0.25	25
6	Pears	$0.59	40
7			
8	Almonds	$2.80	10
9	Cashews	$3.55	16
10	Peanuts	$1.25	20
11	Walnuts	$1.75	12

INDEX(Fruit,2,3) equals the reference C3, containing 38

INDEX(Nuts,1,1) equals the reference A8, containing "Almonds"

INDEX(Fruit,2,4) equals the #REF! error value, because the column_num argument (4) is out of range

INDEX(Stock,1,2) equals the reference B2, containing "Price"

INDEX((A1:C6,A8:C11),2,2,2) equals the reference B9, containing $3.55

SUM(INDEX(Stock,0,3,1)) equals SUM(C1:C11) equals 216

SUM(B2:INDEX(Fruit,5,2)) equals SUM(B2:B6) equals 2.42

Related Functions

CHOOSE	Chooses a value from a list of values
HLOOKUP	Looks in the top row of an array and returns the value of the indicated cell
LOOKUP	Looks up values in a reference or array
MATCH	Looks up values in a reference or array
VLOOKUP	Looks in the first column of an array and moves across the row to return the value of a cell

List of Lookup & Reference Functions

INDEX

Returns the value of an element in an array, selected by the row and column number indexes.

The INDEX function has two syntax forms: reference and array. The reference form always returns a reference; the array form always returns a value or array of values. Use the array form when the first argument to INDEX is an array constant.

Syntax
Array form

INDEX(array, row_num, column_num)

Array   is a range of cells entered as an array.

Row_num   selects the row in array from which to return a value. If row_num is omitted, column_num is required.

Column_num   selects the column in array from which to return a value. If column_num is omitted, row_num is required.

- If both the row_num and column_num arguments are used, INDEX returns the value in the cell at the intersection of row_num and column_num.

- If array contains only one row or column, the corresponding row_num or column_num argument is optional.

- If array has more than one row and more than one column, and only row_num or column_num is used, INDEX returns an array of the entire row or column in array.

- If you set row_num or column_num to 0, INDEX returns the array of values for the entire column or row, respectively. To use values returned as an array, enter the INDEX function as an array in a horizontal array of cells. Arrays are entered by pressing CTRL+SHIFT+ENTER (in Microsoft Excel for Windows) or COMMAND+RETURN (in Microsoft Excel for the Macintosh).

Remarks

Row_num and column_num must point to a cell within array; otherwise, INDEX returns the #REF! error value.

Examples

INDEX({1,2;3,4},2,2) equals 4

If entered as an array formula, then:

INDEX({1,2;3,4},0,2) equals {2;4}

Related Functions

CHOOSE	Chooses a value from a list of values
HLOOKUP	Looks in the top row of an array and returns the value of the indicated cell

LOOKUP	Looks up values in a reference or array
MATCH	Looks up values in a reference or array
VLOOKUP	Looks in the first column of an array and moves across the row to return the value of a cell

List of Lookup & Reference Functions

INDIRECT

Returns the reference specified by ref_text. References are immediately evaluated to display their contents. Use INDIRECT to get the value stored in a cell indicated by a reference in another cell.

Syntax

INDIRECT(ref_text, a1)

Ref_text   is a reference to a cell that contains an A1- style reference, an R1C1-style reference, or a name defined as a reference. If ref_text is not a valid cell reference, INDIRECT returns the #REF! error value.

A1   is a logical value that specifies what type of reference is contained in the cell ref_text.

- If a1 is TRUE or omitted, ref_text is interpreted as an A1-style reference.
- If a1 is FALSE, ref_text is interpreted as an R1C1-style reference.

Examples

If cell A1 contains the text "B2", and cell B2 contains the value 1.333, then:

INDIRECT($A$1) equals 1.333

If the workspace is set to display R1C1-style references, cell R1C1 contains R2C2, and cell R2C2 contains the value 1.333, then:

INT(INDIRECT(R1C1,FALSE)) equals 1

If B3 contains the text "George", and a cell defined as George contains the value 10, then:

INDIRECT($B$3) equals 10

Related Functions   OFFSET   Returns a reference offset from a given reference

List of Lookup & Reference Functions

INFO

Returns information about the current operating environment.

Syntax

INFO(type_text)

Type_text   is text specifying what type of information you want returned.

Type_text	Returns
"directory"	Path of the current directory or folder
"memavail"	Amount of memory available, in bytes
"memused"	Amount of memory being used for data
"numfile"	Number of active worksheets
"origin"	Absolute A1-style reference, as text, prepended with "$A:" for Lotus® 1-2-3® release 3.x compatibility. Returns the cell reference of the top and left most cell visible in the window based on the current scrolling position.
"osversion"	Current operating system version, as text
"recalc"	Current recalculation mode; returns "Automatic" or "Manual"
"release"	Version of Microsoft Excel, as text
"system"	Name of the operating environment:
Macintosh = "mac"	
Windows = "pcdos"	
"totmem"	Total memory available, including memory already in use, in bytes

Examples

The following formula returns 2 if two worksheets are currently open:

```
INFO("numfile")
```

Related Functions

CELL   Returns information about the formatting, location, or contents of a cell

List of Information Functions

INT

Rounds a number down to the nearest integer.

Syntax

INT(number)

Number   is the real number you want to round down to an integer.

Examples

INT(8.9) equals 8

INT(-8.9) equals –9

The following formula returns the decimal part of a positive real number in cell A1:

A1-INT(A1)

Related Functions

CEILING	Rounds a number to the nearest integer or to the nearest multiple of significance
FLOOR	Rounds a number down, toward zero
MOD	Returns the remainder from division
MROUND	Returns a number rounded to the desired multiple
ROUND	Rounds a number to a specified number of digits
TRUNC	Truncates a number to an integer

List of Math & Trigonometry Functions

INTERCEPT

Returns the intercept of the linear regression line through data points in known_x's and known_y's. The intercept is the point at which the regression line through the values in known_x's and known_y's intersects the y-axis. Use the intercept when you want to determine the value of the dependent variable when the independent variable is zero. For example, you can use INTERCEPT to predict a metal's electrical resistance at 0°C when your data points were taken at room temperature and higher.

Syntax

INTERCEPT(known_y's, known_x's)

Known_y's   is the dependent set of observations or data.

Known_x's   is the independent set of observations or data.

Remarks
- The arguments should be numbers, or names, arrays, or references that contain numbers.
- If an array or reference argument contains text, logical values, or empty cells, those values are ignored; however, cells with the value zero are included.
- If known_y's and known_x's contain a different number of data points, or contain no data points, INTERCEPT returns the #N/A error value.

- The equation for the intercept of the regression line is:

$$a = \overline{Y} - b\overline{X}$$

where the slope is calculated as:

$$b = \frac{n\Sigma xy - (\Sigma x)(\Sigma y)}{n\Sigma x^2 - (\Sigma x)^2}$$

Example INTERCEPT({2, 3, 9, 1, 8}, {6, 5, 11, 7, 5}) equals 0.0483871

Related Functions

FORECAST	Returns a value along a linear trend
GROWTH	Returns values along an exponential trend
LINEST	Returns the parameters of a linear trend
LOGEST	Returns the parameters of an exponential trend
PEARSON	Returns the Pearson product moment correlation coefficient
RSQ	Returns the square of the Pearson product moment correlation coefficient
SLOPE	Returns the slope of the linear regression line
STEYX	Returns the standard error of the predicted y-value for each x in the regression
TREND	Returns values along a linear trend

List of Statistical Functions

INTRATE

Returns the interest rate for a fully invested security.

If this function is not available, run the Setup program to install the Analysis ToolPak. After you install the Analysis ToolPak, you must select it in the Add-In Manager. For more information, look up Add-ins in Help.

Syntax   **INTRATE(settlement, maturity, investment, redemption,** basis)

Settlement   is the security's settlement date, expressed as a serial date number.

Maturity   is the security's maturity date, expressed as a serial date number.

Investment   is the amount invested in the security.

Redemption   is the amount to be received at maturity.

Basis   is the type of day count basis to use.

Basis	Day count basis
0 or omitted	US (NASD) 30/360
1	Actual/actual
2	Actual/360
3	Actual/365
4	European 30/360

Remarks
- Settlement, maturity, and basis are truncated to integers.
- If any argument is non-numeric, INTRATE returns the #VALUE! error value.
- If settlement or maturity is not a valid serial date number, INTRATE returns the #NUM! error value.
- If investment ≤ 0 or if redemption ≤ 0, INTRATE returns the #NUM! error value.
- If basis < 0 or if basis > 4, INTRATE returns the #NUM! error value.
- If settlement ≥ maturity, INTRATE returns the #NUM! error value.
- INTRATE is calculated as follows:

$$INTRATE = \frac{redemption - investment}{investment} \times \frac{B}{DIM}$$

Where:

B = number of days in a year, depending on the year basis.

DIM = number of days from settlement to maturity.

Example   A bond has the following terms:

February 15, 1993 settlement (issue) date
May 15, 1993 maturity date
1,000,000 investment
1,014,420 redemption value
Actual/360 basis

The bond discount rate (in the 1900 Date System) is:

`INTRATE(34015,34104,1000000,1014420,2)` equals 0.058328 or 5.8328%

Related Functions   RECEIVED   Returns the amount received at maturity for a fully invested
                                                                 security

List of Financial Functions

IPMT

Returns the interest payment for a given period for an investment based on periodic,
constant payments and a constant interest rate. For a more complete description of
the arguments in IPMT and for more information on annuity functions, see PV.

Syntax   **IPMT(rate, per, nper, pv, fv, type)**

Rate   is the interest rate per period.

Per   is the period for which you want to find the interest, and must be in the range
1 to nper.

Nper   is the total number of payment periods in an annuity.

Pv   is the present value, or the lump-sum amount that a series of future payments
is worth right now.

Fv   is the future value, or a cash balance you want to attain after the last payment
is made. If fv is omitted, it is assumed to be 0 (the future value of a loan, for
example, is 0).

Type   is the number 0 or 1 and indicates when payments are due. If type is
omitted, it is assumed to be 0.

Set type equal to	If payments are due
0	At the end of the period
1	At the beginning of the period

Remarks
- Make sure that you are consistent about the units you use for specifying rate and
  nper. If you make monthly payments on a four-year loan at 12 percent annual
  interest, use 12%/12 for rate and 4*12 for nper. If you make annual payments on
  the same loan, use 12% for rate and 4 for nper.

- For all the arguments, cash you pay out, such as deposits to savings, is
  represented by negative numbers; cash you receive, such as dividend checks, is
  represented by positive numbers.

Examples

The following formula calculates the interest due in the first month of a three-year $8000 loan at 10 percent annual interest:

`IPMT(0.1/12, 1, 36, 8000)` equals –$66.67

The following formula calculates the interest due in the last year of a three-year $8000 loan at 10 percent annual interest, where payments are made yearly:

`IPMT(0.1, 3, 3, 8000)` equals –$292.45

Related Functions

ACCRINT	Returns the accrued interest for a security that pays periodic interest
ACCRINTM	Returns the accrued interest for a security that pays interest at maturity
CUMIPMT	Returns the cumulative interest paid between two periods
INTRATE	Returns the interest rate for a fully invested security
PMT	Returns the periodic payment for an annuity
PPMT	Returns the payment on the principal for an investment for a given period
PV	Returns the present value of an investment
RATE	Returns the interest rate per period of an annuity

List of Financial Functions

IRR

Returns the internal rate of return for a series of cash flows represented by the numbers in values. These cash flows do not have to be even, as they would be for an annuity. The internal rate of return is the interest rate received for an investment consisting of payments (negative values) and income (positive values) that occur at regular periods.

Syntax

IRR(values, guess)

Values   is an array or a reference to cells that contain numbers for which you want to calculate the internal rate of return.

- Values must contain at least one positive value and one negative value to calculate the internal rate of return.

- IRR uses the order of values to interpret the order of cash flows. Be sure to enter your payment and income values in the sequence you want.

- If an array or reference argument contains text, logical values, or empty cells, those values are ignored.

Guess   is a number that you guess is close to the result of IRR.

- Microsoft Excel uses an iterative technique for calculating IRR. Starting with guess, IRR cycles through the calculation until the result is accurate within 0.00001 percent. If IRR can't find a result that works after 20 tries, the #NUM! error value is returned.

- In most cases you do not need to provide guess for the IRR calculation. If guess is omitted, it is assumed to be 0.1 (10 percent).

- If IRR gives the #NUM! error value, or if the result is not close to what you expected, try again with a different value for guess.

Examples

Suppose you want to start a restaurant business. You estimate it will cost $70,000 to start the business and expect to net the following income in the first five years: $12,000, $15,000, $18,000, $21,000, and $26,000. B1:B6 contain the following values: $-70,000, $12,000, $15,000, $18,000, $21,000 and $26,000, respectively.

To calculate the investment's internal rate of return after four years:

IRR(B1:B5) equals −2.12%

To calculate the internal rate of return after five years:

IRR(B1:B6) equals 8.66%

To calculate the internal rate of return after two years, you need to include a guess:

IRR(B1:B3,-10%) equals −44.35%

Remarks

IRR is closely related to NPV, the net present value function. The rate of return calculated by IRR is the interest rate corresponding to a zero net present value. The following macro formula demonstrates how NPV and IRR are related:

NPV(IRR(B1:B6),B1:B6) equals 3.60E-08 (Within the accuracy of the IRR calculation, the value 3.60E-08 is effectively 0.)

Related Functions

MIRR	Returns the internal rate of return where positive and negative cash flows are financed at different rates
NPV	Returns the net present value of an investment based on a series of periodic cash flows and a discount rate
RATE	Returns the interest rate per period of an annuity
XIRR	Returns the internal rate of return for a schedule of cash flows that is not necessarily periodic
XNPV	Returns the net present value for a schedule of cash flows that is not necessarily periodic

List of Financial Functions

IS Functions

This section describes the nine worksheet functions used for testing the type of a value or reference.

Each of these functions, referred to collectively as the IS functions, checks the type of value and returns TRUE or FALSE depending on the outcome. For example, the ISBLANK function returns the logical value TRUE if value is a reference to an empty cell; otherwise it returns FALSE.

Syntax

ISBLANK(value)
ISERR(value)
ISERROR(value)
ISLOGICAL(value)
ISNA(value)
ISNONTEXT(value)
ISNUMBER(value)
ISREF(value)
ISTEXT(value)

Value   is the value you want tested. Value can be a blank (empty cell), error, logical, text, number, or reference value, or name referring to any of these, that you want to test.

Function	Returns TRUE if
ISBLANK	Value refers to an empty cell.
ISERR	Value refers to any error value except #N/A.
ISERROR	Value refers to any error value (#N/A, #VALUE!, #REF!, #DIV/0!, #NUM!, #NAME?, or #NULL!).
ISLOGICAL	Value refers to a logical value.
ISNA	Value refers to the #N/A (value not available) error value.
ISNONTEXT	Value refers to any item that is not text. (Note that this function returns TRUE if value refers to a blank cell.)
ISNUMBER	Value refers to a number.
ISREF	Value refers to a reference.
ISTEXT	Value refers to text.

Remarks

- The value arguments to the IS functions are not converted. For example, in most other functions where a number is required, the text value "19" is converted to the number 19. However, in the formula ISNUMBER("19"), "19" is not converted from a text value, and the ISNUMBER function returns FALSE.

- The IS functions are useful in formulas and macros for testing the outcome of a calculation. When combined with the IF function, they provide a method for locating errors in formulas (see the following examples).

Examples

ISLOGICAL(TRUE) equals TRUE

ISLOGICAL("TRUE") equals FALSE

ISNUMBER(4) equals TRUE

Suppose C1:C5 in a worksheet of Gold prices in different regions shows the following text values, number values and error values: "Gold", "Region1", #REF!, $330.92, #N/A, respectively.

ISBLANK(C1) equals FALSE

ISERROR(C3) equals TRUE

ISNA(C3) equals FALSE

ISNA(C5) equals TRUE

ISERR(C5) equals FALSE

ISNUMBER(C4) equals TRUE (if the $330.92 was entered as a number and not as text)

ISREF(Region1) equals TRUE (if Region1 is defined as a range name)

ISTEXT(C2) equals TRUE (if Region1 is formatted as text)

On another worksheet, suppose you want to calculate the average of the range A1:A4, but you can't be sure that the cells contain numbers. The formula AVERAGE(A1:A4) returns the #DIV/0! error value if A1:A4 does not contain any numbers. To allow for this case, you could use the following formula to locate potential errors:

IF(ISERROR(AVERAGE(A1:A4)),"No Numbers",AVERAGE(A1:A4))

Related Functions

ERROR.TYPE	Returns a number corresponding to an error type
ISEVEN	Returns TRUE if the number is even
ISODD	Returns TRUE if the number is odd
TYPE	Returns a number indicating the data type of a value

List of Information Functions

ISEVEN

Returns TRUE if number is even, or FALSE if number is odd.

If this function is not available, run the Setup program to install the Analysis ToolPak. After you install the Analysis ToolPak, you must select it in the Add-In Manager. For more information, look up Add-ins in Help.

Syntax

ISEVEN(number)

Number   is the value to test. If number is not an integer, it is truncated.

Remarks

If number is non-numeric, ISEVEN returns the #VALUE! error value.

Examples

ISEVEN(-1) equals FALSE

ISEVEN(2.5) equals TRUE

ISEVEN(5) equals FALSE

Related Functions

EVEN	Rounds a number up to the nearest even integer
ISODD	Returns TRUE if the number is odd
ODD	Rounds a number up to the nearest odd integer

List of Information Functions

ISODD

Returns TRUE if number is odd, or FALSE if number is even.

If this function is not available, run the Setup program to install the Analysis ToolPak. After you install the Analysis ToolPak, you must select it in the Add-In Manager. For more information, look up Add-ins in Help.

Syntax

ISODD(number)

Number   is the value to test. If number is not an integer, it is truncated.

Remarks

If number is non-numeric, ISODD returns the #VALUE! error value.

Examples	ISODD(-1) equals TRUE	
	ISODD(2.5) equals FALSE	
	ISODD(5) equals TRUE	
Related Functions	EVEN	Rounds a number up to the nearest even integer
	ISEVEN	Returns TRUE if the number is even
	ODD	Rounds a number up to the nearest odd integer

List of Information Functions

KURT

Returns the kurtosis of a data set. Kurtosis characterizes the relative peakedness or flatness of a distribution compared to the normal distribution. Positive kurtosis indicates a relatively peaked distribution. Negative kurtosis indicates a relatively flat distribution.

Syntax

KURT(number1, number2, ...)

Number1,number2,...　are 1 to 30 arguments for which you want to calculate kurtosis. You can also use a single array or a reference to an array instead of arguments separated by commas.

Remarks

- The arguments should be numbers, or names, arrays, or references that contain numbers.

- If an array or reference argument contains text, logical values, or empty cells, those values are ignored; however, cells with the value zero are included.

- If there are less than four data points, or if the standard deviation of the sample equals zero, KURT returns the #DIV/0! error value.

- Kurtosis is defined as:

$$\left\{ \frac{n(n+1)}{(n-1)(n-2)(n-3)} \sum \left(\frac{x_i - \bar{x}}{s} \right)^4 \right\}$$
$$- \frac{3(n-1)^2}{(n-2)(n-3)}$$

where:

s is the sample standard deviation.

Example   KURT(3,4,5,2,3,4,5,6,4,7) returns -0.1518

Related Functions

SKEW	Returns the skewness of a distribution
STDEV	Estimates standard deviation based on a sample
STDEVP	Calculates standard deviation based on the entire population
VAR	Estimates variance based on a sample
VARP	Calculates variance based on the entire population

List of Statistical Functions

LARGE

Returns the k-th largest value in a data set. You can use this function to select a value based on its relative standing. For example, you can use LARGE to return the highest, runner-up, or third-place score.

Syntax

LARGE(array, k)

Array   is the array or range of data for which you want to determine the k-th largest value.

K   is the position (from the largest) in the array or cell range of data to return.

Remarks

- If array is empty, LARGE returns the #NUM! error value.

- If $k \leq 0$ or if k is greater than the number of data points, LARGE returns the #NUM! error value.

If n is the number of data points in a range, then LARGE(array,1) returns the largest value and LARGE(array,n) returns the smallest value.

Examples

LARGE({3,4,5,2,3,4,5,6,4,7},3) equals 5

LARGE({3,4,5,2,3,4,5,6,4,7},7) equals 4

Related Functions

PERCENTILE	Returns the k-th percentile of values in a range
PERCENTRANK	Returns the percentage rank of a value in a data set
QUARTILE	Returns the quartile of a data set
SMALL	Returns the k-th smallest value in a data set

List of Statistical Functions

LCM

Returns the least common multiple of integers. The least common multiple is the smallest positive integer that is a multiple of all integer arguments number1, number2, and so on. Use LCM to add fractions with different denominators.

If this function is not available, run the Setup program to install the Analysis ToolPak. After you install the Analysis ToolPak, you must select it in the Add-In Manager. For more information, look up Add-ins in Help.

Syntax

LCM(number1, number2, ...)

Number1, number2,...   are 1 to 29 values for which you want the least common multiple. If value is not an integer, it is truncated.

Remarks

- If any argument is non-numeric, LCM returns the #VALUE! error value.
- If any argument is less than one, LCM returns the #NUM! error value.

Examples

LCM(5, 2) equals 10

LCM(24, 36) equals 72

Related Function

GCD   Returns the greatest common divisor

List of Math & Trigonometry Functions

LEFT

Returns the first (or leftmost) character or characters in a text string.

Syntax

LEFT(text, num_chars)

Text   is the text string containing the characters you want to extract.

Num_chars   specifies how many characters you want LEFT to return.

- Num_chars must be greater than or equal to zero.
- If num_chars is greater than the length of text, LEFT returns all of text.
- If num_chars is omitted, it is assumed to be 1.

Examples

LEFT("Sale Price", 4) equals "Sale"

If A1 contains "Sweden", then:

LEFT(A1) equals "S"

Suppose a hardware store assigns stock numbers to its products. The first three characters of the stock number identify the product vendor. On a worksheet, assume that Stock refers to a cell containing a stock number and that VendorTable is a sorted two-column table containing all the vendor numbers in the first column and the corresponding vendor names in the second.

You can use the LEFT function to obtain the first three characters of the stock number (a vendor number) and the VLOOKUP function to return the vendor's name as shown in the following formula:

```
VLOOKUP(VALUE(LEFT(Stock, 3)), VendorTable, 2)
```

Related Functions

MID	Returns a specific number of characters from a text string starting at the position you specify. Returns a specific number of characters from a text string
RIGHT	Returns the rightmost characters from a text value

List of Text Functions

LEN

Returns the number of characters in a text string.

Syntax

LEN(text)

Text   is the text whose length you want to find. Spaces count as characters.

Examples

LEN("Phoenix, AZ") equals 11

LEN("") equals 0

The following macro formula starts a FOR-NEXT loop on a macro sheet. The number of iterations is equal to the length of a string named CheckText:

```
FOR("Counter", 1, LEN(CheckText))
```

Related Functions

EXACT	Checks to see if two text values are identical
SEARCH	Finds one text value within another (not case-sensitive)

List of Text Functions

LINEST

Uses the "least squares" method to calculate a straight line that best fits your data and returns an array that describes the line. The equation for the line is:

$$y = m_1x_1 + m_2x_2 + \cdots + b \text{ or } y = mx + b$$

where the dependent y-value is a function of the independent x-values. The m-values are coefficients corresponding to each x-value, and b is a constant value. Note that y, x, and m can be vectors. The array that LINEST returns is $\{m_n, m_{n-1}, ..., m_1, b\}$. LINEST can also return additional regression statistics.

Syntax

LINEST(known_y's, known_x's, const, stats)

Known_y's   is the set of y-values you already know in the relationship y = mx + b.

- If the array known_y's is in a single column, then each column of known_x's is interpreted as a separate variable.

- If the array known_y's is in a single row, then each row of known_x's is interpreted as a separate variable.

Known_x's   is an optional set of x-values that you may already know in the relationship y = mx + b.

- The array known_x's can include one or more sets of variables. If only one variable is used, known_y's and known_x's can be ranges of any shape, as long as they have equal dimensions. If more than one variable is used, known_y's must be a vector (that is, a range with a height of one row or a width of one column).

- If known_x's is omitted, it is assumed to be the array {1,2,3,...} that is the same size as known_y's.

Const   is a logical value specifying whether to force the constant b to equal 0.

- If const is TRUE or omitted, b is calculated normally.

- If const is FALSE, b is set equal to 0 and the m-values are adjusted to fit y = mx.

Stats   is a logical value specifying whether to return additional regression statistics.

- If stats is TRUE, LINEST returns the additional regression statistics, so the returned array is $\{m_n, m_{n-1}, ..., m_1, b; se_n, se_{n-1}, ..., se_1, se_b; r^2, se_y; F, df; ss_{reg}, ss_{resid}\}$.

- If stats is FALSE or omitted, LINEST returns only the m-coefficients and the constant b.

The additional regression statistics are:

Statistic	Description
$se_1, se_2, ..., se_n$	The standard error values for the coefficients $m_1, m_2, ..., m_n$.
se_b	The standard error value for the constant b (seb = #N/A when const is FALSE).
r^2	The coefficient of determination. Compares estimated and actual y-values and ranges in value from 0 to 1. If it is 1, there is a perfect correlation in the sample—there is no difference between the estimated y-value and the actual y-value. At the other extreme, if the coefficient of determination is 0, the regression equation is not helpful in predicting a y-value. For information about how r^2 is calculated, see "Remarks" later in this topic.
se_y	The standard error for the y estimate.
F	The F statistic, or the F-observed value. Use the F statistic to determine whether the observed relationship between the dependent and independent variables occurs by chance.
df	The degrees of freedom. Use the degrees of freedom to help you find F-critical values in a statistical table. Compare the values you find in the table to the F statistic returned by LINEST to determine a confidence level for the model.
ss_{reg}	The regression sum of squares.
ss_{resid}	The residual sum of squares.

The following illustration shows the order in which the additional regression statistics are returned.

m_n	m_{n-1}	$\cdots$	m_2	m_1	b
se_n	se_{n-1}	$\cdots$	se_2	se_1	se_b
r^2	se_y				
F	df				
ss_{reg}	ss_{resid}				

Remarks

- You can describe any straight line with the slope and the y-intercept:

  Slope (m):
  To find the slope of a line, often written as m, take two points on the line, (x_1,y_1) and (x_2,y_2); the slope is equal to $(y_2 - y_1)/(x_2 - x_1)$.

  Y-intercept (b):
  The y-intercept of a line, often written as b, is the value of y at the point where the line crosses the y-axis.

  The equation of a straight line is y = mx + b. Once you know the values of m and b, you can calculate any point on the line by plugging the y- or x-value into that equation. You can also use the TREND function. For more information, see TREND.

- When you have only one independent x-variable, you can obtain the slope and y-intercept values directly by using the following formulas:

  Slope:
  INDEX(LINEST(known_y's,known_x's),1)

  Y-intercept:
  INDEX(LINEST(known_y's,known_x's),2)

- The accuracy of the line calculated by LINEST depends on the degree of scatter in your data. The more linear the data, the more accurate the LINEST model. LINEST uses the method of least squares for determining the best fit for the data. When you have only one independent x-variable, the calculations for m and b are based on the following formulas:

$$m = \frac{n\left(\sum xy\right)\left(\sum x\right)\left(\sum y\right)}{n\left(\sum \left(x^2\right)\right) - \left(\sum x\right)^2}$$

$$b = \frac{\left(\sum y\right)\left(\sum \left(x^2\right)\right) - \left(\sum x\right)\left(\sum xy\right)}{n\left(\sum \left(x^2\right)\right) - \left(\sum x\right)^2}$$

- The line- and curve-fitting functions LINEST and LOGEST can calculate the best straight line or exponential curve that fits your data. However, you have to decide which of the two results best fits your data. You can calculate TREND(known_y's,known_x's) for a straight line, or GROWTH(known_y's, known_x's) for an exponential curve. These functions, without the new_x's argument, return an array of y-values predicted along that line or curve at your actual data points. You can then compare the predicted values with the actual values. You may want to chart them both for a visual comparison.

- In regression analysis, Microsoft Excel calculates for each point the squared difference between the y-value estimated for that point and its actual y-value. The sum of these squared differences is called the residual sum of squares. Microsoft Excel then calculates the sum of the squared differences between the actual y-values and the average of the y-values, which is called the total sum of squares (regression sum of squares + residual sum of squares). The smaller the residual sum of squares is compared with the total sum of squares, the larger the value of the coefficient of determination, r^2, which is an indicator of how well the equation resulting from the regression analysis explains the relationship among the variables.

- Formulas that return arrays must be entered as array formulas.

- When entering an array constant such as known_x's as an argument, use commas to separate values in the same row and semicolons to separate rows. Separator characters may be different depending on your country settings.

- You should note that the y-values predicted by the regression equation may not be valid if they are outside the range of the y-values you used to determine the equation.

Example 1   Slope and Y-intercept

LINEST({1,9,5,7},{0,4,2,3}) equals {2,1}, the slope = 2 and y-intercept = 1.

Example 2 Simple Linear Regression

Suppose a small business has sales of $3100, $4500, $4400, $5400, $7500, and $8100 during the first six months of the fiscal year. Assuming that the values are entered in the range B2:B7,respectively, you can use the following simple linear regression model to estimate sales for the ninth month.

SUM(LINEST(B2:B7)*{9,1}) equals SUM({1000,2000}*{9,1}) equals $11,000

In general, SUM({m,b}*{x,1}) equals mx + b, the estimated y-value for a given x-value. You can also use the TREND function.

Example 3 Multiple Linear Regression

Suppose a commercial developer is considering purchasing a group of small office buildings in an established business district.

The developer can use multiple linear regression analysis to estimate the value of an office building in a given area based on the following variables.

Variable	Refers to the
y	Assessed value of the office building
x1	Floor space in square feet
x2	Number of offices
x3	Number of entrances
x4	Age of the office building in years

This example assumes that a straight-line relationship exists between each of the independent variables (x_1, x_2, x_3, and x_4) and the dependent variable (y), the value of office buildings in the area.

The developer randomly chooses a sample of 11 office buildings from a possible 1500 office buildings and obtains the following data.

	A	B	C	D	E
1	x1 Floor Space	x2 Offices	x3 Entrances	x4 Age	y Value
2	2,310	2	2	20	$142,000
3	2,333	2	2	12	$144,000
4	2,356	3	1.5	33	$151,000
5	2,379	3	2	43	$150,000
6	2,402	2	3	53	$139,000
7	2,425	4	2	23	$169,000
8	2,448	2	1.5	99	$126,000
9	2,471	2	2	34	$142,900
10	2,494	3	3	23	$163,000
11	2,517	4	4	55	$169,000
12	2,540	2	3	22	$149,000

"Half an entrance" means an entrance for deliveries only. When entered as an array, the following formula:

```
LINEST(E2:E12,A2:D12,TRUE,TRUE)
```

returns the following output.

	A	B	C	D	E
14	-234.23716	2553.21066	12529.7682	27.6413874	52317.8305
15	13.2680115	530.669152	400.066838	5.42937404	12237.3616
16	0.99674799	970.578463	#N/A	#N/A	#N/A
17	459.753674	6	#N/A	#N/A	#N/A
18	1732393319	5652135.32	#N/A	#N/A	#N/A

The multiple regression equation, $y = m_1*x_1 + m_2*x_2 + m_3*x_3 + m_4*x_4 + b$, can now be obtained using the values from row 14:

$$y = 27.64*x_1 + 12,530*x_2 + 2,553*x_3 + 234.24*x_4 + 52,318$$

The developer can now estimate the assessed value of an office building in the same area which has 2500 square feet, three offices, and two entrances, and which is 25 years old, by using the following equation:

$$y = 27.64*2500 + 12530*3 + 2553*2 - 234.24*25 + 52318 = \$158,261$$

You can also use the TREND function to calculate this value. For more information, see TREND.

Example 4
Using the F and R^2
Statistics

In the previous example, the coefficient of determination, or r^2, is 0.99675 (see cell A16 in the output for LINEST), which would indicate a strong relationship between the independent variables and the sale price. You can use the F statistic to determine whether these results, with such a high r^2 value, occurred by chance.

Assume for the moment that in fact there is no relationship among the variables, but that you have drawn a rare sample of 11 office buildings which causes the statistical analysis to demonstrate a strong relationship. The term "Alpha" is used for the probability of erroneously concluding that there is a relationship.

There is a relationship among the variables if the F-observed statistic is greater than the F-critical value. The F-critical value can be obtained by referring to a table of F-critical values in many statistics textbooks. To read the table, assume a single-tailed test, use an Alpha value of 0.05, and for the degrees of freedom (abbreviated in most tables as v1 and v2), use v1 = k = 4 and v2 = n - (k + 1) = 11 - (4 + 1) = 6, where k is the number of variables in the regression analysis and n is the number of data points. The F-critical value is 4.53.

The F-observed value is 459.753674 (cell A17), which is substantially greater than the F-critical value of 4.53. Therefore, the regression equation is useful in predicting the assessed value of office buildings in this area.

Example 5
Calculating the
t-Statistics

Another hypothesis test will determine whether each slope coefficient is useful in estimating the assessed value of an office building in example 3. For example, to test the age coefficient for statistical significance, divide -234.24 (age slope coefficient) by 13.268 (the estimated standard error of age coefficients in cell A15). The following is the t-observed value:

$$t = m_4 \div se_4 = -234.24 \div 13.268 = -17.7$$

If you consult a table in a statistics manual, you will find that t-critical, single tail, with 6 degrees of freedom and Alpha = 0.05 is 1.94 . Since the absolute value of t, 17.7, is greater than 1.94, age is an important variable when estimating the assessed value of an office building. Each of the other independent variables can be tested for statistical significance in a similar manner. The following are the t-observed values for each of the independent variables:

Variable	t-observed value
Floor space	5.1
Number of offices	31.3
Number of entrances	4.8
Age	17.7

These values all have an absolute value greater than 1.94; therefore, all the variables used in the regression equation are useful in predicting the assessed value of office buildings in this area.

Related Functions	GROWTH	Similar to TREND and LINEST, but fits an exponential curve to your data instead of a straight line
	LOGEST	Similar to TREND and LINEST, but fits an exponential curve to your data instead of a straight line
	TREND	Calculates a straight line, but returns an array of predicted y-values instead of the parameters of the line

List of Statistical Functions

LN

Returns the natural logarithm of a number. Natural logarithms are based on the constant e (2.71828182845904).

Syntax   **LN(number)**

Number   is the positive real number for which you want the natural logarithm.

Remarks   LN is the inverse of the EXP function.

Examples   LN(86) equals 4.454347

LN(2.7182818) equals 1

LN(EXP(3)) equals 3

EXP(LN(4)) equals 4

Related Functions	EXP	Returns e raised to the power of a given number
	IMLN	Returns the natural logarithm of a complex number
	IMLOG10	Returns the base-10 logarithm of a complex number
	IMLOG2	Returns the base-2 logarithm of a complex number
	LOG	Returns the logarithm of a number to a specified base
	LOG10	Returns the base-10 logarithm of a number

List of Math & Trigonometry Functions

LOG

Returns the logarithm of a number to the base you specify.

Syntax

LOG(number, base)

Number   is the positive real number for which you want the logarithm.

Base   is the base of the logarithm. If base is omitted, it is assumed to be 10.

Examples

LOG(10) equals 1

LOG(8, 2) equals 3

LOG(86, 2.7182818) equals 4.454347

Related Functions

EXP	Returns e raised to the power of a given number
IMLN	Returns the natural logarithm of a complex number
IMLOG10	Returns the base-10 logarithm of a complex number
IMLOG2	Returns the base-2 logarithm of a complex number
LN	Returns the natural logarithm of a number
LOG10	Returns the base-10 logarithm of a number

List of Math & Trigonometry Functions

LOG10

Returns the base-10 logarithm of a number.

Syntax

LOG10(number)

Number   is the positive real number for which you want the base-10 logarithm.

Examples

LOG10(86) equals 1.934498451

LOG10(10) equals 1

LOG10(1E5) equals 5

LOG10(10^5) equals 5

Related Functions

EXP	Returns e raised to the power of a given number
IMLN	Returns the natural logarithm of a complex number
IMLOG10	Returns the base-10 logarithm of a complex number

IMLOG2	Returns the base-2 logarithm of a complex number
LN	Returns the natural logarithm of a number
LOG	Returns the logarithm of a number to a specified base

List of Math & Trigonometry Functions

LOGEST

Calculates an exponential curve that fits your data and returns an array that describes the curve. The equation for the curve is

$$y = (b*(m_1{}^{\wedge}x_1)*(m_2{}^{\wedge}x_2)*\_) \text{ or } y = b*m^{\wedge}x$$

where the dependent y-value is a function of the independent x-values. The m-values are bases corresponding to each exponent x-value, and b is a constant value. Note that y, x, and m can be vectors. The array that LOGEST returns is $\{m_n,m_{n-1},...,m_1,b\}$.

Syntax

LOGEST(known_y's, known_x's, const, stats)

Known_y's   is the set of y-values you already know in the relationship $y = b*m^{\wedge}x$.

- If the array known_y's is in a single column, then each column of known_x's is interpreted as a separate variable.

- If the array known_y's is in a single row, then each row of known_x's is interpreted as a separate variable.

Known_x's   is an optional set of x-values that you may already know in the relationship $y = b*m^{\wedge}x$.

- The array known_x's can include one or more sets of variables. If only one variable is used, known_y's and known_x's can be ranges of any shape, as long as they have equal dimensions. If more than one variable is used, known_y's must be a vector (that is, a range with a height of one row or width of one column).

- If known_x's is omitted, it is assumed to be the array {1,2,3,...} that is the same size as known_y's.

Const   is a logical value specifying whether to force the constant b to equal 1.

- If const is TRUE or omitted, b is calculated normally.

- If const is FALSE, b is set equal to 1, and the m-values are fitted to $y = m^{\wedge}x$.

Stats   is a logical value specifying whether to return additional regression statistics.

- If stats is TRUE, LOGEST returns the additional regression statistics, so the returned array is $\{m_n,m_{n-1},...,m_1,b;se_n,se_{n-1},...,se_1,se_b;r^2,se_y; F,df;ss_{reg},ss_{resid}\}$.
- If stats is FALSE or omitted, LOGEST returns only the m-coefficients and the constant b.

For more information about the additional regression statistics, see LINEST.

Remarks

- The more a plot of your data resembles an exponential curve, the better the calculated line will fit your data. Like LINEST, LOGEST returns an array of values that describes a relationship among the values, but LINEST fits a straight line to your data; LOGEST fits an exponential curve. For more information, see LINEST.
- When you have only one independent x-variable, you can obtain the m and b values directly by using the following formulas:

m:
INDEX(LOGEST(known_y's,known_x's),1)

b:
INDEX(LOGEST(known_y's,known_x's),2)

You can use the y = b*m^x equation to predict future values of y, but Microsoft Excel provides the GROWTH function to do this for you. For more information, see GROWTH.

- Formulas that return arrays must be entered as array formulas.
- When entering an array constant such as known_x's as an argument, use commas to separate values in the same row and semicolons to separate rows. Separator characters may be different depending on your country setting.
- You should note that the y-values predicted by the regression equation may not be valid if they are outside the range of y-values you used to determine the equation.

Example

After 10 months of sluggish sales, a company experiences exponential growth in sales after putting a new product on the market. In the subsequent 6 months, sales increased to 33,100, 47,300, 69,000, 102,000, 150,000, and 220,000 units per month. Assume that these values are entered into six cells named UnitsSold. When entered as a formula:

```
LOGEST(UnitsSold, {11;12;13;14;15;16}, TRUE, TRUE)
```

generates the following output in, for example, cells D1:E5:

{1.46327563, 495.30477; 0.0026334, 0.03583428; 0.99980862, 0.01101631; 20896.8011, 4; 2.53601883, 0.00048544}

$y = b*m_1^{\wedge}x_1$ or using the values from the array:

$y = 495.3 * 1.4633^x$

You can estimate sales for future months by substituting the month number for x in this equation, or you can use the GROWTH function. For more information, see GROWTH.

You can use the additional regression statistics (cells D2:E5 in the above output array) to determine how useful the equation is for predicting future values.

Important methods you use to test an equation using LOGEST are similar to the methods for LINEST. However, the additional statistics LOGEST returns are based on the following linear model:

$\ln y = x_1 \ln m_1 + \cdots + x_n \ln m_n + \ln b$

You should keep this in mind when you evaluate the additional statistics, especially the se_i and se_b values, which should be compared to $\ln m_i$ and $\ln b$, not to m_i and b. For more information, consult an advanced statistics manual.

Related Functions

GROWTH	Also calculates an exponential curve, but returns an array of predicted y-values instead of the parameters of the curve
LINEST	Similar to LOGEST but fits a straight line instead of an exponential curve to your data
TREND	Similar to GROWTH but fits a straight line instead of an exponential curve to your data

List of Statistical Functions

LOGINV

Returns the inverse of the lognormal cumulative distribution function of x, where $\ln(x)$ is normally distributed with parameters mean and standard_dev. If p = LOGNORMDIST(x,...) then LOGINV(p,...) = x.

Use the lognormal distribution to analyze logarithmically transformed data.

Syntax   **LOGINV(probability, mean, standard_dev)**

Probability   is a probability associated with the lognormal distribution.

Mean   is the mean of ln(x).

Standard_dev   is the standard deviation of ln(x).

The inverse of the lognormal distribution function is:

$$\text{LOGINV}(p, \mu, \sigma) = e^{[\mu + \sigma \times (NORMSINV(p))]}$$

Remarks
- If any argument is non-numeric, LOGINV returns the #VALUE! error value.
- If probability < 0 or probability > 1, LOGINV returns the #NUM! error value.
- If standard_dev ≤ 0, LOGINV returns the #NUM! error value.

Example   `LOGINV(0.039084, 3.5, 1.2)` equals 4.000014

Related Functions

EXP	Returns e raised to the power of a given number
LN	Returns the natural logarithm of a number
LOG	Returns the logarithm of a number to a specified base
LOG10	Returns the base-10 logarithm of a number
LOGNORMDIST	Returns the cumulative lognormal distribution

List of Statistical Functions

LOGNORMDIST

Returns the cumulative lognormal distribution of x, where ln(x) is normally distributed with parameters mean and standard_dev. Use this function to analyze data that has been logarithmically transformed.

Syntax   **LOGNORMDIST(x, mean, standard_dev)**

X   is the value at which to evaluate the function.

Mean   is the mean of ln(x).

Standard_dev   is the standard deviation of ln(x).

Remarks
- If any argument is non-numeric, LOGNORMDIST returns the #VALUE! error value.
- If x ≤ 0 or if standard_dev ≤ 0, LOGNORMDIST returns the #NUM! error value.
- The equation for the lognormal cumulative distribution function is:

$$\text{LOGNORMDIST}(x, \mu, \sigma) =$$
$$\text{NORMSDIST}\left(\frac{\ln(x) - \mu}{\sigma}\right)$$

Example   LOGNORMDIST(4,3.5,1.2) equals 0.039084

Related Functions

EXP	Returns e raised to the power of a given number
LN	Returns the natural logarithm of a number
LOG	Returns the logarithm of a number to a specified base
LOG10	Returns the base-10 logarithm of a number
LOGINV	Returns the inverse of the lognormal distribution

List of Statistical Functions

LOOKUP

The LOOKUP function has two syntax forms, vector and array.

A vector is an array that contains only one row or one column. The vector form of LOOKUP looks in a vector for a value, moves to the corresponding position in a second vector, and returns this value. Use this form of the LOOKUP function when you want to be able to specify the range that contains the values you want to match. The other form of LOOKUP automatically looks in the first column or row.

Syntax 1

Vector form

LOOKUP(lookup_value, lookup_vector, result_vector)

Lookup_value   is a value that LOOKUP searches for in the first vector. Lookup_value can be a number, text, a logical value, or a name or reference that refers to a value.

Lookup_vector   is a range that contains only one row or one column. The values in lookup_vector can be text, numbers, or logical values.

Important The values in lookup_vector must be placed in ascending order: ...,-2, -1, 0, 1, 2, ..., A-Z, FALSE, TRUE; otherwise, LOOKUP may not give the correct value. Uppercase and lowercase text are equivalent.

Result_vector   is a range that contains only one row or column. It should be the same size as lookup_vector.

- If LOOKUP can't find the lookup_value, it matches the largest value in lookup_vector that is less than or equal to lookup_value.

- If lookup_value is smaller than the smallest value in lookup_vector, LOOKUP gives the #N/A error value.

Examples

	A	B	C
1	Frequency	Color	
2	4.14234	red	
3	4.19342	orange	
4	5.17234	yellow	
5	5.77343	green	
6	6.38987	blue	
7	7.31342	violet	

In the preceding worksheet:

LOOKUP(4.91,A2:A7,B2:B7) equals "orange"

LOOKUP(5.00,A2:A7,B2:B7) equals "orange"

LOOKUP(7.66,A2:A7,B2:B7) equals "violet"

LOOKUP(7.66E-14,A2:A7,B2:B7) equals #N/A, because 7.66E-14 is less than the smallest value in the lookup_vector A2:A7

Related Functions	LOOKUP (array)	Looks up values in an array
	HLOOKUP	Looks in the top row of an array and returns the value of the indicated cell
	INDEX	Uses an index to choose a value from a reference or array
	VLOOKUP	Looks in the first column of an array and moves across the row to return the value of a cell

List of Lookup & Reference Functions

LOOKUP

The LOOKUP function has two syntax forms, vector and array.

The array form of LOOKUP looks in the first row or column of an array for the specified value, moves down or across to the last cell, and returns the value of the cell. Use this form of LOOKUP when the values you want to match are in the first row or column of the array. Use the other form of LOOKUP when you want to be able to specify the location of the column or row.

Tip   In general, it's best to use the HLOOKUP or VLOOKUP function instead of the array form of LOOKUP. This form of LOOKUP is provided for compatibility with other spreadsheet programs.

Syntax 2   Array form

LOOKUP(lookup_value, array)

Lookup_value   is a value that LOOKUP searches for in an array. Lookup_value can be a number, text, a logical value, or a name or reference that refers to a value.

- If LOOKUP can't find the lookup_value, it uses the largest value in the array that is less than or equal to lookup_value.
- If lookup_value is smaller than the smallest value in the first row or column (depending on the array dimensions), LOOKUP returns the #N/A error value.

Array   is a range of cells that contains text, numbers, or logical values that you want to compare with lookup_value.

The array form of LOOKUP is very similar to the HLOOKUP and VLOOKUP functions. The difference is that HLOOKUP searches for lookup_value in the first row, VLOOKUP searches in the first column, and LOOKUP searches according to the dimensions of array.

- If array is square, or covers an area that is wider than it is tall (more columns than rows), LOOKUP searches for lookup_value in the first row.

- If array is taller than it is wide (more rows than columns), LOOKUP searches in the first column.

- HLOOKUP and VLOOKUP allow you to index down or across, but LOOKUP always selects the last value in the row or column.

Important   The values must be placed in ascending order: ...,-2, -1, 0, 1, 2, ..., A-Z, FALSE, TRUE; otherwise, LOOKUP may not give the correct value. Uppercase and lowercase text are equivalent.

Examples

LOOKUP("C",{"a","b","c","d";1,2,3,4}) equals 3

LOOKUP("bump",{"a",1;"b",2;"c",3}) equals 2

Related Functions

LOOKUP (vector)	Looks up values in a vector
HLOOKUP	Looks in the top row of an array and returns the value of the indicated cell
INDEX	Uses an index to choose a value from a reference or array
MATCH	Looks up values in a reference or array
VLOOKUP	Looks in the first column of an array and moves across the row to return the value of a cell

List of Lookup & Reference Functions

LOWER

Converts all uppercase letters in a text string to lowercase.

Syntax

LOWER(text)

Text   is the text you want to convert to lowercase. LOWER does not change characters in text that are not letters.

Examples

LOWER("E. E. Cummings") equals "e. e. cummings"

LOWER("Apt. 2B") equals "apt. 2b"

LOWER is similar to PROPER and UPPER. Also see examples for PROPER.

Related Functions   PROPER   Capitalizes the first letter in each word of a text value

UPPER   Converts text to uppercase

List of Text Functions

MATCH

Returns the relative position of an element in an array that matches a specified value in a specified way. Use MATCH instead of one of the LOOKUP functions when you need the position of a matched item instead of the item itself.

Syntax   **MATCH(lookup_value, lookup_array, match_type)**

Lookup_value   is the value you use to find the value you want in a table.

- Lookup_value is the value you want to match in lookup_array. For example, when you look up someone's number in a telephone book, you are using the person's name as the lookup value, but the telephone number is the value you want.

- Lookup_value can be a value (number, text, or logical value) or a cell reference to a number, text, or logical value.

Lookup_array   is a contiguous range of cells containing possible lookup values. Lookup_array can be an array or an array reference.

Match_type   is the number –1, 0, or 1. Match_type specifies how Microsoft Excel matches lookup_value with values in lookup_array.

- If match_type is 1, MATCH finds the largest value that is less than or equal to lookup_value. Lookup_array must be placed in ascending order: ...–2, –1, 0, 1, 2,...A-Z, FALSE, TRUE.

- If match_type is 0, MATCH finds the first value that is exactly equal to lookup_value. Lookup_array can be in any order.

- If match_type is –1, MATCH finds the smallest value that is greater than or equal to lookup_value. Lookup_array must be placed in descending order: TRUE, FALSE, Z-A,...2, 1, 0, –1, –2,..., and so on.

- If match_type is omitted, it is assumed to be 1.

Remarks

- MATCH returns the position of the matched value within lookup_array, not the value itself. For example: MATCH("b",{"a","b","c"},0) returns 2, the relative position of "b" within the array {"a","b","c"}.

- MATCH does not distinguish between uppercase and lowercase letters when matching text values.

- If MATCH is unsuccessful in finding a match, it returns the #N/A error value.

- If match_type is 0 and lookup_value is text, lookup_value can contain the wildcard characters, asterisk (*) and question mark (?). An asterisk matches any sequence of characters; a question mark matches any single character.

Examples

	A	B	C
1	Income (in Yen)	U.S. Dollars	U.S. Tax Rate
2	¥5,365,000.00	$37,000.00	21.50%
3	¥5,510,000.00	$38,000.00	21.67%
4	¥5,655,000.00	$39,000.00	21.84%
5	¥5,800,000.00	$40,000.00	21.99%
6	¥5,945,000.00	$41,000.00	22.14%
7	¥6,090,000.00	$42,000.00	22.28%
8	¥6,235,000.00	$43,000.00	22.41%

Note that C2:C8 contains text formatted as percent numbers.

In the preceding worksheet:

`MATCH(39000,B2:B8,1)` equals 3

`MATCH(38000,B2:B8,0)` equals 2

`MATCH(39000,B2:B8,-1)` equals the #N/A error value because the range B2:B8 is ordered incorrectly for match_type −1 matching (the order must be descending to be correct).

Suppose Yen refers to A2:A8, YenDollar to A2:C8, and MyIncome to a cell containing the number ¥6,301,126.33. This formula:

`"Your tax rate is "&LOOKUP(MyIncome,YenDollar)&", which places you in tax bracket number "&MATCH(MyIncome,Yen)&"."`

produces this result:

"Your tax rate is 22.41%, which places you in tax bracket number 7."

Related Functions   HLOOKUP   Looks in the top row of an array and returns the value of the
                                                  indicated cell

                          VLOOKUP   Looks in the first column of an array and moves across the row
                                                  to return the value of a cell

                          INDEX   Uses an index to choose a value from a reference or array

                          List of Lookup & Reference Functions

---

MAX

Returns the maximum value in a list of arguments.

Syntax   **MAX(number1**, number2, ...)

Number1, number2,...   are 1 to 30 numbers for which you want to find the
maximum value.

- You can specify arguments that are numbers, empty cells, logical values, or text
  representations of numbers. Arguments that are error values or text that cannot
  be translated into numbers cause errors.

- If an argument is an array or reference, only numbers in that array or reference
  are used. Empty cells, logical values, text, or error values in the array or
  reference are ignored.

- If the arguments contain no numbers, MAX returns 0.

Examples   If A1:A5 contains the numbers 10, 7, 9, 27, and 2, then:

MAX(A1:A5) equals 27

MAX(A1:A5,30) equals 30

Related Functions   DMAX   Returns the maximum value from selected database entries
                          MIN   Returns the minimum value in a list of arguments

                          List of Statistical Functions

MDETERM

Returns the matrix determinant of an array.

Syntax

MDETERM(array)

Array   is a numeric array with an equal number of rows and columns.

- Array can be given as a cell range, for example, A1:C3; as an array constant, such as {1,2,3;4,5,6;7,8,9}; or as a name to either of these.
- If any cells in array are empty or contain text, MDETERM returns the #VALUE! error value.
- MDETERM also returns #VALUE! if array does not have an equal number of rows and columns.

Remarks

- The matrix determinant is a number derived from the values in array. For a three-row, three-column array, A1:C3, the determinant is defined as:

  MDETERM(A1:C3) equals
  A1*(B2*C3-B3*C2) + A2*(B3*C1-B1*C3) + A3*(B1*C2-B2*C1)

- Matrix determinants are generally used for solving systems of mathematical equations that involve several variables.
- MDETERM is calculated with an accuracy of approximately 16 digits, which may lead to a small numeric error when the calculation is not complete. For example, the determinant of a singular matrix may differ from zero by 1E–16.

Examples

MDETERM({1,3,8,5;1,3,6,1;1,1,1,0;7,3,10,2}) equals 88

MDETERM({3,6,1;1,1,0;3,10,2}) equals 1

MDETERM({3,6;1,1}) equals –3

MDETERM({1,3,8,5;1,3,6,1}) equals #VALUE! because the array does not have an equal number of rows and columns.

Related Functions

MINVERSE	Returns the matrix inverse of an array
MMULT	Returns the matrix product of two arrays
TRANSPOSE	Returns the transpose of an array

List of Math & Trigonometry Functions

MDURATION

Returns the modified Macauley duration for a security with an assumed par value of $100.

If this function is not available, run the Setup program to install the Analysis ToolPak. After you install the Analysis ToolPak, you must select it in the Add-In Manager. For more information, look up Add-ins in Help.

Syntax

MDURATION(settlement, maturity, coupon, yld, frequency, basis)

Settlement   is the security's settlement date, expressed as a serial date number.

Maturity   is the security's maturity date, expressed as a serial date number.

Coupon   is the security's annual coupon rate.

Yld   is the security's annual yield.

Frequency   is the number of coupon payments per year. For annual payments, frequency = 1; for semiannual, frequency = 2; for quarterly, frequency = 4.

Basis   is the type of day count basis to use.

Basis	Day count basis
0 or omitted	US (NASD) 30/360
1	Actual/actual
2	Actual/360
3	Actual/365
4	European 30/360

Remarks

- Settlement, maturity, frequency, and basis are truncated to integers.
- If any argument is non-numeric, MDURATION returns the #VALUE! error value.
- If settlement or maturity is not a valid serial date number, MDURATION returns the #NUM! error value.
- If yld < 0 or if coupon < 0, MDURATION returns the #NUM! error value.
- If frequency is any number other than 1, 2, or 4, MDURATION returns the #NUM! error value.
- If basis < 0 or if basis > 4, MDURATION returns the #NUM! error value.

- If settlement ≥ maturity, MDURATION returns the #NUM! error value.

- Modified duration is defined as follows:

$$\text{MDURATION} = \frac{\text{DURATION}}{1 + \left(\dfrac{\text{Market yield}}{\text{Coupon payments per year}} \right)}$$

Example

A bond has the following terms:

January 1, 1986 settlement date
January 1, 1994 maturity date
8.0% coupon
9.0% yield
Frequency is semiannual
Actual/actual basis

The modified duration (in the 1900 Date System) is:

`MDURATION(31413,34335,0.08,0.09,2,1)` equals 5.73567

Related Functions

DURATION   Returns the annual duration of a security with
                              periodic interest payments

List of Financial Functions

MEDIAN

Returns the median of the given numbers. The median is the number in the middle of a set of numbers; that is, half the numbers have values that are greater than the median and half have values that are less.

Syntax

MEDIAN(number1, number2, ...)

Number1, number2,... are 1 to 30 numbers for which you want the median.

- The arguments should be numbers or names, arrays, or references that contain numbers. Microsoft Excel examines all the numbers in each reference or array argument.

- If an array or reference argument contains text, logical values, or empty cells, those values are ignored; however, cells with the value zero are included.

Remarks   If there is an even number of numbers in the set, then MEDIAN calculates the average of the two numbers in the middle. See the second example following.

Examples   MEDIAN(1, 2, 3, 4, 5) equals 3

MEDIAN(1, 2, 3, 4, 5, 6) equals 3.5, the average of 3 and 4

Related Functions

AVERAGE	Returns the average of its arguments
COUNT	Counts how many numbers are in the list of arguments
COUNTA	Counts how many values are in the list of arguments
DAVERAGE	Returns the average of selected database entries
MODE	Returns the most common value in a data set
SUM	Adds its arguments

List of Statistical Functions

MID

Returns a specific number of characters from a text string, starting at the position you specify.

Syntax   **MID(text, start_num, num_chars)**

Text   is the text string containing the characters you want to extract.

Start_num   is the position of the first character you want to extract in text. The first character in text has start_num 1, and so on.

- If start_num is greater than the length of text, MID returns "" (empty text).
- If start_num is less than the length of text, but start_num plus num_chars exceeds the length of text, MID returns the characters up to the end of text.
- If start_num is less than 1, MID returns the #VALUE! error value.

Num_chars   specifies how many characters to return from text. If num_chars is negative, MID returns the #VALUE! error value.

Examples   MID("Fluid Flow", 1, 5) equals "Fluid"

MID("Fluid Flow", 7, 20) equals "Flow"

MID("1234", 5, 5) equals "" (empty text)

Also see the examples for CODE and FIND.

Related Functions	CODE	Returns a numeric code for the first character in a text string
	FIND	Finds one text value within another (case-sensitive)
	LEFT	Returns the leftmost characters from a text value
	RIGHT	Returns the rightmost characters from a text value
	SEARCH	Finds one text value within another (not case-sensitive)

List of Text Functions

MIN

Returns the smallest number in the list of arguments.

Syntax

MIN(number1, number2, ...)

Number1, number2,...   are 1 to 30 numbers for which you want to find the minimum value.

- You can specify arguments that are numbers, empty cells, logical values, or text representations of numbers. Arguments that are error values or text that cannot be translated into numbers cause errors.
- If an argument is an array or reference, only numbers in that array or reference are used. Empty cells, logical values, text, or error values in the array or reference are ignored.
- If the arguments contain no numbers, MIN returns 0.

Examples

If A1:A5 contains the numbers 10, 7, 9, 27, and 2, then:

`MIN(A1:A5)` equals 2

`MIN(A1:A5, 0)` equals 0

MIN is similar to MAX. Also see the examples for MAX.

| **Related Functions** | DMIN | Returns the minimum value from selected database entries |
| | MAX | Returns the maximum value in a list of arguments |

List of Statistical Functions

MINUTE

Returns the minute corresponding to serial_number. The minute is given as an integer, ranging from 0 to 59.

Syntax

MINUTE(serial_number)

Serial_number is the date-time code used by Microsoft Excel for date and time calculations. You can give serial_number as text, such as "16:48:00" or "4:48:00 PM", instead of as a number. The text is automatically converted to a serial number. For more information about serial_number, see NOW.

Remarks

Microsoft Excel for Windows and Microsoft Excel for the Macintosh use different date systems as their default. For more information, see NOW.

Examples

MINUTE("4:48:00 PM") equals 48

MINUTE(0.01) equals 14

MINUTE(4.02) equals 28

Related Functions

NOW	Returns the serial number of the current date and time
YEAR, MONTH, DAY, WEEKDAY, HOUR, and SECOND	Convert serial numbers into years, months, days, days of the week, hours, and seconds, respectively

List of Date & Time Functions

MINVERSE

Returns the inverse matrix for the matrix stored in an array.

Syntax

MINVERSE(array)

Array is a numeric array with an equal number of rows and columns.

- Array can be given as a cell range, such as A1:C3; as an array constant, such as {1,2,3;4,5,6;7,8,9}; or as a name for either of these.
- If any cells in array are empty or contain text, MINVERSE returns the #VALUE! error value.
- MINVERSE also returns the #VALUE! error value if array does not have an equal number of rows and columns.

Remarks
- Formulas that return arrays must be entered as array formulas.
- Inverse matrices, like determinants, are generally used for solving systems of mathematical equations involving several variables. The product of a matrix and its inverse is the identity matrix—the square array in which the diagonal values equal 1 and all other values equal 0.
- As an example of how a two-row, two-column matrix is calculated, suppose that the range A1:B2 contains the letters a, b, c, and d that represent any four numbers. The following table shows the inverse of the matrix A1:B2:

	Column A	Column B
Row 1	d/(a*d–b*c)	b/(b*c–a*d)
Row 2	c/(b*c–a*d)	a/(a*d–b*c)

- MINVERSE is calculated with an accuracy of approximately 16 digits, which may lead to a small numeric error when the cancellation is not complete.
- Some square matrices cannot be inverted, and will return the #NUM! error value with MINVERSE. The determinant for a noninvertable matrix is 0.

Examples

MINVERSE({4,-1;2,0}) equals {0,0.5;–1,2}

MINVERSE({1,2,1;3,4,-1;0,2,0}) equals {0.25,0.25,–0.75;0,0,0.5;0.75,–0.25,–0.25}

Tip Use the INDEX function to access individual elements from the inverse matrix.

Related Functions

INDEX	Uses an index to choose a value from a reference or array
MMULT	Returns the matrix product of two arrays
TRANSPOSE	Returns the transpose of an array

List of Math & Trigonometry Functions

MIRR

Returns the modified internal rate of return for a series of periodic cash flows. MIRR considers both the cost of the investment and the interest received on reinvestment of cash.

Syntax

MIRR(values, finance_rate, reinvest_rate)

Values   is an array or a reference to cells that contain numbers. These numbers represent a series of payments (negative values) and income (positive values) occurring at regular periods.

- Values must contain at least one positive value and one negative value to calculate the modified internal rate of return. Otherwise, MIRR returns the #DIV/0! error value.

- If an array or reference argument contains text, logical values, or empty cells, those values are ignored; however, cells with the value zero are included.

Finance_rate   is the interest rate you pay on the money used in the cash flows.

Reinvest_rate   is the interest rate you receive on the cash flows as you reinvest them.

Remarks

- MIRR uses the order of values to interpret the order of cash flows. Be sure to enter your payment and income values in the sequence you want and with the correct signs (positive values for cash received, negative values for cash paid).

- If n is the number of cash flows in values, frate is the finance_rate, and rrate is the reinvest_rate, then the formula for MIRR is:

$$\left(\frac{-NPV(rrate, values[positive]) * (1 + rrate)^n}{NPV(frate, values[negative]) * (1 + frate)} \right)^{\frac{1}{n-1}} - 1$$

Examples

Suppose you're a commercial fisherman just completing your fifth year of operation. Five years ago, you borrowed $120,000 at 10 percent annual interest to purchase a boat. Your catches have yielded $39,000, $30,000, $21,000, $37,000, and $46,000. During these years you reinvested your profits, earning 12% annually. In a worksheet, your loan amount is entered as –$120,000 in B1, and your five annual profits are entered in B2:B6.

To calculate the investment's modified rate of return after five years:

MIRR(B1:B6, 10%, 12%) equals 12.61%

To calculate the modified rate of return after three years:

MIRR(B1:B4, 10%, 12%) equals –4.80%

To calculate the five-year modified rate of return based on a reinvest_rate of 14%

MIRR(B1:B6, 10%, 14%) equals 13.48%

Related Functions RATE   Returns the interest rate per period of an annuity

XIRR   Returns the internal rate of return for a schedule of cash flows
                      that is not necessarily periodic

XNPV   Returns the net present value for a schedule of cash flows that
                      is not necessarily periodic

List of Financial Functions

MMULT

Returns the matrix product of two arrays. The result is an array with the same
number of rows as array1 and the same number of columns as array2.

Syntax

MMULT(array1, array2)

Array1, array2   are the arrays you want to multiply.

- The number of columns in array1 must be the same as the number of rows in
  array2, and both arrays must contain only numbers.
- Array1 and array2 can be given as cell ranges, array constants, or references.
- If any cells are empty or contain text, or if the number of columns in array1 is
  different from the number of rows in array2, MMULT returns the #VALUE!
  error value.

Remarks

- The matrix product array a of two arrays b and c is:

$$a_{ij} = \sum_{k=1}^{n} b_{ik} c_{kj}$$

where i is the row number and j is the column number.

- Formulas that return arrays must be entered as array formulas.

Examples

MMULT({1,3;7,2}, {2,0;0,2}) equals {2,6;14,4}

MMULT({3,0;2,0}, {2,0;0,2}) equals {6,0;4,0}

MMULT({1,3,0;7,2,0;1,0,0}, {2,0;0,2}) equals #VALUE!, because the
first array has three columns and the second array has only two rows.

Related Functions MDETERM   Returns the matrix determinant of an array

MINVERSE   Returns the matrix inverse of an array

TRANSPOSE   Returns the transpose of an array

List of Math & Trigonometry Functions

MOD

Returns the remainder after number is divided by divisor. The result has the same sign as divisor.

Syntax **MOD(number, divisor)**

Number   is the number for which you want to find the remainder.

Divisor   is the number by which you want to divide number. If divisor is 0, MOD returns the #DIV/0! error value.

Remarks The MOD function can be expressed in terms of the INT function:

```
MOD(n, d) = n - d*INT(n/d)
```

Examples MOD(3, 2) equals 1

MOD(-3, 2) equals 1

MOD(3, -2) equals −1

MOD(-3, -2) equals −1

Related Functions INT   Rounds a number down to the nearest integer

ROUND   Rounds a number to a specified number of digits

ROUNDDOWN   Rounds a number down, toward zero

ROUNDUP   Rounds a number up, away from zero

TRUNC   Truncates a number to an integer

List of Math & Trigonometry Functions

MODE

Returns the most frequently occurring value in an array or range of data. Like MEDIAN, MODE is a location measure.

Syntax

MODE(number1, number2, ...)

Number1, number2,...   are 1 to 30 arguments for which you want to calculate the mode. You can also use a single array or a reference to an array instead of arguments separated by commas.

Remarks

- The arguments should be numbers, or names, arrays, or references that contain numbers.

- If an array or reference argument contains text, logical values, or empty cells, those values are ignored; however, cells with the value zero are included.

- If the data set contains no duplicate data points, MODE returns the #N/A error value.

The mode is the most frequently occurring value; the median is the middle value; and the mean is the average value. No single measure of central tendency provides a complete picture of the data. Suppose data is clustered in three areas, half around a single low value, and half around two large values. Both AVERAGE and MEDIAN may return a value in the relatively empty middle, while MODE may return the dominant low value.

Example

MODE({5.6, 4, 4, 3, 2, 4}) equals 4

Related Functions

AVERAGE	Returns the average of its arguments
GEOMEAN	Returns the geometric mean
HARMEAN	Returns the harmonic mean
MEDIAN	Returns the median of the given numbers
TRIMMEAN	Returns the mean of the interior of a data set

List of Statistical Functions

MONTH

Returns the month corresponding to serial_number. The month is given as an integer, ranging from 1 (January) to 12 (December).

Syntax	**MONTH(serial_number)**

Serial_number   is the date-time code used by Microsoft Excel for date and time calculations. You can give serial_number as text, such as "4-15-1993" or "15-Apr-1993", instead of as a number. The text is automatically converted to a serial number. For more information about serial_number, see NOW.

Remarks   Microsoft Excel for Windows and Microsoft Excel for the Macintosh use different date systems as their default. For more information, see NOW.

Examples   MONTH("6-May") equals 5

MONTH(366) equals 12

MONTH(367) equals 1

Related Functions

NOW	Returns the serial number for the current date and time
YEAR, MONTH, DAY, WEEKDAY, HOUR, and MINUTE	Convert serial numbers into years, months, days, days of the week, hours, and minutes
List of Date & Time Functions	

MROUND

Returns a number rounded to the desired multiple.

If this function is not available, run the Setup program to install the Analysis ToolPak. After you install the Analysis ToolPak, you must select it in the Add-In Manager. For more information, look up Add-ins in Help.

Syntax   **MROUND(number, multiple)**

Number   is the value to round.

Multiple   is the multiple to which you want to round number.

Remarks   MROUND rounds up, away from zero, if the remainder of dividing number by multiple is greater than or equal to half the value of multiple.

Examples   MROUND(10, 3) equals 9

MROUND(-10, -3) equals –9

MROUND(1.3, 0.2) equals 1.4

MROUND(5, -2) equals #NUM!

Related Functions	CEILING	Returns the number rounded up to the nearest multiple of significance
	EVEN	Rounds a number up to the nearest even integer
	FLOOR	Rounds a number down, toward zero
	ODD	Rounds a number up to the nearest odd integer
	ROUND	Rounds a number to a specified number of digits
	ROUNDDOWN	Rounds a number down, toward zero
	ROUNDUP	Rounds a number up, away from zero
	TRUNC	Truncates a number to an integer

List of Math & Trigonometry Functions

MULTINOMIAL

Returns the ratio of the factorial of a sum of values to the product of factorials.

If this function is not available, run the Setup program to install the Analysis ToolPak. After you install the Analysis ToolPak, you must select it in the Add-In Manager. For more information, look up Add-ins in Help.

Syntax

MULTINOMIAL(number1, number2, ...)

Number1,number2,...   are 1 to 29 values for which you want the multinomial.

Remarks

- If any argument is non-numeric, MULTINOMIAL returns the #VALUE! error value.
- If any argument is less than one, MULTINOMIAL returns the #NUM! error value.
- The multinomial is:

$$EFFECT = (1 + \frac{No\min al\_Rate}{Nper})^{(Nper-1)}$$

Example

MULTINOMIAL(2, 3, 4) equals 1260

Related Functions	FACT	Returns the factorial of a number
	FACTDOUBLE	Returns the double factorial of a number

List of Math & Trigonometry Functions

N

Returns a value converted to a number.

Syntax

N(value)

Value   is the value you want converted. N converts values listed in the following table.

If value is or refers to	N returns
A number	That number
A date, in one of Microsoft Excel's built-in date formats	The serial number of that date
TRUE	1
Anything else	0

Remarks

It is not generally necessary to use the N function in a formula, since Microsoft Excel automatically converts values as necessary. This function is provided for compatibility with other spreadsheet programs.

Examples

If A1 contains "7", A2 contains "Even", and A3 contains "TRUE", then:

N(A1) equals 7

N(A2) equals 0, because B2 contains text

N(A3) equals 1, because C2 contains TRUE

N("7") equals 0, because "7" is text

N("4/17/91") equals 0, because "4/17/91" is text

Related Functions

T   Converts its arguments to text

List of Information Functions

NA

Returns the error value #N/A. #N/A is the error value that means "no value is available." Use NA to mark empty cells. By entering #N/A in cells where you are missing information, you can avoid the problem of unintentionally including empty cells in your calculations. (When a formula refers to a cell containing #N/A, the formula returns the #N/A error value.)

Syntax	**NA( )**
Remarks	■ You must include the empty parentheses with the function name. Otherwise, Microsoft Excel will not recognize it as a function.
	■ You can also type the value #N/A directly into a cell. The NA function is provided for compatibility with other spreadsheet programs.
Related Function	ISNA Returns TRUE if a value is the #N/A error value
	List of Information Functions

NEGBINOMDIST

Returns the negative binomial distribution. NEGBINOMDIST returns the probability that there will be number_f failures before the number_s-th success, when the constant probability of a success is probability_s. This function is similar to the binomial distribution, except that the number of successes is fixed and the number of trials is variable. Like the binomial, trials are assumed to be independent.

For example, you need to find 10 people with excellent reflexes, and you know the probability that a candidate has these qualifications is 0.3. NEGBINOMDIST calculates the probability that you will interview a certain number of unqualified candidates before finding all 10 qualified candidates.

Syntax

NEGBINOMDIST(number_f, number_s, probability_s)

Number_f   is the number of failures.

Number_s   is the threshold number of successes.

Probability_s   is the probability of a success.

Remarks

■ Number_f and number_s are truncated to integers.

■ If any argument is non-numeric, NEGBINOMDIST returns the #VALUE! error value.

■ If probability_s < 0 or if probability > 1, NEGBINOMDIST returns the #NUM! error value.

- If (number_f + number_s − 1) ≤ 0, NEGBINOMDIST returns the #NUM! error value.

- The equation for the negative binomial distribution is:

$$nb(x; r, p) = \binom{x + r - 1}{r - 1} p^r (1 - p)^x$$

where:

x is number_f, r is number_s, and p is probability_s.

Example NEGBINOMDIST(10,5,0.25) equals 0.055049

Related Functions

BINOMDIST	Returns the individual term binomial distribution probability
COMBIN	Returns the number of combinations for a given number of objects
FACT	Returns the factorial of a number
HYPGEOMDIST	Returns the hypergeometric distribution
PERMUT	Returns the number of permutations for a given number of objects

List of Statistical Functions

NETWORKDAYS

Returns the number of whole working days between start_date and end_date. Working days exclude weekends and any dates identified in holidays. Use NETWORKDAYS to calculate employee benefits that accrue based on the number of days worked during a specific term.

If this function is not available, run the Setup program to install the Analysis ToolPak. After you install the Analysis ToolPak, you must select it in the Add-In Manager. For more information, look up Add-ins in Help.

Syntax **NETWORKDAYS(start_date, end_date, holidays)**

Start_date   is a serial date number that represents the start date.

End_date   is a serial date number that represents the end date.

Holidays   is an optional set of one or more serial date numbers to exclude from the working calendar, such as state and federal holidays and floating holidays.

Remarks
- If any argument is non-numeric, NETWORKDAYS returns the #VALUE! error value.
- If any argument is not a valid serial date number, NETWORKDAYS returns the #NUM! error value.

Example

`NETWORKDAYS(DATEVALUE("10/01/91"), DATEVALUE("12/01/91"), DATEVALUE("11/28/91"))` equals 43

Related Functions

EDATE	Returns the serial number of the date that is the indicated number of months before or after the start date
EOMONTH	Returns the serial number of the last day of the month before or after a specified number of months
NOW	Returns the serial number of the current date and time
WORKDAY	Returns the serial number of the date before or after a specified number of workdays

List of Date & Time Functions

NOMINAL

Returns the nominal annual interest rate given the effective rate and the number of compounding periods per year.

If this function is not available, run the Setup program to install the Analysis ToolPak. After you install the Analysis ToolPak, you must select it in the Add-In Manager. For more information, look up Add-ins in Help.

Syntax

NOMINAL(effect_rate, npery)

Effect_rate   is the effective interest rate.

Npery   is the number of compounding periods per year.

Remarks
- Npery is truncated to an integer.
- If either argument is non-numeric, NOMINAL returns the #VALUE! error value.
- If effect_rate ≤ 0 or if npery < 1, NOMINAL returns the #NUM! error value.
- NOMINAL is related to EFFECT as shown in the following equation:

$$EFFECT = (1 + \frac{No\min al\_Rate}{Nper})^{Npery} - 1$$

Example   NOMINAL(5.3543%,4) equals 0.0525 or 5.25%

Related Function   EFFECT   Returns the effective annual interest rate

List of Financial Functions

NORMDIST

Returns the normal cumulative distribution for the specified mean and standard deviation. This function has a very wide range of applications in statistics, including hypothesis testing.

Syntax

NORMDIST(x, mean, standard_dev, cumulative)

X   is the value for which you want the distribution.

Mean   is the arithmetic mean of the distribution.

Standard_dev   is the standard deviation of the distribution.

Cumulative   is a logical value that determines the form of the function. If cumulative is TRUE, NORMDIST returns the cumulative distribution function; if FALSE, it returns the probability mass function.

Remarks

- If mean or standard_dev is non-numeric, NORMDIST returns the #VALUE! error value.
- If standard_dev ≤ 0, NORMDIST returns the #NUM! error value.
- If mean = 0 and standard_dev = 1, NORMDIST returns the standard normal distribution, NORMSDIST.
- The equation for the normal density function is:

$$f(x;\mu,\sigma) = \frac{1}{\sqrt{2\pi}\sigma} e^{-\left(\frac{(x-\mu)^2}{2\sigma^2}\right)}$$

Example   NORMDIST(42,40,1.5,TRUE) equals 0.908789

Related Functions		
	NORMINV	Returns the inverse of the normal cumulative distribution
	NORMSDIST	Returns the standard normal cumulative distribution
	NORMSINV	Returns the inverse of the standard normal cumulative distribution
	STANDARDIZE	Returns a normalized value
	ZTEST	Returns the two-tailed P-value of a z-test

List of Statistical Functions

NORMINV

Returns the inverse of the normal cumulative distribution for the specified mean and standard deviation.

Syntax

NORMINV(probability, mean, standard_dev)

Probability   is a probability corresponding to the normal distribution.

Mean   is the arithmetic mean of the distribution.

Standard_dev   is the standard deviation of the distribution.

Remarks

- If any argument is non-numeric, NORMINV returns the #VALUE! error value.
- If probability < 0 or if probability > 1, NORMINV returns the #NUM! error value.
- If standard_dev ≤ 0, NORMINV returns the #NUM! error value.

NORMINV uses the standard normal distribution if mean = 0 and standard_dev = 1 (see NORMSINV).

NORMINV uses an iterative technique for calculating the function. Given a probability value, NORMINV iterates until the result is accurate to within ± 3×10^{-7}. If NORMINV does not converge after 100 iterations, the function returns the #N/A error value.

Example

NORMINV(0.908789,40,1.5) equals 42

Related Functions

NORMDIST	Returns the normal cumulative distribution
NORMSDIST	Returns the standard normal cumulative distribution
NORMSINV	Returns the inverse of the standard normal cumulative distribution
STANDARDIZE	Returns a normalized value
ZTEST	Returns the two-tailed P-value of a z-test

List of Statistical Functions

NORMSDIST

Returns the standard normal cumulative distribution function. The distribution has a mean of zero and a standard deviation of one. Use this function in place of a table of standard normal curve areas.

Syntax

NORMSDIST(z)

Z   is the value for which you want the distribution.

Remarks

- If z is non-numeric, NORMSDIST returns the #VALUE! error value.
- The equation for the standard normal density function is:

$$f(z;0,1) = \frac{1}{\sqrt{2\pi}} e^{-\frac{z^2}{2}}$$

Example

NORMSDIST(1.333333) equals 0.908789

Related Functions

NORMDIST	Returns the normal cumulative distribution
NORMINV	Returns the inverse of the standard normal cumulative distribution
NORMSINV	Returns the inverse of the standard normal cumulative distribution
STANDARDIZE	Returns a normalized value
ZTEST	Returns the two-tailed P-value of a z-test

List of Statistical Functions

NORMSINV

Returns the inverse of the standard normal cumulative distribution. The distribution has a mean of zero and a standard deviation of one.

Syntax

NORMSINV(probability)

Probability   is a probability corresponding to the normal distribution.

Remarks

- If probability is non-numeric, NORMSINV returns the #VALUE! error value.
- If probability < 0 or if probability > 1, NORMINV returns the #NUM! error value.

NORMSINV uses an iterative technique for calculating the function. Given a probability value, NORMSINV iterates until the result is accurate to within ± 3×10^{-7}. If NORMSINV does not converge after 100 iterations, the function returns the #N/A error value.

Example

NORMSINV(0.908789) equals 1.3333

Related Functions

NORMDIST	Returns the normal cumulative distribution
NORMSDIST	Returns the standard normal cumulative distribution
NORMINV	Returns the inverse of the standard normal cumulative distribution
STANDARDIZE	Returns a normalized value
ZTEST	Returns the two-tailed P-value of a z-test

List of Statistical Functions

NOT

Reverses the value of its argument. Use NOT when you want to make sure a value is not equal to one particular value.

Syntax

NOT(logical)

Logical   is a value or expression that can be evaluated to TRUE or FALSE. If logical is FALSE, NOT returns TRUE; if logical is TRUE, NOT returns FALSE.

Examples

NOT(FALSE) equals TRUE

NOT(1+1=2) equals FALSE

Related Functions	AND	Returns TRUE if all its arguments are TRUE
	OR	Returns TRUE if any argument is TRUE

List of Logical Functions

NOW

Returns the serial number of the current date and time.

Syntax

NOW( )

Remarks

- Microsoft Excel for Windows and Microsoft Excel for the Macintosh use different default date systems. Microsoft Excel for Windows uses the 1900 Date System, in which serial numbers range from 1 to 65,380, corresponding to the dates January 1, 1900, through December 31, 2078. Microsoft Excel for the Macintosh uses the 1904 Date System, in which serial numbers range from 0 to 63,918, corresponding to the dates January 1, 1904, through December 31, 2078.

- Numbers to the right of the decimal point in the serial number represent the time; numbers to the left represent the date. For example, in the 1900 Date System, the serial number 367.5 represents the date-time combination 12:00 P.M., January 1, 1901.

- You can change the date system by selecting or clearing the 1904 Date System check box in the Calculation tab of the Options dialog box, which appears when you click Options on the Tools menu.

- The date system is changed automatically when you open a document from another platform. For example, if you are working in Microsoft Excel for Windows and you open a document created in Microsoft Excel for the Macintosh, the 1904 Date System check box is selected automatically.

- The NOW function changes only when the worksheet is calculated or when the macro containing the function is run. It is not updated continuously.

Examples

If you are using the 1900 Date System and your computer's built-in clock is set to 12:30:00 P.M., 1-Jan-1987, then:

NOW( ) equals 31778.52083

Ten minutes later:

NOW( ) equals 31778.52778

Related Functions	DATE	Returns the serial number of a particular date
	YEAR, MONTH, DAY, WEEKDAY, HOUR, and MINUTE	Convert serial numbers into years, months, days, days of the week, hours, and minutes
	List of Date & Time Functions	

NPER

Returns the number of periods for an investment based on periodic, constant payments and a constant interest rate.

Syntax

NPER(rate, pmt, pv, fv, type)

For a more complete description of the arguments in NPER and for more information about annuity functions, see PV.

Rate   is the interest rate per period.

Pmt   is the payment made each period; it cannot change over the life of the annuity. Typically, pmt contains principal and interest but no other fees or taxes.

Pv   is the present value, or the lump-sum amount that a series of future payments is worth right now.

Fv   is the future value, or a cash balance you want to attain after the last payment is made. If fv is omitted, it is assumed to be 0 (the future value of a loan, for example, is 0).

Type   is the number 0 or 1 and indicates when payments are due.

Set type equal to	If payments are due
0 or omitted	At the end of the period
1	At the beginning of the period

Examples

NPER(12%/12, -100, -1000, 10000, 1) equals 60

NPER(1%, -100, -1000, 10000) equals 60

NPER(1%, -100, 1000) equals 11

Related Functions	FV	Returns the future value of an investment
	IPMT	Returns the interest payment for an investment for a given period
	PMT	Returns the periodic payment for an annuity
	PPMT	Returns the payment on the principal for an investment for a given period
	PV	Returns the present value of an investment
	RATE	Returns the interest rate per period of an annuity

List of Financial Functions

NPV

Returns the net present value of an investment based on a series of periodic cash flows and a discount rate. The net present value of an investment is today's value of a series of future payments (negative values) and income (positive values).

Syntax

NPV(rate, value1, value2, ...)

Rate   is the rate of discount over the length of one period.

Value1, value2,...   are 1 to 29 arguments representing the payments and income.

- Value1, value2,... must be equally spaced in time and occur at the end of each period.

- NPV uses the order of value1, value2,... to interpret the order of cash flows. Be sure to enter your payment and income values in the correct sequence.

- Arguments that are numbers, empty cells, logical values, or text representations of numbers are counted; arguments that are error values or text that cannot be translated into numbers are ignored.

- If an argument is an array or reference, only numbers in that array or reference are counted. Empty cells, logical values, text, or error values in the array or reference are ignored.

Remarks

- The NPV investment begins one period before the date of the value1 cash flow and ends with the last cash flow in the list. The NPV calculation is based on future cash flows. If your first cash flow occurs at the beginning of the first period, the first value must be added to the NPV result, not included in the values arguments. For more information, see the examples below.

- If n is the number of cash flows in the list of values, the formula for NPV is:

$$NPV = \sum_{i=1}^{n} \frac{values_i}{(1 + rate)^i}$$

- NPV is similar to the PV function (present value). The primary difference between PV and NPV is that PV allows cash flows to begin either at the end or at the beginning of the period. Unlike the variable NPV cash flow values, PV cash flows must be constant throughout the investment. For information about annuities and financial functions, see PV.

- NPV is also related to the IRR function (internal rate of return). IRR is the rate for which NPV equals zero: NPV(IRR(...), ...)=0.

Examples

Suppose you're considering an investment in which you pay $10,000 one year from today and receive an annual income of $3000, $4200, and $6800 in the three years that follow. Assuming an annual discount rate of 10 percent, the net present value of this investment is:

`NPV(10%, -10000, 3000, 4200, 6800)` equals $1188.44

In the preceding example, you include the initial $10,000 cost as one of the values, because the payment occurs at the end of the first period.

Consider an investment that starts at the beginning of the first period. Suppose you're interested in buying a shoe store. The cost of the business is $40,000, and you expect to receive the following income for the first five years of operation: $8000, $9200, $10,000, $12,000, and $14,500. The annual discount rate is 8%. This might represent the rate of inflation or the interest rate of a competing investment.

If the cost and income figures from the shoe store are entered in B1 through B6 respectively, then net present value of the shoe store investment is given by:

`NPV(8%, B2:B6)+B1` equals $1922.06

In the preceding example, you don't include the initial $40,000 cost as one of the values, because the payment occurs at the beginning of the first period.

Suppose your shoe store's roof collapses during the sixth year and you assume a loss of $9000 for that year. The net present value of the shoe store investment after six years is given by:

`NPV(8%, B2:B6, -9000)+B1` equals –$3749.47

Related Functions	FV	Returns the future value of an investment
	IRR	Returns the internal rate of return for a series of cash flows
	PV	Returns the present value of an investment
	XNPV	Returns the net present value for a schedule of cash flows that is not necessarily periodic

List of Financial Functions

OCT2BIN

Converts an octal number to binary.

If this function is not available, run the Setup program to install the Analysis ToolPak. After you install the Analysis ToolPak, you must select it in the Add-In Manager. For more information, look up Add-ins in Help.

Syntax

OCT2BIN(number, places)

Number   is the octal number you want to convert. Number may not contain more than 10 characters. The most significant bit of number is the sign bit. The remaining 29 bits are magnitude bits. Negative numbers are represented using two's-complement notation.

Places   is the number of characters to use. If places is omitted, OCT2BIN uses the minimum number of characters necessary. Places is useful for padding the return value with leading 0s (zeros).

Remarks

- If number is negative, OCT2BIN ignores places and returns a 10-character binary number.
- If number is negative, it cannot be less than equal to 7777777000, and if number is positive, it cannot be greater than 777.
- If number is not a valid octal number, OCT2BIN returns the #NUM! error value.
- If OCT2BIN requires more than places characters, it returns the #NUM! error value.
- If places is not an integer, it is truncated.
- If places is non-numeric, OCT2BIN returns the #VALUE! error value.
- If places is negative, OCT2BIN returns the #NUM! error value.

Examples

OCT2BIN(3, 3) equals 011

OCT2BIN(7777777000) equals 1000000000

Related Functions	BIN2OCT	Converts a binary number to octal
	DEC2OCT	Converts a decimal number to octal
	HEX2OCT	Converts a hexadecimal number to octal

List of Engineering Functions

OCT2DEC

Converts an octal number to decimal.

If this function is not available, run the Setup program to install the Analysis ToolPak. After you install the Analysis ToolPak, you must select it in the Add-In Manager. For more information, look up Add-ins in Help.

Syntax **OCT2DEC(number)**

Number   is the octal number you want to convert. Number may not contain more than 10 octal characters (30 bits). The most significant bit of number is the sign bit. The remaining 29 bits are magnitude bits. Negative numbers are represented using two's-complement notation.

Remarks If number is not a valid octal number, OCT2DEC returns the #NUM! error value.

Examples OCT2DEC(54) equals 44

OCT2DEC(7777777533) equals −165

Related Functions	BIN2OCT	Converts a binary number to octal
	DEC2OCT	Converts a decimal number to octal
	HEX2OCT	Converts a hexadecimal number to octal

List of Engineering Functions

OCT2HEX

Converts an octal number to hexadecimal.

If this function is not available, run the Setup program to install the Analysis ToolPak. After you install the Analysis ToolPak, you must select it in the Add-In Manager. For more information, look up Add-ins in Help.

Syntax	**OCT2HEX(number**, places)

Number   is the octal number you want to convert. Number may not contain more than 10 octal characters (30 bits). The most significant bit of number is the sign bit. The remaining 29 bits are magnitude bits. Negative numbers are represented using two's-complement notation.

Places   is the number of characters to use. If places is omitted, OCT2HEX uses the minimum number of characters necessary. Places is useful for padding the return value with leading 0s (zeros).

Remarks

- If number is negative, OCT2HEX ignores places and returns a 10-character hexadecimal number.
- If number is not a valid octal number, OCT2HEX returns the #NUM! error value.
- If OCT2HEX requires more than places characters, it returns the #NUM! error value.
- If places is not an integer, it is truncated.
- If places is non-numeric, OCT2HEX returns the #VALUE! error value.
- If places is negative, OCT2HEX returns the #NUM! error value.

Examples   OCT2HEX(100, 4) equals 0040

OCT2HEX(7777777533) equals FFFFFFFF5B

Related Functions

BIN2OCT	Converts a binary number to octal
DEC2OCT	Converts a decimal number to octal
HEX2OCT	Converts a hexadecimal number to octal

List of Engineering Functions

ODD

Returns number rounded up to the nearest odd integer.

Syntax	**ODD(number)**

Number   is the value to round.

Remarks

- If number is non-numeric, ODD returns the #VALUE! error value.
- Regardless of the sign of number, a value is rounded up when adjusted away from zero. If number is an odd integer, no rounding occurs.

Examples	ODD(1.5) equals 3
	ODD(3) equals 3
	ODD(2) equals 3
	ODD(-1) equals −1
	ODD(-2) equals −3

Related Functions		
	CEILING	Returns the number rounded up to the nearest multiple of significance
	EVEN	Rounds a number up to the nearest even integer
	FLOOR	Rounds a number down, toward zero
	INT	Rounds a number down to the nearest integer
	ISEVEN	Returns TRUE if the number is even
	ISODD	Returns TRUE if the number is odd
	ROUND	Rounds a number to a specified number of digits
	TRUNC	Truncates a number to an integer

List of Math & Trigonometry Functions

ODDFPRICE

Returns the price per $100 face value of a security having an odd (short or long) first period.

If this function is not available, run the Setup program to install the Analysis ToolPak. After you install the Analysis ToolPak, you must select it in the Add-In Manager. For more information, look up Add-ins in Help.

Syntax   **ODDFPRICE(settlement, maturity, issue, first_coupon, rate, yld, redemption, frequency**, basis)

Settlement   is the security's settlement date, expressed as a serial date number.

Maturity   is the security's maturity date, expressed as a serial date number.

Issue   is the security's issue date, expressed as a serial date number.

First_coupon   is the security's first coupon date, expressed as a serial date number.

Rate   is the security's interest rate.

Yld   is the security's annual yield.

Redemption   is the security's redemption value per $100 face value.

Frequency   is the number of coupon payments per year. For annual payments, frequency = 1; for semiannual, frequency = 2; for quarterly, frequency = 4.

Basis   is the type of day count basis to use.

Basis	Day count basis
0 or omitted	US (NASD) 30/360
1	Actual/actual
2	Actual/360
3	Actual/365
4	European 30/360

Remarks

- Settlement, maturity, issue, first_coupon, and basis are truncated to integers.
- If any argument is non-numeric, ODDFPRICE returns the #VALUE! error value.
- If settlement, maturity, issue, or first_coupon is not a valid serial date number, ODDFPRICE returns the #NUM! error value.
- If rate < 0 or if yld < 0, ODDFPRICE returns the #NUM! error value.
- If basis < 0 or if basis > 4, ODDFPRICE returns the #NUM! error value.
- The following date condition must be satisfied; otherwise, ODDFPRICE returns the #NUM! error value:

maturity > first_coupon > settlement > issue

- ODDFPRICE is calculated as follows:

Odd short first coupon:

$$ODDFPRICE = \left[\frac{redemption}{\left(1 + \dfrac{yld}{frequency}\right)^{\left(N-1+\frac{DSC}{E}\right)}} \right] + \left[\frac{100 \times \dfrac{rate}{frequency} \times \dfrac{DFC}{E}}{\left(1 + \dfrac{yld}{frequency}\right)^{\frac{DSC}{E}}} \right]$$

$$+ \sum_{k=2}^{N} \left[\frac{100 \times \dfrac{rate}{frequency}}{\left(1 + \dfrac{yld}{frequency}\right)^{\left(k-1+\frac{DSC}{E}\right)}} \right]$$

$$- \left[100 \times \frac{rate}{frequency} \times \frac{A}{E} \right]$$

Where:

A = number of days from the beginning of the coupon period to the settlement date (accrued days).

DSC = number of days from the settlement to the next coupon date.

DFC = number of days from the the beginnning of the odd first coupon to the first coupon date.

E = number of days in the coupon period.

N = number of coupon payable between the settlement date and the redemption date. (If this number contains a fraction, it is raised to the next whole number).

Odd long first coupon:

$$ODDFPRICE = \left[\frac{redemption}{\left(1+\dfrac{yld}{frequency}\right)^{\left(N+N_q+\frac{DSC}{E}\right)}} \right]$$

$$+ \left[\frac{100 \times \dfrac{rate}{frequency} \times \left[\displaystyle\sum_{i=1}^{NC} \dfrac{DC_i}{NL_i}\right]}{\left(1+\dfrac{yld}{frequency}\right)^{\left(N_q+\frac{DSC}{E}\right)}} \right]$$

$$+ \sum_{k=2}^{N} \frac{100 \times \dfrac{rate}{frequency}}{\left(1+\dfrac{yld}{frequency}\right)^{\left(k-N_q+\frac{DSC}{E}\right)}}$$

$$- \left[100 \times \frac{rate}{frequency} \times \sum_{i=1}^{NC} \frac{A_i}{NL_i} \right]$$

Where:

A_i = number of days from begining of the ith quasi-coupon period within odd period.

DC_i = number of days from dated date (or issue date) to first quasi-coupon (i=1) or number of days in quasi-coupon (i=2,..., i=NC).

DSC = number of days from settlement to next coupon date.

E = number of days in coupon period.

N = number of coupons payable between the first real coupon date and redemption date. (If this number contains a fraction, it is raised to the next whole number).

NC = number of quasi-coupon periods that fit in odd period. (If this number contains a fraction it will be raised to the next whole number).

NLi = normal length in days of the full ith quasi-coupon period within odd period.

Nq = number of whole quasi-coupon periods between settlement date and first coupon.

Example

A treasury bond has the following terms:

November 11, 1986 settlement date
March 1, 1999 maturity date
October 15, 1986 issue date
March 1, 1987 first coupon date
7.85% coupon
6.25% yield
$100 redemptive value
Frequency is semiannual
Actual/actual basis

the price per $100 face value of a security having an odd (short or long) first period (in the 1900 date system) is:

```
ODDFPRICE(31727,36220,31700,31837,0.0785,0.0625,100,2,1)
```
equals 113.597717

Related Functions

DATE	Returns the serial number of a particular date
ODDFYIELD	Returns the yield of a security with an odd first period
ODDLPRICE	Returns the price per $100 face value of a security with an odd last period
ODDLYIELD	Returns the yield of a security with an odd last period

List of Financial Functions

ODDFYIELD

Returns the yield of a security that has an odd (short or long) first period.

If this function is not available, run the Setup program to install the Analysis ToolPak. After you install the Analysis ToolPak, you must select it in the Add-In Manager. For more information, look up Add-ins in Help.

Syntax

ODDFYIELD(settlement, maturity, issue, first_coupon, rate, pr, redemption, frequency, basis)

Settlement   is the security's settlement date, expressed as a serial date number.

Maturity   is the security's maturity date expressed as a serial date number.

Issue   is the security's issue date, expressed as a serial date number.

First_coupon   is the security's first coupon date, expressed as a serial date number.

Rate   is the security's interest rate.

Pr   is the security's price.

Redemption   is the security's redemption value per $100 face value.

Frequency   is the number of coupon payments per year. For annual payments, frequency = 1; for semiannual, frequency = 2; for quarterly, frequency = 4.

Basis   is the type of day count basis to use.

Basis	Day count basis
0 or omitted	US (NASD) 30/360
1	Actual/actual
2	Actual/360
3	Actual/365
4	European 30/360

Remarks

- Settlement, maturity, issue, first_coupon, and basis are truncated to integers.
- If any argument is non-numeric, ODDFYIELD returns the #VALUE! error value.
- If settlement, maturity, issue, or first_coupon is not a valid serial date number, ODDFYIELD returns the #NUM! error value.
- If rate < 0 or if pr ≤ 0, ODDFYIELD returns the #NUM! error value.
- If basis < 0 or if basis > 4, ODDFYIELD returns the #NUM! error value.
- The following date condition must be satisfied; otherwise, ODDFYIELD returns the #NUM! error value:

  maturity > first_coupon > settlement > issue

- Microsoft Excel uses an iterative technique to calculate ODDFYIELD. This function uses the Newton method based on the formula used for the function ODDFPRICE. The yield is changed through 100 iterations until the estimated price with the given yield is close to the price. See ODDFPRICE for the formula that ODDFYIELD uses.

Example   A bond has the following terms:

January 25, 1991 settlement date
January 1, 1996 maturity date
January 18, 1991 issue date
July 15, 1991 first coupon date
5.75% coupon
$84.50 price
$100 redemptive value
Frequency is semiannual
30/360 basis

The yield of a security that has an odd (short or long) first period is:

ODDFYIELD(33263,35065,33256,33434,0.0575,084.50,100,2,0)
equals .09758 or 9.76%

Related Functions   DATE   Returns the serial number of a particular date

                        ODDFPRICE   Returns the price per $100 face value of a security with
                                               an odd first period

                        ODDLPRICE   Returns the price per $100 face value of a security with
                                               an odd last period

                        ODDLYIELD   Returns the yield of a security with an odd last period

                        List of Financial Functions

ODDLPRICE

Returns the price per $100 face value of a security having an odd (short or long) last coupon period.

If this function is not available, run the Setup program to install the Analysis ToolPak. After you install the Analysis ToolPak, you must select it in the Add-In Manager. For more information, look up Add-ins in Help.

Syntax   **ODDLPRICE(settlement, maturity, last_interest, rate, yld, redemption, frequency**, basis)

Settlement   is the security's settlement date, expressed as a serial date number.

Maturity   is the security's maturity date, expressed as a serial date number.

Last_interest   is the security's last coupon date, expressed as a serial date number.

Rate   is the security's interest rate.

Yld   is the security's annual yield.

Redemption   is the security's redemption value per $100 face value.

Frequency   is the number of coupon payments per year. For annual payments, frequency = 1; for semiannual, frequency = 2; for quarterly, frequency = 4.

Basis   is the type of day count basis to use.

Basis	Day count basis
0 or omitted	US (NASD) 30/360
1	Actual/actual
2	Actual/360
3	Actual/365
4	European 30/360

Remarks

- Settlement, maturity, last_interest, and basis are truncated to integers.
- If any argument is non-numeric, ODDLPRICE returns the #VALUE! error value.
- If settlement, maturity, or last_interest is not a valid serial date number, ODDLPRICE returns the #NUM! error value.
- If rate < 0 or if yld < 0, ODDLPRICE returns the #NUM! error value.
- If basis < 0 or if basis > 4, ODDLPRICE returns the #NUM! error value.
- The following date condition must be satisfied; otherwise, ODDLPRICE returns the #NUM! error value:

  maturity > settlement > last_interest

Example

A bond has the following terms:

February, 7, 1987 settlement date
June 15, 1987 maturity date
October 15, 1986 last interest date
3.75% coupon
4.05% yield
$100 redemptive value
Frequency is semiannual
30/360 basis

The price per $100 of a security having an odd (short or long) last coupon period is:

`ODDLPRICE(31815,31943,31700,0.0375,0.0405,100,2,0)` equals 99.87829

Related Functions

DATE	Returns the serial number of a particular date
ODDFPRICE	Returns the price per $100 face value of a security with an odd first period
ODDFYIELD	Returns the yield of a security with an odd first period
ODDLYIELD	Returns the yield of a security with an odd last period

List of Financial Functions

ODDLYIELD

Returns the yield of a security that has an odd (short or long) last period.

If this function is not available, run the Setup program to install the Analysis ToolPak. After you install the Analysis ToolPak, you must select it in the Add-In Manager. For more information, look up Add-ins in Help.

Syntax

ODDLYIELD(settlement, maturity, last_interest, rate, pr, redemption, frequency, basis)

Settlement   is the security's settlement date, expressed as a serial date number.

Maturity   is the security's maturity date, expressed as a serial date number.

Last_interest   is the security's last coupon date, expressed as a serial date number.

Rate   is the security's interest rate.

Pr   is the security's price.

Redemption   is the security's redemption value per $100 face value.

Frequency   is the number of coupon payments per year. For annual payments, frequency = 1; for semiannual, frequency = 2; for quarterly, frequency = 4.

Basis   is the type of day count basis to use.

Basis	Day count basis
0 or omitted	US (NASD) 30/360
1	Actual/actual
2	Actual/360
3	Actual/365
4	European 30/360

Remarks

- Settlement, maturity, last_interest, and basis are truncated to integers.
- If any argument is non-numeric, ODDLYIELD returns the #VALUE! error value.
- If settlement, maturity, or last_interest is not a valid serial date number, ODDLYIELD returns the #NUM! error value.
- If rate < 0 or if pr ≤ 0, ODDLYIELD returns the #NUM! error value.
- If basis < 0 or if basis > 4, ODDLYIELD returns the #NUM! error value.
- The following date condition must be satisfied; otherwise, ODDLYIELD returns the #NUM! error value:

  maturity > last_interest > settlement

- ODDLYIELD is calculated as follows:

$$ODDLPRICE = \left[\frac{\left(redemption + \left(\left(\sum_{i=1}^{NC} \frac{DC_i}{NL_i} \right) \times \frac{100 \times rate}{frequency} \right) \right) - \left(par + \left(\left(\sum_{i=1}^{NC} \frac{A_i}{NL_i} \right) \times \frac{100 \times rate}{frequency} \right) \right)}{par + \left(\left(\sum_{i=1}^{NC} \frac{A_i}{NL_i} \right) \times \frac{100 \times rate}{frequency} \right)} \right] \times \left[\frac{frequency}{\left(\sum_{i=1}^{NC} \frac{DSC_i}{NL_i} \right)} \right]$$

Where:

Ai = number of accrued days for the ith quasi-coupon period within odd period counting forward from last interest date before redemption.

DCi = number of days counted in each ith quasi-coupon period as delimited by the length of the actual coupon period.

NC = number of quasi-coupon periods that fit in odd period; if this number contains a fraction it will be raised to the next whole number.

NLi = normal length in days of the ith quasi-coupon period within odd coupon period.

Example

A bond has the following terms:

April 20, 1987 settlement date
June 15, 1987 maturity date
December 24, 1986 last interest date
3.75% coupon
$99.875 price
$100 redemptive value
Frequency is semiannual
30/360 basis

The yield of a security that has an odd (short or long) first period is:

ODDLYIELD(31887,31943,31770,0.0375,99.875,100,2,0) equals
0.045192

Related Functions

DATE	Returns the serial number of a particular date
ODDFPRICE	Returns the price per $100 face value of a security with an odd first period
ODDLPRICE	Returns the price per $100 face value of a security with an odd last period
ODDFYIELD	Returns the yield of a security with an odd first period

List of Financial Functions

OFFSET

Returns a reference of a specified height and width, offset from another reference by a specified number of rows and columns.

Syntax

OFFSET(**reference**, **rows**, **cols**, height, width)

Reference   is the reference from which you want to base the offset. If reference is a multiple selection, OFFSET returns the #VALUE! error value.

Rows   is the number of rows, up or down, that you want the upper-left cell to refer to. Using 5 as the rows argument specifies that the upper-left cell in the reference is five rows below reference. Rows can be positive or negative.

Cols   is the number of columns, to the left or right, that you want the upper-left cell of the result to refer to. Using 5 as the cols argument specifies that the upper-left cell in the reference is five columns to the right of reference. Cols can be positive or negative.

If rows and cols offset reference over the edge of the worksheet, OFFSET returns the #REF! error value.

Height   is the height, in number of rows, that you want the returned reference to be. Height must be a positive number.

Width   is the width, in number of columns, that you want the returned reference to be. Width must be a positive number.

If height or width is omitted, it is assumed to be the same height or width as reference.

Remarks

OFFSET doesn't actually move any cells or change the selection; it just returns a reference. OFFSET can be used with any function expecting a reference argument. For example, to select a range offset from the current selection, use OFFSET with the SELECT and SELECTION functions. You can also select a cell offset from the current selection by using a relative reference with the SELECT function, for example, SELECT("R[1]C").

Examples

OFFSET(C3,2,3,1,1) equals F5. If you enter this formula on a worksheet, Microsoft Excel displays the value contained in cell F5.

OFFSET(C3:E5,-1,0,3,3) equals C2:E4

OFFSET(C3:E5,0,-3,3,3) equals #REF!

The following macro formula selects a range of the same size as the current selection one row down:

SELECT(OFFSET(SELECTION(),1,0))

The following macro formula puts the result of the DOCUMENTS function into a range with a height of one row and a width corresponding to the number of columns returned by the COLUMNS function, and offset from the active cell by one row and one column:

FORMULA.ARRAY(DOCUMENTS(),OFFSET(ACTIVE.CELL(),1,1,1,
COLUMNS(DOCUMENTS())))

Related Functions   List of Lookup & Reference Functions

OR

Returns TRUE if any argument is TRUE; returns FALSE if all arguments are FALSE.

Syntax

OR(logical1, logical2, ...)

Logical1, logical2,...   are 1 to 30 conditions you want to test that can be either TRUE or FALSE.

- The arguments should be logical values or arrays or references that contain logical values.

- If an array or reference argument contains text, numbers, or empty cells, those values are ignored.

- If the specified range contains no logical values, OR returns the #VALUE! error value.

- You can use an OR array formula to see if a value occurs in an array. To enter the OR formula as an array, press CTRL+SHIFT (in Microsoft Excel for Windows) or COMMAND+SHIFT (in Microsoft Excel for the Macintosh).

Examples

OR(TRUE) equals TRUE

OR(1+1=1,2+2=5) equals FALSE

If A1:A3 contains the values TRUE, FALSE, and TRUE, then:

OR(A1:A3) equals TRUE

The following macro formula checks the contents of the active cell. If the cell contains the single character "c" or "s", the OR formula returns TRUE and the macro branches to an area named FinishRefresh:

IF(OR(ACTIVE.CELL()="c",ACTIVE.CELL()="s"),GOTO(FinishRefresh))

The preceding example shows how to use the worksheet form of the IF function on a macro sheet. You could also use the macro sheet form. For more information, see IF.

Also see the example for EXACT.

Related Functions

AND	Returns TRUE if all its arguments are TRUE
NOT	Reverses the logic of its argument

List of Logical Functions

PEARSON

Returns the Pearson product moment correlation coefficient, r, a dimensionless index that ranges from –1.0 to 1.0 inclusive, and reflects the extent of a linear relationship between two data sets.

Syntax

PEARSON(array1, array2)

Array1   is a set of independent values.

Array2   is a set of dependent values.

Remarks

- The arguments should be numbers, or names, array constants, or references that contain numbers.

- If an array or reference argument contains text, logical values, or empty cells, those values are ignored; however, cells with the value zero are included.

- If array1 and array2 are empty or have a different number of data points, PEARSON returns the #N/A error value.

- The r value of the regression line is:

$$r = \frac{n(\Sigma XY) - (\Sigma X)(\Sigma Y)}{\sqrt{\left[n\Sigma X^2 - (\Sigma X)^2\right]\left[n\Sigma Y^2 - (\Sigma Y)^2\right]}}$$

Example

PEARSON({9,7,5,3,1},{10,6,1,5,3}) equals 0.699379

Related Functions

INTERCEPT	Returns the intercept of the linear regression line
LINEST	Returns the parameters of a linear trend
RSQ	Returns the square of the Pearson product moment correlatin coefficient
SLOPE	Returns the slope of the linear regression line
STEYX	Returns the standard error of the predicted y-value for each x in the regression

List of Statistical Functions

PERCENTILE

Returns the k-th percentile of values in a range. You can use this function to establish a threshold of acceptance. For example, you can decide to examine candidates that score above the 90th percentile.

Syntax

PERCENTILE(array, k)

Array is the array or range of data that defines relative standing.

K is the percentile value in the range 0..1, inclusive.

Remarks

- If array is empty or contains more than 8191 data points, PERCENTILE returns the #NUM! error value.
- If k is non-numeric, PERCENTILE returns the #VALUE! error value.
- If k is < 0 or if k > 1, PERCENTILE returns the #NUM! error value.
- If k is not a multiple of $1/(n - 1)$, PERCENTILE interpolates to determine the value at the kth percentile.

Example

PERCENTILE({1,2,3,4},0.3) equals 1.9

Related Functions

LARGE	Returns the k-th largest value in a data set
Max	Returns the maximum value in a list of arguments
MEDIAN	Returns the median of the given numbers
Min	Returns the minimum value in a list of arguments
PERCENTRANK	Returns the percentage rank of a value in a data set
QUARTILE	Returns the quartile of a data set
SMALL	Returns the k-th smallest value in a data set

List of Statistical Functions

PERCENTRANK

Returns the percentage rank of a value in a data set. This function can be used to evaluate the relative standing of an observation in a data set. For example, you can use PERCENTRANK to evaluate the standing of an aptitude test score among the population of scores for the test.

Syntax

PERCENTRANK(array, x, significance)

Array is the array or range of data with numeric values that defines relative standing.

X   is the value for which you want to know the rank.

Significance   is an optional value that identifies the number of significant digits for the returned percentage value. If omitted, PERCENTRANK uses three digits (0.xxx%).

Remarks
- If array is empty, PERCENTRANK returns the #NUM! error value.
- If significance < 1, PERCENTRANK returns the #NUM! error value.
- If x does not match one of the values in array, PERCENTRANK interpolates to return the correct percentage rank.

Example   `PERCENTRANK({1,2,3,4,5,6,7,8,9,10},4)` equals 0.333

Related Functions

LARGE	Returns the k-th largest value in a data set
MAX	Returns the maximum value in a list of arguments
MEDIAN	Returns the median of the given numbers
MIN	Returns the minimum value in a list of arguments
PERCENTILE	Returns the k-th percentile of values in a range
QUARTILE	Returns the quartile of a data set
SMALL	Returns the k-th smallest value in a data set

List of Statistical Functions

PERMUT

Returns the number of permutations for a given number of objects that can be selected from number objects. A permutation is any set or subset of objects or events where internal order is significant. Permutations are different than combinations, for which the internal order is not significant. Use this function for lottery-style probability calculations.

Syntax   **PERMUT(number, number_chosen)**

Number   is an integer that describes the number of objects.

Number_chosen   is an integer that describes the number of objects in each permutation.

Remarks   Both arguments are truncated to integers.
- If number or number_chosen is non-numeric, PERMUT returns the #VALUE! error value.

- If number ≤ 0 or if number_chosen < 0, PERMUT returns the #NUM! error value.
- If number < number_chosen, PERMUT returns the #NUM! error value.
- The equation for the number of permutations is:

$$P_{k,n} = \frac{n!}{(n-k)!}$$

Example

Suppose you want to calculate the odds of selecting a winning lottery number. Each lottery number contains three numbers, each of which can be between 0 and 99, inclusive. The following function calculates the number of possible permutations.

PERMUT(100,3) equals 970,200

Related Functions

BINOMDIST	Returns the individual term binomial distribution probability
COMBIN	Returns the number of combinations for a given number of objects
CRITBINOM	Returns the smallest value for which the cumulative binomial distribution is less than or equal to a criterion value
FACT	Returns the factorial of a number
HYPGEOMDIST	Returns the hypergeometric distribution
HEGBINOMDIST	Returns the negative binomial distribution

List of Statistical Functions

PI

Returns the number 3.14159265358979, the mathematical constant π, accurate to 15 digits.

Syntax

PI( )

Examples

PI()/2 equals 1.57079...

SIN(PI()/2) equals 1

If the radius of a circle is stored in a cell named Radius, the following macro formula calculates the area of the circle:

PI()*(Radius^2)

Related Functions

COS	Returns the cosine of a number
SIN	Returns the sine of the given angle
TAN	Returns the tangent of a number

List of Math & Trigonometry Functions

PMT

Returns the periodic payment for an annuity based on constant payments and a constant interest rate.

Syntax

PMT(rate, nper, pv, fv, type)

For a more complete description of the arguments in PMT, see PV.

Rate   is the interest rate per period.

Nper   is the total number of payment periods in an annuity.

Pv   is the present value—the total amount that a series of future payments is worth now.

Fv   is the future value, or a cash balance you want to attain after the last payment is made. If fv is omitted, it is assumed to be 0 (the future value of a loan, for example, is 0).

Type   is the number 0 or 1 and indicates when payments are due.

Set type equal to	If payments are due
0 or omitted	At the end of the period
1	At the beginning of the period

Remarks

- The payment returned by PMT includes principal and interest but no taxes, reserve payments, or fees sometimes associated with annuities.

- Make sure that you are consistent about the units you use for specifying rate and nper. If you make monthly payments on a four-year loan at 12 percent annual interest, use 12%/12 for rate and 4*12 for nper. If you make annual payments on the same loan, use 12% for rate and 4 for nper.

Tip To find the total amount paid over the duration of the annuity, multiply the returned **PMT** value by nper.

Examples The following macro formula returns the monthly payment on a $10,000 loan at an annual rate of 8% that you must pay off in 10 months:

PMT(8%/12, 10, 10000) equals –$1037.03

For the same loan, if payments are due at the beginning of the period, the payment is:

PMT(8%/12, 10, 10000, 0, 1) equals –$1030.16

The following macro formula returns the amount someone must pay to you each month if you loan that person $5000 at 12% and want to be paid back in five months:

PMT(12%/12, 5, -5000) equals $1030.20

Suppose you want to save $50,000 in 18 years by saving a constant amount each month. If you assume you'll be able to earn 6% interest on your savings, you can use PMT to determine how much to save each month:

PMT(6%/12, 18*12, 0, 50000) equals –$129.08

If you pay $129.08 into a 6% savings account every month for 18 years, you will have $50,000.

Related Functions

FV	Returns the future value of an investment
IPMT	Returns the interest payment for an investment for a given period
NPER	Returns the number of periods for an investment
PPMT	Returns the payment on the principal for an investment for a given period
PV	Returns the present value of an investment
RATE	Returns the interest rate per period of an annuity

List of Financial Functions

POISSON

Returns the Poisson distribution. A common application of the Poisson distribution is predicting the number of events over a specific time, such as the number of cars arriving at a toll plaza in one minute.

Syntax **POISSON(x, mean, cumulative)**

X   is the number of events.

Mean   is the expected numeric value.

Cumulative   is a logical value that determines the form of the probability distribution returned. If cumulative is TRUE, POISSON returns the cumulative Poisson probability that the number of random events occurring will be between zero and x inclusive; if FALSE, it returns the Poisson probability mass function that the number of events occurring will be exactly x.

Remarks
- If x is not an integer, it is truncated.
- If x or mean is non-numeric, POISSON returns the #VALUE! error value.
- If x ≤ 0, POISSON returns the #NUM! error value.
- If mean ≤ 0, POISSON returns the #NUM! error value.
- POISSON is calculated as follows.

  For cumulative = FALSE:

$$POISSON = \frac{e^{-\lambda}\lambda^x}{\chi!}$$

  For cumulative =TRUE:

$$CUMPOISSON = \sum_{k=0}^{x} \frac{e^{-\lambda}\lambda^x}{k!}$$

Examples
POISSON(2,5,FALSE) equals 0.084224

POISSON(2,5,TRUE) equals 0.124652

Related Function   EXPONDIST   Returns the exponential distribution

List of Statistical Functions

POWER

Returns the result of a number raised to a power.

Syntax   **POWER(number, power)**

Number   is the base number. It can be any real number.

Power   is the exponent, to which the base number is raised.

Remark   The "^" operator can be used instead of POWER to indicate to what power the base number is to be raised, such as in 5^2.

Examples   POWER(5,2) equals 25

POWER(98.6,3.2) equals 2401077

POWER(4,5/4) equals 5.656854

Related Functions   List of Math & Trigonometry Functions

PPMT

Returns the payment on the principal for a given period for an investment based on periodic, constant payments and a constant interest rate.

Syntax   **PPMT(rate, per, nper, pv,** fv, type)

For a more complete description of the arguments in PPMT, see PV.

Rate   is the interest rate per period.

Per   specifies the period and must be in the range 1 to nper.

Nper   is the total number of payment periods in an annuity.

Pv   is the present value—the total amount that a series of future payments is worth now.

Fv   is the future value, or a cash balance you want to attain after the last payment is made. If fv is omitted, it is assumed to be 0 (the future value of a loan, for example, is 0).

Type   is the number 0 or 1 and indicates when payments are due.

Set type equal to	If payments are due
0 or omitted	At the end of the period
1	At the beginning of the period

Remarks   Make sure that you are consistent about the units you use for specifying rate and nper. If you make monthly payments on a four–year loan at 12 percent annual interest, use 12%/12 for rate and 4*12 for nper. If you make annual payments on the same loan, use 12% for rate and 4 for nper.

Examples

The following formula returns the principal payment for the first month of a two-year $2000 loan at 10% annual interest:

PPMT(10%/12, 1, 24, 2000) equals –$75.62

The following function returns the principal payment for the last year of a 10-year $200,000 loan at 8% annual interest:

PPMT(8%, 10, 10, 200000) equals –$27,598.05

Related Functions

FV	Returns the future value of an investment
IPMT	Returns the interest payment for an investment for a given period
NPER	Returns the number of periods for an investment
PMT	Returns the periodic payment for an annuity
PV	Returns the present value of an investment
RATE	Returns the interest rate per period of an annuity

List of Financial Functions

PRICE

Returns the price per $100 face value of a security that pays periodic interest.

If this function is not available, run the Setup program to install the Analysis ToolPak. After you install the Analysis ToolPak, you must select it in the Add-In Manager. For more information, look up Add-ins in Help.

Syntax

PRICE(settlement, maturity, rate, yld, redemption, frequency, basis)

Settlement   is the security's settlement date, expressed as a serial date number.

Maturity   is the security's maturity date, expressed as a serial date number.

Rate   is the security's annual coupon rate.

Yld   is the security's annual yield.

Redemption   is the security's redemption value per $100 face value.

Frequency   is the number of coupon payments per year. For annual payments, frequency = 1; for semiannual, frequency = 2; for quarterly, frequency = 4.

Basis   is the type of day count basis to use.

Basis	Day count basis
0 or omitted	US (NASD) 30/360
1	Actual/actual
2	Actual/360
3	Actual/365
4	European 30/360

Remarks

- Settlement, maturity, frequency, and basis are truncated to integers.
- If any argument is non-numeric, PRICE returns the #VALUE! error value.
- If settlement or maturity is not a valid serial date number, PRICE returns the #NUM! error value.
- If yld < 0 or if rate < 0, PRICE returns the #NUM! error value.
- If redemption ≤ 0, PRICE returns the #NUM! error value.
- If frequency is any number other than 1, 2, or 4, PRICE returns the #NUM! error value.
- If basis < 0 or if basis > 4, PRICE returns the #NUM! error value.
- If settlement ≥ maturity, PRICE returns the #NUM! error value.
- PRICE is calculated as follows:

$$PRICE = \left[\frac{redemption}{\left(1+\frac{yld}{frequency}\right)^{\left(N-1+\frac{DSC}{E}\right)}}\right] + \left[\sum_{k=1}^{N}\frac{100\times\frac{rate}{frequency}}{\left(1+\frac{yld}{frequency}\right)^{\left(k-1+\frac{DSC}{E}\right)}}\right] - \left(100\times\frac{rate}{frequency}\times\frac{A}{E}\right)$$

Where:

DSC = number of days from settlement to next coupon date.

E = number of days in coupon period in which the settlement date falls.

N = number of coupons payable between settlement date and redemption date.

A = number of days from beginning of coupon period to settlement date.

Example	A bond has the following terms:

February 15, 1991 settlement date
November 15, 1999 maturity date
5.75% semiannual coupon
6.50% yield
$100 redemption value
Frequency in semiannual
30/360 basis

The bond price (in the 1900 Date System) is:

`PRICE(33284,36479,0.0575,0.065,100,2,0)` equals 95.04287

Related Functions	DATE	Returns the serial number of a particular date
	YIELD	Returns the yield on a security that pays periodic interest

List of Financial Functions

PRICEDISC

Returns the price per $100 face value of a discounted security.

If this function is not available, run the Setup program to install the Analysis ToolPak. After you install the Analysis ToolPak, you must select it in the Add-In Manager. For more information, look up Add-ins in Help.

Syntax	**PRICEDISC(settlement, maturity, discount, redemption, basis)**

Settlement   is the security's settlement date, expressed as a serial date number.

Maturity   is the security's maturity date, expressed as a serial date number.

Discount   is the security's discount rate.

Redemption   is the security's redemption value per $100 face value.

Basis   is the type of day count basis to use.

Basis	Day count basis
0 or omitted	US (NASD) 30/360
1	Actual/actual
2	Actual/360
3	Actual/365
4	European 30/360

Remarks

- Settlement, maturity, and basis are truncated to integers.
- If any argument is non-numeric, PRICEDISC returns the #VALUE! error value.
- If settlement or maturity is not a valid serial date number, PRICEDISC returns the #NUM! error value.
- If discount ≤ 0 or if redemption ≤ 0, PRICEDISC returns the #NUM! error value.
- If basis < 0 or if basis > 4, PRICEDISC returns the #NUM! error value.
- If settlement ≥ maturity, PRICEDISC returns the #NUM! error value.
- PRICEDISC is calculated as follows:

$$PRICEDISC = redemption - discount \times redemption \times \frac{DSM}{B}$$

Where:

B = number of days in year, depending on year basis.

DSM = number of days from settlement to maturity.

Example

A bond has the following terms:

February 15, 1993 settlement date
March 1, 1993 maturity date
5.25% discount rate
$100 redemption value
Actual/360 basis

The bond price (in the 1900 Date System) is:

`PRICEDISC(34015,34029,0.0525,100,2)` equals 99.79583

Related Functions

DATE	Returns the serial number of a particular date
DISC	Returns the discount rate for a security
YIELDDISC	Returns the annual yield for a discounted security

List of Financial Functions

PRICEMAT

Returns the price per $100 face value of a security that pays interest at maturity.

If this function is not available, run the Setup program to install the Analysis ToolPak. After you install the Analysis ToolPak, you must select it in the Add-In Manager. For more information, look up Add-ins in Help.

Syntax

PRICEMAT(settlement, maturity, issue, rate, yld, basis)

Settlement is the security's settlement date, expressed as a serial date number.

Maturity is the security's maturity date, expressed as a serial date number.

Issue is the security's issue date, expressed as a serial date number.

Rate is the security's interest rate at date of issue.

Yld is the security's annual yield.

Basis is the type of day count basis to use.

Basis	Day count basis
0 or omitted	US (NASD) 30/360
1	Actual/actual
2	Actual/360
3	Actual/365
4	European 30/360

Remarks

- Settlement, maturity, issue, and basis are truncated to integers.
- If any argument is non-numeric, PRICEMAT returns the #VALUE! error value.
- If settlement, maturity, or issue is not a valid serial date number, PRICEMAT returns the #NUM! error value.
- If rate < 0 or if yld < 0, PRICEMAT returns the #NUM! error value.
- If basis < 0 or if basis > 4, PRICEMAT returns the #NUM! error value.
- If settlement ≥ maturity, PRICEMAT returns the #NUM! error value.
- PRICEMAT is calculated as follows:

$$PRICEMAT = \frac{100 + (\frac{DIM}{B} \times rate \times 100)}{1 + (\frac{DSM}{B} \times yld)} - (\frac{A}{B} \times rate \times 100)$$

Where:

B = number of days in year, depending on year basis.

DSM = number of days from settlement to maturity.

DIM = number of days from issue to maturity.

A = number of days from issue to settlement.

Example

A bond has the following terms:

February 15, 1993 settlement date
April 13, 1993 maturity date
November 11, 1992 issue date
6.1% semiannual coupon
6.1% yield
30/360 basis

The price (in the 1900 Date System) is:

`PRICEMAT(34015,34072,33919,0.061,0.061,0)` equals 99.98449888

Related Functions

DATE	Returns the serial number of a particular date
YIELDMAT	Returns the annual yield of a security that pays interest at maturity

List of Financial Functions

PROB

Returns the probability that values in a range are between two limits. If upper_limit is not supplied, returns the probability that values in x_range are equal to lower_limit.

Syntax

PROB(x_range, prob_range, lower_limit, upper_limit)

X_range   is the range of numeric values of x with which there are associated probabilities.

Prob_range   is a set of probabilities associated with values in x_range.

Lower_limit   is the lower bound on the value for which you want a probability.

Upper_limit   is the optional upper bound on the value for which you want a probability.

Remarks	■ If any value in prob_range ≤ 0 or if any value in prob_range > 1, PROB returns the #NUM! error value.

■ If the sum of the values in prob_range $\neq 1$, PROB returns the #NUM! error value.

■ If upper_limit is omitted, PROB returns the probability of being equal to lower_limit.

■ If x_range and prob_range contain a different number of data points, PROB returns the #N/A error value.

Examples

PROB({0,1,2,3},{0.2,0.3,0.1,0.4},2) equals 0.1

PROB({0,1,2,3},{0.2,0.3,0.1,0.4},1,3) equals 0.8

Related Functions

BINOMDIST	Returns the individual term binomial distribution probability
CRITBINOM	Returns the smallest value for which the cumulative binomial distribution is less than or equal to a criterion value

List of Statistical Functions

PRODUCT

Multiplies all the numbers given as arguments and returns the product.

Syntax

PRODUCT(number1, number2, ...)

Number1, number2,...   are 1 to 30 numbers that you want to multiply.

Remarks

■ Arguments that are numbers, logical values, or text representations of numbers are counted; arguments that are error values or text that cannot be translated into numbers cause errors.

■ If an argument is an array or reference, only numbers in the array or reference are counted. Empty cells, logical values, text, or error values in the array or reference are ignored.

Examples

If cells A2:C2 contain 5, 15, and 30:

PRODUCT(A2:C2) equals 2250

PRODUCT(A2:C2, 2) equals 4500

Related Functions	FACT	Returns the factorial of a number
	SUM	Adds its arguments
	SUMPRODUCT	Returns the sum of the products of corresponding array components

List of Math & Trigonometry Functions

PROPER

Capitalizes the first letter in text and any other letters in text that follow any character other than a letter. Converts all other letters to lowercase.

Syntax

PROPER(text)

Text   is text enclosed in quotation marks, a formula that returns text, or a reference to a cell containing the text you want to partially capitalize.

Examples

PROPER("this is a TITLE") equals "This Is A Title"

PROPER("2-cent's worth") equals "2-Cent'S Worth"

PROPER("76BudGet") equals "76Budget"

Related Functions	LOWER	Converts text to lowercase
	UPPER	Converts text to uppercase

List of Text Functions

PV

Returns the present value of an investment. The present value is the total amount that a series of future payments is worth now. For example, when you borrow money, the loan amount is the present value to the lender.

Syntax

PV(rate, nper, pmt, fv, type)

Rate   is the interest rate per period. For example, if you obtain an automobile loan at a 10% annual interest rate and make monthly payments, your interest rate per month is 10%/12, or 0.83%. You would enter 10%/12, or 0.83%, or 0.0083, into the formula as the rate.

Nper   is the total number of payment periods in an annuity. For example, if you get a four-year car loan and make monthly payments, your loan has 4*12 (or 48) periods. You would enter 48 into the formula for nper.

Pmt   is the payment made each period and cannot change over the life of the annuity. Typically, pmt includes principal and interest but no other fees or taxes. For example, the monthly payments on a $10,000, four-year car loan at 12% are $263.33. You would enter –263.33 into the formula as the pmt.

Fv   is the future value, or a cash balance you want to attain after the last payment is made. If fv is omitted, it is assumed to be 0 (the future value of a loan, for example, is 0). For example, if you want to save $50,000 to pay for a special project in 18 years, then $50,000 is the future value. You could then make a conservative guess at an interest rate and determine how much you must save each month.

Type   is the number 0 or 1 and indicates when payments are due.

Set type equal to	If payments are due
0 or omitted	At the end of the period
1	At the beginning of the period

Remarks

- Make sure that you are consistent about the units you use for specifying rate and nper. If you make monthly payments on a four-year loan at 12% annual interest, use 12%/12 for rate and 4*12 for nper. If you make annual payments on the same loan, use 12% for rate and 4 for nper.

- The following functions apply to annuities:

CUMIPMT	PPMT
CUMPRINC	PV
FV	RATE
FVSCHEDULE	XIRR
IPMT	XNPV
PMT	

An annuity is a series of constant cash payments made over a continuous period. For example, a car loan or a mortgage is an annuity. For more information, see the description for each annuity function.

- In annuity functions, cash you pay out, such as a deposit to savings, is represented by a negative number; cash you receive, such as a dividend check, is represented by a positive number. For example, a $1000 deposit to the bank would be represented by the argument –1000 if you are the depositor and by the argument 1000 if you are the bank.

- Microsoft Excel solves for one financial argument in terms of the others. If rate is not 0, then:

$$pv * (1 + rate)^{nper} + pmt(1 + rate * type) * \left(\frac{(1 + rate)^{nper} - 1}{rate} \right) + fv = 0$$

If rate is 0, then:

(pmt * nper) + pv + fv = 0

Example

Suppose you're thinking of buying an insurance annuity that pays $500 at the end of every month for the next 20 years. The cost of the annuity is $60,000 and the money paid out will earn 8%. You want to determine whether this would be a good investment. Using the PV function you find that the present value of the annuity is:

PV(0.08/12, 12*20, 500, , 0) equals –$59,777.15

The result is negative because it represents money that you would pay, an outgoing cash flow. The present value of the annuity ($59,777.15) is less than what you are asked to pay ($60,000). Therefore, you determine this would not be a good investment.

Related Functions

FV	Returns the future value of an investment
IPMT	Returns the interest payment for an investment for a given period
NPER	Returns the number of periods for an investment
PMT	Returns the periodic payment for an annuity
PPMT	Returns the payment on the principal for an investment for a given period
RATE	Returns the interest rate per period of an annuity

List of Financial Functions

QUARTILE

Returns the quartile of a data set. Quartiles often are used in sales and survey data to divide populations into groups. For example, you can use QUARTILE to find the top 25% of incomes in a population.

Syntax

QUARTILE(array, quart)

Array   is the array or cell range of numeric values for which you want the quartile value.

Quart   indicates which value to return.

If quart equals	QUARTILE returns
0	Minimum value
1	First quartile (25th percentile)
2	Median value (50th percentile)
3	Third quartile (75th percentile)
4	Maximum value

Remarks

- If array is empty or contains more than 8191 data points, QUARTILE returns the #NUM! error value.
- If quart is not an integer, it is truncated.
- If quart < 0 or if quart > 4, QUARTILE returns the #NUM! error value.
- MIN, MEDIAN, and MAX return the same value as QUARTILE when quart is equal to 0,2, and 4. respectively.

Example

QUARTILE({1,2,4,7,8,9,10,12},1) equals 3.5

Related Functions

LARGE	Returns the k-th largest value in a data set
MAX	Returns the maximum value in a list of arguments
MEDIAN	Returns the median of the given numbers
MIN	Returns the minimum value in a list of arguments
PERCENTILE	Returns the k-th percentile of values in a range
PERCENTRANK	Returns the percentage rank of a value in a data set
SMALL	Returns the k-th smallest value in a data set

List of Statistical Functions

QUOTIENT

Returns the integer portion of a division. Use this function when you want to discard the remainder of a division.

If this function is not available, run the Setup program to install the Analysis ToolPak. After you install the Analysis ToolPak, you must select it in the Add-In Manager. For more information, look up Add-ins in Help.

Syntax

QUOTIENT(numerator, denominator)

Numerator   is the dividend.

Denominator   is the divisor.

Remarks

If either argument is non-numeric, QUOTIENT returns the #VALUE! error value.

Examples

QUOTIENT(5, 2) equals 2

QUOTIENT(4.5, 3.1) equals 1

QUOTIENT(-10, 3) equals –3

Related Function

MOD   Returns the remainder from division

List of Math & Trigonometry Functions

RADIANS

Converts degrees to radians.

Syntax

RADIANS(angle)

Angle   is an angle in degrees that you want to convert.

Example

RADIANS(270) equals 4.712389 ($3\pi/2$ radians)

Related Function

DEGREES   Converts radians to degrees

List of Math & Trigonometry Functions

RAND

Returns an evenly distributed random number greater than or equal to 0 and less than 1. A new random number is returned every time the worksheet is calculated.

Syntax

RAND( )

Remarks

- To generate a random real number between a and b, use:
- RAND()*(b–a)+a
- To generate a random integer, use the RANDBETWEEN function.
- If you want to use RAND to generate a random number but don't want the numbers to change every time the cell is calculated, you can enter =RAND( ) in the formula bar and press F9 (or COMMAND + = in Microsoft Excel for the Macintosh) to change the formula to a random number.

Example

To generate a random number greater than or equal to 0 but less than 100:

```
RAND()*100
```

Related Functions

RANDBETWEEN   Returns a random number between the numbers you specify

List of Math & Trigonometry Functions

RANK

Returns the rank of a number in a list of numbers. The rank of a number is its size relative to other values in a list. (If you were to sort the list, the rank of the number would be its position.)

Syntax

RANK(number, ref, order)

Number   is the number whose rank you want to find.

Ref   is an array of, or a reference to, a list of numbers. Non-numeric values in ref are ignored.

Order   is a number specifying how to rank number.

- If order is 0 or omitted, Microsoft Excel ranks number as if ref were a list sorted in descending order.
- If order is any non-zero value, Microsoft Excel ranks number as if ref were a list sorted in ascending order.

Remarks	RANK gives duplicate numbers the same rank. However, the presence of duplicate numbers affects the ranks of subsequent numbers. For example, in a list of integers, if the number 10 appears twice and has a rank of 5, then 11 would have a rank of 7 (no number would have a rank of 6).
Example	If A1:A5 contain the numbers 7, 3.5, 3.5, 1, and 2, respectively, then:
	RANK(A2,A1:A5,1) equals 3 RANK(A1,A1:A5,1) equals 5
Related Functions	List of Statistical Functions

RATE

Returns the interest rate per period of an annuity. RATE is calculated by iteration and can have zero or more solutions. If the successive results of RATE do not converge to within 0.0000001 after 20 iterations, RATE returns the #NUM! error value.

Syntax

RATE(nper, pmt, pv, fv, type, guess)

See PV for a complete description of the arguments nper, pmt, pv, fv, and type.

Nper   is the total number of payment periods in an annuity.

Pmt   is the payment made each period and cannot change over the life of the annuity. Typically, pmt includes principal and interest but no other fees or taxes.

Pv   is the present value—the total amount that a series of future payments is worth now.

Fv   is the future value, or a cash balance you want to attain after the last payment is made. If fv is omitted, it is assumed to be 0 (the future value of a loan, for example, is 0).

Type   is the number 0 or 1 and indicates when payments are due.

Set type equal to	If payments are due
0 or omitted	At the end of the period
1	At the beginning of the period

Guess   is your guess for what the rate will be.

- If you omit guess, it is assumed to be 10%.
- If RATE does not converge, try different values for guess. RATE usually converges if guess is between 0 and 1.

Remarks

Make sure that you are consistent about the units you use for specifying guess and nper. If you make monthly payments on a four-year loan at 12% annual interest, use 12%/12 for guess and 4*12 for nper. If you make annual payments on the same loan, use 12% for guess and 4 for nper.

Example

To calculate the rate of a four-year $8000 loan with monthly payments of $200:

`RATE(48, -200, 8000)` equals 0.77%

This is the monthly rate, because the period is monthly. The annual rate is 0.77%*12, which equals 9.24%.

Related Functions

FV	Returns the future value of an investment
IPMT	Returns the interest payment for an investment for a given period
NPER	Returns the number of periods for an investment
PMT	Returns the periodic payment for an annuity
PPMT	Returns the payment on the principal for an investment for a given period
PV	Returns the present value of an investment

List of Financial Functions

RECEIVED

Returns the amount received at maturity for a fully invested security.

If this function is not available, run the Setup program to install the Analysis ToolPak. After you install the Analysis ToolPak, you must select it in the Add-In Manager. For more information, look up Add-ins in Help.

Syntax

RECEIVED(settlement, maturity, investment, discount, basis)

Settlement   is the security's settlement date, expressed as a serial date number.

Maturity   is the security's maturity date, expressed as a serial date number.

Investment   is the amount invested in the security.

Discount   is the security's discount rate.

Basis   is the type of day count basis to use.

Basis	Day count basis
c0 or omitted	US (NASD) 30/360
1	Actual/actual
2	Actual/360
3	Actual/365
4	European 30/360

Remarks

- Settlement, maturity, and basis are truncated to integers.
- If any argument is non-numeric, RECEIVED returns the #VALUE! error value.
- If settlement or maturity is not a valid serial date number, RECEIVED returns the #NUM! error value.
- If investment ≤ 0 or if discount ≤ 0, RECEIVED returns the #NUM! error value.
- If basis < 0 or if basis > 4, RECEIVED returns the #NUM! error value.
- If settlement ≥ maturity, RECEIVED returns the #NUM! error value.
- RECEIVED is calculated as follows:

$$RECEIVED = \frac{investment}{1 - (discount \times \frac{DIM}{B})}$$

Where:

- B = number of days in a year, depending on the year basis.
- DIM = number of days from issue to maturity.

Example

A bond has the following terms:

February 15, 1993 settlement (issue) date
May 15, 1993 maturity date
1,000,000 investment
5.75% discount rate
Actual/360 basis

The total amount to be received at maturity (in the 1900 Date System) is:

RECEIVED(34015,34104,1000000,0.0575,2) equals 1,014,420.266

Related Functions   DATE   Returns the serial number of a particular date

INTRATE   Returns the interest rate for a fully invested security

List of Financial Functions

REGISTER.ID

Returns the register ID of the specified dynamic link library (DLL) or code resource that has been previously registered. If the DLL or code resource has not been registered, this function registers the DLL or code resource, and then returns the register ID.

REGISTER.ID can be used on worksheets (unlike REGISTER), but you cannot specify a function name and argument names with REGISTER.ID.

For more information about DLLs and code resources and data types, see the "Using the CALL and REGISTER Functions" in the Appendix.

Syntax 1   For Microsoft Excel for Windows

REGISTER.ID(module_text, procedure, type_text)

Syntax 2   For Microsoft Excel for the Macintosh

REGISTER.ID(file_text, resource, type_text)

Module_text   is text specifying the name of the DLL that contains the function in Microsoft Excel for Windows.

Procedure   is text specifying the name of the function in the DLL in Microsoft Excel for Windows. You can also use the ordinal value of the function from the EXPORTS statement in the module-definition file (.DEF). The ordinal value or resource ID number should not be in text form.

Type_text   is text specifying the data type of the return value and the data types of all arguments to the DLL. The first letter of type_text specifies the return value. If the function or code resource is already registered, you can omit this argument.

File_text   is text specifying the name of the file that contains the code resource in Microsoft Excel for the Macintosh.

Resource   is text specifying the name of the function in the code resource in Microsoft Excel for the Macintosh. You can also use the resource ID number. The ordinal value or resource ID number should not be in text form.

Examples (32-bit)   The following formula registers the GetTickCount function from 32-bit Microsoft Windows (Windows 95 or Windows NT), and returns the register ID (In 16-bit Microsoft Excel, substitute "User" for "Kernel32"):

REGISTER.ID("Kernel32", "GetTickCount", "J!")

Assuming that GetTickCount was already registered on another sheet using the preceding formula, the following formula returns the register ID for GetTickCount;

REGISTER.ID("Kernel32", "GetTickCount")

Related Functions   CALL   Calls a procedure in a dynamic link library or code resource

List of DDE/EXTERNAL Functions

REPLACE

Replaces part of a text string with a different text string.

Syntax   **REPLACE(old_text, start_num, num_chars, new_text)**

Old_text   is text in which you want to replace some characters.

Start_num   is the position of the character in old_text that you want to replace with new_text.

Num_chars   is the number of characters in old_text that you want to replace with new_text.

New_text   is the text that will replace characters in old_text.

Examples   The following formula replaces five characters with new_text, starting with the sixth character in old_text:

REPLACE("abcdefghijk", 6, 5, "*") equals "abcde*k"

The sixth through tenth characters are all replaced by "*".

The following formula replaces the last two digits of 1990 with 91:

REPLACE("1990", 3, 2, "91") equals "1991"

If cell A2 contains "123456", then:

REPLACE(A2, 1, 3, "@") equals "@456"

If the RIGHT function returns "ABCDEF", then:

REPLACE(RIGHT(A3, 6), 1, 6, "*") equals "*"

Related Functions	MID	Returns a specific number of characters from a text string
	SEARCH	Finds one text value within another (not case-sensitive)
	SUBSTITUTE	Substitutes new text for old text in a text string
	TRIM	Removes spaces from text

List of Text Functions

REPT

Repeats text a given number of times. Use REPT to fill a cell with a number of instances of a text string.

Syntax

REPT(text, number_times)

Text   is the text you want to repeat.

Number_times   is a positive number specifying the number of times to repeat text. If number_times is 0, REPT returns "" (empty text). If number_times is not an integer, it is truncated. The result of the REPT function cannot be longer than 255 characters.

Tip   You can use this function to create a simple histogram on your worksheet.

Examples

REPT("*-", 3) equals "*-*-*-"

If A3 contains "Sales", then:

REPT($A$3, 2.9) equals "SalesSales"

Related Functions   List of Text Functions

RIGHT

Returns the last (or rightmost) character or characters in a text string.

Syntax

RIGHT(text, num_chars)

Text   is the text string containing the characters you want to extract.

Num_chars   specifies how many characters you want to extract.

- Num_chars must be greater than or equal to zero.
- If num_chars is greater than the length of text, RIGHT returns all of text.
- If num_chars is omitted, it is assumed to be 1.

Examples

RIGHT("Sale Price", 5) equals "Price"

RIGHT("Stock Number") equals "r"

RIGHT is similar to LEFT; for more examples, see LEFT.

Related Functions

LEFT	Returns the leftmost characters from a text value
MID	Returns a specific number of characters from a text string

List of Text Functions

ROMAN

Converts an Arabic numeral to Roman, as text.

Syntax

ROMAN(number, form)

Number   is the Arabic numeral you want converted.

Form   is a number specifying the type of Roman numeral you want. The Roman numeral style ranges from Classic to Simplified, becoming more concise as the value of form increases. See the example following ROMAN(499,0) below.

Form	Type
0 or omitted	Classic
1	More concise. See example below.
2	More concise. See example below.
3	More concise. See example below.
4	Simplified
TRUE	Classic
FALSE	Simplified

Remarks

- If number is negative the #value! error value is returned.
- If number is greater than 3999, the #value error value is returned.

Examples

ROMAN(499,0) equals "CDXCIX"

ROMAN(499,1) equals "LDVLIV"

ROMAN(499,2) equals "XDIX"

ROMAN(499,3) equals "VDIV"

ROMAN(499,4) equals "ID"

ROMAN(1993,0) equals "MCMXCIII"

Related Functions   List of Math & Trigonometry Functions

ROUND

Rounds a number to a specified number of digits.

Syntax   **ROUND(number, num_digits)**

Number   is the number you want to round.

Num_digits   specifies the number of digits to which you want to round number.

- If num_digits is greater than 0, then number is rounded to the specified number of decimal places.
- If num_digits is 0, then number is rounded to the nearest integer.
- If num_digits is less than 0, then number is rounded to the left of the decimal point.

Examples   ROUND(2.15, 1) equals 2.2

ROUND(2.149, 1) equals 2.1

ROUND(-1.475, 2) equals −1.48

ROUND(21.5, -1) equals 20

Related Functions

CEILING	Rounds a number to the nearest integer or to the nearest multiple of significance
FLOOR	Rounds a number down, toward zero
INT	Rounds a number down to the nearest integer
MOD	Returns the remainder from division
MROUND	Returns a number rounded to the desired multiple
ROUNDDOWN	Rounds a number down, toward zero
ROUNDUP	Rounds a number up, away from zero
TRUNC	Truncates a number to an integer

List of Math & Trigonometry Functions

ROUNDDOWN

Rounds a number down, toward zero.

Syntax

ROUNDDOWN(**number**, num_digits)

Number   is any real number that you want rounded down.

Num_digits   is the number of digits to which you want to round number.

Remarks

- ROUNDDOWN behaves like ROUND, except that it always rounds a number down.

- If num_digits is greater than 0, then number is rounded down to the specified number of decimal places.

- If num_digits is 0 or omitted, then number is rounded down to the nearest integer.

- If num_digits is less than 0, then number is rounded down to the left of the decimal point.

Examples

ROUNDDOWN(3.2, 0) equals 3

ROUNDDOWN(76.9,0) equals 76

ROUNDDOWN(3.14159, 3) equals 3.141

ROUNDDOWN(-3.14159, 1) equals -3.1

ROUNDDOWN(31415.92654, -2) equals 31400

Related Functions

CEILING	Rounds a number to the nearest integer or to the nearest multiple of significance
FLOOR	Rounds a number down, toward zero
INT	Rounds a number down to the nearest integer
MOD	Returns the remainder from division
MROUND	Returns a number rounded to the desired multiple
TRUNC	Truncates a number to an integer
ROUND	Rounds a number to a specified number of digits
ROUNDUP	Rounds a number up, away from zero

List of Math & Trigonometry Functions

ROUNDUP

Rounds a number up, away from zero.

Syntax

ROUNDUP(number, num_digits)

Number   is any real number that you want rounded up.

Num_digits   is the number of digits to which you want to round number.

Remarks

- ROUNDUP behaves like ROUND, except that it always rounds a number up.
- If num_digits is greater than 0, then number is rounded up to the specified number of decimal places.
- If num_digits is 0 or omitted, then number is rounded up to the nearest integer.
- If num_digits is less than 0, then number is rounded up to the left of the decimal point.

Examples

ROUNDUP(3.2,0) equals 4

ROUNDUP(76.9,0) equals 77

ROUNDUP(3.14159, 3) equals 3.142

ROUNDUP(-3.14159, 1) equals –3.2

ROUNDUP(31415.92654, -2) equals 31500

Related Functions

CEILING	Rounds a number to the nearest integer or to the nearest multiple of significance
FLOOR	Rounds a number down, toward zero
INT	Rounds a number down to the nearest integer
MOD	Returns the remainder from division
MROUND	Returns a number rounded to the desired multiple
TRUNC	Truncates a number to an integer
ROUND	Rounds a number to a specified number of digits
ROUNDDOWN	Rounds a number down, toward zero

List of Math & Trigonometry Functions

ROW

Returns the row number of a reference.

Syntax   **ROW(reference)**

Reference   is the cell or range of cells for which you want the row number.

- If reference is omitted, it is assumed to be the reference of the cell in which the ROW function appears.
- If reference is a range of cells and if ROW is entered as a vertical array, ROW returns the row numbers of reference as a vertical array.
- Reference cannot refer to multiple areas.

Examples   ROW(A3) equals 3

When entered as an array formula in three vertical cells:

ROW(A3:B5) equals {3;4;5}

If ROW is entered in C5, then:

ROW() equals ROW(C5) equals 5

The following macro formula tells you which row the active cell is in:

ROW(ACTIVE.CELL())

Related Functions   COLUMN   Returns the column number of a reference

ROWS   Returns the number of rows in a reference

List of Lookup & Reference Functions

ROWS

Returns the number of rows in a reference or array.

Syntax   **ROWS(array)**

Array   is an array, an array formula, or a reference to a range of cells for which you want the number of rows.

Examples   ROWS(A1:C4) equals 4

ROWS({1,2,3;4,5,6}) equals 2

The following macro formula calculates the number of rows in the current selection:

```
ROWS|USA|002|001|001|common|UROWS(SELECTION|USA|002|001|001|common|USELE
CTION())
```

The following macro formula calculates the number of rows in the third area in a discontinuous selection (specified by the area_num argument to INDEX) of the current multiple selection:

```
ROWS|USA|002|001|001|common|UROWS(INDEX|USA|002|001|001|common|UINDEX(SE
LECTION|USA|002|001|001|common|USELECTION(),,,3))
```

Related Functions

COLUMNS	Returns the number of columns in a reference
ROW	Returns the row number of a reference

List of Lookup & Reference Functions

RSQ

Returns the square of the Pearson product moment correlatin coefficient through data points in known_y's and known_x's. For more information, see PEARSON. The r-squared value can be interpreted as the proportion of the variance in y attributable to the variance in x.

Syntax

RSQ(known_y's, known_x's)

Known_y's   is an array or range of data points.

Known_x's   is an array or range of data points.

Remarks

- The arguments should be numbers, or names, arrays, or references that contain numbers.

- If an array or reference argument contains text, logical values, or empty cells, those values are ignored; however, cells with the value zero are included.

- If known_y's and known_x's are empty or have a different number of data points, RSQ returns the #N/A error value.

- The equation for the r value of the regression line is:

$$r = \frac{n(\Sigma XY) - (\Sigma X)(\Sigma Y)}{\sqrt{\left[n\Sigma X^2 - (\Sigma X)^2\right]\left[n\Sigma Y^2 - (\Sigma Y)^2\right]}}$$

| **Example** | RSQ({2,3,9,1,8,7,5},{6,5,11,7,5,4,4}) equals 0.05795 |

Related Functions	CORREL	Returns the correlation coefficient between two data sets
	COVAR	Returns covariance, the average of the products of paired deviations
	INTERCEPT	Returns the intercept of the linear regression line
	LINEST	Returns the parameters of a linear trend
	LOGEST	Returns the parameters of an exponential trend
	PEARSON	Returns the Pearson product moment correlation coefficient
	SLOPE	Returns the slope of the linear regression line
	STEYX	Returns the standard error of the predicted y-value for each x in the regression
	TREND	Returns values along a linear trend

List of Statistical Functions

SEARCH

Returns the number of the character at which a specific character or text string is first found, reading from left to right. Use SEARCH to discover the location of a character or text string within another text string, so that you can use the MID or REPLACE functions to change the text.

Syntax

SEARCH(find_text, within_text, start_num)

Find_text   is the text you want to find. You can use the wildcard characters, question mark (?) and asterisk (*), in find_text. A question mark matches any single character; an asterisk matches any sequence of characters. If you want to find an actual question mark or asterisk, type a tilde (~) before the character. If find_text is not found, the #VALUE! error value is returned.

Within_text   is the text in which you want to search for find_text.

Start_num   is the character number in within_text, counting from the left, at which you want to start searching.

- If start_num is omitted, it is assumed to be 1.
- If start_num is not greater than 0 or is greater than the length of within_text, the #VALUE! error value is returned.

Tip   Use start_num to skip a specified number of characters from the left of the text. For example, suppose you are working with a text string such as "AYF0093.YoungMensApparel". To find the number of the first "Y" in the descriptive part of the text string, set start_num equal to 8 so that the serial-number portion of the text is not searched. SEARCH begins with character 8, finds find_text at the next character, and returns the number 9. SEARCH always returns the number of characters from the left of the text string, not from start_num.

Remarks

- SEARCH does not distinguish between uppercase and lowercase letters when searching text.
- SEARCH is similar to FIND, except that FIND is case-sensitive.

Examples

SEARCH("e","Statements",6) equals 7

If cell B17 contains the word "margin" and cell A14 contains "Profit Margin", then:

SEARCH($B$17,$A$14) equals 8

Use SEARCH with the REPLACE function to provide REPLACE with the correct start_num at which to begin inserting new text. Using the same cell references as the previous example:

`REPLACE($A$14,SEARCH($B$17,$A$14),6,"Amount")` returns the text "Profit Amount".

Related Functions

FIND	Finds one text value within another (case-sensitive)
MID	Returns a specific number of characters from a text string
REPLACE	Replaces characters within text
SUBSTITUTE	Substitutes new text for old text in a text string

List of Lookup & Reference Functions

SECOND

Returns the second corresponding to serial_number. The second is given as an integer in the range 0 to 59. Use SECOND to get the time in seconds indicated by a serial number.

Syntax

SECOND(serial_number)

Serial_number   is the date-time code used by Microsoft Excel for date and time calculations. You can give serial_number as text, such as "16:48:23" or "4:48:47 PM", instead of as a number. The text is automatically converted to a serial number. For more information on serial_number, see NOW.

Remarks

Microsoft Excel for Windows and Microsoft Excel for the Macintosh use different date systems as their default. For more information, see NOW.

Examples

`SECOND("4:48:18 PM")` equals 18

`SECOND(0.01)` equals 24

`SECOND(4.02)` equals 48

Related Functions

DATE	Returns the serial number of a particular date
NOW	Returns the serial number of the current date and time
YEAR, MONTH, DAY, WEEKDAY, HOUR, and MINUTE	Convert serial numbers into years, months, days, days of the week, hours, and minutes

List of Date & Time Functions

SERIESSUM

Returns the sum of a power series based on the formula:

$$SERIES(x,n,m,a) = a_1 x^n + a_2 x^{(n+m)} + a_3 x^{(n+2m)}$$
$$+ \ldots + a_i x^{(n+(i-1)m)}$$

Many functions can be approximated by a power series expansion.

If this function is not available, run the Setup program to install the Analysis ToolPak. After you install the Analysis ToolPak, you must select it in the Add-In Manager. For more information, look up Add-ins in Help.

Syntax

SERIESSUM(x, n, m, coefficients)

X   is the input value to the power series.

N   is the initial power to which you want to raise x.

M   is the step by which to increase n for each term in the series.

Coefficients   is a set of coefficients by which each successive power of x is multiplied. The number of values in coefficients determines the number of terms in the power series. For example, if there are three values in coefficients, then there will be three terms in the power series.

Remarks   If any argument is non-numeric, SERIESSUM returns the #VALUE! error value.

Example   Given that cell A1 contains the formula =PI()/4, and cells E1:E4 contain the following set of values for coefficients (calculated using the FACT function):

$$\left[1, -\frac{1}{2!}, \frac{1}{4!}, -\frac{1}{6!} \right]$$

The following macro formula returns an approximation to the cosine of $\pi/4$ radians (45 degrees):

SERIESSUM(A1,0,2,E1:E4) equals .707103

Related Functions   List of Math & Trigonometry Functions

SIGN

Determines the sign of a number. Returns 1 if number is positive, 0 if number is 0, and -1 if number is negative.

Syntax

SIGN(number)

Number   is any real number.

Examples

SIGN(10) equals 1

SIGN(4-4) equals 0

SIGN(-0.00001) equals −1

Related Function

ABS   Returns the absolute value of a number

List of Math & Trigonometry Functions

SIN

Returns the sine of the given angle.

Syntax

SIN(number)

Number   is the angle in radians for which you want the sine. If your argument is in degrees, multiply it by PI()/180 to convert it to radians.

Examples

SIN(PI()) equals 1.22E-16, which is approximately zero. The sine of π is zero.

SIN(PI()/2) equals 1

SIN(30*PI()/180) equals 0.5, the sine of 30 degrees

Related Functions

ASIN   Returns the arcsine of a number

PI   Returns the value π

List of Math & Trigonometry Functions

SINH

Returns the hyperbolic sine of a number.

Syntax

SINH(number)

Number   is any real number.

The formula for the hyperbolic sine is:

$$SINH(z) = \frac{e^z - e^{-z}}{2}$$

Examples

SINH(1) equals 1.175201194

SINH(-1) equals –1.175201194

You can use the hyperbolic sine function to approximate a cumulative probability distribution. Suppose a laboratory test value varies between 0 and 10 seconds. An empirical analysis of the collected history of experiments shows that the probability of obtaining a result, x, of less than t seconds is approximated by the following equation:

P(x<t) = 2.868 * SINH(0.0342 * t), where 0<t<10

To calculate the probability of obtaining a result of less than 1.03 seconds, substitute 1.03 for t:

2.868*SINH(0.0342*1.03) equals 0.101049063

You can expect this result to occur about 101 times for every 1000 experiments.

Related Functions

ASINH	Returns the inverse hyperbolic sine of a number
COSH	Returns the hyperbolic cosine of a number
TANH	Returns the hyperbolic tangent of a number

List of Math & Trigonometry Functions

SKEW

Returns the skewness of a distribution. Skewness characterizes the degree of asymmetry of a distribution around its mean. Positive skewness indicates a distribution with an asymmetric tail extending towards more positive values. Negative skewness indicates a distribution with an asymmetric tail extending towards more negative values.

Syntax

SKEW(number1, number2, ...)

Number1,number2...   are 1 to 30 arguments for which you want to calculate skewness. You can also use a single array or a reference to an array instead of arguments separated by commas.

Remarks

- The arguments should be numbers, or names, arrays, or references that contain numbers.
- If an array or reference argument contains text, logical values, or empty cells, those values are ignored; however, cells with the value zero are included.
- If there are less than three data points, or the sample standard deviation is zero, SKEW returns the #DIV/0! error value.
- The equation for skewness is defined as:

$$\frac{n}{(n-1)(n-2)}\sum\left(\frac{x_i - \bar{x}}{s}\right)^3$$

Example

SKEW(3,4,5,2,3,4,5,6,4,7) equals 0.359543

Related Functions

KURT	Returns the kurtosis of a data set
STDEV	Estimates standard deviation based on a sample
STDEVP	Calculates standard deviation based on the entire population
VAR	Estimates variance based on a sample
VARP	Calculates variance based on the entire population

List of Statistical Functions

SLN

Returns the straight-line depreciation of an asset for one period.

Syntax

SLN(cost, salvage, life)

Cost   is the initial cost of the asset.

Salvage   is the value at the end of the depreciation (sometimes called the salvage value of the asset).

Life   is the number of periods over which the asset is being depreciated (sometimes called the useful life of the asset).

Example   Suppose you've bought a truck for $30,000 that has a useful life of 10 years and a salvage value of $7500. The depreciation allowance for each year is:

SLN(30000, 7500, 10) equals $2250

Related Functions

DDB	Returns the depreciation of an asset for a spcified period using the double-declining balance method or some other method you specify
SYD	Returns the sum-of-years' digits depreciation of an asset for a specified period
VDB	Returns the depreciation of an asset for a specified or partial period using a declining balance method

List of Financial Functions

SLOPE

Returns the slope of the linear regression line through data points in known_y's and known_x's. The slope is the vertical distance divided by the horizontal distance between any two points on the line, which is the rate of change along the regression line.

Syntax   **SLOPE(known_y's, known_x's)**

Known_y's   is an array or cell range of numeric dependent data points.

Known_x's   is the set of independent data points.

Remarks
- The arguments should be numbers, or names, arrays, or references that contain numbers.
- If an array or reference argument contains text, logical values, or empty cells, those values are ignored; however, cells with the value zero are included.
- If known_y's and known_x's are empty or have a different number of data points, SLOPE returns the #N/A error value.
- The equation for the slope of the regression line is:

$$b = \frac{n\sum xy - \left(\sum x\right)\left(\sum y\right)}{n\sum x^2 - \left(\sum x\right)^2}$$

Example   SLOPE({2,3,9,1,8,7,5},{6,5,11,7,5,4,4}) equals 0.305556

Related Functions	INTERCEPT	Returns the intercept of the linear regression line
	LINEST	Returns the parameters of a linear trend
	LOGEST	Returns the parameters of an exponential trend
	PEARSON	Returns the Pearson product moment correlation coefficient
	RSQ	Returns the square of the Pearson product moment correlatin coefficient
	STEYX	Returns the standard error of the predicted y-value for each x in the regression
	TREND	Returns values along a linear trend

List of Statistical Functions

SMALL

Returns the k-th smallest value in a data set. Use this function to return values with a particular relative standing in a data set.

Syntax

SMALL(array, k)

Array   is an array or range of numerical data for which you want to determine the k-th smallest value.

K   is the position (from the smallest) in the array or range of data to return.

Remarks

- If array is empty, SMALL returns the #NUM! error value.
- If k ≤ 0 or if k exceeds the number of data points, SMALL returns the #NUM! error value.
- If n is the number of data points in array, SMALL(array,1) equals the smallest value, and SMALL(array,n) equals the largest value.

Examples

SMALL({3,4,5,2,3,4,5,6,4,7},4) equals 4

SMALL({1,4,8,3,7,12,54,8,23},2) equals 3

Related Functions	LARGE	Returns the k-th largest value in a data set
	MAX	Returns the maximum value in a list of arguments
	MEDIAN	Returns the median of the given numbers
	MIN	Returns the minimum value in a list of arguments

PERCENTILE	Returns the k-th percentile of values in a range
PERCENTRANK	Returns the percentage rank of a value in a data set
QUARTILE	Returns the quartile of a data set

List of Statistical Functions

SQL.REQUEST

Connects with an external data source and runs a query from a worksheet. SQL.REQUEST then returns the result as an array without the need for macro programming. If this function is not available, you must install the Microsoft Excel ODBC add-in (XLODBC.XLA)..

Syntax

SQL.REQUEST(connection_string, output_ref, driver_prompt, **query_text**, column_names_logical)

Connection_string   supplies information, such as the data source name, user ID, and passwords, required by the driver being used to connect to a data source and must follow the driver's format. The following table provides three example connection strings for three drivers.

Driver	connection_string
dBASE®	DSN=NWind;PWD=test
SQL Server	DSN=MyServer;UID=dbayer;PWE=123;Database=Pubs
ORACLE®	DNS=My Oracle Data Source;DBQ=MYSERVER;UID=JohnS;PWD=Sesame

- You must define the data source name (DSN) used in connection_string before you try to connect to it.

- You can enter connection_string as an array or a string. If connection_string exceeds 250 characters, you must enter it as an array.

- If SQL.REQUEST is unable to access the data source using connection_string, it returns the #N/A error value.

Output_ref   is a cell reference where you want the completed connection string placed. If you enter SQL.REQUEST on a worksheet, then Output_ref is ignored.

- Use output_ref when you want SQL.REQUEST to return the completed connection string (you must enter SQL.REQUEST on a macro sheet in this case).

- If you omit the output_ref, SQL.REQUEST does not return a completed connection string.

Driver_prompt   specifies when the driver dialog box is displayed and which options are available. Use one of the numbers described in the following table. If driver_prompt is omitted, SQL.REQUEST uses 2 as the default.

Driver_prompt	Description
1	Driver dialog box is always displayed.
2	Driver dialog box is displayed only if information provided by the connection string and the data source specification is not sufficient to complete the connection. All dialog box options are available.
3	Driver dialog box is displayed only if information provided by the connection string and the data source specification is not sufficient to complete the connection. Dialog box options are dimmed and unavailable if they are not required.
4	Dialog box is not displayed. If the connection is not successful, it returns an error.

Query_text   is the SQL statement that you want to execute on the data source.

- If SQL.REQUEST is unable to execute query_text on the specified data source, it returns the #N/A error value.

- You can update a query by concatenating references into query_text. In the following example, every time $A$3 changes, SQL.REQUEST uses the new value to update the query.

   "SELECT Name FROM Customers WHERE Balance > "'&$A$3'.

   Microsoft Excel limits strings to a length of 255 characters. If query_text exceeds that length, enter the query in a vertical range of cells and use the entire range as the query_text. The values of the cells are concatenated to form the complete SQL statement.

Column_names_logical   indicates whether column names are returned as the first row of the results. Set this argument to TRUE if you want the column names to be returned as the first row of the results. Use FALSE if you do not want the column names returned. If column_names_logical is omitted, SQL.REQUEST does not return column names.

Return Value

- If this function completes all of its actions, it returns an array of query results or the number of rows affected by the query.
- If SQL.REQUEST is unable to access the data source using connection_string, it returns the #N/A error value.

Remarks

- SQL.REQUEST can be entered as an array. When you enter SQL.REQUEST as an array, it returns an array to fit that range.
- If the range of cells is larger than the result set, SQL.REQUEST adds empty cells to the returned array to increase it to the necessary size.
- If the result set is larger than the range entered as an array, SQL.REQUEST returns the whole array.

Examples

Suppose you want to make a query of a dBASE database named DBASE4. When you enter the following formula in a cell, an array of query results is returned, with the first row being the column names.

```
SQL.REQUEST("DSN=NWind;DBQ=c:\msquery;FIL=dBASE4", c15, 2,
"Select Custmr_ID, Due_Date from Orders WHERE order_Amt>100", TRUE)
```

List of DDE and External functions

SQRT

Returns a positive square root.

Syntax

SQRT(number)

Number   is the number for which you want the square root. If number is negative, SQRT returns the #NUM! error value.

Examples

SQRT(16) equals 4

SQRT(-16) equals #NUM!

SQRT(ABS(-16)) equals 4

SQRTPI

Returns the square root of (number * π).

If this function is not available, run the Setup program to install the Analysis ToolPak. After you install the Analysis ToolPak, you must select it in the Add-In Manager. For more information, look up Add-ins in Help.

Syntax **SQRTPI(number)**

Number   is the number by which pi is multiplied.

Remark If number < 0, SQRTPI returns the #NUM! error value.

Examples SQRTPI(1) equals 1.772454

SQRTPI(2) equals 2.506628

Related Functions PI   Returns the value π

SQRT   Returns a positive square root

List of Math & Trigonometry Functions

STANDARDIZE

Returns a normalized value from a distribution characterized by mean and standard_dev.

Syntax **STANDARDIZE(x, mean, standard_dev)**

X   is the value you want to normalize.

Mean   is the arithmetic mean of the distribution.

Standard_dev   is the standard deviation of the distribution.

Remarks ▪ If standard_dev ≤ 0, STANDARDIZE returns the #NUM! error value.

▪ The equation for the normalized value is:

$$Z = \frac{X - \mu}{\sigma}$$

Example STANDARDIZE(42,40,1.5) equals 1.333333

Related Functions	NORMDIST	Returns the normal cumulative distribution
	NORMINV	Returns the inverse of the normal cumulative distribution
	NORMSDIST	Returns the standard normal cumulative distribution
	NORMSINV	Returns the inverse of the standard normal cumulative distribution
	ZTEST	Returns the two-tailed P-value of a z-test

List of Statistical Functions

STDEV

Estimates standard deviation based on a sample. The standard deviation is a measure of how widely values are dispersed from the average value (the mean).

Syntax

STDEV(**number1**,number2,...)

Number1,number2,...   are 1 to 30 number arguments corresponding to a sample of a population. You can also use a single array or a reference to an array instead of arguments separated by commas.

Remarks

- STDEV assumes that its arguments are a sample of the population. If your data represents the entire population, you should compute the standard deviation using STDEVP.

- The standard deviation is calculated using the "nonbiased" or "n-1" method.

- STDEV uses the following formula:

$$\sqrt{\frac{n\sum x^2 - \left(\sum x\right)^2}{n(n-1)}}$$

Example

Suppose 10 tools stamped from the same machine during a production run are collected as a random sample and measured for breaking strength. The sample values (1345, 1301, 1368, 1322, 1310, 1370, 1318, 1350, 1303, 1299) are stored in A2:E3, respectively. STDEV estimates the standard deviation of breaking strengths for all the tools.

STDEV(A2:E3) equals 27.46

Related Functions   List of Statistical Functions

STDEVP

Calculates standard deviation based on the entire population given as arguments. The standard deviation is a measure of how widely values are dispersed from the average value (the mean).

Syntax

STDEVP(**number1**,number2],...

Number1,number2,...   are 1 to 30 number arguments corresponding to a population. You can also use a single array or a reference to an aray instead of arguments separated by commas.

Remarks

- STDEVP assumes that its arguments are the entire population. If your data represents a sample of the population, you should compute the standard deviation using STDEV.

- For large sample sizes, STDEV and STDEVP return approximately equal values.

- The standard deviation is calculated using the "biased" or "n" method.

- STDEVP uses the following formula:

$$\sqrt{\frac{n\sum x^2 - \left(\sum x\right)^2}{n(n-1)}}$$

Example

Using the same data from the STDEV example and assuming that only 10 tools are produced during the production run, STDEVP measures the standard deviation of breaking strengths for all the tools.

STDEVP(A2:E3) equals 26.05

Related Functions   List of Statistical Functions

STEYX

Returns the standard error of the predicted y-value for each x in the regression. The standard error is a measure of the amount of error in the prediction of y for an individual x.

Syntax

STEYX(**known_y's, known_x's**)

Known_y's   is an array or range of dependent data points.

Known_x's   is an array or range of independent data points.

Remarks

- The arguments should be numbers, or names, arrays, or references that contain numbers.

- If an array or reference argument contains text, logical values, or empty cells, those values are ignored; however, cells with the value zero are included.

- If known_y's and known_x's are empty or have a different number of data points, STEYX returns the #N/A error value.

- The equation for the standard error of the predicted y is:

$$S_{y \cdot x} = \sqrt{\left[\frac{1}{n(n-2)}\right]\left[n\Sigma y^2 - (\Sigma y)^2 - \frac{\left[n\Sigma xy - (\Sigma x)(\Sigma y)\right]^2}{n\Sigma x^2 - (\Sigma x)^2}\right]}$$

Example   STEYX({2,3,9,1,8,7,5},{6,5,11,7,5,4,4}) equals 3.305719

Related Functions

INTERCEPT	Returns the intercept of the linear regression line
LINEST	Returns the parameters of a linear trend
LOGEST	Returns the parameters of an exponential trend
PEARSON	Returns the Pearson product moment correlation coefficient
RSQ	Returns the square of the Pearson product moment correlatin coefficient
SLOPE	Returns the slope of the linear regression line

List of Statistical Functions

SUBSTITUTE

Substitutes new_text for old_text in a text string. Use SUBSTITUTE when you want to replace specific text in a text string; use REPLACE when you want to replace any text that occurs in a specific location in a text string.

Syntax   **SUBSTITUTE(text, old_text, new_text,** instance_num)

Text   is the text or the reference to a cell containing text for which you want to substitute characters.

Old_text   is the text you want to replace.

New_text is the text you want to replace old_text with.

Instance_num specifies which occurrence of old_text you want to replace with new_text. If you specify instance_num, only that instance of old_text is replaced. Otherwise, every occurrence of old_text in text is changed to new_text.

Examples

SUBSTITUTE("Sales Data", "Sales", "Cost") equals "Cost Data"

SUBSTITUTE("Quarter 1, 1991", "1", "2", 1) equals "Quarter 2, 1991"

SUBSTITUTE("Quarter 1, 1991", "1", "2", 3) equals "Quarter 1, 1992"

To replace every occurrence of the text constant named Separator in the cell named CellCont2 with square brackets:

SUBSTITUTE(CellCont2, Separator, "] [")

Related Functions

| REPLACE | Replaces characters within text |
| TRIM | Removes spaces from text |

List of Text Functions

SUBTOTAL

Returns a subtotal in a list or database. It is generally easier to create a list with subtotals using the SUBTOTAL command on the Data menu. Once the subtotal list is created, you can modify it by editing the SUBTOTAL formula.

Syntax

SUBTOTAL(function_num, ref)

Function_num is the number 1 to 11 that specifies which function to use in calculating subtotals within a list.

Function_Num	Function
1	AVERAGE
2	COUNT
3	COUNTA
4	MAX
5	MIN

Function_Num	Function
6	PRODUCT
7	STDEV
8	STDEVP
9	SUM
10	VAR
11	VARP

Ref   is range or reference for which you want the subtotal.

Remarks

- If there are other subtotals within ref (or nested subtotals), these nested subtotals are ignored to avoid double counting.
- SUBTOTAL will ignore any hidden rows. This is important when you want to subtotal only the visible data that results from a list that you have filtered.

Example

SUBTOTAL(9,C3:C5) will generate a subtotal of the cells C3:C5 using the SUM function

Related Functions

List of Math & Trigonometry Functions

SUM

Returns the sum of all the numbers in the list of arguments.

Syntax

SUM(number1, number2, ...)

Number1, number2,...   are 1 to 30 arguments for which you want the sum.

- Numbers, logical values, and text representations of numbers that you type directly into the list of arguments are counted. See the first and second examples following.
- If an argument is an array or reference, only numbers in that array or reference are counted. Empty cells, logical values, text, or error values in the array or reference are ignored. See the third example following.
- Arguments that are error values or text that cannot be translated into numbers cause errors.

Examples

SUM(3, 2) equals 5

SUM("3", 2, TRUE) equals 6 because the text values are translated into numbers, and the logical value TRUE is translated into the number 1.

Unlike the previous example, if A1 contains "3" and B1 contains TRUE, then:

SUM(A1, B1, 2) equals 2 because references to non-number values in references are not translated.

If cells A2:E2 contain 5, 15, 30, 40, and 50:

SUM(A2:C2) equals 50

SUM(B2:E2, 15) equals 150

Related Functions	AVERAGE	Returns the average of its arguments
	COUNT or COUNTA	Count how many numbers or values are in a list of arguments
	PRODUCT	Multiplies its arguments
	SUMPRODUCT	Returns the sum of the products of corresponding array components

List of Math & Trigonometry Functions

SUMIF

Adds the cells specified by a given criteria.

Syntax

SUMIF(range, criteria, sum_range)

Range   is the range of cells you want evaluated.

Criteria   is the criteria in the form of a number, expression, or text that defines which cells will be added. For example, Criteria can be expressed as 32, "32", ">32", "apples".

Sum_range   are the actual cells to sum. The cells in sum_range are summed only if their corresponding cells in range match the criteria. If Sum_range is omitted, the cells in range are summed.

Example

Suppose A1:A4 contains the following property values for four homes: $100000, $200000, $300000, $400000, respectively. B1:B4 contains the following sales commissions on each of the corresponding property values: $7000, $14000, $21000, $28000.

SUMIF(A1:A4,">160000",B1:B4) equals $63000

Related Functions	SUM	Adds its arguments
	COUNTIF	Counts the number of non-blank cells within a range which meet the given criteria

List of Math & Trigonometry Functions

SUMPRODUCT

Multiplies corresponding components in the given arrays and returns the sum of those products.

Syntax

SUMPRODUCT(array1, array2, array3, ...)

Array1, array2, array3,...   are 2 to 30 arrays whose components you want to multiply and then add.

- The array arguments must have the same dimensions. If they do not, SUMPRODUCT returns the #VALUE! error value.

- SUMPRODUCT treats array entries that are not numeric as if they were zeros.

Example

	A	B	C	D	E
1	3	4		2	7
2	8	6		6	7
3	1	9		5	3
4					

The following formula multiplies all the components of the two arrays in the preceding worksheet and then adds the products—that is, 3*2 + 4*7 + 8*6 + 6*7 + 1*5 + 9*3.

SUMPRODUCT({3,4;8,6;1,9}, {2,7;6,7;5,3}) equals 156

Remarks

The preceding example returns the same result as the formula SUM(A1:B3*D1:E3) entered as an array. Using arrays provides a more general solution for doing operations similar to SUMPRODUCT. For example, you can calculate the sum of the squares of the elements in A1:B3 by using the formula SUM(A1:B3^2) entered as an array.

Related Functions

MMULT	Returns the matrix product of two arrays
PRODUCT	Multiplies its arguments
SUM	Adds its arguments

List of Math & Trigonometry Functions

SUMSQ

Returns the sum of the squares of the arguments.

Syntax   **SUMSQ(number1**, number2, ...)

Number1, number2,...   are 1 to 30 arguments for which you want the sum of the squares. You can also use a single array or a reference to an array instead of arguments separated by commas.

Example   SUMSQ(3, 4) equals 25

Related Functions   SUM   Adds its arguments

SUMPRODUCT   Returns the sum of the products of corresponding array components

List of Math & Trigonometry Functions

SUMX2MY2

Returns the sum of the difference of squares of corresponding values in two arrays.

Syntax   ·   **SUMX2MY2(array_x, array_y)**

Array_x   is the first array or range of values.

Array_y   is the second array or range of values.

Remarks
- The arguments should be numbers, or names, arrays, or references that contain numbers.
- If an array or reference argument contains text, logical values, or empty cells, those values are ignored; however, cells with the value zero are included.
- If array_x and array_y have a different number of values, SUMX2MY2 returns the #N/A error value.
- The equation for the sum of the difference of squares is:

$$\text{SUMX2MY2} = \sum (x^2 - y^2)$$

Example   SUMX2MY2({2, 3, 9, 1, 8, 7, 5}, {6, 5, 11, 7, 5, 4, 4}) equals -55

Related Functions

SUMPRODUCT	Returns the sum of the products of corresponding array components
SUMX2PY2	Returns the sum of the sum of squares of corresponding values in two arrays
SUMXMY2	Returns the sum of squares of differences of corresponding values in two arrays

List of Math & Trigonometry Functions

SUMX2PY2

Returns the sum of the sum of squares of corresponding values in two arrays. The sum of the sum of squares is a common term in many statistical calculations.

Syntax

SUMX2PY2(array_x, array_y)

Array_x   is the first array or range of values.

Array_y   is the second array or range of values.

Remarks

- The arguments should be numbers, or names, arrays, or references that contain numbers.

- If an array or reference argument contains text, logical values, or empty cells, those values are ignored; however, cells with the value zero are included.

- If array_x and array_y have a different number of values, SUMX2PY2 returns the #N/A error value.

- The equation for the sum of the sum of squares is:

$$SUMX2PY2 = \sum (x^2 + y^2)$$

Example

SUMX2PY2({2, 3, 9, 1, 8, 7, 5}, {6, 5, 11, 7, 5, 4, 4}) equals 521

Related Functions

SUMPRODUCT	Returns the sum of the products of corresponding array components
SUMX2MY2	Returns the sum of the difference of squares of corresponding values in two arrays
	Returns the sum of squares of differences of corresponding values in two arrays

List of Math & Trigonometry Functions

SUMXMY2

Returns the sum of squares of differences of corresponding values in two arrays.

Syntax

SUMXMY2(array_x, array_y)

Array_x   is the first array or range of values.

Array_y   is the second array or range of values.

Remarks

- The arguments should be numbers, or names, arrays, or references that contain numbers.

- If an array or reference argument contains text, logical values, or empty cells, those values are ignored; however, cells with the value zero are included.

- If array_x and array_y have a different number of values, SUMXMY2 returns the #N/A error value.

- The equation for the sum of squared differences is:

$$\text{SUMXMY2} = \sum (x - y)^2$$

Example

SUMXMY2({2, 3, 9, 1, 8, 7, 5}, {6, 5, 11, 7, 5, 4, 4})
equals 79

Related Functions

SUMPRODUCT	Returns the sum of the products of corresponding array components
SUMX2MY2	Returns the sum of the difference of squares of corresponding values in two arrays
SUMXMY2	Returns the sum of the sum of squares of corresponding values in two arrays

List of Math & Trigonometry Functions

SYD

Returns the sum-of-years' digits depreciation of an asset for a specified period.

Syntax

SYD(cost, salvage, life, per)

Cost   is the initial cost of the asset.

Salvage   is the value at the end of the depreciation (sometimes called the salvage value of the asset).

Life   is the number of periods over which the asset is being depreciated (sometimes called the useful life of the asset).

Per   is the period and must use the same units as life.

Remark

- SYD is calculated as follows:

$$SYD = \frac{(\cos t - salvage) * (life - per + 1) * 2}{(life)(life + 1)}$$

Examples

If you've bought a truck for $30,000 that has a useful life of 10 years and a salvage value of $7500, the yearly depreciation allowance for the first year is:

SYD(30000,7500,10,1) equals $4090.91

The yearly depreciation allowance for the 10th year is:

SYD(30000,7500,10,10) equals $409.09

Related Functions

DDB	Returns the depreciation of an asset for a spcified period using the double-declining balance method or some other method you specify
SLN	Returns the straight-line depreciation of an asset for one period
VDB	Returns the depreciation of an asset for a specified or partial period using a declining balance method

List of Financial Functions

T

Returns the text referred to by value.

Syntax

T(value)

Value   is the value you want to test. If value is or refers to text, T returns value. If value does not refer to text, T returns "" (empty text).

Remarks

You do not generally need to use the T function in a formula since Microsoft Excel automatically converts values as necessary. This function is provided for compatibility with other spreadsheet programs.

Examples   If B1 contains the text "Rainfall":

T(B1) equals "Rainfall"

If B2 contains the number 19:

T(B2) equals ""

T("True") equals "True"

T(TRUE) equals ""

Related Functions

CELL	Returns information about the formatting, location, or contents of a cell
N	Returns a value converted to a number
VALUE	Converts a text argument to a number

List of Text Functions

TAN

Returns the tangent of the given angle.

Syntax   **TAN(number)**

Number   is the angle in radians for which you want the tangent. If your argument is in degrees, multiply it by PI()/180 to convert it to radians.

Examples   TAN(0.785) equals 0.99920

TAN(45*PI()/180) equals 1

Related Functions

ATAN	Returns the arctangent of a number
ATAN2	Returns the arctangent from x- and y- coordinates
PI	Returns the value π

List of Math & Trigonometry Functions

TANH

Returns the hyperbolic tangent of a number.

Syntax   **TANH(number)**

Number   is any real number

The formula for the hyperbolic tangent is:

$$TANH(z) = \frac{SINH(z)}{COSH(z)}$$

Examples   TANH(-2) equals –0.96403

TANH(0) equals 0

TANH(0.5) equals 0.462117

Related Functions   ATANH   Returns the inverse hyperbolic tangent of a number

COSH   Returns the hyperbolic cosine of a number

SINH   Returns the hyperbolic sine of a number

List of Math & Trigonometry Functions

TBILLEQ

Returns the bond-equivalent yield for a Treasury bill.

If this function is not available, run the Setup program to install the Analysis ToolPak. After you install the Analysis ToolPak, you must select it in the Add-In Manager. For more information, look up Add-ins in Help.

Syntax   **TBILLEQ(settlement, maturity, discount)**

Settlement   is the Treasury bill's settlement date, expressed as a serial date number.

Maturity   is the Treasury bill's maturity date, expressed as a serial date number.

Discount   is the Treasury bill's discount rate.

Remarks
- Settlement and maturity are truncated to integers.
- If any argument is non-numeric, TBILLEQ returns the #VALUE! error value.
- If settlement or maturity is not a valid serial date number, TBILLEQ returns the #NUM! error value.
- If discount ≤ 0, TBILLEQ returns the #NUM! error value.
- If settlement > maturity, or if maturity is more than one year after settlement, TBILLEQ returns the #NUM! error value.
- TBILLEQ is calucated as TBILLEQ = (365 x rate)/360–(rate x DSM), where DSM is the number of days between settlement and maturity computed according to the 360 days per year basis.

Example

A Treasury bill has the following terms:

March 31, 1993 settlement date
June 1, 1993 maturity date
9.14% discount rate

The bond equivalent yield for a treasury bill (in the 1900 Date System) is:

TBILLEQ(34059,34121,0.0914) equals 0.094151 or 9.4151%

Related Functions

DATE	Returns the serial number of a particular date
TBILLPRICE	Returns the price per $100 face value for a Treasury bill
TBILLYIELD	Returns the yield for a Treasury bill

List of Financial Functions

TBILLPRICE

Returns the price per $100 face value for a Treasury bill.

If this function is not available, run the Setup program to install the Analysis ToolPak. After you install the Analysis ToolPak, you must select it in the Add-In Manager. For more information, look up Add-ins in Help.

Syntax

TBILLPRICE(settlement, maturity, discount)

Settlement   is the Treasury bill's settlement date, expressed as a serial date number.

Maturity   is the Treasury bill's maturity date, expressed as a serial date number.

Discount   is the Treasury bill's discount rate.

Remarks
- Settlement and maturity are truncated to integers.
- If any argument is non-numeric, TBILLPRICE returns the #VALUE! error value.
- If settlement or maturity is not a valid serial date number, TBILLPRICE returns the #NUM! error value.
- If discount ≤ 0, TBILLPRICE returns the #NUM! error value.
- If settlement > maturity, or if maturity is more than one year after settlement, TBILLPRICE returns the #NUM! error value.
- TBILLPRICE is calculated as follows:

$$TBILLPRICE = 100 \times (1 - \frac{discount \times DSM}{360})$$

Where:

- DSM = number of days from settlement to maturity, excluding any maturity date that is more than one calendar year after the settlement date.

Example

A Treasury bill has the following terms:

March 31, 1993 settlement date
June 1, 1993 maturity date
9% discount rate

The Treasury bill price (in the 1900 Date System) is:

TBILLPRICE(34059,34121,0.09) equals 98.45

Related Functions

DATE	Returns the serial number of a particular date
TBILLEQ	Returns the bond-equivalent yield for a Treasury bill
TBILLYIELD	Returns the yield for a Treasury bill

List of Financial Functions

TBILLYIELD

Returns the yield for a Treasury bill.

If this function is not available, run the Setup program to install the Analysis ToolPak. After you install the Analysis ToolPak, you must select it in the Add-In Manager. For more information, look up Add-ins in Help.

Syntax	**TBILLYIELD(settlement, maturity, pr)**

Settlement   is the Treasury bill's settlement date, expressed as a serial date number.

Maturity   is the Treasury bill's maturity date, expressed as a serial date number.

Pr   is the Treasury bill's price per $100 face value.

Remarks

- Settlement and maturity are truncated to integers.
- If any argument is non-numeric, TBILLYIELD returns the #VALUE! error value.
- If settlement or maturity is not a valid serial date number, TBILLYIELD returns the #NUM! error value.
- If pr ≤ 0, TBILLYIELD returns the #NUM! error value.
- If settlement ≥ maturity, or if maturity is more than one year after settlement, TBILLYIELD returns the #NUM! error value.
- TBILLYIELD is calculated as follows:

$$TBILLYIELD = \frac{100 - par}{par} \times \frac{360}{DSM}$$

Where:

- DSM = number of days from settlement to maturity, excluding any maturity date that is more than one calendar year after the settlement date.

Example

A Treasury bill has the following terms:

March 31, 1993 settlement date
June 1, 1993 maturity date
98.45 price per $100 face value

The Treasury bill yield (in the 1900 Date System) is:

`TBILLYIELD(34059,34121,98.45)` equals 9.1417%

Related Functions	DATE	Returns the serial number of a particular date
	TBILLEQ	Returns the bond-equivalent yield for a Treasury bill
	TBILLPRICE	Returns the price per $100 face value for a Treasury bill

List of Financial Functions

TDIST

Returns the Student's t-distribution. The t-distribution is used in the hypothesis testing of small sample data sets. Use this function in place of a table of critical values for the t-distribution.

Syntax

TDIST(x, degrees_freedom, tails)

X   is the numeric value at which to evaluate the distribution.

Degrees_freedom   is an integer indicating the number of degrees of freedom.

Tails   specifies the number of distribution tails to return. If tails = 1, TDIST returns the one-tailed distribution. If tails = 2, TDIST returns the two-tailed distribution.

Remarks

- If any argument is non-numeric, TDIST returns the #VALUE! error value.
- If degrees_freedom < 1, TDIST returns the #NUM! error value.
- The degrees_freedom and tails arguments are truncated to integers.
- If tails is any value other than 1 or 2, TDIST returns the #NUM! error value.
- TDIST is calculated as TDIST=p(x<X), where X is a random variable that follows the t-distribution.

Example

TDIST(1.96,60,2) equals 0.054645

Related Functions

| TINV | Returns the inverse of the Student's t-distribution |
| TTEST | Returns the probability associated with a Student's t-Test |

List of Statistical Functions

TEXT

Converts a value to text in a specific number format.

Syntax

TEXT(value, format_text)

Value   is a numeric value, a formula that evaluates to a numeric value, or a reference to a cell containing a numeric value.

Format_text   is a number format in text form from the Number tab in the Cell Properties dialog box. Format_text cannot contain an asterisk (*) and cannot be "General".

Remarks   Formatting a cell with the command on the number tab from the format cells dialog box changes only the format, not the value. Using the TEXT function converts a value to formatted text, and the result is no longer calculated as a number.

Examples   TEXT(2.715, "$0.00") equals "$2.72"

TEXT("4/15/91", "mmmm dd, yyyy") equals "April 15, 1991"

Related Functions

DOLLAR	Converts a number to text, using currency format
FIXED	Formats a number as text with a fixed number of decimals
T	Converts its arguments to text
VALUE	Converts a text argument to a number

List of Text Functions

TIME

Returns the serial number of a particular time. The serial number returned by TIME is a decimal fraction ranging from 0 to 0.99999999, representing the times from 0:00:00 (12:00:00 A.M.) to 23:59:59 (11:59:59 P.M.).

Syntax   **TIME(hour, minute, second)**

Hour   is a number from 0 to 23 representing the hour.

Minute   is a number from 0 to 59 representing the minute.

Second   is a number from 0 to 59 representing the second.

Remarks   Microsoft Excel for Windows and Microsoft Excel for the Macintosh use different date systems as their default. For more information about date systems and serial numbers, see NOW.

Examples   TIME(12, 0, 0) equals the serial number 0.5, which is equivalent to 12:00:00 P.M.

TIME(16, 48, 10) equals the serial number 0.700115741, which is equivalent to 4:48:10 P.M.

TEXT(TIME(23, 18, 14), "h:mm:ss AM/PM") equals "11:18:14 PM"

Related Functions

HOUR, MINUTE, and SECOND	Convert serial numbers into hours, minutes, and seconds
NOW	Returns the serial number of the current date and time

List of Date & Time Functions

TIMEVALUE

Returns the serial number of the time represented by time_text. The serial number is a decimal fraction ranging from 0 to 0.99999999, representing the times from 0:00:00 (12:00:00 A.M.) to 23:59:59 (11:59:59 P.M.). Use TIMEVALUE to convert a time represented as text into a serial number.

Syntax

TIMEVALUE(time_text)

Time_text   is a text string that gives a time in any one of the Microsoft Excel time formats. Date information in time_text is ignored.

Remarks

Microsoft Excel for Windows and Microsoft Excel for the Macintosh use different date systems as their default. For more information on date systems and serial numbers, see NOW.

Examples

TIMEVALUE("2:24 AM") equals 0.1

TIMEVALUE("22-Aug-55 6:35 AM") equals 0.274305556

Related Functions

DATEVALUE	Converts a date in the form of text to a serial number
HOUR, MINUTE, and SECOND	Convert serial numbers into hours, minutes, and seconds
NOW	Returns the serial number of the current date and time
TIME	Returns the serial number of a particular time

List of Date & Time Functions

TINV

Returns the inverse of the Student's t-distribution for the specified degrees of freedom.

Syntax

TINV(probability, degrees_freedom)

Probability   is the probability associated with the two-tailed Student's t-distribution.

Degrees_freedom   is the number of degrees of freedom to characterize the distribution.

Remarks

- If either argument is non-numeric, TINV returns the #VALUE! error value.
- If probability < 0 or if probability > 1, TINV returns the #NUM! error value.

- If degrees_freedom is not an integer, it is truncated.
- If degrees_freedom < 1, TINV returns the #NUM! error value.
- TINV is calculated as TINV=p(t<X), where X is a random variable that follows the t-distribution.

TINV uses an iterative technique for calculating the function. Given a probability value, TINV iterates until the result is accurate to within ± 3x10^–7. If TINV does not converge after 100 iterations, the function returns the #N/A error value.

Example TINV(0.054645,60) equals 1.96

Related Functions

TDIST	Returns the Student's t-distribution
TTEST	Returns the probability associated with a Student's t-Test

List of Statistical Functions

TODAY

Returns the serial number of the current date. The serial number is the date-time code used by Microsoft Excel for date and time calculations. For more information about serial numbers, see NOW.

Syntax **TODAY( )**

Related Functions

DATE	Returns the serial number of a particular date
DAY	Converts a serial number to a day of the month
NOW	Returns the serial number of the current date and time

List of Date & Time Functions

TRANSPOSE

Returns the transpose of an array. TRANSPOSE must be entered as an array formula in a range that has the same number of rows and columns, respectively, as array has columns and rows. Use TRANSPOSE to shift the vertical and horizontal orientation of an array on a worksheet or macro sheet. For example, some functions, such as DOCUMENTS, return horizontal arrays. The following formula would return a vertical array from DOCUMENTS:

```
TRANSPOSE(DOCUMENTS())
```

Syntax   **TRANSPOSE(array)**

Array   is an array on a worksheet or macro sheet that you want to transpose.
Array can also be a range of cells.

The transpose of an array is created by using the first row of the array as the first
column of the new array, the second row of the array as the second column of the
new array, and so on.

Tip In a macro, you can transpose an array and paste only the values contained in
the array, using the PASTE.SPECIAL macro function with 3 (values) as the
paste_num argument and TRUE as the transpose argument.

Example   Suppose A1:C1 contain 1, 2, 3, respectively. When the following formula is entered
as an array into cells A3:A5:

TRANSPOSE($A$1:$C$1) equals the same respective values in A3:A5

Related Functions   MDETERM   Returns the matrix determinant of an array

MINVERSE   Returns the matrix inverse of an array

MMULT   Returns the matrix product of two arrays

List of Lookup & Reference Functions

TREND

Returns values along a linear trend. Fits a straight line (using the method of least
squares) to the arrays known_y's and known_x's. Returns the y-values along that
line for the array of new_x's that you specify.

Syntax   **TREND(known_y's, known_x's, new_x's, const)**

Known_y's   is the set of y-values you already know in the relationship
$y = mx + b$.

- If the array known_y's is in a single column, then each column of known_x's is
  interpreted as a separate variable.

- If the array known_y's is in a single row, then each row of known_x's is
  interpreted as a separate variable.

Known_x's is an optional set of x-values that you may already know in the relationship y = mx + b.

- The array known_x's can include one or more sets of variables. If only one variable is used, known_y's and known_x's can be ranges of any shape, as long as they have equal dimensions. If more than one variable is used, known_y's must be a vector (that is, a range with a height of one row or a width of one column).

- If known_x's is omitted, it is assumed to be the array {1,2,3,...} that is the same size as known_y's.

New_x's are new x-values for which you want TREND to return corresponding y-values.

- New_x's must include a column (or row) for each independent variable, just as known_x's does. So, if known_y's is in a single column, known_x's and new_x's should have the same number of columns. If known_y's is in a single row, known_x's and new_x's should have the same number of rows.

- If you omit new_x's, it is assumed to be the same as known_x's.

- If you omit both known_x's and new_x's, they are assumed to be the array {1,2,3,...} that is the same size as known_y's.

Const is a logical value specifying whether to force the constant b to equal 0.

- If const is TRUE or omitted, b is calculated normally.

- If const is FALSE, b is set equal to 0 and the m-values are adjusted so that y = mx.

Remarks

- For information on how Microsoft Excel fits a line to data, see LINEST.

- You can use TREND for polynomial curve fitting by regressing against the same variable raised to different powers. For example, suppose column A contained y-values and column B contained x-values. You could enter x^2 in column C, x^3 in column D, and so on, and then regress columns B through D against column A.

- Formulas that return arrays must be entered as array formulas.

- When entering an array constant for an argument such as known_x's, use commas to separate values in the same row and semicolons to separate rows.

Example

Suppose a business wants to purchase a tract of land in July, the start of the next fiscal year. The business collected cost information that covers the most recent 12 months for a typical tract in the desired area. known_y's contains the set of known values ($133,890, $135,000, $135,790, $137,300, $138,130, $139,100, $139900, $141,120, $141,890, $143,230, $144,000, $145,290), and are stored in B2:B13, respectively.

When entered as a vertical array in the range C2:C6, the following formula returns the predicted prices for March, April, May, June, and July:

TREND(B2:B13,,{13;14;15;16;17}) equals
{146172;147190;148208;149226;150244}

The company can expect a typical tract of land to cost about $150,244 if it waits until July. The preceding formula uses the default array {1;2;3;4;5;6;7;8;9;10;11;12} for the known_x's argument, corresponding to the 12 months of sales data. The array {13;14;15;16;17} corresponds to the next five months.

Related Functions	GROWTH	Similar to TREND and LINEST, but fit your data to an exponential curve
	LOGEST	Similar to TREND and LINEST, but fit your data to an exponential curve
	LINEST	Also calculates a line, but returns the parameters of the line instead of an array of y-values

List of Statistical Functions

TRIM

Removes all spaces from text except for single spaces between words. Use TRIM on text that you have received from another application that may have irregular spacing.

Syntax   **TRIM(text)**

Text   is the text from which you want spaces removed.

Example   TRIM(" First   Quarter   Earnings   ") equals "First Quarter Earnings"

Related Functions	CLEAN	Removes all nonprintable characters from text
	MID	Returns a specific number of characters from a text string
	REPLACE	Replaces characters within text
	SUBSTITUTE	Substitutes new text for old text in a text string

List of Text Functions

TRIMMEAN

Returns the mean of the interior of a data set. TRIMMEAN calculates the mean taken by excluding a percentage of data points from the top and bottom tails of a data set. You can use this function when you wish to exclude outlying data from your analysis.

Syntax

TRIMMEAN(array, percent)

Array   is the array or range of values to trim and average.

Percent   is the fractional number of data points to exclude from the calculation. For example, if percent = 0.2, 4 points are trimmed from a data set of 20 points (20 x 0.2), 2 from the top and 2 from the bottom of the set.

Remarks

- If percent < 0 or percent > 1, TRIMMEAN returns the #NUM! error value.
- TRIMMEAN rounds the number of excluded data points down to the nearest multiple of 2. If percent = 0.1, 10% of 30 data points equals 3 points. For symmetry, TRIMMEAN excludes a single value from the top and bottom of the data set.

Example

`TRIMMEAN({4,5,6,7,2,3,4,5,1,2,3},0.2)` equals 3.777778

Related Functions

AVERAGE	Returns the average of its arguments
GECMEAN	Returns the geometric mean
HARMEAN	Returns the harmonic mean
MEDIAN	Returns the median of the given numbers
MODE	Returns the most common value in a data set

List of Statistical Functions

TRUE

Returns the logical value TRUE.

Syntax

TRUE( )

Remarks

You can enter the value TRUE directly into cells and formulas without using this function. The TRUE function is provided primarily for compatibility with other spreadsheet programs.

Related Functions   List of Logical Functions

TRUNC

Truncates a number to an integer by removing the fractional part of the number.

Syntax

TRUNC(number, num_digits)

Number   is the number you want to truncate.

Num_digits   is a number specifying the precision of the truncation. The default value for num_digits is zero.

Remarks

TRUNC and INT are similar in that both return integers. TRUNC removes the fractional part of the number. INT rounds numbers down to the nearest integer based on the value of the fractional part of the number. INT and TRUNC are different only when using negative numbers: TRUNC(-4.3) returns –4, but INT(-4.3) returns –5, because –5 is the lower number.

Examples

TRUNC(8.9) equals 8

TRUNC(-8.9) equals –8

TRUNC(PI()) equals 3

Related Functions

CEILING	Rounds a number to the nearest integer or to the nearest multiple of significance
FLOOR	Rounds a number down, toward zero
INT	Rounds a number down to the nearest integer
MOD	Returns the remainder from division
ROUND	Rounds a number to a specified number of digits

List of Math & Trigonometry Functions

TTEST

Returns the probability associated with a Student's t-Test. Use TTEST to determine whether two samples are likely to have come from the same two underlying populations that have the same mean.

Syntax

TTEST(array1, array2, tails, type)

Array1   is the first data set.

Array2   is the second data set.

Tails   specifies the number of distribution tails. If tails = 1, TTEST uses the one-tailed distribution. If tails = 2, TTEST uses the two-tailed distribution.

Type   is the kind of t-test to perform.

If type equals	This test is performed
1	Paired
2	Two-sample equal variance (homoscedastic)
3	Two-sample unequal variance (heteroscedastic)

Remarks

- If array1 and array2 have a different number of data points, and type = 1 (paired), TTEST returns the #N/A error value.
- The tails and type arguments are truncated to integers.
- If tails or type is non-numeric, TTEST returns the #VALUE! error value.
- If tails is any value other than 1 or 2, TTEST returns the #NUM! error value.

Example

TTEST({3,4,5,8,9,1,2,4,5},{6,19,3,2,14,4,5,17,1},2,1)
equals 0.196016

Related Functions

TDIST	Returns the Student's t-distribution
TINV	Returns the Student's t-distribution

List of Statistical Functions

TYPE

Returns the type of value. Use TYPE when the behavior of another function depends on the type of value in a particular cell.

Syntax

TYPE(value)

Value   can be any Microsoft Excel value, such as a number, text, logical value, and so on.

If value is	TYPE returns
Number	1
Text	2
Logical value	4
Formula	8
Error value	16
Array	64

Remarks	TYPE is most useful when you are using functions that can accept a variety of different types of data, such as ARGUMENT and INPUT. Use TYPE to find out what type of data was returned by the function.
Examples	If A1 contains the text "Smith", then:

TYPE(A1) equals TYPE("Smith") equals 2

TYPE("MR. "&A1) equals 2

TYPE(2+A1) equals TYPE(#VALUE!) equals 16

TYPE({1,2;3,4}) equals 64

UPPER

Converts text to uppercase.

Syntax	**UPPER(text)**

Text   is the text you want converted to uppercase. Text can be a reference or text string.

Examples	UPPER("total") equals "TOTAL"

If E5 contains "yield", then

UPPER(E5) equals "YIELD"

The following macro formula converts the contents of the active cell to uppercase:

FORMULA(UPPER(ACTIVE.CELL()),ACTIVE.CELL())

Related Functions	LOWER	Converts text to lowercase
	PROPER	Capitalizes the first letter in each word of a text value

List of Text Functions

VALUE

Converts text to a number.

Syntax	**VALUE(text)**

Text   is the text enclosed in quotation marks or a reference to a cell containing the text you want to convert. Text can be in any of the constant number, date, or time formats recognized by Microsoft Excel. If text is not in one of these formats, VALUE returns the #VALUE! error value.

Remarks

You do not generally need to use the VALUE function in a formula since Microsoft Excel automatically converts text to numbers as necessary. This function is provided for compatibility with other spreadsheet programs.

Examples

`VALUE("$1, 000")` equals 1,000

`VALUE("16:48:00")-VALUE("12:00:00")` equals "16:48:00"–"12:00:00" equals 0.2, the serial number equivalent to 4 hours and 48 minutes.

Related Functions

DOLLAR	Converts a number to text, using currency format
FIXED	Formats a number as text with a fixed number of decimals
TEXT	Formats a number and converts it to text

List of Text Functions

VAR

Estimates variance based on a sample.

Syntax

VAR(number1, number2, ...)

Number1,number2,...   are 1 to 30 number arguments corresponding to a sample of a population.

Remarks

- VAR assumes that its arguments are a sample of the population. If your data represents the entire population, you should compute the variance using VARP.

- VAR uses the following formula:

$$\frac{n\Sigma x^2 - (\Sigma x)^2}{n(n-1)}$$

Example

Suppose 10 tools stamped from the same machine during a production run are collected as a random sample and measured for breaking strength. The sample values (1345, 1301, 1368, 1322, 1310, 1370, 1318, 1350, 1303, 1299) are stored in A2:E3, respectively. VAR estimates the variance for the breaking strength of the tools.

$VAR(A2:E3)$ equals 754.3

Related Functions   List of Statistical Functions

VARP

Calculates variance based on the entire population.

Syntax   **VARP(number1**, number2, ...)

Number1, number2,...   are 1 to 30 number arguments corresponding to a population.

Remarks   ▪ VARP assumes that its arguments are the entire population. If your data represents a sample of the population, you should compute the variance using VAR.

▪ The equation for VARP is :

$$\frac{n \sum x^2 - \left(\sum x\right)^2}{n(n-1)}$$

Example   Using the data from the VAR example and assuming that only 10 tools are produced during the production run, VARP measures the variance of breaking strengths for all the tools.

$VARP(A2:E3)$ equals 678.8

Related Functions   List of Statistical Functions

VDB

Returns the depreciation of an asset for any period you specify, including partial periods, using the double-declining balance method or some other method you specify. VDB stands for variable declining balance.

Syntax   **VDB(cost, salvage, life, start_period, end_period**, factor, no_switch)

Cost   is the initial cost of the asset.

Salvage   is the value at the end of the depreciation (sometimes called the salvage value of the asset).

Life   is the number of periods over which the asset is being depreciated (sometimes called the useful life of the asset).

Start_period   is the starting period for which you want to calculate the depreciation. Start_period must use the same units as life.

End_period   is the ending period for which you want to calculate the depreciation. End_period must use the same units as life.

Factor   is the rate at which the balance declines. If factor is omitted, it is assumed to be 2 (the double-declining balance method). Change factor if you do not want to use the double-declining balance method. For a description of the double-declining balance method, see DDB.

No_switch   is a logical value specifying whether to switch to straight-line depreciation when depreciation is greater than the declining balance calculation.

- If no_switch is TRUE, Microsoft Excel does not switch to straight-line depreciation even when the depreciation is greater than the declining balance calculation.

- If no_switch is FALSE or omitted, Microsoft Excel switches to straight-line depreciation when depreciation is greater than the declining balance calculation.

All arguments except no_switch must be positive numbers.

Examples

Suppose a factory purchases a new machine. The machine costs $2400 and has a lifetime of 10 years. The salvage value of the machine is $300. The following examples show depreciation over several periods. The results are rounded to two decimal places.

VDB(2400, 300, 3650, 0, 1) equals $1.32, the first day's depreciation. Microsoft Excel automatically assumes that factor is 2.

VDB(2400, 300, 120, 0, 1) equals $40.00, the first month's depreciation.

VDB(2400, 300, 10, 0, 1) equals $480.00, the first year's depreciation.

VDB(2400, 300, 120, 6, 18) equals $396.31, the depreciation between the 6th month and the 18th month.

VDB(2400, 300, 120, 6, 18, 1.5) equals $311.81, the depreciation between the 6th month and the 18th month using a factor of 1.5 instead of the double-declining balance method.

Suppose instead that the $2400 machine is purchased in the middle of the first quarter of the fiscal year. The following macro formula determines the amount of depreciation for the first fiscal year that you own the asset, assuming that tax laws limit you to 150% depreciation of the declining balance:

`VDB(2400, 300, 10, 0, 0.875, 1.5)` equals $315.00

Related Functions

DDB	Returns the depreciation of an asset for a spcified period using the double-declining balance method or some other method you specify
SLN	Returns the straight-line depreciation of an asset for one period
SYD	Returns the sum-of-years' digits depreciation of an asset for a specified period

List of Financial Functions

VLOOKUP

Searches the leftmost column of an array for a particular value, and returns the value in the cell indicated. Use VLOOKUP instead of HLOOKUP when your comparison values are located in a column to the left or right of the data you want to find.

Syntax

VLOOKUP(lookup_value, table_array, col_index_num, range_lookup)

Lookup_value   is the value to be found in the first column of the array. Lookup_value can be a value, a reference, or a text string.

Table_array   is the table of information in which data is looked up. Use a reference to a range or a range name, such as Database or List.

- If range_lookup is TRUE, the values in the first column of table_array must be placed in ascending order: ..., –2, –1, 0, 1, 2, ... , A-Z, FALSE, TRUE; otherwise VLOOKUP may not give the correct value.

- You can put the values in ascending order by choosing the Sort command from the Data menu and selecting Ascending.

- The values in the first column of table_array can be text, numbers, or logical values.

- Uppercase and lowercase text are equivalent.

Col_index_num   is the column number in table_array from which the matching value should be returned. A col_index_num of 1 returns the value in the first column in table_array; a col_index_num of 2 returns the value in the second column in table_array, and so on. If col_index_num is less than 1, VLOOKUP returns the #VALUE! error value; if col_index_num is greater than the number of columns in table_array, VLOOKUP returns the #REF! error value.

Range_lookup   is a logical value that specifies whether you want VLOOKUP to find an exact match or an approximate match. If TRUE or omitted, an approximate match is returned; in other words, if an exact match is not found, the next largest value that is less than lookup_value is returned. If FALSE, VLOOKUP will find an exact match. If one is not found, the error value #N/A is returned.

Remarks

- If VLOOKUP can't find lookup_value, and range_lookup is TRUE, it uses the largest value that is less than or equal to lookup_value.

- If lookup_value is smaller than the smallest value in the first column of table_array, VLOOKUP returns the #N/A error value.

- if VLOOKUP can't find lookup_value and range_lookup is FALSE, VLOOKUP returns the #N/A value.

Examples

	A	B	C	D
1	Air in atm pressure			
2	**Density**	**Viscosity**	**Temp**	
3	(kg/cubic m)	(kg/m*s)*1E+05	(degrees C)	
4	0.457	3.55	500	
5	0.525	3.25	400	
6	0.616	2.93	300	
7	0.675	2.75	250	
8	0.746	2.57	200	
9	0.835	2.38	150	
10	0.946	2.17	100	
11	1.09	1.95	50	
12	1.29	1.71	0	

In the preceding worksheet, where the range A4:C12 is named Range:

VLOOKUP(1,Range,1,TRUE) equals 0.946

VLOOKUP(1,Range,2) equals 2.17

VLOOKUP(1,Range,3,TRUE) equals 100

VLOOKUP(.746,Range,3,FALSE) equals 200

VLOOKUP(0.1,Range,2,TRUE) equals #N/A, because 0.1 is less than the smallest value in column A

VLOOKUP(2,Range,2,TRUE) equals 1.71

Related Functions

HLOOKUP	Looks in the top row of an array and returns the value of the indicated cell
INDEX	Uses an index to choose a value from a reference or array
LOOKUP (array)	Looks up values in an array
LOOKUP (vector)	Looks up values in a vector
MATCH	Looks up values in a reference or array

List of Lookup & Reference Functions

WEEKDAY

Returns the day of the week corresponding to serial_number. The day is given as an integer, ranging from 1 (Sunday) to 7 (Saturday).

Syntax

WEEKDAY(serial_number, return_type)

Serial_number   is the date-time code used by Microsoft Excel for date and time calculations. You can give serial_number as text, such as "15-Apr-1993" or "4-15-93", instead of as a number. The text is automatically converted to a serial number. For more information about serial_number, see NOW.

Return_type   is a number that determines the type of return value.

Return_type	Number returned
1 or omitted	Numbers 1 (Sunday) through 7 (Saturday). Behaves like previous versions of Microsoft Excel.
2	Numbers 1 (Monday) through 7 (Sunday)
3	Numbers 0 (Monday) through 6 (Sunday)

Remarks

- Microsoft Excel for Windows and Microsoft Excel for the Macintosh use different date systems as their default. For more information, see NOW.
- You can also use the TEXT function to convert a value to a specified number format when using the 1900 Date System:
- TEXT("4/16/90", "dddd") equals Monday

Examples   WEEKDAY("2/14/90") equals 4 (Wednesday)

If you are using the 1900 Date System (the default in Microsoft Excel for Windows), then:

WEEKDAY(29747.007) equals 4 (Wednesday)

If you are using the 1904 Date System (the default in Microsoft Excel for the Macintosh), then:

WEEKDAY(29747.007) equals 3 (Tuesday)

Related Functions

DAY	Converts a serial number to a day of the month
NOW	Returns the serial number of the current date and time
TEXT	Formats a number and converts it to text
TODAY	Returns the serial number of today's date

List of Date & Time Functions

WEEKNUM

Returns a number that indicates where the week falls numerically within a year.

If this function is not available, run the Setup program to install the Analysis ToolPak. After you install the Analysis ToolPak, you must select it in the Add-In Manager. For more information, look up Add-ins in Help.

Syntax   **WEEKNUM(date, iflag)**

Date   is the date expressed as a serial date number.

Iflag   is the value zero or 1 that determines on what day the week begins.

Iflag	Week Begins
1	Week begins on Sunday. Weekdays are numbered 1 through 7.
2	Week begins on Monday. Weekdays are numbered 1 through 7.

Examples   If date is Sunday, January 9, 1994, then

WEEKNUM(34343, 0) equals 3

WEEKNUM(34343, 1) equals 2

Related Functions	DAYS360	Returns the number of days between two dates based on a 360-day year (twelve 30-day months)
	WEEKDAY	Returns the day of the week corresponding to serial_number.

WEIBULL

Returns the Weibull distribution. Use this distribution in reliability analysis, such as calculating a device's mean time to failure.

Syntax

WEIBULL(x, alpha, beta, cumulative)

X   is the value at which to evaluate the function.

Alpha   is a parameter to the distribution.

Beta   is a parameter to the distribution.

Cumulative   determines the form of the function.

Remarks

- If x, alpha, or beta is non-numeric, WEIBULL returns the #VALUE! error value.
- If x < 0, WEIBULL returns the #NUM! error value.
- If alpha ≤ 0 or if beta ≤ 0, WEIBULL returns the #NUM! error value.
- The equation for the Weibull cumulative distribution function is:

$$F(x;\alpha,\beta) = 1 - e^{-(x/\beta)^{\alpha}}$$

- The equation for the Weibull probability density function is:

$$f(x;\alpha,\beta) = \frac{\alpha}{\beta^{\alpha}} x^{\alpha-1} e^{-(x/\beta)^{\alpha}}$$

- When alpha = 1, WEIBULL returns the exponential distribution with:

$$\lambda = \frac{1}{\beta}$$

Examples	WEIBULL(105,20,100,TRUE) equals 0.929581
	WEIBULL(105,20,100,FALSE) equals 0.035589
Related Function	EXPONDIST Returns the exponential distribution

List of Statistical Functions

WORKDAY

Returns the serial number date that is the indicated number of working days before or after start_date. Working days exclude weekends and any dates identified in holidays. Use WORKDAY to exclude weekends or holidays when you calculate invoice due dates, expected delivery times, or the number of days of work performed.

If this function is not available, run the Setup program to install the Analysis ToolPak. After you install the Analysis ToolPak, you must select it in the Add-In Manager. For more information, look up Add-ins in Help.

Syntax

WORKDAY(start_date, days, holidays)

Start_date   is a serial date number that represents the start date.

Days   is the number of non-weekend and non-holiday days before or after start_date. A positive value for days yields a future date; a negative value yields a past date.

Holidays   is an optional array of one or more serial date numbers to exclude from the working calendar, such as state and federal holidays and floating holidays.

Remarks

- If any argument is non-numeric, WORKDAY returns the #VALUE! error value.
- If start_date is not a valid serial date number, WORKDAY returns the #NUM! error value.
- If start_date plus days yields an invalid serial date number, WORKDAY returns the #NUM! error value.
- If days is not an integer, it is truncated.

Examples	WORKDAY(DATEVALUE("01/03/91"), 5) equals 33248 or 01/10/91

If January 7, 1991 and January 8, 1991 are holidays, then:
WORKDAY(DATEVALUE("01/03/91"), 5, {33245, 33246}) equals 33252 or 01/14/91

Related Functions	EDATE	Returns the serial number of the date that is the indicated number of months before or after the start date
	EOMONTH	Returns the serial number of the last day of the month before or after a specified number of months
	NETWORKDAYS	Returns the number of whole workdays between two dates
	NOW	Returns the serial number of the current date and time

List of Date & Time Functions

XIRR

Returns the internal rate of return for a schedule of cash flows that is not necessarily periodic.

If this function is not available, run the Setup program to install the Analysis ToolPak. After you install the Analysis ToolPak, you must select it in the Add-In Manager. For more information, look up Add-ins in Help.

Syntax

XIRR(values, dates, guess)

Values   is a series of cash flows that correspond to a schedule of payments in dates. The first payment is optional, and corresponds to a cost or payment that occurs at the beginning of the investment. All succeeding payments are discounted based on a 365-day year.

Dates   is a schedule of payment dates that corresponds to the cash flow payments. The first payment date indicates the beginning of the schedule of payments. All other dates must be later than this date, but they may occur in any order.

Guess   is a number that you guess is close to the result of XIRR.

Remarks

- Numbers in dates are truncated to integers.
- If any argument is non-numeric, XIRR returns the #VALUE! error value.
- XIRR expects at least one positive cash flow and one negative cash flow; otherwise, XIRR returns the #NUM! error value.

- If any number in dates is not a valid serial date number, XIRR returns the #NUM! error value.

- If any number in dates precedes the starting date, XIRR returns the #NUM! error value.

- If values and dates contain a different number of values, XIRR returns the #NUM! error value.

- In most cases you do not need to provide guess for the XIRR calculation. If omitted, guess is assumed to be 0.1 (10%).

- XIRR is closely related to XNPV, the net present value function. The rate of return calculated by XIRR is the interest rate corresponding to XNPV = 0.

- Microsoft Excel uses an iterative technique for calculating XIRR. Using a changing rate (starting with guess), XIRR cycles through the calculation until the result is accurate within 0.000001%. If XIRR can't find a result that works after 100 tries, the #NUM! error value is returned. The rate is changed until:

$$0 = \sum_{i=1}^{N} \frac{P_i}{(1 + rate)^{\frac{(d_i - d_1)}{365}}}$$

Where:

di = the ith payment date.

d_1 = the 0th payment date.

Pi = the ith payment.

Example

Consider an investment that requires a $10,000 cash payment on January 1, 1992, and returns $2750 on March 1, 1992, $4250 on October 30, 1992, $3250 on February 15, 1993, and $2750 on April 1, 1993. The internal rate of return (in the 1900 Date System) is:

XIRR({-10000,2750,4250,3250,2750},
{33604,33664,33907,34015,34060},0.1) equals 0.373363 or 37.3363%

Related Functions

IRR	Returns the internal rate of return for a series of cash flows
MIRR	Returns the internal rate of return where positive and negative cash flows are financed at different rates
NPV	Returns the net present value of an investment based on a series of periodic cash flows and a discount rate
RATE	Returns the interest rate per period of an annuity
XNPV	Returns the net present value for a schedule of cash flows that is not necessarily periodic

List of Financial Functions

XNPV

Returns the net present value for a schedule of cash flows that is not necessarily periodic.

If this function is not available, run the Setup program to install the Analysis ToolPak. After you install the Analysis ToolPak, you must select it in the Add-In Manager. For more information, look up Add-ins in Help.

Syntax

XNPV(rate, values, dates)

Rate   is the discount rate to apply to the cash flows.

Values   is a series of cash flows that correspond to a schedule of payments in dates. The first payment is optional, and corresponds to a cost or payment that occurs at the beginning of the investment. All succeeding payments are discounted based on a 365-day year.

Dates   is a schedule of payment dates that corresponds to the cash flow payments. The first payment date indicates the beginning of the schedule of payments. All other dates must be later than this date, but they may occur in any order.

Remarks

- Numbers in dates are truncated to integers.

- If any argument is non-numeric, XNPV returns the #VALUE! error value.

- If any number in dates is not a valid serial date number, XNPV returns the #NUM! error value.

- If any number in dates precedes the starting date, XNPV returns the #NUM! error value.

- If values and dates contain a different number of values, XNPV returns the #NUM! error value.

- XNPV is calculated as follows:

$$XNPV = \sum_{i=1}^{N} \frac{P_i}{(1 + rate)^{\frac{(d_i - d_1)}{365}}}$$

Where:

d_i = the ith payment date.

d_1 = the 0th payment date.

P_i = the ith payment.

Example Consider an investment that requires a $10,000 cash payment on January 1, 1992, and returns $2750 on March 1, 1992, $4250 on October 30, 1992, $3250 on February 15, 1993, and $2750 on April 1, 1993. Assume that the cash flows are discounted at 9%. The net present value is:

```
XNPV(0.09,{-10000,2750,4250,3250,2750},
{33604,33664,33907,34015,34060}) equals 2086.647602
```

Related Functions

IRR	Returns the internal rate of return for a series of cash flows
MIRR	Returns the internal rate of return where positive and negative cash flows are financed at different rates
NPV	Returns the net present value of an investment based on a series of periodic cash flows and a discount rate
RATE	Returns the interest rate per period of an annuity
XIRR	Returns the internal rate of return for a schedule of cash flows that is not necessarily periodic

List of Financial Functions

YEAR

Returns the year corresponding to serial_number. The year is given as an integer in the range 1900–2078.

Syntax **YEAR(serial_number)**

Serial_number is the date-time code used by Microsoft Excel for date and time calculations. You can give serial_number as text, such as "15-Apr-1993" or "4-15-93", instead of as a number. The text is automatically converted to a serial number. For more information about serial_number, see NOW.

Remarks Microsoft Excel for Windows and Microsoft Excel for the Macintosh use different date systems as their default. For more information, see NOW.

Examples YEAR("7/5/90") equals 1990

If you are using the 1900 Date System (the default in Microsoft Excel for Windows), then:

YEAR(0.007) equals 1900

YEAR(29747.007) equals 1981

If you are using the 1904 Date System (the default in Microsoft Excel for the Macintosh), then:

YEAR(0.007) equals 1904

YEAR(29747.007) equals 1985

Related Functions

MONTH, DAY, WEEKDAY, HOUR, MINUTE, and SECOND	Convert serial numbers into months, days, days of the week, hours, minutes, and seconds
NOW	Returns the serial number of the current date and time
TODAY	Returns the serial number of today's date

List of Date & Time Functions

YEARFRAC

Returns the year fraction representing the number of whole days between start_date and end_date. Use YEARFRAC to identify the proportion of a whole year's benefits or obligations to assign to a specific term.

If this function is not available, run the Setup program to install the Analysis ToolPak. After you install the Analysis ToolPak, you must select it in the Add-In Manager. For more information, look up Add-ins in Help.

Syntax

YEARFRAC(start_date, end_date, basis)

Start_date   is a serial date number that represents the start date.

End_date   is a serial date number that represents the end date.

Basis   is the type of day count basis to use.

Basis	Day count basis
0 or omitted	US (NASD) 30/360
1	Actual/actual
2	Actual/360
3	Actual/365
4	European 30/360

Remarks   All arguments are truncated to integers.

- If any argument is non-numeric, YEARFRAC returns the #VALUE! error value.

- If start_date or end_date are not valid serial date numbers, YEARFRAC returns the #NUM! error value.

- If basis < 0 or if basis > 4, YEARFRAC returns the #NUM! error value.

- If start_date ≥ end_date, YEARFRAC returns the #NUM! error value.

Examples   YEARFRAC(DATEVALUE("01/01/93"),DATEVALUE("06/30/93"),0) equals 0.5

YEARFRAC(DATEVALUE("01/01/93"),DATEVALUE("07/01/93"),3) equals 0.49863

Related Functions

EDATE	Returns the serial number of the date that is the indicated number of months before or after the start date
EOMONTH	Returns the serial number of the last day of the month before or after a specified number of months
NETWORKDAYS	Returns the number of whole workdays between two dates
NOW	Returns the serial number of the current date and time
WORKDAY	Returns the serial number of the date before or after a specified number of workdays

List of Date & Time Functions

YIELD

Returns the yield on a security that pays periodic interest. Use YIELD to calculate bond yield.

If this function is not available, run the Setup program to install the Analysis ToolPak. After you install the Analysis ToolPak, you must select it in the Add-In Manager. For more information, look up Add-ins in Help.

Syntax   **YIELD(settlement, maturity, rate, pr, redemption, frequency, basis)**

Settlement   is the security's settlement date, expressed as a serial date number.

Maturity   is the security's maturity date, expressed as a serial date number.

Rate   is the security's annual coupon rate.

Pr   is the security's price per $100 face value.

Redemption   is the security's redemption value per $100 face value.

Frequency   is the number of coupon payments per year. For annual payments, frequency = 1; for semiannual, frequency = 2; for quarterly, frequency = 4.

Basis   is the type of day count basis to use.

Basis	Day count basis
0 or omitted	US (NASD) 30/360
1	Actual/actual
2	Actual/360
3	Actual/365
4	European 30/360

Remarks   Settlement, maturity, frequency, and basis are truncated to integers.

- If any argument is non-numeric, YIELD returns the #VALUE! error value.

- If settlement or maturity is not a valid serial date number, YIELD returns the #NUM! error value.

- If rate < 0, YIELD returns the #NUM! error value.

- If pr ≤ 0 or if redemption ≤ 0, YIELD returns the #NUM! error value.

- If frequency is any number other than 1, 2, or 4, YIELD returns the #NUM! error value.

- If basis < 0 or if basis > 4, YIELD returns the #NUM! error value.

- If settlement ≥ maturity, YIELD returns the #NUM! error value.

- If there is one coupon period or less until redemption, YIELD is calculated as follows:

$$YIELD = \frac{(\frac{redemption}{100} + \frac{rate}{frequency}) - (\frac{par}{100} + (\frac{A}{E} \times \frac{rate}{frequency}))}{\frac{par}{100} + (\frac{A}{E} \times \frac{rate}{frequency})} \times \frac{frequency \times E}{DSR}$$

Where:

A = number of days from the beginning of the coupon period to the settlement date (accrued days).

DSR = number of days from the settlement date to the redemption date.

E = number of days in the coupon period.

- If there is more than one coupon period until redemption, YIELD is calculated through a hundred iterations. The resolution uses the Newton method based on the formula used for the function PRICE. The yield is changed until the estimated price given the yield is close to price.

Example

A bond has the following terms:

February 15, 1991 settlement date
November 15, 1999 maturity date
5.75% coupon
95.04287 price
$100 redemption value
Frequency is semiannual
30/360 basis

The bond yield (in the 1900 Date System) is:

`YIELD(33284,36479,0.0575,95.04287,100,2,0)` equals 0.065 or 6.5%

Related Functions

NOW	Returns the serial number of the current date and time
PRICE	Returns the price per $100 face value of a security that pays periodic interest

List of Financial Functions

YIELDDISC

Returns the annual yield for a discounted security.

If this function is not available, run the Setup program to install the Analysis ToolPak. After you install the Analysis ToolPak, you must select it in the Add-In Manager. For more information, look up Add-ins in Help.

Syntax

YIELDDISC(settlement, maturity, pr, redemption, basis)

Settlement   is the security's settlement date, expressed as a serial date number.

Maturity   is the security's maturity date, expressed as a serial date number.

Pr   is the security's price per $100 face value.

Redemption   is the security's redemption value per $100 face value.

Basis   is the type of day count basis to use.

Basis	Day count basis
0 or omitted	US (NASD) 30/360
1	Actual/actual
2	Actual/360
3	Actual/365
4	European 30/360

Remarks

- Settlement, maturity, and basis are truncated to integers.
- If any argument is non-numeric, YIELDDISC returns the #VALUE! error value.
- If settlement or maturity is not a valid serial date number, YIELDDISC returns the #NUM! error value.
- If pr ≤ 0 or if redemption ≤ 0, YIELDDISC returns the #NUM! error value.
- If basis < 0 or if basis > 4, YIELDDISC returns the #NUM! error value.
- If settlement ≥ maturity, YIELDDISC returns the #NUM! error value.

Example

A bond has the following terms:

February 15, 1993 settlement date
March 1, 1993 maturity date
99.795 price
$100 redemption value
Actual/360 basis

The bond yield (in the 1900 Date System) is:

`YIELDDISC(34015,34029,99.795,100,2)` equals 5.2823%

Related Functions

DISC	Returns the discount rate for a security
NOW	Returns the serial number of the current date and time
PRICEDISC	Returns the price per $100 face value of a discounted security

List of Financial Functions

YIELDMAT

Returns the annual yield of a security that pays interest at maturity.

If this function is not available, run the Setup program to install the Analysis ToolPak. After you install the Analysis ToolPak, you must select it in the Add-In Manager. For more information, look up Add-ins in Help.

Syntax

YIELDMAT(settlement, maturity, issue, rate, pr, basis)

Settlement   is the security's settlement date, expressed as a serial date number.

Maturity   is the security's maturity date, expressed as a serial date number.

Issue   is the security's issue date, expressed as a serial date number.

Rate   is the security's interest rate at date of issue.

Pr   is the security's price per $100 face value.

Basis   is the type of day count basis to use.

Basis	Day count basis
0 or omitted	US (NASD) 30/360
1	Actual/actual
2	Actual/360
3	Actual/365
4	European 30/360

Remarks

- Settlement, maturity, issue, and basis are truncated to integers.
- If any argument is non-numeric, YIELDMAT returns the #VALUE! error value.
- If settlement, maturity, or issue is not a valid serial date number, YIELDMAT returns the #NUM! error value.
- If rate < 0 or if pr ≤ 0, YIELDMAT returns the #NUM! error value.
- If basis < 0 or if basis > 4, YIELDMAT returns the #NUM! error value.
- If settlement ≥ maturity, YIELDMAT returns the #NUM! error value.

Example

A bond has the following terms:

March 15, 1993 settlement date
November 3, 1993 maturity date
November 8, 1992 issue date
6.25% semiannual coupon
100.0123 price
30/360 basis

The yield (in the 1900 Date System) is:

`YIELDMAT(34043,34276,33916,0.0625,100.0123,0)` equals 0.060954 or 6.0954%

Related Functions   DATE   Returns the serial number of a particular date

PRICEMAT   Returns the price per $100 face value of a security that pays interest at maturity

List of Financial Functions

ZTEST

Returns the two-tailed P-value of a z-test. The z-test generates a standard score for x with respect to the data set, array, and returns the two-tailed probability for the normal distribution. You can use this function to assess the likelihood that a particular observation is drawn from a particular population.

Syntax   **ZTEST(array**, **x**, sigma)

Array   is the array or range of data against which to test x.

X   is the value to test.

Sigma   is the population (known) standard deviation. If omitted, the sample standard deviation is used.

Remarks   ▪ If array is empty, ZTEST returns the #N/A error value.

▪ ZTEST is calculated as follows:

$$ZTEST(array, x) =$$

$$1 - NORMSDIST\left(\frac{\mu - x}{\sigma \div \sqrt{n}}\right)$$

Example   ZTEST({3,6,7,8,6,5,4,2,1,9},4) equals 0.090574

Related Functions   CONFIDENCE   Returns the confidence interval for a population mean

NORMDIST   Returns the normal cumulative distribution

NORMINV   Returns the inverse of the normal cumulative distribution

NORMSDIST   Returns the standard normal cumulative distribution

NORMSINV   Returns the inverse of the standard normal cumulative distribution

STANDARDIZE   Returns a normalized value

List of Statistical Functions

Appendix: Using the CALL and REGISTER Functions

The following describes the argument and return value data types used by the CALL, REGISTER, and REGISTER.ID functions. Arguments and return values differ slightly depending on your operating environment, and these differences are noted in the data type table.

The *Microsoft Excel Developer's Kit* contains detailed information about dynamic link libraries (DLLs) and code resources, the Microsoft Excel application programming interface (API), file formats, and many other technical aspects of Microsoft Excel. It also contains code samples and programming tools that you can use to develop custom applications. To obtain a copy of the Microsoft Excel Developer's Kit, contact your software supplier or Microsoft Corporation. In the United States, contact the Microsoft Developer Services Team at (800) 227-4679 for more information.

Data Types

In the CALL, REGISTER, and REGISTER.ID functions, the type_text argument specifies the data type of the return value and the data types of all arguments to the DLL function or code resource. The first character of type_text specifies the data type of the return value. The remaining characters indicate the data types of all the arguments. For example, a DLL function that returns a floating-point number and takes an integer and a floating-point number as arguments would require "BIB" for the type_text argument.

The following table contains a complete list of the data type codes that Microsoft Excel recognizes, a description of each data type, how the argument or return value is passed, and a typical declaration for the data type in the C programming language.

Code	Descriptions	Pass by	C Declaration
A	Logical (FALSE = 0), TRUE = 1)	Value	short int
B	IEEE 8-byte floating-point number	Value (Windows)	double (Windows)
		Reference (Macintosh)	double * (Macintosh)
C	Null-terminated string (maximum string length = 255)	Reference	char *

Code	Descriptions	Pass by	C Declaration
D	Byte-counted string (first byte contains length of string, maximum string length = 255 characters)	Reference	Unsigned char *
E	IEEE 8-byte floating-point number	Reference	double *
F	Null-terminated string (maximum string length = 255 characters)	Reference (modify in place)	char *
G	Byte-counted string (first byte contains length of string, maximum string length = 255 characters)	Reference (modify in place)	unsigned char *
H	Unsigned 2-byte integer	Value	unsigned short int
I	Signed 2-byte integer	Value	short int
J	Signed 4-byte integer	Value	long int
K	Array	Reference	FP *
L	Logical (FALSE = 0, TRUE = 1)	Reference	short int *
M	Signed 2-byte integer	Reference	short int *
N	Signed 4-byte integer	Reference	long int *
O	Array	Reference	Three arguments are passed: unsigned short int * unsigned short int * double [ ]
P	Microsoft Excel OPER data structure	Reference	OPER *
R	Microsoft Excel XLOPER data structure	Reference	XLOPER *

Remarks

- The C-language declarations are based on the assumption that your compiler defaults to 8-byte doubles, 2-byte short integers, and 4-byte long integers.

- In the Microsoft Windows programming environment, all pointers are far pointers. For example, you should declare the D data type code as `unsigned char far *` in Microsoft Windows.

- All functions in DLLs and code resources are called using the Pascal calling convention. Most C compilers allow you to use the Pascal calling convention by adding the pascal keyword to the function declaration, as shown in the following example:

```
pascal void main (rows,columns,a)
```

- If a function uses a pass-by-reference data type for its return value, you can pass a null pointer as the return value. Microsoft Excel will interpret the null pointer as the #NUM! error value.

Additional Data Type Information

This section contains detailed information about the F, G, K, O, P, and R data types, and other information about the type_text argument.

F and G Data Types

With the F and G data types, a function can modify a string buffer that is allocated by Microsoft Excel. If the return value type code is F or G, then Microsoft Excel ignores the value returned by the function. Instead, Microsoft Excel searches the list of function arguments for the first corresponding data type (F or G) and then takes the current contents of the allocated string buffer as the return value. Microsoft Excel allocates 256 bytes for the argument, so the function may return a larger string than it received.

K Data Type

The K data type uses a pointer to a variable-size FP structure. You should define this structure in the DLL or code resource as follows:

```
typedef struct _FP
{
    unsigned short int rows;
    unsigned short int columns;
    double array[1];    /* Actually, array[rows][columns] */
} FP;
```

The declaration double array[1] allocates storage for only a single-element array. The number of elements in the actual array equals the number of rows multiplied by the number of columns.

O Data Type

The O data type can be used only as an argument, not as a return value. It passes three items: a pointer to the number of rows in an array, a pointer to the number of columns in an array, and a pointer to a two-dimensional array of floating-point numbers.

Instead of returning a value, a function can modify an array passed by the O data type. To do this, you could use ">O" as the type_text argument. For more information, see "Modifying in Place—Functions Declared as Void" below.

The O data type was created for direct compatibility with FORTRAN DLLs, which pass arguments by reference.

P Data Type

The P data type is a pointer to an OPER structure. The OPER structure contains eight bytes of data, followed by a two-byte identifier that specifies the type of data. With the P data type, a DLL function or code resource can take and return any Microsoft Excel data type.

The OPER structure is defined as follows:

```
typedef struct _oper
{
    union
    {
        double num;
        unsigned char *str;
        unsigned short int bool;
        unsigned short int err;
        struct
        {
            struct _oper *lparray;
            unsigned short int rows;
            unsigned short int columns;
        } array;
    } val;
    unsigned short int type;
} OPER;
```

The type field contains one of these values:

Type	Description	Val field to use
1	Numeric	num
2	String (first byte contains length of string)	str
4	Boolean (logical)	bool
16	Error: the error values are:	err
	0 #NULL!	
	7 #DIV/0!	
	15 #Value!	
	23 #REF!	
	29 #NAME?	
	36 #NUM!	
	42 #N/A	
64	Array	array
128	Missing argument	
256	Empty cell	

The last two values can be used only as arguments, not return values. The missing argument value (128) is passed when the caller omits an argument. The empty cell value (256) is passed when the caller passes a reference to an empty cell.

R Data Type— Calling Microsoft Excel Functions from DLLs

The R data type is a pointer to an XLOPER structure, which is an enhanced version of the OPER structure. In Microsoft Excel version 4.0 and later, you can use the R data type to write DLLs and code resources that call Microsoft Excel functions. With the XLOPER structure, a DLL function can pass sheet references and implement flow control, in addition to passing data. A complete description of the R data type and the Microsoft Excel application programming interface (API) is beyond the scope of this topic. The *Microsoft Excel Developer's Kit* contains detailed information about the R data type, the Microsoft Excel API, and many other technical aspects of Microsoft Excel.

Volatile Functions and Recalculation

Microsoft Excel usually calculates a DLL function (or a code resource) only when it is entered into a cell, when one of its precedents changes, or when the cell is calculated during a macro. On a worksheet, you can make a DLL function or code resource volatile, which means that it recalculates every time the worksheet recalculates. To make a function volatile, add an exclamation point (!) as the last character in the type_text argument.

For example, in Microsoft Excel for Windows 95 and Microsoft Excel for Windows NT, the following worksheet formula recalculates every time the worksheet recalculates:

```
CALL("Kernel32","GetTickCount","J!")
```

Modifying in Place—Functions Declared as Void

You can use a single digit n for the return type code in type_text, where n is a number from 1 to 9. This tells Microsoft Excel to modify the variable in the location pointed to by the nth argument in type_text, instead of returning a value. This is also known as modifying in place. The nth argument must be a pass-by-reference data type (C, D, E, F, G, K, L, M, N, O, P, or R). The DLL function or code resource must also be declared with the void keyword in the C language (or the procedure keyword in the Pascal language).

For example, a DLL function that takes a null-terminated string and two pointers to integers as arguments can modify the string in place. Use "1FMM" as the type_text argument, and declare the function as void.

Versions prior to Microsoft Excel 4.0 used the > character to modify the first argument in place—there was no way to modify any argument other than the first. The > character is equivalent to n = 1 in Microsoft Excel version 4.0 and later.

For More Information

The following books provide detailed information on financial, statistical, and engineering methods. For a list of these functions by category, see "Functions Listed by Category".

Milton Abramowitz and Irene A. Stegun, Handbook of Mathematical Functions with Formulas, Graphs, and Mathematical Tables, Tenth Edition. Washington, D. C.: United States Government Printing Office, 1972.

Jay L. Devore, Probability and Statistics for Engineering and the Sciences, Third Edition. Pacific Grove, California: Brooks/Cole Publishing Company, 1991.

Frank J. Fabozzi and Irving M. Pollack, The Handbook of Fixed Income Securities. Homewood, Illinois: Business 1 Irwin, 1986.

Hewlett-Packard Company, HP-12C Owner's Handbook and Problem-Solving Guide, 1981.

John J. Lynch, Jr. and Jan H. Mayle, Standard Securities Calculation Methods, Fixed Income Securities Formulas. New York, New York: Securities Industry Association, 1986.

Robert B. McCall, Fundamental Statistics for the Behavioral Sciences, Fifth Edition. New York, New York: Harcourt Brace Jovanovich, Inc., 1990.

W. H. Press, B. P. Flannery, S. A. Teukolsky, and W. T. Vetterling, Numerical Recipes in C: The Art of Scientific Computing. New York, New York: Cambridge University Press, 1988.

Robert R. Sokal and F. James Rohlf, Biometry: The Principles and Practice of Statistics in Biological Research, Second Edition. New York, New York: W. H. Freeman and Company, 1981.

Marcia Stigum and John Mann, Money Market Calculations: Yields, Break-Evens, and Arbitrage. Homewood, Illinois: Business 1 Irwin, 1989.

Joseph G. Monks, Operations Management: Theory and Problems. New York, New York: McGraw-Hill Book Company, 1987.

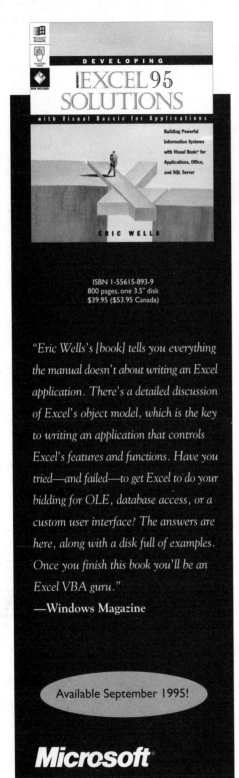
Create industrial-strength business applications for Windows® and the Macintosh® in the Microsoft® Excel object model and in Visual Basic® for Applications.

This book will teach you how to use the powerful tools in Microsoft Excel to create business applications that turn raw data into meaningful, useful information—in a way that could previously be done only by using a high-end development tool such as C or COBOL. You'll save time and money by being able to quickly and efficiently build, maintain, and update these applications within Microsoft Excel, using easy-to-write Visual Basic for Applications macros.

You Have a Powerful Development Tool at Your Fingertips—Microsoft Excel

Microsoft Excel contains more than 125 advanced data analysis objects that you can piece together to create business applications. Not only can you rely on these objects, but because Microsoft Excel supports OLE, you can also integrate a variety of objects from other applications (such as Microsoft Word and Microsoft Access) into your applications.

Learn to Use the Power

After an overview of the Excel object model and Visual Basic for Applications features, you'll learn how to:

- Develop information systems and design custom interfaces

- Take advantage of the powerful Jet database engine to develop database solutions in Excel that can be used with Microsoft Access and Visual Basic

- Develop custom applications with Microsoft Office and other products that support OLE

- Distribute your applications

- Enhance the performance of your applications

Benefit from Expert Advice and Insight

Written by a member of the Microsoft Excel technical team, DEVELOPING MICROSOFT EXCEL 95 SOLUTIONS WITH VISUAL BASIC FOR APPLICATIONS delivers inside strategies, tips, and tricks you won't find anywhere else. The companion disk includes sample Visual Basic for Applications macros and applications covered in the book. This is the only reference you'll need to start creating your own professional-quality data-access and decision-making tools in Microsoft Excel right away.

area A width w base b
perimeter P surface area S circumference C
length l altitude (height) h radius r

Rectangle

$$A = lw \qquad P = 2l + 2w$$

Triangle

$$A = \frac{1}{2}bh$$

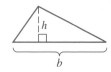

Square

$$A = s^2 \qquad P = 4s$$

Parallelogram

$$A = bh$$

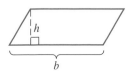

Trapezoid

$$A = \frac{1}{2}h(b_1 + b_2)$$

Circle

$$A = \pi r^2 \qquad C = 2\pi r$$

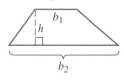

30°–60° Right Triangle

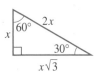

Right Triangle

$$a^2 + b^2 = c^2$$

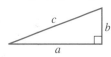

Isosceles Right Triangle

Right Circular Cylinder

$$V = \pi r^2 h \qquad S = 2\pi r^2 + 2\pi rh$$

Sphere

$$S = 4\pi r^2 \qquad V = \frac{4}{3}\pi r^3$$

Right Circular Cone

$$V = \frac{1}{3}\pi r^2 h \qquad S = \pi r^2 + \pi rs$$

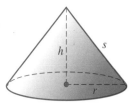

Pyramid

$$V = \frac{1}{3}Bh$$

Prism

$$V = Bh$$

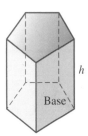

www.brookscole.com

www.brookscole.com is the World Wide Web site for Thomson Brooks/Cole and is your direct source to dozens of online resources.

At *www.brookscole.com* you can find out about supplements, demonstration software, and student resources. You can also send e-mail to many of our authors and preview new publications and exciting new technologies.

www.brookscole.com
Changing the way the world learns®

EIGHTH EDITION

Intermediate Algebra

Jerome E. Kaufmann

Karen L. Schwitters
Seminole Community College

THOMSON

BROOKS/COLE

Australia • Brazil • Canada • Mexico • Singapore • Spain
United Kingdom • United States

THOMSON

BROOKS/COLE

Intermediate Algebra, **Eighth Edition**
Jerome E. Kaufmann, Karen L. Schwitters

Editor: Gary Whalen
Assistant Editor: Rebecca Subity
Editorial Assistants: Katherine Cook and Dianna Muhammad
Technology Project Manager: Sarah Woicicki
Marketing Manager: Greta Kleinert
Marketing Assistant: Brian R. Smith
Marketing Communications Manager: Darlene
  Amidon-Brent
Project Manager, Editorial Production: Harold P. Humphrey
Art Director: Vernon T. Boes
Print Buyer: Barbara Britton

Permissions Editor: Stephanie Lee
Production Service: Susan Graham
Text Designer: John Edeen
Art Editor: Susan Graham
Photo Researcher: Sarah Evertson
Copy Editor: Susan Graham
Illustrator: Network Graphics and G & S Typesetters
Cover Designer: Lisa Henry
Cover Image: Doug Smock/Getty Images
Compositor: G & S Typesetters, Inc.
Text and Cover Printer: Transcontinental Printing/Interglobe

1 2 3 4 5 6 7 10 09 08 07

Library of Congress Control Number: 2005936327

Student Edition ISBN 0-495-10552-X

Thomson Higher Education
10 Davis Drive
Belmont, CA 94002-3098
USA

For more information about our products, contact us at:
Thomson Learning Academic Resource Center
1-800-423-0563
For permission to use material from this text or product, submit a request online at **http://www.thomsonrights.com.**
Any additional questions about permissions can be submitted by e-mail to **thomsonrights@thomson.com.**

Contents

Chapter 1 — **Basic Concepts and Properties** 1

1.1 Sets, Real Numbers, and Numerical Expressions 2
1.2 Operations with Real Numbers 11
1.3 Properties of Real Numbers and the Use of Exponents 22
1.4 Algebraic Expressions 30
Chapter 1 Summary 40
Chapter 1 Review Problem Set 41
Chapter 1 Test 43

Chapter 2 — **Equations, Inequalities, and Problem Solving** 44

2.1 Solving First-Degree Equations 45
2.2 Equations Involving Fractional Forms 53
2.3 Equations Involving Decimals and Problem Solving 61
2.4 Formulas 69
2.5 Inequalities 80
2.6 More on Inequalities and Problem Solving 87
2.7 Equations and Inequalities Involving Absolute Value 96
Chapter 2 Summary 103
Chapter 2 Review Problem Set 104
Chapter 2 Test 107

Chapter 3 — **Polynomials** 108

3.1 Polynomials: Sums and Differences 109
3.2 Products and Quotients of Monomials 115
3.3 Multiplying Polynomials 122
3.4 Factoring: Use of the Distributive Property 129
3.5 Factoring: Difference of Two Squares and Sum or Difference of Two Cubes 137
3.6 Factoring Trinomials 143
3.7 Equations and Problem Solving 151

Chapter 3 Summary   159
Chapter 3 Review Problem Set   160
Chapter 3 Test   162
Cumulative Review Problem Set (Chapters 1–3)   163

Chapter 4   Rational Expressions   165

4.1   Simplifying Rational Expressions   166
4.2   Multiplying and Dividing Rational Expressions   172
4.3   Adding and Subtracting Rational Expressions   177
4.4   More on Rational Expressions and Complex Fractions   185
4.5   Dividing Polynomials   195
4.6   Fractional Equations   201
4.7   More Fractional Equations and Applications   209
Chapter 4 Summary   220
Chapter 4 Review Problem Set   221
Chapter 4 Test   223

Chapter 5   Exponents and Radicals   224

5.1   Using Integers as Exponents   225
5.2   Roots and Radicals   232
5.3   Combining Radicals and Simplifying Radicals That
      Contain Variables   244
5.4   Products and Quotients Involving Radicals   250
5.5   Equations Involving Radicals   256
5.6   Merging Exponents and Roots   261
5.7   Scientific Notation   268
Chapter 5 Summary   274
Chapter 5 Review Problem Set   275
Chapter 5 Test   277

Chapter 6   Quadratic Equations and Inequalities   278

6.1   Complex Numbers   279
6.2   Quadratic Equations   287
6.3   Completing the Square   295
6.4   Quadratic Formula   300
6.5   More Quadratic Equations and Applications   308
6.6   Quadratic and Other Nonlinear Inequalities   320
Chapter 6 Summary   327
Chapter 6 Review Problem Set   328
Chapter 6 Test   330
Cumulative Review Problem Set (Chapters 1–6)   331

Chapter 7 **Linear Equations and Inequalities in Two Variables** 333

7.1 Rectangular Coordinate System and Linear Equations 334
7.2 Graphing Nonlinear Equations 349
7.3 Linear Inequalities in Two Variables 357
7.4 Distance and Slope 362
7.5 Determining the Equation of a Line 374
Chapter 7 Summary 387
Chapter 7 Review Problem Set 388
Chapter 7 Test 390

Chapter 8 **Conic Sections** 391

8.1 Graphing Parabolas 392
8.2 More Parabolas and Some Circles 402
8.3 Graphing Ellipses 410
8.4 Graphing Hyperbolas 415
Chapter 8 Summary 425
Chapter 8 Review Problem Set 425
Chapter 8 Test 427

Chapter 9 **Functions** 428

9.1 Relations and Functions 429
9.2 Functions: Their Graphs and Applications 436
9.3 Graphing Made Easy Via Transformations 450
9.4 Composition of Functions 459
9.5 Inverse Functions 465
9.6 Direct and Inverse Variations 474
Chapter 9 Summary 482
Chapter 9 Review Problem Set 483
Chapter 9 Test 485

Chapter 10 **Systems of Equations** 486

10.1 Systems of Two Linear Equations in Two Variables 487
10.2 Elimination-by-Addition Method 495
10.3 Systems of Three Linear Equations in Three Variables 505
10.4 Matrix Approach to Solving Systems 514
10.5 Determinants 520
10.6 3×3 Determinants and Systems of Three Linear Equations in Three Variables 525
10.7 Systems Involving Nonlinear Equations and Systems of Inequalities 532

Chapter 10 Summary   541
Chapter 10 Review Problem Set   542
Chapter 10 Test   544
Cumulative Review Problem Set (Chapters 1–10)   546

Chapter 11   Exponential and Logarithmic Functions   550

11.1 Exponents and Exponential Functions   551
11.2 Applications of Exponential Functions   558
11.3 Logarithms   568
11.4 Logarithmic Functions   578
11.5 Exponential Equations, Logarithmic Equations, and
       Problem Solving   585
Chapter 11 Summary   594
Chapter 11 Review Problem Set   595
Chapter 11 Test   596

Chapter 12   Sequences and Binomial Expansions   597

12.1 Arithmetic Sequences   598
12.2 Sums of Arithmetic Sequences   603
12.3 Geometric Sequences   608
12.4 Infinite Geometric Sequences   615
12.5 Binomial Expansions   620
Chapter 12 Summary   625
Chapter 12 Review Problem Set   625
Chapter 12 Test   627

Appendix A: Prime Numbers and Operations with Fractions   629

Answers to Odd-Numbered Problems and All Chapter Review, Chapter Test, Cumulative Review, and Appendix A Problems   641

Index I-1

Preface

When preparing *Intermediate Algebra*, Eighth Edition, we wanted to preserve the features that made the previous editions successful, and at the same time, incorporate improvements suggested by reviewers.

This text was written for college students who need an algebra course that bridges the gap between elementary algebra and the more advanced courses in precalculus mathematics. It covers topics that are usually classified as intermediate algebra topics.

The basic concepts of intermediate algebra are presented in this text in a simple, straightforward way. Algebraic ideas are developed in a logical sequence and in an easy-to-read manner without excessive formalism. Concepts are developed through examples, reinforced through additional examples, and then applied in a variety of problem-solving situations.

■ New in This Edition

- Sections 7.1 and 7.2 have been reorganized so that only linear equations in two variables are graphed in Section 7.1. Then, in Section 7.2, the emphasis is on graphing nonlinear equations and using the graphs to motivate tests for *x* axis, *y* axis, and origin symmetry. These symmetry tests are used in Chapters 8 and 9, and will also be used in subsequent mathematics courses as students' graphing skills are enhanced.

- A focal point of every revision is the problem sets. Some users of the previous editions have suggested that the "very good" problem sets could be made even better by adding a few problems in different places. Based on these suggestions we have added approximately 50 new problems and distributed them among ten different problem sets. For example, it was suggested that in Problem Set 6.6 we include a larger variety of quadratic inequalities. We inserted new problems 37–46 in that problem set to satisfy this request.

- In Section 11.2, some of the compound interest rates have been changed to be more in line with predictions for rates in the near future. However, in Section 11.2 and in Problem Set 11.2, we have intentionally used a fairly wide range of interest rates. By varying the rates of interest, the number of compounding periods, and the amount of time, students can begin to see the effect that each variable has on the final result.

- The fact that logarithms are defined for only positive numbers does not imply that logarithmic equations cannot have negative solutions. We added an example at the end of Section 11.3 that shows a logarithmic equation with a negative solution. We also added 5 new logarithmic equations in Problem Set 11.3 that have negative solutions or no solution.

- In Chapter 12, rather than introducing the concept of a "series," we simply work with the indicated sum of a number of terms of a sequence.

■ Other Special Features

- Throughout the book, students are encouraged to (a) learn a skill, (b) use the skill to help solve equations and inequalities, and then (c) use equations and inequalities to solve word problems. This focus has influenced some of the decisions we made in preparing and updating the text.

    1. Approximately 450 word problems are scattered throughout the text. These problems deal with a large variety of applications that show the connection between mathematics and its use in the real world.

    2. Many problem-solving suggestions are offered throughout the text, and there are special discussions in several sections. When appropriate, different methods for solving the same problem are shown. The problem-solving suggestions are demonstrated in more than 85 worked-out examples.

    3. Newly acquired skills are used as soon as possible to solve equations and inequalities, which are, in turn, used to solve word problems. Therefore, the concept of solving equations and inequalities is introduced early and reinforced throughout the text. The concepts of factoring, solving equations, and solving word problems are tied together in Chapter 3.

- As recommended by the American Mathematical Association of Two-Year Colleges, many basic geometric concepts are integrated into a problem-solving setting. This book contains 20 worked-out examples and 100 problems that connect algebra, geometry, and real world applications. Specific discussions of geometric concepts are contained in the following sections:

    (**Section 2.2**) Complementary and supplementary angles; the sum of the measures of the angles of a triangle equals $180°$.
    (**Section 2.4**) Area and volume formulas
    (**Section 3.4**) More on area and volume formulas, perimeter, and circumference formulas
    (**Section 3.7**) The Pythagorean theorem
    (**Section 6.2**) More on the Pythagorean theorem, including work with isosceles right triangles and $30°$–$60°$ right triangles.

- Specific graphing ideas (intercepts, symmetry, restrictions, asymptotes, and transformations) are introduced and used throughout Chapters 7, 8, and 9. In Section 9.3, the work with parabolas from Chapter 8 is used to develop definitions for translations, reflections, stretchings, and shrinkings. These transformations are then applied to the graphs of the following:

$$f(x) = x^3 \qquad f(x) = \frac{1}{x} \qquad f(x) = \sqrt{x} \qquad \text{and} \qquad f(x) = |x|$$

- Problems called **Thoughts into Words** are included in every problem set except the review exercises. These problems are designed to encourage students to express, in written form, their thoughts about various mathematical ideas. See, for examples, Problem Sets 2.1, 3.5, 4.7, 5.5, and 6.6.

- Many problem sets contain a special group of problems called **Further Investigations**, which lend themselves to small-group work. These problems encompass a variety of ideas: some are proofs, some show different approaches to topics covered in the text, some bring in supplementary topics and relationships, and some are more challenging problems. Although these problems add variety and flexibility to the problem sets, they can also be omitted without disrupting the continuity of the text. For examples, see Problem Sets 2.3, 2.7, 3.6, and 7.4.

- The graphing calculator is introduced in Section 7.1. From then on, many of the problem sets contain a group of problems called **Graphing Calculator Activities**. These activities, which are appropriate for either individual or small-group work, have been designed to reinforce concepts already presented and lay groundwork for concepts about to be discussed. In this text the use of a graphing calculator is considered optional.

- Photos and applications are used in the chapter openings to introduce some concepts presented in the chapter.

- Please note the exceptionally pleasing design features of the text, including the functional use of color. The open format makes for a continuous and easy flow of material instead of working through a maze of flags, caution symbols, reminder symbols, and so forth.

- *All* answers for Chapter Review Problem Sets, Chapter Tests, and Cumulative Review Problem Sets appear in the back of the text.

■ Additional Comments about Some of the Chapters

- Chapter 1 is written so that it can be covered quickly, and on an individual basis if necessary, by those who need only a brief review of some basic arithmetic and algebraic concepts.

- Chapter 2 presents an early introduction to the heart of the intermediate algebra course. Problem solving and the solving of equations and inequalities are introduced early so they can be used as unifying themes throughout the text.

- Chapter 6 is organized to give students the opportunity to learn, on a day-by-day basis, different techniques for solving quadratic equations. The process of completing the square is treated as a viable equation-solving tool for certain types of quadratic equations. The emphasis on completing the square in this setting pays off in Chapter 8 when we graph parabolas, circles, ellipses, and hyperbolas. Section 6.5 offers some guidance as to when to use a particular technique for solving a quadratic equation. In addition, the often-overlooked relationships involving the sum and product of roots are discussed and used as an effective checking procedure.

- Chapter 8 is written on the premise that intermediate algebra students should become very familiar with straight lines, parabolas, and circles and should have only limited exposure to ellipses and hyperbolas.
- Chapter 9 is devoted entirely to functions; our treatment of this topic does not jump back and forth between functions and relations that are not functions. This chapter includes some work with the composition of functions and the use of linear and quadratic functions in problem-solving situations. In this chapter domains and ranges are expressed in both interval and set-builder notation. The answers in the back of the text are given in both formats.
- Chapter 10 contains the various techniques for solving systems of linear equations. It is organized so that instructors can use as much of the chapter as they need for their particular course. Section 10.2 presents the elimination-by-addition method, which emphasizes equivalent systems and sets the stage for future work with matrices.
- Chapter 11 presents a modern-day version of the concepts of exponents and logarithms. The emphasis is on making the concepts and their applications meaningful. The calculator is used as a computational tool.
- Appendix A is for students who need a more thorough review of operations with fractions.

■ Ancillaries

For the Instructor

Annotated Instructor's Edition. This special version of the complete student text contains a Resource Integration Guide with answers printed next to all respective exercises. Graphs, tables, and other answers appear in a special answer section at the back of the text. Instructors can quickly identify — by the blue underlines in the instructor's edition — those problems that are available in *iLrn*.

Test Bank. The *Test Bank* includes eight tests per chapter as well as three final exams. The tests are made up of a combination of multiple-choice, free-response, true/false, and fill-in-the-blank questions.

Complete Solutions Manual. The *Complete Solutions Manual* provides worked-out solutions to all of the problems in the text.

iLrn™ Instructor Version. Providing instructors and students with unsurpassed control, variety, and all-in-one utility, *iLrn™* is a powerful and fully integrated teaching and learning system. *iLrn* ties together five fundamental learning activities: diagnostics, tutorials, homework, quizzing, and testing. Easy to use, *iLrn* offers instructors complete control when creating assessments in which they can draw from the wealth of exercises provided or create their own questions. *iLrn* features the greatest variety of problem types — allowing instructors to assess the way they teach. A real timesaver for instructors, *iLrn* offers automatic grading of homework, quizzes, and tests, with results flowing directly into the gradebook. The auto-enrollment feature also saves time with course setup as students self-enroll into the course gradebook. *iLrn* provides seamless integration with Blackboard™ and WebCT™.

Text-Specific Videotapes. These text-specific videotape sets, available at no charge to qualified adopters of the text, feature 10- to 20-minute problem-solving lessons that cover each section of every chapter.

For the Student

Student Solutions Manual. The *Student Solutions Manual* provides worked-out solutions to the odd-numbered problems, and all chapter review, chapter test, and cumulative review problems in the text.

Website (http://mathematics.brookscole.com). Instructors and students have access to a variety of teaching and learning resources. This website features everything from book-specific resources to newsgroups.

iLrn™ Tutorial Student Version. Featuring a variety of approaches that connect with all types of learners, *iLrn™ Tutorial* offers text-specific tutorials that require no setup by instructors. Students can begin exploring active examples from the text by using the access code packaged free with a new book. *iLrn Tutorial* supports students with explanations from the text, examples, step-by-step problem-solving help, unlimited practice, and chapter-by-chapter video lessons. With this self-paced system, students can even check their comprehension along the way by taking quizzes and receiving feedback. If they still are having trouble, students can easily access *vMentor™* for online help from a live math instructor. Students can ask any question and get personalized help through the interactive whiteboard and using their computer microphones to speak with the instructor. While designed for self-study, instructors can also assign the individual tutorial exercises.

Interactive Video Skillbuilder CD-ROM. Think of it as portable office hours. The *Interactive Video Skillbuilder CD-ROM* contains video instruction covering each chapter of the text. The problems worked during each video lesson are shown first so that students can try working them out before watching the solution. To help students evaluate their progress, each section contains a 10-question web quiz (the results of which can be e-mailed to the instructor), and each chapter contains a chapter test, with the answer to each problem on each test. A new learning tool on this CD-ROM is a graphing calculator tutorial for precalculus and college algebra, featuring examples, exercises, and video tutorials. Also new, English/Spanish closed caption translations can be selected to display along with the video instruction. This CD-ROM also features *MathCue* tutorial and testing software. Keyed to the text, *MathCue* offers these components:

- *MathCue Skill Builder*—Presents problems to solve, evaluates answers, and tutors students by displaying complete solutions with step-by-step explanations.

- *MathCue Quiz* — Allows students to generate large numbers of quiz problems keyed to problem types from each section of the book.
- *MathCue Chapter Test* — Also provides large numbers of problems keyed to problem types from each chapter.
- *MathCue Solution Finder* — This unique tool allows students to enter their own basic problems and receive step-by-step help as if they were working with a tutor.
- Score reports for any *MathCue* session can be printed and handed in for credit or extra credit.
- Print or e-mail score reports — Score reports for any *MathCue* session can be printed or sent to instructors via *MathCue's* secure e-mail score system.

vMentor™ Live, Online Tutoring. Packaged free with every text. Accessed seamlessly through *iLrn Tutorial, vMentor* provides tutorial help that can substantially improve student performance, increase test scores, and enhance technical aptitude. Students have access, via the web, to highly qualified tutors with thorough knowledge of our textbooks. When students get stuck on a particular problem or concept, they need only log on to *vMentor*, where they can talk (using their own computer microphones) to *vMentor* tutors who will skillfully guide them through the problem using the interactive whiteboard for illustration. Brooks/Cole also offers *Elluminate Live!*, an online virtual classroom environment that is customizable and easy to use. *Elluminate Live!* keeps students engaged with full two-way audio, instant messaging, and an interactive whiteboard — all in one intuitive, graphical interface. For information about obtaining a *Elluminate Live!* site license, instructors may contact their Thomson representative. *For proprietary, college, and university adopters only. For additional information, instructors may consult their Thomson representative.*

Explorations in Beginning and Intermediate Algebra Using the TI-82/83/83-Plus/85/86 Graphing Calculator, Third Edition (0-534-40644-0)
Deborah J. Cochener and Bonnie M. Hodge both of Austin Peay State University
This user-friendly workbook improves students' understanding and their retention of algebra concepts through a series of activities and guided explorations using the graphing calculator. An ideal supplement for any beginning or intermediate algebra course, *Explorations in Beginning and Intermediate Algebra, Third Edition* is an ideal tool for integrating technology without sacrificing course content. By clearly and succinctly teaching keystrokes, class time is devoted to investigations instead of how to use a graphing calculator.

The Math Student's Guide to the TI-83 Graphing Calculator (0-534-37802-1)
The Math Student's Guide to the TI-86 Graphing Calculator (0-534-37801-3)
The Math Student's Guide to the TI-83 Plus Graphing Calculator (0-534-42021-4)
The Math Student's Guide to the TI-89 Graphing Calculator (0-534-42022-2)
Trish Cabral of Butte College

These videos are designed for students who are new to the graphing calculator or for those who would like to brush up on their skills. Each instructional graphing calculator videotape covers basic calculations, the custom menu, graphing, advanced graphing, matrix operations, trigonometry, parametric equations, polar coordinates, calculus, Statistics I and one-variable data, and Statistics II with linear regression. These wonderful tools are each 105 minutes in length and cover all of the important functions of a graphing calculator.

Mastering Mathematics: How to Be a Great Math Student, Third Edition
(0-534-34947-1)
Richard Manning Smith, Bryant College
Providing solid tips for every stage of study, *Mastering Mathematics* stresses the importance of a positive attitude and gives students the tools to succeed in their math course.

Activities for Beginning and Intermediate Algebra, Second Editon
Instructor Edition (0-534-99874-7); Student Edition (0-534-99873-9)
Debbie Garrison, Judy Jones, and Jolene Rhodes, all of Valencia Community College
Designed as a stand-alone supplement for any beginning or intermediate algebra text, *Activities in Beginning & Intermediate Algebra* is a collection of activities written to incorporate the recommendations from the NCTM and from AMATYC's Crossroads. Activities can be used during class or in a laboratory setting to introduce, teach, or reinforce a topic.

Conquering Math Anxiety: A Self-Help Workbook, Second Edition (0-534-38634-2)
Cynthia Arem, Pima Community College
A comprehensive workbook that provides a variety of exercises and worksheets along with detailed explanations of methods to help "math-anxious" students deal with and overcome math fears. This edition now comes with a free relaxation CD-ROM and a detailed list of Internet resources.

Active Arithmetic and Algebra: Activities for Prealgebra and Beginning Algebra
(0-534-36771-2)
Judy Jones, Valencia Community College
This activities manual includes a variety of approaches to learning mathematical concepts. Sixteen activities, including puzzles, games, data collection, graphing, and writing activities are included.

Math Facts: Survival Guide to Basic Mathematics, Second Edition (0-534-94734-4)
Algebra Facts: Survival Guide to Basic Algebra (0-534-19986-0)
Theodore John Szymanski, Tompkins-Cortland Community College
This booklet gives easy access to the most crucial concepts and formulas in algebra. Although it is bound, this booklet is structured to work like flash cards.

■ Acknowledgments

We would like to take this opportunity to thank the following people who served as reviewers for the new editions of this series of texts:

Yusuf Abdl
Rutgers University

Lynda Fish
St. Louis Community College at Forest Park

Cindy Fleck
Wright State University

James Hodge
Mountain State University

Barbara Laubenthal
University of North Alabama

Karolyn Morgan
University of Montevallo

Jayne Prude
University of North Alabama

Renee Quick
Wallace State Community College

We would like to express our sincere gratitude to the staff of Brooks/Cole, especially Gary Whalen, for his continuous cooperation and assistance throughout this project; and to Susan Graham and Hal Humphrey, who carry out the many details of production. Finally, very special thanks are due to Arlene Kaufmann, who spends numerous hours reading page proofs.

Jerome E. Kaufmann
Karen L. Schwitters

Basic Concepts and Properties

1.1 Sets, Real Numbers, and Numerical Expressions

1.2 Operations with Real Numbers

1.3 Properties of Real Numbers and the Use of Exponents

1.4 Algebraic Expressions

© Alden Pellett / The Image Works

Numbers from the set of integers are used to express temperatures that are below 0°F.

The temperature at 6 p.m. was $-3°$F. By 11 p.m. the temperature had dropped another 5°F. We can use the **numerical expression** $-3 - 5$ to determine the temperature at 11 p.m.

Justin has p pennies, n nickels, and d dimes in his pocket. The **algebraic expression** $p + 5n + 10d$ represents that amount of money in cents.

Algebra is often described as a **generalized arithmetic**. That description may not tell the whole story, but it does convey an important idea: A good understanding of arithmetic provides a sound basis for the study of algebra. In this chapter we use the concepts of **numerical expression** and **algebraic expression** to review some ideas from arithmetic and to begin the transition to algebra. Be sure that you thoroughly understand the basic concepts we review in this first chapter.

1.1 Sets, Real Numbers, and Numerical Expressions

In arithmetic, we use symbols such as 6, $\frac{2}{3}$, 0.27, and π to represent numbers. The symbols $+$, $-$, $\cdot$, and $\div$ commonly indicate the basic operations of addition, subtraction, multiplication, and division, respectively. Thus we can form specific **numerical expressions**. For example, we can write the indicated sum of six and eight as $6 + 8$.

In algebra, the concept of a variable provides the basis for generalizing arithmetic ideas. For example, by using x and y to represent any numbers, we can use the expression $x + y$ to represent the indicated sum of any two numbers. The x and y in such an expression are called **variables**, and the phrase $x + y$ is called an **algebraic expression**.

We can extend to algebra many of the notational agreements we make in arithmetic, with a few modifications. The following chart summarizes the notational agreements that pertain to the four basic operations.

Operation	Arithmetic	Algebra	Vocabulary
Addition	$4 + 6$	$x + y$	The **sum** of x and y
Subtraction	$14 - 10$	$a - b$	The **difference** of a and b
Multiplication	$7 \cdot 5$ or 7×5	$a \cdot b, a(b), (a)b,$ $(a)(b),$ or ab	The **product** of a and b
Division	$8 \div 4, \dfrac{8}{4},$ or $4\overline{)8}$	$x \div y, \dfrac{x}{y},$ or $y\overline{)x}$	The **quotient** of x and y

Note the different ways to indicate a product, including the use of parentheses. The ab form is the simplest and probably the most widely used form. Expressions such as abc, $6xy$, and $14xyz$ all indicate multiplication. We also call your attention to the various forms that indicate division. In algebra, we usually use the fractional form, $\frac{x}{y}$, although the other forms do serve a purpose at times.

■ Use of Sets

We can use some of the basic vocabulary and symbolism associated with the concept of sets in the study of algebra. A **set** is a collection of objects and the objects are called **elements** or **members** of the set. In arithmetic and algebra the elements of a set are usually numbers.

The use of set braces, { }, to enclose the elements (or a description of the elements) and the use of capital letters to name sets provide a convenient way to communicate about sets. For example, we can represent a set A, which consists of the vowels of the alphabet, in any of the following ways:

$$A = \{\text{vowels of the alphabet}\} \quad \text{Word description}$$

$$A = \{a, e, i, o, u\} \qquad\qquad \text{List or roster description}$$

$$A = \{x | x \text{ is a vowel}\} \qquad \text{Set builder notation}$$

We can modify the listing approach if the number of elements is quite large. For example, all of the letters of the alphabet can be listed as

$$\{a, b, c, \ldots, z\}$$

We simply begin by writing enough elements to establish a pattern; then the three dots indicate that the set continues in that pattern. The final entry indicates the last element of the pattern. If we write

$$\{1, 2, 3, \ldots\}$$

the set begins with the counting numbers 1, 2, and 3. The three dots indicate that it continues in a like manner forever; there is no last element. A set that consists of no elements is called the **null set** (written $\varnothing$).

Set builder notation combines the use of braces and the concept of a variable. For example, $\{x | x \text{ is a vowel}\}$ is read "the set of all x such that x is a vowel." Note that the vertical line is read "such that." We can use set builder notation to describe the set $\{1, 2, 3, \ldots\}$ as $\{x | x > 0 \text{ and } x \text{ is a whole number}\}$.

We use the symbol $\in$ to denote set membership. Thus if $A = \{a, e, i, o, u\}$, we can write $e \in A$, which we read as "e is an element of A." The slash symbol, $/$, is commonly used in mathematics as a negation symbol. For example, $m \notin A$ is read as "m is not an element of A."

Two sets are said to be *equal* if they contain exactly the same elements. For example,

$$\{1, 2, 3\} = \{2, 1, 3\}$$

because both sets contain the same elements; the order in which the elements are written doesn't matter. The slash mark through the equality symbol denotes "is not equal to." Thus if $A = \{1, 2, 3\}$ and $B = \{1, 2, 3, 4\}$, we can write $A \neq B$, which we read as "set A is not equal to set B."

■ Real Numbers

We refer to most of the algebra that we will study in this text as the **algebra of real numbers**. This simply means that the variables represent real numbers. Therefore, it is necessary for us to be familiar with the various terms that are used to classify different types of real numbers.

$$\{1, 2, 3, 4, \ldots\} \qquad \text{Natural numbers, counting numbers, positive integers}$$

$$\{0, 1, 2, 3, \ldots\} \qquad \text{Whole numbers, nonnegative integers}$$

$$\{\ldots -3, -2, -1\} \qquad \text{Negative integers}$$

$$\{\ldots -3, -2, -1, 0\} \qquad \text{Nonpositive integers}$$

$$\{\ldots -3, -2, -1, 0, 1, 2, 3, \ldots\} \qquad \text{Integers}$$

We define a **rational number** as any number that can be expressed in the form $\frac{a}{b}$, where a and b are integers and b is not zero. The following are examples of rational numbers.

$$-\frac{3}{4}, \qquad \frac{2}{3}, \qquad -4, \qquad 0, \qquad 0.3, \qquad 6\frac{1}{2}$$

-4 because $-4 = \dfrac{-4}{1} = \dfrac{4}{-1}$ 0 because $0 = \dfrac{0}{1} = \dfrac{0}{2} = \dfrac{0}{3} = \ldots$

0.3 because $0.3 = \dfrac{3}{10}$ $6\dfrac{1}{2}$ because $6\dfrac{1}{2} = \dfrac{13}{2}$

We can also define a rational number in terms of a decimal representation. Before doing so, let's review the different possibilities for decimal representations. We can classify decimals as **terminating**, **repeating**, or **nonrepeating**. Some examples follow.

$$\begin{bmatrix} 0.3 \\ 0.46 \\ 0.789 \\ 0.6234 \end{bmatrix} \begin{array}{l} \text{Terminating} \\ \text{decimals} \end{array} \qquad \begin{bmatrix} 0.6666\ldots \\ 0.141414\ldots \\ 0.694694694\ldots \\ 0.2317171717\ldots \\ 0.5417283283283\ldots \end{bmatrix} \begin{array}{l} \text{Repeating} \\ \text{decimals} \end{array}$$

$$\begin{bmatrix} 0.276314583\ldots \\ 0.21411811161111\ldots \\ 0.673183329333\ldots \end{bmatrix} \begin{array}{l} \text{Nonrepeating} \\ \text{decimals} \end{array}$$

A repeating decimal has a block of digits that repeats indefinitely. This repeating block of digits may be of any number of digits and may or may not begin immediately after the decimal point. A small horizontal bar (overbar) is commonly used to indicate the repeat block. Thus $0.6666\ldots$ is written as $0.\overline{6}$, and $0.2317171717\ldots$ is written as $0.23\overline{17}$.

In terms of decimals, we define a **rational number** as a number that has either a terminating or a repeating decimal representation. The following examples illustrate some rational numbers written in $\frac{a}{b}$ form and in decimal form.

$$\frac{3}{4} = 0.75 \qquad \frac{3}{11} = 0.\overline{27} \qquad \frac{1}{8} = 0.125 \qquad \frac{1}{7} = 0.\overline{142857} \qquad \frac{1}{3} = 0.\overline{3}$$

We define an **irrational number** as a number that *cannot* be expressed in $\frac{a}{b}$ form, where a and b are integers, and b is not zero. Furthermore, an irrational number has a nonrepeating and nonterminating decimal representation. Some examples of irrational numbers and a partial decimal representation for each follow.

$$\sqrt{2} = 1.414213562373095\ldots \qquad \sqrt{3} = 1.73205080756887\ldots$$

$$\pi = 3.14159265358979\ldots$$

The entire set of **real numbers** is composed of the rational numbers along with the irrationals. Every real number is either a rational number or an irrational number. The following tree diagram summarizes the various classifications of the real number system.

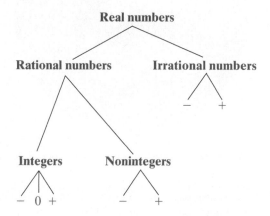

We can trace any real number down through the diagram as follows:

7 is real, rational, an integer, and positive.

$-\dfrac{2}{3}$ is real, rational, noninteger, and negative.

$\sqrt{7}$ is real, irrational, and positive.

0.38 is real, rational, noninteger, and positive.

Remark: We usually refer to the set of nonnegative integers, $\{0, 1, 2, 3, \ldots\}$, as the set of **whole numbers**, and we refer to the set of positive integers, $\{1, 2, 3, \ldots\}$, as the set of **natural numbers**. The set of whole numbers differs from the set of natural numbers by the inclusion of the number zero.

The concept of subset is convenient to use at this time. A set A is a **subset** of a set B if and only if every element of A is also an element of B. This is written as $A \subseteq B$ and read as "A is a subset of B." For example, if $A = \{1, 2, 3\}$ and $B = \{1, 2, 3, 5, 9\}$, then $A \subseteq B$ because every element of A is also an element of B. The slash mark again denotes negation, so if $A = \{1, 2, 5\}$ and $B = \{2, 4, 7\}$, we can say that A is not a subset of B by writing $A \nsubseteq B$. Figure 1.1 represents the subset

Real numbers

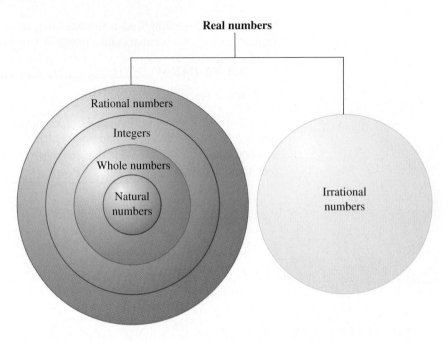

Figure 1.1

relationships for the set of real numbers. Refer to Figure 1.1 as you study the following statements that use subset vocabulary and subset symbolism.

1. The set of whole numbers is a subset of the set of integers.

$$\{0, 1, 2, 3, \ldots\} \subseteq \{\ldots, -2, -1, 0, 1, 2, \ldots\}$$

2. The set of integers is a subset of the set of rational numbers.

$$\{\ldots, -2, -1, 0, 1, 2, \ldots\} \subseteq \{x | x \text{ is a rational number}\}$$

3. The set of rational numbers is a subset of the set of real numbers.

$$\{x | x \text{ is a rational number}\} \subseteq \{y | y \text{ is a real number}\}$$

■ Equality

The relation **equality** plays an important role in mathematics — especially when we are manipulating real numbers and algebraic expressions that represent real numbers. An equality is a statement in which two symbols, or groups of symbols, are names for the same number. The symbol = is used to express an equality. Thus we can write

$$6 + 1 = 7 \qquad 18 - 2 = 16 \qquad 36 \div 4 = 9$$

(The symbol $\neq$ means *is not equal to*.) The following four basic properties of equality are self-evident, but we do need to keep them in mind. (We will expand this list in Chapter 2 when we work with solutions of equations.)

■ Properties of Equality

Reflexive Property

For any real number a,

$a = a$

Examples: $14 = 14$ $x = x$ $a + b = a + b$

Symmetric Property

For any real numbers a and b,

if $a = b$, then $b = a$

Examples :   If $13 + 1 = 14$, then $14 = 13 + 1$.
If $3 = x + 2$, then $x + 2 = 3$.

Transitive Property

For any real numbers a, b, and c,

if $a = b$ and $b = c$,   then $a = c$

Examples: If $3 + 4 = 7$ and $7 = 5 + 2$, then $3 + 4 = 5 + 2$.
If $x + 1 = y$ and $y = 5$, then $x + 1 = 5$.

Substitution Property

For any real numbers a and b: If $a = b$, then a may be replaced by b, or b may be replaced by a, in any statement without changing the meaning of the statement.

Examples: If $x + y = 4$ and $x = 2$, then $2 + y = 4$.
If $a - b = 9$ and $b = 4$, then $a - 4 = 9$.

■ Numerical Expressions

Let's conclude this section by *simplifying some numerical expressions* that involve whole numbers. When simplifying numerical expressions, we perform the operations in the following order. Be sure that you agree with the result in each example.

1. Perform the operations inside the symbols of inclusion (parentheses, brackets, and braces) and above and below each fraction bar. Start with the innermost inclusion symbol.

2. Perform all multiplications and divisions in the order in which they appear from left to right.

3. Perform all additions and subtractions in the order in which they appear from left to right.

E X A M P L E   1

Simplify $20 + 60 \div 10 \cdot 2$

Solution

First do the division.

$$20 + 60 \div 10 \cdot 2 = 20 + 6 \cdot 2$$

Next do the multiplication.

$$20 + 6 \cdot 2 = 20 + 12$$

Then do the addition.

$$20 + 12 = 32$$

Thus $20 + 60 \div 10 \cdot 2$ simplifies to 32. ∎

E X A M P L E   2

Simplify $7 \cdot 4 \div 2 \cdot 3 \cdot 2 \div 4$.

Solution

The multiplications and divisions are to be done from left to right in the order in which they appear.

$$7 \cdot 4 \div 2 \cdot 3 \cdot 2 \div 4 = 28 \div 2 \cdot 3 \cdot 2 \div 4$$
$$= 14 \cdot 3 \cdot 2 \div 4$$
$$= 42 \cdot 2 \div 4$$
$$= 84 \div 4$$
$$= 21$$

Thus $7 \cdot 4 \div 2 \cdot 3 \cdot 2 \div 4$ simplifies to 21. ∎

E X A M P L E   3

Simplify $5 \cdot 3 + 4 \div 2 - 2 \cdot 6 - 28 \div 7$.

Solution

First we do the multiplications and divisions in the order in which they appear. Then we do the additions and subtractions in the order in which they appear. Our work may take on the following format.

$$5 \cdot 3 + 4 \div 2 - 2 \cdot 6 - 28 \div 7 = 15 + 2 - 12 - 4 = 1$$ ∎

EXAMPLE 4   Simplify $(4 + 6)(7 + 8)$.

Solution

We use the parentheses to indicate the *product* of the quantities $4 + 6$ and $7 + 8$. We perform the additions inside the parentheses first and then multiply.

$$(4 + 6)(7 + 8) = (10)(15) = 150$$ ■

EXAMPLE 5   Simplify $(3 \cdot 2 + 4 \cdot 5)(6 \cdot 8 - 5 \cdot 7)$.

Solution

First we do the multiplications inside the parentheses.

$$(3 \cdot 2 + 4 \cdot 5)(6 \cdot 8 - 5 \cdot 7) = (6 + 20)(48 - 35)$$

Then we do the addition and subtraction inside the parentheses.

$$(6 + 20)(48 - 35) = (26)(13)$$

Then we find the final product.

$$(26)(13) = 338$$ ■

EXAMPLE 6   Simplify $6 + 7[3(4 + 6)]$.

Solution

We use brackets for the same purposes as parentheses. In such a problem we need to simplify *from the inside out*; that is, we perform the operations in the innermost parentheses first. We thus obtain

$$
\begin{aligned}
6 + 7[3(4 + 6)] &= 6 + 7[3(10)] \\
&= 6 + 7[30] \\
&= 6 + 210 \\
&= 216
\end{aligned}
$$ ■

EXAMPLE 7   Simplify $\dfrac{6 \cdot 8 \div 4 - 2}{5 \cdot 4 - 9 \cdot 2}$.

Solution

First we perform the operations above and below the fraction bar. Then we find the final quotient.

$$\frac{6 \cdot 8 \div 4 - 2}{5 \cdot 4 - 9 \cdot 2} = \frac{48 \div 4 - 2}{20 - 18} = \frac{12 - 2}{2} = \frac{10}{2} = 5$$ ■

Remark: With parentheses we could write the problem in Example 7 as $(6 \cdot 8 \div 4 - 2) \div (5 \cdot 4 - 9 \cdot 2)$.

Problem Set 1.1

For Problems 1–10, identify each statement as true or false.

1. Every irrational number is a real number.

2. Every rational number is a real number.

3. If a number is real, then it is irrational.

4. Every real number is a rational number.

5. All integers are rational numbers.

6. Some irrational numbers are also rational numbers.

7. Zero is a positive integer.

8. Zero is a rational number.

9. All whole numbers are integers.

10. Zero is a negative integer.

For Problems 11–18, from the list $0, 14, \frac{2}{3}, \pi, \sqrt{7}, -\frac{11}{14},$ $2.34, 3.2\overline{1}, \frac{55}{8}, -\sqrt{17}, -19,$ and -2.6, identify each of the following.

11. The whole numbers

12. The natural numbers

13. The rational numbers

14. The integers

15. The nonnegative integers

16. The irrational numbers

17. The real numbers

18. The nonpositive integers

For Problems 19–28, use the following set designations.

$N = \{x|x \text{ is a natural number}\}$
$Q = \{x|x \text{ is a rational number}\}$
$W = \{x|x \text{ is a whole number}\}$
$H = \{x|x \text{ is an irrational number}\}$
$I = \{x|x \text{ is an integer}\}$
$R = \{x|x \text{ is a real number}\}$

Place $\subseteq$ or $\not\subseteq$ in each blank to make a true statement.

19. R _____ N **20.** N _____ R

21. I _____ Q **22.** N _____ I

23. Q _____ H **24.** H _____ Q

25. N _____ W **26.** W _____ I

27. I _____ N **28.** I _____ W

For Problems 29–32, classify the real number by tracing through the diagram in the text (see page 5).

29. -8 **30.** 0.9

31. $-\sqrt{2}$ **32.** $\frac{5}{6}$

For Problems 33–42, list the elements of each set. For example, the elements of $\{x|x \text{ is a natural number less than 4}\}$ can be listed as $\{1, 2, 3\}$.

33. $\{x|x \text{ is a natural number less than 3}\}$

34. $\{x|x \text{ is a natural number greater than 3}\}$

35. $\{n|n \text{ is a whole number less than 6}\}$

36. $\{y|y \text{ is an integer greater than } -4\}$

37. $\{y|y \text{ is an integer less than 3}\}$

38. $\{n|n \text{ is a positive integer greater than } -7\}$

39. $\{x|x \text{ is a whole number less than 0}\}$

40. $\{x|x \text{ is a negative integer greater than } -3\}$

41. $\{n|n \text{ is a nonnegative integer less than 5}\}$

42. $\{n|n \text{ is a nonpositive integer greater than 3}\}$

For Problems 43–50, replace each question mark to make the given statement an application of the indicated property of equality. For example, $16 = ?$ becomes $16 = 16$ because of the reflexive property of equality.

43. If $y = x$ and $x = -6$, then $y = ?$ (Transitive property of equality)

44. $5x + 7 = ?$ (Reflexive property of equality)

45. If $n = 2$ and $3n + 4 = 10$, then $3(?) + 4 = 10$ (Substitution property of equality)

46. If $y = x$ and $x = z + 2$, then $y = ?$ (Transitive property of equality)

47. If $4 = 3x + 1$, then $? = 4$ (Symmetric property of equality)

PEMDAS

48. If $t = 4$ and $s + t = 9$, then $s + ? = 9$ (Substitution property of equality)

49. $5x = ?$ (Reflexive property of equality)

50. If $5 = n + 3$, then $n + 3 = ?$ (Symmetric property of equality)

For Problems 51–74, simplify each of the numerical expressions.

51. $16 + 9 - 4 - 2 + 8 - 1$

52. $18 + 17 - 9 - 2 + 14 - 11$

53. $9 \div 3 \cdot 4 \div 2 \cdot 14$

54. $21 \div 7 \cdot 5 \cdot 2 \div 6$

55. $7 + 8 \cdot 2$

56. $21 - 4 \cdot 3 + 2$

57. $9 \cdot 7 - 4 \cdot 5 - 3 \cdot 2 + 4 \cdot 7$

58. $6 \cdot 3 + 5 \cdot 4 - 2 \cdot 8 + 3 \cdot 2$

59. $(17 - 12)(13 - 9)(7 - 4)$

60. $(14 - 12)(13 - 8)(9 - 6)$

61. $13 + (7 - 2)(5 - 1)$

62. $48 - (14 - 11)(10 - 6)$

63. $(5 \cdot 9 - 3 \cdot 4)(6 \cdot 9 - 2 \cdot 7)$

64. $(3 \cdot 4 + 2 \cdot 1)(5 \cdot 2 + 6 \cdot 7)$

65. $7[3(6 - 2)] - 64$

66. $12 + 5[3(7 - 4)]$

67. $[3 + 2(4 \cdot 1 - 2)][18 - (2 \cdot 4 - 7 \cdot 1)]$

68. $3[4(6 + 7)] + 2[3(4 - 2)]$

69. $14 + 4\left(\dfrac{8 - 2}{12 - 9}\right) - 2\left(\dfrac{9 - 1}{19 - 15}\right)$

70. $12 + 2\left(\dfrac{12 - 2}{7 - 2}\right) - 3\left(\dfrac{12 - 9}{17 - 14}\right)$

71. $[7 + 2 \cdot 3 \cdot 5 - 5] \div 8$

72. $[27 - (4 \cdot 2 + 5 \cdot 2)][(5 \cdot 6 - 4) - 20]$

73. $\dfrac{3 \cdot 8 - 4 \cdot 3}{5 \cdot 7 - 34} + 19$

74. $\dfrac{4 \cdot 9 - 3 \cdot 5 - 3}{18 - 12}$

75. You must of course be able to do calculations like those in Problems 51–74 both with and without a calculator. Furthermore, different types of calculators handle the priority-of-operations issue in different ways. Be sure you can do Problems 51–74 with *your* calculator.

■ ■ ■ **THOUGHTS INTO WORDS**

76. Explain in your own words the difference between the reflexive property of equality and the symmetric property of equality.

77. Your friend keeps getting an answer of 30 when simplifying $7 + 8(2)$. What mistake is he making and how would you help him?

78. Do you think $3\sqrt{2}$ is a rational or an irrational number? Defend your answer.

79. Explain why every integer is a rational number but not every rational number is an integer.

80. Explain the difference between $1.\overline{3}$ and 1.3.

1.2 Operations with Real Numbers

Before we review the four basic operations with real numbers, let's briefly discuss some concepts and terminology we commonly use with this material. It is often helpful to have a geometric representation of the set of real numbers as indicated in Figure 1.2. Such a representation, called the **real number line**, indicates a one-to-one correspondence between the set of real numbers and the points on a line.

In other words, to each real number there corresponds one and only one point on the line, and to each point on the line there corresponds one and only one real number. The number associated with each point on the line is called the **coordinate** of the point.

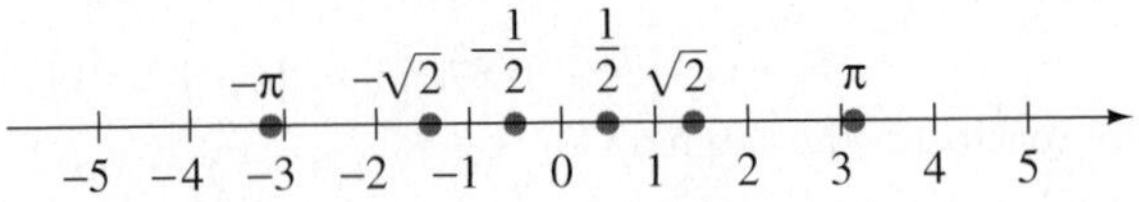

Figure 1.2

Many operations, relations, properties, and concepts pertaining to real numbers can be given a geometric interpretation on the real number line. For example, the addition problem $(-1) + (-2)$ can be depicted on the number line as in Figure 1.3.

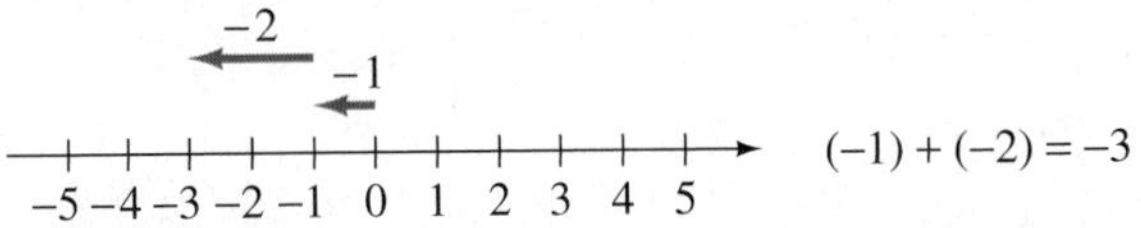

$(-1) + (-2) = -3$

Figure 1.3

The inequality relations also have a geometric interpretation. The statement $a > b$ (which is read "a is greater than b") means that a is to the right of b, and the statement $c < d$ (which is read "c is less than d") means that c is to the left of d as shown in Figure 1.4. The symbol $\leq$ means *is less than or equal to*, and the symbol $\geq$ means *is greater than or equal to*.

Figure 1.4

The property $-(-x) = x$ can be represented on the number line by following the sequence of steps shown in Figure 1.5.

1. Choose a point having a coordinate of x.

2. Locate its opposite, written as $-x$, on the other side of zero.

3. Locate the opposite of $-x$, written as $-(-x)$, on the other side of zero.

Therefore, we conclude that **the opposite of the opposite of any real number is the number itself**, and we symbolically express this by $-(-x) = x$.

Remark: The symbol -1 can be read "negative one," "the negative of one," "the opposite of one," or "the additive inverse of one." The opposite-of and additive-inverse-of terminology is especially meaningful when working with variables. For example, the symbol $-x$, which is read "the opposite of x" or "the additive inverse of x," emphasizes an important issue. Because x can be any real number, $-x$ (the opposite of x) can be zero, positive, or negative. If x is positive, then $-x$ is negative. If x is negative, then $-x$ is positive. If x is zero, then $-x$ is zero.

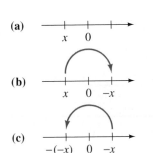

Figure 1.5

■ Absolute Value

We can use the concept of **absolute value** to describe precisely how to operate with positive and negative numbers. Geometrically, the absolute value of any number is the distance between the number and zero on the number line. For example, the absolute value of 2 is 2. The absolute value of -3 is 3. The absolute value of 0 is 0 (see Figure 1.6).

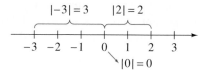

Figure 1.6

Symbolically, absolute value is denoted with vertical bars. Thus we write

$$|2| = 2 \qquad |-3| = 3 \qquad |0| = 0$$

More formally, we define the concept of absolute value as follows:

Definition 1.1

For all real numbers a,

1. If $a \geq 0$, then $|a| = a$.

2. If $a < 0$, then $|a| = -a$.

According to Definition 1.1, we obtain

$|6| = 6$	By applying part 1 of Definition 1.1
$|0| = 0$	By applying part 1 of Definition 1.1
$|-7| = -(-7) = 7$	By applying part 2 of Definition 1.1

Note that the absolute value of a positive number is the number itself, but the absolute value of a negative number is its opposite. Thus the absolute value of any number except zero is positive, and the absolute value of zero is zero. Together, these facts indicate that the absolute value of any real number is equal to the absolute value of its opposite. We summarize these ideas in the following properties.

Properties of Absolute Value

The variables a and b represent any real number.

1. $|a| \geq 0$

2. $|a| = |-a|$

3. $|a - b| = |b - a|$ $a - b$ and $b - a$ are opposites of each other.

■ Adding Real Numbers

We can use various physical models to describe the addition of real numbers. For example, profits and losses pertaining to investments: A loss of \$25.75 (written as -25.75) on one investment, along with a profit of \$22.20 (written as 22.20) on a second investment, produces an overall loss of \$3.55. Thus $(-25.75) + 22.20 = -3.55$. Think in terms of profits and losses for each of the following examples.

$$50 + 75 = 125 \qquad\qquad 20 + (-30) = -10$$

$$-4.3 + (-6.2) = -10.5 \qquad -27 + 43 = 16$$

$$\frac{7}{8} + \left(-\frac{1}{4}\right) = \frac{5}{8} \qquad\qquad -3\frac{1}{2} + \left(-3\frac{1}{2}\right) = -7$$

Though all problems that involve addition of real numbers could be solved using the profit-loss interpretation, it is sometimes convenient to have a more precise description of the addition process. For this purpose we use the concept of absolute value.

Addition of Real Numbers

Two Positive Numbers   The sum of two positive real numbers is the sum of their absolute values.

Two Negative Numbers   The sum of two negative real numbers is the opposite of the sum of their absolute values.

One Positive and One Negative Number   The sum of a positive real number and a negative real number can be found by subtracting the smaller absolute value from the larger absolute value and giving the result the sign of the original number that has the larger absolute value. If the two numbers have the same absolute value, then their sum is 0.

Zero and Another Number   The sum of 0 and any real number is the real number itself.

Now consider the following examples in terms of the previous description of addition. These examples include operations with rational numbers in common fraction form. If you need a review on operations with fractions, see Appendix A.

$$(-6) + (-8) = -(|-6| + |-8|) = -(6 + 8) = -14$$

$$(-1.6) + (-7.7) = -(|-1.6| + |-7.7|) = -(1.6 + 7.7) = -9.3$$

$$6\frac{3}{4} + \left(-2\frac{1}{2}\right) = \left(\left|6\frac{3}{4}\right| - \left|-2\frac{1}{2}\right|\right) = \left(6\frac{3}{4} - 2\frac{1}{2}\right) = \left(6\frac{3}{4} - 2\frac{2}{4}\right) = 4\frac{1}{4}$$

$$14 + (-21) = -(|-21| - |14|) = -(21 - 14) = -7$$
$$-72.4 + 72.4 = 0 \qquad 0 + (-94) = -94$$

■ Subtracting Real Numbers

We can describe the subtraction of real numbers in terms of addition.

Subtraction of Real Numbers

> If a and b are real numbers, then
>
> $$a - b = a + (-b)$$

It may be helpful for you to read $a - b = a + (-b)$ as "a minus b is equal to a plus the opposite of b." In other words, every subtraction problem can be changed to an equivalent addition problem. Consider the following examples.

$$7 - 9 = 7 + (-9) = -2, \qquad -5 - (-13) = -5 + 13 = 8$$
$$6.1 - (-14.2) = 6.1 + 14.2 = 20.3, \qquad -16 - (-11) = -16 + 11 = -5$$
$$-\frac{7}{8} - \left(-\frac{1}{4}\right) = -\frac{7}{8} + \frac{1}{4} = -\frac{7}{8} + \frac{2}{8} = -\frac{5}{8}$$

It should be apparent that addition is a key operation. To simplify numerical expressions that involve addition and subtraction, we can first change all subtractions to additions and then perform the additions.

EXAMPLE 1 Simplify $7 - 9 - 14 + 12 - 6 + 4$.

Solution

$$7 - 9 - 14 + 12 - 6 + 4 = 7 + (-9) + (-14) + 12 + (-6) + 4$$
$$= -6 \qquad\qquad ■$$

EXAMPLE 2 Simplify $-2\frac{1}{8} + \frac{3}{4} - \left(-\frac{3}{8}\right) - \frac{1}{2}$

Solution

$$-2\frac{1}{8} + \frac{3}{4} - \left(-\frac{3}{8}\right) - \frac{1}{2} = -2\frac{1}{8} + \frac{3}{4} + \frac{3}{8} + \left(-\frac{1}{2}\right)$$

$$= -\frac{17}{8} + \frac{6}{8} + \frac{3}{8} + \left(-\frac{4}{8}\right) \quad \text{Change to equivalent fractions with a common denominator.}$$

$$= -\frac{12}{8} = -\frac{3}{2} \qquad\qquad ■$$

It is often helpful to convert subtractions to additions *mentally*. In the next two examples, the work shown in the dashed boxes could be done in your head.

EXAMPLE 3

Simplify $4 - 9 - 18 + 13 - 10$.

Solution

$$4 - 9 - 18 + 13 - 10 = \boxed{4 + (-9) + (-18) + 13 + (-10)}$$

$$= -20 \qquad \blacksquare$$

EXAMPLE 4

Simplify $\left(\dfrac{2}{3} - \dfrac{1}{5}\right) - \left(\dfrac{1}{2} - \dfrac{7}{10}\right)$

Solution

$$\left(\frac{2}{3} - \frac{1}{5}\right) - \left(\frac{1}{2} - \frac{7}{10}\right) = \boxed{\left[\frac{2}{3} + \left(-\frac{1}{5}\right)\right] - \left[\frac{1}{2} + \left(-\frac{7}{10}\right)\right]}$$

$$= \left[\frac{10}{15} + \left(-\frac{3}{15}\right)\right] - \left[\frac{5}{10} + \left(-\frac{7}{10}\right)\right]$$

Within the brackets, change to equivalent fractions with a common denominator.

$$= \left(\frac{7}{15}\right) - \left(-\frac{2}{10}\right)$$

$$= \boxed{\left(\frac{7}{15}\right) + \left(+\frac{2}{10}\right)}$$

$$= \frac{14}{30} + \left(+\frac{6}{30}\right)$$

Change to equivalent fractions with a common denominator.

$$= \frac{20}{30} = \frac{2}{3} \qquad \blacksquare$$

■ Multiplying Real Numbers

We can interpret the multiplication of whole numbers as repeated addition. For example, $3 \cdot 2$ means three 2s; thus $3 \cdot 2 = 2 + 2 + 2 = 6$. This same repeated-addition interpretation of multiplication can be used to find the product of a positive number and a negative number, as shown by the following examples.

$$2(-3) = -3 + (-3) = -6, \qquad 3(-2) = -2 + (-2) + (-2) = -6$$

$$4(-1.2) = -1.2 + (-1.2) + (-1.2) + (-1.2) = -4.8$$

$$3\left(-\frac{1}{8}\right) = -\frac{1}{8} + \left(-\frac{1}{8}\right) + \left(-\frac{1}{8}\right) = -\frac{3}{8}$$

When we are multiplying whole numbers, the order in which we multiply two factors does not change the product. For example, $2(3) = 6$ and $3(2) = 6$. Using this idea, we can handle a negative number times a positive number as follows:

$$(-2)(3) = (3)(-2) = (-2) + (-2) + (-2) = -6$$

$$(-3)(4) = (4)(-3) = (-3) + (-3) + (-3) + (-3) = -12$$

$$\left(-\frac{3}{7}\right)(2) = (2)\left(-\frac{3}{7}\right) = -\frac{3}{7} + \left(-\frac{3}{7}\right) = -\frac{6}{7}$$

Finally, let's consider the product of two negative integers. The following pattern using integers helps with the reasoning.

$$4(-2) = -8 \qquad 3(-2) = -6 \qquad 2(-2) = -4$$

$$1(-2) = -2 \qquad 0(-2) = 0 \qquad (-1)(-2) = \, ?$$

To continue this pattern, the product of -1 and -2 has to be 2. In general, this type of reasoning helps us realize that the product of any two negative real numbers is a positive real number. Using the concept of absolute value, we can describe the **multiplication of real numbers** as follows:

Multiplication of Real Numbers

1. The product of two positive or two negative real numbers is the product of their absolute values.
2. The product of a positive real number and a negative real number (either order) is the opposite of the product of their absolute values.
3. The product of zero and any real number is zero.

The following examples illustrate this description of multiplication. Again, the steps shown in the dashed boxes are usually performed mentally.

$$(-6)(-7) = |-6| \cdot |-7| = 6 \cdot 7 = 42$$

$$(8)(-9) = -(|8| \cdot |-9|) = -(8 \cdot 9) = -72$$

$$\left(-\frac{3}{4}\right)\left(\frac{1}{3}\right) = -\left(\left|-\frac{3}{4}\right| \cdot \left|\frac{1}{3}\right|\right) = -\left(\frac{3}{4} \cdot \frac{1}{3}\right) = -\frac{1}{4}$$

$$(-14.3)(0) = 0$$

The previous examples illustrated a step-by-step process for multiplying real numbers. In practice, however, the key is to remember that the product of two positive or two negative numbers is positive and that the product of a positive number and a negative number (either order) is negative.

■ Dividing Real Numbers

The relationship between multiplication and division provides the basis for dividing real numbers. For example, we know that $8 \div 2 = 4$ because $2 \cdot 4 = 8$. In other words, the quotient of two numbers can be found by looking at a related multiplication problem. In the following examples, we used this same type of reasoning to determine some quotients that involve integers.

$$\frac{6}{-2} = -3 \quad \text{because } (-2)(-3) = 6$$

$$\frac{-12}{3} = -4 \quad \text{because } (3)(-4) = -12$$

$$\frac{-18}{-2} = 9 \quad \text{because } (-2)(9) = -18$$

$$\frac{0}{-5} = 0 \quad \text{because } (-5)(0) = 0$$

$$\frac{-8}{0} \text{ is undefined} \qquad \text{Remember that division by zero is undefined!}$$

A precise description for **division of real numbers** follows.

Division of Real Numbers

1. The quotient of two positive or two negative real numbers is the quotient of their absolute values.
2. The quotient of a positive real number and a negative real number or of a negative real number and a positive real number is the opposite of the quotient of their absolute values.
3. The quotient of zero and any nonzero real number is zero.
4. The quotient of any nonzero real number and zero is undefined.

The following examples illustrate this description of division. Again, for practical purposes, the key is to remember whether the quotient is positive or negative.

$$\frac{-16}{-4} = \frac{|-16|}{|-4|} = \frac{16}{4} = 4 \qquad \frac{28}{-7} = -\left(\frac{|28|}{|-7|}\right) = -\left(\frac{28}{7}\right) = -4$$

$$\frac{-3.6}{4} = -\left(\frac{|-3.6|}{|4|}\right) = -\left(\frac{3.6}{4}\right) = -0.9 \qquad \frac{0}{\frac{7}{8}} = 0$$

Now let's simplify some numerical expressions that involve the four basic operations with real numbers. Remember that multiplications and divisions are done first, from left to right, before additions and subtractions are performed.

EXAMPLE 5

Simplify $-2\frac{1}{3} + 4\left(-\frac{2}{3}\right) - (-5)\left(-\frac{1}{3}\right)$

Solution

$$-2\frac{1}{3} + 4\left(-\frac{2}{3}\right) - (-5)\left(-\frac{1}{3}\right) = -2\frac{1}{3} + \left(-\frac{8}{3}\right) + \left(-\frac{5}{3}\right)$$

$$= -\frac{7}{3} + \left(-\frac{8}{3}\right) + \left(-\frac{5}{3}\right) \quad \text{Change to improper fraction.}$$

$$= -\frac{20}{3} \qquad ■$$

EXAMPLE 6

Simplify $-24 \div 4 + 8(-5) - (-5)(3)$.

Solution

$$-24 \div 4 + 8(-5) - (-5)(3) = -6 + (-40) - (-15)$$

$$= -6 + (-40) + 15$$

$$= -31 \qquad ■$$

EXAMPLE 7

Simplify $-7.3 - 2[-4.6(6 - 7)]$.

Solution

$$-7.3 - 2[-4.6(6 - 7)] = -7.3 - 2[-4.6(-1)] = -7.3 - 2[4.6]$$

$$= -7.3 - 9.2$$

$$= -7.3 + (-9.2)$$

$$= -16.5 \qquad ■$$

EXAMPLE 8

Simplify $[3(-7) - 2(9)][5(-7) + 3(9)]$.

Solution

$$[3(-7) - 2(9)][5(-7) + 3(9)] = [-21 - 18][-35 + 27]$$

$$= [-39][-8]$$

$$= 312 \qquad ■$$

Problem Set 1.2

For Problems 1–50, perform the following operations with real numbers.

1. $8 + (-15)$

2. $9 + (-18)$

3. $(-12) + (-7)$

4. $(-7) + (-14)$

5. $-8 - 14$

6. $-17 - 9$

7. $9 - 16$

8. $8 - 22$

9. $(-9)(-12)$

10. $(-6)(-13)$

11. $(5)(-14)$

12. $(-17)(4)$

13. $(-56) \div (-4)$

14. $(-81) \div (-3)$

15. $\dfrac{-112}{16}$

16. $\dfrac{-75}{5}$

17. $-2\dfrac{3}{8} + 5\dfrac{7}{8}$

18. $-1\dfrac{1}{5} + 3\dfrac{4}{5}$

19. $4\dfrac{1}{3} - \left(-1\dfrac{1}{6}\right)$

20. $1\dfrac{1}{12} - \left(-5\dfrac{3}{4}\right)$

21. $\left(-\dfrac{1}{3}\right)\left(\dfrac{2}{5}\right)$

22. $(-8)\left(\dfrac{1}{3}\right)$

23. $\dfrac{1}{2} \div \left(-\dfrac{1}{8}\right)$

24. $\dfrac{2}{3} \div \left(-\dfrac{1}{6}\right)$

25. $0 \div (-14)$

26. $(-19) \div 0$

27. $(-21) \div 0$

28. $0 \div (-11)$

29. $-21 - 39$

30. $-23 - 38$

31. $-17.3 + 12.5$

32. $-16.3 + 19.6$

33. $21.42 - 7.29$

34. $2.73 - 8.14$

35. $-21.4 - (-14.9)$

36. $-32.6 - (-9.8)$

37. $(5.4)(-7.2)$

38. $(-8.5)(-3.3)$

39. $\dfrac{-1.2}{-6}$

40. $\dfrac{-6.3}{0.7}$

41. $\left(-\dfrac{1}{3}\right) + \left(-\dfrac{3}{4}\right)$

42. $-\dfrac{5}{6} + \dfrac{3}{8}$

43. $-\dfrac{3}{2} - \left(-\dfrac{3}{4}\right)$

44. $\dfrac{5}{8} - \dfrac{11}{12}$

45. $-\dfrac{2}{3} - \dfrac{7}{9}$

46. $\dfrac{5}{6} - \left(-\dfrac{2}{9}\right)$

47. $\left(-\dfrac{3}{4}\right)\left(\dfrac{4}{5}\right)$

48. $\left(\dfrac{1}{2}\right)\left(-\dfrac{4}{5}\right)$

49. $\dfrac{3}{4} \div \left(-\dfrac{1}{2}\right)$

50. $\left(-\dfrac{5}{6}\right) \div \left(-\dfrac{7}{8}\right)$

For Problems 51–90, simplify each numerical expression.

51. $9 - 12 - 8 + 5 - 6$

52. $6 - 9 + 11 - 8 - 7 + 14$

53. $-21 + (-17) - 11 + 15 - (-10)$

54. $-16 - (-14) + 16 + 17 - 19$

55. $7\dfrac{1}{8} - \left(2\dfrac{1}{4} - 3\dfrac{7}{8}\right)$

56. $-4\dfrac{3}{5} - \left(1\dfrac{1}{5} - 2\dfrac{3}{10}\right)$

57. $16 - 18 + 19 - [14 - 22 - (31 - 41)]$

58. $-19 - [15 - 13 - (-12 + 8)]$

59. $[14 - (16 - 18)] - [32 - (8 - 9)]$

60. $[-17 - (14 - 18)] - [21 - (-6 - 5)]$

61. $4\dfrac{1}{12} - \dfrac{1}{2}\left(\dfrac{1}{3}\right)$

62. $-\dfrac{4}{5} - \dfrac{1}{2}\left(-\dfrac{3}{5}\right)$

63. $-5 + (-2)(7) - (-3)(8)$

64. $-9 - 4(-2) + (-7)(6)$

65. $\dfrac{2}{5}\left(-\dfrac{3}{4}\right) - \left(-\dfrac{1}{2}\right)\left(\dfrac{3}{5}\right)$

66. $-\dfrac{2}{3}\left(\dfrac{1}{4}\right) + \left(-\dfrac{1}{3}\right)\left(\dfrac{5}{4}\right)$

67. $(-6)(-9) + (-7)(4)$

68. $(-7)(-7) - (-6)(4)$

69. $3(5 - 9) - 3(-6)$

70. $7(8 - 9) + (-6)(4)$

71. $(6 - 11)(4 - 9)$

72. $(7 - 12)(-3 - 2)$

73. $-6(-3 - 9 - 1)$

74. $-8(-3 - 4 - 6)$

75. $56 \div (-8) - (-6) \div (-2)$

76. $-65 \div 5 - (-13)(-2) + (-36) \div 12$

77. $-3[5 - (-2)] - 2(-4 - 9)$

78. $-2(-7 + 13) + 6(-3 - 2)$

79. $\dfrac{-6 + 24}{-3} + \dfrac{-7}{-6 - 1}$

80. $\dfrac{-12 + 20}{-4} + \dfrac{-7 - 11}{-9}$

81. $14.1 - (17.2 - 13.6)$

82. $-9.3 - (10.4 + 12.8)$

83. $3(2.1) - 4(3.2) - 2(-1.6)$

84. $5(-1.6) - 3(2.7) + 5(6.6)$

85. $7(6.2 - 7.1) - 6(-1.4 - 2.9)$

86. $-3(2.2 - 4.5) - 2(1.9 + 4.5)$

87. $\dfrac{2}{3} - \left(\dfrac{3}{4} - \dfrac{5}{6}\right)$

88. $-\dfrac{1}{2} - \left(\dfrac{3}{8} + \dfrac{1}{4}\right)$

89. $3\left(\dfrac{1}{2}\right) + 4\left(\dfrac{2}{3}\right) - 2\left(\dfrac{5}{6}\right)$

90. $2\left(\dfrac{3}{8}\right) - 5\left(\dfrac{1}{2}\right) + 6\left(\dfrac{3}{4}\right)$

91. Use a calculator to check your answers for Problems 51–86.

92. A scuba diver was 32 feet below sea level when he noticed that his partner had his extra knife. He ascended 13 feet to meet his partner and then continued to dive down for another 50 feet. How far below sea level is the diver?

93. Jeff played 18 holes of golf on Saturday. On each of 6 holes he was 1 under par, on each of 4 holes he was 2 over par, on 1 hole he was 3 over par, on each of 2 holes he shot par, and on each of 5 holes he was 1 over par. How did he finish relative to par?

94. After dieting for 30 days, Ignacio has lost 18 pounds. What number describes his average weight change per day?

95. Michael bet $5 on each of the 9 races at the racetrack. His only winnings were $28.50 on one race. How much did he win (or lose) for the day?

96. Max bought a piece of trim molding that measured $11\dfrac{3}{8}$ feet in length. Because of defects in the wood, he had to trim $1\dfrac{5}{8}$ feet off one end, and he also had to remove $\dfrac{3}{4}$ of a foot off the other end. How long was the piece of molding after he trimmed the ends?

97. Natasha recorded the daily gains or losses for her company stock for a week. On Monday it gained 1.25 dollars; on Tuesday it gained 0.88 dollars; on Wednesday it lost 0.50 dollars; on Thursday it lost 1.13 dollars; on Friday it gained 0.38 dollars. What was the net gain (or loss) for the week?

98. On a summer day in Florida, the afternoon temperature was 96°F. After a thunderstorm, the temperature dropped 8°F. What would be the temperature if the sun came back out and the temperature rose 5°F?

99. In an attempt to lighten a dragster, the racing team exchanged two rear wheels for wheels that each weighed 15.6 pounds less. They also exchanged the crankshaft for one that weighed 4.8 pounds less. They changed the rear axle for one that weighed 23.7 pounds less but had to add an additional roll bar that weighed 10.6 pounds. If they wanted to lighten the dragster by 50 pounds, did they meet their goal?

100. A large corporation has five divisions. Two of the divisions had earnings of $2,300,000 each. The other three divisions had a loss of $1,450,000, a loss of $640,000, and a gain of $1,850,000, respectively. What was the net gain (or loss) of the corporation for the year?

■ ■ ■ THOUGHTS INTO WORDS

101. Explain why $\dfrac{0}{8} = 0$, but $\dfrac{8}{0}$ is undefined.

102. The following simplification problem is incorrect. The answer should be -11. Find and correct the error.

$$8 \div (-4)(2) - 3(4) \div 2 + (-1) = (-2)(2) - 12 \div 1$$
$$= -4 - 12$$
$$= -16$$

1.3   Properties of Real Numbers and the Use of Exponents

At the beginning of this section we will list and briefly discuss some of the basic properties of real numbers. Be sure that you understand these properties, for they not only facilitate manipulations with real numbers but also serve as the basis for many algebraic computations.

Closure Property for Addition

If a and b are real numbers, then $a + b$ is a unique real number.

Closure Property for Multiplication

If a and b are real numbers, then ab is a unique real number.

We say that the set of real numbers is *closed* with respect to addition and also with respect to multiplication. That is, the sum of two real numbers is a unique real number, and the product of two real numbers is a unique real number. We use the word *unique* to indicate *exactly one*.

Commutative Property of Addition

If a and b are real numbers, then

$$a + b = b + a$$

Commutative Property of Multiplication

If a and b are real numbers, then

$$ab = ba$$

We say that addition and multiplication are commutative operations. This means that the order in which we add or multiply two numbers does not affect the result. For example, $6 + (-8) = (-8) + 6$ and $(-4)(-3) = (-3)(-4)$. It is also important to realize that subtraction and division are *not* commutative operations; order *does* make a difference. For example, $3 - 4 = -1$ but $4 - 3 = 1$. Likewise, $2 \div 1 = 2$ but $1 \div 2 = \dfrac{1}{2}$.

Associative Property of Addition

If a, b, and c are real numbers, then

$$(a + b) + c = a + (b + c)$$

Associative Property of Multiplication

If a, b, and c are real numbers, then

$$(ab)c = a(bc)$$

Addition and multiplication are **binary operations**. That is, we add (or multiply) two numbers at a time. The associative properties apply if more than two numbers are to be added or multiplied; they are grouping properties. For example, $(-8 + 9) + 6 = -8 + (9 + 6)$; changing the grouping of the numbers does not affect the final sum. This is also true for multiplication, which is illustrated by $[(-4)(-3)](2) = (-4)[(-3)(2)]$. Subtraction and division are *not* associative operations. For example, $(8 - 6) - 10 = -8$, but $8 - (6 - 10) = 12$. An example showing that division is not associative is $(8 \div 4) \div 2 = 1$, but $8 \div (4 \div 2) = 4$.

Identity Property of Addition

If a is any real number, then

$$a + 0 = 0 + a = a$$

Zero is called the identity element for addition. This merely means that the sum of any real number and zero is identically the same real number. For example, $-87 + 0 = 0 + (-87) = -87$.

Identity Property of Multiplication

If a is any real number, then

$$a(1) = 1(a) = a$$

We call 1 the identity element for multiplication. The product of any real number and 1 is identically the same real number. For example, $(-119)(1) = (1)(-119) = -119$.

Additive Inverse Property

For every real number a, there exists a unique real number $-a$ such that

$$a + (-a) = -a + a = 0$$

The real number $-a$ is called the **additive inverse of a** or the **opposite of a**. For example, 16 and -16 are additive inverses, and their sum is 0. The additive inverse of 0 is 0.

Multiplication Property of Zero

If a is any real number, then

$$(a)(0) = (0)(a) = 0$$

The product of any real number and zero is zero. For example, $(-17)(0) = 0(-17) = 0$.

Multiplication Property of Negative One

If a is any real number, then

$$(a)(-1) = (-1)(a) = -a$$

The product of any real number and -1 is the opposite of the real number. For example, $(-1)(52) = (52)(-1) = -52$.

Multiplicative Inverse Property

For every nonzero real number a, there exists a unique real number $\dfrac{1}{a}$ such that

$$a\left(\frac{1}{a}\right) = \frac{1}{a}(a) = 1$$

The number $\dfrac{1}{a}$ is called the **multiplicative inverse of a** or the **reciprocal of a**. For example, the reciprocal of 2 is $\dfrac{1}{2}$ and $2\left(\dfrac{1}{2}\right) = \dfrac{1}{2}(2) = 1$. Likewise, the reciprocal of $\frac{1}{2}$ is $\frac{1}{\frac{1}{2}} = 2$. Therefore, 2 and $\frac{1}{2}$ are said to be reciprocals (or multiplicative inverses) of each other. Because division by zero is undefined, zero does not have a reciprocal.

Distributive Property

> If a, b, and c are real numbers, then
>
> $$a(b + c) = ab + ac$$

The distributive property ties together the operations of addition and multiplication. We say that **multiplication distributes over addition**. For example, $7(3 + 8) = 7(3) + 7(8)$. Because $b - c = b + (-c)$, it follows that **multiplication also distributes over subtraction**. This can be expressed symbolically as $a(b - c) = ab - ac$. For example, $6(8 - 10) = 6(8) - 6(10)$.

The following examples illustrate the use of the properties of real numbers to facilitate certain types of manipulations.

EXAMPLE 1

Simplify $[74 + (-36)] + 36$.

Solution

In such a problem, it is much more advantageous to group -36 and 36.

$$[74 + (-36)] + 36 = 74 + [(-36) + 36] \quad \text{By using the associative property for addition}$$
$$= 74 + 0 = 74$$

EXAMPLE 2

Simplify $[(-19)(25)](-4)$.

Solution

It is much easier to group 25 and -4. Thus

$$[(-19)(25)](-4) = (-19)[(25)(-4)] \quad \text{By using the associative property for multiplication}$$
$$= (-19)(-100)$$
$$= 1900$$

EXAMPLE 3

Simplify $17 + (-14) + (-18) + 13 + (-21) + 15 + (-33)$.

Solution

We could add in the order in which the numbers appear. However, because addition is commutative and associative, we could change the order and group in any convenient way. For example, we could add all of the positive integers and add all of the negative integers, and then find the sum of these two results. It might be convenient to use the vertical format as follows:

$$
\begin{array}{ccc}
 & -14 & \\
17 & -18 & \\
13 & -21 & -86 \\
\dfrac{15}{45} & \dfrac{-33}{-86} & \dfrac{45}{-41}
\end{array}
$$

∎

EXAMPLE 4

Simplify $-25(-2 + 100)$.

Solution

For this problem, it might be easiest to apply the distributive property first and then simplify.

$$
\begin{aligned}
-25(-2 + 100) &= (-25)(-2) + (-25)(100) \\
&= 50 + (-2500) \\
&= -2450
\end{aligned}
$$

∎

EXAMPLE 5

Simplify $(-87)(-26 + 25)$.

Solution

For this problem, it would be better not to apply the distributive property but instead to add the numbers inside the parentheses first and then find the indicated product.

$$
\begin{aligned}
(-87)(-26 + 25) &= (-87)(-1) \\
&= 87
\end{aligned}
$$

∎

EXAMPLE 6

Simplify $3.7(104) + 3.7(-4)$.

Solution

Remember that the distributive property allows us to change from the form $a(b + c)$ to $ab + ac$ or from the form $ab + ac$ to $a(b + c)$. In this problem, we want to use the latter change. Thus

$$
\begin{aligned}
3.7(104) + 3.7(-4) &= 3.7[104 + (-4)] \\
&= 3.7(100) \\
&= 370
\end{aligned}
$$

∎

Examples 4, 5, and 6 illustrate an important issue. Sometimes the form $a(b + c)$ is more convenient, but at other times the form $ab + ac$ is better. In these cases, as well as in the cases of other properties, you should *think first* and decide whether or not the properties can be used to make the manipulations easier.

■ Exponents

Exponents are used to indicate repeated multiplication. For example, we can write $4 \cdot 4 \cdot 4$ as 4^3, where the "raised 3" indicates that 4 is to be used as a factor 3 times. The following general definition is helpful.

Definition 1.2

If n is a positive integer and b is any real number, then

$$b^n = \underbrace{bbb \cdots b}_{n \text{ factors of } b}$$

We refer to the b as the **base** and to n as the **exponent**. The expression b^n can be read "b to the nth power." We commonly associate the terms *squared* and *cubed* with exponents of 2 and 3, respectively. For example, b^2 is read "b squared" and b^3 as "b cubed." An exponent of 1 is usually not written, so b^1 is written as b. The following examples illustrate Definition 1.2.

$$2^3 = 2 \cdot 2 \cdot 2 = 8 \qquad \left(\frac{1}{2}\right)^5 = \frac{1}{2} \cdot \frac{1}{2} \cdot \frac{1}{2} \cdot \frac{1}{2} \cdot \frac{1}{2} = \frac{1}{32}$$

$$3^4 = 3 \cdot 3 \cdot 3 \cdot 3 = 81 \qquad (0.7)^2 = (0.7)(0.7) = 0.49$$

$$-5^2 = -(5 \cdot 5) = -25 \qquad (-5)^2 = (-5)(-5) = 25$$

Please take special note of the last two examples. Note that $(-5)^2$ means that -5 is the base and is to be used as a factor twice. However, -5^2 means that 5 is the base and that after it is squared, we take the opposite of that result.

Simplifying numerical expressions that contain exponents creates no trouble if we keep in mind that exponents are used to indicate repeated multiplication. Let's consider some examples.

E X A M P L E   7   Simplify $3(-4)^2 + 5(-3)^2$.

Solution

$$3(-4)^2 + 5(-3)^2 = 3(16) + 5(9) \qquad \text{Find the powers.}$$

$$= 48 + 45$$

$$= 93$$

■

EXAMPLE 8 Simplify $(2 + 3)^2$

Solution

$$(2 + 3)^2 = (5)^2 \qquad \text{Add inside the parentheses before applying the exponent.}$$

$$= 25 \qquad \text{Square the 5.} \qquad \blacksquare$$

EXAMPLE 9 Simplify $[3(-1) - 2(1)]^3$.

Solution

$$[3(-1) - 2(1)]^3 = [-3 - 2]^3$$

$$= [-5]^3$$

$$= -125 \qquad \blacksquare$$

EXAMPLE 10 Simplify $4\left(\dfrac{1}{2}\right)^3 - 3\left(\dfrac{1}{2}\right)^2 + 6\left(\dfrac{1}{2}\right) + 2$.

Solution

$$4\left(\frac{1}{2}\right)^3 - 3\left(\frac{1}{2}\right)^2 + 6\left(\frac{1}{2}\right) + 2 = 4\left(\frac{1}{8}\right) - 3\left(\frac{1}{4}\right) + 6\left(\frac{1}{2}\right) + 2$$

$$= \frac{1}{2} - \frac{3}{4} + 3 + 2$$

$$= \frac{19}{4} \qquad \blacksquare$$

Problem Set 1.3

For Problems 1–14, state the property that justifies each of the statements. For example, $3 + (-4) = (-4) + 3$ because of the commutative property of addition.

1. $[6 + (-2)] + 4 = 6 + [(-2) + 4]$

2. $x(3) = 3(x)$

3. $42 + (-17) = -17 + 42$

4. $1(x) = x$

5. $-114 + 114 = 0$

6. $(-1)(48) = -48$

7. $-1(x + y) = -(x + y)$

8. $-3(2 + 4) = -3(2) + (-3)(4)$

9. $12yx = 12xy$

10. $[(-7)(4)](-25) = (-7)[4(-25)]$

11. $7(4) + 9(4) = (7 + 9)4$

12. $(x + 3) + (-3) = x + [3 + (-3)]$

13. $[(-14)(8)](25) = (-14)[8(25)]$

14. $\left(\dfrac{3}{4}\right)\left(\dfrac{4}{3}\right) = 1$

For Problems 15–26, simplify each numerical expression. Be sure to take advantage of the properties whenever they can be used to make the computations easier.

15. $36 + (-14) + (-12) + 21 + (-9) - 4$

16. $-37 + 42 + 18 + 37 + (-42) - 6$

17. $[83 + (-99)] + 18$ **18.** $[63 + (-87)] + (-64)$

19. $(25)(-13)(4)$ **20.** $(14)(25)(-13)(4)$

21. $17(97) + 17(3)$ **22.** $-86[49 + (-48)]$

23. $14 - 12 - 21 - 14 + 17 - 18 + 19 - 32$

24. $16 - 14 - 13 - 18 + 19 + 14 - 17 + 21$

25. $(-50)(15)(-2) - (-4)(17)(25)$

26. $(2)(17)(-5) - (4)(13)(-25)$

For Problems 27–54, simplify each of the numerical expressions.

27. $2^3 - 3^3$ **28.** $3^2 - 2^4$

29. $-5^2 - 4^2$ **30.** $-7^2 + 5^2$

31. $(-2)^3 - 3^2$ **32.** $(-3)^3 + 3^2$

33. $3(-1)^3 - 4(3)^2$ **34.** $4(-2)^3 - 3(-1)^4$

35. $7(2)^3 + 4(-2)^3$ **36.** $-4(-1)^2 - 3(2)^3$

37. $-3(-2)^3 + 4(-1)^5$ **38.** $5(-1)^3 - (-3)^3$

39. $(-3)^2 - 3(-2)(5) + 4^2$

40. $(-2)^2 - 3(-2)(6) - (-5)^2$

41. $2^3 + 3(-1)^3(-2)^2 - 5(-1)(2)^2$

42. $-2(3)^2 - 2(-2)^3 - 6(-1)^5$

43. $(3 + 4)^2$ **44.** $(4 - 9)^2$

45. $[3(-2)^2 - 2(-3)^2]^3$

46. $[-3(-1)^3 - 4(-2)^2]^2$

47. $2(-1)^3 - 3(-1)^2 + 4(-1) - 5$

48. $(-2)^3 + 2(-2)^2 - 3(-2) - 1$

49. $2^4 - 2(2)^3 - 3(2)^2 + 7(2) - 10$

50. $3(-3)^3 + 4(-3)^2 - 5(-3) + 7$

51. $3\left(\dfrac{1}{2}\right)^4 - 2\left(\dfrac{1}{2}\right)^3 + 5\left(\dfrac{1}{2}\right)^2 - 4\left(\dfrac{1}{2}\right) + 1$

52. $4(0.1)^2 - 6(0.1) + 0.7$

53. $-\left(\dfrac{2}{3}\right)^2 + 5\left(\dfrac{2}{3}\right) - 4$

54. $4\left(\dfrac{1}{3}\right)^3 + 3\left(\dfrac{1}{3}\right)^2 + 2\left(\dfrac{1}{3}\right) + 6$

C 55. Use your calculator to check your answers for Problems 27–52.

C For Problems 56–64, use your calculator to evaluate each numerical expression.

56. 2^{10} **57.** 3^7

58. $(-2)^8$ **59.** $(-2)^{11}$

60. -4^9 **61.** -5^6

62. $(3.14)^3$ **63.** $(1.41)^4$

64. $(1.73)^5$

The symbol, **C**, signals a problem that requires a calculator.

■ ■ ■ THOUGHTS INTO WORDS

65. State, in your own words, the multiplication property of negative one.

66. Explain how the associative and commutative properties can help simplify $[(25)(97)](-4)$.

67. Your friend keeps getting an answer of 64 when simplifying -2^6. What mistake is he making, and how would you help him?

68. Write a sentence explaining in your own words how to evaluate the expression $(-8)^2$. Also write a sentence explaining how to evaluate -8^2.

69. For what natural numbers n does $(-1)^n = -1$? For what natural numbers n does $(-1)^n = 1$? Explain your answers.

70. Is the set $\{0, 1\}$ closed with respect to addition? Is the set $\{0, 1\}$ closed with respect to multiplication? Explain your answers.

1.4 Algebraic Expressions

Algebraic expressions such as

$$2x, \qquad 8xy, \qquad 3xy^2, \qquad -4a^2b^3c, \qquad \text{and} \qquad z$$

are called **terms**. A term is an indicated product that may have any number of factors. The variables involved in a term are called **literal factors**, and the numerical factor is called the **numerical coefficient**. Thus in $8xy$, the x and y are literal factors, and 8 is the numerical coefficient. The numerical coefficient of the term $-4a^2bc$ is -4. Because $1(z) = z$, the numerical coefficient of the term z is understood to be 1. Terms that have the same literal factors are called **similar terms** or **like terms**. Some examples of similar terms are

$$3x \quad \text{and} \quad 14x \qquad\qquad 5x^2 \quad \text{and} \quad 18x^2$$

$$7xy \quad \text{and} \quad -9xy \qquad\qquad 9x^2y \quad \text{and} \quad -14x^2y$$

$$2x^3y^2, \quad 3x^3y^2, \quad \text{and} \quad -7x^3y^2$$

By the symmetric property of equality, we can write the distributive property as

$$ab + ac = a(b + c)$$

Then the commutative property of multiplication can be applied to change the form to

$$ba + ca = (b + c)a$$

This latter form provides the basis for simplifying algebraic expressions by **combining similar terms**. Consider the following examples.

$$3x + 5x = (3 + 5)x \qquad\qquad -6xy + 4xy = (-6 + 4)xy$$

$$= 8x \qquad\qquad\qquad\qquad = -2xy$$

$$5x^2 + 7x^2 + 9x^2 = (5 + 7 + 9)x^2 \qquad 4x - x = 4x - 1x$$

$$= 21x^2 \qquad\qquad\qquad\qquad = (4 - 1)x = 3x$$

More complicated expressions might require that we first rearrange the terms by applying the commutative property for addition.

$$7x + 2y + 9x + 6y = 7x + 9x + 2y + 6y$$

$$= (7 + 9)x + (2 + 6)y \qquad \text{Distributive property}$$

$$= 16x + 8y$$

$$6a - 5 - 11a + 9 = 6a + (-5) + (-11a) + 9$$

$$= 6a + (-11a) + (-5) + 9 \qquad \text{Commutative property}$$

$$= (6 + (-11))a + 4 \qquad\qquad \text{Distributive property}$$

$$= -5a + 4$$

As soon as you thoroughly understand the various simplifying steps, you may want to do the steps mentally. Then you could go directly from the given expression to the simplified form, as follows:

$$14x + 13y - 9x + 2y = 5x + 15y$$

$$3x^2y - 2y + 5x^2y + 8y = 8x^2y + 6y$$

$$-4x^2 + 5y^2 - x^2 - 7y^2 = -5x^2 - 2y^2$$

Applying the distributive property to remove parentheses and then to combine similar terms sometimes simplifies an algebraic expression (as the next examples illustrate).

$$
\begin{aligned}
4(x + 2) + 3(x + 6) &= 4(x) + 4(2) + 3(x) + 3(6) \\
&= 4x + 8 + 3x + 18 \\
&= 4x + 3x + 8 + 18 \\
&= (4 + 3)x + 26 \\
&= 7x + 26
\end{aligned}
$$

$$
\begin{aligned}
-5(y + 3) - 2(y - 8) &= -5(y) - 5(3) - 2(y) - 2(-8) \\
&= -5y - 15 - 2y + 16 \\
&= -5y - 2y - 15 + 16 \\
&= -7y + 1
\end{aligned}
$$

$$
\begin{aligned}
5(x - y) - (x + y) &= 5(x - y) - 1(x + y) \qquad \text{Remember, } -a = -1(a). \\
&= 5(x) - 5(y) - 1(x) - 1(y) \\
&= 5x - 5y - 1x - 1y \\
&= 4x - 6y
\end{aligned}
$$

When we are multiplying two terms such as 3 and $2x$, the associative property for multiplication provides the basis for simplifying the product.

$$3(2x) = (3 \cdot 2)x = 6x$$

This idea is put to use in the following example.

$$
\begin{aligned}
3(2x + 5y) + 4(3x + 2y) &= 3(2x) + 3(5y) + 4(3x) + 4(2y) \\
&= 6x + 15y + 12x + 8y \\
&= 6x + 12x + 15y + 8y \\
&= 18x + 23y
\end{aligned}
$$

After you are sure of each step, a more simplified format may be used, as the following examples illustrate.

$$
\begin{aligned}
5(a + 4) - 7(a + 3) &= 5a + 20 - 7a - 21 \qquad \text{Be careful with this sign.} \\
&= -2a - 1
\end{aligned}
$$

$$3(x^2 + 2) + 4(x^2 - 6) = 3x^2 + 6 + 4x^2 - 24$$
$$= 7x^2 - 18$$
$$2(3x - 4y) - 5(2x - 6y) = 6x - 8y - 10x + 30y$$
$$= -4x + 22y$$

■ Evaluating Algebraic Expressions

An algebraic expression takes on a numerical value whenever each variable in the expression is replaced by a real number. For example, if x is replaced by 5 and y by 9, the algebraic expression $x + y$ becomes the numerical expression $5 + 9$, which simplifies to 14. We say that $x + y$ has a value of 14 when x equals 5 and y equals 9. If $x = -3$ and $y = 7$, then $x + y$ has a value of $-3 + 7 = 4$. The following examples illustrate the process of finding a value of an algebraic expression. We commonly refer to the process as **evaluating algebraic expressions**.

EXAMPLE 1

Find the value of $3x - 4y$ when $x = 2$ and $y = -3$.

Solution

$$3x - 4y = 3(2) - 4(-3), \quad \text{when } x = 2 \text{ and } y = -3$$
$$= 6 + 12$$
$$= 18 \qquad \blacksquare$$

EXAMPLE 2

Evaluate $x^2 - 2xy + y^2$ for $x = -2$ and $y = -5$.

Solution

$$x^2 - 2xy + y^2 = (-2)^2 - 2(-2)(-5) + (-5)^2, \quad \text{when } x = -2 \text{ and } y = -5$$
$$= 4 - 20 + 25$$
$$= 9 \qquad \blacksquare$$

EXAMPLE 3

Evaluate $(a + b)^2$ for $a = 6$ and $b = -2$.

Solution

$$(a + b)^2 = [6 + (-2)]^2, \quad \text{when } a = 6 \text{ and } b = -2$$
$$= (4)^2$$
$$= 16 \qquad \blacksquare$$

E X A M P L E   4

Evaluate $(3x + 2y)(2x - y)$ for $x = 4$ and $y = -1$.

Solution

$$(3x + 2y)(2x - y) = [3(4) + 2(-1)][2(4) - (-1)] \quad \text{when } x = 4$$
$$\text{and } y = -1$$

$$= (12 - 2)(8 + 1)$$

$$= (10)(9)$$

$$= 90 \qquad \blacksquare$$

E X A M P L E   5

Evaluate $7x - 2y + 4x - 3y$ for $x = -\dfrac{1}{2}$ and $y = \dfrac{2}{3}$.

Solution

Let's first simplify the given expression.

$$7x - 2y + 4x - 3y = 11x - 5y$$

Now we can substitute $-\dfrac{1}{2}$ for x and $\dfrac{2}{3}$ for y.

$$11x - 5y = 11\left(-\frac{1}{2}\right) - 5\left(\frac{2}{3}\right)$$

$$= -\frac{11}{2} - \frac{10}{3}$$

$$= -\frac{33}{6} - \frac{20}{6} \qquad \text{Change to equivalent fractions}$$
$$\text{with a common denominator.}$$

$$= -\frac{53}{6} \qquad \blacksquare$$

E X A M P L E   6

Evaluate $2(3x + 1) - 3(4x - 3)$ for $x = -6.2$.

Solution

Let's first simplify the given expression.

$$2(3x + 1) - 3(4x - 3) = 6x + 2 - 12x + 9$$

$$= -6x + 11$$

Now we can substitute -6.2 for x.

$$-6x + 11 = -6(-6.2) + 11$$

$$= 37.2 + 11$$

$$= 48.2 \qquad \blacksquare$$

EXAMPLE 7   Evaluate $2(a^2 + 1) - 3(a^2 + 5) + 4(a^2 - 1)$ for $a = 10$.

Solution

Let's first simplify the given expression.

$$2(a^2 + 1) - 3(a^2 + 5) + 4(a^2 - 1) = 2a^2 + 2 - 3a^2 - 15 + 4a^2 - 4$$
$$= 3a^2 - 17$$

Substituting $a = 10$, we obtain

$$3a^2 - 17 = 3(10)^2 - 17$$
$$= 3(100) - 17$$
$$= 300 - 17$$
$$= 283 \qquad \blacksquare$$

■ Translating from English to Algebra

To use the tools of algebra to solve problems, we must be able to translate from English to algebra. This translation process requires that we recognize key phrases in the English language that translate into algebraic expressions (which involve the operations of addition, subtraction, multiplication, and division). Some of these key phrases and their algebraic counterparts are listed in the following table. The variable n represents the number being referred to in each phrase. When translating, remember that the commutative property holds only for the operations of addition and multiplication. Therefore, order will be crucial to algebraic expressions that involve subtraction and division.

English phrase	Algebraic expression
Addition	
The sum of a number and 4	$n + 4$
7 more than a number	$n + 7$
A number plus 10	$n + 10$
A number increased by 6	$n + 6$
8 added to a number	$n + 8$
Subtraction	
14 minus a number	$14 - n$
12 less than a number	$n - 12$
A number decreased by 10	$n - 10$
The difference between a number and 2	$n - 2$
5 subtracted from a number	$n - 5$

English phrase	Algebraic expression
Multiplication	
14 times a number	$14n$
The product of 4 and a number	$4n$
$\dfrac{3}{4}$ of a number	$\dfrac{3}{4}n$
Twice a number	$2n$
Multiply a number by 12	$12n$
Division	
The quotient of 6 and a number	$\dfrac{6}{n}$
The quotient of a number and 6	$\dfrac{n}{6}$
A number divided by 9	$\dfrac{n}{9}$
The ratio of a number and 4	$\dfrac{n}{4}$
Mixture of operations	
4 more than three times a number	$3n + 4$
5 less than twice a number	$2n - 5$
3 times the sum of a number and 2	$3(n + 2)$
2 more than the quotient of a number and 12	$\dfrac{n}{12} + 2$
7 times the difference of 6 and a number	$7(6 - n)$

An English statement may not always contain a key word such as *sum, difference, product*, or *quotient*. Instead, the statement may describe a physical situation, and from this description we must deduce the operations involved. Some suggestions for handling such situations are given in the following examples.

E X A M P L E   8

Sonya can type 65 words per minute. How many words will she type in m minutes?

Solution

The total number of words typed equals the product of the rate per minute and the number of minutes. Therefore, Sonya should be able to type $65m$ words in m minutes. ∎

EXAMPLE 9

Russ has n nickels and d dimes. Express this amount of money in cents.

Solution

Each nickel is worth 5 cents and each dime is worth 10 cents. We represent the amount in cents by $5n + 10d$. ∎

EXAMPLE 10

The cost of a 50-pound sack of fertilizer is d dollars. What is the cost per pound for the fertilizer?

Solution

We calculate the cost per pound by dividing the total cost by the number of pounds. We represent the cost per pound by $\dfrac{d}{50}$. ∎

The English statement we want to translate into algebra may contain some geometric ideas. Tables 1.1 and 1.2 contain some of the basic relationships that pertain to linear measurement in the English and metric systems, respectively.

Table 1.1 English system
12 inches = 1 foot
3 feet = 1 yard
1760 yards = 1 mile
5280 feet = 1 mile

Table 1.2 Metric system	
1 kilometer =	1000 meters
1 hectometer =	100 meters
1 dekameter =	10 meters
1 decimeter =	0.1 meter
1 centimeter =	0.01 meter
1 millimeter =	0.001 meter

EXAMPLE 11

The distance between two cities is k kilometers. Express this distance in meters.

Solution

Because 1 kilometer equals 1000 meters, the distance in meters is represented by $1000k$. ∎

EXAMPLE 12

The length of a rope is y yards and f feet. Express this length in inches.

Solution

Because 1 foot equals 12 inches and 1 yard equals 36 inches, the length of the rope in inches can be represented by $36y + 12f$. ∎

E X A M P L E   1 3   The length of a rectangle is l centimeters and the width is w centimeters. Express the perimeter of the rectangle in meters.

Solution

A sketch of the rectangle may be helpful (Figure 1.7).

l centimeters

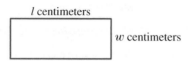

w centimeters

Figure 1.7

The perimeter of a rectangle is the sum of the lengths of the four sides. Thus the perimeter in centimeters is $l + w + l + w$, which simplifies to $2l + 2w$. Now, because 1 centimeter equals 0.01 meter, the perimeter, in meters, is $0.01(2l + 2w)$. This could also be written as $\dfrac{2l + 2w}{100} = \dfrac{2(l + w)}{100} = \dfrac{l + w}{50}$. ■

Problem Set 1.4

Simplify the algebraic expressions in Problems 1–14 by combining similar terms.

1. $-7x + 11x$

2. $5x - 8x + x$

3. $5a^2 - 6a^2$

4. $12b^3 - 17b^3$

5. $4n - 9n - n$

6. $6n + 13n - 15n$

7. $4x - 9x + 2y$

8. $7x - 9y - 10x - 13y$

9. $-3a^2 + 7b^2 + 9a^2 - 2b^2$ **10.** $-xy + z - 8xy - 7z$

11. $15x - 4 + 6x - 9$

12. $5x - 2 - 7x + 4 - x - 1$

13. $5a^2b - ab^2 - 7a^2b$

14. $8xy^2 - 5x^2y + 2xy^2 + 7x^2y$

Simplify the algebraic expressions in Problems 15–34 by removing parentheses and combining similar terms.

15. $3(x + 2) + 5(x + 3)$

16. $5(x - 1) + 7(x + 4)$

17. $-2(a - 4) - 3(a + 2)$

18. $-7(a + 1) - 9(a + 4)$

19. $3(n^2 + 1) - 8(n^2 - 1)$

20. $4(n^2 + 3) + (n^2 - 7)$

21. $-6(x^2 - 5) - (x^2 - 2)$

22. $3(x + y) - 2(x - y)$

23. $5(2x + 1) + 4(3x - 2)$

24. $5(3x - 1) + 6(2x + 3)$

25. $3(2x - 5) - 4(5x - 2)$

26. $3(2x - 3) - 7(3x - 1)$

27. $-2(n^2 - 4) - 4(2n^2 + 1)$

28. $-4(n^2 + 3) - (2n^2 - 7)$

29. $3(2x - 4y) - 2(x + 9y)$

30. $-7(2x - 3y) + 9(3x + y)$

31. $3(2x - 1) - 4(x + 2) - 5(3x + 4)$

32. $-2(x - 1) - 5(2x + 1) + 4(2x - 7)$

33. $-(3x - 1) - 2(5x - 1) + 4(-2x - 3)$

34. $4(-x - 1) + 3(-2x - 5) - 2(x + 1)$

Evaluate the algebraic expressions in Problems 35–57 for the given values of the variables.

35. $3x + 7y$, $x = -1$ and $y = -2$

36. $5x - 9y$, $x = -2$ and $y = 5$

37. $4x^2 - y^2$, $x = 2$ and $y = -2$

38. $3a^2 + 2b^2$, $a = 2$ and $b = 5$

39. $2a^2 - ab + b^2$, $a = -1$ and $b = -2$

40. $-x^2 + 2xy + 3y^2$, $x = -3$ and $y = 3$

41. $2x^2 - 4xy - 3y^2$, $x = 1$ and $y = -1$

42. $4x^2 + xy - y^2$, $x = 3$ and $y = -2$

43. $3xy - x^2y^2 + 2y^2$, $x = 5$ and $y = -1$

44. $x^2y^3 - 2xy + x^2y^2$, $x = -1$ and $y = -3$

45. $7a - 2b - 9a + 3b$, $a = 4$ and $b = -6$

46. $-4x + 9y - 3x - y$, $x = -4$ and $y = 7$

47. $(x - y)^2$, $x = 5$ and $y = -3$

48. $2(a + b)^2$, $a = 6$ and $b = -1$

49. $-2a - 3a + 7b - b$, $a = -10$ and $b = 9$

50. $3(x - 2) - 4(x + 3)$, $x = -2$

51. $-2(x + 4) - (2x - 1)$, $x = -3$

52. $-4(2x - 1) + 7(3x + 4)$, $x = 4$

53. $2(x - 1) - (x + 2) - 3(2x - 1)$, $x = -1$

54. $-3(x + 1) + 4(-x - 2) - 3(-x + 4)$, $x = -\dfrac{1}{2}$

55. $3(x^2 - 1) - 4(x^2 + 1) - (2x^2 - 1)$, $x = \dfrac{2}{3}$

56. $2(n^2 + 1) - 3(n^2 - 3) + 3(5n^2 - 2)$, $n = \dfrac{1}{4}$

57. $5(x - 2y) - 3(2x + y) - 2(x - y)$, $x = \dfrac{1}{3}$ and $y = -\dfrac{3}{4}$

☑ For Problems 58–63, use your calculator and evaluate each of the algebraic expressions for the indicated values. Express the final answers to the nearest tenth.

58. πr^2, $\pi = 3.14$ and $r = 2.1$

59. πr^2, $\pi = 3.14$ and $r = 8.4$

60. $\pi r^2 h$, $\pi = 3.14$, $r = 1.6$, and $h = 11.2$

61. $\pi r^2 h$, $\pi = 3.14$, $r = 4.8$, and $h = 15.1$

62. $2\pi r^2 + 2\pi rh$, $\pi = 3.14$, $r = 3.9$, and $h = 17.6$

63. $2\pi r^2 + 2\pi rh$, $\pi = 3.14$, $r = 7.8$, and $h = 21.2$

For Problems 64–78, translate each English phrase into an algebraic expression and use n to represent the unknown number.

64. The sum of a number and 4

65. A number increased by 12

66. A number decreased by 7

67. Five less than a number

68. A number subtracted from 75

69. The product of a number and 50

70. One-third of a number

71. Four less than one-half of a number

72. Seven more than three times a number

73. The quotient of a number and 8

74. The quotient of 50 and a number

75. Nine less than twice a number

76. Six more than one-third of a number

77. Ten times the difference of a number and 6

78. Twelve times the sum of a number and 7

For Problems 79–99, answer the question with an algebraic expression.

79. Brian is n years old. How old will he be in 20 years?

80. Crystal is n years old. How old was she 5 years ago?

81. Pam is t years old, and her mother is 3 less than twice as old as Pam. What is the age of Pam's mother?

82. The sum of two numbers is 65, and one of the numbers is x. What is the other number?

83. The difference of two numbers is 47, and the smaller number is n. What is the other number?

84. The product of two numbers is 98, and one of the numbers is n. What is the other number?

85. The quotient of two numbers is 8, and the smaller number is y. What is the other number?

86. The perimeter of a square is c centimeters. How long is each side of the square?

87. The perimeter of a square is m meters. How long, in centimeters, is each side of the square?

88. Jesse has n nickels, d dimes, and q quarters in his bank. How much money, in cents, does he have in his bank?

89. Tina has c cents, which is all in quarters. How many quarters does she have?

90. If n represents a whole number, what represents the next larger whole number?

91. If n represents an odd integer, what represents the next larger odd integer?

92. If n represents an even integer, what represents the next larger even integer?

93. The cost of a 5-pound box of candy is c cents. What is the price per pound?

The symbol, **C**, signals a problem that requires a calculator.

94. Larry's annual salary is d dollars. What is his monthly salary?

95. Mila's monthly salary is d dollars. What is her annual salary?

96. The perimeter of a square is i inches. What is the perimeter expressed in feet?

97. The perimeter of a rectangle is y yards and f feet. What is the perimeter expressed in feet?

98. The length of a line segment is d decimeters. How long is the line segment expressed in meters?

99. The distance between two cities is m miles. How far is this, expressed in feet?

C 100. Use your calculator to check your answers for Problems 35–54.

■ ■ ■ **THOUGHTS INTO WORDS**

101. Explain the difference between simplifying a numerical expression and evaluating an algebraic expression.

102. How would you help someone who is having difficulty expressing n nickels and d dimes in terms of cents?

103. When asked to write an algebraic expression for "8 more than a number," you wrote $x + 8$ and another student wrote $8 + x$. Are both expressions correct? Explain your answer.

104. When asked to write an algebraic expression for "6 less than a number," you wrote $x - 6$ and another student wrote $6 - x$. Are both expressions correct? Explain your answer.

(1.1) A **set** is a collection of objects; the objects are called **elements** or **members** of the set. Set A is a subset of set B if and only if every member of A is also a member of B. The sets of **natural numbers, whole numbers, integers, rational numbers**, and **irrational numbers** are all subsets of the set of **real numbers**.

We can evaluate **numerical expressions** by performing the operations in the following order.

1. Perform the operations inside the parentheses and above and below fraction bars.

2. Find all powers or convert them to indicated multiplication.

3. Perform all multiplications and divisions in the order in which they appear from left to right.

4. Perform all additions and subtractions in the order in which they appear from left to right.

(1.2) The **absolute value** of a real number a is defined as follows:

1. If $a \geq 0$, then $|a| = a$.

2. If $a < 0$, then $|a| = -a$.

■ Operations with Real Numbers

Addition

1. The sum of two positive real numbers is the sum of their absolute values.

2. The sum of two negative real numbers is the opposite of the sum of their absolute values.

3. The sum of one positive and one negative number is found as follows:

   a. If the positive number has the larger absolute value, then the sum is the difference of their absolute values when the smaller absolute value is subtracted from the larger absolute value.

   b. If the negative number has the larger absolute value, then the sum is the opposite of the difference of their absolute values when the smaller absolute value is subtracted from the larger absolute value.

Subtraction

Applying the principle that $a - b = a + (-b)$ changes every subtraction problem to an equivalent addition problem. Then the rules for addition can be followed.

Multiplication

1. The product of two positive numbers or two negative real numbers is the product of their absolute values.

2. The product of one positive and one negative real number is the opposite of the product of their absolute values.

Division

1. The quotient of two positive numbers or two negative real numbers is the quotient of their absolute values.

2. The quotient of one positive and one negative real number is the opposite of the quotient of their absolute values.

(1.3) The following basic properties of real numbers help with numerical manipulations and serve as a basis for algebraic computations.

■ Closure properties

$a + b$ is a real number

ab is a real number

■ Commutative properties

$a + b = b + a$

$ab = ba$

■ Associative properties

$(a + b) + c = a + (b + c)$

$(ab)c = a(bc)$

■ Identity properties

$a + 0 = 0 + a = a$

$a(1) = 1(a) = a$

■ Additive inverse property

$$a + (-a) = (-a) + a = 0$$

■ Multiplication property of zero

$$a(0) = 0(a) = 0$$

■ Multiplication property of negative one

$$-1(a) = a(-1) = -a$$

■ Multiplicative inverse property

$$a\left(\frac{1}{a}\right) = \left(\frac{1}{a}\right)a = 1$$

■ Distributive properties

$$a(b + c) = ab + ac$$

$$a(b - c) = ab - ac$$

(1.4) Algebraic expressions such as

$$2x, \quad 8xy, \quad 3xy^2, \quad -4a^2b^3c, \quad \text{and} \quad z$$

are called **terms**. A term is an indicated product and may have any number of factors. We call the variables in a term the **literal factors**, and we call the numerical factor the **numerical coefficient**. Terms that have the same literal factors are called **similar** or **like terms**.

The distributive property in the form $ba + ca = (b + c)a$ serves as the basis for **combining similar terms**. For example,

$$3x^2y + 7x^2y = (3 + 7)x^2y = 10x^2y$$

To translate English phrases into algebraic expressions, we must be familiar with the key phrases that signal whether we are to find a sum, difference, product, or quotient.

Chapter 1   Review Problem Set

1. From the list $0, \sqrt{2}, \dfrac{3}{4}, -\dfrac{5}{6}, \dfrac{25}{3}, -\sqrt{3}, -8, 0.34, 0.2\overline{3},$ 67, and $\dfrac{9}{7}$, identify each of the following.

   a. The natural numbers

   b. The integers

   c. The nonnegative integers

   d. The rational numbers

   e. The irrational numbers

For Problems 2–10, state the property of equality or the property of real numbers that justifies each of the statements. For example, $6(-7) = -7(6)$ because of the commutative property for multiplication; and if $2 = x + 3$, then $x + 3 = 2$ is true because of the symmetric property of equality.

2. $7 + (3 + (-8)) = (7 + 3) + (-8)$

3. If $x = 2$ and $x + y = 9$, then $2 + y = 9$.

4. $-1(x + 2) = -(x + 2)$

5. $3(x + 4) = 3(x) + 3(4)$

6. $[(17)(4)](25) = (17)[(4)(25)]$

7. $x + 3 = 3 + x$

8. $3(98) + 3(2) = 3(98 + 2)$

9. $\left(\dfrac{3}{4}\right)\left(\dfrac{4}{3}\right) = 1$

10. If $4 = 3x - 1$, then $3x - 1 = 4$.

For Problems 11–22, simplify each of the numerical expressions.

11. $-8\dfrac{1}{4} + \left(-4\dfrac{5}{8}\right) - \left(-6\dfrac{3}{8}\right)$

12. $9\dfrac{1}{3} - 12\dfrac{1}{2} + \left(-4\dfrac{1}{6}\right) - \left(-1\dfrac{1}{6}\right)$

13. $-8(2) - 16 \div (-4) + (-2)(-2)$

41

14. $4(-3) - 12 \div (-4) + (-2)(-1) - 8$

15. $-3(2 - 4) - 4(7 - 9) + 6$

16. $[48 + (-73)] + 74$

17. $[5(-2) - 3(-1)][-2(-1) + 3(2)]$

18. $-4^2 - 2^3$

19. $(-2)^4 + (-1)^3 - 3^2$

20. $2(-1)^2 - 3(-1)(2) - 2^2$

21. $[4(-1) - 2(3)]^2$

22. $3 - [-2(3 - 4)] + 7$

For Problems 23–32, simplify each of the algebraic expressions by combining similar terms.

23. $3a^2 - 2b^2 - 7a^2 - 3b^2$

24. $4x - 6 - 2x - 8 + x + 12$

25. $\dfrac{1}{5}ab^2 - \dfrac{3}{10}ab^2 + \dfrac{2}{5}ab^2 + \dfrac{7}{10}ab^2$

26. $-\dfrac{2}{3}x^2y - \left(-\dfrac{3}{4}x^2y\right) - \dfrac{5}{12}x^2y - 2x^2y$

27. $3(2n^2 + 1) + 4(n^2 - 5)$

28. $-2(3a - 1) + 4(2a + 3) - 5(3a + 2)$

29. $-(n - 1) - (n + 2) + 3$

30. $3(2x - 3y) - 4(3x + 5y) - x$

31. $4(a - 6) - (3a - 1) - 2(4a - 7)$

32. $-5(x^2 - 4) - 2(3x^2 + 6) + (2x^2 - 1)$

For Problems 33–42, evaluate each of the algebraic expressions for the given values of the variables.

33. $-5x + 4y$ for $x = \dfrac{1}{2}$ and $y = -1$

34. $3x^2 - 2y^2$ for $x = \dfrac{1}{4}$ and $y = -\dfrac{1}{2}$

35. $-5(2x - 3y)$ for $x = 1$ and $y = -3$

36. $(3a - 2b)^2$ for $a = -2$ and $b = 3$

37. $a^2 + 3ab - 2b^2$ for $a = 2$ and $b = -2$

38. $3n^2 - 4 - 4n^2 + 9$ for $n = 7$

39. $3(2x - 1) + 2(3x + 4)$ for $x = 1.2$

40. $-4(3x - 1) - 5(2x - 1)$ for $x = -2.3$

41. $2(n^2 + 3) - 3(n^2 + 1) + 4(n^2 - 6)$ for $n = -\dfrac{2}{3}$

42. $5(3n - 1) - 7(-2n + 1) + 4(3n - 1)$ for $n = \dfrac{1}{2}$

For Problems 43–50, translate each English phrase into an algebraic expression and use n to represent the unknown number.

43. Four increased by twice a number

44. Fifty subtracted from three times a number

45. Six less than two-thirds of a number

46. Ten times the difference of a number and 14

47. Eight subtracted from five times a number

48. The quotient of a number and three less than the number

49. Three less than five times the sum of a number and 2

50. Three-fourths of the sum of a number and 12

For Problems 51–60, answer the question with an algebraic expression.

51. The sum of two numbers is 37 and one of the numbers is n. What is the other number?

52. Yuriko can type w words in an hour. What is her typing rate per minute?

53. Harry is y years old. His brother is 7 years less than twice as old as Harry. How old is Harry's brother?

54. If n represents a multiple of 3, what represents the next largest multiple of 3?

55. Celia has p pennies, n nickels, and q quarters. How much, in cents, does Celia have?

56. The perimeter of a square is i inches. How long, in feet, is each side of the square?

57. The length of a rectangle is y yards and the width is f feet. What is the perimeter of the rectangle expressed in inches?

58. The length of a piece of wire is d decimeters. What is the length expressed in centimeters?

59. Joan is f feet and i inches tall. How tall is she in inches?

60. The perimeter of a rectangle is 50 centimeters. If the rectangle is c centimeters long, how wide is it?

Chapter 1 Test

1. State the property of equality that justifies writing $x + 4 = 6$ for $6 = x + 4$.

2. State the property of real numbers that justifies writing $5(10 + 2)$ as $5(10) + 5(2)$.

For Problems 3–11, simplify each numerical expression.

3. $-4 - (-3) + (-5) - 7 + 10$

4. $7 - 8 - 3 + 4 - 9 - 4 + 2 - 12$

5. $5\left(-\dfrac{1}{3}\right) - 3\left(-\dfrac{1}{2}\right) + 7\left(-\dfrac{2}{3}\right) + 1$

6. $(-6) \cdot 3 \div (-2) - 8 \div (-4)$

7. $-\dfrac{1}{2}(3 - 7) - \dfrac{2}{5}(2 - 17)$

8. $[48 + (-93)] + (-49)$

9. $3(-2)^3 + 4(-2)^2 - 9(-2) - 14$

10. $[2(-6) + 5(-4)][-3(-4) - 7(6)]$

11. $[-2(-3) - 4(2)]^5$

12. Simplify $6x^2 - 3x - 7x^2 - 5x - 2$ by combining similar terms.

13. Simplify $3(3n - 1) - 4(2n + 3) + 5(-4n - 1)$ by removing parentheses and combining similar terms.

For Problems 14–20, evaluate each algebraic expression for the given values of the variables.

14. $-7x - 3y$ for $x = -6$ and $y = 5$

15. $3a^2 - 4b^2$ for $a = -\dfrac{3}{4}$ and $b = \dfrac{1}{2}$

16. $6x - 9y - 8x + 4y$ for $x = \dfrac{1}{2}$ and $y = -\dfrac{1}{3}$

17. $-5n^2 - 6n + 7n^2 + 5n - 1$ for $n = -6$

18. $-7(x - 2) + 6(x - 1) - 4(x + 3)$ for $x = 3.7$

19. $-2xy - x + 4y$ for $x = -3$ and $y = 9$

20. $4(n^2 + 1) - (2n^2 + 3) - 2(n^2 + 3)$ for $n = -4$

For Problems 21 and 22, translate the English phrase into an algebraic expression using n to represent the unknown number.

21. Thirty subtracted from six times a number

22. Four more than three times the sum of a number and 8

For Problems 23–25, answer each question with an algebraic expression.

23. The product of two numbers is 72 and one of the numbers is n. What is the other number?

24. Tao has n nickels, d dimes, and q quarters. How much money, in cents, does she have?

25. The length of a rectangle is x yards and the width is y feet. What is the perimeter of the rectangle expressed in feet?

2

Equations, Inequalities, and Problem Solving

2.1 Solving First-Degree Equations

2.2 Equations Involving Fractional Forms

2.3 Equations Involving Decimals and Problem Solving

2.4 Formulas

2.5 Inequalities

2.6 More on Inequalities and Problem Solving

2.7 Equations and Inequalities Involving Absolute Value

Most shoppers take advantage of the discounts offered by retailers. When making decisions about purchases, it is beneficial to be able to compute the sale prices.

© James Leynse/CORBIS-SABA

A retailer of sporting goods bought a putter for $18. He wants to price the putter to make a profit of 40% of the selling price. What price should he mark on the putter? The equation $s = 18 + 0.4s$ can be used to determine that the putter should be sold for $30.

Throughout this text, we develop algebraic skills, use these skills to help solve equations and inequalities, and then use equations and inequalities to solve applied problems. In this chapter, we review and expand concepts that are important to the development of problem-solving skills.

2.1   Solving First-Degree Equations

In Section 1.1, we stated that an equality (equation) is a statement where two symbols, or groups of symbols, are names for the same number. It should be further stated that an equation may be true or false. For example, the equation $3 + (-8) = -5$ is true, but the equation $-7 + 4 = 2$ is false.

Algebraic equations contain one or more variables. The following are examples of algebraic equations.

$$3x + 5 = 8 \qquad 4y - 6 = -7y + 9 \qquad x^2 - 5x - 8 = 0$$

$$3x + 5y = 4 \qquad x^3 + 6x^2 - 7x - 2 = 0$$

An algebraic equation such as $3x + 5 = 8$ is neither true nor false as it stands, and we often refer to it as an "open sentence." Each time that a number is substituted for x, the algebraic equation $3x + 5 = 8$ becomes a numerical statement that is true or false. For example, if $x = 0$, then $3x + 5 = 8$ becomes $3(0) + 5 = 8$, which is a false statement. If $x = 1$, then $3x + 5 = 8$ becomes $3(1) + 5 = 8$, which is a true statement. **Solving an equation** refers to the process of finding the number (or numbers) that make(s) an algebraic equation a true numerical statement. We call such numbers the **solutions** or **roots** of the equation, and we say that they **satisfy** the equation. We call the set of all solutions of an equation its **solution set**. Thus $\{1\}$ is the solution set of $3x + 5 = 8$.

In this chapter, we will consider techniques for solving **first-degree equations in one variable**. This means that the equations contain only one variable and that this variable has an exponent of 1. The following are examples of first-degree equations in one variable.

$$3x + 5 = 8 \qquad \frac{2}{3}y + 7 = 9$$

$$7a - 6 = 3a + 4 \qquad \frac{x - 2}{4} = \frac{x - 3}{5}$$

Equivalent equations are equations that have the same solution set. For example,

1. $3x + 5 = 8$
2. $3x = 3$
3. $x = 1$

are all equivalent equations because $\{1\}$ is the solution set of each.

The general procedure for solving an equation is to continue replacing the given equation with equivalent but simpler equations until we obtain an equation of the form *variable = constant* or *constant = variable*. Thus in the example above, $3x + 5 = 8$ was simplified to $3x = 3$, which was further simplified to $x = 1$, from which the solution set $\{1\}$ is obvious.

To solve equations we need to use the various properties of equality. In addition to the reflexive, symmetric, transitive, and substitution properties we listed in Section 1.1, the following properties of equality play an important role.

Addition Property of Equality

For all real numbers a, b, and c,

$$a = b \quad \text{if and only if } a + c = b + c$$

Multiplication Property of Equality

For all real numbers a, b, and c, where $c \neq 0$,

$$a = b \quad \text{if and only if } ac = bc$$

The addition property of equality states that when the same number is added to both sides of an equation, an equivalent equation is produced. The multiplication property of equality states that we obtain an equivalent equation whenever we multiply both sides of an equation by the same *nonzero* real number. The following examples demonstrate the use of these properties to solve equations.

EXAMPLE 1   Solve $2x - 1 = 13$.

Solution

$$2x - 1 = 13$$

$$2x - 1 + 1 = 13 + 1 \qquad \text{Add 1 to both sides.}$$

$$2x = 14$$

$$\frac{1}{2}(2x) = \frac{1}{2}(14) \qquad \text{Multiply both sides by } \frac{1}{2}.$$

$$x = 7$$

The solution set is $\{7\}$. ■

To check an apparent solution, we can substitute it into the original equation and see if we obtain a true numerical statement.

 Check

$$2x - 1 = 13$$

$$2(7) - 1 \stackrel{?}{=} 13$$

$$14 - 1 \stackrel{?}{=} 13$$

$$13 = 13$$

Now we know that $\{7\}$ is the solution set of $2x - 1 = 13$. We will not show our checks for every example in this text, but do remember that checking is a way to detect arithmetic errors.

E X A M P L E   2

Solve $-7 = -5a + 9$.

Solution

$$-7 = -5a + 9$$

$$-7 + (-9) = 5a + 9 + (-9) \qquad \text{Add } -9 \text{ to both sides.}$$

$$-16 = -5a$$

$$-\frac{1}{5}(-16) = -\frac{1}{5}(-5a) \qquad \text{Multiply both sides by } -\frac{1}{5}.$$

$$\frac{16}{5} = a$$

The solution set is $\left\{\dfrac{16}{5}\right\}$.   ■

Note that in Example 2 the final equation is $\dfrac{16}{5} = a$ instead of $a = \dfrac{16}{5}$. Technically, the symmetric property of equality (if $a = b$, then $b = a$) would permit us to change from $\dfrac{16}{5} = a$ to $a = \dfrac{16}{5}$, but such a change is not necessary to determine that the solution is $\dfrac{16}{5}$. Note that we could use the symmetric property at the very beginning to change $-7 = -5a + 9$ to $-5a + 9 = -7$; some people prefer having the variable on the left side of the equation.

Let's clarify another point. We stated the properties of equality in terms of only two operations, addition and multiplication. We could also include the operations of subtraction and division in the statements of the properties. That is, we could think in terms of subtracting the same number from both sides of an equation and also in terms of dividing both sides of an equation by the same nonzero number. For example, in the solution of Example 2, we could subtract 9 from both sides rather than adding -9 to both sides. Likewise, we could divide both sides by -5 instead of multiplying both sides by $-\dfrac{1}{5}$.

E X A M P L E   3

Solve $7x - 3 = 5x + 9$.

Solution

$$7x - 3 = 5x + 9$$

$$7x - 3 + (-5x) = 5x + 9 + (-5x) \qquad \text{Add } -5x \text{ to both sides.}$$

$$2x - 3 = 9$$

$$2x - 3 + 3 = 9 + 3 \qquad \text{Add 3 to both sides.}$$

$$2x = 12$$

$$\frac{1}{2}(2x) = \frac{1}{2}(12) \qquad \text{Multiply both sides by } \frac{1}{2}.$$

$$x = 6$$

The solution set is {6}. ■

EXAMPLE 4

Solve $4(y - 1) + 5(y + 2) = 3(y - 8)$.

Solution

$$4(y - 1) + 5(y + 2) = 3(y - 8)$$

$$4y - 4 + 5y + 10 = 3y - 24 \qquad \text{Remove parentheses by applying the distributive property.}$$

$$9y + 6 = 3y - 24 \qquad \text{Simplify the left side by combining similar terms.}$$

$$9y + 6 + (-3y) = 3y - 24 + (-3y) \qquad \text{Add } -3y \text{ to both sides.}$$

$$6y + 6 = -24$$

$$6y + 6 + (-6) = -24 + (-6) \qquad \text{Add } -6 \text{ to both sides.}$$

$$6y = -30$$

$$\frac{1}{6}(6y) = \frac{1}{6}(-30) \qquad \text{Multiply both sides by } \frac{1}{6}.$$

$$y = -5$$

The solution set is {−5}. ■

We can summarize the process of solving first-degree equations in one variable as follows:

Step 1 Simplify both sides of the equation as much as possible.

Step 2 Use the addition property of equality to isolate a term that contains the variable on one side of the equation and a constant on the other side.

Step 3 Use the multiplication property of equality to make the coefficient of the variable 1; that is, multiply both sides of the equation by the reciprocal of the numerical coefficient of the variable. The solution set should now be obvious.

Step 4 Check each solution by substituting it in the original equation and verifying that the resulting numerical statement is true.

■ Use of Equations to Solve Problems

To use the tools of algebra to solve problems, we must be able to translate back and forth between the English language and the language of algebra. More specifically, we need to translate English sentences into algebraic equations. Such translations allow us to use our knowledge of equation solving to solve word problems. Let's consider an example.

P R O B L E M   1

If we subtract 27 from three times a certain number, the result is 18. Find the number.

Solution

Let n represent the number to be found. The sentence "If we subtract 27 from three times a certain number, the result is 18" translates into the equation $3n - 27 = 18$. Solving this equation, we obtain

$$3n - 27 = 18$$

$$3n = 45 \qquad \text{Add 27 to both sides.}$$

$$n = 15 \qquad \text{Multiply both sides by } \frac{1}{3}.$$

The number to be found is 15.   ■

We often refer to the statement "Let n represent the number to be found" as **declaring the variable**. We need to choose a letter to use as a variable and indicate what it represents for a specific problem. This may seem like an insignificant idea, but as the problems become more complex, the process of declaring the variable becomes even more important. Furthermore, it is true that you could probably solve a problem such as Problem 1 without setting up an algebraic equation. However, as problems increase in difficulty, the translation from English to algebra becomes a key issue. Therefore, even with these relatively easy problems, we suggest that you concentrate on the translation process.

The next example involves the use of integers. Remember that the set of integers consists of $\{\ldots -2, -1, 0, 1, 2, \ldots\}$. Furthermore, the integers can be classified as even, $\{\ldots -4, -2, 0, 2, 4, \ldots\}$, or odd, $\{\ldots -3, -1, 1, 3, \ldots\}$.

P R O B L E M   2

The sum of three consecutive integers is 13 greater than twice the smallest of the three integers. Find the integers.

Solution

Because consecutive integers differ by 1, we will represent them as follows: Let n represent the smallest of the three consecutive integers; then $n + 1$ represents the second largest, and $n + 2$ represents the largest.

The sum of the three
consecutive integers   13 greater than twice the smallest

$$n + (n + 1) + (n + 2) = 2n + 13$$

$$3n + 3 = 2n + 13$$

$$n = 10$$

The three consecutive integers are 10, 11, and 12.   ■

To check our answers for Problem 2, we must determine whether or not they satisfy the conditions stated in the original problem. Because 10, 11, and 12 are consecutive integers whose sum is 33, and because twice the smallest plus 13 is also 33 ($2(10) + 13 = 33$), we know that our answers are correct. (Remember, in checking a result for a word problem, it is *not* sufficient to check the result in the equation set up to solve the problem; the equation itself may be in error!)

In the two previous problems, the equation formed was almost a direct translation of a sentence in the statement of the problem. Now let's consider a situation where we need to think in terms of a guideline not explicitly stated in the problem.

PROBLEM 3

Khoa received a car repair bill for $106. This included $23 for parts, $22 per hour for each hour of labor, and $6 for taxes. Find the number of hours of labor.

Solution

See Figure 2.1. Let h represent the number of hours of labor. Then $22h$ represents the total charge for labor.

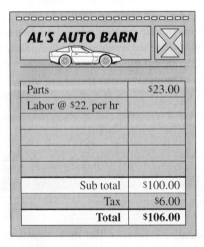

AL'S AUTO BARN

Parts	$23.00
Labor @ $22. per hr	
Sub total	$100.00
Tax	$6.00
Total	**$106.00**

Figure 2.1

We can use a guideline of *charge for parts plus charge for labor plus tax equals the total bill* to set up the following equation.

Parts   Labor   Tax   Total bill

$$23 + 22h + 6 = 106$$

Solving this equation, we obtain

$$22h + 29 = 106$$

$$22h = 77$$

$$h = 3\frac{1}{2}$$

Khoa was charged for $3\frac{1}{2}$ hours of labor. ∎

Problem Set 2.1

For problems 1–50, solve each equation.

1. $3x + 4 = 16$

2. $4x + 2 = 22$

3. $5x + 1 = -14$

4. $7x + 4 = -31$

5. $-x - 6 = 8$

6. $8 - x = -2$

7. $4y - 3 = 21$

8. $6y - 7 = 41$

9. $3x - 4 = 15$

10. $5x + 1 = 12$

11. $-4 = 2x - 6$

12. $-14 = 3a - 2$

13. $-6y - 4 = 16$

14. $-8y - 2 = 18$

15. $4x - 1 = 2x + 7$

16. $9x - 3 = 6x + 18$

17. $5y + 2 = 2y - 11$

18. $9y + 3 = 4y - 10$

19. $3x + 4 = 5x - 2$

20. $2x - 1 = 6x + 15$

21. $-7a + 6 = -8a + 14$

22. $-6a - 4 = -7a + 11$

23. $5x + 3 - 2x = x - 15$

24. $4x - 2 - x = 5x + 10$

25. $6y + 18 + y = 2y + 3$

26. $5y + 14 + y = 3y - 7$

27. $4x - 3 + 2x = 8x - 3 - x$

28. $x - 4 - 4x = 6x + 9 - 8x$

29. $6n - 4 - 3n = 3n + 10 + 4n$

30. $2n - 1 - 3n = 5n - 7 - 3n$

31. $4(x - 3) = -20$

32. $3(x + 2) = -15$

33. $-3(x - 2) = 11$

34. $-5(x - 1) = 12$

35. $5(2x + 1) = 4(3x - 7)$

36. $3(2x - 1) = 2(4x + 7)$

37. $5x - 4(x - 6) = -11$

38. $3x - 5(2x + 1) = 13$

39. $-2(3x - 1) - 3 = -4$

40. $-6(x - 4) - 10 = -12$

41. $-2(3x + 5) = -3(4x + 3)$

42. $-(2x - 1) = -5(2x + 9)$

43. $3(x - 4) - 7(x + 2) = -2(x + 18)$

44. $4(x - 2) - 3(x - 1) = 2(x + 6)$

45. $-2(3n - 1) + 3(n + 5) = -4(n - 4)$

46. $-3(4n + 2) + 2(n - 6) = -2(n + 1)$

47. $3(2a - 1) - 2(5a + 1) = 4(3a + 4)$

48. $4(2a + 3) - 3(4a - 2) = 5(4a - 7)$

49. $-2(n - 4) - (3n - 1) = -2 + (2n - 1)$

50. $-(2n - 1) + 6(n + 3) = -4 - (7n - 11)$

For Problems 51–66, use an algebraic approach to solve each problem.

51. If 15 is subtracted from three times a certain number, the result is 27. Find the number.

52. If 1 is subtracted from seven times a certain number, the result is the same as if 31 is added to three times the number. Find the number.

53. Find three consecutive integers whose sum is 42.

54. Find four consecutive integers whose sum is −118.

55. Find three consecutive odd integers such that three times the second minus the third is 11 more than the first.

56. Find three consecutive even integers such that four times the first minus the third is six more than twice the second.

57. The difference of two numbers is 67. The larger number is three less than six times the smaller number. Find the numbers.

58. The sum of two numbers is 103. The larger number is one more than five times the smaller number. Find the numbers.

59. Angelo is paid double time for each hour he works over 40 hours in a week. Last week he worked 46 hours and earned $572. What is his normal hourly rate?

60. Suppose that a plumbing repair bill, not including tax, was $130. This included $25 for parts and an amount for 5 hours of labor. Find the hourly rate that was charged for labor.

61. Suppose that Maria has 150 coins consisting of pennies, nickels, and dimes. The number of nickels she has is 10 less than twice the number of pennies; the number of dimes she has is 20 less than three times the number of pennies. How many coins of each kind does she have?

62. Hector has a collection of nickels, dimes, and quarters totaling 122 coins. The number of dimes he has is 3 more than four times the number of nickels, and the number of quarters he has is 19 less than the number of dimes. How many coins of each kind does he have?

63. The selling price of a ring is $750. This represents $150 less than three times the cost of the ring. Find the cost of the ring.

64. In a class of 62 students, the number of females is one less than twice the number of males. How many females and how many males are there in the class?

65. An apartment complex contains 230 apartments each having one, two, or three bedrooms. The number of two-bedroom apartments is 10 more than three times the number of three-bedroom apartments. The number of one-bedroom apartments is twice the number of two-bedroom apartments. How many apartments of each kind are in the complex?

66. Barry sells bicycles on a salary-plus-commission basis. He receives a monthly salary of $300 and a commission of $15 for each bicycle that he sells. How many bicycles must he sell in a month to have a total monthly income of $750?

■ ■ ■ THOUGHTS INTO WORDS

67. Explain the difference between a numerical statement and an algebraic equation.

68. Are the equations $7 = 9x - 4$ and $9x - 4 = 7$ equivalent equations? Defend your answer.

69. Suppose that your friend shows you the following solution to an equation.

$$17 = 4 - 2x$$
$$17 + 2x = 4 - 2x + 2x$$
$$17 + 2x = 4$$
$$17 + 2x - 17 = 4 - 17$$

$$2x = -13$$
$$x = \frac{-13}{2}$$

Is this a correct solution? What suggestions would you have in terms of the method used to solve the equation?

70. Explain in your own words what it means to declare a variable when solving a word problem.

71. Make up an equation whose solution set is the null set and explain why this is the solution set.

72. Make up an equation whose solution set is the set of all real numbers and explain why this is the solution set.

■ ■ ■ **FURTHER INVESTIGATIONS**

73. Solve each of the following equations.

(a) $5x + 7 = 5x - 4$

(b) $4(x - 1) = 4x - 4$

(c) $3(x - 4) = 2(x - 6)$

(d) $7x - 2 = -7x + 4$

(e) $2(x - 1) + 3(x + 2) = 5(x - 7)$

(f) $-4(x - 7) = -2(2x + 1)$

74. Verify that for any three consecutive integers, the sum of the smallest and largest is equal to twice the middle integer. [*Hint*: Use n, $n + 1$, and $n + 2$ to represent the three consecutive integers.]

75. Verify that no four consecutive integers can be found such that the product of the smallest and largest is equal to the product of the other two integers.

2.2   Equations Involving Fractional Forms

To solve equations that involve fractions, it is usually easiest to begin by **clearing the equation of all fractions**. This can be accomplished by multiplying both sides of the equation by the least common multiple of all the denominators in the equation. Remember that the least common multiple of a set of whole numbers is the smallest nonzero whole number that is divisible by each of the numbers. For example, the least common multiple of 2, 3, and 6 is 12. When working with fractions, we refer to the least common multiple of a set of denominators as the **least common denominator** (LCD). Let's consider some equations involving fractions.

E X A M P L E   1   Solve $\dfrac{1}{2}x + \dfrac{2}{3} = \dfrac{3}{4}$.

Solution

$$\frac{1}{2}x + \frac{2}{3} = \frac{3}{4}$$

$$12\left(\frac{1}{2}x + \frac{2}{3}\right) = 12\left(\frac{3}{4}\right) \qquad \text{Multiply both sides by 12, which is the LCD of 2, 3, and 4.}$$

$$12\left(\frac{1}{2}x\right) + 12\left(\frac{2}{3}\right) = 12\left(\frac{3}{4}\right) \qquad \text{Apply the distributive property to the left side.}$$

$$6x + 8 = 9$$

$$6x = 1$$

$$x = \frac{1}{6}$$

The solution set is $\left\{\dfrac{1}{6}\right\}$.

✔ **Check**

$$\frac{1}{2}x + \frac{2}{3} = \frac{3}{4}$$

$$\frac{1}{2}\left(\frac{1}{6}\right) + \frac{2}{3} \overset{?}{=} \frac{3}{4}$$

$$\frac{1}{12} + \frac{2}{3} \overset{?}{=} \frac{3}{4}$$

$$\frac{1}{12} + \frac{8}{12} \overset{?}{=} \frac{3}{4}$$

$$\frac{9}{12} \overset{?}{=} \frac{3}{4}$$

$$\frac{3}{4} = \frac{3}{4}$$

■

E X A M P L E   2

Solve $\dfrac{x}{2} + \dfrac{x}{3} = 10$.

Solution

$$\frac{x}{2} + \frac{x}{3} = 10 \qquad \text{Recall that } \frac{x}{2} = \frac{1}{2}x.$$

$$6\left(\frac{x}{2} + \frac{x}{3}\right) = 6(10) \qquad \text{Multiply both sides by the LCD.}$$

$$6\left(\frac{x}{2}\right) + 6\left(\frac{x}{3}\right) = 6(10) \qquad \begin{array}{l}\text{Apply the distributive property to}\\ \text{the left side.}\end{array}$$

$$3x + 2x = 60$$

$$5x = 60$$

$$x = 12$$

The solution set is {12}. ■

As you study the examples in this section, pay special attention to the steps shown in the solutions. There are no hard and fast rules as to which steps should be performed mentally; this is an individual decision. When you solve problems, show enough steps to allow the flow of the process to be understood and to minimize the chances of making careless computational errors.

E X A M P L E   3

Solve $\dfrac{x-2}{3} + \dfrac{x+1}{8} = \dfrac{5}{6}$.

Solution

$$\frac{x-2}{3} + \frac{x+1}{8} = \frac{5}{6}$$

$$24\left(\frac{x-2}{3}+\frac{x+1}{8}\right)=24\left(\frac{5}{6}\right)$$ Multiply both sides by the LCD.

$$24\left(\frac{x-2}{3}\right)+24\left(\frac{x+1}{8}\right)=24\left(\frac{5}{6}\right)$$ Apply the distributive property to the left side.

$$8(x-2)+3(x+1)=20$$

$$8x-16+3x+3=20$$

$$11x-13=20$$

$$11x=33$$

$$x=3$$

The solution set is {3}.   ∎

EXAMPLE 4   Solve $\dfrac{3t-1}{5}-\dfrac{t-4}{3}=1$.

Solution

$$\frac{3t-1}{5}-\frac{t-4}{3}=1$$

$$15\left(\frac{3t-1}{5}-\frac{t-4}{3}\right)=15(1)$$ Multiply both sides by the LCD.

$$15\left(\frac{3t-1}{5}\right)-15\left(\frac{t-4}{3}\right)=15(1)$$ Apply the distributive property to the left side.

$$3(3t-1)-5(t-4)=15$$

$$9t-3-5t+20=15$$ Be careful with this sign!

$$4t+17=15$$

$$4t=-2$$

$$t=-\frac{2}{4}=-\frac{1}{2}$$ Reduce!

The solution set is $\left\{-\dfrac{1}{2}\right\}$.   ∎

■ Problem Solving

As we expand our skills for solving equations, we also expand our capabilities for solving word problems. There is no one definite procedure that will ensure success at solving word problems, but the following suggestions can be helpful.

Suggestions for Solving Word Problems

1. Read the problem carefully and make certain that you understand the meanings of all of the words. Be especially alert for any technical terms used in the statement of the problem.
2. Read the problem a second time (perhaps even a third time) to get an overview of the situation being described. Determine the known facts as well as what is to be found.
3. Sketch any figure, diagram, or chart that might be helpful in analyzing the problem.
4. Choose a meaningful variable to represent an unknown quantity in the problem (perhaps t, if time is an unknown quantity) and represent any other unknowns in terms of that variable.
5. Look for a guideline that you can use to set up an equation. A guideline might be a formula, such as *distance equals rate times time*, or a statement of a relationship, such as "The sum of the two numbers is 28."
6. Form an equation that contains the variable and that translates the conditions of the guideline from English to algebra.
7. Solve the equation, and use the solution to determine all facts requested in the problem.
8. Check all answers back into the **original statement of the problem**.

Keep these suggestions in mind as we continue to solve problems. We will elaborate on some of these suggestions at different times throughout the text. Now let's consider some problems.

PROBLEM 1

Find a number such that three-eighths of the number minus one-half of it is 14 less than three-fourths of the number.

Solution

Let n represent the number to be found.

$$\frac{3}{8}n - \frac{1}{2}n = \frac{3}{4}n - 14$$

$$8\left(\frac{3}{8}n - \frac{1}{2}n\right) = 8\left(\frac{3}{4}n - 14\right)$$

$$8\left(\frac{3}{8}n\right) - 8\left(\frac{1}{2}n\right) = 8\left(\frac{3}{4}n\right) - 8(14)$$

$$3n - 4n = 6n - 112$$

$$-n = 6n - 112$$

$$-7n = -112$$

$$n = 16$$

The number is 16. Check it! ∎

PROBLEM 2

The width of a rectangular parking lot is 8 feet less than three-fifths of the length. The perimeter of the lot is 400 feet. Find the length and width of the lot.

Solution

Let l represent the length of the lot. Then $\frac{3}{5}l - 8$ represents the width (Figure 2.2).

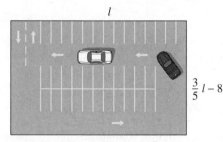

Figure 2.2

A guideline for this problem is the formula, *the perimeter of a rectangle equals twice the length plus twice the width (P = 2l + 2w)*. Use this formula to form the following equation.

$$P = 2l + 2w$$

$$400 = 2l + 2\left(\frac{3}{5}l - 8\right)$$

Solving this equation, we obtain

$$400 = 2l + \frac{6l}{5} - 16$$

$$5(400) = 5\left(2l + \frac{6l}{5} - 16\right)$$

$$2000 = 10l + 6l - 80$$

$$2000 = 16l - 80$$

$$2080 = 16l$$

$$130 = l.$$

The length of the lot is 130 feet, and the width is $\frac{3}{5}(130) - 8 = 70$ feet. ∎

In Problems 1 and 2, note the use of different letters as variables. It is helpful to choose a variable that has significance for the problem you are working on. For example, in Problem 2 the choice of l to represent the length seems natural and meaningful. (Certainly this is another matter of personal preference, but you might consider it.)

In Problem 2 a geometric relationship, ($P = 2l + 2w$), serves as a guideline for setting up the equation. The following geometric relationships pertaining to angle measure may also serve as guidelines.

1. Complementary angles are two angles the sum of whose measures is 90°.

2. Supplementary angles are two angles the sum of whose measures is 180°.

3. The sum of the measures of the three angles of a triangle is 180°.

P R O B L E M   3

One of two complementary angles is 6° larger than one-half of the other angle. Find the measure of each of the angles.

Solution

Let a represent the measure of one of the angles. Then $\frac{1}{2}a + 6$ represents the measure of the other angle. Because they are complementary angles, the sum of their measures is 90°.

$$a + \left(\frac{1}{2}a + 6\right) = 90$$

$$2a + a + 12 = 180$$

$$3a + 12 = 180$$

$$3a = 168$$

$$a = 56$$

If $a = 56$, then $\frac{1}{2}a + 6$ becomes $\frac{1}{2}(56) + 6 = 34$. The angles have measures of 34° and 56°. ■

P R O B L E M   4

Dominic's present age is 10 years more than Michele's present age. In 5 years Michele's age will be three-fifths of Dominic's age. What are their present ages?

Solution

Let x represent Michele's present age. Then Dominic's age will be represented by $x + 10$. In 5 years, everyone's age is increased by 5 years, so we need to add 5 to Michele's present age and 5 to Dominic's present age to represent their ages in 5 years. Therefore, in 5 years Michele's age will be represented by $x + 5$, and Dominic's age will be represented by $x + 15$. Thus we can set up the equation reflecting the fact that in 5 years, Michele's age will be three-fifths of Dominic's age.

$$x + 5 = \frac{3}{5}(x + 15)$$

$$5(x + 5) = 5\left[\frac{3}{5}(x + 15)\right]$$

$$5x + 25 = 3(x + 15)$$

$$5x + 25 = 3x + 45$$

$$2x + 25 = 45$$

$$2x = 20$$

$$x = 10$$

Because x represents Michele's present age, we know her age is 10. Dominic's present age is represented by $x + 10$, so his age is 20.   ■

Keep in mind that the problem-solving suggestions offered in this section simply outline a general algebraic approach to solving problems. You will add to this list throughout this course and in any subsequent mathematics courses that you take. Furthermore, you will be able to pick up additional problem-solving ideas from your instructor and from fellow classmates as you discuss problems in class. Always be on the alert for any ideas that might help you become a better problem solver.

Problem Set 2.2

For Problems 1–40, solve each equation.

1. $\dfrac{3}{4}x = 9$

2. $\dfrac{2}{3}x = -14$

3. $\dfrac{-2x}{3} = \dfrac{2}{5}$

4. $\dfrac{-5x}{4} = \dfrac{7}{2}$

5. $\dfrac{n}{2} - \dfrac{2}{3} = \dfrac{5}{6}$

6. $\dfrac{n}{4} - \dfrac{5}{6} = \dfrac{5}{12}$

7. $\dfrac{5n}{6} - \dfrac{n}{8} = \dfrac{-17}{12}$

8. $\dfrac{2n}{5} - \dfrac{n}{6} = \dfrac{-7}{10}$

9. $\dfrac{a}{4} - 1 = \dfrac{a}{3} + 2$

10. $\dfrac{3a}{7} - 1 = \dfrac{a}{3}$

11. $\dfrac{h}{4} + \dfrac{h}{5} = 1$

12. $\dfrac{h}{6} + \dfrac{3h}{8} = 1$

13. $\dfrac{h}{2} - \dfrac{h}{3} + \dfrac{h}{6} = 1$

14. $\dfrac{3h}{4} + \dfrac{2h}{5} = 1$

15. $\dfrac{x - 2}{3} + \dfrac{x + 3}{4} = \dfrac{11}{6}$

16. $\dfrac{x + 4}{5} + \dfrac{x - 1}{4} = \dfrac{37}{10}$

17. $\dfrac{x + 2}{2} - \dfrac{x - 1}{5} = \dfrac{3}{5}$

18. $\dfrac{2x + 1}{3} - \dfrac{x + 1}{7} = -\dfrac{1}{3}$

19. $\dfrac{n + 2}{4} - \dfrac{2n - 1}{3} = \dfrac{1}{6}$

20. $\dfrac{n - 1}{9} - \dfrac{n + 2}{6} = \dfrac{3}{4}$

21. $\dfrac{y}{3} + \dfrac{y - 5}{10} = \dfrac{4y + 3}{5}$

22. $\dfrac{y}{3} + \dfrac{y - 2}{8} = \dfrac{6y - 1}{12}$

23. $\dfrac{4x - 1}{10} - \dfrac{5x + 2}{4} = -3$

24. $\dfrac{2x - 1}{2} - \dfrac{3x + 1}{4} = \dfrac{3}{10}$

25. $\dfrac{2x - 1}{8} - 1 = \dfrac{x + 5}{7}$

26. $\dfrac{3x + 1}{9} + 2 = \dfrac{x - 1}{4}$

27. $\dfrac{2a - 3}{6} + \dfrac{3a - 2}{4} + \dfrac{5a + 6}{12} = 4$

28. $\dfrac{3a - 1}{4} + \dfrac{a - 2}{3} - \dfrac{a - 1}{5} = \dfrac{21}{20}$

29. $x + \dfrac{3x - 1}{9} - 4 = \dfrac{3x + 1}{3}$

30. $\dfrac{2x + 7}{8} + x - 2 = \dfrac{x - 1}{2}$

31. $\dfrac{x + 3}{2} + \dfrac{x + 4}{5} = \dfrac{3}{10}$

32. $\dfrac{x - 2}{5} - \dfrac{x - 3}{4} = -\dfrac{1}{20}$

33. $n + \dfrac{2n - 3}{9} - 2 = \dfrac{2n + 1}{3}$

34. $n - \dfrac{3n + 1}{6} - 1 = \dfrac{2n + 4}{12}$

35. $\dfrac{3}{4}(t - 2) - \dfrac{2}{5}(2t - 3) = \dfrac{1}{5}$

36. $\dfrac{2}{3}(2t + 1) - \dfrac{1}{2}(3t - 2) = 2$

37. $\dfrac{1}{2}(2x - 1) - \dfrac{1}{3}(5x + 2) = 3$

38. $\dfrac{2}{5}(4x - 1) + \dfrac{1}{4}(5x + 2) = -1$

39. $3x - 1 + \dfrac{2}{7}(7x - 2) = -\dfrac{11}{7}$

40. $2x + 5 + \dfrac{1}{2}(6x - 1) = -\dfrac{1}{2}$

For Problems 41–58, use an algebraic approach to solve each problem.

41. Find a number such that one-half of the number is 3 less than two-thirds of the number.

42. One-half of a number plus three-fourths of the number is 2 more than four-thirds of the number. Find the number.

43. Suppose that the width of a certain rectangle is 1 inch more than one-fourth of its length. The perimeter of the rectangle is 42 inches. Find the length and width of the rectangle.

44. Suppose that the width of a rectangle is 3 centimeters less than two-thirds of its length. The perimeter of the rectangle is 114 centimeters. Find the length and width of the rectangle.

45. Find three consecutive integers such that the sum of the first plus one-third of the second plus three-eighths of the third is 25.

46. Lou is paid $1\dfrac{1}{2}$ times his normal hourly rate for each hour he works over 40 hours in a week. Last week he worked 44 hours and earned $276. What is his normal hourly rate?

47. A board 20 feet long is cut into two pieces such that the length of one piece is two-thirds of the length of the other piece. Find the length of the shorter piece of board.

48. Jody has a collection of 116 coins consisting of dimes, quarters, and silver dollars. The number of quarters is 5 less than three-fourths of the number of dimes. The number of silver dollars is 7 more than five-eighths of the number of dimes. How many coins of each kind are in her collection?

49. The sum of the present ages of Angie and her mother is 64 years. In eight years Angie will be three-fifths as old as her mother at that time. Find the present ages of Angie and her mother.

50. Annilee's present age is two-thirds of Jessie's present age. In 12 years the sum of their ages will be 54 years. Find their present ages.

51. Sydney's present age is one-half of Marcus's present age. In 12 years, Sydney's age will be five-eighths of Marcus's age. Find their present ages.

52. The sum of the present ages of Ian and his brother is 45. In 5 years, Ian's age will be five-sixths of his brother's age. Find their present ages.

53. Aura took three biology exams and has an average score of 88. Her second exam score was 10 points better than her first, and her third exam score was 4 points better than her second exam. What were her three exam scores?

54. The average of the salaries of Tim, Maida, and Aaron is $24,000 per year. Maida earns $10,000 more than Tim, and Aaron's salary is $2000 more than twice Tim's salary. Find the salary of each person.

55. One of two supplementary angles is 4° more than one-third of the other angle. Find the measure of each of the angles.

56. If one-half of the complement of an angle plus three-fourths of the supplement of the angle equals 110°, find the measure of the angle.

57. If the complement of an angle is 5° less than one-sixth of its supplement, find the measure of the angle.

58. In $\triangle ABC$, angle B is 8° less than one-half of angle A and angle C is 28° larger than angle A. Find the measures of the three angles of the triangle.

■ ■ ■ THOUGHTS INTO WORDS

59. Explain why the solution set of the equation $x + 3 = x + 4$ is the null set.

60. Explain why the solution set of the equation $\dfrac{x}{3} + \dfrac{x}{2} = \dfrac{5x}{6}$ is the entire set of real numbers.

61. Why must potential answers to word problems be checked back into the original statement of the problem?

62. Suppose your friend solved the problem, *find two consecutive odd integers whose sum is 28* like this:

$$x + x + 1 = 28$$
$$2x = 27$$
$$x = \frac{27}{2} = 13\frac{1}{2}$$

She claims that $13\frac{1}{2}$ will check in the equation. Where has she gone wrong and how would you help her?

2.3   Equations Involving Decimals and Problem Solving

In solving equations that involve fractions, usually the procedure is to clear the equation of all fractions. For solving equations that involve decimals, there are two commonly used procedures. One procedure is to keep the numbers in decimal form and solve the equation by applying the properties. Another procedure is to multiply both sides of the equation by an appropriate power of 10 to clear the equation of all decimals. Which technique to use depends on your personal preference and on the complexity of the equation. The following examples demonstrate both techniques.

EXAMPLE 1   Solve $0.2x + 0.24 = 0.08x + 0.72$.

Solution

Let's clear the decimals by multiplying both sides of the equation by 100.

$$0.2x + 0.24 = 0.08x + 0.72$$
$$100(0.2x + 0.24) = 100(0.08x + 0.72)$$
$$100(0.2x) + 100(0.24) = 100(0.08x) + 100(0.72)$$
$$20x + 24 = 8x + 72$$
$$12x + 24 = 72$$
$$12x = 48$$
$$x = 4$$

✔ **Check**

$$0.2x + 0.24 = 0.08x + 0.72$$

$$0.2(4) + 0.24 \stackrel{?}{=} 0.08(4) + 0.72$$

$$0.8 + 0.24 \stackrel{?}{=} 0.32 + 0.72$$

$$1.04 = 1.04$$

The solution set is {4}. ■

E X A M P L E   2

Solve $0.07x + 0.11x = 3.6$.

Solution

Let's keep this problem in decimal form.

$$0.07x + 0.11x = 3.6$$

$$0.18x = 3.6$$

$$x = \frac{3.6}{0.18}$$

$$x = 20$$

✔ **Check**

$$0.07x + 0.11x = 3.6$$

$$0.07(20) + 0.11(20) \stackrel{?}{=} 3.6$$

$$1.4 + 2.2 \stackrel{?}{=} 3.6$$

$$3.6 = 3.6$$

The solution set is {20}. ■

E X A M P L E   3

Solve $s = 1.95 + 0.35s$.

Solution

Let's keep this problem in decimal form.

$$s = 1.95 + 0.35s$$

$$s + (-0.35s) = 1.95 + 0.35s + (-0.35s)$$

$$0.65s = 1.95 \qquad \text{Remember, } s = 1.00s.$$

$$s = \frac{1.95}{0.65}$$

$$s = 3$$

The solution set is {3}. Check it! ■

E X A M P L E   4

Solve $0.12x + 0.11(7000 - x) = 790$.

Solution

Let's clear the decimals by multiplying both sides of the equation by 100.

$$0.12x + 0.11(7000 - x) = 790$$

$$100[0.12x + 0.11(7000 - x)] = 100(790) \qquad \text{Multiply both sides by 100.}$$

$$100(0.12x) + 100[0.11(7000 - x)] = 100(790)$$

$$12x + 11(7000 - x) = 79{,}000$$

$$12x + 77{,}000 - 11x = 79{,}000$$

$$x + 77{,}000 = 79{,}000$$

$$x = 2000$$

The solution set is {2000}.   ■

■ Back to Problem Solving

We can solve many consumer problems with an algebraic approach. For example, let's consider some discount sale problems involving the relationship, *original selling price minus discount equals discount sale price*.

Original selling price $-$ Discount $=$ Discount sale price

P R O B L E M   1

Karyl bought a dress at a 35% discount sale for $32.50. What was the original price of the dress?

Solution

Let p represent the original price of the dress. Using the discount sale relationship as a guideline, we find that the problem translates into an equation as follows:

Original selling price	Minus	Discount	Equals	Discount sale price
p	$-$	$(35\%)(p)$	$=$	\$32.50

Switching this equation to decimal form and solving the equation, we obtain

$$p - (35\%)(p) = 32.50$$

$$(65\%)(p) = 32.50$$

$$0.65p = 32.50$$

$$p = 50$$

The original price of the dress was $50.   ■

PROBLEM 2

A pair of jogging shoes that was originally priced at $50 is on sale for 20% off. Find the discount sale price of the shoes.

Solution

Let s represent the discount sale price.

Original price	Minus	Discount	Equals	Sale price
$50	−	(20%)($50)	=	s

Solving this equation we obtain

$$50 - (20\%)(50) = s$$
$$50 - (0.2)(50) = s$$
$$50 - 10 = s$$
$$40 = s$$

The shoes are on sale for $40.   ■

Remark: Keep in mind that if an item is on sale for 35% off, then the purchaser will pay 100% − 35% = 65% of the original price. Thus in Problem 1 you could begin with the equation $0.65p = 32.50$. Likewise in Problem 2 you could start with the equation $s = 0.8(50)$.

Another basic relationship that pertains to consumer problems is *selling price equals cost plus profit*. We can state profit (also called markup, markon, and margin of profit) in different ways. Profit may be stated as a percent of the selling price, as a percent of the cost, or simply in terms of dollars and cents. We shall consider some problems for which the profit is calculated either as a percent of the cost or as a percent of the selling price.

$$\text{Selling price} = \text{Cost} + \text{Profit}$$

PROBLEM 3

A retailer has some shirts that cost $20 each. She wants to sell them at a profit of 60% of the cost. What selling price should be marked on the shirts?

Solution

Let s represent the selling price. Use the relationship *selling price equals cost plus profit* as a guideline.

Selling price	Equals	Cost	Plus	Profit
s	=	$20	+	(60%)($20)

Solving this equation yields

$$s = 20 + (60\%)(20)$$
$$s = 20 + (0.6)(20)$$

$$s = 20 + 12$$

$$s = 32$$

The selling price should be $32.   ■

Remark: A profit of 60% of the cost means that the selling price is 100% of the cost plus 60% of the cost, or 160% of the cost. Thus in Problem 3 we could solve the equation $s = 1.6(20)$.

PROBLEM 4

A retailer of sporting goods bought a putter for $18. He wants to price the putter such that he will make a profit of 40% of the selling price. What price should he mark on the putter?

Solution

Let s represent the selling price.

Selling price	Equals	Cost	Plus	Profit
s	$=$	$18	$+$	$(40\%)(s)$

Solving this equation yields

$$s = 18 + (40\%)(s)$$

$$s = 18 + 0.4s$$

$$0.6s = 18$$

$$s = 30$$

The selling price should be $30.   ■

PROBLEM 5

If a maple tree costs a landscaper $55.00, and he sells it for $80.00, what is his rate of profit based on the cost? Round the rate to the nearest tenth of a percent.

Solution

Let r represent the rate of profit, and use the following guideline.

Selling price	Equals	Cost	Plus	Profit
80.00	$=$	55.00	$+$	$r(55.00)$
25.00	$=$	$r(55.00)$		
$\dfrac{25.00}{55.00}$	$=$	r		
0.455	$\approx$	r		

To change the answer to a percent, multiply 0.455 by 100. Thus his rate of profit is 45.5%.   ■

We can solve certain types of investment and money problems by using an algebraic approach. Consider the following examples.

Erick has 40 coins, consisting only of dimes and nickels, worth $3.35. How many dimes and how many nickels does he have?

Solution

Let x represent the number of dimes. Then the number of nickels can be represented by the total number of coins minus the number of dimes. Hence $40 - x$ represents the number of nickels. Because we know the amount of money Erick has, we need to multiply the number of each coin by its value. Use the following guideline.

Money from the dimes	Plus	Money from the nickels	Equals	Total money	
↓		↓		↓	
$0.10x$	$+$	$0.05(40 - x)$	$=$	3.35	
$10x$	$+$	$5(40 - x)$	$=$	335	Multiply both sides by 100.
$10x$	$+$	$200 - 5x$	$=$	335	
		$5x + 200$	$=$	335	
		$5x$	$=$	135	
		x	$=$	27	

The number of dimes is 27, and the number of nickels is $40 - x = 13$. So, Erick has 27 dimes and 13 nickels.   ■

A man invests $8000, part of it at 11% and the remainder at 12%. His total yearly interest from the two investments is $930. How much did he invest at each rate?

Solution

Let x represent the amount he invested at 11%. Then $8000 - x$ represents the amount he invested at 12%. Use the following guideline.

Interest earned from 11% investment	+	Interest earned from 12% investment	=	Total amount of interest earned
↓		↓		↓
$(11\%)(x)$	$+$	$(12\%)(8000 - x)$	$=$	$\$930$

Solving this equation yields

$$(11\%)(x) + (12\%)(8000 - x) = 930$$

$$0.11x + 0.12(8000 - x) = 930$$

$$11x + 12(8000 - x) = 93{,}000 \qquad \text{Multiply both sides by 100.}$$
$$11x + 96{,}000 - 12x = 93{,}000$$
$$-x + 96{,}000 = 93{,}000$$
$$-x = -3000$$
$$x = 3000$$

Therefore, $3000 was invested at 11%, and $8000 − $3000 = $5000 was invested at 12%.   ■

Don't forget to check word problems; determine whether the answers satisfy the conditions stated in the *original* problem. A check for Problem 7 follows.

 Check

We claim that $3000 is invested at 11% and $5000 at 12%, and this satisfies the condition that $8000 is invested. The $3000 at 11% produces $330 of interest, and the $5000 at 12% produces $600. Therefore, the interest from the investments is $930. The conditions of the problem are satisfied, and our answers are correct.

As you tackle word problems throughout this text, keep in mind that our primary objective is to expand your repertoire of problem-solving techniques. We have chosen problems that provide you with the opportunity to use a variety of approaches to solving problems. Don't fall into the trap of thinking "I will never be faced with this kind of problem." That is not the issue; the goal is to develop problem-solving techniques. In the examples that follow we are sharing some of our ideas for solving problems, but don't hesitate to use your own ingenuity. Furthermore, don't become discouraged — all of us have difficulty with some problems. Give each your best shot!

Problem Set 2.3

For Problems 1–28, solve each equation.

1. $0.14x = 2.8$

2. $1.6x = 8$

3. $0.09y = 4.5$

4. $0.07y = 0.42$

5. $n + 0.4n = 56$

6. $n - 0.5n = 12$

7. $s = 9 + 0.25s$

8. $s = 15 + 0.4s$

9. $s = 3.3 + 0.45s$

10. $s = 2.1 + 0.6s$

11. $0.11x + 0.12(900 - x) = 104$

12. $0.09x + 0.11(500 - x) = 51$

13. $0.08(x + 200) = 0.07x + 20$

14. $0.07x = 152 - 0.08(2000 - x)$

15. $0.12t - 2.1 = 0.07t - 0.2$

16. $0.13t - 3.4 = 0.08t - 0.4$

17. $0.92 + 0.9(x - 0.3) = 2x - 5.95$

18. $0.3(2n - 5) = 11 - 0.65n$

19. $0.1d + 0.11(d + 1500) = 795$

20. $0.8x + 0.9(850 - x) = 715$

21. $0.12x + 0.1(5000 - x) = 560$

22. $0.10t + 0.12(t + 1000) = 560$

23. $0.09(x + 200) = 0.08x + 22$

24. $0.09x = 1650 - 0.12(x + 5000)$

25. $0.3(2t + 0.1) = 8.43$

26. $0.5(3t + 0.7) = 20.6$

27. $0.1(x - 0.1) - 0.4(x + 2) = -5.31$

28. $0.2(x + 0.2) + 0.5(x - 0.4) = 5.44$

For Problems 29–50, use an algebraic approach to solve each problem.

29. Judy bought a coat at a 20% discount sale for $72. What was the original price of the coat?

30. Jim bought a pair of slacks at a 25% discount sale for $24. What was the original price of the slacks?

31. Find the discount sale price of a $64 item that is on sale for 15% off.

32. Find the discount sale price of a $72 item that is on sale for 35% off.

33. A retailer has some skirts that cost $30 each. She wants to sell them at a profit of 60% of the cost. What price should she charge for the skirts?

34. The owner of a pizza parlor wants to make a profit of 70% of the cost for each pizza sold. If it costs $2.50 to make a pizza, at what price should each pizza be sold?

35. If a ring costs a jeweler $200, at what price should it be sold to yield a profit of 50% on the selling price?

36. If a head of lettuce costs a retailer $0.32, at what price should it be sold to yield a profit of 60% on the selling price?

37. If a pair of shoes costs a retailer $24, and he sells them for $39.60, what is his rate of profit based on the cost?

38. A retailer has some skirts that cost her $45 each. If she sells them for $83.25 per skirt, find her rate of profit based on the cost.

39. If a computer costs an electronics dealer $300, and she sells them for $800, what is her rate of profit based on the selling price?

40. A textbook costs a bookstore $45, and the store sells it for $60. Find the rate of profit based on the selling price.

41. Mitsuko's salary for next year is $34,775. This represents a 7% increase over this year's salary. Find Mitsuko's present salary.

42. Don bought a used car for $15,794, with 6% tax included. What was the price of the car without the tax?

43. Eva invested a certain amount of money at 10% interest and $1500 more than that amount at 11%. Her total yearly interest was $795. How much did she invest at each rate?

44. A total of $4000 was invested, part of it at 8% interest and the remainder at 9%. If the total yearly interest amounted to $350, how much was invested at each rate?

45. A sum of $95,000 is split between two investments, one paying 6% and the other 9%. If the total yearly interest amounted to $7290, how much was invested at 9%?

46. If $1500 is invested at 6% interest, how much money must be invested at 9% so that the total return for both investments is $301.50?

47. Suppose that Javier has a handful of coins, consisting of pennies, nickels, and dimes, worth $2.63. The number of nickels is 1 less than twice the number of pennies, and the number of dimes is 3 more than the number of nickels. How many coins of each kind does he have?

48. Sarah has a collection of nickels, dimes, and quarters worth $15.75. She has 10 more dimes than nickels and twice as many quarters as dimes. How many coins of each kind does she have?

49. A collection of 70 coins consisting of dimes, quarters, and half-dollars has a value of $17.75. There are three times as many quarters as dimes. Find the number of each kind of coin.

50. Abby has 37 coins, consisting only of dimes and quarters, worth $7.45. How many dimes and how many quarters does she have?

■ ■ ■ **THOUGHTS INTO WORDS**

51. Go to Problem 39 and calculate the rate of profit based on cost. Compare the rate of profit based on cost to the rate of profit based on selling price. From a consumer's viewpoint, would you prefer that a retailer figure his profit on the basis of the cost of an item or on the basis of its selling price? Explain your answer.

52. Is a 10% discount followed by a 30% discount the same as a 30% discount followed by a 10% discount? Justify your answer.

53. What is wrong with the following solution and how should it be done?

$$1.2x + 2 = 3.8$$
$$10(1.2x) + 2 = 10(3.8)$$
$$12x + 2 = 38$$
$$12x = 36$$
$$x = 3$$

■ ■ ■ **FURTHER INVESTIGATIONS**

For Problems 54–63, solve each equation and express the solutions in decimal form. Be sure to check your solutions. Use your calculator whenever it seems helpful.

54. $1.2x + 3.4 = 5.2$

55. $0.12x - 0.24 = 0.66$

56. $0.12x + 0.14(550 - x) = 72.5$

57. $0.14t + 0.13(890 - t) = 67.95$

58. $0.7n + 1.4 = 3.92$

59. $0.14n - 0.26 = 0.958$

60. $0.3(d + 1.8) = 4.86$

61. $0.6(d - 4.8) = 7.38$

62. $0.8(2x - 1.4) = 19.52$

63. $0.5(3x + 0.7) = 20.6$

64. The following formula can be used to determine the selling price of an item when the profit is based on a percent of the selling price.

$$\text{Selling price} = \frac{\text{Cost}}{100\% - \text{Percent of profit}}$$

Show how this formula is developed.

65. A retailer buys an item for $90, resells it for $100, and claims that she is making only a 10% profit. Is this claim correct?

66. Is a 10% discount followed by a 20% discount equal to a 30% discount? Defend your answer.

2.4 Formulas

To find the distance traveled in 4 hours at a rate of 55 miles per hour, we multiply the rate times the time; thus the distance is $55(4) = 220$ miles. We can state the rule *distance equals rate times time* as a formula: $d = rt$. Formulas are rules we state in symbolic form, usually as equations.

Formulas are typically used in two different ways. At times a formula is solved for a specific variable when we are given the numerical values for the other variables. This is much like evaluating an algebraic expression. At other times we need to change the form of an equation by solving for one variable in terms of the other variables. Throughout our work on formulas, we will use the properties of equality and the techniques we have previously learned for solving equations. Let's consider some examples.

EXAMPLE 1

If we invest P dollars at r percent for t years, the amount of simple interest i is given by the formula $i = Prt$. Find the amount of interest earned by \$500 at 7% for 2 years.

Solution

By substituting \$500 for P, 7% for r, and 2 for t, we obtain

$$i = Prt$$

$$i = (500)(7\%)(2)$$

$$i = (500)(0.07)(2)$$

$$i = 70$$

Thus we earn \$70 in interest.   ■

EXAMPLE 2

If we invest P dollars at a simple rate of r percent, then the amount A accumulated after t years is given by the formula $A = P + Prt$. If we invest \$500 at 8%, how many years will it take to accumulate \$600?

Solution

Substituting \$500 for P, 8% for r, and \$600 for A, we obtain

$$A = P + Prt$$

$$600 = 500 + 500(8\%)(t)$$

Solving this equation for t yields

$$600 = 500 + 500(0.08)(t)$$

$$600 = 500 + 40t$$

$$100 = 40t$$

$$2\frac{1}{2} = t$$

It will take $2\frac{1}{2}$ years to accumulate \$600.   ■

When we are using a formula, it is sometimes convenient first to change its form. For example, suppose we are to use the *perimeter* formula for a rectangle ($P = 2l + 2w$) to complete the following chart.

Perimeter (*P*)	32	24	36	18	56	80	
Length (*l*)	10	7	14	5	15	22	All in centimeters
Width (*w*)	?	?	?	?	?	?	

Because w is the unknown quantity, it would simplify the computational work if we first solved the formula for w in terms of the other variables as follows:

$$P = 2l + 2w$$

$$P - 2l = 2w \qquad \text{Add } -2l \text{ to both sides.}$$

$$\frac{P - 2l}{2} = w \qquad \text{Multiply both sides by } \frac{1}{2}.$$

$$w = \frac{P - 2l}{2} \qquad \text{Apply the symmetric property of equality.}$$

Now for each value for P and l, we can easily determine the corresponding value for w. Be sure you agree with the following values for w: 6, 5, 4, 4, 13, and 18. Likewise we can also solve the formula $P = 2l + 2w$ for l in terms of P and w. The result would be $l = \frac{P - 2w}{2}$.

Let's consider some other often-used formulas and see how we can use the properties of equality to alter their forms. Here we will be solving a formula for a specified variable in terms of the other variables. The key is to isolate the term that contains the variable being solved for. Then, by appropriately applying the multiplication property of equality, we will solve the formula for the specified variable. Throughout this section, we will identify formulas when we first use them. (Some geometric formulas are also given on the endsheets.)

E X A M P L E   3

Solve $A = \frac{1}{2}bh$ for h (area of a triangle).

Solution

$$A = \frac{1}{2}bh$$

$$2A = bh \qquad \text{Multiply both sides by 2.}$$

$$\frac{2A}{b} = h \qquad \text{Multiply both sides by } \frac{1}{b}.$$

$$h = \frac{2A}{b} \qquad \text{Apply the symmetric property of equality.} \qquad \blacksquare$$

E X A M P L E   4

Solve $A = P + Prt$ for t.

Solution

$$A = P + Prt$$

$$A - P = Prt \qquad \text{Add } -P \text{ to both sides.}$$

$$\frac{A - P}{Pr} = t \qquad \text{Multiply both sides by } \frac{1}{Pr}.$$

$$t = \frac{A - P}{Pr} \qquad \text{Apply the symmetric property of equality.} \qquad \blacksquare$$

EXAMPLE 5

Solve $A = P + Prt$ for P.

Solution

$$A = P + Prt$$

$$A = P(1 + rt) \qquad \text{Apply the distributive property to the right side.}$$

$$\frac{A}{1 + rt} = P \qquad \text{Multiply both sides by } \frac{1}{1 + rt}.$$

$$P = \frac{A}{1 + rt} \qquad \text{Apply the symmetric property of equality.} \qquad \blacksquare$$

EXAMPLE 6

Solve $A = \frac{1}{2}h(b_1 + b_2)$ for b_1 (area of a trapezoid).

Solution

$$A = \frac{1}{2}h(b_1 + b_2)$$

$$2A = h(b_1 + b_2) \qquad \text{Multiply both sides by 2.}$$

$$2A = hb_1 + hb_2 \qquad \text{Apply the distributive property to right side.}$$

$$2A - hb_2 = hb_1 \qquad \text{Add } -hb_2 \text{ to both sides.}$$

$$\frac{2A - hb_2}{h} = b_1 \qquad \text{Multiply both sides by } \frac{1}{h}.$$

$$b_1 = \frac{2A - hb_2}{h} \qquad \text{Apply the symmetric property of equality.} \qquad \blacksquare$$

In order to isolate the term containing the variable being solved for, we will apply the distributive property in different ways. In Example 5 you *must* use the distributive property to change from the form $P + Prt$ to $P(1 + rt)$. However, in Example 6 we used the distributive property to change $h(b_1 + b_2)$ to $hb_1 + hb_2$. In both problems the key is to isolate the term that contains the variable being solved for, so that an appropriate application of the multiplication property of equality will produce the desired result. Also note the use of subscripts to identify the two bases of a trapezoid. Subscripts enable us to use the same letter b to identify the bases, but b_1 represents one base and b_2 the other.

Sometimes we are faced with equations such as $ax + b = c$, where x is the variable and a, b, and c are referred to as *arbitrary constants*. Again we can use the properties of equality to solve the equation for x as follows:

$$ax + b = c$$

$$ax = c - b \qquad \text{Add } -b \text{ to both sides.}$$

$$x = \frac{c - b}{a} \qquad \text{Multiply both sides by } \frac{1}{a}.$$

In Chapter 7, we will be working with equations such as $2x - 5y = 7$, which are called equations of two variables in x and y. Often we need to change the form of such equations by solving for one variable in terms of the other variable. The properties of equality provide the basis for doing this.

EXAMPLE 7

Solve $2x - 5y = 7$ for y in terms of x.

Solution

$$2x - 5y = 7$$

$$-5y = 7 - 2x \qquad \text{Add } -2x \text{ to both sides.}$$

$$y = \frac{7 - 2x}{-5} \qquad \text{Multiply both sides by } -\frac{1}{5}.$$

$$y = \frac{2x - 7}{5} \qquad \text{Multiply the numerator and denominator of the fraction on the right by } -1. \text{ (This final step is not absolutely necessary, but usually we prefer to have a positive number as a denominator.)} \qquad ■$$

Equations of two variables may also contain arbitrary constants. For example, the equation $\dfrac{x}{a} + \dfrac{y}{b} = 1$ contains the variables x and y and the arbitrary constants a and b.

EXAMPLE 8

Solve the equation $\dfrac{x}{a} + \dfrac{y}{b} = 1$ for x.

Solution

$$\frac{x}{a} + \frac{y}{b} = 1$$

$$ab\left(\frac{x}{a} + \frac{y}{b}\right) = ab(1) \qquad \text{Multiply both sides by } ab.$$

$$bx + ay = ab$$

$$bx = ab - ay \qquad \text{Add } -ay \text{ to both sides.}$$

$$x = \frac{ab - ay}{b} \qquad \text{Multiply both sides by } \frac{1}{b}. \qquad ■$$

Remark: Traditionally, equations that contain more than one variable, such as those in Examples 3–8, are called **literal equations**. As illustrated, it is sometimes necessary to solve a literal equation for one variable in terms of the other variable(s).

■ Formulas and Problem Solving

We often use formulas as guidelines for setting up an appropriate algebraic equation when solving a word problem. Let's consider an example to illustrate this point.

PROBLEM 1

How long will it take $500 to double itself if we invest it at 8% simple interest?

Solution

For $500 to grow into $1000 (double itself), it must earn $500 in interest. Thus we let t represent the number of years it will take $500 to earn $500 in interest. Now we can use the formula $i = Prt$ as a guideline.

$$i = Prt$$

$$500 = 500(8\%)(t)$$

Solving this equation, we obtain

$$500 = 500(0.08)(t)$$

$$1 = 0.08t$$

$$100 = 8t$$

$$12\frac{1}{2} = t$$

It will take $12\frac{1}{2}$ years.   ■

Sometimes we use formulas in the analysis of a problem but not as the main guideline for setting up the equation. For example, uniform motion problems involve the formula $d = rt$, but the main guideline for setting up an equation for such problems is usually a statement about times, rates, or distances. Let's consider an example to demonstrate.

PROBLEM 2

Mercedes starts jogging at 5 miles per hour. One-half hour later, Karen starts jogging on the same route at 7 miles per hour. How long will it take Karen to catch Mercedes?

Solution

First, let's sketch a diagram and record some information (Figure 2.3).

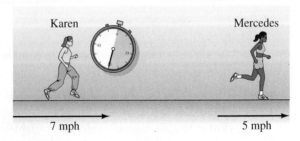

Karen   Mercedes

7 mph   5 mph

Figure 2.3

If we let t represent Karen's time, then $t + \dfrac{1}{2}$ represents Mercedes' time. We can use the statement *Karen's distance equals Mercedes' distance* as a guideline.

Karen's distance   Mercedes' distance

$$7t \quad = \quad 5\left(t + \frac{1}{2}\right)$$

Solving this equation, we obtain

$$7t = 5t + \frac{5}{2}$$

$$2t = \frac{5}{2}$$

$$t = \frac{5}{4}$$

Karen should catch Mercedes in $1\frac{1}{4}$ hours.   ■

Remark: An important part of problem solving is the ability to sketch a meaningful figure that can be used to record the given information and help in the analysis of the problem. Our sketches were done by professional artists for aesthetic purposes. Your sketches can be very roughly drawn as long as they depict the situation in a way that helps you analyze the problem.

Note that in the solution of Problem 2 we used a figure and a simple arrow diagram to record and organize the information pertinent to the problem. Some people find it helpful to use a chart for that purpose. We shall use a chart in Problem 3. Keep in mind that we are not trying to dictate a particular approach; you decide what works best for you.

PROBLEM 3

Two trains leave a city at the same time, one traveling east and the other traveling west. At the end of $9\frac{1}{2}$ hours, they are 1292 miles apart. If the rate of the train traveling east is 8 miles per hour faster than the rate of the other train, find their rates.

Solution

If we let r represent the rate of the westbound train, then $r + 8$ represents the rate of the eastbound train. Now we can record the times and rates in a chart and then use the distance formula ($d = rt$) to represent the distances.

	Rate	Time	Distance ($d = rt$)
Westbound train	r	$9\frac{1}{2}$	$\frac{19}{2}r$
Eastbound train	$r + 8$	$9\frac{1}{2}$	$\frac{19}{2}(r + 8)$

Because the distance that the westbound train travels plus the distance that the eastbound train travels equals 1292 miles, we can set up and solve the following equation.

$$\begin{array}{ccc} \text{Eastbound} & + & \text{Westbound} \\ \text{distance} & & \text{distance} \end{array} = \begin{array}{c} \text{Miles} \\ \text{apart} \end{array}$$

$$\frac{19r}{2} + \frac{19(r + 8)}{2} = 1292$$

$$19r + 19(r + 8) = 2584$$

$$19r + 19r + 152 = 2584$$

$$38r = 2432$$

$$r = 64$$

The westbound train travels at a rate of 64 miles per hour, and the eastbound train travels at a rate of $64 + 8 = 72$ miles per hour. ∎

Now let's consider a problem that is often referred to as a mixture problem. There is no basic formula that applies to all of these problems, but we suggest that you think in terms of a pure substance, which is often helpful in setting up a guideline. Also keep in mind that the phrase "a 40% solution of some substance" means that the solution contains 40% of that particular substance and 60% of something else mixed with it. For example, a 40% salt solution contains 40% salt, and the other 60% is something else, probably water. Now let's illustrate what we mean by suggesting that you think in terms of a pure substance.

P R O B L E M   4

Bryan's Pest Control stocks a 7% solution of insecticide for lawns and also a 15% solution. How many gallons of each should be mixed to produce 40 gallons that is 12% insecticide?

Solution

The key idea in solving such a problem is to recognize the following guideline.

$$\left(\begin{array}{c}\text{Amount of insecticide} \\ \text{in the 7\% solution}\end{array}\right) + \left(\begin{array}{c}\text{Amount of insecticide} \\ \text{in the 15\% solution}\end{array}\right) = \left(\begin{array}{c}\text{Amount of insecticide in} \\ \text{40 gallons of 15\% solution}\end{array}\right)$$

Let x represent the gallons of 7% solution. Then $40 - x$ represents the gallons of 15% solution. The guideline translates into the following equation.

$$(7\%)(x) + (15\%)(40 - x) = (12\%)(40)$$

Solving this equation yields

$$0.07x + 0.15(40 - x) = 0.12(40)$$

$$0.07x + 6 - 0.15x = 4.8$$

$$-0.08x + 6 = 4.8$$

$$-0.08x = -1.2$$
$$x = 15$$

Thus 15 gallons of 7% solution and $40 - x = 25$ gallons of 15% solution need to be mixed to obtain 40 gallons of 12% solution.   ∎

P R O B L E M   5

How many liters of pure alcohol must we add to 20 liters of a 40% solution to obtain a 60% solution?

Solution

The key idea in solving such a problem is to recognize the following guideline.

$$\begin{pmatrix} \text{Amount of pure} \\ \text{alcohol in the} \\ \text{original solution} \end{pmatrix} + \begin{pmatrix} \text{Amount of} \\ \text{pure alcohol} \\ \text{to be added} \end{pmatrix} = \begin{pmatrix} \text{Amount of pure} \\ \text{alcohol in the} \\ \text{final solution} \end{pmatrix}$$

Let l represent the number of liters of pure alcohol to be added, and the guideline translates into the following equation.

$$(40\%)(20) + l = 60\%(20 + l)$$

Solving this equation yields

$$0.4(20) + l = 0.6(20 + l)$$
$$8 + l = 12 + 0.6l$$
$$0.4l = 4$$
$$l = 10$$

We need to add 10 liters of pure alcohol. (Remember to check this answer back into the original statement of the problem.)   ∎

Problem Set 2.4

1. Solve $i = Prt$ for i, given that $P = \$300$, $r = 8\%$, and $t = 5$ years.

2. Solve $i = Prt$ for i, given that $P = \$500$, $r = 9\%$, and $t = 3\frac{1}{2}$ years.

3. Solve $i = Prt$ for t, given that $P = \$400$, $r = 11\%$, and $i = \$132$.

4. Solve $i = Prt$ for t, given that $P = \$250$, $r = 12\%$, and $i = \$120$.

5. Solve $i = Prt$ for r, given that $P = \$600$, $t = 2\frac{1}{2}$ years, and $i = \$90$. Express r as a percent.

6. Solve $i = Prt$ for r, given that $P = \$700$, $t = 2$ years, and $i = \$126$. Express r as a percent.

7. Solve $i = Prt$ for P, given that $r = 9\%$, $t = 3$ years, and $i = \$216$.

8. Solve $i = Prt$ for P, given that $r = 8\frac{1}{2}\%$, $t = 2$ years, and $i = \$204$.

9. Solve $A = P + Prt$ for A, given that $P = \$1000$, $r = 12\%$, and $t = 5$ years.

10. Solve $A = P + Prt$ for A, given that $P = \$850$, $r = 9\frac{1}{2}\%$, and $t = 10$ years.

11. Solve $A = P + Prt$ for r, given that $A = \$1372$, $P = \$700$, and $t = 12$ years. Express r as a percent.

12. Solve $A = P + Prt$ for r, given that $A = \$516$, $P = \$300$, and $t = 8$ years. Express r as a percent.

13. Solve $A = P + Prt$ for P, given that $A = \$326$, $r = 7\%$, and $t = 9$ years.

14. Solve $A = P + Prt$ for P, given that $A = \$720$, $r = 8\%$, and $t = 10$ years.

15. Use the formula $A = \dfrac{1}{2}h(b_1 + b_2)$ and complete the following chart.

A	98	104	49	162	$16\frac{1}{2}$	$38\frac{1}{2}$	square feet
h	14	8	7	9	3	11	feet
b_1	8	12	4	16	4	5	feet
b_2	?	?	?	?	?	?	feet

A = area, h = height, b_1 = one base, b_2 = other base

16. Use the formula $P = 2l + 2w$ and complete the following chart. (You may want to change the form of the formula.)

P	28	18	12	34	68	centimeters
w	6	3	2	7	14	centimeters
l	?	?	?	?	?	centimeters

P = perimeter, w = width, l = length

Solve each of the following for the indicated variable.

17. $V = Bh$ for h (Volume of a prism)

18. $A = lw$ for l (Area of a rectangle)

19. $V = \pi r^2 h$ for h (Volume of a circular cylinder)

20. $V = \dfrac{1}{3}Bh$ for B (Volume of a pyramid)

21. $C = 2\pi r$ for r (Circumference of a circle)

22. $A = 2\pi r^2 + 2\pi rh$ for h (Surface area of a circular cylinder)

23. $I = \dfrac{100M}{C}$ for C (Intelligence quotient)

24. $A = \dfrac{1}{2}h(b_1 + b_2)$ for h (Area of a trapezoid)

25. $F = \dfrac{9}{5}C + 32$ for C (Celsius to Fahrenheit)

26. $C = \dfrac{5}{9}(F - 32)$ for F (Fahrenheit to Celsius)

For Problems 27–36, solve each equation for x.

27. $y = mx + b$

28. $\dfrac{x}{a} + \dfrac{y}{b} = 1$

29. $y - y_1 = m(x - x_1)$

30. $a(x + b) = c$

31. $a(x + b) = b(x - c)$

32. $x(a - b) = m(x - c)$

33. $\dfrac{x - a}{b} = c$

34. $\dfrac{x}{a} - 1 = b$

35. $\dfrac{1}{3}x + a = \dfrac{1}{2}b$

36. $\dfrac{2}{3}x - \dfrac{1}{4}a = b$

For Problems 37–46, solve each equation for the indicated variable.

37. $2x - 5y = 7$ for x

38. $5x - 6y = 12$ for x

39. $-7x - y = 4$ for y

40. $3x - 2y = -1$ for y

41. $3(x - 2y) = 4$ for x

42. $7(2x + 5y) = 6$ for y

43. $\dfrac{y - a}{b} = \dfrac{x + b}{c}$ for x

44. $\dfrac{x - a}{b} = \dfrac{y - a}{c}$ for y

45. $(y + 1)(a - 3) = x - 2$ for y

46. $(y - 2)(a + 1) = x$ for y

Solve each of Problems 47–62 by setting up and solving an appropriate algebraic equation.

47. Suppose that the length of a certain rectangle is 2 meters less than four times its width. The perimeter of the rectangle is 56 meters. Find the length and width of the rectangle.

48. The perimeter of a triangle is 42 inches. The second side is 1 inch more than twice the first side, and the third side is 1 inch less than three times the first side. Find the lengths of the three sides of the triangle.

49. How long will it take $500 to double itself at 9% simple interest?

50. How long will it take $700 to triple itself at 10% simple interest?

51. How long will it take P dollars to double itself at 9% simple interest?

52. How long will it take P dollars to triple itself at 10% simple interest?

53. Two airplanes leave Chicago at the same time and fly in opposite directions. If one travels at 450 miles per hour and the other at 550 miles per hour, how long will it take for them to be 4000 miles apart?

54. Look at Figure 2.4. Tyrone leaves city A on a moped traveling toward city B at 18 miles per hour. At the same time, Tina leaves city B on a bicycle traveling toward city A at 14 miles per hour. The distance between the two cities is 112 miles. How long will it take before Tyrone and Tina meet?

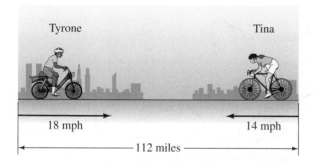

Figure 2.4

55. Juan starts walking at 4 miles per hour. An hour and a half later, Cathy starts jogging along the same route at 6 miles per hour. How long will it take Cathy to catch up with Juan?

56. A car leaves a town at 60 kilometers per hour. How long will it take a second car, traveling at 75 kilometers per hour, to catch the first car if it leaves 1 hour later?

57. Bret started on a 70-mile bicycle ride at 20 miles per hour. After a time he became a little tired and slowed down to 12 miles per hour for the rest of the trip. The entire trip of 70 miles took $4\frac{1}{2}$ hours. How far had Bret ridden when he reduced his speed to 12 miles per hour?

58. How many gallons of a 12%-salt solution must be mixed with 6 gallons of a 20%-salt solution to obtain a 15%-salt solution?

59. Suppose that you have a supply of a 30% solution of alcohol and a 70% solution of alcohol. How many quarts of each should be mixed to produce 20 quarts that is 40% alcohol?

60. How many cups of grapefruit juice must be added to 40 cups of punch that is 5% grapefruit juice to obtain a punch that is 10% grapefruit juice?

61. How many milliliters of pure acid must be added to 150 milliliters of a 30% solution of acid to obtain a 40% solution?

62. A 16-quart radiator contains a 50% solution of antifreeze. How much needs to be drained out and replaced with pure antifreeze to obtain a 60% antifreeze solution?

■ ■ ■ **THOUGHTS INTO WORDS**

63. Some people subtract 32 and then divide by 2 to estimate the change from a Fahrenheit reading to a Celsius reading. Why does this give an estimate and how good is the estimate?

64. One of your classmates analyzes Problem 56 as follows: "The first car has traveled 60 kilometers before the second car starts. Because the second car travels 15 kilometers per hour faster, it will take $\frac{60}{15} = 4$ hours for the second car to overtake the first car." How would you react to this analysis of the problem?

65. Summarize the new ideas relative to problem solving that you have acquired thus far in this course.

For Problems 66–73, use your calculator to help solve each formula for the indicated variable.

66. Solve $i = Prt$ for i, given that $P = \$875, r = 12\frac{1}{2}\%$, and $t = 4$ years.

67. Solve $i = Prt$ for i, given that $P = \$1125, r = 13\frac{1}{4}\%$, and $t = 4$ years.

68. Solve $i = Prt$ for t, given that $i = \$453.25, P = \$925$, and $r = 14\%$.

69. Solve $i = Prt$ for t, given that $i = \$243.75, P = \$1250$, and $r = 13\%$.

70. Solve $i = Prt$ for r, given that $i = \$356.50, P = \$1550$, and $t = 2$ years. Express r as a percent.

71. Solve $i = Prt$ for r, given that $i = \$159.50, P = \$2200$, and $t = 0.5$ of a year. Express r as a percent.

72. Solve $A = P + Prt$ for P, given that $A = \$1423.50$, $r = 9\frac{1}{2}\%$, and $t = 1$ year.

73. Solve $A = P + Prt$ for P, given that $A = \$2173.75$, $r = 8\frac{3}{4}\%$, and $t = 2$ years.

74. If you have access to computer software that includes spreadsheets, go to Problems 15 and 16. You should be able to enter the given information in rows. Then, when you enter a formula in a cell below the information and drag that formula across the columns, the software should produce all the answers.

2.5   Inequalities

We listed the basic inequality symbols in Section 1.2. With these symbols we can make various **statements of inequality**:

$a < b$ means a is less than b.

$a \leq b$ means a is less than or equal to b.

$a > b$ means a is greater than b.

$a \geq b$ means a is greater than or equal to b.

Here are some examples of **numerical statements of inequality**:

$$7 + 8 > 10 \qquad -4 + (-6) \geq -10$$

$$-4 > -6 \qquad 7 - 9 \leq -2$$

$$7 - 1 < 20 \qquad 3 + 4 > 12$$

$$8(-3) < 5(-3) \qquad 7 - 1 < 0$$

Note that only $3 + 4 > 12$ and $7 - 1 < 0$ are *false*; the other six are *true* numerical statements.

Algebraic inequalities contain one or more variables. The following are examples of algebraic inequalities.

$$x + 4 > 8 \qquad 3x + 2y \leq 4$$

$$3x - 1 < 15 \qquad x^2 + y^2 + z^2 \geq 7$$

$$y^2 + 2y - 4 \geq 0$$

An algebraic inequality such as $x + 4 > 8$ is neither true nor false as it stands, and we call it an **open sentence**. For each numerical value we substitute for x, the algebraic inequality $x + 4 > 8$ becomes a numerical statement of inequality that is true or false. For example, if $x = -3$, then $x + 4 > 8$ becomes $-3 + 4 > 8$, which is false. If $x = 5$, then $x + 4 > 8$ becomes $5 + 4 > 8$, which is true. **Solving an inequality** is the process of finding the numbers that make an algebraic inequality a true numerical statement. We call such numbers the *solutions* of the inequality; the solutions *satisfy* the inequality.

The general process for solving inequalities closely parallels the process for solving equations. We continue to replace the given inequality with equivalent, but simpler, inequalities. For example,

$$3x + 4 > 10 \tag{1}$$

$$3x > 6 \tag{2}$$

$$x > 2 \tag{3}$$

are all equivalent inequalities; that is, they all have the same solutions. By inspection we see that the solutions for (3) are all numbers greater than *2*. Thus (1) has the same solutions.

The exact procedure for simplifying inequalities so that we can determine the solutions is based primarily on two properties. The first of these is the addition property of inequality.

Addition Property of Inequality

For all real numbers a, b, and c,

$$a > b \quad \text{if and only if } a + c > b + c$$

The addition property of inequality states that we can add any number to both sides of an inequality to produce an equivalent inequality. We have stated the property in terms of $>$, but analogous properties exist for $<$, $\geq$, and $\leq$.

Before we state the multiplication property of inequality let's look at some numerical examples.

$2 < 5$	Multiply both sides by 4	$4(2) < 4(5)$	$8 < 20$
$-3 > -7$	Multiply both sides by 2	$2(-3) > 2(-7)$	$-6 > -14$
$-4 < 6$	Multiply both sides by 10	$10(-4) < 10(6)$	$-40 < 60$
$4 < 8$	Multiply both sides by -3	$-3(4) > -3(8)$	$-12 > -24$
$3 > -2$	Multiply both sides by -4	$-4(3) < -4(-2)$	$-12 < 8$
$-4 < -1$	Multiply both sides by -2	$-2(-4) > -2(-1)$	$8 > 2$

Notice in the first three examples that when we multiply both sides of an inequality by a *positive number*, we get an inequality of the *same sense*. That means that if the original inequality is *less than*, then the new inequality is *less than*; and if the original inequality is *greater than*, then the new inequality is *greater than*. The last three examples illustrate that when we multiply both sides of an inequality by a *negative number* we get an inequality of the *opposite sense*.

We can state the multiplication property of inequality as follows.

Multiplication Property of Inequality

(a) For all real numbers a, b, and c, with $c > 0$,

$$a > b \quad \text{if and only if} \quad ac > bc$$

(b) For all real numbers a, b, and c, with $c < 0$,

$$a > b \quad \text{if and only if} \quad ac < bc$$

Similar properties hold if we reverse each inequality or if we replace $>$ with $\geq$ and $<$ with $\leq$. For example, if $a \leq b$ and $c < 0$, then $ac \geq bc$.

Now let's use the addition and multiplication properties of inequality to help solve some inequalities.

E X A M P L E   1

Solve $3x - 4 > 8$.

Solution

$$3x - 4 > 8$$
$$3x - 4 + 4 > 8 + 4 \qquad \text{Add 4 to both sides.}$$
$$3x > 12$$
$$\frac{1}{3}(3x) > \frac{1}{3}(12) \qquad \text{Multiply both sides by } \frac{1}{3}.$$
$$x > 4$$

The solution set is $\{x \mid x > 4\}$. (Remember that we read the set $\{x \mid x > 4\}$ as "the set of all x such that x is greater than 4.")   ■

In Example 1, once we obtained the simple inequality $x > 4$, the solution set $\{x \mid x > 4\}$ became obvious. We can also express solution sets for inequalities on a number line graph. Figure 2.5 shows the graph of the solution set for Example 1. The left-hand parenthesis at 4 indicates that 4 is *not* a solution, and the red part of the line to the right of 4 indicates that all numbers greater than 4 are solutions.

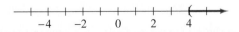

Figure 2.5

It is also convenient to express solution sets of inequalities using **interval notation**. For example, the notation $(4, \infty)$ also refers to the set of real numbers greater than 4. As in Figure 2.5, the left-hand parenthesis indicates that 4 is not to be included. The infinity symbol, ∞, along with the right-hand parenthesis, indicates that there is no right-hand endpoint. Following is a partial list of interval notations, along with the sets of graphs they represent (Figure 2.6). We will add to this list in the next section.

Set	Graph	Interval notation
$\{x \mid x > a\}$		(a, ∞)
$\{x \mid x \geq a\}$		$[a, \infty)$
$\{x \mid x < b\}$		$(-\infty, b)$
$\{x \mid x \leq b\}$		$(-\infty, b]$

Figure 2.6

Note the use of square brackets to indicate the inclusion of endpoints. From now on, we will express the solution sets of inequalities using interval notation.

E X A M P L E   2

Solve $-2x + 1 > 5$ and graph the solutions.

Solution

$$-2x + 1 > 5$$

$$-2x + 1 + (-1) > 5 + (-1) \qquad \text{Add } -1 \text{ to both sides.}$$

$$-2x > 4$$

$$-\frac{1}{2}(-2x) < -\frac{1}{2}(4) \qquad \text{Multiply both sides by } -\frac{1}{2}.$$

$$x < -2 \qquad \begin{array}{l}\text{Note that the sense of the}\\ \text{inequality has been reversed.}\end{array}$$

The solution set is $(-\infty, -2)$, which can be illustrated on a number line as in Figure 2.7.

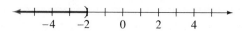

Figure 2.7

Checking solutions for an inequality presents a problem. Obviously, we cannot check all of the infinitely many solutions for a particular inequality. However, by checking at least one solution, especially when the multiplication property has been used, we might catch the common mistake of forgetting to change the sense of an inequality. In Example 2 we are claiming that all numbers less than -2 will satisfy the original inequality. Let's check one such number, say -4.

$$-2x + 1 > 5$$

$$-2(-4) + 1 \overset{?}{>} 5 \quad \text{when } x = -4$$

$$8 + 1 \overset{?}{>} 5$$

$$9 > 5$$

Thus -4 satisfies the original inequality. Had we forgotten to switch the sense of the inequality when both sides were multiplied by $-\dfrac{1}{2}$, our answer would have been $x > -2$, and we would have detected such an error by the check.

Many of the same techniques used to solve equations, such as removing parentheses and combining similar terms, may be used to solve inequalities. However, we must be extremely careful when using the multiplication property of inequality. Study each of the following examples very carefully. The format we used highlights the major steps of a solution.

EXAMPLE 3

Solve $-3x + 5x - 2 \geq 8x - 7 - 9x$.

Solution

$$-3x + 5x - 2 \geq 8x - 7 - 9x$$

$$2x - 2 \geq -x - 7 \qquad \text{Combine similar terms on both sides.}$$

$$3x - 2 \geq -7 \qquad \text{Add } x \text{ to both sides.}$$

$$3x \geq -5 \qquad \text{Add 2 to both sides.}$$

$$\frac{1}{3}(3x) \geq \frac{1}{3}(-5) \qquad \text{Multiply both sides by } \frac{1}{3}.$$

$$x \geq -\frac{5}{3}$$

The solution set is $\left[-\dfrac{5}{3}, \infty \right)$. ∎

EXAMPLE 4

Solve $-5(x - 1) \leq 10$ and graph the solutions.

Solution

$$-5(x - 1) \leq 10$$

$$-5x + 5 \leq 10 \qquad \text{Apply the distributive property on the left.}$$

$$-5x \leq 5 \qquad \text{Add } -5 \text{ to both sides.}$$

$$-\frac{1}{5}(-5x) \ge -\frac{1}{5}(5)$$ Multiply both sides by $-\frac{1}{5}$, which reverses
the inequality.

$$x \ge -1$$

The solution set is $[-1, \infty)$, and it can be graphed as in Figure 2.8.

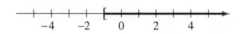

Figure 2.8   ■

EXAMPLE 5   Solve $4(x - 3) > 9(x + 1)$.

Solution

$$4(x - 3) > 9(x + 1)$$

$$4x - 12 > 9x + 9$$ Apply the distributive property.

$$-5x - 12 > 9$$ Add $-9x$ to both sides.

$$-5x > 21$$ Add 12 to both sides.

$$-\frac{1}{5}(-5x) < -\frac{1}{5}(21)$$ Multiply both sides by $-\frac{1}{5}$, which reverses
the inequality.

$$x < -\frac{21}{5}$$

The solution set is $\left(-\infty, -\frac{21}{5}\right)$.   ■

The next example will solve the inequality without indicating the justification for each step. Be sure that you can supply the reasons for the steps.

EXAMPLE 6   Solve $3(2x + 1) - 2(2x + 5) < 5(3x - 2)$.

Solution

$$3(2x + 1) - 2(2x + 5) < 5(3x - 2)$$

$$6x + 3 - 4x - 10 < 15x - 10$$

$$2x - 7 < 15x - 10$$

$$-13x - 7 < -10$$

$$-13x < -3$$

$$-\frac{1}{13}(-13x) > -\frac{1}{13}(-3)$$

$$x > \frac{3}{13}$$

The solution set is $\left(\frac{3}{13}, \infty\right)$.   ■

Problem Set 2.5

For Problems 1–8, express the given inequality in interval notation and sketch a graph of the interval.

1. $x > 1$

2. $x > -2$

3. $x \geq -1$

4. $x \geq 3$

5. $x < -2$

6. $x < 1$

7. $x \leq 2$

8. $x \leq 0$

For Problems 9–16, express each interval as an inequality using the variable x. For example, we can express the interval $[5, \infty)$ as $x \geq 5$.

9. $(-\infty, 4)$

10. $(-\infty, -2)$

11. $(-\infty, -7]$

12. $(-\infty, 9]$

13. $(8, \infty)$

14. $(-5, \infty)$

15. $[-7, \infty)$

16. $[10, \infty)$

For Problems 17–40, solve each of the inequalities and graph the solution set on a number line.

17. $x - 3 > -2$

18. $x + 2 < 1$

19. $-2x \geq 8$

20. $-3x \leq -9$

21. $5x \leq -10$

22. $4x \geq -4$

23. $2x + 1 < 5$

24. $2x + 2 > 4$

25. $3x - 2 > -5$

26. $5x - 3 < -3$

27. $-7x - 3 \leq 4$

28. $-3x - 1 \geq 8$

29. $2 + 6x > -10$

30. $1 + 6x > -17$

31. $5 - 3x < 11$

32. $4 - 2x < 12$

33. $15 < 1 - 7x$

34. $12 < 2 - 5x$

35. $-10 \leq 2 + 4x$

36. $-9 \leq 1 + 2x$

37. $3(x + 2) > 6$

38. $2(x - 1) < -4$

39. $5x + 2 \geq 4x + 6$

40. $6x - 4 \leq 5x - 4$

For Problems 41–70, solve each inequality and express the solution set using interval notation.

41. $2x - 1 > 6$

42. $3x - 2 < 12$

43. $-5x - 2 < -14$

44. $5 - 4x > -2$

45. $-3(2x + 1) \geq 12$

46. $-2(3x + 2) \leq 18$

47. $4(3x - 2) \geq -3$

48. $3(4x - 3) \leq -11$

49. $6x - 2 > 4x - 14$

50. $9x + 5 < 6x - 10$

51. $2x - 7 < 6x + 13$

52. $2x - 3 > 7x + 22$

53. $4(x - 3) \leq -2(x + 1)$

54. $3(x - 1) \geq -(x + 4)$

55. $5(x - 4) - 6(x + 2) < 4$

56. $3(x + 2) - 4(x - 1) < 6$

57. $-3(3x + 2) - 2(4x + 1) \geq 0$

58. $-4(2x - 1) - 3(x + 2) \geq 0$

59. $-(x - 3) + 2(x - 1) < 3(x + 4)$

60. $3(x - 1) - (x - 2) > -2(x + 4)$

61. $7(x + 1) - 8(x - 2) < 0$

62. $5(x - 6) - 6(x + 2) < 0$

63. $-5(x - 1) + 3 > 3x - 4 - 4x$

64. $3(x + 2) + 4 < -2x + 14 + x$

65. $3(x - 2) - 5(2x - 1) \geq 0$

66. $4(2x - 1) - 3(3x + 4) \geq 0$

67. $-5(3x + 4) < -2(7x - 1)$

68. $-3(2x + 1) > -2(x + 4)$

69. $-3(x + 2) > 2(x - 6)$

70. $-2(x - 4) < 5(x - 1)$

■■■ THOUGHTS INTO WORDS

71. Do the *less than* and *greater than* relations possess a symmetric property similar to the symmetric property of equality? Defend your answer.

72. Give a step-by-step description of how you would solve the inequality $-3 > 5 - 2x$.

73. How would you explain to someone why it is necessary to reverse the inequality symbol when multiplying both sides of an inequality by a negative number?

■ ■ ■ **FURTHER INVESTIGATIONS**

74. Solve each of the following inequalities.

   (a) $5x - 2 > 5x + 3$

   (b) $3x - 4 < 3x + 7$

   (c) $4(x + 1) < 2(2x + 5)$

   (d) $-2(x - 1) > 2(x + 7)$

   (e) $3(x - 2) < -3(x + 1)$

   (f) $2(x + 1) + 3(x + 2) < 5(x - 3)$

2.6   More on Inequalities and Problem Solving

When we discussed solving equations that involve fractions, we found that **clearing the equation of all fractions** is frequently an effective technique. To accomplish this, we multiply both sides of the equation by the least common denominator of all the denominators in the equation. This same basic approach also works very well with inequalities that involve fractions, as the next examples demonstrate.

EXAMPLE 1   Solve $\dfrac{2}{3}x - \dfrac{1}{2}x > \dfrac{3}{4}$.

Solution

$$\frac{2}{3}x - \frac{1}{2}x > \frac{3}{4}$$

$$12\left(\frac{2}{3}x - \frac{1}{2}x\right) > 12\left(\frac{3}{4}\right) \qquad \text{Multiply both sides by 12, which is the LCD of 3, 2, and 4.}$$

$$12\left(\frac{2}{3}x\right) - 12\left(\frac{1}{2}x\right) > 12\left(\frac{3}{4}\right) \qquad \text{Apply the distributive property.}$$

$$8x - 6x > 9$$

$$2x > 9$$

$$x > \frac{9}{2}$$

The solution set is $\left(\dfrac{9}{2}, \infty\right)$.   ■

EXAMPLE 2   Solve $\dfrac{x + 2}{4} + \dfrac{x - 3}{8} < 1$.

Solution

$$\frac{x + 2}{4} + \frac{x - 3}{8} < 1$$

$$8\left(\frac{x + 2}{4} + \frac{x - 3}{8}\right) < 8(1) \qquad \text{Multiply both sides by 8, which is the LCD of 4 and 8.}$$

$$8\left(\frac{x+2}{4}\right) + 8\left(\frac{x-3}{8}\right) < 8(1)$$

$$2(x+2) + (x-3) < 8$$

$$2x + 4 + x - 3 < 8$$

$$3x + 1 < 8$$

$$3x < 7$$

$$x < \frac{7}{3}$$

The solution set is $\left(-\infty, \frac{7}{3}\right)$.   ■

EXAMPLE 3   Solve $\dfrac{x}{2} - \dfrac{x-1}{5} \geq \dfrac{x+2}{10} - 4$.

Solution

$$\frac{x}{2} - \frac{x-1}{5} \geq \frac{x+2}{10} - 4$$

$$10\left(\frac{x}{2} - \frac{x-1}{5}\right) \geq 10\left(\frac{x+2}{10} - 4\right)$$

$$10\left(\frac{x}{2}\right) - 10\left(\frac{x-1}{5}\right) \geq 10\left(\frac{x+2}{10}\right) - 10(4)$$

$$5x - 2(x-1) \geq x + 2 - 40$$

$$5x - 2x + 2 \geq x - 38$$

$$3x + 2 \geq x - 38$$

$$2x + 2 \geq -38$$

$$2x \geq -40$$

$$x \geq -20$$

The solution set is $[-20, \infty)$.   ■

The idea of **clearing all decimals** also works with inequalities in much the same way as it does with equations. We can multiply both sides of an inequality by an appropriate power of 10 and then proceed to solve in the usual way. The next two examples illustrate this procedure.

EXAMPLE 4   Solve $x \geq 1.6 + 0.2x$.

Solution

$$x \geq 1.6 + 0.2x$$

$$10(x) \geq 10(1.6 + 0.2x)$$ Multiply both sides by 10.

$$10x \geq 16 + 2x$$

$$8x \geq 16$$

$$x \geq 2$$

The solution set is $[2, \infty)$.   ∎

E X A M P L E   5

Solve $0.08x + 0.09(x + 100) \geq 43$.

Solution

$$0.08x + 0.09(x + 100) \geq 43$$

$$100(0.08x + 0.09(x + 100)) \geq 100(43) \qquad \text{Multiply both sides by 100.}$$

$$8x + 9(x + 100) \geq 4300$$

$$8x + 9x + 900 \geq 4300$$

$$17x + 900 \geq 4300$$

$$17x \geq 3400$$

$$x \geq 200$$

The solution set is $[200, \infty)$.   ∎

■ Compound Statements

We use the words "and" and "or" in mathematics to form **compound statements**. The following are examples of compound numerical statements that use "and." We call such statements **conjunctions**. We agree to call a conjunction true only if all of its component parts are true. Statements 1 and 2 below are true, but statements 3, 4, and 5 are false.

1. $3 + 4 = 7$ and $-4 < -3$.   True

2. $-3 < -2$ and $-6 > -10$.   True

3. $6 > 5$ and $-4 < -8$.   False

4. $4 < 2$ and $0 < 10$.   False

5. $-3 + 2 = 1$ and $5 + 4 = 8$.   False

We call compound statements that use "or" **disjunctions**. The following are examples of disjunctions that involve numerical statements.

6. $0.14 > 0.13$ or $0.235 < 0.237$.   True

7. $\dfrac{3}{4} > \dfrac{1}{2}$ or $-4 + (-3) = 10$.   True

8. $-\dfrac{2}{3} > \dfrac{1}{3}$ or $(0.4)(0.3) = 0.12$.   True

9. $\dfrac{2}{5} < -\dfrac{2}{5}$ or $7 + (-9) = 16$.   False

A disjunction is true if at least one of its component parts is true. In other words, disjunctions are false only if all of the component parts are false. Thus statements 6, 7, and 8 are true, but statement 9 is false.

Now let's consider finding solutions for some compound statements that involve algebraic inequalities. Keep in mind that our previous agreements for labeling conjunctions and disjunctions true or false form the basis for our reasoning.

E X A M P L E   6

Graph the solution set for the conjunction $x > -1$ and $x < 3$.

Solution

The key word is "and," so we need to satisfy both inequalities. Thus all numbers between -1 and 3 are solutions, and we can indicate this on a number line as in Figure 2.9.

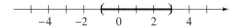

Figure 2.9

Using interval notation, we can represent the interval enclosed in parentheses in Figure 2.9 by $(-1, 3)$. Using set builder notation we can express the same interval as $\{x | -1 < x < 3\}$, where the statement $-1 < x < 3$ is read "Negative one is less than x, and x is less than three." In other words, x is between -1 and 3. ∎

Example 6 represents another concept that pertains to sets. The set of all elements common to two sets is called the **intersection** of the two sets. Thus in Example 6, we found the intersection of the two sets $\{x | x > -1\}$ and $\{x | x < 3\}$ to be the set $\{x | -1 < x < 3\}$. In general, we define the intersection of two sets as follows:

Definition 2.1

> The **intersection** of two sets A and B (written $A \cap B$) is the set of all elements that are in both A and in B. Using set builder notation, we can write
>
> $$A \cap B = \{x | x \in A \text{ and } x \in B\}$$

E X A M P L E   7

Solve the conjunction $3x + 1 > -5$ *and* $2x + 5 > 7$, and graph its solution set on a number line.

Solution

First, let's simplify both inequalities.

$$3x + 1 > -5 \quad \text{and} \quad 2x + 5 > 7$$

$$3x > -6 \quad \text{and} \quad 2x > 2$$

$$x > -2 \quad \text{and} \quad x > 1$$

Because this is a conjunction, we must satisfy both inequalities. Thus all numbers greater than 1 are solutions, and the solution set is $(1, \infty)$. We show the graph of the solution set in Figure 2.10.

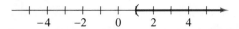

Figure 2.10   ∎

We can solve a conjunction such as $3x + 1 > -3$ and $3x + 1 < 7$, in which the same algebraic expression (in this case $3x + 1$) is contained in both inequalities, by using the **compact form** $-3 < 3x + 1 < 7$ as follows:

$$-3 \; < \; 3x + 1 \; < 7$$

$$-4 \; < \; 3x \; < \; 6 \qquad \text{Add } -1 \text{ to the left side, middle, and right side.}$$

$$-\frac{4}{3} \; < \; x \; < \; 2 \qquad \text{Multiply through by } \frac{1}{3}.$$

The solution set is $\left(-\dfrac{4}{3}, 2\right)$.

The word *and* ties the concept of a conjunction to the set concept of intersection. In a like manner, the word *or* links the idea of a disjunction to the set concept of **union**. We define the union of two sets as follows:

Definition 2.2

> The **union** of two sets A and B (written $A \cup B$) is the set of all elements that are in A or in B, or in both. Using set builder notation, we can write
>
> $$A \cup B = \{x | x \in A \text{ or } x \in B\}$$

E X A M P L E   8

Graph the solution set for the disjunction $x < -1$ *or* $x > 2$, and express it using interval notation.

Solution

The key word is "or," so all numbers that satisfy either inequality (or both) are solutions. Thus all numbers less than -1, along with all numbers greater than 2, are the solutions. The graph of the solution set is shown in Figure 2.11.

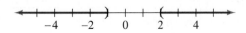

Figure 2.11

Using interval notation and the set concept of union, we can express the solution set as $(-\infty, -1) \cup (2, \infty)$.   ∎

Example 8 illustrates that in terms of set vocabulary, the solution set of a disjunction is the union of the solution sets of the component parts of the disjunction. Note that there is no compact form for writing $x < -1$ or $x > 2$ or for any disjunction.

E X A M P L E   9

Solve the disjunction $2x - 5 < -11$ or $5x + 1 \geq 6$, and graph its solution set on a number line.

Solution

First, let's simplify both inequalities.

$$
\begin{array}{ccc}
2x - 5 < -11 & \text{or} & 5x + 1 \geq 6 \\
2x < -6 & \text{or} & 5x \geq 5 \\
x < -3 & \text{or} & x \geq 1
\end{array}
$$

This is a disjunction, and all numbers less than -3, along with all numbers greater than or equal to 1, will satisfy it. Thus the solution set is $(-\infty, -3) \cup [1, \infty)$. Its graph is shown in Figure 2.12.

Figure 2.12

In summary, to solve a compound sentence involving an inequality, proceed as follows:

1. Solve separately each inequality in the compound sentence.

2. If it is a conjunction, the solution set is the intersection of the solution sets of each inequality.

3. If it is a disjunction, the solution set is the union of the solution sets of each inequality.

The following agreements on the use of interval notation (Figure 2.13) should be added to the list in Figure 2.6.

Set	Graph	Interval notation
$\{x \mid a < x < b\}$	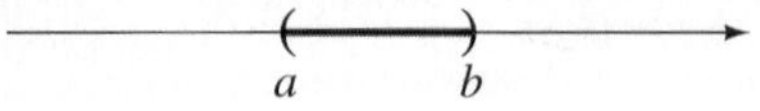 $\overset{a \qquad b}{\longleftarrow (\quad\quad) \longrightarrow}$	(a, b)
$\{x \mid a \leq x < b\}$	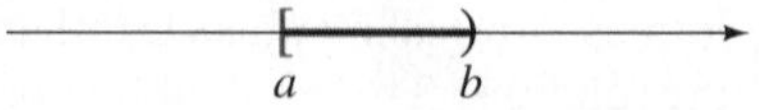 $\overset{a \qquad b}{\longleftarrow [\quad\quad) \longrightarrow}$	$[a, b)$
$\{x \mid a < x \leq b\}$	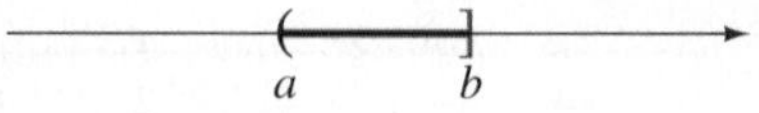 $\overset{a \qquad b}{\longleftarrow (\quad\quad] \longrightarrow}$	$(a, b]$
$\{x \mid a \leq x \leq b\}$	 $\overset{a \qquad b}{\longleftarrow [\quad\quad] \longrightarrow}$	$[a, b]$

Figure 2.13

■ Problem Solving

We will conclude this section with some word problems that contain inequality statements.

Sari had scores of 94, 84, 86, and 88 on her first four exams of the semester. What score must she obtain on the fifth exam to have an average of 90 or better for the five exams?

Solution

Let s represent the score Sari needs on the fifth exam. Because the average is computed by adding all scores and dividing by the number of scores, we have the following inequality to solve.

$$\frac{94 + 84 + 86 + 88 + s}{5} \geq 90$$

Solving this inequality, we obtain

$$\frac{352 + s}{5} \geq 90$$

$$5\left(\frac{352 + s}{5}\right) \geq 5(90) \qquad \text{Multiply both sides by 5.}$$

$$352 + s \geq 450$$

$$s \geq 98$$

Sari must receive a score of 98 or better.   ■

An investor has $1000 to invest. Suppose she invests $500 at 8% interest. At what rate must she invest the other $500 so that the two investments together yield more than $100 of yearly interest?

Solution

Let r represent the unknown rate of interest. We can use the following guideline to set up an inequality.

Interest from 8% investment	+	Interest from r percent investment	>	$100
$(8\%)(\$500)$	+	$r(\$500)$	>	$100

Solving this inequality yields

$$40 + 500r > 100$$

$$500r > 60$$

$$r > \frac{60}{500}$$

$$r > 0.12 \qquad \text{Change to a decimal.}$$

She must invest the other $500 at a rate greater than 12%.   ■

PROBLEM 3

If the temperature for a 24-hour period ranged between 41°F and 59°F, inclusive (that is, $41 \leq F \leq 59$), what was the range in Celsius degrees?

Solution

Use the formula $F = \dfrac{9}{5}C + 32$, to solve the following compound inequality.

$$41 \leq \frac{9}{5}C + 32 \leq 59$$

Solving this yields

$$9 \leq \frac{9}{5}C \leq 27 \qquad \text{Add } -32.$$

$$\frac{5}{9}(9) \leq \frac{5}{9}\left(\frac{9}{5}C\right) \leq \frac{5}{9}(27) \qquad \text{Multiply by } \frac{5}{9}.$$

$$5 \leq C \leq 15$$

The range was between 5°C and 15°C, inclusive. ■

Problem Set 2.6

For Problems 1–18, solve each of the inequalities and express the solution sets in interval notation.

1. $\dfrac{2}{5}x + \dfrac{1}{3}x > \dfrac{44}{15}$

2. $\dfrac{1}{4}x - \dfrac{4}{3}x < -13$

3. $x - \dfrac{5}{6} < \dfrac{x}{2} + 3$

4. $x + \dfrac{2}{7} > \dfrac{x}{2} - 5$

5. $\dfrac{x-2}{3} + \dfrac{x+1}{4} \geq \dfrac{5}{2}$

6. $\dfrac{x-1}{3} + \dfrac{x+2}{5} \leq \dfrac{3}{5}$

7. $\dfrac{3-x}{6} + \dfrac{x+2}{7} \leq 1$

8. $\dfrac{4-x}{5} + \dfrac{x+1}{6} \geq 2$

9. $\dfrac{x+3}{8} - \dfrac{x+5}{5} \geq \dfrac{3}{10}$

10. $\dfrac{x-4}{6} - \dfrac{x-2}{9} \leq \dfrac{5}{18}$

11. $\dfrac{4x-3}{6} - \dfrac{2x-1}{12} < -2$

12. $\dfrac{3x+2}{9} - \dfrac{2x+1}{3} > -1$

13. $0.06x + 0.08(250 - x) \geq 19$

14. $0.08x + 0.09(2x) \geq 130$

15. $0.09x + 0.1(x + 200) > 77$

16. $0.07x + 0.08(x + 100) > 38$

17. $x \geq 3.4 + 0.15x$

18. $x \geq 2.1 + 0.3x$

For Problems 19–34, graph the solution set for each compound inequality, and express the solution sets in interval notation.

19. $x > -1$ and $x < 2$

20. $x > 1$ and $x < 4$

21. $x \leq 2$ and $x > -1$

22. $x \leq 4$ and $x \geq -2$

23. $x > 2$ or $x < -1$

24. $x > 1$ or $x < -4$

25. $x \leq 1$ or $x > 3$

26. $x < -2$ or $x \geq 1$

27. $x > 0$ and $x > -1$

28. $x > -2$ and $x > 2$

29. $x < 0$ and $x > 4$

30. $x > 1$ or $x < 2$

31. $x > -2$ or $x < 3$

32. $x > 3$ and $x < -1$

33. $x > -1$ or $x > 2$

34. $x < -2$ or $x < 1$

For Problems 35–44, solve each compound inequality and graph the solution sets. Express the solution sets in interval notation.

35. $x - 2 > -1$ and $x - 2 < 1$

36. $x + 3 > -2$ and $x + 3 < 2$

37. $x + 2 < -3$ or $x + 2 > 3$

38. $x - 4 < -2$ or $x - 4 > 2$

39. $2x - 1 \geq 5$ and $x > 0$

40. $3x + 2 > 17$ and $x \geq 0$

41. $5x - 2 < 0$ and $3x - 1 > 0$

42. $x + 1 > 0$ and $3x - 4 < 0$

43. $3x + 2 < -1$ or $3x + 2 > 1$

44. $5x - 2 < -2$ or $5x - 2 > 2$

For Problems 45–56, solve each compound inequality using the compact form. Express the solution sets in interval notation.

45. $-3 < 2x + 1 < 5$

46. $-7 < 3x - 1 < 8$

47. $-17 \leq 3x - 2 \leq 10$

48. $-25 \leq 4x + 3 \leq 19$

49. $1 < 4x + 3 < 9$

50. $0 < 2x + 5 < 12$

51. $-6 < 4x - 5 < 6$

52. $-2 < 3x + 4 < 2$

53. $-4 \leq \dfrac{x - 1}{3} \leq 4$

54. $-1 \leq \dfrac{x + 2}{4} \leq 1$

55. $-3 < 2 - x < 3$

56. $-4 < 3 - x < 4$

For Problems 57–67, solve each problem by setting up and solving an appropriate inequality.

57. Suppose that Lance has $500 to invest. If he invests $300 at 9% interest, at what rate must he invest the remaining $200 so that the two investments yield more than $47 in yearly interest?

58. Mona invests $100 at 8% yearly interest. How much does she have to invest at 9% so that the total yearly interest from the two investments exceeds $26?

59. The average height of the two forwards and the center of a basketball team is 6 feet and 8 inches. What must

the average height of the two guards be so that the team average is at least 6 feet and 4 inches?

60. Thanh has scores of 52, 84, 65, and 74 on his first four math exams. What score must he make on the fifth exam to have an average of 70 or better for the five exams?

61. Marsha bowled 142 and 170 in her first two games. What must she bowl in the third game to have an average of at least 160 for the three games?

62. Candace had scores of 95, 82, 93, and 84 on her first four exams of the semester. What score must she obtain on the fifth exam to have an average of 90 or better for the five exams?

63. Suppose that Derwin shot rounds of 82, 84, 78, and 79 on the first four days of a golf tournament. What must he shoot on the fifth day of the tournament to average 80 or less for the five days?

64. The temperatures for a 24-hour period ranged between $-4°F$ and $23°F$, inclusive. What was the range in Celsius degrees? $\left(\text{Use } F = \dfrac{9}{5}C + 32. \right)$

65. Oven temperatures for baking various foods usually range between 325°F and 425°F, inclusive. Express this range in Celsius degrees. (Round answers to the nearest degree.)

66. A person's intelligence quotient (I) is found by dividing mental age (M), as indicated by standard tests, by chronological age (C) and then multiplying this ratio by 100. The formula $I = \dfrac{100M}{C}$ can be used. If the I range of a group of 11-year-olds is given by $80 \leq I \leq 140$, find the range of the mental age of this group.

67. Repeat Problem 66 for an I range of 70 to 125, inclusive, for a group of 9-year-olds.

■ ■ ■ **THOUGHTS INTO WORDS**

68. Explain the difference between a conjunction and a disjunction. Give an example of each (outside the field of mathematics).

69. How do you know by inspection that the solution set of the inequality $x + 3 > x + 2$ is the entire set of real numbers?

70. Find the solution set for each of the following compound statements, and in each case explain your reasoning.

(a) $x < 3$ and $5 > 2$

(b) $x < 3$ or $5 > 2$

(c) $x < 3$ and $6 < 4$

(d) $x < 3$ or $6 < 4$

In Section 1.2, we defined the absolute value of a real number by

$$|a| = \begin{cases} a, & \text{if } a \geq 0 \\ -a, & \text{if } a < 0 \end{cases}$$

We also interpreted the absolute value of any real number to be the distance between the number and zero on a number line. For example, $|6| = 6$ translates to 6 units between 6 and 0. Likewise, $|-8| = 8$ translates to 8 units between -8 and 0.

The interpretation of absolute value as distance on a number line provides a straightforward approach to solving a variety of equations and inequalities involving absolute value. First, let's consider some equations.

EXAMPLE 1   Solve $|x| = 2$.

Solution

Think in terms of distance between the number and zero, and you will see that x must be 2 or -2. That is, the equation $|x| = 2$ is equivalent to

$$x = -2 \quad \text{or} \quad x = 2$$

The solution set is $\{-2, 2\}$. ■

EXAMPLE 2   Solve $|x + 2| = 5$.

Solution

The number, $x + 2$, must be -5 or 5. Thus $|x + 2| = 5$ is equivalent to

$$x + 2 = -5 \quad \text{or} \quad x + 2 = 5$$

Solving each equation of the disjunction yields

$$x + 2 = -5 \quad \text{or} \quad x + 2 = 5$$
$$x = -7 \quad \text{or} \quad x = 3$$

The solution set is $\{-7, 3\}$.

✔ **Check**

$$\begin{array}{ll} |x + 2| = 5 & |x + 2| = 5 \\ |-7 + 2| \stackrel{?}{=} 5 & |3 + 2| \stackrel{?}{=} 5 \\ |-5| \stackrel{?}{=} 5 & |5| \stackrel{?}{=} 5 \\ 5 = 5 & 5 = 5 \end{array}$$

■

The following general property should seem reasonable from the distance interpretation of absolute value.

Property 2.1

$|x| = k$ is equivalent to $x = -k$ or $x = k$, where k is a positive number.

Example 3 demonstrates our format for solving equations of the form $|x| = k$.

E X A M P L E   3

Solve $|5x + 3| = 7$.

Solution

$$|5x + 3| = 7$$

$$5x + 3 = -7 \quad \text{or} \quad 5x + 3 = 7$$

$$5x = -10 \quad \text{or} \quad 5x = 4$$

$$x = -2 \quad \text{or} \quad x = \frac{4}{5}$$

The solution set is $\left\{-2, \dfrac{4}{5}\right\}$. Check these solutions! ■

The distance interpretation for absolute value also provides a good basis for solving some inequalities that involve absolute value. Consider the following examples.

E X A M P L E   4

Solve $|x| < 2$ and graph the solution set.

Solution

The number, x, must be less than two units away from zero. Thus $|x| < 2$ is equivalent to

$$x > -2 \quad \text{and} \quad x < 2$$

The solution set is $(-2, 2)$ and its graph is shown in Figure 2.14.

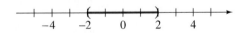

Figure 2.14 ■

EXAMPLE 5   Solve $|x + 3| < 1$ and graph the solutions.

Solution

Let's continue to think in terms of distance on a number line. The number, $x + 3$, must be less than one unit away from zero. Thus $|x + 3| < 1$ is equivalent to

$$x + 3 > -1 \quad \text{and} \quad x + 3 < 1$$

Solving this conjunction yields

$$x + 3 > -1 \quad \text{and} \quad x + 3 < 1$$
$$x > -4 \quad \text{and} \quad x < -2$$

The solution set is $(-4, -2)$ and its graph is shown in Figure 2.15.

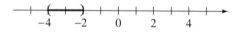

Figure 2.15   ■

Take another look at Examples 4 and 5. The following general property should seem reasonable.

Property 2.2

$|x| < k$ is equivalent to $x > -k$ and $x < k$, where k is a positive number.

Remember that we can write a conjunction such as $x > -k$ and $x < k$ in the compact form $-k < x < k$. The compact form provides a very convenient format for solving inequalities such as $|3x - 1| < 8$, as Example 6 illustrates.

EXAMPLE 6   Solve $|3x - 1| < 8$ and graph the solutions.

Solution

$$|3x - 1| < 8$$
$$-8 < 3x - 1 < 8$$
$$-7 < 3x < 9 \qquad \text{Add 1 to left side, middle, and right side.}$$
$$\frac{1}{3}(-7) < \frac{1}{3}(3x) < \frac{1}{3}(9) \qquad \text{Multiply through by } \frac{1}{3}.$$
$$-\frac{7}{3} < x < 3$$

The solution set is $\left(-\dfrac{7}{3}, 3\right)$, and its graph is shown in Figure 2.16.

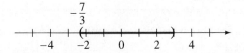

Figure 2.16   ■

  The distance interpretation also clarifies a property that pertains to *greater than* situations involving absolute value. Consider the following examples.

E X A M P L E   7

Solve $|x| > 1$ and graph the solutions.

Solution

The number, x, must be more than one unit away from zero. Thus $|x| > 1$ is equivalent to

$$x < -1 \quad \text{or} \quad x > 1$$

The solution set is $(-\infty, -1) \cup (1, \infty)$, and its graph is shown in Figure 2.17.

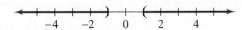

Figure 2.17   ■

E X A M P L E   8

Solve $|x - 1| > 3$ and graph the solutions.

Solution

The number, $x - 1$, must be more than three units away from zero. Thus $|x - 1| > 3$ is equivalent to

$$x - 1 < -3 \quad \text{or} \quad x - 1 > 3$$

Solving this disjunction yields

$$x - 1 < -3 \quad \text{or} \quad x - 1 > 3$$
$$x < -2 \quad \text{or} \quad x > 4$$

The solution set is $(-\infty, -2) \cup (4, \infty)$, and its graph is shown in Figure 2.18.

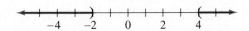

Figure 2.18   ■

Examples 7 and 8 illustrate the following general property.

Property 2.3

$|x| > k$ is equivalent to $x < -k$ or $x > k$, where k is a positive number.

Therefore, solving inequalities of the form $|x| > k$ can take the format shown in Example 9.

E X A M P L E   9

Solve $|3x - 1| > 2$ and graph the solutions.

Solution

$$|3x - 1| > 2$$

$$3x - 1 < -2 \qquad \text{or} \qquad 3x - 1 > 2$$

$$3x < -1 \qquad \text{or} \qquad 3x > 3$$

$$x < -\frac{1}{3} \qquad \text{or} \qquad x > 1$$

The solution set is $\left(-\infty, -\dfrac{1}{3}\right) \cup (1, \infty)$ and its graph is shown in Figure 2.19.

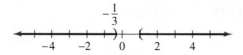

Figure 2.19   ■

   Properties 2.1, 2.2, and 2.3 provide the basis for solving a variety of equations and inequalities that involve absolute value. However, if at any time you become doubtful about what property applies, don't forget the distance interpretation. Furthermore, note that in each of the properties, k is a positive number. If k is a nonpositive number, we can determine the solution sets by inspection, as indicated by the following examples.

$|x + 3| = 0$ has a solution of $x = -3$, because the number $x + 3$ has to be 0. The solution set of $|x + 3| = 0$ is $\{-3\}$.

$|2x - 5| = -3$ has no solutions, because the absolute value (distance) cannot be negative. The solution set is $\varnothing$, the null set.

$|x - 7| < -4$ has no solutions, because we cannot obtain an absolute value less than -4. The solution set is $\varnothing$.

$|2x - 1| > -1$ is satisfied by all real numbers because the absolute value of $(2x - 1)$, regardless of what number is substituted for x, will always be greater than -1. The solution set is the set of all real numbers, which we can express in interval notation as $(-\infty, \infty)$.

Problem Set 2.7

For Problems 1–14, solve each inequality and graph the solutions.

1. $|x| < 5$

2. $|x| < 1$

3. $|x| \leq 2$

4. $|x| \leq 4$

5. $|x| > 2$

6. $|x| > 3$

7. $|x - 1| < 2$

8. $|x - 2| < 4$

9. $|x + 2| \leq 4$

10. $|x + 1| \leq 1$

11. $|x + 2| > 1$

12. $|x + 1| > 3$

13. $|x - 3| \geq 2$

14. $|x - 2| \geq 1$

For Problems 15–54, solve each equation and inequality.

15. $|x - 1| = 8$

16. $|x + 2| = 9$

17. $|x - 2| > 6$

18. $|x - 3| > 9$

19. $|x + 3| < 5$

20. $|x + 1| < 8$

21. $|2x - 4| = 6$

22. $|3x - 4| = 14$

23. $|2x - 1| \leq 9$

24. $|3x + 1| \leq 13$

25. $|4x + 2| \geq 12$

26. $|5x - 2| \geq 10$

27. $|3x + 4| = 11$

28. $|5x - 7| = 14$

29. $|4 - 2x| = 6$

30. $|3 - 4x| = 8$

31. $|2 - x| > 4$

32. $|4 - x| > 3$

33. $|1 - 2x| < 2$

34. $|2 - 3x| < 5$

35. $|5x + 9| \leq 16$

36. $|7x - 6| \geq 22$

37. $\left| x - \dfrac{3}{4} \right| = \dfrac{2}{3}$

38. $\left| x + \dfrac{1}{2} \right| = \dfrac{3}{5}$

39. $|-2x + 7| \leq 13$

40. $|-3x - 4| \leq 15$

41. $\left| \dfrac{x - 3}{4} \right| < 2$

42. $\left| \dfrac{x + 2}{3} \right| < 1$

43. $\left| \dfrac{2x + 1}{2} \right| > 1$

44. $\left| \dfrac{3x - 1}{4} \right| > 3$

45. $|2x - 3| + 2 = 5$

46. $|3x - 1| - 1 = 9$

47. $|x + 2| - 6 = -2$

48. $|x - 3| - 4 = -1$

49. $|4x - 3| + 2 = 2$

50. $|5x + 1| + 4 = 4$

51. $|x + 7| - 3 \geq 4$

52. $|x - 2| + 4 \geq 10$

53. $|2x - 1| + 1 \leq 6$

54. $|4x + 3| - 2 \leq 5$

For Problems 55–64, solve each equation and inequality *by inspection*.

55. $|2x + 1| = -4$

56. $|5x - 1| = -2$

57. $|3x - 1| > -2$

58. $|4x + 3| < -4$

59. $|5x - 2| = 0$

60. $|3x - 1| = 0$

61. $|4x - 6| < -1$

62. $|x + 9| > -6$

63. $|x + 4| < 0$

64. $|x + 6| > 0$

■ ■ ■ THOUGHTS INTO WORDS

65. Explain how you would solve the inequality $|2x + 5| > -3$.

66. Why is 2 the only solution for $|x - 2| \leq 0$?

67. Explain how you would solve the equation $|2x - 3| = 0$.

■ ■ ■ **FURTHER INVESTIGATIONS**

Consider the equation $|x| = |y|$. This equation will be a true statement if x is equal to y, or if x is equal to the opposite of y. Use the following format, $x = y$ or $x = -y$, to solve the equations in Problems 68–73.

For Problems 68–73, solve each equation.

68. $|3x + 1| = |2x + 3|$

69. $|-2x - 3| = |x + 1|$

70. $|2x - 1| = |x - 3|$

71. $|x - 2| = |x + 6|$

72. $|x + 1| = |x - 4|$

73. $|x + 1| = |x - 1|$

74. Use the definition of absolute value to help prove Property 2.1.

75. Use the definition of absolute value to help prove Property 2.2.

76. Use the definition of absolute value to help prove Property 2.3.

Chapter 2   Summary

(2.1) Solving an algebraic equation refers to the process of finding the number (or numbers) that make(s) the algebraic equation a true numerical statement. We call such numbers the **solutions** or **roots** of the equation that **satisfy** the equation. We call the set of all solutions of an equation the **solution set**. The general procedure for solving an equation is to continue replacing the given equation with **equivalent but simpler** equations until we arrive at one that can be solved by inspection. Two properties of equality play an important role in the process of solving equations.

Addition Property of Equality $a = b$ if and only if $a + c = b + c$.

Multiplication Property of Equality For $c \neq 0$, $a = b$ if and only if $ac = bc$.

(2.2) To solve an equation involving fractions, first **clear the equation of all fractions**. It is usually easiest to begin by multiplying both sides of the equation by the least common multiple of all of the denominators in the equation (by the least common denominator, or LCD).

Keep the following suggestions in mind as you solve word problems.

1. Read the problem carefully.
2. Sketch any figure, diagram, or chart that might be helpful.
3. Choose a meaningful variable.
4. Look for a guideline.
5. Form an equation or inequality.
6. Solve the equation or inequality.
7. Check your answers.

(2.3) To solve equations that contain decimals, you can clear the equation of all decimals by multiplying both sides by an appropriate power of 10, or you can keep the problem in decimal form and perform the calculations with decimals.

(2.4) We use equations to put rules in symbolic form; we call these rules **formulas**.

We can solve a formula such as $P = 2l + 2w$ for $l\left(l = \dfrac{P - 2w}{2}\right)$ or for $w\left(w = \dfrac{P - 2l}{2}\right)$ by applying the addition and multiplication properties of equality.

We often use formulas as **guidelines** for solving word problems.

(2.5) Solving an algebraic inequality refers to the process of finding the numbers that make the algebraic inequality a true numerical statement. We call such numbers the **solutions**, and we call the set of all solutions the **solution set**.

The general procedure for solving an inequality is to continue replacing the given inequality with **equivalent, but simpler**, inequalities until we arrive at one that we can solve by inspection. The following properties form the basis for solving algebraic inequalities.

1. $a > b$ if and only if $a + c > b + c$.   (Addition property)
2. **a.** For $c > 0$, $a > b$ if and only if $ac > bc$.
   b. For $c < 0$, $a > b$ if and only if $ac < bc$.   (Multiplication properties)

(2.6) To solve compound sentences that involve inequalities, we proceed as follows:

1. Solve separately each inequality in the compound sentence.
2. If it is a **conjunction**, the solution set is the **intersection** of the solution sets of each inequality.
3. If it is a **disjunction**, the solution set is the **union** of the solution sets of each inequality.

We define the intersection and union of two sets as follows.

Intersection $A \cap B = \{x | x \in A \quad and \quad x \in B\}$

Union $A \cup B = \{x | x \in A \quad or \quad x \in B\}$

The following are some examples of solution sets that we examined in Sections 2.5 and 2.6 (Figure 2.20).

Solution Set	Graph	Interval notation
$\{x\|x > 1\}$	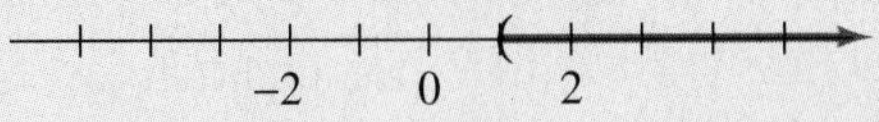	$(1, \infty)$
$\{x\|x \geq 2\}$	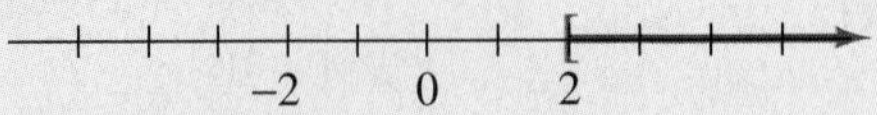	$[2, \infty)$
$\{x\|x < 0\}$	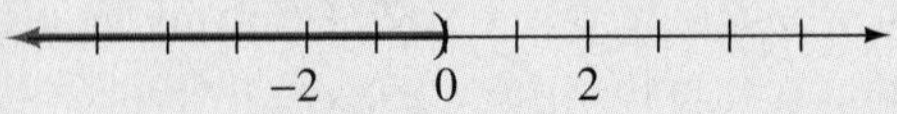	$(-\infty, 0)$
$\{x\|x \leq -1\}$	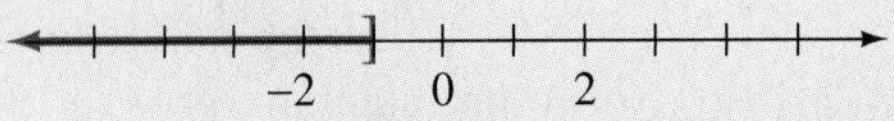	$(-\infty, -1]$
$\{x\|-2 < x \leq 2\}$	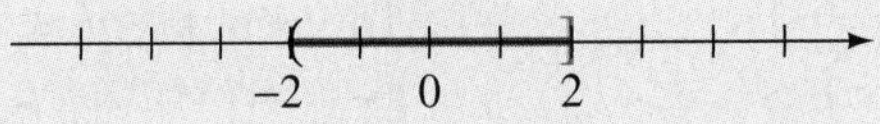	$(-2, 2]$
$\{x\|x \leq -1 \text{ or } x > 1\}$	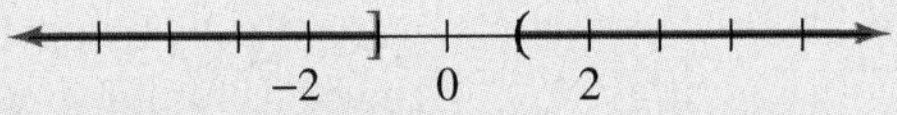	$(-\infty, -1] \cup (1, \infty)$

Figure 2.20

(2.7) We can interpret the **absolute value** of a number on the number line as the distance between that number and zero. The following properties form the basis for solving equations and inequalities involving absolute value.

1. $|x| = k$ is equivalent to $x = -k$ or $x = k$
2. $|x| < k$ is equivalent to $x > -k$ and $x < k$ $\quad\Big\} \; k > 0$
3. $|x| > k$ is equivalent to $x < -k$ or $x > k$

Chapter 2   Review Problem Set

For Problems 1–15, solve each of the equations.

1. $5(x - 6) = 3(x + 2)$

2. $2(2x + 1) - (x - 4) = 4(x + 5)$

3. $-(2n - 1) + 3(n + 2) = 7$

4. $2(3n - 4) + 3(2n - 3) = -2(n + 5)$

5. $\dfrac{3t - 2}{4} = \dfrac{2t + 1}{3}$

6. $\dfrac{x + 6}{5} + \dfrac{x - 1}{4} = 2$

7. $1 - \dfrac{2x - 1}{6} = \dfrac{3x}{8}$

8. $\dfrac{2x + 1}{3} + \dfrac{3x - 1}{5} = \dfrac{1}{10}$

9. $\dfrac{3n - 1}{2} - \dfrac{2n + 3}{7} = 1$

10. $|3x - 1| = 11$

11. $0.06x + 0.08 (x + 100) = 15$

12. $0.4(t - 6) = 0.3(2t + 5)$

13. $0.1(n + 300) = 0.09n + 32$

14. $0.2(x - 0.5) - 0.3(x + 1) = 0.4$

15. $|2n + 3| = 4$

For Problems 16–20, solve each equation for x.

16. $ax - b = b + 2$

17. $ax = bx + c$

18. $m(x + a) = p(x + b)$

19. $5x - 7y = 11$

20. $\dfrac{x - a}{b} = \dfrac{y + 1}{c}$

For Problems 21–24, solve each of the formulas for the indicated variable.

21. $A = \pi r^2 + \pi rs$ for s

22. $A = \dfrac{1}{2}h(b_1 + b_2)$ for b_2

23. $S_n = \dfrac{n(a_1 + a_2)}{2}$ for n

24. $\dfrac{1}{R} = \dfrac{1}{R_1} + \dfrac{1}{R_2}$ for R

For Problems 25–36, solve each of the inequalities.

25. $5x - 2 \geq 4x - 7$

26. $3 - 2x < -5$

27. $2(3x - 1) - 3(x - 3) > 0$

28. $3(x + 4) \leq 5(x - 1)$

29. $\dfrac{5}{6}n - \dfrac{1}{3}n < \dfrac{1}{6}$

30. $\dfrac{n - 4}{5} + \dfrac{n - 3}{6} > \dfrac{7}{15}$

31. $s \geq 4.5 + 0.25s$

32. $0.07x + 0.09(500 - x) \geq 43$

33. $|2x - 1| < 11$

34. $|3x + 1| > 10$

35. $-3(2t - 1) - (t + 2) > -6(t - 3)$

36. $\dfrac{2}{3}(x - 1) + \dfrac{1}{4}(2x + 1) < \dfrac{5}{6}(x - 2)$

For Problems 37–44, graph the solutions of each compound inequality.

37. $x > -1$ and $x < 1$

38. $x > 2$ or $x \leq -3$

39. $x > 2$ and $x > 3$

40. $x < 2$ or $x > -1$

41. $2x + 1 > 3$ or $2x + 1 < -3$

42. $2 \leq x + 4 \leq 5$

43. $-1 < 4x - 3 \leq 9$

44. $x + 1 > 3$ and $x - 3 < -5$

Solve each of Problems 45–56 by setting up and solving an appropriate equation or inequality.

45. The width of a rectangle is 2 meters more than one-third of the length. The perimeter of the rectangle is 44 meters. Find the length and width of the rectangle.

46. A total of $500 was invested, part of it at 7% interest and the remainder at 8%. If the total yearly interest from both investments amounted to $38, how much was invested at each rate?

47. Susan's average score for her first three psychology exams is 84. What must she get on the fourth exam so that her average for the four exams is 85 or better?

48. Find three consecutive integers such that the sum of one-half of the smallest and one-third of the largest is one less than the other integer.

49. Pat is paid time-and-a-half for each hour he works over 36 hours in a week. Last week he worked 42 hours for a total of $472.50. What is his normal hourly rate?

50. Marcela has a collection of nickels, dimes, and quarters worth $24.75. The number of dimes is 10 more than twice the number of nickels, and the number of quarters is 25 more than the number of dimes. How many coins of each kind does she have?

51. If the complement of an angle is one-tenth of the supplement of the angle, find the measure of the angle.

52. A retailer has some sweaters that cost her $38 each. She wants to sell them at a profit of 20% of her cost. What price should she charge for the sweaters?

53. How many pints of a 1% hydrogen peroxide solution should be mixed with a 4% hydrogen peroxide solution to obtain 10 pints of a 2% hydrogen peroxide solution?

54. Gladys leaves a town driving at a rate of 40 miles per hour. Two hours later, Reena leaves from the same place traveling the same route. She catches Gladys in 5 hours and 20 minutes. How fast was Reena traveling?

55. In $1\frac{1}{4}$ hours more time, Rita, riding her bicycle at 12 miles per hour, rode 2 miles farther than Sonya, who was riding her bicycle at 16 miles per hour. How long did each girl ride?

56. How many cups of orange juice must be added to 50 cups of a punch that is 10% orange juice to obtain a punch that is 20% orange juice?

Chapter 2   Test

For Problems 1–10, solve each equation.

1. $5x - 2 = 2x - 11$

2. $6(n - 2) - 4(n + 3) = -14$

3. $-3(x + 4) = 3(x - 5)$

4. $3(2x - 1) - 2(x + 5) = -(x - 3)$

5. $\dfrac{3t - 2}{4} = \dfrac{5t + 1}{5}$

6. $\dfrac{5x + 2}{3} - \dfrac{2x + 4}{6} = -\dfrac{4}{3}$

7. $|4x - 3| = 9$

8. $\dfrac{1 - 3x}{4} + \dfrac{2x + 3}{3} = 1$

9. $2 - \dfrac{3x - 1}{5} = -4$

10. $0.05x + 0.06(1500 - x) = 83.5$

11. Solve $\dfrac{2}{3}x - \dfrac{3}{4}y = 2$ for y

12. Solve $S = 2\pi r(r + h)$ for h

For Problems 13–20, solve each inequality and express the solution set using interval notation.

13. $7x - 4 > 5x - 8$

14. $-3x - 4 \leq x + 12$

15. $2(x - 1) - 3(3x + 1) \geq -6(x - 5)$

16. $\dfrac{3}{5}x - \dfrac{1}{2}x < 1$

17. $\dfrac{x - 2}{6} - \dfrac{x + 3}{9} > -\dfrac{1}{2}$

18. $0.05x + 0.07(800 - x) \geq 52$

19. $|6x - 4| < 10$

20. $|4x + 5| \geq 6$

For Problems 21–25, solve each problem by setting up and solving an appropriate equation or inequality.

21. Dela bought a dress at a 20% discount sale for $57.60. Find the original price of the dress.

22. The length of a rectangle is 1 centimeter more than three times its width. If the perimeter of the rectangle is 50 centimeters, find the length of the rectangle.

23. How many cups of grapefruit juice must be added to 30 cups of a punch that is 8% grapefruit juice to obtain a punch that is 10% grapefruit juice?

24. Rex has scores of 85, 92, 87, 88, and 91 on the first five exams. What score must he make on the sixth exam to have an average of 90 or better for all six exams?

25. If the complement of an angle is $\dfrac{2}{11}$ of the supplement of the angle, find the measure of the angle.

3

Polynomials

3.1 Polynomials: Sums and Differences

3.2 Products and Quotients of Monomials

3.3 Multiplying Polynomials

3.4 Factoring: Use of the Distributive Property

3.5 Factoring: Difference of Two Squares and Sum or Difference of Two Cubes

3.6 Factoring Trinomials

3.7 Equations and Problem Solving

A quadratic equation can be solved to determine the width of a uniform strip trimmed off both sides and ends of a sheet of paper to obtain a specified area for the sheet of paper.

© Tony Freeman /PhotoEdit

A strip of uniform width cut off of both sides and both ends of an 8-inch by 11-inch sheet of paper must reduce the size of the paper to an area of 40 square inches. Find the width of the strip. With the equation $(11 - 2x)(8 - 2x) = 40$, you can determine that the strip should be 1.5 inches wide.

The main object of this text is to help you develop algebraic skills, use these skills to solve equations and inequalities, and use equations and inequalities to solve word problems. The work in this chapter will focus on a class of algebraic expressions called **polynomials**.

Recall that algebraic expressions such as $5x$, $-6y^2$, $7xy$, $14a^2b$, and $-17ab^2c^3$ are called terms. A **term** is an indicated product and may contain any number of factors. The variables in a term are called **literal factors**, and the numerical factor is called the **numerical coefficient**. Thus in $7xy$, the x and y are literal factors, 7 is the numerical coefficient, and the term is in two variables (x and y).

Terms that contain variables with only whole numbers as exponents are called **monomials**. The previously listed terms, $5x$, $-6y^2$, $7xy$, $14a^2b$, and $-17ab^2c^3$, are all monomials. (We shall work later with some algebraic expressions, such as $7x^{-1}y^{-1}$ and $6a^{-2}b^{-3}$, that are not monomials.)

The **degree** of a monomial is the sum of the exponents of the literal factors.

$7xy$ is of degree 2.

$14a^2b$ is of degree 3.

$-17ab^2c^3$ is of degree 6.

$5x$ is of degree 1.

$-6y^2$ is of degree 2.

If the monomial contains only one variable, then the exponent of the variable is the degree of the monomial. The last two examples illustrate this point. We say that any nonzero constant term is of degree zero.

A **polynomial** is a monomial or a finite sum (or difference) of monomials. Thus

$$4x^2, \qquad 3x^2 - 2x - 4, \qquad 7x^4 - 6x^3 + 4x^2 + x - 1,$$

$$3x^2y - 2xy^2, \qquad \frac{1}{5}a^2 - \frac{2}{3}b^2, \qquad \text{and} \qquad 14$$

are examples of polynomials. In addition to calling a polynomial with one term a **monomial**, we also classify polynomials with two terms as **binomials**, and those with three terms as **trinomials**.

The **degree of a polynomial** is the degree of the term with the highest degree in the polynomial. The following examples illustrate some of this terminology.

The polynomial $4x^3y^4$ is a monomial in two variables of degree 7.

The polynomial $4x^2y - 2xy$ is a binomial in two variables of degree 3.

The polynomial $9x^2 - 7x + 1$ is a trinomial in one variable of degree 2.

■ Combining Similar Terms

Remember that *similar terms*, or *like terms*, are terms that have the same literal factors. In the preceding chapters, we have frequently simplified algebraic expressions by combining similar terms, as the next examples illustrate.

$$2x + 3y + 7x + 8y = \boxed{2x + 7x + 3y + 8y}$$
$$= \boxed{(2 + 7)x + (3 + 8)y}$$
$$= 9x + 11y$$

Steps in dashed boxes are usually done mentally.

$$4a - 7 - 9a + 10 = \boxed{4a + (-7) + (-9a) + 10}$$
$$= \boxed{4a + (-9a) + (-7) + 10}$$
$$= \boxed{(4 + (-9))a + (-7) + 10}$$
$$= -5a + 3$$

Both addition and subtraction of polynomials rely on basically the same ideas. The commutative, associative, and distributive properties provide the basis for rearranging, regrouping, and combining similar terms. Let's consider some examples.

EXAMPLE 1   Add $4x^2 + 5x + 1$ and $7x^2 - 9x + 4$.

Solution

We generally use the horizontal format for such work. Thus

$$(4x^2 + 5x + 1) + (7x^2 - 9x + 4) = (4x^2 + 7x^2) + (5x - 9x) + (1 + 4)$$
$$= 11x^2 - 4x + 5 \qquad ■$$

EXAMPLE 2   Add $5x - 3$, $3x + 2$, and $8x + 6$.

Solution

$$(5x - 3) + (3x + 2) + (8x + 6) = (5x + 3x + 8x) + (-3 + 2 + 6)$$
$$= 16x + 5 \qquad ■$$

EXAMPLE 3   Find the indicated sum: $(-4x^2y + xy^2) + (7x^2y - 9xy^2) + (5x^2y - 4xy^2)$.

Solution

$$(-4x^2y + xy^2) + (7x^2y - 9xy^2) + (5x^2y - 4xy^2)$$
$$= (-4x^2y + 7x^2y + 5x^2y) + (xy^2 - 9xy^2 - 4xy^2)$$
$$= 8x^2y - 12xy^2 \qquad ■$$

The idea of subtraction as adding the opposite extends to polynomials in general. Hence the expression $a - b$ is equivalent to $a + (-b)$. We can form the opposite of a polynomial by taking the opposite of each term. For example, the opposite of $3x^2 - 7x + 1$ is $-3x^2 + 7x - 1$. We express this in symbols as

$$-(3x^2 - 7x + 1) = -3x^2 + 7x - 1$$

Now consider the following subtraction problems.

E X A M P L E   4

Subtract $3x^2 + 7x - 1$ from $7x^2 - 2x - 4$.

Solution

Use the horizontal format to obtain

$$(7x^2 - 2x - 4) - (3x^2 + 7x - 1) = (7x^2 - 2x - 4) + (-3x^2 - 7x + 1)$$
$$= (7x^2 - 3x^2) + (-2x - 7x) + (-4 + 1)$$
$$= 4x^2 - 9x - 3 \qquad \blacksquare$$

E X A M P L E   5

Subtract $-3y^2 + y - 2$ from $4y^2 + 7$.

Solution

Because subtraction is not a commutative operation, be sure to perform the subtraction in the correct order.

$$(4y^2 + 7) - (-3y^2 + y - 2) = (4y^2 + 7) + (3y^2 - y + 2)$$
$$= (4y^2 + 3y^2) + (-y) + (7 + 2)$$
$$= 7y^2 - y + 9 \qquad \blacksquare$$

The next example demonstrates the use of the vertical format for this work.

E X A M P L E   6

Subtract $4x^2 - 7xy + 5y^2$ from $3x^2 - 2xy + y^2$.

Solution

$$3x^2 - 2xy + y^2$$
$$\underline{4x^2 - 7xy + 5y^2}$$

Note which polynomial goes on the bottom and how the similar terms are aligned.

Now we can mentally form the opposite of the bottom polynomial and add.

$$3x^2 - 2xy + y^2$$
$$\underline{4x^2 - 7xy + 5y^2}$$
$$-x^2 + 5xy - 4y^2$$

The opposite of $4x^2 - 7xy + 5y^2$ is $-4x^2 + 7xy - 5y^2$.

$\blacksquare$

We can also use the distributive property and the properties $a = 1(a)$ and $-a = -1(a)$ when adding and subtracting polynomials. The next examples illustrate this approach.

E X A M P L E 7

Perform the indicated operations: $(5x - 2) + (2x - 1) - (3x + 4)$.

Solution

$$(5x - 2) + (2x - 1) - (3x + 4) = 1(5x - 2) + 1(2x - 1) - 1(3x + 4)$$
$$= 1(5x) - 1(2) + 1(2x) - 1(1) - 1(3x) - 1(4)$$
$$= 5x - 2 + 2x - 1 - 3x - 4$$
$$= 5x + 2x - 3x - 2 - 1 - 4$$
$$= 4x - 7 \qquad \blacksquare$$

We can do some of the steps mentally and simplify our format, as shown in the next two examples.

E X A M P L E 8

Perform the indicated operations: $(5a^2 - 2b) - (2a^2 + 4) + (-7b - 3)$.

Solution

$$(5a^2 - 2b) - (2a^2 + 4) + (-7b - 3) = 5a^2 - 2b - 2a^2 - 4 - 7b - 3$$
$$= 3a^2 - 9b - 7 \qquad \blacksquare$$

E X A M P L E 9

Simplify $(4t^2 - 7t - 1) - (t^2 + 2t - 6)$.

Solution

$$(4t^2 - 7t - 1) - (t^2 + 2t - 6) = 4t^2 - 7t - 1 - t^2 - 2t + 6$$
$$= 3t^2 - 9t + 5 \qquad \blacksquare$$

Remember that a polynomial in parentheses preceded by a negative sign can be written without the parentheses by replacing each term with its opposite. Thus in Example 9, $-(t^2 + 2t - 6) = -t^2 - 2t + 6$. Finally, let's consider a simplification problem that contains grouping symbols within grouping symbols.

E X A M P L E 1 0

Simplify $7x + [3x - (2x + 7)]$.

Solution

$$7x + [3x - (2x + 7)] = 7x + [3x - 2x - 7] \qquad \text{Remove the innermost}$$
$$\text{parentheses first.}$$
$$= 7x + [x - 7]$$
$$= 7x + x - 7$$
$$= 8x - 7 \qquad \blacksquare$$

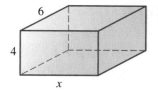

Figure 3.1

Sometimes we encounter polynomials in a geometric setting. For example, we can find a polynomial that represents the total surface area of the rectangular solid in Figure 3.1 as follows:

$$4x \quad + \quad 4x \quad + \quad 6x \quad + \quad 6x \quad + \quad 24 \quad + \quad 24$$

| Area of front | Area of back | Area of top | Area of bottom | Area of left side | Area of right side |

Simplifying $4x + 4x + 6x + 6x + 24 + 24$, we obtain the polynomial $20x + 48$, which represents the total surface area of the rectangular solid. Furthermore, by evaluating the polynomial $20x + 48$ for different positive values of x, we can determine the total surface area of any rectangular solid for which two dimensions are 4 and 6. The following chart contains some specific rectangular solids.

x	4 by 6 by x rectangular solid	Total surface area $(20x + 48)$
2	4 by 6 by 2	$20(2) + 48 = 88$
4	4 by 6 by 4	$20(4) + 48 = 128$
5	4 by 6 by 5	$20(5) + 48 = 148$
7	4 by 6 by 7	$20(7) + 48 = 188$
12	4 by 6 by 12	$20(12) + 48 = 288$

Problem Set 3.1

For Problems 1–10, determine the degree of the given polynomials.

1. $7xy + 6y$

2. $-5x^2y^2 - 6xy^2 + x$

3. $-x^2y + 2xy^2 - xy$

4. $5x^3y^2 - 6x^3y^3$

5. $5x^2 - 7x - 2$

6. $7x^3 - 2x + 4$

7. $8x^6 + 9$

8. $5y^6 + y^4 - 2y^2 - 8$

9. -12

10. $7x - 2y$

For Problems 11–20, add the given polynomials.

11. $3x - 7$ and $7x + 4$

12. $9x + 6$ and $5x - 3$

13. $-5t - 4$ and $-6t + 9$

14. $-7t + 14$ and $-3t - 6$

15. $3x^2 - 5x - 1$ and $-4x^2 + 7x - 1$

16. $6x^2 + 8x + 4$ and $-7x^2 - 7x - 10$

17. $12a^2b^2 - 9ab$ and $5a^2b^2 + 4ab$

18. $15a^2b^2 - ab$ and $-20a^2b^2 - 6ab$

19. $2x - 4$, $-7x + 2$, and $-4x + 9$

20. $-x^2 - x - 4$, $2x^2 - 7x + 9$, and $-3x^2 + 6x - 10$

For Problems 21–30, subtract the polynomials using the horizontal format.

21. $5x - 2$ from $3x + 4$

22. $7x + 5$ from $2x - 1$

23. $-4a - 5$ from $6a + 2$

24. $5a + 7$ from $-a - 4$

25. $3x^2 - x + 2$ from $7x^2 + 9x + 8$

26. $5x^2 + 4x - 7$ from $3x^2 + 2x - 9$

27. $2a^2 - 6a - 4$ from $-4a^2 + 6a + 10$

28. $-3a^2 - 6a + 3$ from $3a^2 + 6a - 11$

29. $2x^3 + x^2 - 7x - 2$ from $5x^3 + 2x^2 + 6x - 13$

30. $6x^3 + x^2 + 4$ from $9x^3 - x - 2$

For Problems 31–40, subtract the polynomials using the vertical format.

31. $5x - 2$ from $12x + 6$

32. $3x - 7$ from $2x + 1$

33. $-4x + 7$ from $-7x - 9$

34. $-6x - 2$ from $5x + 6$

35. $2x^2 + x + 6$ from $4x^2 - x - 2$

36. $4x^2 - 3x - 7$ from $-x^2 - 6x + 9$

37. $x^3 + x^2 - x - 1$ from $-2x^3 + 6x^2 - 3x + 8$

38. $2x^3 - x + 6$ from $x^3 + 4x^2 + 1$

39. $-5x^2 + 6x - 12$ from $2x - 1$

40. $2x^2 - 7x - 10$ from $-x^3 - 12$

For Problems 41–46, perform the operations as described.

41. Subtract $2x^2 - 7x - 1$ from the sum of $x^2 + 9x - 4$ and $-5x^2 - 7x + 10$.

42. Subtract $4x^2 + 6x + 9$ from the sum of $-3x^2 - 9x + 6$ and $-2x^2 + 6x - 4$.

43. Subtract $-x^2 - 7x - 1$ from the sum of $4x^2 + 3$ and $-7x^2 + 2x$.

44. Subtract $-4x^2 + 6x - 3$ from the sum of $-3x + 4$ and $9x^2 - 6$.

45. Subtract the sum of $5n^2 - 3n - 2$ and $-7n^2 + n + 2$ from $-12n^2 - n + 9$.

46. Subtract the sum of $-6n^2 + 2n - 4$ and $4n^2 - 2n + 4$ from $-n^2 - n + 1$.

For Problems 47–56, perform the indicated operations.

47. $(5x + 2) + (7x - 1) + (-4x - 3)$

48. $(-3x + 1) + (6x - 2) + (9x - 4)$

49. $(12x - 9) - (-3x + 4) - (7x + 1)$

50. $(6x + 4) - (4x - 2) - (-x - 1)$

51. $(2x^2 - 7x - 1) + (-4x^2 - x + 6) + (-7x^2 - 4x - 1)$

52. $(5x^2 + x + 4) + (-x^2 + 2x + 4) + (-14x^2 - x + 6)$

53. $(7x^2 - x - 4) - (9x^2 - 10x + 8) + (12x^2 + 4x - 6)$

54. $(-6x^2 + 2x + 5) - (4x^2 + 4x - 1) + (7x^2 + 4)$

55. $(n^2 - 7n - 9) - (-3n + 4) - (2n^2 - 9)$

56. $(6n^2 - 4) - (5n^2 + 9) - (6n + 4)$

For Problems 57–70, simplify by removing the inner parentheses first and working outward.

57. $3x - [5x - (x + 6)]$

58. $7x - [2x - (-x - 4)]$

59. $2x^2 - [-3x^2 - (x^2 - 4)]$

60. $4x^2 - [-x^2 - (5x^2 - 6)]$

61. $-2n^2 - [n^2 - (-4n^2 + n + 6)]$

62. $-7n^2 - [3n^2 - (-n^2 - n + 4)]$

63. $[4t^2 - (2t + 1) + 3] - [3t^2 + (2t - 1) - 5]$

64. $-(3n^2 - 2n + 4) - [2n^2 - (n^2 + n + 3)]$

65. $[2n^2 - (2n^2 - n + 5)] + [3n^2 + (n^2 - 2n - 7)]$

66. $3x^2 - [4x^2 - 2x - (x^2 - 2x + 6)]$

67. $[7xy - (2x - 3xy + y)] - [3x - (x - 10xy - y)]$

68. $[9xy - (4x + xy - y)] - [4y - (2x - xy + 6y)]$

69. $[4x^3 - (2x^2 - x - 1)] - [5x^3 - (x^2 + 2x - 1)]$

70. $[x^3 - (x^2 - x + 1)] - [-x^3 + (7x^2 - x + 10)]$

71. Find a polynomial that represents the perimeter of each of the following figures (Figures 3.2, 3.3, and 3.4).

(a)

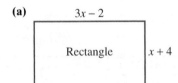

Figure 3.2

(b)

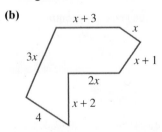

Figure 3.3

(c)

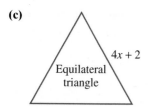

Figure 3.4

72. Find a polynomial that represents the total surface area of the rectangular solid in Figure 3.5.

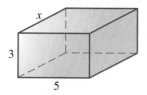

Figure 3.5

Now use that polynomial to determine the total surface area of each of the following rectangular solids.

(a) 3 by 5 by <u>4</u>   **(b)** 3 by 5 by <u>7</u>

(c) 3 by 5 by <u>11</u>   **(d)** 3 by 5 by <u>13</u>

73. Find a polynomial that represents the total surface area of the right circular cylinder in Figure 3.6. Now use that polynomial to determine the total surface area of each of the following right circular cylinders that have a base with a radius of 4. Use 3.14 for π, and express the answers to the nearest tenth.

(a) $h = 5$ **(b)** $h = 7$

(c) $h = 14$ **(d)** $h = 18$

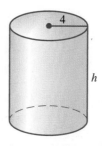

Figure 3.6

■ ■ ■ **THOUGHTS INTO WORDS**

74. Explain how to subtract the polynomial $-3x^2 + 2x - 4$ from $4x^2 + 6$.

75. Is the sum of two binomials always another binomial? Defend your answer.

76. Explain how to simplify the expression

$$7x - [3x - (2x - 4) + 2] - x$$

3.2   Products and Quotients of Monomials

Suppose that we want to find the product of two monomials such as $3x^2y$ and $4x^3y^2$. To proceed, use the properties of real numbers, and keep in mind that exponents indicate repeated multiplication.

$$(3x^2y)(4x^3y^2) = (3 \cdot x \cdot x \cdot y)(4 \cdot x \cdot x \cdot x \cdot y \cdot y)$$
$$= 3 \cdot 4 \cdot x \cdot x \cdot x \cdot x \cdot x \cdot y \cdot y \cdot y$$
$$= 12x^5y^3$$

You can use such an approach to find the product of any two monomials. However, there are some basic properties of exponents that make the process of multiplying monomials a much easier task. Let's consider each of these properties and illustrate its use when multiplying monomials. The following examples demonstrate the first property.

$$x^2 \cdot x^3 = (x \cdot x)(x \cdot x \cdot x) = x^5$$

$$a^4 \cdot a^2 = (a \cdot a \cdot a \cdot a)(a \cdot a) = a^6$$

$$b^3 \cdot b^4 = (b \cdot b \cdot b)(b \cdot b \cdot b \cdot b) = b^7$$

In general,

$$b^n \cdot b^m = \underbrace{(b \cdot b \cdot b \cdot \ldots b)}_{\substack{n \text{ factors} \\ \text{of } b}}\underbrace{(b \cdot b \cdot b \cdot \ldots b)}_{\substack{m \text{ factors} \\ \text{of } b}}$$

$$= \underbrace{b \cdot b \cdot b \cdot \ldots b}_{(n + m) \text{ factors of } b}$$

$$= b^{n+m}$$

We can state the first property as follows:

Property 3.1

If b is any real number, and n and m are positive integers, then

$$b^n \cdot b^m = b^{n+m}$$

Property 3.1 says that to find the product of two positive integral powers of the same base, we add the exponents and use this sum as the exponent of the common base.

$$x^7 \cdot x^8 = x^{7+8} = x^{15} \qquad\qquad y^6 \cdot y^4 = y^{6+4} = y^{10}$$

$$2^3 \cdot 2^8 = 2^{3+8} = 2^{11} \qquad\qquad (-3)^4 \cdot (-3)^5 = (-3)^{4+5} = (-3)^9$$

$$\left(\frac{2}{3}\right)^7 \cdot \left(\frac{2}{3}\right)^5 = \left(\frac{2}{3}\right)^{5+7} = \left(\frac{2}{3}\right)^{12}$$

The following examples illustrate the use of Property 3.1, along with the commutative and associative properties of multiplication, to form the basis for multiplying monomials. The steps enclosed in the dashed boxes could be performed mentally.

EXAMPLE 1

$$(3x^2y)(4x^3y^2) = \overline{3 \cdot 4 \cdot x^2 \cdot x^3 \cdot y \cdot y^2}$$

$$= \overline{12x^{2+3}y^{1+2}}$$

$$= 12x^5y^3$$

EXAMPLE 2

$$(-5a^3b^4)(7a^2b^5) = -5 \cdot 7 \cdot a^3 \cdot a^2 \cdot b^4 \cdot b^5$$

$$= -35a^{3+2}b^{4+5}$$

$$= -35a^5b^9$$

■

EXAMPLE 3

$$\left(\frac{3}{4}xy\right)\left(\frac{1}{2}x^5y^6\right) = \frac{3}{4} \cdot \frac{1}{2} \cdot x \cdot x^5 \cdot y \cdot y^6$$

$$= \frac{3}{8}x^{1+5}y^{1+6}$$

$$= \frac{3}{8}x^6y^7$$

■

EXAMPLE 4

$$(-ab^2)(-5a^2b) = (-1)(-5)(a)(a^2)(b^2)(b)$$

$$= 5a^{1+2}b^{2+1}$$

$$= 5a^3b^3$$

■

EXAMPLE 5

$$(2x^2y^2)(3x^2y)(4y^3) = 2 \cdot 3 \cdot 4 \cdot x^2 \cdot x^2 \cdot y^2 \cdot y \cdot y^3$$

$$= 24x^{2+2}y^{2+1+3}$$

$$= 24x^4y^6$$

■

The following examples demonstrate another useful property of exponents.

$$(x^2)^3 = x^2 \cdot x^2 \cdot x^2 = x^{2+2+2} = x^6$$

$$(a^3)^2 = a^3 \cdot a^3 = a^{3+3} = a^6$$

$$(b^4)^3 = b^4 \cdot b^4 \cdot b^4 = b^{4+4+4} = b^{12}$$

In general,

$$(b^n)^m = \underbrace{b^n \cdot b^n \cdot b^n \cdot \ldots b^n}_{m \text{ factors of } b^n}$$

adding m of these

$$= b^{\overbrace{n+n+n+\cdots+n}}$$

$$= b^{mn}$$

We can state this property as follows:

Property 3.2

If b is any real number, and m and n are positive integers, then

$$(b^n)^m = b^{mn}$$

The following examples show how Property 3.2 is used to find "the power of a power."

$$(x^4)^5 = x^{5(4)} = x^{20} \qquad (y^6)^3 = y^{3(6)} = y^{18}$$

$$(2^3)^7 = 2^{7(3)} = 2^{21}$$

A third property of exponents pertains to raising a monomial to a power. Consider the following examples, which we use to introduce the property.

$$(3x)^2 = (3x)(3x) = 3 \cdot 3 \cdot x \cdot x = 3^2 \cdot x^2$$

$$(4y^2)^3 = (4y^2)(4y^2)(4y^2) = 4 \cdot 4 \cdot 4 \cdot y^2 \cdot y^2 \cdot y^2 = (4)^3(y^2)^3$$

$$(-2a^3b^4)^2 = (-2a^3b^4)(-2a^3b^4) = (-2)(-2)(a^3)(a^3)(b^4)(b^4)$$

$$= (-2)^2(a^3)^2(b^4)^2$$

In general,

$$(ab)^n = \underbrace{(ab)(ab)(ab) \cdot \ldots (ab)}_{n \text{ factors of } ab}$$

$$= \underbrace{(a \cdot a \cdot a \cdot a \cdot \ldots a)}_{\substack{n \text{ factors} \\ \text{of } a}}\underbrace{(b \cdot b \cdot b \cdot \ldots b)}_{\substack{n \text{ factors} \\ \text{of } b}}$$

$$= a^n b^n$$

We can formally state Property 3.3 as follows:

Property 3.3

If a and b are real numbers, and n is a positive integer, then

$$(ab)^n = a^n b^n$$

Property 3.3 and Property 3.2 form the basis for raising a monomial to a power, as in the next examples.

EXAMPLE 6

$$(x^2y^3)^4 = (x^2)^4(y^3)^4 \qquad \text{Use } (ab)^n = a^nb^n.$$
$$= x^8y^{12} \qquad \text{Use } (b^n)^m = b^{mn}.$$ ■

EXAMPLE 7

$$(3a^5)^3 = (3)^3(a^5)^3$$
$$= 27a^{15}$$ ■

EXAMPLE 8

$$(-2xy^4)^5 = (-2)^5(x)^5(y^4)^5$$
$$= -32x^5y^{20}$$ ■

■ Dividing Monomials

To develop an effective process for dividing by a monomial, we need yet another property of exponents. This property is a direct consequence of the definition of an exponent. Study the following examples.

$$\frac{x^4}{x^3} = \frac{x \cdot x \cdot x \cdot x}{x \cdot x \cdot x} = x \qquad\qquad \frac{x^3}{x^3} = \frac{x \cdot x \cdot x}{x \cdot x \cdot x} = 1$$

$$\frac{a^5}{a^2} = \frac{a \cdot a \cdot a \cdot a \cdot a}{a \cdot a} = a^3 \qquad\qquad \frac{y^5}{y^5} = \frac{y \cdot y \cdot y \cdot y \cdot y}{y \cdot y \cdot y \cdot y \cdot y} = 1$$

$$\frac{y^8}{y^4} = \frac{y \cdot y \cdot y \cdot y \cdot y \cdot y \cdot y \cdot y}{y \cdot y \cdot y \cdot y} = y^4$$

We can state the general property as follows:

Property 3.4

> If b is any nonzero real number, and m and n are positive integers, then
>
> **1.** $\dfrac{b^n}{b^m} = b^{n-m}, \quad$ when $n > m$
>
> **2.** $\dfrac{b^n}{b^m} = 1, \quad$ when $n = m$

Applying Property 3.4 to the previous examples yields

$$\frac{x^4}{x^3} = x^{4-3} = x^1 = x \qquad \frac{x^3}{x^3} = 1$$

$$\frac{a^5}{a^2} = a^{5-2} = a^3 \qquad \frac{y^5}{y^5} = 1$$

$$\frac{y^8}{y^4} = y^{8-4} = y^4$$

(We will discuss the situation when $n < m$ in a later chapter.)

Property 3.4, along with our knowledge of dividing integers, provides the basis for dividing monomials. The following examples demonstrate the process.

$$\frac{24x^5}{3x^2} = 8x^{5-2} = 8x^3 \qquad \frac{-36a^{13}}{-12a^5} = 3a^{13-5} = 3a^8$$

$$\frac{-56x^9}{7x^4} = -8x^{9-4} = -8x^5 \qquad \frac{72b^5}{8b^5} = 9 \quad \left(\frac{b^5}{b^5} = 1\right)$$

$$\frac{48y^7}{-12y} = -4y^{7-1} = -4y^6 \qquad \frac{12x^4y^7}{2x^2y^4} = 6x^{4-2}y^{7-4} = 6x^2y^3$$

Problem Set 3.2

For Problems 1–36, find each product.

1. $(4x^3)(9x)$

2. $(6x^3)(7x^2)$

3. $(-2x^2)(6x^3)$

4. $(2xy)(-4x^2y)$

5. $(-a^2b)(-4ab^3)$

6. $(-8a^2b^2)(-3ab^3)$

7. $(x^2yz^2)(-3xyz^4)$

8. $(-2xy^2z^2)(-x^2y^3z)$

9. $(5xy)(-6y^3)$

10. $(-7xy)(4x^4)$

11. $(3a^2b)(9a^2b^4)$

12. $(-8a^2b^2)(-12ab^5)$

13. $(m^2n)(-mn^2)$

14. $(-x^3y^2)(xy^3)$

15. $\left(\frac{2}{5}xy^2\right)\left(\frac{3}{4}x^2y^4\right)$

16. $\left(\frac{1}{2}x^2y^6\right)\left(\frac{2}{3}xy\right)$

17. $\left(-\frac{3}{4}ab\right)\left(\frac{1}{5}a^2b^3\right)$

18. $\left(-\frac{2}{7}a^2\right)\left(\frac{3}{5}ab^3\right)$

19. $\left(-\frac{1}{2}xy\right)\left(\frac{1}{3}x^2y^3\right)$

20. $\left(\frac{3}{4}x^4y^5\right)(-x^2y)$

21. $(3x)(-2x^2)(-5x^3)$

22. $(-2x)(-6x^3)(x^2)$

23. $(-6x^2)(3x^3)(x^4)$

24. $(-7x^2)(3x)(4x^3)$

25. $(x^2y)(-3xy^2)(x^3y^3)$

26. $(xy^2)(-5xy)(x^2y^4)$

27. $(-3y^2)(-2y^2)(-4y^5)$

28. $(-y^3)(-6y)(-8y^4)$

29. $(4ab)(-2a^2b)(7a)$

30. $(3b)(-2ab^2)(7a)$

31. $(-ab)(-3ab)(-6ab)$

32. $(-3a^2b)(-ab^2)(-7a)$

33. $\left(\frac{2}{3}xy\right)(-3x^2y)(5x^4y^5)$

34. $\left(\frac{3}{4}x\right)(-4x^2y^2)(9y^3)$

35. $(12y)(-5x)\left(-\frac{5}{6}x^4y\right)$

36. $(-12x)(3y)\left(-\frac{3}{4}xy^6\right)$

For Problems 37–58, raise each monomial to the indicated power.

37. $(3xy^2)^3$

38. $(4x^2y^3)^3$

39. $(-2x^2y)^5$

40. $(-3xy^4)^3$

41. $(-x^4y^5)^4$

42. $(-x^5y^2)^4$

43. $(ab^2c^3)^6$

44. $(a^2b^3c^5)^5$

45. $(2a^2b^3)^6$

46. $(2a^3b^2)^6$

47. $(9xy^4)^2$

48. $(8x^2y^5)^2$

49. $(-3ab^3)^4$

50. $(-2a^2b^4)^4$

51. $-(2ab)^4$

52. $-(3ab)^4$

53. $-(xy^2z^3)^6$

54. $-(xy^2z^3)^8$

55. $(-5a^2b^2c)^3$

56. $(-4abc^4)^3$

57. $(-xy^4z^2)^7$

58. $(-x^2y^4z^5)^5$

For Problems 59–74, find each quotient.

59. $\dfrac{9x^4y^5}{3xy^2}$

60. $\dfrac{12x^2y^7}{6x^2y^3}$

61. $\dfrac{25x^5y^6}{-5x^2y^4}$

62. $\dfrac{56x^6y^4}{-7x^2y^3}$

63. $\dfrac{-54ab^2c^3}{-6abc}$

64. $\dfrac{-48a^3bc^5}{-6a^2c^4}$

65. $\dfrac{-18x^2y^2z^6}{xyz^2}$

66. $\dfrac{-32x^4y^5z^8}{x^2yz^3}$

67. $\dfrac{a^3b^4c^7}{-abc^5}$

68. $\dfrac{-a^4b^5c}{a^2b^4c}$

69. $\dfrac{-72x^2y^4}{-8x^2y^4}$

70. $\dfrac{-96x^4y^5}{12x^4y^4}$

71. $\dfrac{14ab^3}{-14ab}$

72. $\dfrac{-12abc^2}{12bc}$

73. $\dfrac{-36x^3y^5}{2y^5}$

74. $\dfrac{-48xyz^2}{2xz}$

For Problems 75–90, find each product. Assume that the variables in the exponents represent positive integers. For example,

$$(x^{2n})(x^{3n}) = x^{2n+3n} = x^{5n}$$

75. $(2x^n)(3x^{2n})$

76. $(3x^{2n})(x^{3n-1})$

77. $(a^{2n-1})(a^{3n+4})$

78. $(a^{5n-1})(a^{5n+1})$

79. $(x^{3n-2})(x^{n+2})$

80. $(x^{n-1})(x^{4n+3})$

81. $(a^{5n-2})(a^3)$

82. $(x^{3n-4})(x^4)$

83. $(2x^n)(-5x^n)$

84. $(4x^{2n-1})(-3x^{n+1})$

85. $(-3a^2)(-4a^{n+2})$

86. $(-5x^{n-1})(-6x^{2n+4})$

87. $(x^n)(2x^{2n})(3x^2)$

88. $(2x^n)(3x^{3n-1})(-4x^{2n+5})$

89. $(3x^{n-1})(x^{n+1})(4x^{2-n})$

90. $(-5x^{n+2})(x^{n-2})(4x^{3-2n})$

91. Find a polynomial that represents the total surface area of the rectangular solid in Figure 3.7. Also find a polynomial that represents the volume.

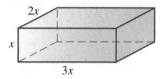

Figure 3.7

92. Find a polynomial that represents the total surface area of the rectangular solid in Figure 3.8. Also find a polynomial that represents the volume.

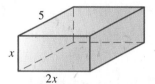

Figure 3.8

93. Find a polynomial that represents the area of the shaded region in Figure 3.9. The length of a radius of the larger circle is r units, and the length of a radius of the smaller circle is 6 units.

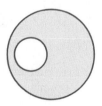

Figure 3.9

■ ■ ■ THOUGHTS INTO WORDS

94. How would you convince someone that $x^6 \div x^2$ is x^4 and not x^3?

95. Your friend simplifies $2^3 \cdot 2^2$ as follows:

$$2^3 \cdot 2^2 = 4^{3+2} = 4^5 = 1024$$

What has she done incorrectly and how would you help her?

3.3 Multiplying Polynomials

We usually state the distributive property as $a(b + c) = ab + ac$; however, we can extend it as follows:

$$a(b + c + d) = ab + ac + ad$$

$$a(b + c + d + e) = ab + ac + ad + ae \quad \text{etc.}$$

We apply the commutative and associative properties, the properties of exponents, and the distributive property together to find the product of a monomial and a polynomial. The following examples illustrate this idea.

EXAMPLE 1

$$3x^2(2x^2 + 5x + 3) = 3x^2(2x^2) + 3x^2(5x) + 3x^2(3)$$
$$= 6x^4 + 15x^3 + 9x^2 \qquad \blacksquare$$

EXAMPLE 2

$$-2xy(3x^3 - 4x^2y - 5xy^2 + y^3) = -2xy(3x^3) - (-2xy)(4x^2y)$$
$$-(-2xy)(5xy^2) + (-2xy)(y^3)$$
$$= -6x^4y + 8x^3y^2 + 10x^2y^3 - 2xy^4 \qquad \blacksquare$$

Now let's consider the product of two polynomials neither of which is a monomial. Consider the following examples.

EXAMPLE 3

$$(x + 2)(y + 5) = x(y + 5) + 2(y + 5)$$
$$= x(y) + x(5) + 2(y) + 2(5)$$
$$= xy + 5x + 2y + 10 \qquad \blacksquare$$

Note that each term of the first polynomial is multiplied by each term of the second polynomial.

EXAMPLE 4

$$(x - 3)(y + z + 3) = x(y + z + 3) - 3(y + z + 3)$$
$$= xy + xz + 3x - 3y - 3z - 9 \qquad \blacksquare$$

Multiplying polynomials often produces similar terms that can be combined to simplify the resulting polynomial.

EXAMPLE 5

$$(x + 5)(x + 7) = x(x + 7) + 5(x + 7)$$
$$= x^2 + 7x + 5x + 35$$
$$= x^2 + 12x + 35 \qquad \blacksquare$$

E X A M P L E   6

$$(x - 2)(x^2 - 3x + 4) = x(x^2 - 3x + 4) - 2(x^2 - 3x + 4)$$
$$= x^3 - 3x^2 + 4x - 2x^2 + 6x - 8$$
$$= x^3 - 5x^2 + 10x - 8 \qquad ∎$$

In Example 6, we are claiming that

$$(x - 2)(x^2 - 3x + 4) = x^3 - 5x^2 + 10x - 8$$

for all real numbers. In addition to going back over our work, how can we verify such a claim? Obviously, we cannot try all real numbers, but trying at least one number gives us a partial check. Let's try the number 4.

$$(x - 2)(x^2 - 3x + 4) = (4 - 2)(4^2 - 3(4) + 4)$$
$$= 2(16 - 12 + 4)$$
$$= 2(8)$$
$$= 16$$

$$x^3 - 5x^2 + 10x - 8 = 4^3 - 5(4)^2 + 10(4) - 8$$
$$= 64 - 80 + 40 - 8$$
$$= 16$$

E X A M P L E   7

$$(3x - 2y)(x^2 + xy - y^2) = 3x(x^2 + xy - y^2) - 2y(x^2 + xy - y^2)$$
$$= 3x^3 + 3x^2y - 3xy^2 - 2x^2y - 2xy^2 + 2y^3$$
$$= 3x^3 + x^2y - 5xy^2 + 2y^3 \qquad ∎$$

It helps to be able to find the product of two binomials without showing all of the intermediate steps. This is quite easy to do with the *three-step shortcut pattern* demonstrated by Figures 3.10 and 3.11 in the following examples.

E X A M P L E   8

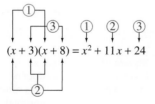

Figure 3.10

Step ①. Multiply $x \cdot x$.

Step ②. Multiply $3 \cdot x$ and $8 \cdot x$ and combine.

Step ③. Multiply $3 \cdot 8$. ∎

EXAMPLE 9

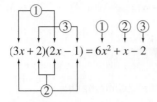

Figure 3.11

Now see if you can use the pattern to find the following products.

$$(x + 2)(x + 6) = ?$$

$$(x - 3)(x + 5) = ?$$

$$(2x + 5)(3x + 7) = ?$$

$$(3x - 1)(4x - 3) = ?$$

Your answers should be $x^2 + 8x + 12$, $x^2 + 2x - 15$, $6x^2 + 29x + 35$, and $12x^2 - 13x + 3$. Keep in mind that this shortcut pattern applies only to finding the product of two binomials.

We can use exponents to indicate repeated multiplication of polynomials. For example, $(x + 3)^2$ means $(x + 3)(x + 3)$, and $(x + 4)^3$ means $(x + 4)(x + 4) \cdot (x + 4)$. To square a binomial, we can simply write it as the product of two equal binomials and apply the shortcut pattern. Thus

$$(x + 3)^2 = (x + 3)(x + 3) = x^2 + 6x + 9$$

$$(x - 6)^2 = (x - 6)(x - 6) = x^2 - 12x + 36 \quad \text{and}$$

$$(3x - 4)^2 = (3x - 4)(3x - 4) = 9x^2 - 24x + 16$$

When squaring binomials, be careful not to forget the middle term. That is to say, $(x + 3)^2 \neq x^2 + 3^2$; instead, $(x + 3)^2 = x^2 + 6x + 9$.

When multiplying binomials, there are some special patterns that you should recognize. We can use these patterns to find products, and later we will use some of them when factoring polynomials.

PATTERN

$$(a + b)^2 = (a + b)(a + b) = a^2 \quad + \quad 2ab \quad + \quad b^2$$

| Square of
first term
of binomial | + | Twice the
product of
the two terms
of binomial | + | Square of
second term
of binomial |

Examples

$$(x + 4)^2 = x^2 + 8x + 16$$

$$(2x + 3y)^2 = 4x^2 + 12xy + 9y^2$$

$$(5a + 7b)^2 = 25a^2 + 70ab + 49b^2$$

PATTERN

$$(a - b)^2 = (a - b)(a - b) = a^2 \quad - \quad 2ab \quad + \quad b^2$$

Square of first term of binomial

− Twice the product of the two terms of binomial

+ Square of second term of binomial

Examples

$$(x - 8)^2 = x^2 - 16x + 64$$

$$(3x - 4y)^2 = 9x^2 - 24xy + 16y^2$$

$$(4a - 9b)^2 = 16a^2 - 72ab + 81b^2$$

∎

PATTERN

$$(a + b)(a - b) = a^2 \quad - \quad b^2$$

Square of first term of binomials

− Square of second term of binomials

Examples

$$(x + 7)(x - 7) = x^2 - 49$$

$$(2x + y)(2x - y) = 4x^2 - y^2$$

$$(3a - 2b)(3a + 2b) = 9a^2 - 4b^2$$

∎

Now suppose that we want to cube a binomial. One approach is as follows:

$$(x + 4)^3 = (x + 4)(x + 4)(x + 4)$$

$$= (x + 4)(x^2 + 8x + 16)$$

$$= x(x^2 + 8x + 16) + 4(x^2 + 8x + 16)$$

$$= x^3 + 8x^2 + 16x + 4x^2 + 32x + 64$$

$$= x^3 + 12x^2 + 48x + 64$$

Another approach is to cube a general binomial and then use the resulting pattern.

PATTERN

$$(a + b)^3 = (a + b)(a + b)(a + b)$$

$$= (a + b)(a^2 + 2ab + b^2)$$

$$= a(a^2 + 2ab + b^2) + b(a^2 + 2ab + b^2)$$

$$= a^3 + 2a^2b + ab^2 + a^2b + 2ab^2 + b^3$$

$$= a^3 + 3a^2b + 3ab^2 + b^3$$

Let's use the pattern $(a + b)^3 = a^3 + 3a^2b + 3ab^2 + b^3$ to cube the binomial $x + 4$.

$$(x + 4)^3 = x^3 + 3x^2(4) + 3x(4)^2 + 4^3$$
$$= x^3 + 12x^2 + 48x + 64 \qquad \blacksquare$$

Because $a - b = a + (-b)$, we can easily develop a pattern for cubing $a - b$.

PATTERN

$$(a - b)^3 = [a + (-b)]^3$$
$$= a^3 + 3a^2(-b) + 3a(-b)^2 + (-b)^3$$
$$= a^3 - 3a^2b + 3ab^2 - b^3$$

Now let's use the pattern $(a - b)^3 = a^3 - 3a^2b + 3ab^2 - b^3$ to cube the binomial $3x - 2y$.

$$(3x - 2y)^3 = (3x)^3 - 3(3x)^2(2y) + 3(3x)(2y)^2 - (2y)^3$$
$$= 27x^3 - 54x^2y + 36xy^2 - 8y^3 \qquad \blacksquare$$

Finally, we need to realize that if the patterns are forgotten or do not apply, then we can revert to applying the distributive property.

$$(2x - 1)(x^2 - 4x + 6) = 2x(x^2 - 4x + 6) - 1(x^2 - 4x + 6)$$
$$= 2x^3 - 8x^2 + 12x - x^2 + 4x - 6$$
$$= 2x^3 - 9x^2 + 16x - 6$$

■ Back to the Geometry Connection

As you might expect, there are geometric interpretations for many of the algebraic concepts we present in this section. We will give you the opportunity to make some of these connections between algebra and geometry in the next problem set. Let's conclude this section with a problem that allows us to use some algebra and geometry.

EXAMPLE 10

A rectangular piece of tin is 16 inches long and 12 inches wide as shown in Figure 3.12. From each corner a square piece x inches on a side is cut out. The flaps are then turned up to form an open box. Find polynomials that represent the volume and outside surface area of the box.

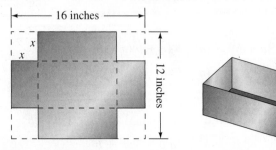

Figure 3.12

Solution

The length of the box will be $16 - 2x$, the width $12 - 2x$, and the height x. With the volume formula $V = lwh$, the polynomial $(16 - 2x)(12 - 2x)(x)$, which simplifies to $4x^3 - 56x^2 + 192x$, represents the volume.

The outside surface area of the box is the area of the original piece of tin minus the four corners that were cut off. Therefore, the polynomial $16(12) - 4x^2$, or $192 - 4x^2$, represents the outside surface area of the box. ∎

Remark: Recall that in Section 3.1 we found the total surface area of a rectangular solid by adding the areas of the sides, top, and bottom. Use this approach for the open box in Example 10 to check our answer of $192 - 4x^2$. Keep in mind that the box has no top.

Problem Set 3.3

For Problems 1–74, find each indicated product. Remember the shortcut for multiplying binomials and the other special patterns we discussed in this section.

1. $2xy(5xy^2 + 3x^2y^3)$

2. $3x^2y(6y^2 - 5x^2y^4)$

3. $-3a^2b(4ab^2 - 5a^3)$

4. $-7ab^2(2b^3 - 3a^2)$

5. $8a^3b^4(3ab - 2ab^2 + 4a^2b^2)$

6. $9a^3b(2a - 3b + 7ab)$

7. $-x^2y(6xy^2 + 3x^2y^3 - x^3y)$

8. $-ab^2(5a + 3b - 6a^2b^3)$

9. $(a + 2b)(x + y)$

10. $(t - s)(x + y)$

11. $(a - 3b)(c + 4d)$

12. $(a - 4b)(c - d)$

13. $(x + 6)(x + 10)$

14. $(x + 2)(x + 10)$

15. $(y - 5)(y + 11)$

16. $(y - 3)(y + 9)$

17. $(n + 2)(n - 7)$

18. $(n + 3)(n - 12)$

19. $(x + 6)(x - 6)$

20. $(t + 8)(t - 8)$

21. $(x - 6)^2$

22. $(x - 2)^2$

23. $(x - 6)(x - 8)$

24. $(x - 3)(x - 13)$

25. $(x + 1)(x - 2)(x - 3)$

26. $(x - 1)(x + 4)(x - 6)$

27. $(x - 3)(x + 3)(x - 1)$

28. $(x - 5)(x + 5)(x - 8)$

29. $(t + 9)^2$

30. $(t + 13)^2$

31. $(y - 7)^2$

32. $(y - 4)^2$

33. $(4x + 5)(x + 7)$

34. $(6x + 5)(x + 3)$

35. $(3y - 1)(3y + 1)$

36. $(5y - 2)(5y + 2)$

37. $(7x - 2)(2x + 1)$

38. $(6x - 1)(3x + 2)$

39. $(1 + t)(5 - 2t)$

40. $(3 - t)(2 + 4t)$

41. $(3t + 7)^2$

42. $(4t + 6)^2$

43. $(2 - 5x)(2 + 5x)$

44. $(6 - 3x)(6 + 3x)$

45. $(7x - 4)^2$

46. $(5x - 7)^2$

47. $(6x + 7)(3x - 10)$

48. $(4x - 7)(7x + 4)$

49. $(2x - 5y)(x + 3y)$

50. $(x - 4y)(3x + 7y)$

51. $(5x - 2a)(5x + 2a)$

52. $(9x - 2y)(9x + 2y)$

53. $(t + 3)(t^2 - 3t - 5)$

54. $(t - 2)(t^2 + 7t + 2)$

55. $(x - 4)(x^2 + 5x - 4)$

56. $(x + 6)(2x^2 - x - 7)$

57. $(2x - 3)(x^2 + 6x + 10)$

58. $(3x + 4)(2x^2 - 2x - 6)$

59. $(4x - 1)(3x^2 - x + 6)$

60. $(5x - 2)(6x^2 + 2x - 1)$

61. $(x^2 + 2x + 1)(x^2 + 3x + 4)$

62. $(x^2 - x + 6)(x^2 - 5x - 8)$

63. $(2x^2 + 3x - 4)(x^2 - 2x - 1)$

64. $(3x^2 - 2x + 1)(2x^2 + x - 2)$

65. $(x + 2)^3$

66. $(x + 1)^3$

67. $(x - 4)^3$

68. $(x - 5)^3$

69. $(2x + 3)^3$

70. $(3x + 1)^3$

71. $(4x - 1)^3$

72. $(3x - 2)^3$

73. $(5x + 2)^3$

74. $(4x - 5)^3$

For Problems 75–84, find the indicated products. Assume all variables that appear as exponents represent positive integers.

75. $(x^n - 4)(x^n + 4)$

76. $(x^{3a} - 1)(x^{3a} + 1)$

77. $(x^a + 6)(x^a - 2)$

78. $(x^a + 4)(x^a - 9)$

79. $(2x^n + 5)(3x^n - 7)$

80. $(3x^n + 5)(4x^n - 9)$

81. $(x^{2a} - 7)(x^{2a} - 3)$

82. $(x^{2a} + 6)(x^{2a} - 4)$

83. $(2x^n + 5)^2$

84. $(3x^n - 7)^2$

85. Explain how Figure 3.13 can be used to demonstrate geometrically that $(x + 2)(x + 6) = x^2 + 8x + 12$.

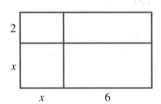

Figure 3.13

86. Find a polynomial that represents the sum of the areas of the two rectangles shown in Figure 3.14.

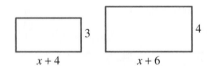

Figure 3.14

87. Find a polynomial that represents the area of the shaded region in Figure 3.15.

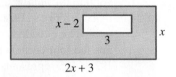

Figure 3.15

88. Explain how Figure 3.16 can be used to demonstrate geometrically that $(x + 7)(x - 3) = x^2 + 4x - 21$.

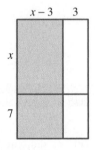

Figure 3.16

89. A square piece of cardboard is 16 inches on a side. A square piece x inches on a side is cut out from each corner. The flaps are then turned up to form an open box. Find polynomials that represent the volume and outside surface area of the box.

■ ■ ■ **THOUGHTS INTO WORDS**

90. How would you simplify $(2^3 + 2^2)^2$? Explain your reasoning.

91. Describe the process of multiplying two polynomials.

92. Determine the number of terms in the product of $(x + y)$ and $(a + b + c + d)$ without doing the multiplication. Explain how you arrived at your answer.

■ ■ ■ **FURTHER INVESTIGATIONS**

93. We have used the following two multiplication patterns.

$$(a + b)^2 = a^2 + 2ab + b^2$$

$$(a + b)^3 = a^3 + 3a^2b + 3ab^2 + b^3$$

By multiplying, we can extend these patterns as follows:

$$(a + b)^4 = a^4 + 4a^3b + 6a^2b^2 + 4ab^3 + b^4$$

$$(a + b)^5 = a^5 + 5a^4b + 10a^3b^2 + 10a^2b^3 + 5a^4 + b^5$$

On the basis of these results, see if you can determine a pattern that will enable you to complete each of the following without using the long-multiplication process.

(a) $(a + b)^6$ **(b)** $(a + b)^7$

(c) $(a + b)^8$ **(d)** $(a + b)^9$

94. Find each of the following indicated products. These patterns will be used again in Section 3.5.

(a) $(x - 1)(x^2 + x + 1)$ **(b)** $(x + 1)(x^2 - x + 1)$

(c) $(x + 3)(x^2 - 3x + 9)$ **(d)** $(x - 4)(x^2 + 4x + 16)$

(e) $(2x - 3)(4x^2 + 6x + 9)$

(f) $(3x + 5)(9x^2 - 15x + 25)$

95. Some of the product patterns can be used to do arithmetic computations mentally. For example, let's use the pattern $(a + b)^2 = a^2 + 2ab + b^2$ to compute 31^2 mentally. Your thought process should be "$31^2 = (30 + 1)^2 = 30^2 + 2(30)(1) + 1^2 = 961$." Compute each

of the following numbers mentally, and then check your answers.

(a) 21^2 **(b)** 41^2 **(c)** 71^2

(d) 32^2 **(e)** 52^2 **(f)** 82^2

96. Use the pattern $(a - b)^2 = a^2 - 2ab + b^2$ to compute each of the following numbers mentally, and then check your answers.

(a) 19^2 **(b)** 29^2 **(c)** 49^2

(d) 79^2 **(e)** 38^2 **(f)** 58^2

97. Every whole number with a units digit of 5 can be represented by the expression $10x + 5$, where x is a whole number. For example, $35 = 10(3) + 5$ and $145 = 10(14) + 5$. Now let's observe the following pattern when squaring such a number.

$$(10x + 5)^2 = 100x^2 + 100x + 25$$

$$= \boxed{100x(x + 1) + 25}$$

The pattern inside the dashed box can be stated as "add 25 to the product of x, $x + 1$, and 100." Thus, to compute 35^2 mentally, we can think "$35^2 = 3(4)(100) + 25 = 1225$." Compute each of the following numbers mentally, and then check your answers.

(a) 15^2 **(b)** 25^2 **(c)** 45^2

(d) 55^2 **(e)** 65^2 **(f)** 75^2

(g) 85^2 **(h)** 95^2 **(i)** 105^2

3.4   Factoring: Use of the Distributive Property

Recall that 2 and 3 are said to be *factors* of 6 because the product of 2 and 3 is 6. Likewise, in an indicated product such as $7ab$, the 7, a, and b are called factors of the product. If a positive integer greater than 1 has no factors that are positive integers other than itself and 1, then it is called a **prime number**. Thus the prime numbers less than 20 are 2, 3, 5, 7, 11, 13, 17, and 19. A positive integer greater than 1 that is not a prime number is called a **composite number**. The composite numbers less than 20 are 4, 6, 8, 9, 10, 12, 14, 15, 16, and 18. Every composite number is the product of prime numbers. Consider the following examples.

$$4 = 2 \cdot 2 \qquad\qquad 63 = 3 \cdot 3 \cdot 7$$

$$12 = 2 \cdot 2 \cdot 3 \qquad 121 = 11 \cdot 11$$

$$35 = 5 \cdot 7$$

The indicated product form that contains only prime factors is called the **prime factorization form** of a number. Thus the prime factorization form of 63 is $3 \cdot 3 \cdot 7$. We also say that the number has been **completely factored** when it is in the prime factorization form.

In general, factoring is the reverse of multiplication. Previously, we have used the distributive property to find the product of a monomial and a polynomial, as in the next examples.

$$3(x + 2) = 3(x) + 3(2) = 3x + 6$$

$$5(2x - 1) = 5(2x) - 5(1) = 10x - 5$$

$$x(x^2 + 6x - 4) = x(x^2) + x(6x) - x(4) = x^3 + 6x^2 - 4x$$

We shall also use the distributive property [in the form $ab + ac = a(b + c)$] to reverse the process — that is, to factor a given polynomial. Consider the following examples. (The steps in the dashed boxes can be done mentally.)

$$3x + 6 = \overline{3(x) + 3(2)} = 3(x + 2),$$

$$10x - 5 = \overline{5(2x) - 5(1)} = 5(2x - 1),$$

$$x^3 + 6x^2 - 4x = \overline{x(x^2) + x(6x) - x(4)} = x(x^2 + 6x - 4)$$

Note that in each example a given polynomial has been factored into the product of a monomial and a polynomial. Obviously, polynomials could be factored in a variety of ways. Consider some factorizations of $3x^2 + 12x$.

$$3x^2 + 12x = 3x(x + 4) \qquad \text{or} \qquad 3x^2 + 12x = 3(x^2 + 4x) \qquad \text{or}$$

$$3x^2 + 12x = x(3x + 12) \qquad \text{or} \qquad 3x^2 + 12x = \frac{1}{2}(6x^2 + 24x)$$

We are, however, primarily interested in the first of the previous factorization forms, which we refer to as the **completely factored form**. A polynomial with integral coefficients is in completely factored form if

1. It is expressed as a product of polynomials with *integral coefficients*, and

2. No polynomial, other than a monomial, within the factored form can be further factored into polynomials with integral coefficients.

Do you see why only the first of the above factored forms of $3x^2 + 12x$ is said to be in completely factored form? In each of the other three forms, the polynomial inside the parentheses can be factored further. Moreover, in the last form, $\frac{1}{2}(6x^2 + 24x)$, the condition of using only integral coefficients is violated.

The factoring process that we discuss in this section, $ab + ac = a(b + c)$, is often referred to as **factoring out the highest common monomial factor**. The key idea in this process is to recognize the monomial factor that is common to all terms. For example, we observe that each term of the polynomial $2x^3 + 4x^2 + 6x$ has a factor of $2x$. Thus we write

$$2x^3 + 4x^2 + 6x = 2x(\qquad)$$

and insert within the parentheses the appropriate polynomial factor. We determine the terms of this polynomial factor by dividing each term of the original polynomial by the factor of $2x$. The final, completely factored form is

$$2x^3 + 4x^2 + 6x = 2x(x^2 + 2x + 3)$$

The following examples further demonstrate this process of factoring out the highest common monomial factor.

$$12x^3 + 16x^2 = 4x^2(3x + 4) \qquad 6x^2y^3 + 27xy^4 = 3xy^3(2x + 9y)$$

$$8ab - 18b = 2b(4a - 9) \qquad 8y^3 + 4y^2 = 4y^2(2y + 1)$$

$$30x^3 + 42x^4 - 24x^5 = 6x^3(5 + 7x - 4x^2)$$

Note that in each example, the common monomial factor itself is not in a completely factored form. For example, $4x^2(3x + 4)$ is not written as $2 \cdot 2 \cdot x \cdot x \cdot (3x + 4)$.

Sometimes there may be a common binomial factor rather than a common monomial factor. For example, each of the two terms of the expression $x(y + 2) + z(y + 2)$ has a binomial factor of $(y + 2)$. Thus we can factor $(y + 2)$ from each term, and our result is

$$x(y + 2) + z(y + 2) = (y + 2)(x + z)$$

Consider a few more examples that involve a common binomial factor.

$$a^2(b + 1) + 2(b + 1) = (b + 1)(a^2 + 2)$$

$$x(2y - 1) - y(2y - 1) = (2y - 1)(x - y)$$

$$x(x + 2) + 3(x + 2) = (x + 2)(x + 3)$$

It may be that the original polynomial exhibits no apparent common monomial or binomial factor, which is the case with $ab + 3a + bc + 3c$. However, by factoring a from the first two terms and c from the last two terms, we get

$$ab + 3a + bc + 3c = a(b + 3) + c(b + 3)$$

Now a common binomial factor of $(b + 3)$ is obvious, and we can proceed as before.

$$a(b + 3) + c(b + 3) = (b + 3)(a + c)$$

We refer to this factoring process as **factoring by grouping**. Let's consider a few more examples of this type.

$$ab^2 - 4b^2 + 3a - 12 = b^2(a - 4) + 3(a - 4)$$

Factor b^2 from the first two terms and 3 from the last two terms.

$$= (a - 4)(b^2 + 3)$$

Factor common binomial from both terms.

$$x^2 - x + 5x - 5 = x(x - 1) + 5(x - 1)$$

Factor x from the first two terms and 5 from the last two terms.

$$= (x - 1)(x + 5)$$

Factor common binomial from both terms.

$$x^2 + 2x - 3x - 6 = x(x + 2) - 3(x + 2)$$

Factor x from the first two terms and -3 from the last two terms.

$$= (x + 2)(x - 3)$$

Factor common binomial factor from both terms.

It may be necessary to rearrange some terms before applying the distributive property. Terms that contain common factors need to be grouped together, and this may be done in more than one way. The next example illustrates this idea.

$$4a^2 - bc^2 - a^2b + 4c^2 = 4a^2 - a^2b + 4c^2 - bc^2$$
$$= a^2(4 - b) + c^2(4 - b)$$
$$= (4 - b)(a^2 + c^2) \quad \text{or}$$
$$4a^2 - bc^2 - a^2b + 4c^2 = 4a^2 + 4c^2 - bc^2 - a^2b$$
$$= 4(a^2 + c^2) - b(c^2 + a^2)$$
$$= 4(a^2 + c^2) - b(a^2 + c^2)$$
$$= (a^2 + c^2)(4 - b)$$

■ Equations and Problem Solving

One reason why factoring is an important algebraic skill is that it extends our techniques for solving equations. Each time we examine a factoring technique, we will then use it to help solve certain types of equations.

We need another property of equality before we consider some equations where the highest-common-factor technique is useful. Suppose that the product of two numbers is zero. Can we conclude that at least one of these numbers must itself be zero? Yes. Let's state a property that formalizes this idea. Property 3.5, along with the highest-common-factor pattern, provides us with another technique for solving equations.

Property 3.5

Let a and b be real numbers. Then

$$ab = 0 \quad \text{if and only if } a = 0 \text{ or } b = 0$$

E X A M P L E   1

Solve $x^2 + 6x = 0$.

Solution

$$x^2 + 6x = 0$$

$$x(x + 6) = 0 \qquad \text{Factor the left side.}$$

$$x = 0 \quad \text{or} \quad x + 6 = 0 \qquad ab = 0 \text{ if and only if } a = 0 \text{ or } b = 0$$

$$x = 0 \quad \text{or} \quad x = -6$$

Thus both 0 and -6 will satisfy the original equation, and the solution set is $\{-6, 0\}$. ∎

E X A M P L E   2

Solve $a^2 = 11a$.

Solution

$$a^2 = 11a$$

$$a^2 - 11a = 0 \qquad \text{Add } -11a \text{ to both sides.}$$

$$a(a - 11) = 0 \qquad \text{Factor the left side.}$$

$$a = 0 \quad \text{or} \quad a - 11 = 0 \qquad ab = 0 \text{ if and only if } a = 0 \text{ or } b = 0$$

$$a = 0 \quad \text{or} \quad a = 11$$

The solution set is $\{0, \ 11\}$. ∎

Remark: Note that in Example 2 we did *not* divide both sides of the equation by a. This would cause us to lose the solution of 0.

E X A M P L E   3

Solve $3n^2 - 5n = 0$.

Solution

$$3n^2 - 5n = 0$$

$$n(3n - 5) = 0$$

$$n = 0 \quad \text{or} \quad 3n - 5 = 0$$

$$n = 0 \quad \text{or} \quad 3n = 5$$

$$n = 0 \quad \text{or} \quad n = \frac{5}{3}$$

The solution set is $\left\{0, \dfrac{5}{3}\right\}$. ∎

E X A M P L E   4   Solve $3ax^2 + bx = 0$ for x.

Solution

$$3ax^2 + bx = 0$$

$$x(3ax + b) = 0$$

$$x = 0 \quad \text{or} \quad 3ax + b = 0$$

$$x = 0 \quad \text{or} \quad 3ax = -b$$

$$x = 0 \quad \text{or} \quad x = -\frac{b}{3a}$$

The solution set is $\left\{0, -\dfrac{b}{3a}\right\}$.   ∎

Many of the problems that we solve in the next few sections have a geometric setting. Some basic geometric figures, along with appropriate formulas, are listed in the inside front cover of this text. You may need to refer to them to refresh your memory.

P R O B L E M   1   The area of a square is three times its perimeter. Find the length of a side of the square.

Solution

Let s represent the length of a side of the square (Figure 3.17). The area is represented by s^2 and the perimeter by $4s$. Thus

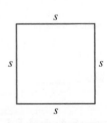

$$s^2 = 3(4s) \qquad \text{The area is to be three}$$
$$\text{times the perimeter.}$$

$$s^2 = 12s$$

$$s^2 - 12s = 0$$

$$s(s - 12) = 0$$

$$s = 0 \quad \text{or} \quad s = 12$$

Figure 3.17

Because 0 is not a reasonable solution, it must be a 12-by-12 square. (Be sure to check this answer in the original statement of the problem!)   ∎

P R O B L E M   2   Suppose that the volume of a right circular cylinder is numerically equal to the total surface area of the cylinder. If the height of the cylinder is equal to the length of a radius of the base, find the height.

Solution

Because $r = h$, the formula for volume $V = \pi r^2 h$ becomes $V = \pi r^3$, and the formula for the total surface area $S = 2\pi r^2 + 2\pi rh$ becomes $S = 2\pi r^2 + 2\pi r^2$, or $S = 4\pi r^2$. Therefore, we can set up and solve the following equation.

$$\pi r^3 = 4\pi r^2$$
$$\pi r^3 - 4\pi r^2 = 0$$
$$\pi r^2(r - 4) = 0$$
$$\pi r^2 = 0 \quad \text{or} \quad r - 4 = 0$$
$$r = 0 \quad \text{or} \quad r = 4$$

Zero is not a reasonable answer, therefore the height must be 4 units. ∎

Problem Set 3.4

For Problems 1–10, classify each number as prime or composite.

1. 63

2. 81

3. 59

4. 83

5. 51

6. 69

7. 91

8. 119

9. 71

10. 101

For Problems 11–20, factor each of the composite numbers into the product of prime numbers. For example, $30 = 2 \cdot 3 \cdot 5$.

11. 28

12. 39

13. 44

14. 49

15. 56

16. 64

17. 72

18. 84

19. 87

20. 91

For Problems 21–46, factor completely.

21. $6x + 3y$

22. $12x + 8y$

23. $6x^2 + 14x$

24. $15x^2 + 6x$

25. $28y^2 - 4y$

26. $42y^2 - 6y$

27. $20xy - 15x$

28. $27xy - 36y$

29. $7x^3 + 10x^2$

30. $12x^3 - 10x^2$

31. $18a^2b + 27ab^2$

32. $24a^3b^2 + 36a^2b$

33. $12x^3y^4 - 39x^4y^3$

34. $15x^4y^2 - 45x^5y^4$

35. $8x^4 + 12x^3 - 24x^2$

36. $6x^5 - 18x^3 + 24x$

37. $5x + 7x^2 + 9x^4$

38. $9x^2 - 17x^4 + 21x^5$

39. $15x^2y^3 + 20xy^2 + 35x^3y^4$

40. $8x^5y^3 - 6x^4y^5 + 12x^2y^3$

41. $x(y + 2) + 3(y + 2)$

42. $x(y - 1) + 5(y - 1)$

43. $3x(2a + b) - 2y(2a + b)$

44. $5x(a - b) + y(a - b)$

45. $x(x + 2) + 5(x + 2)$

46. $x(x - 1) - 3(x - 1)$

For Problems 47–64, factor by grouping.

47. $ax + 4x + ay + 4y$

48. $ax - 2x + ay - 2y$

49. $ax - 2bx + ay - 2by$

50. $2ax - bx + 2ay - by$

51. $3ax - 3bx - ay + by$

52. $5ax - 5bx - 2ay + 2by$

53. $2ax + 2x + ay + y$

54. $3bx + 3x + by + y$

55. $ax^2 - x^2 + 2a - 2$

56. $ax^2 - 2x^2 + 3a - 6$

57. $2ac + 3bd + 2bc + 3ad$

58. $2bx + cy + cx + 2by$

59. $ax - by + bx - ay$

60. $2a^2 - 3bc - 2ab + 3ac$

61. $x^2 + 9x + 6x + 54$

62. $x^2 - 2x + 5x - 10$

63. $2x^2 + 8x + x + 4$

64. $3x^2 + 18x - 2x - 12$

For Problems 65–80, solve each of the equations.

65. $x^2 + 7x = 0$

66. $x^2 + 9x = 0$

67. $x^2 - x = 0$

68. $x^2 - 14x = 0$

69. $a^2 = 5a$

70. $b^2 = -7b$

71. $-2y = 4y^2$

72. $-6x = 2x^2$

73. $3x^2 + 7x = 0$

74. $-4x^2 + 9x = 0$

75. $4x^2 = 5x$

76. $3x = 11x^2$

77. $x - 4x^2 = 0$

78. $x - 6x^2 = 0$

79. $12a = -a^2$

80. $-5a = -a^2$

For Problems 81–86, solve each equation for the indicated variable.

81. $5bx^2 - 3ax = 0$ for x

82. $ax^2 + bx = 0$ for x

83. $2by^2 = -3ay$ for y

84. $3ay^2 = by$ for y

85. $y^2 - ay + 2by - 2ab = 0$ for y

86. $x^2 + ax + bx + ab = 0$ for x

For Problems 87–96, set up an equation and solve each of the following problems.

87. The square of a number equals seven times the number. Find the number.

88. Suppose that the area of a square is six times its perimeter. Find the length of a side of the square.

89. The area of a circular region is numerically equal to three times the circumference of the circle. Find the length of a radius of the circle.

90. Find the length of a radius of a circle such that the circumference of the circle is numerically equal to the area of the circle.

91. Suppose that the area of a circle is numerically equal to the perimeter of a square and that the length of a radius of the circle is equal to the length of a side of the square. Find the length of a side of the square. Express your answer in terms of π.

92. Find the length of a radius of a sphere such that the surface area of the sphere is numerically equal to the volume of the sphere.

93. Suppose that the area of a square lot is twice the area of an adjoining rectangular plot of ground. If the rectangular plot is 50 feet wide, and its length is the same as the length of a side of the square lot, find the dimensions of both the square and the rectangle.

94. The area of a square is one-fourth as large as the area of a triangle. One side of the triangle is 16 inches long, and the altitude to that side is the same length as a side of the square. Find the length of a side of the square.

95. Suppose that the volume of a sphere is numerically equal to twice the surface area of the sphere. Find the length of a radius of the sphere.

96. Suppose that a radius of a sphere is equal in length to a radius of a circle. If the volume of the sphere is numerically equal to four times the area of the circle, find the length of a radius for both the sphere and the circle.

■■■ **THOUGHTS INTO WORDS**

97. Is $2 \cdot 3 \cdot 5 \cdot 7 \cdot 11 + 7$ a prime or a composite number? Defend your answer.

98. Suppose that your friend factors $36x^2y + 48xy^2$ as follows:

$$36x^2y + 48xy^2 = (4xy)(9x + 12y)$$
$$= (4xy)(3)(3x + 4y)$$
$$= 12xy(3x + 4y)$$

Is this a correct approach? Would you have any suggestion to offer your friend?

99. Your classmate solves the equation $3ax + bx = 0$ for x as follows:

$$3ax + bx = 0$$
$$3ax = -bx$$
$$x = \frac{-bx}{3a}$$

How should he know that the solution is incorrect? How would you help him obtain the correct solution?

100. The total surface area of a right circular cylinder is given by the formula $A = 2\pi r^2 + 2\pi rh$, where r represents the radius of a base, and h represents the height of the cylinder. For computational purposes, it may be more convenient to change the form of the right side of the formula by factoring it.

$$A = 2\pi r^2 + 2\pi rh$$
$$= 2\pi r(r + h)$$

Use $A = 2\pi r(r + h)$ to find the total surface area of each of the following cylinders. Also, use $\dfrac{22}{7}$ as an approximation for π.

(a) $r = 7$ centimeters and $h = 12$ centimeters

(b) $r = 14$ meters and $h = 20$ meters

(c) $r = 3$ feet and $h = 4$ feet

(d) $r = 5$ yards and $h = 9$ yards

For Problems 101–106, factor each expression. Assume that all variables that appear as exponents represent positive integers.

101. $2x^{2a} - 3x^a$

102. $6x^{2a} + 8x^a$

103. $y^{3m} + 5y^{2m}$

104. $3y^{5m} - y^{4m} - y^{3m}$

105. $2x^{6a} - 3x^{5a} + 7x^{4a}$

106. $6x^{3a} - 10x^{2a}$

3.5 **Factoring: Difference of Two Squares and Sum or Difference of Two Cubes**

In Section 3.3, we examined some special multiplication patterns. One of these patterns was

$$(a + b)(a - b) = a^2 - b^2$$

This same pattern, viewed as a factoring pattern, is referred to as the difference of two squares.

Difference of Two Squares

$$a^2 - b^2 = (a + b)(a - b)$$

Applying the pattern is fairly simple, as these next examples demonstrate. Again, the steps in dashed boxes are usually performed mentally.

$$x^2 - 16 = (x)^2 - (4)^2 = (x + 4)(x - 4)$$
$$4x^2 - 25 = (2x)^2 - (5)^2 = (2x + 5)(2x - 5)$$
$$16x^2 - 9y^2 = (4x)^2 - (3y)^2 = (4x + 3y)(4x - 3y)$$
$$1 - a^2 = (1)^2 - (a)^2 = (1 + a)(1 - a)$$

Multiplication is commutative, so the order of writing the factors is not important. For example, $(x + 4)(x - 4)$ can also be written as $(x - 4)(x + 4)$.

You must be careful not to assume an analogous factoring pattern for the *sum* of two squares; *it does not exist*. For example, $x^2 + 4 \neq (x + 2)(x + 2)$ because $(x + 2)(x + 2) = x^2 + 4x + 4$. We say that a polynomial such as $x^2 + 4$ is a **prime polynomial** or that it is not factorable using integers.

Sometimes the difference-of-two-squares pattern can be applied more than once, as the next examples illustrate.

$$x^4 - y^4 = (x^2 + y^2)(x^2 - y^2) = (x^2 + y^2)(x + y)(x - y)$$
$$16x^4 - 81y^4 = (4x^2 + 9y^2)(4x^2 - 9y^2) = (4x^2 + 9y^2)(2x + 3y)(2x - 3y)$$

It may also be that the squares are other than simple monomial squares, as in the next three examples.

$$(x + 3)^2 - y^2 = ((x + 3) + y)((x + 3) - y) = (x + 3 + y)(x + 3 - y)$$
$$4x^2 - (2y + 1)^2 = (2x + (2y + 1))(2x - (2y + 1))$$
$$= (2x + 2y + 1)(2x - 2y - 1)$$
$$(x - 1)^2 - (x + 4)^2 = ((x - 1) + (x + 4))((x - 1) - (x + 4))$$
$$= (x - 1 + x + 4)(x - 1 - x - 4)$$
$$= (2x + 3)(-5)$$

It is possible to apply both the technique of factoring out a common monomial factor and the pattern of the difference of two squares to the same problem. In general, it is best to look first for a common monomial factor. Consider the following examples.

$$2x^2 - 50 = 2(x^2 - 25) \qquad\qquad 9x^2 - 36 = 9(x^2 - 4)$$
$$= 2(x + 5)(x - 5) \qquad\qquad = 9(x + 2)(x - 2)$$
$$48y^3 - 27y = 3y(16y^2 - 9)$$
$$= 3y(4y + 3)(4y - 3)$$

Word of Caution   The polynomial $9x^2 - 36$ can be factored as follows:

$$9x^2 - 36 = (3x + 6)(3x - 6)$$
$$= 3(x + 2)(3)(x - 2)$$
$$= 9(x + 2)(x - 2)$$

However, when one takes this approach, there seems to be a tendency to stop at the step $(3x + 6)(3x - 6)$. Therefore, remember the suggestion to *look first for a common monomial factor*.

The following examples should help you summarize all of the factoring techniques we have considered thus far.

$$7x^2 + 28 = 7(x^2 + 4)$$
$$4x^2y - 14xy^2 = 2xy(2x - 7y)$$

$$x^2 - 4 = (x + 2)(x - 2)$$

$$18 - 2x^2 = 2(9 - x^2) = 2(3 + x)(3 - x)$$

$y^2 + 9$ is not factorable using integers.

$5x + 13y$ is not factorable using integers.

$$x^4 - 16 = (x^2 + 4)(x^2 - 4) = (x^2 + 4)(x + 2)(x - 2)$$

■ Sum and Difference of Two Cubes

As we pointed out before, there exists no sum-of-squares pattern analogous to the difference-of-squares factoring pattern. That is, a polynomial such as $x^2 + 9$ is not factorable using integers. However, patterns do exist for both the sum and the difference of two cubes. These patterns are as follows:

Sum and Difference of Two Cubes

$$a^3 + b^3 = (a + b)(a^2 - ab + b^2)$$

$$a^3 - b^3 = (a - b)(a^2 + ab + b^2)$$

Note how we apply these patterns in the next four examples.

$$x^3 + 27 = (x)^3 + (3)^3 = (x + 3)(x^2 - 3x + 9)$$

$$8a^3 + 125b^3 = (2a)^3 + (5b)^3 = (2a + 5b)(4a^2 - 10ab + 25b^2)$$

$$x^3 - 1 = (x)^3 - (1)^3 = (x - 1)(x^2 + x + 1)$$

$$27y^3 - 64x^3 = (3y)^3 - (4x)^3 = (3y - 4x)(9y^2 + 12xy + 16x^2)$$

■ Equations and Problem Solving

Remember that each time we pick up a new factoring technique we also develop more power for solving equations. Let's consider how we can use the difference-of-two-squares factoring pattern to help solve certain types of equations.

EXAMPLE 1

Solve $x^2 = 16$.

Solution

$$x^2 = 16$$

$$x^2 - 16 = 0$$

$$(x + 4)(x - 4) = 0$$

$$x + 4 = 0 \quad \text{or} \quad x - 4 = 0$$

$$x = -4 \quad \text{or} \quad x = 4$$

The solution set is $\{-4, 4\}$. (Be sure to check these solutions in the original equation!)

■

E X A M P L E   2   Solve $9x^2 = 64$.

Solution

$$9x^2 = 64$$

$$9x^2 - 64 = 0$$

$$(3x + 8)(3x - 8) = 0$$

$$3x + 8 = 0 \quad \text{or} \quad 3x - 8 = 0$$

$$3x = -8 \quad \text{or} \quad 3x = 8$$

$$x = -\frac{8}{3} \quad \text{or} \quad x = \frac{8}{3}$$

The solution set is $\left\{ -\dfrac{8}{3}, \dfrac{8}{3} \right\}$.   ■

E X A M P L E   3   Solve $7x^2 - 7 = 0$.

Solution

$$7x^2 - 7 = 0$$

$$7(x^2 - 1) = 0$$

$$x^2 - 1 = 0 \qquad \text{Multiply both sides by } \frac{1}{7}.$$

$$(x + 1)(x - 1) = 0$$

$$x + 1 = 0 \quad \text{or} \quad x - 1 = 0$$

$$x = -1 \quad \text{or} \quad x = 1$$

The solution set is $\{-1, 1\}$.   ■

In the previous examples we have been using the property $ab = 0$ if and only if $a = 0$ or $b = 0$. This property can be extended to any number of factors whose product is zero. Thus for three factors, the property could be stated $abc = 0$ if and only if $a = 0$ or $b = 0$ or $c = 0$. The next two examples illustrate this idea.

E X A M P L E   4   Solve $x^4 - 16 = 0$.

Solution

$$x^4 - 16 = 0$$

$$(x^2 + 4)(x^2 - 4) = 0$$

$$(x^2 + 4)(x + 2)(x - 2) = 0$$

$$x^2 + 4 = 0 \quad \text{or} \quad x + 2 = 0 \quad \text{or} \quad x - 2 = 0$$

$$x^2 = -4 \quad \text{or} \quad x = -2 \quad \text{or} \quad x = 2$$

The solution set is $\{-2, 2\}$. (Because no real numbers, when squared, will produce -4, the equation $x^2 = -4$ yields no additional real number solutions.) ■

EXAMPLE 5

Solve $x^3 - 49x = 0$.

Solution

$$x^3 - 49x = 0$$

$$x(x^2 - 49) = 0$$

$$x(x + 7)(x - 7) = 0$$

$$x = 0 \quad \text{or} \quad x + 7 = 0 \quad \text{or} \quad x - 7 = 0$$

$$x = 0 \quad \text{or} \quad x = -7 \quad \text{or} \quad x = 7$$

The solution set is $\{-7, 0, 7\}$. ■

The more we know about solving equations, the better we are at solving word problems.

PROBLEM 1

The combined area of two squares is 40 square centimeters. Each side of one square is three times as long as a side of the other square. Find the dimensions of each of the squares.

Solution

Let s represent the length of a side of the smaller square. Then $3s$ represents the length of a side of the larger square (Figure 3.18).

$$s^2 + (3s)^2 = 40$$

$$s^2 + 9s^2 = 40$$

$$10s^2 = 40$$

$$s^2 = 4$$

$$s^2 - 4 = 0$$

$$(s + 2)(s - 2) = 0$$

$$s + 2 = 0 \quad \text{or} \quad s - 2 = 0$$

$$s = -2 \quad \text{or} \quad s = 2$$

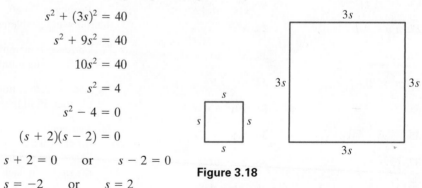

Figure 3.18

Because s represents the length of a side of a square, the solution -2 has to be disregarded. Thus the length of a side of the small square is 2 centimeters, and the large square has sides of length $3(2) = 6$ centimeters. ■

Problem Set 3.5

For Problems 1–20, use the difference-of-squares pattern to factor each of the following.

1. $x^2 - 1$

2. $x^2 - 9$

3. $16x^2 - 25$

4. $4x^2 - 49$

5. $9x^2 - 25y^2$

6. $x^2 - 64y^2$

7. $25x^2y^2 - 36$

8. $x^2y^2 - a^2b^2$

9. $4x^2 - y^4$

10. $x^6 - 9y^2$

11. $1 - 144n^2$

12. $25 - 49n^2$

13. $(x + 2)^2 - y^2$

14. $(3x + 5)^2 - y^2$

15. $4x^2 - (y + 1)^2$

16. $x^2 - (y - 5)^2$

17. $9a^2 - (2b + 3)^2$

18. $16s^2 - (3t + 1)^2$

19. $(x + 2)^2 - (x + 7)^2$

20. $(x - 1)^2 - (x - 8)^2$

For Problems 21–44, factor each of the following polynomials completely. Indicate any that are not factorable using integers. Don't forget to look first for a common monomial factor.

21. $9x^2 - 36$

22. $8x^2 - 72$

23. $5x^2 + 5$

24. $7x^2 + 28$

25. $8y^2 - 32$

26. $5y^2 - 80$

27. $a^3b - 9ab$

28. $x^3y^2 - xy^2$

29. $16x^2 + 25$

30. $x^4 - 16$

31. $n^4 - 81$

32. $4x^2 + 9$

33. $3x^3 + 27x$

34. $20x^3 + 45x$

35. $4x^3y - 64xy^3$

36. $12x^3 - 27xy^2$

37. $6x - 6x^3$

38. $1 - 16x^4$

39. $1 - x^4y^4$

40. $20x - 5x^3$

41. $4x^2 - 64y^2$

42. $9x^2 - 81y^2$

43. $3x^4 - 48$

44. $2x^5 - 162x$

For Problems 45–56, use the sum-of-two-cubes or the difference-of-two-cubes pattern to factor each of the following.

45. $a^3 - 64$

46. $a^3 - 27$

47. $x^3 + 1$

48. $x^3 + 8$

49. $27x^3 + 64y^3$

50. $8x^3 + 27y^3$

51. $1 - 27a^3$

52. $1 - 8x^3$

53. $x^3y^3 - 1$

54. $125x^3 + 27y^3$

55. $x^6 - y^6$

56. $x^6 + y^6$

For Problems 57–70, find all real number solutions for each equation.

57. $x^2 - 25 = 0$

58. $x^2 - 1 = 0$

59. $9x^2 - 49 = 0$

60. $4y^2 = 25$

61. $8x^2 - 32 = 0$

62. $3x^2 - 108 = 0$

63. $3x^3 = 3x$

64. $4x^3 = 64x$

65. $20 - 5x^2 = 0$

66. $54 - 6x^2 = 0$

67. $x^4 - 81 = 0$

68. $x^5 - x = 0$

69. $6x^3 + 24x = 0$

70. $4x^3 + 12x = 0$

For Problems 71–80, set up an equation and solve each of the following problems.

71. The cube of a number equals nine times the same number. Find the number.

72. The cube of a number equals the square of the same number. Find the number.

73. The combined area of two circles is 80π square centimeters. The length of a radius of one circle is twice the length of a radius of the other circle. Find the length of the radius of each circle.

74. The combined area of two squares is 26 square meters. The sides of the larger square are five times as long as the sides of the smaller square. Find the dimensions of each of the squares.

75. A rectangle is twice as long as it is wide, and its area is 50 square meters. Find the length and the width of the rectangle.

76. Suppose that the length of a rectangle is one and one-third times as long as its width. The area of the rectangle is 48 square centimeters. Find the length and width of the rectangle.

77. The total surface area of a right circular cylinder is 54π square inches. If the altitude of the cylinder is twice the length of a radius, find the altitude of the cylinder.

78. The total surface area of a right circular cone is 108π square feet. If the slant height of the cone is twice the length of a radius of the base, find the length of a radius.

79. The sum of the areas of a circle and a square is $(16\pi + 64)$ square yards. If a side of the square is twice the length of a radius of the circle, find the length of a side of the square.

80. The length of an altitude of a triangle is one-third the length of the side to which it is drawn. If the area of the triangle is 6 square centimeters, find the length of that altitude.

■ ■ ■ THOUGHTS INTO WORDS

81. Explain how you would solve the equation $4x^3 = 64x$.

82. What is wrong with the following factoring process?

$$25x^2 - 100 = (5x + 10)(5x - 10)$$

How would you correct the error?

83. Consider the following solution:

$$6x^2 - 24 = 0$$

$$6(x^2 - 4) = 0$$

$$6(x + 2)(x - 2) = 0$$

$6 = 0$	or	$x + 2 = 0$	or	$x - 2 = 0$
$6 = 0$	or	$x = -2$	or	$x = 2$

The solution set is $\{-2, 2\}$.

Is this a correct solution? Would you have any suggestion to offer the person who used this approach?

3.6 Factoring Trinomials

One of the most common types of factoring used in algebra is the expression of a trinomial as the product of two binomials. To develop a factoring technique, we first look at some multiplication ideas. Let's consider the product $(x + a)(x + b)$ and use the distributive property to show how each term of the resulting trinomial is formed.

$$(x + a)(x + b) = x(x + b) + a(x + b)$$

$$= x(x) + x(b) + a(x) + a(b)$$

$$= x^2 + (a + b)x + ab$$

Note that the coefficient of the middle term is the sum of a and b and that the last term is the product of a and b. These two relationships can be used to factor trinomials. Let's consider some examples.

EXAMPLE 1

Factor $x^2 + 8x + 12$.

Solution

We need to complete the following with two integers whose sum is 8 and whose product is 12.

$$x^2 + 8x + 12 = (x + \underline{\quad})(x + \underline{\quad})$$

The possible pairs of factors of 12 are $1(12)$, $2(6)$, and $3(4)$. Because $6 + 2 = 8$, we can complete the factoring as follows:

$$x^2 + 8x + 12 = (x + 6)(x + 2)$$

To check our answer, we find the product of $(x + 6)$ and $(x + 2)$.   ■

EXAMPLE 2

Factor $x^2 - 10x + 24$.

Solution

We need two integers whose product is 24 and whose sum is -10. Let's use a small table to organize our thinking.

Factors	Product of the factors	Sum of the factors
$(-1)(-24)$	24	-25
$(-2)(-12)$	24	-14
$(-3)(-8)$	24	-11
$(-4)(-6)$	24	-10

The bottom line contains the numbers that we need. Thus

$$x^2 - 10x + 24 = (x - 4)(x - 6)$$ ■

EXAMPLE 3

Factor $x^2 + 7x - 30$.

Solution

We need two integers whose product is -30 and whose sum is 7.

Factors	Product of the factors	Sum of the factors
$(-1)(30)$	-30	29
$(1)(-30)$	-30	-29
$(2)(-15)$	-30	-13
$(-2)(15)$	-30	13
$(-3)(10)$	-30	7

No need to search any further

The numbers that we need are -3 and 10, and we can complete the factoring.

$$x^2 + 7x - 30 = (x + 10)(x - 3)$$ ■

EXAMPLE 4   Factor $x^2 + 7x + 16$.

Solution

We need two integers whose product is 16 and whose sum is 7.

Factors	Product of the factors	Sum of the factors
(1)(16)	16	17
(2)(8)	16	10
(4)(4)	16	8

We have exhausted all possible pairs of factors of 16 and no two factors have a sum of 7, so we conclude that $x^2 + 7x + 16$ *is not factorable using integers.*   ■

The tables in Examples 2, 3, and 4 were used to illustrate one way of organizing your thoughts for such problems. Normally you would probably factor such problems mentally without taking the time to formulate a table. Note, however, that in Example 4 the table helped us to be absolutely sure that we tried all the possibilities. Whether or not you use the table, keep in mind that the key ideas are the product and sum relationships.

EXAMPLE 5   Factor $n^2 - n - 72$.

Solution

Note that the coefficient of the middle term is -1. Hence we are looking for two integers whose product is -72, and because their sum is -1, the absolute value of the negative number must be 1 larger than the positive number. The numbers are -9 and 8, and we can complete the factoring.

$$n^2 - n - 72 = (n - 9)(n + 8)$$ ■

EXAMPLE 6   Factor $t^2 + 2t - 168$.

Solution

We need two integers whose product is -168 and whose sum is 2. Because the absolute value of the constant term is rather large, it might help to look at it in prime factored form.

$$168 = 2 \cdot 2 \cdot 2 \cdot 3 \cdot 7$$

Now we can mentally form two numbers by using all of these factors in different combinations. Using two 2s and a 3 in one number and the other 2 and the 7 in the second number produces $2 \cdot 2 \cdot 3 = 12$ and $2 \cdot 7 = 14$. The coefficient of the middle term of the trinomial is 2, so we know that we must use 14 and -12. Thus we obtain

$$t^2 + 2t - 168 = (t + 14)(t - 12)$$ ■

■ Trinomials of the Form $ax^2 + bx + c$

We have been factoring trinomials of the form $x^2 + bx + c$—that is, trinomials where the coefficient of the squared term is 1. Now let's consider factoring trinomials where the coefficient of the squared term is not 1. First, let's illustrate an informal trial-and-error technique that works quite well for certain types of trinomials. This technique is based on our knowledge of multiplication of binomials.

EXAMPLE 7   Factor $2x^2 + 11x + 5$.

Solution

By looking at the first term, $2x^2$, and the positive signs of the other two terms, we know that the binomials are of the form

$$(x + \underline{\quad})(2x + \underline{\quad})$$

Because the factors of the last term, 5, are 1 and 5, we have only the following two possibilities to try.

$$(x + 1)(2x + 5) \quad \text{or} \quad (x + 5)(2x + 1)$$

By checking the middle term formed in each of these products, we find that the second possibility yields the correct middle term of $11x$. Therefore,

$$2x^2 + 11x + 5 = (x + 5)(2x + 1) \qquad ■$$

EXAMPLE 8   Factor $10x^2 - 17x + 3$.

Solution

First, observe that $10x^2$ can be written as $x \cdot 10x$ or $2x \cdot 5x$. Second, because the middle term of the trinomial is negative, and the last term is positive, we know that the binomials are of the form

$$(x - \underline{\quad})(10x - \underline{\quad}) \quad \text{or} \quad (2x - \underline{\quad})(5x - \underline{\quad})$$

The factors of the last term, 3, are 1 and 3, so the following possibilities exist.

$$(x - 1)(10x - 3) \qquad (2x - 1)(5x - 3)$$
$$(x - 3)(10x - 1) \qquad (2x - 3)(5x - 1)$$

By checking the middle term formed in each of these products, we find that the product $(2x - 3)(5x - 1)$ yields the desired middle term of $-17x$. Therefore,

$$10x^2 - 17x + 3 = (2x - 3)(5x - 1) \qquad ■$$

EXAMPLE 9   Factor $4x^2 + 6x + 9$.

Solution

The first term, $4x^2$, and the positive signs of the middle and last terms indicate that the binomials are of the form

$$(x + \underline{\quad})(4x + \underline{\quad}) \quad \text{or} \quad (2x + \underline{\quad})(2x + \underline{\quad}).$$

Because the factors of 9 are 1 and 9 or 3 and 3, we have the following five possibilities to try.

$$(x + 1)(4x + 9) \qquad (2x + 1)(2x + 9)$$
$$(x + 9)(4x + 1) \qquad (2x + 3)(2x + 3)$$
$$(x + 3)(4x + 3)$$

When we try all of these possibilities we find that none of them yields a middle term of $6x$. Therefore, $4x^2 + 6x + 9$ is not factorable using integers. ∎

By now it is obvious that factoring trinomials of the form $ax^2 + bx + c$ can be tedious. The key idea is to organize your work so that you consider all possibilities. We suggested one possible format in the previous three examples. As you practice such problems, you may come across a format of your own. Whatever works best for you is the right approach.

There is another, more systematic technique that you may wish to use with some trinomials. It is an extension of the technique we used at the beginning of this section. To see the basis of this technique, let's look at the following product.

$$(px + r)(qx + s) = px(qx) + px(s) + r(qx) + r(s)$$
$$= (pq)x^2 + (ps + rq)x + rs$$

Note that the product of the coefficient of the x^2 term and the constant term is $pqrs$. Likewise, the product of the two coefficients of x, ps and rq, is also $pqrs$. Therefore, when we are factoring the trinomial $(pq)x^2 + (ps + rq)x + rs$, the two coefficients of x must have a sum of $(ps) + (rq)$ and a product of $pqrs$. Let's see how this works in some examples.

E X A M P L E   1 0

Factor $6x^2 - 11x - 10$

Solution

First, multiply the coefficient of the x^2 term, 6, and the constant term, -10.

$$(6)(-10) = -60$$

Now find two integers whose sum is -11 and whose product is -60. The integers 4 and -15 satisfy these conditions.

Rewrite the original problem, expressing the middle term as a sum of terms with these factors of -60 as their coefficients.

$$6x^2 - 11x - 10 = 6x^2 + 4x - 15x - 10$$

After rewriting the problem, we can factor by grouping — that is, factoring $2x$ from the first two terms and -5 from the last two terms.

$$6x^2 + 4x - 15x - 10 = 2x(3x + 2) - 5(3x + 2)$$

Now a common binomial factor of $(3x + 2)$ is obvious, and we can proceed as follows:

$$2x(3x + 2) - 5(3x + 2) = (3x + 2)(2x - 5)$$

Thus $6x^2 - 11x - 10 = (3x + 2)(2x - 5)$. ∎

EXAMPLE 11   Factor $4x^2 - 29x + 30$

Solution

First, multiply the coefficient of the x^2 term, 4, and the constant term, 30.

$$(4)(30) = 120$$

Now find two integers whose sum is -29 and whose product is 120. The integers -24 and -5 satisfy these conditions.

Rewrite the original problem, expressing the middle term as a sum of terms with these factors of 120 as their coefficients.

$$4x^2 - 29x + 30 = 4x^2 - 24x - 5x + 30$$

After rewriting the problem, we can factor by grouping — that is, factoring $4x$ from the first two terms and -5 from the last two terms.

$$4x^2 - 29x - 5x + 30 = 4x(x - 6) - 5(x - 6)$$

Now a common binomial factor of $(x - 6)$ is obvious, and we can proceed as follows:

$$4x(x - 6) - 5(x - 6) = (x - 6)(4x - 5)$$

Thus $4x^2 - 29x + 30 = (x - 6)(4x - 5)$.   ■

The technique presented in Examples 10 and 11 has concrete steps to follow. Examples 7 through 9 were factored by trial-and-error technique. Both of the techniques we used have their strengths and weaknesses. Which technique to use depends on the complexity of the problem and on your personal preference. The more that you work with both techniques, the more comfortable you will feel using them.

■ Summary of Factoring Techniques

Before we summarize our work with factoring techniques, let's look at two more special factoring patterns. In Section 3.3 we used the following two patterns to square binomials.

$$(a + b)^2 = a^2 + 2ab + b^2 \qquad \text{and} \qquad (a - b)^2 = a^2 - 2ab + b^2$$

These patterns can also be used for factoring purposes.

$$a^2 + 2ab + b^2 = (a + b)^2 \qquad \text{and} \qquad a^2 - 2ab + b^2 = (a - b)^2$$

The trinomials on the left sides are called **perfect-square trinomials**; they are the result of squaring a binomial. We can always factor perfect-square trinomials using the usual techniques for factoring trinomials. However, they are easily recognized by the nature of their terms. For example, $4x^2 + 12x + 9$ is a perfect-square trinomial because

1. The first term is a perfect square. $(2x)^2$

2. The last term is a perfect square. $(3)^2$

3. The middle term is twice the product of the quantities $2(2x)(3)$
being squared in the first and last terms.

Likewise, $9x^2 - 30x + 25$ is a perfect-square trinomial because

1. The first term is a perfect square. $(3x)^2$

2. The last term is a perfect square. $(5)^2$

3. The middle term is the negative of twice the product of $-2(3x)(5)$
the quantities being squared in the first and last terms.

Once we know that we have a perfect-square trinomial, the factors follow immediately from the two basic patterns. Thus

$$4x^2 + 12x + 9 = (2x + 3)^2 \qquad 9x^2 - 30x + 25 = (3x - 5)^2$$

Here are some additional examples of perfect-square trinomials and their
factored forms.

$$x^2 + 14x + 49 = (x)^2 + 2(x)(7) + (7) = (x + 7)^2$$
$$n^2 - 16n + 64 = (n)^2 - 2(n)(8) + (8)^2 = (n - 8)^2$$
$$36a^2 + 60ab + 25b^2 = (6a)^2 + 2(6a)(5b) + (5b)^2 = (6a + 5b)^2$$
$$16x^2 - 8xy + y^2 = (4x)^2 - 2(4x)(y) + (y)^2 = (4x - y)^2$$

Perhaps you will want to do this
step mentally after you feel
comfortable with the process.

As we have indicated, factoring is an important algebraic skill. We learned
some basic factoring techniques one at a time, but you must be able to apply
whichever is (or are) appropriate to the situation. Let's review the techniques and
consider a variety of examples that demonstrate their use.

In this chapter, we have discussed

1. Factoring by using the distributive property to factor out a common monomial
(or binomial) factor.

2. Factoring by applying the difference-of-two-squares pattern.

3. Factoring by applying the sum-of-two-cubes or the difference-of-two-cubes
pattern.

4. Factoring of trinomials into the product of two binomials. (The perfect-square-
trinomial pattern is a special case of this technique.)

As a general guideline, always look for a common monomial factor first and then
proceed with the other techniques. Study the following examples carefully and be
sure that you agree with the indicated factors.

$$2x^2 + 20x + 48 = 2(x^2 + 10x + 24) \qquad 16a^2 - 64 = 16(a^2 - 4)$$
$$= 2(x + 4)(x + 6) \qquad\qquad = 16(a + 2)(a - 2)$$

$$3x^3y^3 + 27xy = 3xy(x^2y^2 + 9) \qquad x^2 + 3x - 21 \text{ is not factorable}$$
$$\text{using integers}$$

$$30n^2 - 31n + 5 = (5n - 1)(6n - 5) \qquad t^4 + 3t^2 + 2 = (t^2 + 2)(t^2 + 1)$$

$$2x^3 - 16 = 2(x^3 - 8) = 2(x - 2)(x^2 + 2x + 4)$$

Problem Set 3.6

For Problems 1–56, factor completely each of the polynomials and indicate any that are not factorable using integers.

1. $x^2 + 9x + 20$

2. $x^2 + 11x + 24$

3. $x^2 - 11x + 28$

4. $x^2 - 8x + 12$

5. $a^2 + 5a - 36$

6. $a^2 + 6a - 40$

7. $y^2 + 20y + 84$

8. $y^2 + 21y + 98$

9. $x^2 - 5x - 14$

10. $x^2 - 3x - 54$

11. $x^2 + 9x + 12$

12. $35 - 2x - x^2$

13. $6 + 5x - x^2$

14. $x^2 + 8x - 24$

15. $x^2 + 15xy + 36y^2$

16. $x^2 - 14xy + 40y^2$

17. $a^2 - ab - 56b^2$

18. $a^2 + 2ab - 63b^2$

19. $15x^2 + 23x + 6$

20. $9x^2 + 30x + 16$

21. $12x^2 - x - 6$

22. $20x^2 - 11x - 3$

23. $4a^2 + 3a - 27$

24. $12a^2 + 4a - 5$

25. $3n^2 - 7n - 20$

26. $4n^2 + 7n - 15$

27. $3x^2 + 10x + 4$

28. $4n^2 - 19n + 21$

29. $10n^2 - 29n - 21$

30. $4x^2 - x + 6$

31. $8x^2 + 26x - 45$

32. $6x^2 + 13x - 33$

33. $6 - 35x - 6x^2$

34. $4 - 4x - 15x^2$

35. $20y^2 + 31y - 9$

36. $8y^2 + 22y - 21$

37. $24n^2 - 2n - 5$

38. $3n^2 - 16n - 35$

39. $5n^2 + 33n + 18$

40. $7n^2 + 31n + 12$

41. $x^2 + 25x + 150$

42. $x^2 + 21x + 108$

43. $n^2 - 36n + 320$

44. $n^2 - 26n + 168$

45. $t^2 + 3t - 180$

46. $t^2 - 2t - 143$

47. $t^4 - 5t^2 + 6$

48. $t^4 + 10t^2 + 24$

49. $10x^4 + 3x^2 - 4$

50. $3x^4 + 7x^2 - 6$

51. $x^4 - 9x^2 + 8$

52. $x^4 - x^2 - 12$

53. $18n^4 + 25n^2 - 3$

54. $4n^4 + 3n^2 - 27$

55. $x^4 - 17x^2 + 16$

56. $x^4 - 13x^2 + 36$

Problems 57–94 should help you pull together all of the factoring techniques of this chapter. Factor completely each polynomial, and indicate any that are not factorable using integers.

57. $2t^2 - 8$

58. $14w^2 - 29w - 15$

59. $12x^2 + 7xy - 10y^2$

60. $8x^2 + 2xy - y^2$

61. $18n^3 + 39n^2 - 15n$

62. $n^2 + 18n + 77$

63. $n^2 - 17n + 60$

64. $(x + 5)^2 - y^2$

65. $36a^2 - 12a + 1$

66. $2n^2 - n - 5$

67. $6x^2 + 54$

68. $x^5 - x$

69. $3x^2 + x - 5$

70. $5x^2 + 42x - 27$

71. $x^2 - (y - 7)^2$

72. $2n^3 + 6n^2 + 10n$

73. $1 - 16x^4$

74. $9a^2 - 30a + 25$

75. $4n^2 + 25n + 36$

76. $x^3 - 9x$

77. $n^3 - 49n$

78. $4x^2 + 16$

79. $x^2 - 7x - 8$

80. $x^2 + 3x - 54$

81. $3x^4 - 81x$

82. $x^3 + 125$

83. $x^4 + 6x^2 + 9$

84. $18x^2 - 12x + 2$

85. $x^4 - 5x^2 - 36$

86. $6x^4 - 5x^2 - 21$

87. $6w^2 - 11w - 35$

88. $10x^3 + 15x^2 + 20x$

89. $25n^2 + 64$

90. $4x^2 - 37x + 40$

91. $2n^3 + 14n^2 - 20n$

92. $25t^2 - 100$

93. $2xy + 6x + y + 3$

94. $3xy + 15x - 2y - 10$

■ ■ ■ THOUGHTS INTO WORDS

95. How can you determine that $x^2 + 5x + 12$ is not factorable using integers?

96. Explain your thought process when factoring $30x^2 + 13x - 56$.

97. Consider the following approach to factoring $12x^2 + 54x + 60$.

$$12x^2 + 54x + 60 = (3x + 6)(4x + 10)$$
$$= 3(x + 2)(2)(2x + 5)$$
$$= 6(x + 2)(2x + 5)$$

Is this a correct factoring process? Do you have any suggestion for the person using this approach?

■ ■ ■ FURTHER INVESTIGATIONS

For Problems 98–103, factor each trinomial and assume that all variables that appear as exponents represent positive integers.

98. $x^{2a} + 2x^a - 24$

99. $x^{2a} + 10x^a + 21$

100. $6x^{2a} - 7x^a + 2$

101. $4x^{2a} + 20x^a + 25$

102. $12x^{2n} + 7x^n - 12$

103. $20x^{2n} + 21x^n - 5$

Consider the following approach to factoring $(x - 2)^2 + 3(x - 2) - 10$.

$$(x - 2)^2 + 3(x - 2) - 10$$
$$= y^2 + 3y - 10 \qquad \text{Replace } x - 2 \text{ with } y.$$
$$= (y + 5)(y - 2) \qquad \text{Factor.}$$
$$= (x - 2 + 5)(x - 2 - 2) \qquad \text{Replace } y \text{ with } x - 2.$$
$$= (x + 3)(x - 4)$$

Use this approach to factor Problems 104–109.

104. $(x - 3)^2 + 10(x - 3) + 24$

105. $(x + 1)^2 - 8(x + 1) + 15$

106. $(2x + 1)^2 + 3(2x + 1) - 28$

107. $(3x - 2)^2 - 5(3x - 2) - 36$

108. $6(x - 4)^2 + 7(x - 4) - 3$

109. $15(x + 2)^2 - 13(x + 2) + 2$

3.7 Equations and Problem Solving

The techniques for factoring trinomials that were presented in the previous section provide us with more power to solve equations. That is, the property "$ab = 0$ if and only if $a = 0$ or $b = 0$" continues to play an important role as we solve equations that contain factorable trinomials. Let's consider some examples.

EXAMPLE 1

Solve $x^2 - 11x - 12 = 0$.

Solution

$$x^2 - 11x - 12 = 0$$
$$(x - 12)(x + 1) = 0$$
$$x - 12 = 0 \quad \text{or} \quad x + 1 = 0$$
$$x = 12 \quad \text{or} \quad x = -1$$

The solution set is $\{-1, 12\}$. ∎

EXAMPLE 2

Solve $20x^2 + 7x - 3 = 0$.

Solution

$$20x^2 + 7x - 3 = 0$$
$$(4x - 1)(5x + 3) = 0$$
$$4x - 1 = 0 \quad \text{or} \quad 5x + 3 = 0$$
$$4x = 1 \quad \text{or} \quad 5x = -3$$
$$x = \frac{1}{4} \quad \text{or} \quad x = -\frac{3}{5}$$

The solution set is $\left\{ -\dfrac{3}{5}, \dfrac{1}{4} \right\}$. ∎

EXAMPLE 3

Solve $-2n^2 - 10n + 12 = 0$.

Solution

$$-2n^2 - 10n + 12 = 0$$
$$-2(n^2 + 5n - 6) = 0$$
$$n^2 + 5n - 6 = 0 \qquad \text{Multiply both sides by } -\frac{1}{2}.$$
$$(n + 6)(n - 1) = 0$$
$$n + 6 = 0 \quad \text{or} \quad n - 1 = 0$$
$$n = -6 \quad \text{or} \quad n = 1$$

The solution set is $\{-6, 1\}$. ∎

EXAMPLE 4

Solve $16x^2 - 56x + 49 = 0$.

Solution

$$16x^2 - 56x + 49 = 0$$
$$(4x - 7)^2 = 0$$

$$(4x - 7)(4x - 7) = 0$$

$$4x - 7 = 0 \quad \text{or} \quad 4x - 7 = 0$$

$$4x = 7 \quad \text{or} \quad 4x = 7$$

$$x = \frac{7}{4} \quad \text{or} \quad x = \frac{7}{4}$$

The only solution is $\frac{7}{4}$; thus the solution set is $\left\{\frac{7}{4}\right\}$. ■

EXAMPLE 5   Solve $9a(a + 1) = 4$.

Solution

$$9a(a + 1) = 4$$

$$9a^2 + 9a = 4$$

$$9a^2 + 9a - 4 = 0$$

$$(3a + 4)(3a - 1) = 0$$

$$3a + 4 = 0 \quad \text{or} \quad 3a - 1 = 0$$

$$3a = -4 \quad \text{or} \quad 3a = 1$$

$$a = -\frac{4}{3} \quad \text{or} \quad a = \frac{1}{3}$$

The solution set is $\left\{-\frac{4}{3}, \frac{1}{3}\right\}$. ■

EXAMPLE 6   Solve $(x - 1)(x + 9) = 11$.

Solution

$$(x - 1)(x + 9) = 11$$

$$x^2 + 8x - 9 = 11$$

$$x^2 + 8x - 20 = 0$$

$$(x + 10)(x - 2) = 0$$

$$x + 10 = 0 \quad \text{or} \quad x - 2 = 0$$

$$x = -10 \quad \text{or} \quad x = 2$$

The solution set is $\{-10, \ 2\}$. ■

■ Problem Solving

As you might expect, the increase in our power to solve equations broadens our base for solving problems. Now we are ready to tackle some problems using equations of the types presented in this section.

PROBLEM 1

A room contains 78 chairs. The number of chairs per row is one more than twice the number of rows. Find the number of rows and the number of chairs per row.

Solution

Let r represent the number of rows. Then $2r + 1$ represents the number of chairs per row.

$$r(2r + 1) = 78 \qquad \text{The number of rows times the number of chairs per row yields the total number of chairs.}$$

$$2r^2 + r = 78$$

$$2r^2 + r - 78 = 0$$

$$(2r + 13)(r - 6) = 0$$

$$2r + 13 = 0 \quad \text{or} \quad r - 6 = 0$$

$$2r = -13 \quad \text{or} \quad r = 6$$

$$r = -\frac{13}{2} \quad \text{or} \quad r = 6$$

The solution $-\dfrac{13}{2}$ must be disregarded, so there are 6 rows and $2r + 1$ or $2(6) + 1$ = 13 chairs per row. ∎

PROBLEM 2

A strip of uniform width cut from both sides and both ends of an 8-inch by 11-inch sheet of paper reduces the size of the paper to an area of 40 square inches. Find the width of the strip.

Solution

Let x represent the width of the strip, as indicated in Figure 3.19.

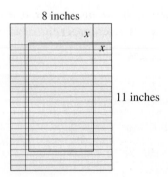

8 inches

x

x

11 inches

Figure 3.19

The length of the paper after the strips of width x are cut from both ends and both sides will be $11 - 2x$, and the width of the newly formed rectangle will be

$8 - 2x$. Because the area ($A = lw$) is to be 40 square inches, we can set up and solve the following equation.

$$(11 - 2x)(8 - 2x) = 40$$

$$88 - 38x + 4x^2 = 40$$

$$4x^2 - 38x + 48 = 0$$

$$2x^2 - 19x + 24 = 0$$

$$(2x - 3)(x - 8) = 0$$

$$2x - 3 = 0 \quad \text{or} \quad x - 8 = 0$$

$$2x = 3 \quad \text{or} \quad x = 8$$

$$x = \frac{3}{2} \quad \text{or} \quad x = 8$$

The solution of 8 must be discarded because the width of the original sheet is only 8 inches. Therefore, the strip to be cut from all four sides must be $1\frac{1}{2}$ inches wide. (Check this answer!) ■

The Pythagorean theorem, an important theorem pertaining to right triangles, can sometimes serve as a guideline for solving problems that deal with right triangles (see Figure 3.20). The Pythagorean theorem states that "in any right triangle, the square of the longest side (called the hypotenuse) is equal to the sum of the squares of the other two sides (called legs)." Let's use this relationship to help solve a problem.

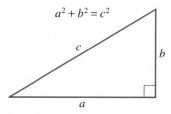

Figure 3.20

PROBLEM 3

One leg of a right triangle is 2 centimeters more than twice as long as the other leg. The hypotenuse is 1 centimeter longer than the longer of the two legs. Find the lengths of the three sides of the right triangle.

Solution

Let l represent the length of the shortest leg. Then $2l + 2$ represents the length of the other leg, and $2l + 3$ represents the length of the hypotenuse. Use the Pythagorean theorem as a guideline to set up and solve the following equation.

$$l^2 + (2l + 2)^2 = (2l + 3)^2$$

$$l^2 + 4l^2 + 8l + 4 = 4l^2 + 12l + 9$$

$$l^2 - 4l - 5 = 0$$

$$(l - 5)(l + 1) = 0$$

$$l - 5 = 0 \quad \text{or} \quad l + 1 = 0$$
$$l = 5 \quad \text{or} \quad l = -1$$

The negative solution must be discarded, so the length of one leg is 5 centimeters; the other leg is $2(5) + 2 = 12$ centimeters long, and the hypotenuse is $2(5) + 3 = 13$ centimeters long. ∎

Problem Set 3.7

For Problems 1–54, solve each equation. You will need to use the factoring techniques that we discussed throughout this chapter.

1. $x^2 + 4x + 3 = 0$

2. $x^2 + 7x + 10 = 0$

3. $x^2 + 18x + 72 = 0$

4. $n^2 + 20n + 91 = 0$

5. $n^2 - 13n + 36 = 0$

6. $n^2 - 10n + 16 = 0$

7. $x^2 + 4x - 12 = 0$

8. $x^2 + 7x - 30 = 0$

9. $w^2 - 4w = 5$

10. $s^2 - 4s = 21$

11. $n^2 + 25n + 156 = 0$

12. $n(n - 24) = -128$

13. $3t^2 + 14t - 5 = 0$

14. $4t^2 - 19t - 30 = 0$

15. $6x^2 + 25x + 14 = 0$

16. $25x^2 + 30x + 8 = 0$

17. $3t(t - 4) = 0$

18. $1 - x^2 = 0$

19. $-6n^2 + 13n - 2 = 0$

20. $(x + 1)^2 - 4 = 0$

21. $2n^3 = 72n$

22. $a(a - 1) = 2$

23. $(x - 5)(x + 3) = 9$

24. $3w^3 - 24w^2 + 36w = 0$

25. $16 - x^2 = 0$

26. $16t^2 - 72t + 81 = 0$

27. $n^2 + 7n - 44 = 0$

28. $2x^3 = 50x$

29. $3x^2 = 75$

30. $x^2 + x - 2 = 0$

31. $15x^2 + 34x + 15 = 0$

32. $20x^2 + 41x + 20 = 0$

33. $8n^2 - 47n - 6 = 0$

34. $7x^2 + 62x - 9 = 0$

35. $28n^2 - 47n + 15 = 0$

36. $24n^2 - 38n + 15 = 0$

37. $35n^2 - 18n - 8 = 0$

38. $8n^2 - 6n - 5 = 0$

39. $-3x^2 - 19x + 14 = 0$

40. $5x^2 = 43x - 24$

41. $n(n + 2) = 360$

42. $n(n + 1) = 182$

43. $9x^4 - 37x^2 + 4 = 0$

44. $4x^4 - 13x^2 + 9 = 0$

45. $3x^2 - 46x - 32 = 0$

46. $x^4 - 9x^2 = 0$

47. $2x^2 + x - 3 = 0$

48. $x^3 + 5x^2 - 36x = 0$

49. $12x^3 + 46x^2 + 40x = 0$

50. $5x(3x - 2) = 0$

51. $(3x - 1)^2 - 16 = 0$

52. $(x + 8)(x - 6) = -24$

53. $4a(a + 1) = 3$

54. $-18n^2 - 15n + 7 = 0$

For Problems 55–70, set up an equation and solve each problem.

55. Find two consecutive integers whose product is 72.

56. Find two consecutive even whole numbers whose product is 224.

57. Find two integers whose product is 105 such that one of the integers is one more than twice the other integer.

58. Find two integers whose product is 104 such that one of the integers is three less than twice the other integer.

59. The perimeter of a rectangle is 32 inches, and the area is 60 square inches. Find the length and width of the rectangle.

60. Suppose that the length of a certain rectangle is two centimeters more than three times its width. If the area of the rectangle is 56 square centimeters, find its length and width.

61. The sum of the squares of two consecutive integers is 85. Find the integers.

62. The sum of the areas of two circles is 65π square feet. The length of a radius of the larger circle is 1 foot less than twice the length of a radius of the smaller circle. Find the length of a radius of each circle.

63. The combined area of a square and a rectangle is 64 square centimeters. The width of the rectangle is 2 centimeters more than the length of a side of the square, and the length of the rectangle is 2 centimeters more than its width. Find the dimensions of the square and the rectangle.

64. The Ortegas have an apple orchard that contains 90 trees. The number of trees in each row is 3 more than twice the number of rows. Find the number of rows and the number of trees per row.

65. The lengths of the three sides of a right triangle are represented by consecutive whole numbers. Find the lengths of the three sides.

66. The area of the floor of the rectangular room shown in Figure 3.21 is 175 square feet. The length of the room is $1\frac{1}{2}$ feet longer than the width. Find the length of the room.

Area = 175 square feet

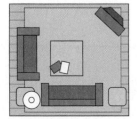

Figure 3.21

67. Suppose that the length of one leg of a right triangle is 3 inches more than the length of the other leg. If the length of the hypotenuse is 15 inches, find the lengths of the two legs.

68. The lengths of the three sides of a right triangle are represented by consecutive even whole numbers. Find the lengths of the three sides.

69. The area of a triangular sheet of paper is 28 square inches. One side of the triangle is 2 inches more than three times the length of the altitude to that side. Find the length of that side and the altitude to the side.

70. A strip of uniform width is shaded along both sides and both ends of a rectangular poster that measures 12 inches by 16 inches (see Figure 3.22). How wide is the shaded strip if one-half of the poster is shaded?

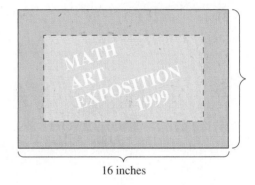

16 inches

Figure 3.22

■ ■ ■ **THOUGHTS INTO WORDS**

71. Discuss the role that factoring plays in solving equations.

72. Explain how you would solve the equation $(x + 6)(x - 4) = 0$ and also how you would solve $(x + 6)(x - 4) = -16$.

73. Explain how you would solve the equation $3(x - 1)(x + 2) = 0$ and also how you would solve the equation $x(x - 1)(x + 2) = 0$.

74. Consider the following two solutions for the equation $(x + 3)(x - 4) = (x + 3)(2x - 1)$.

Solution A

$$(x + 3)(x - 4) = (x + 3)(2x - 1)$$
$$(x + 3)(x - 4) - (x + 3)(2x - 1) = 0$$
$$(x + 3)[x - 4 - (2x - 1)] = 0$$
$$(x + 3)(x - 4 - 2x + 1) = 0$$
$$(x + 3)(-x - 3) = 0$$

$x + 3 = 0$ or $-x - 3 = 0$

$x = -3$ or $-x = 3$

$x = -3$ or $x = -3$

The solution set is $\{-3\}$.

Solution B

$$(x + 3)(x - 4) = (x + 3)(2x - 1)$$
$$x^2 - x - 12 = 2x^2 + 5x - 3$$
$$0 = x^2 + 6x + 9$$
$$0 = (x + 3)^2$$
$$x + 3 = 0$$
$$x = -3$$

The solution set is $\{-3\}$.

Are both approaches correct? Which approach would you use, and why?

(3.1) A **term** is an indicated product and may contain any number of factors. The variables involved in a term are called **literal factors**, and the numerical factor is called the **numerical coefficient**. Terms that contain variables with only nonnegative integers as exponents are called **monomials**. The **degree** of a monomial is the sum of the exponents of the literal factors.

A **polynomial** is a monomial or a finite sum (or difference) of monomials. We classify polynomials as follows:

Polynomial with one term $\longrightarrow$ Monomial

Polynomial with two terms $\longrightarrow$ Binomial

Polynomial with three terms $\longrightarrow$ Trinomial

Similar terms, or **like terms**, have the same literal factors. The commutative, associative, and distributive properties provide the basis for rearranging, regrouping, and combining similar terms.

(3.2) The following properties provide the basis for multiplying and dividing monomials.

1. $b^n \cdot b^m = b^{n+m}$

2. $(b^n)^m = b^{mn}$

3. $(ab)^n = a^n b^n$

4. **(a)** $\dfrac{b^n}{b^m} = b^{n-m}, \quad if \; n > m$

   (b) $\dfrac{b^n}{b^m} = 1, \quad if \; n = m$

(3.3) The commutative and associative properties, the properties of exponents, and the distributive property work together to form a basis for multiplying polynomials. The following can be used as multiplication patterns.

$$(a + b)^2 = a^2 + 2ab + b^2$$

$$(a - b)^2 = a^2 - 2ab + b^2$$

$$(a + b)(a - b) = a^2 - b^2$$

$$(a + b)^3 = a^3 + 3a^2b + 3ab^2 + b^3$$

$$(a - b)^3 = a^3 - 3a^2b + 3ab^2 - b^3$$

(3.4) If a positive integer greater than 1 has no factors that are positive integers other than itself and 1, then it is called a **prime number**. A positive integer greater than 1 that is not a prime number is called a **composite number**.

The indicated product form that contains only prime factors is called the **prime factorization form** of a number.

An expression such as $ax + bx + ay + by$ can be factored as follows:

$$ax + bx + ay + by = x(a + b) + y(a + b)$$

$$= (a + b)(x + y)$$

This is called **factoring by grouping**.

The distributive property in the form $ab + ac = a(b + c)$ is the basis for **factoring out the highest common monomial factor**.

Expressing polynomials in factored form, and then applying the property $ab = 0$ if and only if $a = 0$ or $b = 0$, provides us with another technique for solving equations.

(3.5) The factoring pattern

$$a^2 - b^2 = (a + b)(a - b)$$

is called the **difference of two squares**.

The difference-of-two-squares factoring pattern, along with the property $ab = 0$ if and only if $a = 0$ or $b = 0$, provides us with another technique for solving equations. The factoring patterns

$$a^3 + b^3 = (a + b)(a^2 - ab + b^2) \quad \text{and}$$

$$a^3 - b^3 = (a - b)(a^2 + ab + b^2)$$

are called the **sum and difference of two cubes**.

(3.6) Expressing a trinomial (for which the coefficient of the squared term is 1) as a product of two binomials is based on the relationship

$$(x + a)(x + b) = x^2 + (a + b)x + ab$$

The coefficient of the middle term is the sum of a and b, and the last term is the product of a and b.

If the coefficient of the squared term of a trinomial does not equal 1, then the following relationship holds.

$$(px + r)(qx + s) = (pq)x^2 + (ps + rq)x + rs$$

The two coefficients of x, ps and rq, must have a sum of $(ps) + (rq)$ and a product of $pqrs$. Thus to factor something like $6x^2 + 7x - 3$, we need to find two integers whose product is $6(-3) = -18$ and whose sum is 7. The integers are 9 and -2, and we can factor as follows:

$$6x^2 + 7x - 3 = 6x^2 + 9x - 2x - 3$$

$$= 3x(2x + 3) - 1(2x + 3)$$

$$= (2x + 3)(3x - 1)$$

A **perfect-square trinomial** is the result of squaring a binomial. There are two basic perfect-square trinomial factoring patterns.

$$a^2 + 2ab + b^2 = (a + b)^2$$

$$a^2 - 2ab + b^2 = (a - b)^2$$

(3.7) The factoring techniques we discussed in this chapter, along with the property $ab = 0$ if and only if $a = 0$ or $b = 0$, provide the basis for expanding our repertoire of equation-solving processes.

The ability to solve more types of equations increases our capabilities for problem solving.

Chapter 3　Review Problem Set

For Problems 1–23, perform the indicated operations and simplify each of the following.

1. $(3x - 2) + (4x - 6) + (-2x + 5)$

2. $(8x^2 + 9x - 3) - (5x^2 - 3x - 1)$

3. $(6x^2 - 2x - 1) + (4x^2 + 2x + 5) - (-2x^2 + x - 1)$

4. $(-5x^2y^3)(4x^3y^4)$　　　**5.** $(-2a^2)(3ab^2)(a^2b^3)$

6. $5a^2(3a^2 - 2a - 1)$　　　**7.** $(4x - 3y)(6x + 5y)$

8. $(x + 4)(3x^2 - 5x - 1)$　　**9.** $(4x^2y^3)^4$

10. $(3x - 2y)^2$　　　　　　**11.** $(-2x^2y^3z)^3$

12. $\dfrac{-39x^3y^4}{3xy^3}$

13. $[3x - (2x - 3y + 1)] - [2y - (x - 1)]$

14. $(x^2 - 2x - 5)(x^2 + 3x - 7)$

15. $(7 - 3x)(3 + 5x)$　　　**16.** $-(3ab)(2a^2b^3)^2$

17. $\left(\dfrac{1}{2}ab\right)(8a^3b^2)(-2a^3)$　　**18.** $(7x - 9)(x + 4)$

19. $(3x + 2)(2x^2 - 5x + 1)$　**20.** $(3x^{n+1})(2x^{3n-1})$

21. $(2x + 5y)^2$　　　　　　**22.** $(x - 2)^3$

23. $(2x + 5)^3$

For Problems 24–45, factor each polynomial completely. Indicate any that are not factorable using integers.

24. $x^2 + 3x - 28$　　　　　**25.** $2t^2 - 18$

26. $4n^2 + 9$　　　　　　　**27.** $12n^2 - 7n + 1$

28. $x^6 - x^2$　　　　　　　**29.** $x^3 - 6x^2 - 72x$

30. $6a^3b + 4a^2b^2 - 2a^2bc$　　**31.** $x^2 - (y - 1)^2$

32. $8x^2 + 12$　　　　　　　**33.** $12x^2 + x - 35$

34. $16n^2 - 40n + 25$　　　**35.** $4n^2 - 8n$

36. $3w^3 + 18w^2 - 24w$　　**37.** $20x^2 + 3xy - 2y^2$

38. $16a^2 - 64a$　　　　　　**39.** $3x^3 - 15x^2 - 18x$

40. $n^2 - 8n - 128$　　　　**41.** $t^4 - 22t^2 - 75$

42. $35x^2 - 11x - 6$　　　　**43.** $15 - 14x + 3x^2$

44. $64n^3 - 27$　　　　　　**45.** $16x^3 + 250$

For Problems 46–65, solve each equation.

46. $4x^2 - 36 = 0$

47. $x^2 + 5x - 6 = 0$

48. $49n^2 - 28n + 4 = 0$

49. $(3x - 1)(5x + 2) = 0$

50. $(3x - 4)^2 - 25 = 0$

51. $6a^3 = 54a$

52. $x^5 = x$

53. $-n^2 + 2n + 63 = 0$

54. $7n(7n + 2) = 8$

55. $30w^2 - w - 20 = 0$

56. $5x^4 - 19x^2 - 4 = 0$

57. $9n^2 - 30n + 25 = 0$

58. $n(2n + 4) = 96$

59. $7x^2 + 33x - 10 = 0$

60. $(x + 1)(x + 2) = 42$

61. $x^2 + 12x - x - 12 = 0$

62. $2x^4 + 9x^2 + 4 = 0$

63. $30 - 19x - 5x^2 = 0$

64. $3t^3 - 27t^2 + 24t = 0$

65. $-4n^2 - 39n + 10 = 0$

For Problems 66–75, set up an equation and solve each problem.

66. Find three consecutive integers such that the product of the smallest and the largest is one less than 9 times the middle integer.

67. Find two integers whose sum is 2 and whose product is −48.

68. Find two consecutive odd whole numbers whose product is 195.

69. Two cars leave an intersection at the same time, one traveling north and the other traveling east. Some time later, they are 20 miles apart, and the car going east has traveled 4 miles farther than the other car. How far has each car traveled?

70. The perimeter of a rectangle is 32 meters, and its area is 48 square meters. Find the length and width of the rectangle.

71. A room contains 144 chairs. The number of chairs per row is two less than twice the number of rows. Find the number of rows and the number of chairs per row.

72. The area of a triangle is 39 square feet. The length of one side is 1 foot more than twice the altitude to that side. Find the length of that side and the altitude to the side.

73. A rectangular-shaped pool 20 feet by 30 feet has a side-walk of uniform width around the pool (see Figure 3.23). The area of the sidewalk is 336 square feet. Find the width of the sidewalk.

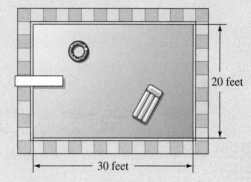

20 feet

30 feet

Figure 3.23

74. The sum of the areas of two squares is 89 square centimeters. The length of a side of the larger square is 3 centimeters more than the length of a side of the smaller square. Find the dimensions of each square.

75. The total surface area of a right circular cylinder is 32π square inches. If the altitude of the cylinder is three times the length of a radius, find the altitude of the cylinder.

For Problems 1–8, perform the indicated operations and simplify each expression.

1. $(-3x - 1) + (9x - 2) - (4x + 8)$

2. $(-6xy^2)(8x^3y^2)$

3. $(-3x^2y^4)^3$ **4.** $(5x - 7)(4x + 9)$

5. $(3n - 2)(2n - 3)$ **6.** $(x - 4y)^3$

7. $(x + 6)(2x^2 - x - 5)$ **8.** $\dfrac{-70x^4y^3}{5xy^2}$

For Problems 9–14, factor each expression completely.

9. $6x^2 + 19x - 20$ **10.** $12x^2 - 3$

11. $64 + t^3$ **12.** $30x + 4x^2 - 16x^3$

13. $x^2 - xy + 4x - 4y$ **14.** $24n^2 + 55n - 24$

For Problems 15–22, solve each equation.

15. $x^2 + 8x - 48 = 0$ **16.** $4n^2 = n$

17. $4x^2 - 12x + 9 = 0$

18. $(n - 2)(n + 7) = -18$

19. $3x^3 + 21x^2 - 54x = 0$

20. $12 + 13x - 35x^2 = 0$

21. $n(3n - 5) = 2$ **22.** $9x^2 - 36 = 0$

For Problems 23–25, set up an equation and solve each problem.

23. The perimeter of a rectangle is 30 inches, and its area is 54 square inches. Find the length of the longest side of the rectangle.

24. A room contains 105 chairs arranged in rows. The number of rows is one more than twice the number of chairs per row. Find the number of rows.

25. The combined area of a square and a rectangle is 57 square feet. The width of the rectangle is 3 feet more than the length of a side of the square, and the length of the rectangle is 5 feet more than the length of a side of the square. Find the length of the rectangle.

For Problems 1–10, evaluate each algebraic expression for the given values of the variables. Don't forget that in some cases it may be helpful to simplify the algebraic expression before evaluating it.

1. $x^2 - 2xy + y^2$ for $x = -2$ and $y = -4$

2. $-n^2 + 2n - 4$ for $n = -3$

3. $2x^2 - 5x + 6$ for $x = 3$

4. $3(2x - 1) - 2(x + 4) - 4(2x - 7)$ for $x = -1$

5. $-(2n - 1) + 5(2n - 3) - 6(3n + 4)$ for $n = 4$

6. $2(a - 4) - (a - 1) + (3a - 6)$ for $a = -5$

7. $(3x^2 - 4x - 7) - (4x^2 - 7x + 8)$ for $x = -4$

8. $-2(3x - 5y) - 4(x + 2y) + 3(-2x - 3y)$ for $x = 2$ and $y = -3$

9. $5(-x^2 - x + 3) - (2x^2 - x + 6) - 2(x^2 + 4x - 6)$ for $x = 2$

10. $3(x^2 - 4xy + 2y^2) - 2(x^2 - 6xy - y^2)$ for $x = -5$ and $y = -2$

For Problems 11–18, perform the indicated operations and express your answers in simplest form.

11. $4(3x - 2) - 2(4x - 1) - (2x + 5)$

12. $(-6ab^2)(2ab)(-3b^3)$

13. $(5x - 7)(6x + 1)$ **14.** $(-2x - 3)(x + 4)$

15. $(-4a^2b^3)^3$ **16.** $(x + 2)(5x - 6)(x - 2)$

17. $(x - 3)(x^2 - x - 4)$

18. $(x^2 + x + 4)(2x^2 - 3x - 7)$

For Problems 19–38, factor each of the algebraic expressions completely.

19. $7x^2 - 7$ **20.** $4a^2 - 4ab + b^2$

21. $3x^2 - 17x - 56$ **22.** $1 - x^3$

23. $xy - 5x + 2y - 10$ **24.** $3x^2 - 24x + 48$

25. $4n^4 - n^2 - 3$ **26.** $32x^4 + 108x$

27. $4x^2 + 36$ **28.** $6x^2 + 5x - 4$

29. $9x^2 - 30x + 25$ **30.** $2x^2 + 6xy + x + 3y$

31. $8a^3 + 27b^3$ **32.** $x^4 - 16$

33. $10m^4n^2 - 2m^3n^3 - 4m^2n^4$

34. $5x(2y + 7z) - 12(2y + 7z)$

35. $3x^2 - x - 10$ **36.** $25 - 4a^2$

37. $36x^2 + 60x + 25$ **38.** $64y^3 + 1$

For Problems 39–42, solve each equation for the indicated variable.

39. $5x - 2y = 6$ for x **40.** $3x + 4y = 12$ for y

41. $V = 2\pi rh + 2\pi r^2$ for h

42. $\dfrac{1}{R} = \dfrac{1}{R_1} + \dfrac{1}{R_2}$ for R_1

43. Solve $A = P + Prt$ for r, given that $A = \$4997$, $P = \$3800$, and $t = 3$ years.

44. Solve $C = \dfrac{5}{9}(F - 32)$ for C, given that $F = 5°$.

For Problems 45–62, solve each of the equations.

45. $(x - 2)(x + 5) = 8$

46. $(5n - 2)(3n + 7) = 0$

47. $-2(n - 1) + 3(2n + 1) = -11$

48. $x^2 + 7x - 18 = 0$

49. $8x^2 - 8 = 0$

50. $\dfrac{3}{4}(x - 2) - \dfrac{2}{5}(2x - 3) = \dfrac{1}{5}$

51. $0.1(x - 0.1) - 0.4(x + 2) = -5.31$

52. $\dfrac{2x - 1}{2} - \dfrac{5x + 2}{3} = 3$

53. $|3n - 2| = 7$

54. $|2x - 1| = |x + 4|$

55. $0.08(x + 200) = 0.07x + 20$

56. $2x^2 - 12x - 80 = 0$

57. $x^3 = 16x$

58. $x(x + 2) - 3(x + 2) = 0$

59. $-12n^2 + 5n + 2 = 0$

60. $3y(y + 1) = 90$

61. $2x^3 + 6x^2 - 20x = 0$

62. $(3n - 1)(2n + 3) = (n + 4)(6n - 5)$

For Problems 63–70, solve each of the inequalities.

63. $-5(3n + 4) < -2(7n - 1)$

64. $7(x + 1) - 8(x - 2) < 0$

65. $|2x - 1| > 7$

66. $|3x + 7| < 14$

67. $0.09x + 0.1(x + 200) > 77$

68. $\dfrac{2x - 1}{4} - \dfrac{x - 2}{6} \le \dfrac{3}{8}$

69. $-(x - 1) + 2(3x - 1) \ge 2(x + 4) - (x - 1)$

70. $\dfrac{1}{4}(x - 2) + \dfrac{3}{7}(2x - 1) < \dfrac{3}{14}$

For Problems 71–84, solve each problem by setting up and solving an appropriate equation or inequality.

71. Find three consecutive odd integers such that three times the first minus the second is one more than the third.

72. Inez has a collection of 48 coins consisting of nickels, dimes, and quarters. The number of dimes is one less than twice the number of nickels, and the number of quarters is ten greater than the number of dimes. How many coins of each denomination are there in the collection?

73. The sum of the present ages of Joey and his mother is 46 years. In 4 years, Joey will be 3 years less than one-half as old as his mother at that time. Find the present ages of Joey and his mother.

74. The difference of the measures of two supplementary angles is 56°. Find the measure of each angle.

75. Norm invested a certain amount of money at 8% interest and $200 more than that amount at 9%. His total yearly interest was $86. How much did he invest at each rate?

76. Sanchez has a collection of pennies, nickels, and dimes worth $9.35. He has five more nickels than pennies and twice as many dimes as pennies. How may coins of each kind does he have?

77. Sandy starts off with her bicycle at 8 miles per hour. Fifty minutes later, Billie starts riding along the same route at 12 miles per hour. How long will it take Billie to overtake Sandy?

78. How many milliliters of pure acid must be added to 150 milliliters of a 30% solution of acid to obtain a 40% solution?

79. A retailer has some carpet that cost him $18.00 a square yard. If he sells it for $30 a square yard, what is his rate of profit based on the selling price?

80. Brad had scores of 88, 92, 93, and 89 on his first four algebra tests. What score must he obtain on the fifth test to have an average better than 90 for the five tests?

81. Suppose that the area of a square is one-half the area of a triangle. One side of the triangle is 16 inches long, and the altitude to that side is the same length as a side of the square. Find the length of a side of the square.

82. A rectangle is twice as long as it is wide, and its area is 98 square meters. Find the length and width of the rectangle.

83. A room contains 96 chairs. The number of chairs per row is four more than the number of rows. Find the number of rows and the number of chairs per row.

84. One leg of a right triangle is 3 feet longer than the other leg. The hypotenuse is 3 feet longer than the longer leg. Find the lengths of the three sides of the right triangle.

Rational Expressions

4.1 Simplifying Rational Expressions

4.2 Multiplying and Dividing Rational Expressions

4.3 Adding and Subtracting Rational Expressions

4.4 More on Rational Expressions and Complex Fractions

4.5 Dividing Polynomials

4.6 Fractional Equations

4.7 More Fractional Equations and Applications

Computers often work together to compile large processing jobs. Rational numbers are used to express the rate of the processing speed of a computer.

AP/Wide World Photos

It takes Pat 12 hours to complete a task. After he had been working on this task for 3 hours, he was joined by his brother, Liam, and together they finished the job in 5 hours. How long would it take Liam to do the job by himself? We can use the **fractional equation** $\frac{5}{12} + \frac{5}{h} = \frac{3}{4}$ to determine that Liam could do the entire job by himself in 15 hours.

Rational expressions are to algebra what rational numbers are to arithmetic. Most of the work we will do with rational expressions in this chapter parallels the work you have previously done with arithmetic fractions. The same basic properties we use to explain reducing, adding, subtracting, multiplying, and dividing arithmetic fractions will serve as a basis for our work with rational expressions. The techniques of factoring that we studied in Chapter 3 will also play an important role in our discussions. At the end of this chapter, we will work with some fractional equations that contain rational expressions.

4.1   Simplifying Rational Expressions

We reviewed the basic operations with rational numbers in an informal setting in Chapter 1. In this review, we relied primarily on your knowledge of arithmetic. At this time, we want to become a little more formal with our review so that we can use the work with rational numbers as a basis for operating with rational expressions. We will define a rational expression shortly.

You will recall that any number that can be written in the form $\frac{a}{b}$, where a and b are integers and $b \neq 0$, is called a rational number. The following are examples of rational numbers.

$$\frac{1}{2} \quad \frac{3}{4} \quad \frac{15}{7} \quad \frac{-5}{6} \quad \frac{7}{-8} \quad \frac{-12}{-17}$$

Numbers such as $6, -4, 0, 4\frac{1}{2}, 0.7,$ and 0.21 are also rational, because we can express them as the indicated quotient of two integers. For example,

$$6 = \frac{6}{1} = \frac{12}{2} = \frac{18}{3} \quad \text{and so on} \qquad 4\frac{1}{2} = \frac{9}{2}$$

$$-4 = \frac{4}{-1} = \frac{-4}{1} = \frac{8}{-2} \quad \text{and so on} \qquad 0.7 = \frac{7}{10}$$

$$0 = \frac{0}{1} = \frac{0}{2} = \frac{0}{3} \quad \text{and so on} \qquad 0.21 = \frac{21}{100}$$

Because a rational number is the quotient of two integers, our previous work with division of integers can help us understand the various forms of rational numbers. If the signs of the numerator and denominator are different, then the rational number is negative. If the signs of the numerator and denominator are the same, then the rational number is positive. The next examples and Property 4.1 show the equivalent forms of rational numbers. Generally, it is preferred to express the denominator of a rational number as a positive integer.

$$\frac{8}{-2} = \frac{-8}{2} = -\frac{8}{2} = -4 \qquad \frac{12}{3} = \frac{-12}{-3} = 4$$

Observe the following general properties.

Property 4.1

1. $\dfrac{-a}{b} = \dfrac{a}{-b} = -\dfrac{a}{b},$ where $b \neq 0$

2. $\dfrac{-a}{-b} = \dfrac{a}{b},$ where $b \neq 0$

Therefore, a rational number such as $\dfrac{-2}{5}$ can also be written as $\dfrac{2}{-5}$ or $-\dfrac{2}{5}$.

We use the following property, often referred to as the **fundamental principle of fractions**, to reduce fractions to lowest terms or express fractions in simplest or reduced form.

Property 4.2

If b and k are nonzero integers and a is any integer, then

$$\frac{a \cdot k}{b \cdot k} = \frac{a}{b}$$

Let's apply Properties 4.1 and 4.2 to the following examples.

EXAMPLE   1

Reduce $\dfrac{18}{24}$ to lowest terms.

Solution

$$\frac{18}{24} = \frac{3 \cdot 6}{4 \cdot 6} = \frac{3}{4}$$ ■

EXAMPLE   2

Change $\dfrac{40}{48}$ to simplest form.

Solution

$$\frac{\overset{5}{\cancel{40}}}{\underset{6}{\cancel{48}}} = \frac{5}{6}$$ A common factor of 8 was divided out of both numerator and denominator.   ■

EXAMPLE   3

Express $\dfrac{-36}{63}$ in reduced form.

Solution

$$\frac{-36}{63} = -\frac{36}{63} = -\frac{4 \cdot 9}{7 \cdot 9} = -\frac{4}{7}$$ ■

EXAMPLE   4

Reduce $\dfrac{72}{-90}$ to simplest form.

Solution

$$\frac{72}{-90} = -\frac{72}{90} = -\frac{2 \cdot 2 \cdot 2 \cdot 3 \cdot 3}{2 \cdot 3 \cdot 3 \cdot 5} = -\frac{4}{5}$$ ■

Note the different terminology used in Examples 1–4. Regardless of the terminology, keep in mind that the number is not being changed, but the form of the numeral representing the number is being changed. In Example 1, $\dfrac{18}{24}$ and $\dfrac{3}{4}$ are equivalent fractions; they name the same number. Also note the use of prime factors in Example 4.

■ Rational Expressions

A **rational expression** is the indicated quotient of two polynomials. The following are examples of rational expressions.

$$\frac{3x^2}{5} \qquad \frac{x-2}{x+3} \qquad \frac{x^2+5x-1}{x^2-9} \qquad \frac{xy^2+x^2y}{xy} \qquad \frac{a^3-3a^2-5a-1}{a^4+a^3+6}$$

Because we must avoid division by zero, no values that create a denominator of zero can be assigned to variables. Thus the rational expression $\dfrac{x-2}{x+3}$ is meaningful for all values of x except $x = -3$. Rather than making restrictions for each individual expression, we will merely assume that all denominators represent nonzero real numbers.

Property 4.2 $\left(\dfrac{a \cdot k}{b \cdot k} = \dfrac{a}{b} \right)$ serves as the basis for simplifying rational expressions, as the next examples illustrate.

E X A M P L E 5

Simplify $\dfrac{15xy}{25y}$.

Solution

$$\frac{15xy}{25y} = \frac{3 \cdot \cancel{5} \cdot x \cdot \cancel{y}}{\cancel{5} \cdot 5 \cdot \cancel{y}} = \frac{3x}{5}$$

■

E X A M P L E 6

Simplify $\dfrac{-9}{18x^2y}$.

Solution

$$\frac{-9}{18x^2y} = -\frac{\overset{1}{\cancel{9}}}{\underset{2}{\cancel{18}}x^2y} = -\frac{1}{2x^2y} \qquad \text{A common factor of 9 was divided out of numerator and denominator.}$$

■

E X A M P L E 7

Simplify $\dfrac{-28a^2b^2}{-63a^2b^3}$.

Solution

$$\frac{-28a^2b^2}{-63a^2b^3} = \frac{4 \cdot \cancel{7} \cdot \cancel{a^2} \cdot \cancel{b^2}}{9 \cdot \cancel{7} \cdot \cancel{a^2} \cdot \underset{b}{\cancel{b^3}}} = \frac{4}{9b}$$

■

The factoring techniques from Chapter 3 can be used to factor numerators and/or denominators so that we can apply the property $\dfrac{a \cdot k}{b \cdot k} = \dfrac{a}{b}$. Examples 8–12 should clarify this process.

E X A M P L E 8

Simplify $\dfrac{x^2 + 4x}{x^2 - 16}$.

Solution

$$\frac{x^2 + 4x}{x^2 - 16} = \frac{x(x+4)}{(x-4)(x+4)} = \frac{x}{x-4}$$ ∎

E X A M P L E 9

Simplify $\dfrac{4a^2 + 12a + 9}{2a + 3}$.

Solution

$$\frac{4a^2 + 12a + 9}{2a + 3} = \frac{(2a+3)(2a+3)}{1(2a+3)} = \frac{2a+3}{1} = 2a + 3$$ ∎

E X A M P L E 1 0

Simplify $\dfrac{5n^2 + 6n - 8}{10n^2 - 3n - 4}$.

Solution

$$\frac{5n^2 + 6n - 8}{10n^2 - 3n - 4} = \frac{(5n-4)(n+2)}{(5n-4)(2n+1)} = \frac{n+2}{2n+1}$$ ∎

E X A M P L E 1 1

Simplify $\dfrac{6x^3y - 6xy}{x^3 + 5x^2 + 4x}$.

Solution

$$\frac{6x^3y - 6xy}{x^3 + 5x^2 + 4x} = \frac{6xy(x^2 - 1)}{x(x^2 + 5x + 4)} = \frac{6xy(x+1)(x-1)}{x(x+1)(x+4)} = \frac{6y(x-1)}{x+4}$$ ∎

Note that in Example 11 we left the numerator of the final fraction in factored form. This is often done if expressions other than monomials are involved. Either $\dfrac{6y(x-1)}{x+4}$ or $\dfrac{6xy - 6y}{x+4}$ is an acceptable answer.

Remember that the quotient of any nonzero real number and its opposite is -1. For example, $\dfrac{6}{-6} = -1$ and $\dfrac{-8}{8} = -1$. Likewise, the indicated quotient of any polynomial and its opposite is equal to -1; that is,

$$\frac{a}{-a} = -1 \quad \text{because } a \text{ and } -a \text{ are opposites}$$

$$\frac{a - b}{b - a} = -1 \quad \text{because } a - b \text{ and } b - a \text{ are opposites}$$

$$\frac{x^2 - 4}{4 - x^2} = -1 \quad \text{because } x^2 - 4 \text{ and } 4 - x^2 \text{ are opposites}$$

Example 12 shows how we use this idea when simplifying rational expressions.

EXAMPLE 12   Simplify $\dfrac{6a^2 - 7a + 2}{10a - 15a^2}$.

Solution

$$\frac{6a^2 - 7a + 2}{10a - 15a^2} = \frac{(2a - 1)\,(3a - 2)}{5a\,(2 - 3a)} \qquad\qquad \frac{3a - 2}{2 - 3a} = -1$$

$$= (-1)\left(\frac{2a - 1}{5a}\right)$$

$$= -\frac{2a - 1}{5a} \quad \text{or} \quad \frac{1 - 2a}{5a} \qquad\qquad ■$$

Problem Set 4.1

For Problems 1–8, express each rational number in reduced form.

1. $\dfrac{27}{36}$ **2.** $\dfrac{14}{21}$ **3.** $\dfrac{45}{54}$

4. $\dfrac{-14}{42}$ **5.** $\dfrac{24}{-60}$ **6.** $\dfrac{45}{-75}$

7. $\dfrac{-16}{-56}$ **8.** $\dfrac{-30}{-42}$

For Problems 9–50, simplify each rational expression.

9. $\dfrac{12xy}{42y}$ **10.** $\dfrac{21xy}{35x}$

11. $\dfrac{18a^2}{45ab}$ **12.** $\dfrac{48ab}{84b^2}$

13. $\dfrac{-14y^3}{56xy^2}$ **14.** $\dfrac{-14x^2y^3}{63xy^2}$

15. $\dfrac{54c^2d}{-78cd^2}$ **16.** $\dfrac{60x^3z}{-64xyz^2}$

17. $\dfrac{-40x^3y}{-24xy^4}$ **18.** $\dfrac{-30x^2y^2z^2}{-35xz^3}$

19. $\dfrac{x^2 - 4}{x^2 + 2x}$ **20.** $\dfrac{xy + y^2}{x^2 - y^2}$

21. $\dfrac{18x + 12}{12x - 6}$ **22.** $\dfrac{20x + 50}{15x - 30}$

23. $\dfrac{a^2 + 7a + 10}{a^2 - 7a - 18}$ **24.** $\dfrac{a^2 + 4a - 32}{3a^2 + 26a + 16}$

25. $\dfrac{2n^2 + n - 21}{10n^2 + 33n - 7}$

26. $\dfrac{4n^2 - 15n - 4}{7n^2 - 30n + 8}$

27. $\dfrac{5x^2 + 7}{10x}$

28. $\dfrac{12x^2 + 11x - 15}{20x^2 - 23x + 6}$

29. $\dfrac{6x^2 + x - 15}{8x^2 - 10x - 3}$

30. $\dfrac{4x^2 + 8x}{x^3 + 8}$

31. $\dfrac{3x^2 - 12x}{x^3 - 64}$

32. $\dfrac{x^2 - 14x + 49}{6x^2 - 37x - 35}$

33. $\dfrac{3x^2 + 17x - 6}{9x^2 - 6x + 1}$

34. $\dfrac{9y^2 - 1}{3y^2 + 11y - 4}$

35. $\dfrac{2x^3 + 3x^2 - 14x}{x^2y + 7xy - 18y}$

36. $\dfrac{3x^3 + 12x}{9x^2 + 18x}$

37. $\dfrac{5y^2 + 22y + 8}{25y^2 - 4}$

38. $\dfrac{16x^3y + 24x^2y^2 - 16xy^3}{24x^2y + 12xy^2 - 12y^3}$

39. $\dfrac{15x^3 - 15x^2}{5x^3 + 5x}$

40. $\dfrac{5n^2 + 18n - 8}{3n^2 + 13n + 4}$

41. $\dfrac{4x^2y + 8xy^2 - 12y^3}{18x^3y - 12x^2y^2 - 6xy^3}$

42. $\dfrac{3 + x - 2x^2}{2 + x - x^2}$

43. $\dfrac{3n^2 + 16n - 12}{7n^2 + 44n + 12}$

44. $\dfrac{x^4 - 2x^2 - 15}{2x^4 + 9x^2 + 9}$

45. $\dfrac{8 + 18x - 5x^2}{10 + 31x + 15x^2}$

46. $\dfrac{6x^4 - 11x^2 + 4}{2x^4 + 17x^2 - 9}$

47. $\dfrac{27x^4 - x}{6x^3 + 10x^2 - 4x}$

48. $\dfrac{64x^4 + 27x}{12x^3 - 27x^2 - 27x}$

49. $\dfrac{-40x^3 + 24x^2 + 16x}{20x^3 + 28x^2 + 8x}$

50. $\dfrac{-6x^3 - 21x^2 + 12x}{-18x^3 - 42x^2 + 120x}$

For Problems 51–58, simplify each rational expression. You will need to use factoring by grouping.

51. $\dfrac{xy + ay + bx + ab}{xy + ay + cx + ac}$

52. $\dfrac{xy + 2y + 3x + 6}{xy + 2y + 4x + 8}$

53. $\dfrac{ax - 3x + 2ay - 6y}{2ax - 6x + ay - 3y}$

54. $\dfrac{x^2 - 2x + ax - 2a}{x^2 - 2x + 3ax - 6a}$

55. $\dfrac{5x^2 + 5x + 3x + 3}{5x^2 + 3x - 30x - 18}$

56. $\dfrac{x^2 + 3x + 4x + 12}{2x^2 + 6x - x - 3}$

57. $\dfrac{2st - 30 - 12s + 5t}{3st - 6 - 18s + t}$

58. $\dfrac{nr - 6 - 3n + 2r}{nr + 10 + 2r + 5n}$

For Problems 59–68, simplify each rational expression. You may want to refer to Example 12 of this section.

59. $\dfrac{5x - 7}{7 - 5x}$

60. $\dfrac{4a - 9}{9 - 4a}$

61. $\dfrac{n^2 - 49}{7 - n}$

62. $\dfrac{9 - y}{y^2 - 81}$

63. $\dfrac{2y - 2xy}{x^2y - y}$

64. $\dfrac{3x - x^2}{x^2 - 9}$

65. $\dfrac{2x^3 - 8x}{4x - x^3}$

66. $\dfrac{x^2 - (y - 1)^2}{(y - 1)^2 - x^2}$

67. $\dfrac{n^2 - 5n - 24}{40 + 3n - n^2}$

68. $\dfrac{x^2 + 2x - 24}{20 - x - x^2}$

■ ■ ■ **THOUGHTS INTO WORDS**

69. Compare the concept of a rational number in arithmetic to the concept of a rational expression in algebra.

70. What role does factoring play in the simplifying of rational expressions?

71. Why is the rational expression $\dfrac{x + 3}{x^2 - 4}$ undefined for $x = 2$ and $x = -2$ but defined for $x = -3$?

72. How would you convince someone that $\dfrac{x - 4}{4 - x} = -1$ for all real numbers except 4?

4.2   Multiplying and Dividing Rational Expressions

We define multiplication of rational numbers in common fraction form as follows:

Definition 4.1

If a, b, c, and d are integers, and b and d are not equal to zero, then

$$\frac{a}{b} \cdot \frac{c}{d} = \frac{a \cdot c}{b \cdot d} = \frac{ac}{bd}$$

To multiply rational numbers in common fraction form, we merely **multiply numerators and multiply denominators**, as the following examples demonstrate. (The steps in the dashed boxes are usually done mentally.)

$$\frac{2}{3} \cdot \frac{4}{5} = \boxed{\frac{2 \cdot 4}{3 \cdot 5}} = \frac{8}{15}$$

$$\frac{-3}{4} \cdot \frac{5}{7} = \boxed{\frac{-3 \cdot 5}{4 \cdot 7} = \frac{-15}{28}} = -\frac{15}{28}$$

$$-\frac{5}{6} \cdot \frac{13}{3} = \boxed{\frac{-5}{6} \cdot \frac{13}{3} = \frac{-5 \cdot 13}{6 \cdot 3} = \frac{-65}{18}} = -\frac{65}{18}$$

We also agree, when multiplying rational numbers, to express the final product in reduced form. The following examples show some different formats used to multiply and simplify rational numbers.

$$\frac{3}{4} \cdot \frac{4}{7} = \frac{3 \cdot \cancel{4}}{\cancel{4} \cdot 7} = \frac{3}{7}$$

$$\frac{\overset{1}{\cancel{8}}}{\underset{1}{\cancel{9}}} \cdot \frac{\overset{3}{\cancel{27}}}{\underset{4}{\cancel{32}}} = \frac{3}{4} \qquad \text{A common factor of 9 was divided out of 9 and 27, and a common factor of 8 was divided out of 8 and 32.}$$

$$\left(-\frac{28}{25}\right)\left(-\frac{65}{78}\right) = \frac{2 \cdot 2 \cdot 7 \cdot \cancel{5} \cdot \cancel{13}}{\cancel{8} \cdot 5 \cdot 2 \cdot 3 \cdot \cancel{13}} = \frac{14}{15}. \qquad \text{We should recognize that a negative times a negative is positive. Also, note the use of prime factors to help us recognize common factors.}$$

Multiplication of rational expressions follows the same basic pattern as multiplication of rational numbers in common fraction form. That is to say, we multiply numerators and multiply denominators and express the final product in simplified or reduced form. Let's consider some examples.

$$\frac{3x}{4y} \cdot \frac{8y^2}{9x} = \frac{\overset{2}{\cancel{3}} \cdot \overset{}{\cancel{8}} \cdot \cancel{x} \cdot \overset{y}{\cancel{y^2}}}{\cancel{4} \cdot \underset{3}{\cancel{9}} \cdot \cancel{x} \cdot \cancel{y}} = \frac{2y}{3}$$

Note that we use the commutative property of multiplication to rearrange the factors in a form that allows us to identify common factors of the numerator and denominator.

$$\frac{-4a}{6a^2b^2} \cdot \frac{9ab}{12a^2} = -\frac{\underset{2}{\cancel{4}} \cdot \overset{3}{\underset{3}{\cancel{9}}} \cdot \overset{}{\cancel{a^2}} \cdot \cancel{b}}{\cancel{6} \cdot \cancel{12} \cdot \underset{a^2}{\cancel{a^4}} \cdot \underset{b}{\cancel{b^2}}} = -\frac{1}{2a^2b}$$

$$\frac{12x^2y}{-18xy} \cdot \frac{-24xy^2}{56y^3} = \frac{\overset{2}{\cancel{12}} \cdot \overset{3}{\cancel{24}} \cdot \overset{x^2}{\cancel{x^3}} \cdot \cancel{y^3}}{\underset{3}{\cancel{18}} \cdot \underset{7}{\cancel{56}} \cdot \cancel{x} \cdot \underset{y}{\cancel{y^4}}} = \frac{2x^2}{7y}$$

You should recognize that the first fraction is equivalent to

$-\dfrac{12x^2y}{18xy}$ and the second to

$-\dfrac{24xy^2}{56y^3}$; thus the product is positive.

If the rational expressions contain polynomials (other than monomials) that are factorable, then our work may take on the following format.

EXAMPLE   1

Multiply and simplify $\dfrac{y}{x^2 - 4} \cdot \dfrac{x + 2}{y^2}$.

Solution

$$\frac{y}{x^2 - 4} \cdot \frac{x + 2}{y^2} = \frac{\cancel{y}(\cancel{x + 2})}{\underset{y}{\cancel{y^2}}(\cancel{x + 2})(x - 2)} = \frac{1}{y(x - 2)}$$

In Example 1, note that we combined the steps of multiplying numerators and denominators and factoring the polynomials. Also note that we left the final answer in factored form. Either $\dfrac{1}{y(x - 2)}$ or $\dfrac{1}{xy - 2y}$ would be an acceptable answer.

EXAMPLE   2

Multiply and simplify $\dfrac{x^2 - x}{x + 5} \cdot \dfrac{x^2 + 5x + 4}{x^4 - x^2}$.

Solution

$$\frac{x^2 - x}{x + 5} \cdot \frac{x^2 + 5x + 4}{x^4 - x^2} = \frac{x(x - 1)}{x + 5} \cdot \frac{(x + 1)(x + 4)}{x^2(x - 1)(x + 1)}$$

$$= \frac{\cancel{x}(\cancel{x - 1})(\cancel{x + 1})(x + 4)}{(x + 5)(\underset{x}{\cancel{x^2}})(\cancel{x - 1})(\cancel{x + 1})} = \frac{x + 4}{x(x + 5)}$$

EXAMPLE 3

Multiply and simplify $\dfrac{6n^2 + 7n - 5}{n^2 + 2n - 24} \cdot \dfrac{4n^2 + 21n - 18}{12n^2 + 11n - 15}$.

Solution

$$\dfrac{6n^2 + 7n - 5}{n^2 + 2n - 24} \cdot \dfrac{4n^2 + 21n - 18}{12n^2 + 11n - 15}$$

$$= \dfrac{(3n + 5)(2n - 1)(4n - 3)(n + 6)}{(n + 6)(n - 4)(3n + 5)(4n - 3)} = \dfrac{2n - 1}{n - 4}$$ ∎

■ Dividing Rational Expressions

We define division of rational numbers in common fraction form as follows:

Definition 4.2

If a, b, c, and d are integers, and b, c, and d are not equal to zero, then

$$\dfrac{a}{b} \div \dfrac{c}{d} = \dfrac{a}{b} \cdot \dfrac{d}{c} = \dfrac{ad}{bc}$$

Definition 4.2 states that to divide two rational numbers in fraction form, we **invert the divisor and multiply.** We call the numbers $\dfrac{c}{d}$ and $\dfrac{d}{c}$ "reciprocals" or "multiplicative inverses" of each other, because their product is 1. Thus we can describe division by saying "to divide by a fraction, multiply by its reciprocal." The following examples demonstrate the use of Definition 4.2.

$$\dfrac{7}{8} \div \dfrac{5}{6} = \dfrac{7}{8} \cdot \dfrac{\overset{3}{\cancel{6}}}{5} = \dfrac{21}{20}, \qquad \dfrac{-5}{9} \div \dfrac{15}{18} = -\dfrac{\cancel{5}}{\cancel{9}} \cdot \dfrac{\overset{2}{\cancel{18}}}{\cancel{15}} = -\dfrac{2}{3}$$

$$\dfrac{14}{-19} \div \dfrac{21}{-38} = \left(-\dfrac{14}{19}\right) \div \left(-\dfrac{21}{38}\right) = \left(-\dfrac{\cancel{14}}{\cancel{19}}\right)\left(-\dfrac{\overset{2}{\cancel{38}}}{\cancel{21}}\right) = \dfrac{4}{3}$$

We define division of algebraic rational expressions in the same way that we define division of rational numbers. That is, the quotient of two rational expressions is the product we obtain when we multiply the first expression by the reciprocal of the second. Consider the following examples.

EXAMPLE 4

Divide and simplify $\dfrac{16x^2y}{24xy^3} \div \dfrac{9xy}{8x^2y^2}$.

Solution

$$\dfrac{16x^2y}{24xy^3} \div \dfrac{9xy}{8x^2y^2} = \dfrac{16x^2y}{24xy^3} \cdot \dfrac{8x^2y^2}{9xy} = \dfrac{16 \cdot 8 \cdot \overset{x^2}{\cancel{x^4}} \cdot \cancel{y^3}}{\underset{3}{\cancel{24}} \cdot 9 \cdot \cancel{x^2} \cdot \underset{y}{\cancel{y^4}}} = \dfrac{16x^2}{27y}$$ ∎

EXAMPLE 5

Divide and simplify $\dfrac{3a^2 + 12}{3a^2 - 15a} \div \dfrac{a^4 - 16}{a^2 - 3a - 10}$.

Solution

$$\frac{3a^2 + 12}{3a^2 - 15a} \div \frac{a^4 - 16}{a^2 - 3a - 10} = \frac{3a^2 + 12}{3a^2 - 15a} \cdot \frac{a^2 - 3a - 10}{a^4 - 16}$$

$$= \frac{3(a^2 + 4)}{3a(a - 5)} \cdot \frac{(a - 5)(a + 2)}{(a^2 + 4)(a + 2)(a - 2)}$$

$$= \frac{\overset{1}{\cancel{3}}(\cancel{a^2 + 4})(\cancel{a - 5})(\cancel{a + 2})}{\underset{1}{\cancel{3}}a(\cancel{a - 5})(\cancel{a^2 + 4})(\cancel{a + 2})(a - 2)}$$

$$= \frac{1}{a(a - 2)} \qquad \blacksquare$$

EXAMPLE 6

Divide and simplify $\dfrac{28t^3 - 51t^2 - 27t}{49t^2 + 42t + 9} \div (4t - 9)$.

Solution

$$\frac{28t^3 - 51t^2 - 27t}{49t^2 + 42t + 9} \div \frac{4t - 9}{1} = \frac{28t^3 - 51t^2 - 27t}{49t^2 + 42t + 9} \cdot \frac{1}{4t - 9}$$

$$= \frac{t(7t + 3)(4t - 9)}{(7t + 3)(7t + 3)} \cdot \frac{1}{(4t - 9)}$$

$$= \frac{t(\cancel{7t + 3})(\cancel{4t - 9})}{(\cancel{7t + 3})(7t + 3)(\cancel{4t - 9})}$$

$$= \frac{t}{7t + 3} \qquad \blacksquare$$

In a problem such as Example 6, it may be helpful to write the divisor with a denominator of 1. Thus we write $4t - 9$ as $\dfrac{4t - 9}{1}$; its reciprocal is obviously $\dfrac{1}{4t - 9}$.

Let's consider one final example that involves both multiplication and division.

EXAMPLE 7

Perform the indicated operations and simplify.

$$\frac{x^2 + 5x}{3x^2 - 4x - 20} \cdot \frac{x^2y + y}{2x^2 + 11x + 5} \div \frac{xy^2}{6x^2 - 17x - 10}$$

Solution

$$\frac{x^2 + 5x}{3x^2 - 4x - 20} \cdot \frac{x^2y + y}{2x^2 + 11x + 5} \div \frac{xy^2}{6x^2 - 17x - 10}$$

$$= \frac{x^2 + 5x}{3x^2 - 4x - 20} \cdot \frac{x^2y + y}{2x^2 + 11x + 5} \cdot \frac{6x^2 - 17x - 10}{xy^2}$$

$$= \frac{x(x + 5)}{(3x - 10)(x + 2)} \cdot \frac{y(x^2 + 1)}{(2x + 1)(x + 5)} \cdot \frac{(2x + 1)(3x - 10)}{xy^2}$$

$$= \frac{x(x + 5)(y)(x^2 + 1)(2x + 1)(3x - 10)}{(3x - 10)(x + 2)(2x + 1)(x + 5)(x)(y^2)} = \frac{x^2 + 1}{y(x + 2)}$$

■

Problem Set 4.2

For Problems 1–12, perform the indicated operations involving rational numbers. Express final answers in reduced form.

1. $\dfrac{7}{12} \cdot \dfrac{6}{35}$

2. $\dfrac{5}{8} \cdot \dfrac{12}{20}$

3. $\dfrac{-4}{9} \cdot \dfrac{18}{30}$

4. $\dfrac{-6}{9} \cdot \dfrac{36}{48}$

5. $\dfrac{3}{-8} \cdot \dfrac{-6}{12}$

6. $\dfrac{-12}{16} \cdot \dfrac{18}{-32}$

7. $\left(-\dfrac{5}{7}\right) \div \dfrac{6}{7}$

8. $\left(-\dfrac{5}{9}\right) \div \dfrac{10}{3}$

9. $\dfrac{-9}{5} \div \dfrac{27}{10}$

10. $\dfrac{4}{7} \div \dfrac{16}{-21}$

11. $\dfrac{4}{9} \cdot \dfrac{6}{11} \div \dfrac{4}{15}$

12. $\dfrac{2}{3} \cdot \dfrac{6}{7} \div \dfrac{8}{3}$

For Problems 13–50, perform the indicated operations involving rational expressions. Express final answers in simplest form.

13. $\dfrac{6xy}{9y^4} \cdot \dfrac{30x^3y}{-48x}$

14. $\dfrac{-14xy^4}{18y^2} \cdot \dfrac{24x^2y^3}{35y^2}$

15. $\dfrac{5a^2b^2}{11ab} \cdot \dfrac{22a^3}{15ab^2}$

16. $\dfrac{10a^2}{5b^2} \cdot \dfrac{15b^3}{2a^4}$

17. $\dfrac{5xy}{8y^2} \cdot \dfrac{18x^2y}{15}$

18. $\dfrac{4x^2}{5y^2} \cdot \dfrac{15xy}{24x^2y^2}$

19. $\dfrac{5x^4}{12x^2y^3} \div \dfrac{9}{5xy}$

20. $\dfrac{7x^2y}{9xy^3} \div \dfrac{3x^4}{2x^2y^2}$

21. $\dfrac{9a^2c}{12bc^2} \div \dfrac{21ab}{14c^3}$

22. $\dfrac{3ab^3}{4c} \div \dfrac{21ac}{12bc^3}$

23. $\dfrac{9x^2y^3}{14x} \cdot \dfrac{21y}{15xy^2} \cdot \dfrac{10x}{12y^3}$

24. $\dfrac{5xy}{7a} \cdot \dfrac{14a^2}{15x} \cdot \dfrac{3a}{8y}$

25. $\dfrac{3x + 6}{5y} \cdot \dfrac{x^2 + 4}{x^2 + 10x + 16}$

26. $\dfrac{5xy}{x + 6} \cdot \dfrac{x^2 - 36}{x^2 - 6x}$

27. $\dfrac{5a^2 + 20a}{a^3 - 2a^2} \cdot \dfrac{a^2 - a - 12}{a^2 - 16}$

28. $\dfrac{2a^2 + 6}{a^2 - a} \cdot \dfrac{a^3 - a^2}{8a - 4}$

29. $\dfrac{3n^2 + 15n - 18}{3n^2 + 10n - 48} \cdot \dfrac{6n^2 - n - 40}{4n^2 + 6n - 10}$

30. $\dfrac{6n^2 + 11n - 10}{3n^2 + 19n - 14} \cdot \dfrac{2n^2 + 6n - 56}{2n^2 - 3n - 20}$

31. $\dfrac{9y^2}{x^2 + 12x + 36} \div \dfrac{12y}{x^2 + 6x}$

32. $\dfrac{7xy}{x^2 - 4x + 4} \div \dfrac{14y}{x^2 - 4}$

33. $\dfrac{x^2 - 4xy + 4y^2}{7xy^2} \div \dfrac{4x^2 - 3xy - 10y^2}{20x^2y + 25xy^2}$

34. $\dfrac{x^2 + 5xy - 6y^2}{xy^2 - y^3} \cdot \dfrac{2x^2 + 15xy + 18y^2}{xy + 4y^2}$

35. $\dfrac{5 - 14n - 3n^2}{1 - 2n - 3n^2} \cdot \dfrac{9 + 7n - 2n^2}{27 - 15n + 2n^2}$

36. $\dfrac{6 - n - 2n^2}{12 - 11n + 2n^2} \cdot \dfrac{24 - 26n + 5n^2}{2 + 3n + n^2}$

37. $\dfrac{3x^4 + 2x^2 - 1}{3x^4 + 14x^2 - 5} \cdot \dfrac{x^4 - 2x^2 - 35}{x^4 - 17x^2 + 70}$

38. $\dfrac{2x^4 + x^2 - 3}{2x^4 + 5x^2 + 2} \cdot \dfrac{3x^4 + 10x^2 + 8}{3x^4 + x^2 - 4}$

39. $\dfrac{3x^2 - 20x + 25}{2x^2 - 7x - 15} \div \dfrac{9x^2 - 3x - 20}{12x^2 + 28x + 15}$

40. $\dfrac{21t^2 + t - 2}{2t^2 - 17t - 9} \div \dfrac{12t^2 - 5t - 3}{8t^2 - 2t - 3}$

41. $\dfrac{10t^3 + 25t}{20t + 10} \cdot \dfrac{2t^2 - t - 1}{t^5 - t}$

42. $\dfrac{t^4 - 81}{t^2 - 6t + 9} \cdot \dfrac{6t^2 - 11t - 21}{5t^2 + 8t - 21}$

43. $\dfrac{4t^2 + t - 5}{t^3 - t^2} \cdot \dfrac{t^4 + 6t^3}{16t^2 + 40t + 25}$

44. $\dfrac{9n^2 - 12n + 4}{n^2 - 4n - 32} \cdot \dfrac{n^2 + 4n}{3n^3 - 2n^2}$

45. $\dfrac{nr + 3n + 2r + 6}{nr + 3n - 3r - 9} \cdot \dfrac{n^2 - 9}{n^3 - 4n}$

46. $\dfrac{xy + xc + ay + ac}{xy - 2xc + ay - 2ac} \cdot \dfrac{2x^3 - 8x}{12x^3 + 20x^2 - 8x}$

47. $\dfrac{x^2 - x}{4y} \cdot \dfrac{10xy^2}{2x - 2} \div \dfrac{3x^2 + 3x}{15x^2y^2}$

48. $\dfrac{4xy^2}{7x} \cdot \dfrac{14x^3y}{12y} \div \dfrac{7y}{9x^3}$

49. $\dfrac{a^2 - 4ab + 4b^2}{6a^2 - 4ab} \cdot \dfrac{3a^2 + 5ab - 2b^2}{6a^2 + ab - b^2} \div \dfrac{a^2 - 4b^2}{8a + 4b}$

50. $\dfrac{2x^2 + 3x}{2x^3 - 10x^2} \cdot \dfrac{x^2 - 8x + 15}{3x^3 - 27x} \div \dfrac{14x + 21}{x^2 - 6x - 27}$

■ ■ ■ **THOUGHTS INTO WORDS**

51. Explain in your own words how to divide two rational expressions.

52. Suppose that your friend missed class the day the material in this section was discussed. How could you draw on her background in arithmetic to explain to her how to multiply and divide rational expressions?

53. Give a step-by-step description of how to do the following multiplication problem.

$$\dfrac{x^2 + 5x + 6}{x^2 - 2x - 8} \cdot \dfrac{x^2 - 16}{16 - x^2}$$

4.3 Adding and Subtracting Rational Expressions

We can define addition and subtraction of rational numbers as follows:

Definition 4.3

If a, b, and c are integers, and b is not zero, then

$$\dfrac{a}{b} + \dfrac{c}{b} = \dfrac{a + c}{b} \qquad \text{Addition}$$

$$\dfrac{a}{b} - \dfrac{c}{b} = \dfrac{a - c}{b} \qquad \text{Subtraction}$$

We can add or subtract rational numbers with a common denominator by adding or subtracting the numerators and placing the result over the common denominator. The following examples illustrate Definition 4.3.

$$\frac{2}{9} + \frac{3}{9} = \frac{2+3}{9} = \frac{5}{9}$$

$$\frac{7}{8} - \frac{3}{8} = \frac{7-3}{8} = \frac{4}{8} = \frac{1}{2} \qquad \text{Don't forget to reduce!}$$

$$\frac{4}{6} + \frac{-5}{6} = \frac{4+(-5)}{6} = \frac{-1}{6} = -\frac{1}{6}$$

$$\frac{7}{10} + \frac{4}{-10} = \frac{7}{10} + \frac{-4}{10} = \frac{7+(-4)}{10} = \frac{3}{10}$$

We use this same *common denominator* approach when adding or subtracting rational expressions, as in these next examples.

$$\frac{3}{x} + \frac{9}{x} = \frac{3+9}{x} = \frac{12}{x}$$

$$\frac{8}{x-2} - \frac{3}{x-2} = \frac{8-3}{x-2} = \frac{5}{x-2}$$

$$\frac{9}{4y} + \frac{5}{4y} = \frac{9+5}{4y} = \frac{14}{4y} = \frac{7}{2y} \qquad \text{Don't forget to simplify the final answer!}$$

$$\frac{n^2}{n-1} - \frac{1}{n-1} = \frac{n^2-1}{n-1} = \frac{(n+1)(n-1)}{n-1} = n+1$$

$$\frac{6a^2}{2a+1} + \frac{13a+5}{2a+1} = \frac{6a^2+13a+5}{2a+1} = \frac{(2a+1)(3a+5)}{2a+1} = 3a+5$$

In each of the previous examples that involve rational expressions, we should technically restrict the variables to exclude division by zero. For example, $\frac{3}{x} + \frac{9}{x} = \frac{12}{x}$ is true for all real number values for x, except $x = 0$. Likewise, $\frac{8}{x-2} - \frac{3}{x-2} = \frac{5}{x-2}$ as long as x does not equal 2. Rather than taking the time and space to write down restrictions for each problem, we will merely assume that such restrictions exist.

If rational numbers that do not have a common denominator are to be added or subtracted, then we apply the fundamental principle of fractions $\left(\dfrac{a}{b} = \dfrac{ak}{bk}\right)$ **to obtain equivalent fractions with a common denominator.** Equivalent fractions are fractions such as $\dfrac{1}{2}$ and $\dfrac{2}{4}$ that name the same number. Consider the following example.

$$\frac{1}{2} + \frac{1}{3} = \frac{3}{6} + \frac{2}{6} = \frac{3+2}{6} = \frac{5}{6}$$

$$\left(\begin{array}{l}\dfrac{1}{2} \text{ and } \dfrac{3}{6} \\ \text{are equivalent} \\ \text{fractions.}\end{array}\right) \quad \left(\begin{array}{l}\dfrac{1}{3} \text{ and } \dfrac{2}{6} \\ \text{are equivalent} \\ \text{fractions.}\end{array}\right)$$

Note that we chose 6 as our common denominator, and 6 is the **least common multiple** of the original denominators 2 and 3. (The least common multiple of a set of whole numbers is the smallest nonzero whole number divisible by each of the numbers.) In general, we use the least common multiple of the denominators of the fractions to be added or subtracted as a **least common denominator** (LCD).

A least common denominator may be found by inspection or by using the prime-factored forms of the numbers. Let's consider some examples and use each of these techniques.

EXAMPLE 1   Subtract $\dfrac{5}{6} - \dfrac{3}{8}$.

Solution

By inspection, we can see that the LCD is 24. Thus both fractions can be changed to equivalent fractions, each with a denominator of 24.

$$\frac{5}{6} - \frac{3}{8} = \left(\frac{5}{6}\right)\left(\frac{4}{4}\right) - \left(\frac{3}{8}\right)\left(\frac{3}{3}\right) = \frac{20}{24} - \frac{9}{24} = \frac{11}{24}$$

$$\uparrow \qquad\qquad \uparrow$$

$$\text{Form of 1} \quad \text{Form of 1}$$

■

In Example 1, note that the fundamental principle of fractions, $\dfrac{a}{b} = \dfrac{a \cdot k}{b \cdot k}$, can be written as $\dfrac{a}{b} = \left(\dfrac{a}{b}\right)\left(\dfrac{k}{k}\right)$. This latter form emphasizes the fact that 1 is the multiplication identity element.

EXAMPLE 2   Perform the indicated operations: $\dfrac{3}{5} + \dfrac{1}{6} - \dfrac{13}{15}$

Solution

Again by inspection, we can determine that the LCD is 30. Thus we can proceed as follows:

$$\frac{3}{5} + \frac{1}{6} - \frac{13}{15} = \left(\frac{3}{5}\right)\left(\frac{6}{6}\right) + \left(\frac{1}{6}\right)\left(\frac{5}{5}\right) - \left(\frac{13}{15}\right)\left(\frac{2}{2}\right)$$

$$= \frac{18}{30} + \frac{5}{30} - \frac{26}{30} = \frac{18 + 5 - 26}{30}$$

$$= \frac{-3}{30} = -\frac{1}{10} \qquad \text{Don't forget to reduce!} \qquad \blacksquare$$

EXAMPLE 3   Add $\dfrac{7}{18} + \dfrac{11}{24}$.

Solution

Let's use the prime-factored forms of the denominators to help find the LCD.

$$18 = 2 \cdot 3 \cdot 3 \qquad 24 = 2 \cdot 2 \cdot 2 \cdot 3$$

The LCD must contain three factors of 2 because 24 contains three 2s. The LCD must also contain two factors of 3 because 18 has two 3s. Thus the LCD $= 2 \cdot 2 \cdot 2 \cdot 3 \cdot 3 = 72$. Now we can proceed as usual.

$$\frac{7}{18} + \frac{11}{24} = \left(\frac{7}{18}\right)\left(\frac{4}{4}\right) + \left(\frac{11}{24}\right)\left(\frac{3}{3}\right) = \frac{28}{72} + \frac{33}{72} = \frac{61}{72} \qquad \blacksquare$$

To add and subtract rational expressions with different denominators, follow the same basic routine that you follow when you add or subtract rational numbers with different denominators. Study the following examples carefully and note the similarity to our previous work with rational numbers.

EXAMPLE 4   Add $\dfrac{x + 2}{4} + \dfrac{3x + 1}{3}$.

Solution

By inspection, we see that the LCD is 12.

$$\frac{x + 2}{4} + \frac{3x + 1}{3} = \left(\frac{x + 2}{4}\right)\left(\frac{3}{3}\right) + \left(\frac{3x + 1}{3}\right)\left(\frac{4}{4}\right)$$

$$= \frac{3(x + 2)}{12} + \frac{4(3x + 1)}{12}$$

$$= \frac{3(x + 2) + 4(3x + 1)}{12}$$

$$= \frac{3x + 6 + 12x + 4}{12}$$

$$= \frac{15x + 10}{12}$$ ∎

Note the final result in Example 4. The numerator, $15x + 10$, could be factored as $5(3x + 2)$. However, because this produces no common factors with the denominator, the fraction cannot be simplified. Thus the final answer can be left as $\frac{15x + 10}{12}$. It would also be acceptable to express it as $\frac{5(3x + 2)}{12}$.

E X A M P L E   5   Subtract $\dfrac{a - 2}{2} - \dfrac{a - 6}{6}$.

Solution

By inspection, we see that the LCD is 6.

$$\frac{a - 2}{2} - \frac{a - 6}{6} = \left(\frac{a - 2}{2}\right)\left(\frac{3}{3}\right) - \frac{a - 6}{6}$$

$$= \frac{3(a - 2)}{6} - \frac{a - 6}{6}$$

$$= \frac{3(a - 2) - (a - 6)}{6}$$ Be careful with this sign as you move to the next step!

$$= \frac{3a - 6 - a + 6}{6}$$

$$= \frac{2a}{6} = \frac{a}{3}$$ Don't forget to simplify.   ∎

E X A M P L E   6   Perform the indicated operations: $\dfrac{x + 3}{10} + \dfrac{2x + 1}{15} - \dfrac{x - 2}{18}$.

Solution

If you cannot determine the LCD by inspection, then use the prime-factored forms of the denominators.

$$10 = 2 \cdot 5 \qquad 15 = 3 \cdot 5 \qquad 18 = 2 \cdot 3 \cdot 3$$

The LCD must contain one factor of 2, two factors of 3, and one factor of 5. Thus the LCD is $2 \cdot 3 \cdot 3 \cdot 5 = 90$.

$$\frac{x + 3}{10} + \frac{2x + 1}{15} - \frac{x - 2}{18} = \left(\frac{x + 3}{10}\right)\left(\frac{9}{9}\right) + \left(\frac{2x + 1}{15}\right)\left(\frac{6}{6}\right) - \left(\frac{x - 2}{18}\right)\left(\frac{5}{5}\right)$$

$$= \frac{9(x + 3)}{90} + \frac{6(2x + 1)}{90} - \frac{5(x - 2)}{90}$$

$$= \frac{9(x + 3) + 6(2x + 1) - 5(x - 2)}{90}$$

$$= \frac{9x + 27 + 12x + 6 - 5x + 10}{90}$$

$$= \frac{16x + 43}{90} \qquad \blacksquare$$

A denominator that contains variables does not create any serious difficulties; our approach remains basically the same.

EXAMPLE 7   Add $\dfrac{3}{2x} + \dfrac{5}{3y}$.

Solution

Using an LCD of $6xy$, we can proceed as follows:

$$\frac{3}{2x} + \frac{5}{3y} = \left(\frac{3}{2x}\right)\left(\frac{3y}{3y}\right) + \left(\frac{5}{3y}\right)\left(\frac{2x}{2x}\right)$$

$$= \frac{9y}{6xy} + \frac{10x}{6xy}$$

$$= \frac{9y + 10x}{6xy} \qquad \blacksquare$$

EXAMPLE 8   Subtract $\dfrac{7}{12ab} - \dfrac{11}{15a^2}$.

Solution

We can prime-factor the numerical coefficients of the denominators to help find the LCD.

$$\left. \begin{array}{l} 12ab = 2 \cdot 2 \cdot 3 \cdot a \cdot b \\[2mm] 15a^2 = 3 \cdot 5 \cdot a^2 \end{array} \right\} \longrightarrow \text{LCD} = 2 \cdot 2 \cdot 3 \cdot 5 \cdot a^2 \cdot b = 60a^2b$$

$$\frac{7}{12ab} - \frac{11}{15a^2} = \left(\frac{7}{12ab}\right)\left(\frac{5a}{5a}\right) - \left(\frac{11}{15a^2}\right)\left(\frac{4b}{4b}\right)$$

$$= \frac{35a}{60a^2b} - \frac{44b}{60a^2b}$$

$$= \frac{35a - 44b}{60a^2b}$$

■

E X A M P L E   9

Add $\dfrac{x}{x-3} + \dfrac{4}{x}$.

Solution

By inspection, the LCD is $x(x-3)$.

$$\frac{x}{x-3} + \frac{4}{x} = \left(\frac{x}{x-3}\right)\left(\frac{x}{x}\right) + \left(\frac{4}{x}\right)\left(\frac{x-3}{x-3}\right)$$

$$= \frac{x^2}{x(x-3)} + \frac{4(x-3)}{x(x-3)}$$

$$= \frac{x^2 + 4(x-3)}{x(x-3)}$$

$$= \frac{x^2 + 4x - 12}{x(x-3)} \qquad \text{or} \qquad \frac{(x+6)(x-2)}{x(x-3)}$$

■

E X A M P L E   1 0

Subtract $\dfrac{2x}{x+1} - 3$.

Solution

$$\frac{2x}{x+1} - 3 = \frac{2x}{x+1} - 3\left(\frac{x+1}{x+1}\right)$$

$$= \frac{2x}{x+1} - \frac{3(x+1)}{x+1}$$

$$= \frac{2x - 3(x+1)}{x+1}$$

$$= \frac{2x - 3x - 3}{x+1}$$

$$= \frac{-x - 3}{x+1}$$

■

Problem Set 4.3

For Problems 1–12, perform the indicated operations involving rational numbers. Be sure to express your answers in reduced form.

1. $\dfrac{1}{4} + \dfrac{5}{6}$

2. $\dfrac{3}{5} + \dfrac{1}{6}$

3. $\dfrac{7}{8} - \dfrac{3}{5}$

4. $\dfrac{7}{9} - \dfrac{1}{6}$

5. $\dfrac{6}{5} + \dfrac{1}{-4}$

6. $\dfrac{7}{8} + \dfrac{5}{-12}$

7. $\dfrac{8}{15} + \dfrac{3}{25}$

8. $\dfrac{5}{9} - \dfrac{11}{12}$

9. $\dfrac{1}{5} + \dfrac{5}{6} - \dfrac{7}{15}$

10. $\dfrac{2}{3} - \dfrac{7}{8} + \dfrac{1}{4}$

11. $\dfrac{1}{3} - \dfrac{1}{4} - \dfrac{3}{14}$

12. $\dfrac{5}{6} - \dfrac{7}{9} - \dfrac{3}{10}$

For Problems 13–66, add or subtract the rational expressions as indicated. Be sure to express your answers in simplest form.

13. $\dfrac{2x}{x-1} + \dfrac{4}{x-1}$

14. $\dfrac{3x}{2x+1} - \dfrac{5}{2x+1}$

15. $\dfrac{4a}{a+2} + \dfrac{8}{a+2}$

16. $\dfrac{6a}{a-3} - \dfrac{18}{a-3}$

17. $\dfrac{3(y-2)}{7y} + \dfrac{4(y-1)}{7y}$

18. $\dfrac{2x-1}{4x^2} + \dfrac{3(x-2)}{4x^2}$

19. $\dfrac{x-1}{2} + \dfrac{x+3}{3}$

20. $\dfrac{x-2}{4} + \dfrac{x+6}{5}$

21. $\dfrac{2a-1}{4} + \dfrac{3a+2}{6}$

22. $\dfrac{a-4}{6} + \dfrac{4a-1}{8}$

23. $\dfrac{n+2}{6} - \dfrac{n-4}{9}$

24. $\dfrac{2n+1}{9} - \dfrac{n+3}{12}$

25. $\dfrac{3x-1}{3} - \dfrac{5x+2}{5}$

26. $\dfrac{4x-3}{6} - \dfrac{8x-2}{12}$

27. $\dfrac{x-2}{5} - \dfrac{x+3}{6} + \dfrac{x+1}{15}$

28. $\dfrac{x+1}{4} + \dfrac{x-3}{6} - \dfrac{x-2}{8}$

29. $\dfrac{3}{8x} + \dfrac{7}{10x}$

30. $\dfrac{5}{6x} - \dfrac{3}{10x}$

31. $\dfrac{5}{7x} - \dfrac{11}{4y}$

32. $\dfrac{5}{12x} - \dfrac{9}{8y}$

33. $\dfrac{4}{3x} + \dfrac{5}{4y} - 1$

34. $\dfrac{7}{3x} - \dfrac{8}{7y} - 2$

35. $\dfrac{7}{10x^2} + \dfrac{11}{15x}$

36. $\dfrac{7}{12a^2} - \dfrac{5}{16a}$

37. $\dfrac{10}{7n} - \dfrac{12}{4n^2}$

38. $\dfrac{6}{8n^2} - \dfrac{3}{5n}$

39. $\dfrac{3}{n^2} - \dfrac{2}{5n} + \dfrac{4}{3}$

40. $\dfrac{1}{n^2} + \dfrac{3}{4n} - \dfrac{5}{6}$

41. $\dfrac{3}{x} - \dfrac{5}{3x^2} - \dfrac{7}{6x}$

42. $\dfrac{7}{3x^2} - \dfrac{9}{4x} - \dfrac{5}{2x}$

43. $\dfrac{6}{5t^2} - \dfrac{4}{7t^3} + \dfrac{9}{5t^3}$

44. $\dfrac{5}{7t} + \dfrac{3}{4t^2} + \dfrac{1}{14t}$

45. $\dfrac{5b}{24a^2} - \dfrac{11a}{32b}$

46. $\dfrac{9}{14x^2y} - \dfrac{4x}{7y^2}$

47. $\dfrac{7}{9xy^3} - \dfrac{4}{3x} + \dfrac{5}{2y^2}$

48. $\dfrac{7}{16a^2b} + \dfrac{3a}{20b^2}$

49. $\dfrac{2x}{x-1} + \dfrac{3}{x}$

50. $\dfrac{3x}{x-4} - \dfrac{2}{x}$

51. $\dfrac{a-2}{a} - \dfrac{3}{a+4}$

52. $\dfrac{a+1}{a} - \dfrac{2}{a+1}$

53. $\dfrac{-3}{4n+5} - \dfrac{8}{3n+5}$

54. $\dfrac{-2}{n-6} - \dfrac{6}{2n+3}$

55. $\dfrac{-1}{x+4} + \dfrac{4}{7x-1}$

56. $\dfrac{-3}{4x+3} + \dfrac{5}{2x-5}$

57. $\dfrac{7}{3x-5} - \dfrac{5}{2x+7}$

58. $\dfrac{5}{x-1} - \dfrac{3}{2x-3}$

59. $\dfrac{5}{3x-2} + \dfrac{6}{4x+5}$

60. $\dfrac{3}{2x+1} + \dfrac{2}{3x+4}$

61. $\dfrac{3x}{2x+5} + 1$

62. $2 + \dfrac{4x}{3x-1}$

63. $\dfrac{4x}{x-5} - 3$

64. $\dfrac{7x}{x+4} - 2$

65. $-1 - \dfrac{3}{2x + 1}$ **66.** $-2 - \dfrac{5}{4x - 3}$

67. Recall that the indicated quotient of a polynomial and its opposite is -1. For example, $\dfrac{x - 2}{2 - x}$ simplifies to -1. Keep this idea in mind as you add or subtract the following rational expressions.

(a) $\dfrac{1}{x - 1} - \dfrac{x}{x - 1}$ **(b)** $\dfrac{3}{2x - 3} - \dfrac{2x}{2x - 3}$

(c) $\dfrac{4}{x - 4} - \dfrac{x}{x - 4} + 1$ **(d)** $-1 + \dfrac{2}{x - 2} - \dfrac{x}{x - 2}$

68. Consider the addition problem $\dfrac{8}{x - 2} + \dfrac{5}{2 - x}$. Note that the denominators are opposites of each other.

If the property $\dfrac{a}{-b} = -\dfrac{a}{b}$ is applied to the second fraction, we have $\dfrac{5}{2 - x} = -\dfrac{5}{x - 2}$. Thus we proceed as follows:

$$\dfrac{8}{x - 2} + \dfrac{5}{2 - x} = \dfrac{8}{x - 2} - \dfrac{5}{x - 2} = \dfrac{8 - 5}{x - 2} = \dfrac{3}{x - 2}$$

Use this approach to do the following problems.

(a) $\dfrac{7}{x - 1} + \dfrac{2}{1 - x}$ **(b)** $\dfrac{5}{2x - 1} + \dfrac{8}{1 - 2x}$

(c) $\dfrac{4}{a - 3} - \dfrac{1}{3 - a}$ **(d)** $\dfrac{10}{a - 9} - \dfrac{5}{9 - a}$

(e) $\dfrac{x^2}{x - 1} - \dfrac{2x - 3}{1 - x}$ **(f)** $\dfrac{x^2}{x - 4} - \dfrac{3x - 28}{4 - x}$

■ ■ ■ THOUGHTS INTO WORDS

69. What is the difference between the concept of least common multiple and the concept of least common denominator?

70. A classmate tells you that she finds the least common multiple of two counting numbers by listing the multiples of each number and then choosing the smallest number that appears in both lists. Is this a correct procedure? What is the weakness of this procedure?

71. For which real numbers does $\dfrac{x}{x - 3} + \dfrac{4}{x}$ equal $\dfrac{(x + 6)(x - 2)}{x(x - 3)}$? Explain your answer.

72. Suppose that your friend does an addition problem as follows:

$$\dfrac{5}{8} + \dfrac{7}{12} = \dfrac{5(12) + 8(7)}{8(12)} = \dfrac{60 + 56}{96} = \dfrac{116}{96} = \dfrac{29}{24}$$

Is this answer correct? If not, what advice would you offer your friend?

4.4
More on Rational Expressions and Complex Fractions

In this section, we expand our work with adding and subtracting rational expressions, and we discuss the process of simplifying complex fractions. Before we begin, however, this seems like an appropriate time to offer a bit of advice regarding your study of algebra. Success in algebra depends on having a good understanding of the concepts as well as on being able to perform the various computations. As for the computational work, you should adopt a carefully organized format that shows as many steps as you need in order to minimize the chances of making careless errors. Don't be eager to find shortcuts for certain computations before you have a thorough understanding of the steps involved in the process. This advice is especially appropriate at the beginning of this section.

Study Examples 1–4 very carefully. Note that the same basic procedure is followed in solving each problem:

Step 1 Factor the denominators.

Step 2 Find the LCD.

Step 3 Change each fraction to an equivalent fraction that has the LCD as its denominator.

Step 4 Combine the numerators and place over the LCD.

Step 5 Simplify by performing the addition or subtraction.

Step 6 Look for ways to reduce the resulting fraction.

EXAMPLE 1 Add $\dfrac{8}{x^2 - 4x} + \dfrac{2}{x}$.

Solution

$$\frac{8}{x^2 - 4x} + \frac{2}{x} = \frac{8}{x(x - 4)} + \frac{2}{x}$$
Factor the denominators.

The LCD is $x(x - 4)$.
Find the LCD.

$$= \frac{8}{x(x - 4)} + \left(\frac{2}{x}\right)\left(\frac{x - 4}{x - 4}\right)$$
Change each fraction to an equivalent fraction that has the LCD as its denominator.

$$= \frac{8 + 2(x - 4)}{x(x - 4)}$$
Combine numerators and place over the LCD.

$$= \frac{8 + 2x - 8}{x(x - 4)}$$
Simplify performing the addition or subtraction.

$$= \frac{2x}{x(x - 4)}$$

$$= \frac{2}{x - 4}$$
Reduce. ∎

EXAMPLE 2   Subtract $\dfrac{a}{a^2 - 4} - \dfrac{3}{a + 2}$.

Solution

$$\frac{a}{a^2 - 4} - \frac{3}{a + 2} = \frac{a}{(a + 2)(a - 2)} - \frac{3}{a + 2} \qquad \text{Factor the denominators.}$$

The LCD is $(a + 2)(a - 2)$.   Find the LCD.

$$= \frac{a}{(a + 2)(a - 2)} - \left(\frac{3}{a + 2}\right)\left(\frac{a - 2}{a - 2}\right)$$

Change each fraction to an equivalent fraction that has the LCD as its denominator.

$$= \frac{a - 3(a - 2)}{(a + 2)(a - 2)}$$

Combine numerators and place over the LCD.

$$= \frac{a - 3a + 6}{(a + 2)(a - 2)}$$

Simplify performing the addition or subtraction.

$$= \frac{-2a + 6}{(a + 2)(a - 2)} \qquad \text{or} \qquad \frac{-2(a - 3)}{(a + 2)(a - 2)} \qquad \blacksquare$$

EXAMPLE 3   Add $\dfrac{3n}{n^2 + 6n + 5} + \dfrac{4}{n^2 - 7n - 8}$.

Solution

$$\frac{3n}{n^2 + 6n + 5} + \frac{4}{n^2 - 7n - 8}$$

$$= \frac{3n}{(n + 5)(n + 1)} + \frac{4}{(n - 8)(n + 1)} \qquad \text{Factor the denominators.}$$

The LCD is $(n + 5)(n + 1)(n - 8)$.   Find the LCD.

$$= \left(\frac{3n}{(n + 5)(n + 1)}\right)\left(\frac{n - 8}{n - 8}\right)$$

$$+ \left(\frac{4}{(n - 8)(n + 1)}\right)\left(\frac{n + 5}{n + 5}\right)$$

Change each fraction to an equivalent fraction that has the LCD as its denominator.

$$= \frac{3n(n - 8) + 4(n + 5)}{(n + 5)(n + 1)(n - 8)}$$

Combine numerators and place over the LCD.

$$= \frac{3n^2 - 24n + 4n + 20}{(n + 5)(n + 1)(n - 8)}$$

Simplify performing the addition or subtraction.

$$= \frac{3n^2 - 20n + 20}{(n + 5)(n + 1)(n - 8)} \qquad \blacksquare$$

EXAMPLE 4

Perform the indicated operations.

$$\frac{2x^2}{x^4 - 1} + \frac{x}{x^2 - 1} - \frac{1}{x - 1}$$

Solution

$$\frac{2x^2}{x^4 - 1} + \frac{x}{x^2 - 1} - \frac{1}{x - 1}$$

$$= \frac{2x^2}{(x^2 + 1)(x + 1)(x - 1)} + \frac{x}{(x + 1)(x - 1)} - \frac{1}{x - 1} \qquad \text{Factor the denominators.}$$

The LCD is $(x^2 + 1)(x + 1)(x - 1)$.   Find the LCD.

$$= \frac{2x^2}{(x^2 + 1)(x + 1)(x - 1)}$$

Change each fraction to an equivalent fraction that has the LCD as its denominator.

$$+ \left(\frac{x}{(x + 1)(x - 1)} \right)\left(\frac{x^2 + 1}{x^2 + 1} \right)$$

$$- \left(\frac{1}{x - 1} \right)\frac{(x^2 + 1)(x + 1)}{(x^2 + 1)(x + 1)}$$

$$= \frac{2x^2 + x(x^2 + 1) - (x^2 + 1)(x + 1)}{(x^2 + 1)(x + 1)(x - 1)}$$

Combine numerators and place over the LCD.

$$= \frac{2x^2 + x^3 + x - x^3 - x^2 - x - 1}{(x^2 + 1)(x + 1)(x - 1)}$$

Simplify performing the addition or subtraction.

$$= \frac{x^2 - 1}{(x^2 + 1)(x + 1)(x - 1)}$$

$$= \frac{(x + 1)(x - 1)}{(x^2 + 1)(x + 1)(x - 1)}$$

$$= \frac{1}{x^2 + 1} \qquad \text{Reduce.} \qquad \blacksquare$$

■ Complex Fractions

Complex fractions are fractional forms that contain rational numbers or rational expressions in the numerators and/or denominators. The following are examples of complex fractions.

$$\frac{\dfrac{4}{x}}{\dfrac{2}{xy}} \qquad \frac{\dfrac{1}{2} + \dfrac{3}{4}}{\dfrac{5}{6} - \dfrac{3}{8}} \qquad \frac{\dfrac{3}{x} + \dfrac{2}{y}}{\dfrac{5}{x} - \dfrac{6}{y^2}} \qquad \frac{\dfrac{1}{x} + \dfrac{1}{y}}{2} \qquad \frac{-3}{\dfrac{2}{x} - \dfrac{3}{y}}$$

It is often necessary to **simplify** a complex fraction. We will take each of these five examples and examine some techniques for simplifying complex fractions.

EXAMPLE 5

Simplify $\dfrac{\dfrac{4}{x}}{\dfrac{2}{xy}}$.

Solution

This type of problem is a simple division problem.

$$\frac{\dfrac{4}{x}}{\dfrac{2}{xy}} = \frac{4}{x} \div \frac{2}{xy}$$

$$= \frac{\overset{2}{\cancel{4}}}{\cancel{x}} \cdot \frac{xy}{2} = 2y \qquad \blacksquare$$

EXAMPLE 6

Simplify $\dfrac{\dfrac{1}{2} + \dfrac{3}{4}}{\dfrac{5}{6} - \dfrac{3}{8}}$.

Let's look at two possible ways to simplify such a problem.

Solution A

Here we will simplify the numerator by performing the addition and simplify the denominator by performing the subtraction. Then the problem is a simple division problem like Example 5.

$$\frac{\dfrac{1}{2} + \dfrac{3}{4}}{\dfrac{5}{6} - \dfrac{3}{8}} = \frac{\dfrac{2}{4} + \dfrac{3}{4}}{\dfrac{20}{24} - \dfrac{9}{24}}$$

$$= \frac{\dfrac{5}{4}}{\dfrac{11}{24}} = \frac{5}{\cancel{4}} \cdot \frac{\overset{6}{\cancel{24}}}{11}$$

$$= \frac{30}{11}$$

Solution B

Here we find the LCD of all four denominators (2, 4, 6, and 8). The LCD is 24. Use this LCD to multiply the entire complex fraction by a form of 1, specifically $\dfrac{24}{24}$.

$$\frac{\dfrac{1}{2}+\dfrac{3}{4}}{\dfrac{5}{6}-\dfrac{3}{8}} = \left(\frac{24}{24}\right)\left(\frac{\dfrac{1}{2}+\dfrac{3}{4}}{\dfrac{5}{6}-\dfrac{3}{8}}\right)$$

$$= \frac{24\left(\dfrac{1}{2}+\dfrac{3}{4}\right)}{24\left(\dfrac{5}{6}-\dfrac{3}{8}\right)}$$

$$= \frac{24\left(\dfrac{1}{2}\right)+24\left(\dfrac{3}{4}\right)}{24\left(\dfrac{5}{6}\right)-24\left(\dfrac{3}{8}\right)}$$

$$= \frac{12+18}{20-9} = \frac{30}{11}$$ ∎

E X A M P L E   7   Simplify $\dfrac{\dfrac{3}{x}+\dfrac{2}{y}}{\dfrac{5}{x}-\dfrac{6}{y^2}}$.

Solution A

Simplify the numerator and the denominator. Then the problem becomes a division problem.

$$\frac{\dfrac{3}{x}+\dfrac{2}{y}}{\dfrac{5}{x}-\dfrac{6}{y^2}} = \frac{\left(\dfrac{3}{x}\right)\left(\dfrac{y}{y}\right)+\left(\dfrac{2}{y}\right)\left(\dfrac{x}{x}\right)}{\left(\dfrac{5}{x}\right)\left(\dfrac{y^2}{y^2}\right)-\left(\dfrac{6}{y^2}\right)\left(\dfrac{x}{x}\right)}$$

$$= \frac{\dfrac{3y}{xy}+\dfrac{2x}{xy}}{\dfrac{5y^2}{xy^2}-\dfrac{6x}{xy^2}}$$

$$= \frac{\dfrac{3y + 2x}{xy}}{\dfrac{5y^2 - 6x}{xy^2}}$$

$$= \frac{3y + 2x}{xy} \div \frac{5y^2 - 6x}{xy^2}$$

$$= \frac{3y + 2x}{\cancel{xy}} \cdot \frac{\cancel{xy^2}^{\,y}}{5y^2 - 6x}$$

$$= \frac{y(3y + 2x)}{5y^2 - 6x}$$

Solution B

Here we find the LCD of all four denominators (x, y, x, and y^2). The LCD is xy^2. Use this LCD to multiply the entire complex fraction by a form of 1, specifically $\dfrac{xy^2}{xy^2}$.

$$\frac{\dfrac{3}{x} + \dfrac{2}{y}}{\dfrac{5}{x} - \dfrac{6}{y^2}} = \left(\frac{xy^2}{xy^2}\right)\left(\frac{\dfrac{3}{x} + \dfrac{2}{y}}{\dfrac{5}{x} - \dfrac{6}{y^2}}\right)$$

$$= \frac{xy^2\left(\dfrac{3}{x} + \dfrac{2}{y}\right)}{xy^2\left(\dfrac{5}{x} - \dfrac{6}{y^2}\right)}$$

$$= \frac{xy^2\left(\dfrac{3}{x}\right) + xy^2\left(\dfrac{2}{y}\right)}{xy^2\left(\dfrac{5}{x}\right) - xy^2\left(\dfrac{6}{y^2}\right)}$$

$$= \frac{3y^2 + 2xy}{5y^2 - 6x} \quad \text{or} \quad \frac{y(3y + 2x)}{5y^2 - 6x} \qquad \blacksquare$$

Certainly either approach (Solution A or Solution B) will work with problems such as Examples 6 and 7. Examine Solution B in both examples carefully. This approach works effectively with complex fractions where the LCD of all the denominators is easy to find. (Don't be misled by the length of Solution B for Example 6; we were especially careful to show every step.)

EXAMPLE 8

Simplify $\dfrac{\dfrac{1}{x}+\dfrac{1}{y}}{2}$.

Solution

The number 2 can be written as $\dfrac{2}{1}$; thus the LCD of all three denominators (x, y, and 1) is xy. Therefore, let's multiply the entire complex fraction by a form of 1, specifically $\dfrac{xy}{xy}$.

$$\left(\dfrac{\dfrac{1}{x}+\dfrac{1}{y}}{\dfrac{2}{1}}\right)\left(\dfrac{xy}{xy}\right)=\dfrac{xy\left(\dfrac{1}{x}\right)+xy\left(\dfrac{1}{y}\right)}{2xy}$$

$$=\dfrac{y+x}{2xy}$$ ∎

EXAMPLE 9

Simplify $\dfrac{-3}{\dfrac{2}{x}-\dfrac{3}{y}}$.

Solution

$$\left(\dfrac{\dfrac{-3}{1}}{\dfrac{2}{x}-\dfrac{3}{y}}\right)\left(\dfrac{xy}{xy}\right)=\dfrac{-3(xy)}{xy\left(\dfrac{2}{x}\right)-xy\left(\dfrac{3}{y}\right)}$$

$$=\dfrac{-3xy}{2y-3x}$$ ∎

Let's conclude this section with an example that has a complex fraction as part of an algebraic expression.

EXAMPLE 10

Simplify $1-\dfrac{n}{1-\dfrac{1}{n}}$.

Solution

First simplify the complex fraction $\dfrac{n}{1-\dfrac{1}{n}}$ by multiplying by $\dfrac{n}{n}$.

$$\left(\dfrac{n}{1-\dfrac{1}{n}}\right)\left(\dfrac{n}{n}\right)=\dfrac{n^2}{n-1}$$

Now we can perform the subtraction.

$$1 - \frac{n^2}{n-1} = \left(\frac{n-1}{n-1}\right)\left(\frac{1}{1}\right) - \frac{n^2}{n-1}$$

$$= \frac{n-1}{n-1} - \frac{n^2}{n-1}$$

$$= \frac{n-1-n^2}{n-1} \quad \text{or} \quad \frac{-n^2+n-1}{n-1} \quad ■$$

Problem Set 4.4

For Problems 1–40, perform the indicated operations, and express your answers in simplest form.

1. $\dfrac{2x}{x^2+4x} + \dfrac{5}{x}$

2. $\dfrac{3x}{x^2-6x} + \dfrac{4}{x}$

3. $\dfrac{4}{x^2+7x} - \dfrac{1}{x}$

4. $\dfrac{-10}{x^2-9x} - \dfrac{2}{x}$

5. $\dfrac{x}{x^2-1} + \dfrac{5}{x+1}$

6. $\dfrac{2x}{x^2-16} + \dfrac{7}{x-4}$

7. $\dfrac{6a+4}{a^2-1} - \dfrac{5}{a-1}$

8. $\dfrac{4a-4}{a^2-4} - \dfrac{3}{a+2}$

9. $\dfrac{2n}{n^2-25} - \dfrac{3}{4n+20}$

10. $\dfrac{3n}{n^2-36} - \dfrac{2}{5n+30}$

11. $\dfrac{5}{x} - \dfrac{5x-30}{x^2+6x} + \dfrac{x}{x+6}$

12. $\dfrac{3}{x+1} + \dfrac{x+5}{x^2-1} - \dfrac{3}{x-1}$

13. $\dfrac{3}{x^2+9x+14} + \dfrac{5}{2x^2+15x+7}$

14. $\dfrac{6}{x^2+11x+24} + \dfrac{4}{3x^2+13x+12}$

15. $\dfrac{1}{a^2-3a-10} - \dfrac{4}{a^2+4a-45}$

16. $\dfrac{6}{a^2-3a-54} - \dfrac{10}{a^2+5a-6}$

17. $\dfrac{3a}{8a^2-2a-3} + \dfrac{1}{4a^2+13a-12}$

18. $\dfrac{2a}{6a^2+13a-5} + \dfrac{a}{2a^2+a-10}$

19. $\dfrac{5}{x^2+3} - \dfrac{2}{x^2+4x-21}$

20. $\dfrac{7}{x^2+1} - \dfrac{3}{x^2+7x-60}$

21. $\dfrac{3x}{x^2-6x+9} - \dfrac{2}{x-3}$

22. $\dfrac{3}{x+4} + \dfrac{2x}{x^2+8x+16}$

23. $\dfrac{5}{x^2-1} + \dfrac{9}{x^2+2x+1}$

24. $\dfrac{6}{x^2-9} - \dfrac{9}{x^2-6x+9}$

25. $\dfrac{2}{y^2+6y-16} - \dfrac{4}{y+8} - \dfrac{3}{y-2}$

26. $\dfrac{7}{y-6} - \dfrac{10}{y+12} + \dfrac{4}{y^2+6y-72}$

27. $x - \dfrac{x^2}{x-2} + \dfrac{3}{x^2-4}$

28. $x + \dfrac{5}{x^2-25} - \dfrac{x^2}{x+5}$

29. $\dfrac{x+3}{x+10} + \dfrac{4x-3}{x^2+8x-20} + \dfrac{x-1}{x-2}$

30. $\dfrac{2x-1}{x+3} + \dfrac{x+4}{x-6} + \dfrac{3x-1}{x^2-3x-18}$

31. $\dfrac{n}{n-6} + \dfrac{n+3}{n+8} + \dfrac{12n+26}{n^2+2n-48}$

32. $\dfrac{n-1}{n+4} + \dfrac{n}{n+6} + \dfrac{2n+18}{n^2+10n+24}$

33. $\dfrac{4x-3}{2x^2+x-1} - \dfrac{2x+7}{3x^2+x-2} - \dfrac{3}{3x-2}$

34. $\dfrac{2x+5}{x^2+3x-18} - \dfrac{3x-1}{x^2+4x-12} + \dfrac{5}{x-2}$

35. $\dfrac{n}{n^2+1} + \dfrac{n^2+3n}{n^4-1} - \dfrac{1}{n-1}$

36. $\dfrac{2n^2}{n^4 - 16} - \dfrac{n}{n^2 - 4} + \dfrac{1}{n + 2}$

37. $\dfrac{15x^2 - 10}{5x^2 - 7x + 2} - \dfrac{3x + 4}{x - 1} - \dfrac{2}{5x - 2}$

38. $\dfrac{32x + 9}{12x^2 + x - 6} - \dfrac{3}{4x + 3} - \dfrac{x + 5}{3x - 2}$

39. $\dfrac{t + 3}{3t - 1} + \dfrac{8t^2 + 8t + 2}{3t^2 - 7t + 2} - \dfrac{2t + 3}{t - 2}$

40. $\dfrac{t - 3}{2t + 1} + \dfrac{2t^2 + 19t - 46}{2t^2 - 9t - 5} - \dfrac{t + 4}{t - 5}$

For Problems 41–64, simplify each complex fraction.

41. $\dfrac{\dfrac{1}{2} - \dfrac{1}{4}}{\dfrac{5}{8} + \dfrac{3}{4}}$

42. $\dfrac{\dfrac{3}{8} + \dfrac{3}{4}}{\dfrac{5}{8} - \dfrac{7}{12}}$

43. $\dfrac{\dfrac{3}{28} - \dfrac{5}{14}}{\dfrac{5}{7} + \dfrac{1}{4}}$

44. $\dfrac{\dfrac{5}{9} + \dfrac{7}{36}}{\dfrac{3}{18} - \dfrac{5}{12}}$

45. $\dfrac{\dfrac{5}{6y}}{\dfrac{10}{3xy}}$

46. $\dfrac{\dfrac{9}{8xy^2}}{\dfrac{5}{4x^2}}$

47. $\dfrac{\dfrac{3}{x} - \dfrac{2}{y}}{\dfrac{4}{y} - \dfrac{7}{xy}}$

48. $\dfrac{\dfrac{9}{x} + \dfrac{7}{x^2}}{\dfrac{5}{y} + \dfrac{3}{y^2}}$

49. $\dfrac{\dfrac{6}{a} - \dfrac{5}{b^2}}{\dfrac{12}{a^2} + \dfrac{2}{b}}$

50. $\dfrac{\dfrac{4}{ab} - \dfrac{3}{b^2}}{\dfrac{1}{a} + \dfrac{3}{b}}$

51. $\dfrac{\dfrac{2}{x} - 3}{\dfrac{3}{y} + 4}$

52. $\dfrac{1 + \dfrac{3}{x}}{1 - \dfrac{6}{x}}$

53. $\dfrac{3 + \dfrac{2}{n + 4}}{5 - \dfrac{1}{n + 4}}$

54. $\dfrac{4 + \dfrac{6}{n - 1}}{7 - \dfrac{4}{n - 1}}$

55. $\dfrac{5 - \dfrac{2}{n - 3}}{4 - \dfrac{1}{n - 3}}$

56. $\dfrac{\dfrac{3}{n - 5} - 2}{1 - \dfrac{4}{n - 5}}$

57. $\dfrac{\dfrac{-1}{y - 2} + \dfrac{5}{x}}{\dfrac{3}{x} - \dfrac{4}{xy - 2x}}$

58. $\dfrac{\dfrac{-2}{x} - \dfrac{4}{x + 2}}{\dfrac{3}{x^2 + 2x} + \dfrac{3}{x}}$

59. $\dfrac{\dfrac{2}{x - 3} - \dfrac{3}{x + 3}}{\dfrac{5}{x^2 - 9} - \dfrac{2}{x - 3}}$

60. $\dfrac{\dfrac{2}{x - y} + \dfrac{3}{x + y}}{\dfrac{5}{x + y} - \dfrac{1}{x^2 - y^2}}$

61. $\dfrac{3a}{2 - \dfrac{1}{a}} - 1$

62. $\dfrac{a}{\dfrac{1}{a} + 4} + 1$

63. $2 - \dfrac{x}{3 - \dfrac{2}{x}}$

64. $1 + \dfrac{x}{1 + \dfrac{1}{x}}$

■ ■ ■ THOUGHTS INTO WORDS

65. Which of the two techniques presented in the text would you use to simplify $\dfrac{\dfrac{1}{4} + \dfrac{1}{3}}{\dfrac{3}{4} - \dfrac{1}{6}}$? Which technique would you use to simplify $\dfrac{\dfrac{3}{8} - \dfrac{5}{7}}{\dfrac{7}{9} + \dfrac{6}{25}}$? Explain your choice for each problem.

66. Give a step-by-step description of how to do the following addition problem.

$$\dfrac{3x + 4}{8} + \dfrac{5x - 2}{12}$$

4.5   Dividing Polynomials

In Chapter 3, we saw how the property $\dfrac{b^n}{b^m} = b^{n-m}$, along with our knowledge of dividing integers, is used to divide monomials. For example,

$$\frac{12x^3}{3x} = 4x^2 \qquad \frac{-36x^4y^5}{4xy^2} = -9x^3y^3$$

In Section 4.3, we used $\dfrac{a}{b} + \dfrac{c}{b} = \dfrac{a+c}{b}$ and $\dfrac{a}{b} - \dfrac{c}{b} = \dfrac{a-c}{b}$ as the basis for adding and subtracting rational expressions. These same equalities, viewed as $\dfrac{a+b}{c} = \dfrac{a}{c} + \dfrac{b}{c}$ and $\dfrac{a-c}{b} = \dfrac{a}{b} - \dfrac{c}{b}$, along with our knowledge of dividing monomials, provide the basis for dividing polynomials by monomials. Consider the following examples.

$$\frac{18x^3 + 24x^2}{6x} = \frac{18x^3}{6x} + \frac{24x^2}{6x} = 3x^2 + 4x$$

$$\frac{35x^2y^3 - 55x^3y^4}{5xy^2} = \frac{35x^2y^3}{5xy^2} - \frac{55x^3y^4}{5xy^2} = 7xy - 11x^2y^2$$

To divide a polynomial by a monomial, we divide each term of the polynomial by the monomial. As with many skills, once you feel comfortable with the process, you may then want to perform some of the steps mentally. Your work could take on the following format.

$$\frac{40x^4y^5 + 72x^5y^7}{8x^2y} = 5x^2y^4 + 9x^3y^6 \qquad \frac{36a^3b^4 - 45a^4b^6}{-9a^2b^3} = -4ab + 5a^2b^3$$

In Section 4.1, we saw that a fraction like $\dfrac{3x^2 + 11x - 4}{x + 4}$ can be simplified as follows:

$$\frac{3x^2 + 11x - 4}{x + 4} = \frac{(3x - 1)(x+4)}{x+4} = 3x - 1$$

We can obtain the same result by using a dividing process similar to long division in arithmetic.

Step 1   Use the conventional long-division format, and arrange both the dividend and the divisor in descending powers of the variable.

$$x + 4 \overline{)3x^2 + 11x - 4}$$

Step 2   Find the first term of the quotient by dividing the first term of the dividend by the first term of the divisor.

$$\begin{array}{r} 3x \phantom{{}+11x-4} \\ x + 4 \overline{)3x^2 + 11x - 4} \end{array}$$

Step 3   Multiply the entire divisor by the term of the quotient found in Step 2, and position the product to be subtracted from the dividend.

$$\begin{array}{r} 3x \phantom{{}+11x-4} \\ x + 4 \overline{)3x^2 + 11x - 4} \\ \underline{3x^2 + 12x} \end{array}$$

Step 4 Subtract.

$$\require{enclose}\begin{array}{r} 3x \\ x + 4 \enclose{longdiv}{3x^2 + 11x - 4} \\ \underline{3x^2 + 12x } \\ -x - 4 \end{array}$$

Remember to add the opposite!
$(3x^2 + 11x - 4) - (3x^2 + 12x) = -x - 4$

Step 5 Repeat the process beginning with Step 2; use the polynomial that resulted from the subtraction in Step 4 as a new dividend.

$$\begin{array}{r} 3x -1 \\ x + 4 \enclose{longdiv}{3x^2 + 11x - 4} \\ \underline{3x^2 + 12x } \\ -x - 4 \\ \underline{-x - 4} \end{array}$$

In the next example, let's *think* in terms of the previous step-by-step procedure but arrange our work in a more compact form.

EXAMPLE 1

Divide $5x^2 + 6x - 8$ by $x + 2$.

Solution

$$\begin{array}{r} 5x - 4 \\ x + 2 \enclose{longdiv}{5x^2 + 6x - 8} \\ \underline{5x^2 + 10x } \\ -4x - 8 \\ \underline{-4x - 8} \\ 0 \end{array}$$

Think Steps

1. $\dfrac{5x^2}{x} = 5x$.

2. $5x(x + 2) = 5x^2 + 10x$.

3. $(5x^2 + 6x - 8) - (5x^2 + 10x) = -4x - 8$.

4. $\dfrac{-4x}{x} = -4$.

5. $-4(x + 2) = -4x - 8$. ∎

Recall that to check a division problem, we can multiply the divisor times the quotient and add the remainder. In other words,

Dividend = (Divisor)(Quotient) + (Remainder)

Sometimes the remainder is expressed as a fractional part of the divisor. The relationship then becomes

$$\frac{\text{Dividend}}{\text{Divisor}} = \text{Quotient} + \frac{\text{Remainder}}{\text{Divisor}}$$

EXAMPLE 2

Divide $2x^2 - 3x + 1$ by $x - 5$.

Solution

$$\begin{array}{r} 2x + 7 \\ x - 5 \enclose{longdiv}{2x^2 - 3x + 1} \\ \underline{2x^2 - 10x } \\ 7x + 1 \\ \underline{7x - 35} \\ 36 \end{array}$$

← Remainder

Thus

$$\frac{2x^2 - 3x + 1}{x - 5} = 2x + 7 + \frac{36}{x - 5} \qquad x \neq 5$$

✔ **Check**

$$(x - 5)(2x + 7) + 36 \stackrel{?}{=} 2x^2 - 3x + 1$$

$$2x^2 - 3x - 35 + 36 \stackrel{?}{=} 2x^2 - 3x + 1$$

$$2x^2 - 3x + 1 = 2x^2 - 3x + 1 \qquad ■$$

Each of the next two examples illustrates another point regarding the division process. Study them carefully, and then you should be ready to work the exercises in the next problem set.

E X A M P L E   3

Divide $t^3 - 8$ by $t - 2$.

Solution

$$
\require{enclose}
\begin{array}{r}
t^2 + 2t + 4 \\
t - 2 \enclose{longdiv}{t^3 + 0t^2 + 0t - 8} \\
\underline{t^3 - 2t^2} \\
2t^2 + 0t - 8 \\
\underline{2t^2 - 4t} \\
4t - 8 \\
\underline{4t - 8} \\
0
\end{array}
$$

⟵ Note the insertion of a "t-squared" term and a "t term" with zero coefficients.

Check this result! ■

E X A M P L E   4

Divide $y^3 + 3y^2 - 2y - 1$ by $y^2 + 2y$.

Solution

$$
\require{enclose}
\begin{array}{r}
y + 1 \\
y^2 + 2y \enclose{longdiv}{y^3 + 3y^2 - 2y - 1} \\
\underline{y^3 + 2y^2} \\
y^2 - 2y - 1 \\
\underline{y^2 + 2y} \\
- 4y - 1
\end{array}
$$

⟵ Remainder of $-4y - 1$

(The division process is complete when the degree of the remainder is less than the degree of the divisor.) Thus

$$\frac{y^3 + 3y^2 - 2y - 1}{y^2 + 2y} = y + 1 + \frac{-4y - 1}{y^2 + 2y} \qquad ■$$

If the divisor is of the form $x - k$, where the coefficient of the x term is 1, then the format of the division process described in this section can be simplified by a procedure called **synthetic division**. This procedure is a shortcut for this type of polynomial division. If you are continuing on to study college algebra, then you will want to know synthetic division. If you are not continuing on to college algebra, then you probably will not need a shortcut and the long-division process will be sufficient.

First, let's consider an example and use the usual division process. Then, in step-by-step fashion, we can observe some shortcuts that will lead us into the synthetic-division procedure. Consider the division problem $(2x^4 + x^3 - 17x^2 + 13x + 2) \div (x - 2)$

$$
\begin{array}{r}
2x^3 + 5x^2 - 7x - 1 \\
x - 2 \overline{\smash{)}\, 2x^4 + x^3 - 17x^2 + 13x + 2} \\
\underline{2x^4 - 4x^3} \\
5x^3 - 17x^2 \\
\underline{5x^3 - 10x^2} \\
-7x^2 + 13x \\
\underline{-7x^2 + 14x} \\
-x + 2 \\
\underline{-x + 2}
\end{array}
$$

Note that because the dividend $(2x^4 + x^3 - 17x^2 + 13x + 2)$ is written in descending powers of x, the quotient $(2x^3 + 5x^2 - 7x - 1)$ is produced, also in descending powers of x. In other words, the numerical coefficients are the important numbers. Thus let's rewrite this problem in terms of its coefficients.

$$
\begin{array}{r}
2 + 5 - 7 - 1 \\
1 - 2 \overline{\smash{)}\, 2 + 1 - 17 + 13 + 2} \\
\underline{②- 4} \\
5 ⊖17 \\
\underline{⑤- 10} \\
-7 \ +⑬ \\
\underline{⊖7 \ + 14} \\
-1 \ +② \\
\underline{⊖1 + 2}
\end{array}
$$

Now observe that the numbers that are circled are simply repetitions of the numbers directly above them in the format. Therefore, by removing the circled numbers, we can write the process in a more compact form as

$$
\begin{array}{r}
2 \ 5 - 7 - 1 \qquad\qquad (1) \\
-2 \overline{\smash{)}\, 2 \ \ 1 - 17 - 13 \ \ 2} \qquad (2) \\
\underline{-4 - 10 \quad 14 \ \ 2} \qquad (3) \\
5 - 7 - 1 \ \ 0 \qquad\qquad (4)
\end{array}
$$

where the repetitions are omitted and where 1, the coefficient of x in the divisor, is omitted.

Note that line (4) reveals all of the coefficients of the quotient, line (1), except for the first coefficient of 2. Thus we can begin line (4) with the first coefficient and then use the following form.

$$
\begin{array}{r}
-2 \overline{\smash{)}\, 2 \ \ 1 - 17 \quad 13 \ \ 2} \qquad (5) \\
\underline{-4 - 10 \quad 14 \ \ 2} \qquad (6) \\
2 \ 5 - 7 - 1 \ \ 0 \qquad (7)
\end{array}
$$

Line (7) contains the coefficients of the quotient, where the 0 indicates the remainder.

Finally, by changing the constant in the divisor to 2 (instead of -2), we can add the corresponding entries in lines (5) and (6) rather than subtract. Thus the final synthetic division form for this problem is

$$
\begin{array}{r}
2)\overline{2 \quad 1 \;-17 \quad 13 \quad 2} \\
4 \quad 10 \;-14 \;-2 \\
\hline
2 \quad 5 \;-\; 7 \;-\; 1 \quad 0
\end{array}
$$

Now let's consider another problem that illustrates a step-by-step procedure for carrying out the synthetic-division process. Suppose that we want to divide $3x^3 - 2x^2 + 6x - 5$ by $x + 4$.

Step 1   Write the coefficients of the dividend as follows:

$$
)\overline{3 \quad -2 \quad 6 \quad -5}
$$

Step 2   In the divisor, $(x + 4)$, use -4 instead of 4 so that later we can add rather than subtract.

$$
-4)\overline{3 \quad -2 \quad 6 \quad -5}
$$

Step 3   Bring down the first coeffecient of the dividend (3).

$$
\begin{array}{r}
-4)\overline{3 \quad -2 \quad 6 \quad -5} \\
\hline
3
\end{array}
$$

Step 4   Multiply$(3)(-4)$, which yields -12; this result is to be added to the second coefficient of the dividend (-2).

$$
\begin{array}{r}
-4)\overline{3 \quad -\; 2 \quad 6 \quad -5} \\
-12 \\
\hline
3 \quad -14
\end{array}
$$

Step 5   Multiply $(-14)(-4)$, which yields 56; this result is to be added to the third coefficient of the dividend (6).

$$
\begin{array}{r}
-4)\overline{3 \quad -\; 2 \quad 6 \quad -5} \\
-12 \quad 56 \\
\hline
3 \quad -14 \quad 62
\end{array}
$$

Step 6   Multiply $(62)(-4)$, which yields -248; this result is added to the last term of the dividend (-5).

$$
\begin{array}{r}
-4)\overline{3 \quad -\; 2 \quad 6 \quad -\; 5} \\
-12 \quad 56 \quad -248 \\
\hline
3 \quad -14 \quad 62 \quad -253
\end{array}
$$

The last row indicates a quotient of $3x^2 - 14x + 62$ and a remainder of -253. Thus we have

$$
\frac{3x^3 - 2x^2 + 6x - 5}{x + 4} = 3x^2 - 14x + 62 - \frac{253}{x + 4}
$$

We will consider one more example, which shows only the final, compact form for synthetic division.

EXAMPLE 5 Find the quotient and remainder for $(4x^4 - 2x^3 + 6x - 1) \div (x - 1)$.

Solution

$$
\begin{array}{r|rrrr}
1) & 4 & -2 & 0 & 6 & -1 \\
  &   & 4 & 2 & 2 & 8 \\
\hline
  & 4 & 2 & 2 & 8 & 7
\end{array}
$$

Note that a zero has been inserted as the coefficient of the missing x^2 term.

Therefore,

$$\frac{4x^4 - 2x^3 + 6x - 1}{x - 1} = 4x^3 + 2x^2 + 2x + 8 + \frac{7}{x - 1}$$ ■

Problem Set 4.5

For Problems 1–10, perform the indicated divisions of polynomials by monomials.

1. $\dfrac{9x^4 + 18x^3}{3x}$

2. $\dfrac{12x^3 - 24x^2}{6x^2}$

3. $\dfrac{-24x^6 + 36x^8}{4x^2}$

4. $\dfrac{-35x^5 - 42x^3}{-7x^2}$

5. $\dfrac{15a^3 - 25a^2 - 40a}{5a}$

6. $\dfrac{-16a^4 + 32a^3 - 56a^2}{-8a}$

7. $\dfrac{13x^3 - 17x^2 + 28x}{-x}$

8. $\dfrac{14xy - 16x^2y^2 - 20x^3y^4}{-xy}$

9. $\dfrac{-18x^2y^2 + 24x^3y^2 - 48x^2y^3}{6xy}$

10. $\dfrac{-27a^3b^4 - 36a^2b^3 + 72a^2b^5}{9a^2b^2}$

For Problems 11–52, perform the indicated divisions.

11. $\dfrac{x^2 - 7x - 78}{x + 6}$

12. $\dfrac{x^2 + 11x - 60}{x - 4}$

13. $(x^2 + 12x - 160) \div (x - 8)$

14. $(x^2 - 18x - 175) \div (x + 7)$

15. $\dfrac{2x^2 - x - 4}{x - 1}$

16. $\dfrac{3x^2 - 2x - 7}{x + 2}$

17. $\dfrac{15x^2 + 22x - 5}{3x + 5}$

18. $\dfrac{12x^2 - 32x - 35}{2x - 7}$

19. $\dfrac{3x^3 + 7x^2 - 13x - 21}{x + 3}$

20. $\dfrac{4x^3 - 21x^2 + 3x + 10}{x - 5}$

21. $(2x^3 + 9x^2 - 17x + 6) \div (2x - 1)$

22. $(3x^3 - 5x^2 - 23x - 7) \div (3x + 1)$

23. $(4x^3 - x^2 - 2x + 6) \div (x - 2)$

24. $(6x^3 - 2x^2 + 4x - 3) \div (x + 1)$

25. $(x^4 - 10x^3 + 19x^2 + 33x - 18) \div (x - 6)$

26. $(x^4 + 2x^3 - 16x^2 + x + 6) \div (x - 3)$

27. $\dfrac{x^3 - 125}{x - 5}$

28. $\dfrac{x^3 + 64}{x + 4}$

29. $(x^3 + 64) \div (x + 1)$

30. $(x^3 - 8) \div (x - 4)$

31. $(2x^3 - x - 6) \div (x + 2)$

32. $(5x^3 + 2x - 3) \div (x - 2)$

33. $\dfrac{4a^2 - 8ab + 4b^2}{a - b}$

34. $\dfrac{3x^2 - 2xy - 8y^2}{x - 2y}$

35. $\dfrac{4x^3 - 5x^2 + 2x - 6}{x^2 - 3x}$

36. $\dfrac{3x^3 + 2x^2 - 5x - 1}{x^2 + 2x}$

37. $\dfrac{8y^3 - y^2 - y + 5}{y^2 + y}$

38. $\dfrac{5y^3 - 6y^2 - 7y - 2}{y^2 - y}$

39. $(2x^3 + x^2 - 3x + 1) \div (x^2 + x - 1)$

40. $(3x^3 - 4x^2 + 8x + 8) \div (x^2 - 2x + 4)$

41. $(4x^3 - 13x^2 + 8x - 15) \div (4x^2 - x + 5)$

42. $(5x^3 + 8x^2 - 5x - 2) \div (5x^2 - 2x - 1)$

43. $(5a^3 + 7a^2 - 2a - 9) \div (a^2 + 3a - 4)$

44. $(4a^3 - 2a^2 + 7a - 1) \div (a^2 - 2a + 3)$

45. $(2n^4 + 3n^3 - 2n^2 + 3n - 4) \div (n^2 + 1)$

46. $(3n^4 + n^3 - 7n^2 - 2n + 2) \div (n^2 - 2)$

47. $(x^5 - 1) \div (x - 1)$ **48.** $(x^5 + 1) \div (x + 1)$

49. $(x^4 - 1) \div (x + 1)$ **50.** $(x^4 - 1) \div (x - 1)$

51. $(3x^4 + x^3 - 2x^2 - x + 6) \div (x^2 - 1)$

52. $(4x^3 - 2x^2 + 7x - 5) \div (x^2 + 2)$

For problems 53–64, use synthetic division to determine the quotient and remainder.

53. $(x^2 - 8x + 12) \div (x - 2)$

54. $(x^2 + 9x + 18) \div (x + 3)$

55. $(x^2 + 2x - 10) \div (x - 4)$

56. $(x^2 - 10x + 15) \div (x - 8)$

57. $(x^3 - 2x^2 - x + 2) \div (x - 2)$

58. $(x^3 - 5x^2 + 2x + 8) \div (x + 1)$

59. $(x^3 - 7x - 6) \div (x + 2)$

60. $(x^3 + 6x^2 - 5x - 1) \div (x - 1)$

61. $(2x^3 - 5x^2 - 4x + 6) \div (x - 2)$

62. $(3x^4 - x^3 + 2x^2 - 7x - 1) \div (x + 1)$

63. $(x^4 + 4x^3 - 7x - 1) \div (x - 3)$

64. $(2x^4 + 3x^2 + 3) \div (x + 2)$

■ ■ ■ **THOUGHTS INTO WORDS**

65. Describe the process of long division of polynomials.

66. Give a step-by-step description of how you would do the following division problem.

$$(4 - 3x - 7x^3) \div (x + 6)$$

67. How do you know by inspection that $3x^2 + 5x + 1$ cannot be the correct answer for the division problem $(3x^3 - 7x^2 - 22x + 8) \div (x - 4)$?

4.6   Fractional Equations

The fractional equations used in this text are of two basic types. One type has only constants as denominators, and the other type contains variables in the denominators.

In Chapter 2, we considered fractional equations that involve only constants in the denominators. Let's briefly review our approach to solving such equations, because we will be using that same basic technique to solve any type of fractional equation.

EXAMPLE 1

Solve $\dfrac{x-2}{3} + \dfrac{x+1}{4} = \dfrac{1}{6}$.

Solution

$$\frac{x-2}{3} + \frac{x+1}{4} = \frac{1}{6}$$

$$12\left(\frac{x-2}{3} + \frac{x+1}{4}\right) = 12\left(\frac{1}{6}\right) \qquad \text{Multiply both sides by 12, which is the LCD of all of the denominators.}$$

$$4(x-2) + 3(x+1) = 2$$

$$4x - 8 + 3x + 3 = 2$$

$$7x - 5 = 2$$

$$7x = 7$$

$$x = 1$$

The solution set is {1}. Check it! ∎

If an equation contains a variable (or variables) in one or more denominators, then we proceed in essentially the same way as in Example 1 **except that we must avoid any value of the variable that makes a denominator zero.** Consider the following examples.

EXAMPLE 2

Solve $\dfrac{5}{n} + \dfrac{1}{2} = \dfrac{9}{n}$.

Solution

First, we need to realize that n cannot equal zero. (Let's indicate this restriction so that it is not forgotten!) Then we can proceed.

$$\frac{5}{n} + \frac{1}{2} = \frac{9}{n}, \qquad n \neq 0$$

$$2n\left(\frac{5}{n} + \frac{1}{2}\right) = 2n\left(\frac{9}{n}\right) \qquad \text{Multiply both sides by the LCD, which is } 2n.$$

$$10 + n = 18$$

$$n = 8$$

The solution set is {8}. Check it! ∎

EXAMPLE 3

Solve $\dfrac{35-x}{x} = 7 + \dfrac{3}{x}$.

Solution

$$\frac{35-x}{x} = 7 + \frac{3}{x}, \qquad x \neq 0$$

$$x\left(\frac{35 - x}{x}\right) = x\left(7 + \frac{3}{x}\right) \qquad \text{Multiply both sides by } x.$$

$$35 - x = 7x + 3$$

$$32 = 8x$$

$$4 = x$$

The solution set is {4}. ∎

E X A M P L E   4

Solve $\dfrac{3}{a - 2} = \dfrac{4}{a + 1}$.

Solution

$$\frac{3}{a - 2} = \frac{4}{a + 1}, \qquad a \neq 2 \text{ and } a \neq -1$$

$$(a - 2)(a + 1)\left(\frac{3}{a - 2}\right) = (a - 2)(a + 1)\left(\frac{4}{a + 1}\right) \qquad \begin{array}{l}\text{Multiply both sides} \\ \text{by } (a - 2)(a + 1).\end{array}$$

$$3(a + 1) = 4(a - 2)$$

$$3a + 3 = 4a - 8$$

$$11 = a$$

The solution set is {11}. ∎

Keep in mind that listing the restrictions at the beginning of a problem does not replace checking the potential solutions. In Example 4, the answer 11 needs to be checked in the original equation.

E X A M P L E   5

Solve $\dfrac{a}{a - 2} + \dfrac{2}{3} = \dfrac{2}{a - 2}$.

Solution

$$\frac{a}{a - 2} + \frac{2}{3} = \frac{2}{a - 2}, \qquad a \neq 2$$

$$3(a - 2)\left(\frac{a}{a - 2} + \frac{2}{3}\right) = 3(a - 2)\left(\frac{2}{a - 2}\right) \qquad \begin{array}{l}\text{Multiply both sides} \\ \text{by } 3(a - 2).\end{array}$$

$$3a + 2(a - 2) = 6$$

$$3a + 2a - 4 = 6$$

$$5a = 10$$

$$a = 2$$

Because our initial restriction was $a \neq 2$, we conclude that this equation has no solution. Thus the solution set is ∅. ∎

■ Ratio and Proportion

A **ratio** is the comparison of two numbers by division. We often use the fractional form to express ratios. For example, we can write the ratio of a to b as $\dfrac{a}{b}$. A statement of equality between two ratios is called a **proportion**. Thus if $\dfrac{a}{b}$ and $\dfrac{c}{d}$ are two equal ratios, we can form the proportion $\dfrac{a}{b} = \dfrac{c}{d}$ $(b \neq 0$ and $d \neq 0)$. We deduce an important property of proportions as follows:

$$\frac{a}{b} = \frac{c}{d}, \qquad b \neq 0 \text{ and } d \neq 0$$

$$bd\left(\frac{a}{b}\right) = bd\left(\frac{c}{d}\right) \qquad \text{Multiply both sides by } bd.$$

$$ad = bc$$

Cross-Multiplication Property of Proportions

> If $\dfrac{a}{b} = \dfrac{c}{d}$ $(b \neq 0$ and $d \neq 0)$, then $ad = bc$.

We can treat some fractional equations as proportions and solve them by using the cross-multiplication idea, as in the next examples.

E X A M P L E   6

Solve $\dfrac{5}{x + 6} = \dfrac{7}{x - 5}$.

Solution

$$\frac{5}{x + 6} = \frac{7}{x - 5}, \qquad x \neq -6 \text{ and } x \neq 5$$

$$5(x - 5) = 7(x + 6) \qquad \text{Apply the cross-multiplication property.}$$

$$5x - 25 = 7x + 42$$

$$-67 = 2x$$

$$-\frac{67}{2} = x$$

The solution set is $\left\{-\dfrac{67}{2}\right\}$.

■

EXAMPLE 7   Solve $\dfrac{x}{7} = \dfrac{4}{x+3}$.

Solution

$$\frac{x}{7} = \frac{4}{x+3}, \qquad x \neq -3$$

$$x(x+3) = 7(4) \qquad \text{Cross-multiplication property}$$

$$x^2 + 3x = 28$$

$$x^2 + 3x - 28 = 0$$

$$(x+7)(x-4) = 0$$

$$x+7 = 0 \qquad \text{or} \qquad x-4 = 0$$

$$x = -7 \qquad \text{or} \qquad x = 4$$

The solution set is $\{-7, 4\}$. Check these solutions in the original equation.   ■

■ Problem Solving

The ability to solve fractional equations broadens our base for solving word problems. We are now ready to tackle some word problems that translate into fractional equations.

PROBLEM 1   The sum of a number and its reciprocal is $\dfrac{10}{3}$. Find the number.

Solution

Let n represent the number. Then $\dfrac{1}{n}$ represents its reciprocal.

$$n + \frac{1}{n} = \frac{10}{3}, \qquad n \neq 0$$

$$3n\left(n + \frac{1}{n}\right) = 3n\left(\frac{10}{3}\right)$$

$$3n^2 + 3 = 10n$$

$$3n^2 - 10n + 3 = 0$$

$$(3n - 1)(n - 3) = 0$$

$$3n - 1 = 0 \qquad \text{or} \qquad n - 3 = 0$$

$$3n = 1 \qquad \text{or} \qquad n = 3$$

$$n = \frac{1}{3} \qquad \text{or} \qquad n = 3$$

If the number is $\dfrac{1}{3}$, then its reciprocal is $\dfrac{1}{\frac{1}{3}} = 3$. If the number is 3, then its reciprocal is $\dfrac{1}{3}$. ■

Now let's consider a problem where we can use the relationship

$$\frac{\text{Dividend}}{\text{Divisor}} = \text{Quotient} + \frac{\text{Remainder}}{\text{Divisor}}$$

as a guideline.

PROBLEM 2

The sum of two numbers is 52. If the larger is divided by the smaller, the quotient is 9, and the remainder is 2. Find the numbers.

Solution

Let n represent the smaller number. Then $52 - n$ represents the larger number. Let's use the relationship we discussed previously as a guideline and proceed as follows:

$$\frac{\text{Dividend}}{\text{Divisor}} = \text{Quotient} + \frac{\text{Remainder}}{\text{Divisor}}$$

$$\frac{52 - n}{n} = 9 + \frac{2}{n}, \qquad n \neq 0$$

$$n\left(\frac{52 - n}{n}\right) = n\left(9 + \frac{2}{n}\right)$$

$$52 - n = 9n + 2$$

$$50 = 10n$$

$$5 = n$$

If $n = 5$, then $52 - n$ equals 47. The numbers are 5 and 47. ■

We can conveniently set up some problems and solve them using the concepts of ratio and proportion. Let's conclude this section with two such examples.

PROBLEM 3

On a certain map $1\dfrac{1}{2}$ inches represents 25 miles. If two cities are $5\dfrac{1}{4}$ inches apart on the map, find the number of miles between the cities (see Figure 4.1).

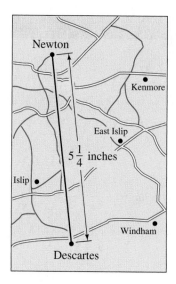

Figure 4.1

Solution

Let m represent the number of miles between the two cities. To set up the proportion, we will use a ratio of inches on the map to miles. Be sure to keep the ratio "inches on the map to miles" the same for both sides of the proportion.

$$\frac{1\frac{1}{2}}{25} = \frac{5\frac{1}{4}}{m}, \qquad m \neq 0$$

$$\frac{\frac{3}{2}}{25} = \frac{\frac{21}{4}}{m}$$

$$\frac{3}{2}m = 25\left(\frac{21}{4}\right) \qquad \text{Cross-multiplication property}$$

$$\frac{2}{3}\left(\frac{3}{2}m\right) = \frac{2}{3}(25)\left(\frac{\overset{7}{\cancel{21}}}{\underset{2}{\cancel{4}}}\right) \qquad \text{Multiply both sides by } \frac{2}{3}.$$

$$m = \frac{175}{2}$$

$$= 87\frac{1}{2}$$

The distance between the two cities is $87\frac{1}{2}$ miles. ∎

PROBLEM 4

A sum of \$750 is to be divided between two people in the ratio of 2 to 3. How much does each person receive?

Solution

Let d represent the amount of money that one person receives. Then $750 - d$ represents the amount for the other person.

$$\frac{d}{750 - d} = \frac{2}{3}, \qquad d \neq 750$$

$$3d = 2(750 - d)$$

$$3d = 1500 - 2d$$

$$5d = 1500$$

$$d = 300$$

If $d = 300$, then $750 - d$ equals 450. Therefore, one person receives \$300 and the other person receives \$450. ∎

Problem Set 4.6

For Problems 1–44, solve each equation.

1. $\dfrac{x+1}{4} + \dfrac{x-2}{6} = \dfrac{3}{4}$

2. $\dfrac{x+2}{5} + \dfrac{x-1}{6} = \dfrac{3}{5}$

3. $\dfrac{x+3}{2} - \dfrac{x-4}{7} = 1$

4. $\dfrac{x+4}{3} - \dfrac{x-5}{9} = 1$

5. $\dfrac{5}{n} + \dfrac{1}{3} = \dfrac{7}{n}$

6. $\dfrac{3}{n} + \dfrac{1}{6} = \dfrac{11}{3n}$

7. $\dfrac{7}{2x} + \dfrac{3}{5} = \dfrac{2}{3x}$

8. $\dfrac{9}{4x} + \dfrac{1}{3} = \dfrac{5}{2x}$

9. $\dfrac{3}{4x} + \dfrac{5}{6} = \dfrac{4}{3x}$

10. $\dfrac{5}{7x} - \dfrac{5}{6} = \dfrac{1}{6x}$

11. $\dfrac{47-n}{n} = 8 + \dfrac{2}{n}$

12. $\dfrac{45-n}{n} = 6 + \dfrac{3}{n}$

13. $\dfrac{n}{65-n} = 8 + \dfrac{2}{65-n}$

14. $\dfrac{n}{70-n} = 7 + \dfrac{6}{70-n}$

15. $n + \dfrac{1}{n} = \dfrac{17}{4}$

16. $n + \dfrac{1}{n} = \dfrac{37}{6}$

17. $n - \dfrac{2}{n} = \dfrac{23}{5}$

18. $n - \dfrac{3}{n} = \dfrac{26}{3}$

19. $\dfrac{5}{7x-3} = \dfrac{3}{4x-5}$

20. $\dfrac{3}{2x-1} = \dfrac{5}{3x+2}$

21. $\dfrac{-2}{x-5} = \dfrac{1}{x+9}$

22. $\dfrac{5}{2a-1} = \dfrac{-6}{3a+2}$

23. $\dfrac{x}{x+1} - 2 = \dfrac{3}{x-3}$

24. $\dfrac{x}{x-2} + 1 = \dfrac{8}{x-1}$

25. $\dfrac{a}{a+5} - 2 = \dfrac{3a}{a+5}$

26. $\dfrac{a}{a-3} - \dfrac{3}{2} = \dfrac{3}{a-3}$

27. $\dfrac{5}{x+6} = \dfrac{6}{x-3}$

28. $\dfrac{3}{x-1} = \dfrac{4}{x+2}$

29. $\dfrac{3x-7}{10} = \dfrac{2}{x}$

30. $\dfrac{x}{-4} = \dfrac{3}{12x-25}$

31. $\dfrac{x}{x-6} - 3 = \dfrac{6}{x-6}$

32. $\dfrac{x}{x+1} + 3 = \dfrac{4}{x+1}$

33. $\dfrac{3s}{s+2} + 1 = \dfrac{35}{2(3s+1)}$

34. $\dfrac{s}{2s-1} - 3 = \dfrac{-32}{3(s+5)}$

35. $2 - \dfrac{3x}{x-4} = \dfrac{14}{x+7}$

36. $-1 + \dfrac{2x}{x+3} = \dfrac{-4}{x+4}$

37. $\dfrac{n+6}{27} = \dfrac{1}{n}$

38. $\dfrac{n}{5} = \dfrac{10}{n-5}$

39. $\dfrac{3n}{n-1} - \dfrac{1}{3} = \dfrac{-40}{3n-18}$

40. $\dfrac{n}{n+1} + \dfrac{1}{2} = \dfrac{-2}{n+2}$

41. $\dfrac{-3}{4x+5} = \dfrac{2}{5x-7}$

42. $\dfrac{7}{x+4} = \dfrac{3}{x-8}$

43. $\dfrac{2x}{x-2} + \dfrac{15}{x^2-7x+10} = \dfrac{3}{x-5}$

44. $\dfrac{x}{x-4} - \dfrac{2}{x+3} = \dfrac{20}{x^2-x-12}$

For Problems 45–60, set up an algebraic equation and solve each problem.

45. A sum of $1750 is to be divided between two people in the ratio of 3 to 4. How much does each person receive?

46. A blueprint has a scale where 1 inch represents 5 feet. Find the dimensions of a rectangular room that measures $3\frac{1}{2}$ inches by $5\frac{3}{4}$ inches on the blueprint.

47. One angle of a triangle has a measure of $60°$ and the measures of the other two angles are in the ratio of 2 to 3. Find the measures of the other two angles.

48. The ratio of the complement of an angle to its supplement is 1 to 4. Find the measure of the angle.

49. The sum of a number and its reciprocal is $\dfrac{53}{14}$. Find the number.

50. The sum of two numbers is 80. If the larger is divided by the smaller, the quotient is 7, and the remainder is 8. Find the numbers.

51. If a home valued at $150,000 is assessed $2500 in real estate taxes, then how much, at the same rate, are the taxes on a home valued at $210,000?

52. The ratio of male students to female students at a certain university is 5 to 7. If there is a total of 16,200 students, find the number of male students and the number of female students.

53. Suppose that, together, Laura and Tammy sold $120.75 worth of candy for the annual school fair. If the ratio of Tammy's sales to Laura's sales was 4 to 3, how much did each sell?

54. The total value of a house and a lot is $168,000. If the ratio of the value of the house to the value of the lot is 7 to 1, find the value of the house.

55. The sum of two numbers is 90. If the larger is divided by the smaller, the quotient is 10, and the remainder is 2. Find the numbers.

56. What number must be added to the numerator and denominator of $\dfrac{2}{5}$ to produce a rational number that is equivalent to $\dfrac{7}{8}$?

57. A 20-foot board is to be cut into two pieces whose lengths are in the ratio of 7 to 3. Find the lengths of the two pieces.

58. An inheritance of $300,000 is to be divided between a son and the local heart fund in the ratio of 3 to 1. How much money will the son receive?

59. Suppose that in a certain precinct, 1150 people voted in the last presidential election. If the ratio of female voters to male voters was 3 to 2, how many females and how many males voted?

60. The perimeter of a rectangle is 114 centimeters. If the ratio of its width to its length is 7 to 12, find the dimensions of the rectangle.

■■■ THOUGHTS INTO WORDS

61. How could you do Problem 57 without using algebra?

62. Now do Problem 59 using the same approach that you used in Problem 61. What difficulties do you encounter?

63. How can you tell by inspection that the equation
$$\frac{x}{x+2} = \frac{-2}{x+2}$$ has no solution?

64. How would you help someone solve the equation
$$\frac{3}{x} - \frac{4}{x} = \frac{-1}{x}?$$

4.7   More Fractional Equations and Applications

Let's begin this section by considering a few more fractional equations. We will continue to solve them using the same basic techniques as in the previous section. That is, we will multiply both sides of the equation by the least common denominator of all of the denominators in the equation, with the necessary restrictions to avoid division by zero. Some of the denominators in these problems will require factoring before we can determine a least common denominator.

EXAMPLE 1   Solve $\dfrac{x}{2x - 8} + \dfrac{16}{x^2 - 16} = \dfrac{1}{2}$.

Solution

$$\frac{x}{2x - 8} + \frac{16}{x^2 - 16} = \frac{1}{2}$$

$$\frac{x}{2(x - 4)} + \frac{16}{(x + 4)(x - 4)} = \frac{1}{2}, \qquad x \neq 4 \text{ and } x \neq -4$$

$$2(x - 4)(x + 4)\left(\frac{x}{2(x - 4)} + \frac{16}{(x + 4)(x - 4)}\right) = 2(x + 4)(x - 4)\left(\frac{1}{2}\right) \qquad \begin{array}{l}\text{Multiply both}\\ \text{sides by the LCD,}\\ 2(x - 4)(x + 4).\end{array}$$

$$x(x + 4) + 2(16) = (x + 4)(x - 4)$$

$$x^2 + 4x + 32 = x^2 - 16$$

$$4x = -48$$

$$x = -12$$

The solution set is $\{-12\}$. Perhaps you should check it!   ∎

In Example 1, note that the restrictions were not indicated until the denominators were expressed in factored form. It is usually easier to determine the necessary restrictions at this step.

EXAMPLE 2   Solve $\dfrac{3}{n - 5} - \dfrac{2}{2n + 1} = \dfrac{n + 3}{2n^2 - 9n - 5}$.

Solution

$$\frac{3}{n - 5} - \frac{2}{2n + 1} = \frac{n + 3}{2n^2 - 9n - 5}$$

$$\frac{3}{n - 5} - \frac{2}{2n + 1} = \frac{n + 3}{(2n + 1)(n - 5)}, \qquad n \neq -\frac{1}{2} \text{ and } n \neq 5$$

$$(2n + 1)(n - 5)\left(\frac{3}{n - 5} - \frac{2}{2n + 1}\right) = (2n + 1)(n - 5)\left(\frac{n + 3}{(2n + 1)(n - 5)}\right) \qquad \begin{array}{l}\text{Multiply both}\\ \text{sides by the LCD,}\\ (2n + 1)(n - 5).\end{array}$$

$$3(2n + 1) - 2(n - 5) = n + 3$$

$$6n + 3 - 2n + 10 = n + 3$$

$$4n + 13 = n + 3$$

$$3n = -10$$

$$n = -\frac{10}{3}$$

The solution set is $\left\{-\dfrac{10}{3}\right\}$.   ∎

E X A M P L E   3

Solve $2 + \dfrac{4}{x-2} = \dfrac{8}{x^2 - 2x}$.

Solution

$$2 + \frac{4}{x-2} = \frac{8}{x^2 - 2x}$$

$$2 + \frac{4}{x-2} = \frac{8}{x(x-2)}, \qquad x \neq 0 \text{ and } x \neq 2$$

$$x(x-2)\left(2 + \frac{4}{x-2}\right) = x(x-2)\left(\frac{8}{x(x-2)}\right) \qquad \begin{array}{l}\text{Multiply both sides}\\ \text{by the LCD, } x(x-2).\end{array}$$

$$2x(x-2) + 4x = 8$$

$$2x^2 - 4x + 4x = 8$$

$$2x^2 = 8$$

$$x^2 = 4$$

$$x^2 - 4 = 0$$

$$(x+2)(x-2) = 0$$

$$x + 2 = 0 \qquad \text{or} \qquad x - 2 = 0$$

$$x = -2 \qquad \text{or} \qquad x = 2$$

Because our initial restriction indicated that $x \neq 2$, the only solution is -2. Thus the solution set is $\{-2\}$.   ■

In Section 2.4, we discussed using the properties of equality to change the form of various formulas. For example, we considered the simple interest formula $A = P + Prt$ and changed its form by solving for P as follows:

$$A = P + Prt$$

$$A = P(1 + rt)$$

$$\frac{A}{1 + rt} = P \qquad \text{Multiply both sides by } \frac{1}{1 + rt}.$$

If the formula is in the form of a fractional equation, then the techniques of these last two sections are applicable. Consider the following example.

E X A M P L E   4

If the original cost of some business property is C dollars and it is depreciated linearly over N years, then its value, V, at the end of T years is given by

$$V = C\left(1 - \frac{T}{N}\right)$$

Solve this formula for N in terms of V, C, and T.

Solution

$$V = C\left(1 - \frac{T}{N}\right)$$

$$V = C - \frac{CT}{N}$$

$$N(V) = N\left(C - \frac{CT}{N}\right) \qquad \text{Multiply both sides by } N.$$

$$NV = NC - CT$$

$$NV - NC = -CT$$

$$N(V - C) = -CT$$

$$N = \frac{-CT}{V - C}$$

$$N = -\frac{CT}{V - C} \qquad\qquad\qquad\qquad\qquad \blacksquare$$

■ Problem Solving

In Section 2.4 we solved some uniform motion problems. The formula $d = rt$ was used in the analysis of the problems, and we used guidelines that involve distance relationships. Now let's consider some uniform motion problems where guidelines that involve either times or rates are appropriate. These problems will generate fractional equations to solve.

P R O B L E M   1

An airplane travels 2050 miles in the same time that a car travels 260 miles. If the rate of the plane is 358 miles per hour greater than the rate of the car, find the rate of each.

Solution

Let r represent the rate of the car. Then $r + 358$ represents the rate of the plane. The fact that the times are equal can be a guideline. Remember from the basic formula, $d = rt$, that $t = \dfrac{d}{r}$.

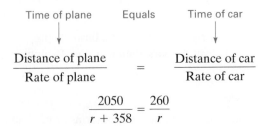

$$\frac{2050}{r + 358} = \frac{260}{r}$$

$$2050r = 260(r + 358)$$
$$2050r = 260r + 93{,}080$$
$$1790r = 93{,}080$$
$$r = 52$$

If $r = 52$, then $r + 358$ equals 410. Thus the rate of the car is 52 miles per hour, and the rate of the plane is 410 miles per hour. ■

PROBLEM 2

It takes a freight train 2 hours longer to travel 300 miles than it takes an express train to travel 280 miles. The rate of the express train is 20 miles per hour greater than the rate of the freight train. Find the times and rates of both trains.

Solution

Let t represent the time of the express train. Then $t + 2$ represents the time of the freight train. Let's record the information of this problem in a table.

	Distance	Time	Rate $= \dfrac{\text{Distance}}{\text{Time}}$
Express train	280	t	$\dfrac{280}{t}$
Freight train	300	$t + 2$	$\dfrac{300}{t + 2}$

The fact that the rate of the express train is 20 miles per hour greater than the rate of the freight train can be a guideline.

Rate of express	Equals	Rate of freight train plus 20
$\dfrac{280}{t}$	$=$	$\dfrac{300}{t + 2} + 20$

$$t(t + 2)\left(\frac{280}{t}\right) = t(t + 2)\left(\frac{300}{t + 2} + 20\right)$$
$$280(t + 2) = 300t + 20t(t + 2)$$
$$280t + 560 = 300t + 20t^2 + 40t$$
$$280t + 560 = 340t + 20t^2$$
$$0 = 20t^2 + 60t - 560$$
$$0 = t^2 + 3t - 28$$
$$0 = (t + 7)(t - 4)$$
$$t + 7 = 0 \quad \text{or} \quad t - 4 = 0$$
$$t = -7 \quad \text{or} \quad t = 4$$

The negative solution must be discarded, so the time of the express train (t) is 4 hours, and the time of the freight train ($t + 2$) is 6 hours. The rate of the express train $\left(\dfrac{280}{t}\right)$ is $\dfrac{280}{4} = 70$ miles per hour, and the rate of the freight train $\left(\dfrac{300}{t + 2}\right)$ is $\dfrac{300}{6} = 50$ miles per hour. ∎

Remark: Note that to solve Problem 1 we went directly to a guideline without the use of a table, but for Problem 2 we used a table. Again, remember that this is a personal preference; we are merely acquainting you with a variety of techniques.

Uniform motion problems are a special case of a larger group of problems we refer to as **rate-time problems**. For example, if a certain machine can produce 150 items in 10 minutes, then we say that the machine is producing at a rate of $\dfrac{150}{10} = 15$ items per minute. Likewise, if a person can do a certain job in 3 hours, then, assuming a constant rate of work, we say that the person is working at a rate of $\dfrac{1}{3}$ of the job per hour. In general, if Q is the quantity of something done in t units of time, then the rate, r, is given by $r = \dfrac{Q}{t}$. We state the rate in terms of *so much quantity per unit of time*. (In uniform motion problems the "quantity" is distance.) Let's consider some examples of rate-time problems.

P R O B L E M   3

If Jim can mow a lawn in 50 minutes, and his son, Todd, can mow the same lawn in 40 minutes, how long will it take them to mow the lawn if they work together?

Solution

Jim's rate is $\dfrac{1}{50}$ of the lawn per minute, and Todd's rate is $\dfrac{1}{40}$ of the lawn per minute.

If we let m represent the number of minutes that they work together, then $\dfrac{1}{m}$ represents their rate when working together. Therefore, because the sum of the individual rates must equal the rate working together, we can set up and solve the following equation.

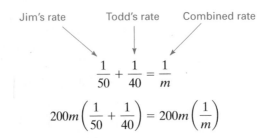

$$\underset{\text{Jim's rate}}{\dfrac{1}{50}} + \underset{\text{Todd's rate}}{\dfrac{1}{40}} = \underset{\text{Combined rate}}{\dfrac{1}{m}}$$

$$200m\left(\dfrac{1}{50} + \dfrac{1}{40}\right) = 200m\left(\dfrac{1}{m}\right)$$

$$4m + 5m = 200$$

$$9m = 200$$

$$m = \frac{200}{9} = 22\frac{2}{9}$$

It should take them $22\frac{2}{9}$ minutes.   ■

P R O B L E M   4   Working together, Linda and Kathy can type a term paper in $3\frac{3}{5}$ hours. Linda can type the paper by herself in 6 hours. How long would it take Kathy to type the paper by herself?

Solution

Their rate working together is $\dfrac{1}{3\frac{3}{5}} = \dfrac{1}{\frac{18}{5}} = \dfrac{5}{18}$ of the job per hour, and Linda's rate

is $\dfrac{1}{6}$ of the job per hour. If we let h represent the number of hours that it would take

Kathy to do the job by herself, then her rate is $\dfrac{1}{h}$ of the job per hour. Thus we have

Linda's rate   Kathy's rate   Combined rate

$$\frac{1}{6} \quad + \quad \frac{1}{h} \quad = \quad \frac{5}{18}$$

Solving this equation yields

$$18h\left(\frac{1}{6} + \frac{1}{h}\right) = 18h\left(\frac{5}{18}\right)$$

$$3h + 18 = 5h$$

$$18 = 2h$$

$$9 = h$$

It would take Kathy 9 hours to type the paper by herself.   ■

Our final example of this section illustrates another approach that some people find meaningful for rate-time problems. For this approach, think in terms of fractional parts of the job. For example, if a person can do a certain job in 5 hours, then at the end of 2 hours, he or she has done $\dfrac{2}{5}$ of the job. (Again, assume a constant rate of work.) At the end of 4 hours, he or she has finished $\dfrac{4}{5}$ of the job;

and, in general, at the end of h hours, he or she has done $\dfrac{h}{5}$ of the job. Then, just as in the motion problems where distance equals rate times the time, here the fractional part done equals the working rate times the time. Let's see how this works in a problem.

PROBLEM 5

It takes Pat 12 hours to complete a task. After he had been working for 3 hours, he was joined by his brother Mike, and together they finished the task in 5 hours. How long would it take Mike to do the job by himself?

Solution

Let h represent the number of hours that it would take Mike to do the job by himself. The fractional part of the job that Pat does equals his working rate times his time. Because it takes Pat 12 hours to do the entire job, his working rate is $\dfrac{1}{12}$. He works for 8 hours (3 hours before Mike and then 5 hours with Mike). Therefore, Pat's part of the job is $\dfrac{1}{12}(8) = \dfrac{8}{12}$. The fractional part of the job that Mike does equals his working rate times his time. Because h represents Mike's time to do the entire job, his working rate is $\dfrac{1}{h}$; he works for 5 hours. Therefore, Mike's part of the job is $\dfrac{1}{h}(5) = \dfrac{5}{h}$. Adding the two fractional parts together results in 1 entire job being done. Let's also show this information in chart form and set up our guideline. Then we can set up and solve the equation.

	Time to do entire job	Working rate	Time working	Fractional part of the job done
Pat	12	$\dfrac{1}{12}$	8	$\dfrac{8}{12}$
Mike	h	$\dfrac{1}{h}$	5	$\dfrac{5}{h}$

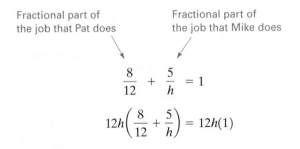

Fractional part of the job that Pat does   Fractional part of the job that Mike does

$$\frac{8}{12} + \frac{5}{h} = 1$$

$$12h\left(\frac{8}{12} + \frac{5}{h}\right) = 12h(1)$$

$$12h\left(\frac{8}{12}\right) + 12h\left(\frac{5}{h}\right) = 12h$$

$$8h + 60 = 12h$$

$$60 = 4h$$

$$15 = h$$

It would take Mike 15 hours to do the entire job by himself.   ■

Problem Set 4.7

For Problems 1–30, solve each equation.

1. $\dfrac{x}{4x - 4} + \dfrac{5}{x^2 - 1} = \dfrac{1}{4}$

2. $\dfrac{x}{3x - 6} + \dfrac{4}{x^2 - 4} = \dfrac{1}{3}$

3. $3 + \dfrac{6}{t - 3} = \dfrac{6}{t^2 - 3t}$

4. $2 + \dfrac{4}{t - 1} = \dfrac{4}{t^2 - t}$

5. $\dfrac{3}{n - 5} + \dfrac{4}{n + 7} = \dfrac{2n + 11}{n^2 + 2n - 35}$

6. $\dfrac{2}{n + 3} + \dfrac{3}{n - 4} = \dfrac{2n - 1}{n^2 - n - 12}$

7. $\dfrac{5x}{2x + 6} - \dfrac{4}{x^2 - 9} = \dfrac{5}{2}$

8. $\dfrac{3x}{5x + 5} - \dfrac{2}{x^2 - 1} = \dfrac{3}{5}$

9. $1 + \dfrac{1}{n - 1} = \dfrac{1}{n^2 - n}$

10. $3 + \dfrac{9}{n - 3} = \dfrac{27}{n^2 - 3n}$

11. $\dfrac{2}{n - 2} - \dfrac{n}{n + 5} = \dfrac{10n + 15}{n^2 + 3n - 10}$

12. $\dfrac{n}{n + 3} + \dfrac{1}{n - 4} = \dfrac{11 - n}{n^2 - n - 12}$

13. $\dfrac{2}{2x - 3} - \dfrac{2}{10x^2 - 13x - 3} = \dfrac{x}{5x + 1}$

14. $\dfrac{1}{3x + 4} + \dfrac{6}{6x^2 + 5x - 4} = \dfrac{x}{2x - 1}$

15. $\dfrac{2x}{x + 3} - \dfrac{3}{x - 6} = \dfrac{29}{x^2 - 3x - 18}$

16. $\dfrac{x}{x - 4} - \dfrac{2}{x + 8} = \dfrac{63}{x^2 + 4x - 32}$

17. $\dfrac{a}{a - 5} + \dfrac{2}{a - 6} = \dfrac{2}{a^2 - 11a + 30}$

18. $\dfrac{a}{a + 2} + \dfrac{3}{a + 4} = \dfrac{14}{a^2 + 6a + 8}$

19. $\dfrac{-1}{2x - 5} + \dfrac{2x - 4}{4x^2 - 25} = \dfrac{5}{6x + 15}$

20. $\dfrac{-2}{3x + 2} + \dfrac{x - 1}{9x^2 - 4} = \dfrac{3}{12x - 8}$

21. $\dfrac{7y + 2}{12y^2 + 11y - 15} - \dfrac{1}{3y + 5} = \dfrac{2}{4y - 3}$

22. $\dfrac{5y - 4}{6y^2 + y - 12} - \dfrac{2}{2y + 3} = \dfrac{5}{3y - 4}$

23. $\dfrac{2n}{6n^2 + 7n - 3} - \dfrac{n - 3}{3n^2 + 11n - 4} = \dfrac{5}{2n^2 + 11n + 12}$

24. $\dfrac{x + 1}{2x^2 + 7x - 4} - \dfrac{x}{2x^2 - 7x + 3} = \dfrac{1}{x^2 + x - 12}$

25. $\dfrac{1}{2x^2 - x - 1} + \dfrac{3}{2x^2 + x} = \dfrac{2}{x^2 - 1}$

26. $\dfrac{2}{n^2 + 4n} + \dfrac{3}{n^2 - 3n - 28} = \dfrac{5}{n^2 - 6n - 7}$

27. $\dfrac{x + 1}{x^3 - 9x} - \dfrac{1}{2x^2 + x - 21} = \dfrac{1}{2x^2 + 13x + 21}$

28. $\dfrac{x}{2x^2 + 5x} - \dfrac{x}{2x^2 + 7x + 5} = \dfrac{2}{x^2 + x}$

29. $\dfrac{4t}{4t^2 - t - 3} + \dfrac{2 - 3t}{3t^2 - t - 2} = \dfrac{1}{12t^2 + 17t + 6}$

30. $\dfrac{2t}{2t^2 + 9t + 10} + \dfrac{1 - 3t}{3t^2 + 4t - 4} = \dfrac{4}{6t^2 + 11t - 10}$

For Problems 31–44, solve each equation for the indicated variable.

31. $y = \dfrac{5}{6}x + \dfrac{2}{9}$ for x

32. $y = \dfrac{3}{4}x - \dfrac{2}{3}$ for x

33. $\dfrac{-2}{x - 4} = \dfrac{5}{y - 1}$ for y

34. $\dfrac{7}{y - 3} = \dfrac{3}{x + 1}$ for y

35. $I = \dfrac{100M}{C}$ for M

36. $V = C\left(1 - \dfrac{T}{N}\right)$ for T

37. $\dfrac{R}{S} = \dfrac{T}{S + T}$ for R

38. $\dfrac{1}{R} = \dfrac{1}{S} + \dfrac{1}{T}$ for R

39. $\dfrac{y - 1}{x - 3} = \dfrac{b - 1}{a - 3}$ for y

40. $y = -\dfrac{a}{b}x + \dfrac{c}{d}$ for x

41. $\dfrac{x}{a} + \dfrac{y}{b} = 1$ for y

42. $\dfrac{y - b}{x} = m$ for y

43. $\dfrac{y - 1}{x + 6} = \dfrac{-2}{3}$ for y

44. $\dfrac{y + 5}{x - 2} = \dfrac{3}{7}$ for y

Set up an equation and solve each of the following problems.

45. Kent drives his Mazda 270 miles in the same time that it takes Dave to drive his Nissan 250 miles. If Kent averages 4 miles per hour faster than Dave, find their rates.

46. Suppose that Wendy rides her bicycle 30 miles in the same time that it takes Kim to ride her bicycle 20 miles. If Wendy rides 5 miles per hour faster than Kim, find the rate of each.

47. An inlet pipe can fill a tank (see Figure 4.2) in 10 minutes. A drain can empty the tank in 12 minutes. If the tank is empty, and both the pipe and drain are open, how long will it take before the tank overflows?

Figure 4.2

48. Barry can do a certain job in 3 hours, whereas it takes Sanchez 5 hours to do the same job. How long would it take them to do the job working together?

49. Connie can type 600 words in 5 minutes less than it takes Katie to type 600 words. If Connie types at a rate of 20 words per minute faster than Katie types, find the typing rate of each woman.

50. Walt can mow a lawn in 1 hour, and his son, Malik, can mow the same lawn in 50 minutes. One day Malik started mowing the lawn by himself and worked for 30 minutes. Then Walt joined him and they finished the lawn. How long did it take them to finish mowing the lawn after Walt started to help?

51. Plane A can travel 1400 miles in 1 hour less time than it takes plane B to travel 2000 miles. The rate of plane B is 50 miles per hour greater than the rate of plane A. Find the times and rates of both planes.

52. To travel 60 miles, it takes Sue, riding a moped, 2 hours less time than it takes Doreen to travel 50 miles riding a bicycle. Sue travels 10 miles per hour faster than Doreen. Find the times and rates of both girls.

53. It takes Amy twice as long to deliver papers as it does Nancy. How long would it take each girl to deliver the papers by herself if they can deliver the papers together in 40 minutes?

54. If two inlet pipes are both open, they can fill a pool in 1 hour and 12 minutes. One of the pipes can fill the pool by itself in 2 hours. How long would it take the other pipe to fill the pool by itself?

55. Rod agreed to mow a vacant lot for $12. It took him an hour longer than he had anticipated, so he earned $1 per hour less than he had originally calculated. How long had he anticipated that it would take him to mow the lot?

56. Last week Al bought some golf balls for $20. The next day they were on sale for $0.50 per ball less, and he bought $22.50 worth of balls. If he purchased 5 more balls on the second day than on the first day, how many did he buy each day and at what price per ball?

57. Debbie rode her bicycle out into the country for a distance of 24 miles. On the way back, she took a much shorter route of 12 miles and made the return trip in one-half hour less time. If her rate out into the country was 4 miles per hour greater than her rate on the return trip, find both rates.

58. Felipe jogs for 10 miles and then walks another 10 miles. He jogs $2\frac{1}{2}$ miles per hour faster than he walks, and the entire distance of 20 miles takes 6 hours. Find the rate at which he walks and the rate at which he jogs.

■ ■ ■ THOUGHTS INTO WORDS

59. Why is it important to consider more than one way to do a problem?

60. Write a paragraph or two summarizing the new ideas about problem solving you have acquired thus far in this course.

(4.1) Any number that can be written in the form $\dfrac{a}{b}$, where a and b are integers and $b \neq 0$, is called a **rational number**.

A **rational expression** is defined as the indicated quotient of two polynomials. The following properties pertain to rational numbers and rational expressions.

1. $\dfrac{-a}{b} = \dfrac{a}{-b} = -\dfrac{a}{b}$

2. $\dfrac{-a}{-b} = \dfrac{a}{b}$

3. $\dfrac{a \cdot k}{b \cdot k} = \dfrac{a}{b}$ Fundamental principle of fractions

(4.2) Multiplication and division of rational expressions are based on the following definitions:

1. $\dfrac{a}{b} \cdot \dfrac{c}{d} = \dfrac{ac}{bd}$ Multiplication

2. $\dfrac{a}{b} \div \dfrac{c}{d} = \dfrac{a}{b} \cdot \dfrac{d}{c} = \dfrac{ad}{bc}$ Division

(4.3) Addition and subtraction of rational expressions are based on the following definitions:

1. $\dfrac{a}{b} + \dfrac{c}{b} = \dfrac{a + c}{b}$ Addition

2. $\dfrac{a}{b} - \dfrac{c}{b} = \dfrac{a - c}{b}$ Subtraction

(4.4) The following basic procedure is used to add or subtract rational expressions.

1. Factor the denominators.
2. Find the LCD.
3. Change each fraction to an equivalent fraction that has the LCD as its denominator.

4. Combine the numerators and place over the LCD.
5. Simplify by performing the addition or subtraction.
6. Look for ways to reduce the resulting fraction.

Fractional forms that contain rational numbers or rational expressions in the numerators and/or denominators are called **complex fractions**. The fundamental principle of fractions serves as a basis for simplifying complex fractions.

(4.5) To divide a polynomial by a monomial, we divide each term of the polynomial by the monomial. The procedure for dividing a polynomial by a polynomial, rather than a monomial, resembles the long-division process in arithmetic. (See the examples in Section 4.5.) Synthetic division is a shortcut to the long-division process when the divisor is of the form $x - k$.

(4.6) To solve a fractional equation, it is often easiest to begin by multiplying both sides of the equation by the LCD of all of the denominators in the equation. If an equation contains a variable in one or more denominators, then we must be careful to avoid any value of the variable that makes the denominator zero.

A **ratio** is the comparison of two numbers by division. A statement of equality between two ratios is a **proportion**.

We can treat some fractional equations as proportions, and we can solve them by applying the following property. This property is often called the **cross-multiplication** property:

$$\text{If } \frac{a}{b} = \frac{c}{d}, \quad \text{then } ad = bc.$$

(4.7) The techniques that we use to solve fractional equations can also be used to change the form of formulas containing rational expressions so that we can use those formulas to solve problems.

Chapter 4   Review Problem Set

For Problems 1–6, simplify each rational expression.

1. $\dfrac{26x^2y^3}{39x^4y^2}$

2. $\dfrac{a^2 - 9}{a^2 + 3a}$

3. $\dfrac{n^2 - 3n - 10}{n^2 + n - 2}$

4. $\dfrac{x^4 - 1}{x^3 - x}$

5. $\dfrac{8x^3 - 2x^2 - 3x}{12x^2 - 9x}$

6. $\dfrac{x^4 - 7x^2 - 30}{2x^4 + 7x^2 + 3}$

For Problems 7–10, simplify each complex fraction.

7. $\dfrac{\dfrac{5}{8} - \dfrac{1}{2}}{\dfrac{1}{6} + \dfrac{3}{4}}$

8. $\dfrac{\dfrac{3}{2x} + \dfrac{5}{3y}}{\dfrac{4}{x} - \dfrac{3}{4y}}$

9. $\dfrac{\dfrac{3}{x - 2} - \dfrac{4}{x^2 - 4}}{\dfrac{2}{x + 2} + \dfrac{1}{x - 2}}$

10. $1 - \dfrac{1}{2 - \dfrac{1}{x}}$

For Problems 11–22, perform the indicated operations, and express your answers in simplest form.

11. $\dfrac{6xy^2}{7y^3} \div \dfrac{15x^2y}{5x^2}$

12. $\dfrac{9ab}{3a + 6} \cdot \dfrac{a^2 - 4a - 12}{a^2 - 6a}$

13. $\dfrac{n^2 + 10n + 25}{n^2 - n} \cdot \dfrac{5n^3 - 3n^2}{5n^2 + 22n - 15}$

14. $\dfrac{x^2 - 2xy - 3y^2}{x^2 + 9y^2} \div \dfrac{2x^2 + xy - y^2}{2x^2 - xy}$

15. $\dfrac{2x + 1}{5} + \dfrac{3x - 2}{4}$

16. $\dfrac{3}{2n} + \dfrac{5}{3n} - \dfrac{1}{9}$

17. $\dfrac{3x}{x + 7} - \dfrac{2}{x}$

18. $\dfrac{10}{x^2 - 5x} + \dfrac{2}{x}$

19. $\dfrac{3}{n^2 - 5n - 36} + \dfrac{2}{n^2 + 3n - 4}$

20. $\dfrac{3}{2y + 3} + \dfrac{5y - 2}{2y^2 - 9y - 18} - \dfrac{1}{y - 6}$

21. $(18x^2 + 9x - 2) \div (3x + 2)$

22. $(3x^3 + 5x^2 - 6x - 2) \div (x + 4)$

For Problems 23–32, solve each equation.

23. $\dfrac{4x + 5}{3} + \dfrac{2x - 1}{5} = 2$

24. $\dfrac{3}{4x} + \dfrac{4}{5} = \dfrac{9}{10x}$

25. $\dfrac{a}{a - 2} - \dfrac{3}{2} = \dfrac{2}{a - 2}$

26. $\dfrac{4}{5y - 3} = \dfrac{2}{3y + 7}$

27. $n + \dfrac{1}{n} = \dfrac{53}{14}$

28. $\dfrac{1}{2x - 7} + \dfrac{x - 5}{4x^2 - 49} = \dfrac{4}{6x - 21}$

29. $\dfrac{x}{2x + 1} - 1 = \dfrac{-4}{7(x - 2)}$

30. $\dfrac{2x}{-5} = \dfrac{3}{4x - 13}$

31. $\dfrac{2n}{2n^2 + 11n - 21} - \dfrac{n}{n^2 + 5n - 14} = \dfrac{3}{n^2 + 5n - 14}$

32. $\dfrac{2}{t^2 - t - 6} + \dfrac{t + 1}{t^2 + t - 12} = \dfrac{t}{t^2 + 6t + 8}$

33. Solve $\dfrac{y - 6}{x + 1} = \dfrac{3}{4}$ for y.

34. Solve $\dfrac{x}{a} - \dfrac{y}{b} = 1$ for y.

For Problems 35–40, set up an equation, and solve the problem.

35. A sum of \$1400 is to be divided between two people in the ratio of $\dfrac{3}{5}$. How much does each person receive?

36. Working together, Dan and Julio can mow a lawn in 12 minutes. Julio can mow the lawn by himself in 10 minutes less time than it takes Dan by himself. How long does it take each of them to mow the lawn alone?

37. Suppose that car A can travel 250 miles in 3 hours less time than it takes car B to travel 440 miles. The rate of car B is 5 miles per hour faster than that of car A. Find the rates of both cars.

38. Mark can overhaul an engine in 20 hours, and Phil can do the same job by himself in 30 hours. If they both work together for a time and then Mark finishes the job by himself in 5 hours, how long did they work together?

39. Kelly contracted to paint a house for $640. It took him 20 hours longer than he had anticipated, so he earned $1.60 per hour less than he had calculated. How long had he anticipated that it would take him to paint the house?

40. Nasser rode his bicycle 66 miles in $4\frac{1}{2}$ hours. For the first 40 miles he averaged a certain rate, and then for the last 26 miles he reduced his rate by 3 miles per hour. Find his rate for the last 26 miles.

For Problems 1–4, simplify each rational expression.

1. $\dfrac{39x^2y^3}{72x^3y}$

2. $\dfrac{3x^2 + 17x - 6}{x^3 - 36x}$

3. $\dfrac{6n^2 - 5n - 6}{3n^2 + 14n + 8}$

4. $\dfrac{2x - 2x^2}{x^2 - 1}$

For Problems 5–13, perform the indicated operations, and express your answers in simplest form.

5. $\dfrac{5x^2y}{8x} \cdot \dfrac{12y^2}{20xy}$

6. $\dfrac{5a + 5b}{20a + 10b} \cdot \dfrac{a^2 - ab}{2a^2 + 2ab}$

7. $\dfrac{3x^2 + 10x - 8}{5x^2 + 19x - 4} \div \dfrac{3x^2 - 23x + 14}{x^2 - 3x - 28}$

8. $\dfrac{3x - 1}{4} + \dfrac{2x + 5}{6}$

9. $\dfrac{5x - 6}{3} - \dfrac{x - 12}{6}$

10. $\dfrac{3}{5n} + \dfrac{2}{3} - \dfrac{7}{3n}$

11. $\dfrac{3x}{x - 6} + \dfrac{2}{x}$

12. $\dfrac{9}{x^2 - x} - \dfrac{2}{x}$

13. $\dfrac{3}{2n^2 + n - 10} + \dfrac{5}{n^2 + 5n - 14}$

14. Divide $3x^3 + 10x^2 - 9x - 4$ by $x + 4$.

15. Simplify the complex fraction $\dfrac{\dfrac{3}{2x} - \dfrac{1}{6}}{\dfrac{2}{3x} + \dfrac{3}{4}}$.

16. Solve $\dfrac{x + 2}{y - 4} = \dfrac{3}{4}$ for y.

For Problems 17–22, solve each equation.

17. $\dfrac{x - 1}{2} - \dfrac{x + 2}{5} = -\dfrac{3}{5}$

18. $\dfrac{5}{4x} + \dfrac{3}{2} = \dfrac{7}{5x}$

19. $\dfrac{-3}{4n - 1} = \dfrac{-2}{3n + 11}$

20. $n - \dfrac{5}{n} = 4$

21. $\dfrac{6}{x - 4} - \dfrac{4}{x + 3} = \dfrac{8}{x - 4}$

22. $\dfrac{1}{3x - 1} + \dfrac{x - 2}{9x^2 - 1} = \dfrac{7}{6x - 2}$

For Problems 23–25, set up an equation and solve the problem.

23. The denominator of a rational number is 9 less than three times the numerator. The number in simplest form is $\dfrac{3}{8}$. Find the number.

24. It takes Jodi three times as long to deliver papers as it does Jannie. Together they can deliver the papers in 15 minutes. How long would it take Jodi by herself?

25. René can ride her bike 60 miles in 1 hour less time than it takes Sue to ride 60 miles. René's rate is 3 miles per hour faster than Sue's rate. Find René's rate.

Exponents and Radicals

5.1 Using Integers as Exponents

5.2 Roots and Radicals

5.3 Combining Radicals and Simplifying Radicals That Contain Variables

5.4 Products and Quotients Involving Radicals

5.5 Equations Involving Radicals

5.6 Merging Exponents and Roots

5.7 Scientific Notation

By knowing the time it takes for the pendulum to swing from one side to the other side and back, the formula, $T = 2\pi\sqrt{\dfrac{L}{32}}$, can be solved to find the length of the pendulum.

© Jonathan Nourok /PhotoEdit

How long will it take a pendulum that is 1.5 feet long to swing from one side to the other side and back? The formula $T = 2\pi\sqrt{\dfrac{L}{32}}$ can be used to determine that it will take approximately 1.4 seconds.

It is not uncommon in mathematics to find two separately developed concepts that are closely related to each other. In this chapter, we will first develop the concepts of exponent and root individually and then show how they merge to become even more functional as a unified idea.

5.1 Using Integers as Exponents

Thus far in the text we have used only positive integers as exponents. In Chapter 1 the expression b^n, where b is any real number and n is a positive integer, was defined by

$$b^n = b \cdot b \cdot b \cdot \ldots \cdot b \qquad n \text{ factors of } b$$

Then, in Chapter 3, some of the parts of the following property served as a basis for manipulation with polynomials.

Property 5.1

If m and n are positive integers, and a and b are real numbers (and $b \neq 0$ whenever it appears in a denominator), then

1. $b^n \cdot b^m = b^{n+m}$ **2.** $(b^n)^m = b^{mn}$

3. $(ab)^n = a^n b^n$

4. $\left(\dfrac{a}{b}\right)^n = \dfrac{a^n}{b^n}$

5. $\dfrac{b^n}{b^m} = b^{n-m}$ when $n > m$

$\dfrac{b^n}{b^m} = 1$ when $n = m$

$\dfrac{b^n}{b^m} = \dfrac{1}{b^{m-n}}$ when $n < m$

We are now ready to extend the concept of an exponent to include the use of zero and the negative integers as exponents.

First, let's consider the use of zero as an exponent. We want to use zero in such a way that the previously listed properties continue to hold. If $b^n \cdot b^m = b^{n+m}$ is to hold, then $x^4 \cdot x^0 = x^{4+0} = x^4$. In other words, x^0 *acts like* 1 because $x^4 \cdot x^0 = x^4$. This line of reasoning suggests the following definition.

Definition 5.1

If b is a nonzero real number, then

$$b^0 = 1$$

According to Definition 5.1, the following statements are all true.

$$5^0 = 1 \qquad\qquad\qquad (-413)^0 = 1$$

$$\left(\frac{3}{11}\right)^0 = 1 \qquad\qquad\qquad n^0 = 1, \quad n \neq 0$$

$$(x^3 y^4)^0 = 1, \qquad x \neq 0, y \neq 0$$

We can use a similar line of reasoning to motivate a definition for the use of negative integers as exponents. Consider the example $x^4 \cdot x^{-4}$. If $b^n \cdot b^m = b^{n+m}$ is to hold, then $x^4 \cdot x^{-4} = x^{4+(-4)} = x^0 = 1$. Thus x^{-4} must be the reciprocal of x^4, because their product is 1. That is,

$$x^{-4} = \frac{1}{x^4}$$

This suggests the following general definition.

Definition 5.2

If n is a positive integer, and b is a nonzero real number, then

$$b^{-n} = \frac{1}{b^n}$$

According to Definition 5.2, the following statements are all true.

$$x^{-5} = \frac{1}{x^5} \qquad\qquad\qquad 2^{-4} = \frac{1}{2^4} = \frac{1}{16}$$

$$10^{-2} = \frac{1}{10^2} = \frac{1}{100} \quad \text{or} \quad 0.01 \qquad\qquad \frac{2}{x^{-3}} = \frac{2}{\dfrac{1}{x^3}} = (2)\left(\frac{x^3}{1}\right) = 2x^3$$

$$\left(\frac{3}{4}\right)^{-2} = \frac{1}{\left(\dfrac{3}{4}\right)^2} = \frac{1}{\dfrac{9}{16}} = \frac{16}{9}$$

It can be verified (although it is beyond the scope of this text) that all of the parts of Property 5.1 hold for *all integers*. In fact, the following equality can replace the three separate statements for part (5).

$$\frac{b^n}{b^m} = b^{n-m} \quad \text{for all integers } n \text{ and } m$$

Let's restate Property 5.1 as it holds for all integers and include, at the right, a "name tag" for easy reference.

Property 5.2

If m and n are integers, and a and b are real numbers (and $b \neq 0$ whenever it appears in a denominator), then

1. $b^n \cdot b^m = b^{n+m}$ Product of two powers

2. $(b^n)^m = b^{mn}$ Power of a power

3. $(ab)^n = a^n b^n$ Power of a product

4. $\left(\dfrac{a}{b} \right)^n = \dfrac{a^n}{b^n}$ Power of a quotient

5. $\dfrac{b^n}{b^m} = b^{n-m}$ Quotient of two powers

Having the use of all integers as exponents enables us to work with a large variety of numerical and algebraic expressions. Let's consider some examples that illustrate the use of the various parts of Property 5.2.

E X A M P L E   1

Simplify each of the following numerical expressions.

(a) $10^{-3} \cdot 10^2$ **(b)** $(2^{-3})^{-2}$ **(c)** $(2^{-1} \cdot 3^2)^{-1}$

(d) $\left(\dfrac{2^{-3}}{3^{-2}} \right)^{-1}$ **(e)** $\dfrac{10^{-2}}{10^{-4}}$

Solution

(a) $10^{-3} \cdot 10^2 = 10^{-3+2}$ Product of two powers

                $= 10^{-1}$

                $= \dfrac{1}{10^1} = \dfrac{1}{10}$

(b) $(2^{-3})^{-2} = 2^{(-2)(-3)}$ Power of a power

                $= 2^6 = 64$

(c) $(2^{-1} \cdot 3^2)^{-1} = (2^{-1})^{-1}(3^2)^{-1}$ Power of a product

                $= 2^1 \cdot 3^{-2}$

                $= \dfrac{2^1}{3^2} = \dfrac{2}{9}$

(d) $\left(\dfrac{2^{-3}}{3^{-2}}\right)^{-1} = \dfrac{(2^{-3})^{-1}}{(3^{-2})^{-1}}$ Power of a quotient

$\qquad\qquad\quad = \dfrac{2^3}{3^2} = \dfrac{8}{9}$

(e) $\dfrac{10^{-2}}{10^{-4}} = 10^{-2-(-4)}$ Quotient of two powers

$\qquad\quad = 10^2 = 100$ ∎

E X A M P L E   2

Simplify each of the following; express final results without using zero or negative integers as exponents.

(a) $x^2 \cdot x^{-5}$ **(b)** $(x^{-2})^4$ **(c)** $(x^2 y^{-3})^{-4}$

(d) $\left(\dfrac{a^3}{b^{-5}}\right)^{-2}$ **(e)** $\dfrac{x^{-4}}{x^{-2}}$

Solution

(a) $x^2 \cdot x^{-5} = x^{2+(-5)}$ Product of two powers

$\qquad\qquad = x^{-3}$

$\qquad\qquad = \dfrac{1}{x^3}$

(b) $(x^{-2})^4 = x^{4(-2)}$ Power of a power

$\qquad\qquad = x^{-8}$

$\qquad\qquad = \dfrac{1}{x^8}$

(c) $(x^2 y^{-3})^{-4} = (x^2)^{-4}(y^{-3})^{-4}$ Power of a product

$\qquad\qquad = x^{-4(2)} y^{-4(-3)}$

$\qquad\qquad = x^{-8} y^{12}$

$\qquad\qquad = \dfrac{y^{12}}{x^8}$

(d) $\left(\dfrac{a^3}{b^{-5}}\right)^{-2} = \dfrac{(a^3)^{-2}}{(b^{-5})^{-2}}$ Power of a quotient

$\qquad\qquad = \dfrac{a^{-6}}{b^{10}}$

$\qquad\qquad = \dfrac{1}{a^6 b^{10}}$

(e) $\dfrac{x^{-4}}{x^{-2}} = x^{-4-(-2)}$ Quotient of two powers

$= x^{-2}$

$= \dfrac{1}{x^2}$ ∎

E X A M P L E   3   Find the indicated products and quotients; express your results using positive integral exponents only.

(a) $(3x^2y^{-4})(4x^{-3}y)$ **(b)** $\dfrac{12a^3b^2}{-3a^{-1}b^5}$ **(c)** $\left(\dfrac{15x^{-1}y^2}{5xy^{-4}}\right)^{-1}$

 Solution

(a) $(3x^2y^{-4})(4x^{-3}y) = 12x^{2+(-3)}y^{-4+1}$

$= 12x^{-1}y^{-3}$

$= \dfrac{12}{xy^3}$

(b) $\dfrac{12a^3b^2}{-3a^{-1}b^5} = -4a^{3-(-1)}b^{2-5}$

$= -4a^4b^{-3}$

$= -\dfrac{4a^4}{b^3}$

(c) $\left(\dfrac{15x^{-1}y^2}{5xy^{-4}}\right)^{-1} = (3x^{-1-1}y^{2-(-4)})^{-1}$ Note that we are first simplifying inside the parentheses.

$= (3x^{-2}y^6)^{-1}$

$= 3^{-1}x^2y^{-6}$

$= \dfrac{x^2}{3y^6}$ ∎

The final examples of this section show the simplification of numerical and algebraic expressions that involve sums and differences. In such cases, we use Definition 5.2 to change from negative to positive exponents so that we can proceed in the usual way.

E X A M P L E   4   Simplify $2^{-3} + 3^{-1}$.

Solution

$$2^{-3} + 3^{-1} = \dfrac{1}{2^3} + \dfrac{1}{3^1}$$

$$= \frac{1}{8} + \frac{1}{3}$$

$$= \frac{3}{24} + \frac{8}{24} \qquad \text{Use 24 as the LCD.}$$

$$= \frac{11}{24}$$

EXAMPLE 5

Simplify $(4^{-1} - 3^{-2})^{-1}$.

Solution

$$(4^{-1} - 3^{-2})^{-1} = \left(\frac{1}{4^1} - \frac{1}{3^2} \right)^{-1} \qquad \text{Apply } b^{-n} = \frac{1}{b^n} \text{ to } 4^{-1} \text{ and to } 3^{-2}.$$

$$= \left(\frac{1}{4} - \frac{1}{9} \right)^{-1}$$

$$= \left(\frac{9}{36} - \frac{4}{36} \right)^{-1} \qquad \text{Use 36 as the LCD.}$$

$$= \left(\frac{5}{36} \right)^{-1}$$

$$= \frac{1}{\left(\frac{5}{36} \right)^1} \qquad \text{Apply } b^{-n} = \frac{1}{b^n}.$$

$$= \frac{1}{\frac{5}{36}} = \frac{36}{5}$$

EXAMPLE 6

Express $a^{-1} + b^{-2}$ as a single fraction involving positive exponents only.

Solution

$$a^{-1} + b^{-2} = \frac{1}{a^1} + \frac{1}{b^2} \qquad \text{Use } ab^2 \text{ as the LCD.}$$

$$= \left(\frac{1}{a} \right) \left(\frac{b^2}{b^2} \right) + \left(\frac{1}{b^2} \right) \left(\frac{a}{a} \right) \qquad \begin{array}{l} \text{Change to equivalent fractions} \\ \text{with } ab^2 \text{ as the LCD.} \end{array}$$

$$= \frac{b^2}{ab^2} + \frac{a}{ab^2}$$

$$= \frac{b^2 + a}{ab^2}$$

Problem Set 5.1

For Problems 1–42, simplify each numerical expression.

1. 3^{-3}

2. 2^{-4}

3. -10^{-2}

4. 10^{-3}

5. $\dfrac{1}{3^{-4}}$

6. $\dfrac{1}{2^{-6}}$

7. $-\left(\dfrac{1}{3}\right)^{-3}$

8. $\left(\dfrac{1}{2}\right)^{-3}$

9. $\left(-\dfrac{1}{2}\right)^{-3}$

10. $\left(\dfrac{2}{7}\right)^{-2}$

11. $\left(-\dfrac{3}{4}\right)^{0}$

12. $\dfrac{1}{\left(\dfrac{4}{5}\right)^{-2}}$

13. $\dfrac{1}{\left(\dfrac{3}{7}\right)^{-2}}$

14. $-\left(\dfrac{5}{6}\right)^{0}$

15. $2^{7} \cdot 2^{-3}$

16. $3^{-4} \cdot 3^{6}$

17. $10^{-5} \cdot 10^{2}$

18. $10^{4} \cdot 10^{-6}$

19. $10^{-1} \cdot 10^{-2}$

20. $10^{-2} \cdot 10^{-2}$

21. $(3^{-1})^{-3}$

22. $(2^{-2})^{-4}$

23. $(5^{3})^{-1}$

24. $(3^{-1})^{3}$

25. $(2^{3} \cdot 3^{-2})^{-1}$

26. $(2^{-2} \cdot 3^{-1})^{-3}$

27. $(4^{2} \cdot 5^{-1})^{2}$

28. $(2^{-3} \cdot 4^{-1})^{-1}$

29. $\left(\dfrac{2^{-1}}{5^{-2}}\right)^{-1}$

30. $\left(\dfrac{2^{-4}}{3^{-2}}\right)^{-2}$

31. $\left(\dfrac{2^{-1}}{3^{-2}}\right)^{2}$

32. $\left(\dfrac{3^{2}}{5^{-1}}\right)^{-1}$

33. $\dfrac{3^{3}}{3^{-1}}$

34. $\dfrac{2^{-2}}{2^{3}}$

35. $\dfrac{10^{-2}}{10^{2}}$

36. $\dfrac{10^{-2}}{10^{-5}}$

37. $2^{-2} + 3^{-2}$

38. $2^{-4} + 5^{-1}$

39. $\left(\dfrac{1}{3}\right)^{-1} - \left(\dfrac{2}{5}\right)^{-1}$

40. $\left(\dfrac{3}{2}\right)^{-1} - \left(\dfrac{1}{4}\right)^{-1}$

41. $(2^{-3} + 3^{-2})^{-1}$

42. $(5^{-1} - 2^{-3})^{-1}$

For Problems 43–62, simplify each expression. Express final results without using zero or negative integers as exponents.

43. $x^{2} \cdot x^{-8}$

44. $x^{-3} \cdot x^{-4}$

45. $a^{3} \cdot a^{-5} \cdot a^{-1}$

46. $b^{-2} \cdot b^{3} \cdot b^{-6}$

47. $(a^{-4})^{2}$

48. $(b^{4})^{-3}$

49. $(x^{2}y^{-6})^{-1}$

50. $(x^{5}y^{-1})^{-3}$

51. $(ab^{3}c^{-2})^{-4}$

52. $(a^{3}b^{-3}c^{-2})^{-5}$

53. $(2x^{3}y^{-4})^{-3}$

54. $(4x^{5}y^{-2})^{-2}$

55. $\left(\dfrac{x^{-1}}{y^{-4}}\right)^{-3}$

56. $\left(\dfrac{y^{3}}{x^{-4}}\right)^{-2}$

57. $\left(\dfrac{3a^{-2}}{2b^{-1}}\right)^{-2}$

58. $\left(\dfrac{2xy^{2}}{5a^{-1}b^{-2}}\right)^{-1}$

59. $\dfrac{x^{-6}}{x^{-4}}$

60. $\dfrac{a^{-2}}{a^{2}}$

61. $\dfrac{a^{3}b^{-2}}{a^{-2}b^{-4}}$

62. $\dfrac{x^{-3}y^{-4}}{x^{2}y^{-1}}$

For Problems 63–74, find the indicated products and quotients. Express final results using positive integral exponents only.

63. $(2xy^{-1})(3x^{-2}y^{4})$

64. $(-4x^{-1}y^{2})(6x^{3}y^{-4})$

65. $(-7a^{2}b^{-5})(-a^{-2}b^{7})$

66. $(-9a^{-3}b^{-6})(-12a^{-1}b^{4})$

67. $\dfrac{28x^{-2}y^{-3}}{4x^{-3}y^{-1}}$

68. $\dfrac{63x^{2}y^{-4}}{7xy^{-4}}$

69. $\dfrac{-72a^{2}b^{-4}}{6a^{3}b^{-7}}$

70. $\dfrac{108a^{-5}b^{-4}}{9a^{-2}b}$

71. $\left(\dfrac{35x^{-1}y^{-2}}{7x^{4}y^{3}}\right)^{-1}$

72. $\left(\dfrac{-48ab^{2}}{-6a^{3}b^{5}}\right)^{-2}$

73. $\left(\dfrac{-36a^{-1}b^{-6}}{4a^{-1}b^{4}}\right)^{-2}$

74. $\left(\dfrac{8xy^{3}}{-4x^{4}y}\right)^{-3}$

For Problems 75–84, express each of the following as a single fraction involving positive exponents only.

75. $x^{-2} + x^{-3}$

76. $x^{-1} + x^{-5}$

77. $x^{-3} - y^{-1}$

78. $2x^{-1} - 3y^{-2}$

79. $3a^{-2} + 4b^{-1}$

80. $a^{-1} + a^{-1}b^{-3}$

81. $x^{-1}y^{-2} - xy^{-1}$

82. $x^2y^{-2} - x^{-1}y^{-3}$

83. $2x^{-1} - 3x^{-2}$

84. $5x^{-2}y + 6x^{-1}y^{-2}$

■ ■ ■ **THOUGHTS INTO WORDS**

85. Is the following simplification process correct?

$$(3^{-2})^{-1} = \left(\frac{1}{3^2}\right)^{-1} = \left(\frac{1}{9}\right)^{-1} = \frac{1}{\left(\frac{1}{9}\right)^1} = 9$$

Could you suggest a better way to do the problem?

86. Explain how to simplify $(2^{-1} \cdot 3^{-2})^{-1}$ and also how to simplify $(2^{-1} + 3^{-2})^{-1}$.

■ ■ ■ **FURTHER INVESTIGATIONS**

87. Use a calculator to check your answers for Problems 1–42.

88. Use a calculator to simplify each of the following numerical expressions. Express your answers to the nearest hundredth.

(a) $(2^{-3} + 3^{-3})^{-2}$

(b) $(4^{-3} - 2^{-1})^{-2}$

(c) $(5^{-3} - 3^{-5})^{-1}$

(d) $(6^{-2} + 7^{-4})^{-2}$

(e) $(7^{-3} - 2^{-4})^{-2}$

(f) $(3^{-4} + 2^{-3})^{-3}$

5.2 Roots and Radicals

To **square a number** means to raise it to the second power — that is, to use the number as a factor twice.

$$4^2 = 4 \cdot 4 = 16 \quad \text{Read "four squared equals sixteen."}$$

$$10^2 = 10 \cdot 10 = 100$$

$$\left(\frac{1}{2}\right)^2 = \frac{1}{2} \cdot \frac{1}{2} = \frac{1}{4}$$

$$(-3)^2 = (-3)(-3) = 9$$

A **square root of a number** is one of its two equal factors. Thus 4 is a square root of 16 because $4 \cdot 4 = 16$. Likewise, -4 is also a square root of 16 because

$(-4)(-4) = 16$. In general, a is a square root of b if $a^2 = b$. The following generalizations are a direct consequence of the previous statement.

1. Every positive real number has two square roots; one is positive and the other is negative. They are opposites of each other.

2. Negative real numbers have no real number square roots because any real number except zero is positive when squared.

3. The square root of 0 is 0.

The symbol $\sqrt{}$, called a **radical sign**, is used to designate the nonnegative square root. The number under the radical sign is called the **radicand**. The entire expression, such as $\sqrt{16}$, is called a **radical**.

$\sqrt{16} = 4$ $\sqrt{16}$ indicates the nonnegative or **principal square root** of 16.

$-\sqrt{16} = -4$ $-\sqrt{16}$ indicates the negative square root of 16.

$\sqrt{0} = 0$ Zero has only one square root. Technically, we could write $-\sqrt{0} = -0 = 0$.

$\sqrt{-4}$ is not a real number.

$-\sqrt{-4}$ is not a real number.

In general, the following definition is useful.

Definition 5.3

If $a \geq 0$ and $b \geq 0$, then $\sqrt{b} = a$ if and only if $a^2 = b$; a is called the **principal square root of b**.

To **cube a number** means to raise it to the third power — that is, to use the number as a factor three times.

$2^3 = 2 \cdot 2 \cdot 2 = 8$ Read "two cubed equals eight."

$4^3 = 4 \cdot 4 \cdot 4 = 64$

$\left(\dfrac{2}{3}\right)^3 = \dfrac{2}{3} \cdot \dfrac{2}{3} \cdot \dfrac{2}{3} = \dfrac{8}{27}$

$(-2)^3 = (-2)(-2)(-2) = -8$

A **cube root of a number** is one of its three equal factors. Thus 2 is a cube root of 8 because $2 \cdot 2 \cdot 2 = 8$. (In fact, 2 is the only real number that is a cube root of 8.) Furthermore, -2 is a cube root of -8 because $(-2)(-2)(-2) = -8$. (In fact, -2 is the only real number that is a cube root of -8.)

In general, a is a cube root of b if $a^3 = b$. The following generalizations are a direct consequence of the previous statement.

1. Every positive real number has one positive real number cube root.

2. Every negative real number has one negative real number cube root.

3. The cube root of 0 is 0.

Remark: Technically, every nonzero real number has three cube roots, but only one of them is a real number. The other two roots are classified as complex numbers. We are restricting our work at this time to the set of real numbers.

The symbol $\sqrt[3]{}$ designates the cube root of a number. Thus we can write

$$\sqrt[3]{8} = 2 \qquad\qquad \sqrt[3]{\frac{1}{27}} = \frac{1}{3}$$

$$\sqrt[3]{-8} = -2 \qquad\qquad \sqrt[3]{-\frac{1}{27}} = -\frac{1}{3}$$

In general, the following definition is useful.

Definition 5.4

$$\sqrt[3]{b} = a \quad \text{if and only if } a^3 = b.$$

In Definition 5.4, if b is a positive number, then a, the cube root, is a positive number; whereas if b is a negative number, then a, the cube root, is a negative number. The number a is called the principal cube root of b or simply the cube root of b.

The concept of root can be extended to fourth roots, fifth roots, sixth roots, and, in general, nth roots.

Definition 5.5

The nth root of b is a,   if and only if $a^n = b$.

We can make the following generalizations.

If n is an even positive integer, then the following statements are true.

1. Every positive real number has exactly two real nth roots — one positive and one negative. For example, the real fourth roots of 16 are 2 and −2.

2. Negative real numbers do not have real nth roots. For example, there are no real fourth roots of −16.

If n is an odd positive integer greater than 1, then the following statements are true.

1. Every real number has exactly one real nth root.

2. The real nth root of a positive number is positive. For example, the fifth root of 32 is 2.

3. The real nth root of a negative number is negative. For example, the fifth root of -32 is -2.

The symbol $\sqrt[n]{\ }$ designates the principal nth root. To complete our terminology, the n in the radical $\sqrt[n]{b}$ is called the index of the radical. If $n = 2$, we commonly write $\sqrt{b}$ instead of $\sqrt[2]{b}$.

The following chart can help summarize this information with respect to $\sqrt[n]{b}$, where n is a positive integer greater than 1.

	If b is		
	Positive	**Zero**	**Negative**
n is even	$\sqrt[n]{b}$ is a positive real number	$\sqrt[n]{b} = 0$	$\sqrt[n]{b}$ is not a real number
n is odd	$\sqrt[n]{b}$ is a positive real number	$\sqrt[n]{b} = 0$	$\sqrt[n]{b}$ is a negative real number

Consider the following examples.

$\sqrt[4]{81} = 3$ because $3^4 = 81$

$\sqrt[5]{32} = 2$ because $2^5 = 32$

$\sqrt[5]{-32} = -2$ because $(-2)^5 = -32$

$\sqrt[4]{-16}$ is not a real number   because any real number, except zero, is positive when raised to the fourth power

The following property is a direct consequence of Definition 5.5.

Property 5.3

1. $(\sqrt[n]{b})^n = b$ n is any positive integer greater than 1.

2. $\sqrt[n]{b^n} = b$ n is any positive integer greater than 1 if $b \geq 0$; n is an odd positive integer greater than 1 if $b < 0$.

Because the radical expressions in parts (1) and (2) of Property 5.3 are both equal to b, by the transitive property they are equal to each other. Hence $\sqrt[n]{b^n} = (\sqrt[n]{b})^n$.

The arithmetic is usually easier to simplify when we use the form $(\sqrt[n]{b})^n$. The following examples demonstrate the use of Property 5.3.

$$\sqrt{144^2} = (\sqrt{144})^2 = 12^2 = 144$$

$$\sqrt[3]{64^3} = (\sqrt[3]{64})^3 = 4^3 = 64$$

$$\sqrt[3]{(-8)^3} = (\sqrt[3]{-8})^3 = (-2)^3 = -8$$

$$\sqrt[4]{16^4} = (\sqrt[4]{16})^4 = 2^4 = 16$$

Let's use some examples to lead into the next very useful property of radicals.

$$\sqrt{4 \cdot 9} = \sqrt{36} = 6 \quad \text{and} \quad \sqrt{4} \cdot \sqrt{9} = 2 \cdot 3 = 6$$

$$\sqrt{16 \cdot 25} = \sqrt{400} = 20 \quad \text{and} \quad \sqrt{16} \cdot \sqrt{25} = 4 \cdot 5 = 20$$

$$\sqrt[3]{8 \cdot 27} = \sqrt[3]{216} = 6 \quad \text{and} \quad \sqrt[3]{8} \cdot \sqrt[3]{27} = 2 \cdot 3 = 6$$

$$\sqrt[3]{(-8)(27)} = \sqrt[3]{-216} = -6 \quad \text{and} \quad \sqrt[3]{-8} \cdot \sqrt[3]{27} = (-2)(3) = -6$$

In general, we can state the following property.

Property 5.4

$$\sqrt[n]{bc} = \sqrt[n]{b}\sqrt[n]{c} \qquad \sqrt[n]{b} \text{ and } \sqrt[n]{c} \text{ are real numbers}$$

Property 5.4 states that **the nth root of a product is equal to the product of the nth roots**.

■ Simplest Radical Form

The definition of nth root, along with Property 5.4, provides the basis for changing radicals to simplest radical form. The concept of **simplest radical form** takes on additional meaning as we encounter more complicated expressions, but for now it simply means that the radicand is not to contain any perfect powers of the index. Let's consider some examples to clarify this idea.

EXAMPLE 1

Express each of the following in simplest radical form.

(a) $\sqrt{8}$ (b) $\sqrt{45}$ (c) $\sqrt[3]{24}$ (d) $\sqrt[3]{54}$

Solution

(a) $\sqrt{8} = \sqrt{4 \cdot 2} = \sqrt{4}\sqrt{2} = 2\sqrt{2}$

4 is a
perfect
square.

(b) $\sqrt{45} = \sqrt{9 \cdot 5} = \sqrt{9}\sqrt{5} = 3\sqrt{5}$

             ↑
9 is a
perfect
square.

(c) $\sqrt[3]{24} = \sqrt[3]{8 \cdot 3} = \sqrt[3]{8}\sqrt[3]{3} = 2\sqrt[3]{3}$

         ↑
8 is a
perfect
cube.

(d) $\sqrt[3]{54} = \sqrt[3]{27 \cdot 2} = \sqrt[3]{27}\sqrt[3]{2} = 3\sqrt[3]{2}$

         ↑
27 is a
perfect
cube.

The first step in each example is to express the radicand of the given radical as the product of two factors, one of which must be a perfect nth power other than 1. Also, observe the radicands of the final radicals. In each case, the radicand cannot have a factor that is a perfect nth power other than 1. We say that the final radicals $2\sqrt{2}, 3\sqrt{5}, 2\sqrt[3]{3}$, and $3\sqrt[3]{2}$ are in **simplest radical form**.

You may vary the steps somewhat in changing to simplest radical form, but the final result should be the same. Consider some different approaches to changing $\sqrt{72}$ to simplest form:

$$\sqrt{72} = \sqrt{9}\sqrt{8} = 3\sqrt{8} = 3\sqrt{4}\sqrt{2} = 3 \cdot 2\sqrt{2} = 6\sqrt{2} \quad \text{or}$$

$$\sqrt{72} = \sqrt{4}\sqrt{18} = 2\sqrt{18} = 2\sqrt{9}\sqrt{2} = 2 \cdot 3\sqrt{2} = 6\sqrt{2} \quad \text{or}$$

$$\sqrt{72} = \sqrt{36}\sqrt{2} = 6\sqrt{2}$$

Another variation of the technique for changing radicals to simplest form is to prime-factor the radicand and then to look for perfect nth powers in exponential form. The following example illustrates the use of this technique.

E X A M P L E   2

Express each of the following in simplest radical form.

    (a) $\sqrt{50}$ **(b)** $3\sqrt{80}$ **(c)** $\sqrt[3]{108}$

Solution

    (a) $\sqrt{50} = \sqrt{2 \cdot 5 \cdot 5} = \sqrt{5^2}\sqrt{2} = 5\sqrt{2}$

    (b) $3\sqrt{80} = 3\sqrt{2 \cdot 2 \cdot 2 \cdot 2 \cdot 5} = 3\sqrt{2^4}\sqrt{5} = 3 \cdot 2^2\sqrt{5} = 12\sqrt{5}$

    (c) $\sqrt[3]{108} = \sqrt[3]{2 \cdot 2 \cdot 3 \cdot 3 \cdot 3} = \sqrt[3]{3^3}\sqrt[3]{4} = 3\sqrt[3]{4}$

Another property of nth roots is demonstrated by the following examples.

$$\sqrt{\frac{36}{9}} = \sqrt{4} = 2 \quad \text{and} \quad \frac{\sqrt{36}}{\sqrt{9}} = \frac{6}{3} = 2$$

$$\sqrt[3]{\frac{64}{8}} = \sqrt[3]{8} = 2 \quad \text{and} \quad \frac{\sqrt[3]{64}}{\sqrt[3]{8}} = \frac{4}{2} = 2$$

$$\sqrt[3]{\frac{-8}{64}} = \sqrt[3]{-\frac{1}{8}} = -\frac{1}{2} \quad \text{and} \quad \frac{\sqrt[3]{-8}}{\sqrt[3]{64}} = \frac{-2}{4} = -\frac{1}{2}$$

In general, we can state the following property.

Property 5.5

$$\sqrt[n]{\frac{b}{c}} = \frac{\sqrt[n]{b}}{\sqrt[n]{c}} \qquad \sqrt[n]{b} \text{ and } \sqrt[n]{c} \text{ are real numbers, and } c \neq 0.$$

Property 5.5 states that **the nth root of a quotient is equal to the quotient of the nth roots**.

To evaluate radicals such as $\sqrt{\dfrac{4}{25}}$ and $\sqrt[3]{\dfrac{27}{8}}$, for which the numerator and denominator of the fractional radicand are perfect nth powers, you may use Property 5.5 or merely rely on the definition of nth root.

$$\sqrt{\frac{4}{25}} = \frac{\sqrt{4}}{\sqrt{25}} = \frac{2}{5} \quad \text{or} \quad \sqrt{\frac{4}{25}} = \frac{2}{5} \quad \text{because} \quad \frac{2}{5} \cdot \frac{2}{5} = \frac{4}{25}$$

↑   ↑
Property 5.5   Definition of nth root
↓   ↓

$$\sqrt[3]{\frac{27}{8}} = \frac{\sqrt[3]{27}}{\sqrt[3]{8}} = \frac{3}{2} \quad \text{or} \quad \sqrt[3]{\frac{27}{8}} = \frac{3}{2} \quad \text{because} \quad \frac{3}{2} \cdot \frac{3}{2} \cdot \frac{3}{2} = \frac{27}{8}$$

Radicals such as $\sqrt{\dfrac{28}{9}}$ and $\sqrt[3]{\dfrac{24}{27}}$, in which only the denominators of the radicand are perfect nth powers, can be simplified as follows:

$$\sqrt{\frac{28}{9}} = \frac{\sqrt{28}}{\sqrt{9}} = \frac{\sqrt{28}}{3} = \frac{\sqrt{4}\sqrt{7}}{3} = \frac{2\sqrt{7}}{3}$$

$$\sqrt[3]{\frac{24}{27}} = \frac{\sqrt[3]{24}}{\sqrt[3]{27}} = \frac{\sqrt[3]{24}}{3} = \frac{\sqrt[3]{8}\sqrt[3]{3}}{3} = \frac{2\sqrt[3]{3}}{3}$$

Before we consider more examples, let's summarize some ideas that pertain to the simplifying of radicals. A radical is said to be in **simplest radical form** if the following conditions are satisfied.

1. No fraction appears with a radical sign. $\sqrt{\dfrac{3}{4}}$ violates this condition.

2. No radical appears in the denominator. $\dfrac{\sqrt{2}}{\sqrt{3}}$ violates this condition.

3. No radicand, when expressed in prime-factored form, contains a factor raised to a power equal to or greater than the index.

$\sqrt{2^3 \cdot 5}$ violates this condition.

Now let's consider an example in which neither the numerator nor the denominator of the radicand is a perfect nth power.

EXAMPLE 3

Simplify $\sqrt{\dfrac{2}{3}}$.

Solution

$$\sqrt{\frac{2}{3}} = \frac{\sqrt{2}}{\sqrt{3}} = \frac{\sqrt{2}}{\sqrt{3}} \cdot \frac{\sqrt{3}}{\sqrt{3}} = \frac{\sqrt{6}}{3}$$

Form of 1 ∎

We refer to the process we used to simplify the radical in Example 3 as **rationalizing the denominator**. Note that the denominator becomes a rational number. The process of rationalizing the denominator can often be accomplished in more than one way, as we will see in the next example.

EXAMPLE 4

Simplify $\dfrac{\sqrt{5}}{\sqrt{8}}$.

Solution A

$$\frac{\sqrt{5}}{\sqrt{8}} = \frac{\sqrt{5}}{\sqrt{8}} \cdot \frac{\sqrt{8}}{\sqrt{8}} = \frac{\sqrt{40}}{8} = \frac{\sqrt{4}\sqrt{10}}{8} = \frac{2\sqrt{10}}{8} = \frac{\sqrt{10}}{4}$$

Solution B

$$\frac{\sqrt{5}}{\sqrt{8}} = \frac{\sqrt{5}}{\sqrt{8}} \cdot \frac{\sqrt{2}}{\sqrt{2}} = \frac{\sqrt{10}}{\sqrt{16}} = \frac{\sqrt{10}}{4}$$

Solution C

$$\frac{\sqrt{5}}{\sqrt{8}} = \frac{\sqrt{5}}{\sqrt{4}\sqrt{2}} = \frac{\sqrt{5}}{2\sqrt{2}} = \frac{\sqrt{5}}{2\sqrt{2}} \cdot \frac{\sqrt{2}}{\sqrt{2}} = \frac{\sqrt{10}}{2\sqrt{4}} = \frac{\sqrt{10}}{2(2)} = \frac{\sqrt{10}}{4} \qquad \blacksquare$$

The three approaches to Example 4 again illustrate the need to think first and only then push the pencil. You may find one approach easier than another. To conclude this section, study the following examples and check the final radicals against the three conditions previously listed for **simplest radical form**.

EXAMPLE 5

Simplify each of the following.

(a) $\dfrac{3\sqrt{2}}{5\sqrt{3}}$ **(b)** $\dfrac{3\sqrt{7}}{2\sqrt{18}}$ **(c)** $\sqrt[3]{\dfrac{5}{9}}$ **(d)** $\dfrac{\sqrt[3]{5}}{\sqrt[3]{16}}$

Solution

(a) $\dfrac{3\sqrt{2}}{5\sqrt{3}} = \dfrac{3\sqrt{2}}{5\sqrt{3}} \cdot \dfrac{\sqrt{3}}{\sqrt{3}} = \dfrac{3\sqrt{6}}{5\sqrt{9}} = \dfrac{3\sqrt{6}}{15} = \dfrac{\sqrt{6}}{5}$

Form of 1

(b) $\dfrac{3\sqrt{7}}{2\sqrt{18}} = \dfrac{3\sqrt{7}}{2\sqrt{18}} \cdot \dfrac{\sqrt{2}}{\sqrt{2}} = \dfrac{3\sqrt{14}}{2\sqrt{36}} = \dfrac{3\sqrt{14}}{12} = \dfrac{\sqrt{14}}{4}$

Form of 1

(c) $\sqrt[3]{\dfrac{5}{9}} = \dfrac{\sqrt[3]{5}}{\sqrt[3]{9}} = \dfrac{\sqrt[3]{5}}{\sqrt[3]{9}} \cdot \dfrac{\sqrt[3]{3}}{\sqrt[3]{3}} = \dfrac{\sqrt[3]{15}}{\sqrt[3]{27}} = \dfrac{\sqrt[3]{15}}{3}$

Form of 1

(d) $\dfrac{\sqrt[3]{5}}{\sqrt[3]{16}} = \dfrac{\sqrt[3]{5}}{\sqrt[3]{16}} \cdot \dfrac{\sqrt[3]{4}}{\sqrt[3]{4}} = \dfrac{\sqrt[3]{20}}{\sqrt[3]{64}} = \dfrac{\sqrt[3]{20}}{4}$

Form of 1 $\qquad \blacksquare$

■ Applications of Radicals

Many real-world applications involve radical expressions. For example, police often use the formula $S = \sqrt{30Df}$ to estimate the speed of a car on the basis of the length of the skid marks at the scene of an accident. In this formula, S represents the speed of the car in miles per hour, D represents the length of the skid marks in feet, and f represents a coefficient of friction. For a particular situation, the coefficient of friction is a constant that depends on the type and condition of the road surface.

E X A M P L E   6

Using 0.35 as a coefficient of friction, determine how fast a car was traveling if it skidded 325 feet.

Solution

Substitute 0.35 for f and 325 for D in the formula.

$$S = \sqrt{30Df} = \sqrt{30(325)(0.35)} = 58, \quad \text{to the nearest whole number}$$

The car was traveling at approximately 58 miles per hour.   ■

The **period** of a pendulum is the time it takes to swing from one side to the other side and back. The formula

$$T = 2\pi\sqrt{\frac{L}{32}}$$

where T represents the time in seconds and L the length in feet, can be used to determine the period of a pendulum (see Figure 5.1).

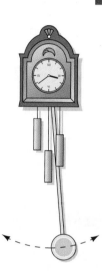

Figure 5.1

E X A M P L E   7

Find, to the nearest tenth of a second, the period of a pendulum of length 3.5 feet.

Solution

Let's use 3.14 as an approximation for π and substitute 3.5 for L in the formula.

$$T = 2\pi\sqrt{\frac{L}{32}} = 2(3.14)\sqrt{\frac{3.5}{32}} = 2.1, \quad \text{to the nearest tenth}$$

The period is approximately 2.1 seconds.   ■

Radical expressions are also used in some geometric applications. For example, the area of a triangle can be found by using a formula that involves a square root. If a, b, and c represent the lengths of the three sides of a triangle, the formula $K = \sqrt{s(s-a)(s-b)(s-c)}$, known as Heron's formula, can be used to determine the area (K) of the triangle. The letter s represents the semiperimeter of the triangle; that is, $s = \dfrac{a+b+c}{2}$.

EXAMPLE 8

Find the area of a triangular piece of sheet metal that has sides of lengths 17 inches, 19 inches, and 26 inches.

Solution

First, let's find the value of s, the semiperimeter of the triangle.

$$s = \frac{17 + 19 + 26}{2} = 31$$

Now we can use Heron's formula.

$$K = \sqrt{s(s-a)(s-b)(s-c)} = \sqrt{31(31-17)(31-19)(31-26)}$$

$$= \sqrt{31(14)(12)(5)}$$

$$= \sqrt{20{,}640}$$

$$= 161.4, \quad \text{to the nearest tenth}$$

Thus the area of the piece of sheet metal is approximately 161.4 square inches. ■

Remark: Note that in Examples 6–8, we did not simplify the radicals. When one is using a calculator to approximate the square roots, there is no need to simplify first.

Problem Set 5.2

For Problems 1–20, evaluate each of the following. For example, $\sqrt{25} = 5$.

1. $\sqrt{64}$

2. $\sqrt{49}$

3. $-\sqrt{100}$

4. $-\sqrt{81}$

5. $\sqrt[3]{27}$

6. $\sqrt[3]{216}$

7. $\sqrt[3]{-64}$

8. $\sqrt[3]{-125}$

9. $\sqrt[4]{81}$

10. $-\sqrt[4]{16}$

11. $\sqrt{\dfrac{16}{25}}$

12. $\sqrt{\dfrac{25}{64}}$

13. $-\sqrt{\dfrac{36}{49}}$

14. $\sqrt{\dfrac{16}{64}}$

15. $\sqrt{\dfrac{9}{36}}$

16. $\sqrt{\dfrac{144}{36}}$

17. $\sqrt[3]{\dfrac{27}{64}}$

18. $\sqrt[3]{-\dfrac{8}{27}}$

19. $\sqrt[3]{8^3}$

20. $\sqrt[4]{16^4}$

For Problems 21–74, change each radical to simplest radical form.

21. $\sqrt{27}$

22. $\sqrt{48}$

23. $\sqrt{32}$

24. $\sqrt{98}$

25. $\sqrt{80}$

26. $\sqrt{125}$

27. $\sqrt{160}$

28. $\sqrt{112}$

29. $4\sqrt{18}$

30. $5\sqrt{32}$

31. $-6\sqrt{20}$

32. $-4\sqrt{54}$

33. $\dfrac{2}{5}\sqrt{75}$

34. $\dfrac{1}{3}\sqrt{90}$

35. $\dfrac{3}{2}\sqrt{24}$

36. $\dfrac{3}{4}\sqrt{45}$

37. $-\dfrac{5}{6}\sqrt{28}$

38. $-\dfrac{2}{3}\sqrt{96}$

39. $\sqrt{\dfrac{19}{4}}$

40. $\sqrt{\dfrac{22}{9}}$

41. $\sqrt{\dfrac{27}{16}}$

42. $\sqrt{\dfrac{8}{25}}$

43. $\sqrt{\dfrac{75}{81}}$

44. $\sqrt{\dfrac{24}{49}}$

45. $\sqrt{\dfrac{2}{7}}$

46. $\sqrt{\dfrac{3}{8}}$

47. $\sqrt{\dfrac{2}{3}}$

48. $\sqrt{\dfrac{7}{12}}$

49. $\dfrac{\sqrt{5}}{\sqrt{12}}$

50. $\dfrac{\sqrt{3}}{\sqrt{7}}$

51. $\dfrac{\sqrt{11}}{\sqrt{24}}$

52. $\dfrac{\sqrt{5}}{\sqrt{48}}$

53. $\dfrac{\sqrt{18}}{\sqrt{27}}$

54. $\dfrac{\sqrt{10}}{\sqrt{20}}$

55. $\dfrac{\sqrt{35}}{\sqrt{7}}$

56. $\dfrac{\sqrt{42}}{\sqrt{6}}$

57. $\dfrac{2\sqrt{3}}{\sqrt{7}}$

58. $\dfrac{3\sqrt{2}}{\sqrt{6}}$

59. $-\dfrac{4\sqrt{12}}{\sqrt{5}}$

60. $\dfrac{-6\sqrt{5}}{\sqrt{18}}$

61. $\dfrac{3\sqrt{2}}{4\sqrt{3}}$

62. $\dfrac{6\sqrt{5}}{5\sqrt{12}}$

63. $\dfrac{-8\sqrt{18}}{10\sqrt{50}}$

64. $\dfrac{4\sqrt{45}}{-6\sqrt{20}}$

65. $\sqrt[3]{16}$

66. $\sqrt[3]{40}$

67. $2\sqrt[3]{81}$

68. $-3\sqrt[3]{54}$

69. $\dfrac{2}{\sqrt[3]{9}}$

70. $\dfrac{3}{\sqrt[3]{3}}$

71. $\dfrac{\sqrt[3]{27}}{\sqrt[3]{4}}$

72. $\dfrac{\sqrt[3]{8}}{\sqrt[3]{16}}$

73. $\dfrac{\sqrt[3]{6}}{\sqrt[3]{4}}$

74. $\dfrac{\sqrt[3]{4}}{\sqrt[3]{2}}$

75. Use a coefficient of friction of 0.4 in the formula from Example 6 and find the speeds of cars that left skid marks of lengths 150 feet, 200 feet, and 350 feet. Express your answers to the nearest mile per hour.

76. Use the formula from Example 7, and find the periods of pendulums of lengths 2 feet, 3 feet, and 4.5 feet. Express your answers to the nearest tenth of a second.

77. Find, to the nearest square centimeter, the area of a triangle that measures 14 centimeters by 16 centimeters by 18 centimeters.

78. Find, to the nearest square yard, the area of a triangular plot of ground that measures 45 yards by 60 yards by 75 yards.

79. Find the area of an equilateral triangle, each of whose sides is 18 inches long. Express the area to the nearest square inch.

80. Find, to the nearest square inch, the area of the quadrilateral in Figure 5.2.

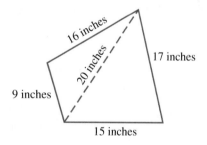

Figure 5.2

■ ■ ■ THOUGHTS INTO WORDS

81. Why is $\sqrt{-9}$ not a real number?

82. Why is it that we say 25 has two square roots (5 and −5), but we write $\sqrt{25} = 5$?

83. How is the multiplication property of 1 used when simplifying radicals?

84. How could you find a whole number approximation for $\sqrt{2750}$ if you did not have a calculator or table available?

■ ■ ■ **FURTHER INVESTIGATIONS**

85. Use your calculator to find a rational approximation, to the nearest thousandth, for (a) through (i).

(a) $\sqrt{2}$ (b) $\sqrt{75}$ (c) $\sqrt{156}$

(d) $\sqrt{691}$ (e) $\sqrt{3249}$ (f) $\sqrt{45,123}$

(g) $\sqrt{0.14}$ (h) $\sqrt{0.023}$ (i) $\sqrt{0.8649}$

86. Sometimes a fairly good estimate can be made of a radical expression by using whole number approximations. For example, $5\sqrt{35} + 7\sqrt{50}$ is approximately $5(6) + 7(7) = 79$. Using a calculator, we find that $5\sqrt{35} + 7\sqrt{50} = 79.1$, to the nearest tenth. In this case

our whole number estimate is very good. For (a) through (f), first make a whole number estimate, and then use your calculator to see how well you estimated.

(a) $3\sqrt{10} - 4\sqrt{24} + 6\sqrt{65}$

(b) $9\sqrt{27} + 5\sqrt{37} - 3\sqrt{80}$

(c) $12\sqrt{5} + 13\sqrt{18} + 9\sqrt{47}$

(d) $3\sqrt{98} - 4\sqrt{83} - 7\sqrt{120}$

(e) $4\sqrt{170} + 2\sqrt{198} + 5\sqrt{227}$

(f) $-3\sqrt{256} - 6\sqrt{287} + 11\sqrt{321}$

5.3 Combining Radicals and Simplifying Radicals That Contain Variables

Recall our use of the distributive property as the basis for combining similar terms. For example,

$$3x + 2x = (3 + 2)x = 5x$$

$$8y - 5y = (8 - 5)y = 3y$$

$$\frac{2}{3}a^2 + \frac{3}{4}a^2 = \left(\frac{2}{3} + \frac{3}{4}\right)a^2 = \left(\frac{8}{12} + \frac{9}{12}\right)a^2 = \frac{17}{12}a^2$$

In a like manner, expressions that contain radicals can often be simplified by using the distributive property, as follows:

$$3\sqrt{2} + 5\sqrt{2} = (3 + 5)\sqrt{2} = 8\sqrt{2}$$

$$7\sqrt[3]{5} - 3\sqrt[3]{5} = (7 - 3)\sqrt[3]{5} = 4\sqrt[3]{5}$$

$$4\sqrt{7} + 5\sqrt{7} + 6\sqrt{11} - 2\sqrt{11} = (4 + 5)\sqrt{7} + (6 - 2)\sqrt{11} = 9\sqrt{7} + 4\sqrt{11}$$

Note that *in order to be added or subtracted, radicals must have the same index and the same radicand.* Thus we cannot simplify an expression such as $5\sqrt{2} + 7\sqrt{11}$.

Simplifying by combining radicals sometimes requires that you first express the given radicals in simplest form and then apply the distributive property. The following examples illustrate this idea.

EXAMPLE 1 Simplify $3\sqrt{8} + 2\sqrt{18} - 4\sqrt{2}$.

Solution

$$\begin{aligned}
3\sqrt{8} + 2\sqrt{18} - 4\sqrt{2} &= 3\sqrt{4}\sqrt{2} + 2\sqrt{9}\sqrt{2} - 4\sqrt{2} \\
&= 3 \cdot 2 \cdot \sqrt{2} + 2 \cdot 3 \cdot \sqrt{2} - 4\sqrt{2} \\
&= 6\sqrt{2} + 6\sqrt{2} - 4\sqrt{2} \\
&= (6 + 6 - 4)\sqrt{2} = 8\sqrt{2}
\end{aligned}$$

EXAMPLE 2 Simplify $\dfrac{1}{4}\sqrt{45} + \dfrac{1}{3}\sqrt{20}$.

Solution

$$\begin{aligned}
\frac{1}{4}\sqrt{45} + \frac{1}{3}\sqrt{20} &= \frac{1}{4}\sqrt{9}\sqrt{5} + \frac{1}{3}\sqrt{4}\sqrt{5} \\
&= \frac{1}{4} \cdot 3 \cdot \sqrt{5} + \frac{1}{3} \cdot 2 \cdot \sqrt{5} \\
&= \frac{3}{4}\sqrt{5} + \frac{2}{3}\sqrt{5} = \left(\frac{3}{4} + \frac{2}{3}\right)\sqrt{5} \\
&= \left(\frac{9}{12} + \frac{8}{12}\right)\sqrt{5} = \frac{17}{12}\sqrt{5}
\end{aligned}$$

EXAMPLE 3 Simplify $5\sqrt[3]{2} - 2\sqrt[3]{16} - 6\sqrt[3]{54}$.

Solution

$$\begin{aligned}
5\sqrt[3]{2} - 2\sqrt[3]{16} - 6\sqrt[3]{54} &= 5\sqrt[3]{2} - 2\sqrt[3]{8}\sqrt[3]{2} - 6\sqrt[3]{27}\sqrt[3]{2} \\
&= 5\sqrt[3]{2} - 2 \cdot 2 \cdot \sqrt[3]{2} - 6 \cdot 3 \cdot \sqrt[3]{2} \\
&= 5\sqrt[3]{2} - 4\sqrt[3]{2} - 18\sqrt[3]{2} \\
&= (5 - 4 - 18)\sqrt[3]{2} \\
&= -17\sqrt[3]{2}
\end{aligned}$$

■ Radicals That Contain Variables

Before we discuss the process of simplifying radicals that contain variables, there is one technicality that we should call to your attention. Let's look at some examples to clarify the point. Consider the radical $\sqrt{x^2}$.

Let $x = 3$; then $\sqrt{x^2} = \sqrt{3^2} = \sqrt{9} = 3$.

Let $x = -3$; then $\sqrt{x^2} = \sqrt{(-3)^2} = \sqrt{9} = 3$.

Thus if $x \geq 0$, then $\sqrt{x^2} = x$, *but* if $x < 0$, then $\sqrt{x^2} = -x$. Using the concept of absolute value, we can state that for all real numbers, $\sqrt{x^2} = |x|$.

Now consider the radical $\sqrt{x^3}$. Because x^3 is negative when x is negative, we need to restrict x to the nonnegative reals when working with $\sqrt{x^3}$. Thus we can write, "if $x \geq 0$, then $\sqrt{x^3} = \sqrt{x^2}\sqrt{x} = x\sqrt{x}$," and no absolute-value sign is necessary. Finally, let's consider the radical $\sqrt[3]{x^3}$.

$$\text{Let } x = 2; \quad \text{then } \sqrt[3]{x^3} = \sqrt[3]{2^3} = \sqrt[3]{8} = 2.$$

$$\text{Let } x = -2; \text{then } \sqrt[3]{x^3} = \sqrt[3]{(-2)^3} = \sqrt[3]{-8} = -2.$$

Thus it is correct to write, "$\sqrt[3]{x^3} = x$ for all real numbers," and again no absolute-value sign is necessary.

The previous discussion indicates that technically, every radical expression involving variables in the radicand needs to be analyzed individually in terms of any necessary restrictions imposed on the variables. To help you gain experience with this skill, examples and problems are discussed under Further Investigations in the problem set. For now, however, to avoid considering such restrictions on a problem-to-problem basis, we shall merely assume that all variables represent positive real numbers. Let's consider the process of simplifying radicals that contain variables in the radicand. Study the following examples, and note that the same basic approach we used in Section 5.2 is applied here.

EXAMPLE 4

Simplify each of the following.

(a) $\sqrt{8x^3}$ **(b)** $\sqrt{45x^3y^7}$ **(c)** $\sqrt{180a^4b^3}$ **(d)** $\sqrt[3]{40x^4y^8}$

Solution

(a) $\sqrt{8x^3} = \sqrt{4x^2}\sqrt{2x} = 2x\sqrt{2x}$

$\uparrow$
$4x^2$ is a
perfect square.

(b) $\sqrt{45x^3y^7} = \sqrt{9x^2y^6}\sqrt{5xy} = 3xy^3\sqrt{5xy}$

$\uparrow$
$9x^2y^6$ is a
perfect square.

(c) If the numerical coefficient of the radicand is quite large, you may want to look at it in the prime-factored form.

$$\sqrt{180a^4b^3} = \sqrt{2 \cdot 2 \cdot 3 \cdot 3 \cdot 5 \cdot a^4 \cdot b^3}$$

$$= \sqrt{36 \cdot 5 \cdot a^4 \cdot b^3}$$

$$= \sqrt{36a^4b^2}\sqrt{5b}$$

$$= 6a^2b\sqrt{5b}$$

(d) $\sqrt[3]{40x^4y^8} = \sqrt[3]{8x^3y^6}\sqrt[3]{5xy^2} = 2xy^2\sqrt[3]{5xy^2}$

$8x^3y^6$ is a
perfect cube.

■

Before we consider more examples, let's restate (in such a way as to include radicands containing variables) the conditions necessary for a radical to be in simplest radical form.

---

1. A radicand contains no polynomial factor raised to a power equal to or greater than the index of the radical.

$\sqrt{x^3}$ violates this condition.

2. No fraction appears within a radical sign.

$\sqrt{\dfrac{2x}{3y}}$ violates this condition.

3. No radical appears in the denominator.

$\dfrac{3}{\sqrt[3]{4x}}$ violates this condition.

EXAMPLE 5

Express each of the following in simplest radical form.

(a) $\sqrt{\dfrac{2x}{3y}}$ **(b)** $\dfrac{\sqrt{5}}{\sqrt{12a^3}}$ **(c)** $\dfrac{\sqrt{8x^2}}{\sqrt{27y^5}}$

(d) $\dfrac{3}{\sqrt[3]{4x}}$ **(e)** $\dfrac{\sqrt[3]{16x^2}}{\sqrt[3]{9y^5}}$

Solution

(a) $\sqrt{\dfrac{2x}{3y}} = \dfrac{\sqrt{2x}}{\sqrt{3y}} = \dfrac{\sqrt{2x}}{\sqrt{3y}} \cdot \dfrac{\sqrt{3y}}{\sqrt{3y}} = \dfrac{\sqrt{6xy}}{3y}$

Form of 1

(b) $\dfrac{\sqrt{5}}{\sqrt{12a^3}} = \dfrac{\sqrt{5}}{\sqrt{12a^3}} \cdot \dfrac{\sqrt{3a}}{\sqrt{3a}} = \dfrac{\sqrt{15a}}{\sqrt{36a^4}} = \dfrac{\sqrt{15a}}{6a^2}$

Form of 1

(c) $\dfrac{\sqrt{8x^2}}{\sqrt{27y^5}} = \dfrac{\sqrt{4x^2}\sqrt{2}}{\sqrt{9y^4}\sqrt{3y}} = \dfrac{2x\sqrt{2}}{3y^2\sqrt{3y}} = \dfrac{2x\sqrt{2}}{3y^2\sqrt{3y}} \cdot \dfrac{\sqrt{3y}}{\sqrt{3y}}$

$$= \dfrac{2x\sqrt{6y}}{(3y^2)(3y)} = \dfrac{2x\sqrt{6y}}{9y^3}$$

(d) $\dfrac{3}{\sqrt[3]{4x}} = \dfrac{3}{\sqrt[3]{4x}} \cdot \dfrac{\sqrt[3]{2x^2}}{\sqrt[3]{2x^2}} = \dfrac{3\sqrt[3]{2x^2}}{\sqrt[3]{8x^3}} = \dfrac{3\sqrt[3]{2x^2}}{2x}$

(e) $\dfrac{\sqrt[3]{16x^2}}{\sqrt[3]{9y^5}} = \dfrac{\sqrt[3]{16x^2}}{\sqrt[3]{9y^5}} \cdot \dfrac{\sqrt[3]{3y}}{\sqrt[3]{3y}} = \dfrac{\sqrt[3]{48x^2y}}{\sqrt[3]{27y^6}} = \dfrac{\sqrt[3]{8}\sqrt[3]{6x^2y}}{3y^2} = \dfrac{2\sqrt[3]{6x^2y}}{3y^2}$ ■

Note that in part (c) we did some simplifying first before rationalizing the denominator, whereas in part (b) we proceeded immediately to rationalize the denominator. This is an individual choice, and you should probably do it both ways a few times to decide which you prefer.

Problem Set 5.3

For Problems 1–20, use the distributive property to help simplify each of the following. For example,

$$3\sqrt{8} - \sqrt{32} = 3\sqrt{4}\sqrt{2} - \sqrt{16}\sqrt{2}$$
$$= 3(2)\sqrt{2} - 4\sqrt{2}$$
$$= 6\sqrt{2} - 4\sqrt{2}$$
$$= (6-4)\sqrt{2} = 2\sqrt{2}$$

1. $5\sqrt{18} - 2\sqrt{2}$

2. $7\sqrt{12} + 4\sqrt{3}$

3. $7\sqrt{12} + 10\sqrt{48}$

4. $6\sqrt{8} - 5\sqrt{18}$

5. $-2\sqrt{50} - 5\sqrt{32}$

6. $-2\sqrt{20} - 7\sqrt{45}$

7. $3\sqrt{20} - \sqrt{5} - 2\sqrt{45}$

8. $6\sqrt{12} + \sqrt{3} - 2\sqrt{48}$

9. $-9\sqrt{24} + 3\sqrt{54} - 12\sqrt{6}$

10. $13\sqrt{28} - 2\sqrt{63} - 7\sqrt{7}$

11. $\dfrac{3}{4}\sqrt{7} - \dfrac{2}{3}\sqrt{28}$

12. $\dfrac{3}{5}\sqrt{5} - \dfrac{1}{4}\sqrt{80}$

13. $\dfrac{3}{5}\sqrt{40} + \dfrac{5}{6}\sqrt{90}$

14. $\dfrac{3}{8}\sqrt{96} - \dfrac{2}{3}\sqrt{54}$

15. $\dfrac{3\sqrt{18}}{5} - \dfrac{5\sqrt{72}}{6} + \dfrac{3\sqrt{98}}{4}$

16. $\dfrac{-2\sqrt{20}}{3} + \dfrac{3\sqrt{45}}{4} - \dfrac{5\sqrt{80}}{6}$

17. $5\sqrt[3]{3} + 2\sqrt[3]{24} - 6\sqrt[3]{81}$

18. $-3\sqrt[3]{2} - 2\sqrt[3]{16} + \sqrt[3]{54}$

19. $-\sqrt[3]{16} + 7\sqrt[3]{54} - 9\sqrt[3]{2}$

20. $4\sqrt[3]{24} - 6\sqrt[3]{3} + 13\sqrt[3]{81}$

For Problems 21–64, express each of the following in simplest radical form. All variables represent positive real numbers.

21. $\sqrt{32x}$

22. $\sqrt{50y}$

23. $\sqrt{75x^2}$

24. $\sqrt{108y^2}$

25. $\sqrt{20x^2y}$

26. $\sqrt{80xy^2}$

27. $\sqrt{64x^3y^7}$

28. $\sqrt{36x^5y^6}$

29. $\sqrt{54a^4b^3}$

30. $\sqrt{96a^7b^8}$

31. $\sqrt{63x^6y^8}$

32. $\sqrt{28x^4y^{12}}$

33. $2\sqrt{40a^3}$

34. $4\sqrt{90a^5}$

35. $\dfrac{2}{3}\sqrt{96xy^3}$

36. $\dfrac{4}{5}\sqrt{125x^4y}$

37. $\sqrt{\dfrac{2x}{5y}}$

38. $\sqrt{\dfrac{3x}{2y}}$

39. $\sqrt{\dfrac{5}{12x^4}}$

40. $\sqrt{\dfrac{7}{8x^2}}$

41. $\dfrac{5}{\sqrt{18y}}$

42. $\dfrac{3}{\sqrt{12x}}$

43. $\dfrac{\sqrt{7x}}{\sqrt{8y^5}}$

44. $\dfrac{\sqrt{5y}}{\sqrt{18x^3}}$

45. $\dfrac{\sqrt{18y^3}}{\sqrt{16x}}$

46. $\dfrac{\sqrt{2x^3}}{\sqrt{9y}}$

47. $\dfrac{\sqrt{24a^2b^3}}{\sqrt{7ab^6}}$

48. $\dfrac{\sqrt{12a^2b}}{\sqrt{5a^3b^3}}$

49. $\sqrt[3]{24y}$

50. $\sqrt[3]{16x^2}$

51. $\sqrt[3]{16x^4}$

52. $\sqrt[3]{54x^3}$

53. $\sqrt[3]{56x^6y^8}$

54. $\sqrt[3]{81x^5y^6}$

55. $\sqrt[3]{\dfrac{7}{9x^2}}$

56. $\sqrt[3]{\dfrac{5}{2x}}$

57. $\dfrac{\sqrt[3]{3y}}{\sqrt[3]{16x^4}}$

58. $\dfrac{\sqrt[3]{2y}}{\sqrt[3]{3x}}$

59. $\dfrac{\sqrt[3]{12xy}}{\sqrt[3]{3x^2y^5}}$

60. $\dfrac{5}{\sqrt[3]{9xy^2}}$

61. $\sqrt{8x + 12y}$ [Hint: $\sqrt{8x + 12y} = \sqrt{4(2x + 3y)}$]

62. $\sqrt{4x + 4y}$

63. $\sqrt{16x + 48y}$

64. $\sqrt{27x + 18y}$

For Problems 65–74, use the distributive property to help simplify each of the following. All variables represent positive real numbers.

65. $-3\sqrt{4x} + 5\sqrt{9x} + 6\sqrt{16x}$

66. $-2\sqrt{25x} - 4\sqrt{36x} + 7\sqrt{64x}$

67. $2\sqrt{18x} - 3\sqrt{8x} - 6\sqrt{50x}$

68. $4\sqrt{20x} + 5\sqrt{45x} - 10\sqrt{80x}$

69. $5\sqrt{27n} - \sqrt{12n} - 6\sqrt{3n}$

70. $4\sqrt{8n} + 3\sqrt{18n} - 2\sqrt{72n}$

71. $7\sqrt{4ab} - \sqrt{16ab} - 10\sqrt{25ab}$

72. $4\sqrt{ab} - 9\sqrt{36ab} + 6\sqrt{49ab}$

73. $-3\sqrt{2x^3} + 4\sqrt{8x^3} - 3\sqrt{32x^3}$

74. $2\sqrt{40x^5} - 3\sqrt{90x^5} + 5\sqrt{160x^5}$

■ ■ ■ THOUGHTS INTO WORDS

75. Is the expression $3\sqrt{2} + \sqrt{50}$ in simplest radical form? Defend your answer.

76. Your friend simplified $\dfrac{\sqrt{6}}{\sqrt{8}}$ as follows:

$$\dfrac{\sqrt{6}}{\sqrt{8}} \cdot \dfrac{\sqrt{8}}{\sqrt{8}} = \dfrac{\sqrt{48}}{8} = \dfrac{\sqrt{16}\sqrt{3}}{8} = \dfrac{4\sqrt{3}}{8} = \dfrac{\sqrt{3}}{2}$$

Is this a correct procedure? Can you show her a better way to do this problem?

77. Does $\sqrt{x + y}$ equal $\sqrt{x} + \sqrt{y}$? Defend your answer.

■ ■ ■ FURTHER INVESTIGATIONS

78. Use your calculator and evaluate each expression in Problems 1–16. Then evaluate the simplified expres-sion that you obtained when doing these problems. Your two results for each problem should be the same.

Consider these problems, where the variables could represent any real number. However, we would still have the restriction that the radical would represent a real number. In other words, the radicand must be nonnegative.

$\sqrt{98x^2} = \sqrt{49x^2}\sqrt{2} = 7|x|\sqrt{2}$ An absolute-value sign is necessary to ensure that the principal root is nonnegative.

$\sqrt{24x^4} = \sqrt{4x^4}\sqrt{6} = 2x^2\sqrt{6}$ Because x^2 is nonnegative, there is no need for an absolute-value sign to ensure that the principal root is nonnegative.

$\sqrt{25x^3} = \sqrt{25x^2}\sqrt{x} = 5x\sqrt{x}$ Because the radicand is defined to be nonnegative, x must be nonnegative, and there is no need for an absolute-value sign to ensure that the principal root is nonnegative.

$\sqrt{18b^5} = \sqrt{9b^4}\sqrt{2b} = 3b^2\sqrt{2b}$ An absolute-value sign is not necessary to ensure that the principal root is nonnegative.

$\sqrt{12y^6} = \sqrt{4y^6}\sqrt{3} = 2|y^3|\sqrt{3}$ An absolute-value sign is necessary to ensure that the principal root is nonnegative.

79. Do the following problems, where the variable could be any real number as long as the radical represents a real number. Use absolute-value signs in the answers as necessary.

(a) $\sqrt{125x^2}$ **(b)** $\sqrt{16x^4}$

(c) $\sqrt{8b^3}$ **(d)** $\sqrt{3y^5}$

(e) $\sqrt{288x^6}$ **(f)** $\sqrt{28m^8}$

(g) $\sqrt{128c^{10}}$ **(h)** $\sqrt{18d^7}$

(i) $\sqrt{49x^2}$ **(j)** $\sqrt{80n^{20}}$

(k) $\sqrt{81h^3}$

5.4   Products and Quotients Involving Radicals

As we have seen, Property 5.4 ($\sqrt[n]{bc} = \sqrt[n]{b}\sqrt[n]{c}$) is used to express one radical as the product of two radicals and also to express the product of two radicals as one radical. In fact, we have used the property for both purposes within the framework of simplifying radicals. For example,

$$\frac{\sqrt{3}}{\sqrt{32}} = \frac{\sqrt{3}}{\sqrt{16}\sqrt{2}} = \frac{\sqrt{3}}{4\sqrt{2}} = \frac{\sqrt{3}}{4\sqrt{2}} \cdot \frac{\sqrt{2}}{\sqrt{2}} = \frac{\sqrt{6}}{8}$$

$$\uparrow \qquad \uparrow \qquad\qquad\qquad \uparrow \qquad \uparrow$$

$$\sqrt[n]{bc} = \sqrt[n]{b}\sqrt[n]{c} \qquad\qquad \sqrt[n]{b}\sqrt[n]{c} = \sqrt[n]{bc}$$

The following examples demonstrate the use of Property 5.4 to multiply radicals and to express the product in simplest form.

E X A M P L E   1

Multiply and simplify where possible.

(a) $(2\sqrt{3})(3\sqrt{5})$ **(b)** $(3\sqrt{8})(5\sqrt{2})$

(c) $(7\sqrt{6})(3\sqrt{8})$ **(d)** $(2\sqrt[3]{6})(5\sqrt[3]{4})$

Solution

(a) $(2\sqrt{3})(3\sqrt{5}) = 2 \cdot 3 \cdot \sqrt{3} \cdot \sqrt{5} = 6\sqrt{15}$

(b) $(3\sqrt{8})(5\sqrt{2}) = 3 \cdot 5 \cdot \sqrt{8} \cdot \sqrt{2} = 15\sqrt{16} = 15 \cdot 4 = 60.$

(c) $(7\sqrt{6})(3\sqrt{8}) = 7 \cdot 3 \cdot \sqrt{6} \cdot \sqrt{8} = 21\sqrt{48} = 21\sqrt{16}\sqrt{3}$

$\qquad\qquad\qquad\qquad = 21 \cdot 4 \cdot \sqrt{3} = 84\sqrt{3}$

(d) $(2\sqrt[3]{6})(5\sqrt[3]{4}) = 2 \cdot 5 \cdot \sqrt[3]{6} \cdot \sqrt[3]{4} = 10\sqrt[3]{24}$

$\qquad\qquad\qquad\qquad\quad = 10\sqrt[3]{8}\sqrt[3]{3}$

$\qquad\qquad\qquad\qquad\quad = 10 \cdot 2 \cdot \sqrt[3]{3}$

$\qquad\qquad\qquad\qquad\quad = 20\sqrt[3]{3}$ ∎

Recall the use of the distributive property when finding the product of a monomial and a polynomial. For example, $3x^2(2x + 7) = 3x^2(2x) + 3x^2(7) = 6x^3 + 21x^2$. In a similar manner, the distributive property and Property 5.4 provide the basis for finding certain special products that involve radicals. The following examples illustrate this idea.

E X A M P L E   2

Multiply and simplify where possible.

(a) $\sqrt{3}(\sqrt{6} + \sqrt{12})$ **(b)** $2\sqrt{2}(4\sqrt{3} - 5\sqrt{6})$

(c) $\sqrt{6x}(\sqrt{8x} + \sqrt{12xy})$ **(d)** $\sqrt[3]{2}(5\sqrt[3]{4} - 3\sqrt[3]{16})$

Solution

(a) $\sqrt{3}(\sqrt{6} + \sqrt{12}) = \sqrt{3}\sqrt{6} + \sqrt{3}\sqrt{12}$

$\qquad\qquad\qquad\quad = \sqrt{18} + \sqrt{36}$

$\qquad\qquad\qquad\quad = \sqrt{9}\sqrt{2} + 6$

$\qquad\qquad\qquad\quad = 3\sqrt{2} + 6$

(b) $2\sqrt{2}(4\sqrt{3} - 5\sqrt{6}) = (2\sqrt{2})(4\sqrt{3}) - (2\sqrt{2})(5\sqrt{6})$

$\qquad\qquad\qquad\qquad\quad = 8\sqrt{6} - 10\sqrt{12}$

$\qquad\qquad\qquad\qquad\quad = 8\sqrt{6} - 10\sqrt{4}\sqrt{3}$

$\qquad\qquad\qquad\qquad\quad = 8\sqrt{6} - 20\sqrt{3}$

(c) $\sqrt{6x}(\sqrt{8x} + \sqrt{12xy}) = (\sqrt{6x})(\sqrt{8x}) + (\sqrt{6x})(\sqrt{12xy})$

$\qquad\qquad\qquad\qquad\quad = \sqrt{48x^2} + \sqrt{72x^2y}$

$\qquad\qquad\qquad\qquad\quad = \sqrt{16x^2}\sqrt{3} + \sqrt{36x^2}\sqrt{2y}$

$\qquad\qquad\qquad\qquad\quad = 4x\sqrt{3} + 6x\sqrt{2y}$

(d) $\sqrt[3]{2}(5\sqrt[3]{4} - 3\sqrt[3]{16}) = (\sqrt[3]{2})(5\sqrt[3]{4}) - (\sqrt[3]{2})(3\sqrt[3]{16})$

$\qquad\qquad\qquad\qquad\quad = 5\sqrt[3]{8} - 3\sqrt[3]{32}$

$\qquad\qquad\qquad\qquad\quad = 5 \cdot 2 - 3\sqrt[3]{8}\sqrt[3]{4}$

$\qquad\qquad\qquad\qquad\quad = 10 - 6\sqrt[3]{4}$ ∎

The distributive property also plays a central role in determining the product of two binomials. For example, $(x + 2)(x + 3) = x(x + 3) + 2(x + 3) = x^2 + 3x + 2x + 6 = x^2 + 5x + 6$. Finding the product of two binomial expressions that involve radicals can be handled in a similar fashion, as in the next examples.

E X A M P L E   3

Find the following products and simplify.

(a) $(\sqrt{3} + \sqrt{5})(\sqrt{2} + \sqrt{6})$ (b) $(2\sqrt{2} - \sqrt{7})(3\sqrt{2} + 5\sqrt{7})$

(c) $(\sqrt{8} + \sqrt{6})(\sqrt{8} - \sqrt{6})$ (d) $(\sqrt{x} + \sqrt{y})(\sqrt{x} - \sqrt{y})$

Solution

(a) $(\sqrt{3} + \sqrt{5})(\sqrt{2} + \sqrt{6}) = \sqrt{3}(\sqrt{2} + \sqrt{6}) + \sqrt{5}(\sqrt{2} + \sqrt{6})$

$$= \sqrt{3}\sqrt{2} + \sqrt{3}\sqrt{6} + \sqrt{5}\sqrt{2} + \sqrt{5}\sqrt{6}$$

$$= \sqrt{6} + \sqrt{18} + \sqrt{10} + \sqrt{30}$$

$$= \sqrt{6} + 3\sqrt{2} + \sqrt{10} + \sqrt{30}$$

(b) $(2\sqrt{2} - \sqrt{7})(3\sqrt{2} + 5\sqrt{7}) = 2\sqrt{2}(3\sqrt{2} + 5\sqrt{7})$

$$- \sqrt{7}(3\sqrt{2} + 5\sqrt{7})$$

$$= (2\sqrt{2})(3\sqrt{2}) + (2\sqrt{2})(5\sqrt{7})$$

$$- (\sqrt{7})(3\sqrt{2}) - (\sqrt{7})(5\sqrt{7})$$

$$= 12 + 10\sqrt{14} - 3\sqrt{14} - 35$$

$$= -23 + 7\sqrt{14}$$

(c) $(\sqrt{8} + \sqrt{6})(\sqrt{8} - \sqrt{6}) = \sqrt{8}(\sqrt{8} - \sqrt{6}) + \sqrt{6}(\sqrt{8} - \sqrt{6})$

$$= \sqrt{8}\sqrt{8} - \sqrt{8}\sqrt{6} + \sqrt{6}\sqrt{8} - \sqrt{6}\sqrt{6}$$

$$= 8 - \sqrt{48} + \sqrt{48} - 6$$

$$= 2$$

(d) $(\sqrt{x} + \sqrt{y})(\sqrt{x} - \sqrt{y}) = \sqrt{x}(\sqrt{x} - \sqrt{y}) + \sqrt{y}(\sqrt{x} - \sqrt{y})$

$$= \sqrt{x}\sqrt{x} - \sqrt{x}\sqrt{y} + \sqrt{y}\sqrt{x} - \sqrt{y}\sqrt{y}$$

$$= x - \sqrt{xy} + \sqrt{xy} - y$$

$$= x - y \qquad\blacksquare$$

Note parts (c) and (d) of Example 3; they fit the special-product pattern $(a + b)(a - b) = a^2 - b^2$. Furthermore, in each case the final product is in rational form. The factors $a + b$ and $a - b$ are called **conjugates**. This suggests a way of rationalizing the denominator in an expression that contains a binomial denominator with radicals. We will multiply by the conjugate of the binomial denominator. Consider the following example.

EXAMPLE 4

Simplify $\dfrac{4}{\sqrt{5} + \sqrt{2}}$ by rationalizing the denominator.

Solution

$$\frac{4}{\sqrt{5} + \sqrt{2}} = \frac{4}{\sqrt{5} + \sqrt{2}} \cdot \left(\frac{\sqrt{5} - \sqrt{2}}{\sqrt{5} - \sqrt{2}}\right) \quad \text{Form of 1.}$$

$$= \frac{4(\sqrt{5} - \sqrt{2})}{(\sqrt{5} + \sqrt{2})(\sqrt{5} - \sqrt{2})} = \frac{4(\sqrt{5} - \sqrt{2})}{5 - 2}$$

$$= \frac{4(\sqrt{5} - \sqrt{2})}{3} \quad \text{or} \quad \frac{4\sqrt{5} - 4\sqrt{2}}{3}$$

Either answer is acceptable. ■

The next examples further illustrate the process of rationalizing and simplifying expressions that contain binomial denominators.

EXAMPLE 5

For each of the following, rationalize the denominator and simplify.

(a) $\dfrac{\sqrt{3}}{\sqrt{6} - 9}$ **(b)** $\dfrac{7}{3\sqrt{5} + 2\sqrt{3}}$

(c) $\dfrac{\sqrt{x} + 2}{\sqrt{x} - 3}$ **(d)** $\dfrac{2\sqrt{x} - 3\sqrt{y}}{\sqrt{x} + \sqrt{y}}$

Solution

(a) $\dfrac{\sqrt{3}}{\sqrt{6} - 9} = \dfrac{\sqrt{3}}{\sqrt{6} - 9} \cdot \dfrac{\sqrt{6} + 9}{\sqrt{6} + 9}$

$$= \frac{\sqrt{3}(\sqrt{6} + 9)}{(\sqrt{6} - 9)(\sqrt{6} + 9)}$$

$$= \frac{\sqrt{18} + 9\sqrt{3}}{6 - 81}$$

$$= \frac{3\sqrt{2} + 9\sqrt{3}}{-75}$$

$$= \frac{3(\sqrt{2} + 3\sqrt{3})}{(-3)(25)}$$

$$= -\frac{\sqrt{2} + 3\sqrt{3}}{25} \quad \text{or} \quad \frac{-\sqrt{2} - 3\sqrt{3}}{25}$$

(b) $\dfrac{7}{3\sqrt{5} + 2\sqrt{3}} = \dfrac{7}{3\sqrt{5} + 2\sqrt{3}} \cdot \dfrac{3\sqrt{5} - 2\sqrt{3}}{3\sqrt{5} - 2\sqrt{3}}$

$= \dfrac{7(3\sqrt{5} - 2\sqrt{3})}{(3\sqrt{5} + 2\sqrt{3})(3\sqrt{5} - 2\sqrt{3})}$

$= \dfrac{7(3\sqrt{5} - 2\sqrt{3})}{45 - 12}$

$= \dfrac{7(3\sqrt{5} - 2\sqrt{3})}{33}$ or $\dfrac{21\sqrt{5} - 14\sqrt{3}}{33}$

(c) $\dfrac{\sqrt{x} + 2}{\sqrt{x} - 3} = \dfrac{\sqrt{x} + 2}{\sqrt{x} - 3} \cdot \dfrac{\sqrt{x} + 3}{\sqrt{x} + 3} = \dfrac{(\sqrt{x} + 2)(\sqrt{x} + 3)}{(\sqrt{x} - 3)(\sqrt{x} + 3)}$

$= \dfrac{x + 3\sqrt{x} + 2\sqrt{x} + 6}{x - 9}$

$= \dfrac{x + 5\sqrt{x} + 6}{x - 9}$

(d) $\dfrac{2\sqrt{x} - 3\sqrt{y}}{\sqrt{x} + \sqrt{y}} = \dfrac{2\sqrt{x} - 3\sqrt{y}}{\sqrt{x} + \sqrt{y}} \cdot \dfrac{\sqrt{x} - \sqrt{y}}{\sqrt{x} - \sqrt{y}}$

$= \dfrac{(2\sqrt{x} - 3\sqrt{y})(\sqrt{x} - \sqrt{y})}{(\sqrt{x} + \sqrt{y})(\sqrt{x} - \sqrt{y})}$

$= \dfrac{2x - 2\sqrt{xy} - 3\sqrt{xy} + 3y}{x - y}$

$= \dfrac{2x - 5\sqrt{xy} + 3y}{x - y}$ ■

Problem Set 5.4

For Problems 1–14, multiply and simplify where possible.

1. $\sqrt{6}\sqrt{12}$

2. $\sqrt{8}\sqrt{6}$

3. $(3\sqrt{3})(2\sqrt{6})$

4. $(5\sqrt{2})(3\sqrt{12})$

5. $(4\sqrt{2})(-6\sqrt{5})$

6. $(-7\sqrt{3})(2\sqrt{5})$

7. $(-3\sqrt{3})(-4\sqrt{8})$

8. $(-5\sqrt{8})(-6\sqrt{7})$

9. $(5\sqrt{6})(4\sqrt{6})$

10. $(3\sqrt{7})(2\sqrt{7})$

11. $(2\sqrt[3]{4})(6\sqrt[3]{2})$

12. $(4\sqrt[3]{3})(5\sqrt[3]{9})$

13. $(4\sqrt[3]{6})(7\sqrt[3]{4})$

14. $(9\sqrt[3]{6})(2\sqrt[3]{9})$

For Problems 15–52, find the following products and express answers in simplest radical form. All variables represent nonnegative real numbers.

15. $\sqrt{2}(\sqrt{3} + \sqrt{5})$

16. $\sqrt{3}(\sqrt{7} + \sqrt{10})$

17. $3\sqrt{5}(2\sqrt{2} - \sqrt{7})$

18. $5\sqrt{6}(2\sqrt{5} - 3\sqrt{11})$

19. $2\sqrt{6}(3\sqrt{8} - 5\sqrt{12})$

20. $4\sqrt{2}(3\sqrt{12} + 7\sqrt{6})$

21. $-4\sqrt{5}(2\sqrt{5} + 4\sqrt{12})$

22. $-5\sqrt{3}(3\sqrt{12} - 9\sqrt{8})$

23. $3\sqrt{x}(5\sqrt{2} + \sqrt{y})$

24. $\sqrt{2x}(3\sqrt{y} - 7\sqrt{5})$

25. $\sqrt{xy}(5\sqrt{xy} - 6\sqrt{x})$ **26.** $4\sqrt{x}(2\sqrt{xy} + 2\sqrt{x})$

27. $\sqrt{5y}(\sqrt{8x} + \sqrt{12y^2})$ **28.** $\sqrt{2x}(\sqrt{12xy} - \sqrt{8y})$

29. $5\sqrt{3}(2\sqrt{8} - 3\sqrt{18})$ **30.** $2\sqrt{2}(3\sqrt{12} - \sqrt{27})$

31. $(\sqrt{3} + 4)(\sqrt{3} - 7)$ **32.** $(\sqrt{2} + 6)(\sqrt{2} - 2)$

33. $(\sqrt{5} - 6)(\sqrt{5} - 3)$ **34.** $(\sqrt{7} - 2)(\sqrt{7} - 8)$

35. $(3\sqrt{5} - 2\sqrt{3})(2\sqrt{7} + \sqrt{2})$

36. $(\sqrt{2} + \sqrt{3})(\sqrt{5} - \sqrt{7})$

37. $(2\sqrt{6} + 3\sqrt{5})(\sqrt{8} - 3\sqrt{12})$

38. $(5\sqrt{2} - 4\sqrt{6})(2\sqrt{8} + \sqrt{6})$

39. $(2\sqrt{6} + 5\sqrt{5})(3\sqrt{6} - \sqrt{5})$

40. $(7\sqrt{3} - \sqrt{7})(2\sqrt{3} + 4\sqrt{7})$

41. $(3\sqrt{2} - 5\sqrt{3})(6\sqrt{2} - 7\sqrt{3})$

42. $(\sqrt{8} - 3\sqrt{10})(2\sqrt{8} - 6\sqrt{10})$

43. $(\sqrt{6} + 4)(\sqrt{6} - 4)$

44. $(\sqrt{7} - 2)(\sqrt{7} + 2)$

45. $(\sqrt{2} + \sqrt{10})(\sqrt{2} - \sqrt{10})$

46. $(2\sqrt{3} + \sqrt{11})(2\sqrt{3} - \sqrt{11})$

47. $(\sqrt{2x} + \sqrt{3y})(\sqrt{2x} - \sqrt{3y})$

48. $(2\sqrt{x} - 5\sqrt{y})(2\sqrt{x} + 5\sqrt{y})$

49. $2\sqrt[3]{3}(5\sqrt[3]{4} + \sqrt[3]{6})$

50. $2\sqrt[3]{2}(3\sqrt[3]{6} - 4\sqrt[3]{5})$

51. $3\sqrt[3]{4}(2\sqrt[3]{2} - 6\sqrt[3]{4})$

52. $3\sqrt[3]{3}(4\sqrt[3]{9} + 5\sqrt[3]{7})$

For Problems 53–76, rationalize the denominator and simplify. All variables represent positive real numbers.

53. $\dfrac{2}{\sqrt{7} + 1}$ **54.** $\dfrac{6}{\sqrt{5} + 2}$

55. $\dfrac{3}{\sqrt{2} - 5}$ **56.** $\dfrac{-4}{\sqrt{6} - 3}$

57. $\dfrac{1}{\sqrt{2} + \sqrt{7}}$ **58.** $\dfrac{3}{\sqrt{3} + \sqrt{10}}$

59. $\dfrac{\sqrt{2}}{\sqrt{10} - \sqrt{3}}$ **60.** $\dfrac{\sqrt{3}}{\sqrt{7} - \sqrt{2}}$

61. $\dfrac{\sqrt{3}}{2\sqrt{5} + 4}$ **62.** $\dfrac{\sqrt{7}}{3\sqrt{2} - 5}$

63. $\dfrac{6}{3\sqrt{7} - 2\sqrt{6}}$ **64.** $\dfrac{5}{2\sqrt{5} + 3\sqrt{7}}$

65. $\dfrac{\sqrt{6}}{3\sqrt{2} + 2\sqrt{3}}$ **66.** $\dfrac{3\sqrt{6}}{5\sqrt{3} - 4\sqrt{2}}$

67. $\dfrac{2}{\sqrt{x} + 4}$ **68.** $\dfrac{3}{\sqrt{x} + 7}$

69. $\dfrac{\sqrt{x}}{\sqrt{x} - 5}$ **70.** $\dfrac{\sqrt{x}}{\sqrt{x} - 1}$

71. $\dfrac{\sqrt{x} - 2}{\sqrt{x} + 6}$ **72.** $\dfrac{\sqrt{x} + 1}{\sqrt{x} - 10}$

73. $\dfrac{\sqrt{x}}{\sqrt{x} + 2\sqrt{y}}$ **74.** $\dfrac{\sqrt{y}}{2\sqrt{x} - \sqrt{y}}$

75. $\dfrac{3\sqrt{y}}{2\sqrt{x} - 3\sqrt{y}}$ **76.** $\dfrac{2\sqrt{x}}{3\sqrt{x} + 5\sqrt{y}}$

■ ■ ■ **THOUGHTS INTO WORDS**

77. How would you help someone rationalize the denominator and simplify $\dfrac{4}{\sqrt{8} + \sqrt{12}}$?

78. Discuss how the distributive property has been used thus far in this chapter.

79. How would you simplify the expression $\dfrac{\sqrt{8} + \sqrt{12}}{\sqrt{2}}$?

■ ■ ■ **FURTHER INVESTIGATIONS**

80. Use your calculator to evaluate each expression in Problems 53–66. Then evaluate the results you obtained when you did the problems.

5.5 Equations Involving Radicals

We often refer to equations that contain radicals with variables in a radicand as **radical equations**. In this section we discuss techniques for solving such equations that contain one or more radicals. To solve radical equations, we need the following property of equality.

Property 5.6

Let a and b be real numbers and n be a positive integer.

If $a = b$, then $a^n = b^n$.

Property 5.6 states that we can raise both sides of an equation to a positive integral power. However, raising both sides of an equation to a positive integral power sometimes produces results that do not satisfy the original equation. Let's consider two examples to illustrate this point.

E X A M P L E 1 Solve $\sqrt{2x - 5} = 7$.

Solution

$$\sqrt{2x - 5} = 7$$
$$(\sqrt{2x - 5})^2 = 7^2 \qquad \text{Square both sides.}$$
$$2x - 5 = 49$$
$$2x = 54$$
$$x = 27$$

 Check

$$\sqrt{2x - 5} = 7$$
$$\sqrt{2(27) - 5} \stackrel{?}{=} 7$$
$$\sqrt{49} \stackrel{?}{=} 7$$
$$7 = 7$$

The solution set for $\sqrt{2x - 5} = 7$ is $\{27\}$. ■

EXAMPLE 2 Solve $\sqrt{3a + 4} = -4$.

Solution

$$\sqrt{3a + 4} = -4$$

$$(\sqrt{3a + 4})^2 = (-4)^2 \qquad \text{Square both sides.}$$

$$3a + 4 = 16$$

$$3a = 12$$

$$a = 4$$

✔ **Check**

$$\sqrt{3a + 4} = -4$$

$$\sqrt{3(4) + 4} \stackrel{?}{=} -4$$

$$\sqrt{16} \stackrel{?}{=} -4$$

$$4 \neq -4$$

Because 4 does not check, the original equation has no real number solution. Thus the solution set is $\varnothing$. ∎

In general, raising both sides of an equation to a positive integral power produces an equation that has all of the solutions of the original equation, but it may also have some extra solutions that do not satisfy the original equation. Such extra solutions are called **extraneous solutions**. Therefore, when using Property 5.6, you *must* check each potential solution in the original equation.

Let's consider some examples to illustrate different situations that arise when we are solving radical equations.

EXAMPLE 3 Solve $\sqrt{2t - 4} = t - 2$.

Solution

$$\sqrt{2t - 4} = t - 2$$

$$(\sqrt{2t - 4})^2 = (t - 2)^2 \qquad \text{Square both sides.}$$

$$2t - 4 = t^2 - 4t + 4$$

$$0 = t^2 - 6t + 8$$

$$0 = (t - 2)(t - 4) \qquad \text{Factor the right side.}$$

$$t - 2 = 0 \quad \text{or} \quad t - 4 = 0 \qquad \text{Apply: } ab = 0 \text{ if and only if}$$
$$\phantom{t - 2 = 0 \quad \text{or} \quad } a = 0 \text{ or } b = 0.$$

$$t = 2 \quad \text{or} \quad t = 4$$

✔ **Check**

$$\sqrt{2t - 4} = t - 2 \qquad\qquad \sqrt{2t - 4} = t - 2$$

$$\sqrt{2(2) - 4} \overset{?}{=} 2 - 2, \quad \text{when } t = 2 \quad \text{or} \quad \sqrt{2(4) - 4} \overset{?}{=} 4 - 2, \quad \text{when } t = 4$$

$$\sqrt{0} \overset{?}{=} 0 \qquad\qquad \sqrt{4} \overset{?}{=} 2$$

$$0 = 0 \qquad\qquad 2 = 2$$

The solution set is $\{2, 4\}$. ∎

E X A M P L E   4   Solve $\sqrt{y} + 6 = y$.

Solution

$$\sqrt{y} + 6 = y$$

$$\sqrt{y} = y - 6$$

$$(\sqrt{y})^2 = (y - 6)^2 \qquad \text{Square both sides.}$$

$$y = y^2 - 12y + 36$$

$$0 = y^2 - 13y + 36$$

$$0 = (y - 4)(y - 9) \qquad \text{Factor the right side.}$$

$$y - 4 = 0 \qquad \text{or} \qquad y - 9 = 0 \qquad\quad \text{Apply: } ab = 0 \text{ if and}$$
$$\qquad\qquad\qquad\qquad\qquad\qquad\qquad\qquad \text{only if } a = 0 \text{ or } b = 0.$$

$$y = 4 \qquad \text{or} \qquad y = 9$$

✔ **Check**

$$\sqrt{y} + 6 = y \qquad\qquad \sqrt{y} + 6 = y$$

$$\sqrt{4} + 6 \overset{?}{=} 4, \quad \text{when } y = 4 \quad \text{or} \quad \sqrt{9} + 6 \overset{?}{=} 9, \quad \text{when } y = 9$$

$$2 + 6 \overset{?}{=} 4 \qquad\qquad 3 + 6 \overset{?}{=} 9$$

$$8 \neq 4 \qquad\qquad 9 = 9$$

The only solution is 9; the solution set is $\{9\}$. ∎

In Example 4, note that we changed the form of the original equation $\sqrt{y} + 6 = y$ to $\sqrt{y} = y - 6$ before we squared both sides. Squaring both sides of $\sqrt{y} + 6 = y$ produces $y + 12\sqrt{y} + 36 = y^2$, which is a much more complex equation that still contains a radical. Here again, it pays to think ahead before carrying out all the steps. Now let's consider an example involving a cube root.

E X A M P L E   5   Solve $\sqrt[3]{n^2 - 1} = 2$.

Solution

$$\sqrt[3]{n^2 - 1} = 2$$

$$(\sqrt[3]{n^2 - 1})^3 = 2^3 \qquad \text{Cube both sides.}$$

$$n^2 - 1 = 8$$

$$n^2 - 9 = 0$$

$$(n + 3)(n - 3) = 0$$

$$n + 3 = 0 \quad \text{or} \quad n - 3 = 0$$

$$n = -3 \quad \text{or} \quad n = 3$$

✔ **Check**

$$\sqrt[3]{n^2 - 1} = 2$$

$$\sqrt[3]{(-3)^2 - 1} \overset{?}{=} 2, \quad \text{when } n = -3 \quad \text{or}$$

$$\sqrt[3]{8} \overset{?}{=} 2$$

$$2 = 2$$

$$\sqrt[3]{n^2 - 1} = 2$$

$$\sqrt[3]{3^2 - 1} \overset{?}{=} 2, \quad \text{when } n = 3$$

$$\sqrt[3]{8} \overset{?}{=} 2$$

$$2 = 2$$

The solution set is $\{-3, 3\}$. ∎

It may be necessary to square both sides of an equation, simplify the resulting equation, and then square both sides again. The next example illustrates this type of problem.

E X A M P L E   6

Solve $\sqrt{x + 2} = 7 - \sqrt{x + 9}$.

Solution

$$\sqrt{x + 2} = 7 - \sqrt{x + 9}$$

$$(\sqrt{x + 2})^2 = (7 - \sqrt{x + 9})^2 \qquad \text{Square both sides.}$$

$$x + 2 = 49 - 14\sqrt{x + 9} + x + 9$$

$$x + 2 = x + 58 - 14\sqrt{x + 9}$$

$$-56 = -14\sqrt{x + 9}$$

$$4 = \sqrt{x + 9}$$

$$(4)^2 = (\sqrt{x + 9})^2 \qquad \text{Square both sides.}$$

$$16 = x + 9$$

$$7 = x$$

✔ **Check**

$$\sqrt{x + 2} = 7 - \sqrt{x + 9}$$

$$\sqrt{7 + 2} \overset{?}{=} 7 - \sqrt{7 + 9}$$

$$\sqrt{9} \overset{?}{=} 7 - \sqrt{16}$$

$$3 \overset{?}{=} 7 - 4$$

$$3 = 3$$

The solution set is $\{7\}$. ∎

■ Another Look at Applications

In Section 5.1 we used the formula $S = \sqrt{30Df}$ to approximate how fast a car was traveling on the basis of the length of skid marks. (Remember that S represents the speed of the car in miles per hour, D represents the length of the skid marks in feet, and f represents a coefficient of friction.) This same formula can be used to estimate the length of skid marks that are produced by cars traveling at different rates on various types of road surfaces. To use the formula for this purpose, let's change the form of the equation by solving for D.

$$\sqrt{30Df} = S$$

$$30Df = S^2 \qquad \text{The result of squaring both sides of the original equation}$$

$$D = \frac{S^2}{30f} \qquad \begin{array}{l}\text{\textit{D, S,} and \textit{f} are positive numbers, so this final equation and}\\ \text{the original one are equivalent.}\end{array}$$

E X A M P L E   7

Suppose that for a particular road surface, the coefficient of friction is 0.35. How far will a car skid when the brakes are applied at 60 miles per hour?

Solution

We can substitute 0.35 for f and 60 for S in the formula $D = \dfrac{S^2}{30f}$.

$$D = \frac{60^2}{30(0.35)} = 343, \quad \text{to the nearest whole number}$$

The car will skid approximately 343 feet.   ■

Remark: Pause for a moment and think about the result in Example 7. The coefficient of friction 0.35 refers to a wet concrete road surface. Note that a car traveling at 60 miles per hour on such a surface will skid more than the length of a football field.

Problem Set 5.5

For Problems 1–56, solve each equation. Don't forget to check each of your potential solutions.

1. $\sqrt{5x} = 10$

2. $\sqrt{3x} = 9$

3. $\sqrt{2x} + 4 = 0$

4. $\sqrt{4x} + 5 = 0$

5. $2\sqrt{n} = 5$

6. $5\sqrt{n} = 3$

7. $3\sqrt{n} - 2 = 0$

8. $2\sqrt{n} - 7 = 0$

9. $\sqrt{3y + 1} = 4$

10. $\sqrt{2y - 3} = 5$

11. $\sqrt{4y - 3} - 6 = 0$

12. $\sqrt{3y + 5} - 2 = 0$

13. $\sqrt{3x - 1} + 1 = 4$

14. $\sqrt{4x - 1} - 3 = 2$

15. $\sqrt{2n + 3} - 2 = -1$

16. $\sqrt{5n + 1} - 6 = -4$

17. $\sqrt{2x - 5} = -1$

18. $\sqrt{4x - 3} = -4$

19. $\sqrt{5x + 2} = \sqrt{6x + 1}$

20. $\sqrt{4x + 2} = \sqrt{3x + 4}$

21. $\sqrt{3x + 1} = \sqrt{7x - 5}$

22. $\sqrt{6x + 5} = \sqrt{2x + 10}$

23. $\sqrt{3x - 2} - \sqrt{x + 4} = 0$

24. $\sqrt{7x - 6} - \sqrt{5x + 2} = 0$

25. $5\sqrt{t - 1} = 6$ **26.** $4\sqrt{t + 3} = 6$

27. $\sqrt{x^2 + 7} = 4$ **28.** $\sqrt{x^2 + 3} - 2 = 0$

29. $\sqrt{x^2 + 13x + 37} = 1$

30. $\sqrt{x^2 + 5x - 20} = 2$

31. $\sqrt{x^2 - x + 1} = x + 1$

32. $\sqrt{n^2 - 2n - 4} = n$

33. $\sqrt{x^2 + 3x + 7} = x + 2$

34. $\sqrt{x^2 + 2x + 1} = x + 3$

35. $\sqrt{-4x + 17} = x - 3$ **36.** $\sqrt{2x - 1} = x - 2$

37. $\sqrt{n + 4} = n + 4$ **38.** $\sqrt{n + 6} = n + 6$

39. $\sqrt{3y} = y - 6$ **40.** $2\sqrt{n} = n - 3$

41. $4\sqrt{x + 5} = x$ **42.** $\sqrt{-x - 6} = x$

43. $\sqrt[3]{x - 2} = 3$ **44.** $\sqrt[3]{x + 1} = 4$

45. $\sqrt[3]{2x + 3} = -3$ **46.** $\sqrt[3]{3x - 1} = -4$

47. $\sqrt[3]{2x + 5} = \sqrt[3]{4 - x}$

48. $\sqrt[3]{3x - 1} = \sqrt[3]{2 - 5x}$

49. $\sqrt{x + 19} - \sqrt{x + 28} = -1$

50. $\sqrt{x + 4} = \sqrt{x - 1} + 1$

51. $\sqrt{3x + 1} + \sqrt{2x + 4} = 3$

52. $\sqrt{2x - 1} - \sqrt{x + 3} = 1$

53. $\sqrt{n - 4} + \sqrt{n + 4} = 2\sqrt{n - 1}$

54. $\sqrt{n - 3} + \sqrt{n + 5} = 2\sqrt{n}$

55. $\sqrt{t + 3} - \sqrt{t - 2} = \sqrt{7 - t}$

56. $\sqrt{t + 7} - 2\sqrt{t - 8} = \sqrt{t - 5}$

57. Use the formula given in Example 7 with a coefficient of friction of 0.95. How far will a car skid at 40 miles per hour? at 55 miles per hour? at 65 miles per hour? Express the answers to the nearest foot.

58. Solve the formula $T = 2\pi\sqrt{\dfrac{L}{32}}$ for L. (Remember that in this formula, which was used in Section 5.2, T represents the period of a pendulum expressed in seconds, and L represents the length of the pendulum in feet.)

59. In Problem 58, you should have obtained the equation $L = \dfrac{8T^2}{\pi^2}$. What is the length of a pendulum that has a period of 2 seconds? of 2.5 seconds? of 3 seconds? Express your answers to the nearest tenth of a foot.

■ ■ ■ **THOUGHTS INTO WORDS**

60. Explain the concept of extraneous solutions.

61. Explain why possible solutions for radical equations *must* be checked.

62. Your friend makes an effort to solve the equation $3 + 2\sqrt{x} = x$ as follows:

$$(3 + 2\sqrt{x})^2 = x^2$$
$$9 + 12\sqrt{x} + 4x = x^2$$

At this step he stops and doesn't know how to proceed. What help would you give him?

5.6   Merging Exponents and Roots

Recall that the basic properties of positive integral exponents led to a definition for the use of negative integers as exponents. In this section, the properties of integral exponents are used to form definitions for the use of rational numbers as exponents. These definitions will tie together the concepts of exponent and root.

Let's consider the following comparisons.

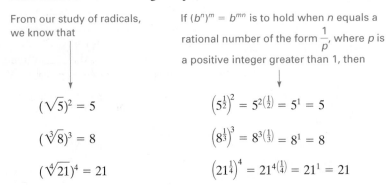

From our study of radicals, we know that

If $(b^n)^m = b^{mn}$ is to hold when n equals a rational number of the form $\dfrac{1}{p}$, where p is a positive integer greater than 1, then

$$(\sqrt{5})^2 = 5 \qquad\qquad \left(5^{\frac{1}{2}}\right)^2 = 5^{2\left(\frac{1}{2}\right)} = 5^1 = 5$$

$$(\sqrt[3]{8})^3 = 8 \qquad\qquad \left(8^{\frac{1}{3}}\right)^3 = 8^{3\left(\frac{1}{3}\right)} = 8^1 = 8$$

$$(\sqrt[4]{21})^4 = 21 \qquad\qquad \left(21^{\frac{1}{4}}\right)^4 = 21^{4\left(\frac{1}{4}\right)} = 21^1 = 21$$

It would seem reasonable to make the following definition.

Definition 5.6

If b is a real number, n is a positive integer greater than 1, and $\sqrt[n]{b}$ exists, then

$$b^{\frac{1}{n}} = \sqrt[n]{b}$$

Definition 5.6 states that $b^{\frac{1}{n}}$ means the nth root of b. We shall assume that b and n are chosen so that $\sqrt[n]{b}$ exists. For example, $(-25)^{\frac{1}{2}}$ is not meaningful at this time because $\sqrt{-25}$ is not a real number. Consider the following examples, which demonstrate the use of Definition 5.6.

$$25^{\frac{1}{2}} = \sqrt{25} = 5 \qquad\qquad 16^{\frac{1}{4}} = \sqrt[4]{16} = 2$$

$$8^{\frac{1}{3}} = \sqrt[3]{8} = 2 \qquad\qquad \left(\frac{36}{49}\right)^{\frac{1}{2}} = \sqrt{\frac{36}{49}} = \frac{6}{7}$$

$$(-27)^{\frac{1}{3}} = \sqrt[3]{-27} = -3$$

The following definition provides the basis for the use of *all* rational numbers as exponents.

Definition 5.7

If $\dfrac{m}{n}$ is a rational number, where n is a positive integer greater than 1, and b is a real number such that $\sqrt[n]{b}$ exists, then

$$b^{\frac{m}{n}} = \sqrt[n]{b^m} = (\sqrt[n]{b})^m$$

In Definition 5.7, note that the denominator of the exponent is the index of the radical and that the numerator of the exponent is either the exponent of the radicand or the exponent of the root.

Whether we use the form $\sqrt[n]{b^m}$ or the form $(\sqrt[n]{b})^m$ for computational purposes depends somewhat on the magnitude of the problem. Let's use both forms on two problems to illustrate this point.

$$8^{\frac{2}{3}} = \sqrt[3]{8^2} \qquad \text{or} \qquad 8^{\frac{2}{3}} = (\sqrt[3]{8})^2$$

$$= \sqrt[3]{64} \qquad\qquad\qquad = 2^2$$

$$= 4 \qquad\qquad\qquad\quad = 4$$

$$27^{\frac{2}{3}} = \sqrt[3]{27^2} \qquad \text{or} \qquad 27^{\frac{2}{3}} = (\sqrt[3]{27})^2$$

$$= \sqrt[3]{729} \qquad\qquad\qquad = 3^2$$

$$= 9 \qquad\qquad\qquad\quad = 9$$

To compute $8^{\frac{2}{3}}$, either form seems to work about as well as the other one. However, to compute $27^{\frac{2}{3}}$, it should be obvious that $(\sqrt[3]{27})^2$ is much easier to handle than $\sqrt[3]{27^2}$.

EXAMPLE 1   Simplify each of the following numerical expressions.

(a) $25^{\frac{3}{2}}$ **(b)** $16^{\frac{3}{4}}$ **(c)** $(32)^{-\frac{2}{5}}$

(d) $(-64)^{\frac{2}{3}}$ **(e)** $-8^{\frac{1}{3}}$

Solution

(a) $25^{\frac{3}{2}} = (\sqrt{25})^3 = 5^3 = 125$

(b) $16^{\frac{3}{4}} = (\sqrt[4]{16})^3 = 2^3 = 8$

(c) $(32)^{-\frac{2}{5}} = \dfrac{1}{(32)^{\frac{2}{5}}} = \dfrac{1}{(\sqrt[5]{32})^2} = \dfrac{1}{2^2} = \dfrac{1}{4}$

(d) $(-64)^{\frac{2}{3}} = (\sqrt[3]{-64})^2 = (-4)^2 = 16$

(e) $-8^{\frac{1}{3}} = -\sqrt[3]{8} = -2$ ■

The basic laws of exponents that we stated in Property 5.2 are true for all rational exponents. Therefore, from now on we will use Property 5.2 for rational as well as integral exponents.

Some problems can be handled better in exponential form and others in radical form. Thus we must be able to switch forms with a certain amount of ease. Let's consider some examples where we switch from one form to the other.

E X A M P L E 2

Write each of the following expressions in radical form.

(a) $x^{\frac{3}{4}}$ (b) $3y^{\frac{2}{5}}$ (c) $x^{\frac{1}{4}}y^{\frac{3}{4}}$ (d) $(x + y)^{\frac{2}{3}}$

Solution

(a) $x^{\frac{3}{4}} = \sqrt[4]{x^3}$ (b) $3y^{\frac{2}{5}} = 3\sqrt[5]{y^2}$

(c) $x^{\frac{1}{4}}y^{\frac{3}{4}} = (xy^3)^{\frac{1}{4}} = \sqrt[4]{xy^3}$ (d) $(x + y)^{\frac{2}{3}} = \sqrt[3]{(x + y)^2}$ ■

E X A M P L E 3

Write each of the following using positive rational exponents.

(a) $\sqrt{xy}$ (b) $\sqrt[4]{a^3b}$ (c) $4\sqrt[3]{x^2}$ (d) $\sqrt[5]{(x + y)^4}$

Solution

(a) $\sqrt{xy} = (xy)^{\frac{1}{2}} = x^{\frac{1}{2}}y^{\frac{1}{2}}$ (b) $\sqrt[4]{a^3b} = (a^3b)^{\frac{1}{4}} = a^{\frac{3}{4}}b^{\frac{1}{4}}$

(c) $4\sqrt[3]{x^2} = 4x^{\frac{2}{3}}$ (d) $\sqrt[5]{(x + y)^4} = (x + y)^{\frac{4}{5}}$ ■

The properties of exponents provide the basis for simplifying algebraic expressions that contain rational exponents, as these next examples illustrate.

E X A M P L E 4

Simplify each of the following. Express final results using positive exponents only.

(a) $\left(3x^{\frac{1}{2}}\right)\left(4x^{\frac{2}{3}}\right)$ (b) $\left(5a^{\frac{1}{3}}b^{\frac{1}{2}}\right)^2$ (c) $\dfrac{12y^{\frac{1}{3}}}{6y^{\frac{1}{2}}}$ (d) $\left(\dfrac{3x^{\frac{2}{5}}}{2y^{\frac{2}{3}}}\right)^4$

Solution

(a) $\left(3x^{\frac{1}{2}}\right)\left(4x^{\frac{2}{3}}\right) = 3 \cdot 4 \cdot x^{\frac{1}{2}} \cdot x^{\frac{2}{3}}$

                  $= 12x^{\frac{1}{2}+\frac{2}{3}}$ $b^n \cdot b^m = b^{n+m}$

                  $= 12x^{\frac{3}{6}+\frac{4}{6}}$ Use 6 as LCD.

                  $= 12x^{\frac{7}{6}}$

(b) $\left(5a^{\frac{1}{3}}b^{\frac{1}{2}}\right)^2 = 5^2 \cdot \left(a^{\frac{1}{3}}\right)^2 \cdot \left(b^{\frac{1}{2}}\right)^2$ $(ab)^n = a^n b^n$

                $= 25a^{\frac{2}{3}}b$ $(b^n)^m = b^{mn}$

(c) $\dfrac{12y^{\frac{1}{3}}}{6y^{\frac{1}{2}}} = 2y^{\frac{1}{3}-\frac{1}{2}}$ $\dfrac{b^n}{b^m} = b^{n-m}$

         $= 2y^{\frac{2}{6}-\frac{3}{6}}$

         $= 2y^{-\frac{1}{6}}$

         $= \dfrac{2}{y^{\frac{1}{6}}}$

(d) $\left(\dfrac{3x^{\frac{2}{5}}}{2y^{\frac{2}{3}}}\right)^{4} = \dfrac{\left(3x^{\frac{2}{5}}\right)^{4}}{\left(2y^{\frac{2}{3}}\right)^{4}}$ $\left(\dfrac{a}{b}\right)^{n} = \dfrac{a^{n}}{b^{n}}$

$= \dfrac{3^{4} \cdot \left(x^{\frac{2}{5}}\right)^{4}}{2^{4} \cdot \left(y^{\frac{2}{3}}\right)^{4}}$ $(ab)^{n} = a^{n}b^{n}$

$= \dfrac{81x^{\frac{8}{5}}}{16y^{\frac{8}{3}}}$ $(b^{n})^{m} = b^{mn}$ ∎

The link between exponents and roots also provides a basis for multiplying and dividing some radicals even if they have different indexes. The general procedure is as follows:

1. Change from radical form to exponential form.
2. Apply the properties of exponents.
3. Then change back to radical form.

The three parts of Example 5 illustrate this process.

Perform the indicated operations and express the answers in simplest radical form.

(a) $\sqrt{2}\sqrt[3]{2}$ **(b)** $\dfrac{\sqrt{5}}{\sqrt[3]{5}}$ **(c)** $\dfrac{\sqrt{4}}{\sqrt[3]{2}}$

Solution

(a) $\sqrt{2}\sqrt[3]{2} = 2^{\frac{1}{2}} \cdot 2^{\frac{1}{3}}$

$= 2^{\frac{1}{2}+\frac{1}{3}}$

$= 2^{\frac{3}{6}+\frac{2}{6}}$ Use 6 as LCD.

$= 2^{\frac{5}{6}}$

$= \sqrt[6]{2^{5}} = \sqrt[6]{32}$

(b) $\dfrac{\sqrt{5}}{\sqrt[3]{5}} = \dfrac{5^{\frac{1}{2}}}{5^{\frac{1}{3}}}$

$= 5^{\frac{1}{2}-\frac{1}{3}}$

$= 5^{\frac{3}{6}-\frac{2}{6}}$ Use 6 as LCD.

$= 5^{\frac{1}{6}} = \sqrt[6]{5}$

(c) $\dfrac{\sqrt{4}}{\sqrt[3]{2}} = \dfrac{4^{\frac{1}{2}}}{2^{\frac{1}{3}}}$

$= \dfrac{(2^{2})^{\frac{1}{2}}}{2^{\frac{1}{3}}}$

$= \dfrac{2^{1}}{2^{\frac{1}{3}}}$

$= 2^{1-\frac{1}{3}}$

$= 2^{\frac{2}{3}} = \sqrt[3]{2^{2}} = \sqrt[3]{4}$ ∎

Problem Set 5.6

For Problems 1–30, evaluate each numerical expression.

1. $81^{\frac{1}{2}}$

2. $64^{\frac{1}{2}}$

3. $27^{\frac{1}{3}}$

4. $(-32)^{\frac{1}{5}}$

5. $(-8)^{\frac{1}{3}}$

6. $\left(-\dfrac{27}{8}\right)^{\frac{1}{3}}$

7. $-25^{\frac{1}{2}}$

8. $-64^{\frac{1}{3}}$

9. $36^{-\frac{1}{2}}$

10. $81^{-\frac{1}{2}}$

11. $\left(\dfrac{1}{27}\right)^{-\frac{1}{3}}$

12. $\left(-\dfrac{8}{27}\right)^{-\frac{1}{3}}$

13. $4^{\frac{3}{2}}$

14. $64^{\frac{2}{3}}$

15. $27^{\frac{4}{3}}$

16. $4^{\frac{7}{2}}$

17. $(-1)^{\frac{7}{3}}$

18. $(-8)^{\frac{4}{3}}$

19. $-4^{\frac{5}{2}}$

20. $-16^{\frac{3}{2}}$

21. $\left(\dfrac{27}{8}\right)^{\frac{4}{3}}$

22. $\left(\dfrac{8}{125}\right)^{\frac{2}{3}}$

23. $\left(\dfrac{1}{8}\right)^{-\frac{2}{3}}$

24. $\left(-\dfrac{1}{27}\right)^{-\frac{2}{3}}$

25. $64^{-\frac{7}{6}}$

26. $32^{-\frac{4}{5}}$

27. $-25^{\frac{3}{2}}$

28. $-16^{\frac{3}{4}}$

29. $125^{\frac{4}{3}}$

30. $81^{\frac{5}{4}}$

For Problems 31–44, write each of the following in radical form. For example,

$$3x^{\frac{2}{3}} = 3\sqrt[3]{x^2}$$

31. $x^{\frac{4}{3}}$

32. $x^{\frac{2}{5}}$

33. $3x^{\frac{1}{2}}$

34. $5x^{\frac{1}{4}}$

35. $(2y)^{\frac{1}{3}}$

36. $(3xy)^{\frac{1}{2}}$

37. $(2x - 3y)^{\frac{1}{2}}$

38. $(5x + y)^{\frac{1}{3}}$

39. $(2a - 3b)^{\frac{2}{3}}$

40. $(5a + 7b)^{\frac{3}{5}}$

41. $x^{\frac{2}{3}}y^{\frac{1}{3}}$

42. $x^{\frac{3}{7}}y^{\frac{5}{7}}$

43. $-3x^{\frac{1}{5}}y^{\frac{2}{5}}$

44. $-4x^{\frac{3}{4}}y^{\frac{1}{4}}$

For Problems 45–58, write each of the following using positive rational exponents. For example,

$$\sqrt{ab} = (ab)^{\frac{1}{2}} = a^{\frac{1}{2}}b^{\frac{1}{2}}$$

45. $\sqrt{5y}$

46. $\sqrt{2xy}$

47. $3\sqrt{y}$

48. $5\sqrt{ab}$

49. $\sqrt[3]{xy^2}$

50. $\sqrt[5]{x^2y^4}$

51. $\sqrt[4]{a^2b^3}$

52. $\sqrt[6]{ab^5}$

53. $\sqrt[5]{(2x - y)^3}$

54. $\sqrt[7]{(3x - y)^4}$

55. $5x\sqrt{y}$

56. $4y\sqrt[3]{x}$

57. $-\sqrt[3]{x + y}$

58. $-\sqrt[5]{(x - y)^2}$

For Problems 59–80, simplify each of the following. Express final results using positive exponents only. For example,

$$\left(2x^{\frac{1}{2}}\right)\left(3x^{\frac{1}{3}}\right) = 6x^{\frac{5}{6}}$$

59. $\left(2x^{\frac{2}{5}}\right)\left(6x^{\frac{1}{4}}\right)$

60. $\left(3x^{\frac{1}{4}}\right)\left(5x^{\frac{1}{3}}\right)$

61. $\left(y^{\frac{2}{3}}\right)\left(y^{-\frac{1}{4}}\right)$

62. $\left(y^{\frac{3}{4}}\right)\left(y^{-\frac{1}{2}}\right)$

63. $\left(x^{\frac{2}{5}}\right)\left(4x^{-\frac{1}{2}}\right)$

64. $\left(2x^{\frac{1}{3}}\right)\left(x^{-\frac{1}{2}}\right)$

65. $\left(4x^{\frac{1}{2}}y\right)^2$

66. $\left(3x^{\frac{1}{4}}y^{\frac{1}{5}}\right)^3$

67. $(8x^6y^3)^{\frac{1}{3}}$

68. $(9x^2y^4)^{\frac{1}{2}}$

69. $\dfrac{24x^{\frac{3}{5}}}{6x^{\frac{1}{3}}}$

70. $\dfrac{18x^{\frac{1}{2}}}{9x^{\frac{1}{3}}}$

71. $\dfrac{48b^{\frac{1}{3}}}{12b^{\frac{3}{4}}}$

72. $\dfrac{56a^{\frac{1}{6}}}{8a^{\frac{1}{4}}}$

73. $\left(\dfrac{6x^{\frac{2}{5}}}{7y^{\frac{2}{3}}}\right)^2$

74. $\left(\dfrac{2x^{\frac{1}{3}}}{3y^{\frac{1}{4}}}\right)^4$

75. $\left(\dfrac{x^2}{y^3}\right)^{-\frac{1}{2}}$

76. $\left(\dfrac{a^3}{b^{-2}}\right)^{-\frac{1}{3}}$

77. $\left(\dfrac{18x^{\frac{1}{3}}}{9x^{\frac{1}{4}}}\right)^{2}$ **78.** $\left(\dfrac{72x^{\frac{3}{4}}}{6x^{\frac{1}{2}}}\right)^{2}$

79. $\left(\dfrac{60a^{\frac{1}{5}}}{15a^{\frac{3}{4}}}\right)^{2}$ **80.** $\left(\dfrac{64a^{\frac{1}{3}}}{16a^{\frac{5}{9}}}\right)^{3}$

For Problems 81–90, perform the indicated operations and express answers in simplest radical form. (See Example 5.)

81. $\sqrt[3]{3}\sqrt{3}$ **82.** $\sqrt{2}\sqrt[4]{2}$

83. $\sqrt[4]{6}\sqrt{6}$ **84.** $\sqrt[3]{5}\sqrt{5}$

85. $\dfrac{\sqrt[3]{3}}{\sqrt{3}}$ **86.** $\dfrac{\sqrt{2}}{\sqrt[3]{2}}$

87. $\dfrac{\sqrt[3]{8}}{\sqrt[4]{4}}$ **88.** $\dfrac{\sqrt{9}}{\sqrt[3]{3}}$

89. $\dfrac{\sqrt[4]{27}}{\sqrt{3}}$ **90.** $\dfrac{\sqrt[3]{16}}{\sqrt[6]{4}}$

■ ■ ■ **THOUGHTS INTO WORDS**

91. Your friend keeps getting an error message when evaluating $-4^{\frac{5}{2}}$ on his calculator. What error is he probably making?

92. Explain how you would evaluate $27^{\frac{2}{3}}$ without a calculator.

■ ■ ■ **FURTHER INVESTIGATIONS**

93. Use your calculator to evaluate each of the following.

(a) $\sqrt[3]{1728}$ (b) $\sqrt[3]{5832}$

(c) $\sqrt[4]{2401}$ (d) $\sqrt[4]{65{,}536}$

(e) $\sqrt[5]{161{,}051}$ (f) $\sqrt[5]{6{,}436{,}343}$

94. Definition 5.7 states that

$$b^{\frac{m}{n}} = \sqrt[n]{b^{m}} = \left(\sqrt[n]{b}\right)^{m}$$

Use your calculator to verify each of the following.

(a) $\sqrt[3]{27^{2}} = \left(\sqrt[3]{27}\right)^{2}$ (b) $\sqrt[3]{8^{5}} = \left(\sqrt[3]{8}\right)^{5}$

(c) $\sqrt[4]{16^{3}} = \left(\sqrt[4]{16}\right)^{3}$ (d) $\sqrt[3]{16^{2}} = \left(\sqrt[3]{16}\right)^{2}$

(e) $\sqrt[5]{9^{4}} = \left(\sqrt[5]{9}\right)^{4}$ (f) $\sqrt[3]{12^{4}} = \left(\sqrt[3]{12}\right)^{4}$

95. Use your calculator to evaluate each of the following.

(a) $16^{\frac{5}{2}}$ (b) $25^{\frac{7}{2}}$

(c) $16^{\frac{9}{4}}$ (d) $27^{\frac{5}{3}}$

(e) $343^{\frac{2}{3}}$ (f) $512^{\frac{4}{3}}$

96. Use your calculator to estimate each of the following to the nearest one-thousandth.

(a) $7^{\frac{4}{3}}$ (b) $10^{\frac{4}{5}}$

(c) $12^{\frac{3}{5}}$ (d) $19^{\frac{2}{5}}$

(e) $7^{\frac{3}{4}}$ (f) $10^{\frac{5}{4}}$

97. (a) Because $\dfrac{4}{5} = 0.8$, we can evaluate $10^{\frac{4}{5}}$ by evaluating $10^{0.8}$, which involves a shorter sequence of "calculator steps." Evaluate parts (b), (c), (d), (e), and (f) of Problem 96 and take advantage of decimal exponents.

(b) What problem is created when we try to evaluate $7^{\frac{4}{3}}$ by changing the exponent to decimal form?

5.7 Scientific Notation

Many applications of mathematics involve the use of very large or very small numbers.

1. The speed of light is approximately 29,979,200,000 centimeters per second.

2. A light year — the distance that light travels in 1 year — is approximately 5,865,696,000,000 miles.

3. A millimicron equals 0.000000001 of a meter.

Working with numbers of this type in standard decimal form is quite cumbersome. It is much more convenient to represent very small and very large numbers in **scientific notation**. The expression $(N)(10)^k$, where N is a number greater than or equal to 1 and less than 10, written in decimal form, and k is any integer, is commonly called scientific notation or the scientific form of a number. Consider the following examples, which show a comparison between ordinary decimal notation and scientific notation.

Ordinary notation	Scientific notation
2.14	$(2.14)(10)^0$
31.78	$(3.178)(10)^1$
412.9	$(4.129)(10)^2$
8,000,000	$(8)(10)^6$
0.14	$(1.4)(10)^{-1}$
0.0379	$(3.79)(10)^{-2}$
0.00000049	$(4.9)(10)^{-7}$

To switch from ordinary notation to scientific notation, you can use the following procedure.

Write the given number as the product of a number greater than or equal to 1 and less than 10, and a power of 10. The exponent of 10 is determined by counting the number of places that the decimal point was moved when going from the original number to the number greater than or equal to 1 and less than 10. This exponent is (a) negative if the original number is less than 1, (b) positive if the original number is greater than 10, and (c) 0 if the original number itself is between 1 and 10.

Thus we can write

$$0.00467 = (4.67)(10)^{-3}$$

$$87,000\; = (8.7)(10)^{4}$$

$$3.1416\; = (3.1416)(10)^{0}$$

We can express the applications given earlier in scientific notation as follows:

Speed of light $29,979,200,000 = (2.99792)(10)^{10}$ centimeters per second.

Light year $5,865,696,000,000 = (5.865696)(10)^{12}$ miles.

Metric units   A millimicron is $0.000000001 = (1)(10)^{-9}$ meter.

To switch from scientific notation to ordinary decimal notation, you can use the following procedure.

> Move the decimal point the number of places indicated by the exponent of 10. The decimal point is moved to the right if the exponent is positive and to the left if the exponent is negative.

Thus we can write

$$(4.78)(10)^{4} = 47,800$$

$$(8.4)(10)^{-3} = 0.0084$$

Scientific notation can frequently be used to simplify numerical calculations. We merely change the numbers to scientific notation and use the appropriate properties of exponents. Consider the following examples.

EXAMPLE   1

Perform the indicated operations.

(a) $(0.00024)(20,000)$

(b) $\dfrac{7,800,000}{0.0039}$

(c) $\dfrac{(0.00069)(0.0034)}{(0.0000017)(0.023)}$

(d) $\sqrt{0.000004}$

Solution

(a) $(0.00024)(20,000) = (2.4)(10)^{-4}(2)(10)^{4}$

$$= (2.4)(2)(10)^{-4}(10)^{4}$$

$$= (4.8)(10)^{0}$$

$$= (4.8)(1)$$

$$= 4.8$$

(b) $\dfrac{7,800,000}{0.0039} = \dfrac{(7.8)(10)^6}{(3.9)(10)^{-3}}$

$= (2)(10)^9$

$= 2,000,000,000$

(c) $\dfrac{(0.00069)(0.0034)}{(0.0000017)(0.023)} = \dfrac{(6.9)(10)^{-4}(3.4)(10)^{-3}}{(1.7)(10)^{-6}(2.3)(10)^{-2}}$

$= \dfrac{(\overset{3}{\cancel{6.9}})(\overset{2}{\cancel{3.4}})(10)^{-7}}{(\cancel{1.7})(\cancel{2.3})(10)^{-8}}$

$= (6)(10)^1$

$= 60$

(d) $\sqrt{0.00004} = \sqrt{(4)(10)^{-6}}$

$= ((4)(10)^{-6})^{\frac{1}{2}}$

$= 4^{\frac{1}{2}}((10)^{-6})^{\frac{1}{2}}$

$= (2)(10)^{-3}$

$= 0.002$ ■

E X A M P L E   2

The speed of light is approximately $(1.86)(10^5)$ miles per second. When the earth is $(9.3)(10^7)$ miles away from the sun, how long does it take light from the sun to reach the earth?

Solution

We will use the formula $t = \dfrac{d}{r}$.

$t = \dfrac{(9.3)(10^7)}{(1.86)(10^5)}$

$t = \dfrac{(9.3)}{(1.86)}(10^2)$ Subtract exponents.

$t = (5)(10^2) = 500$ seconds

At this distance it takes light about 500 seconds to travel from the sun to the earth. To find the answer in minutes, divide 500 seconds by 60 seconds/minute. That gives a result of approximately 8.33 minutes.   ■

Many calculators are equipped to display numbers in scientific notation. The display panel shows the number between 1 and 10 and the appropriate exponent of 10. For example, evaluating $(3,800,000)^2$ yields

$\boxed{1.444\text{E}13}$

Thus $(3,800,000)^2 = (1.444)(10)^{13} = 14,440,000,000,000$.

Similarly, the answer for $(0.000168)^2$ is displayed as

$$\boxed{2.8224\text{E-}8}$$

Thus $(0.000168)^2 = (2.8224)(10)^{-8} = 0.000000028224.$

Calculators vary as to the number of digits displayed in the number between 1 and 10 when scientific notation is used. For example, we used two different calculators to estimate $(6729)^6$ and obtained the following results.

$$\boxed{9.2833\text{E}22}$$

$$\boxed{9.283316768\text{E}22}$$

Obviously, you need to know the capabilities of your calculator when working with problems in scientific notation. Many calculators also allow the entry of a number in scientific notation. Such calculators are equipped with an enter-the-exponent key (often labeled as $\boxed{\text{EE}}$ or $\boxed{\text{EEX}}$). Thus a number such as $(3.14)(10)^8$ might be entered as follows:

Enter	Press	Display		Enter	Press	Display
3.14	$\boxed{\text{EE}}$	3.14E	or	3.14	$\boxed{\text{EE}}$	$3.14^{\,00}$
8		3.14E8		8		$3.14^{\,08}$

A $\boxed{\text{MODE}}$ key is often used on calculators to let you choose normal decimal notation, scientific notation, or engineering notation. (The abbreviations Norm, Sci, and Eng are commonly used.) If the calculator is in scientific mode, then a number can be entered and changed to scientific form by pressing the $\boxed{\text{ENTER}}$ key. For example, when we enter 589 and press the $\boxed{\text{ENTER}}$ key, the display will show 5.89E2. Likewise, when the calculator is in scientific mode, the answers to computational problems are given in scientific form. For example, the answer for $(76)(533)$ is given as 4.0508E4.

It should be evident from this brief discussion that even when you are using a calculator, you need to have a thorough understanding of scientific notation.

Problem Set 5.7

For Problems 1–18, write each of the following in scientific notation. For example

$$27800 = (2.78)(10)^4$$

1. 89

2. 117

3. 4290

4. 812,000

5. 6,120,000

6. 72,400,000

7. 40,000,000

8. 500,000,000

9. 376.4

10. 9126.21

11. 0.347

12. 0.2165

13. 0.0214

14. 0.0037

15. 0.00005

16. 0.00000082

17. 0.00000000194

18. 0.00000000003

For Problems 19–32, write each of the following in ordinary decimal notation. For example,

$$(3.18)(10)^2 = 318$$

19. $(2.3)(10)^1$

20. $(1.62)(10)^2$

21. $(4.19)(10)^3$

22. $(7.631)(10)^4$

23. $(5)(10)^8$

24. $(7)(10)^9$

25. $(3.14)(10)^{10}$

26. $(2.04)(10)^{12}$

27. $(4.3)(10)^{-1}$

28. $(5.2)(10)^{-2}$

29. $(9.14)(10)^{-4}$

30. $(8.76)(10)^{-5}$

31. $(5.123)(10)^{-8}$

32. $(6)(10)^{-9}$

For Problems 33–50, use scientific notation and the properties of exponents to help you perform the following operations.

33. $(0.0037)(0.00002)$

34. $(0.00003)(0.00025)$

35. $(0.00007)(11,000)$

36. $(0.000004)(120,000)$

37. $\dfrac{360,000,000}{0.0012}$

38. $\dfrac{66,000,000,000}{0.022}$

39. $\dfrac{0.000064}{16,000}$

40. $\dfrac{0.00072}{0.0000024}$

41. $\dfrac{(60,000)(0.006)}{(0.0009)(400)}$

42. $\dfrac{(0.00063)(960,000)}{(3,200)(0.0000021)}$

43. $\dfrac{(0.0045)(60,000)}{(1800)(0.00015)}$

44. $\dfrac{(0.00016)(300)(0.028)}{0.064}$

45. $\sqrt{9,000,000}$

46. $\sqrt{0.00000009}$

47. $\sqrt[3]{8000}$

48. $\sqrt[3]{0.001}$

49. $(90,000)^{\frac{3}{2}}$

50. $(8000)^{\frac{2}{3}}$

51. Avogadro's number, 602,000,000,000,000,000,000,000, is the number of atoms in 1 mole of a substance. Express this number in scientific notation.

52. The Social Security program paid out approximately $33,200,000,000 in benefits in May 2000. Express this number in scientific notation.

53. Carlos's first computer had a processing speed of $(1.6)(10^6)$ hertz. He recently purchased a laptop computer with a processing speed of $(1.33)(10^9)$ hertz. Approximately how many times faster is the processing speed of his laptop than that of his first computer? Express the result in decimal form.

54. Alaska has an area of approximately $(6.15)(10^5)$ square miles. In 1999 the state had a population of approximately 619,000 people. Compute the population density to the nearest hundredth. Population density is the number of people per square mile. Express the result in decimal form rounded to the nearest hundredth.

55. In the year 2000 the public debt of the United States was approximately $5,700,000,000,000. For July 2000, the census reported that 275,000,000 people lived in the United States. Convert these figures to scientific notation, and compute the average debt per person. Express the result in scientific notation.

56. The space shuttle can travel at approximately 410,000 miles per day. If the shuttle could travel to Mars, and Mars was 140,000,000 miles away, how many days would it take the shuttle to travel to Mars? Express the result in decimal form.

57. Atomic masses are measured in atomic mass units (amu). The amu, $(1.66)(10^{-27})$ kilograms, is defined as $\dfrac{1}{12}$ the mass of a common carbon atom. Find the mass of a carbon atom in kilograms. Express the result in scientific notation.

58. The field of view of a microscope is $(4)(10^{-4})$ meters. If a single cell organism occupies $\dfrac{1}{5}$ of the field of view, find the length of the organism in meters. Express the result in scientific notation.

59. The mass of an electron is $(9.11)(10^{-31})$ kilogram, and the mass of a proton is $(1.67)(10^{-27})$ kilogram. Approximately how many times more is the weight of a proton than the weight of an electron? Express the result in decimal form.

60. A square pixel on a computer screen has a side of length $(1.17)(10^{-2})$ inches. Find the approximate area of the pixel in inches. Express the result in decimal form.

■ ■ ■ **THOUGHTS INTO WORDS**

61. Explain the importance of scientific notation.

62. Why do we need scientific notation even when using calculators and computers?

■ ■ ■ **FURTHER INVESTIGATIONS**

63. Sometimes it is more convenient to express a number as a product of a power of 10 and a number that is not between 1 and 10. For example, suppose that we want to calculate $\sqrt{640,000}$. We can proceed as follows:

$$\sqrt{640,000} = \sqrt{(64)(10)^4}$$
$$= ((64)(10)^4)^{\frac{1}{2}}$$
$$= (64)^{\frac{1}{2}}(10^4)^{\frac{1}{2}}$$
$$= (8)(10)^2$$
$$= 8(100) = 800$$

Compute each of the following without a calculator, and then use a calculator to check your answers.

(a) $\sqrt{49,000,000}$ **(b)** $\sqrt{0.0025}$

(c) $\sqrt{14,400}$ **(d)** $\sqrt{0.000121}$

(e) $\sqrt[3]{27,000}$ **(f)** $\sqrt[3]{0.000064}$

64. Use your calculator to evaluate each of the following. Express final answers in ordinary notation.

(a) $(27,000)^2$ **(b)** $(450,000)^2$

(c) $(14,800)^2$ **(d)** $(1700)^3$

(e) $(900)^4$ **(f)** $(60)^5$

(g) $(0.0213)^2$ **(h)** $(0.000213)^2$

(i) $(0.000198)^2$ **(j)** $(0.000009)^3$

65. Use your calculator to estimate each of the following. Express final answers in scientific notation with the number between 1 and 10 rounded to the nearest one-thousandth.

(a) $(4576)^4$ **(b)** $(719)^{10}$

(c) $(28)^{12}$ **(d)** $(8619)^6$

(e) $(314)^5$ **(f)** $(145,723)^2$

66. Use your calculator to estimate each of the following. Express final answers in ordinary notation rounded to the nearest one-thousandth.

(a) $(1.09)^5$ **(b)** $(1.08)^{10}$

(c) $(1.14)^7$ **(d)** $(1.12)^{20}$

(e) $(0.785)^4$ **(f)** $(0.492)^5$

Chapter 5 Summary

(5.1) The following properties form the basis for manipulating with exponents.

1. $b^n \cdot b^m = b^{n+m}$ Product of two powers
2. $(b^n)^m = b^{mn}$ Power of a power
3. $(ab)^n = a^n b^n$ Power of a product
4. $\left(\dfrac{a}{b}\right)^n = \dfrac{a^n}{b^n}$ Power of a quotient
5. $\dfrac{b^n}{b^m} = b^{n-m}$ Quotient of two powers

(5.2) and (5.3) The **principal nth root of b** is designated by $\sqrt[n]{b}$, where n is the **index** and b is the **radicand**.

A radical expression is in **simplest radical form** if

1. A radicand contains no polynomial factor raised to a power equal to or greater than the index of the radical,
2. No fraction appears within a radical sign, and
3. No radical appears in the denominator.

The following properties are used to express radicals in simplest form.

$$\sqrt[n]{bc} = \sqrt[n]{b}\sqrt[n]{c} \qquad \sqrt[n]{\frac{b}{c}} = \frac{\sqrt[n]{b}}{\sqrt[n]{c}}$$

Simplifying by combining radicals sometimes requires that we first express the given radicals in simplest form and then apply the distributive property.

(5.4) The distributive property and the property $\sqrt[n]{b}\sqrt[n]{c} = \sqrt[n]{bc}$ are used to find products of expressions that involve radicals.

The special-product pattern $(a + b)(a - b) = a^2 - b^2$ suggests a procedure for **rationalizing the denominator** of an expression that contains a binomial denominator with radicals.

(5.5) Equations that contain radicals with variables in a radicand are called **radical equations**. The property "if $a = b$, then $a^n = b^n$" forms the basis for solving radical equations. Raising both sides of an equation to a positive integral power may produce **extraneous solutions**—that is, solutions that do not satisfy the original equation. Therefore, you must check each potential solution.

(5.6) If b is a real number, n is a positive integer greater than 1, and $\sqrt[n]{b}$ exists, then

$$b^{\frac{1}{n}} = \sqrt[n]{b}$$

Thus $b^{\frac{1}{n}}$ means **the nth root of b**.

If $\dfrac{m}{n}$ is a rational number, n is a positive integer greater than 1, and b is a real number such that $\sqrt[n]{b}$ exists, then

$$b^{\frac{m}{n}} = \sqrt[n]{b^m} = (\sqrt[n]{b})^m$$

Both $\sqrt[n]{b^m}$ and $(\sqrt[n]{b})^m$ can be used for computational purposes.

We need to be able to switch back and forth between **exponential form** and **radical form**. The link between exponents and roots provides a basis for multiplying and dividing some radicals even if they have different indexes.

(5.7) The **scientific form** of a number is expressed as

$$(N)(10)^k$$

where N is a number greater than or equal to 1 and less than 10, written in decimal form, and k is an integer. Scientific notation is often convenient to use with very small and very large numbers. For example, 0.000046 can be expressed as $(4.6)(10^{-5})$, and 92,000,000 can be written as $(9.2)(10)^7$.

Scientific notation can often be used to simplify numerical calculations. For example,

$$(0.000016)(30,000) = (1.6)(10)^{-5}(3)(10)^4$$
$$= (4.8)(10)^{-1} = 0.48$$

Chapter 5   Review Problem Set

For Problems 1–12, evaluate each of the following numerical expressions.

1. 4^{-3}

2. $\left(\dfrac{2}{3}\right)^{-2}$

3. $(3^2 \cdot 3^{-3})^{-1}$

4. $\sqrt[3]{-8}$

5. $\sqrt[4]{\dfrac{16}{81}}$

6. $4^{\frac{5}{2}}$

7. $(-1)^{\frac{2}{3}}$

8. $\left(\dfrac{8}{27}\right)^{\frac{2}{3}}$

9. $-16^{\frac{3}{2}}$

10. $\dfrac{2^3}{2^{-2}}$

11. $(4^{-2} \cdot 4^2)^{-1}$

12. $\left(\dfrac{3^{-1}}{3^2}\right)^{-1}$

For Problems 13–24, express each of the following radicals in simplest radical form. Assume the variables represent positive real numbers.

13. $\sqrt{54}$

14. $\sqrt{48x^3y}$

15. $\dfrac{4\sqrt{3}}{\sqrt{6}}$

16. $\sqrt{\dfrac{5}{12x^3}}$

17. $\sqrt[3]{56}$

18. $\dfrac{\sqrt[3]{2}}{\sqrt[3]{9}}$

19. $\sqrt{\dfrac{9}{5}}$

20. $\sqrt{\dfrac{3x^3}{7}}$

21. $\sqrt[3]{108x^4y^8}$

22. $\dfrac{3}{4}\sqrt{150}$

23. $\dfrac{2}{3}\sqrt{45xy^3}$

24. $\dfrac{\sqrt{8x^2}}{\sqrt{2x}}$

For Problems 25–32, multiply and simplify. Assume the variables represent nonnegative real numbers.

25. $(3\sqrt{8})(4\sqrt{5})$

26. $(5\sqrt[3]{2})(6\sqrt[3]{4})$

27. $3\sqrt{2}(4\sqrt{6} - 2\sqrt{7})$

28. $(\sqrt{x} + 3)(\sqrt{x} - 5)$

29. $(2\sqrt{5} - \sqrt{3})(2\sqrt{5} + \sqrt{3})$

30. $(3\sqrt{2} + \sqrt{6})(5\sqrt{2} - 3\sqrt{6})$

31. $(2\sqrt{a} + \sqrt{b})(3\sqrt{a} - 4\sqrt{b})$

32. $(4\sqrt{8} - \sqrt{2})(\sqrt{8} + 3\sqrt{2})$

For Problems 33–36, rationalize the denominator and simplify.

33. $\dfrac{4}{\sqrt{7} - 1}$

34. $\dfrac{\sqrt{3}}{\sqrt{8} + \sqrt{5}}$

35. $\dfrac{3}{2\sqrt{3} + 3\sqrt{5}}$

36. $\dfrac{3\sqrt{2}}{2\sqrt{6} - \sqrt{10}}$

For Problems 37–42, simplify each of the following, and express the final results using positive exponents.

37. $(x^{-3}y^4)^{-2}$

38. $\left(\dfrac{2a^{-1}}{3b^4}\right)^{-3}$

39. $(4x^{\frac{1}{2}})(5x^{\frac{1}{5}})$

40. $\dfrac{42a^{\frac{3}{4}}}{6a^{\frac{1}{3}}}$

41. $\left(\dfrac{x^3}{y^4}\right)^{-\frac{1}{3}}$

42. $\left(\dfrac{6x^{-2}}{2x^4}\right)^{-2}$

For Problems 43–46, use the distributive property to help simplify each of the following.

43. $3\sqrt{45} - 2\sqrt{20} - \sqrt{80}$

44. $4\sqrt[3]{24} + 3\sqrt[3]{3} - 2\sqrt[3]{81}$

45. $3\sqrt{24} - \dfrac{2\sqrt{54}}{5} + \dfrac{\sqrt{96}}{4}$

46. $-2\sqrt{12x} + 3\sqrt{27x} - 5\sqrt{48x}$

For Problems 47 and 48, express each as a single fraction involving positive exponents only.

47. $x^{-2} + y^{-1}$

48. $a^{-2} - 2a^{-1}b^{-1}$

For Problems 49–56, solve each equation.

49. $\sqrt{7x - 3} = 4$

50. $\sqrt{2y + 1} = \sqrt{5y - 11}$

51. $\sqrt{2x} = x - 4$

52. $\sqrt{n^2 - 4n - 4} = n$

53. $\sqrt[3]{2x - 1} = 3$

54. $\sqrt{t^2 + 9t - 1} = 3$

55. $\sqrt{x^2 + 3x - 6} = x$

56. $\sqrt{x + 1} - \sqrt{2x} = -1$

For Problems 57–64, use scientific notation and the properties of exponents to help perform the following calculations.

57. $(0.00002)(0.0003)$

58. $(120,000)(300,000)$

59. $(0.000015)(400,000)$

60. $\dfrac{0.000045}{0.0003}$

61. $\dfrac{(0.00042)(0.0004)}{0.006}$

62. $\sqrt{0.000004}$

63. $\sqrt[3]{0.000000008}$

64. $(4,000,000)^{\frac{3}{2}}$

For Problems 1–4, simplify each of the numerical expressions.

1. $(4)^{-\frac{5}{2}}$

2. $-16^{\frac{5}{4}}$

3. $\left(\dfrac{2}{3}\right)^{-4}$

4. $\left(\dfrac{2^{-1}}{2^{-2}}\right)^{-2}$

For Problems 5–9, express each radical expression in simplest radical form. Assume the variables represent positive real numbers.

5. $\sqrt{63}$

6. $\sqrt[3]{108}$

7. $\sqrt{52x^4y^3}$

8. $\dfrac{5\sqrt{18}}{3\sqrt{12}}$

9. $\sqrt{\dfrac{7}{24x^3}}$

10. Multiply and simplify: $(4\sqrt{6})(3\sqrt{12})$

11. Multiply and simplify: $(3\sqrt{2}+\sqrt{3})(\sqrt{2}-2\sqrt{3})$

12. Simplify by combining similar radicals:
$2\sqrt{50}-4\sqrt{18}-9\sqrt{32}$

13. Rationalize the denominator and simplify:
$$\dfrac{3\sqrt{2}}{4\sqrt{3}-\sqrt{8}}$$

14. Simplify and express the answer using positive exponents: $\left(\dfrac{2x^{-1}}{3y}\right)^{-2}$

15. Simplify and express the answer using positive exponents: $\dfrac{-84a^{\frac{1}{2}}}{7a^{\frac{4}{5}}}$

16. Express $x^{-1}+y^{-3}$ as a single fraction involving positive exponents.

17. Multiply and express the answer using positive exponents: $\left(3x^{-\frac{1}{2}}\right)\left(4x^{\frac{3}{4}}\right)$

18. Multiply and simplify:
$(3\sqrt{5}-2\sqrt{3})(3\sqrt{5}+2\sqrt{3})$

For Problems 19 and 20, use scientific notation and the properties of exponents to help with the calculations.

19. $\dfrac{(0.00004)(300)}{0.00002}$

20. $\sqrt{0.000009}$

For Problems 21–25, solve each equation.

21. $\sqrt{3x+1}=3$

22. $\sqrt[3]{3x+2}=2$

23. $\sqrt{x}=x-2$

24. $\sqrt{5x-2}=\sqrt{3x+8}$

25. $\sqrt{x^2-10x+28}=2$

6

Quadratic Equations and Inequalities

6.1 Complex Numbers

6.2 Quadratic Equations

6.3 Completing the Square

6.4 Quadratic Formula

6.5 More Quadratic Equations and Applications

6.6 Quadratic and Other Nonlinear Inequalities

The Pythagorean theorem is applied throughout the construction industry when right angles are involved.

© Jeff Greenberg/PhotoEdit

A page for a magazine contains 70 square inches of type. The height of the page is twice the width. If the margin around the type is 2 inches uniformly, what are the dimensions of a page? We can use the quadratic equation $(x - 4)(2x - 4) = 70$ to determine that the page measures 9 inches by 18 inches.

Solving equations is one of the central themes of this text. Let's pause for a moment and reflect on the different types of equations that we have solved in the last five chapters.

As the chart on the next page shows, we have solved second-degree equations in one variable, but only those for which the polynomial is factorable. In this chapter we will expand our work to include more general types of second-degree equations, as well as inequalities in one variable.

Type of Equation	Examples
First-degree equations in one variable	$3x + 2x = x - 4$; $5(x + 4) = 12$; $\dfrac{x + 2}{3} + \dfrac{x - 1}{4} = 2$
Second-degree equations in one variable *that are factorable*	$x^2 + 5x = 0$; $x^2 + 5x + 6 = 0$; $x^2 - 9 = 0$; $x^2 - 10x + 25 = 0$
Fractional equations	$\dfrac{2}{x} + \dfrac{3}{x} = 4$; $\dfrac{5}{a - 1} = \dfrac{6}{a - 2}$; $\dfrac{2}{x^2 - 9} + \dfrac{3}{x + 3} = \dfrac{4}{x - 3}$
Radical equations	$\sqrt{x} = 2$; $\sqrt{3x - 2} = 5$; $\sqrt{5y + 1} = \sqrt{3y + 4}$

6.1   Complex Numbers

Because the square of any real number is nonnegative, a simple equation such as $x^2 = -4$ has no solutions in the set of real numbers. To handle this situation, we can expand the set of real numbers into a larger set called the **complex numbers**. In this section we will instruct you on how to manipulate complex numbers.

To provide a solution for the equation $x^2 + 1 = 0$, we use the number i, such that

$$i^2 = -1$$

The number i is not a real number and is often called the **imaginary unit**, but the number i^2 is the real number -1. The imaginary unit i is used to define a complex number as follows:

Definition 6.1

A **complex number** is any number that can be expressed in the form

$a + bi$

where a and b are real numbers.

The form $a + bi$ is called the **standard form** of a complex number. The real number a is called the **real part** of the complex number, and b is called the **imaginary**

part. (Note that b is a real number even though it is called the imaginary part.) The following list exemplifies this terminology.

1. The number $7 + 5i$ is a complex number that has a real part of 7 and an imaginary part of 5.

2. The number $\frac{2}{3} + i\sqrt{2}$ is a complex number that has a real part of $\frac{2}{3}$ and an imaginary part of $\sqrt{2}$. (It is easy to mistake $\sqrt{2i}$ for $\sqrt{2}i$. Thus we commonly write $i\sqrt{2}$ instead of $\sqrt{2}i$ to avoid any difficulties with the radical sign.)

3. The number $-4 - 3i$ can be written in the standard form $-4 + (-3i)$ and therefore is a complex number that has a real part of -4 and an imaginary part of -3. [The form $-4 - 3i$ is often used, but we know that it means $-4 + (-3i)$.]

4. The number $-9i$ can be written as $0 + (-9i)$; thus it is a complex number that has a real part of 0 and an imaginary part of -9. (Complex numbers, such as $-9i$, for which $a = 0$ and $b \neq 0$ are called **pure imaginary numbers**.)

5. The real number 4 can be written as $4 + 0i$ and is thus a complex number that has a real part of 4 and an imaginary part of 0.

Look at item 5 in this list. We see that the set of real numbers is a subset of the set of complex numbers. The following diagram indicates the organizational format of the complex numbers.

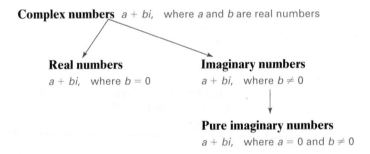

Complex numbers $a + bi$, where a and b are real numbers

Real numbers
$a + bi$, where $b = 0$

Imaginary numbers
$a + bi$, where $b \neq 0$

Pure imaginary numbers
$a + bi$, where $a = 0$ and $b \neq 0$

Two complex numbers $a + bi$ and $c + di$ are said to be **equal** if and only if $a = c$ and $b = d$.

■ Adding and Subtracting Complex Numbers

To **add complex numbers**, we simply add their real parts and add their imaginary parts. Thus

$$(a + bi) + (c + di) = (a + c) + (b + d)i$$

The following examples show addition of two complex numbers.

1. $(4 + 3i) + (5 + 9i) = (4 + 5) + (3 + 9)i = 9 + 12i$

2. $(-6 + 4i) + (8 - 7i) = (-6 + 8) + (4 - 7)i$

$$= 2 - 3i$$

3. $\left(\dfrac{1}{2} + \dfrac{3}{4}i\right) + \left(\dfrac{2}{3} + \dfrac{1}{5}i\right) = \left(\dfrac{1}{2} + \dfrac{2}{3}\right) + \left(\dfrac{3}{4} + \dfrac{1}{5}\right)i$

$$= \left(\dfrac{3}{6} + \dfrac{4}{6}\right) + \left(\dfrac{15}{20} + \dfrac{4}{20}\right)i$$

$$= \dfrac{7}{6} + \dfrac{19}{20}i$$

The set of complex numbers is closed with respect to addition; that is, the sum of two complex numbers is a complex number. Furthermore, the commutative and associative properties of addition hold for all complex numbers. The addition identity element is $0 + 0i$ (or simply the real number 0). The additive inverse of $a + bi$ is $-a - bi$, because

$$(a + bi) + (-a - bi) = 0$$

To **subtract complex numbers**, $c + di$ from $a + bi$, add the additive inverse of $c + di$. Thus

$$(a + bi) - (c + di) = (a + bi) + (-c - di)$$

$$= (a - c) + (b - d)i$$

In other words, we subtract the real parts and subtract the imaginary parts, as in the next examples.

1. $(9 + 8i) - (5 + 3i) = (9 - 5) + (8 - 3)i$

$$= 4 + 5i$$

2. $(3 - 2i) - (4 - 10i) = (3 - 4) + (-2 - (-10))i$

$$= -1 + 8i$$

■ Products and Quotients of Complex Numbers

Because $i^2 = -1$, i is a square root of -1, so we let $i = \sqrt{-1}$. It should also be evident that $-i$ is a square root of -1, because

$$(-i)^2 = (-i)(-i) = i^2 = -1$$

Thus, in the set of complex numbers, -1 has two square roots, i and $-i$. We express these symbolically as

$$\sqrt{-1} = i \qquad \text{and} \qquad -\sqrt{-1} = -i$$

Let us extend our definition so that in the set of complex numbers every negative real number has two square roots. We simply define $\sqrt{-b}$, where b is a positive real number, to be the number whose square is $-b$. Thus

$$(\sqrt{-b})^2 = -b, \quad \text{for } b > 0$$

Furthermore, because $(i\sqrt{b})(i\sqrt{b}) = i^2(b) = -1(b) = -b$, we see that

$$\sqrt{-b} = i\sqrt{b}$$

In other words, a square root of any negative real number can be represented as the product of a real number and the imaginary unit i. Consider the following examples.

$$\sqrt{-4} = i\sqrt{4} = 2i$$

$$\sqrt{-17} = i\sqrt{17}$$

$$\sqrt{-24} = i\sqrt{24} = i\sqrt{4}\sqrt{6} = 2i\sqrt{6} \qquad \text{Note that we simplified the radical } \sqrt{24} \text{ to } 2\sqrt{6}.$$

We should also observe that $-\sqrt{-b}$, where $b > 0$, is a square root of $-b$ because

$$(-\sqrt{-b})^2 = (-i\sqrt{b})^2 = i^2(b) = -1(b) = -b$$

Thus in the set of complex numbers, $-b$ (where $b > 0$) has two square roots, $i\sqrt{b}$ and $-i\sqrt{b}$. We express these symbolically as

$$\sqrt{-b} = i\sqrt{b} \qquad \text{and} \qquad -\sqrt{-b} = -i\sqrt{b}$$

We must be very careful with the use of the symbol $\sqrt{-b}$, where $b > 0$. Some real number properties that involve the square root symbol do not hold if the square root symbol does not represent a real number. For example, $\sqrt{a}\sqrt{b} = \sqrt{ab}$ does not hold if a and b are both negative numbers.

Correct $\sqrt{-4}\sqrt{-9} = (2i)(3i) = 6i^2 = 6(-1) = -6$

Incorrect $\sqrt{-4}\sqrt{-9} = \sqrt{(-4)(-9)} = \sqrt{36} = 6$

To avoid difficulty with this idea, you should rewrite all expressions of the form $\sqrt{-b}$, where $b > 0$, in the form $i\sqrt{b}$ before doing any computations. The following examples further demonstrate this point.

1. $\sqrt{-5}\sqrt{-7} = (i\sqrt{5})(i\sqrt{7}) = i^2\sqrt{35} = (-1)\sqrt{35} = -\sqrt{35}$

2. $\sqrt{-2}\sqrt{-8} = (i\sqrt{2})(i\sqrt{8}) = i^2\sqrt{16} = (-1)(4) = -4$

3. $\sqrt{-6}\sqrt{-8} = (i\sqrt{6})(i\sqrt{8}) = i^2\sqrt{48} = (-1)\sqrt{16}\sqrt{3} = -4\sqrt{3}$

4. $\dfrac{\sqrt{-75}}{\sqrt{-3}} = \dfrac{i\sqrt{75}}{i\sqrt{3}} = \dfrac{\sqrt{75}}{\sqrt{3}} = \sqrt{\dfrac{75}{3}} = \sqrt{25} = 5$

5. $\dfrac{\sqrt{-48}}{\sqrt{12}} = \dfrac{i\sqrt{48}}{\sqrt{12}} = i\sqrt{\dfrac{48}{12}} = i\sqrt{4} = 2i$

Complex numbers have a binomial form, so we find the product of two complex numbers in the same way that we find the product of two binomials. Then, by replacing i^2 with -1, we are able to simplify and express the final result in standard form. Consider the following examples.

6. $(2 + 3i)(4 + 5i) = 2(4 + 5i) + 3i(4 + 5i)$

$$= 8 + 10i + 12i + 15i^2$$

$$= 8 + 22i + 15i^2$$

$$= 8 + 22i + 15(-1) = -7 + 22i$$

7. $(-3 + 6i)(2 - 4i) = -3(2 - 4i) + 6i(2 - 4i)$

$$= -6 + 12i + 12i - 24i^2$$

$$= -6 + 24i - 24(-1)$$

$$= -6 + 24i + 24 = 18 + 24i$$

8. $(1 - 7i)^2 = (1 - 7i)(1 - 7i)$

$$= 1(1 - 7i) - 7i(1 - 7i)$$

$$= 1 - 7i - 7i + 49i^2$$

$$= 1 - 14i + 49(-1)$$

$$= 1 - 14i - 49$$

$$= -48 - 14i$$

9. $(2 + 3i)(2 - 3i) = 2(2 - 3i) + 3i(2 - 3i)$

$$= 4 - 6i + 6i - 9i^2$$

$$= 4 - 9(-1)$$

$$= 4 + 9$$

$$= 13$$

Example 9 illustrates an important situation: The complex numbers $2 + 3i$ and $2 - 3i$ are conjugates of each other. In general, two complex numbers $a + bi$ and $a - bi$ are called **conjugates** of each other. *The product of a complex number and its conjugate is always a real number*, which can be shown as follows:

$$(a + bi)(a - bi) = a(a - bi) + bi(a - bi)$$

$$= a^2 - abi + abi - b^2i^2$$

$$= a^2 - b^2(-1)$$

$$= a^2 + b^2$$

We use conjugates to simplify expressions such as $\dfrac{3i}{5 + 2i}$ that indicate the quotient of two complex numbers. To eliminate i in the denominator and change the indicated quotient to the standard form of a complex number, we can multiply both the numerator and the denominator by the conjugate of the denominator as follows:

$$\frac{3i}{5 + 2i} = \frac{3i(5 - 2i)}{(5 + 2i)(5 - 2i)}$$

$$= \frac{15i - 6i^2}{25 - 4i^2}$$

$$= \frac{15i - 6(-1)}{25 - 4(-1)}$$

$$= \frac{15i + 6}{29}$$

$$= \frac{6}{29} + \frac{15}{29}i$$

The following examples further clarify the process of dividing complex numbers.

10. $\dfrac{2 - 3i}{4 - 7i} = \dfrac{(2 - 3i)(4 + 7i)}{(4 - 7i)(4 + 7i)}$ $4 + 7i$ is the conjugate of $4 - 7i$.

$$= \frac{8 + 14i - 12i - 21i^2}{16 - 49i^2}$$

$$= \frac{8 + 2i - 21(-1)}{16 - 49(-1)}$$

$$= \frac{8 + 2i + 21}{16 + 49}$$

$$= \frac{29 + 2i}{65}$$

$$= \frac{29}{65} + \frac{2}{65}i$$

11. $\dfrac{4 - 5i}{2i} = \dfrac{(4 - 5i)(-2i)}{(2i)(-2i)}$ $-2i$ is the conjugate of $2i$.

$$= \frac{-8i + 10i^2}{-4i^2}$$

$$= \frac{-8i + 10(-1)}{-4(-1)}$$

$$= \frac{-8i - 10}{4}$$

$$= -\frac{5}{2} - 2i$$

In Example 11, where the denominator is a pure imaginary number, we can change to standard form by choosing a multiplier other than the conjugate. Consider the following alternative approach for Example 11.

$$\frac{4 - 5i}{2i} = \frac{(4 - 5i)(i)}{(2i)(i)}$$

$$= \frac{4i - 5i^2}{2i^2}$$

$$= \frac{4i - 5(-1)}{2(-1)}$$

$$= \frac{4i + 5}{-2}$$

$$= -\frac{5}{2} - 2i$$

Problem Set 6.1

For Problems 1–8, label each statement true or false.

1. Every complex number is a real number.

2. Every real number is a complex number.

3. The real part of the complex number $6i$ is 0.

4. Every complex number is a pure imaginary number.

5. The sum of two complex numbers is always a complex number.

6. The imaginary part of the complex number 7 is 0.

7. The sum of two complex numbers is sometimes a real number.

8. The sum of two pure imaginary numbers is always a pure imaginary number.

For Problems 9–26, add or subtract as indicated.

9. $(6 + 3i) + (4 + 5i)$

10. $(5 + 2i) + (7 + 10i)$

11. $(-8 + 4i) + (2 + 6i)$

12. $(5 - 8i) + (-7 + 2i)$

13. $(3 + 2i) - (5 + 7i)$

14. $(1 + 3i) - (4 + 9i)$

15. $(-7 + 3i) - (5 - 2i)$

16. $(-8 + 4i) - (9 - 4i)$

17. $(-3 - 10i) + (2 - 13i)$

18. $(-4 - 12i) + (-3 + 16i)$

19. $(4 - 8i) - (8 - 3i)$

20. $(12 - 9i) - (14 - 6i)$

21. $(-1 - i) - (-2 - 4i)$

22. $(-2 - 3i) - (-4 - 14i)$

23. $\left(\frac{3}{2} + \frac{1}{3}i\right) + \left(\frac{1}{6} - \frac{3}{4}i\right)$

24. $\left(\frac{2}{3} - \frac{1}{5}i\right) + \left(\frac{3}{5} - \frac{3}{4}i\right)$

25. $\left(-\frac{5}{9} + \frac{3}{5}i\right) - \left(\frac{4}{3} - \frac{1}{6}i\right)$

26. $\left(\frac{3}{8} - \frac{5}{2}i\right) - \left(\frac{5}{6} + \frac{1}{7}i\right)$

For Problems 27–42, write each of the following in terms of i and simplify. For example,

$$\sqrt{-20} = i\sqrt{20} = i\sqrt{4}\sqrt{5} = 2i\sqrt{5}$$

27. $\sqrt{-81}$

28. $\sqrt{-49}$

29. $\sqrt{-14}$

30. $\sqrt{-33}$

31. $\sqrt{-\frac{16}{25}}$

32. $\sqrt{-\frac{64}{36}}$

33. $\sqrt{-18}$

34. $\sqrt{-84}$

35. $\sqrt{-75}$

36. $\sqrt{-63}$

37. $3\sqrt{-28}$

38. $5\sqrt{-72}$

39. $-2\sqrt{-80}$

40. $-6\sqrt{-27}$

41. $12\sqrt{-90}$

42. $9\sqrt{-40}$

For Problems 43–60, write each of the following in terms of i, perform the indicated operations, and simplify. For example,

$$\sqrt{-3}\sqrt{-8} = (i\sqrt{3})(i\sqrt{8})$$

$$= i^2\sqrt{24}$$

$$= (-1)\sqrt{4}\sqrt{6}$$

$$= -2\sqrt{6}$$

43. $\sqrt{-4}\sqrt{-16}$

44. $\sqrt{-81}\sqrt{-25}$

45. $\sqrt{-3}\sqrt{-5}$

46. $\sqrt{-7}\sqrt{-10}$

47. $\sqrt{-9}\sqrt{-6}$

48. $\sqrt{-8}\sqrt{-16}$

49. $\sqrt{-15}\sqrt{-5}$

50. $\sqrt{-2}\sqrt{-20}$

51. $\sqrt{-2}\sqrt{-27}$

52. $\sqrt{-3}\sqrt{-15}$

53. $\sqrt{6}\sqrt{-8}$

54. $\sqrt{-75}\sqrt{3}$

55. $\dfrac{\sqrt{-25}}{\sqrt{-4}}$

56. $\dfrac{\sqrt{-81}}{\sqrt{-9}}$

57. $\dfrac{\sqrt{-56}}{\sqrt{-7}}$

58. $\dfrac{\sqrt{-72}}{\sqrt{-6}}$

59. $\dfrac{\sqrt{-24}}{\sqrt{6}}$

60. $\dfrac{\sqrt{-96}}{\sqrt{2}}$

For Problems 61–84, find each of the products and express the answers in the standard form of a complex number.

61. $(5i)(4i)$

62. $(-6i)(9i)$

63. $(7i)(-6i)$

64. $(-5i)(-12i)$

65. $(3i)(2 - 5i)$

66. $(7i)(-9 + 3i)$

67. $(-6i)(-2 - 7i)$

68. $(-9i)(-4 - 5i)$

69. $(3 + 2i)(5 + 4i)$

70. $(4 + 3i)(6 + i)$

71. $(6 - 2i)(7 - i)$

72. $(8 - 4i)(7 - 2i)$

73. $(-3 - 2i)(5 + 6i)$

74. $(-5 - 3i)(2 - 4i)$

75. $(9 + 6i)(-1 - i)$

76. $(10 + 2i)(-2 - i)$

77. $(4 + 5i)^2$

78. $(5 - 3i)^2$

79. $(-2 - 4i)^2$

80. $(-3 - 6i)^2$

81. $(6 + 7i)(6 - 7i)$

82. $(5 - 7i)(5 + 7i)$

83. $(-1 + 2i)(-1 - 2i)$

84. $(-2 - 4i)(-2 + 4i)$

For Problems 85–100, find each of the following quotients and express the answers in the standard form of a complex number.

85. $\dfrac{3i}{2 + 4i}$

86. $\dfrac{4i}{5 + 2i}$

87. $\dfrac{-2i}{3 - 5i}$

88. $\dfrac{-5i}{2 - 4i}$

89. $\dfrac{-2 + 6i}{3i}$

90. $\dfrac{-4 - 7i}{6i}$

91. $\dfrac{2}{7i}$

92. $\dfrac{3}{10i}$

93. $\dfrac{2 + 6i}{1 + 7i}$

94. $\dfrac{5 + i}{2 + 9i}$

95. $\dfrac{3 + 6i}{4 - 5i}$

96. $\dfrac{7 - 3i}{4 - 3i}$

97. $\dfrac{-2 + 7i}{-1 + i}$

98. $\dfrac{-3 + 8i}{-2 + i}$

99. $\dfrac{-1 - 3i}{-2 - 10i}$

100. $\dfrac{-3 - 4i}{-4 - 11i}$

101. Some of the solution sets for quadratic equations in the next sections will contain complex numbers such as $(-4 + \sqrt{-12})/2$ and $(-4 - \sqrt{-12})/2$. We can simplify the first number as follows.

$$\frac{-4 + \sqrt{-12}}{2} = \frac{-4 + i\sqrt{12}}{2} =$$

$$\frac{-4 + 2i\sqrt{3}}{2} = \frac{\cancel{2}(-2 + i\sqrt{3})}{\cancel{2}} = -2 + i\sqrt{3}$$

Simplify each of the following complex numbers.

(a) $\dfrac{-4 - \sqrt{-12}}{2}$

(b) $\dfrac{6 + \sqrt{-24}}{4}$

(c) $\dfrac{-1 - \sqrt{-18}}{2}$

(d) $\dfrac{-6 + \sqrt{-27}}{3}$

(e) $\dfrac{10 + \sqrt{-45}}{4}$

(f) $\dfrac{4 - \sqrt{-48}}{2}$

Let's consider quadratic equations of the form $x^2 = a$, where x is the variable and a is any real number. We can solve $x^2 = a$ as follows:

$$x^2 = a$$

$$x^2 - a = 0$$

$$x^2 - (\sqrt{a})^2 = 0 \qquad\qquad a = (\sqrt{a})^2$$

$$(x - \sqrt{a})(x + \sqrt{a}) = 0 \qquad\qquad \text{Factor the left side.}$$

$$x - \sqrt{a} = 0 \qquad \text{or} \qquad x + \sqrt{a} = 0 \qquad \text{Apply: } ab = 0 \text{ if and}$$
$$\text{only if } a = 0 \text{ or } b = 0.$$

$$x = \sqrt{a} \qquad \text{or} \qquad x = -\sqrt{a}.$$

The solutions are $\sqrt{a}$ and $-\sqrt{a}$. We can state this result as a general property and use it to solve certain types of quadratic equations.

Property 6.1

For any real number a,

$$x^2 = a \quad \text{if and only if } x = \sqrt{a} \text{ or } x = -\sqrt{a}$$

(The statement $x = \sqrt{a}$ or $x = -\sqrt{a}$ can be written as $x = \pm\sqrt{a}$.)

Property 6.1, along with our knowledge of square roots, makes it very easy to solve quadratic equations of the form $x^2 = a$.

EXAMPLE 4

Solve $x^2 = 45$.

Solution

$$x^2 = 45$$

$$x = \pm\sqrt{45}$$

$$x = \pm 3\sqrt{5} \qquad \sqrt{45} = \sqrt{9}\sqrt{5} = 3\sqrt{5}$$

The solution set is $\{\pm 3\sqrt{5}\}$. ■

EXAMPLE 5

Solve $x^2 = -9$.

Solution

$$x^2 = -9$$

$$x = \pm\sqrt{-9}$$

$$x = \pm 3i$$

Thus the solution set is $\{\pm 3i\}$. ■

EXAMPLE 6

Solve $7n^2 = 12$.

Solution

$$7n^2 = 12$$

$$n^2 = \frac{12}{7}$$

$$n = \pm\sqrt{\frac{12}{7}}$$

$$n = \pm\frac{2\sqrt{21}}{7} \qquad \sqrt{\frac{12}{7}} = \frac{\sqrt{12}}{\sqrt{7}} \cdot \frac{\sqrt{7}}{\sqrt{7}} = \frac{\sqrt{84}}{7} = \frac{\sqrt{4}\sqrt{21}}{7} = \frac{2\sqrt{21}}{7}$$

The solution set is $\left\{\pm\dfrac{2\sqrt{21}}{7}\right\}$. ∎

EXAMPLE 7

Solve $(3n + 1)^2 = 25$.

Solution

$$(3n + 1)^2 = 25$$

$$(3n + 1) = \pm\sqrt{25}$$

$$3n + 1 = \pm 5$$

$$3n + 1 = 5 \qquad \text{or} \qquad 3n + 1 = -5$$

$$3n = 4 \qquad \text{or} \qquad 3n = -6$$

$$n = \frac{4}{3} \qquad \text{or} \qquad n = -2$$

The solution set is $\left\{-2, \dfrac{4}{3}\right\}$. ∎

EXAMPLE 8

Solve $(x - 3)^2 = -10$.

Solution

$$(x - 3)^2 = -10$$

$$x - 3 = \pm\sqrt{-10}$$

$$x - 3 = \pm i\sqrt{10}$$

$$x = 3 \pm i\sqrt{10}$$

Thus the solution set is $\{3 \pm i\sqrt{10}\}$. ∎

Remark: Take another look at the equations in Examples 5 and 8. We should immediately realize that the solution sets will consist only of nonreal complex numbers, because any nonzero real number squared is positive.

Sometimes it may be necessary to change the form before we can apply Property 6.1. Let's consider one example to illustrate this idea.

EXAMPLE 9

Solve $3(2x - 3)^2 + 8 = 44$.

Solution

$$3(2x - 3)^2 + 8 = 44$$
$$3(2x - 3)^2 = 36$$
$$(2x - 3)^2 = 12$$
$$2x - 3 = \pm\sqrt{12}$$
$$2x - 3 = \pm2\sqrt{3}$$
$$2x = 3 \pm 2\sqrt{3}$$
$$x = \frac{3 \pm 2\sqrt{3}}{2}$$

The solution set is $\left\{\dfrac{3 \pm 2\sqrt{3}}{2}\right\}$. ∎

■ Back to the Pythagorean Theorem

Our work with radicals, Property 6.1, and the Pythagorean theorem form a basis for solving a variety of problems that pertain to right triangles.

EXAMPLE 10

A 50-foot rope hangs from the top of a flagpole. When pulled taut to its full length, the rope reaches a point on the ground 18 feet from the base of the pole. Find the height of the pole to the nearest tenth of a foot.

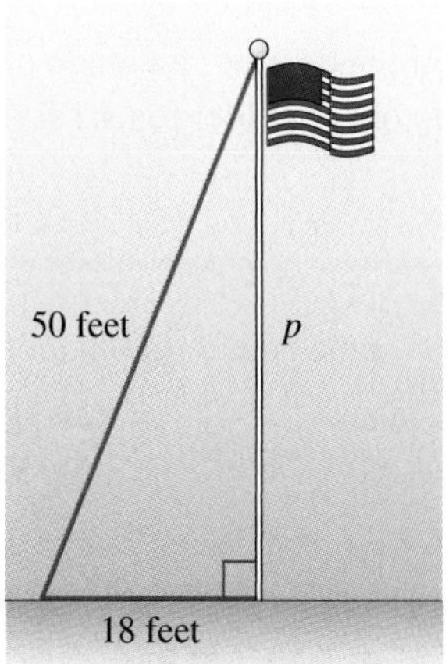

Solution

Let's make a sketch (Figure 6.1) and record the given information.

Use the Pythagorean theorem to solve for p as follows:

$$p^2 + 18^2 = 50^2$$
$$p^2 + 324 = 2500$$
$$p^2 = 2176$$
$$p = \sqrt{2176} = 46.6, \quad \text{to the nearest tenth}$$

The height of the flagpole is approximately 46.6 feet. ∎

50 feet p

18 feet

p represents the height of the flagpole.

Figure 6.1

There are two special kinds of right triangles that we use extensively in later mathematics courses. The first is the **isosceles right triangle**, which is a right triangle that has both legs of the same length. Let's consider a problem that involves an isosceles right triangle.

EXAMPLE   11

Find the length of each leg of an isosceles right triangle that has a hypotenuse of length 5 meters.

Solution

Let's sketch an isosceles right triangle and let x represent the length of each leg (Figure 6.2). Then we can apply the Pythagorean theorem.

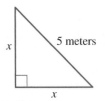

Figure 6.2

$$x^2 + x^2 = 5^2$$
$$2x^2 = 25$$
$$x^2 = \frac{25}{2}$$
$$x = \pm\sqrt{\frac{25}{2}} = \pm\frac{5}{\sqrt{2}} = \pm\frac{5\sqrt{2}}{2}$$

Each leg is $\dfrac{5\sqrt{2}}{2}$ meters long.   ∎

Remark: In Example 10 we made no attempt to express $\sqrt{2176}$ in simplest radical form because the answer was to be given as a rational approximation to the nearest tenth. However, in Example 11 we left the final answer in radical form and therefore expressed it in simplest radical form.

The second special kind of right triangle that we use frequently is one that contains acute angles of 30° and 60°. In such a right triangle, which we refer to as a **30°– 60° right triangle**, the side opposite the 30° angle is equal in length to one-half of the length of the hypotenuse. This relationship, along with the Pythagorean theorem, provides us with another problem-solving technique.

EXAMPLE   12

Suppose that a 20-foot ladder is leaning against a building and makes an angle of 60° with the ground. How far up the building does the top of the ladder reach? Express your answer to the nearest tenth of a foot.

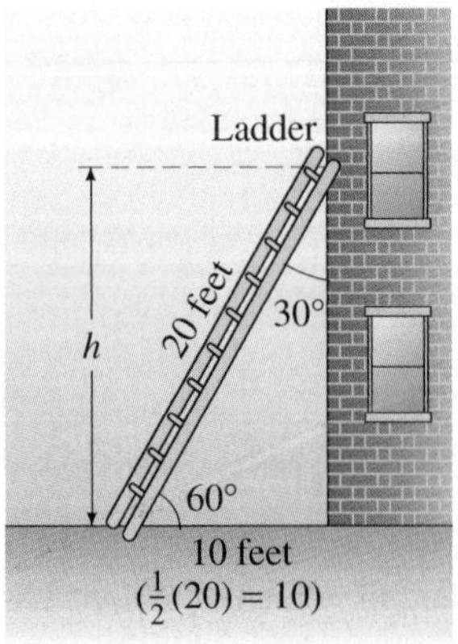

Solution

Figure 6.3 depicts this situation. The side opposite the 30° angle equals one-half of the hypotenuse, so it is of length $\frac{1}{2}(20) = 10$ feet. Now we can apply the Pythagorean theorem.

$$h^2 + 10^2 = 20^2$$
$$h^2 + 100 = 400$$
$$h^2 = 300$$
$$h = \sqrt{300} = 17.3, \quad \text{to the nearest tenth}$$

The top of the ladder touches the building at a point approximately 17.3 feet from the ground.   ∎

Figure 6.3

Problem Set 6.2

For Problems 1–20, solve each of the quadratic equations by factoring and applying the property, $ab = 0$ if and only if $a = 0$ or $b = 0$. If necessary, return to Chapter 3 and review the factoring techniques presented there.

1. $x^2 - 9x = 0$

2. $x^2 + 5x = 0$

3. $x^2 = -3x$

4. $x^2 = 15x$

5. $3y^2 + 12y = 0$

6. $6y^2 - 24y = 0$

7. $5n^2 - 9n = 0$

8. $4n^2 + 13n = 0$

9. $x^2 + x - 30 = 0$

10. $x^2 - 8x - 48 = 0$

11. $x^2 - 19x + 84 = 0$

12. $x^2 - 21x + 104 = 0$

13. $2x^2 + 19x + 24 = 0$

14. $4x^2 + 29x + 30 = 0$

15. $15x^2 + 29x - 14 = 0$

16. $24x^2 + x - 10 = 0$

17. $25x^2 - 30x + 9 = 0$

18. $16x^2 - 8x + 1 = 0$

19. $6x^2 - 5x - 21 = 0$

20. $12x^2 - 4x - 5 = 0$

For Problems 21–26, solve each radical equation. Don't forget, you *must* check potential solutions.

21. $3\sqrt{x} = x + 2$

22. $3\sqrt{2x} = x + 4$

23. $\sqrt{2x} = x - 4$

24. $\sqrt{x} = x - 2$

25. $\sqrt{3x} + 6 = x$

26. $\sqrt{5x} + 10 = x$

For Problems 27–34, solve each equation for x by factoring and applying the property, $ab = 0$ if and only if $a = 0$ or $b = 0$.

27. $x^2 - 5kx = 0$

28. $x^2 + 7kx = 0$

29. $x^2 = 16k^2x$

30. $x^2 = 25k^2x$

31. $x^2 - 12kx + 35k^2 = 0$

32. $x^2 - 3kx - 18k^2 = 0$

33. $2x^2 + 5kx - 3k^2 = 0$

34. $3x^2 - 20kx - 7k^2 = 0$

For Problems 35–70, use Property 6.1 to help solve each quadratic equation.

35. $x^2 = 1$

36. $x^2 = 81$

37. $x^2 = -36$

38. $x^2 = -49$

39. $x^2 = 14$

40. $x^2 = 22$

41. $n^2 - 28 = 0$

42. $n^2 - 54 = 0$

43. $3t^2 = 54$

44. $4t^2 = 108$

45. $2t^2 = 7$

46. $3t^2 = 8$

47. $15y^2 = 20$

48. $14y^2 = 80$

49. $10x^2 + 48 = 0$

50. $12x^2 + 50 = 0$

51. $24x^2 = 36$

52. $12x^2 = 49$

53. $(x - 2)^2 = 9$

54. $(x + 1)^2 = 16$

55. $(x + 3)^2 = 25$

56. $(x - 2)^2 = 49$

57. $(x + 6)^2 = -4$

58. $(3x + 1)^2 = 9$

59. $(2x - 3)^2 = 1$

60. $(2x + 5)^2 = -4$

61. $(n - 4)^2 = 5$

62. $(n - 7)^2 = 6$

63. $(t + 5)^2 = 12$

64. $(t - 1)^2 = 18$

65. $(3y - 2)^2 = -27$

66. $(4y + 5)^2 = 80$

67. $3(x + 7)^2 + 4 = 79$

68. $2(x + 6)^2 - 9 = 63$

69. $2(5x - 2)^2 + 5 = 25$

70. $3(4x - 1)^2 + 1 = -17$

For Problems 71–76, a and b represent the lengths of the legs of a right triangle, and c represents the length of the hypotenuse. Express answers in simplest radical form.

71. Find c if $a = 4$ centimeters and $b = 6$ centimeters.

72. Find c if $a = 3$ meters and $b = 7$ meters.

73. Find a if $c = 12$ inches and $b = 8$ inches.

74. Find a if $c = 8$ feet and $b = 6$ feet.

75. Find b if $c = 17$ yards and $a = 15$ yards.

76. Find b if $c = 14$ meters and $a = 12$ meters.

For Problems 77–80, use the isosceles right triangle in Figure 6.4. Express your answers in simplest radical form.

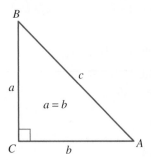

Figure 6.4

77. If $b = 6$ inches, find c.

78. If $a = 7$ centimeters, find c.

79. If $c = 8$ meters, find a and b.

80. If $c = 9$ feet, find a and b.

For Problems 81–86, use the triangle in Figure 6.5. Express your answers in simplest radical form.

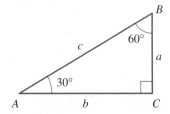

Figure 6.5

81. If $a = 3$ inches, find b and c.

82. If $a = 6$ feet, find b and c.

83. If $c = 14$ centimeters, find a and b.

84. If $c = 9$ centimeters, find a and b.

85. If $b = 10$ feet, find a and c.

86. If $b = 8$ meters, find a and c.

87. A 24-foot ladder resting against a house reaches a windowsill 16 feet above the ground. How far is the foot of the ladder from the foundation of the house? Express your answer to the nearest tenth of a foot.

88. A 62-foot guy-wire makes an angle of 60° with the ground and is attached to a telephone pole (see Figure 6.6). Find the distance from the base of the pole to the point on the pole where the wire is attached. Express your answer to the nearest tenth of a foot.

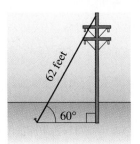

Figure 6.6

89. A rectangular plot measures 16 meters by 34 meters. Find, to the nearest meter, the distance from one corner of the plot to the corner diagonally opposite.

90. Consecutive bases of a square-shaped baseball diamond are 90 feet apart (see Figure 6.7). Find, to the nearest tenth of a foot, the distance from first base diagonally across the diamond to third base.

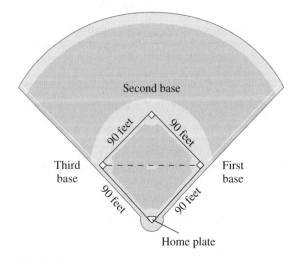

Figure 6.7

91. A diagonal of a square parking lot is 75 meters. Find, to the nearest meter, the length of a side of the lot.

■ ■ ■ THOUGHTS INTO WORDS

92. Explain why the equation $(x + 2)^2 + 5 = 1$ has no real number solutions.

93. Suppose that your friend solved the equation $(x + 3)^2 = 25$ as follows:

$$(x + 3)^2 = 25$$

$$x^2 + 6x + 9 = 25$$

$$x^2 + 6x - 16 = 0$$

$$(x + 8)(x - 2) = 0$$

$$x + 8 = 0 \quad \text{or} \quad x - 2 = 0$$

$$x = -8 \quad \text{or} \quad x = 2$$

Is this a correct approach to the problem? Would you offer any suggestion about an easier approach to the problem?

■ ■ ■ FURTHER INVESTIGATIONS

94. Suppose that we are given a cube with edges 12 centimeters in length. Find the length of a diagonal from a lower corner to the diagonally opposite upper corner. Express your answer to the nearest tenth of a centimeter.

95. Suppose that we are given a rectangular box with a length of 8 centimeters, a width of 6 centimeters, and a height of 4 centimeters. Find the length of a diagonal from a lower corner to the upper corner diagonally opposite. Express your answer to the nearest tenth of a centimeter.

96. The converse of the Pythagorean theorem is also true. It states, "If the measures $a, b,$ and c of the sides of a triangle are such that $a^2 + b^2 = c^2$, then the triangle is a right triangle with a and b the measures of the legs and c the measure of the hypotenuse." Use the converse of the Pythagorean theorem to determine which of the triangles with sides of the following measures are right triangles.

(a) 9, 40, 41   (b) 20, 48, 52

(c) 19, 21, 26   (d) 32, 37, 49

(e) 65, 156, 169   (f) 21, 72, 75

97. Find the length of the hypotenuse (h) of an isosceles right triangle if each leg is s units long. Then use this relationship to redo Problems 77–80.

98. Suppose that the side opposite the 30° angle in a 30°–60° right triangle is s units long. Express the length of the hypotenuse and the length of the other leg in terms of s. Then use these relationships and redo Problems 81–86.

6.3 Completing the Square

Thus far we have solved quadratic equations by factoring and applying the property, $ab = 0$ if and only if $a = 0$ or $b = 0$, or by applying the property, $x^2 = a$ if and only if $x = \pm\sqrt{a}$. In this section we examine another method called **completing the square**, which will give us the power to solve any quadratic equation.

A factoring technique we studied in Chapter 3 relied on recognizing **perfect-square trinomials**. In each of the following, the perfect-square trinomial on the right side is the result of squaring the binomial on the left side.

$$(x + 4)^2 = x^2 + 8x + 16 \qquad (x - 6)^2 = x^2 - 12x + 36$$

$$(x + 7)^2 = x^2 + 14x + 49 \qquad (x - 9)^2 = x^2 - 18x + 81$$

$$(x + a)^2 = x^2 + 2ax + a^2$$

Note that in each of the square trinomials, the constant term is equal to the square of one-half of the coefficient of the x term. This relationship enables us to form a perfect-square trinomial by adding a proper constant term. To find the constant term, take one-half of the coefficient of the x term and then square the result. For example, suppose that we want to form a perfect-square trinomial from $x^2 + 10x$. The coefficient of the x term is 10. Because $\frac{1}{2}(10) = 5$, and $5^2 = 25$, the constant term should be 25. The perfect-square trinomial that can be formed is $x^2 + 10x + 25$. This perfect-square trinomial can be factored and expressed as $(x + 5)^2$. Let's use the previous ideas to help solve some quadratic equations.

E X A M P L E   1

Solve $x^2 + 10x - 2 = 0$.

Solution

$$x^2 + 10x - 2 = 0$$

$$x^2 + 10x = 2 \qquad \text{Isolate the } x^2 \text{ and } x \text{ terms.}$$

$$\frac{1}{2}(10) = 5 \text{ and } 5^2 = 25 \qquad \text{Take } \frac{1}{2} \text{ of the coefficient of the } x \text{ term and then square the result.}$$

$$x^2 + 10x + 25 = 2 + 25 \qquad \text{Add 25 to } \textit{both} \text{ sides of the equation.}$$

$$(x + 5)^2 = 27 \qquad \text{Factor the perfect-square trinomial.}$$

$$x + 5 = \pm\sqrt{27} \qquad \text{Now solve by applying Property 6.1.}$$

$$x + 5 = \pm 3\sqrt{3}$$

$$x = -5 \pm 3\sqrt{3}$$

The solution set is $\{-5 \pm 3\sqrt{3}\}$. ∎

Note from Example 1 that the method of completing the square to solve a quadratic equation is merely what the name implies. A perfect-square trinomial is formed, then the equation can be changed to the necessary form for applying the property "$x^2 = a$ if and only if $x = \pm\sqrt{a}$." Let's consider another example.

E X A M P L E   2

Solve $x(x + 8) = -23$.

Solution

$$x(x + 8) = -23$$

$$x^2 + 8x = -23 \qquad \text{Apply the distributive property.}$$

$$\frac{1}{2}(8) = 4 \text{ and } 4^2 = 16 \qquad \text{Take } \frac{1}{2} \text{ of the coefficient of the } x \text{ term and then square the result.}$$

$$x^2 + 8x + 16 = -23 + 16 \qquad \text{Add 16 to } both \text{ sides of the equation.}$$

$$(x + 4)^2 = -7 \qquad \text{Factor the perfect-square trinomial.}$$

$$x + 4 = \pm\sqrt{-7} \qquad \text{Now solve by applying Property 6.1.}$$

$$x + 4 = \pm i\sqrt{7}$$

$$x = -4 \pm i\sqrt{7}$$

The solution set is $\{-4 \pm i\sqrt{7}\}$.

EXAMPLE 3

Solve $x^2 - 3x + 1 = 0$.

Solution

$$x^2 - 3x + 1 = 0$$

$$x^2 - 3x = -1$$

$$x^2 - 3x + \frac{9}{4} = -1 + \frac{9}{4} \qquad \frac{1}{2}(3) = \frac{3}{2} \text{ and } \left(\frac{3}{2}\right)^2 = \frac{9}{4}$$

$$\left(x - \frac{3}{2}\right)^2 = \frac{5}{4}$$

$$x - \frac{3}{2} = \pm\sqrt{\frac{5}{4}}$$

$$x - \frac{3}{2} = \pm\frac{\sqrt{5}}{2}$$

$$x = \frac{3}{2} \pm \frac{\sqrt{5}}{2}$$

$$x = \frac{3 \pm \sqrt{5}}{2}$$

The solution set is $\left\{\dfrac{3 \pm \sqrt{5}}{2}\right\}$.

In Example 3 note that because the coefficient of the x term is odd, we are forced into the realm of fractions. Using common fractions rather than decimals enables us to apply our previous work with radicals.

The relationship for a perfect-square trinomial that states that the constant term is equal to the square of one-half of the coefficient of the x term holds only if the coefficient of x^2 is 1. Thus we must make an adjustment when solving quadratic equations that have a coefficient of x^2 other than 1. We will need to apply the multiplication property of equality so that the coefficient of the x^2 term becomes 1. The next example shows how to make this adjustment.

EXAMPLE 4   Solve $2x^2 + 12x - 5 = 0$.

Solution

$$2x^2 + 12x - 5 = 0$$

$$2x^2 + 12x = 5$$

$$x^2 + 6x = \frac{5}{2} \qquad \text{Multiply both sides by } \frac{1}{2}.$$

$$x^2 + 6x + 9 = \frac{5}{2} + 9 \qquad \frac{1}{2}(6) = 3, \text{ and } 3^2 = 9$$

$$x^2 + 6x + 9 = \frac{23}{2}$$

$$(x + 3)^2 = \frac{23}{2}$$

$$x + 3 = \pm\sqrt{\frac{23}{2}}$$

$$x + 3 = \pm\frac{\sqrt{46}}{2} \qquad \sqrt{\frac{23}{2}} = \frac{\sqrt{23}}{\sqrt{2}} \cdot \frac{\sqrt{2}}{\sqrt{2}} = \frac{\sqrt{46}}{2}$$

$$x = -3 \pm \frac{\sqrt{46}}{2}$$

$$x = \frac{-6}{2} \pm \frac{\sqrt{46}}{2} \qquad \text{Common denominator of 2}$$

$$x = \frac{-6 \pm \sqrt{46}}{2}$$

The solution set is $\left\{ \dfrac{-6 \pm \sqrt{46}}{2} \right\}$. ■

As we mentioned earlier, we can use the method of completing the square to solve *any* quadratic equation. To illustrate, let's use it to solve an equation that could also be solved by factoring.

EXAMPLE 5   Solve $x^2 - 2x - 8 = 0$ by completing the square.

Solution

$$x^2 - 2x - 8 = 0$$

$$x^2 - 2x = 8$$

$$x^2 - 2x + 1 = 8 + 1 \qquad \frac{1}{2}(-2) = -1 \text{ and } (-1)^2 = 1$$

$$(x - 1)^2 = 9$$

$$x - 1 = \pm 3$$

$$x - 1 = 3 \quad \text{or} \quad x - 1 = -3$$

$$x = 4 \quad \text{or} \quad x = -2$$

The solution set is $\{-2, 4\}$. ▪

Solving the equation in Example 5 by factoring would be easier than completing the square. Remember, however, that the method of completing the square will work with any quadratic equation.

Problem Set 6.3

For Problems 1–14, solve each quadratic equation by using (a) the factoring method and (b) the method of completing the square.

1. $x^2 - 4x - 60 = 0$

2. $x^2 + 6x - 16 = 0$

3. $x^2 - 14x = -40$

4. $x^2 - 18x = -72$

5. $x^2 - 5x - 50 = 0$

6. $x^2 + 3x - 18 = 0$

7. $x(x + 7) = 8$

8. $x(x - 1) = 30$

9. $2n^2 - n - 15 = 0$

10. $3n^2 + n - 14 = 0$

11. $3n^2 + 7n - 6 = 0$

12. $2n^2 + 7n - 4 = 0$

13. $n(n + 6) = 160$

14. $n(n - 6) = 216$

For Problems 15–38, use the method of completing the square to solve each quadratic equation.

15. $x^2 + 4x - 2 = 0$

16. $x^2 + 2x - 1 = 0$

17. $x^2 + 6x - 3 = 0$

18. $x^2 + 8x - 4 = 0$

19. $y^2 - 10y = 1$

20. $y^2 - 6y = -10$

21. $n^2 - 8n + 17 = 0$

22. $n^2 - 4n + 2 = 0$

23. $n(n + 12) = -9$

24. $n(n + 14) = -4$

25. $n^2 + 2n + 6 = 0$

26. $n^2 + n - 1 = 0$

27. $x^2 + 3x - 2 = 0$

28. $x^2 + 5x - 3 = 0$

29. $x^2 + 5x + 1 = 0$

30. $x^2 + 7x + 2 = 0$

31. $y^2 - 7y + 3 = 0$

32. $y^2 - 9y + 30 = 0$

33. $2x^2 + 4x - 3 = 0$

34. $2t^2 - 4t + 1 = 0$

35. $3n^2 - 6n + 5 = 0$

36. $3x^2 + 12x - 2 = 0$

37. $3x^2 + 5x - 1 = 0$

38. $2x^2 + 7x - 3 = 0$

For Problems 39–60, solve each quadratic equation using the method that seems most appropriate.

39. $x^2 + 8x - 48 = 0$

40. $x^2 + 5x - 14 = 0$

41. $2n^2 - 8n = -3$

42. $3x^2 + 6x = 1$

43. $(3x - 1)(2x + 9) = 0$

44. $(5x + 2)(x - 4) = 0$

45. $(x + 2)(x - 7) = 10$

46. $(x - 3)(x + 5) = -7$

47. $(x - 3)^2 = 12$

48. $x^2 = 16x$

49. $3n^2 - 6n + 4 = 0$

50. $2n^2 - 2n - 1 = 0$

51. $n(n + 8) = 240$

52. $t(t - 26) = -160$

53. $3x^2 + 5x = -2$

54. $2x^2 - 7x = -5$

55. $4x^2 - 8x + 3 = 0$

56. $9x^2 + 18x + 5 = 0$

57. $x^2 + 12x = 4$

58. $x^2 + 6x = -11$

59. $4(2x + 1)^2 - 1 = 11$

60. $5(x + 2)^2 + 1 = 16$

61. Use the method of completing the square to solve $ax^2 + bx + c = 0$ for x, where a, b, and c are real numbers and $a \neq 0$.

■ ■ ■ THOUGHTS INTO WORDS

62. Explain the process of completing the square to solve a quadratic equation.

63. Give a step-by-step description of how to solve $3x^2 + 9x - 4 = 0$ by completing the square.

■ ■ ■ FURTHER INVESTIGATIONS

Solve Problems 64–67 for the indicated variable. Assume that all letters represent positive numbers.

64. $\dfrac{x^2}{a^2} - \dfrac{y^2}{b^2} = 1$ for y

65. $\dfrac{x^2}{a^2} + \dfrac{y^2}{b^2} = 1$ for x

66. $s = \dfrac{1}{2}gt^2$ for t

67. $A = \pi r^2$ for r

Solve each of the following equations for x.

68. $x^2 + 8ax + 15a^2 = 0$

69. $x^2 - 5ax + 6a^2 = 0$

70. $10x^2 - 31ax - 14a^2 = 0$

71. $6x^2 + ax - 2a^2 = 0$

72. $4x^2 + 4bx + b^2 = 0$

73. $9x^2 - 12bx + 4b^2 = 0$

6.4   Quadratic Formula

As we saw in the last section, the method of completing the square can be used to solve any quadratic equation. Thus if we apply the method of completing the square to the equation $ax^2 + bx + c = 0$, where a, b, and c are real numbers and $a \neq 0$, we can produce a formula for solving quadratic equations. This formula can then be used to solve any quadratic equation. Let's solve $ax^2 + bx + c = 0$ by completing the square.

$$ax^2 + bx + c = 0$$

$$ax^2 + bx = -c \qquad \text{Isolate the } x^2 \text{ and } x \text{ terms.}$$

$$x^2 + \frac{b}{a}x = -\frac{c}{a} \qquad \text{Multiply both sides by } \frac{1}{a}.$$

$$x^2 + \frac{b}{a}x + \frac{b^2}{4a^2} = -\frac{c}{a} + \frac{b^2}{4a^2} \qquad \frac{1}{2}\left(\frac{b}{a}\right) = \frac{b}{2a} \quad \text{and} \quad \left(\frac{b}{2a}\right)^2 = \frac{b^2}{4a^2}$$

Complete the square by adding $\dfrac{b^2}{4a^2}$ to both sides.

$$x^2 + \frac{b}{a}x + \frac{b^2}{4a^2} = -\frac{4ac}{4a^2} + \frac{b^2}{4a^2} \qquad \text{Common denominator of } 4a^2 \text{ on right side}$$

$$x^2 + \frac{b}{a}x + \frac{b^2}{4a^2} = \frac{b^2}{4a^2} - \frac{4ac}{4a^2} \qquad \text{Commutative property}$$

$$\left(x + \frac{b}{2a}\right)^2 = \frac{b^2 - 4ac}{4a^2}$$

The right side is combined into a single fraction.

$$x + \frac{b}{2a} = \pm\sqrt{\frac{b^2 - 4ac}{4a^2}}$$

$$x + \frac{b}{2a} = \pm\frac{\sqrt{b^2 - 4ac}}{\sqrt{4a^2}}$$

$$x + \frac{b}{2a} = \pm\frac{\sqrt{b^2 - 4ac}}{2a}$$

$\sqrt{4a^2} = |2a|$ but $2a$ can be used because of the use of $\pm$.

$$x + \frac{b}{2a} = \frac{\sqrt{b^2 - 4ac}}{2a} \qquad \text{or} \qquad x + \frac{b}{2a} = -\frac{\sqrt{b^2 - 4ac}}{2a}$$

$$x = -\frac{b}{2a} + \frac{\sqrt{b^2 - 4ac}}{2a} \qquad \text{or} \qquad x = -\frac{b}{2a} - \frac{\sqrt{b^2 - 4ac}}{2a}$$

$$x = \frac{-b + \sqrt{b^2 - 4ac}}{2a} \qquad \text{or} \qquad x = \frac{-b - \sqrt{b^2 - 4ac}}{2a}$$

The quadratic formula is usually stated as follows:

Quadratic Formula

$$x = \frac{-b \pm \sqrt{b^2 - 4ac}}{2a}, \qquad a \neq 0$$

We can use the quadratic formula to solve *any* quadratic equation by expressing the equation in the standard form $ax^2 + bx + c = 0$ and substituting the values for a, b, and c into the formula. Let's consider some examples.

EXAMPLE 1   Solve $x^2 + 5x + 2 = 0$.

Solution

$$x^2 + 5x + 2 = 0$$

The given equation is in standard form with $a = 1$, $b = 5$, and $c = 2$. Let's substitute these values into the formula and simplify.

$$x = \frac{-b \pm \sqrt{b^2 - 4ac}}{2a}$$

$$x = \frac{-5 \pm \sqrt{5^2 - 4(1)(2)}}{2(1)}$$

$$x = \frac{-5 \pm \sqrt{25 - 8}}{2}$$

$$x = \frac{-5 \pm \sqrt{17}}{2}$$

The solution set is $\left\{ \dfrac{-5 \pm \sqrt{17}}{2} \right\}$. ∎

E X A M P L E   2   Solve $x^2 - 2x - 4 = 0$.

Solution

$$x^2 - 2x - 4 = 0$$

We need to think of $x^2 - 2x - 4 = 0$ as $x^2 + (-2)x + (-4) = 0$ to determine the values $a = 1$, $b = -2$, and $c = -4$. Let's substitute these values into the quadratic formula and simplify.

$$x = \frac{-b \pm \sqrt{b^2 - 4ac}}{2a}$$

$$x = \frac{-(-2) \pm \sqrt{(-2)^2 - 4(1)(-4)}}{2(1)}$$

$$x = \frac{2 \pm \sqrt{4 + 16}}{2}$$

$$x = \frac{2 \pm \sqrt{20}}{2}$$

$$x = \frac{2 \pm 2\sqrt{5}}{2}$$

$$x = \frac{2(1 \pm \sqrt{5})}{2} = (1 \pm \sqrt{5})$$

The solution set is $\{1 \pm \sqrt{5}\}$. ∎

E X A M P L E   3   Solve $x^2 - 2x + 19 = 0$.

Solution

$$x^2 - 2x + 19 = 0$$

We can substitute $a = 1$, $b = -2$, and $c = 19$.

$$x = \frac{-b \pm \sqrt{b^2 - 4ac}}{2a}$$

$$x = \frac{-(-2) \pm \sqrt{(-2)^2 - 4(1)(19)}}{2(1)}$$

$$x = \frac{2 \pm \sqrt{4 - 76}}{2}$$

$$x = \frac{2 \pm \sqrt{-72}}{2}$$

$$x = \frac{2 \pm 6i\sqrt{2}}{2} \qquad \sqrt{-72} = i\sqrt{72} = i\sqrt{36}\sqrt{2} = 6i\sqrt{2}$$

$$x = \frac{2(1 \pm 3i\sqrt{2})}{2} = 1 \pm 3i\sqrt{2}$$

The solution set is $\{1 \pm 3i\sqrt{2}\}$.

EXAMPLE 4

Solve $2x^2 + 4x - 3 = 0$.

Solution

$$2x^2 + 4x - 3 = 0$$

Here $a = 2$, $b = 4$, and $c = -3$. Solving by using the quadratic formula is unlike solving by completing the square in that there is no need to make the coefficient of x^2 equal to 1.

$$x = \frac{-b \pm \sqrt{b^2 - 4ac}}{2a}$$

$$x = \frac{-4 \pm \sqrt{4^2 - 4(2)(-3)}}{2(2)}$$

$$x = \frac{-4 \pm \sqrt{16 + 24}}{4}$$

$$x = \frac{-4 \pm \sqrt{40}}{4}$$

$$x = \frac{-4 \pm 2\sqrt{10}}{4}$$

$$x = \frac{2(-2 \pm \sqrt{10})}{4}$$

$$x = \frac{-2 \pm \sqrt{10}}{2}$$

The solution set is $\left\{ \dfrac{-2 \pm \sqrt{10}}{2} \right\}$.

EXAMPLE 5

Solve $n(3n - 10) = 25$.

Solution

$$n(3n - 10) = 25$$

First, we need to change the equation to the standard form $an^2 + bn + c = 0$.

$$n(3n - 10) = 25$$

$$3n^2 - 10n = 25$$

$$3n^2 - 10n - 25 = 0$$

Now we can substitute $a = 3$, $b = -10$, and $c = -25$ into the quadratic formula.

$$n = \frac{-b \pm \sqrt{b^2 - 4ac}}{2a}$$

$$n = \frac{-(-10) \pm \sqrt{(-10)^2 - 4(3)(-25)}}{2(3)}$$

$$n = \frac{10 \pm \sqrt{100 + 300}}{2(3)}$$

$$n = \frac{10 \pm \sqrt{400}}{6}$$

$$n = \frac{10 \pm 20}{6}$$

$$n = \frac{10 + 20}{6} \quad \text{or} \quad n = \frac{10 - 20}{6}$$

$$n = 5 \quad \text{or} \quad n = -\frac{5}{3}$$

The solution set is $\left\{-\frac{5}{3}, 5\right\}$. ∎

In Example 5, note that we used the variable n. The quadratic formula is usually stated in terms of x, but it certainly can be applied to quadratic equations in other variables. Also note in Example 5 that the polynomial $3n^2 - 10n - 25$ can be factored as $(3n + 5)(n - 5)$. Therefore, we could also solve the equation $3n^2 - 10n - 25 = 0$ by using the factoring approach. Section 6.5 will offer some guidance in deciding which approach to use for a particular equation.

■ Nature of Roots

The quadratic formula makes it easy to determine the nature of the roots of a quadratic equation without completely solving the equation. The number

$$b^2 - 4ac$$

which appears under the radical sign in the quadratic formula, is called the **discriminant** of the quadratic equation. The discriminant is the indicator of the kind of roots the equation has. For example, suppose that you start to solve the equation $x^2 - 4x + 7 = 0$ as follows:

$$x = \frac{-b \pm \sqrt{b^2 - 4ac}}{2a}$$

$$x = \frac{-(-4) \pm \sqrt{(-4)^2 - 4(1)(7)}}{2(1)}$$

$$x = \frac{4 \pm \sqrt{16 - 28}}{2}$$

$$x = \frac{4 \pm \sqrt{-12}}{2}$$

At this stage you should be able to look ahead and realize that you will obtain two complex solutions for the equation. (Note, by the way, that these solutions are complex conjugates.) In other words, the discriminant, -12, indicates what type of roots you will obtain.

We make the following general statements relative to the roots of a quadratic equation of the form $ax^2 + bx + c = 0$.

1. If $b^2 - 4ac < 0$, then the equation has two nonreal complex solutions.
2. If $b^2 - 4ac = 0$, then the equation has one real solution.
3. If $b^2 - 4ac > 0$, then the equation has two real solutions.

The following examples illustrate each of these situations. (You may want to solve the equations completely to verify the conclusions.)

Equation	Discriminant	Nature of roots
$x^2 - 3x + 7 = 0$	$b^2 - 4ac = (-3)^2 - 4(1)(7)$ $= 9 - 28$ $= -19$	Two nonreal complex solutions
$9x^2 - 12x + 4 = 0$	$b^2 - 4ac = (-12)^2 - 4(9)(4)$ $= 144 - 144$ $= 0$	One real solution
$2x^2 + 5x - 3 = 0$	$b^2 - 4ac = (5)^2 - 4(2)(-3)$ $= 25 + 24$ $= 49$	Two real solutions

There is another very useful relationship that involves the roots of a quadratic equation and the numbers a, b, and c of the general form $ax^2 + bx + c = 0$. Suppose that we let x_1 and x_2 be the two roots generated by the quadratic formula. Thus we have

$$x_1 = \frac{-b + \sqrt{b^2 - 4ac}}{2a} \quad \text{and} \quad x_2 = \frac{-b - \sqrt{b^2 - 4ac}}{2a}$$

Remark: A clarification is called for at this time. Previously, we made the statement that if $b^2 - 4ac = 0$, then the equation has one real solution. Technically, such an equation has two solutions, but they are equal. For example, each factor of $(x - 2)(x - 2) = 0$ produces a solution, but both solutions are the number 2. We sometimes refer to this as one real solution with a *multiplicity of two*. Using the idea of multiplicity of roots, we can say that every quadratic equation has two roots.

Now let's consider the sum and product of the two roots.

$$\textbf{Sum} \quad x_1 + x_2 = \frac{-b + \sqrt{b^2 - 4ac}}{2a} + \frac{-b - \sqrt{b^2 - 4ac}}{2a} = \frac{-2b}{2a} = \boxed{-\frac{b}{a}}$$

$$\textbf{Product} \quad (x_1)(x_2) = \left(\frac{-b + \sqrt{b^2 - 4ac}}{2a}\right)\left(\frac{-b - \sqrt{b^2 - 4ac}}{2a}\right)$$

$$= \frac{b^2 - (b^2 - 4ac)}{4a^2}$$

$$= \frac{b^2 - b^2 + 4ac}{4a^2}$$

$$= \frac{4ac}{4a^2} = \boxed{\frac{c}{a}}$$

These relationships provide another way of checking potential solutions when solving quadratic equations. For instance, back in Example 3 we solved the equation $x^2 - 2x + 19 = 0$ and obtained solutions of $1 + 3i\sqrt{2}$ and $1 - 3i\sqrt{2}$. Let's check these solutions by using the sum and product relationships.

✔ **Check for Example 3**

Sum of roots $(1 + 3i\sqrt{2}) + (1 - 3i\sqrt{2}) = 2$ and $-\frac{b}{a} = -\frac{-2}{1} = 2$

Product of roots $(1 + 3i\sqrt{2})(1 - 3i\sqrt{2}) = 1 - 18i^2 = 1 + 18 = 19$ and

$$\frac{c}{a} = \frac{19}{1} = 19$$

Likewise, a check for Example 4 is as follows:

✔ **Check for Example 4**

Sum of roots $\left(\dfrac{-2 + \sqrt{10}}{2}\right) + \left(\dfrac{-2 - \sqrt{10}}{2}\right) = -\dfrac{4}{2} = -2$ and

$$-\dfrac{b}{a} = -\dfrac{4}{2} = -2$$

Product of roots $\left(\dfrac{-2 + \sqrt{10}}{2}\right)\left(\dfrac{-2 - \sqrt{10}}{2}\right) = -\dfrac{6}{4} = -\dfrac{3}{2}$ and

$$\dfrac{c}{a} = \dfrac{-3}{2} = -\dfrac{3}{2}$$

Note that for both Examples 3 and 4, it was much easier to check by using the sum and product relationships than it would have been to check by substituting back into the original equation. Don't forget that the values for a, b, and c come from a quadratic equation of the form $ax^2 + bx + c = 0$. In Example 5, if we are going to check the potential solutions by using the sum and product relationships, we must be certain that we made no errors when changing the given equation $n(3n - 10) = 25$ to the form $3n^2 - 10n - 25 = 0$.

Problem Set 6.4

For each quadratic equation in Problems 1–10, first use the discriminant to determine whether the equation has two nonreal complex solutions, one real solution with a multiplicity of two, or two real solutions. Then solve the equation.

1. $x^2 + 4x - 21 = 0$

2. $x^2 - 3x - 54 = 0$

3. $9x^2 - 6x + 1 = 0$

4. $4x^2 + 20x + 25 = 0$

5. $x^2 - 7x + 13 = 0$

6. $2x^2 - x + 5 = 0$

7. $15x^2 + 17x - 4 = 0$

8. $8x^2 + 18x - 5 = 0$

9. $3x^2 + 4x = 2$

10. $2x^2 - 6x = -1$

For Problems 11–50, use the quadratic formula to solve each of the quadratic equations. Check your solutions by using the sum and product relationships.

11. $x^2 + 2x - 1 = 0$

12. $x^2 + 4x - 1 = 0$

13. $n^2 + 5n - 3 = 0$

14. $n^2 + 3n - 2 = 0$

15. $a^2 - 8a = 4$

16. $a^2 - 6a = 2$

17. $n^2 + 5n + 8 = 0$

18. $2n^2 - 3n + 5 = 0$

19. $x^2 - 18x + 80 = 0$

20. $x^2 + 19x + 70 = 0$

21. $-y^2 = -9y + 5$

22. $-y^2 + 7y = 4$

23. $2x^2 + x - 4 = 0$

24. $2x^2 + 5x - 2 = 0$

25. $4x^2 + 2x + 1 = 0$

26. $3x^2 - 2x + 5 = 0$

27. $3a^2 - 8a + 2 = 0$

28. $2a^2 - 6a + 1 = 0$

29. $-2n^2 + 3n + 5 = 0$

30. $-3n^2 - 11n + 4 = 0$

31. $3x^2 + 19x + 20 = 0$

32. $2x^2 - 17x + 30 = 0$

33. $36n^2 - 60n + 25 = 0$

34. $9n^2 + 42n + 49 = 0$

35. $4x^2 - 2x = 3$

36. $6x^2 - 4x = 3$

37. $5x^2 - 13x = 0$

38. $7x^2 + 12x = 0$

39. $3x^2 = 5$

40. $4x^2 = 3$

41. $6t^2 + t - 3 = 0$

42. $2t^2 + 6t - 3 = 0$

43. $n^2 + 32n + 252 = 0$

44. $n^2 - 4n - 192 = 0$

45. $12x^2 - 73x + 110 = 0$

46. $6x^2 + 11x - 255 = 0$

47. $-2x^2 + 4x - 3 = 0$

48. $-2x^2 + 6x - 5 = 0$

49. $-6x^2 + 2x + 1 = 0$

50. $-2x^2 + 4x + 1 = 0$

■ ■ ■ THOUGHTS INTO WORDS

51. Your friend states that the equation $-2x^2 + 4x - 1 = 0$ must be changed to $2x^2 - 4x + 1 = 0$ (by multiplying both sides by -1) before the quadratic formula can be applied. Is she right about this? If not, how would you convince her she is wrong?

52. Another of your friends claims that the quadratic formula can be used to solve the equation $x^2 - 9 = 0$. How would you react to this claim?

53. Why must we change the equation $3x^2 - 2x = 4$ to $3x^2 - 2x - 4 = 0$ before applying the quadratic formula?

■ ■ ■ FURTHER INVESTIGATIONS

The solution set for $x^2 - 4x - 37 = 0$ is $\{2 \pm \sqrt{41}\}$. With a calculator, we found a rational approximation, to the nearest one-thousandth, for each of these solutions.

$$2 - \sqrt{41} = -4.403 \quad \text{and} \quad 2 + \sqrt{41} = 8.403$$

Thus the solution set is $\{-4.403, 8.403\}$, with the answers rounded to the nearest one-thousandth.

Solve each of the equations in Problems 54–63, expressing solutions to the nearest one-thousandth.

54. $x^2 - 6x - 10 = 0$

55. $x^2 - 16x - 24 = 0$

56. $x^2 + 6x - 44 = 0$

57. $x^2 + 10x - 46 = 0$

58. $x^2 + 8x + 2 = 0$

59. $x^2 + 9x + 3 = 0$

60. $4x^2 - 6x + 1 = 0$

61. $5x^2 - 9x + 1 = 0$

62. $2x^2 - 11x - 5 = 0$

63. $3x^2 - 12x - 10 = 0$

For Problems 64–66, use the discriminant to help solve each problem.

64. Determine k so that the solutions of $x^2 - 2x + k = 0$ are complex but nonreal.

65. Determine k so that $4x^2 - kx + 1 = 0$ has two equal real solutions.

66. Determine k so that $3x^2 - kx - 2 = 0$ has real solutions.

6.5   More Quadratic Equations and Applications

Which method should be used to solve a particular quadratic equation? There is no hard and fast answer to that question; it depends on the type of equation and on your personal preference. In the following examples we will state reasons for choosing a specific technique. However, keep in mind that usually this is a decision you must make as the need arises. That's why you need to be familiar with the strengths and weaknesses of each method.

EXAMPLE 1

Solve $2x^2 - 3x - 1 = 0$.

Solution

Because of the leading coefficient of 2 and the constant term of -1, there are very few factoring possibilities to consider. Therefore, with such problems, first try the factoring approach. Unfortunately, this particular polynomial is not factorable using integers. Let's use the quadratic formula to solve the equation.

$$x = \frac{-b \pm \sqrt{b^2 - 4ac}}{2a}$$

$$x = \frac{-(-3) \pm \sqrt{(-3)^2 - 4(2)(-1)}}{2(2)}$$

$$x = \frac{3 \pm \sqrt{9 + 8}}{4}$$

$$x = \frac{3 \pm \sqrt{17}}{4}$$

✔ **Check**

We can use the sum-of-roots and the product-of-roots relationships for our checking purposes.

Sum of roots $\dfrac{3 + \sqrt{17}}{4} + \dfrac{3 - \sqrt{17}}{4} = \dfrac{6}{4} = \dfrac{3}{2}$ and $-\dfrac{b}{a} = -\dfrac{-3}{2} = \dfrac{3}{2}$

Product of roots $\left(\dfrac{3 + \sqrt{17}}{4}\right)\left(\dfrac{3 - \sqrt{17}}{4}\right) = \dfrac{9 - 17}{16} = -\dfrac{8}{16} = -\dfrac{1}{2}$ and

$$\frac{c}{a} = \frac{-1}{2} = -\frac{1}{2}$$

The solution set is $\left\{\dfrac{3 \pm \sqrt{17}}{4}\right\}$.   ■

EXAMPLE 2

Solve $\dfrac{3}{n} + \dfrac{10}{n + 6} = 1$.

Solution

$$\frac{3}{n} + \frac{10}{n + 6} = 1, \qquad n \neq 0 \text{ and } n \neq -6$$

$$n(n + 6)\left(\frac{3}{n} + \frac{10}{n + 6}\right) = 1(n)(n + 6) \qquad \text{Multiply both sides by } n(n + 6), \text{ which is the LCD.}$$

$$3(n + 6) + 10n = n(n + 6)$$
$$3n + 18 + 10n = n^2 + 6n$$
$$13n + 18 = n^2 + 6n$$
$$0 = n^2 - 7n - 18$$

This equation is an easy one to consider for possible factoring, and it factors as follows:

$$0 = (n - 9)(n + 2)$$

$$n - 9 = 0 \quad \text{or} \quad n + 2 = 0$$

$$n = 9 \quad \text{or} \quad n = -2$$

✔ **Check**

Substituting 9 and −2 back into the original equation, we obtain

$$\frac{3}{n} + \frac{10}{n + 6} = 1$$

$$\frac{3}{9} + \frac{10}{9 + 6} \overset{?}{=} 1$$

$$\frac{1}{3} + \frac{10}{15} \overset{?}{=} 1 \qquad \text{or}$$

$$\frac{1}{3} + \frac{2}{3} \overset{?}{=} 1$$

$$1 = 1$$

$$\frac{3}{n} + \frac{10}{n + 6} = 1$$

$$-\frac{3}{2} + \frac{10}{-2 + 6} \overset{?}{=} 1$$

$$-\frac{3}{2} + \frac{10}{4} \overset{?}{=} 1$$

$$-\frac{3}{2} + \frac{5}{2} \overset{?}{=} 1$$

$$\frac{2}{2} = 1$$

The solution set is $\{-2, 9\}$. ∎

We should make two comments about Example 2. First, note the indication of the initial restrictions $n \neq 0$ and $n \neq -6$. Remember that we need to do this when solving fractional equations. Second, the sum-of-roots and product-of-roots relationships were not used for checking purposes in this problem. Those relationships would check the validity of our work only from the step $0 = n^2 - 7n - 18$ to the finish. In other words, an error made in changing the original equation to quadratic form would not be detected by checking the sum and product of potential roots. With such a problem, the only *absolute check* is to substitute the potential solutions back into the original equation.

E X A M P L E   3

Solve $x^2 + 22x + 112 = 0$.

Solution

The size of the constant term makes the factoring approach a little cumbersome for this problem. Furthermore, because the leading coefficient is 1 and the coefficient of the x term is even, the method of completing the square will work effectively.

$$x^2 + 22x + 112 = 0$$

$$x^2 + 22x = -112$$

$$x^2 + 22x + 121 = -112 + 121$$

$$(x + 11)^2 = 9$$

$$x + 11 = \pm\sqrt{9}$$

$$x + 11 = \pm 3$$

$$x + 11 = 3 \quad \text{or} \quad x + 11 = -3$$

$$x = -8 \quad \text{or} \quad x = -14$$

✔ **Check**

Sum of roots $-8 + (-14) = -22$ and $-\dfrac{b}{a} = -22$

Product of roots $(-8)(-14) = 112$ and $\dfrac{c}{a} = 112$

The solution set is $\{-14, -8\}$.   ■

EXAMPLE 4   Solve $x^4 - 4x^2 - 96 = 0$.

Solution

An equation such as $x^4 - 4x^2 - 96 = 0$ is not a quadratic equation, but we can solve it using the techniques that we use on quadratic equations. That is, we can factor the polynomial and apply the property "$ab = 0$ if and only if $a = 0$ or $b = 0$" as follows:

$$x^4 - 4x^2 - 96 = 0$$

$$(x^2 - 12)(x^2 + 8) = 0$$

$$x^2 - 12 = 0 \quad \text{or} \quad x^2 + 8 = 0$$

$$x^2 = 12 \quad \text{or} \quad x^2 = -8$$

$$x = \pm\sqrt{12} \quad \text{or} \quad x = \pm\sqrt{-8}$$

$$x = \pm 2\sqrt{3} \quad \text{or} \quad x = \pm 2i\sqrt{2}$$

The solution set is $\{\pm 2\sqrt{3}, \pm 2i\sqrt{2}\}$. (We will leave the check for this problem for you to do!)   ■

Remark: Another approach to Example 4 would be to substitute y for x^2 and y^2 for x^4. The equation $x^4 - 4x^2 - 96 = 0$ becomes the quadratic equation

$y^2 - 4y - 96 = 0$. Thus we say that $x^4 - 4x^2 - 96 = 0$ is of *quadratic form*. Then we could solve the quadratic equation $y^2 - 4y - 96 = 0$ and use the equation $y = x^2$ to determine the solutions for x.

■ Applications

Before we conclude this section with some word problems that can be solved using quadratic equations, let's restate the suggestions we made in an earlier chapter for solving word problems.

Suggestions for Solving Word Problems

1. Read the problem carefully, and make certain that you understand the meanings of all the words. Be especially alert for any technical terms used in the statement of the problem.
2. Read the problem a second time (perhaps even a third time) to get an overview of the situation being described and to determine the known facts, as well as what is to be found.
3. Sketch any figure, diagram, or chart that might be helpful in analyzing the problem.
4. Choose a meaningful variable to represent an unknown quantity in the problem (perhaps l, if the length of a rectangle is an unknown quantity), and represent any other unknowns in terms of that variable.
5. Look for a guideline that you can use to set up an equation. A guideline might be a formula such as $A = lw$ or a relationship such as "the fractional part of a job done by Bill plus the fractional part of the job done by Mary equals the total job."
6. Form an equation that contains the variable and that translates the conditions of the guideline from English to algebra.
7. Solve the equation and use the solutions to determine all facts requested in the problem.
8. **Check all answers back into the original statement of the problem.**

Keep these suggestions in mind as we now consider some word problems.

PROBLEM 1

A page for a magazine contains 70 square inches of type. The height of a page is twice the width. If the margin around the type is to be 2 inches uniformly, what are the dimensions of a page?

Solution

Let x represent the width of a page. Then $2x$ represents the height of a page. Now let's draw and label a model of a page (Figure 6.8).

Width of typed material   Height of typed material   Area of typed material

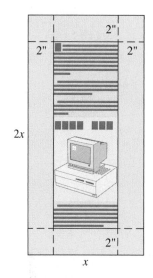

$$(x - 4)(2x - 4) = 70$$

$$2x^2 - 12x + 16 = 70$$

$$2x^2 - 12x - 54 = 0$$

$$x^2 - 6x - 27 = 0$$

$$(x - 9)(x + 3) = 0$$

$$x - 9 = 0 \quad \text{or} \quad x + 3 = 0$$

$$x = 9 \quad \text{or} \quad x = -3$$

Figure 6.8

Disregard the negative solution; the page must be 9 inches wide, and its height is $2(9) = 18$ inches. ∎

Let's use our knowledge of quadratic equations to analyze some applications of the business world. For example, if P dollars is invested at r rate of interest compounded annually for t years, then the amount of money, A, accumulated at the end of t years is given by the formula

$$A = P(1 + r)^t$$

This compound interest formula serves as a guideline for the next problem.

PROBLEM   2

Suppose that $100 is invested at a certain rate of interest compounded annually for 2 years. If the accumulated value at the end of 2 years is $121, find the rate of interest.

Solution

Let r represent the rate of interest. Substitute the known values into the compound interest formula to yield

$$A = P(1 + r)^t$$

$$121 = 100(1 + r)^2$$

Solving this equation, we obtain

$$\frac{121}{100} = (1 + r)^2$$

$$\pm\sqrt{\frac{121}{100}} = (1 + r)$$

$$\pm\frac{11}{10} = 1 + r$$

$$1 + r = \frac{11}{10} \qquad \text{or} \qquad 1 + r = -\frac{11}{10}$$

$$r = -1 + \frac{11}{10} \qquad \text{or} \qquad r = -1 - \frac{11}{10}$$

$$r = \frac{1}{10} \qquad \text{or} \qquad r = -\frac{21}{10}$$

We must disregard the negative solution, so that $r = \frac{1}{10}$ is the only solution.

Change $\frac{1}{10}$ to a percent, and the rate of interest is 10%. ∎

PROBLEM 3

On a 130-mile trip from Orlando to Sarasota, Roberto encountered a heavy thunderstorm for the last 40 miles of the trip. During the thunderstorm he averaged 20 miles per hour slower than before the storm. The entire trip took $2\frac{1}{2}$ hours. How fast did he travel before the storm?

Solution

Let x represent Roberto's rate before the thunderstorm. Then $x - 20$ represents his speed during the thunderstorm. Because $t = \frac{d}{r}$, then $\frac{90}{x}$ represents the time traveling before the storm, and $\frac{40}{x - 20}$ represents the time traveling during the storm. The following guideline sums up the situation.

Time traveling before the storm	Plus	Time traveling after the storm	Equals	Total time
↓		↓		↓
$\dfrac{90}{x}$	$+$	$\dfrac{40}{x - 20}$	$=$	$\dfrac{5}{2}$

Solving this equation, we obtain

$$2x(x - 20)\left(\frac{90}{x} + \frac{40}{x - 20}\right) = 2x(x - 20)\left(\frac{5}{2}\right)$$

$$2x(x - 20)\left(\frac{90}{x}\right) + 2x(x - 20)\left(\frac{40}{x - 20}\right) = 2x(x - 20)\left(\frac{5}{2}\right)$$

$$180(x - 20) + 2x(40) = 5x(x - 20)$$

$$180x - 3600 + 80x = 5x^2 - 100x$$
$$0 = 5x^2 - 360x + 3600$$
$$0 = 5(x^2 - 72x + 720)$$
$$0 = 5(x - 60)(x - 12)$$
$$x - 60 = 0 \quad \text{or} \quad x - 12 = 0$$
$$x = 60 \quad \text{or} \quad x = 12$$

We discard the solution of 12 because it would be impossible to drive 20 miles per hour slower than 12 miles per hour; thus Roberto's rate before the thunderstorm was 60 miles per hour. ∎

PROBLEM 4

A businesswoman bought a parcel of land on speculation for $120,000. She subdivided the land into lots, and when she had sold all but 18 lots at a profit of $6000 per lot, she had regained the entire cost of the land. How many lots were sold and at what price per lot?

Solution

Let x represent the number of lots sold. Then $x + 18$ represents the total number of lots. Therefore, $\dfrac{120,000}{x}$ represents the selling price per lot, and $\dfrac{120,000}{x + 18}$ represents the cost per lot. The following equation sums up the situation.

Selling price per lot	Equals	Cost per lot	Plus	$6000
↓		↓		↓
$\dfrac{120,000}{x}$	=	$\dfrac{120,000}{x + 18}$	+	6000

Solving this equation, we obtain

$$x(x + 18)\left(\frac{120,000}{x}\right) = \left(\frac{120,000}{x + 18} + 6000\right)(x)(x + 18)$$
$$120,000(x + 18) = 120,000x + 6000x(x + 18)$$
$$120,000x + 2,160,000 = 120,000x + 6000x^2 + 108,000x$$
$$0 = 6000x^2 + 108,000x - 2,160,000$$
$$0 = x^2 + 18x - 360$$

The method of completing the square works very well with this equation.

$$x^2 + 18x = 360$$
$$x^2 + 18x + 81 = 441$$
$$(x + 9)^2 = 441$$
$$x + 9 = \pm\sqrt{441}$$

$$x + 9 = \pm 21$$

$$x + 9 = 21 \quad \text{or} \quad x + 9 = -21$$

$$x = 12 \quad \text{or} \quad x = -30$$

We discard the negative solution; thus 12 lots were sold at $\dfrac{120{,}000}{x} = \dfrac{120{,}000}{12} =$ $10,000 per lot. ∎

P R O B L E M   5

Barry bought a number of shares of stock for $600. A week later the value of the stock had increased $3 per share, and he sold all but 10 shares and regained his original investment of $600. How many shares did he sell and at what price per share?

Solution

Let s represent the number of shares Barry sold. Then $s + 10$ represents the number of shares purchased. Therefore, $\dfrac{600}{s}$ represents the selling price per share, and $\dfrac{600}{s + 10}$ represents the cost per share.

Selling price per share		Cost per share
↓		↓
$\dfrac{600}{s}$	$=$	$\dfrac{600}{s + 10} + 3$

Solving this equation yields

$$s(s + 10)\left(\frac{600}{s}\right) = \left(\frac{600}{s + 10} + 3\right)(s)(s + 10)$$

$$600(s + 10) = 600s + 3s(s + 10)$$

$$600s + 6000 = 600s + 3s^2 + 30s$$

$$0 = 3s^2 + 30s - 6000$$

$$0 = s^2 + 10s - 2000$$

Use the quadratic formula to obtain

$$s = \frac{-10 \pm \sqrt{10^2 - 4(1)(-2000)}}{2(1)}$$

$$s = \frac{-10 \pm \sqrt{100 + 8000}}{2}$$

$$s = \frac{-10 \pm \sqrt{8100}}{2}$$

$$s = \frac{-10 \pm 90}{2}$$

$$s = \frac{-10 + 90}{2} \quad \text{or} \quad s = \frac{-10 - 90}{2}$$

$$s = 40 \quad \text{or} \quad s = -50$$

We discard the negative solution, and we know that 40 shares were sold at $\frac{600}{s} = \frac{600}{40} = \$15$ per share. ∎

This next problem set contains a large variety of word problems. Not only are there some business applications similar to those we discussed in this section, but there are also more problems of the types we discussed in Chapters 3 and 4. Try to give them your best shot without referring to the examples in earlier chapters.

Problem Set 6.5

For Problems 1–20, solve each quadratic equation using the method that seems most appropriate to you.

1. $x^2 - 4x - 6 = 0$

2. $x^2 - 8x - 4 = 0$

3. $3x^2 + 23x - 36 = 0$

4. $n^2 + 22n + 105 = 0$

5. $x^2 - 18x = 9$

6. $x^2 + 20x = 25$

7. $2x^2 - 3x + 4 = 0$

8. $3y^2 - 2y + 1 = 0$

9. $135 + 24n + n^2 = 0$

10. $28 - x - 2x^2 = 0$

11. $(x - 2)(x + 9) = -10$

12. $(x + 3)(2x + 1) = -3$

13. $2x^2 - 4x + 7 = 0$

14. $3x^2 - 2x + 8 = 0$

15. $x^2 - 18x + 15 = 0$

16. $x^2 - 16x + 14 = 0$

17. $20y^2 + 17y - 10 = 0$

18. $12x^2 + 23x - 9 = 0$

19. $4t^2 + 4t - 1 = 0$

20. $5t^2 + 5t - 1 = 0$

For Problems 21–40, solve each equation.

21. $n + \frac{3}{n} = \frac{19}{4}$

22. $n - \frac{2}{n} = -\frac{7}{3}$

23. $\frac{3}{x} + \frac{7}{x - 1} = 1$

24. $\frac{2}{x} + \frac{5}{x + 2} = 1$

25. $\frac{12}{x - 3} + \frac{8}{x} = 14$

26. $\frac{16}{x + 5} - \frac{12}{x} = -2$

27. $\frac{3}{x - 1} - \frac{2}{x} = \frac{5}{2}$

28. $\frac{4}{x + 1} + \frac{2}{x} = \frac{5}{3}$

29. $\frac{6}{x} + \frac{40}{x + 5} = 7$

30. $\frac{12}{t} + \frac{18}{t + 8} = \frac{9}{2}$

31. $\frac{5}{n - 3} - \frac{3}{n + 3} = 1$

32. $\frac{3}{t + 2} + \frac{4}{t - 2} = 2$

33. $x^4 - 18x^2 + 72 = 0$

34. $x^4 - 21x^2 + 54 = 0$

35. $3x^4 - 35x^2 + 72 = 0$

36. $5x^4 - 32x^2 + 48 = 0$

37. $3x^4 + 17x^2 + 20 = 0$

38. $4x^4 + 11x^2 - 45 = 0$

39. $6x^4 - 29x^2 + 28 = 0$

40. $6x^4 - 31x^2 + 18 = 0$

For Problems 41–70, set up an equation and solve each problem.

41. Find two consecutive whole numbers such that the sum of their squares is 145.

42. Find two consecutive odd whole numbers such that the sum of their squares is 74.

43. Two positive integers differ by 3, and their product is 108. Find the numbers.

44. Suppose that the sum of two numbers is 20, and the sum of their squares is 232. Find the numbers.

45. Find two numbers such that their sum is 10 and their product is 22.

46. Find two numbers such that their sum is 6 and their product is 7.

47. Suppose that the sum of two whole numbers is 9, and the sum of their reciprocals is $\frac{1}{2}$. Find the numbers.

48. The difference between two whole numbers is 8, and the difference between their reciprocals is $\frac{1}{6}$. Find the two numbers.

49. The sum of the lengths of the two legs of a right triangle is 21 inches. If the length of the hypotenuse is 15 inches, find the length of each leg.

50. The length of a rectangular floor is 1 meter less than twice its width. If a diagonal of the rectangle is 17 meters, find the length and width of the floor.

51. A rectangular plot of ground measuring 12 meters by 20 meters is surrounded by a sidewalk of a uniform width (see Figure 6.9). The area of the sidewalk is 68 square meters. Find the width of the walk.

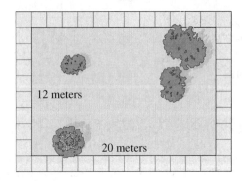

12 meters

20 meters

Figure 6.9

52. A 5-inch by 7-inch picture is surrounded by a frame of uniform width. The area of the picture and frame together is 80 square inches. Find the width of the frame.

53. The perimeter of a rectangle is 44 inches, and its area is 112 square inches. Find the length and width of the rectangle.

54. A rectangular piece of cardboard is 2 units longer than it is wide. From each of its corners a square piece 2 units on a side is cut out. The flaps are then turned up to form an open box that has a volume of 70 cubic units. Find the length and width of the original piece of cardboard.

55. Charlotte's time to travel 250 miles is 1 hour more than Lorraine's time to travel 180 miles. Charlotte drove 5 miles per hour faster than Lorraine. How fast did each one travel?

56. Larry's time to travel 156 miles is 1 hour more than Terrell's time to travel 108 miles. Terrell drove 2 miles per hour faster than Larry. How fast did each one travel?

57. On a 570-mile trip, Andy averaged 5 miles per hour faster for the last 240 miles than he did for the first 330 miles. The entire trip took 10 hours. How fast did he travel for the first 330 miles?

58. On a 135-mile bicycle excursion, Maria averaged 5 miles per hour faster for the first 60 miles than she did for the last 75 miles. The entire trip took 8 hours. Find her rate for the first 60 miles.

59. It takes Terry 2 hours longer to do a certain job than it takes Tom. They worked together for 3 hours; then Tom left and Terry finished the job in 1 hour. How long would it take each of them to do the job alone?

60. Suppose that Arlene can mow the entire lawn in 40 minutes less time with the power mower than she can with the push mower. One day the power mower broke down after she had been mowing for 30 minutes. She finished the lawn with the push mower in 20 minutes. How long does it take Arlene to mow the entire lawn with the power mower?

61. A student did a word processing job for $24. It took him 1 hour longer than he expected, and therefore he earned $4 per hour less than he anticipated. How long did he expect that it would take to do the job?

62. A group of students agreed that each would chip in the same amount to pay for a party that would cost $100. Then they found 5 more students interested in the party and in sharing the expenses. This decreased the amount each had to pay by $1. How many students were involved in the party and how much did each student have to pay?

63. A group of students agreed that each would contribute the same amount to buy their favorite teacher an $80 birthday gift. At the last minute, 2 of the students decided not to chip in. This increased the amount that the remaining students had to pay by $2 per student. How many students actually contributed to the gift?

64. A retailer bought a number of special mugs for $48. She decided to keep two of the mugs for herself but then

had to change the price to $3 a mug above the original cost per mug. If she sells the remaining mugs for $70, how many mugs did she buy and at what price per mug did she sell them?

65. Tony bought a number of shares of stock for $720. A month later the value of the stock increased by $8 per share, and he sold all but 20 shares and received $800. How many shares did he sell and at what price per share?

66. The formula $D = \dfrac{n(n-3)}{2}$ yields the number of diagonals, D, in a polygon of n sides. Find the number of sides of a polygon that has 54 diagonals.

67. The formula $S = \dfrac{n(n+1)}{2}$ yields the sum, S, of the first n natural numbers $1, 2, 3, 4, \ldots$. How many consecutive natural numbers starting with 1 will give a sum of 1275?

68. At a point 16 yards from the base of a tower, the distance to the top of the tower is 4 yards more than the height of the tower (see Figure 6.10). Find the height of the tower.

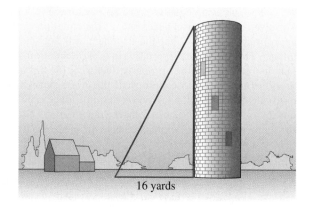

16 yards

Figure 6.10

69. Suppose that $500 is invested at a certain rate of interest compounded annually for 2 years. If the accumulated value at the end of 2 years is $594.05, find the rate of interest.

70. Suppose that $10,000 is invested at a certain rate of interest compounded annually for 2 years. If the accumulated value at the end of 2 years is $12,544, find the rate of interest.

■ ■ ■ THOUGHTS INTO WORDS

71. How would you solve the equation $x^2 - 4x = 252$? Explain your choice of the method that you would use.

72. Explain how you would solve $(x - 2)(x - 7) = 0$ and also how you would solve $(x - 2)(x - 7) = 4$.

73. One of our problem-solving suggestions is to look for a guideline that can be used to help determine an equation. What does this suggestion mean to you?

74. Can a quadratic equation with integral coefficients have exactly one nonreal complex solution? Explain your answer.

■ ■ ■ FURTHER INVESTIGATIONS

For Problems 75–81, solve each equation.

75. $x - 9\sqrt{x} + 18 = 0$ [*Hint:* Let $y = \sqrt{x}$.]

76. $x - 4\sqrt{x} + 3 = 0$

77. $x + \sqrt{x} - 2 = 0$

78. $x^{\frac{2}{3}} + x^{\frac{1}{3}} - 6 = 0$ [*Hint:* Let $y = x^{\frac{1}{3}}$.]

79. $6x^{\frac{2}{3}} - 5x^{\frac{1}{3}} - 6 = 0$

80. $x^{-2} + 4x^{-1} - 12 = 0$

81. $12x^{-2} - 17x^{-1} - 5 = 0$

The following equations are also quadratic in form. To solve, begin by raising each side of the equation to the appropriate power so that the exponent will become an integer. Then, to solve the resulting quadratic equation, you may use the square-root property, factoring, or the quadratic formula, as is most appropriate. Be aware that raising each side of the equation to a power may introduce extraneous roots; therefore, be sure to check your solutions. Study the following example before you begin the problems.

Solve

$$(x + 3)^{\frac{2}{3}} = 1$$

$$\left[(x + 3)^{\frac{2}{3}}\right]^3 = 1^3 \qquad \text{Raise both sides to the third power.}$$

$$(x + 3)^2 = 1$$

$$x^2 + 6x + 9 = 1$$

$$x^2 + 6x + 8 = 0$$

$$(x + 4)(x + 2) = 0$$

$$x + 4 = 0 \quad \text{or} \quad x + 2 = 0$$

$$x = -4 \quad \text{or} \quad x = -2$$

Both solutions do check. The solution set is $\{-4, -2\}$.

For problems 82–90, solve each equation.

82. $(5x + 6)^{\frac{1}{2}} = x$

83. $(3x + 4)^{\frac{1}{2}} = x$

84. $x^{\frac{2}{3}} = 2$

85. $x^{\frac{2}{5}} = 2$

86. $(2x + 6)^{\frac{1}{2}} = x$

87. $(2x - 4)^{\frac{2}{3}} = 1$

88. $(4x + 5)^{\frac{2}{3}} = 2$

89. $(6x + 7)^{\frac{1}{2}} = x + 2$

90. $(5x + 21)^{\frac{1}{2}} = x + 3$

6.6 Quadratic and Other Nonlinear Inequalities

We refer to the equation $ax^2 + bx + c = 0$ as the standard form of a quadratic equation in one variable. Similarly, the following forms express **quadratic inequalities** in one variable.

$$ax^2 + bx + c > 0 \qquad\qquad ax^2 + bx + c < 0$$
$$ax^2 + bx + c \geq 0 \qquad\qquad ax^2 + bx + c \leq 0$$

We can use the number line very effectively to help solve quadratic inequalities where the quadratic polynomial is factorable. Let's consider some examples to illustrate the procedure.

EXAMPLE 1

Solve and graph the solutions for $x^2 + 2x - 8 > 0$.

Solution

First, let's factor the polynomial.

$$x^2 + 2x - 8 > 0$$

$$(x + 4)(x - 2) > 0$$

On a number line (Figure 6.11), we indicate that at $x = 2$ and $x = -4$, the product $(x + 4)(x - 2)$ equals zero. The numbers -4 and 2 divide the number line into three intervals: (1) the numbers less than -4, (2) the numbers between -4 and 2, and (3) the numbers greater than 2. We can choose a **test number** from each of these intervals and see how it affects the signs of the factors $x + 4$ and $x - 2$ and,

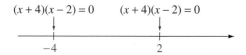

$(x + 4)(x - 2) = 0$ $(x + 4)(x - 2) = 0$

Figure 6.11

consequently, the sign of the product of these factors. For example, if $x < -4$ (try $x = -5$), then $x + 4$ is negative and $x - 2$ is negative, so their product is positive. If $-4 < x < 2$ (try $x = 0$), then $x + 4$ is positive and $x - 2$ is negative, so their product is negative. If $x > 2$ (try $x = 3$), then $x + 4$ is positive and $x - 2$ is positive, so their product is positive. This information can be conveniently arranged using a number line, as shown in Figure 6.12. Note the open circles at -4 and 2 to indicate that they are not included in the solution set.

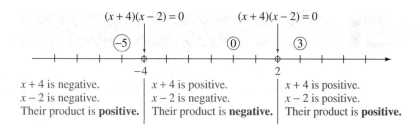

$(x + 4)(x - 2) = 0$ $(x + 4)(x - 2) = 0$

$x + 4$ is negative.	$x + 4$ is positive.	$x + 4$ is positive.
$x - 2$ is negative.	$x - 2$ is negative.	$x - 2$ is positive.
Their product is **positive.**	Their product is **negative.**	Their product is **positive.**

Figure 6.12

Thus the given inequality, $x^2 + 2x - 8 > 0$, is satisfied by numbers less than -4 along with numbers greater than 2. Using interval notation, the solution set is $(-\infty, -4) \cup (2, \infty)$. These solutions can be shown on a number line (Figure 6.13).

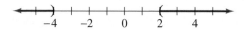

Figure 6.13

We refer to numbers such as -4 and 2 in the preceding example (where the given polynomial or algebraic expression equals zero or is undefined) as **critical numbers**. Let's consider some additional examples that make use of critical numbers and test numbers.

EXAMPLE 2

Solve and graph the solutions for $x^2 + 2x - 3 \leq 0$.

Solution

First, factor the polynomial.

$$x^2 + 2x - 3 \leq 0$$

$$(x + 3)(x - 1) \leq 0$$

Second, locate the values for which $(x + 3)(x - 1)$ equals zero. We put dots at -3 and 1 to remind ourselves that these two numbers are to be included in the solution set because the given statement includes equality. Now let's choose a test number from each of the three intervals, and record the sign behavior of the factors $(x + 3)$ and $(x - 1)$ (Figure 6.14).

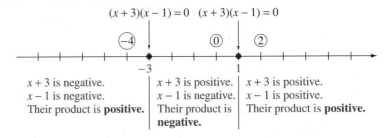

Figure 6.14

Therefore, the solution set is $[-3, 1]$, and it can be graphed as in Figure 6.15.

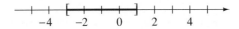

Figure 6.15 ∎

Examples 1 and 2 have indicated a systematic approach for solving quadratic inequalities where the polynomial is factorable. This same type of number line analysis can also be used to solve indicated quotients such as $\dfrac{x + 1}{x - 5} > 0$.

EXAMPLE 3

Solve and graph the solutions for $\dfrac{x+1}{x-5} > 0$.

Solution

First, indicate that at $x = -1$ the given quotient equals zero, and at $x = 5$ the quotient is undefined. Second, choose test numbers from each of the three intervals, and record the sign behavior of $(x + 1)$ and $(x - 5)$ as in Figure 6.16.

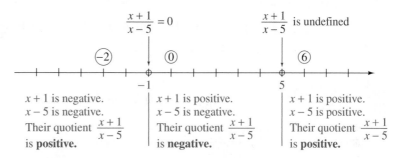

$\dfrac{x+1}{x-5} = 0$ $\dfrac{x+1}{x-5}$ is undefined

$x + 1$ is negative.
$x - 5$ is negative.
Their quotient $\dfrac{x+1}{x-5}$ is **positive**.

$x + 1$ is positive.
$x - 5$ is negative.
Their quotient $\dfrac{x+1}{x-5}$ is **negative**.

$x + 1$ is positive.
$x - 5$ is positive.
Their quotient $\dfrac{x+1}{x-5}$ is **positive**.

Figure 6.16

Therefore, the solution set is $(-\infty, -1) \cup (5, \infty)$, and its graph is shown in Figure 6.17.

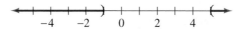

Figure 6.17 ∎

EXAMPLE 4

Solve $\dfrac{x+2}{x+4} \le 0$.

Solution

The indicated quotient equals zero at $x = -2$ and is undefined at $x = -4$. (Note that -2 is to be included in the solution set, but -4 is not to be included.) Now let's choose some test numbers and record the sign behavior of $(x + 2)$ and $(x + 4)$ as in Figure 6.18.

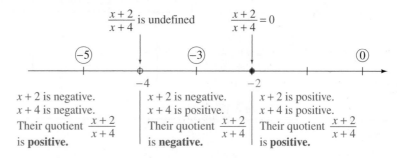

$\dfrac{x+2}{x+4}$ is undefined $\dfrac{x+2}{x+4} = 0$

$x + 2$ is negative.
$x + 4$ is negative.
Their quotient $\dfrac{x+2}{x+4}$ is **positive**.

$x + 2$ is negative.
$x + 4$ is positive.
Their quotient $\dfrac{x+2}{x+4}$ is **negative**.

$x + 2$ is positive.
$x + 4$ is positive.
Their quotient $\dfrac{x+2}{x+4}$ is **positive**.

Figure 6.18

Therefore, the solution set is $(-4, -2]$. ∎

The final example illustrates that sometimes we need to change the form of the given inequality before we use the number line analysis.

E X A M P L E   5

Solve $\dfrac{x}{x+2} \geq 3$.

Solution

First, let's change the form of the given inequality as follows:

$$\frac{x}{x+2} \geq 3$$

$$\frac{x}{x+2} - 3 \geq 0 \qquad \text{Add } -3 \text{ to both sides.}$$

$$\frac{x - 3(x+2)}{x+2} \geq 0 \qquad \text{Express the left side over a common denominator.}$$

$$\frac{x - 3x - 6}{x+2} \geq 0$$

$$\frac{-2x - 6}{x+2} \geq 0$$

Now we can proceed as we did with the previous examples. If $x = -3$, then $\dfrac{-2x-6}{x+2}$ equals zero; and if $x = -2$, then $\dfrac{-2x-6}{x+2}$ is undefined. Then, choosing test numbers, we can record the sign behavior of $(-2x-6)$ and $(x+2)$ as in Figure 6.19.

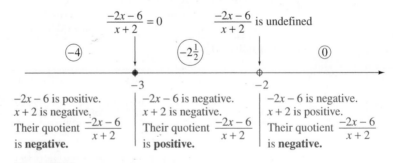

Figure 6.19

Therefore, the solution set is $[-3, -2)$. Perhaps you should check a few numbers from this solution set back into the original inequality! ■

Problem Set 6.6

For Problems 1–20, solve each inequality and graph its solution set on a number line.

1. $(x + 2)(x - 1) > 0$

2. $(x - 2)(x + 3) > 0$

3. $(x + 1)(x + 4) < 0$

4. $(x - 3)(x - 1) < 0$

5. $(2x - 1)(3x + 7) \geq 0$

6. $(3x + 2)(2x - 3) \geq 0$

7. $(x + 2)(4x - 3) \leq 0$

8. $(x - 1)(2x - 7) \leq 0$

9. $(x + 1)(x - 1)(x - 3) > 0$

10. $(x + 2)(x + 1)(x - 2) > 0$

11. $x(x + 2)(x - 4) \leq 0$

12. $x(x + 3)(x - 3) \leq 0$

13. $\dfrac{x + 1}{x - 2} > 0$

14. $\dfrac{x - 1}{x + 2} > 0$

15. $\dfrac{x - 3}{x + 2} < 0$

16. $\dfrac{x + 2}{x - 4} < 0$

17. $\dfrac{2x - 1}{x} \geq 0$

18. $\dfrac{x}{3x + 7} \geq 0$

19. $\dfrac{-x + 2}{x - 1} \leq 0$

20. $\dfrac{3 - x}{x + 4} \leq 0$

For Problems 21–56, solve each inequality.

21. $x^2 + 2x - 35 < 0$

22. $x^2 + 3x - 54 < 0$

23. $x^2 - 11x + 28 > 0$

24. $x^2 + 11x + 18 > 0$

25. $3x^2 + 13x - 10 \leq 0$

26. $4x^2 - x - 14 \leq 0$

27. $8x^2 + 22x + 5 \geq 0$

28. $12x^2 - 20x + 3 \geq 0$

29. $x(5x - 36) > 32$

30. $x(7x + 40) < 12$

31. $x^2 - 14x + 49 \geq 0$

32. $(x + 9)^2 \geq 0$

33. $4x^2 + 20x + 25 \leq 0$

34. $9x^2 - 6x + 1 \leq 0$

35. $(x + 1)(x - 3)^2 > 0$

36. $(x - 4)^2(x - 1) \leq 0$

37. $4 - x^2 < 0$

38. $2x^2 - 18 \geq 0$

39. $4(x^2 - 36) < 0$

40. $-4(x^2 - 36) \geq 0$

41. $5x^2 + 20 > 0$

42. $-3x^2 - 27 \geq 0$

43. $x^2 - 2x \geq 0$

44. $2x^2 + 6x < 0$

45. $3x^3 + 12x^2 > 0$

46. $2x^3 + 4x^2 \leq 0$

47. $\dfrac{2x}{x + 3} > 4$

48. $\dfrac{x}{x - 1} > 2$

49. $\dfrac{x - 1}{x - 5} \leq 2$

50. $\dfrac{x + 2}{x + 4} \leq 3$

51. $\dfrac{x + 2}{x - 3} > -2$

52. $\dfrac{x - 1}{x - 2} < -1$

53. $\dfrac{3x + 2}{x + 4} \leq 2$

54. $\dfrac{2x - 1}{x + 2} \geq -1$

55. $\dfrac{x + 1}{x - 2} < 1$

56. $\dfrac{x + 3}{x - 4} \geq 1$

■ ■ ■ THOUGHTS INTO WORDS

57. Explain how to solve the inequality $(x + 1)(x - 2)(x - 3) > 0$.

58. Explain how to solve the inequality $(x - 2)^2 > 0$ by inspection.

59. Your friend looks at the inequality $1 + \dfrac{1}{x} > 2$ and without any computation states that the solution set is all real numbers between 0 and 1. How can she do that?

60. Why is the solution set for $(x - 2)^2 \geq 0$ the set of all real numbers?

61. Why is the solution set for $(x - 2)^2 \leq 0$ the set $\{2\}$?

■ ■ ■ **FURTHER INVESTIGATIONS**

62. The product $(x - 2)(x + 3)$ is positive if both factors are negative *or* if both factors are positive. Therefore, we can solve $(x - 2)(x + 3) > 0$ as follows:

$$(x - 2 < 0 \text{ and } x + 3 < 0) \text{ or } (x - 2 > 0 \text{ and } x + 3 > 0)$$

$$(x < 2 \text{ and } x < -3) \text{ or } (x > 2 \text{ and } x > -3)$$

$$x < -3 \text{ or } x > 2$$

The solution set is $(-\infty, -3) \cup (2, \infty)$. Use this type of analysis to solve each of the following.

(a) $(x - 2)(x + 7) > 0$

(b) $(x - 3)(x + 9) \geq 0$

(c) $(x + 1)(x - 6) \leq 0$

(d) $(x + 4)(x - 8) < 0$

(e) $\dfrac{x + 4}{x - 7} > 0$

(f) $\dfrac{x - 5}{x + 8} \leq 0$

(6.1) A number of the form $a + bi$, where a and b are real numbers, and i is the imaginary unit defined by $i = \sqrt{-1}$, is a **complex number**.

Two complex numbers $a + bi$ and $c + di$ are said to be equal if and only if $a = c$ and $b = d$.

We describe addition and subtraction of complex numbers as follows:

$$(a + bi) + (c + di) = (a + c) + (b + d)i$$

$$(a + bi) - (c + di) = (a - c) + (b - d)i$$

We can represent a square root of any negative real number as the product of a real number and the imaginary unit i. That is,

$$\sqrt{-b} = i\sqrt{b}, \quad \text{where } b \text{ is a positive real number}$$

The product of two complex numbers conforms with the product of two binomials. The **conjugate** of $a + bi$ is $a - bi$. The product of a complex number and its conjugate is a real number. Therefore, conjugates are used to simplify expressions such as $\dfrac{4 + 3i}{5 - 2i}$, which indicate the quotient of two complex numbers.

(6.2) The **standard form for a quadratic equation** in one variable is

$$ax^2 + bx + c = 0$$

where a, b, and c are real numbers and $a \neq 0$.

Some quadratic equations can be solved by factoring and applying the property, $ab = 0$ if and only if $a = 0$ or $b = 0$.

Don't forget that applying the property, if $a = b$, then $a^n = b^n$ might produce extraneous solutions. Therefore, we *must* check all potential solutions.

We can solve some quadratic equations by applying the property, $x^2 = a$ if and only if $x = \pm\sqrt{a}$.

(6.3) To solve a quadratic equation of the form $x^2 + bx = k$ by **completing the square**, we (1) add $\left(\dfrac{b}{2}\right)^2$ to both sides, (2) factor the left side, and (3) apply the property, $x^2 = a$ if and only if $x = \pm\sqrt{a}$.

(6.4) We can solve any quadratic equation of the form $ax^2 + bx + c = 0$ by the **quadratic formula**, which we usually state as

$$x = \frac{-b \pm \sqrt{b^2 - 4ac}}{2a}$$

The **discriminant**, $b^2 - 4ac$, can be used to determine the nature of the roots of a quadratic equation as follows:

1. If $b^2 - 4ac < 0$, then the equation has two nonreal complex solutions.

2. If $b^2 - 4ac = 0$, then the equation has two equal real solutions.

3. If $b^2 - 4ac > 0$, then the equation has two unequal real solutions.

If x_1 and x_2 are roots of a quadratic equation, then the following relationships exist.

$$x_1 + x_2 = -\frac{b}{a} \quad \text{and} \quad (x_1)(x_2) = \frac{c}{a}$$

These **sum-of-roots** and **product-of-roots relationships** can be used to check potential solutions of quadratic equations.

(6.5) To review the strengths and weaknesses of the three basic methods for solving a quadratic equation (factoring, completing the square, and the quadratic formula), go back over the examples in this section.

Keep the following suggestions in mind as you solve word problems.

1. Read the problem carefully.

2. Sketch any figure, diagram, or chart that might help you organize and analyze the problem.

3. Choose a meaningful variable.

4. Look for a guideline that can be used to set up an equation.

5. Form an equation that translates the guideline from English to algebra.

6. Solve the equation and use the solutions to determine all facts requested in the problem.

7. Check all answers back into the original statement of the problem.

(6.6) The number line, along with **critical numbers** and **test numbers**, provides a good basis for solving **quadratic inequalities** where the polynomial is factorable. We can use this same basic approach to solve inequalities, such as $\dfrac{3x + 1}{x - 4} > 0$, that indicate quotients.

Chapter 6   Review Problem Set

For Problems 1–8, perform the indicated operations and express the answers in the standard form of a complex number.

1. $(-7 + 3i) + (9 - 5i)$

2. $(4 - 10i) - (7 - 9i)$

3. $5i(3 - 6i)$

4. $(5 - 7i)(6 + 8i)$

5. $(-2 - 3i)(4 - 8i)$

6. $(4 - 3i)(4 + 3i)$

7. $\dfrac{4 + 3i}{6 - 2i}$

8. $\dfrac{-1 - i}{-2 + 5i}$

For Problems 9–12, find the discriminant of each equation and determine whether the equation has (1) two nonreal complex solutions, (2) one real solution with a multiplicity of two, or (3) two real solutions. Do not solve the equations.

9. $4x^2 - 20x + 25 = 0$

10. $5x^2 - 7x + 31 = 0$

11. $7x^2 - 2x - 14 = 0$

12. $5x^2 - 2x = 4$

For Problems 13–31, solve each equation.

13. $x^2 - 17x = 0$

14. $(x - 2)^2 = 36$

15. $(2x - 1)^2 = -64$

16. $x^2 - 4x - 21 = 0$

17. $x^2 + 2x - 9 = 0$

18. $x^2 - 6x = -34$

19. $4\sqrt{x} = x - 5$

20. $3n^2 + 10n - 8 = 0$

21. $n^2 - 10n = 200$

22. $3a^2 + a - 5 = 0$

23. $x^2 - x + 3 = 0$

24. $2x^2 - 5x + 6 = 0$

25. $2a^2 + 4a - 5 = 0$

26. $t(t + 5) = 36$

27. $x^2 + 4x + 9 = 0$

28. $(x - 4)(x - 2) = 80$

29. $\dfrac{3}{x} + \dfrac{2}{x + 3} = 1$

30. $2x^4 - 23x^2 + 56 = 0$

31. $\dfrac{3}{n - 2} = \dfrac{n + 5}{4}$

For Problems 32–35, solve each inequality and indicate the solution set on a number line graph.

32. $x^2 + 3x - 10 > 0$

33. $2x^2 + x - 21 \leq 0$

34. $\dfrac{x - 4}{x + 6} \geq 0$

35. $\dfrac{2x - 1}{x + 1} > 4$

For Problems 36–43, set up an equation and solve each problem.

36. Find two numbers whose sum is 6 and whose product is 2.

37. Sherry bought a number of shares of stock for $250. Six months later the value of the stock had increased by $5 per share, and she sold all but 5 shares and regained her original investment plus a profit of $50. How many shares did she sell and at what price per share?

38. Andre traveled 270 miles in 1 hour more time than it took Sandy to travel 260 miles. Sandy drove 7 miles per hour faster than Andre. How fast did each one travel?

39. The area of a square is numerically equal to twice its perimeter. Find the length of a side of the square.

40. Find two consecutive even whole numbers such that the sum of their squares is 164.

41. The perimeter of a rectangle is 38 inches, and its area is 84 square inches. Find the length and width of the rectangle.

42. It takes Billy 2 hours longer to do a certain job than it takes Reena. They worked together for 2 hours; then Reena left, and Billy finished the job in 1 hour. How long would it take each of them to do the job alone?

43. A company has a rectangular parking lot 40 meters wide and 60 meters long. The company plans to increase the area of the lot by 1100 square meters by adding a strip of equal width to one side and one end. Find the width of the strip to be added.

1. Find the product $(3 - 4i)(5 + 6i)$ and express the result in the standard form of a complex number.

2. Find the quotient $\dfrac{2 - 3i}{3 + 4i}$ and express the result in the standard form of a complex number.

For Problems 3–15, solve each equation.

3. $x^2 = 7x$

4. $(x - 3)^2 = 16$

5. $x^2 + 3x - 18 = 0$

6. $x^2 - 2x - 1 = 0$

7. $5x^2 - 2x + 1 = 0$

8. $x^2 + 30x = -224$

9. $(3x - 1)^2 + 36 = 0$

10. $(5x - 6)(4x + 7) = 0$

11. $(2x + 1)(3x - 2) = 55$

12. $n(3n - 2) = 40$

13. $x^4 + 12x^2 - 64 = 0$

14. $\dfrac{3}{x} + \dfrac{2}{x + 1} = 4$

15. $3x^2 - 2x - 3 = 0$

16. Does the equation $4x^2 + 20x + 25 = 0$ have (a) two nonreal complex solutions, (b) two equal real solutions, or (c) two unequal real solutions?

17. Does the equation $4x^2 - 3x = -5$ have (a) two nonreal complex solutions, (b) two equal real solutions, or (c) two unequal real solutions?

For Problems 18–20, solve each inequality and express the solution set using interval notation.

18. $x^2 - 3x - 54 \le 0$

19. $\dfrac{3x - 1}{x + 2} > 0$

20. $\dfrac{x - 2}{x + 6} \ge 3$

For Problems 21–25, set up an equation and solve each problem.

21. A 24-foot ladder leans against a building and makes an angle of $60°$ with the ground. How far up on the building does the top of the ladder reach? Express your answer to the nearest tenth of a foot.

22. A rectangular plot of ground measures 16 meters by 24 meters. Find, to the nearest meter, the distance from one corner of the plot to the diagonally opposite corner.

23. Dana bought a number of shares of stock for a total of $3000. Three months later the stock had increased in value by $5 per share, and she sold all but 50 shares and regained her original investment of $3000. How many shares did she sell?

24. The perimeter of a rectangle is 41 inches and its area is 91 square inches. Find the length of its shortest side.

25. The sum of two numbers is 6 and their product is 4. Find the larger of the two numbers.

Chapters 1–6   Cumulative Review Problem Set

For Problems 1–5, evaluate each algebraic expression for the given values of the variables.

1. $\dfrac{4a^2b^3}{12a^3b}$ for $a = 5$ and $b = -8$

2. $\dfrac{\dfrac{1}{x}+\dfrac{1}{y}}{\dfrac{1}{x}-\dfrac{1}{y}}$ for $x = 4$ and $y = 7$

3. $\dfrac{3}{n}+\dfrac{5}{2n}-\dfrac{4}{3n}$ for $n = 25$

4. $\dfrac{4}{x-1}-\dfrac{2}{x+2}$ for $x = \dfrac{1}{2}$

5. $2\sqrt{2x+y}-5\sqrt{3x-y}$ for $x = 5$ and $y = 6$

For Problems 6–17, perform the indicated operations and express the answers in simplified form.

6. $(3a^2b)(-2ab)(4ab^3)$

7. $(x + 3)(2x^2 - x - 4)$

8. $\dfrac{6xy^2}{14y}\cdot\dfrac{7x^2y}{8x}$

9. $\dfrac{a^2 + 6a - 40}{a^2 - 4a}\div\dfrac{2a^2 + 19a - 10}{a^3 + a^2}$

10. $\dfrac{3x + 4}{6}-\dfrac{5x - 1}{9}$

11. $\dfrac{4}{x^2 + 3x}+\dfrac{5}{x}$

12. $\dfrac{3n^2 + n}{n^2 + 10n + 16}\cdot\dfrac{2n^2 - 8}{3n^3 - 5n^2 - 2n}$

13. $\dfrac{3}{5x^2 + 3x - 2}-\dfrac{2}{5x^2 - 22x + 8}$

14. $\dfrac{y^3 - 7y^2 + 16y - 12}{y - 2}$

15. $(4x^3 - 17x^2 + 7x + 10)\div(4x - 5)$

16. $(3\sqrt{2} + 2\sqrt{5})(5\sqrt{2} - \sqrt{5})$

17. $(\sqrt{x} - 3\sqrt{y})(2\sqrt{x} + 4\sqrt{y})$

For Problems 18–25, evaluate each of the numerical expressions.

18. $-\sqrt{\dfrac{9}{64}}$

19. $\sqrt[3]{-\dfrac{8}{27}}$

20. $\sqrt[3]{0.008}$

21. $32^{-\frac{1}{5}}$

22. $3^0 + 3^{-1} + 3^{-2}$

23. $-9^{\frac{3}{2}}$

24. $\left(\dfrac{3}{4}\right)^{-2}$

25. $\dfrac{1}{\left(\dfrac{2}{3}\right)^{-3}}$

For Problems 26–31, factor each of the algebraic expressions completely.

26. $3x^4 + 81x$

27. $6x^2 + 19x - 20$

28. $12 + 13x - 14x^2$

29. $9x^4 + 68x^2 - 32$

30. $2ax - ay - 2bx + by$

31. $27x^3 - 8y^3$

For Problems 32–55, solve each of the equations.

32. $3(x - 2) - 2(3x + 5) = 4(x - 1)$

33. $0.06n + 0.08(n + 50) = 25$

34. $4\sqrt{x} + 5 = x$

35. $\sqrt[3]{n^2 - 1} = -1$

36. $6x^2 - 24 = 0$

37. $a^2 + 14a + 49 = 0$

38. $3n^2 + 14n - 24 = 0$

39. $\dfrac{2}{5x - 2}=\dfrac{4}{6x + 1}$

40. $\sqrt{2x - 1} - \sqrt{x + 2} = 0$

41. $5x - 4 = \sqrt{5x - 4}$

42. $|3x - 1| = 11$

43. $(3x - 2)(4x - 1) = 0$

331

44. $(2x + 1)(x - 2) = 7$

45. $\dfrac{5}{6x} - \dfrac{2}{3} = \dfrac{7}{10x}$

46. $\dfrac{3}{y + 4} + \dfrac{2y - 1}{y^2 - 16} = \dfrac{-2}{y - 4}$

47. $6x^4 - 23x^2 - 4 = 0$

48. $3n^3 + 3n = 0$

49. $n^2 - 13n - 114 = 0$

50. $12x^2 + x - 6 = 0$

51. $x^2 - 2x + 26 = 0$

52. $(x + 2)(x - 6) = -15$

53. $(3x - 1)(x + 4) = 0$

54. $x^2 + 4x + 20 = 0$

55. $2x^2 - x - 4 = 0$

For Problems 56 – 65, solve each inequality and express the solution set using interval notation.

56. $6 - 2x \geq 10$

57. $4(2x - 1) < 3(x + 5)$

58. $\dfrac{n + 1}{4} + \dfrac{n - 2}{12} > \dfrac{1}{6}$

59. $|2x - 1| < 5$

60. $|3x + 2| > 11$

61. $\dfrac{1}{2}(3x - 1) - \dfrac{2}{3}(x + 4) \leq \dfrac{3}{4}(x - 1)$

62. $x^2 - 2x - 8 \leq 0$

63. $3x^2 + 14x - 5 > 0$

64. $\dfrac{x + 2}{x - 7} \geq 0$

65. $\dfrac{2x - 1}{x + 3} < 1$

For Problems 66–74, solve each problem by setting up and solving an appropriate equation.

66. How many liters of a 60%-acid solution must be added to 14 liters of a 10%-acid solution to produce a 25%-acid solution?

67. A sum of $2250 is to be divided between two people in the ratio of 2 to 3. How much does each person receive?

68. The length of a picture without its border is 7 inches less than twice its width. If the border is 1 inch wide and its area is 62 square inches, what are the dimensions of the picture alone?

69. Working together, Lolita and Doug can paint a shed in 3 hours and 20 minutes. If Doug can paint the shed by himself in 10 hours, how long would it take Lolita to paint the shed by herself?

70. Angie bought some golf balls for $14. If each ball had cost $0.25 less, she could have purchased one more ball for the same amount of money. How many golf balls did Angie buy?

71. A jogger who can run an 8-minute mile starts half a mile ahead of a jogger who can run a 6-minute mile. How long will it take the faster jogger to catch the slower jogger?

72. Suppose that $100 is invested at a certain rate of interest compounded annually for 2 years. If the accumulated value at the end of 2 years is $114.49, find the rate of interest.

73. A room contains 120 chairs arranged in rows. The number of chairs per row is one less than twice the number of rows. Find the number of chairs per row.

74. Bjorn bought a number of shares of stock for $2800. A month later the value of the stock had increased $6 per share, and he sold all but 60 shares and regained his original investment of $2800. How many shares did he sell?

Linear Equations and Inequalities in Two Variables

7.1 Rectangular Coordinate System and Linear Equations

7.2 Graphing Nonlinear Equations

7.3 Linear Inequalities in Two Variables

7.4 Distance and Slope

7.5 Determining the Equation of a Line

René Descartes, a philosopher and mathematician, developed a system for locating a point on a plane. This system is our current rectangular coordinate grid used for graphing; it is named the Cartesian coordinate system.

© Leonard de Selva/CORBIS

René Descartes, a French mathematician of the 17th century, was able to transform geometric problems into an algebraic setting so that he could use the tools of algebra to solve the problems. This connecting of algebraic and geometric ideas is the foundation of a branch of mathematics called **analytic geometry**, today more commonly called **coordinate geometry**. Basically, there are two kinds of problems in coordinate geometry: Given an algebraic equation, find its geometric graph; and given a set of conditions pertaining to a geometric graph, find its algebraic equation. We discuss problems of both types in this chapter.

7.1 **Rectangular Coordinate System and Linear Equations**

Consider two number lines, one vertical and one horizontal, perpendicular to each other at the point we associate with zero on both lines (Figure 7.1). We refer to these number lines as the **horizontal and vertical axes** or, together, as the **coordinate axes**. They partition the plane into four regions called **quadrants**. The quadrants are numbered counterclockwise from I through IV as indicated in Figure 7.1. The point of intersection of the two axes is called the **origin**.

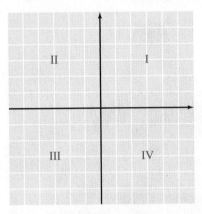

Figure 7.1

It is now possible to set up a one-to-one correspondence between **ordered pairs** of real numbers and the points in a plane. To each ordered pair of real numbers there corresponds a unique point in the plane, and to each point in the plane there corresponds a unique ordered pair of real numbers. A part of this correspondence is illustrated in Figure 7.2. The ordered pair (3, 2) means that the point A is located

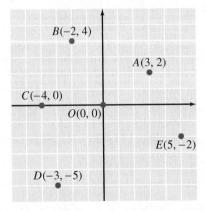

Figure 7.2

three units to the right of, and two units up from, the origin. (The ordered pair $(0, 0)$ is associated with the origin O.) The ordered pair $(-3, -5)$ means that the point D is located three units to the left and five units down from the origin.

Remark: The notation $(-2, 4)$ was used earlier in this text to indicate an interval of the real number line. Now we are using the same notation to indicate an ordered pair of real numbers. This double meaning should not be confusing because the context of the material will always indicate which meaning of the notation is being used. Throughout this chapter, we will be using the ordered-pair interpretation.

In general we refer to the real numbers a and b in an ordered pair (a, b) associated with a point as the **coordinates of the point**. The first number, a, called the **abscissa**, is the directed distance of the point from the vertical axis measured parallel to the horizontal axis. The second number, b, called the **ordinate**, is the directed distance of the point from the horizontal axis measured parallel to the vertical axis (Figure 7.3a). Thus in the first quadrant all points have a positive abscissa and a positive ordinate. In the second quadrant all points have a negative abscissa and a positive ordinate. We have indicated the sign situations for all four quadrants in Figure 7.3(b). This system of associating points in a plane with pairs of real numbers is called the **rectangular coordinate system** or the **Cartesian coordinate system**.

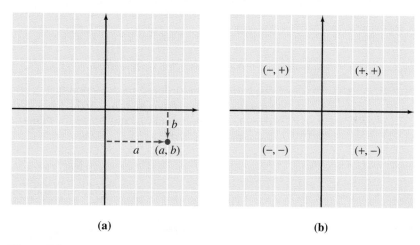

(a)   (b)

Figure 7.3

Historically, the rectangular coordinate system provided the basis for the development of the branch of mathematics called **analytic geometry**, or what we presently refer to as **coordinate geometry**. In this discipline, René Descartes, a French 17th-century mathematician, was able to transform geometric problems into an algebraic setting and then use the tools of algebra to solve the problems. Basically, there are two kinds of problems to solve in coordinate geometry:

1. Given an algebraic equation, find its geometric graph.

2. Given a set of conditions pertaining to a geometric figure, find its algebraic equation.

In this chapter we will discuss problems of both types. Let's begin by considering the solutions for the equation $y = x + 2$. A **solution** of an equation in two variables is an ordered pair of real numbers that satisfies the equation. When using the variables x and y, we agree that the first number of an ordered pair is a value of x, and the second number is a value of y. We see that $(1, 3)$ is a solution for $y = x + 2$ because if x is replaced by 1 and y by 3, the true numerical statement $3 = 1 + 2$ is obtained. Likewise, $(-2, 0)$ is a solution because $0 = -2 + 2$ is a true statement. We can find infinitely many pairs of real numbers that satisfy $y = x + 2$ by arbitrarily choosing values for x, and for each value of x we choose, we can determine a corresponding value for y. Let's use a table to record some of the solutions for $y = x + 2$.

Choose x	Determine y from $y = x + 2$	Solutions for $y = x + 2$
0	2	$(0, 2)$
1	3	$(1, 3)$
3	5	$(3, 5)$
5	7	$(5, 7)$
-2	0	$(-2, 0)$
-4	-2	$(-4, -2)$
-6	-4	$(-6, -4)$

We can plot the ordered pairs as points in a coordinate plane and use the horizontal axis as the x axis and the vertical axis as the y axis, as in Figure 7.4(a). The straight line that contains the points in Figure 7.4(b) is called the **graph of the equation** $y = x + 2$.

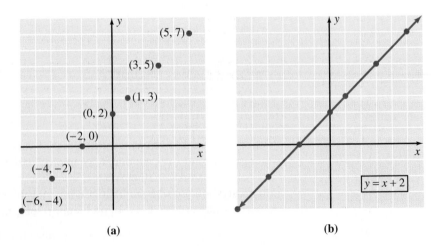

(a)   (b)

Figure 7.4

Remark: It is important to recognize that all points on the x axis have ordered pairs of the form $(a, 0)$ associated with them. That is, the second number in the ordered pair is 0. Likewise, all points on the y axis have ordered pairs of the form $(0, b)$ associated with them.

EXAMPLE 1   Graph $2x + 3y = 6$.

Solution

First, let's find the points of this graph that fall on the coordinate axes. Let $x = 0$; then

$$2(0) + 3y = 6$$

$$3y = 6$$

$$y = 2$$

Thus $(0, 2)$ is a solution and locates a point of the graph on the y axis. Let $y = 0$; then

$$2x + 3(0) = 6$$

$$2x = 6$$

$$x = 3$$

Thus $(3, 0)$ is a solution and locates a point of the graph on the x axis.

Second, let's change the form of the equation to make it easier to find some additional solutions. We can either solve for x in terms of y, or solve for y in terms of x. Let's solve for y in terms of x.

$$2x + 3y = 6$$

$$3y = 6 - 2x$$

$$y = \frac{6 - 2x}{3}$$

Third, a table of values can be formed that includes the two points we found previously.

x	y
0	2
3	0
6	-2
-3	4
-6	6

Plotting these points, we see that they lie in a straight line, and we obtain Figure 7.5.

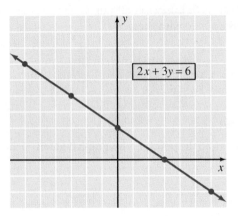

$$2x + 3y = 6$$

Figure 7.5   ∎

Remark: Look again at the table of values in Example 1. Note that values of x were chosen such that integers were obtained for y. That is not necessary, but it does make things easier from a computational standpoint.

The points $(3, 0)$ and $(0, 2)$ in Figure 7.5 are special points. They are the points of the graph that are on the coordinate axes. That is, they yield the x intercept and the y intercept of the graph. Let's define in general the *intercepts* of a graph.

> The x coordinates of the points that a graph has in common with the x axis are called the **x intercepts** of the graph. (To compute the x intercepts, let $y = 0$ and solve for x.)
>
> The y coordinates of the points that a graph has in common with the y axis are called the **y intercepts** of the graph. (To compute the y intercepts, let $x = 0$ and solve for y.)

It is advantageous to be able to recognize the kind of graph that a certain type of equation produces. For example, if we recognize that the graph of $3x + 2y = 12$ is a straight line, then it becomes a simple matter to find two points and sketch the line. Let's pursue the graphing of straight lines in a little more detail.

In general, any equation of the form $Ax + By = C$, where A, B, and C are constants (A and B not both zero) and x and y are variables, is a **linear equation**, and its graph is a straight line. Two points of clarification about this description of a linear equation should be made. First, the choice of x and y for variables is arbitrary. Any two letters could be used to represent the variables. For example, an equation such as $3r + 2s = 9$ can be considered a linear equation in two variables. So that we are not constantly changing the labeling of the coordinate axes when graphing equations, however, it is much easier to use the same two variables in all equations. Thus we will go along with convention and use x and y as variables. Second, the phrase "any equation of the form $Ax + By = C$" technically means "any equation of the form $Ax + By = C$ or equivalent to that form." For example, the equation $y = 2x - 1$ is equivalent to $-2x + y = -1$ and thus is linear and produces a straight-line graph.

The knowledge that any equation of the form $Ax + By = C$ produces a straight-line graph, along with the fact that two points determine a straight line, makes graphing linear equations a simple process. We merely find two solutions (such as the intercepts), plot the corresponding points, and connect the points with a straight line. It is usually wise to find a third point as a check point. Let's consider an example.

E X A M P L E   2

Graph $3x - 2y = 12$.

Solution

First, let's find the intercepts. Let $x = 0$; then

$$3(0) - 2y = 12$$
$$-2y = 12$$
$$y = -6$$

Thus $(0, -6)$ is a solution. Let $y = 0$; then

$$3x - 2(0) = 12$$
$$3x = 12$$
$$x = 4$$

Thus $(4, 0)$ is a solution. Now let's find a third point to serve as a check point. Let $x = 2$; then

$$3(2) - 2y = 12$$
$$6 - 2y = 12$$
$$-2y = 6$$
$$y = -3$$

Thus $(2, -3)$ is a solution. Plot the points associated with these three solutions and connect them with a straight line to produce the graph of $3x - 2y = 12$ in Figure 7.6.

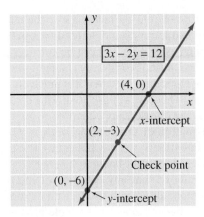

Figure 7.6 ■

Let's review our approach to Example 2. Note that we did not solve the equation for y in terms of x or for x in terms of y. Because we know the graph is a straight line, there is no need for any extensive table of values; thus there is no need to change the form of the original equation. Furthermore, the solution $(2, -3)$ served as a check point. If it had not been on the line determined by the two intercepts, then we would have known that an error had been made.

E X A M P L E   3   Graph $2x + 3y = 7$.

Solution

Without showing all of our work, the following table indicates the intercepts and a check point.

x	y	
0	$\dfrac{7}{3}$	
$\dfrac{7}{2}$	0	Intercepts
2	1	Check point

The points from the table are plotted, and the graph of $2x + 3y = 7$ is shown in Figure 7.7.

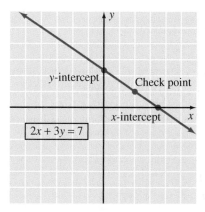

Figure 7.7 ∎

It is helpful to recognize some *special* straight lines. For example, the graph of any equation of the form $Ax + By = C$, where $C = 0$ (the constant term is zero), is a straight line that contains the origin. Let's consider an example.

EXAMPLE 4

Graph $y = 2x$.

Solution

Obviously $(0, 0)$ is a solution. (Also, notice that $y = 2x$ is equivalent to $-2x + y = 0$; thus it fits the condition $Ax + By = C$, where $C = 0$.) Because both the x intercept and the y intercept are determined by the point $(0, 0)$, another point is necessary to determine the line. Then a third point should be found as a check point. The graph of $y = 2x$ is shown in Figure 7.8.

x	y	
0	0	Intercepts
2	4	Additional point
−1	−2	Check point

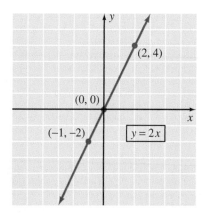

Figure 7.8 ∎

EXAMPLE 5

Graph $x = 2$.

Solution

Because we are considering linear equations in *two variables*, the equation $x = 2$ is equivalent to $x + 0(y) = 2$. Now we can see that any value of y can be used, but the x value must always be 2. Therefore, some of the solutions are $(2, 0)$, $(2, 1)$, $(2, 2)$, $(2, -1)$, and $(2, -2)$. The graph of all solutions of $x = 2$ is the vertical line in Figure 7.9.

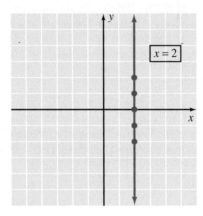

Figure 7.9

EXAMPLE 6

Graph $y = -3$.

Solution

The equation $y = -3$ is equivalent to $0(x) + y = -3$. Thus any value of x can be used, but the value of y must be -3. Some solutions are $(0, -3)$, $(1, -3)$, $(2, -3)$, $(-1, -3)$, and $(-2, -3)$. The graph of $y = -3$ is the horizontal line in Figure 7.10.

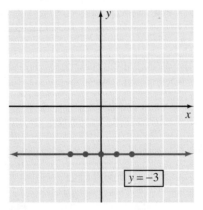

Figure 7.10

In general, the graph of any equation of the form $Ax + By = C$, where $A = 0$ or $B = 0$ (not both), is a line parallel to one of the axes. More specifically, any equation of the form $x = a$, where a is a constant, is a line parallel to the y axis that has an x intercept of a. Any equation of the form $y = b$, where b is a constant, is a line parallel to the x axis that has a y intercept of b.

■ Linear Relationships

There are numerous applications of linear relationships. For example, suppose that a retailer has a number of items that she wants to sell at a profit of 30% of the cost of each item. If we let s represent the selling price and c the cost of each item, then the equation

$$s = c + 0.3c = 1.3c$$

can be used to determine the selling price of each item based on the cost of the item. In other words, if the cost of an item is $4.50, then it should be sold for $s = (1.3)(4.5) = \$5.85$.

The equation $s = 1.3c$ can be used to determine the following table of values. Reading from the table, we see that if the cost of an item is $15, then it should be sold for $19.50 in order to yield a profit of 30% of the cost. Furthermore, because this is a linear relationship, we can obtain exact values between values given in the table.

c	1	5	10	15	20
s	1.3	6.5	13	19.5	26

For example, a c value of 12.5 is halfway between c values of 10 and 15, so the corresponding s value is halfway between the s values of 13 and 19.5. Therefore, a c value of 12.5 produces an s value of

$$s = 13 + \frac{1}{2}(19.5 - 13) = 16.25$$

Thus, if the cost of an item is $12.50, it should be sold for $16.25.

Now let's graph this linear relationship. We can label the horizontal axis c, label the vertical axis s, and use the origin along with one ordered pair from the table to produce the straight-line graph in Figure 7.11. (Because of the type of application, we use only nonnegative values for c and s.)

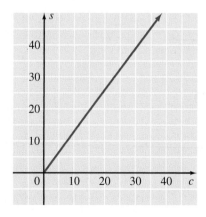

Figure 7.11

From the graph we can approximate s values on the basis of given c values. For example, if $c = 30$, then by reading up from 30 on the c axis to the line and then across to the s axis, we see that s is a little less than 40. (An exact s value of 39 is obtained by using the equation $s = 1.3c$.)

Many formulas that are used in various applications are linear equations in two variables. For example, the formula $C = \dfrac{5}{9}(F - 32)$, which is used to convert temperatures from the Fahrenheit scale to the Celsius scale, is a linear relationship. Using this equation, we can determine that 14°F is equivalent to $C = \dfrac{5}{9}(14 - 32) = \dfrac{5}{9}(-18) = -10°C$. Let's use the equation $C = \dfrac{5}{9}(F - 32)$ to complete the following table.

F	−22	−13	5	32	50	68	86
C	−30	−25	−15	0	10	20	30

Reading from the table, we see, for example, that $-13°F = -25°C$ and $68°F = 20°C$.

To graph the equation $C = \dfrac{5}{9}(F - 32)$ we can label the horizontal axis F, label the vertical axis C, and plot two ordered pairs (F, C) from the table. Figure 7.12 shows the graph of the equation.

From the graph we can approximate C values on the basis of given F values. For example, if $F = 80°$, then by reading up from 80 on the F axis to the line and then across to the C axis, we see that C is approximately 25°. Likewise, we can obtain approximate F values on the basis of given C values. For example, if $C = -25°$, then by reading across from −25 on the C axis to the line and then up to the F axis, we see that F is approximately −15°.

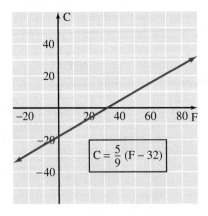

Figure 7.12

■ Graphing Utilities

The term **graphing utility** is used in current literature to refer to either a graphing calculator (see Figure 7.13) or a computer with a graphing software package. (We will frequently use the phrase *use a graphing calculator* to mean "use a graphing calculator or a computer with the appropriate software.")

These devices have a large range of capabilities that enable the user not only to obtain a quick sketch of a graph but also to study various characteristics of it, such as the x intercepts, y intercepts, and turning points of a curve. We will introduce some of these features of graphing utilities as we need them in the text. Because there are so many different types of graphing utilities available, we will use mostly generic terminology and let you consult your user's manual for specific key-punching instructions. We urge you to study the graphing utility examples in this text even if you do not have access to a graphing calculator or a computer. The examples were chosen to reinforce concepts under discussion.

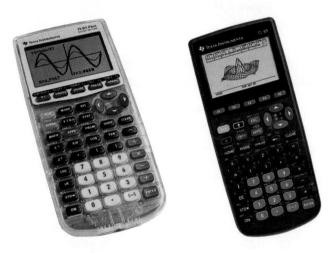

Courtesy Texas Instruments

Figure 7.13

EXAMPLE 7

Use a graphing utility to obtain a graph of the line $2.1x + 5.3y = 7.9$.

Solution

First, let's solve the equation for y in terms of x.

$$2.1x + 5.3y = 7.9$$

$$5.3y = 7.9 - 2.1x$$

$$y = \frac{7.9 - 2.1x}{5.3}$$

Now we can enter the expression $\dfrac{7.9 - 2.1x}{5.3}$ for Y_1 and obtain the graph as shown in Figure 7.14.

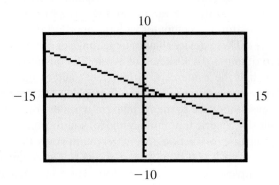

Figure 7.14

Problem Set 7.1

For Problems 1–33, graph each of the linear equations.

1. $x + 2y = 4$

2. $2x + y = 6$

3. $2x - y = 2$

4. $3x - y = 3$

5. $3x + 2y = 6$

6. $2x + 3y = 6$

7. $5x - 4y = 20$

8. $4x - 3y = -12$

9. $x + 4y = -6$

10. $5x + y = -2$

11. $-x - 2y = 3$

12. $-3x - 2y = 12$

13. $y = x + 3$

14. $y = x - 1$

15. $y = -2x - 1$

16. $y = 4x + 3$

17. $y = \dfrac{1}{2}x + \dfrac{2}{3}$

18. $y = \dfrac{2}{3}x - \dfrac{3}{4}$

19. $y = -x$

20. $y = x$

21. $y = 3x$

22. $y = -4x$

23. $x = 2y - 1$

24. $x = -3y + 2$

25. $y = -\dfrac{1}{4}x + \dfrac{1}{6}$

26. $y = -\dfrac{1}{2}x - \dfrac{1}{2}$

27. $2x - 3y = 0$

28. $3x + 4y = 0$

29. $x = 0$

30. $y = 0$

31. $y = 2$

32. $x = -3$

33. $-3y = -x + 3$

34. Suppose that the daily profit from an ice cream stand is given by the equation $p = 2n - 4$, where n represents the number of gallons of ice cream mix used in a day, and p represents the number of dollars of profit. Label the horizontal axis n and the vertical axis p, and graph the equation $p = 2n - 4$ for nonnegative values of n.

35. The cost (c) of playing an online computer game for a time (t) in hours is given by the equation $c = 3t + 5$. Label the horizontal axis t and the vertical axis c, and graph the equation for nonnegative values of t.

36. The area of a sidewalk whose width is fixed at 3 feet can be given by the equation $A = 3l$, where A represents the area in square feet, and l represents the length in feet. Label the horizontal axis l and the vertical axis A, and graph the equation $A = 3l$ for nonnegative values of l.

37. An online grocery store charges for delivery based on the equation $C = 0.30p$, where C represents the cost in dollars, and p represents the weight of the groceries in pounds. Label the horizontal axis p and the vertical axis C, and graph the equation $C = 0.30p$ for non-negative values of p.

38. (a) The equation $F = \dfrac{9}{5}C + 32$ can be used to convert from degrees Celsius to degrees Fahrenheit. Complete the following table.

C	0	5	10	15	20	−5	−10	−15	−20	−25
F										

(b) Graph the equation $F = \dfrac{9}{5}C + 32$.

(c) Use your graph from part (b) to approximate values for F when $C = 25°, 30°, -30°,$ and $-40°$.

(d) Check the accuracy of your readings from the graph in part (c) by using the equation $F = \dfrac{9}{5}C + 32$.

39. (a) Digital Solutions charges for help-desk services according to the equation $c = 0.25m + 10$, where c represents the cost in dollars, and m represents the minutes of service. Complete the following table.

m	5	10	15	20	30	60
c						

(b) Label the horizontal axis m and the vertical axis c, and graph the equation $c = 0.25m + 10$ for non-negative values of m.

(c) Use the graph from part (b) to approximate values for c when $m = 25, 40,$ and 45.

(d) Check the accuracy of your readings from the graph in part (c) by using the equation $c = 0.25m + 10$.

■■■ THOUGHTS INTO WORDS

40. How do we know that the graph of $y = -3x$ is a straight line that contains the origin?

41. How do we know that the graphs of $2x - 3y = 6$ and $-2x + 3y = -6$ are the same line?

42. What is the graph of the conjunction $x = 2$ and $y = 4$? What is the graph of the disjunction $x = 2$ or $y = 4$? Explain your answers.

43. Your friend claims that the graph of the equation $x = 2$ is the point $(2, 0)$. How do you react to this claim?

■■■ FURTHER INVESTIGATIONS

From our work with absolute value, we know that $|x + y| = 1$ is equivalent to $x + y = 1$ or $x + y = -1$. Therefore, the graph of $|x + y| = 1$ consists of the two lines $x + y = 1$ and $x + y = -1$. Graph each of the following.

44. $|x + y| = 1$

45. $|x - y| = 4$

46. $|2x - y| = 4$

47. $|3x + 2y| = 6$

▥ GRAPHING CALCULATOR ACTIVITIES

This is the first of many appearances of a group of problems called graphing calculator activities. These problems are specifically designed for those of you who have access to a graphing calculator or a computer with an appropriate software package. Within the framework of these problems, you will be given the opportunity to reinforce concepts we discussed in the text; lay groundwork for concepts we will introduce later in the text; predict shapes and locations of graphs on the basis of your previous graphing experiences; solve problems that are unreasonable or perhaps impossible to solve without a graphing utility; and in general become familiar with the capabilities and limitations of your graphing utility.

48. (a) Graph $y = 3x + 4$, $y = 2x + 4$, $y = -4x + 4$, and $y = -2x + 4$ on the same set of axes.

(b) Graph $y = \frac{1}{2}x - 3$, $y = 5x - 3$, $y = 0.1x - 3$, and $y = -7x - 3$ on the same set of axes.

(c) What characteristic do all lines of the form $y = ax + 2$ (where a is any real number) share?

49. **(a)** Graph $y = 2x - 3$, $y = 2x + 3$, $y = 2x - 6$, and $y = 2x + 5$ on the same set of axes.

(b) Graph $y = -3x + 1$, $y = -3x + 4$, $y = -3x - 2$, and $y = -3x - 5$ on the same set of axes.

(c) Graph $y = \frac{1}{2}x + 3$, $y = \frac{1}{2}x - 4$, $y = \frac{1}{2}x + 5$, and $y = \frac{1}{2}x - 2$ on the same set of axes.

(d) What relationship exists among all lines of the form $y = 3x + b$, where b is any real number?

50. **(a)** Graph $2x + 3y = 4$, $2x + 3y = -6$, $4x - 6y = 7$, and $8x + 12y = -1$ on the same set of axes.

(b) Graph $5x - 2y = 4$, $5x - 2y = -3$, $10x - 4y = 3$, and $15x - 6y = 30$ on the same set of axes.

(c) Graph $x + 4y = 8$, $2x + 8y = 3$, $x - 4y = 6$, and $3x + 12y = 10$ on the same set of axes.

(d) Graph $3x - 4y = 6$, $3x + 4y = 10$, $6x - 8y = 20$, and $6x - 8y = 24$ on the same set of axes.

(e) For each of the following pairs of lines, (a) predict whether they are parallel lines, and (b) graph each pair of lines to check your prediction.

  (1) $5x - 2y = 10$ and $5x - 2y = -4$
  (2) $x + y = 6$ and $x - y = 4$
  (3) $2x + y = 8$ and $4x + 2y = 2$
  (4) $y = 0.2x + 1$ and $y = 0.2x - 4$
  (5) $3x - 2y = 4$ and $3x + 2y = 4$
  (6) $4x - 3y = 8$ and $8x - 6y = 3$
  (7) $2x - y = 10$ and $6x - 3y = 6$
  (8) $x + 2y = 6$ and $3x - 6y = 6$

51. Now let's use a graphing calculator to get a graph of $C = \frac{5}{9}(F - 32)$. By letting $F = x$ and $C = y$, we obtain Figure 7.15.

Pay special attention to the boundaries on x. These values were chosen so that the fraction

$$\frac{\text{(Maximum value of } x) \text{ minus (Minimum value of } x)}{95}$$

would be equal to 1. The viewing window of the graphing calculator used to produce Figure 7.15 is 95 pixels (dots) wide. Therefore, we use 95 as the denominator

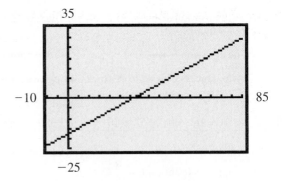

Figure 7.15

of the fraction. We chose the boundaries for y to make sure that the cursor would be visible on the screen when we looked for certain values.

Now let's use the TRACE feature of the graphing calculator to complete the following table. Note that the cursor moves in increments of 1 as we trace along the graph.

F	-5	5	9	11	12	20	30	45	60
C									

(This was accomplished by setting the aforementioned fraction equal to 1.) By moving the cursor to each of the F values, we can complete the table as follows.

F	-5	5	9	11	12	20	30	45	60
C	-21	-15	-13	-12	-11	-7	-1	7	16

The C values are expressed to the nearest degree. Use your calculator and check the values in the table by using the equation $C = \frac{5}{9}(F - 32)$.

52. **(a)** Use your graphing calculator to graph $F = \frac{9}{5}C + 32$. Be sure to set boundaries on the horizontal axis so that when you are using the trace feature, the cursor will move in increments of 1.

(b) Use the TRACE feature and check your answers for part (a) of Problem 38.

7.2   Graphing Nonlinear Equations

Equations such as $y = x^2 - 4$, $x = y^2$, $y = \dfrac{1}{x}$, $x^2y = -2$, and $x = y^3$ are all examples of nonlinear equations. The graphs of these equations are figures other than straight lines that can be determined by plotting a sufficient number of points. Let's plot the points and observe some characteristics of these graphs that we then can use to supplement the point-plotting process.

E X A M P L E   1   Graph $y = x^2 - 4$

Solution

Let's begin by finding the intercepts. If $x = 0$, then

$$y = 0^2 - 4 = -4$$

The point $(0, -4)$ is on the graph. If $y = 0$, then

$$0 = x^2 - 4$$
$$0 = (x + 2)(x - 2)$$
$$x + 2 = 0 \quad \text{or} \quad x - 2 = 0$$
$$x = -2 \quad \text{or} \quad x = 2$$

The points $(-2, 0)$ and $(2, 0)$ are on the graph. The given equation is in a convenient form for setting up a table of values.

Plotting these points and connecting them with a smooth curve produces Figure 7.16.

x	y	
0	−4	
−2	0	Intercepts
2	0	
1	−3	
−1	−3	
3	5	Other points
−3	5	

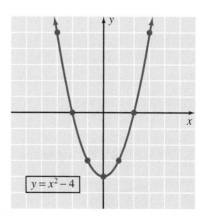

Figure 7.16

The curve in Figure 7.16 is called a parabola; we will study parabolas in more detail in a later chapter. However, at this time we want to emphasize that the parabola in Figure 7.16 is said to be *symmetric with respect to the y axis*. In other words, the y axis is a line of symmetry. Each half of the curve is a mirror image of the other half through the y axis. Note, in the table of values, that for each ordered pair (x, y), the ordered pair $(-x, y)$ is also a solution. A general test for y axis symmetry can be stated as follows:

y Axis Symmetry

The graph of an equation is symmetric with respect to the y axis if replacing x with $-x$ results in an equivalent equation.

The equation $y = x^2 - 4$ exhibits symmetry with respect to the y axis because replacing x with $-x$ produces $y = (-x)^2 - 4 = x^2 - 4$. Let's test some equations for such symmetry. We will replace x with $-x$ and check for an equivalent equation.

Equation	Test for symmetry with respect to the y axis	Equivalent equation	Symmetric with respect to the y axis
$y = -x^2 + 2$	$y = -(-x)^2 + 2 = -x^2 + 2$	Yes	Yes
$y = 2x^2 + 5$	$y = 2(-x)^2 + 5 = 2x^2 + 5$	Yes	Yes
$y = x^4 + x^2$	$y = (-x)^4 + (-x)^2$ $= x^4 + x^2$	Yes	Yes
$y = x^3 + x^2$	$y = (-x)^3 + (-x)^2$ $= -x^3 + x^2$	No	No
$y = x^2 + 4x + 2$	$y = (-x)^2 + 4(-x) + 2$ $= x^2 - 4x + 2$	No	No

Some equations yield graphs that have x axis symmetry. In the next example we will see the graph of a parabola that is symmetric with respect to the x axis.

EXAMPLE 2

Graph $x = y^2$.

Solution

First, we see that $(0, 0)$ is on the graph and determines both intercepts. Second, the given equation is in a convenient form for setting up a table of values.

Plotting these points and connecting them with a smooth curve produces Figure 7.17.

x	y	
0	0	Intercepts
1	1	
1	−1	Other points
4	2	
4	−2	

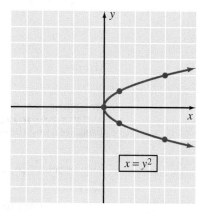

Figure 7.17

The parabola in Figure 7.17 is said to be *symmetric with respect to the x axis*. Each half of the curve is a mirror image of the other half through the x axis. Also note, in the table of values, that for each ordered pair (x, y), the ordered pair $(x, -y)$ is a solution. A general test for x axis symmetry can be stated as follows:

x Axis Symmetry

> The graph of an equation is symmetric with respect to the x axis if replacing y with $-y$ results in an equivalent equation.

The equation $x = y^2$ exhibits x axis symmetry because replacing x with $-y$ produces $y = (-y)^2 = y^2$. Let's test some equations for x axis symmetry. We will replace y with $-y$ and check for an equivalent equation.

Equation	Test for symmetry with respect to the x axis	Equivalent equation	Symmetric with respect to the x axis
$x = y^2 + 5$	$x = (-y)^2 + 5 = y^2 + 5$	Yes	Yes
$x = -3y^2$	$x = -3(-y)^2 = -3y^2$	Yes	Yes
$x = y^3 + 2$	$x = (-y)^3 + 2 = -y^3 + 2$	No	No
$x = y^2 - 5y + 6$	$x = (-y)^2 - 5(-y) + 6$ $= y^2 + 5y + 6$	No	No

In addition to y axis and x axis symmetry, some equations yield graphs that have symmetry with respect to the origin. In the next example we will see a graph that is symmetric with respect to the origin.

EXAMPLE 3

Graph $y = \dfrac{1}{x}$.

Solution

First, let's find the intercepts. Let $x = 0$; then $y = \dfrac{1}{x}$ becomes $y = \dfrac{1}{0}$, and $\dfrac{1}{0}$ is undefined. Thus there is no y intercept. Let $y = 0$; then $y = \dfrac{1}{x}$ becomes $0 = \dfrac{1}{x}$, and there are no values of x that will satisfy this equation. In other words, this graph has no points on either the x axis or the y axis. Second, let's set up a table of values and keep in mind that neither x nor y can equal zero.

In Figure 7.18(a) we plotted the points associated with the solutions from the table. Because the graph does not intersect either axis, it must consist of two branches. Thus connecting the points in the first quadrant with a smooth curve and then connecting the points in the third quadrant with a smooth curve, we obtain the graph shown in Figure 7.18(b).

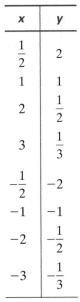

x	y
$\dfrac{1}{2}$	2
1	1
2	$\dfrac{1}{2}$
3	$\dfrac{1}{3}$
$-\dfrac{1}{2}$	-2
-1	-1
-2	$-\dfrac{1}{2}$
-3	$-\dfrac{1}{3}$

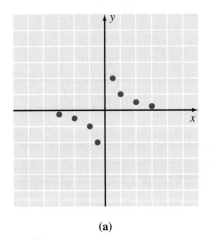

(a)

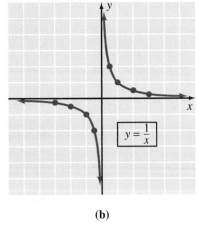

(b)

Figure 7.18

The curve in Figure 7.18 is said to be *symmetric with respect to the origin*. Each half of the curve is a mirror image of the other half through the origin. Note, in the table of values, that for each ordered pair (x, y), the ordered pair $(-x, -y)$ is also a solution. A general test for origin symmetry can be stated as follows:

Origin Symmetry

> The graph of an equation is symmetric with respect to the origin if replacing x with $-x$ and y with $-y$ results in an equivalent equation.

The equation $y = \dfrac{1}{x}$ exhibits symmetry with respect to the origin because replacing y with $-y$ and x with $-x$ produces $-y = \dfrac{1}{-x}$, which is equivalent to $y = \dfrac{1}{x}$. Let's test some equations for symmetry with respect to the origin. We will replace y with $-y$, replace x with $-x$, and then check for an equivalent equation.

Equation	Test for symmetry with respect to the origin	Equivalent equation	Symmetric with respect to the origin
$y = x^3$	$(-y) = (-x)^3$ $-y = -x^3$ $y = x^3$	Yes	Yes
$x^2 + y^2 = 4$	$(-x)^2 + (-y)^2 = 4$ $x^2 + y^2 = 4$	Yes	Yes
$y = x^2 - 3x + 4$	$(-y) = (-x)^2 - 3(-x) + 4$ $-y = x^2 + 3x + 4$ $y = -x^2 - 3x - 4$	No	No

Let's pause for a moment and pull together the graphing techniques that we have introduced thus far. Following is a list of graphing suggestions. The order of the suggestions indicates the order in which we usually attack a new graphing problem.

1. Determine what type of symmetry the equation exhibits.

2. Find the intercepts.

3. Solve the equation for y in terms of x or for x in terms of y if it is not already in such a form.

4. Set up a table of ordered pairs that satisfy the equation. The type of symmetry will affect your choice of values in the table. (We will illustrate this in a moment.)

5. Plot the points associated with the ordered pairs from the table, and connect them with a smooth curve. Then, if appropriate, reflect this part of the curve according to the symmetry shown by the equation.

E X A M P L E   4

Graph $x^2y = -2$.

Solution

Because replacing x with $-x$ produces $(-x)^2y = -2$ or, equivalently, $x^2y = -2$, the equation exhibits y axis symmetry. There are no intercepts because neither x nor y can equal 0. Solving the equation for y produces $y = \dfrac{-2}{x^2}$. The equation exhibits y axis symmetry, so let's use only positive values for x and then reflect the curve across the y axis.

x	y
1	-2
2	$-\dfrac{1}{2}$
3	$-\dfrac{2}{9}$
4	$-\dfrac{1}{8}$
$\dfrac{1}{2}$	-8

Let's plot the points determined by the table, connect them with a smooth curve, and reflect this portion of the curve across the y axis. Figure 7.19 is the result of this process.

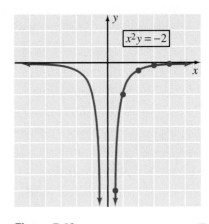

Figure 7.19 ∎

E X A M P L E   5

Graph $x = y^3$.

Solution

Because replacing x with $-x$ and y with $-y$ produces $-x = (-y)^3 = -y^3$, which is equivalent to $x = y^3$, the given equation exhibits origin symmetry. If $x = 0$, then $y = 0$, so the origin is a point of the graph. The given equation is in an easy form for deriving a table of values.

x	y
0	0
8	2
$\dfrac{1}{8}$	$\dfrac{1}{2}$
$\dfrac{27}{64}$	$\dfrac{3}{4}$

Let's plot the points determined by the table, connect them with a smooth curve, and reflect this portion of the curve through the origin to produce Figure 7.20.

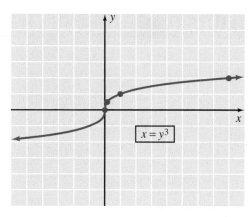

Figure 7.20

EXAMPLE 6

Use a graphing utility to obtain a graph of the equation $x = y^3$.

Solution

First, we may need to solve the equation for y in terms of x. (We say we "may need to" because some graphing utilities are capable of graphing two-variable equations without solving for y in terms of x.)

$$y = \sqrt[3]{x} = x^{1/3}$$

Now we can enter the expression $x^{1/3}$ for Y_1 and obtain the graph shown in Figure 7.21.

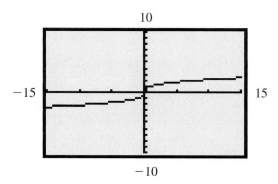

Figure 7.21

As indicated in Figure 7.21, the **viewing rectangle** of a graphing utility is a portion of the xy plane shown on the display of the utility. In this display, the boundaries were set so that $-15 \le x \le 15$ and $-10 \le y \le 10$. These boundaries were set automatically; however, boundaries can be reassigned as necessary, which is an important feature of graphing utilities.

Problem Set 7.2

For each of the points in Problems 1–5, determine the points that are symmetric with respect to (a) the x axis, (b) the y axis, and (c) the origin.

1. $(-3, 1)$

2. $(-2, -4)$

3. $(7, -2)$

4. $(0, -4)$

5. $(5, 0)$

For Problems 6–25, determine the type(s) of symmetry (symmetry with respect to the x axis, y axis, and/or origin) exhibited by the graph of each of the following equations. Do not sketch the graph.

6. $x^2 + 2y = 4$

7. $-3x + 2y^2 = -4$

8. $x = -y^2 + 5$

9. $y = 4x^2 + 13$

10. $xy = -6$

11. $2x^2y^2 = 5$

12. $2x^2 + 3y^2 = 9$

13. $x^2 - 2x - y^2 = 4$

14. $y = x^2 - 6x - 4$

15. $y = 2x^2 - 7x - 3$

16. $y = x$

17. $y = 2x$

18. $y = x^4 + 4$

19. $y = x^4 - x^2 + 2$

20. $x^2 + y^2 = 13$

21. $x^2 - y^2 = -6$

22. $y = -4x^2 - 2$

23. $x = -y^2 + 9$

24. $x^2 + y^2 - 4x - 12 = 0$

25. $2x^2 + 3y^2 + 8y + 2 = 0$

For Problems 26–59, graph each of the equations.

26. $y = x + 1$

27. $y = x - 4$

28. $y = 3x - 6$

29. $y = 2x + 4$

30. $y = -2x + 1$

31. $y = -3x - 1$

32. $y = \dfrac{2}{3}x - 1$

33. $y = -\dfrac{1}{3}x + 2$

34. $y = \dfrac{1}{3}x$

35. $y = \dfrac{1}{2}x$

36. $2x + y = 6$

37. $2x - y = 4$

38. $x + 3y = -3$

39. $x - 2y = 2$

40. $y = x^2 - 1$

41. $y = x^2 + 2$

42. $y = -x^3$

43. $y = x^3$

44. $y = \dfrac{2}{x^2}$

45. $y = \dfrac{-1}{x^2}$

46. $y = 2x^2$

47. $y = -3x^2$

48. $xy = -3$

49. $xy = 2$

50. $x^2y = 4$

51. $xy^2 = -4$

52. $y^3 = x^2$

53. $y^2 = x^3$

54. $y = \dfrac{-2}{x^2 + 1}$

55. $y = \dfrac{4}{x^2 + 1}$

56. $x = -y^3$

57. $y = x^4$

58. $y = -x^4$

59. $x = -y^3 + 2$

■ ■ ■ **THOUGHTS INTO WORDS**

60. How would you convince someone that there are infinitely many ordered pairs of real numbers that satisfy $x + y = 7$?

61. What is the graph of $x = 0$? What is the graph of $y = 0$? Explain your answers.

62. Is a graph symmetric with respect to the origin if it is symmetric with respect to both axes? Defend your answer.

63. Is a graph symmetric with respect to both axes if it is symmetric with respect to the origin? Defend your answer.

 GRAPHING CALCULATOR ACTIVITIES

This set of activities is designed to help you get started with your graphing utility by setting different boundaries for the viewing rectangle; you will notice the effect on the graphs produced. These boundaries are usually set by using a menu displayed by a key marked either WINDOW or RANGE. You may need to consult the user's manual for specific key-punching instructions.

64. Graph the equation $y = \dfrac{1}{x}$ (Example 4) using the following boundaries.
  (a) $-15 \le x \le 15$ and $-10 \le y \le 10$
  (b) $-10 \le x \le 10$ and $-10 \le y \le 10$
  (c) $-5 \le x \le 5$ and $-5 \le y \le 5$

65. Graph the equation $y = \dfrac{-2}{x^2}$ (Example 5), using the following boundaries.
  (a) $-15 \le x \le 15$ and $-10 \le y \le 10$
  (b) $-5 \le x \le 5$ and $-10 \le y \le 10$
  (c) $-5 \le x \le 5$ and $-10 \le y \le 1$

66. Graph the two equations $y = \pm\sqrt{x}$ (Example 3) on the same set of axes, using the following boundaries.

(Let $Y_1 = \sqrt{x}$ and $Y_2 = -\sqrt{x}$)
  (a) $-15 \le x \le 15$ and $-10 \le y \le 10$
  (b) $-1 \le x \le 15$ and $-10 \le y \le 10$
  (c) $-1 \le x \le 15$ and $-5 \le y \le 5$

67. Graph $y = \dfrac{1}{x}$, $y = \dfrac{5}{x}$, $y = \dfrac{10}{x}$, and $y = \dfrac{20}{x}$ on the same set of axes. (Choose your own boundaries.) What effect does increasing the constant seem to have on the graph?

68. Graph $y = \dfrac{10}{x}$ and $y = \dfrac{-10}{x}$ on the same set of axes. What relationship exists between the two graphs?

69. Graph $y = \dfrac{10}{x^2}$ and $y = \dfrac{-10}{x^2}$ on the same set of axes. What relationship exists between the two graphs?

7.3 Linear Inequalities in Two Variables

Linear inequalities in two variables are of the form $Ax + By > C$ or $Ax + By < C$, where A, B, and C are real numbers. (Combined linear equality and inequality statements are of the form $Ax + By \ge C$ or $Ax + By \le C$.)

Graphing linear inequalities is almost as easy as graphing linear equations. The following discussion leads into a simple, step-by-step process. Let's consider the following equation and related inequalities.

$$x + y = 2 \qquad x + y > 2 \qquad x + y < 2$$

The graph of $x + y = 2$ is shown in Figure 7.22. The line divides the plane into two half planes, one above the line and one below the line. In Figure 7.23(a) we

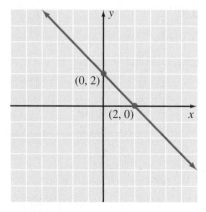

Figure 7.22

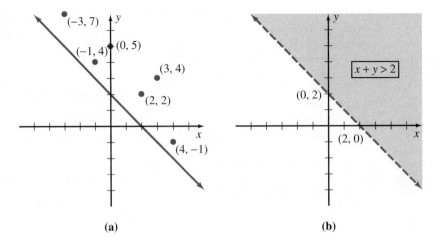

(a) **(b)**

Figure 7.23

indicated several points in the half plane above the line. Note that for each point, the ordered pair of real numbers satisfies the inequality $x + y > 2$. This is true for *all points* in the half plane above the line. Therefore, the graph of $x + y > 2$ is the half plane above the line, as indicated by the shaded portion in Figure 7.23(b). We use a dashed line to indicate that points on the line do *not* satisfy $x + y > 2$. We would use a solid line if we were graphing $x + y \geq 2$.

In Figure 7.24(a) several points were indicated in the half plane below the line, $x + y = 2$. Note that for each point, the ordered pair of real numbers satisfies the inequality $x + y < 2$. This is true for *all points* in the half plane below the line. Thus the graph of $x + y < 2$ is the half plane below the line, as indicated in Figure 7.24(b).

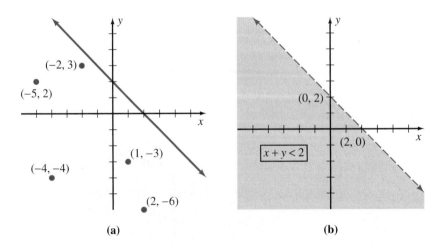

(a) **(b)**

Figure 7.24

To graph a linear inequality, we suggest the following steps.

1. First, graph the corresponding equality. Use a solid line if equality is included in the original statement. Use a dashed line if equality is not included.

2. Choose a "test point" not on the line and substitute its coordinates into the inequality. (The origin is a convenient point to use if it is not on the line.)

3. The graph of the original inequality is
   (a) the half plane that contains the test point if the inequality is satisfied by that point, or
   (b) the half plane that does not contain the test point if the inequality is not satisfied by the point.

Let's apply these steps to some examples.

EXAMPLE   1

Graph $x - 2y > 4$.

Solution

Step 1   Graph $x - 2y = 4$ as a dashed line because equality is not included in $x - 2y > 4$ (Figure 7.25).

Step 2   Choose the origin as a test point and substitute its coordinates into the inequality.

$$x - 2y > 4 \qquad \text{becomes } 0 - 2(0) > 4, \text{ which is false.}$$

Step 3   Because the test point did not satisfy the given inequality, the graph is the half plane that does not contain the test point. Thus the graph of $x - 2y > 4$ is the half plane below the line, as indicated in Figure 7.25.

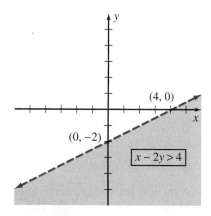

Figure 7.25

EXAMPLE 2

Graph $3x + 2y \leq 6$.

Solution

Step 1 Graph $3x + 2y = 6$ as a solid line because equality is included in $3x + 2y \leq 6$ (Figure 7.26).

Step 2 Choose the origin as a test point and substitute its coordinates into the given statement.

$$3x + 2y \leq 6 \qquad \text{becomes } 3(0) + 2(0) \leq 6, \text{ which is true.}$$

Step 3 Because the test point satisfies the given statement, all points in the same half plane as the test point satisfy the statement. Thus the graph of $3x + 2y \leq 6$ consists of the line and the half plane below the line (Figure 7.26).

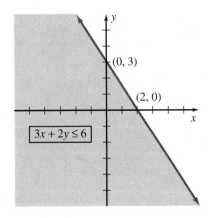

Figure 7.26

■

EXAMPLE 3

Graph $y \leq 3x$.

Solution

Step 1 Graph $y = 3x$ as a solid line because equality is included in the statement $y \leq 3x$ (Figure 7.27).

Step 2 The origin is on the line, so we must choose some other point as a test point. Let's try $(2, 1)$.

$$y \leq 3x \qquad \text{becomes } 1 \leq 3(2), \text{ which is a true statement.}$$

Step 3 Because the test point satisfies the given inequality, the graph is the half plane that contains the test point. Thus the graph of $y \leq 3x$ consists of the line and the half plane below the line, as indicated in Figure 7.27.

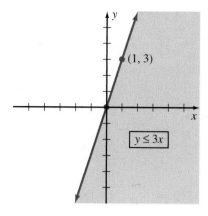

$y \le 3x$

Figure 7.27

Problem Set 7.3

For Problems 1–24, graph each of the inequalities.

1. $x - y > 2$

2. $x + y > 4$

3. $x + 3y < 3$

4. $2x - y > 6$

5. $2x + 5y \ge 10$

6. $3x + 2y \le 4$

7. $y \le -x + 2$

8. $y \ge -2x - 1$

9. $y > -x$

10. $y < x$

11. $2x - y \ge 0$

12. $x + 2y \ge 0$

13. $-x + 4y - 4 \le 0$

14. $-2x + y - 3 \le 0$

15. $y > -\dfrac{3}{2}x - 3$

16. $2x + 5y > -4$

17. $y < -\dfrac{1}{2}x + 2$

18. $y < -\dfrac{1}{3}x + 1$

19. $x \le 3$

20. $y \ge -2$

21. $x > 1$ and $y < 3$

22. $x > -2$ and $y > -1$

23. $x \le -1$ and $y < 1$

24. $x < 2$ and $y \ge -2$

■ ■ ■ THOUGHTS INTO WORDS

25. Why is the point $(-4, 1)$ not a good test point to use when graphing $5x - 2y > -22$?

26. Explain how you would graph the inequality $-3 > x - 3y$.

■ ■ ■ FURTHER INVESTIGATIONS

27. Graph $|x| < 2$. [*Hint*: Remember that $|x| < 2$ is equivalent to $-2 < x < 2$.]

28. Graph $|y| > 1$.

29. Graph $|x + y| < 1$.

30. Graph $|x - y| > 2$.

GRAPHING CALCULATOR ACTIVITIES

31. This is a good time for you to become acquainted with the DRAW features of your graphing calculator. Again, you may need to consult your user's manual for specific key-punching instructions. Return to Examples 1, 2, and 3 of this section, and use your graphing calculator to graph the inequalities.

32. Use a graphing calculator to check your graphs for Problems 1–24.

33. Use the DRAW feature of your graphing calculator to draw each of the following.
  (a) A line segment between $(-2, -4)$ and $(-2, 5)$
  (b) A line segment between $(2, 2)$ and $(5, 2)$
  (c) A line segment between $(2, 3)$ and $(5, 7)$
  (d) A triangle with vertices at $(1, -2)$, $(3, 4)$, and $(-3, 6)$

7.4 Distance and Slope

As we work with the rectangular coordinate system, it is sometimes necessary to express the length of certain line segments. In other words, we need to be able to find the distance between two points. Let's first consider two specific examples and then develop the general distance formula.

EXAMPLE 1

Find the distance between the points $A(2, 2)$ and $B(5, 2)$ and also between the points $C(-2, 5)$ and $D(-2, -4)$.

Solution

Let's plot the points and draw $\overline{AB}$ as in Figure 7.28. Because $\overline{AB}$ is parallel to the x axis, its length can be expressed as $|5 - 2|$ or $|2 - 5|$. (The absolute-value symbol is used to ensure a nonnegative value.) Thus the length of $\overline{AB}$ is 3 units. Likewise, the length of $\overline{CD}$ is $|5 - (-4)| = |-4 - 5| = 9$ units.

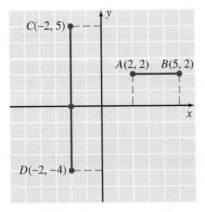

Figure 7.28

EXAMPLE 2

Find the distance between the points $A(2, 3)$ and $B(5, 7)$.

Solution

Let's plot the points and form a right triangle as indicated in Figure 7.29. Note that the coordinates of point C are $(5, 3)$. Because $\overline{AC}$ is parallel to the horizontal axis, its length is easily determined to be 3 units. Likewise, $\overline{CB}$ is parallel to the vertical axis and its length is 4 units. Let d represent the length of $\overline{AB}$, and apply the Pythagorean theorem to obtain

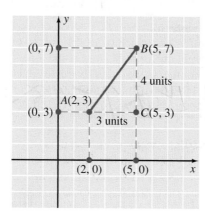

$$d^2 = 3^2 + 4^2$$
$$d^2 = 9 + 16$$
$$d^2 = 25$$
$$d = \pm\sqrt{25} = \pm5$$

"Distance between" is a nonnegative value, so the length of $\overline{AB}$ is 5 units.

Figure 7.29   ■

We can use the approach we used in Example 2 to develop a general distance formula for finding the distance between any two points in a coordinate plane. The development proceeds as follows:

1. Let $P_1(x_1, y_1)$ and $P_2(x_2, y_2)$ represent any two points in a coordinate plane.

2. Form a right triangle as indicated in Figure 7.30. The coordinates of the vertex of the right angle, point R, are (x_2, y_1).

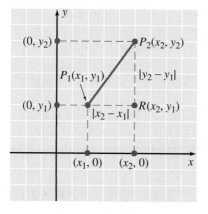

Figure 7.30

The length of $\overline{P_1R}$ is $|x_2 - x_1|$ and the length of $\overline{RP_2}$ is $|y_2 - y_1|$. (The absolute-value symbol is used to ensure a nonnegative value.) Let d represent the length of P_1P_2 and apply the Pythagorean theorem to obtain

$$d^2 = |x_2 - x_1|^2 + |y_2 - y_1|^2$$

Because $|a|^2 = a^2$, the **distance formula** can be stated as

$$d = \sqrt{(x_2 - x_1)^2 + (y_2 - y_1)^2}$$

It makes no difference which point you call P_1 or P_2 when using the distance formula. If you forget the formula, don't panic. Just form a right triangle and apply the Pythagorean theorem as we did in Example 2. Let's consider an example that demonstrates the use of the distance formula.

EXAMPLE 3   Find the distance between $(-1, 4)$ and $(1, 2)$.

Solution

Let $(-1, 4)$ be P_1 and $(1, 2)$ be P_2. Using the distance formula, we obtain

$$d = \sqrt{[(1 - (-1))]^2 + (2 - 4)^2}$$
$$= \sqrt{2^2 + (-2)^2}$$
$$= \sqrt{4 + 4}$$
$$= \sqrt{8} = 2\sqrt{2} \qquad \text{Express the answer in simplest radical form.}$$

The distance between the two points is $2\sqrt{2}$ units.   ■

In Example 3, we did not sketch a figure because of the simplicity of the problem. However, sometimes it is helpful to use a figure to organize the given information and aid in the analysis of the problem, as we see in the next example.

EXAMPLE 4   Verify that the points $(-3, 6)$, $(3, 4)$, and $(1, -2)$ are vertices of an isosceles triangle. (An isosceles triangle has two sides of the same length.)

Solution

Let's plot the points and draw the triangle (Figure 7.31). Use the distance formula to find the lengths d_1, d_2, and d_3, as follows:

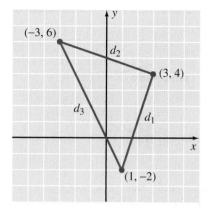

$$d_1 = \sqrt{(3-1)^2 + (4-(-2))^2}$$
$$= \sqrt{2^2 + 6^2} = \sqrt{40} = 2\sqrt{10}$$
$$d_2 = \sqrt{(-3-3)^2 + (6-4)^2}$$
$$= \sqrt{(-6)^2 + 2^2} = \sqrt{40}$$
$$= 2\sqrt{10}$$
$$d_3 = \sqrt{(-3-1)^2 + (6-(-2))^2}$$
$$= \sqrt{(-4)^2 + 8^2} = \sqrt{80} = 4\sqrt{5}$$

Figure 7.31

Because $d_1 = d_2$, we know that it is an isosceles triangle.   ■

■ Slope of a Line

In coordinate geometry, the concept of **slope** is used to describe the "steepness" of lines. The slope of a line is the ratio of the vertical change to the horizontal change as we move from one point on a line to another point. This is illustrated in Figure 7.32 with points P_1 and P_2.

A precise definition for slope can be given by considering the coordinates of the points P_1, P_2, and R as indicated in Figure 7.33. The horizontal change as we move from P_1 to P_2 is $x_2 - x_1$ and the vertical change is $y_2 - y_1$. Thus the following definition for slope is given.

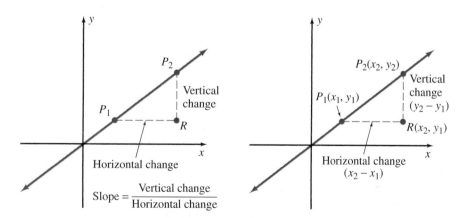

Figure 7.32

Figure 7.33

Definition 7.1

If points P_1 and P_2 with coordinates (x_1, y_1) and (x_2, y_2), respectively, are any two different points on a line, then the slope of the line (denoted by m) is

$$m = \frac{y_2 - y_1}{x_2 - x_1}, \qquad x_2 \neq x_1$$

Because $\dfrac{y_2 - y_1}{x_2 - x_1} = \dfrac{y_1 - y_2}{x_1 - x_2}$, how we designate P_1 and P_2 is not important. Let's use Definition 7.1 to find the slopes of some lines.

EXAMPLE 5

Find the slope of the line determined by each of the following pairs of points, and graph the lines.

(a) $(-1, 1)$ and $(3, 2)$ **(b)** $(4, -2)$ and $(-1, 5)$

(c) $(2, -3)$ and $(-3, -3)$

Solution

(a) Let $(-1, 1)$ be P_1 and $(3, 2)$ be P_2 (Figure 7.34).

$$m = \frac{y_2 - y_1}{x_2 - x_1} = \frac{2 - 1}{3 - (-1)} = \frac{1}{4}$$

(b) Let $(4, -2)$ be P_1 and $(-1, 5)$ be P_2 (Figure 7.35).

$$m = \frac{y_2 - y_1}{x_2 - x_1} = \frac{5 - (-2)}{-1 - 4} = \frac{7}{-5} = -\frac{7}{5}$$

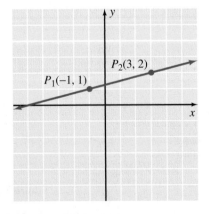

Figure 7.34

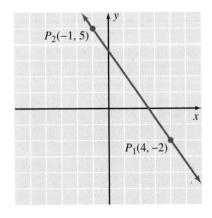

Figure 7.35

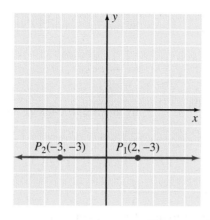

Figure 7.36

(c) Let $(2, -3)$ be P_1 and $(-3, -3)$ be P_2 (Figure 7.36).

$$m = \frac{y_2 - y_1}{x_2 - x_1}$$

$$= \frac{-3 - (-3)}{-3 - 2}$$

$$= \frac{0}{-5} = 0$$

∎

The three parts of Example 5 represent the three basic possibilities for slope; that is, the slope of a line can be positive, negative, or zero. A line that has a positive slope rises as we move from left to right, as in Figure 7.34. A line that has a negative slope falls as we move from left to right, as in Figure 7.35. A horizontal line, as in Figure 7.36, has a slope of zero. Finally, we need to realize that *the concept of slope is undefined for vertical lines*. This is due to the fact that for any vertical line, the horizontal change as we move from one point on the line to another is zero. Thus the ratio $\dfrac{y_2 - y_1}{x_2 - x_1}$ will have a denominator of zero and be undefined. Accordingly, the restriction $x_2 \neq x_1$ is imposed in Definition 7.1.

One final idea pertaining to the concept of slope needs to be emphasized. The slope of a line is a **ratio**, the ratio of vertical change to horizontal change. A slope of $\dfrac{2}{3}$ means that for every 2 units of vertical change there must be a corresponding 3 units of horizontal change. Thus, starting at some point on a line that has a slope of $\dfrac{2}{3}$, we could locate other points on the line as follows:

$\dfrac{2}{3} = \dfrac{4}{6}$ ⟶ by moving 4 units *up* and 6 units to the *right*

$\dfrac{2}{3} = \dfrac{8}{12}$ ⟶ by moving 8 units *up* and 12 units to the *right*

$\dfrac{2}{3} = \dfrac{-2}{-3}$ ⟶ by moving 2 units *down* and 3 units to the *left*

Likewise, if a line has a slope of $-\dfrac{3}{4}$, then by starting at some point on the line we could locate other points on the line as follows:

$-\dfrac{3}{4} = \dfrac{-3}{4}$ ⟶ by moving 3 units *down* and 4 units to the *right*

$$-\frac{3}{4} = \frac{3}{-4}$$ → by moving 3 units *up* and 4 units to the *left*

$$-\frac{3}{4} = \frac{-9}{12}$$ → by moving 9 units *down* and 12 units to the *right*

$$-\frac{3}{4} = \frac{15}{-20}$$ → by moving 15 units *up* and 20 units to the *left*

E X A M P L E   6   Graph the line that passes through the point $(0, -2)$ and has a slope of $\frac{1}{3}$.

Solution

To graph, plot the point $(0, -2)$. Furthermore, because the slope $= \frac{\text{vertical change}}{\text{horizontal change}} = \frac{1}{3}$, we can locate another point on the line by starting from the point $(0, -2)$ and moving 1 unit up and 3 units to the right to obtain the point $(3, -1)$. Because two points determine a line, we can draw the line (Figure 7.37).

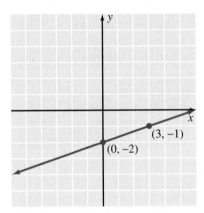

Figure 7.37

Remark: Because $m = \frac{1}{3} = \frac{-1}{-3}$, we can locate another point by moving 1 unit down and 3 units to the left from the point $(0, -2)$. ∎

E X A M P L E   7   Graph the line that passes through the point $(1, 3)$ and has a slope of -2.

Solution

To graph the line, plot the point $(1, 3)$. We know that $m = -2 = \frac{-2}{1}$. Furthermore, because the slope $= \frac{\text{vertical change}}{\text{horizontal change}} = \frac{-2}{1}$, we can locate another point on the line by starting from the point (1, 3) and moving 2 units down and 1 unit to the right to obtain the point (2, 1). Because two points determine a line, we can draw the line (Figure 7.38).

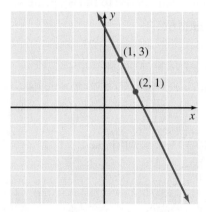

Figure 7.38

Remark: Because $m = -2 = \dfrac{-2}{1} = \dfrac{2}{-1}$ we can locate another point by moving 2 units up and 1 unit to the left from the point (1, 3).   ∎

■ Applications of Slope

The concept of slope has many real-world applications even though the word *slope* is often not used. The concept of slope is used in most situations where an incline is involved. Hospital beds are hinged in the middle so that both the head end and the foot end can be raised or lowered; that is, the slope of either end of the bed can be changed. Likewise, treadmills are designed so that the incline (slope) of the platform can be adjusted. A roofer, when making an estimate to replace a roof, is concerned not only about the total area to be covered but also about the pitch of the roof. (Contractors do not define *pitch* as identical with the mathematical definition of slope, but both concepts refer to "steepness.") In Figure 7.39, the two roofs might require the same amount of shingles, but the roof on the left will take longer to complete because the pitch is so great that scaffolding will be required.

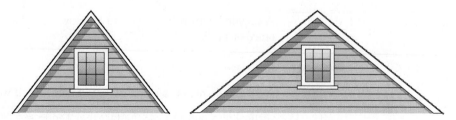

Figure 7.39

The concept of slope is also used in the construction of flights of stairs (Figure 7.40). The terms *rise* and *run* are commonly used, and the steepness (slope) of the stairs can be expressed as the ratio of rise to run. In Figure 7.40, the stairs on the left, where the ratio of rise to run is $\dfrac{10}{11}$, are steeper than the stairs on the right, which have a ratio of $\dfrac{7}{11}$.

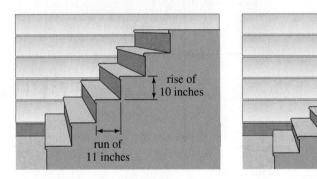

rise of 10 inches

run of 11 inches

rise of 7 inches

run of 11 inches

Figure 7.40

In highway construction, the word *grade* is used for the concept of slope. For example, in Figure 7.41 the highway is said to have a grade of 17%. This means that for every horizontal distance of 100 feet, the highway rises or drops 17 feet. In other words, the slope of the highway is $\dfrac{17}{100}$.

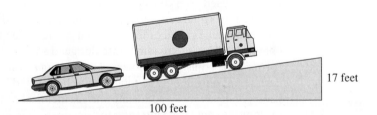

17 feet

100 feet

Figure 7.41

E X A M P L E   8

A certain highway has a 3% grade. How many feet does it rise in a horizontal distance of 1 mile?

Solution

A 3% grade means a slope of $\dfrac{3}{100}$. Therefore, if we let y represent the unknown vertical distance and use the fact that 1 mile = 5280 feet, we can set up and solve the following proportion.

$$\frac{3}{100} = \frac{y}{5280}$$

$$100y = 3(5280) = 15{,}840$$

$$y = 158.4$$

The highway rises 158.4 feet in a horizontal distance of 1 mile. ■

Problem Set 7.4

For Problems 1–12, find the distance between each of the pairs of points. Express answers in simplest radical form.

1. $(-2, -1), (7, 11)$ **2.** $(2, 1), (10, 7)$

3. $(1, -1), (3, -4)$ **4.** $(-1, 3), (2, -2)$

5. $(6, -4), (9, -7)$ **6.** $(-5, 2), (-1, 6)$

7. $(-3, 3), (0, -3)$ **8.** $(-2, -4), (4, 0)$

9. $(1, -6), (-5, -6)$ **10.** $(-2, 3), (-2, -7)$

11. $(1, 7), (4, -2)$ **12.** $(6, 4), (-4, -8)$

13. Verify that the points $(-3, 1)$, $(5, 7)$, and $(8, 3)$ are vertices of a right triangle. [*Hint:* If $a^2 + b^2 = c^2$, then it is a right triangle with the right angle opposite side c.]

14. Verify that the points $(0, 3)$, $(2, -3)$, and $(-4, -5)$ are vertices of an isosceles triangle.

15. Verify that the points $(7, 12)$ and $(11, 18)$ divide the line segment joining $(3, 6)$ and $(15, 24)$ into three segments of equal length.

16. Verify that $(3, 1)$ is the midpoint of the line segment joining $(-2, 6)$ and $(8, -4)$.

For Problems 17–28, graph the line determined by the two points and find the slope of the line.

17. $(1, 2), (4, 6)$ **18.** $(3, 1), (-2, -2)$

19. $(-4, 5), (-1, -2)$ **20.** $(-2, 5), (3, -1)$

21. $(2, 6), (6, -2)$ **22.** $(-2, -1), (2, -5)$

23. $(-6, 1), (-1, 4)$ **24.** $(-3, 3), (2, 3)$

25. $(-2, -4), (2, -4)$ **26.** $(1, -5), (4, -1)$

27. $(0, -2), (4, 0)$ **28.** $(-4, 0), (0, -6)$

29. Find x if the line through $(-2, 4)$ and $(x, 6)$ has a slope of $\frac{2}{9}$.

30. Find y if the line through $(1, y)$ and $(4, 2)$ has a slope of $\frac{5}{3}$.

31. Find x if the line through $(x, 4)$ and $(2, -5)$ has a slope of $-\frac{9}{4}$.

32. Find y if the line through $(5, 2)$ and $(-3, y)$ has a slope of $-\frac{7}{8}$.

For Problems 33–40, you are given one point on a line and the slope of the line. Find the coordinates of three other points on the line.

33. $(2, 5), m = \frac{1}{2}$ **34.** $(3, 4), m = \frac{5}{6}$

35. $(-3, 4), m = 3$ **36.** $(-3, -6), m = 1$

37. $(5, -2), m = -\frac{2}{3}$ **38.** $(4, -1), m = -\frac{3}{4}$

39. $(-2, -4), m = -2$ **40.** $(-5, 3), m = -3$

For Problems 41–48, graph the line that passes through the given point and has the given slope.

41. $(3, 1)$ $m = \dfrac{2}{3}$

42. $(-1, 0)$ $m = \dfrac{3}{4}$

43. $(-2, 3)$ $m = -1$

44. $(1, -4)$ $m = -3$

45. $(0, 5)$ $m = \dfrac{-1}{4}$

46. $(-3, 4)$ $m = \dfrac{-3}{2}$

47. $(2, -2)$ $m = \dfrac{3}{2}$

48. $(3, -4)$ $m = \dfrac{5}{2}$

For Problems 49–58, find the coordinates of two points on the given line, and then use those coordinates to find the slope of the line.

49. $2x + 3y = 6$

50. $4x + 5y = 20$

51. $x - 2y = 4$

52. $3x - y = 12$

53. $4x - 7y = 12$

54. $2x + 7y = 11$

55. $y = 4$

56. $x = 3$

57. $y = -5x$

58. $y - 6x = 0$

59. A certain highway has a 2% grade. How many feet does it rise in a horizontal distance of 1 mile? (1 mile = 5280 feet)

60. The grade of a highway up a hill is 30%. How much change in horizontal distance is there if the vertical height of the hill is 75 feet?

61. Suppose that a highway rises a distance of 215 feet in a horizontal distance of 2640 feet. Express the grade of the highway to the nearest tenth of a percent.

62. If the ratio of rise to run is to be $\dfrac{3}{5}$ for some steps and the rise is 19 centimeters, find the run to the nearest centimeter.

63. If the ratio of rise to run is to be $\dfrac{2}{3}$ for some steps, and the run is 28 centimeters, find the rise to the nearest centimeter.

64. Suppose that a county ordinance requires a $2\dfrac{1}{4}\%$ "fall" for a sewage pipe from the house to the main pipe at the street. How much vertical drop must there be for a horizontal distance of 45 feet? Express the answer to the nearest tenth of a foot.

▪▪▪ THOUGHTS INTO WORDS

65. How would you explain the concept of slope to someone who was absent from class the day it was discussed?

66. If one line has a slope of $\dfrac{2}{5}$, and another line has a slope of $\dfrac{3}{7}$, which line is steeper? Explain your answer.

67. Suppose that a line has a slope of $\dfrac{2}{3}$ and contains the point $(4, 7)$. Are the points $(7, 9)$ and $(1, 3)$ also on the line? Explain your answer.

▪▪▪ FURTHER INVESTIGATIONS

68. Sometimes it is necessary to find the coordinate of a point on a number line that is located somewhere between two given points. For example, suppose that we want to find the coordinate (x) of the point located two-thirds of the distance from 2 to 8. Because the total distance from 2 to 8 is $8 - 2 = 6$ units, we can start at 2 and move $\dfrac{2}{3}(6) = 4$ units toward 8. Thus $x = 2 + \dfrac{2}{3}(6) = 2 + 4 = 6$.

For each of the following, find the coordinate of the indicated point on a number line.
(a) Two-thirds of the distance from 1 to 10
(b) Three-fourths of the distance from -2 to 14
(c) One-third of the distance from -3 to 7
(d) Two-fifths of the distance from -5 to 6
(e) Three-fifths of the distance from -1 to -11
(f) Five-sixths of the distance from 3 to -7

69. Now suppose that we want to find the coordinates of point P, which is located two-thirds of the distance from $A(1, 2)$ to $B(7, 5)$ in a coordinate plane. We have plotted the given points A and B in Figure 7.42 to help with the analysis of this problem. Point D is two-thirds of the distance from A to C because parallel lines cut off proportional segments on every transversal that intersects the lines. Thus $\overline{AC}$ can be treated as a segment of a number line, as shown in Figure 7.43.

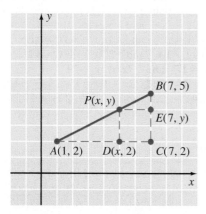

Figure 7.42

Figure 7.43

Therefore,

$$x = 1 + \frac{2}{3}(7 - 1) = 1 + \frac{2}{3}(6) = 5$$

Similarly, $\overline{CB}$ can be treated as a segment of a number line, as shown in Figure 7.44. Therefore,

$$y = 2 + \frac{2}{3}(5 - 2) = 2 + \frac{2}{3}(3) = 4$$

The coordinates of point P are $(5, 4)$.

Figure 7.44

For each of the following, find the coordinates of the indicated point in the xy plane.
(a) One-third of the distance from $(2, 3)$ to $(5, 9)$
(b) Two-thirds of the distance from $(1, 4)$ to $(7, 13)$
(c) Two-fifths of the distance from $(-2, 1)$ to $(8, 11)$
(d) Three-fifths of the distance from $(2, -3)$ to $(-3, 8)$
(e) Five-eighths of the distance from $(-1, -2)$ to $(4, -10)$
(f) Seven-eighths of the distance from $(-2, 3)$ to $(-1, -9)$

70. Suppose we want to find the coordinates of the midpoint of a line segment. Let $P(x, y)$ represent the midpoint of the line segment from $A(x_1, y_1)$ to $B(x_2, y_2)$. Using the method in Problem 68, the formula for the x coordinate of the midpoint is $x = x_1 + \frac{1}{2}(x_2 - x_1)$. This formula can be simplified algebraically to produce a simpler formula.

$$x = x_1 + \frac{1}{2}(x_2 - x_1)$$

$$x = x_1 + \frac{1}{2}x_2 - \frac{1}{2}x_1$$

$$x = \frac{1}{2}x_1 + \frac{1}{2}x_2$$

$$x = \frac{x_1 + x_2}{2}$$

Hence the x coordinate of the midpoint can be interpreted as the average of the x coordinates of the endpoints of the line segment. A similar argument for the y coordinate of the midpoint gives the following formula.

$$y = \frac{y_1 + y_2}{2}$$

For each of the pairs of points, use the formula to find the midpoint of the line segment between the points.
(a) $(3, 1)$ and $(7, 5)$
(b) $(-2, 8)$ and $(6, 4)$
(c) $(-3, 2)$ and $(5, 8)$
(d) $(4, 10)$ and $(9, 25)$
(e) $(-4, -1)$ and $(-10, 5)$
(f) $(5, 8)$ and $(-1, 7)$

GRAPHING CALCULATOR ACTIVITIES

71. Remember that we did some work with parallel lines back in the graphing calculator activities in Problem Set 7.1. Now let's do some work with perpendicular lines. Be sure to set your boundaries so that the distance between tick marks is the same on both axes.

(a) Graph $y = 4x$ and $y = -\dfrac{1}{4}x$ on the same set of axes. Do they appear to be perpendicular lines?

(b) Graph $y = 3x$ and $y = \dfrac{1}{3}x$ on the same set of axes. Do they appear to be perpendicular lines?

(c) Graph $y = \dfrac{2}{5}x - 1$ and $y = -\dfrac{5}{2}x + 2$ on the same set of axes. Do they appear to be perpendicular lines?

(d) Graph $y = \dfrac{3}{4}x - 3$, $y = \dfrac{4}{3}x + 2$, and $y = -\dfrac{4}{3}x + 2$ on the same set of axes. Does there appear to be a pair of perpendicular lines?

(e) On the basis of your results in parts (a) through (d), make a statement about how we can recognize perpendicular lines from their equations.

72. For each of the following pairs of equations, (1) predict whether they represent parallel lines, perpendicular lines, or lines that intersect but are not perpendicular, and (2) graph each pair of lines to check your prediction.
(a) $5.2x + 3.3y = 9.4$ and $5.2x + 3.3y = 12.6$
(b) $1.3x - 4.7y = 3.4$ and $1.3x - 4.7y = 11.6$
(c) $2.7x + 3.9y = 1.4$ and $2.7x - 3.9y = 8.2$
(d) $5x - 7y = 17$ and $7x + 5y = 19$
(e) $9x + 2y = 14$ and $2x + 9y = 17$
(f) $2.1x + 3.4y = 11.7$ and $3.4x - 2.1y = 17.3$

7.5   Determining the Equation of a Line

To review, there are basically two types of problems to solve in coordinate geometry:

1. Given an algebraic equation, find its geometric graph.

2. Given a set of conditions pertaining to a geometric figure, find its algebraic equation.

Problems of type 1 have been our primary concern thus far in this chapter. Now let's analyze some problems of type 2 that deal specifically with straight lines. Given certain facts about a line, we need to be able to determine its algebraic equation. Let's consider some examples.

E X A M P L E   1   Find the equation of the line that has a slope of $\dfrac{2}{3}$ and contains the point $(1, 2)$.

Solution

First, let's draw the line and record the given information. Then choose a point (x, y) that represents any point on the line other than the given point $(1, 2)$. (See Figure 7.45.)

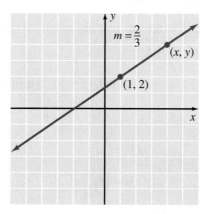

The slope determined by $(1, 2)$ and (x, y) is $\dfrac{2}{3}$. Thus

$$\frac{y - 2}{x - 1} = \frac{2}{3}$$

$$2(x - 1) = 3(y - 2)$$

$$2x - 2 = 3y - 6$$

$$2x - 3y = -4$$

Figure 7.45

E X A M P L E   2

Find the equation of the line that contains $(3, 2)$ and $(-2, 5)$.

Solution

First, let's draw the line determined by the given points (Figure 7.46); if we know two points, we can find the slope.

$$m = \frac{y_2 - y_1}{x_2 - x_1} = \frac{3}{-5} = -\frac{3}{5}$$

Now we can use the same approach as in Example 1.

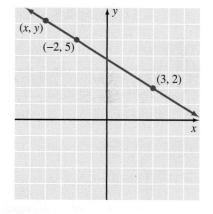

Figure 7.46

Form an equation using a variable point (x, y), one of the two given points, and the slope of $-\dfrac{3}{5}$.

$$\frac{y - 5}{x + 2} = \frac{3}{-5} \qquad \left(-\frac{3}{5} = \frac{3}{-5}\right)$$

$$3(x + 2) = -5(y - 5)$$

$$3x + 6 = -5y + 25$$

$$3x + 5y = 19$$

E X A M P L E   3

Find the equation of the line that has a slope of $\dfrac{1}{4}$ and a y intercept of 2.

Solution

A y intercept of 2 means that the point $(0, 2)$ is on the line (Figure 7.47).

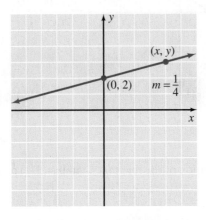

Figure 7.47

Choose a variable point (x, y) and proceed as in the previous examples.

$$\frac{y - 2}{x - 0} = \frac{1}{4}$$

$$1(x - 0) = 4(y - 2)$$

$$x = 4y - 8$$

$$x - 4y = -8$$ ∎

Perhaps it would be helpful to pause a moment and look back over Examples 1, 2, and 3. Note that we used the same basic approach in all three situations. We chose a variable point (x, y) and used it to determine the equation that satisfies the conditions given in the problem. The approach we took in the previous examples can be generalized to produce some special forms of equations of straight lines.

■ Point-Slope Form

E X A M P L E   4

Find the equation of the line that has a slope of m and contains the point (x_1, y_1).

Solution

Choose (x, y) to represent any other point on the line (Figure 7.48), and the slope of the line is therefore given by

$$m = \frac{y - y_1}{x - x_1}, \qquad x \neq x_1$$

from which

$$y - y_1 = m(x - x_1)$$

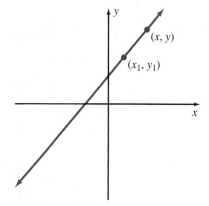

Figure 7.48

We refer to the equation

$$y - y_1 = m(x - x_1)$$

as the **point-slope form** of the equation of a straight line. Instead of the approach we used in Example 1, we could use the point-slope form to write the equation of a line with a given slope that contains a given point. For example, we can determine the equation of the line that has a slope of $\dfrac{3}{5}$ and contains the point (2, 4) as follows:

$$y - y_1 = m(x - x_1)$$

Substitute (2, 4) for (x_1, y_1) and $\dfrac{3}{5}$ for m.

$$y - 4 = \frac{3}{5}(x - 2)$$

$$5(y - 4) = 3(x - 2)$$

$$5y - 20 = 3x - 6$$

$$-14 = 3x - 5y$$

■ Slope-Intercept Form

EXAMPLE 5

Find the equation of the line that has a slope of m and a y intercept of b.

Solution

A y intercept of b means that the line contains the point $(0, b)$, as in Figure 7.49. Therefore, we can use the point-slope form as follows:

$$y - y_1 = m(x - x_1)$$

$$y - b = m(x - 0)$$

$$y - b = mx$$

$$y = mx + b$$

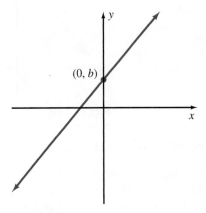

Figure 7.49 ■

We refer to the equation

$$y = mx + b$$

as the **slope-intercept form** of the equation of a straight line. We use it for three primary purposes, as the next three examples illustrate.

EXAMPLE 6

Find the equation of the line that has a slope of $\dfrac{1}{4}$ and a y intercept of 2.

Solution

This is a restatement of Example 3, but this time we will use the slope-intercept form $(y = mx + b)$ of a line to write its equation. Because $m = \dfrac{1}{4}$ and $b = 2$, we can substitute these values into $y = mx + b$.

$$y = mx + b$$

$$y = \frac{1}{4}x + 2$$

$$4y = x + 8 \qquad \text{Multiply both sides by 4.}$$

$$x - 4y = -8 \qquad \text{Same result as in Example 3.}$$ ■

E X A M P L E   7

Find the slope of the line when the equation is $3x + 2y = 6$.

Solution

We can solve the equation for y in terms of x and then compare it to the slope-intercept form to determine its slope. Thus

$$3x + 2y = 6$$

$$2y = -3x + 6$$

$$y = -\frac{3}{2}x + 3$$

$$y = -\frac{3}{2}x + 3 \qquad y = mx + b$$

The slope of the line is $-\dfrac{3}{2}$. Furthermore, the y intercept is 3.   ■

E X A M P L E   8

Graph the line determined by the equation $y = \dfrac{2}{3}x - 1$.

Solution

Comparing the given equation to the general slope-intercept form, we see that the slope of the line is $\dfrac{2}{3}$ and the y intercept is -1. Because the y intercept is -1, we can plot the point $(0, -1)$. Then, because the slope is $\dfrac{2}{3}$, let's move 3 units to the right and 2 units up from $(0, -1)$ to locate the point $(3, 1)$. The two points $(0, -1)$ and $(3, 1)$ determine the line in Figure 7.50. (Again, you should determine a third point as a check point.)

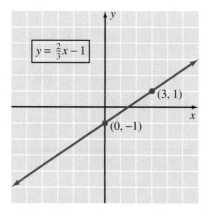

Figure 7.50   ■

> In general, if the equation of a nonvertical line is written in slope-intercept form ($y = mx + b$), the coefficient of x is the slope of the line, and the constant term is the y intercept. (Remember that the concept of slope is not defined for a vertical line.)

■ Parallel and Perpendicular Lines

We can use two important relationships between lines and their slopes to solve certain kinds of problems. It can be shown that nonvertical parallel lines have the same slope and that two nonvertical lines are perpendicular if the product of their slopes is -1. (Details for verifying these facts are left to another course.) In other words, if two lines have slopes m_1 and m_2, respectively, then

1. The two lines are parallel if and only if $m_1 = m_2$.

2. The two lines are perpendicular if and only if $(m_1)(m_2) = -1$.

The following examples demonstrate the use of these properties.

E X A M P L E   9

(a) Verify that the graphs of $2x + 3y = 7$ and $4x + 6y = 11$ are parallel lines.

(b) Verify that the graphs of $8x - 12y = 3$ and $3x + 2y = 2$ are perpendicular lines.

Solution

(a) Let's change each equation to slope-intercept form.

$$2x + 3y = 7 \quad \longrightarrow \quad 3y = -2x + 7$$

$$y = -\frac{2}{3}x + \frac{7}{3}$$

$$4x + 6y = 11 \quad \longrightarrow \quad 6y = -4x + 11$$

$$y = -\frac{4}{6}x + \frac{11}{6}$$

$$y = -\frac{2}{3}x + \frac{11}{6}$$

Both lines have a slope of $-\dfrac{2}{3}$, but they have different y intercepts. Therefore, the two lines are parallel.

(b) Solving each equation for y in terms of x, we obtain

$$8x - 12y = 3 \quad \longrightarrow \quad -12y = -8x + 3$$

$$y = \frac{8}{12}x - \frac{3}{12}$$

$$y = \frac{2}{3}x - \frac{1}{4}$$

$$3x + 2y = 2 \qquad \longrightarrow \qquad 2y = -3x + 2$$

$$y = -\frac{3}{2}x + 1$$

Because $\left(\dfrac{2}{3}\right)\left(-\dfrac{3}{2}\right) = -1$ (the product of the two slopes is -1), the lines are perpendicular.   ■

Remark: The statement "the product of two slopes is -1" is the same as saying that the two slopes are negative reciprocals of each other; that is, $m_1 = -\dfrac{1}{m_2}$.

E X A M P L E   1 0

Find the equation of the line that contains the point $(1, 4)$ and is parallel to the line determined by $x + 2y = 5$.

Solution

First, let's draw a figure to help in our analysis of the problem (Figure 7.51). Because the line through $(1, 4)$ is to be parallel to the line determined by $x + 2y = 5$, it must have the same slope. Let's find the slope by changing $x + 2y = 5$ to the slope-intercept form.

$$x + 2y = 5$$

$$2y = -x + 5$$

$$y = -\frac{1}{2}x + \frac{5}{2}$$

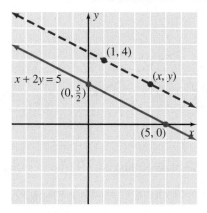

Figure 7.51

The slope of both lines is $-\dfrac{1}{2}$. Now we can choose a variable point (x, y) on the line through $(1, 4)$ and proceed as we did in earlier examples.

$$\frac{y - 4}{x - 1} = \frac{1}{-2}$$

$$1(x - 1) = -2(y - 4)$$

$$x - 1 = -2y + 8$$

$$x + 2y = 9 \qquad\qquad\blacksquare$$

E X A M P L E   1 1

Find the equation of the line that contains the point $(-1, -2)$ and is perpendicular to the line determined by $2x - y = 6$.

Solution

First, let's draw a figure to help in our analysis of the problem (Figure 7.52). Because the line through $(-1, -2)$ is to be perpendicular to the line determined by $2x - y = 6$, its slope must be the negative reciprocal of the slope of $2x - y = 6$. Let's find the slope of $2x - y = 6$ by changing it to the slope-intercept form.

$$2x - y = 6$$

$$-y = -2x + 6$$

$$y = 2x - 6 \qquad\qquad \text{The slope is 2.}$$

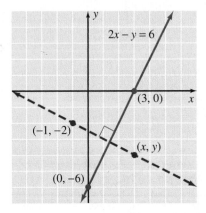

Figure 7.52

The slope of the desired line is $-\dfrac{1}{2}$ (the negative reciprocal of 2), and we can proceed as before by using a variable point (x, y).

$$\frac{y + 2}{x + 1} = \frac{1}{-2}$$

$$1(x + 1) = -2(y + 2)$$

$$x + 1 = -2y - 4$$

$$x + 2y = -5 \qquad\qquad\blacksquare$$

We use two forms of equations of straight lines extensively. They are the **standard form** and the **slope-intercept form**, and we describe them as follows.

Standard Form $Ax + By = C$, where B and C are integers, and A is a nonnegative integer (A and B not both zero).

Slope-Intercept Form $y = mx + b$, where m is a real number representing the slope, and b is a real number representing the y intercept.

Problem Set 7.5

For Problems 1–8, write the equation of the line that has the indicated slope and contains the indicated point. Express final equations in standard form.

1. $m = \dfrac{1}{2}$, $(3, 5)$

2. $m = \dfrac{1}{3}$, $(2, 3)$

3. $m = 3$, $(-2, 4)$

4. $m = -2$, $(-1, 6)$

5. $m = -\dfrac{3}{4}$, $(-1, -3)$

6. $m = -\dfrac{3}{5}$, $(-2, -4)$

7. $m = \dfrac{5}{4}$, $(4, -2)$

8. $m = \dfrac{3}{2}$, $(8, -2)$

For Problems 9–18, write the equation of the line that contains the indicated pair of points. Express final equations in standard form.

9. $(2, 1), (6, 5)$

10. $(-1, 2), (2, 5)$

11. $(-2, -3), (2, 7)$

12. $(-3, -4), (1, 2)$

13. $(-3, 2), (4, 1)$

14. $(-2, 5), (3, -3)$

15. $(-1, -4), (3, -6)$

16. $(3, 8), (7, 2)$

17. $(0, 0), (5, 7)$

18. $(0, 0), (-5, 9)$

For Problems 19–26, write the equation of the line that has the indicated slope (m) and y intercept (b). Express final equations in slope-intercept form.

19. $m = \dfrac{3}{7}$, $b = 4$

20. $m = \dfrac{2}{9}$, $b = 6$

21. $m = 2$, $b = -3$

22. $m = -3$, $b = -1$

23. $m = -\dfrac{2}{5}$, $b = 1$

24. $m = -\dfrac{3}{7}$, $b = 4$

25. $m = 0$, $b = -4$

26. $m = \dfrac{1}{5}$, $b = 0$

For Problems 27–42, write the equation of the line that satisfies the given conditions. Express final equations in standard form.

27. x intercept of 2 and y intercept of -4

28. x intercept of -1 and y intercept of -3

29. x intercept of -3 and slope of $-\dfrac{5}{8}$

30. x intercept of 5 and slope of $-\dfrac{3}{10}$

31. Contains the point $(2, -4)$ and is parallel to the y axis

32. Contains the point $(-3, -7)$ and is parallel to the x axis

33. Contains the point $(5, 6)$ and is perpendicular to the y axis

34. Contains the point $(-4, 7)$ and is perpendicular to the x axis

35. Contains the point $(1, 3)$ and is parallel to the line $x + 5y = 9$

36. Contains the point $(-1, 4)$ and is parallel to the line $x - 2y = 6$

37. Contains the origin and is parallel to the line $4x - 7y = 3$

38. Contains the origin and is parallel to the line $-2x - 9y = 4$

39. Contains the point $(-1, 3)$ and is perpendicular to the line $2x - y = 4$

40. Contains the point $(-2, -3)$ and is perpendicular to the line $x + 4y = 6$

41. Contains the origin and is perpendicular to the line $-2x + 3y = 8$

42. Contains the origin and is perpendicular to the line $y = -5x$

For Problems 43–48, change the equation to slope-intercept form and determine the slope and y intercept of the line.

43. $3x + y = 7$

44. $5x - y = 9$

45. $3x + 2y = 9$

46. $x - 4y = 3$

47. $x = 5y + 12$

48. $-4x - 7y = 14$

For Problems 49–56, use the slope-intercept form to graph the following lines.

49. $y = \dfrac{2}{3}x - 4$

50. $y = \dfrac{1}{4}x + 2$

51. $y = 2x + 1$

52. $y = 3x - 1$

53. $y = -\dfrac{3}{2}x + 4$

54. $y = -\dfrac{5}{3}x + 3$

55. $y = -x + 2$

56. $y = -2x + 4$

For Problems 57–66, graph the following lines using the technique that seems most appropriate.

57. $y = -\dfrac{2}{5}x - 1$

58. $y = -\dfrac{1}{2}x + 3$

59. $x + 2y = 5$

60. $2x - y = 7$

61. $-y = -4x + 7$

62. $3x = 2y$

63. $7y = -2x$

64. $y = -3$

65. $x = 2$

66. $y = -x$

For Problems 67–70, the situations can be described by the use of linear equations in two variables. If two pairs of values are known, then we can determine the equation by using the approach we used in Example 2 of this section. For each of the following, assume that the relationship can be expressed as a linear equation in two variables, and use the given information to determine the equation. Express the equation in slope-intercept form.

67. A company uses 7 pounds of fertilizer for a lawn that measures 5000 square feet and 12 pounds for a lawn that measures 10,000 square feet. Let y represent the pounds of fertilizer and x the square footage of the lawn.

68. A new diet fad claims that a person weighing 140 pounds should consume 1490 daily calories and that a 200-pound person should consume 1700 calories. Let y represent the calories and x the weight of the person in pounds.

69. Two banks on opposite corners of a town square had signs that displayed the current temperature. One bank displayed the temperature in degrees Celsius and the other in degrees Fahrenheit. A temperature of $10°C$ was displayed at the same time as a temperature of $50°F$. On another day, a temperature of $-5°C$ was displayed at the same time as a temperature of $23°F$. Let y represent the temperature in degrees Fahrenheit and x the temperature in degrees Celsius.

70. An accountant has a schedule of depreciation for some business equipment. The schedule shows that after 12 months the equipment is worth \$7600 and that after 20 months it is worth \$6000. Let y represent the worth and x represent the time in months.

■ ■ ■ THOUGHTS INTO WORDS

71. What does it mean to say that two points determine a line?

72. How would you help a friend determine the equation of the line that is perpendicular to $x - 5y = 7$ and contains the point $(5, 4)$?

73. Explain how you would find the slope of the line $y = 4$.

■ ■ ■ FURTHER INVESTIGATIONS

74. The equation of a line that contains the two points (x_1, y_1) and (x_2, y_2) is $\dfrac{y - y_1}{x - x_1} = \dfrac{y_2 - y_1}{x_2 - x_1}$. We often refer to this as the **two-point form** of the equation of a straight line. Use the two-point form and write the equation of the line that contains each of the indicated pairs of points. Express final equations in standard form.

(a) $(1, 1)$ and $(5, 2)$

(b) $(2, 4)$ and $(-2, -1)$

(c) $(-3, 5)$ and $(3, 1)$

(d) $(-5, 1)$ and $(2, -7)$

75. Let $Ax + By = C$ and $A'x + B'y = C'$ represent two lines. Change both of these equations to slope-intercept form, and then verify each of the following properties.

(a) If $\dfrac{A}{A'} = \dfrac{B}{B'} \neq \dfrac{C}{C'}$, then the lines are parallel.

(b) If $AA' = -BB'$, then the lines are perpendicular.

76. The properties in Problem 75 provide us with another way to write the equation of a line parallel or perpendicular to a given line that contains a given point not on the line. For example, suppose that we want the equation of the line perpendicular to $3x + 4y = 6$ that contains the point $(1, 2)$. The form $4x - 3y = k$, where k is a constant, represents a family of lines perpendicular to $3x + 4y = 6$ because we have satisfied the condition $AA' = -BB'$. Therefore, to find what specific line of the family contains $(1, 2)$, we substitute 1 for x and 2 for y to determine k.

$$4x - 3y = k$$
$$4(1) - 3(2) = k$$
$$-2 = k$$

Thus the equation of the desired line is $4x - 3y = -2$.

Use the properties from Problem 75 to help write the equation of each of the following lines.

(a) Contains $(1, 8)$ and is parallel to $2x + 3y = 6$

(b) Contains $(-1, 4)$ and is parallel to $x - 2y = 4$

(c) Contains $(2, -7)$ and is perpendicular to $3x - 5y = 10$

(d) Contains $(-1, -4)$ and is perpendicular to $2x + 5y = 12$

77. The problem of finding the perpendicular bisector of a line segment presents itself often in the study of analytic geometry. As with any problem of writing the equation of a line, you must determine the slope of the line and a point that the line passes through. A perpendicular bisector passes through the midpoint of the line segment and has a slope that is the negative reciprocal of the slope of the line segment. The problem can be solved as follows:

Find the perpendicular bisector of the line segment between the points $(1, -2)$ and $(7, 8)$.

The midpoint of the line segment is $\left(\dfrac{1 + 7}{2}, \dfrac{-2 + 8}{2} \right)$ $= (4, 3)$.

The slope of the line segment is $m = \dfrac{8 - (-2)}{7 - 1}$ $= \dfrac{10}{6} = \dfrac{5}{3}$.

Hence the perpendicular bisector will pass through the point $(4, 3)$ and have a slope of $m = -\dfrac{3}{5}$.

$$y - 3 = -\frac{3}{5}(x - 4)$$
$$5(y - 3) = -3(x - 4)$$
$$5y - 15 = -3x + 12$$
$$3x + 5y = 27$$

Thus the equation of the perpendicular bisector of the line segment between the points $(1, -2)$ and $(7, 8)$ is $3x + 5y = 27$.

Find the perpendicular bisector of the line segment between the points for the following. Write the equation in standard form.

(a) $(-1, 2)$ and $(3, 0)$

(b) $(6, -10)$ and $(-4, 2)$

(c) $(-7, -3)$ and $(5, 9)$

(d) $(0, 4)$ and $(12, -4)$

GRAPHING CALCULATOR ACTIVITIES

78. Predict whether each of the following pairs of equations represents parallel lines, perpendicular lines, or lines that intersect but are not perpendicular. Then graph each pair of lines to check your predictions. (The properties presented in Problem 75 should be very helpful.)

(a) $5.2x + 3.3y = 9.4$ and $5.2x + 3.3y = 12.6$

(b) $1.3x - 4.7y = 3.4$ and $1.3x - 4.7y = 11.6$

(c) $2.7x + 3.9y = 1.4$ and $2.7x - 3.9y = 8.2$

(d) $5x - 7y = 17$ and $7x + 5y = 19$

(e) $9x + 2y = 14$ and $2x + 9y = 17$

(f) $2.1x + 3.4y = 11.7$ and $3.4x - 2.1y = 17.3$

(g) $7.1x - 2.3y = 6.2$ and $2.3x + 7.1y = 9.9$

(h) $-3x + 9y = 12$ and $9x - 3y = 14$

(i) $2.6x - 5.3y = 3.4$ and $5.2x - 10.6y = 19.2$

(j) $4.8x - 5.6y = 3.4$ and $6.1x + 7.6y = 12.3$

Chapter 7 Summary

(7.1) The **Cartesian** (or **rectangular**) **coordinate system** is used to graph ordered pairs of real numbers. The first number, a, of the ordered pair (a, b) is called the **abscissa**, and the second number, b, is called the **ordinate**; together they are referred to as the **coordinates** of a point.

Two basic kinds of problems exist in coordinate geometry:

1. Given an algebraic equation, find its geometric graph.
2. Given a set of conditions that pertains to a geometric figure, find its algebraic equation.

A **solution** of an equation in two variables is an ordered pair of real numbers that satisfies the equation.

Any equation of the form $Ax + By = C$, where A, B, and C are constants (A and B not both zero) and x and y are variables, is a **linear equation**, and its graph is a **straight line**.

Any equation of the form $Ax + By = C$, where $C = 0$, is a straight line that contains the origin.

Any equation of the form $x = a$, where a is a constant, is a line parallel to the y axis that has an x intercept of a.

Any equation of the form $y = b$, where b is a constant, is a line parallel to the x axis that has a y intercept of b.

(7.2) The following suggestions are offered for **graphing an equation** in two variables.

1. Determine what type of symmetry the equation exhibits.
2. Find the intercepts.
3. Solve the equation for y in terms of x or for x in terms of y if it is not already in such a form.
4. Set up a table of ordered pairs that satisfy the equation. The type of symmetry will affect your choice of values in the table.
5. Plot the points associated with the ordered pairs from the table, and connect them with a smooth curve. Then, if appropriate, reflect this part of the curve according to the symmetry shown by the equation.

(7.3) **Linear inequalities** in two variables are of the form $Ax + By > C$ or $Ax + By < C$. To **graph a linear inequality**, we suggest the following steps.

1. First, graph the corresponding equality. Use a solid line if equality is included in the original statement. Use a dashed line if equality is not included.
2. Choose a test point not on the line and substitute its coordinates into the inequality.
3. The graph of the original inequality is
   (a) the half plane that contains the test point if the inequality is satisfied by that point, or
   (b) the half plane that does not contain the test point if the inequality is not satisfied by the point.

(7.4) The distance between any two points (x_1, y_1) and (x_2, y_2) is given by the **distance formula**,

$$d = \sqrt{(x_2 - x_1)^2 + (y_2 - y_1)^2}$$

The **slope** (denoted by m) of a line determined by the points (x_1, y_1) and (x_2, y_2) is given by the slope formula,

$$m = \frac{y_2 - y_1}{x_2 - x_1}, \qquad x_2 \neq x_1$$

(7.5) The equation $y = mx + b$ is referred to as the **slope-intercept form** of the equation of a straight line. If the equation of a nonvertical line is written in this y form, the coefficient of x is the slope of the line and the constant term is the y intercept.

If two lines have slopes m_1 and m_2, respectively, then

1. The two lines are parallel if and only if $m_1 = m_2$.
2. The two lines are perpendicular if and only if $(m_1)(m_2) = -1$.

To determine the equation of a straight line given a set of conditions, we can use the point-slope form, $y - y_1 = m(x - x_1)$, or $\dfrac{y - y_1}{x - x_1} = m$. The conditions generally fall into one of the following four categories.

1. Given the slope and a point contained in the line
2. Given two points contained in the line
3. Given a point contained in the line and that the line is parallel to another line
4. Given a point contained in the line and that the line is perpendicular to another line

The result can then be expressed in standard form or slope-intercept form.

Chapter 7   Review Problem Set

1. Find the slope of the line determined by each pair of points.
    (a) $(3, 4), (-2, -2)$ **(b)** $(-2, 3), (4, -1)$

2. Find y if the line through $(-4, 3)$ and $(12, y)$ has a slope of $\dfrac{1}{8}$.

3. Find x if the line through $(x, 5)$ and $(3, -1)$ has a slope of $-\dfrac{3}{2}$.

4. Find the slope of each of the following lines.
    (a) $4x + y = 7$ **(b)** $2x - 7y = 3$

5. Find the lengths of the sides of a triangle whose vertices are at $(2, 3)$, $(5, -1)$, and $(-4, -5)$.

6. Find the distance between each of the pairs of points.
    (a) $(-1, 4), (1, -2)$ **(b)** $(5, 0), (2, 7)$

7. Verify that $(1, 6)$ is the midpoint of the line segment joining $(3, 2)$ and $(-1, 10)$.

For Problems 8–15, write the equation of the line that satisfies the stated conditions. Express final equations in standard form.

8. Containing the points $(-1, 2)$ and $(3, -5)$

9. Having a slope of $-\dfrac{3}{7}$ and a y intercept of 4

10. Containing the point $(-1, -6)$ and having a slope of $\dfrac{2}{3}$

11. Containing the point $(2, 5)$ and parallel to the line $x - 2y = 4$

12. Containing the point $(-2, -6)$ and perpendicular to the line $3x + 2y = 12$

13. Containing the points $(0, 4)$ and $(2, 6)$

14. Containing the point $(3, -5)$ and having a slope of -1

15. Containing the point $(-8, 3)$ and parallel to the line $4x + y = 7$

For Problems 16–35, graph each equation.

16. $2x - y = 6$ **17.** $y = 2x - 5$

18. $y = -2x - 1$ **19.** $y = -4x$

20. $-3x - 2y = 6$ **21.** $x = 2y + 4$

22. $5x - y = -5$ **23.** $y = -\dfrac{1}{2}x + 3$

24. $y = \dfrac{3x - 4}{2}$ **25.** $y = 4$

26. $2x + 3y = 0$ **27.** $y = \dfrac{3}{5}x - 4$

28. $x = 1$ **29.** $x = -3$

30. $y = -2$ **31.** $2x - 3y = 3$

32. $y = x^3 + 2$ **33.** $y = -x^3$

34. $y = x^2 + 3$ **35.** $y = -2x^2 - 1$

For Problems 36–41, graph each inequality.

36. $-x + 3y < -6$ **37.** $x + 2y \geq 4$

38. $2x - 3y \leq 6$ **39.** $y > -\dfrac{1}{2}x + 3$

40. $y < 2x - 5$ **41.** $y \geq \dfrac{2}{3}x$

42. A certain highway has a 6% grade. How many feet does it rise in a horizontal distance of 1 mile?

43. If the ratio of rise to run is to be $\dfrac{2}{3}$ for the steps of a staircase, and the run is 12 inches, find the rise.

44. Find the slope of any line that is perpendicular to the line $-3x + 5y = 7$.

45. Find the slope of any line that is parallel to the line $4x + 5y = 10$.

46. The taxes for a primary residence can be described by a linear relationship. Find the equation for the relationship if the taxes for a home valued at $200,000 are $2400, and the taxes are $3150 when the home is valued at $250,000. Let y be the taxes and x the value of the home. Write the equation in slope-intercept form.

47. The freight charged by a trucking firm for a parcel under 200 pounds depends on the miles it is being shipped. To ship a 150-pound parcel 300 miles, it costs $40. If the same parcel is shipped 1000 miles, the cost is $180. Assume the relationship between the cost and miles is linear. Find the equation for the relationship. Let y be the cost and x be the miles. Write the equation in slope-intercept form.

48. On a final exam in math class, the number of points earned has a linear relationship with the number of correct answers. John got 96 points when he answered 12 questions correctly. Kimberly got 144 points when she answered 18 questions correctly. Find the equation for the relationship. Let y be the number of points and

x be the number of correct answers. Write the equation in slope-intercept form.

49. The time needed to install computer cables has a linear relationship with the number of feet of cable being installed. It takes $1\frac{1}{2}$ hours to install 300 feet, and 1050 feet can be installed in 4 hours. Find the equation for the relationship. Let y be the feet of cable installed and x be the time in hours. Write the equation in slope-intercept form.

50. Determine the type(s) of symmetry (symmetry with respect to the x axis, y axis, and/or origin) exhibited by the graph of each of the following equations. Do not sketch the graph.
(a) $y = x^2 + 4$ **(b)** $xy = -4$
(c) $y = -x^3$ **(d)** $x = y^4 + 2y^2$

1. Find the slope of the line determined by the points $(-2, 4)$ and $(3, -2)$.

2. Find the slope of the line determined by the equation $3x - 7y = 12$.

3. Find the length of the line segment whose endpoints are $(4, 2)$ and $(-3, -1)$. Express the answer in simplest radical form.

4. Find the equation of the line that has a slope of $-\dfrac{3}{2}$ and contains the point $(4, -5)$. Express the equation in standard form.

5. Find the equation of the line that contains the points $(-4, 2)$ and $(2, 1)$. Express the equation in slope-intercept form.

6. Find the equation of the line that is parallel to the line $5x + 2y = 7$ and contains the point $(-2, -4)$. Express the equation in standard form.

7. Find the equation of the line that is perpendicular to the line $x - 6y = 9$ and contains the point $(4, 7)$. Express the equation in standard form.

8. What kind(s) of symmetry does the graph of $y = 9x$ exhibit?

9. What kind(s) of symmetry does the graph of $y^2 = x^2 + 6$ exhibit?

10. What kind(s) of symmetry does the graph of $x^2 + 6x + 2y^2 - 8 = 0$ exhibit?

11. What is the slope of all lines that are parallel to the line $7x - 2y = 9$?

12. What is the slope of all lines that are perpendicular to the line $4x + 9y = -6$?

13. Find the x intercept of the line $y = \dfrac{3}{5}x - \dfrac{2}{3}$.

14. Find the y intercept of the line $\dfrac{3}{4}x - \dfrac{2}{5}y = \dfrac{1}{4}$.

15. The grade of a highway up a hill is 25%. How much change in horizontal distance is there if the vertical height of the hill is 120 feet?

16. Suppose that a highway rises 200 feet in a horizontal distance of 3000 feet. Express the grade of the highway to the nearest tenth of a percent.

17. If the ratio of rise to run is to be $\dfrac{3}{4}$ for the steps of a staircase, and the rise is 32 centimeters, find the run to the nearest centimeter.

For Problems 18–23, graph each equation.

18. $y = -x^2 - 3$

19. $y = -x - 3$

20. $-3x + y = 5$

21. $3y = 2x$

22. $\dfrac{1}{3}x + \dfrac{1}{2}y = 2$

23. $y = \dfrac{-x - 1}{4}$

For Problems 24 and 25, graph each inequality.

24. $2x - y < 4$

25. $3x + 2y \geq 6$

Conic Sections

8.1 Graphing Parabolas

8.2 More Parabolas and Some Circles

8.3 Graphing Ellipses

8.4 Graphing Hyperbolas

© AFP/Getty Images

Examples of conic sections, in particular parabolas and ellipses, can be found in corporate logos throughout the world.

Parabolas, circles, ellipses, and hyperbolas can be formed when a plane intersects a conical surface as shown in Figure 8.1; we often refer to these curves as the **conic sections**. A flashlight produces a "cone of light" that can be cut by the plane of a wall to illustrate the conic sections. Try shining a flashlight against a wall at different angles to produce a circle, an ellipse, a parabola, and one branch of a hyperbola. (You may find it difficult to distinguish between a parabola and a branch of a hyperbola.)

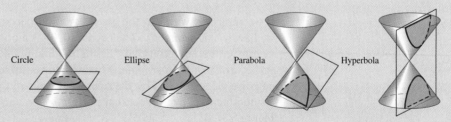

Circle   Ellipse   Parabola   Hyperbola

Figure 8.1

8.1 Graphing Parabolas

In general the graph of any equation of the form $y = ax^2 + bx + c$, where a, b, and c are real numbers and $a \neq 0$, is a parabola. At this time we want to develop a very easy and systematic way of graphing parabolas without the use of a graphing calculator. As we work with parabolas, we will use the vocabulary indicated in Figure 8.2.

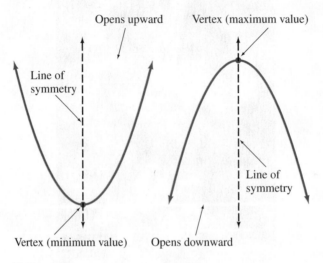

Figure 8.2

Let's begin by using the concepts of intercepts and symmetry to help us sketch the graph of the equation $y = x^2$.

EXAMPLE 1   Graph $y = x^2$.

Solution

If we replace x with $-x$, the given equation becomes $y = (-x)^2 = x^2$; therefore, we have y axis symmetry. The origin, $(0, 0)$, is a point of the graph. We can recognize from the equation that 0 is the minimum value of y; hence the point $(0, 0)$ is the vertex of the parabola. Now we can set up a table of values that uses nonnegative values for x. Plot the points determined by the table, connect them with a smooth curve, and reflect that portion of the curve across the y axis to produce Figure 8.3.

x	y
0	0
$\frac{1}{2}$	$\frac{1}{4}$
1	1
2	4
3	9

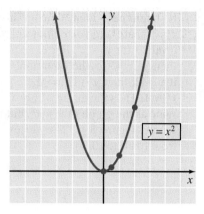

Figure 8.3

To graph parabolas, we need to be able to:

1. Find the vertex.

2. Determine whether the parabola opens upward or downward.

3. Locate two points on opposite sides of the line of symmetry.

4. Compare the parabola to the basic parabola $y = x^2$.

To graph parabolas produced by the various types of equations such as $y = x^2 + k$, $y = ax^2$, $y = (x - h)^2$, and $y = a(x - h)^2 + k$, we can compare these equations to that of the basic parabola, $y = x^2$. First, let's consider some equations of the form $y = x^2 + k$, where k is a constant.

EXAMPLE 2

Graph $y = x^2 + 1$.

Solution

Let's set up a table of values to compare y values for $y = x^2 + 1$ to corresponding y values for $y = x^2$.

x	$y = x^2$	$y = x^2 + 1$
0	0	1
1	1	2
2	4	5
−1	1	2
−2	4	5

It should be evident that y values for $y = x^2 + 1$ are *1 greater than* corresponding y values for $y = x^2$. For example, if $x = 2$, then $y = 4$ for the equation $y = x^2$; but if $x = 2$, then $y = 5$ for the equation $y = x^2 + 1$. Thus the graph of $y = x^2 + 1$ is the same as the graph of $y = x^2$, but moved up 1 unit (Figure 8.4). The vertex will move from $(0, 0)$ to $(0, 1)$.

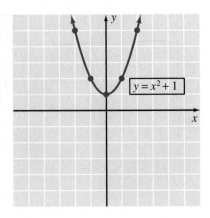

Figure 8.4   ■

EXAMPLE   3

Graph $y = x^2 - 2$.

Solution

The y values for $y = x^2 - 2$ are *2 less than* the corresponding y values for $y = x^2$, as indicated in the following table.

x	$y = x^2$	$y = x^2 - 2$
0	0	-2
1	1	-1
2	4	2
-1	1	-1
-2	4	2

Thus the graph of $y = x^2 - 2$ is the same as the graph of $y = x^2$ but moved down 2 units (Figure 8.5). The vertex will move from $(0, 0)$ to $(0, -2)$.

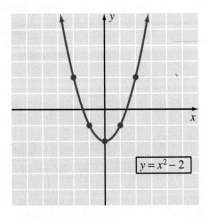

Figure 8.5   ■

In general, the graph of a quadratic equation of the form $y = x^2 + k$ is the same as the graph of $y = x^2$ but moved up or down $|k|$ units, depending on whether k is positive or negative.

Now, let's consider some quadratic equations of the form $y = ax^2$, where a is a nonzero constant.

E X A M P L E   4

Graph $y = 2x^2$.

Solution

Again, let's use a table to make some comparisons of y values.

x	$y = x^2$	$y = 2x^2$
0	0	0
1	1	2
2	4	8
−1	1	2
−2	4	8

Obviously, the y values for $y = 2x^2$ are *twice* the corresponding y values for $y = x^2$. Thus the parabola associated with $y = 2x^2$ has the same vertex (the origin) as the graph of $y = x^2$, but it is narrower (Figure 8.6).

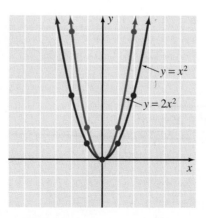

Figure 8.6

E X A M P L E   5   Graph $y = \frac{1}{2}x^2$.

Solution

The following table indicates some comparisons of y values.

x	$y = x^2$	$y = \frac{1}{2}x^2$
0	0	0
1	1	$\frac{1}{2}$
2	4	2
−1	1	$\frac{1}{2}$
−2	4	2

The y values for $y = \frac{1}{2}x^2$ are one half of the corresponding y values for $y = x^2$. Therefore, the graph of $y = \frac{1}{2}x^2$ has the same vertex (the origin) as the graph of $y = x^2$, but it is wider (Figure 8.7).

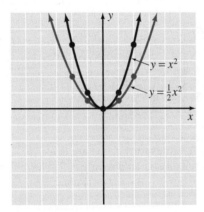

Figure 8.7   ∎

E X A M P L E   6   Graph $y = -x^2$.

Solution

x	$y = x^2$	$y = -x^2$
0	0	0
1	1	−1
2	4	−4
−1	1	−1
−2	4	−4

The y values for $y = -x^2$ are the opposites of the corresponding y values for $y = x^2$. Thus the graph of $y = -x^2$ has the same vertex (the origin) as the graph of $y = x^2$, but it is a reflection across the x axis of the basic parabola (Figure 8.8).

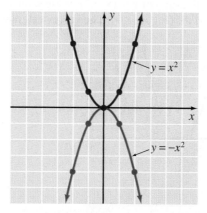

Figure 8.8   ■

> In general, the graph of a quadratic equation of the form $y = ax^2$ has its vertex at the origin and opens upward if a is positive and downward if a is negative. The parabola is narrower than the basic parabola if $|a| > 1$ and wider if $|a| < 1$.

Let's continue our investigation of quadratic equations by considering those of the form $y = (x - h)^2$, where h is a nonzero constant.

EXAMPLE 7   Graph $y = (x - 2)^2$.

Solution

A fairly extensive table of values reveals a pattern.

x	$y = x^2$	$y = (x - 2)^2$
-2	4	16
-1	1	9
0	0	4
1	1	1
2	4	0
3	9	1
4	16	4
5	25	9

Note that $y = (x - 2)^2$ and $y = x^2$ take on the same y values, but for different values of x. More specifically, if $y = x^2$ achieves a certain y value at x equals a constant, then $y = (x - 2)^2$ achieves the same y value at x equals the *constant plus two*. In other words, the graph of $y = (x - 2)^2$ is the same as the graph of $y = x^2$ but moved 2 units to the right (Figure 8.9). The vertex will move from $(0, 0)$ to $(2, 0)$.

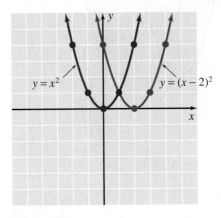

Figure 8.9   ◼

EXAMPLE 8   Graph $y = (x + 3)^2$.

Solution

x	$y = x^2$	$y = (x + 3)^2$
-3	9	0
-2	4	1
-1	1	4
0	0	9
1	1	16
2	4	25
3	9	36

If $y = x^2$ achieves a certain y value at x equals a constant, then $y = (x + 3)^2$ achieves that same y value at x equals that *constant minus three*. Therefore, the graph of $y = (x + 3)^2$ is the same as the graph of $y = x^2$ but moved 3 units to the left (Figure 8.10). The vertex will move from $(0, 0)$ to $(-3, 0)$.

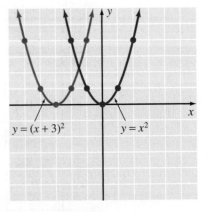

Figure 8.10   ◼

In general, the graph of a quadratic equation of the form $y = (x - h)^2$ is the same as the graph of $y = x^2$ but moved to the right h units if h is positive or moved to the left $|h|$ units if h is negative.

$y = (x - 4)^2$ → Moved to the right 4 units

$y = (x + 2)^2 = (x - (-2))^2$ → Moved to the left 2 units

The following diagram summarizes our work with graphing quadratic equations.

$y = x^2 + \boxed{k}$ → Moves the parabola up or down

$y = x^2$ ⟶ $y = \boxed{a}x^2$ → Affects the width and which way the parabola opens

Basic parabola $y = (x - \boxed{h})^2$ → Moves the parabola right or left

Equations of the form $y = x^2 + k$ and $y = ax^2$ are symmetric about the y axis. The next two examples of this section show how we can combine these ideas to graph a quadratic equation of the form $y = a(x - h)^2 + k$.

EXAMPLE 9

Graph $y = 2(x - 3)^2 + 1$.

Solution

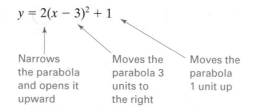

$y = 2(x - 3)^2 + 1$

| Narrows the parabola and opens it upward | Moves the parabola 3 units to the right | Moves the parabola 1 unit up |

The vertex will be located at the point $(3, 1)$. In addition to the vertex, two points are located to determine the parabola. The parabola is drawn in Figure 8.11.

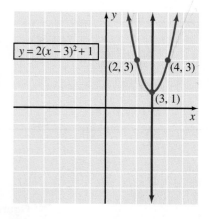

$y = 2(x - 3)^2 + 1$

$(2, 3)$ $(4, 3)$

$(3, 1)$

Figure 8.11

EXAMPLE 10

Graph $y = -\dfrac{1}{2}(x + 1)^2 - 2$.

Solution

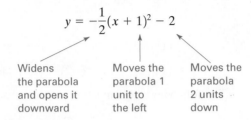

$$y = -\frac{1}{2}(x + 1)^2 - 2$$

Widens the parabola and opens it downward

Moves the parabola 1 unit to the left

Moves the parabola 2 units down

The parabola is drawn in Figure 8.12.

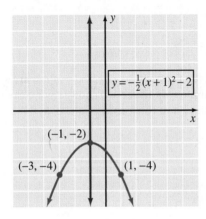

$y = -\frac{1}{2}(x+1)^2 - 2$

$(-1, -2)$

$(-3, -4)$ $(1, -4)$

Figure 8.12

Finally, we can use a graphing utility to demonstrate some of the ideas of this section. Let's graph $y = x^2$, $y = -3(x - 7)^2 - 1$, $y = 2(x + 9)^2 + 5$, and $y = -0.2(x + 8)^2 - 3.5$ on the same set of axes, as shown in Figure 8.13. Certainly, Figure 8.13 is consistent with the ideas we presented in this section.

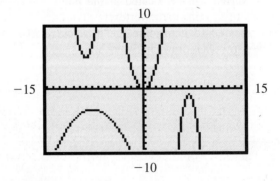

Figure 8.13

Problem Set 8.1

For Problems 1–30, graph each parabola.

1. $y = x^2 + 2$

2. $y = x^2 + 3$

3. $y = x^2 - 1$

4. $y = x^2 - 5$

5. $y = 4x^2$

6. $y = 3x^2$

7. $y = -3x^2$

8. $y = -4x^2$

9. $y = \frac{1}{3}x^2$

10. $y = \frac{1}{4}x^2$

11. $y = -\frac{1}{2}x^2$

12. $y = -\frac{2}{3}x^2$

13. $y = (x - 1)^2$

14. $y = (x - 3)^2$

15. $y = (x + 4)^2$

16. $y = (x + 2)^2$

17. $y = 3x^2 + 2$

18. $y = 2x^2 + 3$

19. $y = -2x^2 - 2$

20. $y = \frac{1}{2}x^2 - 2$

21. $y = (x - 1)^2 - 2$

22. $y = (x - 2)^2 + 3$

23. $y = (x + 2)^2 + 1$

24. $y = (x + 1)^2 - 4$

25. $y = 3(x - 2)^2 - 4$

26. $y = 2(x + 3)^2 - 1$

27. $y = -(x + 4)^2 + 1$

28. $y = -(x - 1)^2 + 1$

29. $y = -\frac{1}{2}(x + 1)^2 - 2$

30. $y = -3(x - 4)^2 - 2$

■ ■ ■ THOUGHTS INTO WORDS

31. Write a few paragraphs that summarize the ideas we presented in this section for someone who was absent from class that day.

32. How would you convince someone that $y = (x + 3)^2$ is the basic parabola moved 3 units to the left but that $y = (x - 3)^2$ is the basic parabola moved 3 units to the right?

33. How does the graph of $-y = x^2$ compare to the graph of $y = x^2$? Explain your answer.

34. How does the graph of $y = 4x^2$ compare to the graph of $y = 2x^2$? Explain your answer.

GRAPHING CALCULATOR ACTIVITIES

35. Use a graphing calculator to check your graphs for Problems 21–30.

36. (a) Graph $y = x^2$, $y = 2x^2$, $y = 3x^2$, and $y = 4x^2$ on the same set of axes.

(b) Graph $y = x^2$, $y = \frac{3}{4}x^2$, $y = \frac{1}{2}x^2$, and $y = \frac{1}{5}x^2$ on the same set of axes.

(c) Graph $y = x^2$, $y = -x^2$, $y = -3x^2$, and $y = -\frac{1}{4}x^2$ on the same set of axes.

37. (a) Graph $y = x^2$, $y = (x - 2)^2$, $y = (x - 3)^2$, and $y = (x - 5)^2$ on the same set of axes.

(b) Graph $y = x^2$, $y = (x + 1)^2$, $y = (x + 3)^2$, and $y = (x + 6)^2$ on the same set of axes.

38. (a) Graph $y = x^2$, $y = (x - 2)^2 + 3$, $y = (x + 4)^2 - 2$, and $y = (x - 6)^2 - 4$ on the same set of axes.

(b) Graph $y = x^2$, $y = 2(x + 1)^2 + 4$, $y = 3(x - 1)^2 - 3$, and $y = \frac{1}{2}(x - 5)^2 + 2$ on the same set of axes.

(c) Graph $y = x^2$, $y = -(x - 4)^2 - 3$, $y = -2(x + 3)^2 - 1$, and $y = -\frac{1}{2}(x - 2)^2 + 6$ on the same set of axes.

39. (a) Graph $y = x^2 - 12x + 41$ and $y = x^2 + 12x + 41$ on the same set of axes. What relationship seems to exist between the two graphs?

(b) Graph $y = x^2 - 8x + 22$ and $y = -x^2 + 8x - 22$ on the same set of axes. What relationship seems to exist between the two graphs?

(c) Graph $y = x^2 + 10x + 29$ and $y = -x^2 + 10x - 29$ on the same set of axes. What relationship seems to exist between the two graphs?

(d) Summarize your findings for parts (a) through (c).

8.2 More Parabolas and Some Circles

We are now ready to graph quadratic equations of the form $y = ax^2 + bx + c$, where a, b, and c are real numbers, and $a \neq 0$. The general approach is one of changing equations of the form $y = ax^2 + bx + c$ to the form $y = a(x - h)^2 + k$. Then we can proceed to graph them as we did in the previous section. The process of *completing the square* is used to make the necessary change in the form of the equations. Let's consider some examples to illustrate the details.

E X A M P L E 1

Graph $y = x^2 + 6x + 8$.

Solution

$$y = x^2 + 6x + 8$$

$$y = (x^2 + 6x + \_\_) - (\_\_) + 8$$

$$y = (x^2 + 6x + 9) - (9) + 8$$

$$y = (x + 3)^2 - 1$$

Complete the square.

$\dfrac{1}{2}(6) = 3$ and $3^2 = 9$. Add 9 and also subtract 9 to compensate for the 9 that was added.

The graph of $y = (x + 3)^2 - 1$ is the basic parabola moved 3 units to the left and 1 unit down (Figure 8.14).

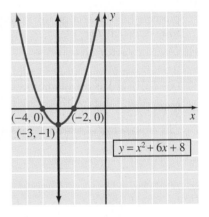

Figure 8.14 ∎

E X A M P L E 2

Graph $y = x^2 - 3x - 1$.

Solution

$$y = x^2 - 3x - 1$$

$$y = (x^2 - 3x + \_\_) - (\_\_) - 1$$

Complete the square.

$$y = \left(x^2 - 3x + \frac{9}{4}\right) - \frac{9}{4} - 1$$

Add and

$$y = \left(x - \frac{3}{2}\right)^2 - \frac{13}{4}$$

subtract $\dfrac{9}{4}$.

The graph of $y = \left(x - \dfrac{3}{2}\right)^2 - \dfrac{13}{4}$ is the basic parabola moved $1\dfrac{1}{2}$ units to the right and $3\dfrac{1}{4}$ units down (Figure 8.15).

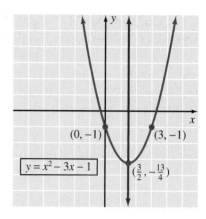

$(0, -1)$ $(3, -1)$

$y = x^2 - 3x - 1$ $\left(\frac{3}{2}, -\frac{13}{4}\right)$

Figure 8.15 ■

If the coefficient of x^2 is not 1, then a slight adjustment has to be made before we apply the process of completing the square. The next two examples illustrate this situation.

EXAMPLE 3

Graph $y = 2x^2 + 8x + 9$.

Solution

$$y = 2x^2 + 8x + 9$$

$$y = 2(x^2 + 4x) + 9 \qquad \text{Factor a 2 from the } x\text{-variable terms.}$$

$$y = 2(x^2 + 4x + \underline{\quad}) - (2)(\underline{\quad}) + 9 \qquad \text{Complete the square. Note that the number being subtracted will be multiplied by a factor of 2.}$$

$$y = 2(x^2 + 4x + 4) - 2(4) + 9 \qquad \tfrac{1}{2}(4) = 2, \text{ and } 2^2 = 4$$

$$y = 2(x^2 + 4x + 4) - 8 + 9$$

$$y = 2(x + 2)^2 + 1$$

See Figure 8.16 for the graph of $y = 2(x + 2)^2 + 1$.

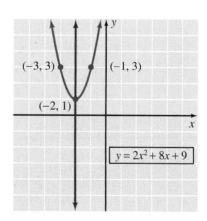

$(-3, 3)$ $(-1, 3)$

$(-2, 1)$

$y = 2x^2 + 8x + 9$

Figure 8.16 ■

E X A M P L E   4   Graph $y = -3x^2 + 6x - 5$.

Solution

$$y = -3x^2 + 6x - 5$$

$$y = -3(x^2 - 2x) - 5 \qquad \text{Factor } -3 \text{ from the } x\text{-variable terms.}$$

$$y = -3(x^2 - 2x + \underline{\quad}) - (-3)(\underline{\quad}) - 5 \qquad \text{Complete the square. Note that the number being subtracted will be multiplied by a factor of } -3.$$

$$y = -3(x^2 - 2x + 1) - (-3)(1) - 5 \qquad \frac{1}{2}(-2) = -1 \text{ and } (-1)^2 = 1$$

$$y = -3(x^2 - 2x + 1) + 3 - 5$$

$$y = -3(x - 1)^2 - 2$$

The graph of $y = -3(x - 1)^2 - 2$ is shown in Figure 8.17.

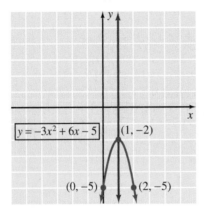

Figure 8.17   ■

■ Circles

The distance formula, $d = \sqrt{(x_2 - x_1)^2 + (y_2 - y_1)^2}$ (developed in Section 7.4), when it applies to the definition of a circle produces what is known as the **standard equation of a circle**. We start with a precise definition of a circle.

Definition 8.1

> A **circle** is the set of all points in a plane equidistant from a given fixed point called the **center**. A line segment determined by the center and any point on the circle is called a **radius**.

Let's consider a circle that has a radius of length r and a center at (h, k) on a coordinate system (Figure 8.18).

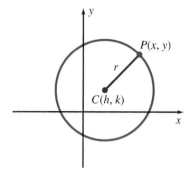

By using the distance formula, we can express the length of a radius (denoted by r) for any point $P(x, y)$ on the circle, as

$$r = \sqrt{(x - h)^2 + (y - k)^2}$$

Figure 8.18

Thus squaring both sides of the equation, we obtain the **standard form of the equation of a circle**:

$$(x - h)^2 + (y - k)^2 = r^2$$

We can use the standard form of the equation of a circle to solve two basic kinds of circle problems:

1. Given the coordinates of the center and the length of a radius of a circle, find its equation.

2. Given the equation of a circle, find its center and the length of a radius.

Let's look at some examples of such problems.

EXAMPLE 5

Write the equation of a circle that has its center at $(3, -5)$ and a radius of length 6 units.

Solution

Let's substitute 3 for h, -5 for k, and 6 for r into the standard form $(x - h)^2 + (y - k)^2 = r^2$ that becomes $(x - 3)^2 + (y + 5)^2 = 6^2$, which we can simplify as follows:

$$(x - 3)^2 + (y + 5)^2 = 6^2$$
$$x^2 - 6x + 9 + y^2 + 10y + 25 = 36$$
$$x^2 + y^2 - 6x + 10y - 2 = 0$$

$\blacksquare$

Note in Example 5 that we simplified the equation to the form $x^2 + y^2 + Dx + Ey + F = 0$, where D, E, and F are integers. This is another form that we commonly use when working with circles.

EXAMPLE 6

Graph $x^2 + y^2 + 4x - 6y + 9 = 0$.

Solution

This equation is of the form $x^2 + y^2 + Dx + Ey + F = 0$, so its graph is a circle. We can change the given equation into the form $(x - h)^2 + (y - k)^2 = r^2$ by completing the square on x and on y as follows:

$$x^2 + y^2 + 4x - 6y + 9 = 0$$

$$(x^2 + 4x + \underline{\quad}) + (y^2 - 6y + \underline{\quad}) = -9$$

$$(x^2 + 4x + 4) + (y^2 - 6y + 9) = -9 + 4 + 9$$

| Added 4 to complete the square on x | Added 9 to complete the square on y | Added 4 and 9 to compensate for the 4 and 9 added on the left side |

$$(x + 2)^2 + (y - 3)^2 = 4$$

$$(x - (-2))^2 + (y - 3)^2 = 2^2$$

$h \qquad k \qquad r$

The center of the circle is at $(-2, 3)$ and the length of a radius is 2 (Figure 8.19).

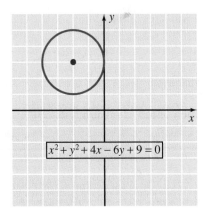

$x^2 + y^2 + 4x - 6y + 9 = 0$

Figure 8.19 ∎

As demonstrated by Examples 5 and 6, both forms, $(x - h)^2 + (y - k)^2 = r^2$ and $x^2 + y^2 + Dx + Ey + F = 0$, play an important role when we are solving problems that deal with circles.

Finally, we need to recognize that the standard form of a circle that has its center at the origin is $x^2 + y^2 = r^2$. This is merely the result of letting $h = 0$ and $k = 0$ in the general standard form.

$$(x - h)^2 + (y - k)^2 = r^2$$
$$(x - 0)^2 + (y - 0)^2 = r^2$$
$$x^2 + y^2 = r^2$$

Thus by inspection we can recognize that $x^2 + y^2 = 9$ is a circle with its center at the origin; the length of a radius is 3 units. Likewise, the equation of a circle that has its center at the origin and a radius of length 6 units is $x^2 + y^2 = 36$.

When using a graphing utility to graph a circle, we need to solve the equation for y in terms of x. This will produce two equations that can be graphed on the same set of axes. Furthermore, as with any graph, it may be necessary to change the boundaries on x or y (or both) to obtain a complete graph. If the circle appears oblong, you may want to use a zoom square option so that the graph will appear as a circle. Let's consider an example.

E X A M P L E   7

Use a graphing utility to graph $x^2 - 40x + y^2 + 351 = 0$.

Solution

First, we need to solve for y in terms of x.

$$x^2 - 40x + y^2 + 351 = 0$$
$$y^2 = -x^2 + 40x - 351$$
$$y = \pm\sqrt{-x^2 + 40x - 351}$$

Now we can make the following assignments.

$$Y_1 = \sqrt{-x^2 + 40x - 351}$$
$$Y_2 = -Y_1$$

(Note that we assigned Y_2 in terms of Y_1. By doing this we avoid repetitive key strokes and thus reduce the chance for errors. You may need to consult your user's manual for instructions on how to keystroke $-Y_1$.) Figure 8.20 shows the graph.

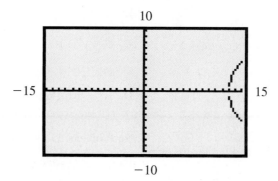

Figure 8.20

Because we know from the original equation that this graph should be a circle, we need to make some adjustments on the boundaries in order to get a complete graph. This can be done by completing the square on the original equation to change its form to $(x - 20)^2 + y^2 = 49$ or simply by a trial-and-error process. By changing the boundaries on x such that $-15 \le x \le 30$, we obtain Figure 8.21.

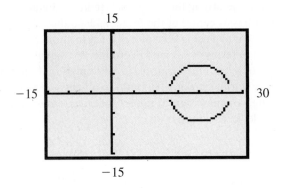

Figure 8.21

Problem Set 8.2

For Problems 1–22, graph each parabola.

1. $y = x^2 - 6x + 13$

2. $y = x^2 - 4x + 7$

3. $y = x^2 + 2x + 6$

4. $y = x^2 + 8x + 14$

5. $y = x^2 - 5x + 3$

6. $y = x^2 + 3x + 1$

7. $y = x^2 + 7x + 14$

8. $y = x^2 - x - 1$

9. $y = 3x^2 - 6x + 5$

10. $y = 2x^2 + 4x + 7$

11. $y = 4x^2 - 24x + 32$

12. $y = 3x^2 + 24x + 49$

13. $y = -2x^2 - 4x - 5$

14. $y = -2x^2 + 8x - 5$

15. $y = -x^2 + 8x - 21$

16. $y = -x^2 - 6x - 7$

17. $y = 2x^2 - x + 2$

18. $y = 2x^2 + 3x + 1$

19. $y = 3x^2 + 2x + 1$

20. $y = 3x^2 - x - 1$

21. $y = -3x^2 - 7x - 2$

22. $y = -2x^2 + x - 2$

For Problems 23–34, find the center and the length of a radius of each circle.

23. $x^2 + y^2 - 2x - 6y - 6 = 0$

24. $x^2 + y^2 + 4x - 12y + 39 = 0$

25. $x^2 + y^2 + 6x + 10y + 18 = 0$

26. $x^2 + y^2 - 10x + 2y + 1 = 0$

27. $x^2 + y^2 = 10$

28. $x^2 + y^2 + 4x + 14y + 50 = 0$

29. $x^2 + y^2 - 16x + 6y + 71 = 0$

30. $x^2 + y^2 = 12$

31. $x^2 + y^2 + 6x - 8y = 0$

32. $x^2 + y^2 - 16x + 30y = 0$

33. $4x^2 + 4y^2 + 4x - 32y + 33 = 0$

34. $9x^2 + 9y^2 - 6x - 12y - 40 = 0$

For Problems 35–44, graph each circle.

35. $x^2 + y^2 = 25$

36. $x^2 + y^2 = 36$

37. $(x - 1)^2 + (y + 2)^2 = 9$

38. $(x + 3)^2 + (y - 2)^2 = 1$

39. $x^2 + y^2 + 6x - 2y + 6 = 0$

40. $x^2 + y^2 - 4x - 6y - 12 = 0$

41. $x^2 + y^2 + 4y - 5 = 0$

42. $x^2 + y^2 - 4x + 3 = 0$

43. $x^2 + y^2 + 4x + 4y - 8 = 0$

44. $x^2 + y^2 - 6x + 6y + 2 = 0$

For Problems 45–54, write the equation of each circle. Express the final equation in the form $x^2 + y^2 + Dx + Ey + F = 0$.

45. Center at $(3, 5)$ and $r = 5$

46. Center at $(2, 6)$ and $r = 7$

47. Center at $(-4, 1)$ and $r = 8$

48. Center at $(-3, 7)$ and $r = 6$

49. Center at $(-2, -6)$ and $r = 3\sqrt{2}$

50. Center at $(-4, -5)$ and $r = 2\sqrt{3}$

51. Center at $(0, 0)$ and $r = 2\sqrt{5}$

52. Center at $(0, 0)$ and $r = \sqrt{7}$

53. Center at $(5, -8)$ and $r = 4\sqrt{6}$

54. Center at $(4, -10)$ and $r = 8\sqrt{2}$

55. Find the equation of the circle that passes through the origin and has its center at $(0, 4)$.

56. Find the equation of the circle that passes through the origin and has its center at $(-6, 0)$.

57. Find the equation of the circle that passes through the origin and has its center at $(-4, 3)$.

58. Find the equation of the circle that passes through the origin and has its center at $(8, -15)$.

■ ■ ■ THOUGHTS INTO WORDS

59. What is the graph of $x^2 + y^2 = -4$? Explain your answer.

60. On which axis does the center of the circle $x^2 + y^2 - 8y + 7 = 0$ lie? Defend your answer.

61. Give a step-by-step description of how you would help someone graph the parabola $y = 2x^2 - 12x + 9$.

■ ■ ■ FURTHER INVESTIGATIONS

62. The points (x, y) and (y, x) are mirror images of each other across the line $y = x$. Therefore, by interchanging

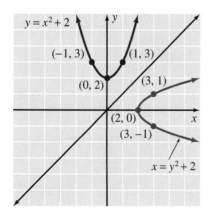

Figure 8.22

x and y in the equation $y = ax^2 + bx + c$, we obtain the equation of its mirror image across the line $y = x$—namely, $x = ay^2 + by + c$. Thus to graph $x = y^2 + 2$, we can first graph $y = x^2 + 2$ and then reflect it across the line $y = x$, as indicated in Figure 8.22.

Graph each of the following parabolas.
(a) $x = y^2$ **(b)** $x = -y^2$
(c) $x = y^2 - 1$ **(d)** $x = -y^2 + 3$
(e) $x = -2y^2$ **(f)** $x = 3y^2$
(g) $x = y^2 + 4y + 7$ **(h)** $x = y^2 - 2y - 3$

63. By expanding $(x - h)^2 + (y - k)^2 = r^2$, we obtain $x^2 - 2hx + h^2 + y^2 - 2ky + k^2 - r^2 = 0$. When we compare this result to the form $x^2 + y^2 + Dx + Ey + F = 0$, we see that $D = -2h$, $E = -2k$, and $F = h^2 + k^2 - r^2$. Therefore, the center and length of a radius of a circle can be found by using $h = \dfrac{D}{-2}$, $k = \dfrac{E}{-2}$, and

$r = \sqrt{h^2 + k^2 - F}$. Use these relationships to find the center and the length of a radius of each of the following circles.

(a) $x^2 + y^2 - 2x - 8y + 8 = 0$

(b) $x^2 + y^2 + 4x - 14y + 49 = 0$

(c) $x^2 + y^2 + 12x + 8y - 12 = 0$

(d) $x^2 + y^2 - 16x + 20y + 115 = 0$

(e) $x^2 + y^2 - 12y - 45 = 0$

(f) $x^2 + y^2 + 14x = 0$

GRAPHING CALCULATOR ACTIVITIES

64. Use a graphing calculator to check your graphs for Problems 1–22.

65. Use a graphing calculator to graph the circles in Problems 23–26. Be sure that your graphs are consistent with the center and the length of a radius that you found when you did the problems.

66. Graph each of the following parabolas and circles. Be sure to set your boundaries so that you get a complete graph.

(a) $x^2 + 24x + y^2 + 135 = 0$

(b) $y = x^2 - 4x + 18$

(c) $x^2 + y^2 - 18y + 56 = 0$

(d) $x^2 + y^2 + 24x + 28y + 336 = 0$

(e) $y = -3x^2 - 24x - 58$

(f) $y = x^2 - 10x + 3$

8.3 Graphing Ellipses

In the previous section, we found that the graph of the equation $x^2 + y^2 = 36$ is a circle of radius 6 units with its center at the origin. More generally, it is true that any equation of the form $Ax^2 + By^2 = C$, where $A = B$ and where A, B, and C are nonzero constants that have the same sign, is a circle with the center at the origin. For example, $3x^2 + 3y^2 = 12$ is equivalent to $x^2 + y^2 = 4$ (divide both sides of the given equation by 3), and thus it is a circle of radius 2 units with its center at the origin.

The general equation $Ax^2 + By^2 = C$ can be used to describe other geometric figures by changing the restrictions on A and B. For example, if A, B, and C are of the same sign, but $A \neq B$, then the graph of the equation $Ax^2 + By^2 = C$ is an **ellipse**. Let's consider two examples.

EXAMPLE 1

Graph $4x^2 + 25y^2 = 100$.

Solution

Let's find the x and y intercepts. Let $x = 0$; then

$$4(0)^2 + 25y^2 = 100$$

$$25y^2 = 100$$

$$y^2 = 4$$

$$y = \pm 2$$

Thus the points $(0, 2)$ and $(0, -2)$ are on the graph. Let $y = 0$; then

$$4x^2 + 25(0)^2 = 100$$

$$4x^2 = 100$$

$$x^2 = 25$$

$$x = \pm 5$$

Thus the points $(5, 0)$ and $(-5, 0)$ are also on the graph. We know that this figure is an ellipse, so we plot the four points and we get a pretty good sketch of the figure (Figure 8.23).

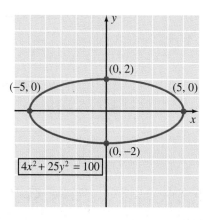

Figure 8.23 ■

In Figure 8.23, the line segment with endpoints at $(-5, 0)$ and $(5, 0)$ is called the **major axis** of the ellipse. The shorter line segment with endpoints at $(0, -2)$ and $(0, 2)$ is called the **minor axis**. Establishing the endpoints of the major and minor axes provides a basis for sketching an ellipse. The point of intersection of the major and minor axes is called the **center** of the ellipse.

E X A M P L E   2

Graph $9x^2 + 4y^2 = 36$.

Solution

Again, let's find the x and y intercepts. Let $x = 0$; then

$$9(0)^2 + 4y^2 = 36$$

$$4y^2 = 36$$

$$y^2 = 9$$

$$y = \pm 3$$

Thus the points $(0, 3)$ and $(0, -3)$ are on the graph. Let $y = 0$; then

$$9x^2 + 4(0)^2 = 36$$

$$9x^2 = 36$$

$$x^2 = 4$$

$$x = \pm 2$$

Thus the points $(2, 0)$ and $(-2, 0)$ are also on the graph. The ellipse is sketched in Figure 8.24.

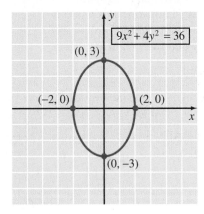

Figure 8.24 ■

In Figure 8.24, the major axis has endpoints at $(0, -3)$ and $(0, 3)$, and the minor axis has endpoints at $(-2, 0)$ and $(2, 0)$. The ellipses in Figures 8.23 and 8.24 are symmetric about the x axis and about the y axis. In other words, both the x axis and the y axis serve as **axes of symmetry**.

Now we turn to some ellipses whose centers are not at the origin but whose major and minor axes are parallel to the x axis and the y axis. We can graph such ellipses in much the same way that we handled circles in Section 8.2. Let's consider two examples to illustrate the procedure.

EXAMPLE 3

Graph $4x^2 + 24x + 9y^2 - 36y + 36 = 0$.

Solution

Let's complete the square on x and y as follows:

$$4x^2 + 24x + 9y^2 - 36y + 36 = 0$$

$$4(x^2 + 6x + \underline{\quad}) + 9(y^2 - 4y + \underline{\quad}) = -36$$

$$4(x^2 + 6x + 9) + 9(y^2 - 4y + 4) = -36 + 36 + 36$$

$$4(x + 3)^2 + 9(y - 2)^2 = 36$$

$$4(x - (-3))^2 + 9(y - 2)^2 = 36$$

Because 4, 9, and 36 are of the same sign and $4 \neq 9$, the graph is an ellipse. The center of the ellipse is at $(-3, 2)$. We can find the endpoints of the major and minor axes as follows: Use the equation $4(x + 3)^2 + 9(y - 2)^2 = 36$ and let $y = 2$ (the y coordinate of the center).

$$4(x + 3)^2 + 9(2 - 2)^2 = 36$$

$$4(x + 3)^2 = 36$$

$$(x + 3)^2 = 9$$

$$x + 3 = \pm 3$$

$$x + 3 = 3 \quad \text{or} \quad x + 3 = -3$$

$$x = 0 \quad \text{or} \quad x = -6$$

This gives the points $(0, 2)$ and $(-6, 2)$. These are the coordinates of the endpoints of the major axis. Now let $x = -3$ (the x coordinate of the center).

$$4(-3 + 3)^2 + 9(y - 2)^2 = 36$$

$$9(y - 2)^2 = 36$$

$$(y - 2)^2 = 4$$

$$y - 2 = \pm 2$$

$$y - 2 = 2 \quad \text{or} \quad y - 2 = -2$$

$$y = 4 \quad \text{or} \quad y = 0$$

This gives the points $(-3, 4)$ and $(-3, 0)$. These are the coordinates of the endpoints of the minor axis. The ellipse is shown in Figure 8.25.

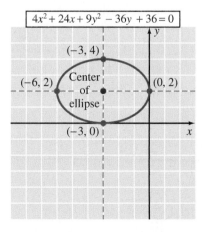

Figure 8.25

EXAMPLE 4

Graph $4x^2 - 16x + y^2 + 6y + 9 = 0$.

Solution

First let's complete the square on x and on y.

$$4x^2 - 16x + y^2 + 6y + 9 = 0$$
$$4(x^2 - 4x + \underline{\ \ }) + (y^2 + 6y + \underline{\ \ }) = -9$$
$$4(x^2 - 4x + 4) + (y^2 + 6y + 9) = -9 + 16 + 9$$
$$4(x - 2)^2 + (y + 3)^2 = 16$$

The center of the ellipse is at $(2, -3)$. Now let $x = 2$ (the x coordinate of the center).

$$4(2 - 2)^2 + (y + 3)^2 = 16$$
$$(y + 3)^2 = 16$$
$$y + 3 = \pm 4$$

$$y + 3 = -4 \quad \text{or} \quad y + 3 = 4$$
$$y = -7 \quad \text{or} \quad y = 1$$

This gives the points $(2, -7)$ and $(2, 1)$. These are the coordinates of the endpoints of the major axis. Now let $y = -3$ (the y coordinate of the center).

$$4(x - 2)^2 + (-3 + 3)^2 = 16$$
$$4(x - 2)^2 = 16$$
$$(x - 2)^2 = 4$$
$$x - 2 = \pm 2$$

$$x - 2 = -2 \quad \text{or} \quad x - 2 = 2$$
$$x = 0 \quad \text{or} \quad x = 4$$

This gives the points $(0, -3)$ and $(4, -3)$. These are the coordinates of the endpoints of the minor axis. The ellipse is shown in Figure 8.26.

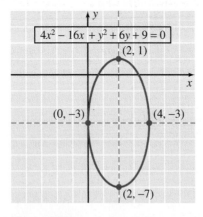

Figure 8.26

Problem Set 8.3

For Problems 1–16, graph each ellipse.

1. $x^2 + 4y^2 = 36$

2. $x^2 + 4y^2 = 16$

3. $9x^2 + y^2 = 36$

4. $16x^2 + 9y^2 = 144$

5. $4x^2 + 3y^2 = 12$

6. $5x^2 + 4y^2 = 20$

7. $16x^2 + y^2 = 16$

8. $9x^2 + 2y^2 = 18$

9. $25x^2 + 2y^2 = 50$

10. $12x^2 + y^2 = 36$

11. $4x^2 + 8x + 16y^2 - 64y + 4 = 0$

12. $9x^2 - 36x + 4y^2 - 24y + 36 = 0$

13. $x^2 + 8x + 9y^2 + 36y + 16 = 0$

14. $4x^2 - 24x + y^2 + 4y + 24 = 0$

15. $4x^2 + 9y^2 - 54y + 45 = 0$

16. $x^2 + 2x + 4y^2 - 15 = 0$

■ ■ ■ THOUGHTS INTO WORDS

17. Is the graph of $x^2 + y^2 = 4$ the same as the graph of $y^2 + x^2 = 4$? Explain your answer.

18. Is the graph of $x^2 + y^2 = 0$ a circle? If so, what is the length of a radius?

19. Is the graph of $4x^2 + 9y^2 = 36$ the same as the graph of $9x^2 + 4y^2 = 36$? Explain your answer.

20. What is the graph of $x^2 + 2y^2 = -16$? Explain your answer.

 ### GRAPHING CALCULATOR ACTIVITIES

21. Use a graphing calculator to graph the ellipses in Examples 1–4 of this section.

22. Use a graphing calculator to check your graphs for Problems 11–16.

8.4   Graphing Hyperbolas

The graph of an equation of the form $Ax^2 + By^2 = C$, where A, B, and C are nonzero real numbers and A and B are of unlike signs, is a **hyperbola**. Let's use some examples to illustrate a procedure for graphing hyperbolas.

E X A M P L E   1

Graph $x^2 - y^2 = 9$.

Solution

If we let $y = 0$, we obtain

$$x^2 - 0^2 = 0$$
$$x^2 = 9$$
$$x = \pm 3$$

Thus the points $(3, 0)$ and $(-3, 0)$ are on the graph. If we let $x = 0$, we obtain

$$0^2 - y^2 = 9$$

$$-y^2 = 9$$

$$y^2 = -9$$

Because $y^2 = -9$ has no real number solutions, there are no points of the y axis on this graph. That is, the graph does not intersect the y axis. Now let's solve the given equation for y so that we have a more convenient form for finding other solutions.

$$x^2 - y^2 = 9$$

$$-y^2 = 9 - x^2$$

$$y^2 = x^2 - 9$$

$$y = \pm\sqrt{x^2 - 9}$$

The radicand, $x^2 - 9$, must be nonnegative, so the values we choose for x must be greater than or equal to 3 or less than or equal to -3. With this in mind, we can form the following table of values.

x	y	
3	0	
-3	0	Intercepts
4	$\pm\sqrt{7}$	
-4	$\pm\sqrt{7}$	
5	± 4	Other points
-5	± 4	

We plot these points and draw the hyperbola as in Figure 8.27. (This graph is also symmetric about both axes.)

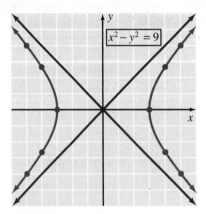

Figure 8.27

Note the blue lines in Figure 8.27; they are called **asymptotes**. Each branch of the hyperbola approaches one of these lines but does not intersect it. Therefore, the ability to sketch the asymptotes of a hyperbola is very helpful when we are graphing the hyperbola. Fortunately, the equations of the asymptotes are easy to determine. They can be found by replacing the constant term in the given equation of the hyperbola with 0 and solving for y. (The reason why this works will become evident in a later course.) Thus for the hyperbola in Example 3, we obtain

$$x^2 - y^2 = 0$$
$$y^2 = x^2$$
$$y = \pm x$$

Thus the two lines $y = x$ and $y = -x$ are the asymptotes indicated by the blue lines in Figure 8.27.

EXAMPLE 2

Graph $y^2 - 5x^2 = 4$.

Solution

If we let $x = 0$, we obtain

$$y^2 - 5(0)^2 = 4$$
$$y^2 = 4$$
$$y = \pm 2$$

The points $(0, 2)$ and $(0, -2)$ are on the graph. If we let $y = 0$, we obtain

$$0^2 - 5x^2 = 4$$
$$-5x^2 = 4$$
$$x^2 = -\frac{4}{5}$$

Because $x^2 = -\dfrac{4}{5}$ has no real number solutions, we know that this hyperbola does not intersect the x axis. Solving the given equation for y yields

$$y^2 - 5x^2 = 4$$
$$y^2 = 5x^2 + 4$$
$$y = \pm\sqrt{5x^2 + 4}$$

The table on the next page shows some additional solutions for the equation. The equations of the asymptotes are determined as follows:

$$y^2 - 5x^2 = 0$$
$$y^2 = 5x^2$$
$$y = \pm\sqrt{5}x$$

x	y	
0	2	Intercepts
0	−2	
1	±3	Other points
−1	±3	
2	±$\sqrt{24}$	
−2	±$\sqrt{24}$	

Sketch the asymptotes and plot the points determined by the table of values to determine the hyperbola in Figure 8.28. (Note that this hyperbola is also symmetric about the x axis and the y axis.)

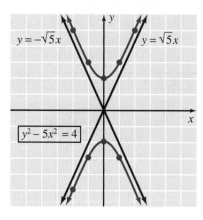

$y = -\sqrt{5}x$ $y = \sqrt{5}x$

$y^2 - 5x^2 = 4$

Figure 8.28   ∎

E X A M P L E   3

Graph $4x^2 - 9y^2 = 36$.

Solution

If we let $x = 0$, we obtain

$$4(0)^2 - 9y^2 = 36$$
$$-9y^2 = 36$$
$$y^2 = -4$$

Because $y^2 = -4$ has no real number solutions, we know that this hyperbola does not intersect the y axis. If we let $y = 0$, we obtain

$$4x^2 - 9(0)^2 = 36$$
$$4x^2 = 36$$
$$x^2 = 9$$
$$x = \pm 3$$

Thus the points $(3, 0)$ and $(-3, 0)$ are on the graph. Now let's solve the equation for y in terms of x and set up a table of values.

$$4x^2 - 9y^2 = 36$$
$$-9y^2 = 36 - 4x^2$$

$$9y^2 = 4x^2 - 36$$

$$y^2 = \frac{4x^2 - 36}{9}$$

$$y = \pm\frac{\sqrt{4x^2 - 36}}{3}$$

x	y	
3	0	Intercepts
−3	0	
4	$\pm\dfrac{2\sqrt{7}}{3}$	
−4	$\pm\dfrac{2\sqrt{7}}{3}$	Other points
5	$\pm\dfrac{8}{3}$	
−5	$\pm\dfrac{8}{3}$	

The equations of the asymptotes are found as follows:

$$4x^2 - 9y^2 = 0$$

$$-9y^2 = -4x^2$$

$$9y^2 = 4x^2$$

$$y^2 = \frac{4x^2}{9}$$

$$y = \pm\frac{2}{3}x$$

Sketch the asymptotes and plot the points determined by the table to determine the hyperbola as shown in Figure 8.29.

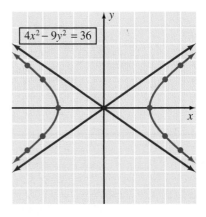

Figure 8.29   ■

Now let's consider hyperbolas that are not symmetric with respect to the origin but are symmetric with respect to lines parallel to one of the axes — that is, vertical and horizontal lines. Again, let's use examples to illustrate a procedure for graphing such hyperbolas.

E X A M P L E 4

Graph $4x^2 - 8x - y^2 - 4y - 16 = 0$.

Solution

Completing the square on x and y, we obtain

$$4x^2 - 8x - y^2 - 4y - 16 = 0$$
$$4(x^2 - 2x + \_\_) - (y^2 + 4y + \_\_) = 16$$
$$4(x^2 - 2x + 1) - (y^2 + 4y + 4) = 16 + 4 - 4$$
$$4(x - 1)^2 - (y + 2)^2 = 16$$
$$4(x - 1)^2 - 1(y - (-2))^2 = 16$$

Because 4 and -1 are of opposite signs, the graph is a hyperbola. The center of the hyperbola is at $(1, -2)$.

Now using the equation $4(x - 1)^2 - (y + 2)^2 = 16$, we can proceed as follows: Let $y = -2$; then

$$4(x - 1)^2 - (-2 + 2)^2 = 16$$
$$4(x - 1)^2 = 16$$
$$(x - 1)^2 = 4$$
$$x - 1 = \pm 2$$

$$x - 1 = 2 \quad \text{or} \quad x - 1 = -2$$
$$x = 3 \quad \text{or} \quad x = -1$$

Thus the hyperbola intersects the horizontal line $y = -2$ at $(3, -2)$ and at $(-1, -2)$. Let $x = 1$; then

$$4(1 - 1)^2 - (y + 2)^2 = 16$$
$$-(y + 2)^2 = 16$$
$$(y + 2)^2 = -16$$

Because $(y + 2)^2 = -16$ has no real number solutions, we know that the hyperbola does not intersect the vertical line $x = 1$. We replace the constant term of $4(x - 1)^2 - (y + 2)^2 = 16$ with 0 and solve for y to produce the equations of the asymptotes as follows:

$$4(x - 1)^2 - (y + 2)^2 = 0$$

The left side can be factored using the pattern of the difference of squares.

$$(2(x - 1) + (y + 2))(2(x - 1) - (y + 2)) = 0$$
$$(2x - 2 + y + 2)(2x - 2 - y - 2) = 0$$

$$(2x + y)(2x - y - 4) = 0$$

$$2x + y = 0 \quad \text{or} \quad 2x - y - 4 = 0$$

$$y = -2x \quad \text{or} \quad 2x - 4 = y$$

Thus the equations of the asymptotes are $y = -2x$ and $y = 2x - 4$. Sketching the asymptotes and plotting the two points $(3, -2)$ and $(-1, -2)$, we can draw the hyperbola as shown in Figure 8.30.

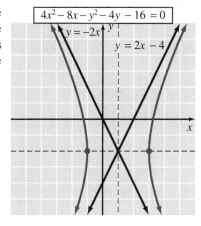

Figure 8.30

E X A M P L E   5

Graph $y^2 - 4y - 4x^2 - 24x - 36 = 0$.

Solution

First let's complete the square on x and on y.

$$y^2 - 4y - 4x^2 - 24x - 36 = 0$$

$$(y^2 - 4y + \underline{\ \ }) - 4(x^2 + 6x + \underline{\ \ }) = 36$$

$$(y^2 - 4y + 4) - 4(x^2 + 6x + 9) = 36 + 4 - 36$$

$$(y - 2)^2 - 4(x + 3)^2 = 4$$

The center of the hyperbola is at $(-3, 2)$. Now let $y = 2$.

$$(2 - 2)^2 - 4(x + 3)^2 = 4$$

$$-4(x + 3)^2 = 4$$

$$(x + 3)^2 = -1$$

Because $(x + 3)^2 = -1$ has no real number solutions, the graph does not intersect the line $y = 2$. Now let $x = -3$.

$$(y - 2)^2 - 4(-3 + 3)^2 = 4$$

$$(y - 2)^2 = 4$$

$$y - 2 = \pm 2$$

$$y - 2 = -2 \quad \text{or} \quad y - 2 = 2$$
$$y = 0 \quad \text{or} \quad y = 4$$

Therefore, the hyperbola intersects the line $x = -3$ at $(-3, 0)$ and $(-3, 4)$. Now, to find the equations of the asymptotes, let's replace the constant term of $(y - 2)^2 - 4(x + 3)^2 = 4$ with 0 and solve for y.

$$(y - 2)^2 - 4(x + 3)^2 = 0$$
$$[(y - 2) + 2(x + 3)][(y - 2) - 2(x + 3)] = 0$$
$$(y - 2 + 2x + 6)(y - 2 - 2x - 6) = 0$$
$$(y + 2x + 4)(y - 2x - 8) = 0$$
$$y + 2x + 4 = 0 \quad \text{or} \quad y - 2x - 8 = 0$$
$$y = -2x - 4 \quad \text{or} \quad y = 2x + 8$$

Therefore, the equations of the asymptotes are $y = -2x - 4$ and $y = 2x + 8$. Drawing the asymptotes and plotting the points $(-3, 0)$ and $(-3, 4)$, we can graph the hyperbola as shown in Figure 8.31.

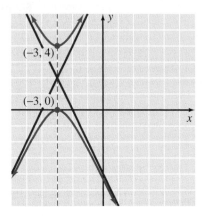

Figure 8.31

As a way of summarizing our work with conic sections, let's focus our attention on the continuity pattern used in this chapter. In Sections 8.1 and 8.2, we studied parabolas by considering variations of the basic quadratic equation $y = ax^2 + bx + c$. Also in Section 8.2, we used the definition of a circle to generate a standard form for the equation of a circle. Then, in Sections 8.3 and 8.4, we discussed ellipses and hyperbolas, not from a definition viewpoint, but by considering variations of the equations $Ax^2 + By^2 = C$ and $A(x - h)^2 + B(y - k)^2 = C$. In a subsequent mathematics course, parabolas, ellipses, and hyperbolas will be developed from a definition viewpoint. That is, first each concept will be defined, and then the definition will be used to generate a standard form of its equation.

Problem Set 8.4

For Problems 1–6, find the intercepts and the equations for the asymptotes.

1. $x^2 - 9y^2 = 16$

2. $16x^2 - y^2 = 25$

3. $y^2 - 9x^2 = 36$

4. $4x^2 - 9y^2 = 16$

5. $25x^2 - 9y^2 = 4$

6. $y^2 - x^2 = 16$

For Problems 7–10, find the equations for the asymptotes.

7. $x^2 + 4x - y^2 - 6y - 30 = 0$

8. $y^2 - 8y - x^2 - 4x + 3 = 0$

9. $9x^2 - 18x - 4y^2 - 24y - 63 = 0$

10. $4x^2 + 24x - y^2 + 4y + 28 = 0$

For Problems 11–28, graph each hyperbola.

11. $x^2 - y^2 = 1$

12. $x^2 - y^2 = 4$

13. $y^2 - 4x^2 = 9$

14. $4y^2 - x^2 = 16$

15. $5x^2 - 2y^2 = 20$

16. $9x^2 - 4y^2 = 9$

17. $y^2 - 16x^2 = 4$

18. $y^2 - 9x^2 = 16$

19. $-4x^2 + y^2 = -4$

20. $-9x^2 + y^2 = -36$

21. $25y^2 - 3x^2 = 75$

22. $16y^2 - 5x^2 = 80$

23. $-4x^2 + 32x + 9y^2 - 18y - 91 = 0$

24. $x^2 - 4x - y^2 + 6y - 14 = 0$

25. $-4x^2 + 24x + 16y^2 + 64y - 36 = 0$

26. $x^2 + 4x - 9y^2 + 54y - 113 = 0$

27. $4x^2 - 24x - 9y^2 = 0$

28. $16y^2 + 64y - x^2 = 0$

29. The graphs of equations of the form $xy = k$, where k is a nonzero constant, are also hyperbolas, sometimes referred to as rectangular hyperbolas. Graph each of the following.
   (a) $xy = 3$ (b) $xy = 5$
   (c) $xy = -2$ (d) $xy = -4$

30. What is the graph of $xy = 0$? Defend your answer.

31. We have graphed various equations of the form $Ax^2 + By^2 = C$, where C is a nonzero constant. Now graph each of the following.
   (a) $x^2 + y^2 = 0$ (b) $2x^2 + 3y^2 = 0$
   (c) $x^2 - y^2 = 0$ (d) $4y^2 - x^2 = 0$

■ ■ ■ THOUGHTS INTO WORDS

32. Explain the concept of an asymptote.

33. Explain how asymptotes can be used to help graph hyperbolas.

34. Are the graphs of $x^2 - y^2 = 0$ and $y^2 - x^2 = 0$ identical? Are the graphs of $x^2 - y^2 = 4$ and $y^2 - x^2 = 4$ identical? Explain your answers.

GRAPHING CALCULATOR ACTIVITIES

35. To graph the hyperbola in Example 1 of this section, we can make the following assignments for the graphing calculator.

$Y_1 = \sqrt{x^2 - 9}$ $Y_2 = -Y_1$

$Y_3 = x$ $Y_4 = -Y_3$

Do this and see if your graph agrees with Figure 8.27. Also graph the asymptotes and hyperbolas for Examples 2 and 3.

36. Use a graphing calculator to check your graphs for Problems 11–16.

37. Use a graphing calculator to check your graphs for Problems 23–28.

38. For each of the following equations, (1) predict the type and location of the graph, and (2) use your graphing calculator to check your predictions.

(a) $x^2 + y^2 = 100$

(b) $x^2 - y^2 = 100$

(c) $y^2 - x^2 = 100$

(d) $y = -x^2 + 9$

(e) $2x^2 + y^2 = 14$

(f) $x^2 + 2y^2 = 14$

(g) $x^2 + 2x + y^2 - 4 = 0$

(h) $x^2 + y^2 - 4y - 2 = 0$

(i) $y = x^2 + 16$

(j) $y^2 = x^2 + 16$

(k) $9x^2 - 4y^2 = 72$

(l) $4x^2 - 9y^2 = 72$

(m) $y^2 = -x^2 - 4x + 6$

(8.1) and **(8.2)** The graph of any quadratic equation of the form $y = ax^2 + bx + c$, where a, b, and c are real numbers and $a \neq 0$, is a **parabola**.

The following diagram summarizes the graphing of parabolas.

$$y = x^2 + \textcircled{k} \longrightarrow \text{Moves the parabola up or down}$$

$$y = x^2 \longrightarrow y = \textcircled{a}x^2 \longrightarrow \text{Affects the width and which way the parabola opens}$$

Basic parabola $\quad y = (x - \textcircled{h})^2 \longrightarrow \text{Moves the parabola right or left}$

The **standard form of the equation of a circle** with its center at (h, k) and a radius of length r is

$$(x - h)^2 + (y - k)^2 = r^2$$

The standard form of the equation of a circle with its center at the origin and a radius of length r is

$$x^2 + y^2 = r^2$$

(8.3) The graph of an equation of the form $Ax^2 + By^2 = C$ or of the form $A(x - h)^2 + B(y - k)^2 = C$, where A, B, and C are nonzero real numbers of the same sign and $A \neq B$, is an **ellipse**.

(8.4) The graph of an equation of the form $Ax^2 + By^2 = C$ or of the form $A(x - h)^2 + B(y - k)^2 = C$, where A, B, and C are nonzero real numbers with A and B of unlike signs, is a **hyperbola**.

The equations of the asymptotes of a hyperbola can be found by replacing the constant term of the equation of the hyperbola with zero and solving the resulting equation for y.

Circles, ellipses, parabolas, and hyperbolas are often referred to as **conic sections**.

Chapter 8   Review Problem Set

For Problems 1–6, find the vertex of each parabola.

1. $y = x^2 + 6$

2. $y = -x^2 - 8$

3. $y = (x + 3)^2 - 1$

4. $y = x^2 - 14x + 54$

5. $y = -x^2 + 12x - 44$

6. $y = 3x^2 + 24x + 39$

For Problems 7–9, write the equation of the circle satisfying the given conditions. Express your answers in the form $x^2 + y^2 + Dx + Ey + F = 0$.

7. Center at $(2, -6)$ and $r = 5$

8. Center at $(-4, -8)$ and $r = 2\sqrt{3}$

9. Center at $(0, 5)$ and passes through the origin.

For Problems 10–13, find the center and the length of a radius for each circle.

10. $x^2 + 14x + y^2 - 8y + 16 = 0$

11. $x^2 + 16x + y^2 + 39 = 0$

12. $x^2 - 12x + y^2 + 16y = 0$

13. $x^2 + y^2 = 24$

For Problems 14–19, find the length of the major axis and the length of the minor axis of each ellipse.

14. $16x^2 + y^2 = 64$

15. $16x^2 + 9y^2 = 144$

16. $4x^2 + 25y^2 = 100$

17. $2x^2 + 7y^2 = 28$

18. $x^2 - 4x + 9y^2 + 54y + 76 = 0$

19. $9x^2 + 72x + 4y^2 - 8y + 112 = 0$

For Problems 20–25, find the equations of the asymptotes of each hyperbola.

20. $x^2 - 9y^2 = 25$

21. $4x^2 - y^2 = 16$

22. $9y^2 - 25x^2 = 36$

23. $16y^2 - 4x^2 = 17$

24. $25x^2 + 100x - 4y^2 + 24y - 36 = 0$

25. $36y^2 - 288y - x^2 + 2x + 539 = 0$

For Problems 26 –39, graph each equation.

26. $9x^2 + y^2 = 81$

27. $9x^2 - y^2 = 81$

28. $y = -2x^2 + 3$

29. $y = 4x^2 - 16x + 19$

30. $x^2 + 4x + y^2 + 8y + 11 = 0$

31. $4x^2 - 8x + y^2 + 8y + 4 = 0$

32. $y^2 + 6y - 4x^2 - 24x - 63 = 0$

33. $y = -2x^2 - 4x - 3$

34. $x^2 - y^2 = -9$

35. $4x^2 + 16y^2 + 96y = 0$

36. $(x - 3)^2 + (y + 1)^2 = 4$

37. $(x + 1)^2 + (y - 2)^2 = 4$

38. $x^2 + y^2 - 6x - 2y + 4 = 0$

39. $x^2 + y^2 - 2y - 8 = 0$

For Problems 1–4, find the vertex of each parabola.

1. $y = -2x^2 + 9$ 2. $y = -x^2 + 2x + 6$

3. $y = 4x^2 + 32x + 62$ 4. $y = x^2 - 6x + 9$

For Problems 5–7, write the equation of the circle that satisfies the given conditions. Express your answers in the form $x^2 + y^2 + Dx + Ey + F = 0$.

5. Center at $(-4, 0)$ and $r = 3\sqrt{5}$

6. Center at $(2, 8)$ and $r = 3$

7. Center at $(-3, -4)$ and $r = 5$

For Problems 8–10, find the center and the length of a radius of each circle.

8. $x^2 + y^2 = 32$

9. $x^2 - 12x + y^2 + 8y + 3 = 0$

10. $x^2 + 10x + y^2 + 2y - 38 = 0$

11. Find the length of the major axis of the ellipse $9x^2 + 2y^2 = 32$.

12. Find the length of the minor axis of the ellipse $8x^2 + 3y^2 = 72$.

13. Find the length of the major axis of the ellipse $3x^2 - 12x + 5y^2 + 10y - 10 = 0$.

14. Find the length of the minor axis of the ellipse $8x^2 - 32x + 5y^2 + 30y + 45 = 0$.

For Problems 15–17, find the equations of the asymptotes for each hyperbola.

15. $y^2 - 16x^2 = 36$ 16. $25x^2 - 16y^2 = 50$

17. $x^2 - 2x - 25y^2 - 50y - 54 = 0$

For Problems 18–25, graph each equation.

18. $x^2 - 4y^2 = -16$ 19. $y = x^2 + 4x$

20. $x^2 + 2x + y^2 + 8y + 8 = 0$ 21. $2x^2 + 3y^2 = 12$

22. $y = 2x^2 + 12x + 22$ 23. $9x^2 - y^2 = 9$

24. $3x^2 - 12x + 5y^2 + 10y - 10 = 0$

25. $x^2 - 4x - y^2 + 4y - 9 = 0$

9

Functions

9.1 Relations and Functions

9.2 Functions: Their Graphs and Applications

9.3 Graphing Made Easy Via Transformations

9.4 Composition of Functions

9.5 Inverse Functions

9.6 Direct and Inverse Variations

The price of goods may be decided by using a function to describe the relationship between the price and the demand. Such a function gives us a means of studying the demand when the price is varied.

© Bill Aron /PhotoEdit

A golf pro-shop operator finds that she can sell 30 sets of golf clubs at \$500 per set in a year. Furthermore, she predicts that for each \$25 decrease in price, 3 additional sets of golf clubs could be sold. At what price should she sell the clubs to maximize gross income? We can use the quadratic function $f(x) = (30 + 3x)(500 - 25x)$ to determine that the clubs should be sold at \$375 per set.

One of the fundamental concepts of mathematics is the concept of a function. Functions are used to unify mathematics and also to apply mathematics to many real-world problems. Functions provide a means of studying quantities that vary with one another — that is, change in one quantity causes a corresponding change in the other.

In this chapter we will (1) introduce the basic ideas that pertain to the function concept, (2) review and extend some concepts from Chapter 8, and (3) discuss some applications of functions.

Mathematically, a function is a special kind of **relation**, so we will begin our discussion with a simple definition of a relation.

Definition 9.1

> A **relation** is a set of ordered pairs.

Thus a set of ordered pairs such as $\{(1, 2), (3, 7), (8, 14)\}$ is a relation. The set of all first components of the ordered pairs is the **domain** of the relation, and the set of all second components is the **range** of the relation. The relation $\{(1, 2), (3, 7), (8, 14)\}$ has a domain of $\{1, 3, 8\}$ and a range of $\{2, 7, 14\}$.

The ordered pairs we refer to in Definition 9.1 may be generated by various means, such as a graph or a chart. However, one of the most common ways of generating ordered pairs is by using equations. Because the solution set of an equation in two variables is a set of ordered pairs, such an equation describes a relation. Each of the following equations describes a relation between the variables x and y. We have listed some of the infinitely many ordered pairs (x, y) of each relation.

1. $x^2 + y^2 = 4$: $(1, \sqrt{3}), (1, -\sqrt{3}), (0, 2), (0, -2)$

2. $y^2 = x^3$: $(0, 0), (1, 1), (1, -1), (4, 8), (4, -8)$

3. $y = x + 2$: $(0, 2), (1, 3), (2, 4), (-1, 1), (5, 7)$

4. $y = \dfrac{1}{x - 1}$: $(0, -1), (2, 1), \left(3, \dfrac{1}{2}\right), \left(-1, -\dfrac{1}{2}\right), \left(-2, -\dfrac{1}{3}\right)$

5. $y = x^2$: $(0, 0), (1, 1), (2, 4), (-1, 1), (-2, 4)$

Now we direct your attention to the ordered pairs associated with equations 3, 4, and 5. Note that in each case, no two ordered pairs have the same first component. Such a set of ordered pairs is called a **function**.

Definition 9.2

> A **function** is a relation in which no two ordered pairs have the same first component.

Stated another way, Definition 9.2 means that a function is a relation wherein each member of the domain is assigned *one and only one* member of the range. Thus it is easy to determine that each of the following sets of ordered pairs is a function.

$$f = \{(x, y)|y = x + 2\}$$

$$g = \left\{(x, y)\middle| y = \frac{1}{x - 1}\right\}$$

$$h = \{(x, y)|y = x^2\}$$

In each case there is one and only one value of y (an element of the range) associated with each value of x (an element of the domain).

Note that we named the previous functions f, g, and h. It is customary to name functions by means of a single letter, and the letters f, g, and h are often used. We would suggest more meaningful choices when functions are used to portray real-world situations. For example, if a problem involves a profit function, then naming the function p or even P would seem natural.

The symbol for a function can be used along with a variable that represents an element in the domain to represent the associated element in the range. For example, suppose that we have a function f specified in terms of the variable x. The symbol $f(x)$, which is read "f of x" or "the value of f at x," represents the element in the range associated with the element x from the domain. The function $f = \{(x, y)| y = x + 2\}$ can be written as $f = \{(x, f(x))| f(x) = x + 2\}$ and is usually shortened to read "f is the function determined by the equation $f(x) = x + 2$."

Remark: Be careful with the notation $f(x)$. As we stated above, it means the value of the function f at x. It does not mean f times x.

This **function notation** is very convenient for computing and expressing various values of the function. For example, the value of the function $f(x) = 3x - 5$ at $x = 1$ is

$$f(1) = 3(1) - 5 = -2$$

Likewise, the functional values for $x = 2$, $x = -1$, and $x = 5$ are

$$f(2) = 3(2) - 5 = 1$$

$$f(-1) = 3(-1) - 5 = -8$$

$$f(5) = 3(5) - 5 = 10$$

Thus this function f contains the ordered pairs $(1, -2)$, $(2, 1)$, $(-1, -8)$, $(5, 10)$, and in general all ordered pairs of the form $(x, f(x))$, where $f(x) = 3x - 5$ and x is any real number.

It may be helpful for you to picture the concept of a function in terms of a *function machine*, as in Figure 9.1. Each time that a value of x is put into the machine, the equation $f(x) = x + 2$ is used to generate one and only one value for $f(x)$ to be ejected from the machine. For example, if 3 is put into this machine, then $f(3) = 3 + 2 = 5$, and 5 is ejected. Thus the ordered pair $(3, 5)$ is one element of the function. Now let's look at some examples to illustrate these ideas about functions.

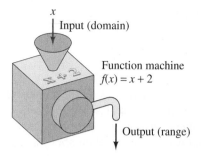

x

Input (domain)

Function machine
$f(x) = x + 2$

Output (range)

Figure 9.1

EXAMPLE 1

Determine whether the relation $\{(x, y) \mid y^2 = x\}$ is a function and specify its domain and range.

Solution

Because $y^2 = x$ is equivalent to $y = \pm\sqrt{x}$, to each value of x there are assigned *two* values for y. Therefore, this relation is not a function. The expression $\sqrt{x}$ requires that x be nonnegative, so the domain (D) is

$$D = \{x \mid x \geq 0\}$$

The domain can also be stated in interval notation as D: $[0, \infty)$. In the next few examples, domain and range will be shown with both set builder notation and interval notation. Consider the advantages and disadvantages of each format so that you can begin to decide, in each case, which format is the most appropriate. The answers given in the back of the book are shown in both set builder notation and interval notation.

To each nonnegative real number, the relation assigns two real numbers, $\sqrt{x}$ and $-\sqrt{x}$. Thus the range (R) is

$$R = \{y \mid y \text{ is a real number}\} \qquad \text{or} \qquad R\text{: } (-\infty, \infty) \qquad \blacksquare$$

EXAMPLE 2

Consider the function $f(x) = x^2$.

(a) Specify its domain.

(b) Determine its range.

(c) Evaluate $f(-2)$, $f(0)$, and $f(4)$.

Solution

(a) Any real number can be squared; therefore, the domain (D) is

$$D = \{x \mid x \text{ is a real number}\} \qquad \text{or} \qquad D\text{: } (-\infty, \infty)$$

(b) Squaring a real number always produces a nonnegative result. Thus the range (R) is

$$R = \{f(x) \mid f(x) \geq 0\} \qquad \text{or} \qquad R\text{: } [0, \infty)$$

(c) $f(-2) = (-2)^2 = 4$

$f(0) = (0)^2 = 0$

$f(4) = (4)^2 = 16$ ∎

For our purposes in this text, if the domain of a function is not specifically indicated or determined by a real-world application, then we assume the domain to be all **real number** replacements for the variable, which represents an element in the domain that will produce **real number** functional values. Consider the following examples.

EXAMPLE 3

Specify the domain for each of the following:

(a) $f(x) = \dfrac{1}{x - 1}$ **(b)** $f(t) = \dfrac{1}{t^2 - 4}$ **(c)** $f(s) = \sqrt{s - 3}$

Solution

(a) We can replace x with any real number except 1, because 1 makes the denominator zero. Thus the domain is given by

$$D = \{x | x \neq 1\} \quad \text{or} \quad D: (-\infty, 1) \cup (1, \infty)$$

Here you may consider set builder notation to be easier than interval notation for expressing the domain.

(b) We need to eliminate any value of t that will make the denominator zero, so let's solve the equation $t^2 - 4 = 0$.

$$t^2 - 4 = 0$$

$$t^2 = 4$$

$$t = \pm 2$$

The domain is the set

$$D = \{t | t \neq -2 \text{ and } t \neq 2\} \quad \text{or} \quad D: (-\infty, -2) \cup (-2, 2) \cup (2, \infty)$$

When the domain is all real numbers except a few numbers, set builder notation is the more compact notation.

(c) The radicand, $s - 3$, must be nonnegative.

$$s - 3 \geq 0$$

$$s \geq 3$$

The domain is the set

$$D = \{s | s \geq 3\} \quad \text{or} \quad D: [3, \infty)$$ ∎

EXAMPLE 4

If $f(x) = -2x + 7$ and $g(x) = x^2 - 5x + 6$, find $f(3), f(-4), f(b), f(3c), g(2), g(-1),$ $g(a)$, and $g(a + 4)$.

Solution

$$f(x) = -2x + 7 \qquad\qquad g(x) = x^2 - 5x + 6$$

$$f(3) = -2(3) + 7 = 1 \qquad\qquad g(2) = (2)^2 - 5(2) + 6 = 0$$

$$f(-4) = -2(-4) + 7 = 15 \qquad g(-1) = (-1)^2 - 5(-1) + 6 = 12$$

$$f(b) = -2(b) + 7 = -2b + 7 \qquad g(a) = (a)^2 - 5(a) + 6 = a^2 - 5a + 6$$

$$f(3c) = -2(3c) + 7 = -6c + 7 \qquad g(a + 4) = (a + 4)^2 - 5(a + 4) + 6$$

$$= a^2 + 8a + 16 - 5a - 20 + 6$$

$$= a^2 + 3a + 2 \qquad \blacksquare$$

In Example 4, note that we are working with two different functions in the same problem. Thus different names, f and g, are used.

The quotient $\dfrac{f(a + h) - f(a)}{h}$ is often called a **difference quotient**, and we use it extensively with functions when studying the limit concept in calculus. The next two examples show how we found the difference quotient for two specific functions.

EXAMPLE 5

If $f(x) = 3x - 5$, find $\dfrac{f(a + h) - f(a)}{h}$.

Solution

$$f(a + h) = 3(a + h) - 5$$

$$= 3a + 3h - 5$$

and

$$f(a) = 3a - 5$$

Therefore,

$$f(a + h) - f(a) = (3a + 3h - 5) - (3a - 5)$$

$$= 3a + 3h - 5 - 3a + 5$$

$$= 3h$$

and

$$\frac{f(a + h) - f(a)}{h} = \frac{3h}{h} = 3 \qquad \blacksquare$$

E X A M P L E   6   If $f(x) = x^2 + 2x - 3$, find $\dfrac{f(a + h) - f(a)}{h}$.

Solution

$$f(a + h) = (a + h)^2 + 2(a + h) - 3$$
$$= a^2 + 2ah + h^2 + 2a + 2h - 3$$

and

$$f(a) = a^2 + 2a - 3$$

Therefore,

$$f(a + h) - f(a) = (a^2 + 2ah + h^2 + 2a + 2h - 3) - (a^2 + 2a - 3)$$
$$= a^2 + 2ah + h^2 + 2a + 2h - 3 - a^2 - 2a + 3$$
$$= 2ah + h^2 + 2h$$

and

$$\frac{f(a + h) - f(a)}{h} = \frac{2ah + h^2 + 2h}{h}$$
$$= \frac{\not{h}(2a + h + 2)}{\not{h}}$$
$$= 2a + h + 2 \qquad\blacksquare$$

Functions and functional notation provide the basis for describing many real-world relationships. The next example illustrates this point.

E X A M P L E   7   Suppose a factory determines that the overhead for producing a quantity of a certain item is $500 and that the cost for each item is $25. Express the total expenses as a function of the number of items produced, and compute the expenses for producing 12, 25, 50, 75, and 100 items.

Solution

Let n represent the number of items produced. Then $25n + 500$ represents the total expenses. Let's use E to represent the expense function, so that we have

$$E(n) = 25n + 500, \quad \text{where } n \text{ is a whole number}$$

from which we obtain

$$E(12) = 25(12) + 500 = 800$$
$$E(25) = 25(25) + 500 = 1125$$
$$E(50) = 25(50) + 500 = 1750$$
$$E(75) = 25(75) + 500 = 2375$$
$$E(100) = 25(100) + 500 = 3000$$

Thus the total expenses for producing 12, 25, 50, 75, and 100 items are $800, $1125, $1750, $2375, and $3000, respectively. $\blacksquare$

Problem Set 9.1

For Problems 1–10, specify the domain and the range for each relation. Also state whether or not the relation is a function.

1. $\{(1, 5), (2, 8), (3, 11), (4, 14)\}$

2. $\{(0, 0), (2, 10), (4, 20), (6, 30), (8, 40)\}$

3. $\{(0, 5), (0, -5), (1, 2\sqrt{6}), (1, -2\sqrt{6})\}$

4. $\{(1, 1), (1, 2), (1, -1), (1, -2), (1, 3)\}$

5. $\{(1, 2), (2, 5), (3, 10), (4, 17), (5, 26)\}$

6. $\{(-1, 5), (0, 1), (1, -3), (2, -7)\}$

7. $\{(x, y)|\, 5x - 2y = 6\}$

8. $\{(x, y)|\, y = -3x\}$

9. $\{(x, y)|\, x^2 = y^3\}$

10. $\{(x, y)|\, x^2 - y^2 = 16\}$

For Problems 11–36, specify the domain for each of the functions.

11. $f(x) = 7x - 2$

12. $f(x) = x^2 + 1$

13. $f(x) = \dfrac{1}{x - 1}$

14. $f(x) = \dfrac{-3}{x + 4}$

15. $g(x) = \dfrac{3x}{4x - 3}$

16. $g(x) = \dfrac{5x}{2x + 7}$

17. $h(x) = \dfrac{2}{(x + 1)(x - 4)}$

18. $h(x) = \dfrac{-3}{(x - 6)(2x + 1)}$

19. $f(x) = \dfrac{14}{x^2 + 3x - 40}$

20. $f(x) = \dfrac{7}{x^2 - 8x - 20}$

21. $f(x) = \dfrac{-4}{x^2 + 6x}$

22. $f(x) = \dfrac{9}{x^2 - 12x}$

23. $f(t) = \dfrac{4}{t^2 + 9}$

24. $f(t) = \dfrac{8}{t^2 + 1}$

25. $f(t) = \dfrac{3t}{t^2 - 4}$

26. $f(t) = \dfrac{-2t}{t^2 - 25}$

27. $h(x) = \sqrt{x + 4}$

28. $h(x) = \sqrt{5x - 3}$

29. $f(s) = \sqrt{4s - 5}$

30. $f(s) = \sqrt{s - 2} + 5$

31. $f(x) = \sqrt{x^2 - 16}$

32. $f(x) = \sqrt{x^2 - 49}$

33. $f(x) = \sqrt{x^2 - 3x - 18}$ **34.** $f(x) = \sqrt{x^2 + 4x - 32}$

35. $f(x) = \sqrt{1 - x^2}$

36. $f(x) = \sqrt{9 - x^2}$

37. If $f(x) = 5x - 2$, find $f(0)$, $f(2)$, $f(-1)$, and $f(-4)$.

38. If $f(x) = -3x - 4$, find $f(-2)$, $f(-1)$, $f(3)$, and $f(5)$.

39. If $f(x) = \dfrac{1}{2}x - \dfrac{3}{4}$, find $f(-2)$, $f(0)$, $f\left(\dfrac{1}{2}\right)$, $f\left(\dfrac{2}{3}\right)$

40. If $g(x) = x^2 + 3x - 1$, find $g(1)$, $g(-1)$, $g(3)$, and $g(-4)$.

41. If $g(x) = 2x^2 - 5x - 7$, find $g(-1)$, $g(2)$, $g(-3)$, and $g(4)$.

42. If $h(x) = -x^2 - 3$, find $h(1)$, $h(-1)$, $h(-3)$, and $h(5)$.

43. If $h(x) = -2x^2 - x + 4$, find $h(-2)$, $h(-3)$, $h(4)$, and $h(5)$.

44. If $f(x) = \sqrt{x - 1}$, find $f(1)$, $f(5)$, $f(13)$, and $f(26)$.

45. If $f(x) = \sqrt{2x + 1}$, find $f(3)$, $f(4)$, $f(10)$, and $f(12)$.

46. If $f(x) = \dfrac{3}{x - 2}$, find $f(3)$, $f(0)$, $f(-1)$, and $f(-5)$.

47. If $f(x) = \dfrac{-4}{x + 3}$, find $f(1)$, $f(-1)$, $f(3)$, and $f(-6)$.

48. If $f(x) = -2x + 7$, find $f(a)$, $f(a + 2)$, and $f(a + h)$.

49. If $f(x) = x^2 - 7x$, find $f(a)$, $f(a - 3)$, and $f(a + h)$.

50. If $f(x) = x^2 - 4x + 10$, find $f(-a)$, $f(a-4)$, and $f(a+h)$.

51. If $f(x) = 2x^2 - x - 1$, find $f(-a)$, $f(a+1)$, and $f(a+h)$.

52. If $f(x) = -x^2 + 3x + 5$, find $f(-a)$, $f(a+6)$, and $f(-a+1)$.

53. If $f(x) = -x^2 - 2x - 7$, find $f(-a)$, $f(-a-2)$, and $f(a+7)$.

54. If $f(x) = 2x^2 - 7$ and $g(x) = x^2 + x - 1$, find $f(-2)$, $f(3)$, $g(-4)$, and $g(5)$.

55. If $f(x) = 5x^2 - 2x + 3$ and $g(x) = -x^2 + 4x - 5$, find $f(-2)$, $f(3)$, $g(-4)$, and $g(6)$.

56. If $f(x) = |3x - 2|$ and $g(x) = |x| + 2$, find $f(1)$, $f(-1)$, $g(2)$, and $g(-3)$.

57. If $f(x) = 3|x| - 1$ and $g(x) = -|x| + 1$, find $f(-2)$, $f(3)$, $g(-4)$, and $g(5)$.

For Problems 58–65, find $\dfrac{f(a+h) - f(a)}{h}$ for each of the given functions.

58. $f(x) = 5x - 4$

59. $f(x) = -3x + 6$

60. $f(x) = x^2 + 5$

61. $f(x) = -x^2 - 1$

62. $f(x) = x^2 - 3x + 7$

63. $f(x) = 2x^2 - x + 8$

64. $f(x) = -3x^2 + 4x - 1$

65. $f(x) = -4x^2 - 7x - 9$

66. Suppose that the cost function for producing a certain item is given by $C(n) = 3n + 5$, where n represents the number of items produced. Compute $C(150)$, $C(500)$, $C(750)$, and $C(1500)$.

67. The height of a projectile fired vertically into the air (neglecting air resistance) at an initial velocity of 64 feet per second is a function of the time (t) and is given by the equation

$$h(t) = 64t - 16t^2$$

Compute $h(1)$, $h(2)$, $h(3)$, and $h(4)$.

68. The profit function for selling n items is given by $P(n) = -n^2 + 500n - 61,500$. Compute $P(200)$, $P(230)$, $P(250)$, and $P(260)$.

69. A car rental agency charges \$50 per day plus \$0.32 a mile. Therefore, the daily charge for renting a car is a function of the number of miles traveled (m) and can be expressed as $C(m) = 50 + 0.32m$. Compute $C(75)$, $C(150)$, $C(225)$, and $C(650)$.

70. The equation $A(r) = \pi r^2$ expresses the area of a circular region as a function of the length of a radius (r). Use 3.14 as an approximation for π and compute $A(2)$, $A(3)$, $A(12)$, and $A(17)$.

71. The equation $I(r) = 500r$ expresses the amount of simple interest earned by an investment of \$500 for 1 year as a function of the rate of interest (r). Compute $I(0.11)$, $I(0.12)$, $I(0.135)$, and $I(0.15)$.

■ ■ ■ THOUGHTS INTO WORDS

72. Are all functions also relations? Are all relations also functions? Defend your answers.

73. What does it mean to say that the domain of a function may be restricted if the function represents a real-world situation? Give two or three examples of such situations.

74. Does $f(a + b) = f(a) + f(b)$ for all functions? Defend your answer.

75. Are there any functions for which $f(a + b) = f(a) + f(b)$? Defend your answer.

9.2 Functions: Their Graphs and Applications

In Section 7.1, we made statements such as "The graph of the solution set of the equation, $y = x - 1$ (or simply the graph of the equation $y = x - 1$), is a line that contains the points $(0, -1)$ and $(1, 0)$." Because the equation $y = x - 1$ (which can be written as $f(x) = x - 1$) can be used to specify a function, that line we previously referred to is also called the **graph of the function specified by the equation** or simply the **graph of the function**. Generally speaking, the graph of any equation that determines a function is also called the graph of the function. Thus the graphing techniques we discussed earlier will continue to play an important role as we graph functions.

As we use the function concept in our study of mathematics, it is helpful to classify certain types of functions and become familiar with their equations, characteristics, and graphs. In this section we will discuss two special types of functions — **linear** and **quadratic functions**. These functions are merely an outgrowth of our earlier study of linear and quadratic equations.

■ Linear Functions

Any function that can be written in the form

$$f(x) = ax + b$$

where a and b are real numbers, is called a **linear function**. The following equations are examples of linear functions.

$$f(x) = -3x + 6 \qquad f(x) = 2x + 4 \qquad f(x) = -\frac{1}{2}x - \frac{3}{4}$$

Graphing linear functions is quite easy because the graph of every linear function is a straight line. Therefore, all we need to do is determine two points of the graph and draw the line determined by those two points. You may want to continue using a third point as a check point.

EXAMPLE 1

Graph the function $f(x) = -3x + 6$.

Solution

Because $f(0) = 6$, the point $(0, 6)$ is on the graph. Likewise, because $f(1) = 3$, the point $(1, 3)$ is on the graph. Plot these two points, and draw the line determined by the two points to produce Figure 9.2.

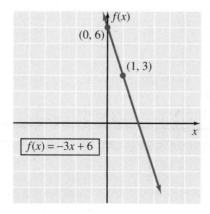

Figure 9.2

Remark: Note in Figure 9.2 that we labeled the vertical axis $f(x)$. We could also label it y, because $f(x) = -3x + 6$ and $y = -3x + 6$ mean the same thing. We will continue to use the label $f(x)$ in this chapter to help you adjust to the function notation.

E X A M P L E   2

Graph the function $f(x) = x$.

Solution

The equation $f(x) = x$ can be written as $f(x) = 1x + 0$; thus it is a linear function. Because $f(0) = 0$ and $f(2) = 2$, the points $(0, 0)$ and $(2, 2)$ determine the line in Figure 9.3. The function $f(x) = x$ is often called the **identity function**.

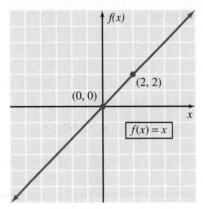

Figure 9.3   ■

As we use function notation to graph functions, it is often helpful to think of the ordinate of every point on the graph as the value of the function at a specific value of x. Geometrically, this functional value is the directed distance of the point from the x axis, as illustrated in Figure 9.4 with the function $f(x) = 2x - 4$. For example, consider the graph of the function $f(x) = 2$. The function $f(x) = 2$ means that every functional value is 2, or, geometrically, that every point on the graph is 2 units above the x axis. Thus the graph is the horizontal line shown in Figure 9.5.

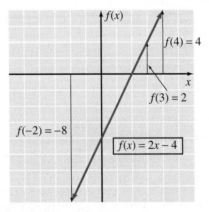

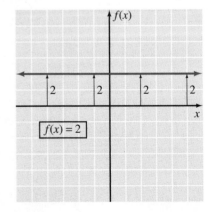

Figure 9.4   **Figure 9.5**

Any linear function of the form $f(x) = ax + b$, where $a = 0$, is called a **constant function**, and its graph is a horizontal line.

■ Applications of Linear Functions

We worked with some applications of linear equations in Section 7.2. Let's consider some additional applications that use the concept of a linear function to connect mathematics to the real world.

E X A M P L E   3   The cost for burning a 60-watt light bulb is given by the function $c(h) = 0.0036h$, where h represents the number of hours that the bulb is burning.

(a) How much does it cost to burn a 60-watt bulb for 3 hours per night for a 30-day month?

(b) Graph the function $c(h) = 0.0036h$.

(c) Suppose that a 60-watt light bulb is left burning in a closet for a week before it is discovered and turned off. Use the graph from part (b) to approximate the cost of allowing the bulb to burn for a week. Then use the function to find the exact cost.

Solution

(a) $c(90) = 0.0036(90) = 0.324$. The cost, to the nearest cent, is $.32.

(b) Because $c(0) = 0$ and $c(100) = 0.36$, we can use the points $(0, 0)$ and $(100, 0.36)$ to graph the linear function $c(h) = 0.0036h$ (Figure 9.6).

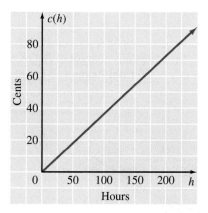

Figure 9.6

(c) If the bulb burns for 24 hours per day for a week, it burns for $24(7) = 168$ hours. Reading from the graph, we can approximate 168 on the horizontal axis, read up to the line, and then read across to the vertical axis. It looks as if it will cost approximately 60 cents. Using $c(h) = 0.0036h$, we obtain exactly $c(168) = 0.0036(168) = 0.6048$.   ■

EXAMPLE 4

The EZ Car Rental charges a fixed amount per day plus an amount per mile for renting a car. For two different day trips, Ed has rented a car from EZ. He paid $70 for 100 miles on one day and $120 for 350 miles on another day. Determine the linear function that the EZ Car Rental uses to determine its daily rental charges.

Solution

The linear function $f(x) = ax + b$, where x represents the number of miles, models this situation. Ed's two day trips can be represented by the ordered pairs (100, 70) and (350, 120). From these two ordered pairs we can determine a, which is the slope of the line.

$$a = \frac{120 - 70}{350 - 100} = \frac{50}{250} = \frac{1}{5} = 0.2$$

Thus $f(x) = ax + b$ becomes $f(x) = 0.2x + b$. Now either ordered pair can be used to determine the value of b. Using (100, 70), we have $f(100) = 70$; therefore,

$$f(100) = 0.2(100) + b = 70$$

$$b = 50$$

The linear function is $f(x) = 0.2x + 50$. In other words, the EZ Car Rental charges a daily fee of $50 plus $.20 per mile. ■

EXAMPLE 5

Suppose that Ed (Example 4) also has access to the A-OK Car Rental agency, which charges a daily fee of $25 plus $0.30 per mile. Should Ed use the EZ Car Rental from Example 4 or A-OK Car Rental?

Solution

The linear function $g(x) = 0.3x + 25$, where x represents the number of miles, can be used to determine the daily charges of A-OK Car Rental. Let's graph this function and $f(x) = 0.2x + 50$ from Example 4 on the same set of axes (Figure 9.7).

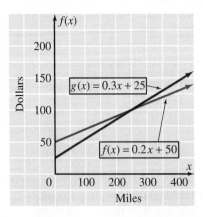

Figure 9.7

Now we see that the two functions have equal values at the point of intersection of the two lines. To find the coordinates of this point, we can set $0.3x + 25$ equal to $0.2x + 50$ and solve for x.

$$0.3x + 25 = 0.2x + 50$$

$$0.1x = 25$$

$$x = 250$$

If $x = 250$, then $0.3(250) + 25 = 100$, and the point of intersection is $(250, 100)$. Again looking at the lines in Figure 9.7, we see that Ed should use A-OK Car Rental for day trips of less than 250 miles, but he should use EZ Car Rental for day trips of more than 250 miles. ∎

■ Quadratic Functions

Any function that can be written in the form

$$f(x) = ax^2 + bx + c$$

where a, b, and c are real numbers with $a \neq 0$, is called a **quadratic function**. The following equations are examples of quadratic functions.

$$f(x) = 3x^2 \qquad f(x) = -2x^2 + 5x \qquad f(x) = 4x^2 - 7x + 1$$

The techniques discussed in Chapter 8 relative to graphing quadratic equations of the form $y = ax^2 + bx + c$ provide the basis for graphing quadratic functions. Let's review some work we did in Chapter 8 with an example.

E X A M P L E   6

Graph the function $f(x) = 2x^2 - 4x + 5$.

Solution

$$f(x) = 2x^2 - 4x + 5$$

$$= 2(x^2 - 2x + \underline{\ \ }) + 5 \qquad \text{Recall the process of completing the square!}$$

$$= 2(x^2 - 2x + 1) + 5 - 2$$

$$= 2(x - 1)^2 + 3$$

From this form we can obtain the following information about the parabola.

$$f(x) = 2(x - 1)^2 + 3$$

Narrows the parabola and opens it upward

Moves the parabola 1 unit to the right

Moves the parabola 3 units up

Thus the parabola can be drawn as shown in Figure 9.8.

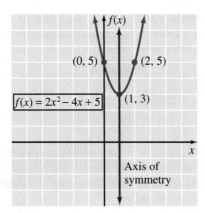

Figure 9.8

In general, if we complete the square on

$$f(x) = ax^2 + bx + c$$

we obtain

$$f(x) = a\left(x^2 + \frac{b}{a}x + \underline{\quad}\right) + c$$

$$= a\left(x^2 + \frac{b}{a}x + \frac{b^2}{4a^2}\right) + c - \frac{b^2}{4a}$$

$$= a\left(x + \frac{b}{2a}\right)^2 + \frac{4ac - b^2}{4a}$$

Therefore, the parabola associated with $f(x) = ax^2 + bx + c$ has its vertex at $\left(-\dfrac{b}{2a}, \dfrac{4ac - b^2}{4a}\right)$ and the equation of its axis of symmetry is $x = -\dfrac{b}{2a}$. These facts are illustrated in Figure 9.9.

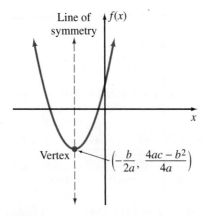

Figure 9.9

By using the information from Figure 9.9, we now have another way of graphing quadratic functions of the form $f(x) = ax^2 + bx + c$, shown by the following steps.

1. Determine whether the parabola opens upward (if $a > 0$) or downward (if $a < 0$).

2. Find $-\dfrac{b}{2a}$, which is the x coordinate of the vertex.

3. Find $f\left(-\dfrac{b}{2a}\right)$, which is the y coordinate of the vertex. $\left(\text{You could also find the } y \text{ coordinate by evaluating } \dfrac{4ac - b^2}{4a}.\right)$

4. Locate another point on the parabola, and also locate its image across the line of symmetry, $x = -\dfrac{b}{2a}$.

The three points in Steps 2, 3, and 4 should determine the general shape of the parabola. Let's use these steps in the following two examples.

E X A M P L E   7

Graph $f(x) = 3x^2 - 6x + 5$.

Solution

Step 1   Because a = 3, the parabola opens upward.

Step 2 $-\dfrac{b}{2a} = -\dfrac{-6}{6} = 1$

Step 3 $f\left(-\dfrac{b}{2a}\right) = f(1) = 3 - 6 + 5 = 2$. Thus the vertex is at $(1, 2)$.

Step 4   Letting $x = 2$, we obtain $f(2) = 12 - 12 + 5 = 5$. Thus $(2, 5)$ is on the graph and so is its reflection $(0, 5)$ across the line of symmetry $x = 1$.

The three points $(1, 2), (2, 5),$ and $(0, 5)$ are used to graph the parabola in Figure 9.10.

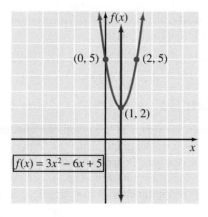

Figure 9.10

<table>
<tr><td>

E X A M P L E   8

</td><td>

Graph $f(x) = -x^2 - 4x - 7$.

</td></tr>
</table>

Solution

Step 1   Because $a = -1$, the parabola opens downward.

Step 2 $-\dfrac{b}{2a} = -\dfrac{-4}{-2} = -2$.

Step 3 $f\left(-\dfrac{b}{2a}\right) = f(-2) = -(-2)^2 - 4(-2) - 7 = -3$. So the vertex is at $(-2, -3)$.

Step 4   Letting $x = 0$, we obtain $f(0) = -7$. Thus $(0, -7)$ is on the graph and so is its reflection $(-4, -7)$ across the line of symmetry $x = -2$.

The three points $(-2, -3)$, $(0, -7)$ and $(-4, -7)$ are used to draw the parabola in Figure 9.11.

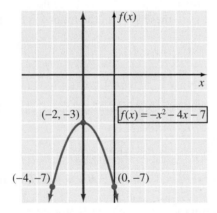

Figure 9.11   ∎

In summary, to graph a quadratic function, we have two methods.

1. We can express the function in the form $f(x) = a(x - h)^2 + k$ and use the values of a, h, and k to determine the parabola.

2. We can express the function in the form $f(x) = ax^2 + bx + c$ and use the approach demonstrated in Examples 7 and 8.

■ Problem Solving Using Quadratic Functions

As we have seen, the vertex of the graph of a quadratic function is either the lowest or the highest point on the graph. Thus the term *minimum value* or *maximum value* of a function is often used in applications of the parabola. The x value of the vertex indicates where the minimum or maximum occurs, and $f(x)$ yields the minimum or maximum value of the function. Let's consider some examples that illustrate these ideas.

E X A M P L E   9

A farmer has 120 rods of fencing and wants to enclose a rectangular plot of land that requires fencing on only three sides because it is bounded by a river on one side. Find the length and width of the plot that will maximize the area.

Solution

Let x represent the width; then $120 - 2x$ represents the length, as indicated in Figure 9.12.

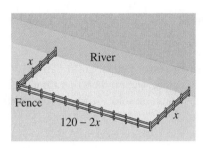

Figure 9.12

The function $A(x) = x(120 - 2x)$ represents the area of the plot in terms of the width x. Because

$$A(x) = x(120 - 2x)$$
$$= 120x - 2x^2$$
$$= -2x^2 + 120x$$

we have a quadratic function with $a = -2$, $b = 120$, and $c = 0$. Therefore, the x value where the maximum value of the function is obtained is

$$-\frac{b}{2a} = -\frac{120}{2(-2)} = 30$$

If $x = 30$, then $120 - 2x = 120 - 2(30) = 60$. Thus the farmer should make the plot 30 rods wide and 60 rods long to maximize the area at $(30)(60) = 1800$ square rods. ■

E X A M P L E   1 0

Find two numbers whose sum is 30, such that the sum of their squares is a minimum.

Solution

Let x represent one of the numbers; then $30 - x$ represents the other number. By expressing the sum of the squares as a function of x, we obtain

$$f(x) = x^2 + (30 - x)^2$$

which can be simplified to

$$f(x) = x^2 + 900 - 60x + x^2$$
$$= 2x^2 - 60x + 900$$

This is a quadratic function with $a = 2$, $b = -60$, and $c = 900$. Therefore, the x value where the minimum occurs is

$$-\frac{b}{2a} = -\frac{-60}{4} = 15$$

If $x = 15$, then $30 - x = 30 - (15) = 15$. Thus the two numbers should both be 15.

■

E X A M P L E   1 1

A golf pro-shop operator finds that she can sell 30 sets of golf clubs at $500 per set in a year. Furthermore, she predicts that for each $25 decrease in price, three more sets of golf clubs could be sold. At what price should she sell the clubs to maximize gross income?

Solution

Sometimes, when we are analyzing such a problem, it helps to set up a table.

	Number of sets	×	Price per set	=	Income
3 additional sets can	30	×	$500	=	$15,000
be sold for a $25	33	×	$475	=	$15,675
decrease in price	36	×	$450	=	$16,200

Let x represent the number of $25 decreases in price. Then we can express the income as a function of x as follows:

$$f(x) = (30 + 3x)(500 - 25x)$$

Number of sets   Price per set

When we simplify, we obtain

$$f(x) = 15,000 - 750x + 1500x - 75x^2$$
$$= -75x^2 + 750x + 15,000$$

Completing the square yields

$$f(x) = -75x^2 + 750x + 15,000$$
$$= -75(x^2 - 10x + \underline{}) + 15,000$$
$$= -75(x^2 - 10x + 25) + 15,000 + 1875$$
$$= -75(x - 5)^2 + 16,875$$

From this form we know that the vertex of the parabola is at (5, 16875). Thus 5 decreases of $25 each—that is, a $125 reduction in price—will give a maximum income of $16,875. The golf clubs should be sold at $375 per set.   ∎

What we know about parabolas and the process of completing the square can be helpful when we are using a graphing utility to graph a quadratic function. Consider the following example.

E X A M P L E   1 2   Use a graphing utility to obtain the graph of the quadratic function

$$f(x) = -x^2 + 37x - 311$$

Solution

First, we know that the parabola opens downward and that its width is the same as that of the basic parabola $f(x) = x^2$. Then we can start the process of completing the square to determine an approximate location of the vertex.

$$f(x) = -x^2 + 37x - 311$$
$$= -(x^2 - 37x + \underline{\quad}) - 311$$
$$= -\left[x^2 - 37x + \left(\frac{37}{2} \right)^2 \right] - 311 + \left(\frac{37}{2} \right)^2$$
$$= -[(x^2 - 37x + (18.5)^2] - 311 + 342.25$$
$$= -(x - 18.5)^2 + 31.25$$

Thus the vertex is near $x = 18$ and $y = 31$. Therefore, setting the boundaries of the viewing rectangle so that $-2 \le x \le 25$ and $-10 \le y \le 35$, we obtain the graph shown in Figure 9.13.

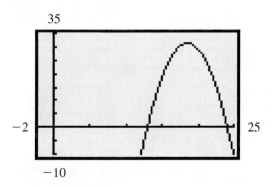

Figure 9.13   ∎

Remark: The graph in Figure 9.13 is sufficient for most purposes, because it shows the vertex and the x intercepts of the parabola. Certainly other boundaries could be used that would also give this information.

Problem Set 9.2

For Problems 1–30, graph each of the following linear and quadratic functions.

1. $f(x) = 2x - 4$

2. $f(x) = 3x + 3$

3. $f(x) = -2x^2$

4. $f(x) = -4x^2$

5. $f(x) = -3x$

6. $f(x) = -4x$

7. $f(x) = -(x + 1)^2 - 2$

8. $f(x) = -(x - 2)^2 + 4$

9. $f(x) = -x + 3$

10. $f(x) = -2x - 4$

11. $f(x) = x^2 + 2x - 2$

12. $f(x) = x^2 - 4x - 1$

13. $f(x) = -x^2 + 6x - 8$

14. $f(x) = -x^2 - 8x - 15$

15. $f(x) = -3$

16. $f(x) = 1$

17. $f(x) = 2x^2 - 20x + 52$

18. $f(x) = 2x^2 + 12x + 14$

19. $f(x) = -3x^2 + 6x$

20. $f(x) = -4x^2 - 8x$

21. $f(x) = x^2 - x + 2$

22. $f(x) = x^2 + 3x + 2$

23. $f(x) = 2x^2 + 10x + 11$

24. $f(x) = 2x^2 - 10x + 15$

25. $f(x) = -2x^2 - 1$

26. $f(x) = -3x^2 + 2$

27. $f(x) = -3x^2 + 12x - 7$

28. $f(x) = -3x^2 - 18x - 23$

29. $f(x) = -2x^2 + 14x - 25$

30. $f(x) = -2x^2 - 10x - 14$

31. The cost for burning a 75-watt bulb is given by the function $c(h) = 0.0045h$, where h represents the number of hours that the bulb burns.
  (a) How much does it cost to burn a 75-watt bulb for 3 hours per night for a 31-day month? Express your answer to the nearest cent.
  (b) Graph the function $c(h) = 0.0045h$.
  (c) Use the graph in part (b) to approximate the cost of burning a 75-watt bulb for 225 hours.
  (d) Use $c(h) = 0.0045h$ to find the exact cost, to the nearest cent, of burning a 75-watt bulb for 225 hours.

32. The Rent-Me Car Rental charges $15 per day plus $0.22 per mile to rent a car. Determine a linear function that can be used to calculate daily car rentals. Then use that function to determine the cost of renting a car for a day and driving 175 miles; 220 miles; 300 miles; 460 miles.

33. The ABC Car Rental uses the function $f(x) = 26$ for any daily use of a car up to and including 200 miles. For driving more than 200 miles per day, ABC uses the function $g(x) = 26 + 0.15(x - 200)$ to determine the charges. How much would ABC charge for daily driving of 150 miles? of 230 miles? of 360 miles? of 430 miles?

34. Suppose that a car rental agency charges a fixed amount per day plus an amount per mile for renting a car. Heidi rented a car one day and paid $80 for 200 miles. On another day she rented a car from the same agency and paid $117.50 for 350 miles. Find the linear function that the agency could use to determine its daily rental charges.

35. A retailer has a number of items that she wants to sell and make a profit of 40% of the cost of each item. The function $s(c) = c + 0.4c = 1.4c$, where c represents the cost of an item, can be used to determine the selling price. Find the selling price of items that cost $1.50, $3.25, $14.80, $21, and $24.20.

36. Zack wants to sell five items that cost him $1.20, $2.30, $6.50, $12, and $15.60. He wants to make a profit of 60% of the cost. Create a function that you can use to determine the selling price of each item, and then use the function to calculate each selling price.

37. "All Items 20% Off Marked Price" is a sign at a local golf course. Create a function and then use it to determine how much one has to pay for each of the following marked items: a $9.50 hat, a $15 umbrella, a $75 pair of golf shoes, a $12.50 golf glove, a $750 set of golf clubs.

38. The linear depreciation method assumes that an item depreciates the same amount each year. Suppose a new piece of machinery costs $32,500 and it depreciates $1950 each year for t years.
  (a) Set up a linear function that yields the value of the machinery after t years.
  (b) Find the value of the machinery after 5 years.
  (c) Find the value of the machinery after 8 years.
  (d) Graph the function from part (a).
  (e) Use the graph from part (d) to approximate how many years it takes for the value of the machinery to become zero.
  (f) Use the function to determine how long it takes for the value of the machinery to become zero.

39. Suppose that the cost function for a particular item is given by the equation $C(x) = 2x^2 - 320x + 12{,}920$, where x represents the number of items. How many items should be produced to minimize the cost?

40. Suppose that the equation $p(x) = -2x^2 + 280x - 1000$, where x represents the number of items sold, describes the profit function for a certain business. How many items should be sold to maximize the profit?

41. Find two numbers whose sum is 30, such that the sum of the square of one number plus ten times the other number is a minimum.

42. The height of a projectile fired vertically into the air (neglecting air resistance) at an initial velocity of 96 feet per second is a function of the time and is given by the equation $f(x) = 96x - 16x^2$, where x represents the time. Find the highest point reached by the projectile.

43. Two hundred and forty meters of fencing is available to enclose a rectangular playground. What should be the dimensions of the playground to maximize the area?

44. Find two numbers whose sum is 50 and whose product is a maximum.

45. A cable TV company has 1000 subscribers, and each pays $15 per month. On the basis of a survey, company managers feel that for each decrease of $0.25 on the monthly rate, they could obtain 20 additional subscribers. At what rate will maximum revenue be obtained and how many subscribers will it take at that rate?

46. A motel advertises that it will provide dinner, dancing, and drinks for $50 per couple at a New Year's Eve party. It must have a guarantee of 30 couples. Furthermore, it will agree that for each couple in excess of 30, it will reduce the price per couple for all attending by $0.50. How many couples will it take to maximize the motel's revenue?

■ ■ ■ **THOUGHTS INTO WORDS**

47. Give a step-by-step description of how you would use the ideas of this section to graph $f(x) = -4x^2 + 16x - 13$.

48. Is $f(x) = (3x - 2) - (2x + 1)$ a linear function? Explain your answer.

49. Suppose that Bianca walks at a constant rate of 3 miles per hour. Explain what it means that the distance Bianca walks is a linear function of the time that she walks.

GRAPHING CALCULATOR ACTIVITIES

50. Use a graphing calculator to check your graphs for Problems 17–30.

51. Graph each of the following parabolas, and keep in mind that you may need to change the dimensions of the viewing window to obtain a good picture.
  (a) $f(x) = x^2 - 2x + 12$ **(b)** $f(x) = -x^2 - 4x - 16$
  (c) $f(x) = x^2 + 12x + 44$ **(d)** $f(x) = x^2 - 30x + 229$
  (e) $f(x) = -2x^2 + 8x - 19$

52. Graph each of the following parabolas, and use the TRACE feature to find whole number estimates of the vertex. Then either complete the square or use $\left(-\dfrac{b}{2a}, \dfrac{4ac - b^2}{4a}\right)$ to find the vertex.

  (a) $f(x) = x^2 - 6x + 3$
  (b) $f(x) = x^2 - 18x + 66$
  (c) $f(x) = -x^2 + 8x - 3$
  (d) $f(x) = -x^2 + 24x - 129$
  (e) $f(x) = 14x^2 - 7x + 1$
  (f) $f(x) = -0.5x^2 + 5x - 8.5$

53. (a) Graph $f(x) = |x|$, $f(x) = 2|x|$, $f(x) = 4|x|$, and $f(x) = \dfrac{1}{2}|x|$ on the same set of axes.

  (b) Graph $f(x) = |x|$, $f(x) = -|x|$, $f(x) = -3|x|$, and $f(x) = -\dfrac{1}{2}|x|$ on the same set of axes.

(c) Use your results from parts (a) and (b) to make a conjecture about the graphs of $f(x) = a|x|$, where a is a nonzero real number.

(d) Graph $f(x) = |x|, f(x) = |x| + 3, f(x) = |x| - 4$, and $f(x) = |x| + 1$ on the same set of axes. Make a conjecture about the graphs of $f(x) = |x| + k$, where k is a nonzero real number.

(e) Graph $f(x) = |x|, f(x) = |x - 3|, f(x) = |x - 1|$, and $f(x) = |x + 4|$ on the same set of axes. Make a conjecture about the graphs of $f(x) = |x - h|$, where h is a nonzero real number.

(f) On the basis of your results from parts (a) through (e), sketch each of the following graphs. Then use a graphing calculator to check your sketches.

(1) $f(x) = |x - 2| + 3$ **(2)** $f(x) = |x + 1| - 4$

(3) $f(x) = 2|x - 4| - 1$ **(4)** $f(x) = -3|x + 2| + 4$

(5) $f(x) = \frac{1}{2}|x - 3| - 2$

9.3   Graphing Made Easy Via Transformations

Figures 9.14–9.16 show the graphs of the functions $f(x) = x^2$, $f(x) = x^3$, and $f(x) = \dfrac{1}{x}$, respectively.

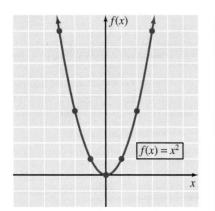

Figure 9.14

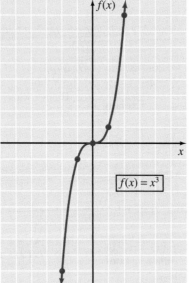

Figure 9.15

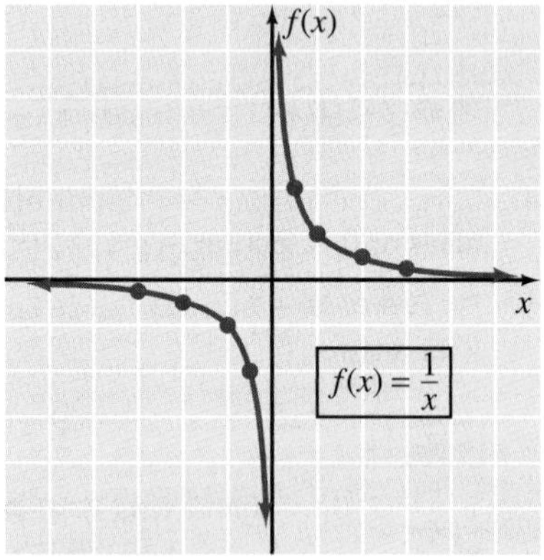

Figure 9.16

To graph a new function — that is, one you are not familiar with — use some of the graphing suggestions we offered in Chapter 7. We will restate those suggestions in terms of function vocabulary and notation. Pay special attention to suggestions 2 and 3, where we have restated the concepts of intercepts and symmetry using function notation.

1. Determine the domain of the function.

2. Determine any types of symmetry that the equation possesses. If $f(-x) = f(x)$, then the function exhibits y axis symmetry. If $f(-x) = -f(x)$, then the function exhibits origin symmetry. (Note that the definition of a function rules out the possibility that the graph of a function has x axis symmetry.)

3. Find the y intercept (we are labeling the y axis with $f(x)$) by evaluating $f(0)$. Find the x intercept by finding the value(s) of x such that $f(x) = 0$.

4. Set up a table of ordered pairs that satisfy the equation. The type of symmetry and the domain will affect your choice of values of x in the table.

5. Plot the points associated with the ordered pairs and connect them with a smooth curve. Then, if appropriate, reflect this part of the curve according to any symmetries the graph exhibits.

Let's consider some examples where we can use some of these suggestions.

EXAMPLE 1

Graph $f(x) = \sqrt{x}$.

Solution

The radicand must be nonnegative, so the domain is the set of nonnegative real numbers. Because $x \geq 0$, $f(-x)$ is not a real number; thus there is no symmetry for this graph. We see that $f(0) = 0$, so both intercepts are 0. That is, the origin $(0, 0)$ is a point of the graph. Now let's set up a table of values, keeping in mind that $x \geq 0$. Plotting these points and connecting them with a smooth curve produces Figure 9.17.

x	$f(x)$
0	0
1	1
4	2
9	3

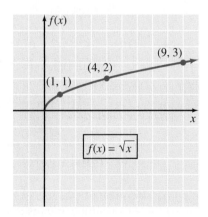

Figure 9.17

Sometimes a new function is defined in terms of old functions. In such cases, the definition plays an important role in the study of the new function. Consider the following example.

E X A M P L E   2

Graph the function $f(x) = |x|$.

Solution

The concept of absolute value is defined for all real numbers as

$$|x| = x \quad \text{if } x \geq 0$$

$$|x| = -x \quad \text{if } x < 0$$

Therefore, we can express the absolute-value function as

$$f(x) = |x| = \begin{cases} x & \text{if } x \geq 0 \\ -x & \text{if } x < 0 \end{cases}$$

The graph of $f(x) = x$ for $x \geq 0$ is the ray in the first quadrant, and the graph of $f(x) = -x$ for $x < 0$ is the half-line in the second quadrant, as indicated in Figure 9.18.

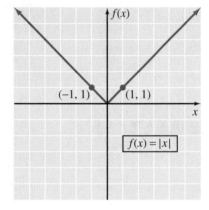

Figure 9.18   ∎

Remark: Note in Example 2 that the equation $f(x) = |x|$ does exhibit y axis symmetry because $f(-x) = |-x| = |x|$. Even though we did not use the symmetry idea to sketch the curve, you should recognize that the symmetry does exist.

∎ Translations of the Basic Curves

From our work in Chapter 8, we know that the graph of $f(x) = x^2 + 3$ is the graph of $f(x) = x^2$ moved up 3 units. Likewise, the graph of $f(x) = x^2 - 2$ is the graph of $f(x) = x^2$ moved down 2 units. Now we will describe in general the concept of **vertical translation**.

Vertical Translation

> The graph of $y = f(x) + k$ is the graph of $y = f(x)$ shifted k units upward if $k > 0$ or shifted $|k|$ units downward if $k < 0$.

In Figure 9.19, we obtain the graph of $f(x) = |x| + 2$ by shifting the graph of $f(x) = |x|$ upward 2 units, and we obtain the graph of $f(x) = |x| - 3$ by shifting the graph of $f(x) = |x|$ downward 3 units. (Remember that we can write $f(x) = |x| - 3$ as $f(x) = |x| + (-3)$.)

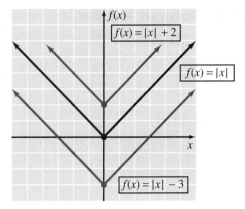

Figure 9.19

We also graphed horizontal translations of the basic parabola in Chapter 8. For example, the graph of $f(x) = (x - 4)^2$ is the graph of $f(x) = x^2$ shifted 4 units to the right, and the graph of $f(x) = (x + 5)^2$ is the graph of $f(x) = x^2$ shifted 5 units to the left. We describe the general concept of a **horizontal translation** as follows:

Horizontal Translation

The graph of $y = f(x - h)$ is the graph of $y = f(x)$ shifted h units to the right if $h > 0$ or shifted $|h|$ units to the left if $h < 0$.

In Figure 9.20, we obtain the graph of $f(x) = (x - 3)^3$ by shifting the graph of $f(x) = x^3$ to the right 3 units. Likewise, we obtain the graph of $f(x) = (x + 2)^3$ by shifting the graph of $f(x) = x^3$ to the left 2 units.

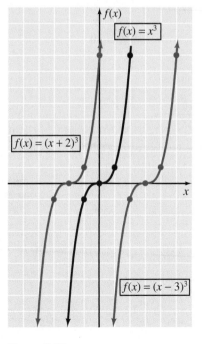

Figure 9.20

■ Reflections of the Basic Curves

From our work in Chapter 8, we know that the graph of $f(x) = -x^2$ is the graph of $f(x) = x^2$ reflected through the x axis. We describe the general concept of an **x axis reflection** as follows:

x Axis Reflection

> The graph of $y = -f(x)$ is the graph of $y = f(x)$ reflected through the x axis.

In Figure 9.21, we obtain the graph of $f(x) = -\sqrt{x}$ by reflecting the graph of $f(x) = \sqrt{x}$ through the x axis. Reflections are sometimes referred to as **mirror images**. Thus, in Figure 9.21, if we think of the x axis as a mirror, the graphs of $f(x) = \sqrt{x}$ and $f(x) = -\sqrt{x}$ are mirror images of each other.

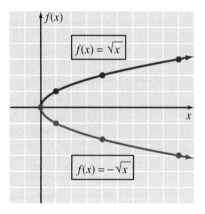

Figure 9.21

In Chapter 8, we did not consider a y axis reflection of the basic parabola $f(x) = x^2$ because it is symmetric with respect to the y axis. In other words, a y axis reflection of $f(x) = x^2$ produces the same figure in the same location. At this time we will describe the general concept of a y axis reflection.

y Axis Reflection

> The graph of $y = f(-x)$ is the graph of $y = f(x)$ reflected through the y axis.

Now suppose that we want to do a y axis reflection of $f(x) = \sqrt{x}$. Because $f(x) = \sqrt{x}$ is defined for $x \geq 0$, the y axis reflection $f(x) = \sqrt{-x}$ is defined for $-x \geq 0$, which is equivalent to $x \leq 0$. Figure 9.22 shows the y axis reflection of $f(x) = \sqrt{x}$.

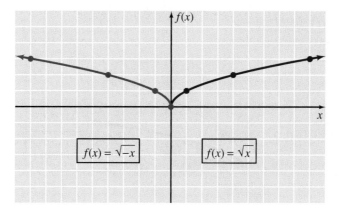

Figure 9.22

■ Vertical Stretching and Shrinking

Translations and reflections are called **rigid transformations** because the basic shape of the curve being transformed is not changed. In other words, only the positions of the graphs are changed. Now we want to consider some transformations that distort the shape of the original figure somewhat.

In Chapter 8, we graphed the equation $y = 2x^2$ by doubling the y coordinates of the ordered pairs that satisfy the equation $y = x^2$. We obtained a parabola with its vertex at the origin, symmetric with respect to the y axis, but narrower than the basic parabola. Likewise, we graphed the equation $y = \frac{1}{2}x^2$ by halving the y coordinates of the ordered pairs that satisfy $y = x^2$. In this case, we obtained a parabola with its vertex at the origin, symmetric with respect to the y axis, but wider than the basic parabola.

We can use the concepts of narrower and wider to describe parabolas, but they cannot be used to describe some other curves accurately. Instead, we use the more general concepts of vertical stretching and shrinking.

Vertical Stretching and Shrinking

> The graph of $y = cf(x)$ is obtained from the graph of $y = f(x)$ by multiplying the y coordinates of $y = f(x)$ by c. If $|c| > 1$, the graph is said to be *stretched* by a factor of $|c|$, and if $0 < |c| < 1$, the graph is said to be *shrunk* by a factor of $|c|$.

In Figure 9.23, the graph of $f(x) = 2\sqrt{x}$ is obtained by doubling the y coordinates of points on the graph of $f(x) = \sqrt{x}$. Likewise, in Figure 9.23, the graph of $f(x) = \frac{1}{2}\sqrt{x}$ is obtained by halving the y coordinates of points on the graph of $f(x) = \sqrt{x}$.

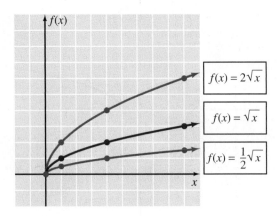

Figure 9.23

■ Successive Transformations

Some curves are the result of performing more than one transformation on a basic curve. Let's consider the graph of a function that involves a stretching, a reflection, a horizontal translation, and a vertical translation of the basic absolute-value function.

E X A M P L E   3

Graph $f(x) = -2|x - 3| + 1$.

Solution

This is the basic absolute-value curve stretched by a factor of two, reflected through the x axis, shifted 3 units to the right, and shifted 1 unit upward. To sketch the graph, we locate the point $(3, 1)$ and then determine a point on each of the rays. The graph is shown in Figure 9.24.

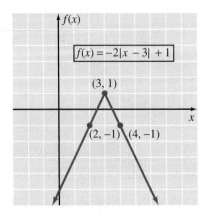

Figure 9.24

Remark: Note in Example 3 that we did not sketch the original basic curve $f(x) = |x|$ or any of the intermediate transformations. However, it is helpful to mentally picture each transformation. This locates the point (3, 1) and establishes the fact that the two rays point downward. Then a point on each ray determines the final graph.

You also need to realize that changing the order of doing the transformations may produce an incorrect graph. In Example 3, performing the translations first, followed by the stretching and x axis reflection, would produce an incorrect graph that has its vertex at (3, −1) instead of (3, 1). Unless parentheses indicate otherwise, stretchings, shrinkings, and x axis reflections should be performed before translations.

EXAMPLE 4

Graph the function $f(x) = \dfrac{1}{x + 2} + 3$.

Solution

This is the basic curve $f(x) = \dfrac{1}{x}$ moved 2 units to the left and 3 units upward. Remember that the x axis is a horizontal asymptote and the y axis a vertical asymptote for the curve $f(x) = \dfrac{1}{x}$. Thus, for this curve, the vertical asymptote is shifted 2 units to the left, and its equation is $x = -2$. Likewise, the horizontal asymptote is shifted 3 units upward, and its equation is $y = 3$. Therefore, in Figure 9.25 we have drawn the asymptotes as dashed lines and then located a few points to help determine each branch of the curve.

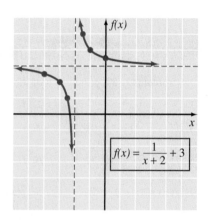

Figure 9.25 ■

Finally, let's use a graphing utility to give another illustration of the concepts of stretching and shrinking a curve.

EXAMPLE 5

If $f(x) = \sqrt{25 - x^2}$, sketch a graph of $y = 2(f(x))$ and $y = \dfrac{1}{2}(f(x))$.

Solution

If $y = f(x) = \sqrt{25 - x^2}$, then

$$y = 2(f(x)) = 2\sqrt{25 - x^2}, \quad \text{and} \quad y = \frac{1}{2}(f(x)) = \frac{1}{2}\sqrt{25 - x^2}$$

Graphing all three of these functions on the same set of axes produces Figure 9.26.

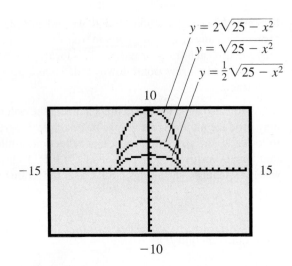

Figure 9.26

Problem Set 9.3

For Problems 1–34, graph each of the functions.

1. $f(x) = -x^3$

2. $f(x) = x^3 - 2$

3. $f(x) = -(x - 4)^2 + 2$

4. $f(x) = -2(x + 3)^2 - 4$

5. $f(x) = \dfrac{1}{x} - 2$

6. $f(x) = \dfrac{1}{x - 2}$

7. $f(x) = |x - 1| + 2$

8. $f(x) = -|x + 2|$

9. $f(x) = \dfrac{1}{2}|x|$

10. $f(x) = -2|x|$

11. $f(x) = -2\sqrt{x}$

12. $f(x) = 2\sqrt{x - 1}$

13. $f(x) = \sqrt{x + 2} - 3$

14. $f(x) = -\sqrt{x + 2} + 2$

15. $f(x) = \dfrac{2}{x - 1} + 3$

16. $f(x) = \dfrac{3}{x + 3} - 4$

17. $f(x) = \sqrt{2 - x}$

18. $f(x) = \sqrt{-1 - x}$

19. $f(x) = -3(x - 2)^2 - 1$

20. $f(x) = (x + 5)^2 - 2$

21. $f(x) = 3(x - 2)^3 - 1$

22. $f(x) = -2(x + 1)^3 + 2$

23. $f(x) = 2x^3 + 3$

24. $f(x) = -2x^3 - 1$

25. $f(x) = -2\sqrt{x + 3} + 4$

26. $f(x) = -3\sqrt{x - 1} + 2$

27. $f(x) = \dfrac{-2}{x + 2} + 2$

28. $f(x) = \dfrac{-1}{x - 1} - 1$

29. $f(x) = \dfrac{x - 1}{x}$

30. $f(x) = \dfrac{x + 2}{x}$

31. $f(x) = -3|x + 4| + 3$

32. $f(x) = -2|x - 3| - 4$

33. $f(x) = 4|x| + 2$

34. $f(x) = -3|x| - 4$

35. Suppose that the graph of $y = f(x)$ with a domain of $-2 \le x \le 2$ is shown in Figure 9.27.

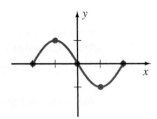

Figure 9.27

Sketch the graph of each of the following transformations of $y = f(x)$.

(a) $y = f(x) + 3$ (b) $y = f(x - 2)$

(c) $y = -f(x)$ (d) $y = f(x + 3) - 4$

36. Use the definition of absolute value to help you sketch the following graphs.

(a) $f(x) = x + |x|$ (b) $f(x) = x - |x|$

(c) $f(x) = |x| - x$ (d) $f(x) = \dfrac{x}{|x|}$ (e) $f(x) = \dfrac{|x|}{x}$

THOUGHTS INTO WORDS

37. Is the graph of $f(x) = x^2 + 2x + 4$ a y axis reflection of $f(x) = x^2 - 2x + 4$? Defend your answer.

38. Is the graph of $f(x) = x^2 - 4x - 7$ an x axis reflection of $f(x) = x^2 + 4x + 7$? Defend your answer.

39. Your friend claims that the graph of $f(x) = \dfrac{2x + 1}{x}$ is the graph of $f(x) = \dfrac{1}{x}$ shifted 2 units upward. How could you verify whether she is correct?

GRAPHING CALCULATOR ACTIVITIES

40. Use a graphing calculator to check your graphs for Problems 12–27.

41. Use a graphing calculator to check your graphs for Problem 36.

42. For each of the following, answer the question on the basis of your knowledge of transformations, and then use a graphing calculator to check your answer.
  (a) Is the graph of $f(x) = 2x^2 + 8x + 13$ a y axis reflection of $f(x) = 2x^2 - 8x + 13$?
  (b) Is the graph of $f(x) = 3x^2 - 12x + 16$ an x axis reflection of $f(x) = -3x^2 + 12x - 16$?
  (c) Is the graph of $f(x) = \sqrt{4 - x}$ a y axis reflection of $f(x) = \sqrt{x + 4}$?
  (d) Is the graph of $f(x) = \sqrt{3 - x}$ a y axis reflection of $f(x) = \sqrt{x - 3}$?
  (e) Is the graph of $f(x) = -x^3 + x + 1$ a y axis reflection of $f(x) = x^3 - x + 1$?

  (f) Is the graph of $f(x) = -(x - 2)^3$ an x axis reflection of $f(x) = (x - 2)^3$?
  (g) Is the graph of $f(x) = -x^3 - x^2 - x + 1$ an x axis reflection of $f(x) = x^3 + x^2 + x - 1$?
  (h) Is the graph of $f(x) = \dfrac{3x + 1}{x}$ a vertical translation of $f(x) = \dfrac{1}{x}$ upward 3 units?
  (i) Is the graph of $f(x) = 2 + \dfrac{1}{x}$ a y axis reflection of $f(x) = \dfrac{2x - 1}{x}$?

43. Are the graphs of $f(x) = 2\sqrt{x}$ and $g(x) = \sqrt{2x}$ identical? Defend your answer.

44. Are the graphs of $f(x) = \sqrt{x + 4}$ and $g(x) = \sqrt{-x + 4}$ y axis reflections of each other? Defend your answer.

| 9.4 | **Composition of Functions** |

The basic operations of addition, subtraction, multiplication, and division can be performed on functions. However, there is an additional operation, called **composition**, that we will use in the next section. Let's start with the definition and an illustration of this operation.

Definition 9.3

The **composition** of functions f and g is defined by

$$(f \circ g)(x) = f(g(x))$$

for all x in the domain of g such that $g(x)$ is in the domain of f.

The left side, $(f \circ g)(x)$, of the equation in Definition 9.3 can be read "the composition of f and g," and the right side, $f(g(x))$, can be read "f of g of x." It may also be helpful for you to picture Definition 9.3 as two function machines hooked together to produce another function (often called a **composite function**) as illustrated in Figure 9.28. Note that what comes out of the function g is substituted into the function f. Thus composition is sometimes called the substitution of functions.

Figure 9.28 also vividly illustrates the fact that $f \circ g$ is defined for all x in the domain of g such that $g(x)$ is in the domain of f. In other words, what comes out of g must be capable of being fed into f. Let's consider some examples.

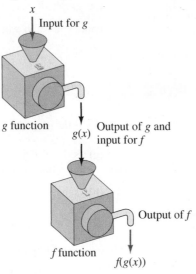

Figure 9.28

E X A M P L E   1

If $f(x) = x^2$ and $g(x) = x - 3$, find $(f \circ g)(x)$ and determine its domain.

Solution

Applying Definition 9.3, we obtain

$$(f \circ g)(x) = f(g(x))$$
$$= f(x - 3)$$
$$= (x - 3)^2$$

Because g and f are both defined for all real numbers, so is $f \circ g$.   ■

E X A M P L E   2

If $f(x) = \sqrt{x}$ and $g(x) = x - 4$, find $(f \circ g)(x)$ and determine its domain.

Solution

Applying Definition 9.3, we obtain

$$(f \circ g)(x) = f(g(x))$$
$$= f(x - 4)$$
$$= \sqrt{x - 4}$$

The domain of g is all real numbers, but the domain of f is only the nonnegative real numbers. Thus $g(x)$, which is $x - 4$, has to be nonnegative. Therefore,

$$x - 4 \geq 0$$

$$x \geq 4$$

and the domain of $f \circ g$ is $D = \{x | x \geq 4\}$ or $D\colon [4, \infty)$. ■

Definition 9.3, with f and g interchanged, defines the composition of g and f as $(g \circ f)(x) = g(f(x))$.

E X A M P L E   3

If $f(x) = x^2$ and $g(x) = x - 3$, find $(g \circ f)(x)$ and determine its domain.

Solution

$$(g \circ f)(x) = g(f(x))$$
$$= g(x^2)$$
$$= x^2 - 3$$

Because f and g are both defined for all real numbers, the domain of $g \circ f$ is the set of all real numbers. ■

The results of Examples 1 and 3 demonstrate an important idea: that the composition of functions is *not a commutative operation*. In other words, it is not true that $f \circ g = g \circ f$ for all functions f and g. However, as we will see in the next section, there is a special class of functions where $f \circ g = g \circ f$.

E X A M P L E   4

If $f(x) = 2x + 3$ and $g(x) = \sqrt{x - 1}$, determine each of the following.

(a) $(f \circ g)(x)$ **(b)** $(g \circ f)(x)$ **(c)** $(f \circ g)(5)$ **(d)** $(g \circ f)(7)$

Solution

(a) $(f \circ g)(x) = f(g(x))$
$$= f(\sqrt{x - 1})$$
$$= 2\sqrt{x - 1} + 3 \qquad D = \{x | x \geq 1\} \text{ or } D\colon [1, \infty)$$

(b) $(g \circ f)(x) = g(f(x))$
$$= g(2x + 3)$$
$$= \sqrt{2x + 3 - 1}$$
$$= \sqrt{2x + 2} \qquad D = \{x | x \geq -1\} \text{ or } D\colon [-1, \infty)$$

(c) $(f \circ g)(5) = 2\sqrt{5 - 1} + 3 = 7$

(d) $(g \circ f)(7) = \sqrt{2(7) + 2} = 4$ ■

E X A M P L E   5   If $f(x) = \dfrac{2}{x-1}$ and $g(x) = \dfrac{1}{x}$, find $(f \circ g)(x)$ and $(g \circ f)(x)$. Determine the domain for each composite function.

Solution

$$(f \circ g)(x) = f(g(x))$$

$$= f\left(\frac{1}{x}\right)$$

$$= \frac{2}{\dfrac{1}{x} - 1} = \frac{2}{\dfrac{1-x}{x}}$$

$$= \frac{2x}{1-x}$$

The domain of g is all real numbers except 0, and the domain of f is all real numbers except 1. Because $g(x)$, which is $\dfrac{1}{x}$, cannot equal 1,

$$\frac{1}{x} \neq 1$$

$$x \neq 1$$

Therefore, the domain of $f \circ g$ is $D = \{x | x \neq 0 \text{ and } x \neq 1\}$ or D: $(-\infty, 0) \cup (0, 1) \cup (1, \infty)$.

$$(g \circ f)(x) = g(f(x))$$

$$= g\left(\frac{2}{x-1}\right)$$

$$= \frac{1}{\dfrac{2}{x-1}}$$

$$= \frac{x-1}{2}$$

The domain of f is all real numbers except 1, and the domain of g is all real numbers except 0. Because $f(x)$, which is $\dfrac{2}{x-1}$, will never equal 0, the domain of $g \circ f$ is $D = \{x | x \neq 1\}$ or D: $(-\infty, 1) \cup (1, \infty)$.   ∎

A graphing utility can be used to find the graph of a composite function without actually forming the function algebraically. Let's see how this works.

EXAMPLE 6

If $f(x) = x^3$ and $g(x) = x - 4$, use a graphing utility to obtain the graph of $y = (f \circ g)(x)$ and the graph of $y = (g \circ f)(x)$.

Solution

To find the graph of $y = (f \circ g)(x)$, we can make the following assignments.

$$Y_1 = x - 4$$

$$Y_2 = (Y_1)^3$$

(Note that we have substituted Y_1 for x in $f(x)$ and assigned this expression to Y_2, much the same way as we would algebraically.) Now, by showing only the graph of Y_2, we obtain Figure 9.29.

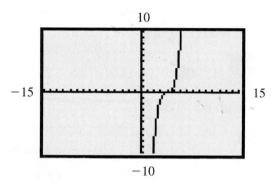

Figure 9.29

To find the graph of $y = (g \circ f)(x)$, we can make the following assignments.

$$Y_1 = x^3$$

$$Y_2 = Y_1 - 4$$

The graph of $y = (g \circ f)(x)$ is the graph of Y_2, as shown in Figure 9.30.

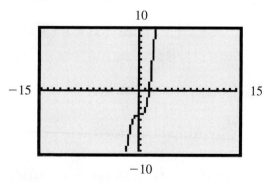

Figure 9.30

Take another look at Figures 9.29 and 9.30. Note that in Figure 9.29 the graph of $y = (f \circ g)(x)$ is the basic cubic curve $f(x) = x^3$ shifted 4 units to the right. Likewise, in Figure 9.30 the graph of $y = (g \circ f)(x)$ is the basic cubic curve shifted 4 units downward. These are examples of a more general concept of using composite functions to represent various geometric transformations.

Problem Set 9.4

For Problems 1–12, determine the indicated functional values.

1. If $f(x) = 9x - 2$ and $g(x) = -4x + 6$, find $(f \circ g)(-2)$ and $(g \circ f)(4)$.

2. If $f(x) = -2x - 6$ and $g(x) = 3x + 10$, find $(f \circ g)(5)$ and $(g \circ f)(-3)$.

3. If $f(x) = 4x^2 - 1$ and $g(x) = 4x + 5$, find $(f \circ g)(1)$ and $(g \circ f)(4)$.

4. If $f(x) = -5x + 2$ and $g(x) = -3x^2 + 4$, find $(f \circ g)(-2)$ and $(g \circ f)(-1)$.

5. If $f(x) = \dfrac{1}{x}$ and $g(x) = \dfrac{2}{x - 1}$, find $(f \circ g)(2)$ and $(g \circ f)(-1)$.

6. If $f(x) = \dfrac{2}{x - 1}$ and $g(x) = -\dfrac{3}{x}$, find $(f \circ g)(1)$ and $(g \circ f)(-1)$.

7. If $f(x) = \dfrac{1}{x - 2}$ and $g(x) = \dfrac{4}{x - 1}$, find $(f \circ g)(3)$ and $(g \circ f)(2)$.

8. If $f(x) = \sqrt{x + 6}$ and $g(x) = 3x - 1$, find $(f \circ g)(-2)$ and $(g \circ f)(-2)$.

9. If $f(x) = \sqrt{3x - 2}$ and $g(x) = -x + 4$, find $(f \circ g)(1)$ and $(g \circ f)(6)$.

10. If $f(x) = -5x + 1$ and $g(x) = \sqrt{4x + 1}$, find $(f \circ g)(6)$ and $(g \circ f)(-1)$.

11. If $f(x) = |4x - 5|$ and $g(x) = x^3$, find $(f \circ g)(-2)$ and $(g \circ f)(2)$.

12. If $f(x) = -x^3$ and $g(x) = |2x + 4|$, find $(f \circ g)(-1)$ and $(g \circ f)(-3)$.

For Problems 13–30, determine $(f \circ g)(x)$ and $(g \circ f)(x)$ for each pair of functions. Also specify the domain of $(f \circ g)(x)$ and $(g \circ f)(x)$.

13. $f(x) = 3x$ and $g(x) = 5x - 1$

14. $f(x) = 4x - 3$ and $g(x) = -2x$

15. $f(x) = -2x + 1$ and $g(x) = 7x + 4$

16. $f(x) = 6x - 5$ and $g(x) = -x + 6$

17. $f(x) = 3x + 2$ and $g(x) = x^2 + 3$

18. $f(x) = -2x + 4$ and $g(x) = 2x^2 - 1$

19. $f(x) = 2x^2 - x + 2$ and $g(x) = -x + 3$

20. $f(x) = 3x^2 - 2x - 4$ and $g(x) = -2x + 1$

21. $f(x) = \dfrac{3}{x}$ and $g(x) = 4x - 9$

22. $f(x) = -\dfrac{2}{x}$ and $g(x) = -3x + 6$

23. $f(x) = \sqrt{x + 1}$ and $g(x) = 5x + 3$

24. $f(x) = 7x - 2$ and $g(x) = \sqrt{2x - 1}$

25. $f(x) = \dfrac{1}{x}$ and $g(x) = \dfrac{1}{x - 4}$

26. $f(x) = \dfrac{2}{x + 3}$ and $g(x) = -\dfrac{3}{x}$

27. $f(x) = \sqrt{x}$ and $g(x) = \dfrac{4}{x}$

28. $f(x) = \dfrac{2}{x}$ and $g(x) = |x|$

29. $f(x) = \dfrac{3}{2x}$ and $g(x) = \dfrac{1}{x + 1}$

30. $f(x) = \dfrac{4}{x - 2}$ and $g(x) = \dfrac{3}{4x}$

For Problems 31–38, show that $(f \circ g)(x) = x$ and $(g \circ f)(x) = x$ for each pair of functions.

31. $f(x) = 3x$ and $g(x) = \dfrac{1}{3}x$

32. $f(x) = -2x$ and $g(x) = -\dfrac{1}{2}x$

33. $f(x) = 4x + 2$ and $g(x) = \dfrac{x - 2}{4}$

34. $f(x) = 3x - 7$ and $g(x) = \dfrac{x + 7}{3}$

35. $f(x) = \dfrac{1}{2}x + \dfrac{3}{4}$ and $g(x) = \dfrac{4x - 3}{2}$

36. $f(x) = \dfrac{2}{3}x - \dfrac{1}{5}$ and $g(x) = \dfrac{3}{2}x + \dfrac{3}{10}$

37. $f(x) = -\dfrac{1}{4}x - \dfrac{1}{2}$ and $g(x) = -4x - 2$

38. $f(x) = -\dfrac{3}{4}x + \dfrac{1}{3}$ and $g(x) = -\dfrac{4}{3}x + \dfrac{4}{9}$

■ ■ ■ THOUGHTS INTO WORDS

39. How would you explain the concept of composition of functions to a friend who missed class the day it was discussed?

40. Explain why the composition of functions is not a commutative operation.

GRAPHING CALCULATOR ACTIVITIES

41. For each of the following, (1) predict the general shape and location of the graph, and then (2) use your graphing calculator to graph the function and thus check your prediction. (Your knowledge of the graphs of the basic functions that are being added or subtracted should be helpful when you make your predictions.)
   (a) $f(x) = x^3 + x^2$ **(b)** $f(x) = x^3 - x^2$
   (c) $f(x) = x^2 - x^3$ **(d)** $f(x) = |x| + \sqrt{x}$
   (e) $f(x) = |x| - \sqrt{x}$ **(f)** $f(x) = \sqrt{x} - |x|$

42. For each of the following, use your graphing calculator to find the graph of $y = (f \circ g)(x)$ and $y = (g \circ f)(x)$. Then algebraically find $(f \circ g)(x)$ and $(g \circ f)(x)$ to see whether your results agree.
   (a) $f(x) = x^2$ and $g(x) = x - 3$
   (b) $f(x) = x^3$ and $g(x) = x + 4$
   (c) $f(x) = x - 2$ and $g(x) = -x^3$
   (d) $f(x) = x + 6$ and $g(x) = \sqrt{x}$
   (e) $f(x) = \sqrt{x}$ and $g(x) = x - 5$

9.5 Inverse Functions

Graphically, the distinction between a relation and a function can be easily recognized. In Figure 9.31, we sketched four graphs. Which of these are graphs of functions and which are graphs of relations that are not functions? Think in terms of the principle that to each member of the domain there is assigned one and only one member of the range; this is the basis for what is known as the **vertical-line test** for functions. Because each value of x produces only one value of $f(x)$, any vertical line drawn through a graph of a function must not intersect the graph in more than one point. Therefore, parts (a) and (c) of Figure 9.31 are graphs of functions, and parts (b) and (d) are graphs of relations that are not functions.

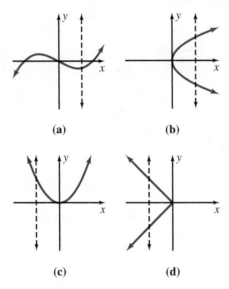

(a)   **(b)**

(c)   **(d)**

Figure 9.31

We can also make a useful distinction between two basic types of functions. Consider the graphs of the two functions $f(x) = 2x - 1$ and $f(x) = x^2$ in Figure 9.32. In part (a), any *horizontal line* will intersect the graph in no more than one point.

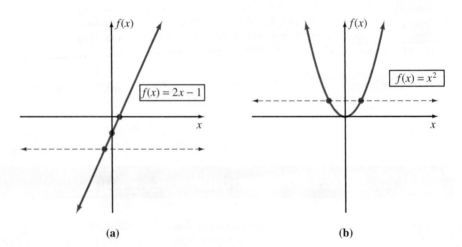

(a)   **(b)**

Figure 9.32

Therefore, every value of $f(x)$ has only one value of x associated with it. Any function that has the additional property of having only one value of x associated with each value of $f(x)$ is called a **one-to-one function**. The function $f(x) = x^2$ is not a one-to-one function because the horizontal line in part (b) of Figure 9.32 intersects the parabola in two points.

   In terms of ordered pairs, a one-to-one function does not contain any ordered pairs that have the same second component. For example,

$$f = \{(1, 3), (2, 6), (4, 12)\}$$

is a one-to-one function, but

$$g = \{(1, 2), (2, 5), (-2, 5)\}$$

is not a one-to-one function.

   If the components of each ordered pair of a given one-to-one function are interchanged, the resulting function and the given function are called **inverses** of each other. Thus

$$\{(1, 3), (2, 6), (4, 12)\} \quad \text{and} \quad \{(3, 1), (6, 2), (12, 4)\}$$

are **inverse functions**. The inverse of a function f is denoted by f^{-1} (which is read "f inverse" or "the inverse of f"). If (a, b) is an ordered pair of f, then (b, a) is an ordered pair of f^{-1}. The domain and range of f^{-1} are the range and domain, respectively, of f.

Remark: Do not confuse the -1 in f^{-1} with a negative exponent. The symbol f^{-1} does not mean $\dfrac{1}{f^1}$ but, rather, refers to the inverse function of function f.

   Graphically, two functions that are inverses of each other are mirror images with reference to the line $y = x$. This is due to the fact that ordered pairs (a, b) and (b, a) are mirror images with respect to the line $y = x$, as illustrated in Figure 9.33. Therefore, if we know the graph of a function f, as in Figure 9.34(a), then we can determine the graph of f^{-1} by reflecting f across the line $y = x$ (Figure 9.34b).

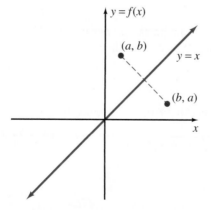

Figure 9.33

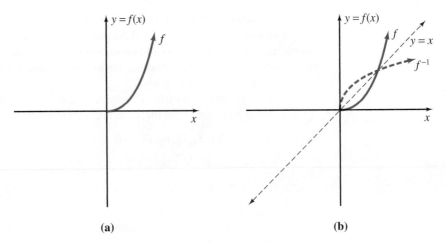

(a)   (b)

Figure 9.34

Another useful way of viewing inverse functions is in terms of composition. Basically, inverse functions *undo* each other, and this can be more formally stated as follows: If *f* and *g* are inverses of each other, then

1. $(f \circ g)(x) = f(g(x)) = x$ for all x in domain of g

2. $(g \circ f)(x) = g(f(x)) = x$ for all x in domain of f

As we will see in a moment, this relationship of inverse functions can be used to verify whether two functions are indeed inverses of each other.

■ Finding Inverse Functions

The idea of inverse functions undoing each other provides the basis for a rather informal approach to finding the inverse of a function. Consider the function

$$f(x) = 2x + 1$$

To each x this function assigns *twice x plus 1*. To undo this function, we could *subtract 1 and divide by 2*. Thus the inverse should be

$$f^{-1}(x) = \frac{x-1}{2}$$

Now let's verify that f and f^{-1} are inverses of each other.

$$(f \circ f^{-1})(x) = f(f^{-1}(x)) = f\left(\frac{x-1}{2}\right) = 2\left(\frac{x-1}{2}\right) + 1 = x$$

and

$$(f^{-1} \circ f)(x) = f^{-1}(f(x)) = f^{-1}(2x+1) = \frac{2x+1-1}{2} = x$$

Thus the inverse of f is given by

$$f^{-1}(x) = \frac{x - 1}{2}$$

Let's consider another example of finding an inverse function by the undoing process.

E X A M P L E   1

Find the inverse of $f(x) = 3x - 5$.

Solution

To each x, the function f assigns *three times x minus 5*. To undo this, we can *add 5 and then divide by 3*, so the inverse should be

$$f^{-1}(x) = \frac{x + 5}{3}$$

To verify that f and f^{-1} are inverses, we can show that

$$(f \circ f^{-1})(x) = f(f^{-1}(x)) = f\left(\frac{x + 5}{3}\right)$$

$$= 3\left(\frac{x + 5}{3}\right) - 5 = x$$

and

$$(f^{-1} \circ f)(x) = f^{-1}(f(x)) = f^{-1}(3x - 5)$$

$$= \frac{3x - 5 + 5}{3} = x$$

Thus f and f^{-1} are inverses, and we can write

$$f^{-1}(x) = \frac{x + 5}{3}$$ ∎

This informal approach may not work very well with more complex functions, but it does emphasize how inverse functions are related to each other. A more formal and systematic technique for finding the inverse of a function can be described as follows:

1. Replace the symbol $f(x)$ by y.

2. Interchange x and y.

3. Solve the equation for y in terms of x.

4. Replace y by the symbol $f^{-1}(x)$.

Now let's use two examples to illustrate this technique.

EXAMPLE 2

Find the inverse of $f(x) = -3x + 11$.

Solution

When we replace $f(x)$ by y, the given equation becomes

$$y = -3x + 11$$

Interchanging x and y produces

$$x = -3y + 11$$

Now, solving for y yields

$$x = -3y + 11$$

$$3y = -x + 11$$

$$y = \frac{-x + 11}{3}$$

Finally, replacing y by $f^{-1}(x)$, we can express the inverse function as

$$f^{-1}(x) = \frac{-x + 11}{3}$$

∎

EXAMPLE 3

Find the inverse of $f(x) = \dfrac{3}{2}x - \dfrac{1}{4}$.

Solution

When we replace $f(x)$ by y, the given equation becomes

$$y = \frac{3}{2}x - \frac{1}{4}$$

Interchanging x and y produces

$$x = \frac{3}{2}y - \frac{1}{4}$$

Now, solving for y yields

$$x = \frac{3}{2}y - \frac{1}{4}$$

$$4(x) = 4\left(\frac{3}{2}y - \frac{1}{4}\right) \qquad \text{Multiply both sides by the LCD.}$$

$$4x = 4\left(\frac{3}{2}y\right) - 4\left(\frac{1}{4}\right)$$

$$4x = 6y - 1$$

$$4x + 1 = 6y$$

$$\frac{4x + 1}{6} = y$$

$$\frac{2}{3}x + \frac{1}{6} = y$$

Finally, replacing y by $f^{-1}(x)$, we can express the inverse function as

$$f^{-1}(x) = \frac{2}{3}x + \frac{1}{6}$$ ■

For both Examples 2 and 3, you should be able to show that $(f \circ f^{-1})(x) = x$ and $(f^{-1} \circ f)(x) = x$.

Problem Set 9.5

For Problems 1–8 (Figures 9.35–9.42), identify each graph as (a) the graph of a function or (b) the graph of a relation that is not a function. Use the vertical-line test.

1.

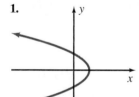

Figure 9.35

2.

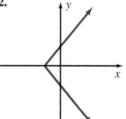

Figure 9.36

5.

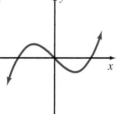

Figure 9.39

6.

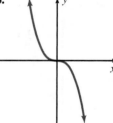

Figure 9.40

3.

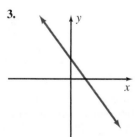

Figure 9.37

4.

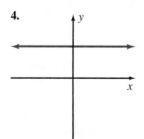

Figure 9.38

7.

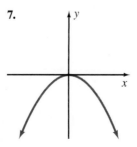

Figure 9.41

8.

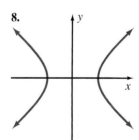

Figure 9.42

For Problems 9–16 (Figures 9.43–9.50), identify each graph as (a) the graph of a one-to-one function or (b) the graph of a function that is not one-to-one. Use the horizontal-line test.

9.

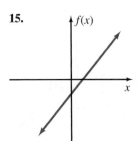

Figure 9.43

10.

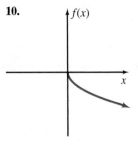

Figure 9.44

11.

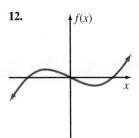

Figure 9.45

12.

Figure 9.46

13.

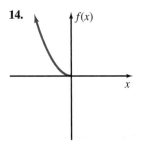

Figure 9.47

14.

Figure 9.48

15.

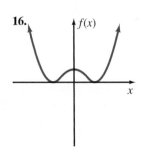

Figure 9.49

16.

Figure 9.50

For Problems 17–20, (a) list the domain and range of the given function, (b) form the inverse function, and (c) list the domain and range of the inverse function.

17. $f = \{(1, 3), (2, 6), (3, 11), (4, 18)\}$

18. $f = \{(0, -4), (1, -3), (4, -2)\}$

19. $f = \{(-2, -1), (-1, 1), (0, 5), (5, 10)\}$

20. $f = \{(-1, 1), (-2, 4), (1, 9), (2, 12)\}$

For Problems 21–30, find the inverse of the given function by using the "undoing process," and then verify that $(f \circ f^{-1})(x) = x$ and $(f^{-1} \circ f)(x) = x$.

21. $f(x) = 5x - 4$

22. $f(x) = 7x + 9$

23. $f(x) = -2x + 1$

24. $f(x) = -4x - 3$

25. $f(x) = \dfrac{4}{5}x$

26. $f(x) = -\dfrac{2}{3}x$

27. $f(x) = \dfrac{1}{2}x + 4$

28. $f(x) = \dfrac{3}{4}x - 2$

29. $f(x) = \dfrac{1}{3}x - \dfrac{2}{5}$

30. $f(x) = \dfrac{2}{5}x + \dfrac{1}{3}$

For Problems 31–40, find the inverse of the given function by using the process illustrated in Examples 2 and 3 of this section, and then verify that $(f \circ f^{-1})(x) = x$ and $(f^{-1} \circ f)(x) = x$.

31. $f(x) = 9x + 4$

32. $f(x) = 8x - 5$

33. $f(x) = -5x - 4$

34. $f(x) = -6x + 2$

35. $f(x) = -\dfrac{2}{3}x + 7$

36. $f(x) = -\dfrac{3}{5}x + 1$

37. $f(x) = \dfrac{4}{3}x - \dfrac{1}{4}$

38. $f(x) = \dfrac{5}{2}x + \dfrac{2}{7}$

39. $f(x) = -\dfrac{3}{7}x - \dfrac{2}{3}$

40. $f(x) = -\dfrac{3}{5}x + \dfrac{3}{4}$

For Problems 41–50, (a) find the inverse of the given function, and (b) graph the given function and its inverse on the same set of axes.

41. $f(x) = 4x$

42. $f(x) = \dfrac{2}{5}x$

43. $f(x) = -\dfrac{1}{3}x$ **44.** $f(x) = -6x$

45. $f(x) = 3x - 3$ **46.** $f(x) = 2x + 2$

47. $f(x) = -2x - 4$ **48.** $f(x) = -3x + 9$

49. $f(x) = x^2, x \geq 0$ **50.** $f(x) = x^2 + 2, x \geq 0$

■ ■ ■ THOUGHTS INTO WORDS

51. Does the function $f(x) = 4$ have an inverse? Explain your answer.

52. Explain why every nonconstant linear function has an inverse.

■ ■ ■ FURTHER INVESTIGATIONS

53. The composition idea can also be used to find the inverse of a function. For example, to find the inverse of $f(x) = 5x + 3$, we could proceed as follows:

$$f(f^{-1}(x)) = 5(f^{-1}(x)) + 3 \quad \text{and} \quad f(f^{-1}(x)) = x$$

Therefore, equating the two expressions for $f(f^{-1}(x))$, we obtain

$$5(f^{-1}(x)) + 3 = x$$

$$5(f^{-1}(x)) = x - 3$$

$$f^{-1}(x) = \frac{x - 3}{5}$$

Use this approach to find the inverse of each of the following functions.

(a) $f(x) = 2x + 1$

(b) $f(x) = 3x - 2$

(c) $f(x) = -4x + 5$

(d) $f(x) = -x + 1$

(e) $f(x) = 2x$

(f) $f(x) = -5x$

GRAPHING CALCULATOR ACTIVITIES

54. For Problems 31–40, graph the given function, the inverse function that you found, and $f(x) = x$ on the same set of axes. In each case the given function and its inverse should produce graphs that are reflections of each other through the line $f(x) = x$.

55. Let's use a graphing calculator to show that $(f \circ g)(x) = x$ and $(g \circ f)(x) = x$ for two functions that we think are inverses of each other. Consider the functions $f(x) = 3x + 4$ and $g(x) = \dfrac{x - 4}{3}$. We can make the following assignments.

$$f: Y_1 = 3x + 4$$

$$g: Y_2 = \frac{x - 4}{3}$$

$$f \circ g: Y_3 = 3Y_2 + 4$$

$$g \circ f: Y_4 = \frac{Y_1 - 4}{3}$$

Now we can graph Y_3 and Y_4 and show that they both produce the line $f(x) = x$.

Use this approach to check your answers for Problems 41–50.

56. Use the approach demonstrated in Problem 55 to show that $f(x) = x^2 - 2$ (for $x \geq 0$) and $g(x) = \sqrt{x + 2}$ (for $x \geq -2$) are inverses of each other.

9.6   Direct and Inverse Variations

"The distance a car travels at a fixed rate varies directly as the time." "At a constant temperature, the volume of an enclosed gas varies inversely as the pressure." Such statements illustrate two basic types of functional relationships, called **direct** and **inverse variation**, that are widely used, especially in the physical sciences. These relationships can be expressed by equations that specify functions. The purpose of this section is to investigate these special functions.

The statement "y varies directly as x" means

$$y = kx$$

where k is a nonzero constant called the **constant of variation**. The phrase "y is directly proportional to x" is also used to indicate direct variation; k is then referred to as the **constant of proportionality**.

Remark: Note that the equation $y = kx$ defines a function and could be written as $f(x) = kx$ by using function notation. However, in this section it is more convenient to avoid the function notation and use variables that are meaningful in terms of the physical entities involved in the problem.

Statements that indicate direct variation may also involve powers of x. For example, "y varies directly as the square of x" can be written as

$$y = kx^2$$

In general, "y varies directly as the nth power of x ($n > 0$)" means

$$y = kx^n$$

The three types of problems that deal with direct variation are

1. To translate an English statement into an equation that expresses the direct variation

2. To find the constant of variation from given values of the variables

3. To find additional values of the variables once the constant of variation has been determined

Let's consider an example of each of these types of problems.

EXAMPLE 1   Translate the statement, "the tension on a spring varies directly as the distance it is stretched," into an equation, and use k as the constant of variation.

Solution

If we let t represent the tension and d the distance, the equation becomes

$$t = kd$$

■

EXAMPLE 2   If A varies directly as the square of s, and $A = 28$ when $s = 2$, find the constant of variation.

Solution

Because A varies directly as the square of s, we have

$$A = ks^2$$

Substituting $A = 28$ and $s = 2$, we obtain

$$28 = k(2)^2$$

Solving this equation for k yields

$$28 = 4k$$

$$7 = k$$

The constant of variation is 7.   ■

EXAMPLE 3   If y is directly proportional to x, and if $y = 6$ when $x = 9$, find the value of y when $x = 24$.

Solution

The statement "y is directly proportional to x" translates into

$$y = kx$$

If we let $y = 6$ and $x = 9$, the constant of variation becomes

$$6 = k(9)$$

$$6 = 9k$$

$$\frac{6}{9} = k$$

$$\frac{2}{3} = k$$

Thus the specific equation is $y = \frac{2}{3}x$. Now, letting $x = 24$, we obtain

$$y = \frac{2}{3}(24) = 16$$

The required value of y is 16.   ■

■ Inverse Variation

We define the second basic type of variation, called **inverse variation**, as follows:
The statement "y varies inversely as x" means

$$y = \frac{k}{x}$$

where k is a nonzero constant; again we refer to it as the constant of variation. The phrase "y is inversely proportional to x" is also used to express inverse variation. As with direct variation, statements that indicate inverse variation may involve powers of x. For example, "y varies inversely as the square of x" can be written as

$$y = \frac{k}{x^2}$$

In general, "y varies inversely as the nth power of x ($n > 0$)" means

$$y = \frac{k}{x^n}$$

The following examples illustrate the three basic kinds of problems we run across that involve inverse variation.

EXAMPLE 4

Translate the statement "the length of a rectangle of a fixed area varies inversely as the width" into an equation that uses k as the constant of variation.

Solution

Let l represent the length and w the width, and the equation is

$$l = \frac{k}{w}$$ ∎

EXAMPLE 5

If y is inversely proportional to x, and $y = 4$ when $x = 12$, find the constant of variation.

Solution

Because y is inversely proportional to x, we have

$$y = \frac{k}{x}$$

Substituting $y = 4$ and $x = 12$, we obtain

$$4 = \frac{k}{12}$$

Solving this equation for k by multiplying both sides of the equation by 12 yields

$$k = 48$$

The constant of variation is 48.   ∎

EXAMPLE 6

Suppose the number of days it takes to complete a construction job varies inversely as the number of people assigned to the job. If it takes 7 people 8 days to do the job, how long would it take 14 people to complete the job?

Solution

Let d represent the number of days and p the number of people. The phrase "number of days . . . varies inversely as the number of people" translates into

$$d = \frac{k}{p}$$

Let $d = 8$ when $p = 7$, and the constant of variation becomes

$$8 = \frac{k}{7}$$

$$k = 56$$

Thus the specific equation is

$$d = \frac{56}{p}$$

Now, let $p = 14$ to obtain

$$d = \frac{56}{14}$$

$$d = 4$$

It should take 14 people 4 days to complete the job.   ■

The terms *direct* and *inverse*, as applied to variation, refer to the relative behavior of the variables involved in the equation. That is, in *direct* variation ($y = kx$), an assignment of *increasing* absolute values for x produces increasing absolute values for y, whereas in *inverse* variation $\left(y = \frac{k}{x}\right)$, an assignment of increasing absolute values for x produces *decreasing* absolute values for y.

■ Joint Variation

Variation may involve more than two variables. The following table illustrates some variation statements and their equivalent algebraic equations that use k as the constant of variation.

Statements 1, 2, and 3 illustrate the concept of **joint variation**. Statements 4 and 5 show that both direct and inverse variation may occur in the same problem. Statement 6 combines joint variation with inverse variation.

The two final examples of this section illustrate some of these variation situations.

Variation statement	Algebraic equation
1. y varies jointly as x and z.	$y = kxz$
2. y varies jointly as x, z, and w.	$y = kxzw$
3. V varies jointly as h and the square of r.	$V = khr^2$
4. h varies directly as V and inversely as w.	$h = \dfrac{kV}{w}$
5. y is directly proportional to x and inversely proportional to the square of z.	$y = \dfrac{kx}{z^2}$
6. y varies jointly as w and z and inversely as x.	$y = \dfrac{kwz}{x}$

E X A M P L E   7   The length of a rectangular box with a fixed height varies directly as the volume and inversely as the width. If the length is 12 centimeters when the volume is 960 cubic centimeters and the width is 8 centimeters, find the length when the volume is 700 centimeters and the width is 5 centimeters.

Solution

Use l for length, V for volume, and w for width, and the phrase "length varies directly as the volume and inversely as the width" translates into

$$l = \frac{kV}{w}$$

Substitute $l = 12$, $V = 960$, and $w = 8$, and the constant of variation becomes

$$12 = \frac{k(960)}{8}$$

$$12 = 120k$$

$$\frac{1}{10} = k$$

Thus the specific equation is

$$l = \frac{\frac{1}{10}V}{w} = \frac{V}{10w}$$

Now let $V = 700$ and $w = 5$ to obtain

$$l = \frac{700}{10(5)} = \frac{700}{50} = 14$$

The length is 14 centimeters.   ∎

E X A M P L E   8

Suppose that y varies jointly as x and z and inversely as w. If $y = 154$ when $x = 6$, $z = 11$, and $w = 3$, find the constant of variation.

Solution

The statement "y varies jointly as x and z and inversely as w" translates into

$$y = \frac{kxz}{w}$$

Substitute $y = 154$, $x = 6$, $z = 11$, and $w = 3$ to obtain

$$154 = \frac{k(6)(11)}{3}$$

$$154 = 22k$$

$$7 = k$$

The constant of variation is 7.

Problem Set 9.6

For Problems 1–10, translate each statement of variation into an equation, and use k as the constant of variation.

1. y varies inversely as the square of x.

2. y varies directly as the cube of x.

3. C varies directly as g and inversely as the cube of t.

4. V varies jointly as l and w.

5. The volume (V) of a sphere is directly proportional to the cube of its radius (r).

6. At a constant temperature, the volume (V) of a gas varies inversely as the pressure (P).

7. The surface area (S) of a cube varies directly as the square of the length of an edge (e).

8. The intensity of illumination (I) received from a source of light is inversely proportional to the square of the distance (d) from the source.

9. The volume (V) of a cone varies jointly as its height and the square of its radius.

10. The volume (V) of a gas varies directly as the absolute temperature (T) and inversely as the pressure (P).

For Problems 11–24, find the constant of variation for each of the stated conditions.

11. y varies directly as x, and $y = 8$ when $x = 12$.

12. y varies directly as x, and $y = 60$ when $x = 24$.

13. y varies directly as the square of x, and $y = -144$ when $x = 6$.

14. y varies directly as the cube of x, and $y = 48$ when $x = -2$.

15. V varies jointly as B and h, and $V = 96$ when $B = 24$ and $h = 12$.

16. A varies jointly as b and h, and $A = 72$ when $b = 16$ and $h = 9$.

17. y varies inversely as x, and $y = -4$ when $x = \dfrac{1}{2}$.

18. y varies inversely as x, and $y = -6$ when $x = \dfrac{4}{3}$.

19. r varies inversely as the square of t, and $r = \dfrac{1}{8}$ when $t = 4$.

20. r varies inversely as the cube of t, and $r = \dfrac{1}{16}$ when $t = 4$.

21. y varies directly as x and inversely as z, and $y = 45$ when $x = 18$ and $z = 2$.

22. y varies directly as x and inversely as z, and $y = 24$ when $x = 36$ and $z = 18$.

23. y is directly proportional to x and inversely proportional to the square of z, and $y = 81$ when $x = 36$ and $z = 2$.

24. y is directly proportional to the square of x and inversely proportional to the cube of z, and $y = 4\frac{1}{2}$ when $x = 6$ and $z = 4$.

Solve each of the following problems.

25. If y is directly proportional to x, and $y = 36$ when $x = 48$, find the value of y when $x = 12$.

26. If y is directly proportional to x, and $y = 42$ when $x = 28$, find the value of y when $x = 38$.

27. If y is inversely proportional to x, and $y = \frac{1}{9}$ when $x = 12$, find the value of y when $x = 8$.

28. If y is inversely proportional to x, and $y = \frac{1}{35}$ when $x = 14$, find the value of y when $x = 16$.

29. If A varies jointly as b and h, and $A = 60$ when $b = 12$ and $h = 10$, find A when $b = 16$ and $h = 14$.

30. If V varies jointly as B and h, and $V = 51$ when $B = 17$ and $h = 9$, find V when $B = 19$ and $h = 12$.

31. The volume of a gas at a constant temperature varies inversely as the pressure. What is the volume of a gas under pressure of 25 pounds if the gas occupies 15 cubic centimeters under a pressure of 20 pounds?

32. The time required for a car to travel a certain distance varies inversely as the rate at which it travels. If it takes 4 hours at 50 miles per hour to travel the distance, how long will it take at 40 miles per hour?

33. The volume (V) of a gas varies directly as the temperature (T) and inversely as the pressure (P). If $V = 48$ when $T = 320$ and $P = 20$, find V when $T = 280$ and $P = 30$.

34. The distance that a freely falling body falls varies directly as the square of the time it falls. If a body falls 144 feet in 3 seconds, how far will it fall in 5 seconds?

35. The period (the time required for one complete oscillation) of a simple pendulum varies directly as the square root of its length. If a pendulum 12 feet long has a period of 4 seconds, find the period of a pendulum 3 feet long.

36. The simple interest earned by a certain amount of money varies jointly as the rate of interest and the time (in years) that the money is invested. If the money is invested at 12% for 2 years, $120 is earned. How much is earned if the money is invested at 14% for 3 years?

37. The electrical resistance of a wire varies directly as its length and inversely as the square of its diameter. If the resistance of 200 meters of wire that has a diameter of $\frac{1}{2}$ centimeter is 1.5 ohms, find the resistance of 400 meters of wire with a diameter of $\frac{1}{4}$ centimeter.

38. The volume of a cylinder varies jointly as its altitude and the square of the radius of its base. If the volume of a cylinder is 1386 cubic centimeters when the radius of the base is 7 centimeters and its altitude is 9 centimeters, find the volume of a cylinder that has a base of radius 14 centimeters. The altitude of the cylinder is 5 centimeters.

39. The simple interest earned by a certain amount of money varies jointly as the rate of interest and the time (in years) that the money is invested.
   (a) If some money invested at 11% for 2 years earns $385, how much would the same amount earn at 12% for 1 year?
   (b) If some money invested at 12% for 3 years earns $819, how much would the same amount earn at 14% for 2 years?
   (c) If some money invested at 14% for 4 years earns $1960, how much would the same amount earn at 15% for 2 years?

40. The period (the time required for one complete oscillation) of a simple pendulum varies directly as the square root of its length. If a pendulum 9 inches long has a period of 2.4 seconds, find the period of a pendulum 12 inches long. Express your answer to the nearest tenth of a second.

41. The volume of a cylinder varies jointly as its altitude and the square of the radius of its base. If a cylinder that has a base with a radius of 5 meters and has an altitude of 7 meters has a volume of 549.5 cubic meters, find the volume of a cylinder that has a base with a radius of 9 meters and has an altitude of 14 meters.

42. If y is directly proportional to x and inversely proportional to the square of z, and if $y = 0.336$ when $x = 6$ and $z = 5$, find the constant of variation.

43. If y is inversely proportional to the square root of x, and if $y = 0.08$ when $x = 225$, find y when $x = 625$.

■ ■ ■ THOUGHTS INTO WORDS

44. How would you explain the difference between direct variation and inverse variation?

45. Suppose that y varies directly as the square of x. Does doubling the value of x also double the value of y? Explain your answer.

46. Suppose that y varies inversely as x. Does doubling the value of x also double the value of y? Explain your answer.

(9.1) A **relation** is a set of ordered pairs; a **function** is a relation in which no two ordered pairs have the same first component. The **domain** of a relation (or function) is the set of all first components, and the **range** is the set of all second components.

Single symbols such as f, g, and h are commonly used to name functions. The symbol $f(x)$ represents the element in the range associated with x from the domain. Thus if $f(x) = 3x + 7$, then $f(1) = 3(1) + 7 = 10$.

(9.2) Any function that can be written in the form

$$f(x) = ax + b$$

where a and b are real numbers, is a **linear function**. The graph of a linear function is a straight line.

Any function that can be written in the form

$$f(x) = ax^2 + bx + c$$

where a, b, and c are real numbers and $a \neq 0$, is a **quadratic function**. The graph of any quadratic function is a **parabola**, which can be drawn using either of the following methods.

1. Express the function in the form $f(x) = a(x - h)^2 + k$ and use the values of a, h, and k to determine the parabola.

2. Express the function in the form $f(x) = ax^2 + bx + c$ and use the fact that the vertex is at

$$\left(-\frac{b}{2a}, f\left(-\frac{b}{2a} \right) \right)$$

and the axis of symmetry is

$$x = -\frac{b}{2a}$$

We can solve some applications that involve maximum and minimum values with our knowledge of parabolas that are generated by quadratic functions.

(9.3) Another important graphing technique is to be able to recognize equations of the transformations of basic curves. We have worked with the following transformations in this chapter.

Vertical Translation   The graph of $y = f(x) + k$ is the graph of $y = f(x)$ shifted k units upward if $k > 0$ or shifted $|k|$ units downward if $k < 0$.

Horizontal Translation   The graph of $y = f(x - h)$ is the graph of $y = f(x)$ shifted h units to the right if $h > 0$ or shifted $|h|$ units to the left if $h < 0$.

x Axis Reflection   The graph of $y = -f(x)$ is the graph of $y = f(x)$ reflected through the x axis.

y Axis Reflection   The graph of $y = f(-x)$ is the graph of $y = f(x)$ reflected through the y axis.

Vertical Stretching and Shrinking   The graph of $y = cf(x)$ is obtained from the graph of $y = f(x)$ by multiplying the y coordinates of $y = f(x)$ by c. If $|c| > 1$, the graph is said to be **stretched** by a factor of $|c|$, and if $0 < |c| < 1$, the graph is said to be **shrunk** by a factor of $|c|$.

We list the following suggestions for graphing functions you are not familiar with.

1. Determine the domain of the function.
2. Determine any type of symmetry exhibited by the equation.
3. Find the intercepts.
4. Set up a table of values that satisfy the equation.
5. Plot the points associated with the ordered pairs and connect them with a smooth curve. Then, if appropriate, reflect this part of the curve according to any symmetry the graph exhibits.

(9.4) The **composition** of two functions f and g is defined by

$$(f \circ g)(x) = f(g(x))$$

for all x in the domain of g such that $g(x)$ is in the domain of f. Remember that the composition of functions is not a commutative operation.

(9.5) A **one-to-one function** is a function such that no two ordered pairs have the same second component.

If the components of each ordered pair of a given one-to-one function are interchanged, the resulting function and the given function are **inverses** of each other. The inverse of a function f is denoted by f^{-1}.

Graphically, two functions that are inverses of each other are mirror images with reference to the line $y = x$.

We can show that two functions f and f^{-1} are inverses of each other by verifying that

1. $(f^{-1} \circ f)(x) = x$ for all x in the domain of f.
2. $(f \circ f^{-1})(x) = x$ for all x in the domain of f^{-1}.

A technique for finding the inverse of a function is as follows:

1. Let $y = f(x)$.
2. Interchange x and y.
3. Solve the equation for y in terms of x.
4. $f^{-1}(x)$ is determined by the final equation.

(9.6) The equation $y = kx$ (k is a nonzero constant) defines a function called **direct variation**. The equation $y = \dfrac{k}{x}$ defines a function called **inverse variation**. In both cases, k is called the **constant of variation**.

Chapter 9   Review Problem Set

For Problems 1–4, specify the domain of each function.

1. $f = \{(1, 3), (2, 5), (4, 9)\}$

2. $f(x) = \dfrac{4}{x - 5}$

3. $f(x) = \dfrac{3}{x^2 + 4x}$

4. $f(x) = \sqrt{x^2 - 25}$

5. If $f(x) = x^2 - 2x - 1$, find $f(2), f(-3)$, and $f(a)$.

6. If $f(x) = 2x^2 + x - 7$, find $\dfrac{f(a + h) - f(a)}{h}$.

For Problems 7–16, graph each of the functions.

7. $f(x) = 4$

8. $f(x) = -3x + 2$

9. $f(x) = x^2 + 2x + 2$

10. $f(x) = |x| + 4$

11. $f(x) = -|x - 2|$

12. $f(x) = \sqrt{x - 2} - 3$

13. $f(x) = \dfrac{1}{x^2}$

14. $f(x) = -\dfrac{1}{2}x^2$

15. $f(x) = -3x^2 + 6x - 2$

16. $f(x) = -\sqrt{x + 1} - 2$

17. Find the coordinates of the vertex and the equation of the line of symmetry for each of the following parabolas.
    (a) $f(x) = x^2 + 10x - 3$
    (b) $f(x) = -2x^2 - 14x + 9$

For Problems 18–20, determine $(f \circ g)(x)$ and $(g \circ f)(x)$ for each pair of functions.

18. $f(x) = 2x - 3$ and $g(x) = 3x - 4$

19. $f(x) = x - 4$ and $g(x) = x^2 - 2x + 3$

20. $f(x) = x^2 - 5$ and $g(x) = -2x + 5$

For Problems 21–23, find the inverse (f^{-1}) of the given function.

21. $f(x) = 6x - 1$

22. $f(x) = \dfrac{2}{3}x + 7$

23. $f(x) = -\dfrac{3}{5}x - \dfrac{2}{7}$

24. If y varies directly as x and inversely as z, and if $y = 21$ when $x = 14$ and $z = 6$, find the constant of variation.

25. If y varies jointly as x and the square root of z, and if $y = 60$ when $x = 2$ and $z = 9$, find y when $x = 3$ and $z = 16$.

26. The weight of a body above the surface of the earth varies inversely as the square of its distance from the center of the earth. Assume that the radius of the earth is 4000 miles. How much would a man weigh 1000 miles above the earth's surface if he weighs 200 pounds on the surface?

27. Find two numbers whose sum is 40 and whose product is a maximum.

28. Find two numbers whose sum is 50 such that the square of one number plus six times the other number is a minimum.

29. Suppose that 50 students are able to raise $250 for a party when each one contributes $5. Furthermore, they figure that for each additional student they can find to contribute, the cost per student will decrease by a nickel. How many additional students will they need to maximize the amount of money they will have for a party?

30. The surface area of a cube varies directly as the square of the length of an edge. If the surface area of a cube that has edges 8 inches long is 384 square inches, find the surface area of a cube that has edges 10 inches long.

31. The cost for burning a 100-watt bulb is given by the function $c(h) = 0.006h$, where h represents the number of hours that the bulb burns. How much, to the nearest cent, does it cost to burn a 100-watt bulb for 4 hours per night for a 30-day month?

32. "All Items 30% Off Marked Price" is a sign in a local department store. Form a function and then use it to determine how much one has to pay for each of the following marked items: a $65 pair of shoes, a $48 pair of slacks, a $15.50 belt.

1. Determine the domain of the function $f(x) = \dfrac{-3}{2x^2 + 7x - 4}$.

2. Determine the domain of the function $f(x) = \sqrt{5 - 3x}$.

3. If $f(x) = -\dfrac{1}{2}x + \dfrac{1}{3}$, find $f(-3)$.

4. If $f(x) = -x^2 - 6x + 3$, find $f(-2)$.

5. Find the vertex of the parabola $f(x) = -2x^2 - 24x - 69$.

6. If $f(x) = 3x^2 + 2x - 5$, find $\dfrac{f(a + h) - f(a)}{h}$.

7. If $f(x) = -3x + 4$ and $g(x) = 7x + 2$, find $(f \circ g)(x)$.

8. If $f(x) = 2x + 5$ and $g(x) = 2x^2 - x + 3$, find $(g \circ f)(x)$.

9. If $f(x) = \dfrac{3}{x - 2}$ and $g(x) = \dfrac{2}{x}$, find $(f \circ g)(x)$.

For Problems 10–12, find the inverse of the given function.

10. $f(x) = 5x - 9$

11. $f(x) = -3x - 6$

12. $f(x) = \dfrac{2}{3}x - \dfrac{3}{5}$

13. If y varies inversely as x, and if $y = \dfrac{1}{2}$ when $x = -8$, find the constant of variation.

14. If y varies jointly as x and z, and if $y = 18$ when $x = 8$ and $z = 9$, find y when $x = 5$ and $z = 12$.

15. Find two numbers whose sum is 60, such that the sum of the square of one number plus twelve times the other number is a minimum.

16. The simple interest earned by a certain amount of money varies jointly as the rate of interest and the time (in years) that the money is invested. If \$140 is earned for a certain amount of money invested at 7% for 5 years, how much is earned if the same amount is invested at 8% for 3 years?

For Problems 17–19, use the concepts of translation and/or reflection to describe how the second curve can be obtained from the first curve.

17. $f(x) = x^3$, $f(x) = (x - 6)^3 - 4$

18. $f(x) = |x|$, $f(x) = -|x| + 8$

19. $f(x) = \sqrt{x}$, $f(x) = -\sqrt{x + 5} + 7$

For Problems 20–25, graph each function.

20. $f(x) = -x - 1$

21. $f(x) = -2x^2 - 12x - 14$

22. $f(x) = 2\sqrt{x} - 2$

23. $f(x) = 3|x - 2| - 1$

24. $f(x) = -\dfrac{1}{x} + 3$

25. $f(x) = \sqrt{-x + 2}$

10

Systems of Equations

10.1 Systems of Two Linear Equations in Two Variables

10.2 Elimination-by-Addition Method

10.3 Systems of Three Linear Equations in Three Variables

10.4 Matrix Approach to Solving Systems

10.5 Determinants

10.6 3 × 3 Determinants and Systems of Three Linear Equations in Three Variables

10.7 Systems Involving Nonlinear Equations and Systems of Inequalities

When mixing different solutions, a chemist could use a system of equations to determine how much of each solution is needed to produce a specific concentration.

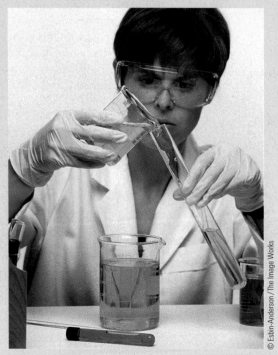

© Esbin-Anderson / The Image Works

A 10%-salt solution is to be mixed with a 20%-salt solution to produce 20 gallons of a 17.5%-salt solution. How many gallons of the 10% solution and how many gallons of the 20% solution will be needed? The two equations $x + y = 20$ and $0.10x + 0.20y = 0.175(20)$, where x represents the number of gallons of the 10% solution, and y represents the number of gallons of the 20% solution, algebraically represent the conditions of the problem. The two equations considered together form a **system of linear equations**, and the problem can be solved by solving this system of equations.

Throughout most of this chapter, we will consider systems of linear equations and their applications. We will discuss various techniques for solving systems of linear equations.

10.1   Systems of Two Linear Equations in Two Variables

In Chapter 7, we stated that any equation of the form $Ax + By = C$, where A, B, and C are real numbers (A and B not both zero) is a *linear equation* in the two variables x and y, and its graph is a straight line. Two linear equations in two variables considered together form a **system of two linear equations in two variables**. Here are a few examples:

$$\begin{pmatrix} x + y = 6 \\ x - y = 2 \end{pmatrix} \qquad \begin{pmatrix} 3x + 2y = 1 \\ 5x - 2y = 23 \end{pmatrix} \qquad \begin{pmatrix} 4x - 5y = 21 \\ 3x + 7y = -38 \end{pmatrix}$$

To **solve a system**, such as one of the above, means to find all of the ordered pairs that satisfy both equations in the system. For example, if we graph the two equations $x + y = 6$ and $x - y = 2$ on the same set of axes, as in Figure 10.1, then the ordered pair associated with the point of intersection of the two lines is the solution of the system. Thus we say that $\{(4, 2)\}$ is the solution set of the system

$$\begin{pmatrix} x + y = 6 \\ x - y = 2 \end{pmatrix}$$

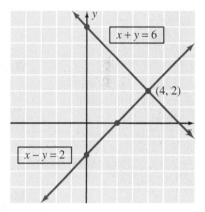

Figure 10.1

To check, substitute 4 for x and 2 for y in the two equations, which yields

$x + y$ becomes $4 + 2 = 6$ A true statement

$x - y$ becomes $4 - 2 = 2$ A true statement

Because the graph of a linear equation in two variables is a straight line, there are three possible situations that can occur when we solve a system of two linear equations in two variables. We illustrate these cases in Figure 10.2.

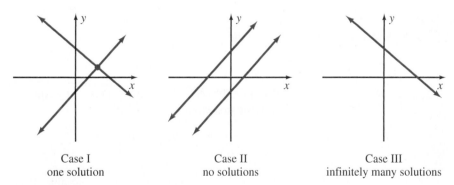

Case I	Case II	Case III
one solution	no solutions	infinitely many solutions

Figure 10.2

Case I The graphs of the two equations are two lines intersecting in *one* point. There is *one solution*, and the system is called a **consistent system**.

Case II The graphs of the two equations are parallel lines. There is *no solution*, and the system is called an **inconsistent system**.

Case III The graphs of the two equations are the same line, and there are *infinitely many solutions* to the system. Any pair of real numbers that satisfies one of the equations will also satisfy the other equation, and we say that the equations are **dependent**.

Thus as we solve a system of two linear equations in two variables, we know what to expect. The system will have no solutions, one ordered pair as a solution, or infinitely many ordered pairs as solutions.

■ Substitution Method

It should be evident that solving systems of equations by graphing requires accurate graphs. In fact, unless the solutions are integers, it is quite difficult to obtain exact solutions from a graph. Thus we will consider some other methods for solving systems of equations.

We describe the **substitution method**, which works quite well with systems of two linear equations in two unknowns, as follows:

Step 1 Solve one of the equations for one variable in terms of the other variable if neither equation is in such a form. (If possible, make a choice that will avoid fractions.)

Step 2 Substitute the expression obtained in Step 1 into the other equation to produce an equation with one variable.

Step 3 Solve the equation obtained in Step 2.

Step 4 Use the solution obtained in Step 3, along with the expression obtained in Step 1, to determine the solution of the system.

Now let's look at some examples that illustrate the substitution method.

E X A M P L E   1

Solve the system $\left(\begin{array}{l} x + y = 16 \\ y = x + 2 \end{array} \right)$.

Solution

Because the second equation states that y equals $x + 2$, we can substitute $x + 2$ for y in the first equation.

$$x + y = 16 \xrightarrow{\text{Substitute } x + 2 \text{ for } y} x + (x + 2) = 16$$

Now we have an equation with one variable that we can solve in the usual way.

$$x + (x + 2) = 16$$
$$2x + 2 = 16$$
$$2x = 14$$
$$x = 7$$

Substituting 7 for x in one of the two original equations (let's use the second one) yields

$$y = 7 + 2 = 9$$

To check, we can substitute 7 for x and 9 for y in both of the original equations.

$$7 + 9 = 16 \qquad \text{A true statement}$$
$$9 = 7 + 2 \qquad \text{A true statement}$$

The solution set is $\{(7, 9)\}$. ∎

EXAMPLE 2

Solve the system $\left(\begin{array}{l} x = 3y - 25 \\ 4x + 5y = 19 \end{array} \right)$.

Solution

In this case the first equation states that x equals $3y - 25$. Therefore, we can substitute $3y - 25$ for x in the second equation.

$$4x + 5y = 19 \xrightarrow{\text{Substitute } 3y - 25 \text{ for } x} 4(3y - 25) + 5y = 19$$

Solving this equation yields

$$4(3y - 25) + 5y = 19$$
$$12y - 100 + 5y = 19$$
$$17y = 119$$
$$y = 7$$

Substituting 7 for y in the first equation produces

$$x = 3(7) - 25$$
$$= 21 - 25 = -4$$

The solution set is $\{(-4, 7)\}$; check it. ∎

EXAMPLE 3

Solve the system $\left(\begin{array}{l} 3x - 7y = 2 \\ x + 4y = 1 \end{array} \right)$.

Solution

Let's solve the second equation for x in terms of y.

$$x + 4y = 1$$
$$x = 1 - 4y$$

Now we can substitute $1 - 4y$ for x in the first equation.

$$3x - 7y = 2 \xrightarrow{\text{Substitute } 1 - 4y \text{ for } x} 3(1 - 4y) - 7y = 2$$

Let's solve this equation for y.

$$3(1 - 4y) - 7y = 2$$

$$3 - 12y - 7y = 2$$

$$-19y = -1$$

$$y = \frac{1}{19}$$

Finally, we can substitute $\frac{1}{19}$ for y in the equation $x = 1 - 4y$.

$$x = 1 - 4\left(\frac{1}{19}\right)$$

$$= 1 - \frac{4}{19}$$

$$= \frac{15}{19}$$

The solution set is $\left\{\left(\frac{15}{19}, \frac{1}{19}\right)\right\}$. ∎

E X A M P L E   4

Solve the system $\begin{pmatrix} 5x - 6y = -4 \\ 3x + 2y = -8 \end{pmatrix}$.

Solution

Note that solving either equation for either variable will produce a fractional form. Let's solve the second equation for y in terms of x.

$$3x + 2y = -8$$

$$2y = -8 - 3x$$

$$y = \frac{-8 - 3x}{2}$$

Now we can substitute $\dfrac{-8 - 3x}{2}$ for y in the first equation.

$$5x - 6y = -4 \xrightarrow{\text{Substitute } \frac{-8 - 3x}{2} \text{ for } y} 5x - 6\left(\frac{-8 - 3x}{2}\right) = -4$$

Solving this equation yields

$$5x - 6\left(\frac{-8 - 3x}{2}\right) = -4$$

$$5x - 3(-8 - 3x) = -4$$

$$5x + 24 + 9x = -4$$

$$14x = -28$$

$$x = -2$$

Substituting -2 for x in $y = \dfrac{-8 - 3x}{2}$ yields

$$y = \frac{-8 - 3(-2)}{2}$$

$$= \frac{-8 + 6}{2}$$

$$= \frac{-2}{2}$$

$$= -1$$

The solution set is $\{(-2, -1)\}$.   ■

■ Problem Solving

Many word problems that we solved earlier in this text using one variable and one equation can also be solved using a system of two linear equations in two variables. In fact, in many of these problems you may find it more natural to use two variables. Let's consider some examples.

E X A M P L E   5

Anita invested some money at 8% and $400 more than that amount at 9%. The yearly interest from the two investments was $87. How much did Anita invest at each rate?

Solution

Let x represent the amount invested at 8% and let y represent the amount invested at 9%. The problem translates into the following system.

Amount invested at 9% was $400 more than at 8%. ⟶ $\left(\begin{array}{l} y = x + 400 \\ 0.08x + 0.09y = 87 \end{array}\right)$
Yearly interest from the two investments was $87. ⟶

From the first equation we can substitute $x + 400$ for y in the second equation and solve for x.

$$0.08x + 0.09(x + 400) = 87$$

$$0.08x + 0.09x + 36 = 87$$

$$0.17x = 51$$

$$x = 300$$

Therefore, $300 is invested at 8% and $300 + $400 = $700 is invested at 9%. ■

The two-variable expression $10t + u$ can be used to represent any two-digit number. The t represents the tens digit, and the u represents the units digit. For example, if $t = 5$ and $u = 2$, then $10t + u$ becomes $10(5) + 2 = 52$. We use this general representation for a two-digit number in the next problem.

E X A M P L E   6

The tens digit of a two-digit number is 2 more than twice the units digit. The number with the digits reversed is 45 less than the original number. Find the original number.

Solution

Let u represent the units digit of the original number. Let t represent the tens digit of the original number. Then $10t + u$ represents the original number and $10u + t$ represents the number with the digits reversed. The problem translates into the following system.

$$\left(\begin{array}{c} t = 2u + 2 \\ 10u + t = 10t + u - 45 \end{array} \right)$$

The tens digit is 2 more than twice the units digit.
The number with the digits reversed is 45 less than the original number.

When we simplify the second equation, the system becomes

$$\left(\begin{array}{c} t = 2u + 2 \\ t - u = 5 \end{array} \right)$$

From the first equation, we can substitute $2u + 2$ for t in the second equation and solve.

$$t - u = 5$$

$$2u + 2 - u = 5$$

$$u = 3$$

Substitute 3 for u in $t = 2u + 2$ to obtain

$$t = 2u + 2$$

$$= 2(3) + 2 = 8$$

The tens digit is 8 and the units digit is 3, so the number is 83. (You should check to see whether 83 satisfies the original conditions stated in the problem.) ■

In our final example of this section, we will use a graphing utility to help solve a system of equations.

E X A M P L E   7

Solve the system $\begin{pmatrix} 1.14x + 2.35y = -7.12 \\ 3.26x - 5.05y = 26.72 \end{pmatrix}$.

Solution

First, we need to solve each equation for y in terms of x. Thus the system becomes

$$\begin{pmatrix} y = \dfrac{-7.12 - 1.14x}{2.35} \\ y = \dfrac{3.26x - 26.72}{5.05} \end{pmatrix}.$$

Now we can enter both of these equations into a graphing utility and obtain Figure 10.3. In this figure it appears that the point of intersection is at approximately $x = 2$ and $y = -4$. By direct substitution into the given equations, we can verify that the point of intersection is exactly $(2, -4)$.

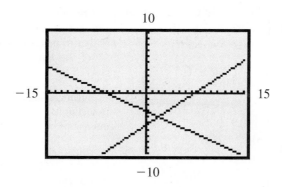

Figure 10.3

Problem Set 10.1

For Problems 1–10, use the graphing approach to determine whether the system is consistent, the system is inconsistent, or the equations are dependent. If the system is consistent, find the solution set from the graph and check it.

1. $\begin{pmatrix} x - y = 1 \\ 2x + y = 8 \end{pmatrix}$

2. $\begin{pmatrix} 3x + y = 0 \\ x - 2y = -7 \end{pmatrix}$

3. $\begin{pmatrix} 4x + 3y = -5 \\ 2x - 3y = -7 \end{pmatrix}$

4. $\begin{pmatrix} 2x - y = 9 \\ 4x - 2y = 11 \end{pmatrix}$

5. $\begin{pmatrix} \dfrac{1}{2}x + \dfrac{1}{4}y = 9 \\ 4x + 2y = 72 \end{pmatrix}$

6. $\begin{pmatrix} 5x + 2y = -9 \\ 4x - 3y = 2 \end{pmatrix}$

7. $\begin{pmatrix} \dfrac{1}{2}x - \dfrac{1}{3}y = 3 \\ x + 4y = -8 \end{pmatrix}$

8. $\begin{pmatrix} 4x - 9y = -60 \\ \dfrac{1}{3}x - \dfrac{3}{4}y = -5 \end{pmatrix}$

9. $\begin{pmatrix} x - \dfrac{y}{2} = -4 \\ 8x - 4y = -1 \end{pmatrix}$

10. $\begin{pmatrix} 3x - 2y = 7 \\ 6x + 5y = -4 \end{pmatrix}$

For Problems 11–36, solve each system by using the substitution method.

11. $\begin{pmatrix} x + y = 20 \\ x = y - 4 \end{pmatrix}$

12. $\begin{pmatrix} x + y = 23 \\ y = x - 5 \end{pmatrix}$

13. $\begin{pmatrix} y = -3x - 18 \\ 5x - 2y = -8 \end{pmatrix}$

14. $\begin{pmatrix} 4x - 3y = 33 \\ x = -4y - 25 \end{pmatrix}$

15. $\begin{pmatrix} x = -3y \\ 7x - 2y = -69 \end{pmatrix}$

16. $\begin{pmatrix} 9x - 2y = -38 \\ y = -5x \end{pmatrix}$

17. $\begin{pmatrix} 2x + 3y = 11 \\ 3x - 2y = -3 \end{pmatrix}$

18. $\begin{pmatrix} 3x - 4y = -14 \\ 4x + 3y = 23 \end{pmatrix}$

19. $\begin{pmatrix} 3x - 4y = 9 \\ x = 4y - 1 \end{pmatrix}$

20. $\begin{pmatrix} y = 3x - 5 \\ 2x + 3y = 6 \end{pmatrix}$

21. $\begin{pmatrix} y = \dfrac{2}{5}x - 1 \\ 3x + 5y = 4 \end{pmatrix}$

22. $\begin{pmatrix} y = \dfrac{3}{4}x - 5 \\ 5x - 4y = 9 \end{pmatrix}$

23. $\begin{pmatrix} 7x - 3y = -2 \\ x = \dfrac{3}{4}y + 1 \end{pmatrix}$

24. $\begin{pmatrix} 5x - y = 9 \\ x = \dfrac{1}{2}y - 3 \end{pmatrix}$

25. $\begin{pmatrix} 2x + y = 12 \\ 3x - y = 13 \end{pmatrix}$

26. $\begin{pmatrix} -x + 4y = -22 \\ x - 7y = 34 \end{pmatrix}$

27. $\begin{pmatrix} 4x + 3y = -40 \\ 5x - y = -12 \end{pmatrix}$

28. $\begin{pmatrix} x - 5y = 33 \\ -4x + 7y = -41 \end{pmatrix}$

29. $\begin{pmatrix} 3x + y = 2 \\ 11x - 3y = 5 \end{pmatrix}$

30. $\begin{pmatrix} 2x - y = 9 \\ 7x + 4y = 1 \end{pmatrix}$

31. $\begin{pmatrix} 3x + 5y = 22 \\ 4x - 7y = -39 \end{pmatrix}$

32. $\begin{pmatrix} 2x - 3y = -16 \\ 6x + 7y = 16 \end{pmatrix}$

33. $\begin{pmatrix} 4x - 5y = 3 \\ 8x + 15y = -24 \end{pmatrix}$

34. $\begin{pmatrix} 2x + 3y = 3 \\ 4x - 9y = -4 \end{pmatrix}$

35. $\begin{pmatrix} 6x - 3y = 4 \\ 5x + 2y = -1 \end{pmatrix}$

36. $\begin{pmatrix} 7x - 2y = 1 \\ 4x + 5y = 2 \end{pmatrix}$

For Problems 37–50, solve each problem by setting up and solving an appropriate system of equations.

37. Doris invested some money at 7% and some money at 8%. She invested $6000 more at 8% than she did at 7%. Her total yearly interest from the two investments was $780. How much did Doris invest at each rate?

38. Suppose that Gus invested a total of $8000, part of it at 8% and the remainder at 9%. His yearly income from the two investments was $690. How much did he invest at each rate?

39. The sum of the digits of a two-digit number is 11. The tens digit is one more than four times the units digit. Find the number.

40. The units digit of a two-digit number is one less than three times the tens digit. If the sum of the digits is 11, find the number.

41. Find two numbers whose sum is 131 such that one number is five less than three times the other.

42. The difference of two numbers is 75. The larger number is three less than four times the smaller number. Find the numbers.

43. In a class of 50 students, the number of females is two more than five times the number of males. How many females are there in the class?

44. In a recent survey, one thousand registered voters were asked about their political preferences. The number of males in the survey was five less than one-half of the number of females. Find the number of males in the survey.

45. The perimeter of a rectangle is 94 inches. The length of the rectangle is 7 inches more than the width. Find the dimensions of the rectangle.

46. Two angles are supplementary, and the measure of one of them is 20° less than three times the measure of the other angle. Find the measure of each angle.

47. A deposit slip listed $700 in cash to be deposited. There were 100 bills, some of them five-dollar bills and the remainder ten-dollar bills. How many bills of each denomination were deposited?

48. Cindy has 30 coins, consisting of dimes and quarters, that total $5.10. How many coins of each kind does she have?

49. The income from a student production was $10,000. The price of a student ticket was $3, and nonstudent tickets were sold at $5 each. Three thousand tickets were sold. How many tickets of each kind were sold?

50. Sue bought 3 packages of cookies and 2 sacks of potato chips for $3.65. Later she bought 2 more packages of cookies and 5 additional sacks of potato chips for $4.23. Find the price of a package of cookies.

■ ■ ■ THOUGHTS INTO WORDS

51. Give a general description of how to use the substitution method to solve a system of two linear equations in two variables.

52. Is it possible for a system of two linear equations in two variables to have exactly two solutions? Defend your answer.

53. Explain how you would solve the system $\begin{pmatrix} 2x + 5y = 5 \\ 5x - y = 9 \end{pmatrix}$ using the substitution method.

GRAPHING CALCULATOR ACTIVITIES

54. Use your graphing calculator to help determine whether, in Problems 1–10, the system is consistent, the system is inconsistent, or the equations are dependent.

55. Use your graphing calculator to help determine the solution set for each of the following systems. Be sure to check your answers.

(a) $\begin{pmatrix} 3x - y = 30 \\ 5x - y = 46 \end{pmatrix}$

(b) $\begin{pmatrix} 1.2x + 3.4y = 25.4 \\ 3.7x - 2.3y = 14.4 \end{pmatrix}$

(c) $\begin{pmatrix} 1.98x + 2.49y = 13.92 \\ 1.19x + 3.45y = 16.18 \end{pmatrix}$

(d) $\begin{pmatrix} 2x - 3y = 10 \\ 3x + 5y = 53 \end{pmatrix}$

(e) $\begin{pmatrix} 4x - 7y = -49 \\ 6x + 9y = 219 \end{pmatrix}$

(f) $\begin{pmatrix} 3.7x - 2.9y = -14.3 \\ 1.6x + 4.7y = -30 \end{pmatrix}$

10.2   Elimination-by-Addition Method

We found in the previous section that the substitution method for solving a system of two equations and two unknowns works rather well. However, as the number of equations and unknowns increases, the substitution method becomes quite unwieldy. In this section we are going to introduce another method, called the **elimination-by-addition** method. We shall introduce it here using systems of two linear equations in two unknowns and then, in the next section, extend its use to three linear equations in three unknowns.

The elimination-by-addition method involves replacing systems of equations with simpler, equivalent systems until we obtain a system whereby we can easily extract the solutions. **Equivalent systems of equations are systems that have exactly the same solution set**. We can apply the following operations or transformations to a system of equations to produce an equivalent system.

1. Any two equations of the system can be interchanged.

2. Both sides of an equation of the system can be multiplied by any nonzero real number.

3. Any equation of the system can be replaced by the *sum* of that equation and a nonzero multiple of another equation.

Now let's see how to apply these operations to solve a system of two linear equations in two unknowns.

E X A M P L E   1

Solve the system $\begin{pmatrix} 3x + 2y = & 1 \\ 5x - 2y = & 23 \end{pmatrix}$.

$$(1)$$
$$(2)$$

Solution

Let's replace equation (2) with an equation we form by multiplying equation (1) by 1 and then adding that result to equation (2).

$$\begin{pmatrix} 3x + 2y = & 1 \\ 8x & = 24 \end{pmatrix}$$

$$(3)$$
$$(4)$$

From equation (4) we can easily obtain the value of x.

$$8x = 24$$

$$x = 3$$

Then we can substitute 3 for x in equation (3).

$$3x + 2y = 1$$

$$3(3) + 2y = 1$$

$$2y = -8$$

$$y = -4$$

The solution set is $\{(3, -4)\}$. Check it! ∎

E X A M P L E   2

Solve the system $\begin{pmatrix} x + 5y = & -2 \\ 3x - 4y = & -25 \end{pmatrix}$.

$$(1)$$
$$(2)$$

Solution

Let's replace equation (2) with an equation we form by multiplying equation (1) by -3 and then adding that result to equation (2).

$$\begin{pmatrix} x + 5y = & -2 \\ -19y = & -19 \end{pmatrix}$$

$$(3)$$
$$(4)$$

From equation (4) we can obtain the value of y.

$$-19y = -19$$

$$y = 1$$

Now we can substitute 1 for y in equation (3).

$$x + 5y = -2$$

$$x + 5(1) = -2$$

$$x = -7$$

The solution set is $\{(-7, 1)\}$. ∎

Note that our objective has been to produce an equivalent system of equations whereby one of the variables can be *eliminated* from one equation. We accomplish this by multiplying one equation of the system by an appropriate number and then *adding* that result to the other equation. Thus the method is called **elimination by addition**. Let's look at another example.

E X A M P L E   3

Solve the system $\left(\begin{array}{rl} 2x + 5y = & 4 \\ 5x - 7y = & -29 \end{array}\right)$.

(1)
(2)

Solution

Let's form an equivalent system where the second equation has no x term. First, we can multiply equation (2) by -2.

$$\left(\begin{array}{rl} 2x + 5y = & 4 \\ -10x + 14y = & 58 \end{array}\right)$$

(3)
(4)

Now we can replace equation (4) with an equation that we form by multiplying equation (3) by 5 and then adding that result to equation (4).

$$\left(\begin{array}{rl} 2x + 5y = & 4 \\ 39y = & 78 \end{array}\right)$$

(5)
(6)

From equation (6) we can find the value of y.

$$39y = 78$$

$$y = 2$$

Now we can substitute 2 for y in equation (5).

$$2x + 5y = 4$$

$$2x + 5(2) = 4$$

$$2x = -6$$

$$x = -3$$

The solution set is $\{(-3, 2)\}$. ■

E X A M P L E   4

Solve the system $\left(\begin{array}{rl} 3x - 2y = & 5 \\ 2x + 7y = & 9 \end{array}\right)$.

(1)
(2)

Solution

We can start by multiplying equation (2) by -3.

$$\left(\begin{array}{rl} 3x - 2y = & 5 \\ -6x - 21y = & -27 \end{array}\right)$$

(3)
(4)

Now we can replace equation (4) with an equation we form by multiplying equation (3) by 2 and then adding that result to equation (4).

$$\left(\begin{array}{rl} 3x - 2y = & 5 \\ -25y = & -17 \end{array}\right)$$

(5)
(6)

From equation (6) we can find the value of y.

$$-25y = -17$$

$$y = \frac{17}{25}$$

Now we can substitute $\frac{17}{25}$ for y in equation (5).

$$3x - 2y = 5$$

$$3x - 2\left(\frac{17}{25}\right) = 5$$

$$3x - \frac{34}{25} = 5$$

$$3x = 5 + \frac{34}{25}$$

$$3x = \frac{125}{25} + \frac{34}{25}$$

$$3x = \frac{159}{25}$$

$$x = \left(\frac{159}{25}\right)\left(\frac{1}{3}\right) = \frac{53}{25}$$

The solution set is $\left\{\left(\frac{53}{25}, \frac{17}{25}\right)\right\}$. (Perhaps you should check this result!) ■

■ Which Method To Use

Both the elimination-by-addition and the substitution methods can be used to obtain exact solutions for any system of two linear equations in two unknowns. Sometimes the issue is that of deciding which method to use on a particular system. As we have seen with the examples thus far in this section and those of the previous section, many systems lend themselves to one or the other method by the original format of the equations. Let's emphasize that point with some more examples.

EXAMPLE 5

Solve the system $\begin{pmatrix} 4x - 3y = 4 \\ 10x + 9y = -1 \end{pmatrix}$.

(1)
(2)

Solution

Because changing the form of either equation in preparation for the substitution method would produce fractional form, we are probably better off using the elimination-by-addition method. Let's replace equation (2) with an equation we form by multiplying equation (1) by 3 and then adding that result to equation (2).

$$\begin{pmatrix} 4x - 3y = 4 \\ 22x \quad\quad = 11 \end{pmatrix} \quad\quad\quad (3) \\ (4)$$

From equation (4) we can determine the value of x.

$$22x = 11$$

$$x = \frac{11}{22} = \frac{1}{2}$$

Now we can substitute $\frac{1}{2}$ for x in equation (3).

$$4x - 3y = 4$$

$$4\left(\frac{1}{2}\right) - 3y = 4$$

$$2 - 3y = 4$$

$$-3y = 2$$

$$y = -\frac{2}{3}$$

The solution set is $\left\{\left(\frac{1}{2}, -\frac{2}{3}\right)\right\}$. ∎

EXAMPLE 6 Solve the system $\begin{pmatrix} 6x + 5y = -3 \\ y = -2x - 7 \end{pmatrix}$. $\quad\quad (1) \\ (2)$

Solution

Because the second equation is of the form "y equals," let's use the substitution method. From the second equation we can substitute $-2x - 7$ for y in the first equation.

$$6x + 5y = -3 \xrightarrow{\text{Substitute } -2x - 7 \text{ for } y} 6x + 5(-2x - 7) = -3$$

Solving this equation yields

$$6x + 5(-2x - 7) = -3$$

$$6x - 10x - 35 = -3$$

$$-4x - 35 = -3$$

$$-4x = 32$$

$$x = -8$$

Substitute -8 for x in the second equation to obtain

$$y = -2(-8) - 7 = 16 - 7 = 9$$

The solution set is $\{(-8, 9)\}$. ∎

Sometimes we need to simplify the equations of a system before we can decide which method to use for solving the system. Let's consider an example of that type.

E X A M P L E   7

Solve the system $\left(\begin{array}{l} \dfrac{x-2}{4} + \dfrac{y+1}{3} = 2 \\ \dfrac{x+1}{7} + \dfrac{y-3}{2} = \dfrac{1}{2} \end{array} \right)$.

(1)

(2)

Solution

First, we need to simplify the two equations. Let's multiply both sides of equation (1) by 12 and simplify.

$$12\left(\frac{x-2}{4} + \frac{y+1}{3} \right) = 12(2)$$

$$3(x-2) + 4(y+1) = 24$$

$$3x - 6 + 4y + 4 = 24$$

$$3x + 4y - 2 = 24$$

$$3x + 4y = 26$$

Let's multiply both sides of equation (2) by 14.

$$14\left(\frac{x+1}{7} + \frac{y-3}{2} \right) = 14\left(\frac{1}{2} \right)$$

$$2(x+1) + 7(y-3) = 7$$

$$2x + 2 + 7y - 21 = 7$$

$$2x + 7y - 19 = 7$$

$$2x + 7y = 26$$

Now we have the following system to solve.

$$\left(\begin{array}{l} 3x + 4y = 26 \\ 2x + 7y = 26 \end{array} \right)$$

(3)

(4)

Probably the easiest approach is to use the elimination-by-addition method. We can start by multiplying equation (4) by -3.

$$\left(\begin{array}{r} 3x + 4y = 26 \\ -6x - 21y = -78 \end{array} \right)$$

(5)

(6)

Now we can replace equation (6) with an equation we form by multiplying equation (5) by 2 and then adding that result to equation (6).

$$\left(\begin{array}{r} 3x + 4y = 26 \\ -13y = -26 \end{array} \right)$$

(7)

(8)

From equation (8) we can find the value of y.

$$-13y = -26$$

$$y = 2$$

Now we can substitute 2 for y in equation (7).

$$3x + 4y = 26$$

$$3x + 4(2) = 26$$

$$3x = 18$$

$$x = 6$$

The solution set is $\{(6, 2)\}$.   ■

Remark: Don't forget that to check a problem like Example 7 you must check the potential solutions back in the original equations.

In Section 10.1, we discussed the fact that you can tell whether a system of two linear equations in two unknowns has no solution, one solution, or infinitely many solutions by graphing the equations of the system. That is, the two lines may be parallel (no solution), or they may intersect in one point (one solution), or they may coincide (infinitely many solutions).

From a practical viewpoint, the systems that have one solution deserve most of our attention. However, we need to be able to deal with the other situations; they do occur occasionally. Let's use two examples to illustrate the type of thing that happens when we encounter *no solution* or *infinitely many solutions* when using either the elimination-by-addition method or the substitution method.

EXAMPLE 8

Solve the system $\begin{pmatrix} y = 3x - 1 \\ -9x + 3y = 4 \end{pmatrix}$.   (1)
                                                                                             (2)

Solution

Using the substitution method, we can proceed as follows:

Substitute $3x - 1$ for y

$$-9x + 3y = 4 \longrightarrow -9x + 3(3x - 1) = 4$$

Solving this equation yields

$$-9x + 3(3x - 1) = 4$$

$$-9x + 9x - 3 = 4$$

$$-3 = 4$$

The *false numerical statement*, $-3 = 4$, implies that the system has *no solution*. (You may want to graph the two lines to verify this conclusion!)   ■

E X A M P L E   9

Solve the system $\begin{pmatrix} 5x + y = 2 \\ 10x + 2y = 4 \end{pmatrix}$.

(1)
(2)

Solution

Use the elimination-by-addition method and proceed as follows: Let's replace equation (2) with an equation we form by multiplying equation (1) by -2 and then adding that result to equation (2).

$$\begin{pmatrix} 5x + y = 2 \\ 0 + 0 = 0 \end{pmatrix}$$

(3)
(4)

The *true numerical statement*, $0 + 0 = 0$, implies that the system has *infinitely many solutions*. Any ordered pair that satisfies one of the equations will also satisfy the other equation. Thus the solution set can be expressed as

$$\{(x, y) | 5x + y = 2\}$$ ∎

Problem Set 10.2

For Problems 1–16, use the elimination-by-addition method to solve each system.

1. $\begin{pmatrix} 2x + 3y = -1 \\ 5x - 3y = 29 \end{pmatrix}$

2. $\begin{pmatrix} 3x - 4y = -30 \\ 7x + 4y = 10 \end{pmatrix}$

3. $\begin{pmatrix} 6x - 7y = 15 \\ 6x + 5y = -21 \end{pmatrix}$

4. $\begin{pmatrix} 5x + 2y = -4 \\ 5x - 3y = 6 \end{pmatrix}$

5. $\begin{pmatrix} x - 2y = -12 \\ 2x + 9y = 2 \end{pmatrix}$

6. $\begin{pmatrix} x - 4y = 29 \\ 3x + 2y = -11 \end{pmatrix}$

7. $\begin{pmatrix} 4x + 7y = -16 \\ 6x - y = -24 \end{pmatrix}$

8. $\begin{pmatrix} 6x + 7y = 17 \\ 3x + y = -4 \end{pmatrix}$

9. $\begin{pmatrix} 3x - 2y = 5 \\ 2x + 5y = -3 \end{pmatrix}$

10. $\begin{pmatrix} 4x + 3y = -4 \\ 3x - 7y = 34 \end{pmatrix}$

11. $\begin{pmatrix} 7x - 2y = 4 \\ 7x - 2y = 9 \end{pmatrix}$

12. $\begin{pmatrix} 5x - y = 6 \\ 10x - 2y = 12 \end{pmatrix}$

13. $\begin{pmatrix} 5x + 4y = 1 \\ 3x - 2y = -1 \end{pmatrix}$

14. $\begin{pmatrix} 2x - 7y = -2 \\ 3x + y = 1 \end{pmatrix}$

15. $\begin{pmatrix} 8x - 3y = 13 \\ 4x + 9y = 3 \end{pmatrix}$

16. $\begin{pmatrix} 10x - 8y = -11 \\ 8x + 4y = -1 \end{pmatrix}$

For Problems 17–44, solve each system by using either the substitution or the elimination-by-addition method, whichever seems more appropriate.

17. $\begin{pmatrix} 5x + 3y = -7 \\ 7x - 3y = 55 \end{pmatrix}$

18. $\begin{pmatrix} 4x - 7y = 21 \\ -4x + 3y = -9 \end{pmatrix}$

19. $\begin{pmatrix} x = 5y + 7 \\ 4x + 9y = 28 \end{pmatrix}$

20. $\begin{pmatrix} 11x - 3y = -60 \\ y = -38 - 6x \end{pmatrix}$

21. $\begin{pmatrix} x = -6y + 79 \\ x = 4y - 41 \end{pmatrix}$

22. $\begin{pmatrix} y = 3x + 34 \\ y = -8x - 54 \end{pmatrix}$

23. $\begin{pmatrix} 4x - 3y = 2 \\ 5x - y = 3 \end{pmatrix}$

24. $\begin{pmatrix} 3x - y = 9 \\ 5x + 7y = 1 \end{pmatrix}$

25. $\begin{pmatrix} 5x - 2y = 1 \\ 10x - 4y = 7 \end{pmatrix}$

26. $\begin{pmatrix} 4x + 7y = 2 \\ 9x - 2y = 1 \end{pmatrix}$

27. $\begin{pmatrix} 3x - 2y = 7 \\ 5x + 7y = 1 \end{pmatrix}$

28. $\begin{pmatrix} 2x - 3y = 4 \\ y = \dfrac{2}{3}x - \dfrac{4}{3} \end{pmatrix}$

29. $\begin{pmatrix} -2x + 5y = -16 \\ x = \dfrac{3}{4}y + 1 \end{pmatrix}$

30. $\begin{pmatrix} y = \dfrac{2}{3}x - \dfrac{3}{4} \\ 2x + 3y = 11 \end{pmatrix}$

31. $\begin{pmatrix} y = \dfrac{2}{3}x - 4 \\ 5x - 3y = 9 \end{pmatrix}$

32. $\begin{pmatrix} 5x - 3y = 7 \\ x = \dfrac{3y}{4} - \dfrac{1}{3} \end{pmatrix}$

33. $\begin{pmatrix} \dfrac{x}{6} + \dfrac{y}{3} = 3 \\ \dfrac{5x}{2} - \dfrac{y}{6} = -17 \end{pmatrix}$

34. $\begin{pmatrix} \dfrac{3x}{4} - \dfrac{2y}{3} = 31 \\ \dfrac{7x}{5} + \dfrac{y}{4} = 22 \end{pmatrix}$

35. $\begin{pmatrix} -(x - 6) + 6(y + 1) = 58 \\ 3(x + 1) - 4(y - 2) = -15 \end{pmatrix}$

36. $\begin{pmatrix} -2(x + 2) + 4(y - 3) = -34 \\ 3(x + 4) - 5(y + 2) = 23 \end{pmatrix}$

37. $\begin{pmatrix} 5(x + 1) - (y + 3) = -6 \\ 2(x - 2) + 3(y - 1) = 0 \end{pmatrix}$

38. $\begin{pmatrix} 2(x - 1) - 3(y + 2) = 30 \\ 3(x + 2) + 2(y - 1) = -4 \end{pmatrix}$

39. $\begin{pmatrix} \dfrac{1}{2}x - \dfrac{1}{3}y = 12 \\ \dfrac{3}{4}x + \dfrac{2}{3}y = 4 \end{pmatrix}$ **40.** $\begin{pmatrix} \dfrac{2}{3}x + \dfrac{1}{5}y = 0 \\ \dfrac{3}{2}x - \dfrac{3}{10}y = -15 \end{pmatrix}$

41. $\begin{pmatrix} \dfrac{2x}{3} - \dfrac{y}{2} = -\dfrac{5}{4} \\ \dfrac{x}{4} + \dfrac{5y}{6} = \dfrac{17}{16} \end{pmatrix}$ **42.** $\begin{pmatrix} \dfrac{x}{2} + \dfrac{y}{3} = \dfrac{5}{72} \\ \dfrac{x}{4} + \dfrac{5y}{2} = -\dfrac{17}{48} \end{pmatrix}$

43. $\begin{pmatrix} \dfrac{3x + y}{2} + \dfrac{x - 2y}{5} = 8 \\ \dfrac{x - y}{3} - \dfrac{x + y}{6} = \dfrac{10}{3} \end{pmatrix}$

44. $\begin{pmatrix} \dfrac{x - y}{4} - \dfrac{2x - y}{3} = -\dfrac{1}{4} \\ \dfrac{2x + y}{3} + \dfrac{x + y}{2} = \dfrac{17}{6} \end{pmatrix}$

For Problems 45–57, solve each problem by setting up and solving an appropriate system of equations.

45. A 10%-salt solution is to be mixed with a 20%-salt solution to produce 20 gallons of a 17.5%-salt solution. How many gallons of the 10% solution and how many gallons of the 20% solution will be needed?

46. A small-town library buys a total of 35 books that cost $462. Some of the books cost $12 each, and the remainder cost $14 each. How many books of each price did the library buy?   14 books at $12 and 21 books at $14

47. Suppose that on a particular day the cost of 3 tennis balls and 2 golf balls is $7. The cost of 6 tennis balls and 3 golf balls is $12. Find the cost of 1 tennis ball and the cost of 1 golf ball.

48. For moving purposes, the Hendersons bought 25 cardboard boxes for $97.50. There were two kinds of boxes; the large ones cost $7.50 per box and the small ones

were $3 per box. How many boxes of each kind did they buy?

49. A motel in a suburb of Chicago rents double rooms for $75 per day and single rooms for $42 per day. If a total of 55 rooms were rented for $3630, how many of each kind were rented?

50. Suppose that one solution contains 50% alcohol and another solution contains 80% alcohol. How many liters of each solution should be mixed to make 10.5 liters of a 70%-alcohol solution?

51. Suppose that a fulcrum is placed so that weights of 40 pounds and 80 pounds are in balance. Furthermore, suppose that when 20 pounds are added to the 40-pound weight, the 80-pound weight must be moved $1\dfrac{1}{2}$ feet farther from the fulcrum to preserve the balance. Find the original distance between the two weights.

52. If a certain two-digit number is divided by the sum of its digits, the quotient is 2. If the digits are reversed, the new number is nine less than five times the original number. Find the original number.

53. If the numerator of a certain fraction is increased by 5, and the denominator is decreased by 1, the resulting fraction is $\dfrac{8}{3}$. However, if the numerator of the original fraction is doubled, and the denominator is increased by 7, then the resulting fraction is $\dfrac{6}{11}$. Find the original fraction.

54. A man bought 2 pounds of coffee and 1 pound of butter for a total of $9.25. A month later, the prices had not changed (this makes it a fictitious problem), and he bought 3 pounds of coffee and 2 pounds of butter for $15.50. Find the price per pound of both the coffee and the butter.

55. Suppose that we have a rectangular-shaped book cover. If the width is increased by 2 centimeters, and the length is decreased by 1 centimeter, the area is increased by 28 square centimeters. However, if the width is decreased by 1 centimeter, and the length is increased by 2 centimeters, then the area is increased by 10 square centimeters. Find the dimensions of the book cover.

56. A blueprint indicates a master bedroom in the shape of a rectangle. If the width is increased by 2 feet and the length remains the same, then the area is increased by 36 square feet. However, if the width is increased by 1 foot and the length is increased by 2 feet, then the area is increased by 48 square feet. Find the dimensions of the room as indicated on the blueprint.

57. A fulcrum is placed so that weights of 60 pounds and 100 pounds are in balance. If 20 pounds are subtracted from the 100-pound weight, then the 60-pound weight must be moved 1 foot closer to the fulcrum to preserve the balance. Find the original distance between the 60-pound and 100-pound weights.

■ ■ ■ THOUGHTS INTO WORDS

58. Give a general description of how to use the elimination-by-addition method to solve a system of two linear equations in two variables.

59. Explain how you would solve the system

$$\begin{pmatrix} 3x - 4y = -1 \\ 2x - 5y = 9 \end{pmatrix}$$

using the elimination-by-addition method.

60. How do you decide whether to solve a system of linear equations in two variables by using the substitution method or by using the elimination-by-addition method?

■ ■ ■ FURTHER INVESTIGATIONS

61. There is another way of telling whether a system of two linear equations in two unknowns is consistent or inconsistent, or whether the equations are dependent, without taking the time to graph each equation. It can be shown that any system of the form

$$a_1x + b_1y = c_1$$

$$a_2x + b_2y = c_2$$

has one and only one solution if

$$\frac{a_1}{a_2} \neq \frac{b_1}{b_2} \qquad \text{Consistent}$$

that it has no solution if

$$\frac{a_1}{a_2} = \frac{b_1}{b_2} \neq \frac{c_1}{c_2} \qquad \text{Inconsistent}$$

and that it has infinitely many solutions if

$$\frac{a_1}{a_2} = \frac{b_1}{b_2} = \frac{c_1}{c_2} \qquad \text{Dependent}$$

For each of the following systems, determine whether the system is consistent, the system is inconsistent, or the equations are dependent.

(a) $\begin{pmatrix} 4x - 3y = 7 \\ 9x + 2y = 5 \end{pmatrix}$ (b) $\begin{pmatrix} 5x - y = 6 \\ 10x - 2y = 19 \end{pmatrix}$

(c) $\begin{pmatrix} 5x - 4y = 11 \\ 4x + 5y = 12 \end{pmatrix}$ (d) $\begin{pmatrix} x + 2y = 5 \\ x - 2y = 9 \end{pmatrix}$

(e) $\begin{pmatrix} x - 3y = 5 \\ 3x - 9y = 15 \end{pmatrix}$ (f) $\begin{pmatrix} 4x + 3y = 7 \\ 2x - y = 10 \end{pmatrix}$

(g) $\begin{pmatrix} 3x + 2y = 4 \\ y = -\dfrac{3}{2}x - 1 \end{pmatrix}$ (h) $\begin{pmatrix} y = \dfrac{4}{3}x - 2 \\ 4x - 3y = 6 \end{pmatrix}$

62. A system such as

$$\begin{pmatrix} \dfrac{3}{x} + \dfrac{2}{y} = 2 \\ \dfrac{2}{x} - \dfrac{3}{y} = \dfrac{1}{4} \end{pmatrix}$$

is not a system of linear equations but can be transformed into a linear system by changing variables. For example, when we substitute u for $\dfrac{1}{x}$ and v for $\dfrac{1}{y}$, the system cited becomes

$$\begin{pmatrix} 3u + 2v = 2 \\ 2u - 3v = \dfrac{1}{4} \end{pmatrix}$$

We can solve this "new" system either by elimination by addition or by substitution (we will leave the details for you) to produce $u = \dfrac{1}{2}$ and $v = \dfrac{1}{4}$. Therefore, because $u = \dfrac{1}{x}$ and $v = \dfrac{1}{y}$, we have

$$\dfrac{1}{x} = \dfrac{1}{2} \quad \text{and} \quad \dfrac{1}{y} = \dfrac{1}{4}$$

Solving these equations yields

$$x = 2 \quad \text{and} \quad y = 4$$

The solution set of the original system is $\{(2, 4)\}$. Solve each of the following systems.

(a) $\begin{pmatrix} \dfrac{1}{x} + \dfrac{2}{y} = \dfrac{7}{12} \\ \dfrac{3}{x} - \dfrac{2}{y} = \dfrac{5}{12} \end{pmatrix}$
(b) $\begin{pmatrix} \dfrac{2}{x} + \dfrac{3}{y} = \dfrac{19}{15} \\ \dfrac{2}{x} + \dfrac{1}{y} = -\dfrac{7}{15} \end{pmatrix}$

(c) $\begin{pmatrix} \dfrac{3}{x} - \dfrac{2}{y} = \dfrac{13}{6} \\ \dfrac{2}{x} + \dfrac{3}{y} = 0 \end{pmatrix}$
(d) $\begin{pmatrix} \dfrac{4}{x} + \dfrac{1}{y} = 11 \\ \dfrac{3}{x} - \dfrac{5}{y} = -9 \end{pmatrix}$

(e) $\begin{pmatrix} \dfrac{5}{x} - \dfrac{2}{y} = 23 \\ \dfrac{4}{x} + \dfrac{3}{y} = \dfrac{23}{2} \end{pmatrix}$
(f) $\begin{pmatrix} \dfrac{2}{x} - \dfrac{7}{y} = \dfrac{9}{10} \\ \dfrac{5}{x} + \dfrac{4}{y} = -\dfrac{41}{20} \end{pmatrix}$

63. Solve the following system for x and y.

$$\begin{pmatrix} a_1x + b_1y = c_1 \\ a_2x + b_2y = c_2 \end{pmatrix}$$

GRAPHING CALCULATOR ACTIVITIES

64. Use a graphing calculator to check your answers for Problem 61.

65. Use a graphing calculator to check your answers for Problem 62.

10.3 Systems of Three Linear Equations in Three Variables

Consider a linear equation in three variables x, y, and z, such as $3x - 2y + z = 7$. Any **ordered triple** (x, y, z) that makes the equation a true numerical statement is said to be a solution of the equation. For example, the ordered triple $(2, 1, 3)$ is a solution because $3(2) - 2(1) + 3 = 7$. However, the ordered triple $(5, 2, 4)$ is not a solution because $3(5) - 2(2) + 4 \neq 7$. There are infinitely many solutions in the solution set.

Remark: The concept of a *linear* equation is generalized to include equations of more than two variables. Thus an equation such as $5x - 2y + 9z = 8$ is called a linear equation in three variables; the equation $5x - 7y + 2z - 11w = 1$ is called a linear equation in four variables; and so on.

To *solve* a system of three linear equations in three variables, such as

$$\begin{pmatrix} 3x - y + 2z = 13 \\ 4x + 2y + 5z = 30 \\ 5x - 3y - z = 3 \end{pmatrix}$$

means to find all of the ordered triples that satisfy all three equations. In other words, the solution set of the system is the intersection of the solution sets of all three equations in the system.

The graph of a linear equation in three variables is a **plane**, not a line. In fact, graphing equations in three variables requires the use of a three-dimensional co-ordinate system. Thus using a graphing approach to solve systems of three linear equations in three variables is not at all practical. However, a simple graphical analysis does give us some idea of what we can expect as we begin solving such systems.

In general, because each linear equation in three variables produces a plane, a system of three such equations produces three planes. There are various ways in which three planes can be related. For example, they may be mutually parallel, or two of the planes may be parallel and the third one intersect each of the two. (You may want to analyze all of the other possibilities for the three planes!) However, for our purposes at this time, we need to realize that from a solution set viewpoint, a system of three linear equations in three variables produces one of the following possibilities.

Figure 10.4

1. There is *one ordered triple* that satisfies all three equations. The three planes have a common point of intersection, as indicated in Figure 10.4.

2. There are *infinitely many* ordered triples in the solution set, all of which are coordinates of points on a line common to the planes. This can happen if three planes have a common line of intersection (Figure 10.5a) or if two of the planes coincide, and the third plane intersects them (Figure 10.5b).

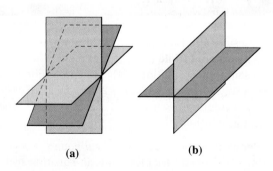

(a)   (b)

Figure 10.5

3. There are *infinitely many* ordered triples in the solution set, all of which are co-ordinates of points on a plane. This happens if the three planes coincide, as il-lustrated in Figure 10.6.

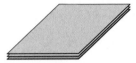

Figure 10.6

4. The solution set is *empty*; it is ∅. This can happen in various ways, as we see in Figure 10.7. Note that in each situation there are no points common to all three planes.

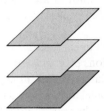

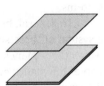

(a) Three parallel planes

(b) Two planes coincide and the third one is parallel to the coinciding planes.

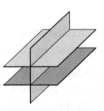

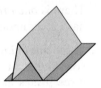

(c) Two planes are parallel and the third intersects them in parallel lines.

(d) No two planes are parallel, but two of them intersect in a line that is parallel to the third plane.

Figure 10.7

Now that we know what possibilities exist, let's consider finding the solution sets for some systems. Our approach will be the elimination-by-addition method, whereby we replace systems with equivalent systems until we obtain a system where we can easily determine the solution set. Let's start with an example that allows us to determine the solution set without changing to another, equivalent system.

E X A M P L E   1

Solve the system $\begin{pmatrix} 2x - 3y + 5z = -5 \\ 2y - 3z = 4 \\ 4z = -8 \end{pmatrix}$.

$\quad$ (1)
$\quad$ (2)
$\quad$ (3)

Solution

From equation (3) we can find the value of z.

$$4z = -8$$

$$z = -2$$

Now we can substitute -2 for z in equation (2).

$$2y - 3z = 4$$

$$2y - 3(-2) = 4$$

$$2y + 6 = 4$$

$$2y = -2$$

$$y = -1$$

Finally, we can substitute -2 for z and -1 for y in equation (1).

$$2x - 3y + 5z = -5$$

$$2x - 3(-1) + 5(-2) = -5$$

$$2x + 3 - 10 = -5$$

$$2x - 7 = -5$$

$$2x = 2$$

$$x = 1$$

The solution set is $\{(1, -1, -2)\}$. $\qquad\blacksquare$

$\quad$ Note the format of the equations in the system of Example 1. The first equation contains all three variables, the second equation has only two variables, and the third equation has only one variable. This allowed us to solve the third equation and then to use "back-substitution" to find the values of the other variables. Now let's consider an example where we have to make one replacement of an equivalent system.

E X A M P L E   2

Solve the system $\begin{pmatrix} 3x + 2y - 7z = -34 \\ y + 5z = 21 \\ 3y - 2z = -22 \end{pmatrix}$.

$\quad$ (1)
$\quad$ (2)
$\quad$ (3)

Solution

Let's replace equation (3) with an equation we form by multiplying equation (2) by -3 and then adding that result to equation (3).

$$\begin{pmatrix} 3x + 2y - 7z = -34 \\ y + 5z = 21 \\ -17z = -85 \end{pmatrix}.$$

$\quad$ (4)
$\quad$ (5)
$\quad$ (6)

From equation (6), we can find the value of z.

$$-17z = -85$$

$$z = 5$$

Now we can substitute 5 for z in equation (5).

$$y + 5z = 21$$

$$y + 5(5) = 21$$

$$y = -4$$

Finally, we can substitute 5 for z and -4 for y in equation (4).

$$3x + 2y - 7z = -34$$

$$3x + 2(-4) - 7(5) = -34$$

$$3x - 8 - 35 = -34$$

$$3x - 43 = -34$$

$$3x = 9$$

$$x = 3$$

The solution set is $\{(3, -4, 5)\}$. ■

Now let's consider some examples where we have to make more than one replacement of equivalent systems.

EXAMPLE 3   Solve the system $\begin{pmatrix} x - & y + 4z = -29 \\ 3x - & 2y - & z = & -6 \\ 2x - & 5y + 6z = -55 \end{pmatrix}$.

(1)
(2)
(3)

Solution

Let's replace equation (2) with an equation we form by multiplying equation (1) by -3 and then adding that result to equation (2). Let's also replace equation (3) with an equation we form by multiplying equation (1) by -2 and then adding that result to equation (3).

$$\begin{pmatrix} x - y + & 4z = -29 \\ & y - 13z = & 81 \\ -3y - & 2z = & 3 \end{pmatrix}$$

(4)
(5)
(6)

Now let's replace equation (6) with an equation we form by multiplying equation (5) by 3 and then adding that result to equation (6).

$$\begin{pmatrix} x - y + & 4z = -29 \\ & y - 13z = & 81 \\ & - 41z = & 246 \end{pmatrix}$$

(7)
(8)
(9)

From equation (9) we can determine the value of z.

$$-41z = 246$$

$$z = -6$$

Now we can substitute -6 for z in equation (8).

$$y - 13z = 81$$

$$y - 13(-6) = 81$$

$$y + 78 = 81$$

$$y = 3$$

Finally, we can substitute -6 for z and 3 for y in equation (7).

$$x - y + 4z = -29$$

$$x - 3 + 4(-6) = -29$$

$$x - 3 - 24 = -29$$

$$x - 27 = -29$$

$$x = -2$$

The solution set is $\{(-2, 3, -6)\}$. ∎

E X A M P L E   4

Solve the system $\begin{pmatrix} 3x - 4y + z = 14 \\ 5x + 3y - 2z = 27 \\ 7x - 9y + 4z = 31 \end{pmatrix}$.

(1)
(2)
(3)

Solution

A glance at the coefficients in the system indicates that eliminating the z terms from equations (2) and (3) would be easy. Let's replace equation (2) with an equation we form by multiplying equation (1) by 2 and then adding that result to equation (2). Let's also replace equation (3) with an equation we form by multiplying equation (1) by -4 and then adding that result to equation (3).

$$\begin{pmatrix} 3x - 4y + z = 14 \\ 11x - 5y = 55 \\ -5x + 7y = -25 \end{pmatrix}$$

(4)
(5)
(6)

Now let's eliminate the y terms from equations (5) and (6). First let's multiply equation (6) by 5.

$$\begin{pmatrix} 3x - 4y + z = 14 \\ 11x - 5y = 55 \\ -25x + 35y = -125 \end{pmatrix}$$

(7)
(8)
(9)

Now we can replace equation (9) with an equation we form by multiplying equation (8) by 7 and then adding that result to equation (9).

$$\begin{pmatrix} 3x - 4y + z = & 14 \\ 11x - 5y \quad\ = & 55 \\ 52x \qquad\quad\ = & 260 \end{pmatrix}$$

$\qquad$ (10)
$\qquad$ (11)
$\qquad$ (12)

From equation (12), we can determine the value of x.

$$52x = 260$$

$$x = 5$$

Now we can substitute 5 for x in equation (11).

$$11x - 5y = 55$$

$$11(5) - 5y = 55$$

$$-5y = 0$$

$$y = 0$$

Finally, we can substitute 5 for x and 0 for y in equation (10).

$$3x - 4y + z = 14$$

$$3(5) - 4(0) + z = 14$$

$$15 - 0 + z = 14$$

$$z = -1$$

The solution set is $\{(5, 0, -1)\}$. $\qquad\qquad$ ■

EXAMPLE 5 Solve the system $\begin{pmatrix} x - 2y + 3z = 1 \\ 3x - 5y - 2z = 4 \\ 2x - 4y + 6z = 7 \end{pmatrix}$.

$\qquad$ (1)
$\qquad$ (2)
$\qquad$ (3)

Solution

A glance at the coefficients indicates that it should be easy to eliminate the x terms from equations (2) and (3). We can replace equation (2) with an equation we form by multiplying equation (1) by -3 and then adding that result to equation (2). Likewise, we can replace equation (3) with an equation we form by multiplying equation (1) by -2 and then adding that result to equation (3).

$$\begin{pmatrix} x - 2y + 3z = 1 \\ y - 11z = 1 \\ 0 + 0 + 0 = 5 \end{pmatrix}$$

$\qquad$ (4)
$\qquad$ (5)
$\qquad$ (6)

The false statement, $0 = 5$, indicates that the system is inconsistent and that the solution set is therefore ∅. (If you were to graph this system, equations (1) and (3) would produce parallel planes, which is the situation depicted back in Figure 10.7c.) $\qquad\qquad$ ■

E X A M P L E   6

Solve the system $\begin{pmatrix} 2x - y + 4z = 1 \\ 3x + 2y - z = 5 \\ 5x - 6y + 17z = -1 \end{pmatrix}$.

(1)
(2)
(3)

Solution

A glance at the coefficients indicates that it is easy to eliminate the y terms from equations (2) and (3). We can replace equation (2) with an equation we form by multiplying equation (1) by 2 and then adding that result to equation (2). Likewise, we can replace equation (3) with an equation we form by multiplying equation (1) by -6 and then adding that result to equation (3).

$\begin{pmatrix} 2x - y + 4z = 1 \\ 7x \qquad + 7z = 7 \\ -7x \qquad - 7z = -7 \end{pmatrix}$

(4)
(5)
(6)

Now let's replace equation (6) with an equation we form by multiplying equation (5) by 1 and then adding that result to equation (6).

$\begin{pmatrix} 2x - y + 4z = 1 \\ 7x \qquad + 7z = 7 \\ 0 + 0 = 0 \end{pmatrix}$

(7)
(8)
(9)

The true numerical statement, $0 + 0 = 0$, indicates that the system has infinitely many solutions. (The graph of this system is shown in Figure 10.5a). ■

Remark: It can be shown that the solutions for the system in Example 6 are of the form $(t, 3 - 2t, 1 - t)$, where t is any real number. For example, if we let $t = 2$, then we get the ordered triple $(2, -1, -1)$, and this triple will satisfy all three of the original equations. For our purposes in this text, we shall simply indicate that such a system has infinitely many solutions.

Problem Set 10.3

Solve each of the following systems. If the solution set is $\varnothing$ or if it contains infinitely many solutions, then so indicate.

1. $\begin{pmatrix} x + 2y - 3z = 2 \\ 3y - z = 13 \\ 3y + 5z = 25 \end{pmatrix}$

2. $\begin{pmatrix} 2x + 3y - 4z = -10 \\ 2y + 3z = 16 \\ 2y - 5z = -16 \end{pmatrix}$

3. $\begin{pmatrix} 3x + 2y - 2z = 14 \\ x \qquad - 6z = 16 \\ 2x \qquad + 5z = -2 \end{pmatrix}$

4. $\begin{pmatrix} 3x + 2y - z = -11 \\ 2x - 3y \qquad = -1 \\ 4x + 5y \qquad = -13 \end{pmatrix}$

5. $\begin{pmatrix} 2x - y + z = 0 \\ 3x - 2y + 4z = 11 \\ 5x + y - 6z = -32 \end{pmatrix}$

6. $\begin{pmatrix} x - 2y + 3z = 7 \\ 2x + y + 5z = 17 \\ 3x - 4y - 2z = 1 \end{pmatrix}$

7. $\begin{pmatrix} 4x - y + z = 5 \\ 3x + y + 2z = 4 \\ x - 2y - z = 1 \end{pmatrix}$

8. $\begin{pmatrix} 2x - y + 3z = -14 \\ 4x + 2y - z = 12 \\ 6x - 3y + 4z = -22 \end{pmatrix}$

9. $\begin{pmatrix} x - y + 2z = 4 \\ 2x - 2y + 4z = 7 \\ 3x - 3y + 6z = 1 \end{pmatrix}$

10. $\begin{pmatrix} x + y - z = 2 \\ 3x - 4y + 2z = 5 \\ 2x + 2y - 2z = 7 \end{pmatrix}$

11. $\begin{pmatrix} x - 2y + z = -4 \\ 2x + 4y - 3z = -1 \\ -3x - 6y + 7z = 4 \end{pmatrix}$

12. $\begin{pmatrix} 2x - y + 3z = 1 \\ 4x + 7y - z = 7 \\ x + 4y - 2z = 3 \end{pmatrix}$

13. $\begin{pmatrix} 3x - 2y + 4z = 6 \\ 9x + 4y - z = 0 \\ 6x - 8y - 3z = 3 \end{pmatrix}$

14. $\begin{pmatrix} 2x - y + 3z = 0 \\ 3x + 2y - 4z = 0 \\ 5x - 3y + 2z = 0 \end{pmatrix}$

15. $\begin{pmatrix} 3x - y + 4z = 9 \\ 3x + 2y - 8z = -12 \\ 9x + 5y - 12z = -23 \end{pmatrix}$ **16.** $\begin{pmatrix} 5x - 3y + z = 1 \\ 2x - 5y = -2 \\ 3x - 2y - 4z = -27 \end{pmatrix}$

17. $\begin{pmatrix} 4x - y + 3z = -12 \\ 2x + 3y - z = 8 \\ 6x + y + 2z = -8 \end{pmatrix}$ **18.** $\begin{pmatrix} x + 3y - 2z = 19 \\ 3x - y - z = 7 \\ -2x + 5y + z = 2 \end{pmatrix}$

19. $\begin{pmatrix} x + y + z = 1 \\ 2x - 3y + 6z = 1 \\ -x + y + z = 0 \end{pmatrix}$ **20.** $\begin{pmatrix} 3x + 2y - 2z = -2 \\ x - 3y + 4z = -13 \\ -2x + 5y + 6z = 29 \end{pmatrix}$

Solve each of the following problems by setting up and solving a system of three linear equations in three variables.

21. The sum of the digits of a three-digit number is 14. The number is 14 larger than 20 times the tens digit. The sum of the tens digit and the units digit is 12 larger than the hundreds digit. Find the number.

22. The sum of the digits of a three-digit number is 13. The sum of the hundreds digit and the tens digit is 1 less than the units digit. The sum of three times the hundreds digit and four times the units digit is 26 more than twice the tens digit. Find the number.

23. Two bottles of catsup, 2 jars of peanut butter, and 1 jar of pickles cost $7.78. Three bottles of catsup, 4 jars of peanut butter, and 2 jars of pickles cost $14.34. Four bottles of catsup, 3 jars of peanut butter, and 5 jars of pickles cost $19.19. Find the cost per bottle of catsup, the cost per jar of peanut butter, and the cost per jar of pickles.

24. Five pounds of potatoes, 1 pound of onions, and 2 pounds of apples cost $3.80. Two pounds of potatoes, 3 pounds of onions, and 4 pounds of apples cost $5.78. Three pounds of potatoes, 4 pounds of onions, and 1 pound of apples cost $4.08. Find the price per pound for each item.

25. The sum of three numbers is 20. The sum of the first and third numbers is 2 more than twice the second number. The third number minus the first yields three times the second number. Find the numbers.

26. The sum of three numbers is 40. The third number is 10 less than the sum of the first two numbers. The second number is 1 larger than the first. Find the numbers.

27. The sum of the measures of the angles of a triangle is 180°. The largest angle is twice the smallest angle. The sum of the smallest and the largest angle is twice the other angle. Find the measure of each angle.

28. A box contains $2 in nickels, dimes, and quarters. There are 19 coins in all, and there are twice as many nickels as dimes. How many coins of each kind are there?

29. Part of $3000 is invested at 12%, another part at 13%, and the remainder at 14%. The total yearly income from the three investments is $400. The sum of the amounts invested at 12% and 13% equals the amount invested at 14%. Determine how much is invested at each rate.

30. The perimeter of a triangle is 45 centimeters. The longest side is 4 centimeters less than twice the shortest side. The sum of the lengths of the shortest and longest sides is 7 centimeters less than three times the length of the remaining side. Find the lengths of all three sides of the triangle.

■ ■ ■ **THOUGHTS INTO WORDS**

31. Give a step-by-step description of how to solve the system

$$\begin{pmatrix} x - 2y + 3z = -23 \\ 5y - 2z = 32 \\ 4z = -24 \end{pmatrix}$$

32. Describe how you would solve the system

$$\begin{pmatrix} x - 3z = 4 \\ 3x - 2y + 7z = -1 \\ 2x + z = 9 \end{pmatrix}$$

10.4 Matrix Approach to Solving Systems

The primary objective of this chapter is to introduce a variety of techniques for solving systems of linear equations. The techniques we have discussed thus far lend themselves to "small" systems. As the number of equations and variables increases, the systems become more difficult to solve and require other techniques. In these next three sections we will continue to work with small systems for the sake of convenience, but you will learn some techniques that can be extended to larger systems. This section introduces a matrix approach to solving systems.

A **matrix** is simply an array of numbers arranged in horizontal rows and vertical columns. For example, the matrix

$$2 \text{ rows} \longrightarrow \begin{bmatrix} 2 & 1 & -4 \\ 5 & -7 & 6 \end{bmatrix}$$

$$\uparrow \quad \uparrow \quad \uparrow$$

$$3 \text{ columns}$$

has 2 rows and 3 columns, which we refer to as a 2×3 (read "two-by-three") matrix. Some additional examples of matrices (*matrices* is the plural of *matrix*) are as follows:

$$
\begin{array}{cccc}
3 \times 2 & 2 \times 2 & 1 \times 4 & 5 \times 1 \\[4pt]
\begin{bmatrix} 3 & 2 \\ -1 & 4 \\ 5 & 7 \end{bmatrix} &
\begin{bmatrix} 4 & 1 \\ 0 & -5 \end{bmatrix} &
\begin{bmatrix} 1 & 2 & 6 & 8 \end{bmatrix} &
\begin{bmatrix} 3 \\ 7 \\ 10 \\ 2 \\ -4 \end{bmatrix}
\end{array}
$$

In general, a matrix of m rows and n columns is called a matrix of dimension $m \times n$. With every system of linear equations we can associate a matrix that consists of the coefficients and constant terms. For example, with the system

$$\begin{pmatrix} x - 3y = -17 \\ 2x + 7y = 31 \end{pmatrix}$$

we can associate the matrix

$$\begin{bmatrix} 1 & -3 & \vdots & -17 \\ 2 & 7 & \vdots & 31 \end{bmatrix}$$

which is called the **augmented matrix** of the system. The dashed line separates the coefficients from the constant terms; technically the dashed line is not necessary.

Because augmented matrices represent systems of equations, we can operate with them as we do with systems of equations. Our previous work with systems of equations was based on the following properties.

1. Any two equations of a system may be interchanged.

Example   When we interchange the two equations, the system $\begin{pmatrix} 2x - 5y = 9 \\ x + 3y = 4 \end{pmatrix}$ is equivalent to the system $\begin{pmatrix} x + 3y = 4 \\ 2x - 5y = 9 \end{pmatrix}$.

2. Any equation of the system may be multiplied by a nonzero constant.

Example   When we multiply the top equation by -2, the system $\begin{pmatrix} x + 3y = 4 \\ 2x - 5y = 9 \end{pmatrix}$ is equivalent to the system $\begin{pmatrix} -2x - 6y = -8 \\ 2x - 5y = 9 \end{pmatrix}$.

3. Any equation of the system can be replaced by adding a nonzero multiple of another equation to that equation.

Example   When we add -2 times the first equation to the second equation, the system $\begin{pmatrix} x + 3y = 4 \\ 2x - 5y = 9 \end{pmatrix}$ is equivalent to the system $\begin{pmatrix} x + 3y = 4 \\ -11y = 1 \end{pmatrix}$.

Each of the properties geared to solving a system of equations produces a corresponding property of the augmented matrix of the system. For example, exchanging two equations of a system corresponds to exchanging two rows of the augmented matrix that represents the system. We usually refer to these properties as elementary row operations, and we can state them as follows:

Elementary Row Operations

1. Any two rows of an augmented matrix can be interchanged.
2. Any row can be multiplied by a nonzero constant.
3. Any row of the augmented matrix can be replaced by adding a nonzero multiple of another row to that row.

Using the elementary row operations on an augmented matrix provides a basis for solving systems of linear equations. Study the following examples very carefully; keep in mind that the general scheme, called **Gaussian elimination**, is one of using elementary row operations on a matrix to continue replacing a system of equations with an equivalent system until a system is obtained where the solutions are easily determined. We will use a format similar to the one we used in the previous section, except that we will represent systems of equations by matrices.

E X A M P L E   1   Solve the system $\begin{pmatrix} x - 3y = -17 \\ 2x + 7y = 31 \end{pmatrix}$.

Solution

The augmented matrix of the system is

$$\begin{bmatrix} 1 & -3 & \vdots & -17 \\ 2 & 7 & \vdots & 31 \end{bmatrix}$$

We can multiply row one by -2 and add this result to row two to produce a new row two.

$$\begin{bmatrix} 1 & -3 & \vdots & -17 \\ 0 & 13 & \vdots & 65 \end{bmatrix}$$

This matrix represents the system

$$\begin{pmatrix} x - 3y = -17 \\ 13y = 65 \end{pmatrix}$$

From the last equation we can determine the value of y.

$$13y = 65$$

$$y = 5$$

Now we can substitute 5 for y in the equation $x - 3y = -17$.

$$x - 3(5) = -17$$

$$x - 15 = -17$$

$$x = -2$$

The solution set is $\{(-2, 5)\}$. ■

E X A M P L E   2   Solve the system $\begin{pmatrix} 3x + 2y = 3 \\ 30x - 6y = 17 \end{pmatrix}$.

Solution

The augmented matrix of the system is

$$\begin{bmatrix} 3 & 2 & \vdots & 3 \\ 30 & -6 & \vdots & 17 \end{bmatrix}$$

We can multiply row one by -10 and add this result to row two to produce a new row two.

$$\begin{bmatrix} 3 & 2 & \vdots & 3 \\ 0 & -26 & \vdots & -13 \end{bmatrix}$$

This matrix represents the system

$$\begin{pmatrix} 3x + 2y = 3 \\ -26y = -13 \end{pmatrix}$$

From the last equation we can determine the value of y.

$$-26y = -13$$

$$y = \frac{-13}{-26} = \frac{1}{2}$$

Now we can substitute $\dfrac{1}{2}$ for y in the equation $3x + 2y = 3$.

$$3x + 2\left(\dfrac{1}{2}\right) = 3$$

$$3x + 1 = 3$$

$$3x = 2$$

$$x = \dfrac{2}{3}$$

The solution set is $\left\{\left(\dfrac{2}{3}, \dfrac{1}{2}\right)\right\}$.   ■

EXAMPLE 3   Solve the system $\begin{pmatrix} 2x - 3y - z = -2 \\ x - 2y + 3z = 9 \\ 3x + y - 5z = -8 \end{pmatrix}$.

Solution

The augmented matrix of the system is

$$\begin{bmatrix} 2 & -3 & -1 & \vdots & -2 \\ 1 & -2 & 3 & \vdots & 9 \\ 3 & 1 & -5 & \vdots & -8 \end{bmatrix}$$

Let's begin by interchanging the top two rows.

$$\begin{bmatrix} 1 & -2 & 3 & \vdots & 9 \\ 2 & -3 & -1 & \vdots & -2 \\ 3 & 1 & -5 & \vdots & -8 \end{bmatrix}$$

Now we can multiply row one by -2 and add this result to row two to produce a new row two. Also, we can multiply row one by -3 and add this result to row three to produce a new row three.

$$\begin{bmatrix} 1 & -2 & 3 & \vdots & 9 \\ 0 & 1 & -7 & \vdots & -20 \\ 0 & 7 & -14 & \vdots & -35 \end{bmatrix}$$

Now we can multiply row two by -7 and add this result to row three to produce a new row three.

$$\begin{bmatrix} 1 & -2 & 3 & \vdots & 9 \\ 0 & 1 & -7 & \vdots & -20 \\ 0 & 0 & 35 & \vdots & 105 \end{bmatrix}$$

This last matrix represents the system $\begin{pmatrix} x - 2y + 3z = & 9 \\ y - 7z = & -20 \\ 35z = & 105 \end{pmatrix}$, which is said to be in **triangular form**. We can use the third equation to determine the value of z.

$$35z = 105$$

$$z = 3$$

Now we can substitute 3 for z in the second equation.

$$y - 7z = -20$$

$$y - 7(3) = -20$$

$$y - 21 = -20$$

$$y = 1$$

Finally, we can substitute 3 for z and 1 for y in the first equation.

$$x - 2y + 3z = 9$$

$$x - 2(1) + 3(3) = 9$$

$$x - 2 + 9 = 9$$

$$x + 7 = 9$$

$$x = 2$$

The solution set is $\{(2, 1, 3)\}$.   ■

At this time it might be very helpful for you to look back at Example 3 of Section 10.3 and then to take another look at Example 3 of this section. Note that our approach to both problems is basically the same, except that in this section we are using matrices to represent the systems of equations.

Problem Set 10.4

Solve each of the following systems and use matrices as we did in the examples of this section.

1. $\begin{pmatrix} x - 2y = 14 \\ 4x + 5y = 4 \end{pmatrix}$

2. $\begin{pmatrix} x + 5y = -3 \\ 3x - 2y = -26 \end{pmatrix}$

3. $\begin{pmatrix} 3x + 7y = -40 \\ x + 4y = -20 \end{pmatrix}$

4. $\begin{pmatrix} 7x - 9y = 53 \\ x - 3y = 11 \end{pmatrix}$

5. $\begin{pmatrix} x - 3y = 4 \\ 4x - 5y = 3 \end{pmatrix}$

6. $\begin{pmatrix} x + 3y = 7 \\ 2x - 4y = 9 \end{pmatrix}$

7. $\begin{pmatrix} 6x + 7y = -15 \\ 4x - 9y = 31 \end{pmatrix}$

8. $\begin{pmatrix} 5x - 3y = -16 \\ 6x + 5y = -2 \end{pmatrix}$

9. $\begin{pmatrix} x + 3y - 4z = & 5 \\ -2x - 5y + z = & 9 \\ 7x - y - z = & -2 \end{pmatrix}$

10. $\begin{pmatrix} x - y + 5z = & -2 \\ -3x + 2y + z = & 17 \\ 4x - 5y - 3z = & -36 \end{pmatrix}$

11. $\begin{pmatrix} x - 2y - 3z = -11 \\ 2x - 3y + z = 7 \\ -3x - 5y + 7z = 14 \end{pmatrix}$

12. $\begin{pmatrix} x + y + 3z = -8 \\ 3x + 2y - 5z = 19 \\ 5x - y - 4z = 23 \end{pmatrix}$

13. $\begin{pmatrix} y + 3z = -3 \\ 2x - 5z = 18 \\ 3x - y + 2z = 5 \end{pmatrix}$

14. $\begin{pmatrix} x - z = -1 \\ -2x + y + 3z = 4 \\ 3x - 4y = 31 \end{pmatrix}$

15. $\begin{pmatrix} -x - 5y + 2z = -5 \\ 3x + 14y - z = 13 \\ 4x - 3y + 5z = -26 \end{pmatrix}$

16. $\begin{pmatrix} -x - 3y + 4z = -3 \\ 3x + 8y - z = 27 \\ 5x - y + 2z = -5 \end{pmatrix}$

17. $\begin{pmatrix} x + 2y - z = -5 \\ 3x + 4y + 2z = -8 \\ -2x - y + 5z = 10 \end{pmatrix}$

18. $\begin{pmatrix} x - 3y + 2z = 0 \\ 2x - 4y - 3z = 19 \\ -3x - y + z = -11 \end{pmatrix}$

19. $\begin{pmatrix} -3x + 2y - z = 12 \\ 5x + 2y - 3z = 6 \\ x - y + 5z = -10 \end{pmatrix}$

20. $\begin{pmatrix} -2x - 3y + 5z = 15 \\ 4x - y + 2z = -4 \\ x + y - 3z = -7 \end{pmatrix}$

21. $\begin{pmatrix} -2x + 5y - z = -1 \\ 4x + y - 5z = 23 \\ x - 2y + 3z = -7 \end{pmatrix}$

22. $\begin{pmatrix} 2x + 5y + z = 1 \\ x + 2y - 3z = -13 \\ 3x - y - 2z = -4 \end{pmatrix}$

■■■ THOUGHTS INTO WORDS

23. What is a matrix? What is an augmented matrix of a system of linear equations?

24. Describe how to use matrices to solve the system $\begin{pmatrix} x - 2y = 5 \\ 2x + 7y = 9 \end{pmatrix}$.

■■■ FURTHER INVESTIGATIONS

25. Solve the system $\begin{pmatrix} x - 3y - 2z + w = -3 \\ -2x + 7y + z - 2w = -1 \\ 3x - 7y - 3z + 3w = -5 \\ 5x + y + 4z - 2w = 18 \end{pmatrix}$.

26. Solve the system $\begin{pmatrix} x - 2y + 2z - w = -2 \\ -3x + 5y - z - 3w = 2 \\ 2x + 3y + 3z + 5w = -9 \\ 4x - y - z - 2w = 8 \end{pmatrix}$.

27. Suppose that the augmented matrix of a system of three equations in three variables can be changed to the following matrix.

28. Suppose that the augmented matrix of a system of three linear equations in three variables can be changed to the following matrix.

$\begin{bmatrix} 1 & 1 & -2 & \vdots & 4 \\ 0 & -5 & 11 & \vdots & -13 \\ 0 & 0 & 0 & \vdots & -9 \end{bmatrix}$

What can be said about the solution set of the system?

$\begin{bmatrix} 1 & 0 & 1 & \vdots & 1 \\ 0 & 1 & -1 & \vdots & 0 \\ 0 & 0 & 0 & \vdots & 0 \end{bmatrix}$

What can be said about the solution set of the system?

GRAPHING CALCULATOR ACTIVITIES

29. If your graphing calculator has the capability to manipulate matrices, this is a good time to become familiar with those operations. You may need to refer to your calculator manual for the specific instructions. To begin the familiarization process, load your calculator with the three augmented matrices in Examples 1, 2, and 3 of this section. Then, for each one, carry out the row operations as described in the text.

10.5 Determinants

A **square matrix** is one that has the same number of rows as columns. Associated with each square matrix that has real number entries is a real number called the **determinant** of the matrix. For a 2×2 matrix

$$\begin{bmatrix} a_1 & b_1 \\ a_2 & b_2 \end{bmatrix}$$

the determinant is written as

$$\begin{vmatrix} a_1 & b_1 \\ a_2 & b_2 \end{vmatrix}$$

and defined by

$$\begin{vmatrix} a_1 & b_1 \\ a_2 & b_2 \end{vmatrix} = a_1 b_2 - a_2 b_1 \tag{1}$$

Note that a determinant is simply a number and that the determinant notation used on the left side of equation (1) is a way of expressing the number on the right side.

E X A M P L E   1   Find the determinant of the matrix $\begin{bmatrix} 3 & -2 \\ 5 & 8 \end{bmatrix}$.

Solution

In this case, $a_1 = 3$, $b_1 = -2$, $a_2 = 5$, and $b_2 = 8$. Thus we have

$$\begin{vmatrix} 3 & -2 \\ 5 & 8 \end{vmatrix} = 3(8) - 5(-2) = 24 + 10 = 34 \qquad \blacksquare$$

Finding the determinant of a square matrix is commonly called *evaluating the determinant*, and the matrix notation is sometimes omitted.

EXAMPLE 2

Evaluate $\begin{vmatrix} -3 & 5 \\ 1 & 2 \end{vmatrix}$.

Solution

$$\begin{vmatrix} -3 & 5 \\ 1 & 2 \end{vmatrix} = -3(2) - 1(5) = -11$$

∎

■ Cramer's Rule

Determinants provide the basis for another method of solving linear systems. Consider the system

$$\begin{pmatrix} a_1x + b_1y = c_1 \\ a_2x + b_2y = c_2 \end{pmatrix} \qquad (1) \\ (2)$$

We shall solve this system by using the elimination method; observe that our solutions can be conveniently written in determinant form. To solve for x, we can multiply equation (1) by b_2 and equation (2) by $-b_1$ and then add.

$$a_1b_2x + b_1b_2y = c_1b_2$$
$$-a_2b_1x - b_1b_2y = -c_2b_1$$
$$\overline{a_1b_2x - a_2b_1x = c_1b_2 - c_2b_1}$$
$$(a_1b_2 - a_2b_1)x = c_1b_2 - c_2b_1$$
$$x = \frac{c_1b_2 - c_2b_1}{a_1b_2 - a_2b_1} \qquad \text{If } a_1b_2 - a_2b_1 \neq 0$$

To solve for y, we can multiply equation (1) by $-a_2$ and equation (2) by a_1 and add.

$$-a_1a_2x - a_2b_1y = -a_2c_1$$
$$a_1a_2x + a_1b_2y = a_1c_2$$
$$\overline{a_1b_2y - a_2b_1y = a_1c_2 - a_2c_1}$$
$$(a_1b_2 - a_2b_1)y = a_1c_2 - a_2c_1$$
$$y = \frac{a_1c_2 - a_2c_1}{a_1b_2 - a_2b_1} \qquad \text{If } a_1b_2 - a_2b_1 \neq 0$$

We can express the solutions for x and y in determinant form as follows:

$$x = \frac{c_1b_2 - c_2b_1}{a_1b_2 - a_2b_1} = \frac{\begin{vmatrix} c_1 & b_1 \\ c_2 & b_2 \end{vmatrix}}{\begin{vmatrix} a_1 & b_1 \\ a_2 & b_2 \end{vmatrix}} \qquad y = \frac{a_1c_2 - a_2c_1}{a_1b_2 - a_2b_1} = \frac{\begin{vmatrix} a_1 & c_1 \\ a_2 & c_2 \end{vmatrix}}{\begin{vmatrix} a_1 & b_1 \\ a_2 & b_2 \end{vmatrix}}$$

For convenience, we shall denote the three determinants in the solution as

$$\begin{vmatrix} a_1 & b_1 \\ a_2 & b_2 \end{vmatrix} = D \qquad \begin{vmatrix} c_1 & b_1 \\ c_2 & b_2 \end{vmatrix} = D_x \qquad \begin{vmatrix} a_1 & c_1 \\ a_2 & c_2 \end{vmatrix} = D_y.$$

Note that the elements of D are the coefficients of the variables in the given system. In D_x, we obtain the elements by replacing the coefficients of x with the respective constants. In D_y, we replace the coefficients of y with the respective constants. This method of using determinants to solve a system of two linear equations in two variables is called **Cramer's rule**. We state it as follows:

Cramer's Rule

Given the system

$$\begin{pmatrix} a_1x + b_1 y = c_1 \\ a_2x + b_2 y = c_2 \end{pmatrix} \quad \text{with } a_1b_2 - a_2b_1 \neq 0$$

then

$$x = \frac{\begin{vmatrix} c_1 & b_1 \\ c_2 & b_2 \end{vmatrix}}{\begin{vmatrix} a_1 & b_1 \\ a_2 & b_2 \end{vmatrix}} = \frac{D_x}{D} \quad \text{and} \quad y = \frac{\begin{vmatrix} a_1 & c_1 \\ a_2 & c_2 \end{vmatrix}}{\begin{vmatrix} a_1 & b_1 \\ a_2 & b_2 \end{vmatrix}} = \frac{D_y}{D}$$

Let's use Cramer's rule to solve some systems.

EXAMPLE 3 Solve the system $\begin{pmatrix} x + 2y = 11 \\ 2x - y = 2 \end{pmatrix}$.

Solution

Let's find D, D_x, and D_y.

$$D = \begin{vmatrix} 1 & 2 \\ 2 & -1 \end{vmatrix} = -1 - 4 = -5$$

$$D_x = \begin{vmatrix} 11 & 2 \\ 2 & -1 \end{vmatrix} = -11 - 4 = -15$$

$$D_y = \begin{vmatrix} 1 & 11 \\ 2 & 2 \end{vmatrix} = 2 - 22 = -20$$

Thus we have

$$x = \frac{D_x}{D} = \frac{-15}{-5} = 3$$

$$y = \frac{D_y}{D} = \frac{-20}{-5} = 4$$

The solution set is $\{(3, 4)\}$, which we can verify, as always, by substituting back into the original equations. ∎

Remark: Note that Cramer's rule has a restriction, $a_1b_2 - a_2b_1 \neq 0$; that is, $D \neq 0$. Thus it is a good idea to find D first. Then if $D = 0$, Cramer's rule does not apply, and you must use one of the other methods to determine whether the solution set is empty or has infinitely many solutions.

EXAMPLE 4   Solve the system $\begin{pmatrix} 2x - 3y = -8 \\ 3x + 5y = 7 \end{pmatrix}$.

Solution

$$D = \begin{vmatrix} 2 & -3 \\ 3 & 5 \end{vmatrix} = 10 - (-9) = 19$$

$$D_x = \begin{vmatrix} -8 & -3 \\ 7 & 5 \end{vmatrix} = -40 - (-21) = -19$$

$$D_y = \begin{vmatrix} 2 & -8 \\ 3 & 7 \end{vmatrix} = 14 - (-24) = 38$$

Thus we obtain

$$x = \frac{D_x}{D} = \frac{-19}{19} = -1 \quad \text{and} \quad y = \frac{D_y}{D} = \frac{38}{19} = 2$$

The solution set is $\{(-1, 2)\}$.   ■

EXAMPLE 5   Solve the system $\begin{pmatrix} y = -2x - 2 \\ 4x - 5y = 17 \end{pmatrix}$.

Solution

First, we must change the form of the first equation so that the system fits the form given in Cramer's rule. The equation $y = -2x - 2$ can be written as $2x + y = -2$. The system now becomes

$$\begin{pmatrix} 2x + y = -2 \\ 4x - 5y = 17 \end{pmatrix}$$

and we can proceed as before.

$$D = \begin{vmatrix} 2 & 1 \\ 4 & -5 \end{vmatrix} = -10 - 4 = -14$$

$$D_x = \begin{vmatrix} -2 & 1 \\ 17 & -5 \end{vmatrix} = 10 - 17 = -7$$

$$D_y = \begin{vmatrix} 2 & -2 \\ 4 & 17 \end{vmatrix} = 34 - (-8) = 42$$

Thus the solutions are

$$x = \frac{D_x}{D} = \frac{-7}{-14} = \frac{1}{2} \quad \text{and} \quad y = \frac{D_y}{D} = \frac{42}{-14} = -3.$$

The solution set is $\left\{ \left(\frac{1}{2}, -3 \right) \right\}$.   ■

Problem Set 10.5

Evaluate each of the following determinants.

1. $\begin{vmatrix} 6 & 2 \\ 4 & 3 \end{vmatrix}$

2. $\begin{vmatrix} 7 & 6 \\ 2 & 5 \end{vmatrix}$

3. $\begin{vmatrix} 4 & 7 \\ 8 & 2 \end{vmatrix}$

4. $\begin{vmatrix} 3 & 9 \\ 6 & 4 \end{vmatrix}$

5. $\begin{vmatrix} -3 & 2 \\ 7 & 5 \end{vmatrix}$

6. $\begin{vmatrix} 5 & 1 \\ 8 & -4 \end{vmatrix}$

7. $\begin{vmatrix} 8 & -3 \\ 6 & 4 \end{vmatrix}$

8. $\begin{vmatrix} 5 & 9 \\ -3 & 6 \end{vmatrix}$

9. $\begin{vmatrix} -3 & 2 \\ 5 & -6 \end{vmatrix}$

10. $\begin{vmatrix} -2 & 4 \\ 9 & -7 \end{vmatrix}$

11. $\begin{vmatrix} 3 & -3 \\ -6 & 8 \end{vmatrix}$

12. $\begin{vmatrix} 6 & -5 \\ -8 & 12 \end{vmatrix}$

13. $\begin{vmatrix} -7 & -2 \\ -2 & 4 \end{vmatrix}$

14. $\begin{vmatrix} 6 & -1 \\ -8 & -3 \end{vmatrix}$

15. $\begin{vmatrix} -2 & -3 \\ -4 & -5 \end{vmatrix}$

16. $\begin{vmatrix} -9 & -7 \\ -6 & -4 \end{vmatrix}$

17. $\begin{vmatrix} \dfrac{1}{4} & -2 \\ \dfrac{3}{2} & 8 \end{vmatrix}$

18. $\begin{vmatrix} -\dfrac{2}{3} & 10 \\ -\dfrac{1}{2} & 6 \end{vmatrix}$

19. $\begin{vmatrix} \dfrac{3}{2} & -\dfrac{1}{2} \\ \dfrac{1}{2} & -\dfrac{2}{5} \end{vmatrix}$

20. $\begin{vmatrix} -\dfrac{1}{4} & \dfrac{1}{3} \\ \dfrac{3}{2} & \dfrac{2}{3} \end{vmatrix}$

Use Cramer's rule to find the solution set for each of the following systems.

21. $\begin{pmatrix} 2x + y = 14 \\ 3x - y = 1 \end{pmatrix}$

22. $\begin{pmatrix} 4x - y = 11 \\ 2x + 3y = 23 \end{pmatrix}$

23. $\begin{pmatrix} -x + 3y = 17 \\ 4x - 5y = -33 \end{pmatrix}$

24. $\begin{pmatrix} 5x + 2y = -15 \\ 7x - 3y = 37 \end{pmatrix}$

25. $\begin{pmatrix} 9x + 5y = -8 \\ 7x - 4y = -22 \end{pmatrix}$

26. $\begin{pmatrix} 8x - 11y = 3 \\ -x + 4y = -3 \end{pmatrix}$

27. $\begin{pmatrix} x + 5y = 4 \\ 3x + 15y = -1 \end{pmatrix}$

28. $\begin{pmatrix} 4x - 7y = 0 \\ 7x + 2y = 0 \end{pmatrix}$

29. $\begin{pmatrix} 6x - y = 0 \\ 5x + 4y = 29 \end{pmatrix}$

30. $\begin{pmatrix} 3x - 4y = 2 \\ 9x - 12y = 6 \end{pmatrix}$

31. $\begin{pmatrix} -4x + 3y = 3 \\ 4x - 6y = -5 \end{pmatrix}$

32. $\begin{pmatrix} x - 2y = -1 \\ x = -6y + 5 \end{pmatrix}$

33. $\begin{pmatrix} 6x - 5y = 1 \\ 4x + 7y = 2 \end{pmatrix}$

34. $\begin{pmatrix} y = 3x + 5 \\ y = 6x + 6 \end{pmatrix}$

35. $\begin{pmatrix} 7x + 2y = -1 \\ y = -x + 2 \end{pmatrix}$

36. $\begin{pmatrix} 9x - y = -2 \\ y = 4 - 8x \end{pmatrix}$

37. $\begin{pmatrix} -\dfrac{2}{3}x + \dfrac{1}{2}y = -7 \\ \dfrac{1}{3}x - \dfrac{3}{2}y = 6 \end{pmatrix}$

38. $\begin{pmatrix} \dfrac{1}{2}x + \dfrac{2}{3}y = -6 \\ \dfrac{1}{4}x - \dfrac{1}{3}y = -1 \end{pmatrix}$

39. $\begin{pmatrix} x + \dfrac{2}{3}y = -6 \\ -\dfrac{1}{4}x + 3y = -8 \end{pmatrix}$

40. $\begin{pmatrix} 3x - \dfrac{1}{2}y = 6 \\ -2x + \dfrac{1}{3}y = -4 \end{pmatrix}$

■ ■ ■ **THOUGHTS INTO WORDS**

41. Explain the difference between a matrix and a determinant.

42. Give a step-by-step description of how you would solve the system $\begin{pmatrix} 3x - 2y = 7 \\ 5x + 9y = 14 \end{pmatrix}$ using determinants.

■ ■ ■ FURTHER INVESTIGATIONS

43. Verify each of the following. The variables represent real numbers.

(a) $\begin{vmatrix} a & b \\ a & b \end{vmatrix} = 0$ **(b)** $\begin{vmatrix} a & a \\ b & b \end{vmatrix} = 0$

(c) $\begin{vmatrix} a & b \\ c & d \end{vmatrix} = -\begin{vmatrix} b & a \\ d & c \end{vmatrix}$ **(d)** $\begin{vmatrix} a & b \\ c & d \end{vmatrix} = -\begin{vmatrix} c & d \\ a & b \end{vmatrix}$

(e) $k\begin{vmatrix} a & b \\ c & d \end{vmatrix} = \begin{vmatrix} ka & b \\ kc & d \end{vmatrix}$ **(f)** $k\begin{vmatrix} a & b \\ c & d \end{vmatrix} = \begin{vmatrix} ka & kb \\ c & d \end{vmatrix}$

GRAPHING CALCULATOR ACTIVITIES

44. Use the determinant function of your graphing calculator to check your answers for Problems 1–16.

45. Make up two or three examples for each part of Problem 43, and evaluate the determinants using your graphing calculator.

10.6   3 × 3 Determinants and Systems of Three Linear Equations in Three Variables

This section will extend the concept of a determinant to include 3 × 3 determinants and then extend the use of determinants to solve systems of three linear equations in three variables.

For a 3 × 3 matrix

$$\begin{bmatrix} a_1 & b_1 & c_1 \\ a_2 & b_2 & c_2 \\ a_3 & b_3 & c_3 \end{bmatrix}$$

the determinant is written as

$$\begin{vmatrix} a_1 & b_1 & c_1 \\ a_2 & b_2 & c_2 \\ a_3 & b_3 & c_3 \end{vmatrix}$$

and defined by

$$\begin{vmatrix} a_1 & b_1 & c_1 \\ a_2 & b_2 & c_2 \\ a_3 & b_3 & c_3 \end{vmatrix} = a_1b_2c_3 + b_1c_2a_3 + c_1a_2b_3 - a_3b_2c_1 - b_3c_2a_1 - c_3a_2b_1 \tag{1}$$

It is evident that the definition given by equation (1) is a bit complicated to be very useful in practice. Fortunately, there is a method called **expansion of a determinant by minors** that we can use to calculate such a determinant.

The **minor** of an element in a determinant is the determinant that remains after deleting the row and column in which the element appears. For example, consider the determinant of equation (1).

The minor of a_1 is $\begin{vmatrix} b_2 & c_2 \\ b_3 & c_3 \end{vmatrix}$.

The minor of a_2 is $\begin{vmatrix} b_1 & c_1 \\ b_3 & c_3 \end{vmatrix}$.

The minor of a_3 is $\begin{vmatrix} b_1 & c_1 \\ b_2 & c_2 \end{vmatrix}$.

Now let's consider the terms, in pairs, of the right side of equation (1) and show the tie-in with minors.

$$a_1 b_2 c_3 - b_3 c_2 a_1 = a_1(b_2 c_3 - b_3 c_2)$$

$$= a_1 \begin{vmatrix} b_2 & c_2 \\ b_3 & c_3 \end{vmatrix}$$

$$c_1 a_2 b_3 - c_3 a_2 b_1 = -(c_3 a_2 b_1 - c_1 a_2 b_3)$$

$$= -a_2(b_1 c_3 - b_3 c_1)$$

$$= -a_2 \begin{vmatrix} b_1 & c_1 \\ b_3 & c_3 \end{vmatrix}$$

$$b_1 c_2 a_3 - a_3 b_2 c_1 = a_3(b_1 c_2 - b_2 c_1)$$

$$= a_3 \begin{vmatrix} b_1 & c_1 \\ b_2 & c_2 \end{vmatrix}$$

Therefore, we have

$$\begin{vmatrix} a_1 & b_1 & c_1 \\ a_2 & b_2 & c_2 \\ a_3 & b_3 & c_3 \end{vmatrix} = a_1 \begin{vmatrix} b_2 & c_2 \\ b_3 & c_3 \end{vmatrix} - a_2 \begin{vmatrix} b_1 & c_1 \\ b_3 & c_3 \end{vmatrix} + a_3 \begin{vmatrix} b_1 & c_1 \\ b_2 & c_2 \end{vmatrix}$$

and this is called the **expansion of the determinant by minors about the first column**.

E X A M P L E   1

Evaluate $\begin{vmatrix} 1 & 2 & -1 \\ 3 & 1 & -2 \\ 2 & 4 & 3 \end{vmatrix}$ by expanding by minors about the first column.

Solution

$$\begin{vmatrix} 1 & 2 & -1 \\ 3 & 1 & -2 \\ 2 & 4 & 3 \end{vmatrix} = 1\begin{vmatrix} 1 & -2 \\ 4 & 3 \end{vmatrix} - 3\begin{vmatrix} 2 & -1 \\ 4 & 3 \end{vmatrix} + 2\begin{vmatrix} 2 & -1 \\ 1 & -2 \end{vmatrix}$$

$$= 1[3 - (-8)] - 3[6 - (-4)] + 2[(-4 - (-1)]$$

$$= 1(11) - 3(10) + 2(-3) = -25 \quad \blacksquare$$

It is possible to expand a determinant by minors about any row or any column. To help determine the signs of the terms in the expansions, the following *sign array* is very useful.

$$+ \ - \ +$$

$$- \ + \ -$$

$$+ \ - \ +$$

For example, let's expand the determinant in Example 1 by minors about the second row. The second row in the sign array is $- \ + \ -$. Therefore,

$$\begin{vmatrix} 1 & 2 & -1 \\ 3 & 1 & -2 \\ 2 & 4 & 3 \end{vmatrix} = -3 \begin{vmatrix} 2 & -1 \\ 4 & 3 \end{vmatrix} + 1 \begin{vmatrix} 1 & -1 \\ 2 & 3 \end{vmatrix} - (-2) \begin{vmatrix} 1 & 2 \\ 2 & 4 \end{vmatrix}$$

$$= -3[6 - (-4)] + 1[3 - (-2)] + 2(4 - 4)$$

$$= -3(10) + 1(5) + 2(0)$$

$$= -25$$

Your decision as to which row or column to use for expanding a particular determinant by minors may depend on the numbers involved in the determinant. A row or column with one or more zeros is frequently a good choice, as the next example illustrates.

EXAMPLE 2   Evaluate $\begin{vmatrix} 3 & -1 & 4 \\ 5 & 2 & 0 \\ -2 & 6 & 0 \end{vmatrix}$.

Solution

Because the third column has two zeros, we shall expand about it.

$$\begin{vmatrix} 3 & -1 & 4 \\ 5 & 2 & 0 \\ -2 & 6 & 0 \end{vmatrix} = 4 \begin{vmatrix} 5 & 2 \\ -2 & 6 \end{vmatrix} - 0 \begin{vmatrix} 3 & -1 \\ -2 & 6 \end{vmatrix} + 0 \begin{vmatrix} 3 & -1 \\ 5 & 2 \end{vmatrix}$$

$$= 4[30 - (-4)] - 0 + 0 = 136$$

(Note that because of the zeros, there is no need to evaluate the last two minors.) ■

Remark 1: The expansion-by-minors method can be extended to determinants of size 4 × 4, 5 × 5, and so on. However, it should be obvious that it becomes increasingly tedious with bigger determinants. Fortunately, the computer handles the calculation of such determinants with a different technique.

Remark 2: There is another method for evaluating 3 × 3 determinants. This method is demonstrated in Problem 36 of the next problem set. If you choose to use that method, keep in mind that it works *only* for 3 × 3 determinants.

Without showing all of the details, we will simply state that Cramer's rule also applies to solving systems of three linear equations in three variables. It can be stated as follows:

Cramer's Rule

Given the system

$$\begin{pmatrix} a_1x + b_1 y + c_1z = d_1 \\ a_2x + b_2 y + c_2z = d_2 \\ a_3x + b_3 y + c_3z = d_3 \end{pmatrix}$$

with

$$D = \begin{vmatrix} a_1 & b_1 & c_1 \\ a_2 & b_2 & c_2 \\ a_3 & b_3 & c_3 \end{vmatrix} \neq 0 \qquad D_x = \begin{vmatrix} d_1 & b_1 & c_1 \\ d_2 & b_2 & c_2 \\ d_3 & b_3 & c_3 \end{vmatrix}$$

$$D_y = \begin{vmatrix} a_1 & d_1 & c_1 \\ a_2 & d_2 & c_2 \\ a_3 & d_3 & c_3 \end{vmatrix} \qquad D_z = \begin{vmatrix} a_1 & b_1 & d_1 \\ a_2 & b_2 & d_2 \\ a_3 & b_3 & d_3 \end{vmatrix}$$

then $x = \dfrac{D_x}{D}, y = \dfrac{D_y}{D}$, and $z = \dfrac{D_z}{D}$.

Note that the elements of D are the coefficients of the variables in the given system. Then D_x, D_y, and D_z are formed by replacing the elements in the x, y, and z columns, respectively, by the constants of the system d_1, d_2, and d_3. Again, note the restriction $D \neq 0$. As before, if $D = 0$, then Cramer's rule does not apply, and you can use the elimination method to determine whether the system has no solution or infinitely many solutions.

EXAMPLE 3

Use Cramer's rule to solve the system $\begin{pmatrix} x - 2y + z = -4 \\ 2x + y - z = 5 \\ 3x + 2y + 4z = 3 \end{pmatrix}$.

Solution

To find D, let's expand about row 1.

$$D = \begin{vmatrix} 1 & -2 & 1 \\ 2 & 1 & -1 \\ 3 & 2 & 4 \end{vmatrix} = 1\begin{vmatrix} 1 & -1 \\ 2 & 4 \end{vmatrix} - (-2)\begin{vmatrix} 2 & -1 \\ 3 & 4 \end{vmatrix} + 1\begin{vmatrix} 2 & 1 \\ 3 & 2 \end{vmatrix}$$

$$= 1[4 - (-2)] + 2[8 - (-3)] + 1(4 - 3)$$

$$= 1(6) + 2(11) + 1(1) = 29$$

To find D_x, let's expand about column 3.

$$D_x = \begin{vmatrix} -4 & -2 & 1 \\ 5 & 1 & -1 \\ 3 & 2 & 4 \end{vmatrix} = 1\begin{vmatrix} 5 & 1 \\ 3 & 2 \end{vmatrix} - (-1)\begin{vmatrix} -4 & -2 \\ 3 & 2 \end{vmatrix} + 4\begin{vmatrix} -4 & -2 \\ 5 & 1 \end{vmatrix}$$

$$= 1(10 - 3) + 1[-8 - (-6)] + 4[-4 - (-10)]$$

$$= 1(7) + 1(-2) + 4(6)$$

$$= 29$$

To find D_y, let's expand about row 1.

$$D_y = \begin{vmatrix} 1 & -4 & 1 \\ 2 & 5 & -1 \\ 3 & 3 & 4 \end{vmatrix} = 1\begin{vmatrix} 5 & -1 \\ 3 & 4 \end{vmatrix} - (-4)\begin{vmatrix} 2 & -1 \\ 3 & 4 \end{vmatrix} + 1\begin{vmatrix} 2 & 5 \\ 3 & 3 \end{vmatrix}$$

$$= 1[20 - (-3)] + 4[8 - (-3)] + 1(6 - 15)$$

$$= 1(23) + 4(11) + 1(-9)$$

$$= 58$$

To find D_z, let's expand about column 1.

$$D_z = \begin{vmatrix} 1 & -2 & -4 \\ 2 & 1 & 5 \\ 3 & 2 & 3 \end{vmatrix} = 1\begin{vmatrix} 1 & 5 \\ 2 & 3 \end{vmatrix} - 2\begin{vmatrix} -2 & -4 \\ 2 & 3 \end{vmatrix} + 3\begin{vmatrix} -2 & -4 \\ 1 & 5 \end{vmatrix}$$

$$= 1(3 - 10) - 2[-6 - (-8)] + 3[-10 - (-4)]$$

$$= 1(-7) - 2(2) + 3(-6)$$

$$= -29$$

Thus

$$x = \frac{D_x}{D} = \frac{29}{29} = 1$$

$$y = \frac{D_y}{D} = \frac{58}{29} = 2$$

$$z = \frac{D_z}{D} = \frac{-29}{29} = -1$$

The solution set is $\{(1, 2, -1)\}$. (Be sure to check it!)   ■

E X A M P L E   4   Use Cramer's rule to solve the system $\begin{pmatrix} 2x - y + 3z = -17 \\ 3y + z = 5 \\ x - 2y - z = -3 \end{pmatrix}$.

Solution

To find D, let's expand about column 1.

$$D = \begin{vmatrix} 2 & -1 & 3 \\ 0 & 3 & 1 \\ 1 & -2 & -1 \end{vmatrix} = 2\begin{vmatrix} 3 & 1 \\ -2 & -1 \end{vmatrix} - 0\begin{vmatrix} -1 & 3 \\ -2 & -1 \end{vmatrix} + 1\begin{vmatrix} -1 & 3 \\ 3 & 1 \end{vmatrix}$$

$$= 2[-3 - (-2)] - 0 + 1(-1 - 9)$$

$$= 2(-1) - 0 - 10 = -12$$

To find D_x, let's expand about column 3.

$$D_x = \begin{vmatrix} -17 & -1 & 3 \\ 5 & 3 & 1 \\ -3 & -2 & -1 \end{vmatrix} = 3\begin{vmatrix} 5 & 3 \\ -3 & -2 \end{vmatrix} - 1\begin{vmatrix} -17 & -1 \\ -3 & -2 \end{vmatrix} + (-1)\begin{vmatrix} -17 & -1 \\ 5 & 3 \end{vmatrix}$$

$$= 3[-10 - (-9)] - 1(34 - 3) - 1[-51 - (-5)]$$

$$= 3(-1) - 1(31) - 1(-46) = 12$$

To find D_y, let's expand about column 1.

$$D_y = \begin{vmatrix} 2 & -17 & 3 \\ 0 & 5 & 1 \\ 1 & -3 & -1 \end{vmatrix} = 2\begin{vmatrix} 5 & 1 \\ -3 & -1 \end{vmatrix} - 0\begin{vmatrix} -17 & 3 \\ -3 & -1 \end{vmatrix} + 1\begin{vmatrix} -17 & 3 \\ 5 & 1 \end{vmatrix}$$

$$= 2[-5 - (-3)] - 0 + 1(-17 - 15)$$

$$= 2(-2) - 0 + 1(-32) = -36$$

To find D_z, let's expand about column 1.

$$D_z = \begin{vmatrix} 2 & -1 & -17 \\ 0 & 3 & 5 \\ 1 & -2 & -3 \end{vmatrix} = 2\begin{vmatrix} 3 & 5 \\ -2 & -3 \end{vmatrix} - 0\begin{vmatrix} -1 & -17 \\ -2 & -3 \end{vmatrix} + 1\begin{vmatrix} -1 & -17 \\ 3 & 5 \end{vmatrix}$$

$$= 2[-9 - (-10)] - 0 + 1[-5 - (-51)]$$

$$= 2(1) - 0 + 1(46) = 48$$

Thus

$$x = \frac{D_x}{D} = \frac{12}{-12} = -1 \qquad y = \frac{D_y}{D} = \frac{-36}{-12} = 3$$

$$z = \frac{D_z}{D} = \frac{48}{-12} = -4.$$

The solution set is $\{(-1, 3, -4)\}$. ∎

Problem Set 10.6

For Problems 1–10, use expansion by minors to evaluate each determinant.

1. $\begin{vmatrix} 2 & 7 & 5 \\ 1 & -1 & 1 \\ -4 & 3 & 2 \end{vmatrix}$

2. $\begin{vmatrix} 2 & 4 & 1 \\ -1 & 5 & 1 \\ -3 & 6 & 2 \end{vmatrix}$

3. $\begin{vmatrix} 3 & -2 & 1 \\ 2 & 1 & 4 \\ -1 & 3 & 5 \end{vmatrix}$

4. $\begin{vmatrix} 1 & -1 & 2 \\ 2 & 1 & 3 \\ -1 & -2 & 1 \end{vmatrix}$

5. $\begin{vmatrix} -3 & -2 & 1 \\ 5 & 0 & 6 \\ 2 & 1 & -4 \end{vmatrix}$

6. $\begin{vmatrix} -5 & 1 & -1 \\ 3 & 4 & 2 \\ 0 & 2 & -3 \end{vmatrix}$

7. $\begin{vmatrix} 3 & -4 & -2 \\ 5 & -2 & 1 \\ 1 & 0 & 0 \end{vmatrix}$

8. $\begin{vmatrix} -6 & 5 & 3 \\ 2 & 0 & -1 \\ 4 & 0 & 7 \end{vmatrix}$

9. $\begin{vmatrix} 4 & -2 & 7 \\ 1 & -1 & 6 \\ 3 & 5 & -2 \end{vmatrix}$

10. $\begin{vmatrix} -5 & 2 & 6 \\ 1 & -1 & 3 \\ 4 & -2 & -4 \end{vmatrix}$

For Problems 11–30, use Cramer's rule to find the solution set of each system.

11. $\begin{pmatrix} 2x - y + 3z = -10 \\ x + 2y - 3z = 2 \\ 3x - 2y + 5z = -16 \end{pmatrix}$ **12.** $\begin{pmatrix} -x + y - z = 1 \\ 2x + 3y - 4z = 10 \\ -3x - y + z = -5 \end{pmatrix}$

13. $\begin{pmatrix} x - y + 2z = -8 \\ 2x + 3y - 4z = 18 \\ -x + 2y - z = 7 \end{pmatrix}$ **14.** $\begin{pmatrix} x - 2y + z = 3 \\ 3x + 2y + z = -3 \\ 2x - 3y - 3z = -5 \end{pmatrix}$

15. $\begin{pmatrix} 3x - 2y - 3z = -5 \\ x + 2y + 3z = -3 \\ -x + 4y - 6z = 8 \end{pmatrix}$ **16.** $\begin{pmatrix} 2x - 3y + 3z = -3 \\ -2x + 5y - 3z = 5 \\ 3x - y + 6z = -1 \end{pmatrix}$

17. $\begin{pmatrix} -x + y + z = -1 \\ x - 2y + 5z = -4 \\ 3x + 4y - 6z = -1 \end{pmatrix}$ **18.** $\begin{pmatrix} x - 2y + 3z = 1 \\ 2x + y + z = 4 \\ 4x - 3y + 7z = 6 \end{pmatrix}$

19. $\begin{pmatrix} x - y + 2z = 4 \\ 3x - 2y + 4z = 6 \\ 2x - 2y + 4z = -1 \end{pmatrix}$ **20.** $\begin{pmatrix} -x - 2y + z = 8 \\ 3x + y - z = 5 \\ 5x - y + 4z = 33 \end{pmatrix}$

21. $\begin{pmatrix} 2x - y + 3z = -5 \\ 3x + 4y - 2z = -25 \\ -x + z = 6 \end{pmatrix}$ **22.** $\begin{pmatrix} 3x - 2y + z = 11 \\ 5x + 3y = 17 \\ x + y - 2z = 6 \end{pmatrix}$

23. $\begin{pmatrix} 2y - z = 10 \\ 3x + 4y = 6 \\ x - y + z = -9 \end{pmatrix}$ **24.** $\begin{pmatrix} 6x - 5y + 2z = 7 \\ 2x + 3y - 4z = -21 \\ 2y + 3z = 10 \end{pmatrix}$

25. $\begin{pmatrix} -2x + 5y - 3z = -1 \\ 2x - 7y + 3z = 1 \\ 4x - y - 6z = -6 \end{pmatrix}$

26. $\begin{pmatrix} 7x - 2y + 3z = -4 \\ 5x + 2y - 3z = 4 \\ -3x - 6y + 12z = -13 \end{pmatrix}$

27. $\begin{pmatrix} -x - y + 5z = 4 \\ x + y - 7z = -6 \\ 2x + 3y + 4z = 13 \end{pmatrix}$ **28.** $\begin{pmatrix} x + 7y - z = -1 \\ -x - 9y + z = 3 \\ 3x + 4y - 6z = 5 \end{pmatrix}$

29. $\begin{pmatrix} 5x - y + 2z = 10 \\ 7x + 2y - 2z = -4 \\ -3x - y + 4z = 1 \end{pmatrix}$ **30.** $\begin{pmatrix} 4x - y - 3z = -12 \\ 5x + y + 6z = 4 \\ 6x - y - 3z = -14 \end{pmatrix}$

■ ■ ■ **THOUGHTS INTO WORDS**

31. How would you explain the process of evaluating 3 × 3 determinants to a friend who missed class the day it was discussed?

32. Explain how to use determinants to solve the system
$$\begin{pmatrix} x - 2y + z = 1 \\ 2x - y - z = 5 \\ 5x + 3y + 4z = -6 \end{pmatrix}$$

■ ■ ■ **FURTHER INVESTIGATIONS**

33. Evaluate the following determinant by expanding about the second column.

$$\begin{vmatrix} a & e & a \\ b & f & b \\ c & g & c \end{vmatrix}$$

Make a conjecture about determinants that contain two identical columns.

34. Show that $\begin{vmatrix} 1 & -1 & 2 \\ 2 & 3 & -1 \\ -1 & 2 & 4 \end{vmatrix} = -\begin{vmatrix} -1 & 1 & 2 \\ 3 & 2 & -1 \\ 2 & -1 & 4 \end{vmatrix}$.

Make a conjecture about the result of interchanging two columns of a determinant.

35. (a) Show that $\begin{vmatrix} 2 & 1 & 2 \\ 4 & -1 & -2 \\ 6 & 3 & 1 \end{vmatrix} = 2\begin{vmatrix} 1 & 1 & 2 \\ 2 & -1 & -2 \\ 3 & 3 & 1 \end{vmatrix}$.

Make a conjecture about the result of factoring a common factor from each element of a column in a determinant.

(b) Use your conjecture from part (a) to help evaluate the following determinant.

$$\begin{vmatrix} 2 & 4 & -1 \\ -3 & -4 & -2 \\ 5 & 4 & 3 \end{vmatrix}$$

36. We can describe another technique for evaluating 3×3 determinants as follows: First, let's write the given determinant with its first two columns repeated on the right.

$$\begin{vmatrix} a_1 & b_1 & c_1 \\ a_2 & b_2 & c_2 \\ a_3 & b_3 & c_3 \end{vmatrix}\begin{matrix} a_1 & b_1 \\ a_2 & b_2 \\ a_3 & b_3 \end{matrix}$$

Then we can add the three products shown with $+$ and subtract the three products shown with $-$.

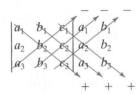

(a) Be sure that the previous description will produce equation (1) on page 525.

(b) Use this technique to do Problems 1–10.

GRAPHING CALCULATOR ACTIVITIES

37. Use your graphing calculator to check your answers for Problems 1–10.

38. Return to Problem 43 of Problem Set 10.5. Make up two examples using 3×3 determinants for each part of

Problem 43. Use your graphing calculator to evaluate the determinants.

10.7   Systems Involving Nonlinear Equations and Systems of Inequalities

Thus far in this chapter, we have solved systems of linear equations. In this section, we shall consider some systems of **linear inequalities** and also some systems where at least one of the equations is *nonlinear*. Let's begin by considering a system of one linear equation and one quadratic equation.

EXAMPLE 1   Solve the system $\begin{pmatrix} x^2 + y^2 = 17 \\ x + y = 5 \end{pmatrix}$.

Solution

First, let's graph the system so that we can predict approximate solutions. From our previous graphing experiences in Chapters 8 and 9, we should recognize

$x^2 + y^2 = 17$ as a circle and $x + y = 5$ as a straight line (Figure 10.8).

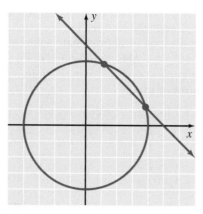

Figure 10.8

The graph indicates that there should be two ordered pairs with positive components (the points of intersection occur in the first quadrant) as solutions for this system. In fact, we could guess that these solutions are (1, 4) and (4, 1), and verify our guess by checking them in the given equations.

Let's also solve the system analytically using the substitution method as follows: Change the form of $x + y = 5$ to $y = 5 - x$ and substitute $5 - x$ for y in the first equation.

$$x^2 + y^2 = 17$$
$$x^2 + (5 - x)^2 = 17$$
$$x^2 + 25 - 10x + x^2 = 17$$
$$2x^2 - 10x + 8 = 0$$
$$x^2 - 5x + 4 = 0$$
$$(x - 4)(x - 1) = 0$$
$$x - 4 = 0 \quad \text{or} \quad x - 1 = 0$$
$$x = 4 \quad \text{or} \quad x = 1$$

Substitute 4 for x and then 1 for x in the second equation of the system to produce

$$x + y = 5 \qquad x + y = 5$$
$$4 + y = 5 \qquad 1 + y = 5$$
$$y = 1 \qquad\qquad y = 4$$

Therefore, the solution set is $\{(1, 4), (4, 1)\}$. ■

EXAMPLE 2

Solve the system $\begin{pmatrix} y = -x^2 + 1 \\ y = x^2 - 2 \end{pmatrix}$.

Solution

Again, let's get an idea of approximate solutions by graphing the system. Both equations produce parabolas, as indicated in Figure 10.9. From the graph, we can predict two nonintegral ordered-pair solutions, one in the third quadrant and the other in the fourth quadrant.

Substitute $-x^2 + 1$ for y in the second equation to obtain

$$y = x^2 - 2$$
$$-x^2 + 1 = x^2 - 2$$
$$3 = 2x^2$$
$$\frac{3}{2} = x^2$$
$$\pm\sqrt{\frac{3}{2}} = x$$
$$\pm\frac{\sqrt{6}}{2} = x$$

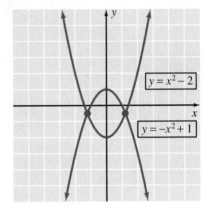

Figure 10.9

Substitute $\dfrac{\sqrt{6}}{2}$ for x in the second equation to yield

$$y = x^2 - 2$$
$$y = \left(\frac{\sqrt{6}}{2}\right)^2 - 2$$
$$= \frac{6}{4} - 2$$
$$= -\frac{1}{2}$$

Substitute $-\dfrac{\sqrt{6}}{2}$ for x in the second equation to yield

$$y = x^2 - 2$$
$$y = \left(-\frac{\sqrt{6}}{2}\right)^2 - 2$$
$$= \frac{6}{4} - 2 = -\frac{1}{2}$$

The solution set is $\left\{\left(-\dfrac{\sqrt{6}}{2}, -\dfrac{1}{2}\right), \left(\dfrac{\sqrt{6}}{2}, -\dfrac{1}{2}\right)\right\}$. Check it! ■

E X A M P L E   3

Solve the system $\left(\begin{array}{l} y = x^2 + 2 \\ 6x - 4y = -5 \end{array} \right)$.

Solution

From previous graphing experiences, we recognize that $y = x^2 + 2$ is the basic parabola shifted upward 2 units and that $6x - 4y = -5$ is a straight line (see Figure 10.10). Because of the close proximity of the curves, it is difficult to tell whether they intersect. In other words, the graph does not definitely indicate any real number solutions for the system.

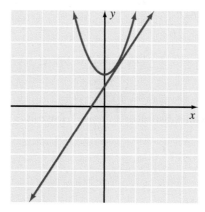

Figure 10.10

Let's solve the system using the substitution method. We can substitute $x^2 + 2$ for y in the second equation, which produces two values for x.

$$6x - 4(x^2 + 2) = -5$$

$$6x - 4x^2 - 8 = -5$$

$$-4x^2 + 6x - 3 = 0$$

$$4x^2 - 6x + 3 = 0$$

$$x = \frac{6 \pm \sqrt{36 - 48}}{8}$$

$$x = \frac{6 \pm \sqrt{-12}}{8}$$

$$x = \frac{6 \pm 2i\sqrt{3}}{8}$$

$$x = \frac{3 \pm i\sqrt{3}}{4}$$

It is now obvious that the system has no real number solutions. That is, the line and the parabola do not intersect in the real number plane. However, there will be two pairs of complex numbers in the solution set. We can substitute $\dfrac{(3 + i\sqrt{3})}{4}$ for x in the first equation.

$$
\begin{aligned}
y &= \left(\frac{3 + i\sqrt{3}}{4}\right)^2 + 2 \\
&= \frac{6 + 6i\sqrt{3}}{16} + 2 \\
&= \frac{6 + 6i\sqrt{3} + 32}{16} \\
&= \frac{38 + 6i\sqrt{3}}{16} = \frac{19 + 3i\sqrt{3}}{8}
\end{aligned}
$$

Likewise, we can substitute $\dfrac{(3 - i\sqrt{3})}{4}$ for x in the first equation.

$$
\begin{aligned}
y &= \left(\frac{3 - i\sqrt{3}}{4}\right)^2 + 2 \\
&= \frac{6 - 6i\sqrt{3}}{16} + 2 \\
&= \frac{6 - 6i\sqrt{3} + 32}{16} \\
&= \frac{38 - 6i\sqrt{3}}{16} \\
&= \frac{19 - 3i\sqrt{3}}{8}
\end{aligned}
$$

The solution set is $\left\{\left(\dfrac{3 + i\sqrt{3}}{4}, \dfrac{19 + 3i\sqrt{3}}{4}\right), \left(\dfrac{3 - i\sqrt{3}}{4}, \dfrac{19 - 3i\sqrt{3}}{4}\right)\right\}.$ ∎

In Example 3, the use of a graphing utility may not, at first, indicate whether or not the system has any real number solutions. Suppose that we graph the system using a viewing rectangle such that $-15 \leq x \leq 15$ and $-10 \leq y \leq 10$. In Figure 10.11, we cannot tell whether or not the line and parabola intersect. However, if we change the viewing rectangle so that $0 \leq x \leq 2$ and $0 \leq y \leq 4$, as shown in Figure 10.12, then it becomes apparent that the two graphs do not intersect.

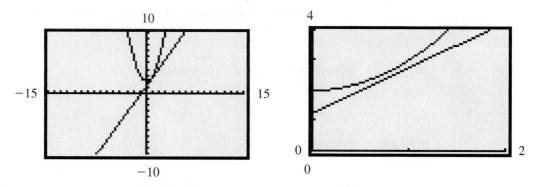

Figure 10.11   **Figure 10.12**

■ Systems of Linear Inequalities

Finding solution sets for systems of linear inequalities relies heavily on the graphing approach. The solution set of a system of linear inequalities, such as

$$\begin{pmatrix} x + y > 2 \\ x - y < 2 \end{pmatrix}$$

is the intersection of the solution sets of the individual inequalities. In Figure 10.13(a) we indicated the solution set for $x + y > 2$, and in Figure 10.13(b) we indicated the solution set for $x - y < 2$. Then, in Figure 10.13(c), we shaded the region that represents the intersection of the two solution sets from parts (a) and (b); thus it is the graph of the system. Remember that dashed lines are used to indicate that the points on the lines are not included in the solution set.

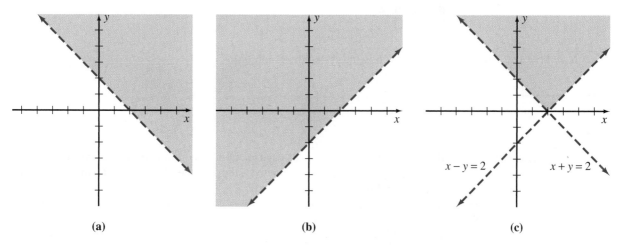

(a)   (b)   (c)

Figure 10.13

In the following examples, we indicated only the final solution set for the system.

E X A M P L E   4

Solve the following system by graphing.

$$\begin{pmatrix} 2x - y \geq 4 \\ x + 2y < 2 \end{pmatrix}$$

Solution

The graph of $2x - y \geq 4$ consists of all points *on or below* the line $2x - y = 4$. The graph of $x + 2y < 2$ consists of all points *below* the line $x + 2y = 2$. The graph of the system is indicated by the shaded region in Figure 10.14. Note that all points in the shaded region are on or below the line $2x - y = 4$ *and* below the line $x + 2y = 2$.

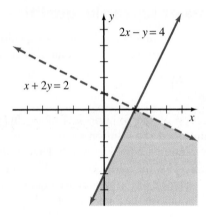

Figure 10.14   ∎

E X A M P L E   5

Solve the following system by graphing.

$$\begin{pmatrix} x \leq 2 \\ y \geq -1 \end{pmatrix}$$

Solution

Remember that even though each inequality contains only one variable, we are working in a rectangular coordinate system that involves ordered pairs. That is, the system could be written as

$$\begin{pmatrix} x + 0(y) \leq 2 \\ 0(x) + y \geq -1 \end{pmatrix}$$

The graph of the system is the shaded region in Figure 10.15. Note that all points in the shaded region are on or to the left of the line $x = 2$ and on or above the line $y = -1$.

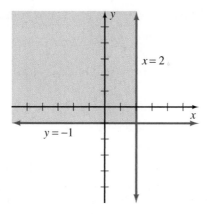

Figure 10.15

Problem Set 10.7

For Problems 1–16, (a) graph each system so that approximate real number solutions (if there are any) can be predicted, and (b) solve each system using the substitution method or the elimination-by-addition method.

1. $\begin{pmatrix} y = (x+2)^2 \\ y = -2x - 4 \end{pmatrix}$
2. $\begin{pmatrix} y = x^2 \\ y = x + 2 \end{pmatrix}$

3. $\begin{pmatrix} x^2 + y^2 = 13 \\ 3x + 2y = 0 \end{pmatrix}$
4. $\begin{pmatrix} x^2 + y^2 = 26 \\ x + y = 6 \end{pmatrix}$

5. $\begin{pmatrix} y = x^2 + 6x + 7 \\ 2x + y = -5 \end{pmatrix}$
6. $\begin{pmatrix} y = x^2 - 4x + 5 \\ -x + y = 1 \end{pmatrix}$

7. $\begin{pmatrix} y = x^2 \\ y = x^2 - 4x + 4 \end{pmatrix}$
8. $\begin{pmatrix} y = -x^2 + 3 \\ y = x^2 + 1 \end{pmatrix}$

9. $\begin{pmatrix} x + y = -8 \\ x^2 - y^2 = 16 \end{pmatrix}$
10. $\begin{pmatrix} x - y = 2 \\ x^2 - y^2 = 16 \end{pmatrix}$

11. $\begin{pmatrix} y = x^2 + 2x - 1 \\ y = x^2 + 4x + 5 \end{pmatrix}$
12. $\begin{pmatrix} 2x^2 + y^2 = 8 \\ x^2 + y^2 = 4 \end{pmatrix}$

13. $\begin{pmatrix} xy = 4 \\ y = x \end{pmatrix}$
14. $\begin{pmatrix} y = x^2 + 2 \\ y = 2x^2 + 1 \end{pmatrix}$

15. $\begin{pmatrix} x^2 + y^2 = 2 \\ x - y = 4 \end{pmatrix}$
16. $\begin{pmatrix} y = -x^2 + 1 \\ x + y = 2 \end{pmatrix}$

For Problems 17–32, indicate the solution set for each system of inequalities by shading the appropriate region.

17. $\begin{pmatrix} 3x - 4y \geq 0 \\ 2x + 3y \leq 0 \end{pmatrix}$
18. $\begin{pmatrix} 3x + 2y \leq 6 \\ 2x - 3y \geq 6 \end{pmatrix}$

19. $\begin{pmatrix} x - 3y < 6 \\ x + 2y \geq 4 \end{pmatrix}$
20. $\begin{pmatrix} 2x - y \leq 4 \\ 2x + y > 4 \end{pmatrix}$

21. $\begin{pmatrix} x + y < 4 \\ x - y > 2 \end{pmatrix}$
22. $\begin{pmatrix} x + y > 1 \\ x - y < 1 \end{pmatrix}$

23. $\begin{pmatrix} y < x + 1 \\ y \geq x \end{pmatrix}$
24. $\begin{pmatrix} y > x - 3 \\ y < x \end{pmatrix}$

25. $\begin{pmatrix} y > x \\ y > 2 \end{pmatrix}$
26. $\begin{pmatrix} 2x + y > 6 \\ 2x + y < 2 \end{pmatrix}$

27. $\begin{pmatrix} x \geq -1 \\ y < 4 \end{pmatrix}$
28. $\begin{pmatrix} x < 3 \\ y > 2 \end{pmatrix}$

29. $\begin{pmatrix} 2x - y > 4 \\ 2x - y > 0 \end{pmatrix}$
30. $\begin{pmatrix} x + y > 4 \\ x + y > 6 \end{pmatrix}$

31. $\begin{pmatrix} 3x - 2y < 6 \\ 2x - 3y < 6 \end{pmatrix}$
32. $\begin{pmatrix} 2x + 5y > 10 \\ 5x + 2y > 10 \end{pmatrix}$

▪▪▪ THOUGHTS INTO WORDS

33. What happens if you try to graph the system

$$\begin{pmatrix} x^2 + 4y^2 = 16 \\ 2x^2 + 5y^2 = -12 \end{pmatrix}?$$

34. Explain how you would solve the system

$$\begin{pmatrix} x^2 + y^2 = 9 \\ y^2 = x^2 + 4 \end{pmatrix}.$$

35. How do you know by inspection, without graphing, that the solution set of the system $\begin{pmatrix} 3x - 2y > 5 \\ 3x - 2y < 2 \end{pmatrix}$ is the null set?

GRAPHING CALCULATOR ACTIVITIES

36. Use a graphing calculator to graph the systems in Problems 1–16, and check the reasonableness of your answers.

37. For each of the following systems, (a) use your graphing calculator to show that there are no real number solutions, and (b) solve the system by the substitution method or the elimination-by-addition method to find the complex solutions.

(a) $\begin{pmatrix} y = x^2 + 1 \\ y = -3 \end{pmatrix}$ **(b)** $\begin{pmatrix} y = -x^2 + 1 \\ y = 3 \end{pmatrix}$

(c) $\begin{pmatrix} y = x^2 \\ x - y = 4 \end{pmatrix}$ **(d)** $\begin{pmatrix} y = x^2 + 1 \\ y = -x^2 \end{pmatrix}$

(e) $\begin{pmatrix} x^2 + y^2 = 1 \\ x + y = 2 \end{pmatrix}$ **(f)** $\begin{pmatrix} x^2 + y^2 = 2 \\ x^2 - y^2 = 6 \end{pmatrix}$

38. Graph the system $\begin{pmatrix} y = x^2 + 2 \\ 6x - 4y = -5 \end{pmatrix}$ and use the TRACE and ZOOM features of your calculator to demonstrate clearly that this system has no real number solutions.

(10.1) Graphing a **system of two linear equations in two variables** produces one of the following results.

1. The graphs of the two equations are two intersecting lines, which indicates that there is **one unique solution** of the system. Such a system is called a **consistent system**.

2. The graphs of the two equations are two parallel lines, which indicates that there is **no solution** for the system. It is called an **inconsistent system**.

3. The graphs of the two equations are the same line, which indicates **infinitely many solutions** for the system. The equations are called **dependent** equations.

We can describe the **substitution method** of solving a system of equations as follows:

Step 1 Solve one of the equations for one variable in terms of the other variable if neither equation is in such a form. (If possible, make a choice that will avoid fractions.)

Step 2 Substitute the expression obtained in Step 1 into the other equation to produce an equation with one variable.

Step 3 Solve the equation obtained in Step 2.

Step 4 Use the solution obtained in Step 3, along with the expression obtained in Step 1, to determine the solution of the system.

(10.2) The **elimination-by-addition method** involves the replacement of a system of equations with equivalent systems until a system is obtained whereby the solutions can be easily determined. The following operations or transformations can be performed on a system to produce an equivalent system.

1. Any two equations of the system can be interchanged.

2. Both sides of any equation of the system can be multiplied by any nonzero real number.

3. Any equation of the system can be replaced by the *sum* of that equation and a nonzero multiple of another equation.

(10.3) Solving **a system of three linear equations in three variables** produces one of the following results.

1. There is **one ordered triple** that satisfies all three equations.

2. There are **infinitely many ordered triples** in the solution set, all of which are coordinates of points on a line common to the planes.

3. There are **infinitely many ordered triples** in the solution set, all of which are coordinates of points on a plane.

4. The solution set is empty; it is $\varnothing$.

(10.4) A **matrix** is an array of numbers arranged in horizontal rows and vertical columns. A matrix of m rows and n columns is called an $m \times n$ ("m-by-n") matrix. The **augmented matrix** of the system

$$\begin{pmatrix} 5x - 2y - z = 4 \\ 3x - y - z = 7 \\ 2x + 3y + 7z = 9 \end{pmatrix}$$

is

$$\begin{bmatrix} 5 & -2 & -1 & \vdots & 4 \\ 3 & -1 & -1 & \vdots & 7 \\ 2 & 3 & 7 & \vdots & 9 \end{bmatrix}$$

The following **elementary row operations** provide the basis for transforming matrices.

1. Any two rows of an augmented matrix can be interchanged.

2. Any row can be multiplied by a nonzero constant.

3. Any row can be replaced by adding a nonzero multiple of another row to that row.

Transforming an augmented matrix to **triangular form** and then using back-substitution provides a systematic technique for solving systems of linear equations.

(10.5) A rectangular array of numbers is called a **matrix**. A **square matrix** has the same number of rows as columns. For a 2×2 matrix,

$$\begin{bmatrix} a_1 & b_1 \\ a_2 & b_2 \end{bmatrix}$$

the **determinant** of the matrix is written as

$$\begin{vmatrix} a_1 & b_1 \\ a_2 & b_2 \end{vmatrix}$$

and defined by

$$\begin{vmatrix} a_1 & b_1 \\ a_2 & b_2 \end{vmatrix} = a_1 b_2 - a_2 b_1$$

Cramer's rule for solving a system of two linear equations in two variables is stated as follows:

Given the system $\begin{pmatrix} a_1 x + b_1 y = c_1 \\ a_2 x + b_2 y = c_2 \end{pmatrix}$ with

$$D = \begin{vmatrix} a_1 & b_1 \\ a_2 & b_2 \end{vmatrix} \neq 0 \qquad D_x = \begin{vmatrix} c_1 & b_1 \\ c_2 & b_2 \end{vmatrix} \qquad D_y = \begin{vmatrix} a_1 & c_1 \\ a_2 & c_2 \end{vmatrix}$$

then

$$x = \frac{D_x}{D} \qquad \text{and} \qquad y = \frac{D_y}{D}$$

(10.6) A 3×3 determinant is defined by

$$\begin{vmatrix} a_1 & b_1 & c_1 \\ a_2 & b_2 & c_2 \\ a_3 & b_3 & c_3 \end{vmatrix} = a_1 b_2 c_3 + b_1 c_2 a_3 + c_1 a_2 b_3 \\ - a_3 b_2 c_1 - b_3 c_2 a_1 - c_3 a_2 b_1$$

The **minor** of an element in a determinant is the determinant that remains after deleting the row and column in which the element appears. A determinant can be evaluated by **expansion by minors** of the elements of any row or any column.

Cramer's rule for solving a system of three linear equations in three variables is stated as follows:

Given the system $\begin{pmatrix} a_1 x + b_1 y + c_1 z = d_1 \\ a_2 x + b_2 y + c_2 z = d_2 \\ a_3 x + b_3 y + c_3 z = d_3 \end{pmatrix}$ with

$$D = \begin{vmatrix} a_1 & b_1 & c_1 \\ a_2 & b_2 & c_2 \\ a_3 & b_3 & c_3 \end{vmatrix} \neq 0 \qquad D_x = \begin{vmatrix} d_1 & b_1 & c_1 \\ d_2 & b_2 & c_2 \\ d_3 & b_3 & c_3 \end{vmatrix}$$

$$D_y = \begin{vmatrix} a_1 & d_1 & c_1 \\ a_2 & d_2 & c_2 \\ a_3 & d_3 & c_3 \end{vmatrix} \qquad D_z = \begin{vmatrix} a_1 & b_1 & d_1 \\ a_2 & b_2 & d_2 \\ a_3 & b_3 & d_3 \end{vmatrix}$$

then $x = \dfrac{D_x}{D}$, $y = \dfrac{D_y}{D}$, and $z = \dfrac{D_z}{D}$.

(10.7) The substitution and elimination methods can also be used to solve systems involving **nonlinear equations**.

The solution set of a system of **linear inequalities** is the intersection of the solution sets of the individual inequalities.

Chapter 10   Review Problem Set

For Problems 1–4, solve each system of equations using (a) the substitution method, (b) the elimination method, (c) a matrix approach, and (d) Cramer's rule.

1. $\begin{pmatrix} 3x - 2y = -6 \\ 2x + 5y = 34 \end{pmatrix}$ **2.** $\begin{pmatrix} x + 4y = 25 \\ y = -3x - 2 \end{pmatrix}$

3. $\begin{pmatrix} x = 5y - 49 \\ 4x + 3y = -12 \end{pmatrix}$ **4.** $\begin{pmatrix} x - 6y = 7 \\ 3x + 5y = 9 \end{pmatrix}$

For Problems 5–14, solve each system using the method that seems most appropriate to you.

5. $\begin{pmatrix} x - 3y = 25 \\ -3x + 2y = -26 \end{pmatrix}$ **6.** $\begin{pmatrix} 5x - 7y = -66 \\ x + 4y = 30 \end{pmatrix}$

7. $\begin{pmatrix} 4x + 3y = -9 \\ 3x - 5y = 15 \end{pmatrix}$ **8.** $\begin{pmatrix} 2x + 5y = 47 \\ 4x - 7y = -25 \end{pmatrix}$

9. $\begin{pmatrix} 7x - 3y = 25 \\ y = 3x - 9 \end{pmatrix}$ **10.** $\begin{pmatrix} x = -4 - 5y \\ y = 4x + 16 \end{pmatrix}$

11. $\begin{pmatrix} \dfrac{1}{2}x + \dfrac{2}{3}y = 6 \\ \dfrac{3}{4}x - \dfrac{5}{6}y = -24 \end{pmatrix}$ **12.** $\begin{pmatrix} \dfrac{3}{4}x - \dfrac{1}{2}y = 14 \\ \dfrac{5}{12}x + \dfrac{3}{4}y = 16 \end{pmatrix}$

13. $\begin{pmatrix} 6x - 4y = 7 \\ 9x + 8y = 0 \end{pmatrix}$ **14.** $\begin{pmatrix} 4x - 5y = -5 \\ 6x - 10y = -9 \end{pmatrix}$

For Problems 15 –18, evaluate each of the determinants.

15. $\begin{vmatrix} 3 & 5 \\ 6 & 4 \end{vmatrix}$ **16.** $\begin{vmatrix} -1 & -5 \\ 4 & 9 \end{vmatrix}$

17. $\begin{vmatrix} 4 & -1 & -3 \\ 2 & 1 & 4 \\ -3 & 2 & 2 \end{vmatrix}$ **18.** $\begin{vmatrix} 5 & 3 & 4 \\ -2 & 0 & 1 \\ -1 & -2 & 6 \end{vmatrix}$

For Problems 19 and 20, solve each system of equations using (a) the elimination method, (b) a matrix approach, and (c) Cramer's rule.

19. $\begin{pmatrix} x - 2y + 4z = -14 \\ 3x - 5y + z = 20 \\ -2x + y - 5z = 22 \end{pmatrix}$

20. $\begin{pmatrix} x + 3y - 2z = 28 \\ 2x - 8y + 3z = -63 \\ 3x + 8y - 5z = 72 \end{pmatrix}$

For Problems 21–24, solve each system using the method that seems most appropriate to you.

21. $\begin{pmatrix} x + y - z = -2 \\ 2x - 3y + 4z = 17 \\ -3x + 2y + 5z = -7 \end{pmatrix}$ **22.** $\begin{pmatrix} -x - y + z = -3 \\ 3x + 2y - 4z = 12 \\ 5x + y + 2z = 5 \end{pmatrix}$

23. $\begin{pmatrix} 3x + y - z = -6 \\ 3x + 2y + 3z = 9 \\ 6x - 2y + 2z = 8 \end{pmatrix}$ **24.** $\begin{pmatrix} x - 3y + z = 2 \\ 2x - 5y - 3z = 22 \\ -4x + 3y + 5z = -26 \end{pmatrix}$

25. Graph the following system, and then find the solution set by using either the substitution or the elimination method.

$$\begin{pmatrix} y = 2x^2 - 1 \\ 2x + y = 3 \end{pmatrix}$$

26. Indicate the solution set of the following system of inequalities by graphing the system and shading the appropriate region.

$$\begin{pmatrix} 3x + y > 6 \\ x - 2y \le 4 \end{pmatrix}$$

For Problems 27–33, solve each problem by setting up and solving a system of two equations and two unknowns.

27. The sum of the squares of two numbers is 13. If one number is 1 larger than the other number, find the numbers.

28. The sum of the squares of two numbers is 34. The difference of the squares of the same two numbers is 16. Find the numbers.

29. A number is 1 larger than the square of another number. The sum of the two numbers is 7. Find the numbers.

30. The area of a rectangular region is 54 square meters and its perimeter is 30 meters. Find the length and width of the rectangle.

31. At a local confectionery, 7 pounds of cashews and 5 pounds of Spanish peanuts cost $88, and 3 pounds of cashews and 2 pounds of Spanish peanuts cost $37. Find the price per pound for cashews and for Spanish peanuts.

32. We bought 2 cartons of pop and 4 pounds of candy for $12. The next day we bought 3 cartons of pop and 2 pounds of candy for $9. Find the price of a carton of pop and also the price of a pound of candy.

33. Suppose that a mail-order company charges a fixed fee for shipping merchandise that weighs 1 pound or less, plus an additional fee for each pound over 1 pound. If the shipping charge for 5 pounds is $2.40 and for 12 pounds is $3.10, find the fixed fee and the additional fee.

For Problems 1–4, refer to the following systems of equations:

I. $\begin{pmatrix} 5x - 2y = 12 \\ 2x + 5y = 7 \end{pmatrix}$ **II.** $\begin{pmatrix} x - 4y = 1 \\ 2x - 8y = 2 \end{pmatrix}$

III. $\begin{pmatrix} 4x - 5y = 6 \\ 4x - 5y = 1 \end{pmatrix}$ **IV.** $\begin{pmatrix} 2x + 3y = 9 \\ 7x - 4y = 9 \end{pmatrix}$

1. For which of these systems are the equations said to be dependent?

2. For which of these systems does the solution set consist of a single ordered pair?

3. For which of these systems are the graphs parallel lines?

4. For which of these systems are the graphs perpendicular lines?

5. Evaluate $\begin{vmatrix} -4 & 3 \\ 2 & 8 \end{vmatrix}$.

6. Evaluate $\begin{vmatrix} 2 & -1 & 1 \\ 3 & 2 & 1 \\ 2 & 4 & -1 \end{vmatrix}$.

7. Use the elimination-by-addition method to solve the system $\begin{pmatrix} 2x - 3y = -17 \\ 5x + y = 17 \end{pmatrix}$.

8. Use the substitution method to solve the system $\begin{pmatrix} -5x + 4y = 35 \\ x - 3y = -18 \end{pmatrix}$.

9. Use Cramer's rule to solve the system $\begin{pmatrix} 6x + 7y = -40 \\ 4x - 3y = 4 \end{pmatrix}$.

10. Use a matrix approach to solve the system $\begin{pmatrix} x - 4y = 15 \\ 3x + 8y = -15 \end{pmatrix}$.

For Problems 11–14, solve each of the systems using the method that seems most appropriate to you.

11. $\begin{pmatrix} 2x - 7y = -8 \\ 4x + 5y = 3 \end{pmatrix}$

12. $\begin{pmatrix} \dfrac{2}{3}x - \dfrac{1}{2}y = 7 \\ \dfrac{1}{4}x + \dfrac{1}{3}y = 12 \end{pmatrix}$

13. $\begin{pmatrix} x - 2y - z = 2 \\ 2x + y + z = 3 \\ 3x - 4y - 2z = 5 \end{pmatrix}$

14. $\begin{pmatrix} x - 2y + z = -8 \\ 2x + y - z = 3 \\ -3x - 4y + 2z = -11 \end{pmatrix}$

15. Find the value of x in the solution for the system $\begin{pmatrix} x = -2y + 5 \\ 7x + 3y = 46 \end{pmatrix}$.

16. Find the value of y in the solution for the system $\begin{pmatrix} x - y + 4z = 25 \\ 3x + 2y - z = 5 \\ 5y + 2z = 5 \end{pmatrix}$.

17. Find the value of z in the solution for the system $\begin{pmatrix} x - y - z = -6 \\ 4x + y + 3z = -4 \\ 5x - 2y - 4z = -18 \end{pmatrix}$.

For Problems 18–20, determine how many ordered pairs of real numbers are in the solution set for each of the systems.

18. $\begin{pmatrix} y = 2x^2 + 1 \\ 3x + 4y = 12 \end{pmatrix}$ **19.** $\begin{pmatrix} x^2 + 2y^2 = 8 \\ 2x^2 + y^2 = 8 \end{pmatrix}$

20. $\begin{pmatrix} y = x^3 \\ y = (x - 1)^2 - 1 \end{pmatrix}$

21. Solve the system $\begin{pmatrix} y = x^2 - 4x + 7 \\ y = -2x^2 + 8x - 5 \end{pmatrix}$.

22. Graph the solution set for the system $\begin{pmatrix} x + 3y < 3 \\ 2x - y > 2 \end{pmatrix}$.

For Problems 23–25, set up and solve a system of equations to help solve each problem.

23. A box contains $7.80 in nickels, dimes, and quarters. There are 6 more dimes than nickels and three times as many quarters as nickels. Find the number of quarters.

24. One solution contains 30% alcohol and another solution contains 80% alcohol. Some of each of the two solutions is mixed to produce 5 liters of a 60%-alcohol solution. How many liters of the 80%-alcohol solution are used?

25. The units digit of a two-digit number is one more than three times the tens digit. If the digits are reversed, the new number formed is 45 larger than the original number. Find the original number.

For Problems 1–5, evaluate each algebraic expression for the given values of the variables.

1. $-5(x - 1) - 3(2x + 4) + 3(3x - 1)$ for $x = -2$

2. $\dfrac{14a^3b^2}{7a^2b}$ for $a = -1$ and $b = 4$

3. $\dfrac{2}{n} - \dfrac{3}{2n} + \dfrac{5}{3n}$ for $n = 4$

4. $-4\sqrt{2x - y} + 5\sqrt{3x + y}$ for $x = 16$ and $y = 16$

5. $\dfrac{3}{x - 2} - \dfrac{5}{x + 3}$ for $x = 3$

For Problems 6–15, perform the indicated operations and express the answers in simplified form.

6. $(-5\sqrt{6})(3\sqrt{12})$

7. $(2\sqrt{x} - 3)(\sqrt{x} + 4)$

8. $(3\sqrt{2} - \sqrt{6})(\sqrt{2} + 4\sqrt{6})$

9. $(2x - 1)(x^2 + 6x - 4)$

10. $\dfrac{x^2 - x}{x + 5} \cdot \dfrac{x^2 + 5x + 4}{x^4 - x^2}$

11. $\dfrac{16x^2y}{24xy^3} \div \dfrac{9xy}{8x^2y^2}$

12. $\dfrac{x + 3}{10} + \dfrac{2x + 1}{15} - \dfrac{x - 2}{18}$

13. $\dfrac{7}{12ab} - \dfrac{11}{15a^2}$

14. $\dfrac{8}{x^2 - 4x} + \dfrac{2}{x}$

15. $(8x^3 - 6x^2 - 15x + 4) \div (4x - 1)$

For Problems 16–19, simplify each of the complex fractions.

16. $\dfrac{\dfrac{5}{x^2} - \dfrac{3}{x}}{\dfrac{1}{y} + \dfrac{2}{y^2}}$

17. $\dfrac{\dfrac{2}{x} - 3}{\dfrac{3}{y} + 4}$

18. $\dfrac{2 - \dfrac{1}{n + 2}}{3 + \dfrac{4}{n + 3}}$

19. $\dfrac{3a}{2 - \dfrac{1}{a}} - 1$

For Problems 20–25, factor each of the algebraic expressions completely.

20. $20x^2 + 7x - 6$

21. $16x^3 + 54$

22. $4x^4 - 25x^2 + 36$

23. $12x^3 - 52x^2 - 40x$

24. $xy - 6x + 3y - 18$

25. $10 + 9x - 9x^2$

For Problems 26–33, evaluate each of the numerical expressions.

26. $\left(\dfrac{2}{3}\right)^{-4}$

27. $\dfrac{3}{\left(\dfrac{4}{3}\right)^{-1}}$

28. $\sqrt[3]{-\dfrac{27}{64}}$

29. $-\sqrt{0.09}$

30. $(27)^{-\frac{4}{3}}$

31. $4^0 + 4^{-1} + 4^{-2}$

32. $\left(\dfrac{3^{-1}}{2^{-3}}\right)^{-2}$

33. $(2^{-3} - 3^{-2})^{-1}$

For Problems 34–36, find the indicated products and quotients, and express the final answers with positive integral exponents only.

34. $(-3x^{-1}y^2)(4x^{-2}y^{-3})$

35. $\dfrac{48x^{-4}y^2}{6xy}$

36. $\left(\dfrac{27a^{-4}b^{-3}}{-3a^{-1}b^{-4}}\right)^{-1}$

For Problems 37–44, express each radical expression in simplest radical form.

37. $\sqrt{80}$

38. $-2\sqrt{54}$

39. $\sqrt{\dfrac{75}{81}}$

40. $\dfrac{4\sqrt{6}}{3\sqrt{8}}$

41. $\sqrt[3]{56}$

42. $\dfrac{\sqrt[3]{3}}{\sqrt[3]{4}}$

43. $4\sqrt{52x^3y^2}$

44. $\sqrt{\dfrac{2x}{3y}}$

For Problems 45–47, use the distributive property to help simplify each of the following.

45. $-3\sqrt{24} + 6\sqrt{54} - \sqrt{6}$

46. $\dfrac{\sqrt{8}}{3} - \dfrac{3\sqrt{18}}{4} - \dfrac{5\sqrt{50}}{2}$

47. $8\sqrt[3]{3} - 6\sqrt[3]{24} - 4\sqrt[3]{81}$

For Problems 48 and 49, rationalize the denominator and simplify.

48. $\dfrac{\sqrt{3}}{\sqrt{6} - 2\sqrt{2}}$

49. $\dfrac{3\sqrt{5} - \sqrt{3}}{2\sqrt{3} + \sqrt{7}}$

For Problems 50–52, use scientific notation to help perform the indicated operations.

50. $\dfrac{(0.00016)(300)(0.028)}{0.064}$

51. $\dfrac{0.00072}{0.0000024}$

52. $\sqrt{0.00000009}$

For Problems 53–56, find each of the indicated products or quotients, and express the answers in standard form.

53. $(5 - 2i)(4 + 6i)$

54. $(-3 - i)(5 - 2i)$

55. $\dfrac{5}{4i}$

56. $\dfrac{-1 + 6i}{7 - 2i}$

57. Find the slope of the line determined by the points $(2, -3)$ and $(-1, 7)$.

58. Find the slope of the line determined by the equation $4x - 7y = 9$.

59. Find the length of the line segment whose endpoints are $(4, 5)$ and $(-2, 1)$.

60. Write the equation of the line that contains the points $(3, -1)$ and $(7, 4)$.

61. Write the equation of the line that is perpendicular to the line $3x - 4y = 6$ and contains the point $(-3, -2)$.

62. Find the center and the length of a radius of the circle $x^2 + 4x + y^2 - 12y + 31 = 0$.

63. Find the coordinates of the vertex of the parabola $y = x^2 + 10x + 21$.

64. Find the length of the major axis of the ellipse $x^2 + 4y^2 = 16$.

For Problems 65–70, graph each of the equations.

65. $-x + 2y = -4$

66. $x^2 + y^2 = 9$

67. $x^2 - y^2 = 9$

68. $x^2 + 2y^2 = 8$

69. $y = -3x$

70. $x^2y = 4$

For Problems 71–76, graph each of the functions.

71. $f(x) = -2x - 4$

72. $f(x) = -2x^2 - 2$

73. $f(x) = x^2 - 2x - 2$

74. $f(x) = \sqrt{x + 1} + 2$

75. $f(x) = 2x^2 + 8x + 9$

76. $f(x) = -|x - 2| + 1$

77. If $f(x) = x - 3$ and $g(x) = 2x^2 - x - 1$, find $(g \circ f)(x)$ and $(f \circ g)(x)$.

78. Find the inverse (f^{-1}) of $f(x) = 3x - 7$.

79. Find the inverse of $f(x) = -\dfrac{1}{2}x + \dfrac{2}{3}$.

80. Find the constant of variation if y varies directly as x, and $y = 2$ when $x = -\dfrac{2}{3}$.

81. If y is inversely proportional to the square of x, and $y = 4$ when $x = 3$, find y when $x = 6$.

82. The volume of a gas at a constant temperature varies inversely as the pressure. What is the volume of a gas under a pressure of 25 pounds if the gas occupies 15 cubic centimeters under a pressure of 20 pounds?

For Problems 83 and 84, evaluate each of the determinants.

83. $\begin{vmatrix} -2 & 4 \\ 7 & 6 \end{vmatrix}$

84. $\begin{vmatrix} 1 & -2 & -1 \\ 2 & 1 & 3 \\ -1 & -3 & 4 \end{vmatrix}$

For Problems 85–105, solve each of the equations.

85. $3(2x - 1) - 2(5x + 1) = 4(3x + 4)$

86. $n + \dfrac{3n - 1}{9} - 4 = \dfrac{3n + 1}{3}$

87. $0.92 + 0.9(x - 0.3) = 2x - 5.95$

88. $|4x - 1| = 11$

89. $3x^2 = 7x$

90. $x^3 - 36x = 0$

91. $30x^2 + 13x - 10 = 0$

92. $8x^3 + 12x^2 - 36x = 0$

93. $x^4 + 8x^2 - 9 = 0$

94. $(n + 4)(n - 6) = 11$

95. $2 - \dfrac{3x}{x - 4} = \dfrac{14}{x + 7}$

96. $\dfrac{2n}{6n^2 + 7n - 3} - \dfrac{n - 3}{3n^2 + 11n - 4} = \dfrac{5}{2n^2 + 11n + 12}$

97. $\sqrt{3y} - y = -6$

98. $\sqrt{x + 19} - \sqrt{x + 28} = -1$

99. $(3x - 1)^2 = 45$

100. $(2x + 5)^2 = -32$

101. $2x^2 - 3x + 4 = 0$

102. $3n^2 - 6n + 2 = 0$

103. $\dfrac{5}{n - 3} - \dfrac{3}{n + 3} = 1$

104. $12x^4 - 19x^2 + 5 = 0$

105. $2x^2 + 5x + 5 = 0$

For Problems 106 –115, solve each of the inequalities.

106. $-5(y - 1) + 3 > 3y - 4 - 4y$

107. $0.06x + 0.08(250 - x) \geq 19$

108. $|5x - 2| > 13$

109. $|6x + 2| < 8$

110. $\dfrac{x - 2}{5} - \dfrac{3x - 1}{4} \leq \dfrac{3}{10}$

111. $(x - 2)(x + 4) \leq 0$

112. $(3x - 1)(x - 4) > 0$

113. $x(x + 5) < 24$

114. $\dfrac{x - 3}{x - 7} \geq 0$

115. $\dfrac{2x}{x + 3} > 4$

For Problems 116 –120, solve each of the systems of equations.

116. $\begin{pmatrix} 4x - 3y = 18 \\ 3x - 2y = 15 \end{pmatrix}$

117. $\begin{pmatrix} y = \dfrac{2}{5}x - 1 \\ 3x + 5y = 4 \end{pmatrix}$

118. $\begin{pmatrix} \dfrac{x}{2} - \dfrac{y}{3} = 1 \\ \dfrac{2x}{5} + \dfrac{y}{2} = 2 \end{pmatrix}$

119. $\begin{pmatrix} 4x - y + 3z = -12 \\ 2x + 3y - z = 8 \\ 6x + y + 2z = -8 \end{pmatrix}$

120. $\begin{pmatrix} x - y + 5z = -10 \\ 5x + 2y - 3z = 6 \\ -3x + 2y - z = 12 \end{pmatrix}$

For Problems 121–135, set up an equation, an inequality, or a system of equations to help solve each problem.

121. Find three consecutive odd integers whose sum is 57.

122. Suppose that Eric has a collection of 63 coins consisting of nickels, dimes, and quarters. The number of dimes is 6 more than the number of nickels, and the number of quarters is 1 more than twice the number of nickels. How many coins of each kind are in the collection?

123. One of two supplementary angles is 4° more than one-third of the other angle. Find the measure of each of the angles.

124. If a ring costs a jeweler $300, at what price should it be sold for the jeweler to make a profit of 50% on the selling price?

125. Last year Beth invested a certain amount of money at 8% and $300 more than that amount at 9%. Her total yearly interest was $316. How much did she invest at each rate?

126. Two trains leave the same depot at the same time, one traveling east and the other traveling west. At the end of $4\frac{1}{2}$ hours, they are 639 miles apart. If the rate of the train traveling east is 10 miles per hour greater than that of the other train, find their rates.

127. Suppose that a 10-quart radiator contains a 50% solution of antifreeze. How much needs to be drained out and replaced with pure antifreeze to obtain a 70%-antifreeze solution?

128. Sam shot rounds of 70, 73, and 76 on the first three days of a golf tournament. What must he shoot on the fourth day of the tournament to average 72 or less for the four days?

129. The cube of a number equals nine times the same number. Find the number.

130. A strip of uniform width is to be cut off of both sides and both ends of a sheet of paper that is 8 inches by 14 inches to reduce the size of the paper to an area of 72 square inches. (See Figure 10.16.) Find the width of the strip.

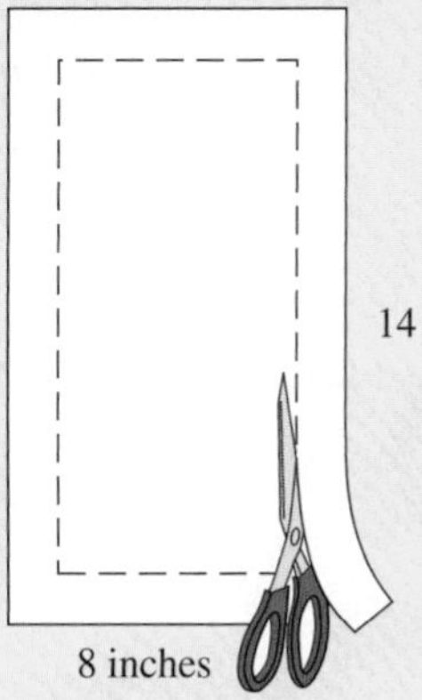

131. A sum of $2450 is to be divided between two people in the ratio of 3 to 4. How much does each person receive?

132. Working together, Crystal and Dean can complete a task in $1\frac{1}{5}$ hours. Dean can do the task by himself in 2 hours. How long would it take Crystal to complete the task by herself?

133. Dudley bought a number of shares of stock for $300. A month later he sold all but 10 shares at a profit of $5 per share and regained his original investment of $300. How many shares did he originally buy and at what price per share?

134. The units digit of a two-digit number is 1 more than twice the tens digit. The sum of the digits is 10. Find the number.

135. The sum of the two smallest angles of a triangle is 40° less than the other angle. The sum of the smallest and largest angles is twice the other angle. Find the measures of the three angles of the triangle.

14 inches

8 inches

Figure 10.16

11

Exponential and Logarithmic Functions

11.1 Exponents and Exponential Functions

11.2 Applications of Exponential Functions

11.3 Logarithms

11.4 Logarithmic Functions

11.5 Exponential Equations, Logarithmic Equations, and Problem Solving

Because the Richter number for reporting the intensity of an earthquake is calculated from a logarithm, it is referred to as a logarithmic scale. Logarithmic scales are commonly used in science and mathematics to transform very large numbers to a smaller scale.

AP/Wide World Photos

How long will it take $100 to triple itself if it is invested at 8% interest compounded continuously? We can use the formula $A = Pe^{rt}$ to generate the equation $300 = 100e^{0.08t}$, which can be solved for t by using logarithms. It will take approximately 13.7 years for the money to triple itself.

This chapter will expand the meaning of an exponent and introduce the concept of a logarithm. We will (1) work with some exponential functions, (2) work with some logarithmic functions, and (3) use the concepts of exponent and logarithm to expand our capabilities for solving problems. Your calculator will be a valuable tool throughout this chapter.

11.1   Exponents and Exponential Functions

In Chapter 1, the expression b^n was defined as n factors of b, where n is any positive integer and b is any real number. For example,

$$4^3 = 4 \cdot 4 \cdot 4 = 64$$

$$\left(\frac{1}{2}\right)^4 = \left(\frac{1}{2}\right)\left(\frac{1}{2}\right)\left(\frac{1}{2}\right)\left(\frac{1}{2}\right) = \frac{1}{16}$$

$$(-0.3)^2 = (-0.3)(-0.3) = 0.09$$

In Chapter 5, by defining $b^0 = 1$ and $b^{-n} = \dfrac{1}{b^n}$, where n is any positive integer and b is any nonzero real number, we extended the concept of an exponent to include all integers. For example,

$$2^{-3} = \frac{1}{2^3} = \frac{1}{2 \cdot 2 \cdot 2} = \frac{1}{8} \qquad \left(\frac{1}{3}\right)^{-2} = \frac{1}{\left(\frac{1}{3}\right)^2} = \frac{1}{\frac{1}{9}} = 9$$

$$(0.4)^{-1} = \frac{1}{(0.4)^1} = \frac{1}{0.4} = 2.5 \qquad (-0.98)^0 = 1$$

In Chapter 5 we also provided for the use of all rational numbers as exponents by defining $b^{\frac{m}{n}} = \sqrt[n]{b^m}$, where n is a positive integer greater than 1, and b is a real number such that $\sqrt[n]{b}$ exists. For example,

$$8^{\frac{2}{3}} = \sqrt[3]{8^2} = \sqrt[3]{64} = 4$$

$$16^{\frac{1}{4}} = \sqrt[4]{16^1} = 2$$

$$32^{-\frac{1}{5}} = \frac{1}{32^{\frac{1}{5}}} = \frac{1}{\sqrt[5]{32}} = \frac{1}{2}$$

To extend the concept of an exponent formally to include the use of irrational numbers requires some ideas from calculus and is therefore beyond the scope of this text. However, here's a glance at the general idea involved. Consider the number $2^{\sqrt{3}}$. By using the nonterminating and nonrepeating decimal representation $1.73205\ldots$ for $\sqrt{3}$, form the sequence of numbers 2^1, $2^{1.7}$, $2^{1.73}$, $2^{1.732}$, $2^{1.7320}$, $2^{1.73205}\ldots$. It would seem reasonable that each successive power gets closer to $2^{\sqrt{3}}$. This is precisely what happens if b^n, where n is irrational, is properly defined by using the concept of a limit.

From now on, then, we can use any real number as an exponent, and the basic properties stated in Chapter 5 can be extended to include all real numbers as exponents. Let's restate those properties at this time with the restriction that the bases a and b are to be positive numbers (to avoid expressions such as $(-4)^{\frac{1}{2}}$, which do not represent real numbers).

Property 11.1

If a and b are positive real numbers and m and n are any real numbers, then

1. $b^n \cdot b^m = b^{n+m}$ Product of two powers

2. $(b^n)^m = b^{mn}$ Power of a power

3. $(ab)^n = a^n b^n$ Power of a product

4. $\left(\dfrac{a}{b}\right)^n = \dfrac{a^n}{b^n}$ Power of a quotient

5. $\dfrac{b^n}{b^m} = b^{n-m}$ Quotient of two powers

Another property that can be used to solve certain types of equations involving exponents can be stated as follows:

Property 11.2

If $b > 0$, $b \neq 1$, and m and n are real numbers, then

$$b^n = b^m \quad \text{if and only if } n = m$$

The following examples illustrate the use of Property 11.2.

EXAMPLE 1

Solve $2^x = 32$.

Solution

$$2^x = 32$$
$$2^x = 2^5 \qquad 32 = 2^5$$
$$x = 5 \qquad \text{Property 11.2}$$

The solution set is $\{5\}$.

E X A M P L E   2

Solve $3^{2x} = \dfrac{1}{9}$.

Solution

$$3^{2x} = \frac{1}{9} = \frac{1}{3^2}$$

$$3^{2x} = 3^{-2}$$

$$2x = -2 \qquad \text{Property 11.2}$$

$$x = -1$$

The solution set is $\{-1\}$. ■

E X A M P L E   3

Solve $\left(\dfrac{1}{5}\right)^{x-2} = \dfrac{1}{125}$.

Solution

$$\left(\frac{1}{5}\right)^{x-2} = \frac{1}{125} = \left(\frac{1}{5}\right)^3$$

$$x - 2 = 3 \qquad \text{Property 11.2}$$

$$x = 5$$

The solution set is $\{5\}$. ■

E X A M P L E   4

Solve $8^x = 32$.

Solution

$$8^x = 32$$

$$(2^3)^x = 2^5 \qquad 8 = 2^3$$

$$2^{3x} = 2^5$$

$$3x = 5 \qquad \text{Property 11.2}$$

$$x = \frac{5}{3}$$

The solution set is $\left\{\dfrac{5}{3}\right\}$. ■

E X A M P L E   5

Solve $(3^{x+1})(9^{x-2}) = 27$.

Solution

$$(3^{x+1})(9^{x-2}) = 27$$

$$(3^{x+1})(3^2)^{x-2} = 3^3$$

$$(3^{x+1})(3^{2x-4}) = 3^3$$

$$3^{3x-3} = 3^3$$

$$3x - 3 = 3 \qquad \text{Property 11.2}$$

$$3x = 6$$

$$x = 2$$

The solution set is {2}.   ∎

■ Exponential Functions

If b is any positive number, then the expression b^x designates exactly one real number for every real value of x. Thus the equation $f(x) = b^x$ defines a function whose domain is the set of real numbers. Furthermore, if we impose the additional restriction $b \neq 1$, then any equation of the form $f(x) = b^x$ describes a one-to-one function and is called an **exponential function**. This leads to the following definition.

Definition 11.1

If $b > 0$ and $b \neq 1$, then the function f defined by

$$f(x) = b^x$$

where x is any real number, is called the **exponential function with base b**.

Remark: The function $f(x) = 1^x$ is a constant function whose graph is a horizontal line, and therefore it is not a one-to-one function. Remember from Chapter 9 that one-to-one functions have inverses; this becomes a key issue in a later section.

Now let's consider graphing some exponential functions.

E X A M P L E   6

Graph the function $f(x) = 2^x$.

Solution

First, let's set up a table of values.

x	$f(x) = 2^x$
-2	$\dfrac{1}{4}$
-1	$\dfrac{1}{2}$
0	1
1	2
2	4
3	8

Plot these points and connect them with a smooth curve to produce Figure 11.1.

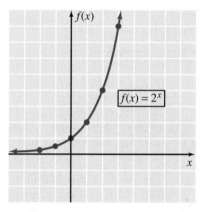

Figure 11.1   ■

E X A M P L E   7   Graph $f(x) = \left(\dfrac{1}{2}\right)^x$.

Solution

Again, let's set up a table of values. Plot these points and connect them with a smooth curve to produce Figure 11.2.

x	$f(x) = \left(\dfrac{1}{2}\right)^x$
-2	4
-1	2
0	1
1	$\dfrac{1}{2}$
2	$\dfrac{1}{4}$
3	$\dfrac{1}{8}$

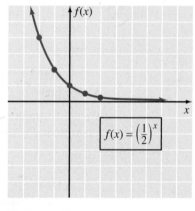

Figure 11.2   ■

In the tables for Examples 6 and 7 we chose integral values for x to keep the computation simple. However, with the use of a calculator, we could easily acquire functional values by using nonintegral exponents. Consider the following additional values for each of the tables.

$f(x) = 2^x$	
$f(0.5) \approx 1.41$	$f(-0.5) \approx 0.71$
$f(1.7) \approx 3.25$	$f(-2.6) \approx 0.16$

$f(x) = \left(\dfrac{1}{2}\right)^x$	
$f(0.7) \approx 0.62$	$f(-0.8) \approx 1.74$
$f(2.3) \approx 0.20$	$f(-2.1) \approx 4.29$

Use your calculator to check these results. Also, it would be worthwhile for you to go back and see that the points determined do fit the graphs in Figures 11.1 and 11.2.

The graphs in Figures 11.1 and 11.2 illustrate a general behavior pattern of exponential functions. That is, if $b > 1$, then the graph of $f(x) = b^x$ goes *up to the right* and the function is called an **increasing function**. If $0 < b < 1$, then the graph of $f(x) = b^x$ goes *down to the right* and the function is called a **decreasing function**. These facts are illustrated in Figure 11.3. Note that because $b^0 = 1$ for any $b > 0$, all graphs of $f(x) = b^x$ contain the point $(0, 1)$.

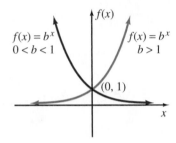

Figure 11.3

As you graph exponential functions, don't forget your previous graphing experiences.

1. The graph of $f(x) = 2^x - 4$ is the graph of $f(x) = 2^x$ moved down 4 units.
2. The graph of $f(x) = 2^{x+3}$ is the graph of $f(x) = 2^x$ moved 3 units to the left.
3. The graph of $f(x) = -2^x$ is the graph of $f(x) = 2^x$ reflected across the x axis.

We used a graphing calculator to graph these four functions on the same set of axes, as shown in Figure 11.4.

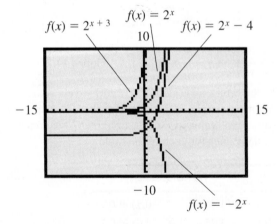

Figure 11.4

Problem Set 11.1

For Problems 1–34, solve each equation.

1. $3^x = 27$

2. $2^x = 64$

3. $2^{2x} = 16$

4. $3^{2x} = 81$

5. $\left(\dfrac{1}{4}\right)^x = \dfrac{1}{256}$

6. $\left(\dfrac{1}{2}\right)^x = \dfrac{1}{128}$

7. $5^{x+2} = 125$

8. $4^{x-3} = 16$

9. $3^{-x} = \dfrac{1}{243}$

10. $5^{-x} = \dfrac{1}{25}$

11. $6^{3x-1} = 36$

12. $2^{2x+3} = 32$

13. $4^x = 8$

14. $16^x = 64$

15. $8^{2x} = 32$

16. $9^{3x} = 27$

17. $\left(\dfrac{1}{2}\right)^{2x} = 64$

18. $\left(\dfrac{1}{3}\right)^{5x} = 243$

19. $\left(\dfrac{3}{4}\right)^x = \dfrac{64}{27}$

20. $\left(\dfrac{2}{3}\right)^x = \dfrac{9}{4}$

21. $9^{4x-2} = \dfrac{1}{81}$

22. $8^{3x+2} = \dfrac{1}{16}$

23. $6^{2x} + 3 = 39$

24. $5^{2x} - 2 = 123$

25. $10^x = 0.1$

26. $10^x = 0.0001$

27. $32^x = \dfrac{1}{4}$

28. $9^x = \dfrac{1}{27}$

29. $(2^{x+1})(2^x) = 64$

30. $(2^{2x-1})(2^{x+2}) = 32$

31. $(27)(3^x) = 9^x$

32. $(3^x)(3^{5x}) = 81$

33. $(4^x)(16^{3x-1}) = 8$

34. $(8^{2x})(4^{2x-1}) = 16$

For Problems 35–52, graph each exponential function.

35. $f(x) = 4^x$

36. $f(x) = 3^x$

37. $f(x) = 6^x$

38. $f(x) = 5^x$

39. $f(x) = \left(\dfrac{1}{3}\right)^x$

40. $f(x) = \left(\dfrac{1}{4}\right)^x$

41. $f(x) = \left(\dfrac{3}{4}\right)^x$

42. $f(x) = \left(\dfrac{2}{3}\right)^x$

43. $f(x) = 2^{x-2}$

44. $f(x) = 2^{x+1}$

45. $f(x) = 3^{-x}$

46. $f(x) = 2^{-x}$

47. $f(x) = 3^{2x}$

48. $f(x) = 2^{2x}$

49. $f(x) = 3^x - 2$

50. $f(x) = 2^x + 1$

51. $f(x) = 2^{-x-2}$

52. $f(x) = 3^{-x+1}$

■■■ THOUGHTS INTO WORDS

53. Explain how you would solve the equation $(2^{x+1})(8^{2x-3}) = 64$.

54. Why is the base of an exponential function restricted to positive numbers not including 1?

55. Explain how you would graph the function $f(x) = -\left(\dfrac{1}{3}\right)^x$.

GRAPHING CALCULATOR ACTIVITIES

56. Use a graphing calculator to check your graphs for Problems 35–52.

57. Graph $f(x) = 2^x$. Where should the graphs of $f(x) = 2^{x-5}$, $f(x) = 2^{x-7}$, and $f(x) = 2^{x+5}$ be located? Graph all three functions on the same set of axes with $f(x) = 2^x$.

58. Graph $f(x) = 3^x$. Where should the graphs of $f(x) = 3^x + 2$, $f(x) = 3^x - 3$, and $f(x) = 3^x - 7$ be located? Graph all three functions on the same set of axes with $f(x) = 3^x$.

59. Graph $f(x) = \left(\dfrac{1}{2}\right)^x$. Where should the graphs of

$f(x) = -\left(\dfrac{1}{2}\right)^x$, $f(x) = \left(\dfrac{1}{2}\right)^{-x}$, and $f(x) = -\left(\dfrac{1}{2}\right)^{-x}$

be located? Graph all three functions on the same set of axes with $f(x) = \left(\dfrac{1}{2}\right)^x$.

60. Graph $f(x) = (1.5)^x$, $f(x) = (5.5)^x$, $f(x) = (0.3)^x$, and $f(x) = (0.7)^x$ on the same set of axes. Are these graphs consistent with Figure 11.3?

61. What is the solution for $3^x = 5$? Do you agree that it is between 1 and 2 because $3^1 = 3$ and $3^2 = 9$? Now graph $f(x) = 3^x - 5$ and use the ZOOM and TRACE features of your graphing calculator to find an approximation, to the nearest hundredth, for the x intercept. You should get an answer of 1.46, to the nearest hundredth. Do you see that this is an approximation for the solution of $3^x = 5$? Try it; raise 3 to the 1.46 power.

Find an approximate solution, to the nearest hundredth, for each of the following equations by graphing the appropriate function and finding the x intercept.

(a) $2^x = 19$ (b) $3^x = 50$
(c) $4^x = 47$ (d) $5^x = 120$
(e) $2^x = 1500$ (f) $3^{x-1} = 34$

11.2   Applications of Exponential Functions

Equations that describe exponential functions can represent many real-world situations that exhibit growth or decay. For example, suppose that an economist predicts an annual inflation rate of 5% for the next 10 years. This means an item that presently costs $8 will cost $8(105\%) = 8(1.05) = \$8.40$ a year from now. The same item will cost $(105\%)[8(105\%)] = 8(1.05)^2 = \$8.82$ in 2 years. In general, the equation

$$P = P_0(1.05)^t$$

yields the predicted price P of an item in t years at the annual inflation rate of 5%, where that item presently costs P_0. By using this equation, we can look at some future prices based on the prediction of a 5% inflation rate.

A $0.79 jar of mustard will cost $0.79(1.05)^3 = \$0.91$ in 3 years.
A $2.69 bag of potato chips will cost $2.69(1.05)^5 = \$3.43$ in 5 years.
A $6.69 can of coffee will cost $6.69(1.05)^7 = \$9.41$ in 7 years.

■ Compound Interest

Compound interest provides another illustration of exponential growth. Suppose that $500 (called the **principal**) is invested at an interest rate of 8% **compounded annually**. The interest earned the first year is $500(0.08) = \$40$, and this amount is added to the original $500 to form a new principal of $540 for the second year. The interest earned during the second year is $540(0.08) = \$43.20$, and this amount is added to $540 to form a new principal of $583.20 for the third year. Each year a new principal is formed by reinvesting the interest earned that year.

In general, suppose that a sum of money P (called the principal) is invested at an interest rate of r percent compounded annually. The interest earned the first year is Pr, and the new principal for the second year is $P + Pr$ or $P(1 + r)$. Note that the new principal for the second year can be found by multiplying the original principal P by $(1 + r)$. In like fashion, the new principal for the third year can be found by multiplying the previous principal $P(1 + r)$ by $(1 + r)$, thus obtaining $P(1 + r)^2$. If this process is continued, then after t years the total amount of money accumulated, A, is given by

$$A = P(1 + r)^t$$

Consider the following examples of investments made at a certain rate of interest compounded annually.

1. $750 invested for 5 years at 9% compounded annually produces

$$A = \$750(1.09)^5 = \$1153.97$$

2. $1000 invested for 10 years at 7% compounded annually produces

$$A = \$1000(1.07)^{10} = \$1967.15$$

3. $5000 invested for 20 years at 6% compounded annually produces

$$A = \$5000(1.06)^{20} = \$16{,}035.68$$

If we invest money at a certain rate of interest to be compounded more than once a year, then we can adjust the basic formula, $A = P(1 + r)^t$, according to the number of compounding periods in the year. For example, for **compounding semiannually**, the formula becomes $A = P\left(1 + \dfrac{r}{2}\right)^{2t}$ and for **compounding quarterly**, the formula becomes $A = P\left(1 + \dfrac{r}{4}\right)^{4t}$. In general, we have the following formula, where n represents the number of compounding periods in a year.

$$A = P\left(1 + \frac{r}{n}\right)^{nt}$$

The following examples should clarify the use of this formula.

1. $750 invested for 5 years at 9% compounded semiannually produces

$$A = \$750\left(1 + \frac{0.09}{2}\right)^{2(5)} = \$750(1.045)^{10} = \$1164.73$$

2. $1000 invested for 10 years at 7% compounded quarterly produces

$$A = \$1000\left(1 + \frac{0.07}{4}\right)^{4(10)} = \$1000(1.0175)^{40} = \$2001.60$$

3. $5000 invested for 20 years at 6% compounded monthly produces

$$A = \$5000\left(1 + \frac{0.06}{12}\right)^{12(20)} = \$5000(1.005)^{240} = \$16{,}551.02$$

You may find it interesting to compare these results with those obtained earlier for compounding annually.

■ Exponential Decay

Suppose it is estimated that the value of a car depreciates 15% per year for the first 5 years. Thus a car that costs $19,500 will be worth $19500(100\% - 15\%) = 19500(85\%) = 19500(0.85) = \$16{,}575$ in 1 year. In 2 years the value of the car will have depreciated to $19500(0.85)^2 = \$14{,}089$ (nearest dollar). The equation

$$V = V_0(0.85)^t$$

yields the value V of a car in t years at the annual depreciation rate of 15%, where the car initially cost V_0. By using this equation, we can estimate some car values, to the nearest dollar, as follows:

A $17,000 car will be worth $\$17{,}000(0.85)^5 = \$7543$ in 5 years.

A $25,000 car will be worth $\$25{,}000(0.85)^4 = \$13{,}050$ in 4 years.

A $40,000 car will be worth $\$40{,}000(0.85)^3 = \$24{,}565$ in 3 years.

Another example of exponential decay is associated with radioactive substances. We can describe the rate of decay exponentially, on the basis of the half-life of a substance. The *half-life* of a radioactive substance is the amount of time that it takes for one-half of an initial amount of the substance to disappear as the result of decay. For example, suppose that we have 200 grams of a certain substance that has a half-life of 5 days. After 5 days, $200\left(\frac{1}{2}\right) = 100$ grams remain. After 10 days, $200\left(\frac{1}{2}\right)^2 = 50$ grams remain. After 15 days, $200\left(\frac{1}{2}\right)^3 = 25$ grams remain. In general, after t days, $200\left(\frac{1}{2}\right)^{\frac{t}{5}}$ grams remain.

This discussion leads us to the following half-life formula. Suppose there is an initial amount, Q_0, of a radioactive substance with a half-life of h. The amount of substance remaining, Q, after a time period of t, is given by the formula

$$Q = Q_0\left(\frac{1}{2}\right)^{\frac{t}{h}}$$

The units of measure for t and h must be the same.

EXAMPLE 1

Barium-140 has a half-life of 13 days. If there are 500 milligrams of barium initially, how many milligrams remain after 26 days? After 100 days?

Solution

When we use $Q_0 = 500$ and $h = 13$, the half-life formula becomes

$$Q = 500\left(\frac{1}{2}\right)^{\frac{t}{13}}$$

If $t = 26$, then

$$Q = 500\left(\frac{1}{2}\right)^{\frac{26}{13}}$$

$$= 500\left(\frac{1}{2}\right)^{2}$$

$$= 500\left(\frac{1}{4}\right)$$

$$= 125$$

Thus 125 milligrams remain after 26 days. If $t = 100$, then

$$Q = 500\left(\frac{1}{2}\right)^{\frac{100}{13}}$$

$$= 500(0.5)^{\frac{100}{13}}$$

$$= 2.4, \quad \text{to the nearest tenth of a milligram}$$

Thus approximately 2.4 milligrams remain after 100 days. ■

Remark: The solution to Example 1 clearly demonstrates one facet of the role of the calculator in the application of mathematics. We solved the first part of the problem easily without the calculator, but the calculator certainly was helpful for the second part of the problem.

■ Number *e*

An interesting situation occurs if we consider the compound interest formula for $P = \$1$, $r = 100\%$, and $t = 1$ year. The formula becomes $A = 1\left(1 + \frac{1}{n}\right)^{n}$. The accompanying table shows some values, rounded to eight decimal places, of $\left(1 + \frac{1}{n}\right)^{n}$ for different values of n.

n	$\left(1 + \dfrac{1}{n}\right)^{n}$
1	2.00000000
10	2.59374246
100	2.70481383
1000	2.71692393
10,000	2.71814593
100,000	2.71826824
1,000,000	2.71828047
10,000,000	2.71828169
100,000,000	2.71828181
1,000,000,000	2.71828183

The table suggests that as n increases, the value of $\left(1 + \dfrac{1}{n}\right)^{n}$ gets closer and closer to some fixed number. This does happen, and the fixed number is called e. To five decimal places, $e = 2.71828$.

The function defined by the equation $f(x) = e^{x}$ is the **natural exponential function**. It has a great many real-world applications; some we will look at in a moment. First, however, let's get a picture of the natural exponential function. Because $2 < e < 3$, the graph of $f(x) = e^{x}$ must fall between the graphs of $f(x) = 2^{x}$ and $f(x) = 3^{x}$. To be more specific, let's use our calculator to determine a table of values. Use the $\boxed{e^{x}}$ key, and round the results to the nearest tenth to obtain the following table. Plot the points determined by this table, and connect them with a smooth curve to produce Figure 11.5.

x	$f(x) = e^{x}$
0	1.0
1	2.7
2	7.4
-1	0.4
-2	0.1

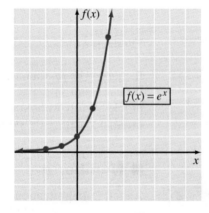

Figure 11.5

Let's return to the concept of compound interest. If the number of compounding periods in a year is increased indefinitely, we arrive at the concept of **compounding continuously**. Mathematically, this can be accomplished by applying the limit concept to the expression $P\left(1 + \dfrac{r}{n}\right)^{nt}$. We will not show the details here, but the following result is obtained. The formula

$$A = Pe^{rt}$$

yields the accumulated value, A, of a sum of money, P, that has been invested for t years at a rate of r percent compounded continuously. The following examples show the use of the formula.

1. \$750 invested for 5 years at 9% compounded continuously produces

$$A = \$750e^{(0.09)(5)} = 750e^{0.45} = \$1176.23$$

2. \$1000 invested for 10 years at 7% compounded continuously produces

$$A = \$1000e^{(0.07)(10)} = 1000e^{0.7} = \$2013.75$$

3. \$5000 invested for 20 years at 6% compounded continuously produces

$$A = \$5000e^{(0.06)(20)} = 5000e^{1.2} = \$16,600.58$$

Again you may find it interesting to compare these results with those you obtained earlier when using a different number of compounding periods.

The ideas behind compounding continuously carry over to other growth situations. The law of exponential growth,

$$Q(t) = Q_0e^{kt}$$

is used as a mathematical model for numerous growth-and-decay applications. In this equation, $Q(t)$ represents the quantity of a given substance at any time t; Q_0 is the initial amount of the substance (when $t = 0$); and k is a constant that depends on the particular application. If $k < 0$, then $Q(t)$ decreases as t increases, and we refer to the model as the **law of decay**. Let's consider some growth-and-decay applications.

E X A M P L E   2

Suppose that in a certain culture, the equation $Q(t) = 15000e^{0.3t}$ expresses the number of bacteria present as a function of the time t, where t is expressed in hours. Find (a) the initial number of bacteria, and (b) the number of bacteria after 3 hours.

Solution

(a) The initial number of bacteria is produced when $t = 0$.

$$Q(0) = 15,000e^{0.3(0)}$$

$$= 15,000e^0$$

$$= 15,000 \qquad e^0 = 1$$

(b) $Q(3) = 15,000e^{0.3(3)}$

$$= 15,000e^{0.9}$$

$$= 36,894, \quad \text{to the nearest whole number}$$

Therefore, there should be approximately 36,894 bacteria present after 3 hours. ∎

EXAMPLE 3

Suppose the number of bacteria present in a certain culture after t minutes is given by the equation $Q(t) = Q_0 e^{0.05t}$, where Q_0 represents the initial number of bacteria. If 5000 bacteria are present after 20 minutes, how many bacteria were present initially?

Solution

If 5000 bacteria are present after 20 minutes, then $Q(20) = 5000$.

$$5000 = Q_0 e^{0.05(20)}$$

$$5000 = Q_0 e^1$$

$$\frac{5000}{e} = Q_0$$

$$1839 = Q_0, \quad \text{to the nearest whole number}$$

Therefore, there were approximately 1839 bacteria present initially. ∎

EXAMPLE 4

The number of grams Q of a certain radioactive substance present after t seconds is given by $Q(t) = 200e^{-0.3t}$. How many grams remain after 7 seconds?

Solution

We need to evaluate $Q(7)$.

$$Q(7) = 200e^{-0.3(7)}$$

$$= 200e^{-2.1}$$

$$= 24, \quad \text{to the nearest whole number}$$

Thus approximately 24 grams remain after 7 seconds. ∎

Finally, let's use a graphing calculator to graph a special exponential function.

EXAMPLE 5

Graph the function

$$y = \frac{1}{\sqrt{2\pi}} e^{-x^2/2}$$

and find its maximum value.

Solution

If $x = 0$, then $y = \dfrac{1}{\sqrt{2\pi}} e^0 = \dfrac{1}{\sqrt{2\pi}} \approx 0.4$. Let's set the boundaries of the viewing rectangle so that $-5 \leq x \leq 5$ and $0 \leq y \leq 1$ with a y scale of 0.1; the graph of the function is shown in Figure 11.6. From the graph, we see that the maximum value of the function occurs at $x = 0$, which we have already determined to be approximately 0.4.

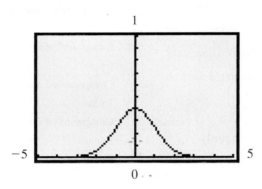

Figure 11.6   ■

Remark: The curve in Figure 11.6 is called the standard normal distribution curve. You may want to ask your instructor to explain what it means to assign grades on the basis of the normal distribution curve.

Problem Set 11.2

1. Assuming that the rate of inflation is 4% per year, the equation $P = P_0(1.04)^t$ yields the predicted price P, in t years, of an item that presently costs P_0. Find the predicted price of each of the following items for the indicated years ahead.

(a) $0.77 can of soup in 3 years
(b) $3.43 container of cocoa mix in 5 years
(c) $1.99 jar of coffee creamer in 4 years
(d) $1.05 can of beans and bacon in 10 years
(e) $18,000 car in 5 years (nearest dollar)
(f) $120,000 house in 8 years (nearest dollar)
(g) $500 TV set in 7 years (nearest dollar)

2. Suppose it is estimated that the value of a car depreciates 30% per year for the first 5 years. The equation $A = P_0(0.7)^t$ yields the value (A) of a car after t years if the original price is P_0. Find the value (to the nearest

dollar) of each of the following cars after the indicated time.

(a) $16,500 car after 4 years
(b) $22,000 car after 2 years
(c) $27,000 car after 5 years
(d) $40,000 car after 3 years

For Problems 3–14, use the formula $A = P\left(1 + \dfrac{r}{n}\right)^{nt}$ to find the total amount of money accumulated at the end of the indicated time period for each of the following investments.

3. $200 for 6 years at 6% compounded annually

4. $250 for 5 years at 7% compounded annually

5. $500 for 7 years at 8% compounded semiannually

6. $750 for 8 years at 8% compounded semiannually

7. $800 for 9 years at 9% compounded quarterly

8. $1200 for 10 years at 10% compounded quarterly

9. $1500 for 5 years at 12% compounded monthly

10. $2000 for 10 years at 9% compounded monthly

11. $5000 for 15 years at 8.5% compounded annually

12. $7500 for 20 years at 9.5% compounded semiannually

13. $8000 for 10 years at 10.5% compounded quarterly

14. $10,000 for 25 years at 9.25% compounded monthly

For Problems 15–23, use the formula $A = Pe^{rt}$ to find the total amount of money accumulated at the end of the indicated time period by compounding continuously.

15. $400 for 5 years at 7%

16. $500 for 7 years at 6%

17. $750 for 8 years at 8%

18. $1000 for 10 years at 9%

19. $2000 for 15 years at 10%

20. $5000 for 20 years at 11%

21. $7500 for 10 years at 8.5%

22. $10,000 for 25 years at 9.25%

23. $15,000 for 10 years at 7.75%

24. Complete the following chart, which illustrates what happens to $1000 invested at various rates of interest for different lengths of time but always compounded continuously. Round your answers to the nearest dollar.

$1000 compounded continuously			
8%	**10%**	**12%**	**14%**
5 years			
10 years			
15 years			
20 years			
25 years			

25. Complete the following chart, which illustrates what happens to $1000 invested at 12% for different lengths of time and different numbers of compounding periods. Round all of your answers to the nearest dollar.

$1000 at 12%			
Compounded annually			
1 year	5 years	10 years	20 years
Compounded semiannually			
1 year	5 years	10 years	20 years
Compounded quarterly			
1 year	5 years	10 years	20 years
Compounded monthly			
1 year	5 years	10 years	20 years
Compounded continuously			
1 year	5 years	10 years	20 years

26. Complete the following chart, which illustrates what happens to $1000 in 10 years for different rates of interest and different numbers of compounding periods. Round your answers to the nearest dollar.

$1000 for 10 years			
Compounded annually			
8%	10%	12%	14%
Compounded semiannually			
8%	10%	12%	14%
Compounded quarterly			
8%	10%	12%	14%
Compounded monthly			
8%	10%	12%	14%
Compounded continuously			
8%	10%	12%	14%

27. Suppose that Nora invested $500 at 8.25% compounded annually for 5 years and Patti invested $500 at 8% compounded quarterly for 5 years. At the end of 5 years, who will have the most money and by how much?

28. Two years ago Daniel invested some money at 8% interest compounded annually. Today it is worth $758.16. How much did he invest two years ago?

29. What rate of interest (to the nearest hundredth of a percent) is needed so that an investment of $2500 will yield $3000 in 2 years if the money is compounded annually?

30. Suppose that a certain radioactive substance has a half-life of 20 years. If there are presently 2500 milligrams of the substance, how much, to the nearest milligram, will remain after 40 years? After 50 years?

31. Strontium-90 has a half-life of 29 years. If there are 400 grams of strontium initially, how much, to the nearest gram, will remain after 87 years? After 100 years?

32. The half-life of radium is approximately 1600 years. If the present amount of radium in a certain location is 500 grams, how much will remain after 800 years? Express your answer to the nearest gram.

For Problems 33–38, graph each of the exponential functions.

33. $f(x) = e^x + 1$

34. $f(x) = e^x - 2$

35. $f(x) = 2e^x$

36. $f(x) = -e^x$

37. $f(x) = e^{2x}$

38. $f(x) = e^{-x}$

For Problems 39–44, express your answers to the nearest whole number.

39. Suppose that in a certain culture, the equation $Q(t) = 1000e^{0.4t}$ expresses the number of bacteria present as a function of the time t, where t is expressed in hours. How many bacteria are present at the end of 2 hours? 3 hours? 5 hours?

40. The number of bacteria present at a given time under certain conditions is given by the equation $Q = 5000e^{0.05t}$,

where t is expressed in minutes. How many bacteria are present at the end of 10 minutes? 30 minutes? 1 hour?

41. The number of bacteria present in a certain culture after t hours is given by the equation $Q = Q_0e^{0.3t}$, where Q_0 represents the initial number of bacteria. If 6640 bacteria are present after 4 hours, how many bacteria were present initially?

42. The number of grams Q of a certain radioactive substance present after t seconds is given by the equation $Q = 1500e^{-0.4t}$. How many grams remain after 5 seconds? 10 seconds? 20 seconds?

43. Suppose that the present population of a city is 75,000. Using the equation $P(t) = 75,000e^{0.01t}$ to estimate future growth, estimate the population
   (a) 10 years from now
   (b) 15 years from now
   (c) 25 years from now

44. Suppose that the present population of a city is 150,000. Use the equation $P(t) = 150,000e^{0.032t}$ to estimate future growth. Estimate the population
   (a) 10 years from now
   (b) 20 years from now
   (c) 30 years from now

45. The atmospheric pressure, measured in pounds per square inch, is a function of the altitude above sea level. The equation $P(a) = 14.7e^{-0.21a}$, where a is the altitude measured in miles, can be used to approximate atmospheric pressure. Find the atmospheric pressure at each of the following locations. Express each answer to the nearest tenth of a pound per square inch.
   (a) Mount McKinley in Alaska—altitude of 3.85 miles
   (b) Denver, Colorado—the "mile-high" city
   (c) Asheville, North Carolina—altitude of 1985 feet (5280 feet = 1 mile)
   (d) Phoenix, Arizona—altitude of 1090 feet

■ ■ ■ **THOUGHTS INTO WORDS**

46. Explain the difference between simple interest and compound interest.

47. Would it be better to invest $5000 at 6.25% interest compounded annually for 5 years or to invest $5000 at 6% interest compounded continuously for 5 years? Defend your answer.

GRAPHING CALCULATOR ACTIVITIES

48. Use a graphing calculator to check your graphs for Problems 33–38.

49. Graph $f(x) = 2^x$, $f(x) = e^x$, and $f(x) = 3^x$ on the same set of axes. Are these graphs consistent with the discussion prior to Figure 11.5?

50. Graph $f(x) = e^x$. Where should the graphs of $f(x) = e^{x-4}$, $f(x) = e^{x-6}$, and $f(x) = e^{x+5}$ be located? Graph all three functions on the same set of axes with $f(x) = e^x$.

51. Graph $f(x) = e^x$. Now predict the graphs for $f(x) = -e^x$, $f(x) = e^{-x}$, and $f(x) = -e^{-x}$. Graph all three functions on the same set of axes with $f(x) = e^x$.

52. How do you think the graphs of $f(x) = e^x$, $f(x) = e^{2x}$, and $f(x) = 2e^x$ will compare? Graph them on the same set of axes to see whether you were correct.

11.3 Logarithms

In Sections 11.1 and 11.2, (1) we learned about exponential expressions of the form b^n, where b is any positive real number and n is any real number, (2) we used exponential expressions of the form b^n to define exponential functions, and (3) we used exponential functions to help solve problems. In the next three sections we will follow the same basic pattern with respect to a new concept, that of a **logarithm**. Let's begin with the following definition.

Definition 11.2

If r is any positive real number, then the unique exponent t such that $b^t = r$ is called the **logarithm of r with base b** and is denoted by $\log_b r$.

According to Definition 11.2, the logarithm of 8 base 2 is the exponent t such that $2^t = 8$; thus we can write $\log_2 8 = 3$. Likewise, we can write $\log_{10} 100 = 2$ because $10^2 = 100$. In general, we can remember Definition 11.2 in terms of the statement

$$\log_b r = t \quad \text{is equivalent to} \quad b^t = r$$

Thus we can easily switch back and forth between exponential and logarithmic forms of equations, as the next examples illustrate.

$$\log_3 81 = 4 \quad \text{is equivalent to} \quad 3^4 = 81$$
$$\log_{10} 100 = 2 \quad \text{is equivalent to} \quad 10^2 = 100$$
$$\log_{10} 0.001 = -3 \quad \text{is equivalent to} \quad 10^{-3} = 0.001$$
$$\log_2 128 = 7 \quad \text{is equivalent to} \quad 2^7 = 128$$

$$\log_m n = p \quad \text{is equivalent to } m^p = n$$

$$2^4 = 16 \quad \text{is equivalent to } \log_2 16 = 4$$

$$5^2 = 25 \quad \text{is equivalent to } \log_5 25 = 2$$

$$\left(\frac{1}{2}\right)^4 = \frac{1}{16} \quad \text{is equivalent to } \log_{\frac{1}{2}}\left(\frac{1}{16}\right) = 4$$

$$10^{-2} = 0.01 \quad \text{is equivalent to } \log_{10} 0.01 = -2$$

$$a^b = c \quad \text{is equivalent to } \log_a c = b$$

We can conveniently calculate some logarithms by changing to exponential form, as in the next examples.

EXAMPLE 1

Evaluate $\log_4 64$.

Solution

Let $\log_4 64 = x$. Then, by switching to exponential form, we have $4^x = 64$, which we can solve as we did back in Section 11.1.

$$4^x = 64$$

$$4^x = 4^3$$

$$x = 3$$

Therefore, we can write $\log_4 64 = 3$. ∎

EXAMPLE 2

Evaluate $\log_{10} 0.1$.

Solution

Let $\log_{10} 0.1 = x$. Then, by switching to exponential form, we have $10^x = 0.1$, which we can solve as follows:

$$10^x = 0.1$$

$$10^x = \frac{1}{10}$$

$$10^x = 10^{-1}$$

$$x = -1$$

Thus we obtain $\log_{10} 0.1 = -1$ ∎

The link between logarithms and exponents also provides the basis for solving some equations that involve logarithms, as the next two examples illustrate.

E X A M P L E 3

Solve $\log_8 x = \dfrac{2}{3}$.

Solution

$$\log_8 x = \frac{2}{3}$$

$$8^{\frac{2}{3}} = x \qquad \text{By switching to exponential form}$$

$$\sqrt[3]{8^2} = x$$

$$(\sqrt[3]{8})^2 = x$$

$$4 = x$$

The solution set is {4}. ∎

E X A M P L E 4

Solve $\log_b 1000 = 3$.

Solution

$$\log_b 1000 = 3$$

$$b^3 = 1000$$

$$b = 10$$

The solution set is {10}. ∎

■ Properties of Logarithms

There are some properties of logarithms that are a direct consequence of Definition 11.2 and our knowledge of exponents. For example, writing the exponential equations $b^1 = b$ and $b^0 = 1$ in logarithmic form yields the following property.

Property 11.3

For $b > 0$ and $b \neq 1$,

1. $\log_b b = 1$ **2.** $\log_b 1 = 0$

Thus we can write

$$\log_{10} 10 = 1$$

$$\log_2 2 = 1$$

$$\log_{10} 1 = 0$$

$$\log_5 1 = 0$$

By Definition 11.2, $\log_b r$ is the exponent t such that $b^t = r$. Therefore, raising b to the $\log_b r$ power must produce r. We state this fact in Property 11.4.

Property 11.4

For $b > 0$, $b \neq 1$, and $r > 0$

$$b^{\log_b r} = r$$

The following examples illustrate Property 11.4.

$$10^{\log_{10} 19} = 19$$

$$2^{\log_2 14} = 14$$

$$e^{\log_e 5} = 5$$

Because a logarithm is by definition an exponent, it would seem reasonable to predict that there are some properties of logarithms that correspond to the basic exponential properties. This is an accurate prediction; these properties provide a basis for computational work with logarithms. Let's state the first of these properties and show how it can be verified by using our knowledge of exponents.

Property 11.5

For positive real numbers b, r, and s, where $b \neq 1$,

$$\log_b rs = \log_b r + \log_b s$$

To verify Property 11.5 we can proceed as follows: Let $m = \log_b r$ and $n = \log_b s$. Change each of these equations to exponential form.

$$m = \log_b r \quad \text{becomes } r = b^m$$

$$n = \log_b s \quad \text{becomes } s = b^n$$

Thus the product rs becomes

$$rs = b^m \cdot b^n = b^{m+n}$$

Now, by changing $rs = b^{m+n}$ back to logarithmic form, we obtain

$$\log_b rs = m + n$$

Replacing m with $\log_b r$ and n with $\log_b s$ yields

$$\log_b rs = \log_b r + \log_b s$$

The following three examples demonstrate a use of Property 11.5.

EXAMPLE 5   If $\log_2 5 = 2.3222$ and $\log_2 3 = 1.5850$, evaluate $\log_2 15$.

Solution

Because $15 = 5 \cdot 3$, we can apply Property 11.5.

$$\log_2 15 = \log_2(5 \cdot 3)$$
$$= \log_2 5 + \log_2 3$$
$$= 2.3222 + 1.5850$$
$$= 3.9072$$ ∎

EXAMPLE 6   If $\log_{10} 178 = 2.2504$ and $\log_{10} 89 = 1.9494$, evaluate $\log_{10}(178 \cdot 89)$.

Solution   *add #'s*

$$\log_{10}(178 \cdot 89) = \log_{10} 178 + \log_{10} 89$$
$$= 2.2504 + 1.9494$$
$$= 4.1998$$ ∎

EXAMPLE 7   If $\log_3 8 = 1.8928$, evaluate $\log_3 72$.

Solution

$$\log_3 72 = \log_3(9 \cdot 8)$$
$$= \log_3 9 + \log_3 8$$
$$= 2 + 1.8928 \qquad \log_3 9 = 2 \text{ because } 3^2 = 9.$$
$$= 3.8928$$ ∎

Because $\dfrac{b^m}{b^n} = b^{m-n}$, we would expect a corresponding property pertaining to logarithms. There is such a property, Property 11.6.

Property 11.6

For positive numbers b, r, and s, where $b \neq 1$,

$$\log_b\left(\frac{r}{s}\right) = \log_b r - \log_b s$$

This property can be verified by using an approach similar to the one we used to verify Property 11.5. We leave it for you to do in an exercise in the next problem set.

We can use Property 11.6 to change a division problem into a subtraction problem, as in the next two examples.

E X A M P L E   8

If $\log_5 36 = 2.2265$ and $\log_5 4 = 0.8614$, evaluate $\log_5 9$.

Solution

Because $9 = \dfrac{36}{4}$, we can use Property 11.6.

$$\log_5 9 = \log_5\left(\frac{36}{4}\right)$$

$$= \log_5 36 - \log_5 4$$

$$= 2.2265 - 0.8614$$

$$= 1.3651$$

E X A M P L E   9

Evaluate $\log_{10}\left(\dfrac{379}{86}\right)$ given that $\log_{10} 379 = 2.5786$ and $\log_{10} 86 = 1.9345$.

Solution

$$\log_{10}\left(\frac{379}{86}\right) = \log_{10} 379 - \log_{10} 86$$

$$= 2.5786 - 1.9345$$

$$= 0.6441$$

The next property of logarithms provides the basis for evaluating expressions such as $3^{\sqrt{2}}$, $(\sqrt{5})^{\frac{2}{3}}$, and $(0.076)^{\frac{2}{3}}$. We cite the property, consider a basis for its justification, and offer illustrations of its use.

Property 11.7

If r is a positive real number, b is a positive real number other than 1, and p is any real number, then

$$\log_b r^p = p(\log_b r)$$

As you might expect, the exponential property $(b^n)^m = b^{mn}$ plays an important role in the verification of Property 11.7. This is an exercise for you in the next problem set. Let's look at some uses of Property 11.7.

E X A M P L E   1 0

Evaluate $\log_2 22^{\frac{1}{3}}$ given that $\log_2 22 = 4.4598$.

Solution

$$\log_2 22^{\frac{1}{3}} = \frac{1}{3}\log_2 22 \qquad \text{Property 11.7}$$

$$= \frac{1}{3}(4.4598)$$

$$= 1.4866 \qquad\qquad\qquad \blacksquare$$

E X A M P L E   1 1

Evaluate $\log_{10}(8540)^{\frac{3}{5}}$ given that $\log_{10} 8540 = 3.9315$.

Solution

$$\log_{10}(8540)^{\frac{3}{5}} = \frac{3}{5}\log_{10} 8540 \qquad \text{Property 11.7}$$

$$= \frac{3}{5}(3.9315)$$

$$= 2.3589 \qquad\qquad\qquad \blacksquare$$

Together, the properties of logarithms enable us to change the forms of various logarithmic expressions. For example, an expression such as $\log_b\sqrt{\dfrac{xy}{z}}$ can be rewritten in terms of sums and differences of simpler logarithmic quantities as follows:

$$\log_b\sqrt{\frac{xy}{z}} = \log_b\left(\frac{xy}{z}\right)^{\frac{1}{2}}$$

$$= \frac{1}{2}\log_b\left(\frac{xy}{z}\right) \qquad\qquad \text{Property 11.7}$$

$$= \frac{1}{2}(\log_b xy - \log_b z) \qquad\quad \text{Property 11.6}$$

$$= \frac{1}{2}(\log_b x + \log_b y - \log_b z) \qquad \text{Property 11.5}$$

Sometimes we need to change from an indicated sum or difference of logarithmic quantities to an indicated product or quotient. This is especially helpful when solving certain kinds of equations that involve logarithms. Note in these next two examples how we can use the properties, along with the process of changing from logarithmic form to exponential form, to solve some equations.

not doing

E X A M P L E   1 2

Solve $\log_{10} x + \log_{10}(x + 9) = 1$.

Solution

$$\log_{10} x + \log_{10}(x + 9) = 1$$

$$\log_{10}[x(x + 9)] = 1 \qquad \text{Property 11.5}$$

$$10^1 = x(x + 9) \quad \text{Change to exponential form.}$$

$$10 = x^2 + 9x$$

$$0 = x^2 + 9x - 10$$

$$0 = (x + 10)(x - 1)$$

$$x + 10 = 0 \qquad \text{or} \qquad x - 1 = 0$$

$$x = -10 \qquad \text{or} \qquad x = 1$$

Because logarithms are defined only for positive numbers, x and $x + 9$ have to be positive. Therefore, the solution of -10 must be discarded. The solution set is $\{1\}$. ■

E X A M P L E   1 3

Solve $\log_5(x + 4) - \log_5 x = 2$.

Solution

$$\log_5(x + 4) - \log_5 x = 2$$

$$\log_5\left(\frac{x + 4}{x}\right) = 2 \qquad \text{Property 11.6}$$

$$5^2 = \frac{x + 4}{x} \qquad \text{Change to exponential form.}$$

$$25 = \frac{x + 4}{x}$$

$$25x = x + 4$$

$$24x = 4$$

$$x = \frac{4}{24} = \frac{1}{6}$$

The solution set is $\left\{\dfrac{1}{6}\right\}$. ■

Because logarithms are defined only for positive numbers, we should realize that some logarithmic equations may not have any solutions. (The solution set is the null set.) It is also possible that a logarithmic equation has a negative solution, as the next example illustrates.

EXAMPLE 14   Solve $\log_2 3 + \log_2(x + 4) = 3$.

Solution

$$\log_2 3 + \log_2(x + 4) = 3$$

$$\log_2 3(x + 4) = 3 \qquad \text{Property 11.5}$$

$$3(x + 4) = 2^3 \qquad \text{Change to exponential form.}$$

$$3x + 12 = 8$$

$$3x = -4$$

$$x = -\frac{4}{3}$$

The only restriction is that $x + 4 > 0$ or $x > -4$. Therefore, the solution set is $\left\{-\dfrac{4}{3}\right\}$. Perhaps you should check this answer. ∎

Problem Set 11.3

For Problems 1–10, write each of the following in logarithmic form. For example, $2^3 = 8$ becomes $\log_2 8 = 3$ in logarithmic form.

1. $2^7 = 128$

2. $3^3 = 27$

3. $5^3 = 125$

4. $2^6 = 64$

5. $10^3 = 1000$

6. $10^1 = 10$

7. $2^{-2} = \left(\dfrac{1}{4}\right)$

8. $3^{-4} = \left(\dfrac{1}{81}\right)$

9. $10^{-1} = 0.1$

10. $10^{-2} = 0.01$

For Problems 11–20, write each of the following in exponential form. For example, $\log_2 8 = 3$ becomes $2^3 = 8$ in exponential form.

11. $\log_3 81 = 4$

12. $\log_2 256 = 8$

13. $\log_4 64 = 3$

14. $\log_5 25 = 2$

15. $\log_{10} 10{,}000 = 4$

16. $\log_{10} 100{,}000 = 5$

17. $\log_2\left(\dfrac{1}{16}\right) = -4$

18. $\log_5\left(\dfrac{1}{125}\right) = -3$

19. $\log_{10} 0.001 = -3$

20. $\log_{10} 0.000001 = -6$

For Problems 21–40, evaluate each expression.

21. $\log_2 16$

22. $\log_3 9$

23. $\log_3 81$

24. $\log_2 512$

25. $\log_6 216$

26. $\log_4 256$

27. $\log_7 \sqrt{7}$

28. $\log_2 \sqrt[3]{2}$

29. $\log_{10} 1$

30. $\log_{10} 10$

31. $\log_{10} 0.1$

32. $\log_{10} 0.0001$

33. $10^{\log_{10} 5}$

34. $10^{\log_{10} 14}$

35. $\log_2\left(\dfrac{1}{32}\right)$

36. $\log_5\left(\dfrac{1}{25}\right)$

37. $\log_5 (\log_2 32)$

38. $\log_2 (\log_4 16)$

39. $\log_{10} (\log_7 7)$

40. $\log_2 (\log_5 5)$

For Problems 41–50, solve each equation.

41. $\log_7 x = 2$

42. $\log_2 x = 5$

43. $\log_8 x = \dfrac{4}{3}$

44. $\log_{16} x = \dfrac{3}{2}$

45. $\log_9 x = \dfrac{3}{2}$

46. $\log_8 x = -\dfrac{2}{3}$

47. $\log_4 x = -\dfrac{3}{2}$

48. $\log_9 x = -\dfrac{5}{2}$

49. $\log_x 2 = \dfrac{1}{2}$

50. $\log_x 3 = \dfrac{1}{2}$

For Problems 51–59, you are given that $\log_2 5 = 2.3219$ and $\log_2 7 = 2.8074$. Evaluate each expression using Properties 11.5–11.7.

51. $\log_2 35$

52. $\log_2\left(\dfrac{7}{5}\right)$

53. $\log_2 125$

54. $\log_2 49$

55. $\log_2 \sqrt{7}$

56. $\log_2 \sqrt[3]{5}$

57. $\log_2 175$

58. $\log_2 56$

59. $\log_2 80$

For Problems 60 – 68, you are given that $\log_8 5 = 0.7740$ and $\log_8 11 = 1.1531$. Evaluate each expression using Properties 11.5–11.7.

60. $\log_8 55$

61. $\log_8\left(\dfrac{5}{11}\right)$

62. $\log_8 25$

63. $\log_8 \sqrt{11}$

64. $\log_8 (5)^{\frac{2}{3}}$

65. $\log_8 88$

66. $\log_8 320$

67. $\log_8\left(\dfrac{25}{11}\right)$

68. $\log_8\left(\dfrac{121}{25}\right)$

For Problems 69–80, express each of the following as the sum or difference of simpler logarithmic quantities. Assume that all variables represent positive real numbers. For example,

$$\log_b \frac{x^3}{y^2} = \log_b x^3 - \log_b y^2$$

$$= 3\log_b x - 2\log_b y$$

69. $\log_b xyz$

70. $\log_b 5x$

71. $\log_b\left(\dfrac{y}{z}\right)$

72. $\log_b\left(\dfrac{x^2}{y}\right)$

73. $\log_b y^3 z^4$

74. $\log_b x^2 y^3$

75. $\log_b\left(\dfrac{x^{\frac{1}{2}} y^{\frac{1}{3}}}{z^4}\right)$

76. $\log_b x^{\frac{2}{3}} y^{\frac{3}{4}}$

77. $\log_b \sqrt[3]{x^2 z}$

78. $\log_b \sqrt{xy}$

79. $\log_b\left(x\sqrt{\dfrac{x}{y}}\right)$

80. $\log_b\sqrt{\dfrac{x}{y}}$

For Problems 81–97, solve each of the equations.

81. $\log_3 x + \log_3 4 = 2$

82. $\log_7 5 + \log_7 x = 1$

83. $\log_{10} x + \log_{10}(x - 21) = 2$

84. $\log_{10} x + \log_{10}(x - 3) = 1$

85. $\log_2 x + \log_2(x - 3) = 2$

86. $\log_3 x + \log_3(x - 2) = 1$

87. $\log_{10}(2x - 1) - \log_{10}(x - 2) = 1$

88. $\log_{10}(9x - 2) = 1 + \log_{10}(x - 4)$

89. $\log_5(3x - 2) = 1 + \log_5(x - 4)$

90. $\log_6 x + \log_6(x + 5) = 2$

91. $\log_8(x + 7) + \log_8 x = 1$

92. $\log_6(x + 1) + \log_6(x - 4) = 2$

93. $\log_2 5 + \log_2(x + 6) = 3$

94. $\log_2(x - 1) - \log_2(x + 3) = 2$

95. $\log_5 x = \log_5(x + 2) + 1$

96. $\log_3(x + 3) + \log_3(x + 5) = 1$

97. $\log_2(x + 2) = 1 - \log_2(x + 3)$

98. Verify Property 11.6.

99. Verify Property 11.7.

▨▨▨ THOUGHTS INTO WORDS

100. Explain, without using Property 11.4, why $4^{\log_4 9}$ equals 9.

101. How would you explain the concept of a logarithm to someone who had just completed an elementary algebra course?

102. In the next section we will show that the logarithmic function $f(x) = \log_2 x$ is the inverse of the exponential function $f(x) = 2^x$. From that information, how could you sketch a graph of $f(x) = \log_2 x$?

11.4   Logarithmic Functions

We can now use the concept of a logarithm to define a new function.

Definition 11.3

> If $b > 0$ and $b \neq 1$, then the function f defined by
>
> $$f(x) = \log_b x$$
>
> where x is any positive real number, is called the **logarithmic function with base b**.

We can obtain the graph of a specific logarithmic function in various ways. For example, we can change the equation $y = \log_2 x$ to the exponential equation $2^y = x$, where we can determine a table of values. The next set of exercises asks you to graph some logarithmic functions with this approach.

We can obtain the graph of a logarithmic function by setting up a table of values directly from the logarithmic equation. Example 1 illustrates this approach.

E X A M P L E   1

Graph $f(x) = \log_2 x$.

Solution

Let's choose some values for x where the corresponding values for $\log_2 x$ are easily determined. (Remember that logarithms are defined only for the positive real numbers.)

x	$f(x)$
$\dfrac{1}{8}$	-3
$\dfrac{1}{4}$	-2
$\dfrac{1}{2}$	-1
1	0
2	1
4	2
8	3

$\log_2 \dfrac{1}{8} = -3$ because $2^{-3} = \dfrac{1}{2^3} = \dfrac{1}{8}$

$\log_2 1 = 0$ because $2^0 = 1$

Plot these points and connect them with a smooth curve to produce Figure 11.7.

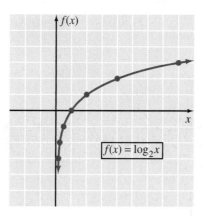

Figure 11.7   ∎

Suppose that we consider the following two functions f and g.

$f(x) = b^x$ Domain: all real numbers
                    Range: positive real numbers

$g(x) = \log_b x$ Domain: positive real numbers
                    Range: all real numbers

Furthermore, suppose that we consider the composition of f and g and the composition of g and f.

$$(f \circ g)(x) = f(g(x)) = f(\log_b x) = b^{\log_b x} = x$$

$$(g \circ f)(x) = g(f(x)) = g(b^x) = \log_b b^x = x \log_b b = x(1) = x$$

Therefore, because the domain of f is the range of g, the range of f is the domain of g, $f(g(x)) = x$, and $g(f(x)) = x$, the two functions f and g are inverses of each other.

Remember also from Chapter 9 that the graphs of a function and its inverse are reflections of each other through the line $y = x$. Thus the graph of a logarithmic function can also be determined by reflecting the graph of its inverse exponential function through the line $y = x$. We see this in Figure 11.8, where the graph of $y = 2^x$ has been reflected across the line $y = x$ to produce the graph of $y = \log_2 x$.

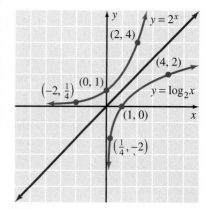

Figure 11.8

The general behavior patterns of exponential functions were illustrated by two graphs back in Figure 11.3. We can now reflect each of those graphs through the line $y = x$ and observe the general behavior patterns of logarithmic functions, as shown in Figure 11.9.

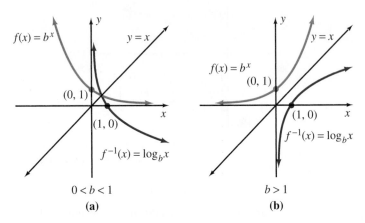

Figure 11.9

Finally, when graphing logarithmic functions, don't forget about variations of the basic curves.

1. The graph of $f(x) = 3 + \log_2 x$ is the graph of $f(x) = \log_2 x$ moved up 3 units. (Because $\log_2 x + 3$ is apt to be confused with $\log_2(x + 3)$, we commonly write $3 + \log_2 x$.)

2. The graph of $f(x) = \log_2(x - 4)$ is the graph of $f(x) = \log_2 x$ moved 4 units to the right.

3. The graph of $f(x) = -\log_2 x$ is the graph of $f(x) = \log_2 x$ reflected across the x axis.

■ Common Logarithms—Base 10

The properties of logarithms we discussed in Section 11.3 are true for any valid base. For example, because the Hindu-Arabic numeration system that we use is a base-10 system, logarithms to base 10 have historically been used for computational purposes. Base-10 logarithms are called **common logarithms**.

Originally, common logarithms were developed to assist in complicated numerical calculations that involved products, quotients, and powers of real numbers. Today they are seldom used for that purpose, because the calculator and computer can much more effectively handle the messy computational problems. However, common logarithms do still occur in applications; they are deserving of our attention.

As we know from earlier work, the definition of a logarithm provides the basis for evaluating $\log_{10} x$ for values of x that are integral powers of 10. Consider the following examples.

$$\log_{10} 1000 = 3 \quad \text{because } 10^3 = 1000$$
$$\log_{10} 100 = 2 \quad \text{because } 10^2 = 100$$
$$\log_{10} 10 = 1 \quad \text{because } 10^1 = 10$$
$$\log_{10} 1 = 0 \quad \text{because } 10^0 = 1$$
$$\log_{10} 0.1 = -1 \quad \text{because } 10^{-1} = \frac{1}{10} = 0.1$$
$$\log_{10} 0.01 = -2 \quad \text{because } 10^{-2} = \frac{1}{10^2} = 0.01$$
$$\log_{10} 0.001 = -3 \quad \text{because } 10^{-3} = \frac{1}{10^3} = 0.001$$

When working with base-10 logarithms, it is customary to omit writing the numeral 10 to designate the base. Thus the expression $\log_{10} x$ is written as $\log x$, and a statement such as $\log_{10} 1000 = 3$ becomes $\log 1000 = 3$. We will follow this practice from now on in this chapter, but don't forget that the base is understood to be 10.

$$\log_{10} x = \log x$$

To find the common logarithm of a positive number that is not an integral power of 10, we can use an appropriately equipped calculator. Using a calculator equipped with a common logarithm function (ordinarily a key labeled $\boxed{\log}$ is used), we obtained the following results, rounded to four decimal places.

$$\log 1.75 = 0.2430$$
$$\log 23.8 = 1.3766$$
$$\log 134 = 2.1271$$
$$\log 0.192 = -0.7167$$
$$\log 0.0246 = -1.6091$$

(Be sure that you can use a calculator and obtain these results.)

In order to use logarithms to solve problems, we sometimes need to be able to determine a number when the logarithm of the number is known. That is, we may need to determine x when $\log x$ is known. Let's consider an example.

EXAMPLE 2

Find x if $\log x = 0.2430$.

Solution

If $\log x = 0.2430$, then by changing to exponential form, we have $10^{0.2430} = x$. Therefore, using the $\boxed{10^x}$ key, we can find x.

$$x = 10^{0.2430} \approx 1.749846689$$

Therefore, $x = 1.7498$, rounded to five significant digits.   ∎

Be sure that you can use your calculator to obtain the following results. We have rounded the values for x to five significant digits.

If $\log x = 0.7629$, then $x = 10^{0.7629} = 5.7930$.

If $\log x = 1.4825$, then $x = 10^{1.4825} = 30.374$.

If $\log x = 4.0214$, then $x = 10^{4.0214} = 10{,}505$.

If $\log x = -1.5162$, then $x = 10^{-1.5162} = 0.030465$.

If $\log x = -3.8921$, then $x = 10^{-3.8921} = 0.00012820$.

The **common logarithmic function** is defined by the equation $f(x) = \log x$. It should now be a simple matter to set up a table of values and sketch the function. We will have you do this in the next set of exercises. Remember that $f(x) = 10^x$ and $g(x) = \log x$ are inverses of each other. Therefore, we could also get the graph of $g(x) = \log x$ by reflecting the exponential curve $f(x) = 10^x$ across the line $y = x$.

■ Natural Logarithms—Base *e*

In many practical applications of logarithms, the number e (remember that $e \approx 2.71828$) is used as a base. Logarithms with a base of e are called **natural logarithms**, and the symbol $\ln x$ is commonly used instead of $\log_e x$.

$$\log_e x = \ln x$$

Natural logarithms can be found with an appropriately equipped calculator. Using a calculator with a natural logarithm function (ordinarily a key labeled $\boxed{\ln x}$), we can obtain the following results, rounded to four decimal places.

$\ln 3.21 = 1.1663$

$\ln 47.28 = 3.8561$

$\ln 842 = 6.7358$

$\ln 0.21 = -1.5606$

$\ln 0.0046 = -5.3817$

$\ln 10 = 2.3026$

Be sure that you can use your calculator to obtain these results. Keep in mind the significance of a statement such as $\ln 3.21 = 1.1663$. By changing to exponential form, we are claiming that e raised to the 1.1663 power is approximately 3.21. Using a calculator, we obtain $e^{1.1663} = 3.210093293$.

Let's do a few more problems and find x when given $\ln x$. Be sure that you agree with these results.

If $\ln x = 2.4156$, then $x = e^{2.4156} = 11.196$.

If $\ln x = 0.9847$, then $x = e^{0.9847} = 2.6770$.

If $\ln x = 4.1482$, then $x = e^{4.1482} = 63.320$.

If $\ln x = -1.7654$, then $x = e^{-1.7654} = 0.17112$.

The **natural logarithmic function** is defined by the equation $f(x) = \ln x$. It is the inverse of the natural exponential function $f(x) = e^x$. Thus one way to graph $f(x) = \ln x$ is to reflect the graph of $f(x) = e^x$ across the line $y = x$. We will have you do this in the next set of problems.

Problem Set 11.4

For Problems 1–10, use a calculator to find each common logarithm. Express answers to four decimal places.

1. log 7.24

2. log 2.05

3. log 52.23

4. log 825.8

5. log 3214.1

6. log 14,189

7. log 0.729

8. log 0.04376

9. log 0.00034

10. log 0.000069

For Problems 11–20, use your calculator to find x when given log x. Express answers to five significant digits.

11. $\log x = 2.6143$

12. $\log x = 1.5263$

13. $\log x = 4.9547$

14. $\log x = 3.9335$

15. $\log x = 1.9006$

16. $\log x = 0.5517$

17. $\log x = -1.3148$

18. $\log x = -0.1452$

19. $\log x = -2.1928$

20. $\log x = -2.6542$

For Problems 21–30, use your calculator to find each natural logarithm. Express answers to four decimal places.

21. ln 5

22. ln 18

23. ln 32.6

24. ln 79.5

25. ln 430

26. ln 371.8

27. ln 0.46

28. ln 0.524

29. ln 0.0314

30. ln 0.008142

For Problems 31–40, use your calculator to find x when given ln x. Express answers to five significant digits.

31. $\ln x = 0.4721$

32. $\ln x = 0.9413$

33. $\ln x = 1.1425$

34. $\ln x = 2.7619$

35. $\ln x = 4.6873$

36. $\ln x = 3.0259$

37. $\ln x = -0.7284$

38. $\ln x = -1.6246$

39. $\ln x = -3.3244$

40. $\ln x = -2.3745$

41. (a) Complete the following table and then graph $f(x) = \log x$. (Express the values for log x to the nearest tenth.)

x	0.1	0.5	1	2	4	8	10
log x							

(b) Complete the following table and express values for 10^x to the nearest tenth.

x	−1	−0.3	0	0.3	0.6	0.9	1
10^x							

Then graph $f(x) = 10^x$ and reflect it across the line $y = x$ to produce the graph for $f(x) = \log x$.

42. (a) Complete the following table and then graph $f(x) = \ln x$. (Express the values for ln x to the nearest tenth.)

x	0.1	0.5	1	2	4	8	10
ln x							

(b) Complete the following table and express values for e^x to the nearest tenth.

x	−2.3	−0.7	0	0.7	1.4	2.1	2.3
e^x							

Then graph $f(x) = e^x$ and reflect it across the line $y = x$ to produce the graph for $f(x) = \ln x$.

43. Graph $y = \log_{\frac{1}{2}} x$ by graphing $\left(\dfrac{1}{2}\right)^y = x$.

44. Graph $y = \log_2 x$ by graphing $2^y = x$.

45. Graph $f(x) = \log_3 x$ by reflecting the graph of $g(x) = 3^x$ across the line $y = x$.

46. Graph $f(x) = \log_4 x$ by reflecting the graph of $g(x) = 4^x$ across the line $y = x$.

For Problems 47–53, graph each of the functions. Remember that the graph of $f(x) = \log_2 x$ is given in Figure 11.7.

47. $f(x) = 3 + \log_2 x$

48. $f(x) = -2 + \log_2 x$

49. $f(x) = \log_2(x + 3)$

50. $f(x) = \log_2(x - 2)$

51. $f(x) = \log_2 2x$

52. $f(x) = -\log_2 x$

53. $f(x) = 2 \log_2 x$

For Problems 54–61, perform the following calculations and express answers to the nearest hundredth. (These calculations are in preparation for our work in the next section.)

54. $\dfrac{\log 7}{\log 3}$

55. $\dfrac{\ln 2}{\ln 7}$

56. $\dfrac{2 \ln 3}{\ln 8}$

57. $\dfrac{\ln 5}{2 \ln 3}$

58. $\dfrac{\ln 3}{0.04}$

59. $\dfrac{\ln 2}{0.03}$

60. $\dfrac{\log 2}{5 \log 1.02}$

61. $\dfrac{\log 5}{3 \log 1.07}$

■■■ **THOUGHTS INTO WORDS**

62. Why is the number 1 excluded from being a base of a logarithmic function?

63. How do we know that $\log_2 6$ is between 2 and 3?

 GRAPHING CALCULATOR ACTIVITIES

64. Graph $f(x) = x$, $f(x) = e^x$, and $f(x) = \ln x$ on the same set of axes.

65. Graph $f(x) = x$, $f(x) = 10^x$, and $f(x) = \log x$ on the same set of axes.

66. Graph $f(x) = \ln x$. How should the graphs of $f(x) = 2 \ln x$, $f(x) = 4 \ln x$, and $f(x) = 6 \ln x$ compare to the graph of $f(x) = \ln x$? Graph the three functions on the same set of axes with $f(x) = \ln x$.

67. Graph $f(x) = \log x$. Now predict the graphs for $f(x) = 2 + \log x$, $f(x) = -2 + \log x$, and $f(x) = -6 + \log x$. Graph the three functions on the same set of axes with $f(x) = \log x$.

68. Graph $\ln x$. Now predict the graphs for $f(x) = \ln (x - 2)$, $f(x) = \ln (x - 6)$, and $f(x) = \ln (x + 4)$. Graph the three functions on the same set of axes with $f(x) = \ln x$.

69. For each of the following, (a) predict the general shape and location of the graph, and (b) use your graphing calculator to graph the function and thus check your prediction.
  (a) $f(x) = \log x + \ln x$
  (b) $f(x) = \log x - \ln x$
  (c) $f(x) = \ln x - \log x$
  (d) $f(x) = \ln x^2$

Exponential Equations, Logarithmic Equations, and Problem Solving

In Section 11.1 we solved exponential equations such as $3^x = 81$ when we expressed both sides of the equation as a power of 3 and then applied the property "if $b^n = b^m$, then $n = m$." However, if we try to use this same approach with an equation such as $3^x = 5$, we face the difficulty of expressing 5 as a power of 3. We can solve this type of problem by using the properties of logarithms and the following property of equality.

Property 11.8

> If $x > 0$, $y > 0$, and $b \neq 1$, then
>
> $$x = y \quad \text{if and only if } \log_b x = \log_b y$$

Property 11.8 is stated in terms of any valid base b; however, for most applications we use either common logarithms (base 10) or natural logarithms (base e). Let's consider some examples.

EXAMPLE 1   Solve $3^x = 5$ to the nearest hundredth.

Solution

By using common logarithms, we can proceed as follows:

$$3^x = 5$$
$$\log 3^x = \log 5 \qquad \text{Property 11.8}$$
$$x \log 3 = \log 5 \qquad \log r^p = p \log r$$
$$x = \frac{\log 5}{\log 3}$$
$$x = 1.46, \qquad \text{to the nearest hundredth}$$

 Check

Because $3^{1.46} \approx 4.972754647$, we say that, to the nearest hundredth, the solution set for $3^x = 5$ is $\{1.46\}$. ∎

EXAMPLE 2   Solve $e^{x+1} = 5$ to the nearest hundredth.

Solution

The base e is used in the exponential expression, so let's use natural logarithms to help solve this equation.

$$e^{x+1} = 5$$

$$\ln e^{x+1} = \ln 5 \qquad \text{Property 11.8}$$

$$(x + 1) \ln e = \ln 5 \qquad \ln r^p = p \ln r$$

$$(x + 1)(1) = \ln 5 \qquad \ln e = 1$$

$$x = \ln 5 - 1$$

$$x \approx 0.609437912$$

$$x = 0.61, \quad \text{to the nearest hundredth}$$

The solution set is {0.61}. Check it! ∎

■ Logarithmic Equations

In Example 12 of Section 11.3 we solved the logarithmic equation

$$\log_{10} x + \log_{10}(x + 9) = 1$$

by simplifying the left side of the equation to $\log_{10}[x(x + 9)]$ and then changing the equation to exponential form to complete the solution. Now, using Property 11.8, we can solve such a logarithmic equation another way and also expand our equation-solving capabilities. Let's consider some examples.

EXAMPLE 3

Solve $\log x + \log(x - 15) = 2$.

Solution

Because log 100 = 2, the given equation becomes

$$\log x + \log(x - 15) = \log 100$$

Now simplify the left side, apply Property 11.8, and proceed as follows:

$$\log(x)(x - 15) = \log 100$$

$$x(x - 15) = 100$$

$$x^2 - 15x - 100 = 0$$

$$(x - 20)(x + 5) = 0$$

$$x - 20 = 0 \qquad \text{or} \qquad x + 5 = 0$$

$$x = 20 \qquad \text{or} \qquad x = -5$$

The domain of a logarithmic function must contain only positive numbers, so x and $x - 15$ must be positive in this problem. Therefore, we discard the solution -5; the solution set is {20}. ∎

E X A M P L E   4

Solve $\ln(x + 2) = \ln(x - 4) + \ln 3$.

Solution

$$\ln(x + 2) = \ln(x - 4) + \ln 3$$

$$\ln(x + 2) = \ln[3(x - 4)]$$

$$x + 2 = 3(x - 4)$$

$$x + 2 = 3x - 12$$

$$14 = 2x$$

$$7 = x$$

The solution set is {7}. ∎

■ Problem Solving

In Section 11.2 we used the compound interest formula

$$A = P\left(1 + \frac{r}{n}\right)^{nt}$$

to determine the amount of money (A) accumulated at the end of t years if P dollars is invested at r rate of interest compounded n times per year. Now let's use this formula to solve other types of problems that deal with compound interest.

E X A M P L E   5

How long will $500 take to double itself if it is invested at 12% interest compounded quarterly?

Solution

To "double itself" means that the $500 will grow into $1000. Thus

$$1000 = 500\left(1 + \frac{0.12}{4}\right)^{4t}$$

$$= 500(1 + 0.03)^{4t}$$

$$= 500(1.03)^{4t}$$

Multiply both sides of $1000 = 500(1.03)^{4t}$ by $\dfrac{1}{500}$ to yield

$$2 = (1.03)^{4t}$$

Therefore,

$$\log 2 = \log(1.03)^{4t} \qquad \text{Property 11.8}$$

$$\log 2 = 4t \log 1.03 \qquad \log r^p = p \log r$$

Solve for t to obtain

$$\log 2 = 4t \log 1.03$$

$$\frac{\log 2}{\log 1.03} = 4t$$

$$\frac{\log 2}{4 \log 1.03} = t \qquad \qquad \text{Multiply both sides by } \frac{1}{4}.$$

$$t \approx 5.862443063$$

$$t = 5.9, \qquad \text{to the nearest tenth}$$

Therefore, we are claiming that $500 invested at 12% interest compounded quarterly will double itself in approximately 5.9 years.

✔ **Check**

$500 invested at 12% compounded quarterly for 5.9 years will produce

$$A = \$500\left(1 + \frac{0.12}{4}\right)^{4(5.9)}$$

$$= \$500(1.03)^{23.6}$$

$$= \$1004.45 \qquad\qquad\qquad ■$$

In Section 11.2, we also used the formula $A = Pe^{rt}$ when money was to be compounded continuously. At this time, with the help of natural logarithms, we can extend our use of this formula.

E X A M P L E   6

How long will it take $100 to triple itself if it is invested at 8% interest compounded continuously?

Solution

To "triple itself" means that the $100 will grow into $300. Thus, using the formula for interest that is compounded continuously, we can proceed as follows:

$$A = Pe^{rt}$$

$$\$300 = \$100e^{(0.08)t}$$

$$3 = e^{0.08t}$$

$$\ln 3 = \ln e^{0.08t} \qquad \text{Property 11.8}$$

$$\ln 3 = 0.08t \ln e \qquad \ln r^p = p \ln r$$

$$\ln 3 = 0.08t \qquad \ln e = 1$$

$$\frac{\ln 3}{0.08} = t$$

$$t \approx 13.73265361$$

$$t = 13.7, \quad \text{to the nearest tenth}$$

Therefore, $100 invested at 8% interest compounded continuously will triple itself in approximately 13.7 years.

✔ **Check**

$100 invested at 8% compounded continuously for 13.7 years produces

$$A = Pe^{rt}$$
$$= \$100e^{0.08(13.7)}$$
$$= \$100e^{1.096}$$
$$\approx \$299.22$$

■

■ Richter Numbers

Seismologists use the Richter scale to measure and report the magnitude of earthquakes. The equation

$$R = \log \frac{I}{I_0}$$ *R* is called a Richter number.

compares the intensity I of an earthquake to a minimum or reference intensity I_0. The reference intensity is the smallest earth movement that can be recorded on a seismograph. Suppose that the intensity of an earthquake was determined to be 50,000 times the reference intensity. In this case, $I = 50,000I_0$, and the Richter number is calculated as follows:

$$R = \log \frac{50,000I_0}{I_0}$$
$$R = \log 50,000$$
$$R \approx 4.698970004$$

Thus a Richter number of 4.7 would be reported. Let's consider two more examples that involve Richter numbers.

E X A M P L E   7

An earthquake in San Francisco in 1989 was reported to have a Richter number of 6.9. How did its intensity compare to the reference intensity?

Solution

$$6.9 = \log \frac{I}{I_0}$$
$$10^{6.9} = \frac{I}{I_0}$$
$$I = (10^{6.9})(I_0)$$
$$I \approx 7943282I_0$$

Thus its intensity was a little less than 8 million times the reference intensity.   ■

EXAMPLE 8

An earthquake in Iran in 1990 had a Richter number of 7.7. Compare the intensity level of that earthquake to the one in San Francisco (Example 7).

Solution

From Example 7 we have $I = (10^{6.9})(I_0)$ for the earthquake in San Francisco. Using a Richter number of 7.7, we obtain $I = (10^{7.7})(I_0)$ for the earthquake in Iran. Therefore, by comparison,

$$\frac{(10^{7.7})(I_0)}{(10^{6.9})(I_0)} = 10^{7.7-6.9} = 10^{0.8} \approx 6.3$$

The earthquake in Iran was about 6 times as intense as the one in San Francisco. ■

■ Change-of-Base for Logarithms with Bases Other Than 10 or *e*

Now let's use either common or natural logarithms to evaluate logarithms that have bases other than 10 or *e*. Consider the following example.

EXAMPLE 9

Evaluate $\log_3 41$.

Solution

Let $x = \log_3 41$. Change to exponential form to obtain

$$3^x = 41$$

Now we can apply Property 11.8 and proceed as follows:

$$\log 3^x = \log 41$$

$$x \log 3 = \log 41$$

$$x = \frac{\log 41}{\log 3}$$

$$x = \frac{1.6128}{0.4771} = 3.3804, \quad \text{rounded to four decimal places} \qquad ■$$

Using the method of Example 9 to evaluate $\log_a r$ produces the following formula, which we often refer to as the **change-of-base** formula for logarithms.

Property 11.9

If a, b, and r are positive numbers with $a \neq 1$ and $b \neq 1$, then

$$\log_a r = \frac{\log_b r}{\log_b a}$$

By using Property 11.9, we can easily determine a relationship between logarithms of different bases. For example, suppose that in Property 11.9 we let $a = 10$ and $b = e$. Then

$$\log_a r = \frac{\log_b r}{\log_b a}$$

becomes

$$\log_{10} r = \frac{\log_e r}{\log_e 10}$$

which can be written as

$$\log_e r = (\log_e 10)(\log_{10} r)$$

Because $\log_e 10 = 2.3026$, rounded to four decimal places, we have

$$\log_e r = (2.3026)(\log_{10} r)$$

Thus the natural logarithm of any positive number is approximately equal to the common logarithm of the number times 2.3026.

Now we can use a graphing utility to graph logarithmic functions such as $f(x) = \log_2 x$. Using the change-of-base formula, we can express this function as $f(x) = \dfrac{\log x}{\log 2}$ or as $f(x) = \dfrac{\ln x}{\ln 2}$. The graph of $f(x) = \log_2 x$ is shown in Figure 11.10.

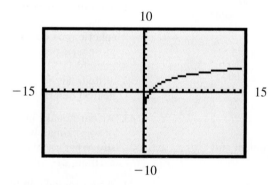

Figure 11.10

Problem Set 11.5

For Problems 1–14, solve each exponential equation and express solutions to the nearest hundredth.

1. $3^x = 32$

2. $2^x = 40$

3. $4^x = 21$

4. $5^x = 73$

5. $3^{x-2} = 11$

6. $2^{x+1} = 7$

7. $5^{3x+1} = 9$

8. $7^{2x-1} = 35$

9. $e^x = 5.4$

10. $e^x = 45$

11. $e^{x-2} = 13.1$

12. $e^{x-1} = 8.2$

13. $3e^x = 35.1$

14. $4e^x - 2 = 26$

For Problems 15–22, solve each logarithmic equation.

15. $\log x + \log(x + 21) = 2$

16. $\log x + \log(x + 3) = 1$

17. $\log(3x - 1) = 1 + \log(5x - 2)$

18. $\log(2x - 1) - \log(x - 3) = 1$

19. $\log(x + 2) - \log(2x + 1) = \log x$

20. $\log(x + 1) - \log(x + 2) = \log\dfrac{1}{x}$

21. $\ln(2t + 5) = \ln 3 + \ln(t - 1)$

22. $\ln(3t - 4) - \ln(t + 1) = \ln 2$

For Problems 23–32, approximate each of the following logarithms to three decimal places.

23. $\log_2 23$

24. $\log_3 32$

25. $\log_6 0.214$

26. $\log_5 1.4$

27. $\log_7 421$

28. $\log_8 514$

29. $\log_9 0.0017$

30. $\log_4 0.00013$

31. $\log_3 720$

32. $\log_2 896$

For Problems 33–41, solve each problem and express answers to the nearest tenth.

33. How long will it take $750 to be worth $1000 if it is invested at 12% interest compounded quarterly?

34. How long will it take $1000 to double itself if it is invested at 9% interest compounded semiannually?

35. How long will it take $2000 to double itself if it is invested at 13% interest compounded continuously?

36. How long will it take $500 to triple itself if it is invested at 9% interest compounded continuously?

37. For a certain strain of bacteria, the number present after t hours is given by the equation $Q = Q_0 e^{0.34t}$, where Q_0 represents the initial number of bacteria. How long will it take 400 bacteria to increase to 4000 bacteria?

38. A piece of machinery valued at $30,000 depreciates at a rate of 10% yearly. How long will it take until it has a value of $15,000?

39. The number of grams of a certain radioactive substance present after t hours is given by the equation $Q = Q_0 e^{-0.45t}$, where Q_0 represents the initial number of grams. How long will it take 2500 grams to be reduced to 1250 grams?

40. For a certain culture the equation $Q(t) = Q_0 e^{0.4t}$, where Q_0 is an initial number of bacteria and t is time measured in hours, yields the number of bacteria as a function of time. How long will it take 500 bacteria to increase to 2000?

41. Suppose that the equation $P(t) = P_0 e^{0.02t}$, where P_0 represents an initial population, and t is the time in years, is used to predict population growth. How long does this equation predict it would take a city of 50,000 to double its population?

Solve each of Problems 42–46.

42. The equation $P(a) = 14.7e^{-0.21a}$, where a is the altitude above sea level measured in miles, yields the atmospheric pressure in pounds per square inch. If the atmospheric pressure at Cheyenne, Wyoming is approximately 11.53 pounds per square inch, find that city's altitude above sea level. Express your answer to the nearest hundred feet.

43. An earthquake in Los Angeles in 1971 had an intensity of approximately five million times the reference intensity. What was the Richter number associated with that earthquake?

44. An earthquake in San Francisco in 1906 was reported to have a Richter number of 8.3. How did its intensity compare to the reference intensity?

45. Calculate how many times more intense an earthquake with a Richter number of 7.3 is than an earthquake with a Richter number of 6.4.

46. Calculate how many times more intense an earthquake with a Richter number of 8.9 is than an earthquake with a Richter number of 6.2.

■ ■ ■ THOUGHTS INTO WORDS

47. Explain how to determine $\log_7 46$ without using Property 11.9.

48. Explain the concept of a Richter number.

49. Explain how you would solve the equation $2^x = 64$ and also how you would solve the equation $2^x = 53$.

50. How do logarithms with a base of 9 compare to logarithms with a base of 3? Explain how you reached this conclusion.

GRAPHING CALCULATOR ACTIVITIES

51. Graph $f(x) = x$, $f(x) = 2^x$, and $f(x) = \log_2 x$ on the same set of axes.

52. Graph $f(x) = x$, $f(x) = (0.5)^x$, and $f(x) = \log_{0.5} x$ on the same set of axes.

53. Graph $f(x) = \log_2 x$. Now predict the graphs for $f(x) = \log_3 x$, $f(x) = \log_4 x$, and $f(x) = \log_8 x$. Graph these three functions on the same set of axes with $f(x) = \log_2 x$.

54. Graph $f(x) = \log_5 x$. Now predict the graphs for $f(x) = 2 \log_5 x$, $f(x) = -4 \log_5 x$, and $f(x) = \log_5(x + 4)$. Graph these three functions on the same set of axes with $f(x) = \log_5 x$.

Chapter 11 Summary

(11.1) If a and b are positive real numbers, and m and n are any real numbers, then

1. $b^n \cdot b^m = b^{m+n}$ Product of two powers

2. $(b^n)^m = b^{mn}$ Power of a power

3. $(ab)^n = a^n b^n$ Power of a product

4. $\left(\dfrac{a}{b}\right)^n = \dfrac{a^n}{b^n}$ Power of a quotient

5. $\dfrac{b^n}{b^m} = b^{n-m}$ Quotient of two powers

If $b > 0$, $b \neq 1$, and m and n are real numbers, then

$$b^n = b^m \quad \text{if and only if } n = m$$

A function defined by an equation of the form

$$f(x) = b^x, \qquad b > 0 \text{ and } b \neq 1$$

is called an **exponential function**.

(11.2) A general formula for any principal, P, invested for any number of years (t) at a rate of r percent compounded n times per year is

$$A = P\left(1 + \frac{r}{n}\right)^{nt}$$

where A represents the total amount of money accumulated at the end of t years. The value of $\left(1 + \dfrac{1}{n}\right)^n$ as n gets infinitely large, approaches the number e, where e equals 2.71828 to five decimal places.

The formula

$$A = Pe^{rt}$$

yields the accumulated value, A, of a sum of money, P, that has been invested for t years at a rate of r percent **compounded continuously**.

The equation

$$Q(t) = Q_0 e^{kt}$$

is used as a mathematical model for many growth-and-decay applications.

(11.3) If r is any positive real number, then the unique exponent t such that $b^t = r$ is called the **logarithm of r with base b** and is denoted by $\log_b r$.

For $b > 0$ and $b \neq 1$, and $r > 0$,

1. $\log_b b = 1$

2. $\log_b 1 = 0$

3. $r = b^{\log_b r}$

The following properties of logarithms are derived from the definition of a logarithm and the properties of exponents. For positive real numbers b, r, and s, where $b \neq 1$,

1. $\log_b rs = \log_b r + \log_b s$

2. $\log_b\left(\dfrac{r}{s}\right) = \log_b r - \log_b s$

3. $\log_b r^p = p \log_b r$ p is any real number.

(11.4) A function defined by an equation of the form

$$f(x) = \log_b x, \qquad b > 0 \text{ and } b \neq 1$$

is called a **logarithmic function**. The equation $y = \log_b x$ is equivalent to $x = b^y$. The two functions $f(x) = b^x$ and $g(x) = \log_b x$ are inverses of each other.

Logarithms with a base of 10 are called **common logarithms**. The expression $\log_{10} x$ is usually written as $\log x$.

Natural logarithms are logarithms that have a base of e, where e is an irrational number whose decimal approximation to eight digits is 2.7182818. Natural logarithms are denoted by $\log_e x$ or **ln x**.

(11.5) The properties of equality and the properties of exponents and logarithms combine to help us solve a variety of exponential and logarithmic equations. Using these properties, we can now solve problems that deal with various applications, including compound interest and growth problems.

The formula

$$\log_a r = \frac{\log_b r}{\log_b a}$$

is often called the **change-of-base** formula.

Chapter 11   Review Problem Set

For Problems 1–8, evaluate each expression without using a calculator.

1. $\log_2 128$

2. $\log_4 64$

3. $\log 10{,}000$

4. $\log 0.001$

5. $\ln e^2$

6. $5^{\log_5 13}$

7. $\log(\log_3 3)$

8. $\log_2\left(\dfrac{1}{4}\right)$

For Problems 9–16, solve each equation without using your calculator.

9. $2^x = \dfrac{1}{16}$

10. $3^x - 4 = 23$

11. $16^x = \dfrac{1}{8}$

12. $\log_8 x = \dfrac{2}{3}$

13. $\log_x 3 = \dfrac{1}{2}$

14. $\log_5 2 + \log_5 (3x + 1) = 1$

15. $\log_2(x + 5) - \log_2 x = 1$

16. $\log_2 x + \log_2 (x - 4) = 5$

For Problems 17–20, use your calculator to find each logarithm. Express answers to four decimal places.

17. $\log 73.14$

18. $\ln 114.2$

19. $\ln 0.014$

20. $\log 0.00235$

For Problems 21–24, use your calculator to find x when given $\log x$ or $\ln x$. Express answers to five significant digits.

21. $\ln x = 0.1724$

22. $\log x = 3.4215$

23. $\log x = -1.8765$

24. $\ln x = -2.5614$

For Problems 25–28, use your calculator to help solve each equation. Express solutions to the nearest hundredth.

25. $3^x = 42$

26. $2e^x = 14$

27. $2^{x+1} = 79$

28. $e^{x-2} = 37$

For Problems 29–32, graph each of the functions.

29. $f(x) = 2^x - 3$

30. $f(x) = -3^x$

31. $f(x) = -1 + \log_2 x$

32. $f(x) = \log_2(x + 1)$

33. Approximate a value for $\log_5 97$ to three decimal places.

34. Suppose that \$800 is invested at 9% interest compounded annually. How much money has accumulated at the end of 15 years?

35. If \$2500 is invested at 10% interest compounded quarterly, how much money has accumulated at the end of 12 years?

36. If \$3500 is invested at 8% interest compounded continuously, how much money will accumulate in 6 years?

37. Suppose that a certain radioactive substance has a half-life of 40 days. If there are presently 750 grams of the substance, how much, to the nearest gram, will remain after 100 days?

38. How long will it take \$100 to double itself if it is invested at 14% interest compounded annually?

39. How long will it take \$1000 to be worth \$3500 if it is invested at 10.5% interest compounded quarterly?

40. Suppose that the present population of a city is 50,000. Use the equation $P(t) = P_0 e^{0.02t}$, where P_0 represents an initial population, to estimate future populations. Estimate the population of that city in 10 years, 15 years, and 20 years.

41. The number of bacteria present in a certain culture after t hours is given by the equation $Q = Q_0 e^{0.29t}$, where Q_0 represents the initial number of bacteria. How long will it take 500 bacteria to increase to 2000 bacteria?

42. An earthquake in Mexico City in 1985 had an intensity level about 125,000,000 times the reference intensity. Find the Richter number for that earthquake.

For Problems 1– 4, evaluate each expression.

1. $\log_3 \sqrt{3}$

2. $\log_2(\log_2 4)$

3. $-2 + \ln e^3$

4. $\log_2(0.5)$

For Problems 5 –10, solve each equation.

5. $4^x = \dfrac{1}{64}$

6. $9^x = \dfrac{1}{27}$

7. $2^{3x-1} = 128$

8. $\log_9 x = \dfrac{5}{2}$

9. $\log x + \log(x + 48) = 2$

10. $\ln x = \ln 2 + \ln(3x - 1)$

For Problems 11–14, given that $\log_3 4 = 1.2619$ and $\log_3 5 = 1.4650$, evaluate each of the following.

11. $\log_3 100$

12. $\log_3 1.25$

13. $\log_3 \sqrt{5}$

14. $\log_3(16 \cdot 25)$

15. Solve $e^x = 176$ to the nearest hundredth.

16. Solve $2^{x-2} = 314$ to the nearest hundredth.

17. Determine $\log_5 632$ to four decimal places.

18. Express $3 \log_b x + 2 \log_b y - \log_b z$ as a single logarithm with a coefficient of 1.

19. If \$3500 is invested at 7.5% interest compounded quarterly, how much money has accumulated at the end of 8 years?

20. How long will it take \$5000 to be worth \$12,500 if it is invested at 7% compounded annually? Express your answer to the nearest tenth of a year.

21. The number of bacteria present in a certain culture after t hours is given by $Q(t) = Q_0 e^{0.23t}$, where Q_0 represents the initial number of bacteria. How long will it take 400 bacteria to increase to 2400 bacteria? Express your answer to the nearest tenth of an hour.

22. Suppose that a certain radioactive substance has a half-life of 50 years. If there are presently 7500 grams of the substance, how much will remain after 32 years? Express your answer to the nearest gram.

For Problems 23 –25, graph each of the functions.

23. $f(x) = e^x - 2$

24. $f(x) = -3^{-x}$

25. $f(x) = \log_2(x - 2)$

Sequences and Binomial Expansions

12.1 Arithmetic Sequences

12.2 Sums of Arithmetic Sequences

12.3 Geometric Sequences

12.4 Infinite Geometric Sequences

12.5 Binomial Expansions

Royalty-Free/CORBIS

When objects are arranged in a sequence, the total number of objects is the sum of the terms of the sequence.

Suppose that an auditorium has 35 seats in the first row, 40 seats in the second row, 45 seats in the third row, and so on for ten rows. The numbers 35, 40, 45, 50, . . . , 80 represent the number of seats per row from row 1 through row 10. The list of numbers has a constant difference of 5 between any two successive numbers in the list; such a list is called an arithmetic sequence.

Suppose that a fungus culture growing under controlled conditions doubles in size each day. If today the size of the culture is 6 units, then the numbers 12, 24, 48, 96, 192 represent the size of the culture for the next five days. In this list of numbers, each number after the first is two times the previous number; such a list is called a geometric sequence. Arithmetic and geometric sequences will be our focus in this chapter.

12.1 Arithmetic Sequences

An **infinite sequence** is a function whose domain is the set of positive integers. For example, consider the function defined by the equation

$$f(n) = 3n + 2$$

where the domain is the set of positive integers. Furthermore, let's substitute the numbers of the domain, in order, starting with 1. We list the resulting ordered pairs as

$$(1, 5), (2, 8), (3, 11), (4, 14), (5, 17)$$

and so on. Because we have agreed to use the domain of positive integers in order, starting with 1, there is no need to use ordered pairs. We can simply express the infinite sequence as

$$5, 8, 11, 14, 17, \ldots .$$

Frequently, we use the letter a to represent *sequential functions*, and we write the functional value at n as a_n (read "a sub n") instead of $a(n)$. The sequence is then

$$a_1, a_2, a_3, a_4, \ldots, a_n, \ldots$$

where a_1 is the first term, a_2 the second term, a_3 the third term, and so on. The expression a_n, which defines the sequence, is called the **general term** of the sequence. Knowing the general term of a sequence allows us to find as many terms of the sequence as needed and also to find any specific terms. Consider the following examples.

EXAMPLE 1

Find the first five terms of each of the following sequences.

(a) $a_n = n^2 + 1$ **(b)** $a_n = 2^n$

Solution

(a) The first five terms are found by replacing n with 1, 2, 3, 4, and 5.

$$a_1 = 1^2 + 1 = 2 \qquad a_2 = 2^2 + 1 = 5$$
$$a_3 = 3^2 + 1 = 10 \qquad a_4 = 4^2 + 1 = 17$$
$$a_5 = 5^2 + 1 = 26$$

Thus the first five terms are 2, 5, 10, 17, and 26.

(b)
$$a_1 = 2^1 = 2 \qquad a_2 = 2^2 = 4$$
$$a_3 = 2^3 = 8 \qquad a_4 = 2^4 = 16$$
$$a_5 = 2^5 = 32$$

The first five terms are 2, 4, 8, 16, and 32. ■

EXAMPLE 2   Find the 12th and 25th terms of the sequence $a_n = 5n - 1$.

Solution

$$a_{12} = 5(12) - 1 = 59$$

$$a_{25} = 5(25) - 1 = 124$$

The 12th term is 59, and the 25th term is 124.   ■

An **arithmetic sequence** (also called an *arithmetic progression*) is a sequence in which there is a **common difference** between successive terms. The following are examples of arithmetic sequences.

(a) $1, 4, 7, 10, 13, \ldots$

(b) $6, 11, 16, 21, 26, \ldots$

(c) $14, 25, 36, 47, 58, \ldots$

(d) $4, 2, 0, -2, -4, \ldots$

(e) $-1, -7, -13, -19, -25, \ldots$

The common difference in (a) of the previous list is 3. That is to say, $4 - 1 = 3$, $7 - 4 = 3, 10 - 7 = 3, 13 - 10 = 3$, and so on. The common differences for (b), (c), (d), and (e) are 5, 11, -2, and -6, respectively. It is sometimes stated that arithmetic sequences exhibit *constant growth*. This is an accurate description if we keep in mind that this "growth" may be in a negative direction, which is illustrated by (d) and (e) above.

In a more general setting, we say that the sequence

$$a_1, a_2, a_3, a_4, \ldots, a_n, \ldots$$

is an arithmetic sequence if and only if there is a real number d such that

$$a_{k+1} - a_k = d \qquad\qquad (1)$$

for every positive integer k. The number d is called the **common difference**.

From equation (1) we see that $a_{k+1} = a_k + d$. In other words, we can generate an arithmetic sequence that has a common difference of d by starting with a first term of a_1 and then simply adding d to each successive term as follows:

First term	a_1	
Second term	$a_1 + d$	
Third term	$a_1 + 2d$	$(a_1 + d) + d = a_1 + 2d$
Fourth term	$a_1 + 3d$	$(a_1 + 2d) + d = a_1 + 3d$
$\cdot$		
$\cdot$		
$\cdot$		
nth term	$a_1 + (n - 1)d$	

Thus the *general term of an arithmetic sequence* is given by

$$a_n = a_1 + (n - 1)d$$

where a_1 is the first term and d the common difference. This general-term formula provides the basis for doing a variety of problems that involve arithmetic sequences.

E X A M P L E   3

Find the general term for each of the following arithmetic sequences.

(a) $1, 5, 9, 13, \ldots$ **(b)** $5, 2, -1, -4, \ldots$

Solution

(a) The common difference is 4 and the first term is 1. Substituting these values into $a_n = a_1 + (n - 1)d$ and simplifying, we obtain

$$a_n = a_1 + (n - 1)d$$
$$= 1 + (n - 1)4$$
$$= 1 + 4n - 4$$
$$= 4n - 3$$

(Perhaps you should verify that the general term $a_n = 4n - 3$ does produce the sequence $1, 5, 9, 13, \ldots$.)

(b) Because the first term is 5 and the common difference is -3, we obtain

$$a_n = a_1 + (n - 1)d$$
$$= 5 + (n - 1)(-3)$$
$$= 5 - 3n + 3 = -3n + 8$$ ∎

E X A M P L E   4

Find the 50th term of the arithmetic sequence $2, 6, 10, 14, \ldots$.

Solution

Certainly we could simply continue to write the terms of the given sequence until the 50th term is reached. However, let's use the general-term formula, $a_n = a_1 + (n - 1)d$, to find the 50th term without determining all of the other terms.

$$a_{50} = 2 + (50 - 1)4$$
$$= 2 + 49(4) = 2 + 196 = 198$$ ∎

E X A M P L E   5

Find the first term of the arithmetic sequence where the third term is 13 and the tenth term is 62.

Solution

Using $a_n = a_1 + (n - 1)d$ with $a_3 = 13$ (the third term is 13) and $a_{10} = 62$ (the tenth term is 62), we have

$$13 = a_1 + (3 - 1)d = a_1 + 2d$$
$$62 = a_1 + (10 - 1)d = a_1 + 9d$$

Solve the system of equations

$$\left(\begin{array}{l} a_1 + 2d = 13 \\ a_1 + 9d = 62 \end{array} \right)$$

to yield $a_1 = -1$. Thus the first term is -1. ∎

Remark: Perhaps you can think of another way to solve the problem in Example 5 without using a system of equations. [*Hint:* How many "differences" are there between the third and tenth terms of an arithmetic sequence?]

Phrases such as "the set of odd whole numbers," "the set of even whole numbers," and "the set of positive multiples of 5" are commonly used in mathematical literature to refer to various subsets of the whole numbers. Though no specific ordering of the numbers is implied by these phrases, most of us would probably react with a natural ordering. For example, if we were asked to list the set of odd whole numbers, our answer probably would be $1, 3, 5, 7, \ldots$. Using such an ordering, we can think of the set of odd whole numbers as an arithmetic sequence. Therefore, we can formulate a general representation for the set of odd whole numbers by using the general-term formula. Thus

$$a_n = a_1 + (n - 1)d$$
$$= 1 + (n - 1)2$$
$$= 1 + 2n - 2$$
$$= 2n - 1$$

The final example of this section illustrates the use of an arithmetic sequence to solve a problem that deals with the constant growth of a man's yearly salary.

E X A M P L E   6

A man started to work in 1970 at an annual salary of $9500. He received a $700 raise each year. How much was his annual salary in 1991?

Solution

The following arithmetic sequence represents the annual salary beginning in 1970.

$9500, 10{,}200, 10{,}900, 11{,}600, \ldots$

The general term of this sequence is

$$a_n = a_1 + (n - 1)d$$

$$= 9500 + (n - 1)700$$

$$= 9500 + 700n - 700$$

$$= 700n + 8800$$

The man's 1991 salary is the 22nd term of this sequence. Thus,

$$a_{22} = 700(22) + 8800 = 24{,}200$$

His salary in 1991 was $24,200. ∎

Problem Set 12.1

For Problems 1–14, write the first five terms of each sequence that has the indicated general term.

1. $a_n = 3n - 4$

2. $a_n = 2n + 3$

3. $a_n = -2n + 5$

4. $a_n = -3n - 2$

5. $a_n = n^2 - 2$

6. $a_n = n^2 + 3$

7. $a_n = -n^2 + 1$

8. $a_n = -n^2 - 2$

9. $a_n = 2n^2 - 3$

10. $a_n = 3n^2 + 2$

11. $a_n = 2^{n-2}$

12. $a_n = 3^{n+1}$

13. $a_n = -2(3)^{n-2}$

14. $a_n = -3(2)^{n-3}$

15. Find the 8th and 12th terms of the sequence where $a_n = n^2 - n - 2$.

16. Find the 10th and 15th terms of the sequence where $a_n = -n^2 - 2n + 3$.

17. Find the 7th and 8th terms of the sequence where $a_n = (-2)^{n-2}$.

18. Find the 6th and 7th terms of the sequence where $a_n = -(3)^{n-3}$.

For Problems 19–28, find the general term (*n*th term) for each of the arithmetic sequences.

19. $1, 3, 5, 7, 9, \ldots$

20. $2, 4, 6, 8, 10, \ldots$

21. $-2, 2, 6, 10, 14, \ldots$

22. $-3, 2, 7, 12, 17, \ldots$

23. $5, 3, 1, -1, -3, \ldots$

24. $2, -1, -4, -7, -10, \ldots$

25. $-7, -10, -13, -16, -19, \ldots$

26. $-3, -5, -7, -9, -11, \ldots$

27. $1, \dfrac{3}{2}, 2, \dfrac{5}{2}, 3, \ldots$

28. $\dfrac{3}{2}, 3, \dfrac{9}{2}, 6, \dfrac{15}{2}, \ldots$

For Problems 29–34, find the indicated term of the arithmetic sequence.

29. The 10th term of $7, 10, 13, 16, \ldots$

30. The 12th term of $9, 11, 13, 15, \ldots$

31. The 20th term of $2, 6, 10, 14, \ldots$

32. The 50th term of $-1, 4, 9, 14, \ldots$

33. The 75th term of $-7, -9, -11, -13, \ldots$

34. The 100th term of $-7, -10, -13, -16, \ldots$

For Problems 35–40, find the number of terms in each of the finite arithmetic sequences.

35. $1, 3, 5, 7, \ldots, 211$

36. $2, 4, 6, 8, \ldots, 312$

37. 10, 13, 16, 19, . . . , 157

38. 9, 13, 17, 21, . . . , 849

39. −7, −9, −11, −13, . . . , −345

40. −4, −7, −10, −13, . . . , −331

41. If the 6th term of an arithmetic sequence is 24, and the 10th term is 44, find the first term.

42. If the 5th term of an arithmetic sequence is 26 and the 12th term is 75, find the first term.

43. If the 4th term of an arithmetic sequence is −9 and the 9th term is −29, find the 5th term.

44. If the 6th term of an arithmetic sequence is −4 and the 14th term is −20, find the 10th term.

45. In the arithmetic sequence 0.97, 1.00, 1.03, 1.06, . . . , which term is 5.02?

46. In the arithmetic sequence 1, 1.2, 1.4, 1.6, . . . , which term is 35.4?

For Problems 47–50, set up an arithmetic sequence and use $a_n = a_1 + (n - 1)d$ to solve each problem.

47. A woman started to work in 1975 at an annual salary of $12,500. She received a $900 raise each year. How much was her annual salary in 1992?

48. Math University had an enrollment of 8500 students in 1976. Each year the enrollment has increased by 350 students. What was the enrollment in 1990?

49. Suppose you are offered a job starting at $900 a month with a guaranteed increase of $30 a month every 6 months for the next 5 years. What will your monthly salary be for the last 6 months of the fifth year of your employment?

50. Between 1976 and 1990 a person invested $500 at 14% simple interest at the beginning of each year. By the end of 1990, how much interest had been earned by the $500 that was invested at the beginning of 1982?

■ ■ ■ **THOUGHTS INTO WORDS**

51. How would you explain the concept of an arithmetic sequence to someone taking an elementary algebra course?

52. Is the sequence whose nth term is $a_n = 2^n$ an arithmetic sequence? Defend your answer.

12.2 Sums of Arithmetic Sequences

Let's begin this section with a problem to solve. Study the solution very carefully.

PROBLEM 1

Find the sum of the first one hundred positive integers.

Solution

We are being asked to find the sum of $1 + 2 + 3 + 4 + \cdots + 100$. Rather than adding in the usual way, we will find the sum in the following manner. Let's simply write the indicated sum forward and backward, and then add in a column fashion.

$$
\begin{array}{cccccc}
1 + & 2 + & 3 + & 4 + & \cdots + & 100 \\
100 + & 99 + & 98 + & 97 + & \cdots + & 1 \\
\hline
101 + & 101 + & 101 + & 101 + & \cdots + & 101
\end{array}
$$

In so doing, we have produced 100 sums of 101. However, this sum is double the amount we want, because we wrote the sum twice. To find the sum of just the numbers 1 to 100, we need to multiply 100 by 101 and then divide by 2.

$$\frac{100(101)}{2} = \frac{\overset{50}{\cancel{100}}\,(101)}{2} = 5050$$

Thus the sum of the first 100 positive integers is 5050.

We could have stated Problem 1 as "Find the sum of the first one hundred terms of the arithmetic sequence that has a general term (nth term) of $a_n = n$." In fact, the forward–backward approach used to solve the problem can be applied to the general arithmetic sequence.

$$a_1 + a_2 + a_3 + \cdots + a_n$$

to produce a formula for finding the sum of the first n terms of any arithmetic sequence. Use S_n to represent the sum of the first n terms and proceed as follows:

$$S_n = a_1 + (a_1 + d) + (a_1 + 2d) + \cdots + (a_n - 2d) + (a_n - d) + a_n$$

Now write this sum in reverse as

$$S_n = a_n + (a_n - d) + (a_n - 2d) + \cdots + (a_1 + 2d) + (a_1 + d) + a_1$$

Add the two equations to produce

$$2S_n = (a_1 + a_n) + (a_1 + a_n) + (a_1 + a_n) + \cdots + (a_1 + a_n)$$
$$+ (a_1 + a_n) + (a_1 + a_n)$$

That is, we have n sums of $(a_1 + a_n)$, so

$$2S_n = n(a_1 + a_n)$$

from which we obtain

$$S_n = \frac{n(a_1 + a_n)}{2}$$

Using the nth-term formula $a_n = a_1 + (n - 1)d$ and the sum formula $\frac{n(a_1 + a_n)}{2}$, we can solve a variety of problems that involve arithmetic sequences.

E X A M P L E   1

Find the sum of the first 50 terms of the sequence

$$2, 5, 8, 11, \ldots.$$

Solution

Using $a_n = a_1 + (n - 1)d$, we find the 50th term to be

$$a_{50} = 2 + 49(3) = 149$$

Then using $S_n = \dfrac{n(a_1 + a_n)}{2}$, we obtain

$$S_{50} = \frac{50(2 + 149)}{2} = 3775$$

∎

EXAMPLE 2

Find the sum of all odd numbers between 7 and 433, inclusive.

Solution

We need to find the sum $7 + 9 + 11 + \cdots + 433$. To use $S_n = \dfrac{n(a_1 + a_n)}{2}$, we need the number of terms, n. Perhaps you could figure this out without a formula (try it), but suppose we use the nth-term formula.

$$a_n = a_1 + (n - 1)d$$
$$433 = 7 + (n - 1)2$$
$$433 = 7 + 2n - 2$$
$$433 = 2n + 5$$
$$428 = 2n$$
$$214 = n$$

Then use $n = 214$ in the sum formula to yield

$$S_{214} = \frac{214(7 + 433)}{2} = 47{,}080$$

∎

EXAMPLE 3

Find the sum of the first 75 terms of the sequence that has a general term of $a_n = -5n + 9$.

Solution

Using $a_n = -5n + 9$, we can generate the sequence as follows:

$$a_1 = -5(1) + 9 = 4$$
$$a_2 = -5(2) + 9 = -1$$
$$a_3 = -5(3) + 9 = -6$$
$$\cdot$$
$$\cdot$$
$$\cdot$$
$$a_{75} = -5(75) + 9 = -366$$

Thus we have the indicated sum of the sequence

$$4 + (-1) + (-6) + \cdots + (-366)$$

Using the sum formula, we obtain

$$S_{75} = \frac{75[4 + (-366)]}{2} = -13{,}575$$

∎

E X A M P L E   4

Sue is saving quarters. She saves 1 quarter the first day, 2 quarters the second day, 3 quarters the third day, and so on. How much money will she have saved in 30 days?

Solution

The total number of quarters will be the sum of the sequence

$$1, 2, 3, \ldots, 30$$

Using the sum formula yields

$$S_{30} = \frac{30(1 + 30)}{2} = 465$$

Thus Sue will have saved $(465)(0.25) = \$116.25$ at the end of 30 days. ∎

Remark: The sum formula, $S_n = \dfrac{n(a_1 + a_n)}{2}$, was developed by using the **forward–backward** technique that we previously used on a specific problem. Now that we have the sum formula, we have two choices as we meet problems where the formula applies. We can memorize the formula and use it as it applies, or we can disregard the formula and use the forward–backward approach. Furthermore, even if you use the formula, and some day you forget it, you can use the forward–backward technique. In other words, once you understand the development of a formula, you can do some problems even if you have forgotten the formula itself.

Problem Set 12.2

For Problems 1–10, find the indicated sum.

1. First 50 terms of $2 + 4 + 6 + 8 + \cdots$

2. First 45 terms of $1 + 3 + 5 + 7 + \cdots$

3. First 60 terms of $3 + 8 + 13 + 18 + \cdots$

4. First 80 terms of $2 + 6 + 10 + 14 + \cdots$

5. First 65 terms of $(-1) + (-3) + (-5) + (-7) + \cdots$

6. First 100 terms of $(-1) + (-4) + (-7) + (-10) + \cdots$

7. First 40 terms of $\dfrac{1}{2} + 1 + \dfrac{3}{2} + 2 + \cdots$

8. First 50 terms of $1 + \dfrac{5}{2} + 4 + \dfrac{11}{2} + \cdots$

9. First 75 terms of $7 + 10 + 13 + 16 + \cdots$

10. First 90 terms of $(-8) + (-1) + 6 + 13 + \cdots$

For Problems 11–16, find the indicated sum.

11. $4 + 8 + 12 + 16 + \cdots + 212$

12. $7 + 9 + 11 + 13 + \cdots + 179$

13. $(-4) + (-1) + 2 + 5 + \cdots + 173$

14. $5 + 10 + 15 + 20 + \cdots + 495$

15. $2.5 + 3.0 + 3.5 + 4.0 + \cdots + 18.5$

16. $1 + (-6) + (-13) + (-20) + \cdots + (-202)$

For Problems 17–22, find the sum of the indicated number of terms of the sequence with the given nth term.

17. First 50 terms of sequence with $a_n = 3n - 1$

18. First 150 terms of sequence with $a_n = 2n - 7$

19. First 125 terms of sequence with $a_n = 5n + 1$

20. First 75 terms of sequence with $a_n = 4n + 3$

21. First 65 terms of sequence with $a_n = -4n - 1$

22. First 90 terms of sequence with $a_n = -3n - 2$

For Problems 23–34, use arithmetic sequences to help solve the problem.

23. Find the sum of the first 350 positive even whole numbers.

24. Find the sum of the first 200 odd whole numbers.

25. Find the sum of all odd whole numbers between 15 and 397, inclusive.

26. Find the sum of all even whole numbers between 14 and 286, inclusive.

27. An auditorium has 20 seats in the front row, 24 seats in the second row, 28 seats in the third row, and so on, for 15 rows. How many seats are there in the last row? How many seats are there in the auditorium?

28. A pile of wood has 15 logs in the bottom row, 14 logs in the row next to the bottom, and so on, with one less log in each row until the top row, which consists of 1 log. How many logs are there in the pile?

29. A raffle is organized so that the amount paid for each ticket is determined by a number on the ticket. The tickets are numbered with the consecutive odd whole numbers 1, 3, 5, 7, ... Each participant pays as many cents as the number on the ticket drawn. How much money will the raffle take in if 1000 tickets are sold?

30. A woman invests $700 at 13% simple interest at the beginning of each year for a period of 15 years. Find the total accumulated value of all of the investments at the end of the 15-year period.

31. A man started to work in 1970 at an annual salary of $18,500. He received a $1500 raise each year through 1982. What were his total earnings for the 13-year period?

32. A well driller charges $9.00 per foot for the first 10 feet, $9.10 per foot for the next 10 feet, $9.20 per foot for the next 10 feet, and so on; he continues to increase the price by $.10 per foot for succeeding intervals of 10 feet. How much would it cost to drill a well with a depth of 150 feet?

33. A display in a grocery store has cans stacked with 25 cans in the bottom row, 23 cans in the second row from the bottom, 21 cans in the third row from the bottom, and so on until there is only 1 can in the top row. How many cans are there in the display?

34. Suppose that a person starts on the first day of August and saves a dime the first day, $.20 the second day, and $.30 the third day and continues to save $.10 more per day than the previous day. How much could be saved in the 31 days of August?

■ ■ ■ **THOUGHTS INTO WORDS**

35. Explain how to find the sum $1 + 2 + 3 + \cdots + 150$ without using the sum formula.

36. Explain how you would find the sum of the first 150 terms of the arithmetic sequence that has a general term of $a_n = -3n + 7$.

■ ■ ■ **FURTHER INVESTIGATIONS**

37. We can express the sum of a sequence where the general term is known in a convenient and compact form using the symbol Σ along with the general-term expression. For example, consider the finite sum.

$1 + 3 + 5 + 7 + 9 + 11$

where the general term is $a_n = 2n - 1$. This indicated sum can be expressed in *summation notation* as

$$\sum_{i=1}^{6} (2i - 1)$$

where the letter i is used as the **index of summation**. The individual terms of the sequence can be generated by successively replacing i in the expression $(2i - 1)$ with the numbers 1, 2, 3, 4, 5, and 6. Thus the first term is $2(1) - 1 = 1$, the second term $2(2) - 1 = 3$, the third term $2(3) - 1 = 5$, and so on. Write out the terms and find the sum of each of the following sequences.

(a) $\displaystyle\sum_{i=1}^{3} (5i + 2)$ **(b)** $\displaystyle\sum_{i=1}^{4} (6i - 7)$

(c) $\displaystyle\sum_{i=1}^{6} (-2i - 1)$ **(d)** $\displaystyle\sum_{i=1}^{5} (-3i + 4)$

(e) $\displaystyle\sum_{i=1}^{5} 3i$ **(f)** $\displaystyle\sum_{i=1}^{6} -4i$

38. Write each of the following in summation notation. For example, because $3 + 8 + 13 + 18 + 23 + 28$ is the indicated sum of an arithmetic sequence, the general-term formula $a_n = a_1 + (n - 1)d$ yields

$$a_n = 3 + (n - 1)5$$
$$= 3 + 5n - 5$$
$$= 5n - 2$$

Now, using i as an index of summation, we can write

$$\sum_{i=1}^{6} (5i - 2)$$

(a) $2 + 5 + 8 + 11 + 14$
(b) $8 + 15 + 22 + 29 + 36 + 43$
(c) $1 + (-1) + (-3) + (-5) + (-7)$
(d) $(-5) + (-9) + (-13) + (-17) + (-21) + (-25) + (-29)$

12.3 Geometric Sequences

A **geometric sequence** or **geometric progression** is a sequence in which each term after the first is obtained by multiplying the preceding term by a common multiplier. The common multiplier is called the **common ratio** of the sequence. The following geometric sequences have common ratios of $2, 3, \dfrac{1}{2}$, and -4, respectively.

$$1, 2, 4, 8, 16, \ldots \qquad 3, 9, 27, 81, 243, \ldots$$

$$8, 4, 2, 1, \frac{1}{2}, \ldots \qquad 1, -4, 16, -64, 256, \ldots$$

We find the common ratio of a geometric sequence by dividing a term (other than the first term) by the preceding term. In a more general setting, we say that the sequence

$$a_1, a_2, a_3, a_4, \ldots, a_n, \ldots$$

is a geometric sequence if and only if there is a nonzero real number r such that

$$a_{k+1} = ra_k \tag{1}$$

for every positive integer k. The nonzero real number r is called the common ratio.

Equation (1) can be used to generate a general geometric sequence that has a_1 as a first term and r as a common ratio. We can proceed as follows:

First term	a_1	
Second term	$a_1 r$	
Third term	$a_1 r^2$	$(a_1 r)(r) = a_1 r^2$
Fourth term	$a_1 r^3$	$(a_1 r^2)(r) = a_1 r^3$
$\cdot$		
$\cdot$		
$\cdot$		
nth term	$a_1 r^{n-1}$	

Thus the *general term of a geometric sequence* is given by

$$a_n = a_1 r^{n-1}$$

where a_1 is the first term, and r is the common ratio.

E X A M P L E   1

Find the general term for the geometric sequence 2, 4, 8, 16, . . .

Solution

Using $a_n = a_1 r^{n-1}$, we obtain

$$a_n = 2(2)^{n-1} \qquad r = \frac{4}{2} = \frac{8}{4} = \frac{16}{8} = 2$$

$$= 2^n \qquad 2^1(2)^{n-1} = 2^{1+n-1} = 2^n$$

∎

E X A M P L E   2

Find the tenth term of the geometric sequence 9, 3, 1, ...

Solution

Using $a_n = a_1 r^{n-1}$, we can find the tenth term as follows:

$$a_{10} = 9\left(\frac{1}{3}\right)^{10-1}$$

$$= 9\left(\frac{1}{3}\right)^{9}$$

$$= 9\left(\frac{1}{19{,}683}\right)$$

$$= \frac{1}{2187}$$

∎

As with arithmetic sequences, we often need to find the sum of a certain number of terms of a geometric sequence. Before we develop a general-sum formula for geometric sequences, let's consider an approach to a specific problem that we can then use in a general setting.

E X A M P L E   3

Find the sum of $1 + 2 + 4 + 8 + \cdots + 512$.

Solution

Let S represent the sum and we can proceed as follows:

$$S = 1 + 2 + 4 + 8 + \cdots + 512, \tag{1}$$

$$2S = \quad 2 + 4 + 8 + \cdots + 512 + 1024 \tag{2}$$

Equation (2) is the result of multiplying both sides of equation (1) by 2. Subtract equation (1) from equation (2) to yield

$$S = 1024 - 1 = 1023 \qquad\qquad \blacksquare$$

Now let's consider the general geometric sequence

$$a_1, a_1r, a_1r^2, \ldots, a_1r^{n-1}$$

By applying a procedure similar to the one used in Example 3, we can develop a formula for finding the sum of the first n terms of any geometric sequence.

Let S_n represent the sum of the first n terms. Thus

$$S_n = a_1 + a_1r + a_1r^2 + \cdots + a_1r^{n-1} \tag{3}$$

Multiply both sides of equation (3) by the common ratio r to produce

$$rS_n = a_1r + a_1r^2 + a_1r^3 + \cdots + a_1r^{n-1} + a_1r^n \tag{4}$$

Subtract equation (3) from equation (4) to yield

$$rS_n - S_n = a_1r^n - a_1$$

Apply the distributive property on the left side and then solve for S_n to obtain

$$S_n(r - 1) = a_1r^n - a_1$$

$$S_n = \frac{a_1r^n - a_1}{r - 1}, \quad r \neq 1$$

Therefore, the sum of the first n terms of a geometric sequence that has a first term of a_1 and a common ratio of r is given by

$$S_n = \frac{a_1r^n - a_1}{r - 1}, \quad r \neq 1$$

EXAMPLE 4

Find the sum of the first seven terms of the geometric sequence $2, 6, 18, \ldots$.

Solution

Use the sum formula to obtain

$$S_7 = \frac{2(3)^7 - 2}{3 - 1}$$

$$= \frac{2(3^7 - 1)}{2}$$

$$= 3^7 - 1$$

$$= 2187 - 1$$

$$= 2186 \quad \blacksquare$$

If the common ratio of a geometric sequence is less than 1, it may be more convenient to change the form of the sum formula. That is, we can change the fraction $\frac{a_1 r^n - a_1}{r - 1}$ to $\frac{a_1 - a_1 r^n}{1 - r}$ by multiplying both the numerator and the denominator by -1. Thus, if we use $S_n = \frac{a_1 - a_1 r^n}{1 - r}$ when $r < 1$, we can sometimes avoid unnecessary work with negative numbers, as the next example illustrates.

EXAMPLE 5

Find the sum $1 + \dfrac{1}{2} + \dfrac{1}{4} + \cdots + \dfrac{1}{256}$.

Solution A

To use the sum formula, we need to know the number of terms, which can be found by simply counting them or by applying the nth-term formula as follows:

$$a_n = a_1 r^{n-1}$$

$$\frac{1}{256} = 1\left(\frac{1}{2}\right)^{n-1}$$

$$\left(\frac{1}{2}\right)^8 = \left(\frac{1}{2}\right)^{n-1}$$

$$8 = n - 1 \qquad \text{Remember that if } b^n = b^m, \text{ then } n = m.$$

$$9 = n$$

Using $n = 9$, $a_1 = 1$, and $r = \dfrac{1}{2}$ in the form of the sum formula

$$S_n = \frac{a_1 - a_1 r^n}{1 - r}$$

we obtain

$$S_9 = \frac{1 - 1\left(\dfrac{1}{2}\right)^9}{1 - \dfrac{1}{2}}$$

$$= \frac{1 - \dfrac{1}{512}}{\dfrac{1}{2}}$$

$$= \frac{\dfrac{511}{512}}{\dfrac{1}{2}}$$

$$= \left(\frac{511}{512}\right)\left(\frac{2}{1}\right) = \frac{511}{256} \quad \text{or} \quad 1\frac{255}{256}$$

You should realize that a problem such as Example 5 can be done without using the sum formula; you can apply the general technique used to develop the formula. Solution B illustrates this approach.

Solution B

Let S represent the desired sum. Thus

$$S = 1 + \frac{1}{2} + \frac{1}{4} + \cdots + \frac{1}{256}$$

Multiply both sides by $\dfrac{1}{2}$ (the common ratio).

$$\frac{1}{2}S = \frac{1}{2} + \frac{1}{4} + \cdots + \frac{1}{256} + \frac{1}{512}$$

Subtract the second equation from the first equation to produce

$$\frac{1}{2}S = 1 - \frac{1}{512}$$

$$\frac{1}{2}S = \frac{511}{512}$$

$$S = \frac{511}{256}$$

$$= 1\frac{255}{256}$$

EXAMPLE 6

Suppose your employer agrees to pay you a penny for your first day's wages and then to double your pay on each succeeding day. How much will you earn on the 15th day? What will be your total earnings for the first 15 days?

Solution

The terms of the geometric sequence $1, 2, 4, 8, \ldots$ depict your daily wages, and the sum of the first 15 terms is your total earnings for the 15 days. The formula $a_n = a_1 r^{n-1}$ can be used to find the 15th day's wages.

$$a_{15} = (1)(2)^{14} = 16{,}384$$

Because the terms of the sequence are expressed in cents, your wages for the 15th day will be \$163.84. Now, using the sum formula, we can find your total earnings as follows:

$$S_n = \frac{a_1 r^n - a_1}{r - 1}$$

$$S_{15} = \frac{1(2)^{15} - 1}{1} = 32{,}768 - 1 = 32{,}767$$

Thus, for the 15 days, you will earn a total of \$327.67. ■

Problem Set 12.3

For Problems 1–12, find the general term (nth term) of each geometric sequence.

1. $1, 3, 9, 27, \ldots$

2. $1, 2, 4, 8, \ldots$

3. $2, 8, 32, 128, \ldots$

4. $3, 9, 27, 81, \ldots$

5. $1, \dfrac{1}{3}, \dfrac{1}{9}, \dfrac{1}{27}, \ldots$

6. $\dfrac{1}{2}, \dfrac{1}{4}, \dfrac{1}{8}, \dfrac{1}{16}, \ldots$

7. $0.2, 0.04, 0.008, 0.0016, \ldots$

8. $1, 0.3, 0.09, 0.027, \ldots$

9. $9, 6, 4, \dfrac{8}{3}, \ldots$

10. $6, 2, \dfrac{2}{3}, \dfrac{2}{9}, \ldots$

11. $1, -4, 16, -64, \ldots$

12. $1, -2, 4, -8, \ldots$

For Problems 13–18, find the indicated term of the geometric sequence.

13. 12th term of $\dfrac{1}{9}, \dfrac{1}{3}, 1, 3, \ldots$

14. 9th term of $2, 4, 8, 16, \ldots$

15. 10th term of $1, -2, 4, -8, \ldots$

16. 8th term of $\dfrac{1}{2}, \dfrac{1}{8}, \dfrac{1}{32}, \dfrac{1}{128}, \ldots$

17. 9th term of $-1, -\dfrac{3}{2}, -\dfrac{9}{4}, -\dfrac{27}{8}, \ldots$

18. 11th term of $1, \dfrac{2}{3}, \dfrac{4}{9}, \dfrac{8}{27}, \ldots$

For Problems 19–24, find the indicated sum.

19. First 10 terms of $\dfrac{1}{2} + \dfrac{3}{2} + \dfrac{9}{2} + \dfrac{27}{2} + \cdots$

20. First 9 terms of $1 + 2 + 4 + 8 + \cdots$

21. First 9 terms of $-2 + 6 + (-18) + 54 + \cdots$

22. First 10 terms of $-4 + 8 + (-16) + 32 + \cdots$

23. First 7 terms of $1 + 3 + 9 + 27 + \cdots$

24. First 8 terms of $4 + 2 + 1 + \dfrac{1}{2} + \cdots$

For Problems 25–30, find the sum of the indicated number of terms of the geometric sequence with the given nth term.

25. First 9 terms of sequence where $a_n = 2^{n-1}$

26. First 8 terms of sequence where $a_n = 3^n$

27. First 8 terms of sequence where $a_n = 2(3)^n$

28. First 10 terms of sequence where $a_n = \dfrac{1}{2^{n-4}}$

29. First 12 terms of sequence where $a_n = (-2)^n$

30. First 9 terms of sequence where $a_n = (-3)^{n-1}$

For Problems 31–36, find the indicated sum.

31. $1 + 3 + 9 + \cdots + 729$

32. $2 + 8 + 32 + \cdots + 2048$

33. $1 + \dfrac{1}{2} + \dfrac{1}{4} + \cdots + \dfrac{1}{1024}$

34. $1 + (-2) + 4 + \cdots + (-128)$

35. $8 + 4 + 2 + \cdots + \dfrac{1}{32}$

36. $2 + 6 + 18 + \cdots + 4374$

For Problems 37–48, use geometric sequences to help solve the problem.

37. Find the common ratio of a geometric sequence if the second term is $\dfrac{1}{6}$, and the fifth term is $\dfrac{1}{48}$.

38. Find the first term of a geometric sequence if the fifth term is $\dfrac{32}{3}$, and the common ratio is 2.

39. Find the sum of the first 16 terms of the geometric sequence where $a_n = (-1)^n$. Also find the sum of the first 19 terms.

40. A fungus culture growing under controlled conditions doubles in size each day. How many units will the culture contain after 7 days if it originally contained 5 units?

41. A tank contains 16,000 liters of water. Each day one-half of the water in the tank is removed and not replaced. How much water remains in the tank at the end of the seventh day?

42. Suppose that you save 25 cents the first day of a week, 50 cents the second day, $1 the third day, and you continue to double your savings each day. How much will you save on the seventh day? What will be your total savings for the week?

43. Suppose you save a nickel the first day of a month, a dime the second day, 20 cents the third day, and you continue to double your savings each day. How much will you save on the 12th day of the month? What will be your total savings for the first 12 days?

44. Suppose an element has a half-life of 3 hours. This means that if n grams of it exist at a specific time, then only $\dfrac{1}{2}n$ grams remain 3 hours later. If at a particular moment we have 40 grams of the element, how much of it will remain 24 hours later?

45. A rubber ball is dropped from a height of 486 meters, and each time it rebounds one-third of the height from which it last fell (see Figure 12.1). How far has the ball traveled by the time it strikes the ground for the seventh time?

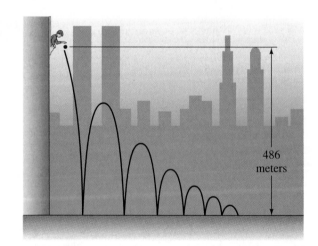

486 meters

Figure 12.1

46. A pump is attached to a container for the purpose of creating a vacuum. For each stroke of the pump, one-fourth of the air remaining in the container is removed.
   (a) Form a geometric sequence where each term represents the fractional part of the air *that still remains* in the container after each stroke. Then use

this sequence to find out how much of the air remains after 6 strokes.

(b) Form a geometric sequence where each term represents the fractional part of the air *being removed* from the container on each stroke of the pump. Then use this sequence to find out how much of the air remains after 6 strokes.

47. If you pay $9500 for a car, and its value depreciates 10% per year, how much will it be worth in 5 years?

48. Suppose that you could get a job that pays only a penny for the first day of employment but doubles your wages each succeeding day. How much would you be earning on the 31st day of your employment?

■ ■ ■ THOUGHTS INTO WORDS

49. Explain the difference between an arithmetic sequence and a geometric sequence.

50. Consider the sequence whose *n*th term is $a_n = 3n$. How can you determine whether this is an arithmetic sequence or a geometric sequence?

■ ■ ■ FURTHER INVESTIGATIONS

For Problems 51–56, use your calculator to help find the indicated term of each geometric sequence.

51. 20th term of 2, 4, 8, 16, . . .

52. 15th term of 3, 9, 27, 81, . . .

53. 12th term of $\dfrac{2}{3}, \dfrac{4}{9}, \dfrac{8}{27}, \dfrac{16}{81}, \ldots$

54. 10th term of $-\dfrac{3}{4}, \dfrac{9}{16}, -\dfrac{27}{64}, \dfrac{81}{256}, \ldots$

55. 11th term of $-\dfrac{3}{2}, \dfrac{9}{4}, -\dfrac{27}{8}, \dfrac{81}{16}, \ldots$

56. 6th term of the sequence where $a_n = (0.1)^n$

57. In Problem 37 of Problem Set 12.2 we introduced the summation notation, which can also be used with geometric sequences. For example, the indicated sum

$$2 + 4 + 8 + 16 + 32$$

can be expressed as

$$\sum_{i=1}^{5} 2^i$$

Write out the terms and find the sum of each of the following.

(a) $\displaystyle\sum_{i=1}^{6} 2^i$

(b) $\displaystyle\sum_{i=1}^{5} 3^i$

(c) $\displaystyle\sum_{i=1}^{5} 2^{i-1}$

(d) $\displaystyle\sum_{i=1}^{6} \left(\dfrac{1}{2}\right)^{i+1}$

(e) $\displaystyle\sum_{i=1}^{4} \left(\dfrac{2}{3}\right)^{i}$

(f) $\displaystyle\sum_{i=1}^{5} \left(-\dfrac{3}{4}\right)^{i}$

12.4 Infinite Geometric Sequences

In Section 12.3 we used the formula

$$S_n = \frac{a_1 - a_1 r^n}{1 - r}, \quad r \neq 1 \tag{1}$$

to find the sum of the first n terms of a geometric sequence. By using the property $\dfrac{a-b}{c} = \dfrac{a}{c} - \dfrac{b}{c}$, we can express the right side of equation (1) in terms of two fractions as follows:

$$S_n = \frac{a_1 - a_1 r^n}{1 - r} = \frac{a_1}{1 - r} - \frac{a_1 r^n}{1 - r}, \quad r \neq 1 \tag{2}$$

Now let's examine the behavior of r^n for $|r| < 1$, that is, for $-1 < r < 1$. For example, suppose that $r = \dfrac{1}{3}$; then

$$r^2 = \left(\frac{1}{3}\right)^2 = \frac{1}{9} \qquad r^3 = \left(\frac{1}{3}\right)^3 = \frac{1}{27}$$

$$r^4 = \left(\frac{1}{3}\right)^4 = \frac{1}{81} \qquad r^5 = \left(\frac{1}{3}\right)^5 = \frac{1}{243}$$

and so on. We can make $\left(\dfrac{1}{3}\right)^n$ as close to 0 as we please by taking sufficiently large values for n. In general, for values of r such that $|r| < 1$, the expression r^n will approach 0 as n increases. Therefore, in equation (2) the fraction $\dfrac{a_1 r^n}{1 - r}$ will approach 0 as n increases, and we say that the *sum of an infinite geometric sequence* is given by

$$S_\infty = \frac{a_1}{1 - r}, \quad |r| < 1$$

EXAMPLE 1

Find the sum of the infinite geometric sequence

$$1, \frac{2}{3}, \frac{4}{9}, \frac{8}{27}, \cdots$$

Solution

Because $a_1 = 1$ and $r = \dfrac{2}{3}$, we obtain

$$S_\infty = \frac{1}{1 - \dfrac{2}{3}}$$

$$= \frac{1}{\dfrac{1}{3}} = 3$$

■

In Example 1, by stating $S_\infty = 3$ we mean that as we add more and more terms, the sum approaches 3.

First term:	1
Sum of first 2 terms:	$1 + \dfrac{2}{3} = 1\dfrac{2}{3}$
Sum of first 3 terms:	$1 + \dfrac{2}{3} + \dfrac{4}{9} = 2\dfrac{1}{9}$
Sum of first 4 terms:	$1 + \dfrac{2}{3} + \dfrac{4}{9} + \dfrac{8}{27} = 2\dfrac{11}{27}$
Sum of first 5 terms:	$1 + \dfrac{2}{3} + \dfrac{4}{9} + \dfrac{8}{27} + \dfrac{16}{81} = 2\dfrac{49}{81}$, etc.

EXAMPLE 2

Find the sum of the infinite geometric sequence

$$\frac{1}{2}, -\frac{1}{4}, \frac{1}{8}, -\frac{1}{16}, \ldots$$

Solution

Because $a_1 = \dfrac{1}{2}$ and $r = -\dfrac{1}{2}$, we obtain

$$S_\infty = \frac{\dfrac{1}{2}}{1 - \left(-\dfrac{1}{2}\right)} = \frac{\dfrac{1}{2}}{\dfrac{3}{2}} = \frac{1}{3}$$

■

If $|r| > 1$, the absolute value of r^n increases without bound as n increases. Consider the following two examples, and note the unbounded growth of the absolute value of r^n.

Let $r = 2$	Let $r = -3$	
$r^2 = 2^2 = 4$	$r^2 = (-3)^2 = 9$	
$r^3 = 2^3 = 8$	$r^3 = (-3)^3 = -27$	$|-27| = 27$
$r^4 = 2^4 = 16$	$r^4 = (-3)^4 = 81$	
$r^5 = 2^5 = 32$	$r^5 = (-3)^5 = -243$	$|-243| = 243$
etc.	etc.	

If $r = 1$, then $S_n = na_1$, and as n increases without bound, $|S_n|$ also increases without bound. If $r = -1$, then S_n will be either a_1 or 0. Therefore, we say that the sum of any infinite geometric sequence where $|r| \geq 1$ does not exist.

■ Repeating Decimals as Sums of Infinite Geometric Sequences

In Section 1.1 we learned that a rational number is a number that can be represented as either a terminating decimal or a repeating decimal. For example,

$$0.23, \quad 0.147, \quad 0.\overline{3}, \quad 0.\overline{14}, \quad \text{and} \quad 0.5\overline{81}$$

are rational numbers. (Remember that $0.\overline{3}$ means 0.333 . . . .) Our knowledge of place value provides the basis for changing terminating decimals such as 0.23 and 0.147 to $\dfrac{a}{b}$ form, where a and b are integers, $b \neq 0$.

$$0.23 = \frac{23}{100}$$

$$0.147 = \frac{147}{1000}$$

However, changing repeating decimals to $\dfrac{a}{b}$ form requires a different technique, and our work with infinite geometric sequences provides the basis for one such approach. Consider the following examples.

EXAMPLE 3

Change $0.\overline{3}$ to $\dfrac{a}{b}$ form, where a and b are integers, $b \neq 0$.

Solution

We can write the repeating decimal $0.\overline{3}$ as the indicated sum of the infinite geometric sequence

$$0.3 + 0.03 + 0.003 + 0.0003 + \cdots$$

with $a_1 = 0.3$ and $r = 0.1$. Therefore, we can use the sum formula and obtain

$$S_\infty = \frac{a_1}{1 - r} = \frac{0.3}{1 - 0.1} = \frac{0.3}{0.9} = \frac{3}{9} = \frac{1}{3}$$

Thus $0.\overline{3} = \dfrac{1}{3}$. ■

EXAMPLE 4

Change $0.\overline{14}$ to $\dfrac{a}{b}$ form, where a and b are integers, $b \neq 0$.

Solution

We can write the repeating decimal $0.\overline{14}$ as the indicated sum of the infinite geometric sequence

$$0.14 + 0.0014 + 0.000014 + \cdots$$

with $a_1 = 0.14$ and $r = 0.01$. The sum formula produces

$$S_\infty = \frac{0.14}{1 - 0.01} = \frac{0.14}{0.99} = \frac{14}{99}$$

Thus $0.\overline{14} = \dfrac{14}{99}$. ■

If the repeating block of digits does not begin immediately after the decimal point, we can make a slight adjustment, as the final example illustrates.

EXAMPLE 5   Change $0.5\overline{81}$ to $\dfrac{a}{b}$ form, where a and b are integers, $b \neq 0$.

Solution

We can write the repeating decimal $0.5\overline{81}$ as

$$[0.5] + [0.081 + 0.00081 + 0.0000081 + \cdots]$$

where

$$0.081 + 0.00081 + 0.0000081 + \cdots$$

is the indicated sum of the infinite geometric sequence with $a_1 = 0.081$ and $r = 0.01$. Thus

$$S_\infty = \frac{0.081}{1 - 0.01} = \frac{0.081}{0.99} = \frac{81}{990} = \frac{9}{110}$$

Therefore,

$$0.5\overline{81} = 0.5 + \frac{9}{110}$$

$$= \frac{5}{10} + \frac{9}{110}$$

$$= \frac{55}{110} + \frac{9}{110}$$

$$= \frac{64}{110}$$

$$= \frac{32}{55}$$

■

Problem Set 12.4

For Problems 1–20, find the sum of each geometric sequence. If the sequence has no sum, so state.

1. $1, \dfrac{3}{4}, \dfrac{9}{16}, \dfrac{27}{64}, \cdots$

2. $\dfrac{2}{3}, \dfrac{2}{9}, \dfrac{2}{27}, \dfrac{2}{81}, \cdots$

3. $\dfrac{1}{2}, \dfrac{1}{4}, \dfrac{1}{8}, \dfrac{1}{16}, \cdots$

4. $1, \dfrac{1}{2}, \dfrac{1}{4}, \dfrac{1}{8}, \cdots$

5. $\dfrac{2}{3}, \dfrac{4}{9}, \dfrac{8}{27}, \dfrac{16}{81}, \cdots$

6. $\dfrac{1}{3}, \dfrac{1}{9}, \dfrac{1}{27}, \dfrac{1}{81}, \cdots$

7. $1, -\dfrac{1}{2}, \dfrac{1}{4}, -\dfrac{1}{8}, \cdots$

8. $1, 2, 4, 8, \cdots$

9. $6, 2, \dfrac{2}{3}, \dfrac{2}{9}, \cdots$

10. $4, -2, 1, -\dfrac{1}{2}, \cdots$

11. $2, -6, 18, -54, \cdots$

12. $4, 2, 1, \dfrac{1}{2}, \cdots$

13. $1, -\dfrac{3}{4}, \dfrac{9}{16}, -\dfrac{27}{64}, \cdots$

14. $9, -3, 1, -\dfrac{1}{3}, \cdots$ **15.** $8, -4, 2, -1, \cdots$

16. $5, 3, \dfrac{9}{5}, \dfrac{27}{5}, \cdots$ **17.** $1, \dfrac{3}{2}, \dfrac{9}{4}, \dfrac{27}{8}, \cdots$

18. $1, -\dfrac{4}{3}, \dfrac{16}{9}, -\dfrac{64}{27}, \cdots$ **19.** $27, 9, 3, 1, \cdots$

20. $9, 3, 1, \dfrac{1}{3}, \cdots$

For Problems 21–34, change each repeating decimal to $\dfrac{a}{b}$ form, where a and b are integers, $b \neq 0$. Express $\dfrac{a}{b}$ in reduced form.

21. $0.\overline{4}$ **22.** $0.\overline{7}$ **23.** $0.\overline{47}$

24. $0.\overline{23}$ **25.** $0.\overline{45}$ **26.** $0.\overline{72}$

27. $0.\overline{427}$ **28.** $0.\overline{129}$ **29.** $0.4\overline{6}$

30. $0.8\overline{6}$ **31.** $2.1\overline{8}$ **32.** $2.9\overline{6}$

33. $0.4\overline{27}$ **34.** $0.2\overline{36}$

■ ■ ■ THOUGHTS INTO WORDS

35. What does it mean to say that the sum of the infinite geometric sequence $1, \dfrac{1}{2}, \dfrac{1}{4}, \dfrac{1}{8}, \cdots$ is 2?

36. What do we mean when we say that the infinite geometric sequence $1, 2, 4, 8, \cdots$ has no sum?

37. Why don't we discuss the sum of an infinite arithmetic sequence?

12.5   Binomial Expansions

In Chapter 3, we used the pattern $(x + y)^2 = x^2 + 2xy + y^2$ to square binomials and the pattern $(x + y)^3 = x^3 + 3x^2y + 3xy^2 + y^3$ to cube binomials. At this time, we can extend those ideas to arrive at a pattern that will allow us to write the expansion of $(x + y)^n$, where n is *any* positive integer. Let's begin by looking at some specific expansions that we can verify by direct multiplication.

$$(x + y)^1 = x + y$$
$$(x + y)^2 = x^2 + 2xy + y^2$$
$$(x + y)^3 = x^3 + 3x^2y + 3xy^2 + y^3$$
$$(x + y)^4 = x^4 + 4x^3y + 6x^2y^2 + 4xy^3 + y^4$$
$$(x + y)^5 = x^5 + 5x^4y + 10x^3y^2 + 10x^2y^3 + 5xy^4 + y^5$$

First, note the patterns of the exponents for x and y on a term-by-term basis. The exponents of x begin with the exponent of the binomial and term-by-term decrease by 1 until the last term has x^0, which is 1. The exponents of y begin with 0 ($y^0 = 1$) and term-by-term increase by 1 until the last term contains y to the power of the original binomial. In other words, the variables in the expansion of $(x + y)^n$ exhibit the following pattern.

$$x^n, \qquad x^{n-1}y, \qquad x^{n-2}y^2, \qquad x^{n-3}y^3, \qquad \dots, \qquad xy^{n-1}, \qquad y^n$$

Note that the sum of the exponents of x and y for each term is n.

Next, let's arrange the **coefficients** in the following triangular formation that yields an easy-to-remember pattern.

$$
\begin{array}{ccccccccccc}
 & & & & 1 & & 1 & & & & \\
 & & & 1 & & 2 & & 1 & & & \\
 & & 1 & & 3 & & 3 & & 1 & & \\
 & 1 & & 4 & & 6 & & 4 & & 1 & \\
1 & & 5 & & 10 & & 10 & & 5 & & 1
\end{array}
$$

The number of the row of the formation contains the coefficients of the expansion of $(x + y)$ to that power. For example, the fifth row contains 1 5 10 10 5 1, which are the coefficients of the terms of the expansion of $(x + y)^5$. Furthermore, each row can be formed from the previous row as follows:

1. Start and end each row with 1.

2. All other entries result from adding the two numbers in the row immediately above, one number to the left and one number to the right.

Thus, from row 5 we can form row 6 as follows:

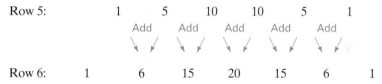

Row 5:   1   5   10   10   5   1
                       Add   Add   Add   Add   Add

Row 6:   1   6   15   20   15   6   1

We can use the row-6 coefficients and our previous discussion relative to the exponents and write out the expansion for $(x + y)^6$.

$$(x + y)^6 = x^6 + 6x^5y + 15x^4y^2 + 20x^3y^3 + 15x^2y^4 + 6xy^5 + y^6$$

Remark: We often refer to the triangular formation of numbers that we have been discussing as Pascal's triangle. This is in honor of Blaise Pascal, a 17th-century mathematician, to whom the discovery of this pattern is attributed.

Although Pascal's triangle will work for any positive integral power of a binomial, it does become somewhat impractical for large powers, so we need another technique for determining the coefficients. Let's look at the following notational agreements. $n!$ (read "n factorial") means $n(n - 1)(n - 2) \dots 1$, where n is any positive integer. For example,

$3!$ means $3 \cdot 2 \cdot 1 = 6$

$5!$ means $5 \cdot 4 \cdot 3 \cdot 2 \cdot 1 = 120$

We also agree that $0! = 1$. (Note that both $0!$ and $1!$ equal 1.)

Let us now use the factorial notation and state the expression of the general case $(x + y)^n$, where n is any positive integer.

$$(x + y)^n = x^n + nx^{n-1}y + \frac{n(n-1)}{2!}x^{n-2}y^2 + \frac{n(n-1)(n-2)}{3!}x^{n-3}y^3$$
$$+ \cdots + y^n$$

The binomial expansion for the general case may look a little confusing, but actually it is quite easy to apply once you try it a few times on some specific examples. Remember the decreasing pattern for the exponents of x and the increasing pattern for the exponents of y. Furthermore, note the pattern of the coefficients:

$$1, \quad n, \quad \frac{n(n-1)}{2!}, \quad \frac{n(n-1)(n-2)}{3!}, \quad \text{etc.}$$

Keep these ideas in mind as you study the following examples.

E X A M P L E   1

Expand $(x + y)^7$.

Solution

We can expand as follows:

$$(x + y)^7 = x^7 + 7x^6y + \frac{7 \cdot 6}{2!}x^5y^2 + \frac{7 \cdot 6 \cdot 5}{3!}x^4y^3 + \frac{7 \cdot 6 \cdot 5 \cdot 4}{4!}x^3y^4 + \frac{7 \cdot 6 \cdot 5 \cdot 4 \cdot 3}{5!}x^2y^5$$

$$+ \frac{7 \cdot 6 \cdot 5 \cdot 4 \cdot 3 \cdot 2}{6!}xy^6 + y^7$$

$$= x^7 + 7x^6y + 21x^5y^2 + 35x^4y^3 + 35x^3y^4 + 21x^2y^5 + 7xy^6 + y^7 \qquad \blacksquare$$

E X A M P L E   2

Expand $(x - y)^5$.

Solution

We shall treat $(x - y)^5$ as $[x + (-y)]^5$.

$$[x + (-y)]^5 = x^5 + 5x^4(-y) + \frac{5 \cdot 4}{2!}x^3(-y)^2 + \frac{5 \cdot 4 \cdot 3}{3!}x^2(-y)^3$$

$$+ \frac{5 \cdot 4 \cdot 3 \cdot 2}{4!}x(-y)^4 + (-y)^5$$

$$= x^5 - 5x^4y + 10x^3y^2 - 10x^2y^3 + 5xy^4 - y^5 \qquad \blacksquare$$

EXAMPLE 3   Expand and simplify $(2a + 3b)^4$.

Solution

Let $x = 2a$ and $y = 3b$.

$$(2a + 3b)^4 = (2a)^4 + 4(2a)^3(3b) + \frac{4 \cdot 3}{2!}(2a)^2(3b)^2 + \frac{4 \cdot 3 \cdot 2}{3!}(2a)(3b)^3 + (3b)^4$$

$$= 16a^4 + 96a^3b + 216a^2b^2 + 216ab^3 + 81b^4 \qquad \blacksquare$$

■ Finding Specific Terms

Sometimes it is convenient to find a specific term of a binomial expansion without writing out the entire expansion. For example, suppose that we need the sixth term of the expansion $(x + y)^{12}$. We could proceed as follows:

The sixth term will contain y^5. (Note in the general expansion that the **exponent of y is always 1 less than the number of the term**.) Because the sum of the exponents for x and y must be 12 (the exponent of the binomial), the sixth term will also contain x^7. Again looking back at the general binomial expansion, note that the **denominators of the coefficients** are of the form $r!$, where the value of r agrees with the exponent of y for each term. Thus if we have y^5, the denominator of the coefficient is 5!. In the general expansion, each **numerator of a coefficient** contains r factors, where the first factor is the exponent of the binomial and each succeeding factor is 1 less than the preceding one. Thus the sixth term of $(x + y)^{12}$ is $\dfrac{12 \cdot 11 \cdot 10 \cdot 9 \cdot 8}{5!}x^7y^5$, which simplifies to $792x^7y^5$.

EXAMPLE 4   Find the fourth term of $(3a + 2b)^7$.

Solution

The fourth term will contain $(2b)^3$ and thus $(3a)^4$. The coefficient is $\dfrac{7 \cdot 6 \cdot 5}{3!}$. Therefore, the fourth term is

$$\frac{7 \cdot 6 \cdot 5}{3!}(3a)^4(2b)^3$$

which simplifies to $22{,}680a^4b^3$. $\qquad \blacksquare$

Problem Set 12.5

For Problems 1–6, use Pascal's triangle to help expand each of the following.

1. $(x + y)^8$

2. $(x + y)^7$

3. $(3x + y)^4$

4. $(x + 2y)^4$

5. $(x - y)^5$

6. $(x - y)^4$

For Problems 7–20, expand and simplify.

7. $(x + y)^{10}$

8. $(x + y)^9$

9. $(2x + y)^6$

10. $(x + 3y)^5$

11. $(x - 3y)^5$

12. $(2x - y)^6$

13. $(3a - 2b)^5$

14. $(2a - 3b)^4$

15. $(x + y^3)^6$

16. $(x^2 + y)^5$

17. $(x + 2)^7$

18. $(x + 3)^6$

19. $(x - 3)^4$

20. $(x - 1)^9$

For Problems 21–24, write the first four terms of the expansion.

21. $(x + y)^{15}$

22. $(x + y)^{12}$

23. $(a - 2b)^{13}$

24. $(x - y)^{20}$

For Problems 25–30, find the indicated term of the expansion.

25. Seventh term of $(x + y)^{11}$

26. Fourth term of $(x + y)^8$

27. Fourth term of $(x - 2y)^6$

28. Fifth term of $(x - y)^9$

29. Third term of $(2x - 5y)^5$

30. Sixth term of $(3a + b)^7$

■ ■ ■ **THOUGHTS INTO WORDS**

31. How would you explain binomial expansions to an elementary algebra student?

32. Explain how to find the fifth term of the expansion of $(2x + 3y)^9$ without writing out the entire expansion.

(12.1) An **infinite sequence** is a function whose domain is the set of positive integers. We frequently express a general infinite sequence as

$$a_1, a_2, a_3, \ldots, a_n, \ldots$$

where a_1 is the first term, a_2 the second term, and so on, and a_n represents the general, or nth, term.

An **arithmetic sequence** is a sequence where there is a **common difference** between successive terms.

The **general term of an arithmetic sequence** is given by

$$a_n = a_1 + (n - 1)d$$

where a_1 is the first term and d is the common difference.

(12.2) The sum of the first n terms of an arithmetic sequence is given by

$$S_n = \frac{n(a_1 + a_n)}{2}$$

(12.3) A **geometric sequence** is a sequence in which each term after the first is obtained by multiplying the preceding term by a common multiplier. The common multiplier is called the **common ratio** of the sequence.

The **general term of a geometric sequence** is given by

$$a_n = a_1 r^{n-1}$$

where a_1 is the first term and r is the common ratio.

The sum of the first n terms of a geometric sequence is given by

$$S_n = \frac{a_1 r^n - a_1}{r - 1}, \qquad r \neq 1$$

(12.4) The sum of an infinite geometric sequence is given by

$$S_\infty = \frac{a_1}{1 - r}, \qquad |r| < 1$$

Any infinite geometric sequence where $|r| \geq 1$ has no sum.

This sum formula can be used to change repeating decimals to $\dfrac{a}{b}$ form.

(12.5) The expansion of $(x + y)^n$, where n is a positive integer, is given by

$$(x + y)^n = x^n + nx^{n-1}y + \frac{n(n - 1)}{2!}x^{n-2}y^2$$

$$+ \frac{n(n - 1)(n - 2)}{3!}x^{n-3}y^3 + \cdots + y^n$$

To find a specific term of a binomial expansion, review Example 4 of Section 12.5.

Chapter 12 **Review Problem Set**

For Problems 1–10, find the general term (nth term) for each of the following sequences. These problems contain a mixture of arithmetic and geometric sequences.

1. $3, 9, 15, 21, \ldots$

2. $\dfrac{1}{3}, 1, 3, 9, \ldots$

3. $10, 20, 40, 80, \ldots$

4. $5, 2, -1, -4, \ldots$

5. $-5, -3, -1, 1, \ldots$

6. $9, 3, 1, \dfrac{1}{3}, \ldots$

7. $-1, 2, -4, 8, \ldots$

8. $12, 15, 18, 21, \ldots$

9. $\dfrac{2}{3}, 1, \dfrac{4}{3}, \dfrac{5}{3}, \ldots$

10. $1, 4, 16, 64, \ldots$

For Problems 11–16, find the indicated term of each of the sequences.

11. The 19th term of $1, 5, 9, 13, \ldots$

12. The 28th term of $-2, 2, 6, 10, \ldots$

13. The 9th term of $8, 4, 2, 1, \ldots$

14. The 8th term of $\dfrac{243}{32}, \dfrac{81}{16}, \dfrac{27}{8}, \dfrac{9}{4}, \ldots$

15. The 34th term of $7, 4, 1, -2, \ldots$

16. The 10th term of $-32, 16, -8, 4, \ldots$

17. If the 5th term of an arithmetic sequence is -19, and the 8th term is -34, find the common difference of the sequence.

18. If the 8th term of an arithmetic sequence is 37 and the 13th term is 57, find the 20th term.

19. Find the first term of a geometric sequence if the 3rd term is 5 and the 6th term is 135.

20. Find the common ratio of a geometric sequence if the 2nd term is $\dfrac{1}{2}$ and the 6th term is 8.

21. Find the sum of the first 9 terms of the sequence $81, 27, 9, 3, \cdots$.

22. Find the sum of the first 70 terms of the sequence $-3, 0, 3, 6, \cdots$.

23. Find the sum of the first 75 terms of the sequence $5, 1, -3, -7, \cdots$.

24. Find the sum of the first 10 terms of the sequence for which $a_n = 2^{5-n}$.

25. Find the sum of the first 95 terms of the sequence for which $a_n = 7n + 1$.

26. Find the sum $5 + 7 + 9 + \cdots + 137$.

27. Find the sum $64 + 16 + 4 + \cdots + \dfrac{1}{64}$.

28. Find the sum of all even numbers between 8 and 384, inclusive.

29. Find the sum of all multiples of 3 between 27 and 276, inclusive.

30. Find the sum of the infinite geometric sequence $64, 16, 4, 1, \cdots$.

31. Change $0.\overline{36}$ to reduced $\dfrac{a}{b}$ form, where a and b are integers, $b \neq 0$.

32. Change $0.4\overline{5}$ to reduced $\dfrac{a}{b}$ form, where a and b are integers, $b \neq 0$.

Solve Problems 33–37 by using your knowledge of arithmetic and geometric sequences.

33. Suppose that at the beginning of the year your savings account contains $3750. If you withdraw $250 per month from the account, how much will it contain at the end of the year?

34. Sonya has decided to start saving dimes. She plans to save 1 dime the first day of April, 2 dimes the second day, 3 dimes the third day, 4 dimes the fourth day, and so on, for the 30 days of April. How much money will she save in April?

35. Nancy has decided to start saving dimes. She plans to save 1 dime the first day of April, 2 dimes the second day, 4 dimes the third day, 8 dimes the fourth day, and so on, for the first 15 days of April. How much will she save in 15 days?

36. A tank contains 61,440 gallons of water. Each day one-fourth of the water is to be drained out. How much will remain in the tank at the end of 6 days?

37. An object, falling from rest in a vacuum, falls 16 feet the first second, 48 feet the second second, 80 feet the third second, 112 feet the fourth second, and so on. How far will the object fall in 15 seconds?

38. Expand $(2x + y)^7$.

39. Expand $(x - 3y)^4$.

40. Find the 5th term of the expansion of $(x + 2y)^8$.

1. Find the 15th term of the sequence for which $a_n = -3n - 1$.

2. Find the 5th term of the sequence for which $a_n = 3(2)^{n-1}$.

3. Find the general term of the sequence $-3, 1, 5, 9, \ldots$.

4. Find the general term of the sequence $5, \dfrac{5}{2}, \dfrac{5}{4}, \dfrac{5}{8}, \ldots$.

5. Find the general term of the sequence $6, 3, 0, -3, \ldots$.

6. Find the 7th term of the sequence $8, 12, 18, 27, \ldots$.

7. Find the 75th term of the sequence $1, 4, 7, 10, \ldots$.

8. Find the number of terms in the sequence $7, 11, 15, \ldots, 243$.

9. If the 4th term of an arithmetic sequence is 13, and the 7th term is 22, find the 15th term.

10. Find the sum of the first 40 terms of the sequence $1, 4, 7, 10, \cdots$.

11. Find the sum of the first 8 terms of the sequence $3, 6, 12, 24, \cdots$.

12. Find the sum of the sequence $3, 1, -1, \cdots, -55$.

13. Find the sum of the sequence $3, 9, 27, \cdots, 2187$.

14. Find the sum of the first 45 terms of the sequence for which $a_n = 7n - 2$.

15. Find the sum of the first 10 terms of the sequence for which $a_n = 3(2)^n$.

16. Find the sum of the first 150 positive even whole numbers.

17. Find the sum of the odd numbers between 11 and 193, inclusive.

18. A woman invests \$350 at 12% simple interest at the beginning of each year for a period of 10 years. Find the total accumulated value of all the investments at the end of the 10-year period.

19. Suppose you save a dime the first day of a month, \$0.20 the second day, and \$0.40 the third day and continue to double how much you save per day for 15 days. Find the total amount that you will have saved at the end of 15 days.

20. Find the sum of the infinite geometric sequence $9, 3, 1, \dfrac{1}{3}, \cdots$.

21. Change the repeating decimal $0.\overline{37}$ to $\dfrac{a}{b}$ form, where a and b are integers and $b \neq 0$.

22. Change the repeating decimal $0.2\overline{6}$ to $\dfrac{a}{b}$ form, where a and b are integers and $b \neq 0$.

23. Expand $(x - 3y)^5$.

24. Write the first three terms of the expansion of $(2x + y)^7$.

25. Find the 5th term of the expansion of $(a + b)^{12}$.

Appendix

A Prime Numbers and Operations with Fractions

This appendix reviews the operations with rational numbers in common fraction form. Throughout this section, we will speak of "multiplying fractions." Be aware that this phrase means multiplying rational numbers in common fraction form. A strong foundation here will simplify your later work in rational expressions. Because prime numbers and prime factorization play an important role in the operations with fractions, let's begin by considering two special kinds of whole numbers, prime numbers and composite numbers.

Definition A.1

A **prime number** is a whole number greater than 1 that has no factors (divisors) other than itself and 1. Whole numbers greater than 1 that are not prime numbers are called **composite numbers**.

The prime numbers less than 50 are 2, 3, 5, 7, 11, 13, 17, 19, 23, 29, 31, 37, 41, 43, and 47. Note that each of these has no factors other than itself and 1. We can express every composite number as the indicated product of prime numbers. Consider the following examples:

$$4 = 2 \cdot 2 \qquad 6 = 2 \cdot 3 \qquad 8 = 2 \cdot 2 \cdot 2 \qquad 10 = 2 \cdot 5 \qquad 12 = 2 \cdot 2 \cdot 3$$

In each case we express a composite number as the indicated product of prime numbers. The indicated-product form is called the prime-factored form of the number. There are various procedures to find the prime factors of a given composite number. For our purposes, the simplest technique is to factor the given composite number into any two easily recognized factors and then continue to factor each of these until we obtain only prime factors. Consider these examples:

$$18 = 2 \cdot 9 = 2 \cdot 3 \cdot 3 \qquad\qquad 27 = 3 \cdot 9 = 3 \cdot 3 \cdot 3$$

$$24 = 4 \cdot 6 = 2 \cdot 2 \cdot 2 \cdot 3 \qquad\qquad 150 = 10 \cdot 15 = 2 \cdot 5 \cdot 3 \cdot 5$$

It does not matter which two factors we choose first. For example, we might start by expressing 18 as $3 \cdot 6$ and then factor 6 into $2 \cdot 3$, which produces a final result of $18 = 3 \cdot 2 \cdot 3$. Either way, 18 contains two prime factors of 3 and one prime factor of 2. The order in which we write the prime factors is not important.

■ Least Common Multiple

It is sometimes necessary to determine the smallest common nonzero multiple of two or more whole numbers. We call this nonzero number the **least common multiple**. In our work with fractions, there will be problems where it will be necessary to find the least common multiple of some numbers, usually the denominators of fractions. So let's review the concepts of multiples. We know that 35 is a multiple of 5 because $5 \cdot 7 = 35$. The set of all whole numbers that are multiples of 5 consists of 0, 5, 10, 15, 20, 25, and so on. In other words, 5 times each successive whole number ($5 \cdot 0 = 0, 5 \cdot 1 = 5, 5 \cdot 2 = 10, 5 \cdot 3 = 15$, etc.) produces the multiples of 5. In a like manner, the set of multiples of 4 consists of 0, 4, 8, 12, 16, and so on. We can illustrate the concept of least common multiple and find the least common multiple of 5 and 4 by using a simple listing of the multiples of 5 and the multiples of 4.

Multiples of 5 are 0, 5, 10, 15, 20, 25, 30, 35, 40, 45, . . .

Multiples of 4 are 0, 4, 8, 12, 16, 20, 24, 28, 32, 36, 40, 44, 48, . . .

The nonzero numbers in common on the lists are 20 and 40. The least of these, 20, is the least common multiple. Stated another way, 20 is the smallest nonzero whole number that is divisible by both 4 and 5.

Often, from your knowledge of arithmetic, you will be able to determine the least common multiple by inspection. For instance, the least common multiple of 6 and 8 is 24. Therefore, 24 is the smallest nonzero whole number that is divisible by both 6 and 8. If we cannot determine the least common multiple by inspection, then using the prime-factorized form of composite numbers is helpful. The procedure is as follows.

Step 1   Express each number as a product of prime factors.

Step 2   The least common multiple contains each different prime factor as many times as the most times it appears in any one of the factorizations from Step 1.

The following examples illustrate this technique for finding the least common multiple of two or more numbers.

EXAMPLE 1   Find the least common multiple of 24 and 36.

Solution

Let's first express each number as a product of prime factors.

$24 = 2 \cdot 2 \cdot 2 \cdot 3$

$36 = 2 \cdot 2 \cdot 3 \cdot 3$

The prime factor 2 occurs the most times (three times) in the factorization of 24. Because the factorization of 24 contains three 2s, the least common multiple must have three 2s. The prime factor 3 occurs the most times (two times) in the factorization of 36. Because the factorization of 36 contains two 3s, the least common multiple must have two 3s. The least common multiple of 24 and 36 is therefore $2 \cdot 2 \cdot 2 \cdot 3 \cdot 3 = 72$. ∎

E X A M P L E   2

Find the least common multiple of 48 and 84.

Solution

$$48 = 2 \cdot 2 \cdot 2 \cdot 2 \cdot 3$$

$$84 = 2 \cdot 2 \cdot 3 \cdot 7$$

We need four 2s in the least common multiple because of the four 2s in 48. We need one 3 because of the 3 in each of the numbers, and we need one 7 because of the 7 in 84. The least common multiple of 48 and 84 is $2 \cdot 2 \cdot 2 \cdot 2 \cdot 3 \cdot 7 = 336$. ∎

E X A M P L E   3

Find the least common multiple of 12, 18, and 28.

Solution

$$28 = 2 \cdot 2 \cdot 7$$

$$18 = 2 \cdot 3 \cdot 3$$

$$12 = 2 \cdot 2 \cdot 3$$

The least common multiple is $2 \cdot 2 \cdot 3 \cdot 3 \cdot 7 = 252$. ∎

E X A M P L E   4

Find the least common multiple of 8 and 9.

Solution

$$9 = 3 \cdot 3$$

$$8 = 2 \cdot 2 \cdot 2$$

The least common multiple is $2 \cdot 2 \cdot 2 \cdot 3 \cdot 3 = 72$. ∎

■ Multiplying Fractions

We can define the multiplication of fractions in common fractional form as follows:

Multiplying Fractions

If a, b, c, and d are integers, with b and d not equal to zero, then $\dfrac{a}{b} \cdot \dfrac{c}{d} = \dfrac{a \cdot c}{b \cdot d}$.

To multiply fractions in common fractional form, we simply multiply numerators and multiply denominators. The following examples illustrate the multiplying of fractions.

$$\frac{1}{3} \cdot \frac{2}{5} = \frac{1 \cdot 2}{3 \cdot 5} = \frac{2}{15}$$

$$\frac{3}{4} \cdot \frac{5}{7} = \frac{3 \cdot 5}{4 \cdot 7} = \frac{15}{28}$$

$$\frac{3}{5} \cdot \frac{5}{3} = \frac{15}{15} = 1$$

The last of these examples is a very special case. If the product of two numbers is 1, then the numbers are said to be reciprocals of each other.

Before we proceed too far with multiplying fractions, we need to learn about reducing fractions. The following property is applied throughout our work with fractions. We call this property the fundamental property of fractions.

Fundamental Property of Fractions

If b and k are nonzero integers, and a is any integer, then $\dfrac{a \cdot k}{b \cdot k} = \dfrac{a}{b}$.

The fundamental property of fractions provides the basis for what is often called reducing fractions to lowest terms, or expressing fractions in simplest or reduced form. Let's apply the property to a few examples.

E X A M P L E   5

Reduce $\dfrac{12}{18}$ to lowest terms.

Solution

$$\frac{12}{18} = \frac{2 \cdot \cancel{6}}{3 \cdot \cancel{6}} = \frac{2}{3}$$ A common factor of 6 has been divided out of both numerator and denominator. ∎

E X A M P L E   6

Change $\dfrac{14}{35}$ to simplest form.

Solution

$$\frac{14}{35} = \frac{2 \cdot \cancel{7}}{5 \cdot \cancel{7}} = \frac{2}{5}$$ A common factor of 7 has been divided out of both numerator and denominator. ∎

EXAMPLE 7

Reduce $\dfrac{72}{90}$.

Solution

$$\frac{72}{90} = \frac{2 \cdot 2 \cdot 2 \cdot 3 \cdot 3}{2 \cdot 3 \cdot 3 \cdot 5} = \frac{4}{5}$$ The prime-factored forms of the numerator and denominator may be used to find common factors.   ■

We are now ready to consider multiplication problems with the understanding that the final answer should be expressed in reduced form. Study the following examples carefully; we use different methods to simplify the problems.

EXAMPLE 8

Multiply $\left(\dfrac{9}{4}\right)\left(\dfrac{14}{15}\right)$.

Solution

$$\left(\frac{9}{4}\right)\left(\frac{14}{15}\right) = \frac{3 \cdot 3 \cdot 2 \cdot 7}{2 \cdot 2 \cdot 3 \cdot 5} = \frac{21}{10}$$ ■

EXAMPLE 9

Find the product of $\dfrac{8}{9}$ and $\dfrac{18}{24}$.

Solution

$$\frac{\overset{1}{\cancel{8}}}{\underset{1}{\cancel{9}}} \cdot \frac{\overset{2}{\cancel{18}}}{\underset{3}{\cancel{24}}} = \frac{2}{3}$$ A common factor of 8 has been divided out of 8 and 24, and a common factor of 9 has been divided out of 9 and 18.   ■

■ Dividing Fractions

The next example motivates a definition for division of rational numbers in fractional form:

$$\frac{\frac{3}{4}}{\frac{2}{3}} = \left(\frac{\frac{3}{4}}{\frac{2}{3}}\right)\left(\frac{\frac{3}{2}}{\frac{3}{2}}\right) = \frac{\left(\frac{3}{4}\right)\left(\frac{3}{2}\right)}{1} = \left(\frac{3}{4}\right)\left(\frac{3}{2}\right) = \frac{9}{8}$$

Note that $\left(\dfrac{\frac{3}{2}}{\frac{3}{2}}\right)$ is a form of 1, and $\dfrac{3}{2}$ is the reciprocal of $\dfrac{2}{3}$. In other words,

$\dfrac{3}{4}$ divided by $\dfrac{2}{3}$ is equivalent to $\dfrac{3}{4}$ times $\dfrac{3}{2}$. The following definition for division now should seem reasonable.

Division of Fractions

> If b, c, and d are nonzero integers, and a is any integer, then $\dfrac{a}{b} \div \dfrac{c}{d} = \dfrac{a}{b} \cdot \dfrac{d}{c}$.

Note that to divide $\dfrac{a}{b}$ by $\dfrac{c}{d}$, we multiply $\dfrac{a}{b}$ times the reciprocal of $\dfrac{c}{d}$, which is $\dfrac{d}{c}$. The next examples demonstrate the important steps of a division problem.

$$\frac{2}{3} \div \frac{1}{2} = \frac{2}{3} \cdot \frac{2}{1} = \frac{4}{3}$$

$$\frac{5}{6} \div \frac{3}{4} = \frac{5}{6} \cdot \frac{4}{3} = \frac{5 \cdot 4}{6 \cdot 3} = \frac{5 \cdot 2 \cdot 2}{2 \cdot 3 \cdot 3} = \frac{10}{9}$$

$$\frac{\frac{6}{7}}{\frac{3}{2}} = \frac{\cancel{6}^{3}}{7} \cdot \frac{1}{\cancel{2}_{1}} = \frac{3}{7}$$

■ Adding and Subtracting Fractions

Suppose that it is one-fifth of a mile between your dorm and the union and two-fifths of a mile between the union and the library along a straight line, as indicated in Figure A.1. The total distance between your dorm and the library is three-fifths of a mile, and we write $\dfrac{1}{5} + \dfrac{2}{5} = \dfrac{3}{5}$.

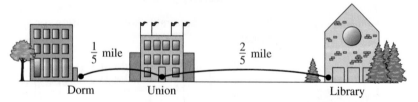

Dorm   Union   Library

Figure A.1

A pizza is cut into seven equal pieces and you eat two of the pieces (see Figure A.2). How much of the pizza remains? We represent the whole pizza by $\dfrac{7}{7}$ and conclude that $\dfrac{7}{7} - \dfrac{2}{7} = \dfrac{5}{7}$ of the pizza remains.

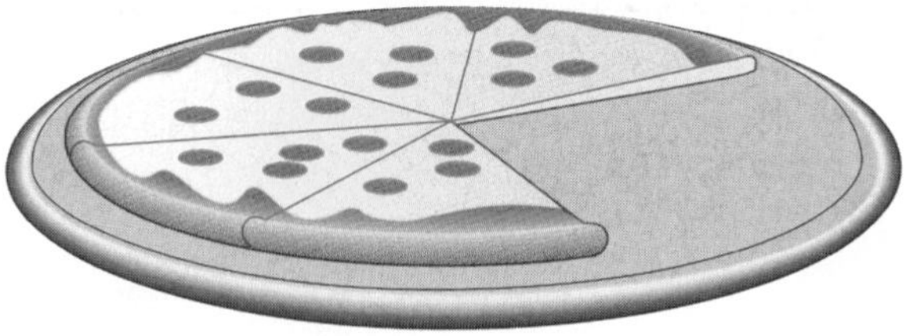

Figure A.2

These examples motivate the following definition for addition and subtraction of rational numbers in $\dfrac{a}{b}$ form.

Addition and Subtraction of Fractions

If a, b, and c are integers, and b is not zero, then

$$\frac{a}{b} + \frac{c}{b} = \frac{a+c}{b} \qquad \text{Addition}$$

$$\frac{a}{b} - \frac{c}{b} = \frac{a-c}{b} \qquad \text{Subtraction}$$

We say that fractions with common denominators can be added or subtracted by adding or subtracting the numerators and placing the results over the common denominator. Consider the following examples:

$$\frac{3}{7} + \frac{2}{7} = \frac{3+2}{7} = \frac{5}{7}$$

$$\frac{7}{8} - \frac{2}{8} = \frac{7-2}{8} = \frac{5}{8}$$

$$\frac{5}{6} - \frac{1}{6} = \frac{5-1}{6} = \frac{4}{6} = \frac{2}{3} \qquad \text{We agree to reduce the final answer.}$$

How do we add or subtract if the fractions do not have a common denominator? We use the fundamental principle of fractions, $\dfrac{a \cdot k}{b \cdot k} = \dfrac{a}{b}$, to get equivalent fractions that have a common denominator. **Equivalent fractions** are fractions that name the same number. Consider the next example, which shows the details.

EXAMPLE 10

Add $\dfrac{1}{4} + \dfrac{2}{5}$.

Solution

$$\frac{1}{4} = \frac{1 \cdot 5}{4 \cdot 5} = \frac{5}{20} \qquad \frac{1}{4} \text{ and } \frac{5}{20} \text{ are equivalent fractions.}$$

$$\frac{2}{5} = \frac{2 \cdot 4}{5 \cdot 4} = \frac{8}{20} \qquad \frac{2}{5} \text{ and } \frac{8}{20} \text{ are equivalent fractions.}$$

$$\frac{5}{20} + \frac{8}{20} = \frac{13}{20}$$

■

Note that in Example 10 we chose 20 as the common denominator, and 20 is the least common multiple of the original denominators 4 and 5. (Recall that the least common multiple is the smallest nonzero whole number divisible by the given numbers.) In general, we use the least common multiple of the denominators of the fractions to be added or subtracted as a **least common denominator** (LCD).

Recall that the least common multiple may be found either by inspection or by using prime factorization forms of the numbers. Consider some examples involving these procedures.

EXAMPLE 11

Subtract $\dfrac{5}{8} - \dfrac{7}{12}$.

Solution

By inspection the LCD is 24.

$$\frac{5}{8} - \frac{7}{12} = \frac{5 \cdot 3}{8 \cdot 3} - \frac{7 \cdot 2}{12 \cdot 2} = \frac{15}{24} - \frac{14}{24} = \frac{1}{24}$$

■

If the LCD is not obvious by inspection, then we can use the technique of prime factorization to find the least common multiple.

EXAMPLE 12

Add $\dfrac{5}{18} + \dfrac{7}{24}$.

Solution

If we cannot find the LCD by inspection, then we can use the prime-factorized forms.

$$\left. \begin{array}{l} 18 = 2 \cdot 3 \cdot 3 \\ \\ 24 = 2 \cdot 2 \cdot 2 \cdot 3 \end{array} \right\} \longrightarrow \text{LCD} = 2 \cdot 2 \cdot 2 \cdot 3 \cdot 3 = 72$$

$$\frac{5}{18} + \frac{7}{24} = \frac{5 \cdot 4}{18 \cdot 4} + \frac{7 \cdot 3}{24 \cdot 3} = \frac{20}{72} + \frac{21}{72} = \frac{41}{72}$$

■

EXAMPLE 13

Marcey put $\dfrac{5}{8}$ pound of chemicals in the spa to adjust the water quality. Michael, not realizing Marcey had already put in chemicals, put $\dfrac{3}{14}$ pound of chemicals in the spa. The chemical manufacturer states that you should never add more than 1 pound of chemicals. Have Marcey and Michael together put in more than 1 pound of chemicals?

Solution

Add $\dfrac{5}{8} + \dfrac{3}{14}$.

$$\left.\begin{array}{l} 8 = 2 \cdot 2 \cdot 2 \\[4pt] 14 = 2 \cdot 7 \end{array}\right\} \longrightarrow \text{LCD} = 2 \cdot 2 \cdot 2 \cdot 7 = 56$$

$$\frac{5}{8} + \frac{3}{14} = \frac{5 \cdot 7}{8 \cdot 7} + \frac{3 \cdot 4}{14 \cdot 4} = \frac{35}{56} + \frac{12}{56} = \frac{47}{56}$$

No, Marcey and Michael have not added more than 1 pound of chemicals. ■

■ Simplifying Numerical Expressions

We now consider simplifying numerical expressions that contain fractions. In agreement with the order of operations, first multiplications and divisions are done as they appear from left to right, and then additions and subtractions are performed as they appear from left to right. In these next examples, we show only the major steps. Be sure you can fill in all the details.

EXAMPLE 14

Simplify $\dfrac{3}{4} + \dfrac{2}{3} \cdot \dfrac{3}{5} - \dfrac{1}{2} \cdot \dfrac{1}{5}$.

Solution

$$\frac{3}{4} + \frac{2}{3} \cdot \frac{3}{5} - \frac{1}{2} \cdot \frac{1}{5} = \frac{3}{4} + \frac{2}{5} - \frac{1}{10}$$

$$= \frac{15}{20} + \frac{8}{20} - \frac{2}{20} = \frac{15 + 8 - 2}{20} = \frac{21}{20}$$ ■

EXAMPLE 15

Simplify $\dfrac{5}{8}\left(\dfrac{1}{2} + \dfrac{1}{3}\right)$.

Solution

$$\frac{5}{8}\left(\frac{1}{2} + \frac{1}{3}\right) = \frac{5}{8}\left(\frac{3}{6} + \frac{2}{6}\right) = \frac{5}{8}\left(\frac{5}{6}\right) = \frac{25}{48}$$ ■

Practice Exercises

For Problems 1–12, factor each composite number into a product of prime numbers; for example, $18 = 2 \cdot 3 \cdot 3$.

1. 26   **2.** 16

3. 36   **4.** 80

5. 49   **6.** 92

7. 56   **8.** 144

9. 120   **10.** 84

11. 135   **12.** 98

For Problems 13–24, find the least common multiple of the given numbers.

13. 6 and 8   **14.** 8 and 12

15. 12 and 16   **16.** 9 and 12

17. 28 and 35   **18.** 42 and 66

19. 49 and 56   **20.** 18 and 24

21. 8, 12, and 28   **22.** 6, 10, and 12

23. 9, 15, and 18   **24.** 8, 14, and 24

For Problems 25–30, reduce each fraction to lowest terms.

25. $\dfrac{8}{12}$ **26.** $\dfrac{12}{16}$

27. $\dfrac{16}{24}$ **28.** $\dfrac{18}{32}$

29. $\dfrac{15}{9}$ **30.** $\dfrac{48}{36}$

For Problems 31–36, multiply or divide as indicated, and express answers in reduced form.

31. $\dfrac{3}{4} \cdot \dfrac{5}{7}$ **32.** $\dfrac{4}{5} \cdot \dfrac{3}{11}$

33. $\dfrac{2}{7} \div \dfrac{3}{5}$ **34.** $\dfrac{5}{6} \div \dfrac{11}{13}$

35. $\dfrac{3}{8} \cdot \dfrac{12}{15}$ **36.** $\dfrac{4}{9} \cdot \dfrac{3}{2}$

37. A certain recipe calls for $\dfrac{3}{4}$ cup of milk. To make half of the recipe, how much milk is needed?

38. John is adding a diesel fuel additive to his fuel tank, which is half full. The directions say to add $\dfrac{1}{3}$ of the bottle to a full fuel tank. What portion of the bottle should he add to the fuel tank?

39. Mark shares a computer with his roommates. He has partitioned the hard drive in such a way that he gets $\dfrac{1}{3}$ of the disk space. His part of the hard drive is currently $\dfrac{2}{3}$ full. What portion of the computer's hard drive space is he currently taking up?

40. Angelina teaches $\dfrac{2}{3}$ of the deaf children in her local school. Her local school educates $\dfrac{1}{2}$ of the deaf children in the school district. What portion of the school district's deaf children is Angelina teaching?

For Problems 41–57, add or subtract as indicated and express answers in lowest terms.

41. $\dfrac{2}{7} + \dfrac{3}{7}$ **42.** $\dfrac{3}{11} + \dfrac{5}{11}$

43. $\dfrac{7}{9} - \dfrac{2}{9}$ **44.** $\dfrac{11}{13} - \dfrac{6}{13}$

45. $\dfrac{3}{4} + \dfrac{9}{4}$ **46.** $\dfrac{5}{6} + \dfrac{7}{6}$

47. $\dfrac{11}{12} - \dfrac{3}{12}$ **48.** $\dfrac{13}{16} - \dfrac{7}{16}$

49. $\dfrac{5}{24} + \dfrac{11}{24}$ **50.** $\dfrac{7}{36} + \dfrac{13}{36}$

51. $\dfrac{1}{3} + \dfrac{1}{5}$ **52.** $\dfrac{1}{6} + \dfrac{1}{8}$

53. $\dfrac{15}{16} - \dfrac{3}{8}$ **54.** $\dfrac{13}{12} - \dfrac{1}{6}$

55. $\dfrac{7}{10} + \dfrac{8}{15}$ **56.** $\dfrac{7}{12} + \dfrac{5}{8}$

57. $\dfrac{11}{24} + \dfrac{5}{32}$

58. Alicia and her brother Jeff shared a pizza. Alicia ate $\frac{1}{8}$ of the pizza, while Jeff ate $\frac{2}{3}$ of the pizza. How much of the pizza has been eaten?

59. Rosa has $\frac{1}{3}$ pound of blueberries, $\frac{1}{4}$ pound of strawberries, and $\frac{1}{2}$ pound of raspberries. If she combines these for a fruit salad, how many pounds of these berries will be in the salad?

60. A chemist has $\frac{11}{16}$ of an ounce of dirt residue to perform crime lab tests. He needs $\frac{3}{8}$ of an ounce to perform a test for iron content. How much of the dirt residue will be left for the chemist to use in other testing?

For Problems 61–68, simplify each numerical expression, expressing answers in reduced form.

61. $\frac{1}{4} - \frac{3}{8} + \frac{5}{12} - \frac{1}{24}$

62. $\frac{3}{4} + \frac{2}{3} - \frac{1}{6} + \frac{5}{12}$

63. $\frac{5}{6} + \frac{2}{3} \cdot \frac{3}{4} - \frac{1}{4} \cdot \frac{2}{5}$

64. $\frac{2}{3} + \frac{1}{2} \cdot \frac{2}{5} - \frac{1}{3} \cdot \frac{1}{5}$

65. $\frac{3}{4} \cdot \frac{6}{9} - \frac{5}{6} \cdot \frac{8}{10} + \frac{2}{3} \cdot \frac{6}{8}$

66. $\frac{3}{5} \cdot \frac{5}{7} + \frac{2}{3} \cdot \frac{3}{5} - \frac{1}{7} \cdot \frac{2}{5}$

67. $\frac{7}{13}\left(\frac{2}{3} - \frac{1}{6}\right)$

68. $48\left(\frac{5}{12} - \frac{1}{6} + \frac{3}{8}\right)$

69. Blake Scott leaves $\frac{1}{4}$ of his estate to the Boy Scouts, $\frac{2}{5}$ to the local cancer fund, and the rest to his church. What fractional part of the estate does the church receive?

70. Franco has $\frac{7}{8}$ of an ounce of gold. He wants to give $\frac{3}{16}$ of an ounce to his friend Julie. He plans to divide the remaining amount of his gold in half to make two rings. How much gold will he have for each ring?

Answers to Odd-Numbered Problems and All Chapter Review, Chapter Test, Cumulative Review, and Appendix Problems

CHAPTER 1

Problem Set 1.1 (page 10)

1. True **3.** False **5.** True **7.** False **9.** True
11. 0 and 14 **13.** $0, 14, \frac{2}{3}, -\frac{11}{14}, 2.34, 3.2\overline{1}, \frac{55}{8}, -19$, and
-2.6 **15.** 0 and 14 **17.** All of them **19.** $\not\subseteq$ **21.** $\subseteq$
23. $\not\subseteq$ **25.** $\subseteq$ **27.** $\not\subseteq$ **29.** Real, rational, an integer,
and negative **31.** Real, irrational, and negative
33. $\{1, 2\}$ **35.** $\{0, 1, 2, 3, 4, 5\}$ **37.** $\{\ldots, -1, 0, 1, 2\}$
39. $\varnothing$ **41.** $\{0, 1, 2, 3, 4\}$ **43.** -6 **45.** 2 **47.** $3x + 1$
49. $5x$ **51.** 26 **53.** 84 **55.** 23 **57.** 65 **59.** 60 **61.** 33
63. 1320 **65.** 20 **67.** 119 **69.** 18 **71.** 4 **73.** 31

Problem Set 1.2 (page 20)

1. -7 **3.** -19 **5.** -22 **7.** -7 **9.** 108 **11.** -70
13. 14 **15.** -7 **17.** $3\frac{1}{2}$ **19.** $5\frac{1}{2}$ **21.** $-\frac{2}{15}$ **23.** -4
25. 0 **27.** Undefined **29.** -60 **31.** -4.8 **33.** 14.13
35. -6.5 **37.** -38.88 **39.** 0.2 **41.** $-\frac{13}{12}$ **43.** $-\frac{3}{4}$
45. $-\frac{13}{9}$ **47.** $-\frac{3}{5}$ **49.** $-\frac{3}{2}$ **51.** -12 **53.** -24 **55.** $\frac{35}{4}$
57. 15 **59.** -17 **61.** $\frac{47}{12}$ **63.** 5 **65.** 0 **67.** 26 **69.** 6
71. 25 **73.** 78 **75.** -10 **77.** 5 **79.** -5 **81.** 10.5
83. -3.3 **85.** 19.5 **87.** $\frac{3}{4}$ **89.** $\frac{5}{2}$ **93.** 10 over par
95. Lost \$16.50 **97.** A gain of 0.88 dollar
99. No; they made it 49.1 pounds lighter

Problem Set 1.3 (page 28)

1. Associative property of addition
3. Commutative property of addition
5. Additive inverse property

7. Multiplication property of negative one
9. Commutative property of multiplication
11. Distributive property
13. Associative property of multiplication
15. 18 **17.** 2 **19.** -1300 **21.** 1700 **23.** -47 **25.** 3200
27. -19 **29.** -41 **31.** -17 **33.** -39 **35.** 24 **37.** 20
39. 55 **41.** 16 **43.** 49 **45.** -216 **47.** -14 **49.** -8
51. $\frac{3}{16}$ **53.** $-\frac{10}{9}$ **57.** 2187 **59.** -2048 **61.** $-15,625$
63. 3.9525416

Problem Set 1.4 (page 37)

1. $4x$ **3.** $-a^2$ **5.** $-6n$ **7.** $-5x + 2y$ **9.** $6a^2 + 5b^2$
11. $21x - 13$ **13.** $-2a^2b - ab^2$ **15.** $8x + 21$
17. $-5a + 2$ **19.** $-5n^2 + 11$ **21.** $-7x^2 + 32$
23. $22x - 3$ **25.** $-14x - 7$ **27.** $-10n^2 + 4$
29. $4x - 30y$ **31.** $-13x - 31$ **33.** $-21x - 9$ **35.** -17
37. 12 **39.** 4 **41.** 3 **43.** -38 **45.** -14 **47.** 64
49. 104 **51.** 5 **53.** 4 **55.** $-\frac{22}{3}$ **57.** $\frac{29}{4}$
59. 221.6 **61.** 1092.4 **63.** 1420.5 **65.** $n + 12$
67. $n - 5$ **69.** $50n$ **71.** $\frac{1}{2}n - 4$ **73.** $\frac{n}{8}$ **75.** $2n - 9$
77. $10(n - 6)$ **79.** $n + 20$ **81.** $2t - 3$ **83.** $n + 47$
85. $8y$ **87.** 25 cm **89.** $\frac{c}{25}$ **91.** $n + 2$ **93.** $\frac{c}{5}$
95. $12d$ **97.** $3y + f$ **99.** $5280m$

Chapter 1 Review Problem Set (page 41)

1. (a) 67 **(b)** $0, -8$, and 67 **(c)** 0 and 67
(d) $0, \frac{3}{4}, -\frac{5}{6}, \frac{25}{3}, -8, 0.34, 0.2\overline{3}, 67$, and $\frac{9}{7}$
(e) $\sqrt{2}$ and $-\sqrt{3}$
2. Associative property for addition
3. Substitution property of equality
4. Multiplication property of negative one

5. Distributive property
6. Associative property for multiplication
7. Commutative property for addition
8. Distributive property
9. Multiplicative inverse property
10. Symmetric property of equality

11. $-6\frac{1}{2}$ 12. $-6\frac{1}{6}$ 13. -8 14. -15 15. 20 16. 49

17. -56 18. -24 19. 6 20. 4 21. 100 22. 8

23. $-4a^2 - 5b^2$ 24. $3x - 2$ 25. ab^2 26. $-\frac{7}{3}x^2y$

27. $10n^2 - 17$ 28. $-13a + 4$ 29. $-2n + 2$

30. $-7x - 29y$ 31. $-7a - 9$ 32. $-9x^2 + 7$ 33. $-6\frac{1}{2}$

34. $-\frac{5}{16}$ 35. -55 36. 144 37. -16 38. -44

39. 19.4 40. 59.6 41. $-\frac{59}{3}$ 42. $\frac{9}{2}$ 43. $4 + 2n$

44. $3n - 50$ 45. $\frac{2}{3}n - 6$ 46. $10(n - 14)$ 47. $5n - 8$

48. $\frac{n}{n-3}$ 49. $5(n + 2) - 3$ 50. $\frac{3}{4}(n + 12)$

51. $37 - n$ 52. $\frac{w}{60}$ 53. $2y - 7$ 54. $n + 3$

55. $p + 5n + 25q$ 56. $\frac{i}{48}$ 57. $24f + 72y$ 58. $10d$

59. $12f + i$ 60. $25 - c$

Chapter 1 Test (page 43)

1. Symmetric property   2. Distributive property   3. -3

4. -23 5. $-\frac{23}{6}$ 6. 11 7. 8 8. -94 9. -4 10. 960

11. -32 12. $-x^2 - 8x - 2$ 13. $-19n - 20$ 14. 27

15. $\frac{11}{16}$ 16. $\frac{2}{3}$ 17. 77 18. -22.5 19. 93 20. -5

21. $6n - 30$ 22. $3n + 28$ or $3(n + 8) + 4$ 23. $\frac{72}{n}$

24. $5n + 10d + 25q$ 25. $6x + 2y$

CHAPTER 2

Problem Set 2.1 (page 51)

1. $\{4\}$ 3. $\{-3\}$ 5. $\{-14\}$ 7. $\{6\}$ 9. $\left\{\frac{19}{3}\right\}$ 11. $\{1\}$

13. $\left\{-\frac{10}{3}\right\}$ 15. $\{4\}$ 17. $\left\{-\frac{13}{3}\right\}$ 19. $\{3\}$ 21. $\{8\}$

23. $\{-9\}$ 25. $\{-3\}$ 27. $\{0\}$ 29. $\left\{-\frac{7}{2}\right\}$ 31. $\{-2\}$

33. $\left\{-\frac{5}{3}\right\}$ 35. $\left\{\frac{33}{2}\right\}$ 37. $\{-35\}$ 39. $\left\{\frac{1}{2}\right\}$ 41. $\left\{\frac{1}{6}\right\}$

43. $\{5\}$ 45. $\{-1\}$ 47. $\left\{-\frac{21}{16}\right\}$ 49. $\left\{\frac{12}{7}\right\}$ 51. 14

53. $13, 14,$ and 15 55. $9, 11,$ and 13 57. 14 and 81

59. $\$11$ per hour   61. 30 pennies, 50 nickels, and 70 dimes

63. $\$300$ 65. 20 three-bedroom, 70 two-bedroom, and 140 one-bedroom   73. **(a)** $\varnothing$ **(c)** $\{0\}$ **(e)** $\varnothing$

Problem Set 2.2 (page 59)

1. $\{12\}$ 3. $\left\{-\frac{3}{5}\right\}$ 5. $\{3\}$ 7. $\{-2\}$ 9. $\{-36\}$ 11. $\left\{\frac{20}{9}\right\}$

13. $\{3\}$ 15. $\{3\}$ 17. $\{-2\}$ 19. $\left\{\frac{8}{5}\right\}$ 21. $\{-3\}$

23. $\left\{\frac{48}{17}\right\}$ 25. $\left\{\frac{103}{6}\right\}$ 27. $\{3\}$ 29. $\left\{\frac{40}{3}\right\}$ 31. $\left\{-\frac{20}{7}\right\}$

33. $\left\{\frac{24}{5}\right\}$ 35. $\{-10\}$ 37. $\left\{-\frac{25}{4}\right\}$ 39. $\{0\}$ 41. 18

43. 16 inches long and 5 inches wide   45. $14, 15,$ and 16

47. 8 feet   49. Angie is 22 and her mother is 42.

51. Sydney is 18 and Marcus is 36.   53. $80, 90,$ and 94

55. $48°$ and $132°$ 57. $78°$

Problem Set 2.3 (page 67)

1. $\{20\}$ 3. $\{50\}$ 5. $\{40\}$ 7. $\{12\}$ 9. $\{6\}$ 11. $\{400\}$

13. $\{400\}$ 15. $\{38\}$ 17. $\{6\}$ 19. $\{3000\}$ 21. $\{3000\}$

23. $\{400\}$ 25. $\{14\}$ 27. $\{15\}$ 29. $\$90$ 31. $\$54.40$

33. $\$48$ 35. $\$400$ 37. 65% 39. 62.5% 41. $\$32,500$

43. $\$3000$ at 10% and $\$4500$ at 11% 45. $\$53,000$

47. 8 pennies, 15 nickels, and 18 dimes

49. 15 dimes, 45 quarters, and 10 half-dollars   55. $\{7.5\}$

57. $\{-4775\}$ 59. $\{8.7\}$ 61. $\{17.1\}$ 63. $\{13.5\}$

Problem Set 2.4 (page 77)

1. $\$120$ 3. 3 years   5. 6% 7. $\$800$ 9. $\$1600$

11. 8% 13. $\$200$ 15. 6 feet; 14 feet; 10 feet; 20 feet; 7 feet; 2 feet   17. $h = \frac{V}{B}$ 19. $h = \frac{V}{\pi r^2}$ 21. $r = \frac{C}{2\pi}$

23. $C = \frac{100M}{I}$ 25. $C = \frac{5}{9}(F - 32)$ or $C = \frac{5F - 160}{9}$

27. $x = \frac{y - b}{m}$ 29. $x = \frac{y - y_1 + mx_1}{m}$

31. $x = \frac{ab + bc}{b - a}$ 33. $x = a + bc$ 35. $x = \frac{3b - 6a}{2}$

37. $x = \frac{5y + 7}{2}$ 39. $y = -7x - 4$ 41. $x = \frac{6y + 4}{3}$

43. $x = \dfrac{cy - ac - b^2}{b}$ **45.** $y = \dfrac{x - a + 1}{a - 3}$

47. 22 meters long and 6 meters wide   **49.** $11\frac{1}{9}$ years

51. $11\frac{1}{9}$ years   **53.** 4 hours   **55.** 3 hours   **57.** 40 miles

59. 15 quarts of 30% solution and 5 quarts of 70% solution
61. 25 milliliters   **67.** $596.25   **69.** 1.5 years   **71.** 14.5%
73. $1850

Problem Set 2.5 (page 86)
1. $(1, \infty)$

3. $[-1, \infty)$

5. $(-\infty, -2)$

7. $(-\infty, 2]$

9. $x < 4$ **11.** $x \leq -7$ **13.** $x > 8$ **15.** $x \geq -7$
17. $(1, \infty)$

19. $(-\infty, -4]$

21. $(-\infty, -2]$

23. $(-\infty, 2)$

25. $(-1, \infty)$

27. $[-1, \infty)$

29. $(-2, \infty)$

31. $(-2, \infty)$

33. $(-\infty, -2)$

35. $[-3, \infty)$

37. $(0, \infty)$

39. $[4, \infty)$

41. $\left(\dfrac{7}{2}, \infty\right)$ **43.** $\left(\dfrac{12}{5}, \infty\right)$ **45.** $\left(-\infty, -\dfrac{5}{2}\right]$

47. $\left[\dfrac{5}{12}, \infty\right)$ **49.** $(-6, \infty)$ **51.** $(-5, \infty)$

53. $\left(-\infty, \dfrac{5}{3}\right)$ **55.** $(-36, \infty)$ **57.** $\left(-\infty, -\dfrac{8}{17}\right]$

59. $\left(-\dfrac{11}{2}, \infty\right)$ **61.** $(23, \infty)$ **63.** $(-\infty, 3)$

65. $\left(-\infty, -\dfrac{1}{7}\right]$ **67.** $(-22, \infty)$ **69.** $\left(-\infty, \dfrac{6}{5}\right)$

Problem Set 2.6 (page 94)
1. $(4, \infty)$ **3.** $\left(-\infty, \dfrac{23}{3}\right)$ **5.** $[5, \infty)$ **7.** $[-9, \infty)$

9. $\left(-\infty, -\dfrac{37}{3}\right]$ **11.** $\left(-\infty, -\dfrac{19}{6}\right)$ **13.** $(-\infty, 50]$

15. $(300, \infty)$ **17.** $[4, \infty)$
19. $(-1, 2)$

21. $(-1, 2]$

23. $(-\infty, -1) \cup (2, \infty)$

25. $(-\infty, 1] \cup (3, \infty)$

27. $(0, \infty)$

29. $\varnothing$

31. $(-\infty, \infty)$

33. $(-1, \infty)$

35. $(1, 3)$

37. $(-\infty, -5) \cup (1, \infty)$

39. $[3, \infty)$

41. $\left(\dfrac{1}{3}, \dfrac{2}{5}\right)$

43. $(-\infty, -1) \cup \left(-\dfrac{1}{3}, \infty\right)$

45. $(-2, 2)$ **47.** $[-5, 4]$ **49.** $\left(-\dfrac{1}{2}, \dfrac{3}{2}\right)$

51. $\left(-\dfrac{1}{4}, \dfrac{11}{4}\right)$ **53.** $[-11, 13]$ **55.** $(-1, 5)$

57. More than 10% **59.** 5 feet and 10 inches or better
61. 168 or better **63.** 77 or less **65.** $163°F \le C \le 218°F$
67. $6.3 \le M \le 11.25$

Problem Set 2.7 (page 101)
1. $(-5, 5)$

3. $[-2, 2]$

5. $(-\infty, -2) \cup (2, \infty)$

7. $(-1, 3)$

9. $[-6, 2]$

11. $(-\infty, -3) \cup (-1, \infty)$

13. $(-\infty, 1] \cup [5, \infty)$

15. $\{-7, 9\}$ **17.** $(-\infty, -4) \cup (8, \infty)$ **19.** $(-8, 2)$
21. $\{-1, 5\}$ **23.** $[-4, 5]$ **25.** $\left(-\infty, -\dfrac{7}{2}\right] \cup \left[\dfrac{5}{2}, \infty\right)$
27. $\left\{-5, \dfrac{7}{3}\right\}$ **29.** $\{-1, 5\}$ **31.** $(-\infty, -2) \cup (6, \infty)$
33. $\left(-\dfrac{1}{2}, \dfrac{3}{2}\right)$ **35.** $\left[-5, \dfrac{7}{5}\right]$ **37.** $\left\{\dfrac{1}{12}, \dfrac{17}{12}\right\}$ **39.** $[-3, 10]$
41. $(-5, 11)$ **43.** $\left(-\infty, -\dfrac{3}{2}\right) \cup \left(\dfrac{1}{2}, \infty\right)$ **45.** $\{0, 3\}$
47. $\{-6, 2\}$ **49.** $\left\{\dfrac{3}{4}\right\}$ **51.** $(-\infty, -14] \cup [0, \infty)$
53. $[-2, 3]$ **55.** $\varnothing$ **57.** $(-\infty, \infty)$ **59.** $\left\{\dfrac{2}{5}\right\}$ **61.** $\varnothing$
63. $\varnothing$ **69.** $\left\{-2, -\dfrac{4}{3}\right\}$ **71.** $\{-2\}$ **73.** $\{0\}$

Chapter 2 Review Problem Set (page 104)

1. $\{18\}$ **2.** $\{-14\}$ **3.** $\{0\}$ **4.** $\left\{\dfrac{1}{2}\right\}$ **5.** $\{10\}$ **6.** $\left\{\dfrac{7}{3}\right\}$
7. $\left\{\dfrac{28}{17}\right\}$ **8.** $\left\{-\dfrac{1}{38}\right\}$ **9.** $\left\{\dfrac{27}{17}\right\}$ **10.** $\left\{-\dfrac{10}{3}, 4\right\}$
11. $\{50\}$ **12.** $\left\{-\dfrac{39}{2}\right\}$ **13.** $\{200\}$ **14.** $\{-8\}$
15. $\left\{-\dfrac{7}{2}, \dfrac{1}{2}\right\}$ **16.** $x = \dfrac{2b + 2}{a}$ **17.** $x = \dfrac{c}{a - b}$

18. $x = \dfrac{pb - ma}{m - p}$ **19.** $x = \dfrac{11 + 7y}{5}$

20. $x = \dfrac{by + b + ac}{c}$ **21.** $s = \dfrac{A - \pi r^2}{\pi r}$

22. $b_2 = \dfrac{2A - hb_1}{h}$ **23.** $n = \dfrac{2S_n}{a_1 + a_2}$ **24.** $R = \dfrac{R_1 R_2}{R_1 + R_2}$

25. $[-5, \infty)$ **26.** $(4, \infty)$ **27.** $\left(-\dfrac{7}{3}, \infty\right)$ **28.** $\left[\dfrac{17}{2}, \infty\right)$

29. $\left(-\infty, \dfrac{1}{3}\right)$ **30.** $\left(\dfrac{53}{11}, \infty\right)$ **31.** $[6, \infty)$ **32.** $(-\infty, 100]$

33. $(-5, 6)$ **34.** $\left(-\infty, -\dfrac{11}{3}\right) \cup (3, \infty)$ **35.** $(-\infty, -17)$

36. $\left(-\infty, -\dfrac{15}{4}\right)$

37. ⟨number line with open interval between -1 and 1⟩

38. ⟨number line, -3 and 2⟩

39. ⟨number line, 3⟩

40. ⟨number line⟩

41. ⟨number line, -2 and 1⟩

42. ⟨number line, -2 and 1⟩

43. ⟨number line, $\frac{1}{2}$ and 3⟩

44. $\varnothing$ **45.** The length is 15 meters and the width is 7 meters. **46.** $200 at 7% and $300 at 8% **47.** 88 or better **48.** 4, 5, and 6 **49.** $10.50 per hour **50.** 20 nickels, 50 dimes, and 75 quarters **51.** $80°$ **52.** $45.60

53. $6\dfrac{2}{3}$ pints **54.** 55 miles per hour **55.** Sonya for $3\dfrac{1}{4}$ hours and Rita for $4\dfrac{1}{2}$ hours **56.** $6\dfrac{1}{4}$ cups

Chapter 2 Test (page 107)

1. $\{-3\}$ **2.** $\{5\}$ **3.** $\left\{\dfrac{1}{2}\right\}$ **4.** $\left\{\dfrac{16}{5}\right\}$ **5.** $\left\{-\dfrac{14}{5}\right\}$ **6.** $\{-1\}$

7. $\left\{-\dfrac{3}{2}, 3\right\}$ **8.** $\{3\}$ **9.** $\left\{\dfrac{31}{3}\right\}$ **10.** $\{650\}$

11. $y = \dfrac{8x - 24}{9}$ **12.** $h = \dfrac{S - 2\pi r^2}{2\pi r}$

14. $[-4, \infty)$ **15.** $(-\infty, -35]$ **16.** $(-\infty, 10)$

18. $(-\infty, 200]$ **19.** $\left(-1, \dfrac{7}{3}\right)$ **20.** $\left(-\infty, -\dfrac{11}{4}\right] \cup \left[\dfrac{}{4}, \right)$

21. $72 **22.** 19 centimeters **23.** $\dfrac{2}{3}$ of a cup

24. 97 or better **25.** $70°$

CHAPTER 3

Problem Set 3.1 (page 113)

1. 2 **3.** 3 **5.** 2 **7.** 6 **9.** 0 **11.** $10x - 3$
13. $-11t + 5$ **15.** $-x^2 + 2x - 2$ **17.** $17a^2b^2 - 5ab$
19. $-9x + 7$ **21.** $-2x + 6$ **23.** $10a + 7$
25. $4x^2 + 10x + 6$ **27.** $-6a^2 + 12a + 14$
29. $3x^3 + x^2 + 13x - 11$ **31.** $7x + 8$ **33.** $-3x - 16$
35. $2x^2 - 2x - 8$ **37.** $-3x^3 + 5x^2 - 2x + 9$
39. $5x^2 - 4x + 11$ **41.** $-6x^2 + 9x + 7$
43. $-2x^2 + 9x + 4$ **45.** $-10n^2 + n + 9$ **47.** $8x - 2$
49. $8x - 14$ **51.** $-9x^2 - 12x + 4$ **53.** $10x^2 + 13x - 18$
55. $-n^2 - 4n - 4$ **57.** $-x + 6$ **59.** $6x^2 - 4$
61. $-7n^2 + n + 6$ **63.** $t^2 - 4t + 8$ **65.** $4n^2 - n - 12$
67. $-4x - 2y$ **69.** $-x^3 - x^2 + 3x$ **71.** (a) $8x + 4$
(c) $12x + 6$ **73.** $8\pi h + 32\pi$ (a) 226.1 (c) 452.2

Problem Set 3.2 (page 120)

1. $36x^4$ **3.** $-12x^5$ **5.** $4a^3b^4$ **7.** $-3x^3y^2z^6$ **9.** $-30xy^4$

11. $27a^4b^5$ **13.** $-m^3n^3$ **15.** $\dfrac{3}{10}x^3y^6$ **17.** $-\dfrac{3}{20}a^3b^4$

19. $-\dfrac{1}{6}x^3y^4$ **21.** $30x^6$ **23.** $-18x^9$ **25.** $-3x^6y^6$

27. $-24y^9$ **29.** $-56a^4b^2$ **31.** $-18a^3b^3$ **33.** $-10x^7y^7$
35. $50x^5y^2$ **37.** $27x^3y^6$ **39.** $-32x^{10}y^5$ **41.** $x^{16}y^{20}$
43. $a^6b^{12}c^{18}$ **45.** $64a^{12}b^{18}$ **47.** $81x^2y^8$ **49.** $81a^4b^{12}$
51. $-16a^4b^4$ **53.** $-x^6y^{12}z^{18}$ **55.** $-125a^6b^6c^3$
57. $-x^7y^{28}z^{14}$ **59.** $3x^3y^3$ **61.** $-5x^3y^2$ **63.** $9bc^2$
65. $-18xyz^4$ **67.** $-a^2b^3c^2$ **69.** 9 **71.** $-b^2$ **73.** $-18x^3$
75. $6x^{3n}$ **77.** a^{5n+3} **79.** x^{4n} **81.** a^{5n+1} **83.** $-10x^{2n}$
85. $12a^{n+4}$ **87.** $6x^{3n+2}$ **89.** $12x^{n+2}$ **91.** $22x^2; 6x^3$
93. $\pi r^2 - 36\pi$

Problem Set 3.3 (page 127)

1. $10x^2y^3 + 6x^3y^4$ **3.** $-12a^3b^3 + 15a^5b$
5. $24a^4b^5 - 16a^4b^6 + 32a^5b^6$ **7.** $-6x^3y^3 - 3x^4y^4 + x^5y^2$
9. $ax + ay + 2bx + 2by$ **11.** $ac + 4ad - 3bc - 12bd$
13. $x^2 + 16x + 60$ **15.** $y^2 + 6y - 55$ **17.** $n^2 - 5n - 14$

$x^2 - 36$ **21.** $x^2 - 12x + 36$ **23.** $x^2 - 14x + 48$
25. $x^3 - 4x^2 + x + 6$ **27.** $x^3 - x^2 - 9x + 9$
29. $t^2 + 18t + 81$ **31.** $y^2 - 14y + 49$
33. $4x^2 + 33x + 35$ **35.** $9y^2 - 1$ **37.** $14x^2 + 3x - 2$
39. $5 + 3t - 2t^2$ **41.** $9t^2 + 42t + 49$ **43.** $4 - 25x^2$
45. $49x^2 - 56x + 16$ **47.** $18x^2 - 39x - 70$
49. $2x^2 + xy - 15y^2$ **51.** $25x^2 - 4a^2$ **53.** $t^3 - 14t - 15$
55. $x^3 + x^2 - 24x + 16$ **57.** $2x^3 + 9x^2 + 2x - 30$
59. $12x^3 - 7x^2 + 25x - 6$
61. $x^4 + 5x^3 + 11x^2 + 11x + 4$
63. $2x^4 - x^3 - 12x^2 + 5x + 4$
65. $x^3 + 6x^2 + 12x + 8$ **67.** $x^3 - 12x^2 + 48x - 64$
69. $8x^3 + 36x^2 + 54x + 27$ **71.** $64x^3 - 48x^2 + 12x - 1$
73. $125x^3 + 150x^2 + 60x + 8$ **75.** $x^{2n} - 16$
77. $x^{2a} + 4x^a - 12$ **79.** $6x^{2n} + x^n - 35$
81. $x^{4a} - 10x^{2a} + 21$ **83.** $4x^{2n} + 20x^n + 25$
87. $2x^2 + 6$ **89.** $4x^3 - 64x^2 + 256x$; $256 - 4x^2$
93. (a) $a^6 + 6a^5b + 15a^4b^2 + 20a^3b^3 + 15a^2b^4 + 6ab^5 + b^6$
(c) $a^8 + 8a^7b + 28a^6b^2 + 56a^5b^3 + 70a^4b^4 + 56a^3b^5 + 28a^2b^6 + 8ab^7 + b^8$

Problem Set 3.4 (page 135)

1. Composite **3.** Prime **5.** Composite **7.** Composite
9. Prime **11.** $2 \cdot 2 \cdot 7$ **13.** $2 \cdot 2 \cdot 11$ **15.** $2 \cdot 2 \cdot 2 \cdot 7$
17. $2 \cdot 2 \cdot 2 \cdot 3 \cdot 3$ **19.** $3 \cdot 29$ **21.** $3(2x + y)$
23. $2x(3x + 7)$ **25.** $4y(7y - 1)$ **27.** $5x(4y - 3)$
29. $x^2(7x + 10)$ **31.** $9ab(2a + 3b)$ **33.** $3x^3y^3(4y - 13x)$
35. $4x^2(2x^2 + 3x - 6)$ **37.** $x(5 + 7x + 9x^3)$
39. $5xy^2(3xy + 4 + 7x^2y^2)$ **41.** $(y + 2)(x + 3)$
43. $(2a + b)(3x - 2y)$ **45.** $(x + 2)(x + 5)$
47. $(a + 4)(x + y)$ **49.** $(a - 2b)(x + y)$
51. $(a - b)(3x - y)$ **53.** $(a + 1)(2x + y)$
55. $(a - 1)(x^2 + 2)$ **57.** $(a + b)(2c + 3d)$
59. $(a + b)(x - y)$ **61.** $(x + 9)(x + 6)$
63. $(x + 4)(2x + 1)$ **65.** $\{-7, 0\}$ **67.** $\{0, 1\}$
69. $\{0, 5\}$ **71.** $\left\{-\dfrac{1}{2}, 0\right\}$ **73.** $\left\{-\dfrac{7}{3}, 0\right\}$ **75.** $\left\{0, \dfrac{5}{4}\right\}$
77. $\left\{0, \dfrac{1}{4}\right\}$ **79.** $\{-12, 0\}$ **81.** $\left\{0, \dfrac{3a}{5b}\right\}$ **83.** $\left\{-\dfrac{3a}{2b}, 0\right\}$
85. $\{a, -2b\}$ **87.** 0 or 7 **89.** 6 units **91.** $\dfrac{4}{\pi}$ units
93. The square is 100 feet by 100 feet, and the rectangle is 50 feet by 100 feet.
95. 6 units **101.** $x^a(2x^a - 3)$ **103.** $y^{2m}(y^m + 5)$
105. $x^{4a}(2x^{2a} - 3x^a + 7)$

Problem Set 3.5 (page 142)

1. $(x + 1)(x - 1)$ **3.** $(4x + 5)(4x - 5)$
5. $(3x + 5y)(3x - 5y)$ **7.** $(5xy + 6)(5xy - 6)$
9. $(2x + y^2)(2x - y^2)$ **11.** $(1 + 12n)(1 - 12n)$

13. $(x + 2 + y)(x + 2 - y)$ **15.** $(2x + y + 1)(2x - y - 1)$
17. $(3a + 2b + 3)(3a - 2b - 3)$ **19.** $-5(2x + 9)$
21. $9(x + 2)(x - 2)$ **23.** $5(x^2 + 1)$ **25.** $8(y + 2)(y - 2)$
27. $ab(a + 3)(a - 3)$ **29.** Not factorable
31. $(n + 3)(n - 3)(n^2 + 9)$ **33.** $3x(x^2 + 9)$
35. $4xy(x + 4y)(x - 4y)$ **37.** $6x(1 + x)(1 - x)$
39. $(1 + xy)(1 - xy)(1 + x^2y^2)$ **41.** $4(x + 4y)(x - 4y)$
43. $3(x + 2)(x - 2)(x^2 + 4)$ **45.** $(a - 4)(a^2 + 4a + 16)$
47. $(x + 1)(x^2 - x + 1)$
49. $(3x + 4y)(9x^2 - 12xy + 16y^2)$
51. $(1 - 3a)(1 + 3a + 9a^2)$ **53.** $(xy - 1)(x^2y^2 + xy + 1)$
55. $(x + y)(x - y)(x^2 - xy + y^2)(x^2 + xy + y^2)$
57. $\{-5, 5\}$ **59.** $\left\{-\dfrac{7}{3}, \dfrac{7}{3}\right\}$ **61.** $\{-2, 2\}$ **63.** $\{-1, 0, 1\}$
65. $\{-2, 2\}$ **67.** $\{-3, 3\}$ **69.** $\{0\}$ **71.** $-3, 0,$ or 3
73. 4 centimeters and 8 centimeters **75.** 10 meters long and 5 meters wide **77.** 6 inches **79.** 8 yards

Problem Set 3.6 (page 150)

1. $(x + 5)(x + 4)$ **3.** $(x - 4)(x - 7)$ **5.** $(a + 9)(a - 4)$
7. $(y + 6)(y + 14)$ **9.** $(x - 7)(x + 2)$ **11.** Not factorable **13.** $(6 - x)(1 + x)$ **15.** $(x + 3y)(x + 12y)$
17. $(a - 8b)(a + 7b)$ **19.** $(3x + 1)(5x + 6)$
21. $(4x - 3)(3x + 2)$ **23.** $(a + 3)(4a - 9)$
25. $(n - 4)(3n + 5)$ **27.** Not factorable
29. $(2n - 7)(5n + 3)$ **31.** $(4x - 5)(2x + 9)$
33. $(1 - 6x)(6 + x)$ **35.** $(5y + 9)(4y - 1)$
37. $(12n + 5)(2n - 1)$ **39.** $(5n + 3)(n + 6)$
41. $(x + 10)(x + 15)$ **43.** $(n - 16)(n - 20)$
45. $(t + 15)(t - 12)$ **47.** $(t^2 - 3)(t^2 - 2)$
49. $(2x^2 - 1)(5x^2 + 4)$ **51.** $(x + 1)(x - 1)(x^2 - 8)$
53. $(3n + 1)(3n - 1)(2n^2 + 3)$
55. $(x + 1)(x - 1)(x + 4)(x - 4)$ **57.** $2(t + 2)(t - 2)$
59. $(4x + 5y)(3x - 2y)$ **61.** $3n(2n + 5)(3n - 1)$
63. $(n - 12)(n - 5)$ **65.** $(6a - 1)^2$ **67.** $6(x^2 + 9)$
69. Not factorable **71.** $(x + y - 7)(x - y + 7)$
73. $(1 + 4x^2)(1 + 2x)(1 - 2x)$ **75.** $(4n + 9)(n + 4)$
77. $n(n + 7)(n - 7)$ **79.** $(x - 8)(x + 1)$
81. $3x(x - 3)(x^2 + 3x + 9)$ **83.** $(x^2 + 3)^2$
85. $(x + 3)(x - 3)(x^2 + 4)$ **87.** $(2w - 7)(3w + 5)$
89. Not factorable **91.** $2n(n^2 + 7n - 10)$
93. $(2x + 1)(y + 3)$ **99.** $(x^a + 3)(x^a + 7)$
101. $(2x^a + 5)^2$ **103.** $(5x^n - 1)(4x^n + 5)$
105. $(x - 4)(x - 2)$ **107.** $(3x - 11)(3x + 2)$
109. $(3x + 4)(5x + 9)$

Problem Set 3.7 (page 156)

1. $\{-3, -1\}$ **3.** $\{-12, -6\}$ **5.** $\{4, 9\}$ **7.** $\{-6, 2\}$
9. $\{-1, 5\}$ **11.** $\{-13, -12\}$ **13.** $\left\{-5, \dfrac{1}{3}\right\}$

15. $\left\{-\dfrac{7}{2}, -\dfrac{2}{3}\right\}$ **17.** $\{0, 4\}$ **19.** $\left\{\dfrac{1}{6}, 2\right\}$ **21.** $\{-6, 0, 6\}$

23. $\{-4, 6\}$ **25.** $\{-4, 4\}$ **27.** $\{-11, 4\}$ **29.** $\{-5, 5\}$

31. $\left\{-\dfrac{5}{3}, -\dfrac{3}{5}\right\}$ **33.** $\left\{-\dfrac{1}{8}, 6\right\}$ **35.** $\left\{\dfrac{3}{7}, \dfrac{5}{4}\right\}$ **37.** $\left\{-\dfrac{2}{7}, \dfrac{4}{5}\right\}$

39. $\left\{-7, \dfrac{2}{3}\right\}$ **41.** $\{-20, 18\}$ **43.** $\left\{-2, -\dfrac{1}{3}, \dfrac{1}{3}, 2\right\}$

45. $\left\{-\dfrac{2}{3}, 16\right\}$ **47.** $\left\{-\dfrac{3}{2}, 1\right\}$ **49.** $\left\{-\dfrac{5}{2}, -\dfrac{4}{3}, 0\right\}$

51. $\left\{-1, \dfrac{5}{3}\right\}$ **53.** $\left\{-\dfrac{3}{2}, \dfrac{1}{2}\right\}$ **55.** 8 and 9 or -9 and -8

57. 7 and 15   **59.** 10 inches by 6 inches
61. -7 and -6 or 6 and 7   **63.** 4 centimeters by
4 centimeters and 6 centimeters by 8 centimeters
65. 3, 4, and 5 units   **67.** 9 inches and 12 inches
69. An altitude of 4 inches and a side 14 inches long
77. (a) 0.28 and 3.73   **(c)** 2.27 and 5.76   **(e)** 0.71

Chapter 3 Review Problem Set (page 160)

1. $5x - 3$ **2.** $3x^2 + 12x - 2$ **3.** $12x^2 - x + 5$
4. $-20x^5y^7$ **5.** $-6a^5b^5$ **6.** $15a^4 - 10a^3 - 5a^2$
7. $24x^2 + 2xy - 15y^2$ **8.** $3x^3 + 7x^2 - 21x - 4$
9. $256x^8y^{12}$ **10.** $9x^2 - 12xy + 4y^2$ **11.** $-8x^6y^9z^3$
12. $-13x^2y$ **13.** $2x + y - 2$
14. $x^4 + x^3 - 18x^2 - x + 35$ **15.** $21 + 26x - 15x^2$
16. $-12a^5b^7$ **17.** $-8a^7b^3$ **18.** $7x^2 + 19x - 36$
19. $6x^3 - 11x^2 - 7x + 2$ **20.** $6x^{4n}$
21. $4x^2 + 20xy + 25y^2$ **22.** $x^3 - 6x^2 + 12x - 8$
23. $8x^3 + 60x^2 + 150x + 125$ **24.** $(x + 7)(x - 4)$
25. $2(t + 3)(t - 3)$ **26.** Not factorable
27. $(4n - 1)(3n - 1)$ **28.** $x^2(x^2 + 1)(x + 1)(x - 1)$
29. $x(x - 12)(x + 6)$ **30.** $2a^2b(3a + 2b - c)$
31. $(x - y + 1)(x + y - 1)$ **32.** $4(2x^2 + 3)$
33. $(4x + 7)(3x - 5)$ **34.** $(4n - 5)^2$ **35.** $4n(n - 2)$
36. $3w(w^2 + 6w - 8)$ **37.** $(5x + 2y)(4x - y)$
38. $16a(a - 4)$ **39.** $3x(x + 1)(x - 6)$
40. $(n + 8)(n - 16)$ **41.** $(t + 5)(t - 5)(t^2 + 3)$
42. $(5x - 3)(7x + 2)$ **43.** $(3 - x)(5 - 3x)$
44. $(4n - 3)(16n^2 + 12n + 9)$
45. $2(2x + 5)(4x^2 - 10x + 25)$ **46.** $\{-3, 3\}$

47. $\{-6, 1\}$ **48.** $\left\{\dfrac{2}{7}\right\}$ **49.** $\left\{-\dfrac{2}{5}, \dfrac{1}{3}\right\}$

50. $\left\{-\dfrac{1}{3}, 3\right\}$ **51.** $\{-3, 0, 3\}$ **52.** $\{-1, 0, 1\}$

53. $\{-7, 9\}$ **54.** $\left\{-\dfrac{4}{7}, \dfrac{2}{7}\right\}$ **55.** $\left\{-\dfrac{4}{5}, \dfrac{5}{6}\right\}$

56. $\{-2, 2\}$ **57.** $\left\{\dfrac{5}{3}\right\}$ **58.** $\{-8, 6\}$

59. $\left\{-5, \dfrac{2}{7}\right\}$ **60.** $\{-8, 5\}$ **61.** $\{-12, 1\}$ **62.** $\varnothing$

63. $\left\{-5, \dfrac{6}{5}\right\}$ **64.** $\{0, 1, 8\}$ **65.** $\left\{-10, \dfrac{1}{4}\right\}$

66. 8, 9, and 10 or -1, 0, and 1   **67.** -6 and 8
68. 13 and 15   **69.** 12 miles and 16 miles   **70.** 4 meters by
12 meters   **71.** 9 rows and 16 chairs per row
72. The side is 13 feet long and the altitude is 6 feet.
73. 3 feet   **74.** 5 centimeters by 5 centimeters and
8 centimeters by 8 centimeters   **75.** 6 inches

Chapter 3 Test (page 162)

1. $2x - 11$ **2.** $-48x^4y^4$ **3.** $-27x^6y^{12}$
4. $20x^2 + 17x - 63$ **5.** $6n^2 - 13n + 6$
6. $x^3 - 12x^2y + 48xy^2 - 64y^3$ **7.** $2x^3 + 11x^2 - 11x - 30$
8. $-14x^3y$ **9.** $(6x - 5)(x + 4)$ **10.** $3(2x + 1)(2x - 1)$
11. $(4 + t)(16 - 4t + t^2)$ **12.** $2x(3 - 2x)(5 + 4x)$
13. $(x - y)(x + 4)$ **14.** $(3n + 8)(8n - 3)$ **15.** $\{-12, 4\}$
16. $\left\{0, \dfrac{1}{4}\right\}$ **17.** $\left\{\dfrac{3}{2}\right\}$ **18.** $\{-4, -1\}$ **19.** $\{-9, 0, 2\}$
20. $\left\{-\dfrac{3}{7}, \dfrac{4}{5}\right\}$ **21.** $\left\{-\dfrac{1}{3}, 2\right\}$ **22.** $\{-2, 2\}$ **23.** 9 inches
24. 15 rows   **25.** 8 feet

Cumulative Review Problem Set (page 163)

1. 4   **2.** -19 **3.** 9   **4.** 21   **5.** -78 **6.** -33 **7.** -43
8. -11 **9.** -39 **10.** 57   **11.** $2x - 11$ **12.** $36a^2b^6$
13. $30x^2 - 37x - 7$ **14.** $-2x^2 - 11x - 12$ **15.** $-64a^6b^9$
16. $5x^3 - 6x^2 - 20x + 24$ **17.** $x^3 - 4x^2 - x + 12$
18. $2x^4 - x^3 - 2x^2 - 19x - 28$ **19.** $7(x + 1)(x - 1)$
20. $(2a - b)^2$ **21.** $(3x + 7)(x - 8)$
22. $(1 - x)(1 + x + x^2)$ **23.** $(y - 5)(x + 2)$
24. $3(x - 4)^2$ **25.** $(4n^2 + 3)(n + 1)(n - 1)$
26. $4x(2x + 3)(4x^2 - 6x + 9)$ **27.** $4(x^2 + 9)$
28. $(3x + 4)(2x - 1)$ **29.** $(3x - 5)^2$
30. $(x + 3y)(2x + 1)$ **31.** $(2a + 3b)(4a^2 - 6ab + 9b^2)$
32. $(x^2 + 4)(x + 2)(x - 2)$ **33.** $2m^2n^2(5m^2 - mn - 2n^2)$
34. $(2y + 7z)(5x - 12)$ **35.** $(3x + 5)(x - 2)$
36. $(5 - 2a)(5 + 2a)$ **37.** $(6x + 5)^2$
38. $(4y + 1)(16y^2 - 4y + 1)$ **39.** $x = \dfrac{2y + 6}{5}$

40. $y = \dfrac{12 - 3x}{4}$ **41.** $h = \dfrac{V - 2\pi r^2}{2\pi r}$ **42.** $R_1 = \dfrac{RR_2}{R_2 - R}$

43. 10.5%   **44.** $-15°$ **45.** $\{-6, 3\}$ **46.** $\left\{-\dfrac{7}{3}, \dfrac{2}{5}\right\}$

47. $\{-4\}$ **48.** $\{-9, 2\}$ **49.** $\{-1, 1\}$ **50.** $\{-10\}$

51. $\{15\}$ **52.** $\left\{-\dfrac{25}{4}\right\}$ **53.** $\left\{-\dfrac{5}{3}, 3\right\}$ **54.** $\{-1, 5\}$

55. $\{400\}$ **56.** $\{-4, 10\}$ **57.** $\{-4, 0, 4\}$

58. $\{-2, 3\}$ **59.** $\left\{-\dfrac{1}{4}, \dfrac{2}{3}\right\}$ **60.** $\{-6, 5\}$ **61.** $\{-5, 0, 2\}$

62. $\left\{\dfrac{17}{12}\right\}$ **63.** $(-22, \infty)$ **64.** $(23, \infty)$

65. $(-\infty, -3) \cup (4, \infty)$ **66.** $\left(-7, \dfrac{7}{3}\right)$ **67.** $(300, \infty)$

68. $\left(-\infty, \dfrac{7}{8}\right]$ **69.** $\left[\dfrac{5}{2}, \infty\right)$ **70.** $\left(-\infty, \dfrac{32}{31}\right)$

71. 7, 9, and 11   **72.** 8 nickels, 15 dimes, 25 quarters
73. 12 and 34   **74.** 62° and 118°   **75.** $400 at 8% and $600
at 9%   **76.** 35 pennies, 40 nickels, 70 dimes
77. 1 hour and 40 minutes   **78.** 25 milliliters
79. 40%   **80.** Better than 88   **81.** 4 inches
82. 7 meters by 14 meters   **83.** 8 rows and 12 chairs
per row   **84.** 9 feet, 12 feet, and 15 feet

CHAPTER 4

Problem Set 4.1 (page 170)

1. $\dfrac{3}{4}$ **3.** $\dfrac{5}{6}$ **5.** $-\dfrac{2}{5}$ **7.** $\dfrac{2}{7}$ **9.** $\dfrac{2x}{7}$ **11.** $\dfrac{2a}{5b}$ **13.** $-\dfrac{y}{4x}$

15. $-\dfrac{9c}{13d}$ **17.** $\dfrac{5x^2}{3y^3}$ **19.** $\dfrac{x-2}{x}$ **21.** $\dfrac{3x+2}{2x-1}$ **23.** $\dfrac{a+5}{a-9}$

25. $\dfrac{n-3}{5n-1}$ **27.** $\dfrac{5x^2+7}{10x}$ **29.** $\dfrac{3x+5}{4x+1}$

31. $\dfrac{3x}{x^2+4x+16}$ **33.** $\dfrac{x+6}{3x-1}$ **35.** $\dfrac{x(2x+7)}{y(x+9)}$

37. $\dfrac{y+4}{5y-2}$ **39.** $\dfrac{3x(x-1)}{x^2+1}$ **41.** $\dfrac{2(x+3y)}{3x(3x+y)}$

43. $\dfrac{3n-2}{7n+2}$ **45.** $\dfrac{4-x}{5+3x}$ **47.** $\dfrac{9x^2+3x+1}{2(x+2)}$

49. $\dfrac{-2(x-1)}{x+1}$ **51.** $\dfrac{y+b}{y+c}$ **53.** $\dfrac{x+2y}{2x+y}$ **55.** $\dfrac{x+1}{x-6}$

57. $\dfrac{2s+5}{3s+1}$ **59.** -1 **61.** $-n-7$ **63.** $-\dfrac{2}{x+1}$

65. -2 **67.** $-\dfrac{n+3}{n+5}$

Problem Set 4.2 (page 176)

1. $\dfrac{1}{10}$ **3.** $-\dfrac{4}{15}$ **5.** $\dfrac{3}{16}$ **7.** $-\dfrac{5}{6}$ **9.** $-\dfrac{2}{3}$

11. $\dfrac{10}{11}$ **13.** $-\dfrac{5x^3}{12y^2}$ **15.** $\dfrac{2a^3}{3b}$ **17.** $\dfrac{3x^3}{4}$

19. $\dfrac{25x^3}{108y^2}$ **21.** $\dfrac{ac^2}{2b^2}$ **23.** $\dfrac{3x}{4y}$ **25.** $\dfrac{3(x^2+4)}{5y(x+8)}$

27. $\dfrac{5(a+3)}{a(a-2)}$ **29.** $\dfrac{3}{2}$ **31.** $\dfrac{3xy}{4(x+6)}$

33. $\dfrac{5(x-2y)}{7y}$ **35.** $\dfrac{5+n}{3-n}$ **37.** $\dfrac{x^2+1}{x^2-10}$

39. $\dfrac{6x+5}{3x+4}$ **41.** $\dfrac{2t^2+5}{2(t^2+1)(t+1)}$ **43.** $\dfrac{t(t+6)}{4t+5}$

45. $\dfrac{n+3}{n(n-2)}$ **47.** $\dfrac{25x^3y^3}{4(x+1)}$ **49.** $\dfrac{2(a-2b)}{a(3a-2b)}$

Problem Set 4.3 (page 184)

1. $\dfrac{13}{12}$ **3.** $\dfrac{11}{40}$ **5.** $\dfrac{19}{20}$ **7.** $\dfrac{49}{75}$ **9.** $\dfrac{17}{30}$ **11.** $-\dfrac{11}{84}$

13. $\dfrac{2x+4}{x-1}$ **15.** 4   **17.** $\dfrac{7y-10}{7y}$ **19.** $\dfrac{5x+3}{6}$

21. $\dfrac{12a+1}{12}$ **23.** $\dfrac{n+14}{18}$ **25.** $-\dfrac{11}{15}$ **27.** $\dfrac{3x-25}{30}$

29. $\dfrac{43}{40x}$ **31.** $\dfrac{20y-77x}{28xy}$ **33.** $\dfrac{16y+15x-12xy}{12xy}$

35. $\dfrac{21+22x}{30x^2}$ **37.** $\dfrac{10n-21}{7n^2}$ **39.** $\dfrac{45-6n+20n^2}{15n^2}$

41. $\dfrac{11x-10}{6x^2}$ **43.** $\dfrac{42t+43}{35t^3}$ **45.** $\dfrac{20b^2-33a^3}{96a^2b}$

47. $\dfrac{14-24y^3+45xy}{18xy^3}$ **49.** $\dfrac{2x^2+3x-3}{x(x-1)}$

51. $\dfrac{a^2-a-8}{a(a+4)}$ **53.** $\dfrac{-41n-55}{(4n+5)(3n+5)}$

55. $\dfrac{-3x+17}{(x+4)(7x-1)}$ **57.** $\dfrac{-x+74}{(3x-5)(2x+7)}$

59. $\dfrac{38x+13}{(3x-2)(4x+5)}$ **61.** $\dfrac{5x+5}{2x+5}$ **63.** $\dfrac{x+15}{x-5}$

65. $\dfrac{-2x-4}{2x+1}$ **67. (a)** -1 **(c)** 0

Problem Set 4.4 (page 193)

1. $\dfrac{7x+20}{x(x+4)}$ **3.** $\dfrac{-x-3}{x(x+7)}$ **5.** $\dfrac{6x-5}{(x+1)(x-1)}$

7. $\dfrac{1}{a+1}$ **9.** $\dfrac{5n+15}{4(n+5)(n-5)}$ **11.** $\dfrac{x^2+60}{x(x+6)}$

13. $\dfrac{11x+13}{(x+2)(x+7)(2x+1)}$ **15.** $\dfrac{-3a+1}{(a-5)(a+2)(a+9)}$

17. $\dfrac{3a^2+14a+1}{(4a-3)(2a+1)(a+4)}$ **19.** $\dfrac{3x^2+20x-111}{(x^2+3)(x+7)(x-3)}$

21. $\dfrac{x+6}{(x-3)^2}$ **23.** $\dfrac{14x-4}{(x-1)(x+1)^2}$

25. $\dfrac{-7y-14}{(y+8)(y-2)}$ **27.** $\dfrac{-2x^2-4x+3}{(x+2)(x-2)}$

29. $\dfrac{2x^2+14x-19}{(x+10)(x-2)}$ **31.** $\dfrac{2n+1}{n-6}$

33. $\dfrac{2x^2 - 32x + 16}{(x+1)(2x-1)(3x-2)}$ **35.** $\dfrac{1}{(n^2+1)(n+1)}$

37. $\dfrac{-16x}{(5x-2)(x-1)}$ **39.** $\dfrac{t+1}{t-2}$ **41.** $\dfrac{2}{11}$

43. $-\dfrac{7}{27}$ **45.** $\dfrac{x}{4}$ **47.** $\dfrac{3y-2x}{4x-7}$ **49.** $\dfrac{6ab^2-5a}{12b^2+2a^2b}$

51. $\dfrac{2y-3xy}{3x+4xy}$ **53.** $\dfrac{3n+14}{5n+19}$ **55.** $\dfrac{5n-17}{4n-13}$

57. $\dfrac{-x+5y-10}{3y-10}$ **59.** $\dfrac{-x+15}{-2x-1}$ **61.** $\dfrac{3a^2-2a+1}{2a-1}$

63. $\dfrac{-x^2+6x-4}{3x-2}$

Problem Set 4.5 (page 200)

1. $3x^3 + 6x^2$ **3.** $-6x^4 + 9x^6$ **5.** $3a^2 - 5a - 8$
7. $-13x^2 + 17x - 28$ **9.** $-3xy + 4x^2y - 8xy^2$
11. $x - 13$ **13.** $x + 20$ **15.** $2x + 1 - \dfrac{3}{x-1}$
17. $5x - 1$ **19.** $3x^2 - 2x - 7$ **21.** $x^2 + 5x - 6$
23. $4x^2 + 7x + 12 + \dfrac{30}{x-2}$ **25.** $x^3 - 4x^2 - 5x + 3$
27. $x^2 + 5x + 25$ **29.** $x^2 - x + 1 + \dfrac{63}{x+1}$
31. $2x^2 - 4x + 7 - \dfrac{20}{x+2}$ **33.** $4a - 4b$
35. $4x + 7 + \dfrac{23x-6}{x^2-3x}$ **37.** $8y - 9 + \dfrac{8y+5}{y^2+y}$
39. $2x - 1$ **41.** $x - 3$ **43.** $5a - 8 + \dfrac{42a-41}{a^2+3a-4}$
45. $2n^2 + 3n - 4$ **47.** $x^4 + x^3 + x^2 + x + 1$
49. $x^3 - x^2 + x - 1$ **51.** $3x^2 + x + 1 + \dfrac{7}{x^2-1}$
53. $x - 6$ **55.** $x + 6$, R $= 14$ **57.** $x^2 - 1$
59. $x^2 - 2x - 3$ **61.** $2x^2 - x - 6$, R $= -6$
63. $x^3 + 7x^2 + 21x + 56$, R $= 167$

Problem Set 4.6 (page 208)

1. $\{2\}$ **3.** $\{-3\}$ **5.** $\{6\}$ **7.** $\left\{-\dfrac{85}{18}\right\}$ **9.** $\left\{\dfrac{7}{10}\right\}$

11. $\{5\}$ **13.** $\{58\}$ **15.** $\left\{\dfrac{1}{4}, 4\right\}$ **17.** $\left\{-\dfrac{2}{5}, 5\right\}$ **19.** $\{-16\}$

21. $\left\{-\dfrac{13}{3}\right\}$ **23.** $\{-3, 1\}$ **25.** $\left\{-\dfrac{5}{2}\right\}$ **27.** $\{-51\}$

29. $\left\{-\dfrac{5}{3}, 4\right\}$ **31.** $\varnothing$ **33.** $\left\{-\dfrac{11}{8}, 2\right\}$ **35.** $\{-29, 0\}$

37. $\{-9, 3\}$ **39.** $\left\{-2, \dfrac{23}{8}\right\}$ **41.** $\left\{\dfrac{11}{23}\right\}$ **43.** $\left\{3, \dfrac{7}{2}\right\}$

45. \$750 and \$1000   **47.** $48°$ and $72°$ **49.** $\dfrac{2}{7}$ or $\dfrac{7}{2}$

51. \$3500   **53.** \$69 for Tammy and \$51.75 for Laura
55. 8 and 82   **57.** 14 feet and 6 feet
59. 690 females and 460 males

Problem Set 4.7 (page 217)

1. $\{-21\}$ **3.** $\{-1, 2\}$ **5.** $\{2\}$ **7.** $\left\{\dfrac{37}{15}\right\}$ **9.** $\{-1\}$

11. $\{-1\}$ **13.** $\left\{0, \dfrac{13}{2}\right\}$ **15.** $\left\{-2, \dfrac{19}{2}\right\}$ **17.** $\{-2\}$

19. $\left\{-\dfrac{1}{5}\right\}$ **21.** $\varnothing$ **23.** $\left\{\dfrac{7}{2}\right\}$ **25.** $\{-3\}$ **27.** $\left\{-\dfrac{7}{9}\right\}$

29. $\left\{-\dfrac{7}{6}\right\}$ **31.** $x = \dfrac{18y-4}{15}$ **33.** $y = \dfrac{-5x+22}{2}$

35. $M = \dfrac{IC}{100}$ **37.** $R = \dfrac{ST}{S+T}$

39. $y = \dfrac{bx-x-3b+a}{a-3}$ **41.** $y = \dfrac{ab-bx}{a}$

43. $y = \dfrac{-2x-9}{3}$

45. 50 miles per hour for Dave and 54 miles per hour for Kent
47. 60 minutes
49. 60 words per minute for Connie and 40 words per minute for Katie
51. Plane B could travel at 400 miles per hour for 5 hours and plane A at 350 miles per hour for 4 hours, or plane B could travel at 250 miles per hour for 8 hours and plane A at 200 miles per hour for 7 hours.
53. 60 minutes for Nancy and 120 minutes for Amy
55. 3 hours
57. 16 miles per hour on the way out and 12 miles per hour on the way back, or 12 miles per hour out and 8 miles per hour back

Chapter 4 Review Problem Set (page 221)

1. $\dfrac{2y}{3x^2}$ **2.** $\dfrac{a-3}{a}$ **3.** $\dfrac{n-5}{n-1}$ **4.** $\dfrac{x^2+1}{x}$ **5.** $\dfrac{2x+1}{3}$

6. $\dfrac{x^2-10}{2x^2+1}$ **7.** $\dfrac{3}{22}$ **8.** $\dfrac{18y+20x}{48y-9x}$ **9.** $\dfrac{3x+2}{3x-2}$

10. $\dfrac{x-1}{2x-1}$ **11.** $\dfrac{2x}{7y^2}$ **12.** $3b$ **13.** $\dfrac{n(n+5)}{n-1}$

14. $\dfrac{x(x-3y)}{x^2+9y^2}$ **15.** $\dfrac{23x-6}{20}$ **16.** $\dfrac{57-2n}{18n}$

17. $\dfrac{3x^2 - 2x - 14}{x(x + 7)}$ **18.** $\dfrac{2}{x - 5}$

19. $\dfrac{5n - 21}{(n - 9)(n + 4)(n - 1)}$ **20.** $\dfrac{6y - 23}{(2y + 3)(y - 6)}$

21. $6x - 1$ **22.** $3x^2 - 7x + 22 - \dfrac{90}{x + 4}$ **23.** $\left\{\dfrac{4}{13}\right\}$

24. $\left\{\dfrac{3}{16}\right\}$ **25.** $\varnothing$ **26.** $\{-17\}$ **27.** $\left\{\dfrac{2}{7}, \dfrac{7}{2}\right\}$ **28.** $\{22\}$

29. $\left\{-\dfrac{6}{7}, 3\right\}$ **30.** $\left\{\dfrac{3}{4}, \dfrac{5}{2}\right\}$ **31.** $\left\{\dfrac{9}{7}\right\}$ **32.** $\left\{-\dfrac{5}{4}\right\}$

33. $y = \dfrac{3x + 27}{4}$ **34.** $y = \dfrac{bx - ab}{a}$ **35.** $525 and $875

36. 20 minutes for Julio and 30 minutes for Dan
37. 50 miles per hour and 55 miles per hour or 8⅓ miles per hour and 13⅓ miles per hour
38. 9 hours **39.** 80 hours **40.** 13 miles per hour

Chapter 4 Test (page 223)

1. $\dfrac{13y^2}{24x}$ **2.** $\dfrac{3x - 1}{x(x - 6)}$ **3.** $\dfrac{2n - 3}{n + 4}$ **4.** $-\dfrac{2x}{x + 1}$ **5.** $\dfrac{3y^2}{8}$

6. $\dfrac{a - b}{4(2a + b)}$ **7.** $\dfrac{x + 4}{5x - 1}$ **8.** $\dfrac{13x + 7}{12}$ **9.** $\dfrac{3x}{2}$

10. $\dfrac{10n - 26}{15n}$ **11.** $\dfrac{3x^2 + 2x - 12}{x(x - 6)}$ **12.** $\dfrac{11 - 2x}{x(x - 1)}$

13. $\dfrac{13n + 46}{(2n + 5)(n - 2)(n + 7)}$ **14.** $3x^2 - 2x - 1$

15. $\dfrac{18 - 2x}{8 + 9x}$ **16.** $y = \dfrac{4x + 20}{3}$ **17.** $\{1\}$ **18.** $\left\{\dfrac{1}{10}\right\}$

19. $\{-35\}$ **20.** $\{-1, 5\}$ **21.** $\left\{\dfrac{5}{3}\right\}$ **22.** $\left\{-\dfrac{9}{13}\right\}$ **23.** $\dfrac{27}{72}$

24. 1 hour **25.** 15 miles per hour

CHAPTER 5

Problem Set 5.1 (page 231)

1. $\dfrac{1}{27}$ **3.** $-\dfrac{1}{100}$ **5.** 81 **7.** -27 **9.** -8 **11.** 1 **13.** $\dfrac{9}{49}$

15. 16 **17.** $\dfrac{1}{1000}$ **19.** $\dfrac{1}{1000}$ **21.** 27 **23.** $\dfrac{1}{125}$ **25.** $\dfrac{9}{8}$

27. $\dfrac{256}{25}$ **29.** $\dfrac{2}{25}$ **31.** $\dfrac{81}{4}$ **33.** 81 **35.** $\dfrac{1}{10,000}$ **37.** $\dfrac{13}{36}$

39. $\dfrac{1}{2}$ **41.** $\dfrac{72}{17}$ **43.** $\dfrac{1}{x^6}$ **45.** $\dfrac{1}{a^3}$ **47.** $\dfrac{1}{a^8}$ **49.** $\dfrac{y^6}{x^2}$

51. $\dfrac{c^8}{a^4 b^{12}}$ **53.** $\dfrac{y^{12}}{8x^9}$ **55.** $\dfrac{x^3}{y^{12}}$ **57.** $\dfrac{4a^4}{9b^2}$ **59.** $\dfrac{1}{x^2}$ **61.** $a^5 b^2$

63. $\dfrac{6y^3}{x}$ **65.** $7b^2$ **67.** $\dfrac{7x}{y^2}$ **69.** $-\dfrac{12b^3}{a}$ **71.** $\dfrac{x^5 y^5}{5}$

73. $\dfrac{b^{20}}{81}$ **75.** $\dfrac{x + 1}{x^3}$ **77.** $\dfrac{y - x^3}{x^3 y}$ **79.** $\dfrac{3b + 4a^2}{a^2 b}$

81. $\dfrac{1 - x^2 y}{xy^2}$ **83.** $\dfrac{2x - 3}{x^2}$

Problem Set 5.2 (page 242)

1. 8 **3.** -10 **5.** 3 **7.** -4 **9.** 3 **11.** $\dfrac{4}{5}$ **13.** $-\dfrac{6}{7}$

15. $\dfrac{1}{2}$ **17.** $\dfrac{3}{4}$ **19.** 8 **21.** $3\sqrt{3}$ **23.** $4\sqrt{2}$ **25.** $4\sqrt{5}$

27. $4\sqrt{10}$ **29.** $12\sqrt{2}$ **31.** $-12\sqrt{5}$ **33.** $2\sqrt{3}$

35. $3\sqrt{6}$ **37.** $-\dfrac{5}{3}\sqrt{7}$ **39.** $\dfrac{\sqrt{19}}{2}$ **41.** $\dfrac{3\sqrt{3}}{4}$ **43.** $\dfrac{5\sqrt{3}}{9}$

45. $\dfrac{\sqrt{14}}{7}$ **47.** $\dfrac{\sqrt{6}}{3}$ **49.** $\dfrac{\sqrt{15}}{6}$ **51.** $\dfrac{\sqrt{66}}{12}$ **53.** $\dfrac{\sqrt{6}}{3}$

55. $\sqrt{5}$ **57.** $\dfrac{2\sqrt{21}}{7}$ **59.** $-\dfrac{8\sqrt{15}}{5}$ **61.** $\dfrac{\sqrt{6}}{4}$ **63.** $-\dfrac{12}{25}$

65. $2\sqrt[3]{2}$ **67.** $6\sqrt[3]{3}$ **69.** $\dfrac{2\sqrt[3]{3}}{3}$ **71.** $\dfrac{3\sqrt[3]{2}}{2}$ **73.** $\dfrac{\sqrt[3]{12}}{2}$

75. 42 miles per hour; 49 miles per hour; 65 miles per hour
77. 107 square centimeters **79.** 140 square inches
85. (a) 1.414 **(c)** 12.490 **(e)** 57.000 **(g)** 0.374
(i) 0.930

Problem Set 5.3 (page 248)

1. $13\sqrt{2}$ **3.** $54\sqrt{3}$ **5.** $-30\sqrt{2}$ **7.** $-\sqrt{5}$ **9.** $-21\sqrt{6}$

11. $-\dfrac{7\sqrt{7}}{12}$ **13.** $\dfrac{37\sqrt{10}}{10}$ **15.** $\dfrac{41\sqrt{2}}{20}$ **17.** $-9\sqrt[3]{3}$

19. $10\sqrt[3]{2}$ **21.** $4\sqrt{2x}$ **23.** $5x\sqrt{3}$ **25.** $2x\sqrt{5y}$

27. $8xy^3\sqrt{xy}$ **29.** $3a^2 b\sqrt{6b}$ **31.** $3x^3 y^4\sqrt{7}$

33. $4a\sqrt{10a}$ **35.** $\dfrac{8y}{3}\sqrt{6xy}$ **37.** $\dfrac{\sqrt{10xy}}{5y}$ **39.** $\dfrac{\sqrt{15}}{6x^2}$

41. $\dfrac{5\sqrt{2y}}{6y}$ **43.** $\dfrac{\sqrt{14xy}}{4y^3}$ **45.** $\dfrac{3y\sqrt{2xy}}{4x}$ **47.** $\dfrac{2\sqrt{42ab}}{7b^2}$

49. $2\sqrt[3]{3y}$ **51.** $2x\sqrt[3]{2x}$ **53.** $2x^2 y^2\sqrt[3]{7y^2}$ **55.** $\dfrac{\sqrt[3]{21x}}{3x}$

57. $\dfrac{\sqrt[3]{12x^2 y}}{4x^2}$ **59.** $\dfrac{\sqrt[3]{4x^2 y^2}}{xy^2}$ **61.** $2\sqrt{2x} + 3y$

63. $4\sqrt{x + 3y}$ **65.** $33\sqrt{x}$ **67.** $-30\sqrt{2x}$ **69.** $7\sqrt{3n}$

71. $-40\sqrt{ab}$ **73.** $-7x\sqrt{2x}$ **79. (a)** $5|x|\sqrt{5}$ **(b)** $4x^2$
(c) $2b\sqrt{2b}$ **(d)** $y^2\sqrt{3y}$ **(e)** $12|x^3|\sqrt{2}$ **(f)** $2m^4\sqrt{7}$

(g) $8|c^5|\sqrt{2}$ **(h)** $3d^3\sqrt{2d}$ **(i)** $7|x|$ **(j)** $4n^{10}\sqrt{5}$
(k) $9h\sqrt{h}$

Problem Set 5.4 (page 254)

1. $6\sqrt{2}$ **3.** $18\sqrt{2}$ **5.** $-24\sqrt{10}$ **7.** $24\sqrt{6}$ **9.** 120
11. 24 **13.** $56\sqrt[3]{3}$ **15.** $\sqrt{6}+\sqrt{10}$
17. $6\sqrt{10}-3\sqrt{35}$ **19.** $24\sqrt{3}-60\sqrt{2}$
21. $-40-32\sqrt{15}$ **23.** $15\sqrt{2x}+3\sqrt{xy}$
25. $5xy-6x\sqrt{y}$ **27.** $2\sqrt{10xy}+2y\sqrt{15y}$
29. $-25\sqrt{6}$ **31.** $-25-3\sqrt{3}$ **33.** $23-9\sqrt{5}$
35. $6\sqrt{35}+3\sqrt{10}-4\sqrt{21}-2\sqrt{6}$
37. $8\sqrt{3}-36\sqrt{2}+6\sqrt{10}-18\sqrt{15}$
39. $11+13\sqrt{30}$ **41.** $141-51\sqrt{6}$ **43.** -10 **45.** -8
47. $2x-3y$ **49.** $10\sqrt[3]{12}+2\sqrt[3]{18}$ **51.** $12-36\sqrt[3]{2}$
53. $\dfrac{\sqrt{7}-1}{3}$ **55.** $\dfrac{-3\sqrt{2}-15}{23}$ **57.** $\dfrac{\sqrt{7}-\sqrt{2}}{5}$
59. $\dfrac{2\sqrt{5}+\sqrt{6}}{7}$ **61.** $\dfrac{\sqrt{15}-2\sqrt{3}}{2}$ **63.** $\dfrac{6\sqrt{7}+4\sqrt{6}}{13}$
65. $\sqrt{3}-\sqrt{2}$ **67.** $\dfrac{2\sqrt{x}-8}{x-16}$ **69.** $\dfrac{x+5\sqrt{x}}{x-25}$
71. $\dfrac{x-8\sqrt{x}+12}{x-36}$ **73.** $\dfrac{x-2\sqrt{xy}}{x-4y}$ **75.** $\dfrac{6\sqrt{xy}+9y}{4x-9y}$

Problem Set 5.5 (page 260)

1. {20} **3.** $\varnothing$ **5.** $\left\{\dfrac{25}{4}\right\}$ **7.** $\left\{\dfrac{4}{9}\right\}$ **9.** {5} **11.** $\left\{\dfrac{39}{4}\right\}$
13. $\left\{\dfrac{10}{3}\right\}$ **15.** $\{-1\}$ **17.** $\varnothing$ **19.** {1} **21.** $\left\{\dfrac{3}{2}\right\}$ **23.** {3}
25. $\left\{\dfrac{61}{25}\right\}$ **27.** $\{-3,3\}$ **29.** $\{-9,-4\}$ **31.** {0} **33.** {3}
35. {4} **37.** $\{-4,-3\}$ **39.** {12} **41.** {25} **43.** {29}
45. $\{-15\}$ **47.** $\left\{-\dfrac{1}{3}\right\}$ **49.** $\{-3\}$ **51.** {0} **53.** {5}
55. {2, 6} **57.** 56 feet; 106 feet; 148 feet
59. 3.2 feet; 5.1 feet; 7.3 feet

Problem Set 5.6 (page 266)

1. 9 **3.** 3 **5.** -2 **7.** -5 **9.** $\dfrac{1}{6}$ **11.** 3 **13.** 8 **15.** 81
17. -1 **19.** -32 **21.** $\dfrac{81}{16}$ **23.** 4 **25.** $\dfrac{1}{128}$ **27.** -125
29. 625 **31.** $\sqrt[3]{x^4}$ **33.** $3\sqrt{x}$ **35.** $\sqrt[3]{2y}$ **37.** $\sqrt{2x-3y}$
39. $\sqrt[3]{(2a-3b)^2}$ **41.** $\sqrt[3]{x^2y}$ **43.** $-3\sqrt[5]{xy^2}$ **45.** $5^{\frac{1}{2}}y^{\frac{1}{2}}$
47. $3y^{\frac{1}{2}}$ **49.** $x^{\frac{1}{3}}y^{\frac{2}{3}}$ **51.** $a^{\frac{1}{2}}b^{\frac{3}{4}}$ **53.** $(2x-y)^{\frac{3}{5}}$ **55.** $5xy^{\frac{1}{2}}$

57. $-(x+y)^{\frac{1}{3}}$ **59.** $12x^{\frac{13}{20}}$ **61.** $y^{\frac{5}{12}}$ **63.** $\dfrac{4}{x^{\frac{1}{10}}}$ **65.** $16xy^2$

67. $2x^2y$ **69.** $4x^{\frac{4}{15}}$ **71.** $\dfrac{4}{b^{\frac{5}{12}}}$ **73.** $\dfrac{36x^{\frac{4}{5}}}{49y^3}$ **75.** $\dfrac{y^{\frac{3}{2}}}{x}$ **77.** $4x^{\frac{1}{6}}$

79. $\dfrac{16}{a^{\frac{11}{10}}}$ **81.** $\sqrt[6]{243}$ **83.** $\sqrt[4]{216}$ **85.** $\sqrt[12]{3}$ **87.** $\sqrt{2}$

89. $\sqrt[4]{3}$ **93. (a)** 12 **(c)** 7 **(e)** 11 **95. (a)** 1024
(c) 512 **(e)** 49

Problem Set 5.7 (page 271)

1. $(8.9)(10)^1$ **3.** $(4.29)(10)^3$ **5.** $(6.12)(10)^6$ **7.** $(4)(10)^7$
9. $(3.764)(10)^2$ **11.** $(3.47)(10)^{-1}$ **13.** $(2.14)(10)^{-2}$
15. $(5)(10)^{-5}$ **17.** $(1.94)(10)^{-9}$ **19.** 23 **21.** 4190
23. 500,000,000 **25.** 31,400,000,000 **27.** 0.43
29. 0.000914 **31.** 0.00000005123 **33.** 0.000000074
35. 0.77 **37.** 300,000,000,000 **39.** 0.000000004
41. 1000 **43.** 1000 **45.** 3000 **47.** 20 **49.** 27,000,000
51. $(6.02)(10^{23})$ **53.** 831 **55.** $(2.07)(10^4)$ dollars
57. $(1.99)(10^{-26})$ kg **59.** 1833 **63. (a)** 7000 **(c)** 120
(e) 30 **65. (a)** $(4.385)(10)^{14}$ **(c)** $(2.322)(10)^{17}$
(e) $(3.052)(10)^{12}$

Chapter 5 Review Problem Set (page 275)

1. $\dfrac{1}{64}$ **2.** $\dfrac{9}{4}$ **3.** 3 **4.** -2 **5.** $\dfrac{2}{3}$ **6.** 32 **7.** 1 **8.** $\dfrac{4}{9}$
9. -64 **10.** 32 **11.** 1 **12.** 27 **13.** $3\sqrt{6}$
14. $4x\sqrt{3xy}$ **15.** $2\sqrt{2}$ **16.** $\dfrac{\sqrt{15x}}{6x^2}$ **17.** $2\sqrt[3]{7}$
18. $\dfrac{\sqrt[3]{6}}{3}$ **19.** $\dfrac{3\sqrt{5}}{5}$ **20.** $\dfrac{x\sqrt{21x}}{7}$ **21.** $3xy^2\sqrt[3]{4xy^2}$
22. $\dfrac{15\sqrt{6}}{4}$ **23.** $2y\sqrt{5xy}$ **24.** $2\sqrt{x}$ **25.** $24\sqrt{10}$
26. 60 **27.** $24\sqrt{3}-6\sqrt{14}$ **28.** $x-2\sqrt{x}-15$
29. 17 **30.** $12-8\sqrt{3}$ **31.** $6a-5\sqrt{ab}-4b$ **32.** 70
33. $\dfrac{2(\sqrt{7}+1)}{3}$ **34.** $\dfrac{2\sqrt{6}-\sqrt{15}}{3}$ **35.** $\dfrac{3\sqrt{5}-2\sqrt{3}}{11}$
36. $\dfrac{6\sqrt{3}+3\sqrt{5}}{7}$ **37.** $\dfrac{x^6}{y^8}$ **38.** $\dfrac{27a^3b^{12}}{8}$ **39.** $20x^{\frac{7}{10}}$
40. $7a^{\frac{5}{12}}$ **41.** $\dfrac{y^{\frac{4}{3}}}{x}$ **42.** $\dfrac{x^{12}}{9}$ **43.** $\sqrt{5}$ **44.** $5\sqrt[3]{3}$
45. $\dfrac{29\sqrt{6}}{5}$ **46.** $-15\sqrt{3x}$ **47.** $\dfrac{y+x^2}{x^2y}$ **48.** $\dfrac{b-2a}{a^2b}$
49. $\left\{\dfrac{19}{7}\right\}$ **50.** {4} **51.** {8} **52.** $\varnothing$ **53.** {14}
54. $\{-10, 1\}$ **55.** {2} **56.** {8} **57.** 0.000000006

58. 36,000,000,000 **59.** 6 **60.** 0.15 **61.** 0.000028
62. 0.002 **63.** 0.002 **64.** 8,000,000,000

Chapter 5 Test (page 277)

1. $\dfrac{1}{32}$ **2.** -32 **3.** $\dfrac{81}{16}$ **4.** $\dfrac{1}{4}$ **5.** $3\sqrt{7}$ **6.** $3\sqrt[3]{4}$

7. $2x^2y\sqrt{13y}$ **8.** $\dfrac{5\sqrt{6}}{6}$ **9.** $\dfrac{\sqrt{42x}}{12x^2}$ **10.** $72\sqrt{2}$

11. $-5\sqrt{6}$ **12.** $-38\sqrt{2}$ **13.** $\dfrac{3\sqrt{6}+3}{10}$ **14.** $\dfrac{9x^2y^2}{4}$

15. $-\dfrac{12}{a^{\frac{3}{10}}}$ **16.** $\dfrac{y^3+x}{xy^3}$ **17.** $-12x^{\frac{1}{4}}$ **18.** 33 **19.** 600

20. 0.003 **21.** $\left\{\dfrac{8}{3}\right\}$ **22.** {2} **23.** {4} **24.** {5}

25. {4, 6}

CHAPTER 6

Problem Set 6.1 (page 285)

1. False **3.** True **5.** True **7.** True **9.** $10+8i$
11. $-6+10i$ **13.** $-2-5i$ **15.** $-12+5i$ **17.** $-1-23i$

19. $-4-5i$ **21.** $1+3i$ **23.** $\dfrac{5}{3}-\dfrac{5}{12}i$ **25.** $-\dfrac{17}{9}+\dfrac{23}{30}i$

27. $9i$ **29.** $i\sqrt{14}$ **31.** $\dfrac{4}{5}i$ **33.** $3i\sqrt{2}$ **35.** $5i\sqrt{3}$

37. $6i\sqrt{7}$ **39.** $-8i\sqrt{5}$ **41.** $36i\sqrt{10}$ **43.** -8
45. $-\sqrt{15}$ **47.** $-3\sqrt{6}$ **49.** $-5\sqrt{3}$ **51.** $-3\sqrt{6}$

53. $4i\sqrt{3}$ **55.** $\dfrac{5}{2}$ **57.** $2\sqrt{2}$ **59.** $2i$ **61.** $-20+0i$

63. $42+0i$ **65.** $15+6i$ **67.** $-42+12i$ **69.** $7+22i$
71. $40-20i$ **73.** $-3-28i$ **75.** $-3-15i$
77. $-9+40i$ **79.** $-12+16i$ **81.** $85+0i$

83. $5+0i$ **85.** $\dfrac{3}{5}+\dfrac{3}{10}i$ **87.** $\dfrac{5}{17}-\dfrac{3}{17}i$ **89.** $2+\dfrac{2}{3}i$

91. $0-\dfrac{2}{7}i$ **93.** $\dfrac{22}{25}-\dfrac{4}{25}i$ **95.** $-\dfrac{18}{41}+\dfrac{39}{41}i$ **97.** $\dfrac{9}{2}-\dfrac{5}{2}i$

99. $\dfrac{4}{13}-\dfrac{1}{26}i$ **101. (a)** $-2-i\sqrt{3}$ **(c)** $\dfrac{-1-3i\sqrt{2}}{2}$

(e) $\dfrac{10+3i\sqrt{5}}{4}$

Problem Set 6.2 (page 293)

1. {0, 9} **3.** {−3, 0} **5.** {−4, 0} **7.** $\left\{0,\dfrac{9}{5}\right\}$ **9.** {−6, 5}

11. {7, 12} **13.** $\left\{-8,-\dfrac{3}{2}\right\}$ **15.** $\left\{-\dfrac{7}{3},\dfrac{2}{5}\right\}$ **17.** $\left\{\dfrac{3}{5}\right\}$

19. $\left\{-\dfrac{3}{2},\dfrac{7}{3}\right\}$ **21.** {1, 4} **23.** {8} **25.** {12} **27.** {0, 5k}

29. {0, 16k²} **31.** {5k, 7k} **33.** $\left\{\dfrac{k}{2},-3k\right\}$ **35.** {±1}

37. {±6i} **39.** $\{\pm\sqrt{14}\}$ **41.** $\{\pm 2\sqrt{7}\}$ **43.** $\{\pm 3\sqrt{2}\}$

45. $\left\{\pm\dfrac{\sqrt{14}}{2}\right\}$ **47.** $\left\{\pm\dfrac{2\sqrt{3}}{3}\right\}$ **49.** $\left\{\pm\dfrac{2i\sqrt{30}}{5}\right\}$

51. $\left\{\pm\dfrac{\sqrt{6}}{2}\right\}$ **53.** {−1, 5} **55.** {−8, 2} **57.** {−6 ± 2i}

59. {1, 2} **61.** $\{4\pm\sqrt{5}\}$ **63.** $\{-5\pm 2\sqrt{3}\}$

65. $\left\{\dfrac{2\pm 3i\sqrt{3}}{3}\right\}$ **67.** {−12, −2} **69.** $\left\{\dfrac{2\pm\sqrt{10}}{5}\right\}$

71. $2\sqrt{13}$ centimeters **73.** $4\sqrt{5}$ inches **75.** 8 yards
77. $6\sqrt{2}$ inches **79.** $a=b=4\sqrt{2}$ meters
81. $b=3\sqrt{3}$ inches and $c=6$ inches
83. $a=7$ centimeters and $b=7\sqrt{3}$ centimeters
85. $a=\dfrac{10\sqrt{3}}{3}$ feet and $c=\dfrac{20\sqrt{3}}{3}$ feet **87.** 17.9 feet
89. 38 meters **91.** 53 meters **95.** 10.8 centimeters
97. $h=s\sqrt{2}$

Problem Set 6.3 (page 299)

1. {−6, 10} **3.** {4, 10} **5.** {−5, 10} **7.** {−8, 1}

9. $\left\{-\dfrac{5}{2},3\right\}$ **11.** $\left\{-3,\dfrac{2}{3}\right\}$ **13.** {−16, 10}

15. $\{-2\pm\sqrt{6}\}$ **17.** $\{-3\pm 2\sqrt{3}\}$ **19.** $\{5\pm\sqrt{26}\}$
21. $\{4\pm i\}$ **23.** $\{-6\pm 3\sqrt{3}\}$ **25.** $\{-1\pm i\sqrt{5}\}$

27. $\left\{\dfrac{-3\pm\sqrt{17}}{2}\right\}$ **29.** $\left\{\dfrac{-5\pm\sqrt{21}}{2}\right\}$ **31.** $\left\{\dfrac{7\pm\sqrt{37}}{2}\right\}$

33. $\left\{\dfrac{-2\pm\sqrt{10}}{2}\right\}$ **35.** $\left\{\dfrac{3\pm i\sqrt{6}}{3}\right\}$ **37.** $\left\{\dfrac{-5\pm\sqrt{37}}{6}\right\}$

39. {−12, 4} **41.** $\left\{\dfrac{4\pm\sqrt{10}}{2}\right\}$ **43.** $\left\{-\dfrac{9}{2},\dfrac{1}{3}\right\}$

45. {−3, 8} **47.** $\{3\pm 2\sqrt{3}\}$ **49.** $\left\{\dfrac{3\pm i\sqrt{3}}{3}\right\}$

51. {−20, 12} **53.** $\left\{-1,-\dfrac{2}{3}\right\}$ **55.** $\left\{\dfrac{1}{2},\dfrac{3}{2}\right\}$

57. $\{-6\pm 2\sqrt{10}\}$ **59.** $\left\{\dfrac{-1\pm\sqrt{3}}{2}\right\}$

61. $\left\{\dfrac{-b\pm\sqrt{b^2-4ac}}{2a}\right\}$ **65.** $x=\dfrac{a\sqrt{b^2-y^2}}{b}$

67. $r=\dfrac{\sqrt{A\pi}}{\pi}$ **69.** {2a, 3a} **71.** $\left\{\dfrac{a}{2},-\dfrac{2a}{3}\right\}$

73. $\left\{\dfrac{2b}{3}\right\}$

Problem Set 6.4 (page 307)

1. Two real solutions; $\{-7, 3\}$ **3.** One real solution; $\left\{\dfrac{1}{3}\right\}$

5. Two complex solutions; $\left\{\dfrac{7 \pm i\sqrt{3}}{2}\right\}$

7. Two real solutions; $\left\{-\dfrac{4}{3}, \dfrac{1}{5}\right\}$

9. Two real solutions; $\left\{\dfrac{-2 \pm \sqrt{10}}{3}\right\}$ **11.** $\{-1 \pm \sqrt{2}\}$

13. $\left\{\dfrac{-5 \pm \sqrt{37}}{2}\right\}$ **15.** $\{4 \pm 2\sqrt{5}\}$ **17.** $\left\{\dfrac{-5 \pm i\sqrt{7}}{2}\right\}$

19. $\{8, 10\}$ **21.** $\left\{\dfrac{9 \pm \sqrt{61}}{2}\right\}$ **23.** $\left\{\dfrac{-1 \pm \sqrt{33}}{4}\right\}$

25. $\left\{\dfrac{-1 \pm i\sqrt{3}}{4}\right\}$ **27.** $\left\{\dfrac{4 \pm \sqrt{10}}{3}\right\}$ **29.** $\left\{-1, \dfrac{5}{2}\right\}$

31. $\left\{-5, -\dfrac{4}{3}\right\}$ **33.** $\left\{\dfrac{5}{6}\right\}$ **35.** $\left\{\dfrac{1 \pm \sqrt{13}}{4}\right\}$

37. $\left\{0, \dfrac{13}{5}\right\}$ **39.** $\left\{\pm\dfrac{\sqrt{15}}{3}\right\}$ **41.** $\left\{\dfrac{-1 \pm \sqrt{73}}{12}\right\}$

43. $\{-18, -14\}$ **45.** $\left\{\dfrac{11}{4}, \dfrac{10}{3}\right\}$ **47.** $\left\{\dfrac{2 \pm i\sqrt{2}}{2}\right\}$

49. $\left\{\dfrac{1 \pm \sqrt{7}}{6}\right\}$ **55.** $\{-1.381, 17.381\}$

57. $\{-13.426, 3.426\}$ **59.** $\{-0.347, -8.653\}$

61. $\{0.119, 1.681\}$ **63.** $\{-0.708, 4.708\}$

65. $k = 4$ or $k = -4$

Problem Set 6.5 (page 317)

1. $\{2 \pm \sqrt{10}\}$ **3.** $\left\{-9, \dfrac{4}{3}\right\}$ **5.** $\{9 \pm 3\sqrt{10}\}$

7. $\left\{\dfrac{3 \pm i\sqrt{23}}{4}\right\}$ **9.** $\{-15, -9\}$ **11.** $\{-8, 1\}$

13. $\left\{\dfrac{2 \pm i\sqrt{10}}{2}\right\}$ **15.** $\{9 \pm \sqrt{66}\}$ **17.** $\left\{-\dfrac{5}{4}, \dfrac{2}{5}\right\}$

19. $\left\{\dfrac{-1 \pm \sqrt{2}}{2}\right\}$ **21.** $\left\{\dfrac{3}{4}, 4\right\}$ **23.** $\left\{\dfrac{11 \pm \sqrt{109}}{2}\right\}$

25. $\left\{\dfrac{3}{7}, 4\right\}$ **27.** $\left\{\dfrac{7 \pm \sqrt{129}}{10}\right\}$ **29.** $\left\{-\dfrac{10}{7}, 3\right\}$

31. $\{1 \pm \sqrt{34}\}$ **33.** $\{\pm\sqrt{6}, \pm 2\sqrt{3}\}$

35. $\left\{\pm 3, \pm\dfrac{2\sqrt{6}}{3}\right\}$ **37.** $\left\{\pm\dfrac{i\sqrt{15}}{3}, \pm 2i\right\}$

39. $\left\{\pm\dfrac{\sqrt{14}}{2}, \pm\dfrac{2\sqrt{3}}{3}\right\}$ **41.** 8 and 9   **43.** 9 and 12

45. $5 + \sqrt{3}$ and $5 - \sqrt{3}$ **47.** 3 and 6

49. 9 inches and 12 inches   **51.** 1 meter

53. 8 inches by 14 inches   **55.** 20 miles per hour for Lorraine and 25 miles per hour for Charlotte, or 45 miles per hour for Lorraine and 50 miles per hour for Charlotte

57. 55 miles per hour   **59.** 6 hours for Tom and 8 hours for Terry   **61.** 2 hours   **63.** 8 students   **65.** 40 shares at $20 per share   **67.** 50 numbers   **69.** 9%   **75.** $\{9, 36\}$

77. $\{1\}$ **79.** $\left\{-\dfrac{8}{27}, \dfrac{27}{8}\right\}$ **81.** $\left\{-4, \dfrac{3}{5}\right\}$ **83.** $\{4\}$

85. $\{\pm 4\sqrt{2}\}$ **87.** $\left\{\dfrac{3}{2}, \dfrac{5}{2}\right\}$ **89.** $\{-1, 3\}$

Problem Set 6.6 (page 325)

1. $(-\infty, -2) \cup (1, \infty)$

3. $(-4, -1)$

5. $\left(-\infty, -\dfrac{7}{3}\right] \cup \left[\dfrac{1}{2}, \infty\right)$

7. $\left[-2, \dfrac{3}{4}\right]$

9. $(-1, 1) \cup (3, \infty)$

11. $(-\infty, -2] \cup [0, 4]$

13. $(-\infty, -1) \cup (2, \infty)$

15. $(-2, 3)$

17. $(-\infty, 0) \cup \left[\dfrac{1}{2}, \infty\right)$

19. $(-\infty, 1) \cup [2, \infty)$

21. $(-7, 5)$ **23.** $(-\infty, 4) \cup (7, \infty)$ **25.** $\left[-5, \dfrac{2}{3}\right]$

27. $\left(-\infty, -\dfrac{5}{2}\right] \cup \left[-\dfrac{1}{4}, \infty\right)$ **29.** $\left(-\infty, -\dfrac{4}{5}\right) \cup (8, \infty)$

31. $(-\infty, \infty)$ **33.** $\left\{-\dfrac{5}{2}\right\}$ **35.** $(-1, 3) \cup (3, \infty)$

37. $(-\infty, -2) \cup (2, \infty)$ **39.** $(-6, 6)$ **41.** $(-\infty, \infty)$

43. $(-\infty, 0] \cup [2, \infty)$ **45.** $(-4, 0) \cup (0, \infty)$ **47.** $(-6, -3)$

49. $(-\infty, 5) \cup [9, \infty)$ **51.** $\left(-\infty, \dfrac{4}{3}\right) \cup (3, \infty)$

53. $(-4, 6]$ **55.** $(-\infty, 2)$

Chapter 6 Review Problem Set (page 328)

1. $2 - 2i$ **2.** $-3 - i$ **3.** $30 + 15i$ **4.** $86 - 2i$

5. $-32 + 4i$ **6.** $25 + 0i$ **7.** $\dfrac{9}{20} + \dfrac{13}{20}i$ **8.** $-\dfrac{3}{29} + \dfrac{7}{29}i$

9. One real solution with a multiplicity of 2.
10. Two nonreal complex solutions
11. Two unequal real solutions
12. Two unequal real solutions   **13.** $\{0, 17\}$ **14.** $\{-4, 8\}$

15. $\left\{\dfrac{1 \pm 8i}{2}\right\}$ **16.** $\{-3, 7\}$ **17.** $\{-1 \pm \sqrt{10}\}$

18. $\{3 \pm 5i\}$ **19.** $\{25\}$ **20.** $\left\{-4, \dfrac{2}{3}\right\}$ **21.** $\{-10, 20\}$

22. $\left\{\dfrac{-1 \pm \sqrt{61}}{6}\right\}$ **23.** $\left\{\dfrac{1 \pm i\sqrt{11}}{2}\right\}$

24. $\left\{\dfrac{5 \pm i\sqrt{23}}{4}\right\}$ **25.** $\left\{\dfrac{-2 \pm \sqrt{14}}{2}\right\}$ **26.** $\{-9, 4\}$

27. $\{-2 \pm i\sqrt{5}\}$ **28.** $\{-6, 12\}$ **29.** $\{1 \pm \sqrt{10}\}$

30. $\left\{\pm\dfrac{\sqrt{14}}{2}, \pm 2\sqrt{2}\right\}$ **31.** $\left\{\dfrac{-3 \pm \sqrt{97}}{2}\right\}$

32. $(-\infty, -5) \cup (2, \infty)$ **33.** $\left[-\dfrac{7}{2}, 3\right]$

34. $(-\infty, -6) \cup [4, \infty)$ **35.** $\left(-\dfrac{5}{2}, -1\right)$

36. $3 + \sqrt{7}$ and $3 - \sqrt{7}$ **37.** 20 shares at \$15 per share
38. 45 miles per hour and 52 miles per hour   **39.** 8 units
40. 8 and 10   **41.** 7 inches by 12 inches   **42.** 4 hours for
Reena and 6 hours for Billy   **43.** 10 meters

Chapter 6 Test (page 330)

1. $39 - 2i$ **2.** $-\dfrac{6}{25} - \dfrac{17}{25}i$ **3.** $\{0, 7\}$ **4.** $\{-1, 7\}$

5. $\{-6, 3\}$ **6.** $\{1 - \sqrt{2}, 1 + \sqrt{2}\}$ **7.** $\left\{\dfrac{1 - 2i}{5}, \dfrac{1 + 2i}{5}\right\}$

8. $\{-16, -14\}$ **9.** $\left\{\dfrac{1 - 6i}{3}, \dfrac{1 + 6i}{3}\right\}$ **10.** $\left\{-\dfrac{7}{4}, \dfrac{6}{5}\right\}$

11. $\left\{-3, \dfrac{19}{6}\right\}$ **12.** $\left\{-\dfrac{10}{3}, 4\right\}$ **13.** $\{-2, 2, -4i, 4i\}$

14. $\left\{-\dfrac{3}{4}, 1\right\}$ **15.** $\left\{\dfrac{1 - \sqrt{10}}{3}, \dfrac{1 + \sqrt{10}}{3}\right\}$

16. Two equal real solutions   **17.** Two nonreal complex

solutions   **18.** $[-6, 9]$ **19.** $(-\infty, -2) \cup \left(\dfrac{1}{3}, \infty\right)$

20. $[-10, -6)$ **21.** 20.8 feet   **22.** 29 meters

23. 150 shares   **24.** $6\dfrac{1}{2}$ inches   **25.** $3 + \sqrt{5}$

Cumulative Review Problem Set (page 331)

1. $\dfrac{64}{15}$ **2.** $\dfrac{11}{3}$ **3.** $\dfrac{1}{6}$ **4.** $-\dfrac{44}{5}$ **5.** -7 **6.** $-24a^4b^5$

7. $2x^3 + 5x^2 - 7x - 12$ **8.** $\dfrac{3x^2y^2}{8}$ **9.** $\dfrac{a(a + 1)}{2a - 1}$

10. $\dfrac{-x + 14}{18}$ **11.** $\dfrac{5x + 19}{x(x + 3)}$ **12.** $\dfrac{2}{n + 8}$

13. $\dfrac{x - 14}{(5x - 2)(x + 1)(x - 4)}$ **14.** $y^2 - 5y + 6$

15. $x^2 - 3x - 2$ **16.** $20 + 7\sqrt{10}$

17. $2x - 2\sqrt{xy} - 12y$ **18.** $-\dfrac{3}{8}$ **19.** $-\dfrac{2}{3}$ **20.** 0.2

21. $\dfrac{1}{2}$ **22.** $\dfrac{13}{9}$ **23.** -27 **24.** $\dfrac{16}{9}$ **25.** $\dfrac{8}{27}$

26. $3x(x + 3)(x^2 - 3x + 9)$ **27.** $(6x - 5)(x + 4)$
28. $(4 + 7x)(3 - 2x)$ **29.** $(3x + 2)(3x - 2)(x^2 + 8)$
30. $(2x - y)(a - b)$ **31.** $(3x - 2y)(9x^2 + 6xy + 4y^2)$

32. $\left\{-\dfrac{12}{7}\right\}$ **33.** $\{150\}$ **34.** $\{25\}$ **35.** $\{0\}$ **36.** $\{-2, 2\}$

37. $\{-7\}$ **38.** $\left\{-6, \dfrac{4}{3}\right\}$ **39.** $\left\{\dfrac{5}{4}\right\}$ **40.** $\{3\}$ **41.** $\left\{\dfrac{4}{5}, 1\right\}$

42. $\left\{-\dfrac{10}{3}, 4\right\}$ **43.** $\left\{\dfrac{1}{4}, \dfrac{2}{3}\right\}$ **44.** $\left\{-\dfrac{3}{2}, 3\right\}$ **45.** $\left\{\dfrac{1}{5}\right\}$

46. $\left\{\dfrac{5}{7}\right\}$ **47.** $\{-2, 2\}$ **48.** $\{0\}$ **49.** $\{-6, 19\}$

50. $\left\{-\dfrac{3}{4}, \dfrac{2}{3}\right\}$ **51.** $\{1 \pm 5i\}$ **52.** $\{1, 3\}$ **53.** $\left\{-4, \dfrac{1}{3}\right\}$

54. $\{-2 \pm 4i\}$ **55.** $\left\{\dfrac{1 \pm \sqrt{33}}{4}\right\}$ **56.** $(-\infty, -2]$

57. $\left(-\infty, \dfrac{19}{5}\right)$ **58.** $\left(\dfrac{1}{4}, \infty\right)$ **59.** $(-2, 3)$

60. $\left(-\infty, -\dfrac{13}{3}\right) \cup (3, \infty)$ **61.** $(-\infty, 29]$ **62.** $[-2, 4]$

63. $(-\infty, -5) \cup \left(\dfrac{1}{3}, \infty\right)$ **64.** $(-\infty, -2] \cup (7, \infty)$

65. $(-3, 4)$ **66.** 6 liters   **67.** $900 and $1350

68. 12 inches by 17 inches   **69.** 5 hours   **70.** 7 golf balls

71. 12 minutes   **72.** 7%   **73.** 15 chairs per row

74. 140 shares

CHAPTER 7

Problem Set 7.1 (page 346)

1.
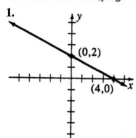

3.
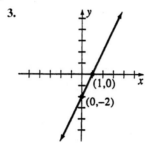

5.
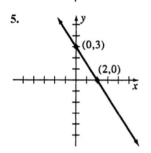

7.
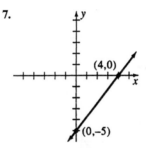

9.
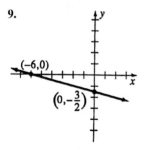

11.
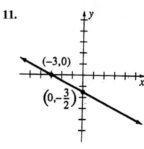

13.
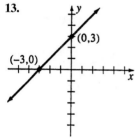

15.
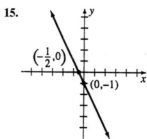

17.
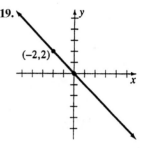

19.
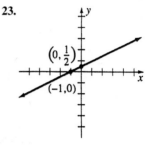

21.
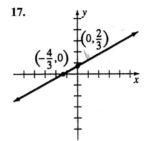

23.
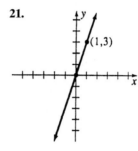

25.
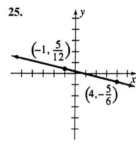

27.
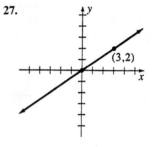

29.
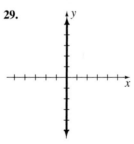

31.
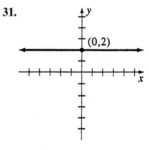

33.
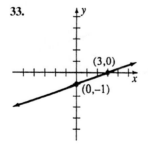

35.
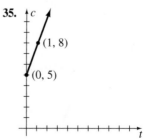

37.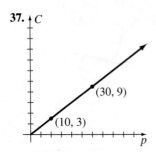

39.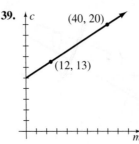

35.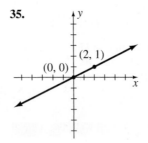

37.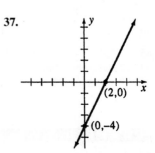

45.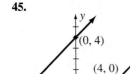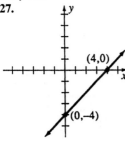

47.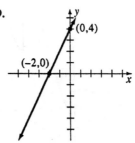

39.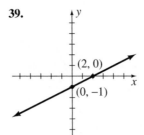

41.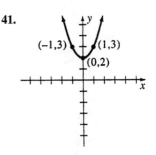

Problem Set 7.2 (page 356)

1. $(-3, -1); (3, 1); (3, -1)$ **3.** $(7, 2); (-7, -2); (-7, 2)$
5. $(5, 0); (-5, 0); (-5, 0)$ **7.** x axis   **9.** y axis
11. x axis, y axis, and origin   **13.** x axis   **15.** None
17. Origin   **19.** y axis   **21.** All three   **23.** x axis
25. y axis

27.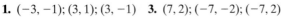

29.

43.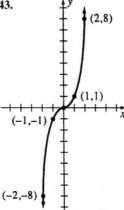

45.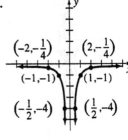

31.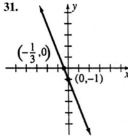

33.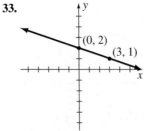

47.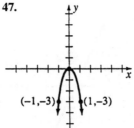

49.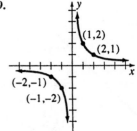

51.

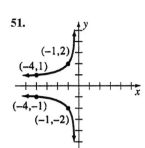

53.

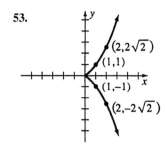

5.

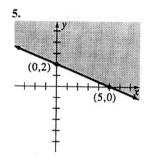

7.

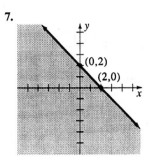

55.

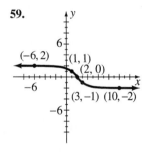

57.

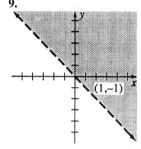

9.

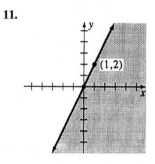

11.

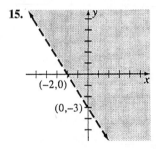

59.

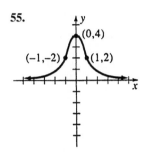

13.

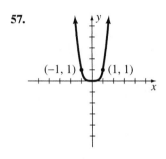

15.

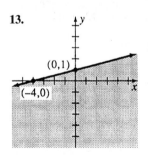

Problem Set 7.3 (page 361)

1.

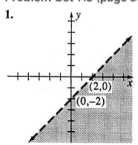

3.

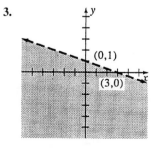

17.

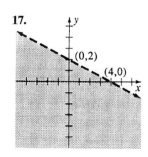

19.

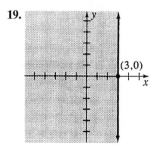

21.

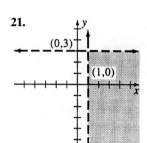

23.

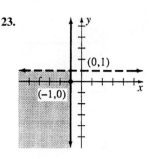

49. $-\dfrac{2}{3}$ **51.** $\dfrac{1}{2}$ **53.** $\dfrac{4}{7}$ **55.** 0 **57.** -5 **59.** 105.6 feet

61. 8.1% **63.** 19 centimeters **69. (a)** $(3, 5)$ **(c)** $(2, 5)$

(e) $\left(\dfrac{17}{8}, -7\right)$

27.

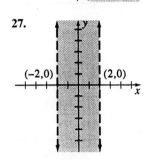

29.

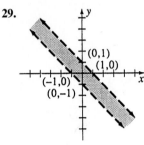

Problem Set 7.5 (page 383)

1. $x - 2y = -7$ **3.** $3x - y = -10$ **5.** $3x + 4y = -15$
7. $5x - 4y = 28$ **9.** $x - y = 1$ **11.** $5x - 2y = -4$
13. $x + 7y = 11$ **15.** $x + 2y = -9$ **17.** $7x - 5y = 0$
19. $y = \dfrac{3}{7}x + 4$ **21.** $y = 2x - 3$ **23.** $y = -\dfrac{2}{5}x + 1$
25. $y = 0(x) - 4$ **27.** $2x - y = 4$ **29.** $5x + 8y = -15$
31. $x + 0(y) = 2$ **33.** $0(x) + y = 6$ **35.** $x + 5y = 16$
37. $4x - 7y = 0$ **39.** $x + 2y = 5$ **41.** $3x + 2y = 0$
43. $m = -3$ and $b = 7$ **45.** $m = -\dfrac{3}{2}$ and $b = \dfrac{9}{2}$
47. $m = \dfrac{1}{5}$ and $b = -\dfrac{12}{5}$

Problem Set 7.4 (page 371)

1. 15 **3.** $\sqrt{13}$ **5.** $3\sqrt{2}$ **7.** $3\sqrt{5}$ **9.** 6 **11.** $3\sqrt{10}$
13. The lengths of the sides are 10, $5\sqrt{5}$, and 5. Because $10^2 + 5^2 = (5\sqrt{5})^2$, it is a right triangle.
15. The distances between (3, 6), and (7, 12), between (7, 12) and (11, 18), and between (11, 18) and (15, 24) are all $2\sqrt{13}$ units.

17. $\dfrac{4}{3}$ **19.** $-\dfrac{7}{3}$ **21.** -2 **23.** $\dfrac{3}{5}$ **25.** 0 **27.** $\dfrac{1}{2}$
29. 7 **31.** -2 **33–39.** Answers will vary.

49.

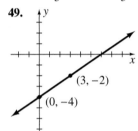

51.

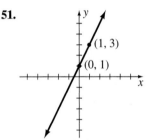

41.

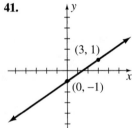

43.

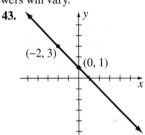

53.

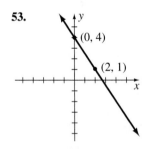

55.

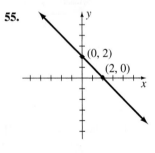

45.

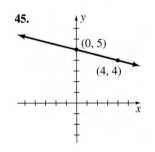

47.

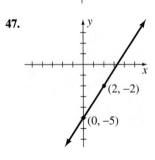

57.

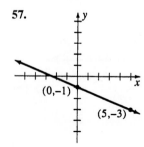

59.

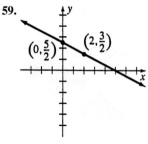

61.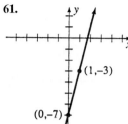

63.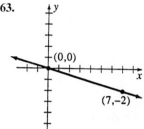

65.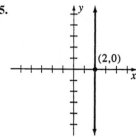

67. $y = \dfrac{1}{1000}x + 2$ **69.** $y = \dfrac{9}{5}x + 32$

77. (a) $2x - y = 1$ **(b)** $5x - 6y = 29$ **(c)** $x + y = 2$
(d) $3x - 2y = 18$

Chapter 7 Review Problem Set (page 388)

1. (a) $\dfrac{6}{5}$ **(b)** $-\dfrac{2}{3}$ **2.** 5   **3.** -1

4. (a) $m = -4$ **(b)** $m = \dfrac{2}{7}$ **5.** 5, 10, and $\sqrt{97}$

6. (a) $2\sqrt{10}$ **(b)** $\sqrt{58}$ **8.** $7x + 4y = 1$
9. $3x + 7y = 28$ **10.** $2x - 3y = 16$
11. $x - 2y = -8$ **12.** $2x - 3y = 14$
13. $x - y = -4$ **14.** $x + y = -2$
15. $4x + y = -29$

16.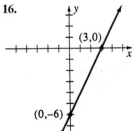

17.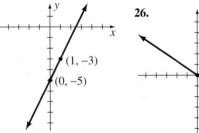

18.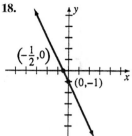

19.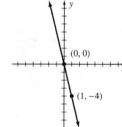

20.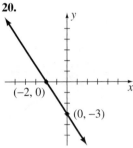

21.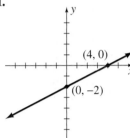

22.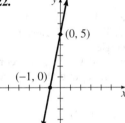

23.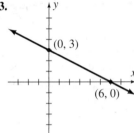

24.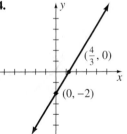

25.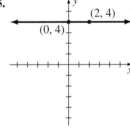

26.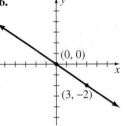

27.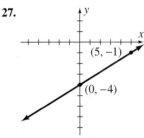

28.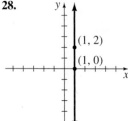

29.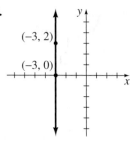

38.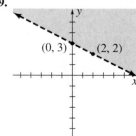

39.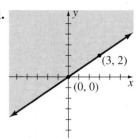

30.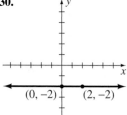

31.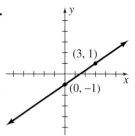

40.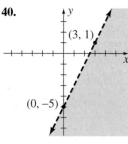

41.

42. 316.8 feet   **43.** 8 inches   **44.** $-\dfrac{5}{3}$ **45.** $-\dfrac{4}{5}$

46. $y = \dfrac{3}{200}x - 600$ **47.** $y = \dfrac{1}{5}x - 20$ **48.** $y = 8x$

49. $y = 300x - 150$ **50. (a)** y axis   **(b)** Origin
(c) Origin   **(d)** x axis

32.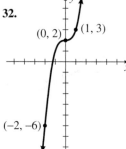

33.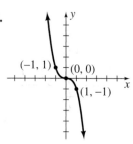

Chapter 7 Test (page 390)

1. $-\dfrac{6}{5}$ **2.** $\dfrac{3}{7}$ **3.** $\sqrt{58}$ **4.** $3x + 2y = 2$ **5.** $y = -\dfrac{1}{6}x + \dfrac{4}{3}$

6. $5x + 2y = -18$ **7.** $6x + y = 31$ **8.** Origin symmetry
9. x axis, y axis, and origin symmetry

10. x axis symmetry   **11.** $\dfrac{7}{2}$ **12.** $\dfrac{9}{4}$ **13.** $\dfrac{10}{9}$

14. $-\dfrac{5}{8}$ **15.** 480 feet   **16.** 6.7%   **17.** 43 centimeters

34.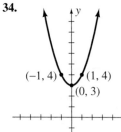

35.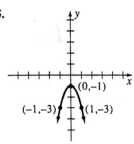

18.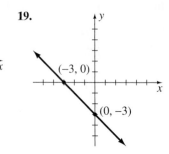

19.

36.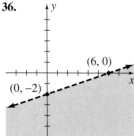

37.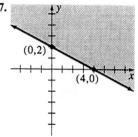

20.

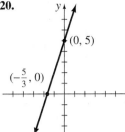

21.

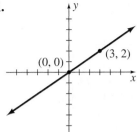

5.

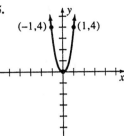

7.

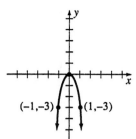

9.

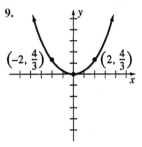

11.

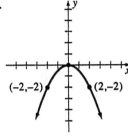

22.

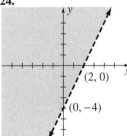

23.

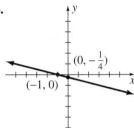

13.

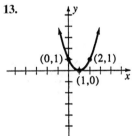

15.

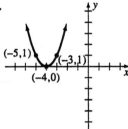

24.

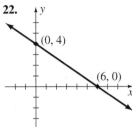

25.

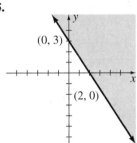

17.

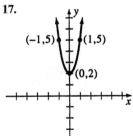

19.

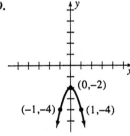

CHAPTER 8

Problem Set 8.1 (page 401)

1.

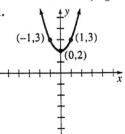

3.

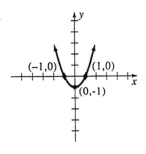

21.

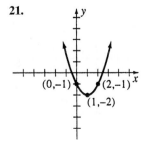

23.

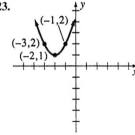

25.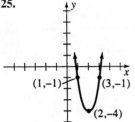

27.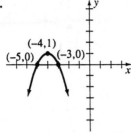

13.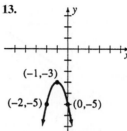

15.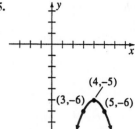

29.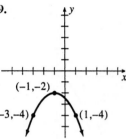

17.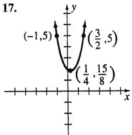

19.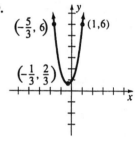

Problem Set 8.2 (page 408)

1.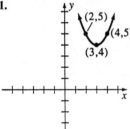

3.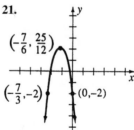

21.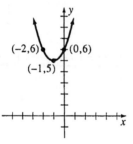

23. $(1, 3), r = 4$

5.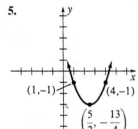

7.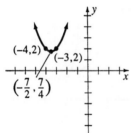

25. $(-3, -5), r = 4$ **27.** $(0, 0), r = \sqrt{10}$
29. $(8, -3), r = \sqrt{2}$ **31.** $(-3, 4), r = 5$
33. $\left(-\dfrac{1}{2}, 4\right), r = 2\sqrt{2}$

9.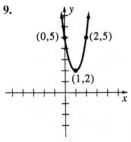

11.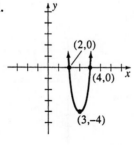

35.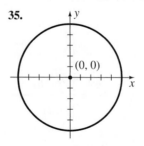

37.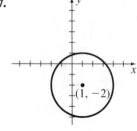

39.

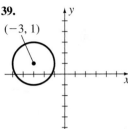

41.

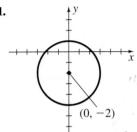

7.

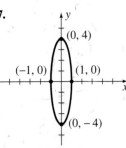

9.

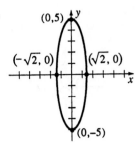

43.

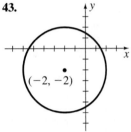

11.

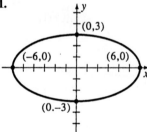

45. $x^2 + y^2 - 6x - 10y + 9 = 0$
47. $x^2 + y^2 + 8x - 2y - 47 = 0$
49. $x^2 + y^2 + 4x + 12y + 22 = 0$ **51.** $x^2 + y^2 - 20 = 0$
53. $x^2 + y^2 - 10x + 16y - 7 = 0$
55. $x^2 + y^2 - 8y = 0$ **57.** $x^2 + y^2 + 8x - 6y = 0$
63. (a) $(1, 4), r = 3$ **(c)** $(-6, -4), r = 8$
(e) $(0, 6), r = 9$

13.

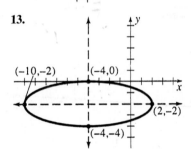

Problem Set 8.3 (page 415)

1.

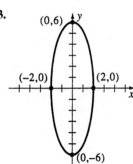

15.

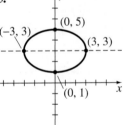

3.

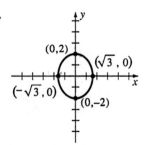

5.

Problem Set 8.4 (page 423)

1. $(4, 0), (-4, 0),$ $y = \dfrac{1}{3}x$ and $y = -\dfrac{1}{3}x$
3. $(0, 6), (0, -6)$ $y = 3x$ and $y = -3x$
5. $\left(\dfrac{2}{5}, 0\right), \left(-\dfrac{2}{5}, 0\right),$ $y = \dfrac{5}{3}x$ and $y = -\dfrac{5}{3}x$
7. $y = -x - 5$ and $y = x - 1$
9. $y = \dfrac{3}{2}x - \dfrac{9}{2}$ and $y = -\dfrac{3}{2}x - \dfrac{3}{2}$

11.

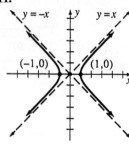

13.

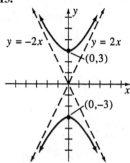

25.

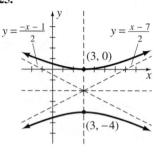

27.

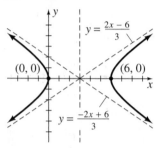

15.

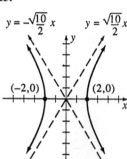

17.

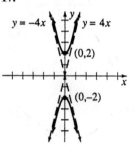

29.

(a)

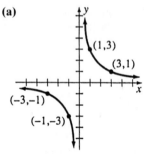

(c)

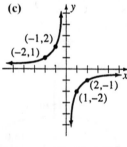

19.

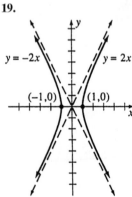

21.

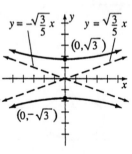

31. (a) Origin

(c)

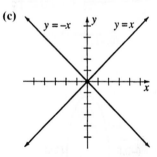

23.

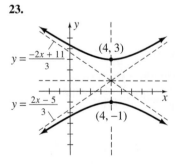

Chapter 8 Review Problem Set (page 425)

1. $(0, 6)$ **2.** $(0, -8)$ **3.** $(-3, -1)$ **4.** $(7, 5)$ **5.** $(6, -8)$
6. $(-4, -9)$ **7.** $x^2 + y^2 - 4x + 12y + 15 = 0$
8. $x^2 + y^2 + 8x + 16y + 68 = 0$

9. $x^2 + y^2 - 10y = 0$ **10.** $(-7, 4)$ and $r = 7$
11. $(-8, 0)$ and $r = 5$ **12.** $(6, -8)$ and $r = 10$
13. $(0, 0)$ and $r = 2\sqrt{6}$ **14.** 16 and 4   **15.** 8 and 6
16. 10 and 4   **17.** $2\sqrt{14}$ and 4   **18.** 6 and 2   **19.** 6 and 4
20. $y = \pm\frac{1}{3}x$ **21.** $y = \pm 2x$ **22.** $y = \pm\frac{5}{3}x$
23. $y = \pm\frac{1}{2}x$ **24.** $y = -\frac{5}{2}x - 2$ and $y = \frac{5}{2}x + 8$
25. $y = -\frac{1}{6}x + \frac{25}{6}$ and $y = \frac{1}{6}x + \frac{23}{6}$

26.

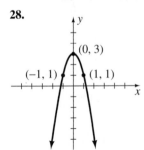

27.

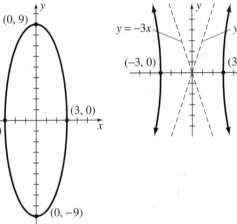

28.

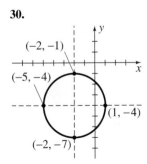

29.

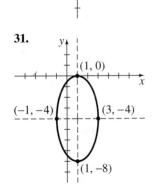

30.

31.

32.

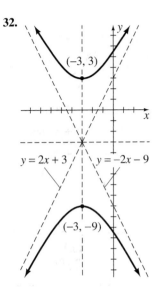

33.

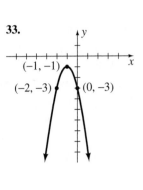

34.

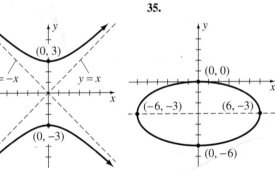

35.

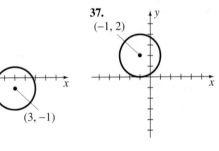

36.

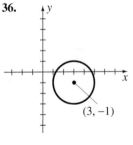

37.

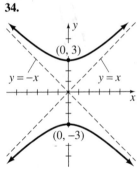

38.

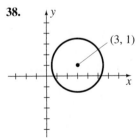

39.

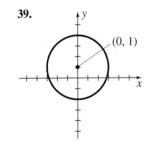

Chapter 8 Test (page 427)

1. $(0, 9)$ **2.** $(1, 7)$ **3.** $(-4, -2)$

4. $(3, 0)$ **5.** $x^2 + 8x + y^2 - 29 = 0$

6. $x^2 + y^2 - 4x - 16y + 59 = 0$

7. $x^2 + y^2 + 6x + 8y = 0$

8. $(0, 0)$ and $r = 4\sqrt{2}$ **9.** $(6, -4)$ and $r = 7$

10. $(-5, -1)$ and $r = 8$ **11.** 8 units **12.** 6 units

13. 6 units **14.** 4 units **15.** $y = \pm 4x$ **16.** $y = \pm \dfrac{5}{4}x$

17. $y = \dfrac{1}{5}x - \dfrac{6}{5}$ and $y = -\dfrac{1}{5}x - \dfrac{4}{5}$

18.

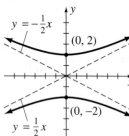

19.

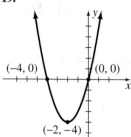

20.

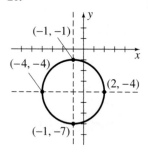

21.

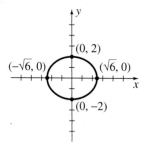

22.

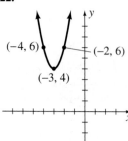

23.

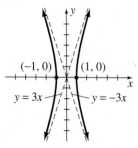

24.

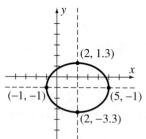

25.

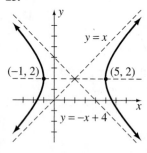

CHAPTER 9

Problem Set 9.1 (page 435)

1. $D = \{1, 2, 3, 4\}$, $R = \{5, 8, 11, 14\}$ It is a function.

3. $D = \{0, 1\}$, $R = \{-2\sqrt{6}, -5, 5, 2\sqrt{6}\}$ It is not a function.

5. $D = \{1, 2, 3, 4, 5\}$, $R = \{2, 5, 10, 17, 26\}$ It is a function.

7. $D = \{\text{all reals}\}$ or $D\colon (-\infty, \infty)$, $R = \{\text{all reals}\}$ or $R\colon (-\infty, \infty)$, yes

9. $D = \{\text{all reals}\}$ or $D\colon (-\infty, \infty)$, $R = \{y \mid y \geq 0\}$ or $R\colon [0, \infty)$, yes **11.** $\{\text{all reals}\}$ or $(-\infty, \infty)$

13. $\{x \mid x \neq 1\}$ or $(-\infty, 1) \cup (1, \infty)$

15. $\left\{ x \mid x \neq \dfrac{3}{4} \right\}$ or $\left(-\infty, \dfrac{3}{4} \right) \cup \left(\dfrac{3}{4}, \infty \right)$

17. $\{x \mid x \neq -1, x \neq 4\}$ or $(-\infty, -1) \cup (-1, 4) \cup (4, \infty)$

19. $\{x \mid x \neq -8, x \neq 5\}$ or $(-\infty, -8) \cup (-8, 5) \cup (5, \infty)$

21. $\{x \mid x \neq -6, x \neq 0\}$ or $(-\infty, -6) \cup (-6, 0) \cup (0, \infty)$

23. $\{\text{all reals}\}$ or $(-\infty, \infty)$

25. $\{t \mid t \neq -2, t \neq 2\}$ or $(-\infty, -2) \cup (-2, 2) \cup (2, \infty)$

27. $\{x \mid x \geq -4\}$ or $[-4, \infty)$ **29.** $\left\{ s \mid s \geq \dfrac{5}{4} \right\}$ or $\left[\dfrac{5}{4}, \infty \right)$

31. $\{x \mid x \leq -4 \text{ or } x \geq 4\}$ or $(-\infty, -4] \cup [4, \infty)$

33. $\{x \mid x \leq -3 \text{ or } x \geq 6\}$ or $(-\infty, -3] \cup [6, \infty)$

35. $\{x \mid -1 \leq x \leq 1\}$ or $[-1, 1]$

37. $f(0) = -2, f(2) = 8, f(-1) = -7, f(-4) = -22$

39. $f(-2) = -\dfrac{7}{4}, f(0) = -\dfrac{3}{4}, f\left(\dfrac{1}{2}\right) = -\dfrac{1}{2}, f\left(\dfrac{2}{3}\right) = -\dfrac{5}{12}$

41. $g(-1) = 0; g(2) = -9; g(-3) = 26; g(4) = 5$

43. $h(-2) = -2; h(-3) = -11; h(4) = -32; h(5) = -51$

45. $f(3) = \sqrt{7}; f(4) = 3; f(10) = \sqrt{21}; f(12) = 5$

47. $f(1) = -1; f(-1) = -2; f(3) = -\dfrac{2}{3}; f(-6) = \dfrac{4}{3}$

49. $f(a) = a^2 - 7a, f(a - 3) = a^2 - 13a + 30$,
$f(a + h) = a^2 + 2ah + h^2 - 7a - 7h$

51. $f(-a) = 2a^2 + a - 1, f(a + 1) = 2a^2 + 3a$,
$f(a + h) = 2a^2 + 4ah + 2h^2 - a - h - 1$

53. $f(-a) = -a^2 + 2a - 7, f(-a - 2) =$
$-a^2 - 2a - 7, f(a + 7) = -a^2 - 16a - 70$
55. $f(-2) = 27; f(3) = 42; g(-4) = -37; g(6) = -17$
57. $f(-2) = 5; f(3) = 8; g(-4) = -3; g(5) = -4$
59. -3 **61.** $-2a - h$ **63.** $4a - 1 + 2h$
65. $-8a - 7 - 4h$
67. $h(1) = 48; h(2) = 64; h(3) = 48; h(4) = 0$
69. $C(75) = \$74; C(150) = \$98; C(225) = \$122; C(650) = \$258$
71. $I(0.11) = 55; I(0.12) = 60; I(0.135) = 67.5; I(0.15) = 75$

13.
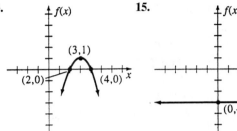

15.

Problem Set 9.2 (page 448)

1.
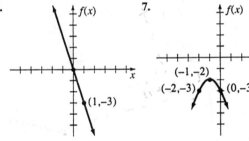

3.

17.
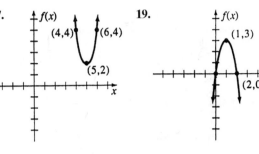

19.

5.
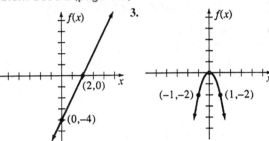

7.

21.
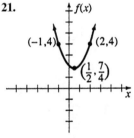

23.
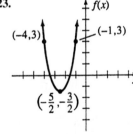

9.
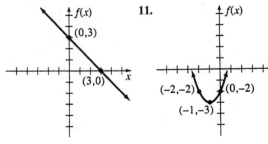

11.

25.
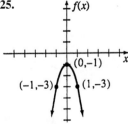

27.
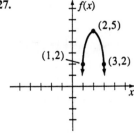

29.

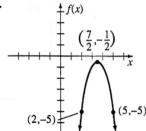

$\left(\frac{7}{2}, -\frac{1}{2}\right)$

$(2, -5)$ $(5, -5)$

13.

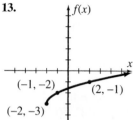

$(-1, -2)$ $(2, -1)$

$(-2, -3)$

15.

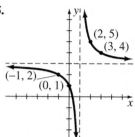

$(2, 5)$
$(3, 4)$

$(-1, 2)$
$(0, 1)$

31. (a) $.42 **(c)** Answers will vary.
33. $26; $30.50; $50; $60.50
35. $2.10; $4.55; $20.72; $29.40; $33.88
37. $f(p) = 0.8p$; $7.60; $12; $60; $10; $600
39. 80 items **41.** 5 and 25 **43.** 60 meters by 60 meters
45. 1100 subscribers at $13.75 per month

Problem Set 9.3 (page 458)

1.

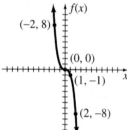

$(-2, 8)$
$(0, 0)$
$(1, -1)$
$(2, -8)$

3.

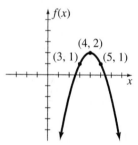

$(4, 2)$
$(3, 1)$ $(5, 1)$

17.

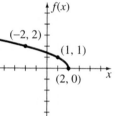

$(-2, 2)$
$(1, 1)$
$(2, 0)$

19.

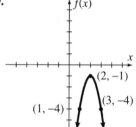

$(2, -1)$
$(1, -4)$ $(3, -4)$

5.

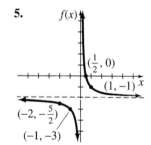

$\left(\frac{1}{2}, 0\right)$
$(1, -1)$
$\left(-2, -\frac{5}{2}\right)$
$(-1, -3)$

7.

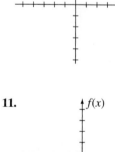

$(-1, 4)$ $(3, 4)$
$(1, 2)$

21.

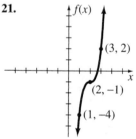

$(3, 2)$
$(2, -1)$
$(1, -4)$

23.

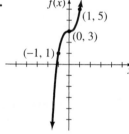

$(1, 5)$
$(0, 3)$
$(-1, 1)$

9.

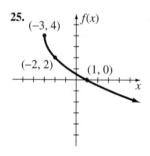

$(-2, 1)$ $(2, 1)$

11.

$(1, -2)$
$(4, -4)$

25.

$(-3, 4)$
$(-2, 2)$
$(1, 0)$

27.

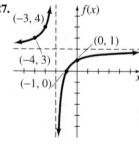

$(-3, 4)$
$(0, 1)$
$(-4, 3)$
$(-1, 0)$

29.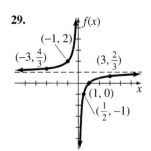

31.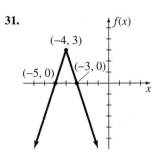

$(g \circ f)(x) = \dfrac{12 - 9x}{x}, D = \{x \mid x \neq 0\}$ or

$D: (-\infty, 0) \cup (0, \infty)$

23. $(f \circ g)(x) = \sqrt{5x + 4}, D = \left\{x \mid x \geq -\dfrac{4}{5}\right\}$

or $D: \left[-\dfrac{4}{5}, \infty\right)$

$(g \circ f)(x) = 5\sqrt{x + 1} + 3, D = \{x \mid x \geq -1\}$ or
$D: [-1, \infty)$

25. $(f \circ g)(x) = x - 4, D = \{x \mid x \neq 4\}$ or
$D: (-\infty, 4) \cup (4, \infty)$

$(g \circ f)(x) = \dfrac{x}{1 - 4x}, D = \left\{x \mid x \neq 0 \text{ and } x \neq \dfrac{1}{4}\right\}$ or

$D: (-\infty, 0) \cup \left(0, \dfrac{1}{4}\right) \cup \left(\dfrac{1}{4}, \infty\right)$

33.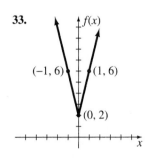

35. (a)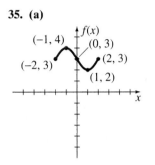

27. $(f \circ g)(x) = \dfrac{2\sqrt{x}}{x}, D = \{x \mid x > 0\}$ or $D: (0, \infty)$

$(g \circ f)(x) = \dfrac{4\sqrt{x}}{x}, D = \{x \mid x > 0\}$ or $D: (0, \infty)$

29. $(f \circ g)(x) = \dfrac{3x + 3}{2}, D = \{x \mid x \neq -1\}$ or

$D: (-\infty, -1) \cup (-1, \infty)$

$(g \circ f)(x) = \dfrac{2x}{2x + 3}, D = \left\{x \mid x \neq 0 \text{ and } x \neq -\dfrac{3}{2}\right\}$ or

$D: \left(-\infty, -\dfrac{3}{2}\right) \cup \left(-\dfrac{3}{2}, 0\right) \cup (0, \infty)$

35. (c)

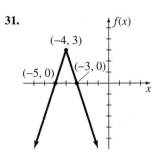

Problem Set 9.5 (page 471)

1. Not a function **3.** Function **5.** Function
7. Function **9.** One-to-one function
11. Not a one-to-one function
13. Not a one-to-one function **15.** One-to-one function
17. Domain of f: $\{1, 2, 3, 4\}$
Range of f: $\{3, 6, 11, 18\}$
f^{-1}: $\{(3, 1), (6, 2), (11, 3), (18, 4)\}$
Domain of f^{-1}: $\{3, 6, 11, 18\}$
Range of f^{-1}: $\{1, 2, 3, 4\}$
19. Domain of f: $\{-2, -1, 0, 5\}$
Range of f: $\{-1, 1, 5, 10\}$
f^{-1}: $\{(-1, -2), (1, -1), (5, 0), (10, 5)\}$
Domain of f^{-1}: $\{-1, 1, 5, 10\}$
Range of f^{-1}: $\{-2, -1, 0, 5\}$
21. $f^{-1}(x) = \dfrac{x + 4}{5}$ **23.** $f^{-1}(x) = \dfrac{1 - x}{2}$
25. $f^{-1}(x) = \dfrac{5}{4}x$ **27.** $f^{-1}(x) = 2x - 8$

Problem Set 9.4 (page 464)

1. 124 and -130 **3.** 323 and 257 **5.** $\dfrac{1}{2}$ and -1

7. Undefined and undefined **9.** $\sqrt{7}$ and 0
11. 37 and 27 **13.** $(f \circ g)(x) = 15x - 3, D = \{\text{all reals}\}$
or $D: (-\infty, \infty)$ $(g \circ f)(x) = 15x - 1, D = \{\text{all reals}\}$
or $D: (-\infty, \infty)$
15. $(f \circ g)(x) = -14x - 7, D = \{\text{all reals}\}$ or $D: (-\infty, \infty)$
$(g \circ f)(x) = -14x + 11, D = \{\text{all reals}\}$ or $D: (-\infty, \infty)$
17. $(f \circ g)(x) = 3x^2 + 11, D = \{\text{all reals}\}$ or $D: (-\infty, \infty)$
$(g \circ f)(x) = 9x^2 + 12x + 7, D = \{\text{all reals}\}$ or $D: (-\infty, \infty)$
19. $(f \circ g)(x) = 2x^2 - 11x + 17, D = \{\text{all reals}\}$ or $D: (-\infty, \infty)$
$(g \circ f)(x) = -2x^2 + x + 1, D = \{\text{all reals}\}$ or $D: (-\infty, \infty)$

21. $(f \circ g)(x) = \dfrac{3}{4x - 9}, D = \left\{x \mid x \neq \dfrac{9}{4}\right\}$ or

$D: \left(-\infty, \dfrac{9}{4}\right) \cup \left(\dfrac{9}{4}, \infty\right)$

29. $f^{-1}(x) = \dfrac{15x + 6}{5}$ **31.** $f^{-1}(x) = \dfrac{x - 4}{9}$

33. $f^{-1}(x) = \dfrac{-x - 4}{5}$ **35.** $f^{-1}(x) = \dfrac{-3x + 21}{2}$

37. $f^{-1}(x) = \dfrac{3}{4}x + \dfrac{3}{16}$ **39.** $f^{-1}(x) = -\dfrac{7}{3}x - \dfrac{14}{9}$

41. $f^{-1}(x) = \dfrac{1}{4}x$ **43.** $f^{-1}(x) = -3x$

45. $f^{-1}(x) = \dfrac{x + 3}{3}$ **47.** $f^{-1}(x) = \dfrac{-x - 4}{2}$

49. $f^{-1}(x) = \sqrt{x},\, x \geq 0$ **53. (a)** $f^{-1}(x) = \dfrac{x - 1}{2}$

(c) $f^{-1}(x) = \dfrac{-x + 5}{4}$ **(e)** $f^{-1}(x) = \dfrac{1}{2}x$

9.
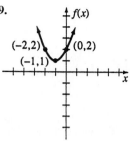

10.
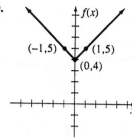

Problem Set 9.6 (page 479)

1. $y = \dfrac{k}{x^2}$ **3.** $C = \dfrac{kg}{t^3}$ **5.** $V = kr^3$ **7.** $S = ke^2$

9. $V = khr^2$ **11.** $\dfrac{2}{3}$ **13.** -4 **15.** $\dfrac{1}{3}$ **17.** -2 **19.** 2

21. 5   **23.** 9   **25.** 9   **27.** $\dfrac{1}{6}$ **29.** 112

31. 12 cubic centimeters   **33.** 28   **35.** 2 seconds
37. 12 ohms   **39. (a)** \$210   **(c)** \$1050
41. 3560.76 cubic meters   **43.** 0.048

11.
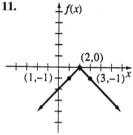

12.
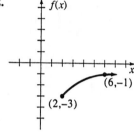

Chapter 9 Review Problem Set (page 483)

1. $D = \{1, 2, 4\}$ **2.** $D = \{x | x \neq 5\}$ or
$D: (-\infty, 5) \cup (5, \infty)$
3. $D = \{x | x \neq 0 \text{ and } x \neq -4\}$ or
$D: (-\infty, -4) \cup (-4, 0) \cup (0, \infty)$
4. $D = \{x | x \geq 5 \text{ or } x \leq -5\}$ or $D: (-\infty, -5] \cup [5, \infty)$
5. $f(2) = -1, f(-3) = 14; f(a) = a^2 - 2a - 1$
6. $4a + 2h + 1$

13.
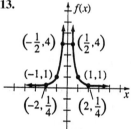

14.
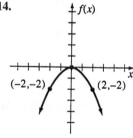

7.

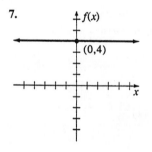

8.
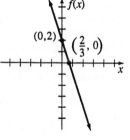

15.
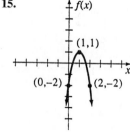

16.
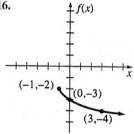

17. (a) $(-5, -28); x = -5$ **(b)** $\left(-\dfrac{7}{6}, \dfrac{67}{2}\right); x = -\dfrac{7}{2}$

18. $(f \circ g)(x) = 6x - 11$ and $(g \circ f)(x) = 6x - 13$

19. $(f \circ g)(x) = x^2 - 2x - 1$ and $(g \circ f)(x) = x^2 - 10x + 27$

20. $(f \circ g)(x) = 4x^2 - 20x + 20$ and $(g \circ f)(x) = -2x^2 + 15$

21. $f^{-1}(x) = \dfrac{x + 1}{6}$ **22.** $f^{-1}(x) = \dfrac{3x - 21}{2}$

23. $f^{-1}(x) = \dfrac{-35x - 10}{21}$ **24.** $k = 9$ **25.** $y = 120$

26. 128 pounds **27.** 20 and 20 **28.** 3 and 47

29. 25 students **30.** 600 square inches **31.** $.72

32. $f(x) = 0.7x$; $45.50; $33.60; $10.85

Chapter 9 Test (page 485)

1. $D = \left\{x \mid x \neq -4 \text{ and } x \neq \dfrac{1}{2}\right\}$ or

$D: (-\infty, -4) \cup \left(-4, \dfrac{1}{2}\right) \cup \left(\dfrac{1}{2}, \infty\right)$

2. $D = \left\{x \mid x \leq \dfrac{5}{3}\right\}$ or $D: \left(-\infty, \dfrac{5}{3}\right]$ **3.** $\dfrac{11}{6}$ **4.** 11

5. $(-6, 3)$ **6.** $6a + 3h + 2$ **7.** $(f \circ g)(x) = -21x - 2$

8. $(g \circ f)(x) = 8x^2 + 38x + 48$ **9.** $(f \circ g)(x) = \dfrac{3x}{2 - 2x}$

10. $f^{-1}(x) = \dfrac{x + 9}{5}$ **11.** $f^{-1}(x) = \dfrac{-x - 6}{3}$

12. $f^{-1}(x) = \dfrac{15x + 9}{10}$ **13.** -4 **14.** 15

15. 6 and 54 **16.** $96

17. The graph of $f(x) = (x - 6)^3 - 4$ is the graph of $f(x) = x^3$ translated 6 units to the right and 4 units downward.

18. The graph of $f(x) = -|x| + 8$ is the graph of $f(x) = |x|$ reflected across the x axis and translated 8 units upward.

19. The graph of $f(x) = -\sqrt{x + 5} + 7$ is the graph of $f(x) = \sqrt{x}$ reflected across the x axis and translated 5 units to the left and 7 units upward.

20.

21.

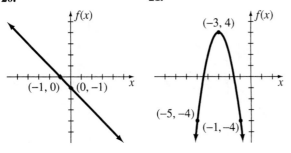

22.

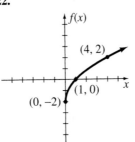

23.

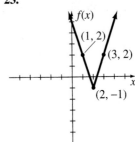

24.

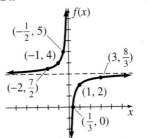

25.

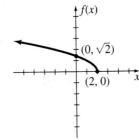

CHAPTER 10

Problem Set 10.1 (page 493)

1. $\{(3, 2)\}$ **3.** $\{(-2, 1)\}$ **5.** Dependent **7.** $\{(4, -3)\}$

9. Inconsistent **11.** $\{(8, 12)\}$ **13.** $\{(-4, -6)\}$

15. $\{(-9, 3)\}$ **17.** $\{(1, 3)\}$ **19.** $\left\{\left(5, \dfrac{3}{2}\right)\right\}$

21. $\left\{\left(\dfrac{9}{5}, -\dfrac{7}{25}\right)\right\}$ **23.** $\{(-2, -4)\}$ **25.** $\{(5, 2)\}$

27. $\{(-4, -8)\}$ **29.** $\left\{\left(\dfrac{11}{20}, \dfrac{7}{20}\right)\right\}$ **31.** $\{(-1, 5)\}$

33. $\left\{\left(-\dfrac{3}{4}, -\dfrac{6}{5}\right)\right\}$ **35.** $\left\{\left(\dfrac{5}{27}, -\dfrac{26}{27}\right)\right\}$

37. $2000 at 7% and $8000 at 8% **39.** 92 **41.** 34 and 97

43. 42 females **45.** 20 inches by 27 inches

47. 60 five-dollar bills and 40 ten-dollar bills

49. 2500 student tickets and 500 nonstudent tickets

Problem Set 10.2 (page 502)

1. $\{(4, -3)\}$ **3.** $\{(-1, -3)\}$ **5.** $\{(-8, 2)\}$ **7.** $\{(-4, 0)\}$

9. $\{(1, -1)\}$ **11.** Inconsistent **13.** $\left\{\left(-\dfrac{1}{11}, \dfrac{4}{11}\right)\right\}$

15. $\left\{\left(\dfrac{3}{2}, -\dfrac{1}{3}\right)\right\}$ **17.** $\{(4, -9)\}$ **19.** $\{(7, 0)\}$ **21.** $\{(7, 12)\}$

23. $\left\{\left(\frac{7}{11}, \frac{2}{11}\right)\right\}$ **25.** Inconsistent **27.** $\left\{\left(\frac{51}{31}, -\frac{32}{31}\right)\right\}$

29. $\{(-2, -4)\}$ **31.** $\left\{\left(-1, -\frac{14}{3}\right)\right\}$ **33.** $\{(-6, 12)\}$

35. $\{(2, 8)\}$ **37.** $\{(-1, 3)\}$ **39.** $\{(16, -12)\}$

41. $\left\{\left(-\frac{3}{4}, \frac{3}{2}\right)\right\}$ **43.** $\{(5, -5)\}$

45. 5 gallons of 10% solution and 15 gallons of 20% solution

47. $1 for a tennis ball and $2 for a golf ball

49. 40 double rooms and 15 single rooms **51.** 9 feet

53. $\frac{3}{4}$ **55.** 18 centimeters by 24 centimeters **57.** 8 feet

61. (a) Consistent **(c)** Consistent **(e)** Dependent **(g)** Inconsistent

Problem Set 10.3 (page 512)

1. $\{(-2, 5, 2)\}$ **3.** $\{(4, -1, -2)\}$ **5.** $\{(-1, 3, 5)\}$

7. Infinitely many solutions **9.** $\varnothing$ **11.** $\left\{\left(-2, \frac{3}{2}, 1\right)\right\}$

13. $\left\{\left(\frac{1}{3}, -\frac{1}{2}, 1\right)\right\}$ **15.** $\left\{\left(\frac{2}{3}, -4, \frac{3}{4}\right)\right\}$ **17.** $\{(-2, 4, 0)\}$

19. $\left\{\left(\frac{1}{2}, \frac{1}{3}, \frac{1}{6}\right)\right\}$ **21.** 194

23. $1.22 per bottle of catsup, $1.77 per jar of peanut butter, and $1.80 per jar of pickles

25. $-2, 6$, and 16 **27.** 40°, 60°, and 80°

29. $500 at 12%, $1000 at 13%, and $1500 at 14%

Problem Set 10.4 (page 518)

1. $\{(6, -4)\}$ **3.** $\{(-4, -4)\}$ **5.** $\left\{\left(-\frac{11}{7}, -\frac{13}{7}\right)\right\}$

7. $\{(1, -3)\}$ **9.** $\{(-1, -2, -3)\}$ **11.** $\{(3, 1, 4)\}$

13. $\{(4, 3, -2)\}$ **15.** $\{(-5, 2, 0)\}$ **17.** $\{(-2, -1, 1)\}$

19. $\{(-1, 4, -1)\}$ **21.** $\{(2, 0, -3)\}$ **25.** $\{(1, -1, 2, -3)\}$

27. $\varnothing$

Problem Set 10.5 (page 524)

1. 10 **3.** -48 **5.** -29 **7.** 50 **9.** 8 **11.** 6 **13.** -32

15. -2 **17.** 5 **19.** $-\frac{7}{20}$ **21.** $\{(3, 8)\}$ **23.** $\{(-2, 5)\}$

25. $\{(-2, 2)\}$ **27.** $\varnothing$ **29.** $\{(1, 6)\}$ **31.** $\left\{\left(-\frac{1}{4}, \frac{2}{3}\right)\right\}$

33. $\left\{\left(\frac{17}{62}, \frac{4}{31}\right)\right\}$ **35.** $\{(-1, 3)\}$ **37.** $\{(9, -2)\}$

39. $\{(-4, -3)\}$

Problem Set 10.6 (page 530)

1. -57 **3.** 14 **5.** -41 **7.** -8 **9.** -96

11. $\{(-3, 1, -1)\}$ **13.** $\{(0, 2, -3)\}$ **15.** $\left\{\left(-2, \frac{1}{2}, -\frac{2}{3}\right)\right\}$

17. $\{(-1, -1, -1)\}$ **19.** $\varnothing$ **21.** $\{(-5, -2, 1)\}$

23. $\{(-2, 3, -4)\}$ **25.** $\left\{\left(-\frac{1}{2}, 0, \frac{2}{3}\right)\right\}$ **27.** $\{(-6, 7, 1)\}$

29. $\left\{\left(1, -6, -\frac{1}{2}\right)\right\}$ **33.** 0 **35. (b)** -20

Problem Set 10.7 (page 539)

1. $\{(-2, 0), (-4, 4)\}$ **3.** $\{(2, -3), (-2, 3)\}$

5. $\{(-6, 7), (-2, -1)\}$ **7.** $\{(1, 1)\}$ **9.** $\{(-5, -3)\}$

11. $\{(-3, 2)\}$ **13.** $\{(2, 2), (-2, -2)\}$

15. $\{(2 + i\sqrt{3}, -2 + i\sqrt{3}), (2 - i\sqrt{3}, -2 - i\sqrt{3})\}$

17.
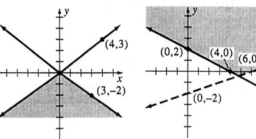

19.

21.

23.
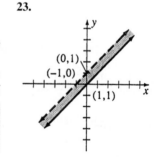

25.
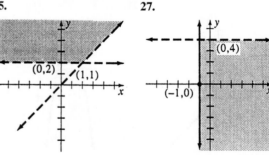

27.

29.

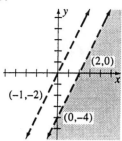

31.

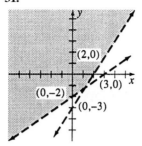

14. $\{(-1, 2, -3)\}$ **15.** $x = 7$ **16.** $y = -1$ **17.** $z = 0$
18. Two   **19.** Four   **20.** One   **21.** $\{(2, 3)\}$
22.

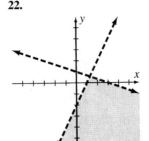

Chapter 10 Review Problem Set (page 542)

1. $\{(2, 6)\}$ **2.** $\{(-3, 7)\}$ **3.** $\{(-9, 8)\}$ **4.** $\left\{\left(\dfrac{89}{23}, -\dfrac{12}{23}\right)\right\}$

5. $\{(4, -7)\}$ **6.** $\{(-2, 8)\}$ **7.** $\{(0, -3)\}$ **8.** $\{(6, 7)\}$

9. $\{(1, -6)\}$ **10.** $\{(-4, 0)\}$ **11.** $\{(-12, 18)\}$ **12.** $\{(24, 8)\}$

13. $\left\{\left(\dfrac{2}{3}, -\dfrac{3}{4}\right)\right\}$ **14.** $\left\{\left(-\dfrac{1}{2}, \dfrac{3}{5}\right)\right\}$ **15.** -18 **16.** 11

17. -29 **18.** 59 **19.** $\{(2, -4, -6)\}$ **20.** $\{(-1, 5, -7)\}$

21. $\{(2, -3, 1)\}$ **22.** $\{(2, -1, -2)\}$ **23.** $\left\{\left(-\dfrac{1}{3}, -1, 4\right)\right\}$

24. $\{(0, -2, -4)\}$
25. $\{(1, 1), (-2, 7)\}$ **26.**

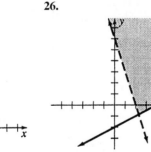

27. 2 and 3 or -3 and -2
28. 5 and 3 or 5 and -3 or -5 and 3 or -5 and -3
29. 2 and 5 or -3 and 10   **30.** 6 meters by 9 meters
31. $9 per pound for cashews and $5 per pound for Spanish peanuts
32. $1.50 for a carton of pop and $2.25 for a pound of candy
33. The fixed fee is $2, and the additional fee is $.10 per pound.

Chapter 10 Test (page 544)

1. II   **2.** I and IV   **3.** III   **4.** I   **5.** -38 **6.** -9
7. $\{(2, 7)\}$ **8.** $\{(-3, 5)\}$ **9.** $\{(-2, -4)\}$ **10.** $\{(3, -3)\}$
11. $\left\{\left(-\dfrac{1}{2}, 1\right)\right\}$ **12.** $\{(24, 18)\}$ **13.** $\{(1, -2, 3)\}$

23. 24 quarters   **24.** 3 liters   **25.** 27

Cumulative Review Problem Set (page 546)

1. -6 **2.** -8 **3.** $\dfrac{13}{24}$ **4.** 24 **5.** $\dfrac{13}{6}$ **6.** $-90\sqrt{2}$

7. $2x + 5\sqrt{x} - 12$ **8.** $-18 + 22\sqrt{3}$

9. $2x^3 + 11x^2 - 14x + 4$ **10.** $\dfrac{x + 4}{x(x + 5)}$ **11.** $\dfrac{16x^2}{27y}$

12. $\dfrac{16x + 43}{90}$ **13.** $\dfrac{35a - 44b}{60a^2b}$ **14.** $\dfrac{2}{x - 4}$

15. $2x^2 - x - 4$ **16.** $\dfrac{5y^2 - 3xy^2}{x^2y + 2x^2}$ **17.** $\dfrac{2y - 3xy}{3x + 4xy}$

18. $\dfrac{(2n + 3)(n + 3)}{(n + 2)(3n + 13)}$ **19.** $\dfrac{3a^2 - 2a + 1}{2a - 1}$

20. $(5x - 2)(4x + 3)$ **21.** $2(2x + 3)(4x^2 - 6x + 9)$
22. $(2x + 3)(2x - 3)(x + 2)(x - 2)$
23. $4x(3x + 2)(x - 5)$ **24.** $(y - 6)(x + 3)$

25. $(5 - 3x)(2 + 3x)$ **26.** $\dfrac{81}{16}$ **27.** 4 **28.** $-\dfrac{3}{4}$ **29.** -0.3

30. $\dfrac{1}{81}$ **31.** $\dfrac{21}{16}$ **32.** $\dfrac{9}{64}$ **33.** 72 **34.** $-\dfrac{12}{x^3y}$ **35.** $\dfrac{8y}{x^5}$

36. $-\dfrac{a^3}{9b}$ **37.** $4\sqrt{5}$ **38.** $-6\sqrt{6}$ **39.** $\dfrac{5\sqrt{3}}{9}$ **40.** $\dfrac{2\sqrt{3}}{3}$

41. $2\sqrt[3]{7}$ **42.** $\dfrac{\sqrt[3]{6}}{2}$ **43.** $8xy\sqrt{13x}$ **44.** $\dfrac{\sqrt{6xy}}{3y}$

45. $11\sqrt{6}$ **46.** $-\dfrac{169\sqrt{2}}{12}$ **47.** $-16\sqrt[3]{3}$

48. $\dfrac{-3\sqrt{2} - 2\sqrt{6}}{2}$ **49.** $\dfrac{6\sqrt{15} - 3\sqrt{35} - 6 + \sqrt{21}}{5}$

50. 0.021 **51.** 300 **52.** 0.0003 **53.** $32 + 22i$

54. $-17 + i$ **55.** $0 - \dfrac{5}{4}i$ **56.** $-\dfrac{19}{53} + \dfrac{40}{53}i$

57. $-\dfrac{10}{3}$ **58.** $\dfrac{4}{7}$ **59.** $2\sqrt{13}$ **60.** $5x - 4y = 19$

61. $4x + 3y = -18$ **62.** $(-2, 6)$ and $r = 3$

63. $(-5, -4)$ **64.** 8 units

65.

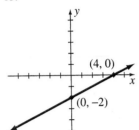

66.

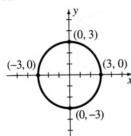

67.

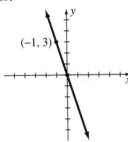

68.

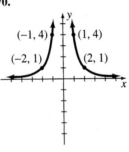

69.

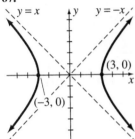

70.

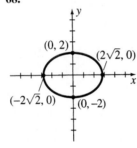

71.

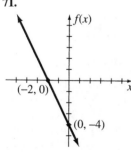

72.

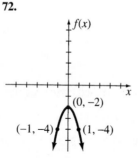

73.

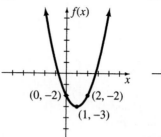

74.

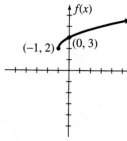

75.

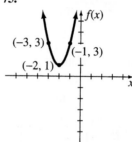

76.

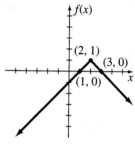

77. $(g \circ f)(x) = 2x^2 - 13x + 20$

$(f \circ g)(x) = 2x^2 - x - 4$ **78.** $f^{-1}(x) = \dfrac{x + 7}{3}$

79. $f^{-1}(x) = -2x + \dfrac{4}{3}$ **80.** $k = -3$ **81.** $y = 1$

82. 12 cubic centimeters **83.** -40 **84.** 40 **85.** $\left\{ -\dfrac{21}{16} \right\}$

86. $\left\{ \dfrac{40}{3} \right\}$ **87.** $\{6\}$ **88.** $\left\{ -\dfrac{5}{2}, 3 \right\}$ **89.** $\left\{ 0, \dfrac{7}{3} \right\}$

90. $\{-6, 0, 6\}$ **91.** $\left\{ -\dfrac{5}{6}, \dfrac{2}{5} \right\}$ **92.** $\left\{ -3, 0, \dfrac{3}{2} \right\}$

93. $\{\pm 1, \pm 3i\}$ **94.** $\{-5, 7\}$ **95.** $\{-29, 0\}$ **96.** $\left\{ \dfrac{7}{2} \right\}$

97. $\{12\}$ **98.** $\{-3\}$ **99.** $\left\{ \dfrac{1 \pm 3\sqrt{5}}{3} \right\}$

100. $\left\{ \dfrac{-5 \pm 4i\sqrt{2}}{2} \right\}$ **101.** $\left\{ \dfrac{3 \pm i\sqrt{23}}{4} \right\}$

102. $\left\{ \dfrac{3 \pm \sqrt{3}}{3} \right\}$ **103.** $\{1 \pm \sqrt{34}\}$

104. $\left\{ \pm \dfrac{\sqrt{5}}{2}, \pm \dfrac{\sqrt{3}}{3} \right\}$ **105.** $\left\{ \dfrac{-5 \pm i\sqrt{15}}{4} \right\}$

106. $(-\infty, 3)$ **107.** $(-\infty, 50]$ **108.** $\left(-\infty -\dfrac{11}{5} \right) \cup (3, \infty)$

109. $\left(-\dfrac{5}{3}, 1\right)$ **110.** $\left[-\dfrac{9}{11}, \infty\right)$ **111.** $[-4, 2]$

112. $\left(-\infty, \dfrac{1}{3}\right) \cup (4, \infty)$ **113.** $(-8, 3)$

114. $(-\infty, 3] \cup (7, \infty)$ **115.** $(-6, -3)$ **116.** $\{(9, 6)\}$

117. $\left\{\left(\dfrac{9}{5}, -\dfrac{7}{25}\right)\right\}$ **118.** $\left\{\left(\dfrac{70}{23}, \dfrac{36}{23}\right)\right\}$ **119.** $\{(-2, 4, 0)\}$

120. $\{(-1, 4, -1)\}$ **121.** 17, 19, and 21

122. 14 nickels, 20 dimes, and 29 quarters

123. 48° and 132°   **124.** \$600

125. \$1700 at 8% and \$2000 at 9%

126. 66 miles per hour and 76 miles per hour

127. 4 quarts   **128.** 69 or less   **129.** $-3, 0,$ or 3

130. 1 inch   **131.** \$1050 and \$1400

132. 3 hours   **133.** 30 shares at \$10 per share

134. 37   **135.** 10°, 60°, and 110°

CHAPTER 11

Problem Set 11.1 (page 557)

1. $\{3\}$ **3.** $\{2\}$ **5.** $\{4\}$ **7.** $\{1\}$ **9.** $\{5\}$ **11.** $\{1\}$ **13.** $\left\{\dfrac{3}{2}\right\}$

15. $\left\{\dfrac{5}{6}\right\}$ **17.** $\{-3\}$ **19.** $\{-3\}$ **21.** $\{0\}$ **23.** $\{1\}$

25. $\{-1\}$ **27.** $\left\{-\dfrac{2}{5}\right\}$ **29.** $\left\{\dfrac{5}{2}\right\}$ **31.** $\{3\}$ **33.** $\left\{\dfrac{1}{2}\right\}$

35.
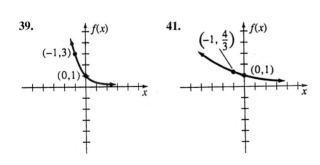

37.

39.
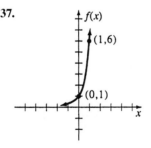

41.

43.
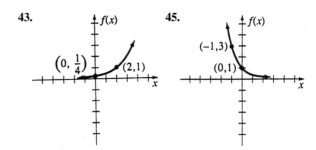

45.

47.
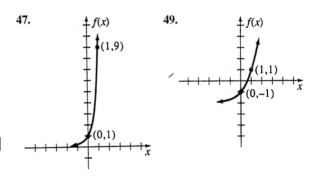

49.

51.
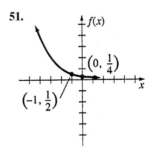

Problem Set 11.2 (page 565)

1. (a) \$0.87   **(c)** \$2.33   **(e)** \$21,900   **(g)** \$658

3. \$283.70   **5.** \$865.84   **7.** \$1782.25   **9.** \$2725.05

11. \$16,998.71   **13.** \$22,553.65   **15.** \$567.63

17. \$1422.36   **19.** \$8963.38   **21.** \$17,547.35

23. \$32,558.88

25.

	1 yr	5 yr	10 yr	20 yr
Compounded annually	\$1120	1762	3106	9,646
Compounded semiannually	1124	1791	3207	10,286
Compounded quarterly	1126	1806	3262	10,641
Compounded monthly	1127	1817	3300	10,893
Compounded continuously	1127	1822	3320	11,023

27. Nora will have $.24 more.   **29.** 9.54%
31. 50 grams; 37 grams

33. 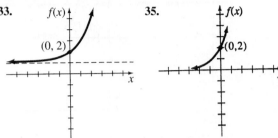 **35.**

37.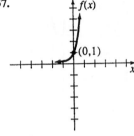

39. 2226; 3320; 7389   **41.** 2000   **43. (a)** 82,888
(c) 96,302   **45. (a)** 6.5 pounds per square inch
(c) 13.6 pounds per square inch

Problem Set 11.3 (page 576)
1. $\log_2 128 = 7$ **3.** $\log_5 125 = 3$ **5.** $\log_{10} 1000 = 3$
7. $\log_2\left(\dfrac{1}{4}\right) = -2$ **9.** $\log_{10} 0.1 = -1$ **11.** $3^4 = 81$
13. $4^3 = 64$ **15.** $10^4 = 10,000$ **17.** $2^{-4} = \dfrac{1}{16}$
19. $10^{-3} = 0.001$ **21.** 4   **23.** 4   **25.** 3   **27.** $\dfrac{1}{2}$ **29.** 0
31. -1 **33.** 5   **35.** -5 **37.** 1   **39.** 0   **41.** {49}
43. {16}   **45.** {27}   **47.** $\left\{\dfrac{1}{8}\right\}$ **49.** {4}   **51.** 5.1293
53. 6.9657   **55.** 1.4037   **57.** 7.4512   **59.** 6.3219
61. -0.3791 **63.** 0.5766   **65.** 2.1531   **67.** 0.3949
69. $\log_b x + \log_b y + \log_b z$ **71.** $\log_b y - \log_b z$
73. $3\log_b y + 4\log_b z$ **75.** $\dfrac{1}{2}\log_b x + \dfrac{1}{3}\log_b y - 4\log_b z$
77. $\dfrac{2}{3}\log_b x + \dfrac{1}{3}\log_b z$ **79.** $\dfrac{3}{2}\log_b x - \dfrac{1}{2}\log_b y$

81. $\left\{\dfrac{9}{4}\right\}$ **83.** {25}   **85.** {4}   **87.** $\left\{\dfrac{19}{8}\right\}$ **89.** {9}
91. {1}   **93.** $\left\{-\dfrac{22}{5}\right\}$ **95.** $\varnothing$ **97.** $\{-1\}$

Problem Set 11.4 (page 583)
1. 0.8597   **3.** 1.7179   **5.** 3.5071   **7.** -0.1373 **9.** -3.4685
11. 411.43   **13.** 90,095   **15.** 79.543   **17.** 0.048440
19. 0.0064150   **21.** 1.6094   **23.** 3.4843   **25.** 6.0638
27. -0.7765 **29.** -3.4609 **31.** 1.6034   **33.** 3.1346
35. 108.56   **37.** 0.48268   **39.** 0.035994

41. 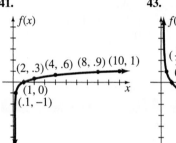 **43.**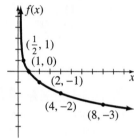

45. 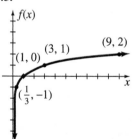 **47.**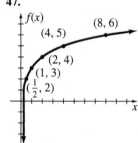

49. 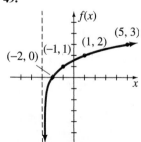 **51.**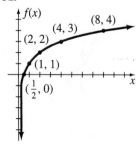

53.

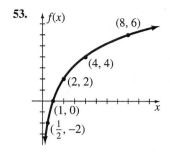

55. 0.36   **57.** 0.73   **59.** 23.10   **61.** 7.93

31.   **32.**

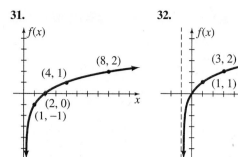

33. 2.842   **34.** $2913.99   **35.** $8178.72   **36.** $5656.26
37. 133 grams   **38.** Approximately 5.3 years
39. Approximately 12.1 years   **40.** 61,070; 67,493; 74,591
41. Approximately 4.8 hours   **42.** 8.1

Problem Set 11.5 (page 591)
1. {3.15}   **3.** {2.20}   **5.** {4.18}   **7.** {0.12}   **9.** {1.69}
11. {4.57}   **13.** {2.46}   **15.** {4}   **17.** $\left\{\dfrac{19}{47}\right\}$
19. {1}   **21.** {8}   **23.** 4.524   **25.** −0.860   **27.** 3.105
29. −2.902   **31.** 5.989   **33.** 2.4 years
35. 5.3 years   **37.** 6.8 hours   **39.** 1.5 hours
41. 34.7 years   **43.** 6.7
45. Approximately 8 times

Chapter 11 Test (page 596)
1. $\dfrac{1}{2}$ **2.** 1   **3.** 1   **4.** −1   **5.** {−3}   **6.** $\left\{-\dfrac{3}{2}\right\}$ **7.** $\left\{\dfrac{8}{3}\right\}$

8. {243}   **9.** {2}   **10.** $\left\{\dfrac{2}{5}\right\}$ **11.** 4.1919   **12.** 0.2031

13. 0.7325   **14.** 5.4538   **15.** {5.17}   **16.** {10.29}

17. 4.0069   **18.** $\log_b\left(\dfrac{x^3 y^2}{z}\right)$ **19.** $6342.08

20. 13.5 years   **21.** 7.8 hours   **22.** 4813 grams

Chapter 11 Review Problem Set (page 595)
1. 7   **2.** 3   **3.** 4   **4.** −3   **5.** 2   **6.** 13   **7.** 0
8. −2   **9.** {−4}   **10.** {3}   **11.** $\left\{-\dfrac{3}{4}\right\}$ **12.** {4}

13. {9}   **14.** $\left\{\dfrac{1}{2}\right\}$ **15.** {5}   **16.** {8}

17. 1.8642   **18.** 4.7380   **19.** −4.2687
20. −2.6289   **21.** 1.1882   **22.** 2639.4   **23.** 0.013289
24. 0.077197   **25.** {3.40}   **26.** {1.95}   **27.** {5.30}
28. {5.61}

23.   **24.**

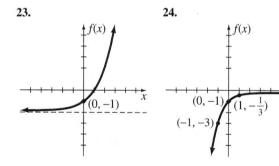

25.

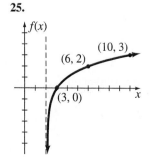

29.   **30.**

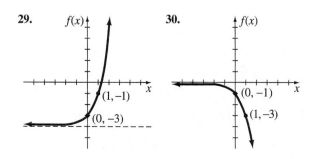

CHAPTER 12

Problem Set 12.1 (page 602)

1. $-1, 2, 5, 8, 11$ **3.** $3, 1, -1, -3, -5$ **5.** $-1, 2, 7, 14, 23$
7. $0, -3, -8, -15, -24$ **9.** $-1, 5, 15, 29, 47$
11. $\frac{1}{2}, 1, 2, 4, 8$ **13.** $-\frac{2}{3}, -2, -6, -18, -54$
15. $a_8 = 54$ and $a_{12} = 130$ **17.** $a_7 = -32$ and $a_8 = 64$
19. $a_n = 2n - 1$ **21.** $a_n = 4n - 6$ **23.** $a_n = -2n + 7$
25. $a_n = -3n - 4$ **27.** $a_n = \frac{1}{2}(n + 1)$ **29.** 34 **31.** 78
33. -155 **35.** 106 **37.** 50 **39.** 170 **41.** -1 **43.** -13
45. 136 **47.** \$27,800 **49.** \$1170

Problem Set 12.2 (page 606)

1. 2550 **3.** 9030 **5.** -4225 **7.** 410 **9.** 8850 **11.** 5724
13. 5070 **15.** 346.5 **17.** 3775 **19.** $39,500$
21. -8645 **23.** $122,850$ **25.** $39,552$
27. 76 seats, 720 seats **29.** \$10,000 **31.** \$357,500
33. 169 **37. (a)** $7 + 12 + 17; 36$
(c) $(-3) + (-5) + (-7) + (-9) + (-11) + (-13); -48$
(e) $3 + 6 + 9 + 12 + 15; 45$

Problem Set 12.3 (page 613)

1. $a_n = 3^{n-1}$ **3.** $a_n = 2^{2n-1}$
5. $a_n = \left(\frac{1}{3}\right)^{n-1}$ or $a_n = \frac{1}{3^{n-1}}$
7. $a_n = 0.2(0.2)^{n-1}$ or $a_n = (0.2)^n$
9. $a_n = 9\left(\frac{2}{3}\right)^{n-1}$ or $a_n = (3^{-n+3})(2)^{n-1}$ **11.** $a_n = (-4)^{n-1}$
13. $19,683$ **15.** -512 **17.** $-\frac{6561}{256}$ **19.** $14,762$
21. -9842 **23.** 1093 **25.** 511 **27.** $19,680$ **29.** 2730
31. 1093 **33.** $1\frac{1023}{1024}$ **35.** $15\frac{31}{32}$ **37.** $\frac{1}{2}$ **39.** $0; -1$
41. 125 liters **43.** \$102.40; \$204.75 **45.** $971.\overline{3}$ meters
47. \$5609.66 **51.** $1,048,576$ **53.** $\frac{4096}{531,441}$ **55.** $-\frac{177,147}{2048}$
57. (a) 126 **(c)** 31 **(e)** $1\frac{49}{81}$

Problem Set 12.4 (page 619)

1. 4 **3.** 1 **5.** 2 **7.** $\frac{2}{3}$ **9.** 9 **11.** No sum **13.** $\frac{4}{7}$
15. $\frac{16}{3}$ **17.** No sum **19.** $\frac{81}{2}$ **21.** $\frac{4}{9}$ **23.** $\frac{47}{99}$ **25.** $\frac{5}{11}$
27. $\frac{427}{999}$ **29.** $\frac{7}{15}$ **31.** $\frac{24}{11}$ **33.** $\frac{47}{110}$

Problem Set 12.5 (page 623)

1. $x^8 + 8x^7y + 28x^6y^2 + 56x^5y^3 + 70x^4y^4 + 56x^3y^5$
$+ 28x^2y^6 + 8xy^7 + y^8$
3. $81x^4 + 108x^3y + 54x^2y^2 + 12xy^3 + y^4$
5. $x^5 - 5x^4y + 10x^3y^2 - 10x^2y^3 + 5xy^4 - y^5$
7. $x^{10} + 10x^9y + 45x^8y^2 + 120x^7y^3 + 210x^6y^4 + 252x^5y^5$
$+ 210x^4y^6 + 120x^3y^7 + 45x^2y^8 + 10xy^9 + y^{10}$
9. $64x^6 + 192x^5y + 240x^4y^2 + 160x^3y^3 + 60x^2y^4$
$+ 12xy^5 + y^6$
11. $x^5 - 15x^4y + 90x^3y^2 - 270x^2y^3 + 405xy^4 - 243y^5$
13. $243a^5 - 810a^4b + 1080a^3b^2 - 720a^2b^3 + 240ab^4 - 32b^5$
15. $x^6 + 6x^5y^3 + 15x^4y^6 + 20x^3y^9 + 15x^2y^{12} + 6xy^{15} + y^{18}$
17. $x^7 + 14x^6 + 84x^5 + 280x^4 + 560x^3 + 672x^2 + 448x + 128$
19. $x^4 - 12x^3 + 54x^2 - 108x + 81$
21. $x^{15} + 15x^{14}y + 105x^{13}y^2 + 455x^{12}y^3$
23. $a^{13} - 26a^{12}b + 312a^{11}b^2 - 2288a^{10}b^3$ **25.** $462x^5y^6$
27. $-160x^3y^3$ **29.** $2000x^3y^2$

Chapter 12 Review Problem Set (page 625)

1. $a_n = 6n - 3$ **2.** $a_n = 3^{n-2}$ **3.** $a_n = 5 \cdot 2^n$
4. $a_n = -3n + 8$ **5.** $a_n = 2n - 7$ **6.** $a_n = 3^{3-n}$
7. $a_n = -(-2)^{n-1}$ **8.** $a_n = 3n + 9$ **9.** $a_n = \frac{n + 1}{3}$
10. $a_n = 4^{n-1}$ **11.** 73 **12.** 106 **13.** $\frac{1}{32}$ **14.** $\frac{4}{9}$ **15.** -92
16. $\frac{1}{16}$ **17.** -5 **18.** 85 **19.** $\frac{5}{9}$ **20.** 2 or -2 **21.** $121\frac{40}{81}$
22. 7035 **23.** $-10,725$ **24.** $31\frac{31}{32}$ **25.** $32,015$
26. 4757 **27.** $85\frac{21}{64}$ **28.** $37,044$ **29.** $12,726$ **30.** $85\frac{1}{3}$
31. $\frac{4}{11}$ **32.** $\frac{41}{90}$ **33.** \$750 **34.** \$46.50 **35.** \$3276.70
36. 10,935 gallons **37.** 3600 feet
38. $128x^7 + 448x^6y + 672x^5y^2 + 560x^4y^3 + 280x^3y^4$
$+ 84x^2y^5 + 14xy^6 + y^7$
39. $x^4 - 12x^3y + 54x^2y^2 - 108xy^3 + 81y^4$ **40.** $1120x^4y^4$

Chapter 12 Test (page 627)

1. -46 **2.** 48 **3.** $a_n = 4n - 7$ **4.** $a_n = 5(2)^{1-n}$
5. $a_n = -3n + 9$ **6.** $\frac{729}{8}$ or $91\frac{1}{8}$ **7.** 223 **8.** 60 terms
9. 46 **10.** 2380 **11.** 765 **12.** -780 **13.** 3279
14. 7155 **15.** 6138 **16.** $22,650$ **17.** 9384 **18.** \$5810
19. \$3276.70 **20.** $13\frac{1}{2}$ **21.** $\frac{37}{99}$ **22.** $\frac{4}{15}$

23. $x^5 - 15x^4y + 90x^3y^2 - 270x^2y^3 + 405xy^4 - 243y^5$
24. $128x^7 + 448x^6y + 672x^5y^2$ **25.** $495a^8b^4$

APPENDIX A

Practice Exercises (page 638)

1. $2 \cdot 13$ **2.** $2 \cdot 2 \cdot 2 \cdot 2$ **3.** $2 \cdot 2 \cdot 3 \cdot 3$
4. $2 \cdot 2 \cdot 2 \cdot 2 \cdot 5$ **5.** $7 \cdot 7$ **6.** $2 \cdot 2 \cdot 23$
7. $2 \cdot 2 \cdot 2 \cdot 7$ **8.** $2 \cdot 2 \cdot 2 \cdot 2 \cdot 3 \cdot 3$
9. $2 \cdot 2 \cdot 2 \cdot 3 \cdot 5$ **10.** $2 \cdot 2 \cdot 3 \cdot 7$ **11.** $3 \cdot 3 \cdot 3 \cdot 5$
12. $2 \cdot 7 \cdot 7$ **13.** 24   **14.** 24   **15.** 48   **16.** 36   **17.** 140
18. 462   **19.** 392   **20.** 72   **21.** 168   **22.** 60   **23.** 90
24. 168   **25.** $\frac{2}{3}$ **26.** $\frac{3}{4}$ **27.** $\frac{2}{3}$ **28.** $\frac{9}{16}$ **29.** $\frac{5}{3}$ **30.** $\frac{4}{3}$

31. $\frac{15}{28}$ **32.** $\frac{12}{55}$ **33.** $\frac{10}{21}$ **34.** $\frac{65}{66}$ **35.** $\frac{3}{10}$ **36.** $\frac{2}{3}$
37. $\frac{3}{8}$ cup   **38.** $\frac{1}{6}$ of the bottle   **39.** $\frac{2}{9}$ of the disk space
40. $\frac{1}{3}$ **41.** $\frac{5}{7}$ **42.** $\frac{8}{11}$ **43.** $\frac{5}{9}$ **44.** $\frac{5}{13}$ **45.** 3   **46.** 2
47. $\frac{2}{3}$ **48.** $\frac{3}{8}$ **49.** $\frac{2}{3}$ **50.** $\frac{5}{9}$ **51.** $\frac{8}{15}$ **52.** $\frac{7}{24}$ **53.** $\frac{9}{16}$
54. $\frac{11}{12}$ **55.** $\frac{37}{30}$ **56.** $\frac{29}{24}$ **57.** $\frac{59}{96}$ **58.** $\frac{19}{24}$ **59.** $\frac{13}{12}$
60. $\frac{5}{16}$ **61.** $\frac{1}{4}$ **62.** $\frac{5}{3}$ **63.** $\frac{37}{30}$ **64.** $\frac{4}{5}$ **65.** $\frac{1}{3}$ **66.** $\frac{27}{35}$
67. $\frac{7}{26}$ **68.** 30   **69.** $\frac{7}{20}$ **70.** $\frac{11}{32}$

Index

Abscissa, 335
Absolute value:
  definition of, 13, 96
  equations involving, 96
  inequalities involving, 98
  properties of, 13
Addition:
  of complex numbers, 280
  of polynomials, 110
  of radical expressions, 244
  of rational expressions, 178
  of real numbers, 14
Addition property of equality, 46
Addition property of inequality, 81
Additive inverse property, 24
Algebraic equation, 45
Algebraic expression, 30
Algebraic inequality, 80
Analytic geometry, 335
Arithmetic sequence, 599
Associative, property:
  of addition, 23
  of multiplication, 23
Asymptotes, 417
Augmented matrix, 514
Axes of a coordinate system, 335
Axis of symmetry, 412

Base of a logarithm, 568
Base of a power, 27, 554
Binary operations, 23
Binomial, 109
Binomial expansion, 622

Cartesian coordinate system, 335
Change-of-base formula, 590
Checking:
  solutions of equations, 46
  solutions of inequalities, 83
  solutions of word problems, 50

Circle, 404
Circle, equation of 405
Circumference, 78
Closure property:
  for addition, 22
  for multiplication, 22
Coefficient, numerical, 109
Common difference of an arithmetic
  sequence, 599
Common logarithm, 580
Common ratio of a geometric
  sequence, 608
Commutative property:
  of addition, 22
  of multiplication, 22
Complementary angles, 58
Completely factored form:
  of a composite number, 130
  of a polynomial, 130
Completing the square, 295
Complex fraction, 188
Complex number, 279
Composite function, 460
Composite number, 129
Composition of functions, 459
Compound interest, 558
Compound statement, 89
Conic section, 391
Conjugate, 252, 283
Conjunction, 89
Consecutive integers, 48
Consistent system of equations, 488
Constant function, 439
Constant of variation, 474
Coordinate geometry, 335
Coordinates of a point, 12, 335
Counting numbers, 3
Cramer's rule, 522, 528
Critical numbers, 322
Cross-multiplication property, 204

Cube root, 233
Cylinder, right circular, 78

Decimals:
  nonrepeating, 4
  repeating, 4
  terminating, 4
Decreasing function, 556
Degree:
  of a monomial, 109
  of a polynomial, 109
Denominator:
  least common, 53
  rationalizing a, 239
Dependent equations, 488
Descartes, René, 333
Determinant, 520
Difference of squares, 137
Difference of two cubes, 139
Difference quotient, 433
Dimension of a matrix, 514
Direct variation, 474
Discriminant, 305
Disjunction, 89
Distance formula, 364
Distributive property, 25
Division:
  of complex numbers, 281
  of polynomials, 195
  of radical expressions, 253
  of rational expressions, 174
  of real numbers, 18
Domain of a relation, 429

e, 561
Elementary row operations, 515
Element of a set, 2
Elimination-by-addition method, 495
Ellipse, 410
Empty set, 3

English system of measure, 36
Equal complex numbers, 279
Equality:
  addition property of, 46
  multiplication property of, 46
  reflexive property of, 7
  substitution property of, 7
  symmetric property of, 7
  transitive property of, 7
Equation(s):
  definition of, 45
  dependent, 488
  equivalent, 45
  exponential, 552
  first-degree in one variable, 45
  first-degree in two variables, 338
  first-degree in three variables, 505
  inconsistent, 488
  linear, 338
  logarithmic, 575
  quadratic, 287
  radical, 256
Equivalent equations, 45
Equivalent fractions, 635
Equivalent inequalities, 81
Equivalent systems, 495
Evaluating algebraic expressions, 32
Expansion of a binomial, 622
Expansion of a determinant by
  minors, 526
Exponents:
  integers, as, 226
  natural numbers as, 27
  negative, 226
  properties of, 225, 227, 552
  rational numbers as, 262
  zero as an, 235
Exponential equation, 552
Exponential function, 554
Extraneous solution or root, 257

Factor, 130
Factoring:
  complete, 130
  difference of cubes, 139
  difference of squares, 137
  by grouping, 131
  sum of cubes, 139
  trinomials, 143, 146

First-degree equations:
  in one variable, 45
  in two variables, 338
  in three variables, 505
Formulas, 69
Function(s):
  constant, 439
  definition of, 429
  domain of a, 429
  exponential, 554
  graph of a, 437
  identity, 438
  inverse of a, 467
  linear, 437
  logarithmic, 578
  one-to-one, 467
  quadratic, 441
  range of a, 429
Functional notation, 430
Fundamental principle of fractions,
  167, 632

Gaussian elimination, 515
General term of a sequence, 598,
  600
Geometric sequence, 608
Graph:
  of an equation, 336
  of a function, 437
  of an inequality, 83
Graphing suggestions, 443, 451
Graphing utilities, 345, 347

Half-life, 560
Heron's formula, 241
Horizontal line test, 466
Horizontal translation, 453
Hyperbola, 415

i, 279
identity element:
  for addition, 23
  for multiplication, 23
Identity function, 438
Imaginary number, 280
Inconsistent equations, 488
Increasing function, 556
Index of a radical, 235
Index of summation, 608

Inequalities:
  involving absolute value, 98
  equivalent, 81
  graphs of, 83
  linear in one variable, 357
  linear in two variables, 357
  quadratic, 320
  sense of an, 82
  solutions of, 81
Infinite sequence, 598
Integers, 3
Intercepts, 338
Intersection of sets, 90
Interval notation, 83, 92
Inverse of a function, 467
Inverse variation, 475
Irrational numbers, 4
Isosceles right triangle, 291
Isosceles triangle, 364

Joint variation, 477

Law of decay, 563
Least common denominator, 53
Least common multiple, 53, 179
Like terms, 30
Linear equations:
  graph of 336
  slope-intercept form for, 378
  standard form for, 338
Linear function:
  definition of, 437
  graph of a, 437
Linear inequality, 357
Linear systems of equations, 487
Line of symmetry, 392
Literal equation, 73
Literal factor, 29, 109
Logarithm(s):
  base of a, 568
  common, 580
  definition of, 568
  natural, 582
  properties of, 570-573
Logarithmic equation, 586
Logarithmic function, 578

Major axis of ellipse, 411
Matrix, 514

Maximum value, 392
Metric system of measure, 36
Minimum value, 392
Minor axis of ellipse, 411
Minors, expansion of a determinant
    by, 526
Monomial(s):
    definition of, 109
    degree of, 109
    division of, 119
    multiplication of, 116
Multiple, least common, 53, 179
Multiplication:
    of complex numbers, 281
    of polynomials, 122
    of radical expressions, 250
    of rational expressions, 172
    of real numbers, 16
Multiplication property of equality,
    46
Multiplication property of inequality,
    82
Multiplication property of negative
    one, 24
Multiplication property of zero, 24
Multiplicative inverse property, 24

nth root, 234
Natural exponential function, 562
Natural logarithm, 582
Natural logarithmic function, 583
Natural numbers, 3
Normal distribution curve, 565
Notation:
    functional, 430
    interval, 83, 92
    scientific, 268
    set, 3
    set-builder, 3
    summation, 608
Null set, 3
Number(s):
    absolute value of, 13
    complex, 279
    composite, 129
    counting, 3
    imaginary, 280
    integers, 3
    irrational, 4

    natural, 3
    prime, 129
    rational, 4
    real, 3
    whole, 3
Numerical coefficient, 109
Numerical expression, 2

One, multiplication property of, 24
One-to-one function, 467
Open sentence, 45
Operations, order of, 7
Ordered pair, 334
Ordered triple, 505
Ordinate, 335
Origin, 334
Origin symmetry, 352, 353

Parabola, 392
Parallel lines, 380
Pascal's triangle, 621
Perfect square trinomial, 295
Perpendicular lines, 380
Point-slope form, 377
Polynomial(s):
    addition of, 110
    completely factored form of, 130
    definition of, 109
    degree of a, 109
    division of, 195
    multiplication of, 122
    subtraction of, 111
Prime factor, 130
Prime number, 129
Principal root, 233
Problem-solving suggestions, 56, 214,
    215, 312
Properties of absolute value, 13
Properties of equality, 7, 46
Properties of inequality, 81
Properties of real numbers, 22-24
Proportion, 204
Pure imaginary number, 280
Pythagorean theorem, 155, 291

Quadrant, 334
Quadratic equation(s):
    definition of, 287
    discriminant of a, 305

    formula, 301
    nature of solutions of, 304
    standard form of, 287
Quadratic formula, 301
Quadratic, function:
    definition of, 441
    graph of a, 441
Quadratic inequality, 320

Radical(s):
    addition of, 244
    changing form of, 236
    definition of, 233
    division of, 253
    index of a, 235
    multiplication of, 250
    simplest form of, 237, 239, 247
    subtraction of, 244
Radical equation, 256
Radicand, 233
Radius of a circle, 404
Range of a relation, 429
Ratio, 204
Ratio of a geometric sequence, 608
Rational exponents, 262
Rational expression, 168
Rationalizing a denominator, 239
Rational number, 4
Real number, 5
Real number line, 12
Reciprocal, 174
Rectangle 77
Rectangular coordinate system, 335
Reducing fractions, 167
Reflexive property of, equality, 7
Relation, 429
Richter number, 589
Roots of an equation, 45

Scientific notation, 268
Sense of an inequality, 82
Sequence:
    arithmetic, 599
    definition of, 598
    general term of, 598, 609
    geometric, 608
    infinite, 598
Set(s):
    element of a, 2

Set(s) (*continued*)
  empty, 3
  equal, 3
  intersection of, 90
  notation, 3
  null, 3
  solution, 45
  union of, 91
Similar terms, 30
Simplest radical form, 237, 239, 243
Simplifying numerical expressions, 7
Simplifying rational expressions, 166
Slope, 365
Slope-intercept form, 378
Solution(s):
  of equations, 45
  extraneous, 257
  of inequalities, 81
  of systems, 487
Solution set:
  of an equation, 45
  of an inequality, 81
  of a system, 487
Square matrix, 520
Square root, 232
Standard form:
  of complex numbers, 279
  of equation of a circle, 405
  of equation of a straight line, 383
  of a linear equation, 383
  of a quadratic equation, 287
Subscripts, 72
Subset, 5
Substitution method, 488
Substitution property of equality, 7

Subtraction:
  of complex numbers, 280
  of polynomials, 111
  of radical expressions, 248
  of rational expressions, 178
  of real numbers, 15
Suggestions for solving word problems, 56, 214, 215, 312
Sum:
  of an arithmetic sequence, 604
  of geometric sequence, 610
  of infinite geometric sequence, 616
Sum of two cubes, 139
Summation notation, 608
Supplementary angles, 58
Symmetric property of equality, 7
Symmetry, 350
Synthetic division, 197
System(s):
  of linear equations in two variables, 487
  of linear equations in three variables, 506
  of linear inequalities, 537
  of nonlinear equations, 532

Term(s):
  addition of like, 30, 110
  of an algebraic expression, 30, 110
  like, 30, 110
  similar, 30, 110
Test numbers, 321
Transformations, 455
Transitive property of equality, 7
Translating from English to algebra, 34

Trapezoid, 72
Triangle, 71
Triangular form, 518
Trinomial, 109

Union of sets, 91

Variable, 2
Variation:
  constant of, 474
  direct, 474
  inverse, 475
  joint, 477
Vertex of a parabola, 392
Vertical line test, 466
Vertical shrinking, 455
Vertical stretching, 455
Vertical translation, 452

Whole numbers, 3

x axis reflection, 454
x axis symmetry, 351
x intercept, 338

y axis reflection, 454
y axis symmetry, 350
y intercept, 338

Zero:
  addition property of, 23
  as an exponent, 225
  multiplication property of, 24